Handbook of Adolescent Psychopathology

Handbook of Adolescent Psycopathology

A Guide to Diagnosis and Treatment

edited by

Vincent B. Van Hasselt

Michel Hersen

LEXINGTON BOOKS
An Imprint of The Free Press
NEW YORK   LONDON   TORONTO   SYDNEY   TOKYO   SINGAPORE

To: Phyllis
Vicki

Library of Congress Cataloging-in-Publication Data

Handbook of adolescent psychopathology : a guide to diagnosis and treatment/edited by Vincent B. Van Hasselt, Michel Hersen.
   p. cm.—(Series in scientific foundations of clinical and counseling psychology)
   Includes index.
   ISBN 0-669-27677-4
   1. Adolescent psychopathology. I. Van Hasselt, Vincent B.
II. Hersen, Michel. III. Series: Scientific foundations of clinical counseling and psychology.
[DNLM: 1. Mental Disorders—in adolescence. 2. Adolescent Behavior. WS 463 H2363
1995]
RJ503.H268 1995   for Library of Congress
616.89'022—dc20   94-31679
DNLM/DLC   CIP

Lexington Books
An Imprint of The Free Press
A Division of Simon & Schuster Inc.
866 Third Avenue, New York, N. Y. 10022

Printed in the United States of America

printing number

1 2 3 4 5 6 7 8 9 10

Contents

iii

Preface

In recent years there has been a dramatic acceleration of clinical and investigative activity in the area of adolescent psychopathology, in part fueled by the desire to demystify this developmental stage in an individual's life. We therefore were convinced that the time was ripe for a comprehensive handbook on adolescent psychopathology. Indeed, we felt that our handbook would appeal to a very wide audience and would cut across several disciplines and theoretical orientations. Included among our intended readers are professionals and graduate students in the fields of clinical psychology, psychiatry, psychiatric social work, psychiatric nursing, counseling, and rehabilitation; we designed the book so that it could also be adopted for graduate-level courses. While some books on adolescent development and adjustment have appeared, they have not covered the topic of adolescent psychopathology in as thorough a manner as in the present tome.

The book is divided into four parts with a total of 23 chapters. Part One (Overview) contains a historical perspective, conceptual models of adolescent psychopathology, and discussions of major aspects of adolescent development and adjustment. In Part Two (Assessment), current strategies and issues in adolescent diagnosis and evaluation are presented. Part Three (Specific Disorders) focuses on the diagnostic classifications relevant to adolescent psychopathology. Given the particular importance of this section, we have provided comprehensive coverage of a wide range of problem areas that should be of considerable interest to the reader.

To the extent possible, and in consideration of interchapter consistency, the material in Chapters 10 through 19 in Part Three follows a standard format:

Description of the Disorder
Historical Background
Clinical Picture

Course and Prognosis
Complications
Epidemiology
Familial Pattern
Differential Diagnosis and Assessment
Clinical Management

Many individuals have contributed to the fruition of this handbook, and we wish to acknowledge their efforts. First and foremost are the contributors, who agreed to share their expertise with us. Second are Burt Bolton, Alissa Miller, and Christine Ryan, who provided the necessary technical assistance. Third, but hardly least of all, we are appreciative of the support and encouragement of Margaret Zusky at Lexington Books, who was willing to tolerate the inevitable delays encountered when producing a large and varied compendium of chapters.

Vincent B. Van Hasselt
Michel Hersen
Fort Lauderdale, Florida

Part I
Overview

1
Cultural and Historical Foundations

Horacio Fabrega, Jr.
Barbara Miller

To most people who will use this handbook, the term *adolescent psychopathology* suggests a coherent domain of mental and behavioral problems in a clearly defined age group. The domain encompasses such seemingly well-marked psychiatric disorders as schizophrenia and depression, as well as such other problems of adaptation as substance abuse, delinquency, and teenage pregnancy. The population group refers, roughly, to individuals of the teenage years.

To those who examine behavioral phenomena from a cultural or historical point of view, however, the distinctiveness of psychopathology and adolescence is less evident. Two interrelated factors linked to the meanings of the descriptors *cultural* and *historical* account for this arbitrariness.

A cultural approach is holistic, comparative, and draws attention to the relativism of phenomena. In particular, it emphasizes differences found across societies with respect to worldviews, notions of self and personhood, and behavioral conventions; these in turn are associated with differences in structural features of the society—the political/economic/material conditions of living. All these parameters shape behavior and its problems, including what may be labeled as adolescent psychopathology. The causes, definition, prevalence, and manifestations of such problems vary in relation to culture. The very terms *adolescent* and *psychopathology* are based on biomedical conventions that are themselves cultural constructs.

A historical approach also challenges the universalism of phenomena labeled as adolescent psychopathology. This approach seeks to understand how, when, and why such phenomena acquired their contemporary shape, form, and meaning. As noted by Foucault (1965, 1978), a historical approach is genealogical: it traces the symbolic and structural (political/economic) factors that, in their integration, provided the conditions for the development, visibility, and seeming naturalness of an area of contemporary life such as adolescent psychopathology. A historical approach is holistic and draws attention to factors that bring about different conditionings of social phenomena through time.

The field of adolescent psychopathology and the discipline of adolescent psychiatry/psychology are recent creations of Western biomedicine. Why have they come about? Some reasons are discussed in this chapter. Since there is comparatively little historical or cross-cultural information pertaining to adolescent psychopathology per se, this chapter concentrates on key theoretical issues with reference to illustrative empirical work. Some information on national differences in adolescent mental health and interethnic comparisons carried out within nations is reviewed. Finally, we consider in more depth three topics—anorexia nervosa, spirit possession, and social aggression—that exemplify the cultural and historical boundedness of adolescent psychopathology. Our goal is to contribute to a fuller understanding of the contemporary Western picture of adolescent psychopathology through which some of its taken-for-granted features lose their apparent necessity and immutability.

Concepts and Definitions

Adolescence

Adolescence in Western society is a distinct period in the life cycle beginning with events associated with puberty and continuing through the high school years (Bogin, 1988; Elder, 1975; MacDonald, 1988; Rutter, 1980). Universal biological changes linked to this phase of the life cycle are associated with changes in social relationships and psychological experience that mark the movement toward adulthood.

Psychopathology

The term psychopathology is used in a general sense in this chapter. It encompasses problems linked to social and psychological behavior as well as psychiatric disorders. Disturbances associated with depression, mania, schizophrenia, and anxiety that conform to criteria defined by psychologists and psychiatrists are classic examples. Our broad interpretation of the term includes phenomena such as substance abuse and juvenile delinquency.

Culture

Culture means learned and widely shared ideas (attitudes, values, beliefs) that influence behavior. Culture is a system of standards for behavior, a fabric of meanings that serve to interpret experience and guide action (D'Andrade, 1984; Geertz, 1973). It is transmitted through verbal and nonverbal learning, whereas genetic information is passed on by inheritance of genes. Culture has a history because values, knowledge, and beliefs are handed down, learned, and transformed from prior forms.

Ethnicity and culture are concepts often used interchangeably in biomedicine. In a strict sense, *culture* refers purely to ideational material, information that is learned. In affecting basic conceptualizations (such as those of self, other, and the world) culture exerts a strong influence on mental contents and experiences, and hence on behavior and its problems. *Ethnicity* is a term derived from *ethos* (meaning culture), but it is also used to describe a social group's country of origin. Because of differences in the genetic structure of populations the term *ethnicity* also implies genetic and other biological factors that are distinctive of an individual given his or her population of origin (the same, of course, could be said of *culture*, if the latter were viewed broadly). Both *culture* and *ethnicity* draw attention to lifestyle differences, including ways of thinking, feeling, and ways of programming the daily cycle—including the conceptualization and care of the body and how it is experienced.

Culture (like ethnicity) influences psychopathology, neurovegetative functioning, and somatic experience. Culture shapes child-rearing patterns, family styles of interaction, social class mores, the ethos of schools, social networks and peer relations, general societal standards, and individual cognitive styles and personality structures. It defines basic conventions about the self, emotion, morality, stages of life, personal goals, and acceptable behavior. Physical environmental factors and material conditions affect adolescent behavior and psychopathology, but these influences are always contextualized by the cultural meanings ascribed to them.

History

In discussing historical factors we take into consideration ideologies, social activities, and structures found mainly in early modern and modern Western societies (roughly from the sixteenth through the nineteenth centuries). In particular, our concern is the social history of what has been termed *mentalities*, or cultural factors affecting mental outlook and social behavior as they pertain to adolescence and its problems (Chartier, 1988; Hunt, 1989; Whiting & Whiting, in press). Much of the previous description of culture also pertains to the historical perspective, because the terms *adolescent* and *psychopathology* are treated as problematic from a diachronic point of view.

The Larger Context

Ecological, social, and political/economic factors also affect human development (Bronfenbrenner, 1977). Super and Harkness (1986) provide a model of the developmental niche in which biological, cultural, and familial factors together create special conditions for rearing infants and children. Child-rearing traditions are realized in distinctive social settings and are characterized by distinctive modes of interacting with infants and children. This model was designed to apply to young children but is relevant to all important transitional and developmental phases, including adolescence (Whiting, 1980). In this framework, cultural values and historical context each receive emphasis in a naturalistic picture of development grounded in biology and ecology. Ideally, material pertaining to all these factors should be integrated in order to understand adolescent psychopathology in its complex totality.

Cultural Anthropological Perspective

From a cultural anthropological point of view, adolescent psychopathology is treated as an *etic* category following standards drawn from psychology/psychiatry (this approach parallels the way a linguist performs a phon*etic* analysis of language; see Headland, Pike, & Harris, 1990; Pike, 1967). Etic analyses allow comparative studies of a preselected and predefined problem. But in various societies we also seek to discover *emic* understandings that are analogous to adolescent psychopathology (just as a linguist, through phon*emic* analyses of language, seeks to understand basic sound units of meaning in a different language community). Emic analyses identify locally defined categories and their meanings.

An etic, scientific observer can safely claim that all societies harbor forms of psychopathology in each of their population subgroups. Genetic vulnerabilities and social environmental stresses can bring about biological changes termed anxiety, schizophrenia, and depression. Some forms of adolescent psychopathology—such as excessive aggression, disturbances in mood regulation, and psychotic disturbances—are human universals since they are based on panhuman genetic vulnerabilities and environmental stressors. But cultures vary in the way they construct social behavior and psychological experience, and so adolescent psychopathology is subject to the intellectual challenge of cultural relativism (Fabrega, 1989, 1992; Spiro, 1986).

Adolescence As a Life Stage

Biologically determined bodily changes initiated by puberty are universal (MacDonald, 1988). Boys and girls in all societies go through the endocrine-based growth and sexual maturational changes of puberty (Adams, Montemayor, & Gullotta, 1989). Even among nonhuman primates, puberty has behavioral visibility traceable to endocrine changes (Montemayor, 1990). Seeing a biological basis in pubertal changes, some scholars have reasoned that psychosocial aspects of adolescence—including features suggesting "storm and stress"—must also be deemed universal (Schlegel & Barry, 1991). The timing of the maturational changes in humans varies across individuals and societies, given differences in nutrition, ecology, physical activities, and differential survival of fast-developing children (Whiting & Whiting, 1975; Worthman, 1991), but the biological characteristics of the transitional period indicate that puberty is a universal life stage (Montemayor, 1990).

Societies, though, vary with respect to whether—and, if so, how strongly—they mark adolescence as a distinct phase of life. A well-marked and elaborated social category of adolescence characterizes contemporary Western societies. But evidence from other cultural contexts adds complexity to the global picture.

According to a study by Davis and Davis (1989) in Morocco, both puberty and something like adolescence are recognized conceptually, and lexical units mark the transition from childhood to adulthood. But it is not clear that these Moroccans set adolescence apart as a life stage possessing distinctive behavioral features. Furthermore, Davis and Davis found much variation among their Moroccan informants in word choice for people between the categories of childhood and adulthood, with some choosing the words *'azri/'azba* (bachelor/virgin), and others the term *shabb/shabba* (youth; p. 51). People also disagreed as to which years in the life cycle corresponded to these categories. With such a low degree of consensus as to labels and ages for adolescence, one wonders how formalized a stage it is. Puberty, with its physical markers, seems a more key phase, a turning point at which such behavioral changes as the child listening less to the parents are noticed.

A situation more clearly and consistently like our concept of adolescence exists among the Australian aborigines who Burbank (1988) studied. Their indigenous language includes terms that translate as "young girls" or "single girls," as well as "young boys" or "single boys" (p. 4). Importantly, however, the period of maidenhood for girls has only recently become one of some duration (3 to 4 years) due to girls beginning to attend school.

Among the group of Eskimos with whom Condon (1987) worked the term *inuhaag* denoted young people making the transition from childhood to adulthood. This phase is associated with the marks of physical maturation surrounding puberty, as well as functional markers: traditionally, a young boy would hunt his first small game during this time, and a young girl would do more household chores and her own sewing.

One of the most differentiated life-cycle structures is found in the Nigerian village reported on by Hollos and Leis (1989). Only two phases (from birth to 2 years, and 60 years and over) are shared by males and females. The differing phases that include adolescents are as follows:

kala awou (male, 6 to 14 years)

kala pesi (male, 15 to 25 years)

ereso (female, 13 to 19 years)

erera (female, 19 to 14 years)

Note that the breaks in categories for males occur after 14 and 25 years, while crucial divides occur for females at 12 and 19 years. As in many other contexts, major changes in children/adolescents roles and responsibilities—as well in the content of these life-cycle stages—are changing rapidly due to the spread of schooling.

One of the life cycles with the least marking of a Western-style adolescence is documented by Fricke (1986), who reported on Tamang villagers of Nepal. For the Tamang, life is a predictable process, with events marking changes in social status at more or less the same time for everybody. The important transitions after birth move without trauma from the first hair cutting to receiving one's inheritance after marriage, establishing a new household, and eventually death. By the age of 8, rural Tamang children of both genders are in a transitional phase to adult roles as they gradually take up tasks such as cooking and farming. Adolescence is neither a named nor a ritually marked phase.

Whiting, Burbank, and Ratner (1986), along with Schlegel and Barry (1991), contrast the amplification of the category of adolescence in preindustrial societies and industrial societies. In the former, preadolescents generally undergo gradual behavioral changes as they begin to learn adult roles and tasks. Gender segregation increases, and boys and girls spend more time with same-sex adults. Peer groups become more important. The educational mode is "learning while doing," directly under adult supervision, since there is little that resembles formal schooling. Special rituals for young males and females commonly—but not universally—mark the transition from childhood to adulthood. In preindustrial societies, a smooth continuum seems to exist between developing cognitive and neuromuscular abilities, actual skills required, and role behaviors expected in adulthood (which are learned progressively). The ethnographic evidence argues against a socially marked stage of adolescence as is found in contemporary Western society.

Historical analyses also support the position that preindustrial societies lack a marked phase comparable to adolescence in the industrial West. In a comparative analysis of the transition to adulthood in the United States and Japan during the first half of the twentieth century, Hogan and Michozuki (1988) argue that structural changes affecting labor force participation, education, and family formation patterns in contemporary times delayed the attainment of adulthood and created an adolescent phase where none previously existed in both societies.

Culture and Adolescent Psychopathology: Theoretical Issues

According to Western biomedicine, psychopathology encompasses specific psychiatric disorders and general problems of adaptation. From a cultural anthropological standpoint, psychopathology can be equated with behavior that in local systems of meaning is judged as deviant and/or as a breakdown in adaptation. There is a logical discontinuity between the biomedical and the local cultural frames of reference. Human behavioral breakdowns that are handled as medical according to local cultural criteria constitute analogues of psychiatric disorders or illnesses; for example, psychosis and some types of spirit possession (Fabrega, 1992). Behavioral breakdowns that are defined psychiatrically are examples of cultural universals, although these may or may not be handled locally as illness. Conversely, some problems of behavior that by local criteria are defined and treated as medical may or may not conform to the pattern of psychiatric disorders (Fabrega, 1992).

Each facet of what is viewed as psychopathological in any society is under the sway of culture (Fabrega, 1989a, b, 1993). The manifestations of psychopathology—especially content, but also form—bear the impact of culture. Anxiety, depression, and psychosis can be viewed from physiological and neuropsychological standpoints as universal, but how they are realized reflects cultural influences: what an individual is anxious about or troubled over, how he or she behaves when anxious or depressed, or his or her picture of reality as distorted by the psychotic process all vary in relation to cultural dictates (Fabrega, 1993). How much cultural variability exists with respect to syndromes of behavior (the exact line separating the universal from the culturally relative) across societies varies depending on the type of problem being considered (e.g., psychosis versus general anxiety). The delineation of pathology from what is normal (or acceptable) across and within societies is also highly fluid.

The preceding implies two varieties of cultural relativism: the universal versus culturally relative appearance or manifestations of psychopathology, and the universal versus culturally relative labeling of behavioral phenomena as normal or pathological. These generalizations are basic to cultural psychiatry and, while controversial, can be applied to adolescent psychopathology as well (Fabrega, 1992, 1993).

Cultural Shaping. Cultural anthropologists have proposed two approaches to the study of how culture shapes psychopathology. One approach, dating from the early decades of the twentieth century, focuses on the links between culture and personality (Singer, 1961). In this tradition, the family structure and child-rearing practices prevailing in a society are held to lead to the formation of personalities characterized by distinctive styles of psychological and social function, malfunction, and conflicts (LeVine, 1973, 1989, 1990; Singer, 1961). Moreover, the personalities are seen as fitted to the projective institutions, values, and guidelines of the culture. A correspondence is posited between developmental influences, personality organization or function, behavioral malfunctions (or psychopathology), and the form and meaning of cultural institutions. This approach is psychodynamic in that theories of development and personality function stemming from psychoanalysis are important, although it is eclectic enough to encompass principles from cognitive psychology and behavioral analysis. The key point is that this view operates in terms of principles of Western psychology.

A newer emphasis, termed "cultural psychology" (Shweder, 1990, 1991), examines human psychologies in terms of the logic and meaning of a particular culture. Self and personhood as culturally shaped are dominant concerns. The concept of personality seems less important, perhaps because of its Western and especially psychodynamic overtones. Cultural psychology views emotion, as an example, not as a phenomenon packaged in terms of such concepts as unconscious defenses pertaining to anxiety and depression, but in terms of local categories that mark and explain the connection between meaningful social activity and persons and their reactions to those activities (Jenkins, 1991; Lutz, 1988). In this perspective, adolescent psychopathology encompasses culturally defined behavioral anomalies that are locally judged as deviant and/or disvalued among persons entering adult roles. The cultural psychology approach emphasizes less the dynamics of how behavior and "pathology" are produced (as explained by Western psychological science) but attends more to the construction, meaning, and organization of culturally appropriate behavior. In this approach, culture is seen as pervasively manifest in child rearing and modes of socializing the young (which are locally implicit or emphasized as explanations of how persons and selves are formed and when, how, and why they might possibly deviate from the acceptable; Schieffelin & Ochs, 1986).

Two Perspectives on the Self. A critical feature of adolescence in contemporary Western thinking about mental health involves the concepts of self and identity. The latter means, as in the work of Erickson (1963, 1980), an adolescent's acquisition of a distinct sense of himself or herself as unique and separate. In contemporary Western societies, the sense of self or identity is said to be individualistic. Establishment of this sense of an individualist self-identity—in the context of a world that is construed as secular, rational, and impersonal and where challenges, expectations, and demands appear prohibitive and formidable—is assumed to underlie decisions and life career pathways that contribute to the prevalence of many of the behavioral and psychological problems labeled as adolescent psychopathology (this position is discussed in more detail below). This kind of developmental framework is used in cross-cultural studies but requires an accommodation to indigenous psychologies, selves, and worldviews.

According to some cultural psychologists, however, preindustrial societies produce more socially oriented selves, and the behavioral environment of the person is not necessarily perceived of as impersonal, secular, and/or disconnected from the individual (Shweder, 1990, 1991). Instead, the concept of a person is articulated with emphases placed on situational factors, where morality, social responsibility, and group solidarity are dominant.

In contrast, the universalist, biomedical view emphasizes that adolescence (and childhood more generally) is a period when distinctive forms of biological disorders become manifest. In this view, adolescent psychopathology is concerned with the form and appearance of disorders that are generic to humans, but which appear during the period of development when biological maturation takes on an adult cast. Important descriptive parameters are seen as universal, with minor surface variations in content. Moreover, similarities and differences between adolescent and adult disorders (indeed, the continuity of such disorders across the life span) are an important concern to psychiatrists (Rutter & Garmezy, 1983).

The centrality of concepts pertaining to the self, person, and identity in any formulation of adolescence generally—and adolescent psychopathology more specifically—cannot be overestimated. These concepts are devices in terms of which a researcher makes analytical sense of adolescent behavior and psychopathology. They are also concepts that pertain to how the adolescent himself or herself makes sense of phenomena in the social world. The problem of cultural variability divides into two questions. First, is what Western analysts mean by *adolescent* different cross-culturally from what others mean by analogous terms? Second, is the adolescent himself or herself different (in a social-psychological-behavioral sense) as a function of culture? The first question involves possible differences in modes of construal, a weaker claim about cultural variability. The second question involves possible differences in the materiality of the entity being referred to (e.g., adolescents or adolescent psychopathology), a stronger claim about cultural variability. The culture-and-personality perspective and the Eriksonian perspective argue for universal social psychological characteristics and rely on Western conventions. Cultural psychology argues for social psychological *and* constructionist differences that vary significantly across societies.

Cultural variability pertaining to the self (in terms of construal and, by implication, materiality as well) has strongly been challenged by cultural anthropologist Melford Spiro. In a theoretical paper, Spiro (1986) argues against strong universalist claims, pointing out some negative implications and drawing on an informed history of anthropological reasoning. While remaining open to the possibility of cultural variability, Spiro suggests that "classic" studies in fact reveal that researchers are comparing "apples and pears" instead of disclosing putative cultural variability on perspectives of the self. By implication, Spiro raises the question that the manifestations of psychiatric disorders and social maladaptation more generally across societies may not necessarily be filtered or expressed through highly discrepant psychological structures pertaining to selves and persons. Spiro's analysis leads us to challenge the claim of variability in our understanding of adolescent psychopathology and to consider the possibility of greater commonality in the construal and material nature of self, identity, and behaviors pertaining to adolescent psychopathology.

Culture and Adolescent Psychopathology: Empirical Approaches

The Adolescent Phase. The range of opinion on the social and cultural recognition of an adolescent phase—one that is neither childhood or adulthood—extends from Schlegel and Barry's (1991) treatment of "adolescence as a universal social and cultural phenomenon" (p. vii) to Whiting et al.'s (1986) exploration of variation in the duration of what is to them a transitional phase. The latter authors consider the example of "maidenhood" for females (a phase like adolescence in that it extends from menarche to marriage) and find cross-cultural differences that extend from very long phases to nonexistence. Both studies, notably, rely on the same standard cross-cultural sample of preindustrial rural societies. Extending our purview to studies of industrial urban societies, we find analyses such as that of Hogan and Michozuki (1988) comparing the preadult stages in the life cycle of a sample of North Americans and Japanese. They find striking differences in the length of the postchild/preadult phases in the two populations, and between males and females. Overall, our assessment is that the anthropological and sociological evidence supports the side of variation, with some societies not recognizing or elaborating the adolescent phase, while others have notable differences in the marking and elaboration of this phase for males and females.

The universalists and the relativists, logically, have different explanations for their findings. Universalists, largely biological determinists, point to the determining role of surging hormones and the possibly adaptive function that the marking and elaborating of adolescence may serve by allowing a society to provide better training for the adult phases (Barry, 1991). Relativists look to cultural factors (e.g., child training, ethos) or the larger social/economic context (e.g., labor markets) as affecting the existence, marking, duration, and elaboration of adolescence.

The cross-cultural picture of adult identity formation entails some separation of preadults from parents and family and the establishment of bonds and relations with persons of similar age and social status. Whiting and Whiting (1975) find that social customs cross-culturally encourage the separation of boys from girls before the beginning of the growth spurt: "Although the data are scanty, it is probably that in many [preindustrial] societies cross-sex interaction is infrequent until a year or two into adolescence, and even then will be significantly less frequent than same-sex inter-action" (p. 4). In addition, societies have well established norms for the division of labor between boys and girls.

Schlegel and Barry (1991) state that in preindustrial societies cross-cul-turally, preadults spend more time with age peers than than they did in ear-lier stages. This trend is more common in males (who often play and congregate in groups) than females (who tend to stay within their natal family, where relations with older female relatives continue to be impor-tant). Relying on literature from child development, ethology, and prima-tology, Schlegel and Barry propose a model that points to "(1) self-imposed or self-segregation of the sexes that commonly occurs in preindustrial soci-eties by adolescence if not before, and (2) the greater extension of boys than girls from close relations with same-sex adults and, consequently, the greater salience of peer groups for boys than girls" (p. 199). In drawing on nonhuman primate studies and emphasizing universalism, this approach suggests sociobiologic roots for the kinds of peer relations that provide opportunities for experiences that can contribute to a sense of self identity and separateness.

Adolescent Psychopathology. If adolescence, in a social and cultural sense, does not exist in all societies, then the "storm and stress"—and psy-chopathologies—associated in some cultures with adolescence would not always be found, at least not to the same extent. This possibility inspired Margaret Mead's research on adolescence in Samoa, published in her book *Coming of Age in Samoa: A Psychological Study of Primitive Youth for Western Civilization* (1928). Mead conducted local-level field research, observing child behavior, peer group interaction, training for adult skills, and boy-girl relationships in the premarital phase. Her conclusion was that in Samoa adolescence as a phase did exist, but that it was not extremely stressful and turbulent as it was said to be in the United States. She depict-ed adolescence as the "best" phase in the life cycle, since adult responsibili-ties had not yet landed on the shoulders of the young, and they were therefore free to enjoy life.

A sharp critique of Mead's work came decades later in Derek Freeman's *Margaret Mead and Samoa: The Making and Unmaking of an Anthropologi-cal Myth (1983)* Freeman attacked Mead's methodology as inadequate, claiming that she had been deluded by her informants and had otherwise overlooked evidence that would have contradicted her results, especially in terms of child punishment practices, male-male competition for rank, ado-lescent male violence, suicide, and rape of females by males. Freeman dis-misses Mead's judgment of nonstressful adolescence in Samoa as a false "negative instance" and attempts to reaffirm the biological basis of adoles-cence as universally stressful.

In turn, Freeman's critique has been the subject of numerous rebuttals. In one of the most thorough, Leacock (1993) claims that Freeman ignores both history and gender relations: for example, his use of 1960s data on violence and delinquency among Samoan youths cannot be taken as indicative of social conditions that prevailed when Mead did her fieldwork. Leacock examines several phases of Samoan history and discusses the rapid and profound changes following World War II that produced the context of Freeman's findings on adolescent turmoil.

The universalist position on stress in adolescence is strongly stated by Schlegel and Barry (1991).

> We consider it unlikely that adolescence can be a stress-free time for young people or their parents, as relationships in the family constellation are changing rapidly at the same time that the child's body is taking on new conformations and capabilities. With the accompanying internal stresses, both the originating hormonal changes and those involving unlearning and relearning, it seems to us implausible that adolescence would be experienced without ambiguities in family attachments. However, these reactions need not be of such magnitude as to result in physical or mental pathology nor need they erupt into antisocial behavior. (pp. 12–13)

The wording in this statement gives an ambiguous message. First is the supposition that adolescence cannot be "stress-free" (an undefined term), and then comes a retrenchment to the concept of "ambiguities in family attachments." The implication overall, however, is that some form of storm and stress is an expectable behavioral outcome for adolescents, with the possibility always lurking of something more pathological.

Little anthropological research deals directly with adolescent psychopathology, viewed as either a local construct or as a clinical phenomenon. In medical/psychological anthropology, scholars who have done excellent research on local categories of illness and their general meaning (Good, 1977; Kleinman, 1988; Obeyesekere, 1981) have tended to overlook children and adolescents.

Recent analyses of such local syndromes as "brain fag" (Prince, 1985) and *ataques de nervios* (Guarnaccia, de la Cancela, & Carrillo, 1989)—including Low's (1985) comparison of *nervios* in different settings of Latin America—delineate the varying form and content of such syndromes among adults. Several other studies, although not concentrating on adolescents per se, contribute to our understanding of what psychopathology means within particular local cultural systems (see Littlewood & Lipsedge, 1985, for a review). Scheper-Hughes's (1979) study of schizophrenia in Ireland is notable in that, although using a Western diagnostic category, she emphasizes the relationship between social organization, kinship, and child socialization patterns that appear to place certain offspring at greater risk for psychopathology than others, especially high-parity sons. The view of psychopathology as medical involves studying categories of illness (e.g., depression, anxiety, schizophrenia) with a view to clarifying their "natural history." These studies are epidemiologically inspired and concentrate on the effect of culture on such things as cause, manifestations, and course. Researchers working in this mode usually handle an etic category of illness as fixed in content and form, requiring only elaboration with respect to distribution, prevalence, and duration or course (see below for fuller elaboration). Manson, Shore, and Bloom (1985) followed this approach in their study of depression among Native American adults, though this study did also attempt to discern Native American categories of feeling and experience.

Another example is the problem of illicit drug use among adolescents, which has become prominent in recent decades (Bailey, 1989; Johnston, O'Malley, & Bachman, 1987; Stiffman & Davis, 1990). Paton and Kandel (1978) conducted a large study in New York State and showed that depressive mood and normlessness were positively associated with use of illicit drugs (other than marijuana) and that the association varied in relation to ethnicity. This study and many others conducted within nations have an epidemiological focus and seek to show correlates of ethnicity or minority status (related epidemiological studies are reviewed below).

An excellent illustration of how culture and society interact to shape behavior in ways that bear on the topic of adolescent psychopathology is provided by Grob and de Rios (1992), who analyze adolescent hallucinogenic plant ingestion during initiation rituals among Australian aboriginal males, Tshogana Tsonga females of Mozambique, and Chumash youths of Southern California. In these preindustrial, traditional tribal societies, a "psychotechnology" operates to manage successful transitions into adulthood. This institutional means, explicit in its directives, creates altered states of consciousness that promote a death of childhood and a rebirth as an adult. Elders supervise initiation rituals in which plant hallucinogens are used to attain visionary quests. By instructing youths on the consequences of ingestion, elders are able to induce expectations; in carrying out sometimes painful mutilation practices they facilitate receptivity in the adolescents. The sacred character of the plants, the honored status accorded the rituals, and the socially valued transition into an adult status that is strongly sought and cherished imbue the whole experience with cultural significance and meaning. Absence of abuse of these substances in tribal societies is emphasized:

> Such drugs have been accepted to be of sacred origin and have been treated with awe and reverence. In tribal societies, plant hallucinogens were in limited supply and protected from abuse and profanation by deviants insofar as they remained under adult control and administration. . . . Thus, psychoactive substances in tribal societies were not abused, but perceived as sacraments facilitating controlled entry into valuable states of consciousness in which "visions" essential for the continued existence of the society could be assessed. (pp. 133–134)

Grob and de Rios compare this institution for adolescent transition and initiation with the absence of meaning pertaining to such transitions in contemporary Western society:

> Contemporary society no longer possesses viable, pre-established paths to initiation. The tribal process of initiation culminates as rebirth into a new life, endowed with special qualities and new meaning. The coming of age in non-state level tribal societies was a solemn rite of passage with the initiates consecrated into adulthood. In the absence of such initiations, we are left with widespread alienation and despair. (p. 135)

An implication of the analysis is that the erosion of values and purposes in the minds of many contemporary Western adolescents, the absence of institutions concerned with promoting and managing a culturally meaningful transition into adulthood, and the ready availability of drugs with no link to sacred or socially celebratory functions are key factors that promote substance abuse, a prominent form of contemporary adolescent psychopathology.

Historical Frame of Reference

Theoretical Background

The contemporary Western idea of adolescence as a period in the life cycle marked by conflicts and disturbances is viewed by many historians as a creation of the late nineteenth and early twentieth centuries. The writings and related social activities of child advocates and persons like G. Stanley Hall (1904) were instrumental in drawing attention to adolescence as a special period in the life career (Demos, 1972; Demos & Demos, 1969; Modell, Furstenberg, & Hershberg, 1976; Parry-Jones, 1989; Walk, 1964). Hall's (1904) emphasis on the peculiarities of the emotional experiences of adolescents contributed to the picture of psychological storm and stress.

The historical study of adolescence is guided by the concept of the self and its social identity (Erickson, 1968; Demos & Demos, 1969; Gillis, 1981; Kett, 1971). To appreciate the historical relevance of this concept for the comparative study of adolescence, one must consider the changes that have taken place in the meanings surrounding personhood and self-identity in European culture since the end of the seventeenth century. Such changes are dialectally related to changes in the political, economic, and social structure, the family, and values related to religion and secularization. Effects on the self are chronicled in the writings of literary historians, social psychologists, social philosophers, and social historians (Anderson, 1971; Gergen, 1971; Hanning, 1977; Langbaum, 1979; MacIntyre, 1981; Morris, 1972; Putz, 1979; Sennett, 1974; Sypher, 1962; Trilling, 1971;

Weintraub, 1978). This literature and its relevance to the study of a histori-cal transformation in adolescents' sense of identity and their experience of self is superbly summarized by Baumeister (1986, 1987) and Baumeister and Tice (1986). The following summary draws on Baumeister's schema and involves looking at influences taking place during the late medieval, Puritan (sixteenth to eighteenth centuries), Romantic (late eighteenth and early nineteenth centuries), Victorian (middle and late nineteenth century), modern (early twentieth century) and postmodern (late twentieth century) eras.

Evidence suggests that during the late medieval era in Europe knowl-edge of the self was not regarded as an important problem. Introspection and the experiencing of inner struggles seems not to have been a promi-nent mode of self-awareness; instead, selfhood seems to have involved purely functional considerations related to one's work and place in society. "Incipient introspection, awareness of separateness of different persons, and sense of unity of each single life all may be regarded as prerequisites for making self-knowledge into a problem. The late Middle Ages satisfied these prerequisites" (Baumeister, 1987, p. 165).

A crucial next step involved divorcing the self from its outer appear-ances and station in life and allowing that the self constituted an inner and private space that could be elaborated and had a private basis. "The inner nature of selfhood, which is regarded as axiomatic by much modern psy-chological thought, seems to have become a common conception first in the 16th century" (Baumeister, 1987, p. 165). The Puritan and Victorian eras added to these developments concerns about sincerity and self-decep-tion that rendered self-knowledge tentative and uncertain. The modern and postmodern periods have further weakened notions of authenticity and inner coherence.

Paralleling these changes was a breakup in the unity of the way the social world was conceptualized—that is, of the "great chain of being" that precisely structured every person's location in society. Concomitant changes in the structure and function of the family and opportunities for independent work played complementary roles in effecting a transforma-tion of selfhood toward entailing self-knowledge, criteria of self-definition, the ideas of self-potential and self-fulfillment, and the relation of the self to society.

As summarized by Baumeister (1986), the cultural conception of adoles-cence changed from that of a period with no striking defining psychologi-cal markers (in an agricultural society, physical size and development were all-important) to one where adolescents required extensive supervision by adults because of the former's putative indecision, awkwardness, and vul-nerability. Socioeconomically, adolescents prior to the Victorian era were semidependent on their parents, had few but well-defined responsibilities (they frequently were "fostered out," were apprenticed, or worked as domestic servants), lacked power to choose their spouse or vocation, were channeled by parents into distinct adult roles, and could support themselves by work but had little control of money. By the turn of the twentieth century, they lived and were economically dependent on their parents, had few or no responsibilities outside of school, and slowly acquired the power of choosing their own occupation and mate. "Teenagers of past centuries were generally occupied with preparations for fixed, particular adult roles that had been chosen for them. Their developmental task involved finishing the highly specific training for the allotted adult role, and otherwise just passing the time until the adult role would become available—such as by an offer of marriage, successful graduation from apprentice to master, or inheritance" (Baumeister, 1986, pp. 188–189). Eventually, multiple options regarding occupation and marriage came to characterize the adolescent experience.

Religious conversions and reawakenings had been characteristic of the developmental process leading to adolescence. Inner virtues and decisions to pursue a life of character as clearly dictated by society were paramount. But this changed, as "the modern adolescent is permitted or required to choose and develop his or her own values. Identity crisis has replaced decision of character" (Baumeister, 1986, p. 188). In short, the adult identity has come to be a matter of choice and definition for adolescents themselves. As alluded to above, this was paralleled by changes in the structure and social psychology of the family: the family no longer constituted a self-sufficient unit economically; children and adolescents became potential wage earners, emotional relationships became increasingly important, the private life of home and family replaced the public life in the society, families consisted of fewer children that tended to be of similar age, and the average age of leaving home increased.

All of these developments contributed to new intergenerational conflicts and raised the salience of such adolescent problems as moodiness, developing sexuality, and penchant for mischief. The presence of the adolescent in the home, for example, may have rekindled so-called oedipal conflicts and heightened sexual awareness among adolescents, as well as parental concerns over masturbation. The structural developments in society and the changes in the experiences of adolescents contributed to the creation of the psychological moratorium which was emphasized by Erikson. Along with this came an extreme age segregation of adolescents in schools, the prominence of peer groups in their daily lives, and the postponing of an adult identity. Finally, the increasing secularization and loss of ideological consensus in society deprived adolescents of accepted and traditional religious/and spiritual symbols that could be used as models of how to resolve crises and conflicts created by the modern, capitalist world's new set of expectations and demands.

In summary, the attention given by psychologists and social critics to adolescence and its perceived pathology during the late nineteenth century was possible because of historical changes, including transformations in Western society associated with increasing industrialization, urbanization, and population growth. Requirements of a capitalist-industrial society had the effect of subjecting children and adolescents to increasingly longer periods of formal schooling as preparation for adult role functioning, yet economic pressures increased the value of these groups in the work place. Child labor laws were enacted, compulsory education became widespread, and the schooling period increased. These transformations contributed to the creation of a distinct period in the life career when children and youths became isolated from family settings and work responsibilities. This allegedly new period of enforced transition and restraint, the argument runs, created a group characterized by distinctive outlooks, expectations, conflicts, and social maladjustments (Bakan, 1972; Gillis, 1981, Springhall, 1986).

This picture of contemporary adolescence is partly substantive and partly constructionist. It refers to real changes in society and to symbols that elaborate on and explicate the consequences of the changes. Implicit in this new picture of adolescence and its psychopathology are four related ideas. First is the idea of a new structural formation—a social group (adolescents) created as a by-product of social differentiation and complexity linked to industrial capitalism. A necessary feature was the intervention of the state in the control and regulation of the process of capitalist development and the protection of exploited population subgroups (i.e., children), as well as the imposition of educational standards required by capitalism. Second is the idea of self-consciousness. In response to their social sequestration, adolescents became more aware of their unique position in society and of themselves as a group. Distinctive outlooks, challenges, and expectations (for placement in adult roles) came to characterize them. Ordeals created by biology and society made for a forging of a new social identity with a potential and momentum for anticipated achievement. Opportunities arose for adolescents to experiment with new configurations of the self. Third is the idea that this group was exploited and manipulated. Capitalists discovered a new teenage market for leisure; stimulations initiated by the market played on the biological and maturational strings of adolescents to create rhythms of sexuality, diet, aggression, and (eventually) substance abuse that proved injurious. Fourth is the idea of pathology linked to adolescence as a social stage, a theme explicit in the writings of Hall and still prevalent in much of the literature. Thus adolescents came to be seen as oppressed, conflicted, burdened by their ordeals, and psychologically disturbed if not ill.

Revisions and elaborations have been made of this historiographical account of adolescence as a distinct pathology of modern industrial society. It gained visibility and momentum in the 1960s when Demos and Demos (1969) wrote their classic article, the ideas of Erikson involving identity had an important initial impact, and social historians began to examine critically the early modern period for clues about adolescence and its possible associated disturbances. Many new empirical studies arose to challenge the idea that adolescence was created in the late nineteenth century and, more specifically, the picture of disturbance, despair, and dissatisfaction.

Empirical Findings

On Adolescence. Social historians have sought to clarify how adolescents fared in an era when no institution existed that separated the adolescent from active participation in the society and (later) when formal schooling was not compulsory. Did opportunities exist that allowed the adolescent time off from structured work routines, time for self-examination regarding future prospects, and time for experimentation regarding their own identity? Is adolescence universally a period during which boys and girls are challenged psychologically by social transitions and the prospect of emerging adult responsibilities? How much of what we know of adolescence today is historically and culturally tied to capitalist, industrial society, and how much is general and intrinsic to the developmental stage itself (and hence likely to have been present in earlier societies)?

Some of the travails of adolescence for boys and girls during the medieval era are clearly spelled out by Weinstein and Bell (1982) in their study of the life careers of saints. Although admittedly based on later reconstructed (hagiographical) accounts of the early lives of those destined for saintliness, their second chapter on adolescents nonetheless offers a cultural portrait of this period. In it they provide a vivid account of the expectations carried into and later encountered:

> The life of religion, whether in a monastery, in a hermitage, or on the pilgrim road, was a compelling alternative . . . and countless young men and women responded to its attractions during their years of formation and decision. . . . The death of a parent abruptly ended this time of growth and telescoped the normal period of adolescence into the confines of a "sudden" conversion. . . . the crisis of youth cut short was a very common one in this age of early and sudden death. . . . Many . . . took the death of a parent as a call to religion, even if only a few became saints. (p. 56)

In her book on the life and trial of a lesbian nun in Italy during the later medieval period, Brown (1986) echoes a similar theme:

> From the moment of her birth, Bennedetta was destined to become a nun. . . . It may be difficult for us to understand and accept [the father's] decision about his daughter's future—a decision made in total disregard for what her wishes might be once she grew up. . . . She was not alone in

being denied a say in what to do with her own life. Most girls of her day were not consulted about the major decision of their lives, whether to enter a convent or marriage. That judgement was made by parents when their daughters were too young either to assent or object. (p. 22)

In her study, Brown goes on to detail the ordeals of young girls confined in convents and discusses the pressures and demands that frequently had their expression in altered states of consciousness and dissociation. These were not regarded as pathological, but they nonetheless entail social disruptions and clearly seem to be a result of privations and stresses encountered. Similar experiences characterized adolescent boys, whether they were destined for a role in religion or in the chivalric life of the time.

Davis's (1971) account of youth groups and *charivaris* (gangs associated with rebellion and unruliness) in late medieval France provides one example of an institution that provided young, unmarried males opportunities to examine and challenge existing traditions. The groups banded together and mocked social institutions, elders, and events of social importance in their respective communities. The activities of the youth groups constituted "a carnival treatment of reality, with an important function in the village" (p. 53). The license of the youths was not rebellious; rather, "it was very much in the service of the village community, clarifying the responsibilities that the youth would have when they were married men and fathers, helping to maintain proper order within marriage, and to sustain the biological continuity of the village" (p. 54). Such groups shared some of the functions attributed to adolescence in the contemporary Western model. The youths had rituals to help control their sexual instincts and to allow them some limited sphere of jurisdiction or autonomy in the interval before they were married. The rituals socialized them to the conscience of the community by making them the raucous voice of that conscience.

Elsewhere, Davis (1986) indicates that in preindustrial Europe, young males were sometimes provided settings in which they were allowed to wander beyond the strict confines of role prescriptions. Apprenticeships for males and domestic employment for females prepared youths for adult roles in a controlled setting of authority and work. Davis demonstrates that notions of self were linked to parents and to a hierarchical society where the family played a dominant role. Nevertheless, even where the youths were embedded "in the powerful and structured field of the family" (p. 55), there were avenues for self-definition and self-expression; "the line drawn around the self was not firmly closed" (p. 56). The individual could creatively use his or her family to bring about enhancement and fortune, manipulating the language of love and family to bring about some separation and identity ("strategies for achieving some personal autonomy in a world where in principle parents and husbands ruled"; p. 59). A boy's nature or temperament tended to be invoked in career placements, although in the face of conflicts the threat of disinheritance must have played an important role in securing compliance with parental directives. Women, according to Davis, used their reproductive worth in promoting favored relationships with suitors.

Evidence presented by Davis (1986) indicates that some degree of personal freedom and autonomy was more prevalent among groups of wandering youths in rural French communities—young men searching for odd jobs as shepherds or farmers. In these groups, male youths sought opportunities to learn about themselves, career opportunities, and social and heterosexual relationships. They strayed from conventional modes of conduct and experimented with alternative lifestyles. Conflicts involving aggression, morality, and gender identity had freer expression, which promoted psychological growth and identity stabilization. Pathologies in the Western sense may have existed but were contained by existing social structures and/or resolved in the course of time. These experiences, Davis contends, provided male adolescents with informal periods (analogous to the school years in the modern West) that allowed the resolution of conflicts and the consolidation of psychological identity.

Similar patterns existed elsewhere in preindustrial Europe. Ingram's (1984) study, although not centered on youths, emphasizes that *charivari*-like forms of protest and criticism existed in England. Trexler's (1974) account of urban confraternities of male adolescents in Renaissance Florence demonstrates that contemporaries saw adolescents as a special social group needing direction and control because of their potential for unsocialized aggression and sexuality.

Yarbrough's (1979) description of sixteenth-century Bristol male apprentices asserts that school was not a boundary separating adolescence from adulthood society, nor was it the context in which adolescent identity was formed. The urban adolescent experience was typically one of integration with the adult culture: "His daily participation in the master's household and in the public round of urban life provided him constant and intimate contact with both ideal and real expressions of the burgess identity to which he aspired" (p. 70).

Yarbrough, like Smith (1973), seems intent on refuting the opinion that adolescence is a social stage of psychological turmoil and that social maladjustment emerged only in the nineteenth century. To this end Yarbrough (1979) reports evidence of society's awareness of the need to control the apprentice's sexual attitudes and behavior. Hiner (1975) seems motivated by similar concerns. He analyzed essays published in New England in the first part of the eighteenth century that show an awareness of how social transformations linked to "population growth and migration, the development of a commercialized economy, ecclesiastical disputes and political factionalism" (p. 255) produced a picture of adolescence not unlike the contemporary Western one. Youths were viewed as particularly vulnerable and prone to misrule, and they were targets of revivalist efforts:

> Normally . . . the rebellion of New England youth tended to be less direct, more subtle and individualistic and therefore at times even more difficult for adults to comprehend than the open defiance of modern adolescents. . . . Still, the essential characteristics of youth as described by writers of the early 18th century have a familiar ring to students of modern adolescence. Pride, sensitivity, sociability and spiritual promise are nicely paralleled by modern portrayals of youth as defiant, sexually active, peer oriented, and idealistic; and the delay of consummation of genital maturity may have produced the regressive revival of auto eroticism, grandiosity, and playfulness among New England youth in much the same way that Erik Erickson claims it does in today's young people. (p. 272).

Analogues of Adolescent Psychopathology

The power of the historical approach to understanding a biomedical or psychological problem is demonstrated when the problem in question is shown to be conditioned by prevailing cultural/historical circumstances. A clear example of this constructionist theme is provided by anorexia nervosa and bulimia nervosa (discussed in a later section). For purposes of illustration here, we consider the disease chlorosis, which afflicted adolescent girls during the late nineteenth and early twentieth centuries.

As Brumberg (1982) shows, chlorosis was a form of anemia that was widely reported in female adolescents in the United States during this period. In her study she shows how this diagnosis related to physiology of female adolescents, the medical profession's understanding of menstruation and the female body, and girls' experiences at this point in history.

> In large part, chlorosis was a cultural construction embedded in the context of Victorian medicine and family life. Physicians expected to see chlorosis in adolescent girls in the process of sexual maturation; girls learned to have the disease from family, friends, the popular press, and their doctors. Changes in diet and nutrition after 1900, coupled with increased understanding of ovarian function and iron deficiency anemia, provided only a partial explanation of the disease's eventual decline. By 1920, a changed social environment made chlorosis a social liability for girls and their mothers. (p. 1468).

In short, the diagnosis and treatment of chlorosis can be viewed as a "cultural artifact and somatic phenomenon."

Elsewhere Brumberg (1991) has extended her analysis to the physiology and social psychology of menstruation per se, showing how orientations of the medical profession, traditional lay views pertaining to ordeals of menstruation, and developments in the capitalist economy related to the potential of a teenage market came together to transform meanings and attitudes about menstruation and the behaviors of adolescent girls.

Clearly Brumberg's (1991) studies on menstruation do not relate centrally to the topic of psychopathology as defined today. Nevertheless, they show dramatically how social cultural factors pertinent to a historical period can lead to the production of distinctive disorders. In a fundamental way, the culture of the period as it pertained to adolescent girls provided influential models in shaping illness behaviors and the medical profession. What is termed a disease thus rests on the fragile fabric of medical knowledge and social valuations pertaining to the body and its processes that a society—including its professional, scientific elite—has at the time.

A Wider View

Social historians have reacted to the idea that adolescence and its pathologies are distinctive creations of the late nineteenth and twentieth centuries. While not overtly pathologizing adolescent behaviors, their writings suggest the prevalence of personal difficulties related to sexuality, vocational pursuits, and the control of aggression well before the nineteenth century.

These studies do not concern diagnosable disorders per se but rather activities that go against expected norms and "prosocial" pursuits. For example, using empirical studies, Jessor (1984, 1991) has written about the ways in which social, psychological, and situational factors predict an array of deviant problem behaviors in adolescents. Petersen (1986, 1987) and coworkers (Petersen & Ebata, 1987; Petersen, Susman, & Beard, 1989) have constructed an elaborate model to demonstrate analytically how changes in the family, the individual, and society can produce a range of psychological and social difficulties in adolescents. In the model many variables—social (ethnicity, religion, social class), family (marital status of parents), and school (commitment, grades)—are assessed in relation to adolescent drug use, delinquency, and psychological well-being. Typically these researchers do not deal with clinical populations but with adolescents in school, and their aim is not to diagnose or establish an etiology of disorders but to understand adolescence as a psychosocial experience influenced by a large array of variables that can contribute to deviance and maladjustment. Since the variables employed are very general, the schemas help one to contextualize how analogous conditions in earlier societies might have promoted social maladjustments and behavioral anomalies in the adolescent.

Social historians do not always handle adolescence so pessimistically. Springhall (1986) offers a useful corrective to the claim that adolescence is always marked by psychopathology. Examining the portrait of adolescence in Britain from 1860 to 1960, he reviews critically the tendency of historians to pathologize adolescence and assembles social science literature countering this view. The final chapter of his book is aptly titled: "Conclusions: The Myth of the Adolescent 'Storm and Stress' Syndrome." He claims that "the misleading image of the disturbed adolescent . . . can be blamed for its longevity . . . on such factors as: unrepresentative sampling techniques, the threat posed to the adult by certain deviant forms of adolescent behavior, or on the role of the professional hand-wringers of the mass media . . . in publicizing minority and sensational behavior among the young" (p. 228). In sum, he claims that "adolescence is not to be thought of as an unduly stressful stage in the life cycle. Yet, it is still possible for the historian to conclude that this age group does indeed represent a meaningful and distinctive stage of human development worthy of scholarly investigation" (p. 234).

Selected Epidemiological Approaches

General Issues

Researchers employing an epidemiological strategy, concentrating on the role of social factors in adolescent psychopathology, constitute a third perspective on cultural influences. This approach, as we define it here, is characterized by reliance on biomedical definitions of adolescent psychiatric disorders (e.g., depression, anorexia nervosa) and/or well-publicized social maladjustments (e.g., juvenile delinquency, substance abuse), as well as quantitative data gathered with standard assessment instruments. Two versions of the epidemiological strategy are the intranational and the cross-national approaches. In the former, the researcher examines a particular problem area in one nation, concentrating on cultural differences operationalized in terms of ethnicity or minority status. In the latter, the focus is on rates or correlates of a disorder or problem area across nations or groups of nations. Goals implicit in all intranational and cross-national epidemiological studies include establishing sound prevalence figures of clinically meaningful disorders in order to plan for effective clinical services and finding correlates and properties of disorders resulting from cultural differences or so-called national traditions.

Problems arise in the handling of culture in both approaches. As indicated earlier, one traditional Western approach to studying culture is in the emically oriented study of a preindustrial or non-Western (clearly "other") society. In this way the anthropologist experiences highly contrastive symbolic systems pertaining to the self and social environment, including language, worldview, and religion. The Western anthropologist is thus challenged to unravel the logic of this other culture and to understand local meanings of such concepts as adolescent psychopathology.

In contrast, the epidemiological focus is on differences among minority or ethnic groups within a particular nation. Such differences are not equivalent with culture as understood by emically oriented anthropologists. African Americans as an ethnic group originated in different African societies characterized by different cultures; their identity in American society is conditioned by their background but also by the ecological setting, their socioeconomic status, and their interaction with the Euro-American population. The same can be said for Hispanic Americans, Asian Americans, and Native Americans. In all these examples of putative cultural groups and cultural differences, a range of biological, social, economic, and environmental—as well as cultural and symbolic—factors operate to contribute to identity and behavior.

In a cross-national study of adolescent psychopathology, in contrast, researchers may be confronted with adolescents who speak different languages and embody different national traditions. Cultural differences are nonetheless diluted because adolescents of both nations are usually socialized in highly urbanized and industrial settings where Western secular conventions pertaining to education, occupational choice, and lifestyle pursuits prevail. In cross-national studies of cultural differences in adolescence, shared conventions, traditions, and even contradictions intrinsic to industrial and postindustrial societies operate to reduce differences as they do in the intrasocietal approach.

Community-centered empirical studies that seek to measure the amount and distribution of adolescent psychopathology often employ the logic used in studies involving the epidemiology of childhood (which often includes adolescent) disorders (Anderson, Williams, McGee, & Silva, 1987; Bird et al., 1988; Brandenburg, 1987; Costello, 1989a, b; Costello & Benjamin, 1989; Kashani et al., 1987). Earlier approaches to the measurement of psychopathology in children and adolescents relied on such global Western categories as "maladjusted" or "disturbed" (Gould, Wursch-Hitzig, & Dohrenwend, 1981). A single dimension or continuum extending between positive (wellness) and negative (maladjusted) was the reference for establishing cases, with individual children and adolescents classified on the basis of their scores on a clinical instrument. Newer approaches in epidemiology employ a more rigorous procedure (e.g., Bird et al., 1988).

In epidemiological approaches in general, a psychiatric case is defined as one that involves psychopathology pervasive across settings and persistent over time. Ideally, case ascertainment depends on a categorical diagnosis reached following a clinical examination by a psychiatrist who relies on a standard system of taxonomy and classification of childhood and adolescent disorders. Alternatively, the ascertainment is accomplished via the use of highly structured interviews that conform to systems of classification used in child and adolescent psychiatry. In preadolescents, parents and teachers are sources of information, whereas with adolescents, the subject has also been interviewed because otherwise some (mainly depressive) disorders can be missed (Kovacs, 1989; Kovacs, Gatsonis, Paulaskas, & Richards, 1989).

Individual cases are determined by a two stage–two method approach. First, a sample of population is assessed through the use of a suitable instrument, and individuals at risk are identified during this first stage based on their scores. In the second stage, individuals at risk (together with a random sample of those not scoring above the established cutoff point) are further assessed (Rutter & Sandberg, 1985). Clinical interviews by psychiatrists or lay-administered structured interviews based on symptom inventories are used to arrive at categorical diagnoses.

Empirical Findings

Intrasocietal Studies. A classic epidemiological study of adolescent psychopathology was conducted on the Isle of Wight and focused on 14- and 15-year-olds (Graham & Rutter, 1973; Rutter, Chadwick, & Yule, 1986). It employed the methodology outlined above and established a baseline regarding prevalence figures for psychiatric disorders. In pointing to details of functional adjustment and parent-child relations, this study contradicted many myths about the alienation of adolescents and the high prevalence of psychopathology. Instances of turmoil and pain, though clearly documented, were not of the anticipated scope. Results also allowed appreciation of the continuity between childhood and adolescent problems. In underscoring the importance of child-parent relations in a number of areas and the meaning of alienation, the researchers touched on cultural factors, but the study's emphasis was more on documenting turmoil, new and old disorders, causative factors, and other traditional epidemiologic questions than with cultural considerations (Rutter, 1986).

A study by Kashani et al. (1987) conducted in the United States focused on adolescents ranging from 14 to 16 years old. The two method–two stage procedure was used, with the Child Behavior Checklist (CBCL) serving as the initial screening instrument and categorical diagnoses based on the Diagnostic Interview Schedule for Children (DISC), which was developed through sponsorship of the National Institute of Mental Health. The sample was predominantly white and middle- to upper middle-class. Of the 150 adolescents studied, 41% were found to have at least one DSM-III diagnosis; the researchers obtained a prevalence rate of 17.7% relying on the criterion of severity reflecting the need for treatment. No differences in prevalence between social classes were recorded. A study by Anderson et al. (1987) conducted in New Zealand and focusing on preadolescents (aged 11 years) followed a similar rationale and procedure, though the researchers used a different screening instrument. This study found a comparable prevalence of disorder (17.6%).

Research conducted in Puerto Rico by Bird et al. (1988) illustrates the strengths and weaknesses of the standard epidemiological approach when used cross-nationally to study prevalence of psychiatric disorders in community settings (although this study concentrated on children aged 4 to 16 years, it encompassed a significant number of adolescents and is thus relevant to this discussion). The study employed the CBCL and DISC in the two stage–two method procedure and yielded an overall prevalence rate of 15.8% to 17.9%, strikingly similar to results in comparable epidemiological studies.

Studies of this genre rely on a comprehensive and complex definition of disorder widely shared among the academic community of clinicians/epidemiologists. Bird et al. (1988) illustrate this "standardization emphasis" by reporting alternative measures of maladjustment based on different conventions. The authors imply that in their interpretation of results they rely on empirical (actual correlations with scores) as well as intuitive ("clinical status") notions in defining cases. They report that the "response rate was higher (93.1%) in the San Juan metropolitan area than in the remaining three zones that were farther and less accessible (83%)" (p. 1122). It is possible that in these zones subjects are from less educated, more indigenous households, although the authors point out clearly that "the high population density of Puerto Rico, and the proximity and easy accessibility of practically every point in the island to larger urban areas, makes the concept of 'rurality' virtually meaningless in that setting" (p. 1124).

The authors indicate that the published cutoff points of the CBCL are too low for their sample, since "inordinately high prevalence rates would be obtained if one were to use published cut-off points as a categoric definition or disorder" (p. 1124). This judgment was based on comparison of raw scores among subjects studied in other national settings. In explanation, the authors suggest that (a) culturally, Puerto Rican mothers may overreport symptoms; (b) the instrument's application in Spanish may result in higher scores; (c) differences may be due to the method of administration of the instrument; (d) established norms (based on a population of nonreferred children in Baltimore) may simply be inappropriate for Puerto Rico, which lacks child mental health services (and thus Puerto Rican cases in the community would be referred in other settings); and (e) Puerto Rican children may in fact have a very high prevalence rate based on the DISC. Indeed, if one is to rely entirely on published cutoff points, 50% of Puerto Rican children have a DSM-III diagnosis, a figure not unlike that produced by Kashani et al. (1987).

The epidemiological study by Bird et al. (1988) illustrates the standard rationale of biomedicine. Western-trained and strongly American-influenced clinicians and researchers from a Latin American society use scientifically impeccable strategies and methods to measure prevalence of disorder. The researchers translate key screening and structured interview procedures into Spanish, attempting always to maintain a conceptual equivalence among categories of symptoms and behaviors. Their awareness of epidemiological knowledge allows them also to influence the selection of case criteria that will yield rates of (comparably screened and assessed) disorders similar to those obtained in other national settings. The thrust of their explanatory model, which relies on traditional scientific categories and principles, implicitly assumes an expectation of similar prevalence levels. Cutoff points on clinical measures seem selected to obtain understandable (i.e., roughly comparable) prevalence levels of disorder. When striking differences are obtained, reasons are offered that take into consideration standard alternatives (employing equally standard conceptual categories), or these differences are not explained.

Little in this model uses the concepts of culture or national identity creatively to analyze what child or adolescent psychopathology might mean in the light of local traditions and/or how the identified cases are labeled and handled in community settings. Similarly, little effort has been made to take into account distinctive historical and/or political economic factors pertaining to Puerto Rico that may either contextualize childhood and adolescent psychopathology differently or explain its results. All possible aspects of cultural historical singularity are eliminated in the methods of procedure.

Cross-National Studies. Achenbach, Verhulst, Baron, Dana, and Grard (1987) conducted an informative study using community samples. We review here the results involving responses of parents and teachers about children's behavior. Standard instruments (the CBCL and Teacher's Report Form) were used and accurate translation was emphasized. The study allowed comparison of how parents and teachers in the United States and the Netherlands evaluate the behavior of children from the standpoint of their manifest problems (rated by both parents and teachers) and their manifest competencies (only parents rated these).

American and Dutch parents rated their children's problems similarly. They produced similar overall scores: although scores on many individual items differed significantly across nations, the magnitude of differences in most instances accounted for small amounts of variance, and parents from the two nations produced roughly similar numbers of higher and lower scores. Moreover, when problems were classified as internalizing or externalizing (based on factor analytic studies), no differences were found across parent groups. Teachers' ratings tended to conform to the same pattern. Overall problem scores, while higher for American children, did not differ significantly between the groups; few individual-item score differences accounted for much variability; and although American parents produced a larger number of significantly higher scores on items than did Dutch teachers, the difference was not statistically significant. Again, there were no national differences when items were classified as internalizing versus externalizing.

American parents rated their children's competence higher than did Dutch parents, but in some instances these differences were not culturally meaningful, since they reflected differences in schooling policies in the two nations. Many differences appeared to "reflect American parents' more favorable bias in reporting how well their children do things, as a majority of American parents reported that their children were better than average on a number of items" (Achenbach, et al., 1987, p. 324). Results suggested that "nationality differences indicate that reports of children's competencies may be more culture bound and less subject to cross-cultural standardization than reports of behavioral/emotional problems" (p. 324).

These last two quotations and the published material in the articles are interesting. As in the study done in Puerto Rico (Bird et al., 1988) discussed above, the researchers seek comparability and appear to judge cultural differences as something to be explained away or minimized. The first quotation does not elaborate on why or how Americans come to rate their children more favorably. The second quotation appears to view cultural boundedness or lack of cultural standardization as a problem for the methodology.

An apparent emphasis on methodology, rigor, and comparability of results at the expense of cultural meaning is reflected in the way the authors analyzed certain items. They examined items that both Dutch teachers and parents rated higher in Dutch children than American parents did in their children and, conversely, those items that both American teachers and parents rated higher on their children than did their Dutch peers. The items are provocative; for example, American children were scored higher (by American parents and teachers) on "argues a lot," "fears impulses," "showing off," and "threatens people," whereas Dutch parents and teachers seemed to single out such things as "underactive," "sulks a lot," "likes to be alone," "too dependent," and "feels persecuted." These profiles suggest differences in children's modal behavior or differences in social control strategies, or differences in parental norms and preoccupations. Though their meaning is ambiguous, the differences indicate underlying cultural meanings.

In a clinical study involving referred Dutch and American boys in two age groups (6 to 11 years and 12 to 16 years), Achenbach, Verhulst, Althaus, and Akkerhuis (1988) found great cross-national similarity in the kinds of syndromes characterizing the two nations. This highly complex study compared two national samples in terms of scores on syndrome scales derived from factor analyses of raw scores from each nation. Most syndromes identified in one nation appeared to have their analogue in the other, although even in the most similar scales some items were not shared cross-nationally, and some syndrome scales seemed to have little correspondence across nations. The authors used the syndromal patterns identified in the clinical sample to compare normative data (obtained in previous studies) pertaining to nonreferred Dutch and American boys. They found no differences between nations on any of the scales. All in all, the authors argue for commonality and comparability in the clinical implications of their comprehensive studies. At each phase of their analysis, however, it is possible to show striking cultural differences that are either ignored or minimized in the discussion, reflecting the "standardization emphasis" mentioned earlier.

This group of investigators has been involved in a series of additional cross-national studies that have relied on the CBCL and involve children and adolescents from Australia, Puerto Rico, and Thailand (Achenbach, et al., 1990; Achenbach, Chaiyasit, et al., 1987; Achenbach, Hensley, Phares, & Grayson, 1990; Weiss et al., 1989). In some of these studies, interesting national differences were observed. For example, Puerto Rican children were scored higher by their parents and teachers than were their peers on the mainland of the United States, whereas adolescents in both cultures scored themselves higher than their parents and teachers did. This led the investigators to suggest that different cutoff points may have to be used to compare problems in these two nations. In another study Australian children and adolescents scored significantly higher than Americans on a large number of problem items, and in still another Thai children (only 6- to 11-year-olds were studied there) scored higher than their American cohorts on nearly all problem scores. In the studies of Thai children the authors show convincingly the differences that can be obtained when teachers, instead of parents, do the reporting. All of these studies are notable for their rigorous methodology and sound reasoning about child and adolescent psychopathology. They illustrate that even when one follows standard procedures of method, prominent national differences emerge even between nations that share many values and historical traditions.

The line of research and data produced by Achenbach and collaborators has to be viewed as potentially one of the most important in the area of cultural differences in child and adolescent psychopathology. The complexity of the material and diversity of themes that it touches on with respect to cultural factors, however, is staggering. The instruments tap three perspectives on behavior of a psychiatric nature: the subject (in the case of adolescents), the teacher, and the parent. These perspectives also reflect different settings in which behavior occurs (i.e., the school and the home). The content of the items used in the evaluations differs greatly in several respects; social behavior (item 74, "showing off or clowning"); frankly psychological phenomena (item 27, "easily jealous"); things that can be regarded as symptoms (item 47, "nightmares"; item 35, "feels worthless or inferior"); and physical symptoms (item 54, "overweight"; item 49, "constipated, doesn't move bowels"). In some instances, the regions of the nation that were studied may contribute special variation (e.g., highly urbanized versus less urbanized). Finally, and equally if not more important, the items can refer to behavior per se (item 59, "plays with own sex parts in public") or to evaluations or judgments about behavior (item 60, "plays with own sex parts too much"). This array of variables allows for many different snapshots of pathology viewed in relation to culture.

A considerable degree of similarity has been obtained across the United States, Holland, Puerto Rico, and Thailand. As an example, correlations of the mean scores on the items of the CBCL across nations ranged from a low of .69 for Holland versus Thailand to a high of .92 for Washington, D.C., versus Sydney, Australia (Achenbach, Howell, Quay, & Connors, 1991). All of the cross-nation correlations produced were significant ($p <$ .01). The mean correlation between Thailand (the only non-Western nation) and other nations was the lowest of all the mean correlations of the remaining nations (71.4 versus a range of 78.4 to 84.0). These gross figures underscore commonality but also potentially interesting cultural differences. Nevertheless, although one expects high correlations between Western nations, given a common social, political, and intellectual history, this is not the case with a non-Western one. The high correlation of this nation with Western ones underscores the powerful effects of Western values and traditions.

The growing number of countries included in such research allows cross-cultural comparisons of the sexes with respect to areas of adolescent behavior and psychopathology. This look at the data involved general populations, not clinical ones. Twelve items were isolated which tended to show consistent sex differences across nations (besides the countries already mentioned, samples from Chile and Canada were also included). Only 1 of the 12 items produced higher scores in females (item 29, "fears certain animals, situations, or places, other than school"). In almost all instances, this item accounted for only a small percent of variance; however, in the case of Puerto Rico, it was substantial (4%). The remaining 11 items produced higher scores in males. In Holland, the item referring to bragging produced large gender differences (12% of variance), whereas in Thailand "can't sit still" and "teases a lot" explained much variation (4% and 5%, respectively). Of the 11 items on which boys outscored girls significantly, 8 were classified by Achenbach as externalizing; this analysis suggests that boys tend toward undercontrol as contrasted with girls, who overcontrol. In general, while these 12 items were associated with gender-related cross-cultural commonalities, specific nations differed substantially on any number of other items in terms of how the sexes were evaluated by parents.

Studies relying on the CBCL have produced a complex body of data pertaining to cultural differences in how parents and teachers rate behavior that is clinically significant. The evolving nature of this research does not allow one to generalize, since (a) different respondents have been used in different nations, (b) in only some nations have both clinical and nonclinical samples been tested, and (c) the data from all of the nations have not been presented in complete form. Despite the diversity of content of material, it is often difficult to determine whether a cultural difference reflects a difference in behavior per se or a difference in parents' or teachers' perception of behavior. Nevertheless, these studies allow a glimpse at how modern Western culture tends to homogenize norms, standards, (possibly) actual behavior, and parent/teacher perceptions about behavior. The content of the items of the CBCL gives a distinctive clinical or biomedical cast to the emerging picture of childhood and adolescence. Although there is great consistency in how parents and teachers rate different areas of behavior that are considered problematic, there nevertheless is much variation linked to national traditions. Finally, the items that are used all reflect a Western and possibly Anglo-American bias. It is not clear whether researchers have made a systematic effort to elicit from informants in each nation what would be seen as problem behaviors within the respective national traditions.

Comment

The field of psychiatric epidemiology of children and adolescents is growing and attaining a level of sophistication comparable to that of adult psychiatry. The pursuit of rigor, standardization, and control ("elegant parsimony"), however, has trapped epidemiological studies into a form of reductionism. In these studies, cultural factors appear to be bleached out in the analysis and reporting. When such factors surface, they are explained away rather than taken into account. These studies fail to depict the variation with which adolescent psychopathology is played out across cultures.

Cultural and Historical Boundedness of Adolescent Psychopathology

An important term in cultural psychiatry, *culture-bound disorders*, refers to psychiatric disorders (behavioral syndromes) shaped and made important by local cultural factors. We extend the concept of culture-bound disorders to include historically bound disorders. Although the concept originally referred to unusual and stereotypical disorders prevalent in non-Western societies (e.g., amok, arctic hysteria; Littlewood & Lipsedge, 1971; Simons & Hughes, 1985), it is applicable to disorders found in Western industrialized societies. Some disorders included in the taxonomy of contemporary biomedical psychiatry may in effect constitute culture-bound disorders of

Western societies (see the provocative discussion of depression in Obeyeskere, 1985). In this section we address this topic through a discussion of three areas of culture-bound psychopathology: anorexia nervosa, possession syndromes, and social aggression.

Anorexia Nervosa

Controversies surround the historical origins, essential features, and underlying causes of anorexia nervosa. A range of endocrinological and other physiological factors have been shown to be influential in anorexia nervosa, and psychological factors also have been emphasized (Russell & Treasure, 1989). What one can view as the models in terms of which people explain disorders of eating have varied considerably. Historical and cultural factors in anorexia nervosa are briefly discussed below.

Historical Considerations. The key study consulted here is *Fasting Girls: The History of Anorexia Nervosa* (Brumberg, 1988), which provides a cultural history of disorders involving eating and fasting in western European societies. Emphasizing the complexity of the subject, Brumberg reviews female fasting's association with important historically conditioned symbols, "from sainthood to patienthood [in late modern contemporary times]. . . . Thus, medieval culture promoted a specific form of appetite control in women, anorexia mirabilis, which symbolized the collective values of that age. Anorexia nervosa expresses the individualism of *our* time" (pp. 45–46).

Taking a historical relativist position, Brumberg asserts that anorexia nervosa constitutes a modern and contemporary disease or disorder:

> In the modern period, female control of appetite is embedded in patterns of class, gender and family relations established in the 19th century; the modern anorectic strives for perfection in terms of society's ideal of physical, rather than spiritual beauty. . . . To describe pre-modern women such as Catherine as anoretic is to flatten differences in female experience across time and discredit the special quality of eucharistic fervor and penitential asceticism as it was lived and perceived. To insist that medieval holy women had anorexia nervosa is, ultimately, a reductionist argument because it converts a complex human behavior into a simple biomedical mechanism. To conflate the two is to ignore the cultural context and the distinction between sainthood and patienthood. (p. 46)

Cultural Considerations. The interplay between culture, history, and biology grounds Brumberg's argument. Culture recruits vulnerable persons and gives them reasons to fast, and the resulting endocrinal and physiological changes entrap them in medical careers that prove difficult to change.

A review of diagnostic criteria for anorexia nervosa illustrates how it changes its appearance in response to cultural circumstances. Anorexia nervosa lacks unequivocal genetic markers or biological indicators; its status as a diagnosable disorder rests primarily on the constancy of association of its clinical features and on the similarity of its course and outcome (Russell, 1970). Recent studies reveal a consistent core of clinical features (Garfinkel & Gardner, 1982) and a similarity in outcome among anorexia nervosa patients treated at different centers (Hsu, 1988).

It is instructive to examine the matter of form versus content with respect to anorexia nervosa. Although disturbances involving food intake, weight status, and menstrual function are characteristic form or structural elements, the fear of fatness, the sine qua non content element of anorexia nervosa in the West, did not emerge as a predominant feature of the illness until about 1930 (Casper, 1983; Russell, 1985). Clinicians interested in cultural and historical factors disagree about the reason for this change in the content of the illness. Russell (1985) states that it is unlikely that Gull and Lasegue (who are viewed as originally describing the condition) could have overlooked their patients' weight concerns, and that "a more likely explanation for the substantially different contemporary psychopathology is that the illness itself has changed since their descriptions of 110 years ago" (p. 102). Casper (1983) offers a similar explanation: "The drive towards thinness does not emerge as a common and predominant motive until about 1960" (p. 10). Habermas (1989), however, believes that clinicians' bias and negligence, rather than transformation of psychopathology, caused the apparent change in the content of anorexia nervosa. He suggests that the observations of the early writers were influenced by their expectations and by the patients' tendency to hide their goal of losing weight.

Despite its relative antiquity and the interest it has aroused in the West, anorexia nervosa is comparatively understudied in non-Western populations. A recent review of literature has found only 35 studies of anorexia and bulimia nervosa among Native Americans, African Americans, Hispanics, Asians, Africans, and Middle Easterners (Davis & Yaeger, 1992; Holden & Robinson, 1988). Most of these were qualitative case reports. The review drew attention to inconsistent diagnostic criteria and the absence of studies validating standard instruments outside of North America. Although anorexia nervosa is classically associated with Western conventions (e.g., body image, size), few studies of non-Western people have attempted to study directly acculturation to such conventions.

Even in contemporary studies, fear of fatness is absent among many anorectic patients in Hong Kong (Lee, Chiu, & Chen, 1989, 1991) and India (Khandelwal & Saxena, 1990). It is possible that a definition and inquiry mode that connected more directly with traditional Chinese or Indian conceptions of body weight, personal effectiveness, alimentation and body shape (e.g., the awareness that patients may adopt a somatic rather than a psychological "idiom of distress") may uncover additional cases of early, evolving or "atypical" anorexia nervosa. It is striking that few quantitative culturally oriented studies have focused on anorexia nervosa in non-Western populations.

Analysis. Variation in the manifest content or symbolic appearance of anorexia nervosa in some contemporary non-Western subjects is intriguing. At least three possible explanations arise for the historical and cross-cultural findings. The first is that patients who do not demonstrate a definite fear of fatness are in fact suffering from atypical anorexia nervosa (or "eating disorders not otherwise specified," or "secondary anorexia nervosa"). This explanation is conceptually the cleanest since it excludes cases that do not meet current diagnostic criteria, but it is the most ethnocentric position because it stipulates that the current Western rationale for food refusal constitutes the universally defining feature of anorexia nervosa.

The second explanation is that the fat phobia has been overlooked or concealed. Clinicians are often influenced by expectations. The tendency for anorexia nervosa patients to conceal their fat phobia could not explain the findings from Hong Kong and India noted above, though, since these clinicians specifically looked for the presence of fat phobia and did not find it in many patients.

The third explanation is that there has been a transformation in the content of anorexia nervosa in the West since around 1930, and that an analogous situation may be occurring in developing countries where a cultural emphasis on female slimness is not yet widely prevalent. Therefore we find in these developing countries a mixture of anorexia nervosa cases that do and do not demonstrate a fat phobia.

Russell (1985) and Russell and Treasure (1989) invoke the concept of pathoplasticity to explain the change in anorexia nervosa. Pathoplastic factors, according to Russell (1985) are "causal factors that contributed to the structure of an illness. . . . They not only influence the content, but also its coloring and its form. . . . [They] are to be distinguished from the main fundamental causes of a psychiatric illness, but they include causes which exert a predisposing tendency, a formative or modeling role, or act as provoking or triggering agents" (p. 7). He then suggests that the current Western pre-occupation with female slimness acts as a pathoplastic factor that leads to "the appearance of relatively new forms of psychiatric disorders—anorexia nervosa and bulimia—in which the central psychopathology is a dread of fatness. Not only the content but the very form of these illnesses would have become changed" (Russell, 1985, p. 107).

If the fear of fatness were the "coloring" of the illness and not its central feature, then we would need to rethink the diagnostic criteria for anorexia nervosa. We would also have to reconsider the central features of the illness, how they can apparently become amplified or triggered by the fashionable emphasis on slimness, and whether these features are the same or different in patients with and without a fear of fatness. There is some indirect support for this view. Japanese anorectics apparently all demonstrate a fear of fatness (Nogami & Yabana 1977; Suematsu, Ishikawa, Kuboki, & Ito, 1985), which is consistent with a pathoplastic view since Japan is highly industrialized and presumably has adopted the cultural emphasis on slimness. Likewise, Arab, Asian, Indian, or Pakistani women who develop an eating disorder while living in the West also uniformly demonstrate a fear of fatness (Bhadrivath 1990; Markantonakis, 1990; Nasser, 1986); presumably they have come under the same cultural emphasis on slimness that affect their Western counterparts. If so, it may be that as Hong Kong, India, and other nations become more industrialized, their anorectic patients will also increasingly adopt the fear of fatness.

Spirit Possession

Spirit possession, according to Kakar (1982), "has been the historically dominant theory of illness and especially of conditions we call mental illness. The Arabs and the Chinese, the Hebrews and the Greeks, have all believed in some form of spirit possession" (p. 24). He also comments on the various manifestations of spirit possessions, from alterations in the possessed person's state of well-being (physical and mental) to trances and other dramatic statements.

In Western psychology and psychiatry, dissociation is defined as a psychological mechanism that splits apart aspects of mental experience. From a cross-cultural standpoint, dissociation constitutes a normal psychological capacity (a human universal) and underlies such altered states of consciousness as trance, hypnosis, and the routine automatization of behavior (e.g., driving while performing unrelated cognitive tasks or conducting conversations; Brown, 1991; Ludwig, 1983). Disturbances in this capacity for dissociation lead to changes or breakups in the flow of behavior, memory, and identity.

Disorders in which dissociation figures importantly are among the most prevalent cross-culturally. Trance and possession have long been an important topic in psychological anthropology (Bourguignon, 1979; Lewis, 1989; Prince, 1968). In American society, behaviors traceable to dissociation have received much attention. In American psychiatry, however, the topic of dissociative disorders—and, in particular, multiple personality disorders (MPD)—has recently dominated attention (Putnam, 1991a; Tasman & Goldfinger, 1991).

The phenomenon of embodied alternative identities constitutes a subject of unparalleled interest to the psychiatrist, psychologist, and anthropologist. That external and culturally validated spirits should possess non-Western peoples (usually in highly dramatized, social settings) whereas distinctive personalities privately command personal awareness and behavior in Western societies is an intriguing topic that is unquestionably linked to cultural and historical traditions involving personhood (Mulhern, 1991).

A characteristic feature of dissociative disorders and MPD is their onset in childhood and adolescence (Putnam, 1991a, b). Psychological trauma due to abuse of various types appears to be a regular accompaniment of these disorders (the discussion of child/adolescent abuse in the following section thus is germane to this topic as well). In this setting of unbearable pain and devastation, the developing self capitalizes on its (biologically derived) propensity for imagination, fantasy, and flexible constraints on reality in order to create psychological entities that can act as walled-off compartments for unwanted, unacceptable intentions, feelings and actions.

Data gathered on adult MPD patients in Western societies suggest that adolescent girls, more often than boys, resort to the strategy of exaggerated dissociation in order to cope with psychological trauma (Putnam, 1991a, b). Studies of MPD in children and adolescents largely confirm this picture of trauma at the root of pathological dissociation (Dell & Eisenhower, 1990). Interestingly, in the latter studies, males tend to be overrepresented as compared to studies of adults. This suggests either that boys are more likely to be brought to the attention of therapists than men, or that boys with MPD may go on to develop other kinds of psychopathology that mask pathological varieties of dissociation.

From the standpoint of culture and the construction of personhood and self, the alternative selves described in MPD provide potentially important information. It is interesting indeed that the alter personalities tend to possess rather standard and conventional forms. In the recent study by Dell and Eisenhower (1990), alter personalities "were quite similar from case to case. All patients had child alters, scared alters, depressed alters, and angry protector alters. Persecutors and internal helpers were found in 82% of the cases. Alters of the opposite sex from the patient were found in 73% of the cases, violent alters in 64% of the cases, sexualized alters in 55% of the cases, and suicidal alters in 50% of the cases" (p. 362). This variety of alter selves closely parallels what is found clinically in adults.

An alter self may be viewed in part as a cultural stereotype—that is, as manifesting a cluster of related traits that embody univalent dispositions that the culture provides as a model (valued or disvalued) of behavior. Such models, although configured by the traumatized individual for personal reasons to play important roles in his or her life, are nonetheless largely constructions of the culture. Alter selves present anthropologists with a profile of types that serve important functions in the psychological economy of the developing adolescent. Perhaps these selves, like the possessing spirits and entities of preindustrial societies, help adolescents to resolve their crises of adjustment (see below). The hypotheses that selves operate as symbols drawn from the culture and that social institutions play an important role (often appropriately called iatrogenic) in constructing and shaping dissociation phenomena have been discussed by Orne and Bauer-Manley (1991), Orne and Bates (1992), and Merskey (1992).

In preindustrial societies, childhood and adolescence must likewise be viewed as providing the initial setting for learning ways to use and mold the universal human potential for dissociation. The syndromes of possession behavior that are learned cannot be equated with the pathological varieties of dissociation seen in industrialized societies. Nevertheless, in these syndromes one encounters paradigmatic illustrations of the role that culture plays in personality functioning and social adaptation more generally. The symbols clustered in the identity of a possessing spirit vary in content and organization and relate importantly to the everyday conflicts of the adolescent who serves as their host. When examined in relation to symbols embodied in the alternative selves of MPD patients, those of possessing spirits provide the cultural anthropologist with an opportunity to analyze and compare psychological mechanisms in adolescents, the ways personality organization is maintained, and how personal crises are resolved by the use of devices that extend the composition of the self.

Cross-Cultural Evidence. The particular type of dissociative disorders termed possession are uncommon in Euro-American societies but are common in South Asia (India, Bangladesh, Nepal, Pakistan, and Sri Lanka) and East and Southeast Asia. Several studies by cultural anthropologists (Boddy, 1988, on Sudan; Freed & Freed, 1985, 1990, on India; Kakar, 1982, on India; Ong, 1987, 1988, on Malaysia; Sharp, 1990, on Madagascar) attest to the pervasiveness of spirit possession of young women in non-Western societies. As elaborated below, these syndromes involve the temporary takeover of the self by spirits, usually at a time of crisis. In their incarnated form, the spirits often make demands and express feelings to which family members acquiesce.

Conversely, multiple personality disorder is relatively common in the United States, yet rare in Asian contexts. Adityanjee, Rajy, and Kandelwal (1989) reported three cases of multiple personality disorder in India that had accumulated over a 3-year period. All three cases involved adolescents, two of whom were females. Each woman presented only one alternate self, and in each case the transitions between personalities occurred suddenly following awakening in the morning. The authors also raise the question that cultural differences pertaining to the construction of social identity might play a role in the way this disorder is expressed across societies. Thus, in Indian culture, dependence and *interdependence* are crucial in identity as compared to dependence versus *independence*, as in the Western ones.

Kakar (1982) reports on several varieties of spirit possession of young Hindu and Muslim women in India. Local terminology for possession conditions varies: *dar* (fear) resembles the Western category of anxiety neurosis, anxiety state, or anxiety reaction (pp. 22–23), and *sankat* (distress) refers to possession by a *bhuta* (malignant spirit) and corresponds roughly to the Western category of hysteria. Spirit possession, Kakar states, is "more than hysteria," but hysterical personalities seem to "make the best use of possession states" (p. 75).

In many respects, the Indian cases of MPD are atypical and conventionalized, as though they were less evolved, less scripted, and less incorporated into the individualistic psychology of alternate selves. This pattern is not surprising insofar as the culture's code regarding autonomy, voluntarism, and separation does not foster full individuation as this is expected and played out in Western-influenced societies. Instead, the self in India is said to be sociocentric, and the culture stipulates the existence of numerous spirits that can provide vehicles for the expression of wishes and actions. These spirits play important roles in resolving psychological, interpersonal, and intrafamilial stress. A similar blending of individualistic and sociocentric themes in the manifestations of MPD, with consequent atypical results clinically, is described for Brazil by Krippner (1987). In this instance, however, Western spiritualism associated with Allen Kardec (a French spiritualist whose ideas were brought to Brazil in the mid-nineteenth Century) merges with traditional West African beliefs to structure the dissociation syndromes.

Sharp's (1990) study of spirit possession among young female migrants in northwest Madagascar illustrates a pattern of stress-related spirit possession related to social change. In the town of Ambanja, volatile and dangerous spirits afflict adolescent schoolgirls who have migrated from rural areas to town to attend school. Sharp comments that these girls, more than other members of this society, experience simultaneously the conflicts involved with the transition from rural to urban life and from childhood to adulthood.

Shame is a key aspect of some possession syndromes in non-Western cultures. An important finding about gender differences in mental illness and familial responses to it in western India is that mental illness among young women is the most stigmatizing of all problems (Skultans, 1991, pp. 329–330). Men's mental illness causes sorrow, while such illness among women causes shame. Young women are especially stigmatized because of the possibilities of their sexual exploitation and the issue of who will care for them (in-laws or natal family). The result is that "the family closes in upon itself to contain the stigma and family sympathies contract" (p. 329).

Historical Evidence. Dissociative phenomena in relation to religious cults and possession behaviors have a long history in Western and Middle Eastern societies (Burkert, 1987). Walker (1981) provides information on states of possession, trance, and exorcism during the early modern period. He focuses on the significance of demonic possession in playing out religious and other political conflicts of the period. The study is unusually rich in its descriptions of individual cases; it is also special because it documents clearly that adolescent girls figured importantly in the cases that achieved notoriety during this time, when witchcraft accusations and executions were common. Walker shows that many cases of possession in adolescent girls raised the question of mental illness and/or epilepsy and that physicians were frequently called in to render differential assessments (as to whether these were authentic cases of demonic possession, episodes of illness, or cases of what we would today view as malingering).

Klaits (1985), in his historical study of the witch hunts in Europe, indicates that adolescent girls were prone to experience dissociation and that during such conditions functioned as accusers of "witches," who were in turn subjected to investigation and sometimes execution. Similarly, he stresses that female adolescents in convents frequently experienced so-called mass possession episodes. His formulation is consistent with that of the historians already mentioned: "Constant exhortations to develop habits of introspection, to detect every forbidden thought, and to confess all prohibited feelings could produce a charged atmosphere of repressed desires and deep guilt, stemming from the nuns' sensations of failure, hopelessness, and fear of damnation. These explosive conditions often found their spark in a male authority figure, either the nuns' confessor and spiritual director or a surrogate" (p. 118).

As mentioned above, Brown (1986) indicated that what can safely be termed syndromes of possession were common in convents and involved the working out of conflicts of spirituality that frequently involved themes of sexuality. Bennedetta, the nun who is the focus of Brown's study, was possessed by a much younger girl, Bartolomea, possibly a late adolescent. Bennedetta's life story illustrates the arduous careers of female adolescents and young adults of early modern Western societies caught in environments that constrained and limited their sexual choices; it illustrates dramatically the shaping of dissociation by religious tenets and moral constraints.

Despite prevalence of adolescent identity crises during the early modern period that involved what can loosely be termed dissociative disorders, few such problems were encountered in the medical-psychiatric practice of Richard Napier, the astrological physician of the Midlands of England, whose exhaustive case notes were analyzed by Michael MacDonald (1988). His case descriptions of adults refer to persons that one can confidently assume suffered from disorders of dissociation. Yet few cases of children and adolescents are recorded in his practice; the reasons for this are not known.

Analysis. Anthropologists who study spirit possession see it as not generally pathological in local terms and valuations (Crapanzano, 1977). Many anthropologists view it as a creative and adaptive response to deprivation by those of marginal status. Another prominent trend in anthropological interpretation is to interpret spirit possession as an expression of protest, especially by women, through which the possessed individuals can make sense of their lives. In this framework, powerlessness becomes the key to understanding spirit possession, and it may prove useful in examining cases of youth stress worldwide.

For example, Ong's (1987, 1988) research on young women workers in a Malaysian electronics factory subscribes to a protest interpretation of spirit possession among these workers. Before industrialization in Malaysia, spirit possession predominantly affected married women, but recently it has begun to occur primarily among unmarried young women workers. Ong ties this shift in affliction to the combined processes of these women's overall powerlessness: their ambiguous social status as unmarried working females in a male-dominated society that values female modesty, oppressive work conditions in the factories, and the women's inability to protest directly any of these conditions.

A dominant thread in Kakar's (1982) interpretation of female-predominant afflictions in India is that of sexual repression (see p. 48). Recurrent in many afflicted women's dreams is the appearance of a strange man who insists on having sexual intercourse (see also Obeyesekere, 1981, on Sri Lanka). Kakar (1982) links the strong taboos against women's expression of sexuality with women's guilt and need to displace this guilt on the stranger in the dream. The author is struck by the "accumulated and expressed rage, the helpless anger of young women at the lack of their social emancipation" (p. 76).

Is spirit possession among youths a case of adolescent psychopathology? There is no clear answer to this question. Much of the anthropological literature portrays a distinction between voluntary possession (mediumship) and involuntary possession (illness; Skultans, 1991). Kakar (1982) indicates that in India, a continuum stretches from acceptable interactions with the spirit world to those that are considered pathological and lead to the individual seeking treatment. Skultans (1991) found in her research in western India that afflicted persons themselves have contradictory interpretations of trance and affliction.

Adolescent Social Aggression and Delinquency

We define social aggression and delinquency as behavior that violates social norms and is considered socially offensive. The term covers acts of violence directed at other people and at property; these may be associated with such things as substance abuse and teenage pregnancy. The scope of this topic is enormous, and no effort is made here to cover it thoroughly. Our goal is to illustrate how culture and history shape what comes to be viewed as adolescent psychopathology in the area of social aggression and delinquency.

Scholars disagree as to the nature and causes of social aggression. Some emphasize its panhuman biological roots, taking it as a natural trait that evolved as social groups became larger and more competitive (Hinde, 1974). Many psychologists argue that social aggression is also learned (Bandura, 1973; Berkowitz, 1962; Buss, 1961; Eron & Huesmann, 1984; Lefkowitz, Eron, Waler, & Huesmann, 1977). Social aggression and delinquency have been particularly associated with adolescence. In anthropology, this emphasis is apparent in the Margaret Mead–Derek Freeman debate discussed earlier. Aggression and delinquency of adolescents has also been a prominent concern of historians (e.g., Davis, 1971) and a central focus of psychiatry.

Western Medical Views. The notions of social aggression, criminality, and delinquency have played an important role in the growth and development of Western psychiatry. One concern of mental health professionals involved protecting and serving individuals whose mental illness was manifested in actions falling within the purview of the criminal justice system. The development of a special objective or technical language of psychopathology (Berrios, 1984) has been integral to the growth of the discipline of psychiatry; it also helped to depoliticize deviant or antisocial behaviors by strengthening the claim that these behaviors also reflected elements of mental illness. A critical perspective on this rise of psychiatry and the growth of the mental health professions generally argues the claim of the medicalization of deviance as put forward by some social scientists (e.g., Conrad & Schneider, 1980; Foucault, 1978; Kittrie, 1971; Scull, 1979).

Although the history of child and adolescent psychiatry is yet to be written, we know that a focusing of interest on the psychopathology of youth occurred during the late eighteenth and early nineteenth centuries, when the harmful effects of urbanization, industrialization, and early capitalism were becoming visible (Dennis, 1949; Gontard, 1988; Hersov, 1986; Keir, 1952; Parry-Jones, 1989; Walk, 1964) In Britain, important social influences in this rising consciousness about the young included theories of education, the development of compulsory education, the mental hygiene and child guidance movements, and philanthropic activities concerned with child welfare. Thus social problems, not diseases per se, played a central role in the growth of awareness about child and adolescent mental health (Levy, 1968).

Psychiatrists did have a concern over the topic of insanity (i.e., psychosis) as it related to juvenile delinquency and the evolution of a juvenile court system. With respect to insanity, the concepts of reasons and unreason—as influenced by the ideas of Locke and applied to children by Haslam—were particularly relevant in focusing attention on children and youths (Binder, 1984, 1987, 1988; Platt, 1977).

Special institutions for disturbed children evolved during the latter half of the nineteenth century, with children segregated from adults and provided with some education. An important (indeed, foundational) influence in the work and interests of the early "alienists" was thus activities and behaviors of deviant, marginal, and delinquent populations, among which problems of children and adolescents were important.

Interest in the psychopathology of children and adolescents increased in England and Europe as a result of the introduction and spread of the concept of "moral insanity" by Prichard (1835). This term signified a behavioral condition characterized by gross disturbances in feelings, conduct, and behavior that were not accompanied by evident intellectual insanity. Later, as a result of Darwin's influence, ideas of degeneration and heredity became associated with moral insanity. The possibility that delinquent, criminal elements who were not psychotic could pass on their disease spurred interest in childhood and adolescent psychopathology. Eventually, as in the writings of Maudsley (1868), these ideas were elaborated in terms of cerebral pathology.

Thus the idea that psychopathology was not limited to the intellectual realm but could manifest itself in disorders of the moral faculties (aggression, opposition, criminality, etc.) played an extremely influential role in the evolution of childhood and adolescent psychopathology. A historical link exists between psychiatric concepts pertaining to moral insanity, sociopathy, psychopathy, conduct disorders, and juvenile delinquency (Werlinder, 1978). These concepts played a central role in psychiatry's involvement in the criminal justice system and in the evolution of its own language about behavioral anomalies that involve criminality. The broadening of what psychopathology encompasses has involved psychiatrists and psychologists in evaluations of adolescent conduct for social institutions not classically concerned with disease; clearly the state plays an important role in controlling child and adolescent behavior, including social aggression (Foucault, 1978; Meyer, 1983).

Mental health researchers who concentrate on social aggression emphasize its persistence and career aspects. A range of factors—biological (genetic or hormonal), social, economic, personal, familial, and ecological—are seen to influence age of first offending, frequency of offending, variety of offending, and persistence of offending (e.g., Loeber, 1982, 1990, 1991). A career perspective on antisocial behavior highlights the possibility that critical periods of development play a significant role in whether a child adopts a deviant, antisocial mode, which in turn influences how malleable he or she is to future change.

This literature is vast and complex, and researchers have constructed models describing a range of factors that interact to produce socially aggressive acts and criminal careers in adolescents and the young (see also Farrington, Loeber, & Elliott, 1990; Jessor, 1984, 1991; Patterson, DeBaryshe, & Ramsey, 1989; Petersen, 1986, 1987; Petersen & Ebata, 1987; Petersen & Hamburg, 1988; Petersen et al., 1989; Robins, 1991). Analyses have included biological, socioeconomic, and psychological variables, as well as family structure, school commitment, and ecology of the environment (Rutter, 1980). Little research, however, has concentrated on cultural and ethnic factors.

Historical Evidence. Social historians differ with respect to how much and what form adolescent aggression has taken in previous times. Aside from the perspective that precludes examination of this topic due to the claim that adolescence had no currency in preindustrial contexts, other scholars (reviewed earlier) have documented forms of ritualized and outright social opposition and misrule in adolescents as far back as the sixteenth century. A larger literature pertains to the marginal and poor and the effects of socioeconomic upheavals associated with industrialism and early capitalism (Cohen & Scull, 1983; Garland, 1990; Weisser, 1982). An extensive literature focuses on youths and young adults involved in vagrancy, protest, and opposition to the social order (Beier, 1985; Mollat, 1986).

The voluminous literature on the social history of crime rarely focuses on adolescence per se; however, one can infer, that adolescents were included among the many deviant individuals described. As an example, studies of prostitution in the late medieval and early modern periods refer to young females who resorted to this line of work. Rather than being viewed as psychopathology, prostitution was considered a form of deviance that affected adolescent and young females (Otis, 1985; Rossiaud, 1984). Scholars (Chesney, 1970; Geremek, 1987; Salgado, 1977) have also looked at marginalized groups of paupers and beggars that included apprentices and domestic workers who had lost their jobs. These groups were traditionally involved in crime and deviance and included individuals now classified as juvenile delinquents (e.g., Sharpe, 1984). In England in the nineteenth century, during the period when the police evolved and crime was a central issue in evolving state policies, juvenile offenders were an important concern of committees reporting on social problems (Emsley, 1987).

Gillis (1975) sees developments in England during the period from 1890 to 1915 as critical in shifting the focus on juvenile delinquency from a social problem involving poor youths to include youths of all social classes. All adolescents came to be viewed as showing a propensity toward delinquency: "A stage of life, adolescence, had replaced station in life, class, as perceived cause of misbehavior" (p. 97). Gillis traces the dialectal interplay during this period between the stereotype of the organized, conforming adolescent and the disorganized, maladjusted one. It was a period during which child labor laws were modified, the legal age for leaving school was extended, and adolescence became institutionalized in home, school, and youth organizations. "By 1910 the dialectic had abated considerably and anxiety about delinquency diminished correspondingly, but not before an entire age group was perceived as prone to delinquency and the traditional 'maladjusted adolescent' enshrined as a major social stereotype" (p. 98).

Hall's (1904) writings on adolescence played a key role in the new visibility and special character of adolescence in general and juvenile delinquency specifically. For information and historical developments involving the concept of juvenile delinquency and recent legal changes in approaches to children and adolescents, the reader is referred to the works of Binder (1984, 1988).

Cross-Cultural Evidence. Adolescent aggression has been studied by anthropologists with emphasis on how youths are trained in adult styles of hostility and violence (Gadpaille, 1984). For example, Herdt (1990, 1993) provides vivid material on rites among the Sambia of Highland Papua New Guinea, where adolescent males undergo a lengthy period of initiation involving practices such as oral insemination by adult males and induced nosebleeds. Herdt (1990) interprets these practices as functioning to sever the boy from maternal attachments, transfer his loyalties to males, and condition the boy to the sight of blood and to aggressive boldness—"leading and killing in battle without compunctions" (p. 389). Herdt emphasizes that such aggressiveness, far from being "natural" for Sambia males, takes years of training to instill.

Another example of active socialization of aggression (as well as sexuality) is provided by Mayer and Mayer (1970), who review material pertaining to the Red Xhosa of South Africa and their strong militaristic tradition:

"Adolescence is seen as a time when both sex and fighting would be practiced actively." (p. 159)

"Xhosa hold that boys are naturally pugnacious; like dogs . . . [and] to that extent boyish fights and battles have to be tolerated." (p. 165)

"Training in the use and control of fighting behavior . . . simultaneously elicits fighting behavior in the boys, directs it against approved antagonists, and regulates it by fair-play rules and conventions." (p. 165)

Importantly, this pattern of education, and youth activities in general, "operates autonomously, without adult guidance or supervision, and away from adult activities" (p. 182); furthermore, as elders freely concede, the behaviors in question "are *neither* uncontrolled, *nor* rebellious, *nor* radical" (p. 183; emphasis in original). Here, then, one observes actual training in fighting and sexuality that is socially contained and does not cross the line to the socially offensive or delinquent.

Ward's (1970) study of temper tantrums in Kan Sai, a fishing village in Hong Kong, reveals how adults of preindustrial communities may cope with the expression of aggression in children. The values of the village emphasize harmony and getting along:

"To push oneself forward in an open effort to dominate others is considered wrong in much the same way that any openly aggressive behavior, including verbally aggressive behavior, is considered wrong." (p. 118)

"Problems of adolescent adjustment appear to be minimal, especially for boys." (p. 115)

"Children grew up with a clear idea of exactly what their place in the socioeconomic system was to be. . . . There were virtually no alternatives offered to adolescents, no choices they could make, and for boys there were no sharp discontinuities at any stage." (p. 115)

Ward noticed that obvious tantrums in children would tend to be ignored: "The child fairly quickly learns that such rages bring no reward . . . and learns that he can expect no sympathy . . . to accept frustrations, and to be peculiarly self composed and in emotional matters self-reliant" (p. 114). What is described, then, is a "structural situation which offers few effective sanctions against aggressive behavior; the people rely mainly upon the successful repression of aggressive impulses. . . . This is secured during the period of socialization partly by physical restraint and partly . . . through the kinds of childhood experience of frustration and the failure of aggressive behavior to obtain its objectives" (p. 120).

A study carried out in a village in South Sulawesi, Indonesia (Broch, 1990), reaffirms the position that adolescence can be free of aggression and violence. Among the Bonerate, the worst that happens is that boys experience more identity confusion than do girls, since girls "follow a shorter path to feminine role-security than the boys follow to reach the same level of confidence in their self-identity" (pp. 144–145). The daily life of adolescent boys is characterized by more leisure time than in their childhood years and "a remarkably high level of passivity. . . . They sit around chatting in the village. They are not discussing important political matters, nor are they training in rhetorical skills. They are relaxing to the point of boredom. The leisure is sometimes broken when a boy goes on an occasional fishing trip or works for a while" (p. 145).

A review of the cross-cultural evidence reveals much variety in the distribution of adolescent antisocial activity (Barry, 1989). Of the 186 societies examined, regular antisocial behavior by boys is coded as absent in 26 societies and present in 24. Such deviant behavior occurs in a reliably higher proportion of the societies where adolescent boys undertake adult roles in the family and in the community, where they own productive property, and where adolescence ends at an early age. The same trends apply also to adolescent girls but are not statistically significant because of less information: regular antisocial behavior by girls is coded as absent in 27 societies, but present in only 6. Other concomitants of regular antisocial behavior by adolescent boys are fewer social relationships with members of the household and with adult males, less emphasis on training to do productive work, and occurrence of antisocial behavior by adults.

The cross-cultural gender distribution of social aggression is of interest here. Recent research in several contexts reveals a wider variety of aggressive behaviors among females than previously believed (Burbank, 1991; Cummings, 1991; Lauer, 1991). Whether such gender patterning is the result of biological or cultural factors, or a combination of both, is a continuing subject of debate.

A key finding is that initiation rituals linked to puberty and preadulthood appear to allow for socially approved expression of aggression. For example, Rosaldo's (1988) study of headhunting among preadult males in a remote area of the Philippines reveals that killing someone is the socially approved means of attaining adulthood. Parallels exist in many societies in which males particularly, but perhaps also females (who are less studied in this domain), must perform some violent or aggressive acts in order to be considered adults. Such anthropological studies focus on the aggressive activities as culturally programmed rites of passage. It is difficult to draw the conclusion from such descriptions that the adolescent himself (rarely are females described) is aggressive or violent, for he is seen as one of several age-mates who are "actors" following a script (Gadpaille, 1984).

Anthropologists have paid little attention to aggression and its provocation in everyday life other than during ritual sequences or warfare. The well-known Six Cultures Study of the 1960s is one exception. Whiting and Whiting (1975) gathered data on aggressive behavior of children and found patterned differences: males tended to be more often aggressive than did females, and aggression was more prominent in the three cultures that were intensively either agricultural or industrial than in the societies characterized by small-scale agriculture. No such study has been done on adolescents, and scant information is available on local definitions of aggression. From the available literature it is not possible to state surely whether aggression in adolescents constitutes a pancultural problem similar to that of juvenile delinquency in Western society, but universality does not appear to be the case, given the counterevidence discussed above.

Research on this topic is again hampered by the lack of consensus on how to define aggression. Psychodynamically oriented researchers (see references in Gadpaille, 1984) often subscribe to a broad view, including child-rearing patterns that contribute to fantasies, beliefs, and rituals that may reflect unconscious hostility and aggression. Even seemingly placid, egalitarian, socialized groups can reveal an intense preoccupation with aggression or opposition in their fantasies. Other researchers concentrate on overt ritualized behaviors whose content is implicitly aggressive and hostile; however, they do *not* address behavior in everyday social situations, nor do they take into account psychodynamic or personality considerations (see also Gadpaille, 1984; Herdt, 1990). A review of the cultural anthropology literature suggests that adolescents across cultures, do not pose a problem to social order. Traditional means of social control situated in family groups of elders and/or clan organizations manage to contain and regulate adolescent expressions of social aggressiveness; these efforts are backed up by traditional religious and moral values that retain great power.

A large literature addresses factors contributing to the social identity and associated problems of adolescence among American ethnic minorities (DeVos, 1980; Jones, 1989; Manson, 1990; Spencer & Dornbusch, 1990; Stiffman & Davis, 1990). This body of research refers to demoralization, psychological distress, and problems in the control of aggressive feelings. Most studies are not controlled and quantitative, nor do they deal with social aggression or delinquency exclusively. The problems addressed illustrate the complex interplay of urbanization, modernization, ethnicity, socioeconomic status, racism, and governmental policy in contemporary Western society, and they span nations with diverse political systems (e.g., Dobson, 1991; Kleinman & Lin, 1981). No effort is made here to review this vast literature. Shelley (1981) emphasizes that modern societies are characterized by distinctive varieties of crime as compared to preindustrial or developing societies, and that juvenile crime is a particular concomitant of modernization.

Junger (1990) offers an interesting study with a specific focus on social aggression and deviance. This study involves social factors relating to delinquency in Moroccan, Surinamese, Turkish, and Dutch boys living in Holland. The ethnic-minority adolescents constituted a random sample of their population in the Netherlands; the control group was derived by interviewing one Dutch boy from the same street or block of every third minority subject interviewed. All three ethnic-minority groups had a higher level of involvement in the criminal justice system (the dependent variable) than the socially comparable Dutch group. No support was found for the social strain theory of delinquency, since socioeconomic position and unemployment bore no relationship to delinquency. Junger tested whether cultural dissonance theory could explain the results and concluded that this was not the case, as level of traditionalism was unrelated to delinquency. No support was found for the idea that these subjects were members of delinquent subcultures, although it was clear that in each ethnic group those with delinquent friends tended to have higher rates of delinquency. Greatest support was found for the social control theory; in each ethnic group, lower level of delinquency was associated with strong bonds to family, school, and conventional values, and lessened participation in unconventional pursuits. In this study, a sociological interpretation best accounted for the pattern of results. Junger does not emphasize cultural and psychological aspects of minority status, and it was not possible to determine either what delinquency meant or the reasons for or consequences of delinquency in these very disparate adolescents.

Child Rearing and Aggression. Many researchers explain child and adolescent aggression/violence as an outcome of psychological neglect or physical abuse. Explanatory models rely on the idea of so-called cycles of violence to draw attention to the important role played by physically abusive adults in producing children who later become abusive (Dodge, Bales, & Pettil, 1990). Important intrapersonal theories of development (e.g., attachment and social learning theory) are used to explain the effects of child abuse on adult violent behavior.

In searching for information on cross-cultural manifestations of physical abuse and neglect of children (and their relation to behavioral outcomes of adolescents), we should note that from the point of view of moral ethnocentrism, many patterns of rearing and ordeals of initiation recorded in the ethnographic literature could be construed as forms of socially sanctioned (i.e., cultural) abuse. These meaning-based, ritually structured, and symbolically encoded patterns teach children and adolescents the adult behavioral vocabulary of the culture, however brutal it may seem to outsiders. Given the ethnocentricity of how such abuse is defined, it is interesting to ask whether schools constitute forms of cultural abuse in contemporary Western societies (Hurrelmann, 1987; Rothstein, 1984). In contrast, personal abuse—characterized by ill feelings and the intention to thwart or subdue—would have no well-articulated representation in the symbolic code of the society.

This discussion raises several important questions that point to the value of anthropological studies for understanding problems of aggression in children and adolescents. Do patterns of rearing and initiation that (etically) qualify as culturally abusive cause chronic aggressive behavior in children and adolescents? Is personal abuse of children and adolescents common in preindustrial societies? Do cultures that are sociocentric, enjoin aggressive (even violent) adult behavior, and systematically instill this in ritualized ways produce children and adolescents that are prone toward personal abuse of others?

Television and Aggression. An issue related to child socialization for aggressive behavior is that of the media, of which television is a particularly powerful form in contemporary Western societies and increasingly throughout the world. Television presents material that plays out, challenges, and elaborates upon traditional cultural themes, stories, and dilemmas. It can also be a vehicle for the learning of antisocial behavior; in fact, some argue that in contemporary Western societies television viewing has had a strong effect on aggressive behavior. As summarized by Eron (1982): "The relation between television violence and aggression in children has been corroborated in two different geographical areas of the United States as well as in Finland, Poland, and Australia and has been found to hold for both boys and girls. . . . The casual effect is seen as circular, with television violence affecting children's aggression and aggressive children watching more and more violent television" (p. 197).

This influence illustrates powerfully how cultural attributes of any modern contemporary society affect behavior. A dialectical interplay between culture, technology, learning, and ultimately behavior creates circumstances that lead to further stress in the adolescent's attempt to manage the transition to adulthood. This type of learning about how situations of conflict can be resolved operates as a structural factor that shapes what is already a difficult passage to adulthood in contemporary societies.

Analytical Considerations. Cross-national studies of delinquency in Western nations have tended to find similar rates and similar overall patterns, including such career aspects as age of first offending, stability of offending, and variety of offending (see Klein, 1989). The nations compared are typically Western and industrial: for example, New Zealand, England, Canada, Finland, and Holland. In analyses of nations with low crime rates, Western and non-Western nations are included (Adler, 1983).

Cross-national researchers handle findings from the different sites and settings as more or less equally relevant to theory development. This is the case because similar-aged children and adolescents attending similar educational systems in similar urban complexes characterized by similar social ecological features provide the material of study. Moreover, a similar rationale and procedure guide the researcher regardless of country of origin, country studied, or countries compared.

What one can term normal science in the study of juvenile delinquency (and adolescent social aggression generally) treats the phenomena in question in a universalistic way, describing them as attributes of complex industrial societies. The problems in question are handled as though they constituted human universals when in fact they seem intrinsic to contemporary nation-states. Thus the style of inquiry in the study of the developmental aspects of adolescent social aggression parallels that of adolescent psychiatric epidemiology: a paramount preoccupation is with measurement and obtaining comparable results, to the detriment of revealing underlying characteristics and meanings pertaining to culture and historical tradition. Nowhere to be found is consideration of what role local religious and cultural traditions, patterns of conflict resolution, or models of personhood and emotional expression might play in producing, shaping, or giving cultural significance to antisocial behavior. Instead, such cultural factors are taken as reducible to age, gender, school, and social class.

Nations have distinctive historical and cultural traditions affecting all types of social behavior, including socially aggressive acts and the means for their expression and regulation. But such differences are bleached out of studies on this topic. Nations also have differing types of political, educational, and criminal justice systems that are characterized by different degrees of secularism, impersonality, and arbitrariness. These disparate in social structure are associated with differing beliefs, values, notions of self, and perspectives on social life, and they play influential roles in controlling behavior and resolving conflicts. But the question of whether forms of social aggression and delinquency are preceded by different means of education and enforcement about norms and the law is overlooked, as is the extent to which social aggression is directed at native sacred objects or traditions rather than impersonal property structures. Social aggression can be directed at culturally respected persons and institutions, impersonal authority figures, or innocent victims, but these possibilities are not considered in the analysis of a nation's juvenile delinquency problem.

Type of school is frequently cited as influential in affecting delinquency and antisocial behavior more generally in the West (Hurrelmann, 1987; Rutter, 1980; Rutter, Maugham, Mortimore, Ouston, & Smith, 1979; Rutter, Tizard, & Whitmore, 1970). Moreover, schools are often discussed as though they constituted differing (sub)cultures that have a determinate effect on the nature, variety, or amount of social aggression. While cultural factors thus are being considered and handled as independently influential in shaping forms of adolescent psychopathology, the system of symbolic categories implicitly used to delimit culture is again Western and universal: it is concerned with what in a school system is rational, efficient, rewarding, considerate, and so forth.

Generalizations that have been reached from the study of nations that are widely recognized for their low crime rates are germane to the topic of adolescent psychopathology, particularly as this applies to cultural factors. Adler (1983) analyzed material bearing on criminality in two nations from five regions of the world: western Europe (Switzerland, Ireland), socialist Europe (Bulgaria, German Democratic Republic), Latin America (Costa Rica, Peru), Islamic northern Africa and the Middle East (Algeria, Saudi Arabia), and Asia and the Pacific (Japan, Nepal). Socioeconomic and demographic predictors provided little help in understanding the levels of crime. However, careful analysis of the criminal justice systems and of the more informal, social systems of control were illuminating.

Adler concluded that lay involvement in crime control and in the criminal justice system as a whole—including the apparent popularity of such involvement—appeared to be influential in accounting for low levels of crime. Similarly important was the extent to which a country's system of social control and justice was anchored in traditional community values and locally based enforcement agencies that drew on shared cultural traditions:

> It is noteworthy that among [the] . . . countries, family controls have been maintained even in the wake of modernization. . . . Each has responded

with imagination and within the context of its own cultural traditions and ideological commitments. Each has made a deliberate and costly governmental effort to keep the family intact as a strong social control organ. . . . All of the successful countries felt challenged to provide communal surrogates for the vanishing clan. . . . The point is that all ten countries with low crime rates have developed social control agencies which, in their proper cultural setting, are popularly accepted and then serve as successful agents in maintaining social solidarity. To reiterate: successful crime control appears to go hand in hand with the existence of effective systems of popularly accepted and culturally harmonious social controls, of which the criminal justice system is one, capable of maintaining, generating, and transmitting shared values. (pp. 131–133)

Japan is said to have low delinquency rates (Adler, 1983; Martin & Conger, 1980), but Yamazaki, Inomata, and Mackenzie (1987) point to an increase in youth unrest and behavior problems of children and adolescents. The authors emphasize that changes brought on by urbanization and modernization, affecting in particular family size and the roles of parents, play important roles in this increase. This study stands out for its attempt to probe into national traditions and values predating the modern transition in order to explain recent changes in child and adolescent psychopathology.

Comment. A first point is that adolescent social aggression is common in Western societies, whether it is playful, ritualized, normative (socially controlled and channelled), or oppositional and subversive (socially destructive and legally incriminating). The content and form of adolescent social aggression depend on prevailing social conditions and cultural orientations.

Another point is that there is no intrinsic universal drive toward aggression and/or violence in adolescence. Rather, such behaviors are the product of the complex interplay of biological, social, and cultural factors. A more apt generalization is that adolescent aggression is widely found because conditions that affect adolescents adversely are common. The form the aggression takes will reflect cultural conventions directly by either affirming or contravening them.

If one posits that adolescents are endowed with quanta of social aggression as part of the natural process of maturation, then one could look for reasons behind differences between preindustrial and industrial societies in the way this aggression is expressed. In the former, (a) adolescent social aggression is provided group sanctioned means of expression in rituals, (b) sanctions and controls in the family and extended group are powerfully enforced and manage to contain most individualized forms of aggression, and (c) rituals and institutions that mark the transition allow youths to move gradually into roles where social aggression is used constructively to maintain group solidarity.

In contrast, adolescents in contemporary Western societies are forced to perform and compete in special educational settings in ways that stimulate aggressive feelings. These settings separate adolescents from meaningful participation in the wider society, and they concentrate cohorts in ways that contribute to stress and disappointments. Schools thus may have pernicious effects on adolescent psychology. Anomalous roles within the family (also the result of structural constraints of modern industrialized society) also contribute to the development of social conflicts and frustrations.

In contemporary Western societies, adolescent psychopathology related to social aggression therefore appears more widespread and visible than it does elsewhere, and it results in phenomena ordinarily labeled as conduct or oppositional problems, antisocial behavior, and juvenile delinquency. These behaviors are correlated with other forms of deviance that also are associated with Western industrialized societies, such as suicide and substance abuse.

Summary

We have ended this chapter by concentrating on problems surrounding (a) eating and bodily appearance, (b) psychological identity or selfhood, and (c) social aggression and delinquency. These problems are represented as conditions in the official diagnostic schema of Western psychiatry under the headings of anorexia nervosa, dissociative disorders (in particular, multiple personality disorder), and oppositional and conduct disorders.

We believe that the three conditions discussed above can be viewed as products of social and cultural changes linked to Western industrial capitalism. Prominent in the manifestations of these disorders are symbols or idioms intrinsic to the culture of our times; for example, physical attractiveness and slimness as markers of femininity; the positive value attached to commodities and their acquisition; an appeal to secularism and rationality (rather than spirituality) as sanctioning human action; the self as a discrete and active entity; and an expectation that behavior should be morally consistent.

Paralleling these symbolic changes are the societal changes loosely referred to as modernization (involving educational requirements and occupational specialization) that place new demands and pressures on adolescents, as well as changes in patterns of socialization and mechanisms for ensuring social control that have eroded traditional and communally based institutions. The result of these cultural/historical changes is the production of the three adolescent problems analyzed above (as well as others) and their prominent psychologization and medicalization.

The following propositions summarize and attempt to model the changes that have conditioned these varieties of adolescent psychopathology:

A. Political economic developments linked to industrial capitalism and interventions by the state apparatus break apart the locally and culturally sanctioned smooth transition from childhood to adulthood.

1. The family becomes less exclusively influential in delineating life course, providing social guidance, and supplying emotional controls and reinforcements.

2. The creation of schools and the stipulation of educational requirements lead to psychological stress.

3. Social complexity, signaled by occupational differentiation and the creation of special labor markets, results in disparate opportunity structures for adolescents leaving school.

4. Competition in schools and for valued future occupations contributes to added psychological stress in adolescents generally, especially those who are less intellectually and socially advantaged.

5. An ethos that emphasizes autonomy, and individual achievement is created.

B. The culture of Western industrial capitalism evolves models regarding bodily appearance, prosocial behavior, social goals, and personal identity that clash with sociobiological (evolutionarily derived) imperatives, inherited physiological/physical traits, and social realities.

1. An emphasis on rationality leads to the dictum that persons are unitary and self-consistent entities, despite the resulting breakup in the solidarity of self and community typically found in preindustrial societies.

2. Attractiveness, commodification, and money value become dominant properties of physical objects, and acquisitiveness becomes a pervasive objective in terms of which self-worth is calibrated.

3. The bodily self is commodified as a physical object whose appearance can be manipulated and enhanced; this becomes a sought-after goal and a marker of personal identity and self-worth.

4. Moral imperatives and sanctions are loosened from religious/sacred roots; moral directives are rendered more complex, more fluid, and hence less binding; a need is created for negotiating moral consistency in behavior and personal identity.

5. The need for maintaining the myth of a consistent, moral self in the context of complex rules, conflicting values, and stimulating directives/technologies of self-indulgence leads to problems in behavior and self-identity.

6. The supernatural domain becomes devalued in a secularized society; spirits are no longer held to intrude freely into personal affairs, being

confined instead to discrete locations and institutional settings. Spirits become less available to the self as vehicles for the resolution of conflicts in behavior and personal identity.

C. Adolescents are presented with complex and inconsistent symbolic codes pertaining to the self and behavior; valued goals are created that cannot easily be achieved. Stress is created by the above propositions in conjunction with biological imperatives involving alimentation, bodily development, aggression/competition, and sexuality.

1. Social identity is no longer clearly defined and culturally salient but intricate and manifold, in the process becoming highly problematized.
2. Psychological identity loses its anchors in the culture and becomes a difficult achievement.
3. Problems such as those embodied in anorexia nervosa, multiple personality disorder, and oppositional disorder are created as categories in a medicalized society.

References

Achenbach, T. M., Bird, H. R., Canino, G., Phares, V., Gould, M. S., & Rubio-Stipec, M. (1990). Epidemiological comparisons of Puerto Rican and U.S. mainland children: Parent, teacher, self reports. *Journal of the American Academy of Child and Adolescent Psychiatry, 29,* 84–93.

Achenbach, T. M., Chaiyasit, W., Suwanlert, S., Walter, B. R., Weiss, B., & Weisz, J. R. (1987). Epidemiology of behavior and emotional problems among Thai and American children: Parent reports for ages 6 to 11. *Journal of American Academy of Child and Adolescent Psychiatry, 26,* 890–897.

Achenbach, T. M., Hensley, V. R., Phares, V., & Grayson, G. (1990). Problems and competencies reported by parents of Australian and American children. *Journal of Child and Adolescent Psychiatry, 31,* 265–286.

Achenbach, T. M., Howell, C. T., Quay, H. C., & Conners, C. K. (1991). National survey of problems and competencies among four to sixteen year olds. *Monographs of the Society for Research in Child Development, 56*(3).

Achenbach, T. M., Verhulst, F. C., Althaus, M., & Akkerhuis, G. W. (1988). A comparison of syndromes derived from the Child Behavior Checklist for American and Dutch boys aged 6–11 and 12–16. *Journal of Child Psychology and Psychiatry, 29,* 879–895.

Achenbach T. M., Verhulst, F. C., Baron, G., Dana, A., & Grard, W. (1987). Epidemiological comparisons of American and Dutch children: I. Behavioral/emotional competencies reported by parents for ages 4 to 16. *Journal of the American Academy of Child and Adolescent Psychiatry, 26,* 317–325.

Adams, G. R., Montemayor, R., & Gullotta, T. G. (1989). *Biology of adolescent behavior and development*. Newbury Park, CA: Sage.

Adityanjee, G. S., Rajy, P., & Kandelwal, S. K. (1989). Current status of multiple personality disorders in India. *American Journal of Psychiatry, 146*, 1607–1610.

Adler, F. (1983). *Nations not obsessed with crime*. Col: Rothman. *Littleton*

Anderson, J. C., Williams, S., McGee, R., & Silva, P. A. (1987). DSM-III disorders in pre-adolescent children. *Archives of General Psychiatry, 44*, 69–76.

Anderson, Q. (1971). *The imperial self*. New York: Knopf.

Aries, P. (1962). *Centuries of childhood*. New York: Random House.

Bailey, G. W. (1989). Current perspectives on substance abuse in youth. *Journal of the American Academy of Child and Adolescent Psychiatry, 28*, 151–162.

Bakan, D. (1972). Adolescence in America: From idea to social fact. In J. Kagan & R. Coles (Eds.), *Twelve to sixteen: Early adolescence* (pp. 73–89). New York: Norton.

Bandura, A. (1973). *Aggression: A Social learning analysis*. Englewood Cliffs, NJ: Prentice-Hall.

Barry, H. (1989). *Adolescent antisocial attitudes associated with accelerated adulthood*. Paper presented at the annual meeting of the Society for Cross-Cultural Research, New Haven, CT.

Barry, H. (1991, October). *A survey of adolescence*. Paper presented at a seminar on Special Topics in Biological Anthropology, Department of Anthropology, University of Pittsburgh.

Baumeister, R. F. (1986). *Identity*. London: Oxford University Press.

Baumeister, R. F. (1987). How the self became a problem: A psychological review of historical research. *Journal of Personality and Social Psychology, 52*, 163–176.

Baumeister, R. F., & Tice, D. M. (1986). How adolescence became the struggle for self: A historical transformation of psychological development. In J. Suls & A. G. Greenwald (Eds.), *Psychological perspectives of the self* (Vol. 3, pp. 103–201). Hillsdale, NJ: Erlbaum.

Beier, A. L. (1985). *Masterless men: The vagrancy problem in England 1560–1640*. New York: Methuen.

Berkowitz, L. (1962). *Aggression: A social psychological analysis*. New York: McGraw-Hill.

Berrios, G. E. (1984). Descriptive psychopathology: Conceptual and historical aspects. *Psychological Medicine, 14*, 303–313.

Bhadrivath, B. R. (1990). Anorexia nervosa in adolescents of Asian extraction. *British Journal of Psychiatry, 156*, 565–568.

Binder, A. (1984). The juvenile court, the U.S. Constitution and when the twain meet. *Journal of Criminal Justice, 12*, 355–366.

Binder, A. (1987). An historical and theoretical introduction. In H. C. Quay (Ed.), *Handbook of juvenile delinquency* (pp. 1–32). New York: Wiley.

Binder, A. (1988). Juvenile delinquency. *Annual Review of Psychology, 39*, 253–282.

Bird, H. R., Canino, G., Rubio-Stipec, G., Madelyn, S., Ribera, J., Sesman, M., Woodbury, M., Huertas-Goldman, S., Pagan, A., Sancher-Lacay, A., &

Moscoso, M. (1988). Estimates of the prevalence of childhood maladjustment in a community survey in Puerto Rico. *Archives of General Psychiatry, 45,* 1120–1126.

Boddy, J. (1988). Spirits and selves in northern Sudan: The cultural therapeutics of possession and trance. *American Ethnologist, 15,* 4–27.

Bogin, B. (1988). *Patterns of human growth.* New York: Cambridge University Press.

Bourguignon, E. (1979). *Psychological anthropology.* New York: Holt, Rinehart & Winston.

Brandenburg, N. A., Friedman, R. M., & Silver, S. (1990). The epidemiology of childhood psychiatric disorders: Prevalent findings from recent studies. *Journal of the American Academy of Child and Adolescent Psychiatry, 29,* 76–83.

Broch, H. B. (1990). *Growing up agreeably: Bonerate childhood observed.* Honolulu: University of Hawaii Press.

Bronfenbrenner, U. (1977). Toward an experimental ecology of human development. *American Psychologist, 32,* 513–531.

Brown, D. (1991). *Human universals.* Philadelphia: Temple University Press.

Brown, J. (1986). *Immodest acts: The life of a lesbian nun in Renaissance Italy.* New York: Oxford University Press.

Brumberg, J. J. (1982). Chlorotic girls, 1870–1920: A historical perspective on female adolescence. *Child Development, 53,* 1468–1477.

Brumberg, J. J. (1988). *Fasting girls: The emergence of anorexia nervosa as a modern disease.* Cambridge, MA: Harvard University Press.

Brumberg, J. J. (1991). *Something happens to girls: The changing experience of menarche.* Paper presented at the biennial meeting of the International Society for the Study of Behavioral Development, Minneapolis.

Burbank, V. K. (1988). *Aboriginal adolescence: Maidenhood in an Australian community.* New Brunswick, NJ: Rutgers University Press.

Burbank, V. K. (1991). Comments on the panel on *"Female aggression: Motives, strategies and tactics."* Presented at the annual meeting of the American Anthropological Association, Chicago.

Burkert, W. (1987). *Ancient mystery cults.* Cambridge, MA: Harvard University Press.

Buss, A. (1961). *The psychology of aggression.* New York: Wiley.

Casper, R. C. (1983). On the engess of bulimic nervosa as a syndrome: A historic view. *International Journal of Eating Disorders, 3,* 3–16.

Chartier, R. (1988). *Cultural history: Between practices and representations.* Ithaca, NY: Cornell University Press.

Chesney, K. (1970). *The Victorian underworld.* Middleserp: England: Penguin.

Cohen, S., & Scull, A. (1983). *Social control and the state.* New York: St. Martin's.

Condon, R. G. (1987). *Inuit youth: Growth and change in the Canadian Arctic.* New Brunswick, NJ: Rutgers University Press.

Conrad, P., & Schneider, J. W. (1980). *Deviance and medicalization: From badness to sickness.* St. Louis, MO: Mosby.

Costello, E. J. (1989a). Developments in child psychiatric epidemiology. *Journal of the American Academy of Child and Adolescent Psychiatry, 28,* 836–841.

Costello, E. J. (1989b). *The status of epidemiologic research into psychiatric disorders of childhood and adolescence.* Paper presented at the annual meeting of the Research and Training Center of Children's Mental Health, Florida Mental Health Institute, University of South Florida, Tampa.

Costello, E. J., & Benjamin, R. (1989). Epidemiology and child diagnosis. In G. G. Last & M. Hersen (Eds.), *Handbook of child psychiatric diagnosis* (pp. 496–516) New York: Wiley.

Crapanzano, V. (1977). Introduction. In V. Crapanzano & V. Garrison (Eds.), *Case studies in spirit possession* (pp. 1–40). New York: Wiley.

Cummings, L. L. (1991). *Reported and observed participation of females in street-fighting in Chihuahua, Mexico.* Paper presented at the annual meeting of the American Anthropological Association, Chicago.

D'Andrade, R. (1984). Cultural meaning systems. In R. Shweder & R. LeVine (Eds.), *Culture theory* (pp. 88–119). Cambridge, England: Cambridge University Press.

Davis, C., & Yaeger, J. (1992). Transcultural aspects of eating disorders: A critical literature review. *Culture, Medicine and Psychiatry, 16,* 377–394.

Davis, N. Z. (1971). The reasons of misrule: Youth groups and *charivaris* in sixteenth century France. *Past and Present, 51,* 41–75.

Davis, N. Z. (1986). Boundaries and the sense of self in sixteenth century France. In T. C. Heller, M. Sosna, & D. E. Wellbery (Eds.), *Reconstructing individualism: Autonomy, individuality and the self in Western thought* (pp. 53–63). Stanford, CA: Stanford University Press.

Davis, S., & Davis, D. A. (1989). *Adolescence in a Moroccan town: Making social sense.* New Brunswick, NJ: Rutgers University Press.

Dell, P. F., & Eisenhower, J. W. (1990). Adolescent multiple personality disorder: A preliminary study of eleven cases. *Journal of the American Academy of Child and Adolescent Psychiatry, 29,* 359–366.

deMause, L. (1974). *The history of childhood.* New York: Harper and Row.

Demos, J. (1972). Developmental perspective on the history of childhood. *Journal of Interdisciplinary History, 2,* 215–237.

Demos, J., & Demos, V. (1969). Adolescence in historical perspective. *Journal of Marriage and the Family, 31,* 632–638.

Dennis, W. (1949). Historical beginnings of child psychology. *Psychological Bulletin, 46,* 224–235.

Dobson, R. B. (1991). Youth problems in the Soviet Union. In A. Jones, W. D. Connor, & D. E. Powell (Eds.), *Soviet social problems* Boulder, CO: Westview.

Dodge, K. A., Bales, J. E., & Pettil, G. S. (1990). Mechanism in the cycle of violence. *Science, 250,* 1678–1683.

Elder, G. H. (1975). Adolescence in the life cycle: An introduction. *Adolescence in the life cycle: Psychological change and social context* (pp. 1–22). New York: Wiley.

Emsley, C. (1987). *Crime and society in England, 1750–1900.* New York: Longman.

Erickson, E. H. (1963). *Childhood and society* (2nd ed.). New York: Norton.

Erickson, E. H. (1968). *Identity, youth and crisis.* New York: Norton.

Erickson, E. H. (1980). *Identity and the life cycle.* New York: Norton.

Eron, C. D. (1982). Parent-child interaction, television violence, and aggression of children. *American Psychologist, 37,* 197–211.

Eron, L. D., & Huesmann, L. R. (1984). The relation of prosocial behavior to the development of aggression and psychopathology. *Aggressive Behavior, 10,* 201–211.

Fabrega, H. (1989a). The self and schizophrenia: A cultural perspective. *Schizophrenia Bulletin,* 15, 277–290.

Fabrega, H. (1989b). Cultural relativism and psychiatric illness. *Journal of Nervous and Mental Disease,* 177, 415–425.

Fabrega, H., Jr. (1992) The role of culture in a theory of psychiatric illness. *Social Science and Medicine,* 35,91–103.

Fabrega, H., Jr. (1993) A cultural analysis of human behavioral breakdowns: An approach to the ontology and epistemology of psychiatric phenomena. *Culture, Medicine and Psychiatry,* 17, 99–132.

Farrington, D. P., Loeber, R., & Elliot, D. S. (1988). Advancing knowledge about delinquency and crime: The need for a coordinated program of longitudinal research. *Behavioral Sciences and the Law,* 6, 307–331.

Foucault, M. (1965). *Madness and civilization: A history of insanity in the age of reason.* New York: Random House.

Foucault, M. (1978). *Discipline and punish.* New York: Pantheon.

Freed, R., & Freed, S. (1985). *The psychomedical case history of a low-caste woman of north India.* (Anthropological Papers of the American Museum of Natural History, Vol. 60, P. 2). New York: American Museum of Natural History.

Freed, R., & Freed, S. (1990). Ghost illness of children in north India. *Medical Anthropology,* 12, 401–417.

Freeman, D. (1983). *Margaret Mead and Samoa: The making and unmaking of an anthropological myth.* New York: Penguin.

Fricke, T. E. (1986). *Himalayan households: Tamang demography and domestic processes.* Ann Arbor: University of Michigan Research Press.

Gadpaille, W. J. (1984). Adolescent aggression from the perspective of cultural anthropology. In C. R. Keith (Ed.), *The aggressive adolescent* (pp. 432–454). New York: Free Press.

Garfinkel, P. E., & Gardner, D. M. (1982). *Anorexia nervosa: A multidimensional perspective.* New York: Basic Books.

Garland, D. (1990). *Punishment and modern society: A study in social theory.* Chicago: University of Chicago Press.

Geertz, C. (1973). *The interpretation of cultures.* New York: Basic Books.

Geremek, B. (1987). *The margins of society in late medieval Paris.* Cambridge, England: Cambridge University Press.

Gergen, K. J. (1971). *The concept of self.* New York: Holt, Rinehart & Winston.

Gillis, J. (1975). The evolution of juvenile delinquency in England 1890–1914. *Past and Present,* 67, 96–126.

Gillis, J. (1981). *Youth and history: Tradition and change in European age relations, 1770–present.* New York: Academic Press.

Gontard, A. von. (1988). The development of child psychiatry in 19th century Britain. *Journal of Child Psychology and Psychiatry,* 29, 569–588.

Good, B. (1977). The heart of what is the matter: The semantics of illness in Iran. *Culture, Medicine and Psychiatry,* 1, 25–28.

Gould, M. S., Wunsch-Hitzig, R., & Dohrenwend, B. (1981). Estimating the prevalence of childhood psychopathology. *Journal of the American Academy of Child Psychiatry, 20,* 462–476.

Graham, P., & Rutter, M. (1973). Psychiatric disorder in the young adolescent: A follow-up study. *Proceeds of the Royal Society of Medicine, 66,* 1226–1229.

Grob, C., & de Rios, D. (1992). Adolescent drug use in cross-cultural perspective. *Journal of Drug Issues, 22,* 121–138.

Guarnaccia, P. J., de la Cancela, V., & Carrillo, E. (1989). The multiple meanings of *ataques de nervios* in the Latino community. *Medical Anthropology, 11,* 47–62.

Habermas, T. (1989). The psychiatric history of anorexia nervosa and bulimia nervosa: Weight concerns and bulimic symptoms in early case reports. *International Journal of Eating Disorders, 8,* 259–273.

Hall, G. S. (1904). *Adolescence: Its psychology and its relations to physiology, anthropology, sociology, sex, crime, religion and education.* New York: Appleton.

Hanning, R. W. (1977). *The individual in twelfth century romance.* New Haven, CT: Yale University Press.

Headland, T., Pike, K., & Harris, M. (Eds.). (1990). *Emics and etics: The insider/outsider debate.* Newbury Park, CA: Sage.

Herdt, G. (1990). Sambia nosebleeding rites and male proximity to women. In J. W. Stigler, R. A. Shweder, & G. Herdt (Eds.), *Cultural psychology: Essays on comparative human development* (pp. 367–400). New York: Cambridge University Press.

Herdt, G. (1993). Sexual repression, social control, and gender hierarchy in Sambia culture. In B. D. Miller (Ed.) *Sex and gender hierarchies* (pp. 193–211). New York: Cambridge University Press.

Hersov, L. (1986). Child psychiatry in Britain—the last 30 years. *Journal of Child Psychology and Psychiatry, 27,* 781–801.

Hinde, R. A. (1974). *Biological basis of human social behavior.* New York: McGraw-Hill.

Hiner, N. R. (1975). Adolescence in eighteenth century America. *History of Childhood Quarterly, 3,* 253–280.

Hogan, D. P., & Michozuki, T. (1988). Demographic transitions and the life course: Lessons from Japanese and American comparisons. *Journal of Family History, 13,* 291–305.

Holden, N. L., & Robinson, P. H. (1988). Anorexia nervosa and bulimia nervosa in British blacks. *British Journal of Psychiatry, 152,* 544–549.

Hollos, M., & P. E. Leis (1989). *Becoming Nigerian in Ijo society.* New Brunswick, NJ: Rutgers University Press.

Hsu, L. K. (1988). The outcome of anorexia nervosa: A reappraisal. *Psychological Medicine, 18,* 807–812.

Hunt, L. (1989). *The new cultural history.* Berkeley: University of California Press.

Hurrelmann, K. (1987). The importance of school in the life course. *Journal of Adolescent Research, 2,* 111–125.

Ingram, J. (1984). Riding, rough music and the reform of popular culture in early modern England. *Past and Present, 105,* 179–213.

Jenkins, J. H. (1991). Anthropology, expressed emotion, and schizophrenia. *Ethos, 19,* 387–431.

Jessor, R. (1984). Adolescent development and behavioral health. In J. D. Matarazzo, S. M. Weiss, J. A. Herd, N. E. Miller, & S. M. Weiss (Eds.), *Behavioral health: A handbook of health enhancement and disease prevention.* New York: Wiley.

Jessor, R. (1991). Risk behavior in adolescence: A psychosocial framework for understanding and action. *Journal of Adolescent Health, 12,* 597–605.

Jones, R. L. (1989). *Black adolescents.* Berkeley, CA: Cobb and Henry.

Johnston, L. D., O'Malley, P. M., & Bachman, J. G. (1987). Psychotherapeutic, licit and illicit drug use of drugs among adolescents: An epidemiological perspective. *Journal of Adolescent Health Care, 8,* 36–51.

Junger, M. (1990). *Delinquency and ethnicity.* Boston: Kluwer Law and Taxation Publishers.

Kakar, S. (1982). *Shamans, mystics and doctors: A psychological inquiry into India and its healing traditions.* Chicago: University of Chicago Press.

Kashani, J. H., Beck, N. C., Hoeper, E. W., Fallahi, C., Corcoran, C. M., McAllister, J. A., Rosenberg, T. K., & Reid, J. C. (1987). Psychiatric disorders in a community sample of adolescents. *American Journal of Psychiatry, 144,* 584–589.

Keir, G. (1952). Symposium on psychologists and psychiatrists in the child guidance service: III. A history of child guidance. *British Journal of Educational Psychology, 22,* 5–29.

Kett, J. (1971). Adolescence and youth in nineteenth century America. *Journal of Interdisciplinary History, 2,* 283–298.

Khandelwal, S. K., & Saxena, S. (1990). Anorexia nervosa in adolescents of Asian extraction. *British Journal of Psychiatry, 157,* 784.

Kittrie, N. N. (1971). *The right to be different.* Baltimore, MD: Johns Hopkins University Press.

Klaits, J. (1985). *Servants of Satan: The age of the witch hunts.* Bloomington: Indiana University Press.

Kleinman, A. (1988). *Rethinking psychiatry: From cultural category to personal experience.* New York: Free Press.

Kleinman, A., & Lin, T. (1981) *Normal and abnormal behavior in Chinese culture.* Dordrecht, Netherlands: Reidel.

Kovacs, M. (1989) Affective disorders in children and adolescents. *American Psychologist, 44,* 209–215.

Kovacs, M., Gatsonis, G., Paulauskas, S. L., & Richards, C. (1989). Depressive disorders in childhood. *Archives of General Psychiatry, 46,* 776–782.

Krippner, S. (1987). Cross cultural approaches to personality disorder: Practices in Brazilian spiritualism. *Ethos, 15,* 273–295.

Langbaum, R. (1979). *The mysteries of identity: A theme in modern literature.* New York: Oxford University Press.

Lauer, C. (1991). *A comparison of aggressive behavior in pre-school girls and boys.* Paper presented at the annual meeting of the American Anthropological Association, Chicago.

Leacock, E. (1993). Women in Samoan history: A further critique of Derek Freeman. In B. D. Miller (Ed.), *Sex and gender hierarchies* (pp. 351–365). New York: Cambridge University Press.

Lee, S. (1991). Anorexia nervosa in Hong Kong: A Chinese perspective. *Psychological Medicine, 21,* 703–711.

Lee, S., Chiu, H. F. K., & Chen, C. N. (1989). Anorexia in Hong Kong: Why not more in Chinese? *British Journal of Psychiatry, 154,* 683–688.

Lefkowitz, M. M., Eron, L. D., Waler, L. O., & Huesmann, L. R. (1977). *Growing up to be violent.* New York: Pergamon.

LeVine, R. A. (1973). *Culture, behavior and personality.* Chicago: Aldine.

LeVine, R. A. (1990). Cultural environments in child development. In W. Damon (Ed.), *Child development today and tomorrow.* San Francisco: Jossey-Bass.

LeVine, R. A. (1989). Infant environments in psychoanalysis: A cross-cultural view. In J. W. Stigler, R. A. Shweder & G. Herdt (Eds.), *Cultural psychology* (pp. 454–474). Cambridge, England: Cambridge University Press.

Levy, D. (1968). Beginnings of the child guidance movement. *American Journal of Orthopsychiatry, 38,* 799–804.

Lewis, I. M. (1989). *Ecstatic religion* (2nd ed.). London: Routledge.

Littlewood, R., & Lipsedge, M. (1971). Culture-bound syndromes. In K. Granville-Grossman (Ed.), *Recent advances in clinical psychiatry* (pp. 105–142). London: Churchill-Livingstone.

Loeber, R. (1982). The stability of antisocial and delinquent child behavior: A review. *Child Development, 53,* 1431–1446.

Loeber, R. (1990). Development and risk factors of juvenile antisocial behavior and delinquency. *Clinical Psychology Review, 10,* 1–14.

Loeber, R. (1991). Antisocial behavior: More enduring than changeable? *Journal of American Academy of Child and Adolescent Psychiatry, 30,* 393–397.

Low, S. M. (1985). Culturally interpreted symptoms or culture-bound syndromes: A cross-cultural review of nerves. *Social Science and Medicine, 21,* 187–196.

Ludwig, A. M. (1983). The psychological functions of dissociation. *American Journal of Clinical Hypnosis, 26,* 93–99.

Lutz, C. (1988). *Unnatural emotions: Everyday sentiments on a Micronesian atoll and their challenge to western theory.* Chicago: University of Chicago Press.

MacDonald, K. B. (1988). *Social and personality development: An evolutionary synthesis.* New York: Plenum.

MacDonald, M. (1988). *Mystical bedlam: Madness, anxiety and healing in seventeenth century England.* Cambridge, England: Cambridge University Press.

MacIntyre, A. (1981). *After virtue.* Notre Dame, IN: University of Notre Dame Press.

Manson, S. M. (1990). *Indian adolescent mental health* (U.S. Congress Office of Technology Publication No. OTA-H-46). Washington, DC: U.S. Government Printing Office.

Manson, S. M., Shore, J. H., & Bloom, J. D. (1985). The depressive experience in American Indian communities: A challenge for psychiatric theory and diagnosis. In A. Kleinman & B. Good (Eds.), *Culture and depression* (pp. 331–368). Berkeley: University of California Press.

Markantonakis, A. (1990). Letter to the editor. *British Journal of Psychiatry, 157,* 783–784.

Maudsley, H. (1868). *The physiology and pathology of the mind* (2nd ed.). London: Macmillan.

Mayer, P., & Mayer, I. (1970). Socialization by peers. In P. Mayer (Ed.), *Socialization: The approach from social anthropology* (pp. 159–189). London: Tavistock.

Martin, R. G., & Conger, R. D. (1980). A comparison of delinquency trends: Japan and the United States. *Criminology, 18,* 53–61.

Mead, M. (1928). *Coming of age in Samoa: A psychological study of primitive youth for Western civilization.* New York: Dell.

Merskey, H. (1992). The manufacture of personalities: The production of multiple personality disorders. *British Journal of Psychiatry, 160,* 327–340.

Meyer, P. (1983). *The child and the state: The intervention of the state in family life.* Cambridge, England: Cambridge University Press.

Modell, J., Furstenberg, F. F., & Hershberg, T. (1976). Social change and transitions to adulthood in historical perspective: Journal of family history. In C. H. Mindel & R. W. Habenstein (Eds.), *Ethnic families in America* (pp. 7–32). New York: Elsevier.

Mollat, M. (1986). *The poor in the Middle Ages.* New Haven, CT: Yale University Press.

Montemayor, R. (1990). Continuity and change in the behavior of non-human primates during the transition to adolescence. In R. Montemayor, G. R. Adams & T. Gullotta (Eds.), *From childhood to adolescence: A transitional period?* Newbury Park, CA: Sage.

Morris, C. (1972). *The discovery of the individual: 1050–1200.* New York: Harper & Row.

Mulhern, S. (1991). Embodied alternative identities: Bearing witness to a world that might have been. *Psychiatric Clinics of North America, 14,* 769–786.

Nasser, M. (1986). Comparative study of the prevalence of abnormal eating attitudes among Arab female students of both London and Cairo universities. *Psychological Medicine, 16,* 621–625.

Nogami, Y., & Yabana, F. (1977). On Kibarashi-Qui. *Folia Psychiatric Neurology Japan, 31,* 159–166.

Obeyesekere, G. (1981). *Medusa's hair: An essay on personal symbols and religious experience.* Chicago: University of Chicago Press.

Obeyesekere, G. (1985). Depression, Buddhism and the work of culture in Sri Lanka. In A. Kleinman & B. Good (Eds.), *Culture and depression* (pp. 134–152). Berkeley: University of California Press.

Ong, A. (1987). *Spirits of resistance and capitalist discipline: Factory women in Malaysia.* Albany: State University of New York Press.

Ong, A. (1988) The production of possession: Spirits and the multinational corporation in Malaysia. *American Ethnologist, 15,* 28–42.

Orne, M. T., & Bates, B. L. (1992). Reflections on personality disorder: A view from the looking-glass of hypnosis past. In C. Pierce, M. Greenblatt, & A. Kales (Eds.), *The mosaic of contemporary psychiatry.* New York: Springer-Verlag.

Orne, M. T., & Bauer-Manley, N. K. (1991). Disorders of self: Myths, metaphors and the demand characteristics of treatment. In J. Strauss & C. R. Goethals (Eds.), *The self: Interdisciplinary approaches* (pp. 93–106). New York: Springer-Verlag.

Otis, L. L. (1985). *Prostitution in medieval society.* Chicago: University of Chicago Press.

Parry-Jones, W. I. (1989). Annotation: The history of child and adolescent psychiatry: Its present day relevance. *Journal of Child Psychology and Psychiatry, 30,* 3–11.

Patterson, G. R., DeBaryshe, B. D., & Ramsey, E. (1989). A developmental perspective on antisocial behavior. *American Psychologist, 49,* 329–335.

Paton, S. M., & Kandel, D. B. (1978). Psychological factors and adolescent illicit drug use: Ethnicity and sex differences. *Adolescence, 40,* 187–200.

Petersen, A. C. (1986). Adolescence: A developmental approach to problems and psychopathology. *Behavior Therapy, 17,* 480–499.

Petersen, A. C. (1987). The nature of biological-psychosocial interactions: The sample case of early adolescence. In R. M. Lerner & T. T. Foch (Eds.), *Biological-psychosocial interactions in early adolescence: A life-span perspective* (pp. 35–61). Hillsdale, NJ: Erlbaum.

Petersen, A. C., & Ebata, A. T. (1987). Developmental transitions and adolescent problem behavior: Implications for prevention and intervention. In K. Jurrelmann, F. X. Kaufmann, & F. Losel (Eds.), *Social intervention: Potential and constraints* (pp. 167–184). New York: Aldine de Gruyter.

Petersen, A. C., & Hamburg, B. A. (1988). Adolescent development. *Annual Review of Psychology, 39,* 583–608.

Petersen, A. C., Susman, E., & Beard, J. L. (1989). The development of coping responses during adolescence: Endocrine and behavioral aspects. In D. Palermo (Ed.), *Coping with uncertainty: Behavioral and developmental perspectives* (pp. 151–172). Hillsdale, NJ: Erlbaum.

Pike, K. L (1967). *Language in relation to a united theory of the structure of human behavior.* The Hague, Netherlands: Mouton.

Platt, A. J. (1977). *The child savers: The invention of delinquency.* Chicago: University of Chicago Press.

Prichard, J. C. (1835). *A treatise on insanity in relation to jurisprudence.* London: Bailliaere.

Prince, R. (1968). *Trance and possession states.* Montreal: Bucke Memorial Society.

Prince, R. (1985). The concept of culture-bound syndromes: Anorexia nervosa and brain-fag. *Social Science and Medicine, 21,* 197–203.

Putnam, F. W. (1991a). Recent research on multiple personality disorders. *Psychiatric Clinics of North America, 14,* 769–787.

Putnam, F. W. (1991b). Dissociative disorders in children and adolescents. *Psychiatric Clinics of North America, 14,* 519–531.

Putz, M. (1979). *The story of identity: American fiction of the sixties.* Stuttgart, Germany: Metzler.

Robins, L. (1991). Conduct disorder. *Journal of Child Psychology and Psychiatry, 32,* 193–212.

Rosaldo, R. (1988). *Ilongot headhunting, 1883–1974: A study in society and history.* Stanford, CA: Stanford University Press.

Rossiaud, J. (1984). *Medieval prostitution.* Oxford, England: Blackwell.

Rothstein, S. W. (1984) *The power to punish: A social inquiry into coercion and control in urban schools.* Leave in LAN HAM, MD: University Press.

Russell, G. F. M. (1970). Anorexia nervosa: Its identity as an illness and its treatment. In J. H. Price (Ed.), *Modern trends in psychological medicine* (Vol. 2, pp. 131–164). London: Butterworth.

Russell, G. F. M. (1985). The changing nature of anorexia nervosa: An introduction to the conference. *Journal of Psychiatric Research, 19,* 101–109.

Russell, G. F. M., & Treasure, J. (1989). The modern history of anorexia nervosa: An interpretation of why the illness has changed. In L. H. Schneider, S. J. Coopera, & K. A. Halmi (Eds.), *The psychobiology of human eating disorders* (pp. 13–30). New York: New York Academy of Sciences.

Rutter, M. (1980). *Changing youth in a changing society.* Cambridge, MA: Harvard University Press.

Rutter, M. (1986). Child psychiatry: Looking 30 years ahead. *Journal of Child Psychology and Psychiatry, 27,* 803–840.

Rutter, M., Chadwick, D. F. D., & Yule, W. (1986). Adolescent turmoil: Fact or fiction. *Journal of Child Psychology and Psychiatry, 17,* 35–56.

Rutter, M., & Garmezy, N. (1983). Developmental psychopathology. In E. M. Hetherington (Ed.), *Socialization, personality and social development* (Vol. 4). New York: Wiley.

Rutter, M., Maugham, B., Mortimore, P., Ouston, J., & Smith, A. (1979). *Fifteen thousand hours: Secondary schools and their effects on children.* London: Open Books.

Rutter, M., & Sandberg, S. (1985). Epidemiology of child psychiatric disorders: Methodological issues and some substantive findings. *Child Psychiatry and Human Development, 15,* 209–233.

Rutter, M., Tizard, J., & Whitmore, K. (1970). *Education, health and behavior.* London: Longman.

Salgado, G. (1977). *The Elizabethan underworld.* London: Dent.

Scheper-Hughes, N. (1979). *Saints, scholars and schizophrenics: Mental illness in rural Ireland.* Berkeley: University of California Press.

Schieffelin, B., & Ochs, E. (1986). *Language socialization across cultures.* Cambridge: Cambridge University Press.

Schlegel, A., & Barry, H. (1991). *Adolescence: An anthropological inquiry.* New York: Free Press.

Scull, A. T. (1979). *Museums of madness.* New York: St. Martin's.

Sennett, R. (1974). *The fall of public man.* New York: Random House.

Sharp, L. A. (1990). Possessed and dispossessed youth: Spirit possession of school children in northwest Madagascar. *Ethos, 14,* 339–364.

Sharpe, J. A. (1984). *Crime in early modern England 1550–1750.* London: Longman.

Shelley, L. (1981). *Crime and modernization: The impact of industrialization and urbanization on crime.* Carbondale: Southern Illinois Press.

Shweder, R. A. (1990). Cultural psychology—what is it? In J. W. Stigler, R. A. Shweder, & G. Herdt (Eds.), *Cultural psychology: Essays on comparative human development* (pp. 1–43). New York: Cambridge University Press.

Shweder, R. A. (1991). *Thinking through cultures.* Cambridge: Harvard University Press.

Skultans, V. (1991). Women and affliction in Maharashtra: A hydraulic model of health and illness. *Culture, Medicine and Psychiatry, 15,* 321–359.

Simons, R. C., & Hughes, C. C. (1985). *The culture-bound syndromes: Folk illnesses of psychiatric and anthropological interest.* Boston: Reidel.

Singer, M. (1961). A survey of culture and personality theory and research. In B.

Kaplan (Ed.), *Studying personality cross-culturally* (pp. 9–92). Evanston, IL: Harper & Row.

Smith, S. R. (1973). The London apprentices in seventeenth century adolescents. *Past and Present, 61,* 149–161.

Spencer, M. B. & Dornbusch, S. M. (1990). Challenges in studying minority youth. In S. S. Feldmand & G. R. Elliott (Eds.), *At the threshold: The developing adolescent* (pp. 123–146). Cambridge: Harvard University Press.

Spiro, M. E. (1986). Cultural relativism and the future of anthropology. *Cultural Anthropology, 1,* 259–286.

Springhall, J. (1986). *Coming of age: Adolescence in Britain 1860–1960.* Dublin: Gill & MacMillan.

Stiffman, R. R., & Davis, L. E. (1990). *Ethnic issues in adolescent mental health.* Newbury Park, CA: Sage.

Suematsu, H., Ishikawa, H., Kuboki, T., & Ito, T. (1985). Statistical studies on anorexia nervosa in Japan. *Psychotherapy and Psychosomatics, 43,* 96–103.

Super, C. M., & Harkness, S. (1986). The developmental niche: A conceptualization of the interface of child and culture. *International Journal of Behavioral Development, 9,* 545–569.

Sypher, W. (1962). *Loss of self in modern literature and art.* New York: Random House.

Tasman, A., & Goldfinger, S. M. (1991). *Review of psychiatry* (Vol. 10). Washington, DC: American Psychiatric Press.

Trexler, R. C. (1974). Ritual in Florence: Adolescence and salvation in the renaissance. In C. Trinkaus & H. A. Hoberman (Eds.), *The pursuit of holiness in late medieval and Renaissance religion.* Kinderhook, N.Y.: E. J. Brill

Trilling, L. (1971). *Sincerity and authenticity.* Cambridge, MA: Harvard University Press.

Walk, A. (1964). The pre-history of child psychiatry. *British Journal of Psychiatry, 110,* 754–767.

Walker, D. P. (1981). *Unclean spirits: Possession and exorcism in the late sixteenth and early seventeenth century.* Philadelphia: University of Pennsylvania.

Ward, B. E. (1970). Temper tantrums in Kau Sai. In P. Mayer (Ed.), *Socialization the view from social anthropology* (pp. 109–125). London: Tavistock.

Weinstein, D., & Bell, R. M. (1982). *Saints and society.* Chicago: University of Chicago Press.

Weintraub, K. J. (1978). *The value of the individual: Self and circumstance in autobiography.* Chicago: University of Chicago Press.

Weiss, J. R., Suwanlest, S., Chaiyasit, W., Weiss, B., Achenbach, T. M., & Trevathan, D. (1989). Epidemiology of behavioral and emotional problems among Thai and American children: Teacher reports for ages 6–11. *Journal of Child Psychology and Psychiatry, 30,* 471–484.

Weisser, M. R. (1982). *Crime and punishment in early modern Europe.* Sussex, England: Harvester.

Werlinder, H. (1978). *Psychopathy: A history of the concepts.* Stockholm: Almqvist and Wiksell.

Whiting, B. B. (1980). Culture and social behavior. *Ethos, 8,* 95–116.

Whiting, B. B., & Whiting, J. W. M. (1975). *Children of six cultures.* Cambridge: Harvard University Press.

Whiting, B. B., & Whiting, J. W. M. (in press). Adolescence in the pre-industrial world. In R. M. Lerner, A. C. Petersen, & J. Brooks-Gunn (Eds.), *The encyclopedia of adolescence.*

Whiting, J. W. M., Burbank, V. K., & Ratner, M. S. (1986). The duration of maidenhood across cultures. In J. Lancaster (Ed.), *School-age pregnancy and parenthood: Biosocial dimensions* (pp. 273–302). New York: Aldine de Gruyter.

Worthman, C. M. (1991, October). *Adolescents and the embodiment of culture.* Paper presented at the biennial meeting of the Society for Psychological Anthropology, Chicago.

Yamazaki, K., Inomata, J. and Mackenzie, J. A. (1987). Self expression, interpersonal relations and juvenile delinquency in Japan. In C. M. Super (ed.) *The Role of Culture in Developmental Disorder.* Boston, Academic Press, pp. 179–204.

Yarbrough, A. (1979). Apprentices as adolescents in sixteenth century Bristol. *Journal of Social History*, 13(1) 67–81, 1979.

2
Biological and Maturational Factors in Development

Julia A. Graber
Jeanne Brooks-Gunn

P ubertal development marks the end of childhood and the entry into adolescence. From the beginning of adolescence until the transition to adulthood, adolescents' lives undergo pervasive changes across nearly every domain (Brooks-Gunn, 1984; Lewin, 1939). During adolescence, social roles, expectations, and relationships are restructured within the family, peer group, and school environment; cognitive and socioemotional changes alter fundamental beliefs about the self as well as levels of psychological adjustment; and the physical changes of puberty produce the outward appearance of an individual who must be viewed—both by the individual or by her or his environment—as no longer a child, but instead as someone who will soon assume adult roles. The pubertal transition has been viewed as the impetus for other behavioral and social changes with which puberty co-occurs and that it precedes (Brooks-Gunn & Petersen, 1983; Petersen & Taylor, 1980).

For example, changes within an individual's social environment are in some part attributable to the response of family, friends, and teachers to his or her more adultlike appearance. Feelings about oneself are also subject to the satisfaction or anxiety one experiences about a changing appearance; puberty has been compared to a game of chance, as the individual can not be certain of how she or he will look when the process is complete (Petersen, 1987). Internal rather than external pubertal processes have also been ascribed as the cause for behavioral change: increases in cognitive skills and abilities have been associated with brain development at adolescence (e.g., Waber, 1977), and emotional lability has been associated with hor-

The authors were supported by a grant from the National Institutes of Health (NICHA) during the writing of this paper. Correspondence should be addressed to Julia A. Graber at the Adolescent Study Program, Box 39, Teachers College, Columbia University, 525 W. 120th Street, New York, NY 10027.

monal changes (e.g., Susman, Dorn, & Chrousos, 1991). Given the range and possibilities for interaction among the biological, social, and psychological substrates of development, it is clear that how pubertal development is traversed may be a potent determinant of the path an individual's life will take during and beyond adolescence. Multiple physical changes and social challenges may be overwhelming for some adolescents, especially those who enter the pubertal transition with poor coping skills (Brooks-Gunn & Reiter, 1990). Hence pubertal changes may be directly and indirectly linked to the development of psychopathology in some adolescents.

In this overview of the role of puberty in adolescent development, the physiological processes that constitute pubertal development are reviewed, followed by a discussion of the behavioral correlates of puberty. Behavioral correlates include individual or internal psychological interpretation of pubertal development (which is often linked to a specific level of development or pubertal status), as well as the influences stemming from the social context of the development (which is often related to the timing of puberty). In addition, because of the salience to adolescent behavior ascribed to hormonal changes, models for examining the direct, indirect, and bidirectional influences among hormonal, psychological, and social changes are presented. Through integration of these models, it is possible to delineate paths for the development of the continuum of adaptive to maladaptive behaviors over the adolescent decade.

The Physiological Changes of Puberty

In order to understand the psychological and social effects of puberty, it is necessary to describe the pubertal process. Pubertal change is not itself a singular process but a term used for the interrelated internal and external physical changes occurring during adolescence. In terms of evolutionary considerations, puberty can be defined as the growth processes that result in the attainment of reproductive capability (Brooks-Gunn & Petersen, 1983; Marshall & Tanner, 1986). In addition, pubertal development includes physical growth and alterations not directly associated with reproduction. The general areas of internal and external changes during the pubertal process are (a) maturation of the reproductive organs and the development of secondary sexual characteristics; (b) the growth spurt, defined as the acceleration and subsequent deceleration of skeletal growth; (c) changes in the composition and distribution of fat and muscle tissue in the body; (d) circulatory and respiratory system development leading to increases in strength and endurance; and (e) changes in specific areas of the nervous system and endocrine system, which through their interaction result in the regulation of the other pubertal developmental processes (Marshall & Tanner, 1986). The culmination of these changes is the attainment of an adult body in appearance and functioning. Extensive delineation of each aspect of physical development has been documented in the medical literature; an overview of this research is presented here.

Pubertal maturation is controlled by the reproductive endocrine system. This system consists primarily of the hypothalamus, the pituitary gland, and the gonads. The hypothalamus is a small area of the brain located below the cortex in the forebrain area and is responsible for regulation of several physiological functions. In particular, portions of the hypothalamus monitor hormone levels in the bloodstream and convey messages to the pituitary gland via hormones and neural pathways in order to alter hormonal levels in the body. The pituitary gland lies at the base of the hypothalamus and secretes hormones into the bloodstream in response to these messages. The gonads are the sex organs (ovaries in females and testes in males), which receive hormonal information from the pituitary and in response produce hormones (e.g., estrogen and testosterone) that are subsequently monitored by the hypothalamus. The hormones and neural pathways are the means through which messages are passed through the body regulating growth and body functioning. Through these feedback loops for transmitting physiological information, the components of this system monitor one another.

The adrenal glands are also influenced by the hypothalamus and pituitary gland and also produce sex hormones (e.g., estrogen, testosterone). In addition, they are responsive to stress. The role of the hypothalamus-pituitary-adrenal (HPA) axis in pubertal maturation is not understood as well as the functioning of the hypothalamus-pituitary-gonadal (HPG) axis.

During the prenatal period of development, hormones—specifically, androgens—"organize" the reproductive system (Goy & McEwen, 1980); that is, when the gonads develop prenatally, hormones are secreted that create the HPG axis and subsequently result in the development of the external genitalia. Androgen levels remain elevated through the first few months of postnatal life. After hormone levels drop postnatally, the reproductive endocrine system remains dormant until middle to late childhood, when the system is "activated" and pubertal development begins (Reiter & Grumbach, 1982). Activation involves increases in sex-steroid hormone secretion through adrenarche and gonadarche, two closely linked but independent processes. *Adrenarche*, which occurs first, refers to the maturation of the adrenal gland resulting in the production of androgens. *Gonadarche*, which occurs approximately 2 years after adrenarche, refers to the activation of the HPG system with activation of hormone secretion by the gonads. Even though many of the hormones produced by the gonads are also produced by the adrenal glands, the two lines are separate, with several aspects of pubertal development along the HPG axis capable of continuing in the absence of increases in androgens (Reiter & Grumbach, 1982).

The physical changes of puberty that occur subsequent to adrenarche

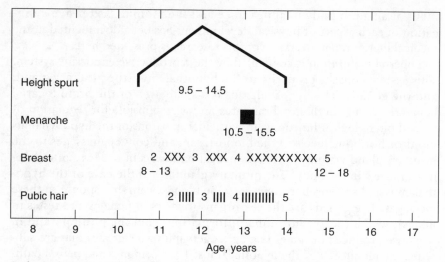

Redrawn from *Growth at adolescence*, p. 36, by Tanner, 1962, Oxford, England: Blackwell Scientific. Copyright 1962 by Blackwell Scientific. Reprinted with permission.

Figure 2–1. The development course of four pubertal processes for girls.

and gonadarche have been described by Marshall and Tanner (1969, 1970). Figures 2–1 and 2–2 show schematically the temporal relationships of the development of primary and secondary sexual characteristics for girls and boys, respectively. Marshall and Tanner (1969, 1970) have defined stages for breast and pubic hair development for girls and gonadal and pubic hair development for boys, as depicted in the figures. Five stages, ranging from no development to mature status, were defined in order to quantify levels of growth; because pubertal development is a continuous process, though, the stages are merely a method for quantifying qualitative change (Brooks-Gunn & Warren, 1985).

Most adolescents will take 4 to 5 years to traverse pubertal development (Petersen, 1987). Ages for initiation of development and attainment of completed growth for specific pubertal events, shown in Figures 2–1 and 2–2, are approximate and are based on British samples obtained during the 1950s. While slight sample variations are expected due to historical change as well as between-sample variations within a historical time period, the sequencing and progression of development is relatively stable across individuals (Marshall & Tanner, 1969, 1970, 1986). Ranges for the ages shown indicate the breadth of normal development; for example, girls reaching menarche at either 9.5 or 15.5 years of age are still within the range of normal development. The timing of the onset of development and the rate at which individuals progress through puberty varies greatly

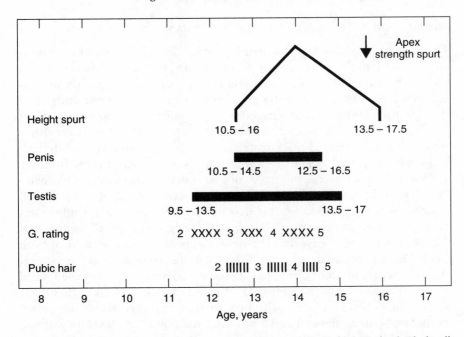

Redrawn from: *Growth at adolescence*, p. 30, by Tanner, 1962, Oxford, England: Blackwell Scientific. Copyright 1962 by Blackwell Scientific. Reprinted with permission.

Figure 2–2. **The development course of four pubertal processes for boys.**

among individuals (Marshall & Tanner, 1969, 1970). As between-individual variations are common in onset and rate and as asynchronies are not uncommon among different pubertal processes within an individual (Brooks-Gunn, Petersen, & Eichorn, 1985; Eichorn, 1975), it has been estimated that it takes 10 or more years to follow a single birth cohort through puberty (Petersen, 1987).

Since this imposes a substantial practical constraint, most investigations of the psychological significance of pubertal development do not examine the entire process. Often only a single indicator (or subset of indicators) is collected either over a brief period of adolescence or at a single point in time, with the expectation that the indicators chosen represent the global pubertal process. In other words, knowing when one or a few events occur, or how advanced certain processes are, is used to indicate the general level of development. While this approach is valid for the majority of adolescents, individual differences do occur for a minority of unknown size (Eichorn, 1975). In order to understand the measurement and meaning of pubertal development, it is worthwhile to consider each of the pubertal processes in more detail.

Development of Secondary Sexual Characteristics

For most girls, breast development begins around 10.5 years of age and is followed by the appearance of pubic hair (Marshall & Tanner, 1969, 1974). Individual variations are common in pubertal development, however, such that pubic hair appears prior to breast budding in one-fifth of all girls (Warren, 1983). These variations may be attributable to differences in hormonal control of breast and pubic hair development: breast growth is predominantly related to estrogen secreted by the ovaries, while hair growth is stimulated by androgen secretions (some of which come from the HPA axis). Girls traverse the stages of breast development in approximately 4.5 years, with this progression encompassing most of the pubertal process. Adult patterns of pubic hair growth are attained in slightly less time. An acceleration in growth in height (or "growth spurt") begins 6 to 12 months before breast development and peaks during stage 3 of both pubic hair and breast development. Just after the peak in height velocity is passed, menarche occurs, at approximately 12.5 years of age in the United States (Brooks-Gunn & Reiter, 1990). As can be seen in Figure 2–1, menarche is reached late in the progression of pubertal development, occurring between stages 4 and 5 of breast and pubic hair development and in the middle of the weight or fat spurt.

Boys' development is typically 1 to 2 years later than girls' development. For boys, development usually begins with growth of the testes, which occurs between 11 and 11.5 years of age and takes about 3 years until adult male genitalia are developed. Growth in size of the testes is associated with the tissue changes that result in reproductive and endocrine functioning. Testicular growth is most frequently assessed via measurements of testicular volume, the most common methods of which are calculating an index of volume (by averaging the length x width of the right and left testes) and comparison of the testes with ellipsoids of known volume. Both the index and ellipsoid measurements produce assessments that correlate with stages of pubertal development. Pubic hair development lags genital development by about one stage, on average. Acceleration in growth in height begins around 11.7 years of age, shortly after initial testicular growth, and peaks around 14 years of age.

Changes in Skeletal Growth, Height, Weight and Body Composition

The adolescent growth spurt in height is associated with changes in the bones, with growth occurring at the epiphyseal growing plates (rings of cartilage located at the ends of bones). During pubertal development, high concentrations of sex-steroid hormones, especially estrogen, cause the epiphyseals to fuse and harden. After ossification of the cartilage, only limited growth occurs.

Acceleration in growth of the skeleton is not uniform across the body (Marshall & Tanner, 1986); often, the spurt of growth in the legs begins more than 6 months before that of the trunk. Closure of the epiphyseals begins distally, with hands and feet reaching maturity first. In addition, the trunk will increase in length over time more than will the legs, leading to changes in body proportions. Such changes in body proportions may be disturbing to adolescents during the process of developing, as they will experience disproportionate shapes and may not be aware that these conditions are transient.

Nearly all girls reach their mature height by 18 years of age, whereas most boys attain adult stature by age 20. Almost 50% of growth in bones, including length and mass, occurs during adolescence and young adulthood. Gender differences in adult height are predominantly attributable to differences in timing of the growth spurt (Marshall & Tanner, 1986; Thissen & Bock, 1990). The overall amount of height gained (10 to 14 inches) during this time does not differ greatly between the sexes (Tanner, Whitehouse, & Takaishi, 1966); rather, it is the amount of childhood growth preceding the adolescent growth spurt that contributes most to overall size and appears to reflect the genetic component of adult height (Thissen & Bock, 1990). Adolescents who mature earlier than other adolescents (e.g., girls) have their childhood growth curtailed earlier and are on average shorter than adolescents who mature later (e.g., boys). Marshall and Tanner (1986), however note that within gender, maturational timing differences in height do not exist (i.e., early and late maturers reach similar average adult stature), although there is some debate as to whether this is true across studies (Malina, 1990).

Measuring the maturity of the bones of the body was previously considered one of the best ways to measure pubertal development (Petersen, 1983), and this method has been extensively studied (Styne & Grumbach, 1978) and used in psychological research (Jones & Bayley, 1950; Jones & Mussen, 1958). Skeletal age is assessed through examination of radiographs of the long bones of the body (most often of the hand and wrist) in order to determine extent of fusion and ossification; the amount of fusion and ossification exhibited in the X-ray is compared with norms for age published in atlases (e.g., Greulich & Pyle, 1959; Tanner & Whitehouse, 1982). The advantages of skeletal age are that (a) it can be used for both girls and boys, (b) it is related to other aspects of physical development (e.g., menarche, growth spurt, height, and weight), and (c) it is related to development of the secondary sexual characteristics (Jones & Bayley, 1950), although it is not predictive of their development (Marshall, 1974). The reliability of the assessment of radiographs and comparisons with norms has been disputed, however, (Roche, Wainer, & Thissen, 1975) and the use of X-rays in order to determine the level of development—while still practiced by physicians treating abnormal cases of development—has been discontinued in social science research due to health risks (Petersen, 1983).

Mathematical modeling (Bock et al., 1973; Thissen & Bock, 1990) and graphic methods of curve fitting (Tanner, Whitehouse, Marshall, Healy, & Goldstein, 1975) have been used to obtain the growth curves for individuals from which specific parameters (e.g., the age at peak height velocity and expected adult height) can be extracted. As this type of curve fitting does not involve X-rays but instead is derived from multiple measures of height, it involves no health risk. Height is often easily obtained by researchers, school nurses, or physicians, or it may already be available from school or physician records (Brooks-Gunn, Warren, Rosso, & Gargiulo, 1987; Petersen & Crockett, 1985). Even though the estimated value of age at peak height velocity has the same advantages in research of skeletal age as noted by Jones and Bayley (1950), estimation of growth curves has usually required numerous points of data collection (Brooks-Gunn & Warren, 1985), beginning in midchildhood. The estimation procedures developed by Bock and his colleagues (Bock et al., 1973; Thissen & Bock, 1990) allow for the use of fewer points of measurement while still calculating fairly accurate estimates (Graber, 1991) because their method incorporates normative data from the population in the estimation procedure. Unfortunately, use of population norms can result in the "overnormalization" of curves for individuals with unusual patterns of growth, such as very tall or very short individuals (Graber, 1991). The overnormalization may not be detected unless other pubertal or growth measures are obtained.

The growth spurt in weight has not been assessed as extensively but is known to occur concurrently with or just after the spurt in height for most individuals (see Malina, 1990; Tanner, 1962, 1972, for reviews). Weight has been examined as an absolute measure, as a ratio in relation to height, or as a percentile. The rapid weight gain observed at puberty is associated with increases in both fat and muscle, with girls accumulating more weight in the form of body fat and with boys accumulating more weight in the form of muscle mass (Tanner, 1962, 1972). Typically for both girls and boys, peak velocity for increases of fat occur between Tanner stages 4 and 5, with peak velocity for increases in muscle mass occurring between Tanner stages 3 and 4 (Gross, 1984).

Timing differences in weight spurt among individuals have been associated with different resultant body types, with early maturers tending to have a higher percentage of fat in their body composition and later maturers having leaner builds (Marshall & Tanner, 1986; Thissen & Bock, 1990). Malina (1990), however, has suggested that these differences may be due to measurement strategies (i.e., obtaining measurements during adolescence rather than after all individuals have completed development) instead of actual differences in final adult build. As with variations across the body in skeletal growth, regional differences in the timing of the weight spurt have been observed (Malina, 1990; Tanner, 1962). Variations in the onset of weight and height gain for different areas of the body, viewed cumulatively, result in substantial variations in the shape changes that occur during puberty (Tanner, Whitehouse, Marubini, & Resele, 1976), further emphasizing the extent of between- and within-individual differences in development over the pubertal years.

Measurements of body fat are commonly based on skinfold thickness from parts of the body (e.g., the upper arm), hydrostatic weighing, and mathematical estimation calculated from measures of height and weight. Mathematical procedures have also been developed to estimate percentage of body fat from measurements of height and weight (Mellits & Cheek, 1970). Regression equations can be used to predict total body water, which is then divided by total weight to obtain an index of fat in the body. While these equations have been criticized because of idiosyncracies in the sample from which they were derived, several researchers (Frisch, 1974, 1983; Newcombe & Bandura, 1983; Waber, 1977) have found this procedure to be useful for assessing relative pubertal development in their samples. Estimates of percentage of body fat correlate with menarcheal status (Frisch, Revelle, & Cook, 1973), but little evidence suggests that this is a meaningful index of development for boys (Graber, 1991).

Circulatory and Respiratory Growth

Along with skeletal growth and changes in muscle and fat distribution at puberty are changes in the internal organs, particularly the lungs and heart. A growth spurt in the heart and lungs is coincidental with the growth spurt in height (Beunen et al., 1988; Marshall & Tanner, 1974, 1986). Whereas some evidence demonstrates that the spurt in heart growth is more marked in boys (Maresh, 1948), other research (Simon, Reid, Tanner, Goldstein, & Benjamin, 1972) suggests that magnitude of the spurt does not differ for boys and girls; rather, boys have larger hearts throughout development. The growth spurt in the heart and lungs is distinct from growth in other organs at this time, as the heart and lungs not only increase in size but in proportion to the rest of the body. Increases in the size of the heart and lungs, coupled with increased muscle mass and the endocrinological changes at puberty, result in greater physical endurance and strength. In addition, a testosterone-related increase in hemoglobin in the blood allows for more oxygen-carrying capacity in red blood cells. The greatest increases in strength occur at the end of pubertal development, at least 1 year after peak height velocity and after sexual development is complete. Improvements in physical performance and capacity occur for both boys and girls, but changes are thought to be more pronounced for boys because of the links to muscle mass development and testosterone production.

Central Nervous System Development

Via recent advances in research methods and technology, changes in the brain across the life span have been studied and documented. Although several alterations in neural structure are thought to develop during adolescence, possibly in relation to the hormonal changes of puberty, specific changes during puberty are only beginning to be confirmed. Postnatal brain growth peaks between birth and 2 to 3 years of age, with a doubling in mass during these years (Dobbing & Sands, 1973). Subsequent structural changes within the brain are associated with changes in myelination, dendrite growth, and synaptogenesis rather than increases in mass; the timing, rate, and nature of these changes varies by region of the brain (Thatcher, Walker, & Giudice, 1987).

Across the brain and central nervous system, increases in myelination—the process of insulation of the nerve (specifically, the axon)—result in faster transmission of neural messages; development in myelination continues into the second decade of life and beyond (Yakovlev & Lecours, 1967). The branching of dendrites (the portion of the neuron that extends and connects to other neural cells) also exhibits developmental changes in a process of growth and "pruning." The connections between cells occur at synapses, hence the term *synaptogenesis* for the production of connections. It is believed that new connections occur across the life span in response to environmental stimulation (Greenough, Black, & Wallace, 1987). Connections are pruned at the same time, however, resulting in cell death. In the first years of life, neural connections are overproduced in the central nervous system (Goldman-Rakic, 1987); this is believed to be genetically controlled to ensure that essential connections among regions of the central nervous system are made.

Environmental conditions within and external to the individual determine which pathways develop and which connections are not made or used (Greenough et al., 1987). Over time, these excess synaptic connections disappear, and specific dendritic paths and neurons die off. Though it has been suggested that increases in synaptogenesis are associated with cognitive advances (Fischer, 1987), evidence supports the hypothesis that the fine-tuning of pathways through the elimination of excess connections is involved in advances in cognition and the attainment of adult patterns of neural functioning (Goldman-Rakic, 1987).

The greatest amount of fine-tuning of the neural system ensues between the ages of 10 and 15 (Feinberg, 1987). Neural changes occurring during this period include the steepest declines in oxygen consumption in the brain (from elevated childhood levels to normal adult levels; Chugani, Phelps, & Mazziotta, 1988), along with declines in synaptic density (Huttenlocher, 1979). Feinberg (1987) makes two observations about the result of these processes. First, these alterations in functioning and structure coincide with advances in cognition. Second, disturbances in what is probably a genetically controlled process may result in perturbations of mental health at this time, suggesting a biological base to the onset of at least certain types of psychopathology during early adolescence.

How early adolescent changes in the central nervous system may relate specifically to pubertal development has not been well studied. Previously it was suggested that hormonal changes at puberty curtail brain development, resulting in differences in certain cognitive abilities (e.g., verbal versus spatial skills) among individuals based on the timing of their development (Waber, 1977). Subsequent research found few if any influences of timing of pubertal development on specific cognitive abilities (Newcombe & Dubas, 1987), with only small effects limited to extreme samples (Graber & Petersen, 1991). Suggestions that the brain exhibits "spurts" in growth comparable to the adolescent growth spurt (Epstein, 1978) have also not been supported (Graber & Petersen, 1991; Greenough et al., 1987).

As specific brain structures (e.g., the hypothalamus and pituitary gland) have primary roles in pubertal development and are receptive to reproductive hormones, it is possible that other areas of the brain are also receptive to pubertal hormones. Advances in research methods such as brain imaging will be instrumental in charting structural and functional changes in the central nervous system at puberty as well as the interaction of biological and behavioral changes.

Endocrine Changes at Puberty

Several of the major hormonal changes at puberty have already been noted. As indicated, the reproductive system (as controlled by the HPG axis) remains dormant through the childhood years and is activated in late childhood. Maturation of the reproductive system results in the production of gonadotropin-releasing hormone (GnRH) by the medial basal hypothalamus. GnRH acts as a chemical signal to the pituitary, which responds by releasing pulsatile bursts of gonadotropins—luteinizing hormone (LH) and follicle-stimulating hormone (FSH). These in turn influence the gonads and the release of sex steroids.

Inhibition of the reproductive system during childhood is most likely controlled by the central nervous system via the temporary discontinuation of the production (or synthesis at low levels) and pulsatile release of GnRH (Grumbach, 1980). The first hormonal changes of pubertal development begin with increases in release of GnRH in late childhood. LH and FSH are secreted at low levels by the pituitary during childhood. Episodic low-amplitude nocturnal bursts of LH are characteristic of the early pubertal stages (Boyar et al., 1972); it is only during the later stages of pubertal development that LH is released throughout the day in adultlike patterns. This sequence of events is similar for boys and girls. For boys, FSH rises gradually throughout puberty, while LH exhibits an early spurt followed by gradual increases. For girls, FSH levels rise early and plateau, whereas LH rises in the later stages of development. This pattern is reflective of tonic release of the gonadotropins. In tonic release, changes in the levels of circulating sex steroids (as monitored by the hypothalamus) result in changes in pituitary release of the gonadotropins.

In addition to tonic release of gonadotropins, girls develop cyclic release of gonadotropins as the menstrual cycle matures. After menarche, tonic secretion becomes characteristic of only particular phases of the menstrual cycle. The positive feedback loop responsible for cyclic secretion in girls matures late in the pubertal process and is related to the stimulatory effect of estradiol on gonadotropin secretion. In order for the positive feedback loop—and subsequently the menstrual cycle—to be functional, the ovaries must be sufficiently primed by FSH to secrete enough estradiol into the bloodstream to maintain "adult" levels, the pituitary must be sensitized by estrogen, and GnRH production must be sufficient to respond to the increased estradiol stimulation. When each of these conditions has been met, enough estradiol is produced to stimulate an ovulatory LH surge. Even after menarche is reached, estradiol, GnRH, and/or pituitary sensitization may not be consistently maintained, such that 50% to 90% of menstrual cycles may be anovulatory in the first two years after menarche. By 5 years after menarche, this has decreased to 20% of menstrual cycles.

Behavioral Correlates of Pubertal Change

Psychological and social developmental changes at puberty have most often been related to only a few indicators of the pubertal process, most often the development of secondary sexual characteristics or age at menarche. Recently the association between hormonal and behavioral changes has also drawn interest. Most pubertal processes have been investigated as antecedents to behavioral change and in terms of how specific processes are experienced by the developing adolescent.

Secondary sexual characteristics in combination with one or two other dimensions of pubertal development have been used to form general ratings of the stage of development (usually based on Tanner's stage system, e.g., Crockett & Petersen, 1987) or have been examined individually (e.g., Brooks-Gunn, 1984) in relation to psychological constructs. Associations with behavior are examined in the context of either the present status of an individual's pubertal growth or the timing of that growth in relation to the pubertal development of most adolescents or one's peers. Gender differences in the onset of pubertal development make it necessary to define timing within gender; for example, boys who mature earlier than other boys are beginning puberty at about the same time as girls who are on-time maturers. Confusion between status and timing is frequent in the literature (Dubas, Graber, & Petersen, 1991). Dubas et al. (1991) make the following distinction:

> Pubertal timing is an individual-differences variable that is often used in examining between-subjects variations on some outcome variable. Pubertal status is a developmental variable that is used to examine whether a certain stage of development is needed before the occurrence of a certain behavior. For example, Steinberg (1987) has found that boys maturing early experienced more conflict with mothers than on-time or late maturers and that for most adolescents, conflict with parents peaks during the midpubertal stage. (pp. 583–584)

During the course of pubertal development, it is difficult to separate status from timing. Timing by definition involves an assessment of status or an assessment of when a pubertal process was begun or traversed. If adolescents do not maintain their rank ordering from assessment to assessment, timing classifications will change rather than remain stable. As within- and between-individual variations in onset and rate of development are not uncommon (Eichorn, 1975; Tanner, 1972), changes in rank ordering also arise. Despite some confounding of these constructs, both timing and status influences on behavior have been reported.

Pubertal Status: Measurement and Meaning

A variety of methods have been employed to assess pubertal status. These include physician (or other health care professional) ratings, parental (usually maternal) ratings, self-ratings based on viewing photographs or drawings depicting each stage of puberty, and self-ratings without visual cues (Brooks-Gunn et al., 1987; Dorn, Susman, Nottelmann, Inoff-Germain, & Chrousos, 1990; Duke, Litt, & Gross, 1980; Petersen, Crockett, Richards, & Boxer, 1988). Self-ratings from photographs and drawings and maternal ratings correspond well with physicians' ratings of pubertal status (Brooks-Gunn et al., 1987; Duke et al., 1980; Morris & Udry, 1980), with some variation by specific pubertal process being assessed (Dorn et al., 1990). Self-reports of status not based on visually presented material have a lower correspondence with physician ratings (Brooks-Gunn et al., 1987) but exhibit acceptable reliability and validity (Petersen et al., 1988).

Age at menarche is perhaps the most commonly measured pubertal process, especially because it can be obtained retrospectively. Both adult women and adolescent girls are accurate and relatively uninhibited in reporting their age at menarche (Bean, Leeper, Wallace, Sherman, & Jagger, 1979; Brooks-Gunn et al., 1987; Rierdan & Koff, 1985). Inaccurate reports by adolescent girls of their age at menarche have been noted; in these cases, girls reported that they had not begun to menstruate whereas their mothers indicated that the girls were postmenarcheal (Petersen, 1983). These discrepancies were usually due to initial denial or hiding of the event, with accuracy improving in subsequent interviews.

Because puberty involves different processes for boys and girls, pubertal status may be experienced differently in the psychological context as well. For example, menarche and breast development are considered to be particularly salient events for girls. Breast development is an outward sign of maturation that presumably elicits a social response to the changing adolescent, whereas menarche—although not outwardly visible—has been considered the single pivotal transition from childhood to adulthood for girls across cultures (Paige, 1983; Weideger, 1975).

The meaning of the processes varies greatly, with most attention focusing on the significance of the menarcheal experience (e.g., Brooks-Gunn & Petersen, 1983; Golub, 1983). Different theoretical perspectives within the psychoanalytic literature had suggested that menarche acts as either an anxiety-provoking and/or a traumatic event or may elicit positive social cues as an indicator of maturity (Blos, 1962; Kestenberg, 1967). Research with adolescent girls during the pubertal years supports both types of responses (Ruble & Brooks-Gunn, 1982). The psychological experience of menarche varies by context, with some girls reporting negative experiences while others have positive or neutral feelings (Petersen, 1983; Rierdan & Koff, 1985; Ruble & Brooks-Gunn, 1982). Most notably, girls who reached menarche earlier than their peers and girls who reported being unprepared for it had more negative experiences than other girls (Brooks-Gunn & Ruble, 1982; Koff, Rierdan, & Sheingold, 1982).

In contrast with research on menarche, little research has focused on the significance of breast development. This is unusual, as breast development is outwardly visible and (as one of the first indicators that puberty has begun) presumably would act as a social cue of the girl's changing status from childhood to adulthood. Conversely, menarche occurs late in the pubertal process and is not outwardly visible; girls are also likely to tell only a few individuals (their mother and/or closest friends) that they have reached menarche (Brooks-Gunn & Ruble, 1982; Brooks-Gunn, Warren, Samelson, & Fox, 1986). Research that has examined correlates of breast development found that girls with more advanced development were higher on self-reported measures of adjustment and had more positive peer relations (Brooks-Gunn, 1984). However, 50% of girls with Tanner stage 3 breast development (which reflects more noticeable physical changes) indicated that they had been teased about their breast development; in no cases was the teasing viewed positively by the girls (Brooks-Gunn, 1984). These results, in combination, suggest that advancing pubertal development does provide social cues and alters internal feelings about the self.

Salience of comparable events for boys remains virtually unstudied. While one group of researchers has defined first nocturnal emission in boys as an event comparable to menarche in girls (as it is hypothetically a psy-chologically significant event for boys that may be experienced both posi-tively and negatively; Sanders & Soares, 1986), the same researchers found that only 60% of the adult men in their sample were either willing to report or able to recall the age when this event occurred. The low response rate, though, may also be due to the narrowness of the question. In a small study of adolescent boys in which the subjects reported the context of their first ejaculatory experience and their feelings about it, first ejaculation was more common during masturbation than during sleep (Gaddis & Brooks-Gunn, 1985); hence, asking about nocturnal emissions may be less relevant for many adult males.

In this same study of adolescent boys, most experienced positive feelings about their first ejaculation, although they also indicated feeling at least a little scared. In contrast with experiences of menarche, few boys express feeling totally unprepared for the experience even though only a handful discussed the experience with family or peers at the time. It is likely that the association between first ejaculation and masturbation inhibits boys and possibly their families from discussing the event. Families, however, may still respond to this transition in boys through changes in interactions, expectations, and attributions made about the adolescent without overtly discussing the stimulus for such relational changes.

Pubertal Timing: Measurement and Meaning

As previously noted, pubertal timing is usually determined from an indica-tor of pubertal status. Classification into early, late, or on-time matura-tional groups is based on national norms for the average age of attaining a specific level of development (Duke et al., 1982) or on sample characteris-tics. An alternative to assessing status or asking for recollections of a puber-tal event (e.g., age at menarche) is to obtain self-reports of pubertal timing (e.g., Berzonsky & Lombardo, 1983; Silbereisen, Petersen, Albrecht, & Kracke, 1989; Tobin-Richards, Boxer, & Petersen, 1983); this strategy is congruent with self-report measures of status.

Perceptions of one's pubertal timing, like retrospective reports of age at menarche, have been especially useful with adult investigations of possible long-term behavioral effects of off-time development (Sanders & Soares, 1986). In a recent investigation of the accuracy of perceptions of pubertal timing, Dubas et al. (1991) compared perceptions of pubertal timing with an objective measure during 7th and 8th grades, the peak pubertal years, and in 12th grade, when most pubertal development is complete. Accuracy was highest in the postpubertal years, indicating that adolescents may have difficulty making assessments of how their own development compares with peers or most adolescents when both they and the referent are chang-ing. Even in the postpubertal years, size of the correspondence between the perceived and objective measures suggested that perceptions were influenced by processes and beliefs—yet to be identified—that were not completely accurate. One possible conclusion is that many adolescents and adults are not as knowledgeable about their pubertal development, and puberty in general, as researchers may be expecting.

Rutter (1989) has emphasized that the timing of any developmental transition might affect behavioral outcomes through biological, psychological, or social paths; in each case, this would be true of behavioral correlates of the timing of the pubertal transition. For both biological and psychological paths, the status of development at the time of the transition will affect the outcome of the transition. For example, in the case of biological development, how hormones affect the neural system depends on the level or extent of neural development at that specific time (Meyer-Bahlburg, Ehrhardt, & Feldman, 1986). This type of timing effect remains relatively unstudied. In the case of psychological development, how individuals cope with and are influenced by puberty depends upon their emotional and cognitive skills when the transition occurs; this has also been called the stage-termination hypothesis (Peskin & Livson, 1972; Petersen & Taylor, 1980). Along similar lines, Coleman's (1978) focal theory suggested that when the multiple changes faced by adolescents occur sequentially, individuals are able to adapt and develop appropriate coping strategies; however, coincidental challenges (e.g., pubertal changes) coupled with changes in the family and/or school environment may overtax psychological resources (Petersen, Sarigiani, & Kennedy, 1991; Simmons & Blyth, 1987).

Timing effects on behavior via social paths or contexts are less related to the individual's development than on a social referent that places a value on normative versus nonnormative development; this has also been conceptualized as a deviancy hypothesis (Neugarten, 1979; Petersen & Taylor, 1980). For example, a societal emphasis on thinness may result in lowered self-esteem for girls who mature earlier than other girls—and hence gain weight when most girls have a "boyish" physical appearance (Faust, 1983; Tobin-Richards et al., 1983). Deviancy models for pubertal timing effects on psychosocial development hypothesize, for example, that girls who mature earlier than their peers will be at an increased risk for negative developmental outcomes, as they mature earlier than any other group of adolescents; hence, they are the most "deviant" from a social perspective and have had the least time to develop psychologically (Brooks-Gunn et al., 1985).

Timing of puberty has been associated with cognitive, emotional, and social development during adolescence with an emphasis on the development of self-esteem and body image, gender role, problem behaviors, heterosocial relations, and family relations (Duke et al., 1982; Newcombe & Bandura, 1983; Silbereisen et al., 1989; Simmons, Blyth, Van Cleave, & Bush, 1979; Stattin & Magnusson, 1990; Steinberg, 1987; Tobin-Richards et al., 1983). The existence and pervasiveness of pubertal timing effects have not been uniform across investigations due to measurement, sample, and contextual differences among studies, as well as the varying strength of the effects (Brooks-Gunn et al., 1985; Newcombe & Dubas, 1987; Susman et al., 1985; Tobin-Richards et al., 1983).

Evidence supporting specific models such as stage termination or deviancy has been mixed. Research with boys has generally found that maturing earlier than one's peers leads to several advantages in social and emotional functioning (Duncan, Ritter, Dornbusch, Gross, & Carlsmith, 1985; Mussen & Jones, 1957; Simmons et al., 1979). Advantages of early pubertal development have been attributed to the social desirability of being taller and stronger (and hence often more athletically skilled) than less developed peers (Jones, 1965; Susman et al., 1985). Possibly because of the value placed on athletic ability in the peer group, more advanced pubertal development has also been associated with increased popularity and more heterosocial interactions. Even though other boys catch up to early maturers over time, longitudinal examination of long-term timing effects has found evidence that even in adulthood early maturers continued to have social advantages—including greater confidence and poise—over men who had been late maturers (Jones, 1965). In other samples these effects appear to be stronger in boys from lower socioeconomic groups (Clausen, 1975), in which athletics may be more highly valued. In more recent investigations early-maturing boys were more satisfied with their weight and height than other boys (Duncan et al., 1985; Simmons & Blyth, 1987), but these differences dissipated by midadolescence (Simmons & Blyth, 1987). Overall, early-maturing boys do not experience difficulty due to stage termination or curtailed psychological development but rather appear to receive positive social feedback that, in some cases, may help them build lasting adaptive skills. The disadvantages in social skills for late-maturing boys reported by Jones (1965) gives some support to social deviancy as a risk for adolescents, as late-maturing boys traverse puberty later than any other group of adolescents. Few subsequent studies, however, have reported disadvantages for late-maturing boys (e.g., Duncan et al., 1985; Graber, Petersen, & Brooks-Gunn, in press; Simmons & Blyth, 1987).

More support for maturational timing effects has been documented for girls, with a predominance of negative outcomes for early-maturing girls (Brooks-Gunn & Reiter, 1990; Jones & Mussen, 1958; Stattin & Magnusson, 1990). Both deviancy and/or stage termination (i.e., social and psychological) mechanisms may be involved. Girls who mature earlier than their peers have a poorer body image than other girls (Blyth, Simmons, & Zakin, 1985; Duncan et al., 1985). In some cases these differences were attributable to weight-related concerns, as the early-maturing girls weighed more than their same-age peers during early adolescence (Simmons & Blyth, 1987). In longitudinal analyses continuing into the postpubertal years, however, girls who had matured earlier than their peers experienced a poorer body image that was not accounted for by differences in actual weight (Graber, Petersen, & Brooks-Gunn, in press; Simmons & Blyth, 1987). This suggests that early maturation for girls may be the beginning of a trajectory that is associated with increased exposure to other contextual risks to adjustment.

Other longer-term effects of timing of maturation demonstrate that early development puts girls in different contextual situations that alter their educational and career trajectories. In a longitudinal investigation of girls' development in Sweden, Stattin and Magnusson (1990) found that despite similar abilities among girls, early-maturing girls did not enjoy school as much as their peers, were less popular with their classmates, and associated more with older peers during the early and midadolescent years than other girls. Association with older peers was linked to increased heterosocial and delinquent behaviors. Most interesting, when interviewed again as adults in their mid-20s, women who had been early maturers had more children, had lower levels of educational attainment, and held lower-prestige jobs than other women. Often they reported not continuing with their education due to child-care difficulties (Stattin & Magnusson, 1990). For these women early maturation, while not associated with poorer adjustment during adolescence, appeared to be a venue for entry onto a lower achievement trajectory. Even though older peers (especially older boys) may have provided social support during adolescence, they may also have modeled or encouraged less emphasis on academic achievement and aspirations. Little is known about the nature of older adolescents who associate with younger girls.

Even though Magnusson and his colleagues do not find long-term influences of timing of maturation on psychological adjustment, other studies have found that early-maturing girls experience higher levels of depressive affect (Petersen et al., 1991) and disturbed eating behaviors across adolescence (Graber, Brooks-Gunn, Paikoff, & Warren, 1994). For depression, earlier maturation along with other stressful adolescent transitions at school and in the family during the middle-school years led to increased depressive affect into late adolescence (Petersen et al., 1991). In our own research, dieting and eating behavior problems were predicted by pubertal status and social relationships during early and middle adolescence; at late adolescence, subclinical eating problems were predicted by family relationships and psychopathology (Attie & Brooks-Gunn, 1989). In an analysis of patterns of eating behaviors across adolescence, however, those girls who reported disturbed eating behaviors repeatedly over the adolescent years were earlier maturers than girls with either intermittent or no problems during adolescence (Graber et al., 1994). As in Magnusson's sample, pubertal development was salient in determining entry onto a particular behavioral trajectory.

Hormones and Behavior

Pubertal status and timing are often thought to influence behavior via social paths emphasizing the importance of the response and attributions of the individual's social milieu, as well as his or her own feelings toward pubertal changes. Alternately, phrases such as *raging hormones* have filled the literature and popular press when adolescent behavior is discussed. While increases in hormonal activity have long been cited as the cause for disturbances in mood and heightened emotionality in early adolescents, formal tests of these assertions have only recently begun. Much of this work has focused on the hormonal correlates of arousal (in particular sexual arousal, aggressive behavior, and affect) and psychopathology (especially depression, depressive affect, and eating disorders and problems). Interest in hormonal bases to aggression and arousal have stemmed from psychoanalytic theory (Deutsch, 1944) as well as animal models of behavior (Rose, Holaday, & Bernstein, 1971). Interest in correlates and causes of psychopathology is spurred by the increases in incidence of depression, eating disorders, and lesser affective disturbances during the adolescent decade (Attie, Brooks-Gunn, & Petersen, 1990; Petersen et al., 1993).

Direct and Indirect Effects. Because the hormone–behavior field is relatively new, research has mostly tested the simplest models, examining direct effects of hormones on affective response; this is shown at the top of Figure 2–3. Indirect effects (through hormone effects on arousal and/or reactivity or via effects on secondary sexual characteristics) are also frequently tested (also shown in Figure 2–3). At this time, little evidence confirms that pubertal status reduces or mediates hormonal effects on behavior (Paikoff & Brooks-Gunn, 1990a, 1990b), although (as already discussed) many studies measuring secondary sexual characteristics along with an affective outcome make inferences about hormonal activity in the absence of hormonal data. The research teams who have published studies on hormone–behavior associations during adolescence vary in subjects studied (boys versus girls), period of adolescence studied (early versus middle), affective outcome of interest, and method of hormonal assessment (circulating in blood, urinary excretion, or salivary output). (See Paikoff & Brooks-Gunn, 1990a, or Halpern & Udry, 1992, for a more extensive review of these methods.)

Associations between aggression and hormonal activity have been reported for adolescent boys, with Olweus, Mattsson, Schalling, and Low (1980, 1988) reporting a direct effect of testosterone on provoked or responsive aggressive behavior. This group also identified indirect effects along the internal-states path such that testosterone influenced impatience and irritability, which was related to aggressive-destructive behavior. In a younger sample of adolescent boys, aggressive behaviors were associated with lower levels of estradiol and higher levels of adrenal androgens (Sus-

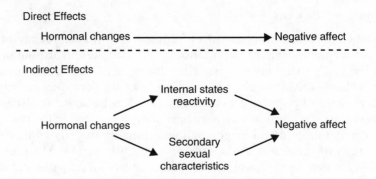

Figure 2–3. Direct and indirect effects of hormones on affect.

man et al., 1987). In contrast, Udry and his colleagues (Halpern, Udry, Campbell, & Suchindran, 1994) did not find a direct or indirect association between boys' aggression and testosterone or changes in testosterone over time, although testosterone was predictive of subsequent problem behavior in their sample (Drigotas & Udry, in press). Instead, Udry and his colleagues note that for boys, even though developmental changes are exhibited in the context for the expression of aggression, individual differences in aggressive behaviors and attitudes are fairly stable across childhood and adolescence (Cairns, Cairns, Neckerman, Ferguson, & Gariepy, 1989). Hence developmental links to changing hormones would not necessarily be expected.

For girls, adrenal androgens (DHEA and DHEAS) have demonstrated small, negative associations with aggression (Brooks-Gunn & Warren, 1989; Susman et al., 1987). Associations between higher levels of estradiol and increased verbal aggression (e.g., dominance, defiance, and anger) toward parents (Inoff-Germain et al., 1988) have also been reported, along with associations between global hormonal functioning and aggressive affect (Warren & Brooks-Gunn, 1989).

Given that the results are mixed for boys and girls with different hormones relating to aggressive behaviors and feelings, it is more likely that rather than increases in a single hormone leading to aggression, hormones lead to arousal, which stimulates an emotional response. Such arousal may be interpreted differently among adolescents and therefore could be expressed as aggression or another emotion (e.g., anxiety, depressive affect). For example, even though boys experience greater increases in testosterone during puberty, girls may be more emotionally or psychologically responsive to small increases in testosterone (Udry & Talbert, 1988). This type of differential response to hormones would account for differences among studies and between genders.

Direct effects of androgens and indirect effects of androgens through an arousal mechanism are more clearly evidenced for sexual feelings and subsequent sexual behaviors, especially for boys (Udry, Billy, Morris, Groff, & Raj, 1985). Testosterone predicted nearly all sexual behaviors and feelings reported by boys (Udry et al., 1985; Udry & Billy, 1987). While adrenal androgens (testosterone, DHEA, and DHEAS) were predictive of masturbation and noncoital sexual activities for girls, intercourse was predicted by social factors rather than hormones (Udry, Talbert, & Morris, 1986). Girls may experience arousal effects, but direct associations between hormones and intercourse appear to be curtailed by a greater adherence to social controls.

For depressive affect, less evidence supports a direct or indirect (again, through reactivity or arousal) link with pubertal hormones. For boys, Susman et al. (1987) identified an association between lower adrenal androgens and positive emotional responses. For girls, Warren and Brooks-Gunn (1989) demonstrated a similar association with hormonal changes linked to increases in depressive affect. In this case, the association was curvilinear such that the highest depression was exhibited by girls who had increased hormone levels as indexed by estradiol categories[*] but who had not reached adult levels of hormonal functioning. In both samples of adolescents, initial hormone levels were associated with negative affect 1 year later, suggesting that hormonal effects may lead to more permanent behavioral changes rather than causing temporary perturbations to the individual.

Interestingly, in their sample, Brooks-Gunn and Warren (1989) found that social events and pubertal development interacted to influence depressive and aggressive affect. In models that included the occurrence of negative and positive life events, hormones accounted for only 4% of the variance in negative affect, whereas social factors accounted for 8% to 18% of the variance. The interaction of pubertal development with negative life events also contributed more to the model than hormones alone. These findings suggest the need to expand simple models to include social and environmental contexts of pubertal development.

Bidirectional Influences Between Internal States and Hormones. Examination of more complex models delineating the interrelationship among hormones, behavior, and environmental factors may account for the variability in contexts under which hormonal effects are or are not demonstrated. In Figure 2–4, bidirectional effects with internal states and environmental contexts are added to the indirect-effects models from Figure 2–3. For example, pubertal development is affected by behaviors such as nutritional

---

[*]Because estradiol is highly correlated with levels of LH and FSH, it is a useful indicator of overall hormonal states. Estradiol levels also correspond to specific levels of reproductive functioning. For example, levels of circulating estradiol between 50 and 75 pg/ml are representative of the middle to late pubertal phases (just after menarche but before regular adult cycles are maintained; see Warren & Brooks-Gunn, 1989, for a discussion of these levels).

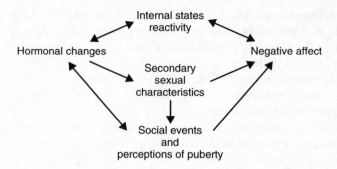

Figure 2–4. **Hormonal and social effects on affect with bidirectional influences.**

intake, exercise, and dieting. It has long been accepted that hormones are receptive to environmental stressors (e.g., starvation induces hormonal changes via hypothalamic regulation), but the importance and influence of behavioral stressors on the developing hormonal system has only recently been considered.

For adolescent girls and young women who were competitive athletes and dancers, the demands of their exercise regimens resulted in delays in pubertal development and/or the disruption and cessation of menstrual functioning (amenorrhea) in many cases (Calabrese et al., 1983; Malina, 1983; Warren et al., 1991; Warren, Brooks-Gunn, Hamilton, Hamilton, & Warren, 1986). Subtle fluctuations in menstrual cycles have also been documented (Warren, 1980) such that exercise affected the hormonal system irrespective of changes in weight. As would be expected, amenorrheic girls have lower estrogen levels (Dhuper, Warren, Brooks-Gunn, & Fox, 1990). Even before amenorrhea has occurred, excessive exercise affects LH and FSH activity (McArthur et al., 1980).

Disturbed eating habits also influence hormonal functioning in the absence of exercise effects. Clinical eating disorders (e.g., anorexia) result in the cessation of menses or a delay in the onset of menarche. Disruption of normal menstrual cycling is accompanied by a return to prepubertal levels and diurnal cycles of LH and FSH secretion (Katz, Boyar, Roffwarg, Hellman, & Weiner, 1978) as well as alterations in the adrenal hormone cortisol (Boyar et al., 1977; Brown, Garfinkel, Jeuniewic, Moldofsky, & Stancer, 1977). In addition, though, girls and women who do not have frank eating disorders but who engage in dieting or have poor nutritional habits are also likely to have irregular menstrual cycles.

Bidirectional Influences Between Hormones and Social Context. Behaviors such as exercise and eating habits that have exhibited influences on the hormonal system can be characterized by a physical component, as well as by the fact that they are under the control by the individual. In contrast, social events and context provide another domain of influence on affective development. As already noted, interactions between negative life events and pubertal development were related to depressive affect (Brooks-Gunn & Warren, 1989). In Figure 2–4, social contexts are added to simple models to include the possibility for bidirectional influences between hormones and social events. This model, one of several that could be proposed (e.g., Brooks-Gunn, Graber, & Paikoff, 1994; Paikoff & Brooks-Gunn, 1990b), represents current advances in research in the field.

Social context factors in the family have recently been linked to the timing of pubertal development (Graber, Brooks-Gunn, & Warren, in press; Moffitt, Caspi, Belsky, & Silva, 1992; Surbey, 1990). In two separate studies (Surbey, 1990; Moffitt et al., 1992), earlier ages of menarche were reported for girls living in households in which no father was residing in the home. Both research groups also reported earlier ages of menarche for girls whose households were intact but exhibited high levels of family conflict. Moffitt and her colleagues found that these effects were not attributable to socioeconomic or weight differences among the girls.

Additional investigation of family relationship influences on age at menarche in our own research indicated that earlier maturation was predicted by conflict and lack of approval in families with both parents residing in the home, even after controlling for weight, height, and hereditary factors (Graber et al., in press). These effects were not attributable to family response to pubertal development, as controlling for amount of visible development (i.e., stage of breast development) did not diminish the amount of variance explained by family relations. Further analysis of this sample found that emotions such as aggressive affect predicted pubic hair development (Graber et al., in press). In combination, these effects indicate that multiple hormonal pathways may be influenced by internal and external environments. Such complex interactions may account to some extent for the inter-and intraindividual variation in pubertal development previously noted.

As yet the hormonal mechanisms linking family context to pubertal development have not been identified. The disrupted family environment may be acting as a stressor on the adolescent's physiological system. As the adrenal glands produce both androgens and cortisol, and as increased cortisol secretion has been associated with stressful conditions, the HPA axis would be indicated as the path through which family stress and maturation are linked. Elevated secretion of cortisol suppresses androgen secretion in the HPG system, however, and development therefore should be slowed rather than accelerated. Since little information exists on the HPA axis and its interaction with the HPG axis, conclusions are tenuous at best.

It is unclear whether boys' development is also responsive to contextual and affective stress or whether menstrual functioning is particularly vulnerable to these influences. Hypothetically, if it is the adrenal or HPA axis that is likely to be influenced by stress, similar models may apply for both boys and girls. Alternatively, if stress influences age at menarche or the menstrual cycle through an influence on cyclic gonadotropin release, boys would not be affected.

Hormonal Links to the Development of Psychopathology. Thus far a variety of hormonal, social, and affective interactions have been presented. Most of the research on hormonal influences on behavior has focused on affective responses (e.g., aggressive or depressive affect) that fall within the range of normal behaviors. While some of the literature reviewed indicates that hormones may interact with other factors to account for some of the changes in affective response during adolescence, research has generally not studied pubertal hormonal changes and the development of psychopathology such as clinical depression or eating disorders. (See Brooks-Gunn, Petersen, & Compas, in press, for a more detailed review of the biological substrates of adolescent depression.)

In the case of depression, this gap is striking for several reasons. First, incidence of clinical depression (disregarding type of depressive mood disorder) increases between childhood and adolescence. Second, in childhood, either no gender differences are found in rate of depression or a somewhat higher incidence is reported for boys; by adulthood, though, the rate for women is twice the rate for men (Brooks-Gunn, Petersen, & Compas, in press; Petersen et al., 1993). A recent epidemiological study found that by age 16 girls were twice as likely as boys to report depressive symptoms (Angold & Rutter, 1992); however, no association was found with pubertal status. Third, an extensive and ongoing literature has examined the biological substrates of clinical depression in adults. This literature has reported dysregulation in the HPG and HPA axes as well as several other hypothalamus-pituitary systems linked to the thyroid and central nervous system neurotransmitters. Some of this work has also been conducted with depressed children and adolescents. While there are indications that thyroid functioning may be lower in depressed than in nondepressed children and adolescents, and that secretion of growth hormone is suppressed in depressed groups across ages, few findings indicate developmental shifts in the biological substrate of depression between childhood and adolescence (Puig-Antich, 1987). An exception has been the investigation by Puig-Antich and colleagues (Dahl et al., 1992; Puig-Antich, 1987) of alterations in hypothalamic-pituitary axes exhibited during sleep among depressed adolescents and children. As yet, these investigations have not consistently identified shifts in the biological substrate of depression with pubertal development, indicating that biological processes may be similar in many respects. Such work does not address why depression increases during adolescence. Rather than being due to changes in hormonal responsivity, increases in depression during adolescence may be linked to maturation of neurotransmitter systems. For example, researchers working with animal models have reported that catecholemine systems are not fully functional until adulthood (Goldman-Rakic & Brown, 1982) and, as previously noted, synaptic connections continue to be formed and altered into adulthood and across the life span (Goldman-Rakic, 1987; Greenough et al., 1987).

Finally, as already noted, depressive affect is influenced to some extent by hormonal changes at puberty. Despite indications that biological changes at puberty may be associated with changes in depression, especially as a causal path for the increased rate of depression in girls, investigations of biological markers of depression have not directly examined puberty or taken a developmental approach. Most of the research conducted in this area has compared children with adolescents without accounting for pubertal development (i.e., the transition between childhood and adolescence); an exception is the Angold and Rutter (1992) epidemiological study of pubertal status and depression. Even less attention has been focused on possible pubertal correlates of eating disorders despite increases in these disorders for adolescent girls that have paralleled increases in depression.

Summary

The models presented depict the interconnections among the biological, psychological, and social realms of influence on and by behavior. Research that incorporates information on internal physiological changes at puberty along with the social context for pubertal development has demonstrated that such interactional models are essential for understanding individual development and adaptive and maladaptive outcomes. Current research on pubertal development has identified several areas for further investigation. To test these models more effectively, additional research must consider pubertal processes at their inception through the longitudinal investigation of prepubertal children. Consideration of a broader range of behavioral outcomes may also prove fruitful for understanding the possible breadth and depth of biosocial interactions. In addition, advances in technology and method raise the exciting possibility of detecting subtle interconnections between pubertal developmental processes and behavior.

References

Angold, A., & Rutter, M. (1992). Effects of age and pubertal status on depression in a large clinical sample. *Development and Psychopathology, 4,* 5–28.

Attie, I. & Brooks-Gunn, J. (1989). Development of eating problems in adolescent girls: A longitudinal study. *Developmental Psychology, 25,* 70–79.

Attie, I., Brooks-Gunn, J., & Petersen, A. C. (1990). A developmental perspective on eating disorders and eating problems. In M. Lewis & S. Miller (Eds.), *Handbook of developmental psychopathology* (pp. 409–420). New York: Plenum.

Bean, J. A., Leeper, J. D., Wallace, R. B., Sherman, B. M., & Jagger, H. J. (1979). Variations in the reporting of menstrual histories. *American Journal of Epidemiology, 109,* 181–185.

Berzonsky, M. D., & Lombardo, J. P. (1983). Pubertal timing and identity crisis: A preliminary investigation. *Journal of Early Adolescence, 3,* 239–246.

Beunen, G., Malina, R. M., Van't Hof, M. A., Simons, J., Ostyn, M., Renson, R., & Van Gerven, D. (1988). *Adolescent growth and motor performance: A longitudinal study of Belgian boys.* Champaign, IL: Human Kinetics.

Blos, P. (1962). *On adolescence: A psychoanalytic interpretation.* New York: Free Press.

Blyth, D. A., Simmons, R. G., & Zakin, D. F. (1985). Satisfaction with body-image for early adolescent females: The impact of pubertal timing within different school environments. *Journal of Youth and Adolescence, 14,* 207–225.

Bock, R. D., Wainer, H., Petersen, A. C., Thissen, D., Murray, J. S., & Roche, A. (1973). A parameterization of human growth curves. *Human Biology, 45,* 63–80.

Boyar, R. M., Finkelstein, J., Roffwarg, H., Kapan, S., Wertzman, E., & Hellman, L. (1972). Synchronizations of augmented luteinizing hormone secretion with sleep during puberty. *New England Journal of Medicine, 287,* 582–586.

Boyar, R. M., Hellman, L. D., Roffwarg, H., Katz, J., Zumoff, B., O'Connor, J., Bradlow, H. L., & Fukushima, D. K. (1977). Cortisol secretion and metabolism in anorexia nervosa. *New England Journal of Medicine, 296,* 190–193.

Brooks-Gunn, J. (1984). The psychological significance of different pubertal events to young girls. *Journal of Early Adolescence, 4,* 315–327.

Brooks-Gunn, J., Graber, J. A., & Paikoff, R. L. (1994). Studying links between hormones and negative affect: Models and measures. *Journal of Research on Adolescence, 4,* 469–486.

Brooks-Gunn, J., & Petersen, A. C. (Eds.). (1983). *Girls at puberty: Biological and psychosocial perspectives.* New York: Plenum.

Brooks-Gunn, J., Petersen, A. C., & Compas, B. E. (in press). Physiological processes and the development of childhood and adolescent depression. In I. M. Goodyer (Ed.), *Mood disorders in childhood and adolescence.* New York: Cambridge University Press.

Brooks-Gunn, J., Petersen, A. C., & Eichorn, D. (1985). The study of maturational timing effects in adolescence. *Journal of Youth and Adolescence, 14,* 149–161.

Brooks-Gunn, J., & Reiter, E. O. (1990). The role of pubertal processes in the early adolescent transition. In S. Feldman & G. Elliott (Eds.), *At the threshold: The developing adolescent* (pp. 16–53). Cambridge, MA: Harvard University Press.

Brooks-Gunn, J., & Ruble, D. N. (1982). The development of menstrual-related beliefs and behaviors during early adolescence. *Child Development, 53,* 1567–1577.

Brooks-Gunn, J., & Warren, M. P. (1985). Measuring physical status and timing in early adolescence: A developmental perspective. *Journal of Youth and Adolescence, 14,* 163–189.

Brooks-Gunn, J., & Warren, M. P. (1989). Biological contributions to affective expression in young adolescent girls. *Child Development, 60,* 372–385.

Brooks-Gunn, J., Warren, M. P., Rosso, J., & Gargiulo, J. (1987). Validity of self-report measures of girls' pubertal status. *Child Development, 58,* 829–841.

Brooks-Gunn, J., Warren, M. P., Samelson, M., & Fox, R. (1986). Physical similarity of and disclosure of menarcheal status to friends: Effects of age and pubertal status. *Journal of Early Adolescence, 6,* 3–14.

Brown, G. M., Garfinkel, P. E., Jeuniewic, N., Moldofsky, H., & Stancer, H. C. (1977). Endocrine profiles in anorexia nervosa. In R. Vigersky (Ed.), *Anorexia nervosa* (pp. 123–136). New York: Raven.

Cairns, R. B., Cairns, B. D., Neckerman, H. J., Ferguson, L. L., & Gariepy, J. L. (1989). Growth and aggression: I. Childhood to early adolescence. *Developmental Psychology, 25,* 320–330.

Calabrese, L. H., Kirkendall, D. T., Floyd, M., Rapoport, S., Williams, G. W., Weiker, G. F., & Bergfeld, J. A. (1983). Menstrual abnormalities, nutritional patterns, and body composition in female classical ballet dancers. *Physician and Sports Medicine, 11,* 86–98.

Chugani, H. T., Phelps, M. E., & Mazziotta, J. C. (1988). Metabolic brain changes in adolescence—one aspect of a global reorganization. *Annals of Neurology, 24,* 465.

Clausen, J. A. (1975). The social meaning of differential physical and sexual maturation. In S. E. Dragastin & G. H. Elder, Jr. (Eds.), *Adolescence in the life cycle: Psychological change and social context* (pp. 25–47). Washington, DC: Hemisphere.

Coleman, J. C. (1978). Current contradictions in adolescent theory. *Journal of Youth and Adolescence, 7,* 1–11.

Crockett, L. J., & Petersen, A. C. (1987). Pubertal status and psychosocial development: Findings from the Early Adolescence Study. In R. M. Lerner & T. T. Foch (Eds.), *Biological-psychosocial interactions in early adolescence: A lifespan perspective* (pp. 173–188). Hillsdale, NJ: Erlbaum.

Dahl, R. E., Ryan, N. D., Williamson, D. E., Ambrosini, P. J., Rabinovich, H., Novachenko, H., Nelson, B., & Puig-Antich, J. (1992). Regulation of sleep and growth hormone in adolescent depression. *Journal of the American Academy of Child and Adolescent Psychiatry, 31,* 615–621.

Deutsch, H. (1944). *The psychology of women* (Vol. 1). New York: Grune & Stratton.

Dhuper, S., Warren, M. P., Brooks-Gunn, J., & Fox, R. (1990). Effects of hormonal status on bone density at maturity in adolescent girls. *Journal of Clinical Endocrinology and Metabolism, 71,* 1083–1087.

Dobbing, J., & Sands, J. (1973). Quantitative growth and development of the human brain. *Archives of Diseases in Childhood, 48,* 757–767.

Dorn, L. D., Susman, E. J., Nottelmann, E. D., Inoff-Germain, G., & Chrousos, G. P. (1990). Perceptions of puberty: Adolescent, parent, and health care personnel. *Developmental Psychology, 26,* 322–329.

Drigotas, S. M., & Udry, J. R. (in press). Biosocial models of adolescent problem behavior: Extension to panel design. *Social Biology.*

Dubas, J. S., Graber, J. A., & Petersen, A. C. (1991). A longitudinal investigation of adolescents' changing perceptions of pubertal timing. *Developmental Psychology, 27,* 580–586.

Duke, P. M., Carlsmith, J. M., Jennings, D., Martin, J. A., Dornbusch, S. M., Gross, R. T., & Siegel-Gorelick, B. (1982). Educational correlates of early and late sexual maturation in adolescence. *Journal of Pediatrics, 100*, 633–637.

Duke, P. M., Litt, I. F., & Gross, R. T. (1980). Adolescents' self-assessment of sexual maturation. *Pediatrics, 66*, 918–920.

Duncan, P. D., Ritter, P. L., Dornbusch, S. M., Gross, R. T., & Carlsmith, J. M. (1985). The effects of pubertal timing on body image, school behavior, and deviance. *Journal of Youth and Adolescence, 14*, 227–235.

Eichorn, D. H. (1975). Asynchronizations in adolescent development. In S. E. Dragastin & G. H. Elder, Jr. (Eds.), *Adolescence in the life cycle: Psychological change and social context*, (pp. 81–96). Washington, DC: Hemisphere.

Epstein, H. T. (1978). Growth spurts during brain development: Implications for educational policy and practice. In J. S. Chall & A. F. Mirsky (Eds.), *Education and the brain* (pp. 345–370). Chicago: Society for the Study of Education.

Faust, M.S. (1983). Alternative constructions of adolescent growth. In J. Brooks-Gunn & A. C. Petersen (Eds.), *Girls at puberty: Biological and psychosocial perspectives* (pp. 105–126). New York: Plenum.

Feinberg, J. (1987). Adolescence and mental illness [Letter]. *Science, 236*, 507–508.

Fischer, K. W. (1987). Relations between brain and cognitive development. *Child Development, 58*, 623–632.

Frisch, R. E. (1974). A method of prediction of age of menarche from height and weight at ages 9 through 13 years. *Pediatrics, 53*, 384–390.

Frisch, R. E. (1983). Fatness, puberty, and fertility: The effects of nutrition and physical training on menarche and ovulation. In J. Brooks-Gunn & A. C. Petersen (Eds.), *Girls at puberty: Biological and psychosocial perspectives* (pp. 29–50). New York: Plenum.

Frisch, R. E., Revelle, R., & Cook, S. (1973). Components of weight at menarche and the initiation of the adolescent growth spurt in girls: Estimated total water, lean body weight and fat. *Human Biology, 45*, 469–483.

Gaddis, A., & Brooks-Gunn, J. (1985). The male experience of pubertal change. *Journal of Youth and Adolescence, 14*, 61–69.

Goldman-Rakic, P. S. (1987). Development of cortical circuitry and cognitive function. *Child Development, 58*, 601–622.

Goldman-Rakic, P. S., & Brown, R. M. (1982). Post-natal development of monoamine content and synthesis in the cerebral cortex of the rhesus monkey. *Brain Research Bulletin, 256*, 339–349.

Golub, S. (Ed.). (1983). *Menarche*. Lexington, MA: Lexington Books.

Goy, R. W., & McEwen, B. S. (1980). *Sexual differentiation of the brain*. Cambridge: MIT Press.

Graber, J. A. (1991). *The measurement of timing of pubertal development: Use of a triple-logistic growth function*. Unpublished doctoral dissertation, Pennsylvania State University, University Park.

Graber, J. A., Brooks-Gunn, J., Paikoff, R. L., & Warren, M. P. (1994). Prediction of eating problems: An eight-year study of adolescent girls. *Developmental Psychology, 30*.

Graber, J. A., Brooks-Gunn, J., & Warren, M. P. (in press). The antecedents of menarcheal age: Heredity, family environment, and stressful life events. *Child Development*.

Graber, J. A., & Petersen, A. C. (1991). Cognitive changes at adolescence: Biological perspectives. In K. R. Gibson & A. C. Petersen (Eds.), *Brain maturation and cognitive development: Comparative and cross-cultural perspectives* (pp. 253–279). Hawthorne, NY: Aldine de Gruyter.

Graber, J. A., Petersen, A. C., & Brooks-Gunn, J. (in press). Transition to puberty. In J. A. Graber, J. Brooks-Gunn, & A. C. Petersen (Eds.), *Transitions through adolescence: Interpersonal domains and context.* Hillsdale, NJ: Erlbaum.

Greenough, W. T., Black, J. E., & Wallace, C. S. (1987). Experience in brain development. *Child Development, 58,* 539–559.

Greulich, W. W., & Pyle, S. I. (1959). *Radiographic atlas of skeletal development of the hand and wrist* (2nd ed.). Stanford, CA: Stanford University Press.

Gross, R. T. (1984). Patterns of maturation: Their effects on behavior and development. In M. D. Levine & P. Satz (Eds.), *Middle childhood: Development and dysfunction* (pp. 47–62). Baltimore, MD: University Park Press.

Grumbach, M. M. (1980). The neuroendocrinology of puberty. In D. T. Krieger & J. C. Hughes (Eds.), *Neuroendocrinology* (pp. 249–258). Sunderland, MA: Sinauer Associates.

Halpern, C. T., & Udry, J. R. (1992). Variation in adolescent hormone measures and implications for behavioral research. *Journal of Research on Adolescence, 2,* 103–122.

Halpern, C. T., Udry, J. R., Campbell, B., & Suchindran, C. (1994). Relationships between aggression and pubertal increases in testosterone: A panel analysis of adolescent males. *Social Biology, 40,* 8–24.

Huttenlocher, P. R. (1979). Synaptic density in human frontal cortex—developmental changes and effects of aging. *Brain Research, 163,* 195–205.

Inoff-Germain, G., Arnold, G. S., Nottelmann, E. D., Susman, E. J., Cutler, G. B., & Chrousos, G. P. (1988). Relations between hormone levels and observational measures of aggressive behavior of young adolescents in family interactions. *Developmental Psychology, 24,* 129–139.

Jones, M. C. (1965). Psychological correlates of somatic development. *Child Development, 56,* 899–911.

Jones, M. C., & Bayley, N. (1950). Physical maturing among boys as related to behavior. *Journal of Educational Psychology, 41,* 129–148.

Jones, M. C., & Mussen, P. H. (1958). Self-conceptions, motivations, and interpersonal attitudes of early- and late-maturing girls. *Child Development, 29,* 491–501.

Katz, J. L., Boyar, R. M., Roffwarg, H., Hellman, L., & Weiner, H. (1978). Weight and circadian luteinizing hormone secretory pattern in anorexia nervosa. *Psychosomatic Medicine, 40,* 549–567.

Kestenberg, J. (1967). Phases of adolescence with suggestions for correlations of psychic and hormonal organizations: II. Prepuberty, diffusion, and reintegration. *Journal of the American Academy of Child Psychiatry, 6,* 577–614.

Koff, E., Rierdan, J., & Sheingold, K. (1982). Memories of menarche: Age, preparation, and prior knowledge as determinants of initial menstrual experience. *Journal of Youth and Adolescence, 11,* 1–9.

Lewin, K. (1939). Field theory and experiment in social psychology: Concepts and methods. *American Journal of Sociology, 44,* 868–896.

Malina, R. M. (1983). Menarche in athletes: A synthesis and hypothesis. *Annals of Human Biology, 10,* 1–24.

Malina, R. M. (1990). Physical growth and performance during the transitional years (9–16). In R. Montemayor, G. R. Adams, & T. P. Gullotta (Eds.), *From childhood to adolescence: Vol. 2. Advances in adolescent development* (pp. 41–62). Newbury Park, CA: Sage.

Maresh, M. M. (1948). Growth of the heart related to bodily growth during childhood and adolescence. *Pediatrics, 2,* 382–404.

Marshall, W. A. (1974). Interrelationships of skeletal maturation, sexual development and somatic growth in man. *Annals of Human Biology, 1,* 29–40.

Marshall, W. A., & Tanner, J. M. (1969). Variations in the pattern of pubertal changes in girls. *Archives of Disease in Childhood, 44,* 291–303.

Marshall, W. A., & Tanner, J. M. (1970). Variations in the pattern of pubertal changes in boys. *Archives of Disease in Childhood, 45,* 13–23.

Marshall, W. A., & Tanner, J. M. (1974). Puberty. In J. D. Douvis & J. Drobeing (Eds.), *Scientific foundation of pediatrics* (pp. 124–151). London: William Heinemann Medical Books.

Marshall, W. A., & Tanner, J. M. (1986). Puberty. In F. Falkner & J. M. Tanner (Eds.), *Human growth: Vol. 2. Postnatal growth neurobiology* (pp. 171–209). New York: Plenum.

McArthur, J. W., Bullen, B. A., Beitins, J. Z., Pagano, M., Badger, T. M., & Klibanski, A. (1980). Hypothalamic amenorrhea in runners of normal body composition. *Endocrine Research Communications, 7,* 13–25.

Mellits, B. D., & Cheek, D. G. (1970). Assessment of body water and fatness from infancy to childhood. *Monographs of the Society for Research in Child Development, 35* (7, Serial No. 140), 12–26.

Meyer-Bahlberg, H. F. L., Ehrhardt, A. A., & Feldman, J. F. (1986). Long-term implications of the prenatal endocrine milieu for sex-dimorphic behavior. In L. Erlenmeyer-Kimling & N. E. Miller (Eds.), *Life-span research on the prediction of psychopathology* (pp. 17–30). Hillsdale, NJ: Erlbaum.

Moffitt, T. E., Caspi, A., Belsky, J., & Silva, P. A. (1992). Childhood experience and the onset of menarche: A test of a sociobiological model. *Child Development, 63,* 47–58.

Morris, N. M., & Udry, J. R. (1980). Validation of a self-administered instrument to assess stage of adolescent development. *Journal of Youth and Adolescence, 9,* 271–280.

Mussen, P. H., & Jones, M. C. (1957). Self-conceptions, motivations, and interpersonal attitudes of late- and early-maturing boys. *Child Development, 28,* 243–256.

Neugarten, B. L. (1979). Time, age and life cycle. *American Journal of Psychiatry, 136,* 887–894.

Newcombe, N., & Bandura, M. M. (1983). Effect of age of puberty on spatial ability in girls: A question of mechanism. *Developmental Psychology, 19,* 215–224.

Newcombe, N., & Dubas, J. S. (1987). Individual differences in cognitive ability: Are they related to timing of puberty? In R. M. Lerner & T. T. Foch (Eds.), *Biological-psychosocial interactions in early adolescence: A life-span perspective* (pp. 249–302). Hillsdale, NJ: Erlbaum.

Olweus, D., Mattsson, A., Schalling, D., & Low, H. (1980). Testosterone, aggression, physical and personality dimensions in normal adolescent males. *Psychosomatic Medicine, 42,* 253–269.

Olweus, D., Mattsson, A., Schalling, D., & Low, H. (1988). Circulating testosterone levels and aggression in adolescent males: A casual analysis. *Psychosomatic Medicine, 50,* 261–272.

Paige, K. E. (1983). A bargaining theory of menarcheal responses in preindustrial cultures. In J. Brooks-Gunn & A. C. Petersen (Eds.), *Girls at puberty: Biological and psychosocial perspectives* (pp. 301–322). New York: Plenum.

Paikoff, R. L., & Brooks-Gunn, J. (1990a). Associations between pubertal hormones and behavioral and affective expression. In C. S. Holmes (Ed.), *Psychoneuroendocrinology: Brain, behavior, and hormonal interactions* (pp. 205–226). New York: Springer-Verlag.

Paikoff, R. L., & Brooks-Gunn, J. (1990b). Physiological processes: What role do they play during the transition to adolescence? In R. Montemayor, G. Adams, & T. Gullotta (Eds.), *From childhood to adolescence: Vol. 2, Advances in adolescent development* (pp. 63–81). Newbury Park, CA: Sage.

Peskin, H., & Livson, N. (1972). Pre- and postpubertal personality and adult psychological functioning. *Seminars in Psychiatry, 4,* 343–355.

Petersen, A. C. (1983). Menarche: Meaning of measures and measuring meaning. In S. Golub (Ed.), *Menarche: The transition from girl to woman* (pp. 63–76). Lexington, MA: Lexington Books.

Petersen, A. C. (1987). The nature of biological-psychosocial interactions: The sample case of early adolescence. In R. M. Lerner & T. T. Foch (Eds.), *Biological-psychosocial interactions in early adolescence: A life-span perspective* (pp. 35–61). Hillsdale, NJ: Erlbaum.

Petersen, A. C., Compas, B. E., Brooks-Gunn, J., Stemmler, M., Ey, S., & Grant, K. E. (1993). Depression in adolescence. *American Psychologist, 48,* 155–168.

Petersen, A. C., & Crockett, L. J. (1985). Pubertal timing and grade effects on adjustment. *Journal of Youth and Adolescence, 14,* 191–206.

Petersen, A. C., Crockett, L. J., Richards, M., & Boxer, A. (1988). A self-report measure of pubertal status: Reliability, validity, and initial norms. *Journal of Youth and Adolescence, 17,* 117–133.

Petersen, A. C., Sarigiani, P. A., & Kennedy, R. E. (1991). Adolescent depression: Why more girls? *Journal of Youth and Adolescence, 20,* 247–271.

Petersen, A. C., & Taylor, B. (1980). The biological approach to adolescence: Biological change and psychological adaptation. In J. Adelson (Ed.), *Handbook of adolescent psychology* (pp. 117–155). New York: Wiley.

Puig-Antich, J. (1987). Sleep and neuroendocrine correlates of affective illness in childhood and adolescence. *Journal of Adolescent Health Care, 8,* 505–529.

Reiter, E. O., & Grumbach, M. M. (1982). Neuroendocrine control mechanisms and the onset of puberty. *Annual Review of Physiology, 44,* 595–613.

Rierdan, J., & Koff, E. (1985). Timing of menarche and initial menstrual experience. *Journal of Youth and Adolescence, 14,* 237–244.

Roche, A. F., Wainer, H., & Thissen, D. (1975). The RWT method for the prediction of adult stature. *Pediatrics, 46,* 1016–1033.

Rose, R. M., Holaday, J. W., & Bernstein, I. S. (1971). Plasma testosterone, dominance rank, and aggressive behavior in male rhesus monkeys. *Nature, 231,* 366–368.

Ruble, D. N., & Brooks-Gunn, J. (1982). The experience of menarche. *Child Development, 53,* 1557–1566.

Rutter, M. (1989). Pathways from childhood to adult life. *Journal of Child Psychology and Psychiatry and Applied Disciplines, 30,* 23–51.

Sanders, B., & Soares, M. P. (1986). Sexual maturation and spatial ability in college students. *Developmental Psychology, 22,* 199–203.

Silbereisen, R. K., Petersen, A. C., Albrecht, H. T., & Kracke, B. (1989). Maturational timing and the development of problem behavior: Longitudinal studies in adolescence. *Journal of Early Adolescence, 9,* 247–268.

Simmons, R. G., & Blyth, D. A. (1987). *Moving into adolescence: The impact of pubertal change and school context.* New York: Aldine.

Simmons, R. G., Blyth, D. A., Van Cleave, E. F., & Bush, D. M. (1979). Entry into early adolescence: The impact of school structure, puberty, and early dating on self-esteem. *American Sociological Review, 44,* 948–967.

Simon, G., Reid, L., Tanner, J. M., Goldstein, H., & Benjamin, B. (1972). Growth of radiologically determined heart diameter, lung width, lung length from 5 to 19 years with standards for clinical use. *Archives of Disease in Childhood, 47,* 373–381.

Stattin, H., & Magnusson, D. (1990). *Paths through life: Vol. 2. Pubertal maturation in female development.* Hillsdale, NJ: Erlbaum.

Steinberg, L. (1987). Impact of puberty on family relations: Effects of pubertal status and pubertal timing. *Developmental Psychology, 23,* 451–460.

Styne, D. M., & Grumbach, M. M. (1978). Puberty in the male and female: Its physiology and disorders. In S. S. C. Yen & R. B. Jaffe (Eds.), *Reproductive endocrinology, physiology, pathophysiology, and clinical management* (pp. 189–240). Philadelphia: Saunders.

Surbey, M. K. (1990). Family composition, stress, and the timing of human menarche. In T. E. Ziegler & F. B. Bercovitch (Eds.), *Socioendocrinology of primate reproduction* (pp. 11–32). New York: Wiley.

Susman, E. J., Dorn, L. D., & Chrousos, G. P. (1991). Negative affect and hormone levels in young adolescents: Concurrent and predictive perspectives. *Journal of Youth and Adolescence, 20,* 167–190.

Susman, E. J., Inoff-Germain, G. E., Nottelmann, E. D., Cutler, G. B., Jr., Loriaux, D. L., & Chrousos, G. P. (1987). Hormones, emotional dispositions, and aggressive attributes in early adolescents. *Child Development, 58,* 1114–1134.

Susman, E. J., Nottelmann, E. D., Inoff, G. E., Dorn, L. D., Cutler, G. B., Jr., Loriaux, D. L., & Chrousos, G. P. (1985). The relation of relative hormone levels and physical development and social-emotional behavior in young adolescents. *Journal of Youth and Adolescence, 14,* 245–264.

Tanner, J. M. (1962). *Growth at adolescence.* Springfield, IL: Thomas.

Tanner, J. M. (1972). Sequence, tempo, and individual variation in growth and development of boys and girls aged twelve to sixteen. In J. Kagan & R. Coles (Eds.), *Twelve to sixteen: Early adolescence.* New York: Norton.

Tanner, J. M., & Whitehouse, R. H. (1982). *Atlas of children's growth: Normal variation and growth disorders.* New York: Academic Press.

Tanner, J. M., Whitehouse, R. H., Marshall, W. A., Healy, M. J. R., & Goldstein, H. (1975). *Assessment of skeletal maturity and prediction of adult height.* London: Academic Press.

Tanner, J. M., Whitehouse, R. H., Marubini, E., & Resele, F. (1976). The adolescent growth spurt of boys and girls in the Harpenden Growth Study. *Annals of Human Biology, 3,* 109–126.

Tanner, J. M., Whitehouse, R. H., & Takaishi, M. (1966). Standards from birth to maturity for height, weight, height velocity, and weight velocity: British children, 1965. *Archives of Disease in Childhood, 41,* 613–635.

Thatcher, R. W., Walker, R. A., & Guidice, S. (1987). Human cerebral hemispheres develop at different rates and ages. *Science, 236,* 1110–1113.

Thissen, D., & Bock, R. D. (1990). Linear and nonlinear curve fitting. In A. von Eye (Ed.), *Statistical methods in longitudinal research: Vol. 2. Time series and categorical longitudinal data* (pp. 289–318). New York: Academic Press.

Tobin-Richards, M. H., Boxer, A. M., & Petersen, A. C. (1983). The psychological significance of pubertal change: Sex differences in perceptions of self during early adolescence. In J. Brooks-Gunn & A. C. Petersen (Eds.), *Girls at puberty: Biological and psychosocial perspectives* (pp. 127–154). New York: Plenum.

Udry, J. R., & Billy, J. O. G. (1987). Initiation of coitus in early adolescence. *American Sociological Review, 52,* 841–855.

Udry, J. R., Billy, J. O. G., Morris, N. M., Groff, T. R., & Raj, M. H. (1985). Serum androgenic hormones motivate sexual behavior in boys. *Fertility and Sterility, 43,* 90–94.

Udry, J. R., & Talbert, L. M. (1988). Sex hormone effects on personality at puberty. *Journal of Personality and Social Psychology, 54,* 291–295.

Udry, J. R., Talbert, L. M., & Morris, N. M. (1986). Biosocial foundations for adolescent female sexuality. *Demography, 23,* 217–230.

Waber, D. P. (1977). Sex differences in mental abilities, hemispheric lateralization, and rate of physical growth at adolescence. *Developmental Psychology, 13,* 29–38.

Warren, M. P. (1980). The effects of exercise on pubertal progression and reproductive function in girls. *Journal of Clinical Endocrinology Metabolism, 51,* 1150–1157.

Warren, M. P. (1983). Physical and biological aspects of puberty. In J. Brooks-Gunn & A. C. Petersen (Eds.), *Girls at puberty: Biological and psychosocial perspectives* (pp. 3–28). New York: Plenum.

Warren, M. P., & Brooks-Gunn, J. (1989). Mood and behavior at adolescence: Evidence for hormonal factors. *Journal of Clinical Endocrinology and Metabolism, 69,* 77–83.

Warren, M. P., Brooks-Gunn, J., Fox, R. P., Lancelot, C., Newman, D., & Hamilton, W. G. (1991). Lack of bone accretion and amenorrhea in young dancers: Evidence for a relative osteopenia in weight bearing bones. *Journal of Clinical Endocrinology and Metabolism, 72,* 847–853.

Warren, M. P., Brook-Gunn, J., Hamilton, L. H., Hamilton, W. G., & Warren, L. F. (1986). Scoliosis and fractures in young ballet dancers: Relationships to delayed menarcheal age and secondary amenorrhea. *New England Journal of Medicine, 314,* 1348–1353.

Weideger, P. (1975). *Menstruation and menopause.* New York: Knopf.

Yakovlev, P. I., & Lecours, A. R. (1967). The myelogenetic cycles of regional maturation in the brain. In A. Minkowski (Ed.), *Regional development of the brain in early life* (pp. 3–70). Oxford, England: Blackwell.

3
Social Interactions and Adjustment

David J. Hansen
Angela M. Giacoletti
Douglas W. Nangle

D uring adolescence, social interactions and relationships become increasingly complicated and adultlike. The peer group becomes larger and more complex, more time is spent with peers, and interactions with opposite-sex peers increase (Berndt, 1982; Csikszentmihalyi & Larson, 1984; Petersen & Hamburg, 1986). There is a greater desire for close friends as adolescents turn to their peers for support formerly provided by the family, and the primarily same-sex interests and playmates of childhood give way to opposite-sex interests and friendships (Csikszentmihalyi & Larson, 1984; Kelly & Hansen, 1987).

The many developmental events that occur during adolescence have a significant impact on an adolescent's interpersonal interactions. The more advanced cognitive and verbal abilities, as well as the physical and emotional changes associated with puberty, alter the adolescent's interactions with both same-sex and opposite-sex peers (Damon, 1983; Kelly & Hansen, 1987). In addition, adolescents may experience a variety of other changes that affect interpersonal interactions, including peer group changes, school moves, changes in family structure or functioning, and alterations in societal and community expectations (Hansen, Watson-Perczel, & Christopher, 1989; Petersen & Hamburg, 1986).

Effective social interactions are necessary for successful functioning at home, school, work, and social settings, as well as to facilitate emotional and behavioral adjustment (Csikszentmihalyi & Larson, 1984; Kelly & Hansen, 1987; Hansen, Christopher, & Nangle, 1992; Kelly & Hansen, 1987; Petersen & Hamburg, 1986). Social interactions may be critical for an adolescent's adjustment in a number of ways, including (a) establishing support systems for emotional and social needs; (b) developing moral judgment and social values; (c) improving or maintaining self-esteem; (d) promotion of interpersonal competence and adultlike social behavior; (e) development of independence assertion that aids in separation from the family; (f) recreation, including entertainment and sexual stimulation; (g) enhancement of status within the peer group; (h) developing sexual attitudes, interests, and sex-role behaviors; (i) experimentation, particularly with sex-role behaviors and sexual activity; and (j) courtship and mate selection (Damon, 1983; Hansen et al., 1992; Kelly & Hansen, 1987).

A great deal of empirical and theoretical literature suggests that social interactions during childhood and adolescence play an important role in later psychological adjustment (Kelly & Hansen, 1987; Parker & Asher, 1987; Petersen & Hamburg, 1986). Correlational research has found a relation between interactional difficulties and social isolation during childhood and a variety of concurrent and later psychosocial difficulties. In a comprehensive review of the literature, Parker and Asher (1987) found support for the hypothesis that children with poor peer adjustment are at risk for such later life difficulties as dropping out of school in adolescence and criminality during adolescence and adulthood. Most of the support comes from research on children with low peer acceptance and aggression; shyness or withdrawal has not been shown to be a good predictor of later maladjustment. Evidence for the link between peer relations in childhood and later psychopathology is incomplete and conflicting (Parker & Asher, 1987).

The purpose of this chapter is to examine the relation between social interactions and adjustment in adolescence. The full range of adolescent development is discussed, from young adolescents (approximately age 12) to adolescents in college. The literature on the relationship between social interaction problems and adjustment is examined, including the role of social behaviors in psychopathology and the social influences on emotional and behavioral adjustment. The literature on the assessment and treatment of social interaction problems is also reviewed.

Social Aspects of Adolescent Psychopathology

Social behaviors play an important role in the identification of adolescent psychopathology. Many of the of diagnostic categories included in the current *Diagnostic and Statistical Manual of Mental Disorders* (DSM-IV; American Psychiatric Association, 1994) include social functioning as a component of the disorder. Approximately 45 percent of the Axis I clinical syndromes and nearly all of the Axis II personality disorders have problematic social functioning as a possible criterion, and the majority of the others have social implications. Among the diagnostic grouping of "disorders first evident in infancy, childhood, or adolescence," the following are the primary Axis I clinical syndromes (followed by their DSM-IV codes) that have social factors as a possible criterion: mental retardation (317.0 to 319.0), autistic disorder (299.0), Rett's disorder (299.8), childhood disintegrative disorder (299.1), attention-deficit/hyperactivity disorder (314.0 to 314.9), conduct disorder (312.8), oppositional defiant disorder (313.81), selective mutism (313.23), and reactive attachment disorder (313.89). In addition, the following Axis I syndromes are usually diagnosed in adulthood but may occur or begin in adolescence and may have social components: major depressive disorder (296.2 to 296.3), dysthymic disorder (300.4), bipolar I and II disorders (296.0 to 296.89), cyclothymic disorder (301.13), schizophrenia (295.1 to 295.9), social phobia (300.23), and adjustment disorder (309.0 to 309.9). Axis II personality disorders with significant social components are paranoid (301.0), schizoid (301.2), schizotypal (301.22), antisocial (301.7), histrionic (301.5), narcissistic (301.81), avoidant (301.82), dependent (301.6), and borderline (301.83) personality disorders.

A number of other disorders do not specifically include interpersonal difficulties as part of the diagnostic criteria but probably have an interpersonal component (see Dodge, 1989). These include learning disorders (315.0 to 315.9), communication disorders and stuttering (315.31 to 315.9, 307.0), elimination disorders (307.6 to 307.7), anorexia nervosa (307.1), bulimia nervosa (307.51), gender identity disorders (302.6 to 302.85), stereotypic movement disorder (307.30), tic disorders (397.20 to 307.23), agoraphobia (300.22), and the many substance-related disorders (291.0 to 305.9). Further, Axis V of the DSM-IV multiaxial rating system provides a mechanism for the global assessment of psychological functioning, particularly with respect to interpersonal situations. Lack of competence in social situations is therefore a core feature of psychological maladjustment. It follows that the quality and extent of an adolescent's interpersonal relationships have important implications for current and future psychological well-being.

A variety of mechanisms may facilitate the development of the social and heterosocial skills necessary for competent interactions during adolescence. Briefly, these include (a) exposure to appropriate social skill models; (b) the consequences (e.g., reinforcement, punishment, extinction) associated with an adolescent's social behavior; (c) exposure to, and participation in, peer social activities; and (d) such "cognitive" factors as self-statements and attributional processes (Kelly, 1982; Kelly & Hansen, 1987). Thus an adolescent's behavioral repertoire is the result of a lengthy process of learning through modeling and contingencies occurring within multiple social contexts. In turn, the adolescent's behavior influences other individuals' responses to his or her behavior. Relations between social influences and adolescent psychopathology are therefore likely to be bidirectional and interactive, rather than unidirectional, in nature. Because opportunities for peer interaction are probably necessary for an adolescent to develop social skills, initial deficits in social skills may limit the opportunity for interaction and, consequently, further limit skill development.

The following section briefly reviews literature relating social interaction variables and psychopathology in adolescence. This discussion has been organized according to three major influences on psychological adjustment: (a) social skills, (b) social anxiety, and (c) social context.

Social Skills

During adolescence, individuals are exposed to new social situations and need different social interaction skills than those required in earlier childhood interactions. Adolescents may begin working with others in a part-time job, spending time with peers without adult supervision, and dating. The extent of the similarity between skills needed for social and heterosocial interactions and between same- and opposite-sex peer relations is unclear but assumed to be significant (Hansen et al., 1992; Kelly, 1982).

Ford (1982) highlights the situational specificity of which behaviors are viewed as "socially competent" during adolescence by defining social competence as "the attainment of relevant social goals in specified social contexts, using appropriate means, and resulting in positive developmental outcomes" (p. 323). Behaviors that are considered socially competent by teachers and parents may not facilitate the adolescent's popularity among his or her peers (Allen, Weissberg, & Hawkins, 1989).

Social competence is related to a wide range of psychological problems in adolescence. For example, social skills deficits are often present among adolescents who exhibit disruptive, externalizing behavior disorders. Freedman, Rosenthal, Donahue, Schlundt, and McFall (1978) examined differences in social skills between delinquent and nondelinquent adolescent males in response to role-play scenarios simulating problematic interpersonal situations. Delinquent adolescents proposed a more limited range of solutions, tended to solve problems by using verbal or physical aggression, and were rated as less socially competent. Dishion, Loeber, Stouthamer-Loeber, and Patterson (1984) also found lower levels of interpersonal problem-solving skills among delinquent males during role-play situations that primarily involved refusals to take part in antisocial behaviors with peers. In a study of conversational competence, Hansen, St. Lawrence, and Christoff (1988) found that impatient conduct-disordered youth were deficient in a variety of conversational skill component behaviors when compared with nonpatient peers.

Social skills deficits have also been associated with a number of internalizing disorders, including depression, schizophrenia, and anxiety (e.g., Christoff et al., 1985; Platt, Spivack, Altman, Altman, & Peizer, 1974; Sarason & Sarason, 1984). The interactional styles of individuals with depressive behaviors may actually elicit negative emotional states (e.g., depression, anxiety, hostility) in other individuals with whom they interact (Coyne, 1976). In analyses of conversational content, depressive patients were found to display inappropriate levels of self-disclosure, primarily with respect to negative and highly personal life events (Coyne, 1976). Young women interacting with depressed peers over the telephone (Coyne, 1976) or in face-to-face conversations (Howes & Hokanson, 1979) voiced significantly less desire to interact with these peers at a later time. Thus social skills deficits may cause previous sources of reinforcements to withdraw, creating a deficit in positive reinforcement and an inability to form new friendships, heterosocial relationships, and support systems. In addition, there is evidence to suggest that interpersonal conflict with significant others in an adolescent's life may be a precipitant to a suicide attempt (e.g., Withers & Kaplan, 1987).

Both retrospective and prospective studies suggest a relation between adolescent social competence and substance abuse (e.g., Hops, Tildesley, Lichtenstein, Ary, & Sherman, 1990; Lindquist, Lindsay, & White, 1979; Van Hasselt, Hersen, & Milliones, 1978). Wills, Baker, and Botvin (1989) assessed a multiracial sample of 7,650 urban and suburban 12- to 14-year-olds using a self-report measure of assertiveness, saliva samples (for cigarette use), and a self-report questionnaire regarding psychosocial variables and substance use (smoking, drinking, and marijuana use). Lower assertiveness related to substance-use situations was found to relate to high substance use. This association was stronger for females than for males and for Caucasians than for African Americans. Adolescents who reported higher levels of social and dating assertiveness were also found to report higher levels of substance use. Thus it appears that social activities provide strong contingencies for substance use, that assertiveness skills specific to substance use are important for refraining from use, and that these relations may differ between genders and ethnic groups. Overall, the research suggests that both social skills (e.g., social problem solving, assertiveness) and social contingencies (e.g., peers, family) play a role in the development and maintenance of substance abuse problems among adolescents.

As with other populations, social skills deficits may negatively affect the performance of adolescents with mental retardation in school, social, and work settings. Matson, Kazdin, and Esveldt-Dawson (1980), for example, examined the social skills of two adolescent males with moderate mental retardation and found the adolescents to be deficient in maintaining appropriate levels of a number of discrete social behaviors (e.g., eye contact, physical gesturing, number of words spoken, appropriate facial expression, speech intonation, verbal content) when compared to nonretarded adolescents matched for age and gender. Bradlyn et al. (1983) found their sample of five adolescents with mental retardation to be deficient in identifying and discussing appropriate conversational topics that are of interest to nonretarded peers. In addition, adolescents with mental retardation may have deficits in the nonverbal and paralinguistic behaviors that could facilitate expressive communication (Matson, Manikam, Coe, Raymond, & Taras, 1988), deficiencies in the interpersonal skills necessary for effective job interviewing (e.g., Kelly, Wildman, & Berler, 1980), and a lack of requisite skills for establishing dating relationships (e.g., Mueser, Valenti-Hein, & Yarnold, 1987). These deficits may be part of a vicious cycle in which the adolescent has little opportunity to interact with nonretarded peers and, therefore, limited exposure to the modeling and consequent-control experiences through which social skills are learned. In turn, nonretarded peers may further withdraw from adolescents with retardation because of the inappropriateness of their social behavior.

There is also a relationship between social skills deficits and other developmental problems. Children with learning disabilities have been found to exhibit fewer positive behaviors (e.g., complimenting, praising, and initiating interactions with peers) and more distracting nonverbal behaviors (see La Greca, 1981). These children also tend to experience more negative peer interactions than nondisabled children. Adolescents with learning disabilities are rated by teachers as exhibiting higher levels of maladaptive behaviors and less socially competent behavior than nondisabled adolescents (e.g., Center & Wascom, 1986). These behaviors appear to influence negatively the relationship between students with learning disabilities and their teachers (e.g., Garrett & Crump, 1980).

As might be expected, research indicates that social skills deficits within both same-sex and opposite-sex interactions are also highly related to the degree of loneliness experienced by adolescents and young adults (e.g., Jones, Hobbs, & Hockenbury, 1982; Solano, Batten, & Parish, 1982). In addition, lonely individuals may make negative attributions about social interactions, and these attributions interfere with the formation of relationships (e.g., Jones, Freeman, & Goswick, 1981). While social isolation and loneliness are not classified as specific psychological disorders according to *DSM-IV* criteria, they do significantly affect psychological adjustment and quality of life. These problems are related to the frequency, extent, and quality of interactions with others (particularly peers) of either gender. Relationships with peers are an important, common concern during adolescence (Kelly & Hansen, 1987), and loneliness has been associated with a range of psychological disorders, including anxiety and depression (Anderson, Horowitz, & French, 1983; Jones et al., 1981).

Problems related to heterosocial interactions appear to be relatively prevalent among adolescents and young adults (Arkowitz, Hinton, Perl, & Himadi, 1978; Borkovec, Stone, O'Brien, & Kaloupek, 1974; Hansen et al., 1992). Deficits in heterosocial competence have been found to relate to such psychosocial problems as less frequent dating, fewer and less varied sexual experiences, decreased satisfaction during sexual activity, greater frequency of sexual dysfunction, and differences in the type and patterns of use of contraception (e.g., Bruch & Hynes, 1987; Leary & Dobbins, 1983). Social skills within heterosocial interactions have also been found to discriminate between male sex offenders and normal control subjects (e.g., Overholser & Beck, 1986); along with social isolation, social anxiety, and general psychosocial maladjustment, it may predispose certain adolescent males toward sexually abusing children (e.g., Katz, 1990).

Sexual interactions are a specific form of social interaction, and research suggests that many adolescents have sexual interaction skills deficits (Nangle & Hansen, 1993). For example, use of a particular contraceptive method involves a complex interaction of many types of behaviors, including sexual and contraceptive knowledge, procedural behaviors (i.e., behaviors required for adequate use of a particular method), and social behaviors (Nangle, Giacoletti, Ellis, Aljazireh, & Hansen, 1994; Nangle & Hansen, 1993). Inadequate contraceptive behavior is widely prevalent among adolescents, as is evidenced by high rates of sexually transmitted diseases (STDs) and pregnancy (Hansen et al., 1992). Koenig and Zelnik (1982) found that within the first 2 years of initial intercourse, as many as 35.9% of sexually active teenage girls become pregnant (33.2% of unmarried Caucasian teens and 43.3% of unmarried African-American teens). MacDonald et al. (1990) found that approximately 70% of college students were sexually active, and of these 5.5% reported a previous STD. Only 24.8% of the college males and 15.6% of the college females sampled always used a condom during sexual intercourse. In a study that examined self-report of specific contraceptive behaviors, Nangle et al. (1994) found that male and female college students were deficient in a number of procedural skills required for uncompromised effectiveness of the contraceptive method. Compared to females, males took less responsibility for contraception, used contraception less consistently, reported greater difficulty engaging in contraceptive-related social behaviors, and were less likely to communicate to a partner that they wanted to use contraception.

Adolescents seldom complain about sexual dysfunction, possibly because of embarrassment, fear of adult reactions, or lack of knowledge about normal human sexual responses (Hansen et al., 1992). As with adults, however, problems may include premature ejaculation or lack of erection for males and painful intercourse or lack of orgasm for females (American Psychiatric Association, 1994). Although little is known about the psychological consequences of early sexual activity and intercourse, the literature suggests that they may include self-devaluation, unsatisfactory sexual experiences, substitution of intercourse for intimacy, anorgasmia, and promiscuity (Hansen et al., 1992).

Additional problems that have been increasingly recognized in heterosocial relationships and that may be related to skill deficits and peer influences are dating violence and date rape (Hansen et al., 1992; Nangle & Hansen, 1993). Estimates of involvement in dating violence (either expressed or sustained) are speculative and extremely varied, ranging from approximately 9% to 65%, with females more likely to report that they have not been a victim of expressed violence in a dating relationship

(Hansen et al., 1992; Sugarman & Hotaling, 1989). Estimates of the incidence of date rape are also alarmingly high. In a survey of 380 female and 368 male undergraduates, Muehlenhard and Linton (1987) found that 14.7% of the females and 7.1% of the males had been involved in unwanted sexual intercourse.

Social Anxiety

Social anxiety is highly influenced by a learning history of conditioned avoidance of social interactions and maladaptive cognitions related to social evaluation (Kelly, 1982; Kelly & Hansen, 1987). Adolescents commonly encounter social situations and pressures that are novel and unfamiliar, leading to heightened physiological responding and subjective feelings of distress. Anxiety and arousal may also be elicited because of a history of failure in similar situations, which may be the result of skill deficits. In any event, social anxiety appears to be relatively common among adolescents and young adults. Arkowitz et al. (1978) reported that 31% of 3,800 college students (37% of the males and 25% of the females) evaluated themselves as anxious about dating. Borkovec et al. (1974) found that 15.5% of the males and 11.5% of the females in introductory psychology classes reported at least some anxiety within heterosocial situations. The greater incidence in males may be due to their more common role as initiators of heterosocial dating (Hansen et al., 1992; Kelly, 1982). Himadi, Arkowitz, Hinton, and Perl (1980) found that socially anxious, low-dating men, but not low-dating women, exhibited general adjustment problems and difficulties in same-sex friendship interactions. Compared to social skills deficits and social anxiety, which are more prevalent for males, the more extreme social phobia appears to be equally prevalent between genders, has a sudden onset during adolescence, is more focused on one or more specific phobic stimuli, and is more occasional and situation-specific in nature (Marks, 1985).

In addition to interfering with the development of relationships, social anxiety and avoidance may be related to such problems as depression, alcoholism, and sexual dysfunction (Arkowitz et al., 1978; Dodge, Heimberg, Nyman, & O'Brien, 1987; Hansen et al., 1992). In recent years, research has also supported the role of anxiety in inadequate contraceptive behavior (Bruch & Hynes, 1987; Leary & Dobbins, 1983). Although survey data demonstrate that social anxiety is a problem for many teenagers, less is known about its severity, the frequency with which it is a transient concern rather than a long-standing developmental pattern, and the degree to which teenagers are able to overcome social anxiety or inhibition on their own through increased exposure to naturally occurring social interactions (Hansen et al., 1992; Kelly & Hansen, 1987).

Social Context

In addition to social skills and anxiety, the social context in which an adolescent functions can influence adjustment. The social influence of peers and family members has been shown to relate to the emotional and behavioral adjustment of adolescents.

Peer Influences. Over time, peers come to play a more central role in influencing an adolescent's behavior, with other social agents (e.g., parents, teachers) continuing to influence behavior but to a lesser degree than in childhood. Adolescents spend a great deal of time in one another's company, increasingly conform to peer norms in order to gain acceptance, and are greatly concerned over their self-presentation and status among peers (Jessor & Jessor, 1977). Social contingencies by peers may take several forms. For example, peers provide models for behavior, and they apply direct social consequences for conformist and deviant behavior. The verbal and nonverbal behavior of the peer group also provides rules or norms that are followed. Such peer influences may have a direct relation to the development and maintenance of many of the disorders evidenced by adolescents.

Aggressive and rule-breaking behaviors appear to be highly influenced by peers. Research suggests that early peer socialization results in the acquisition of both aggressive behavior (Patterson, Littman, & Bricker, 1967) and the skills necessary for controlling such behavior (Hartup & DeWitt, 1974). This socialization process appears to continue throughout adolescence. The majority of adolescent delinquent behaviors are exhibited in the context of small groups of peers (Zimring, 1981); many adolescents arrested for violent offenses and homicides are gang members, and the numbers of youths in gangs is on the rise (Miller, 1975; Zimring, 1981). Peer influences on delinquent behavior by female adolescents have received considerably less attention and are less clear.

Research has also found a significant relation between an adolescent's substance use and similar use by his or her friends (e.g., Ary, Tildesley, Hops, Lichtenstein, & Andrews, 1988; Jessor & Jessor, 1977). Heavy-drinking adolescents tend to select friends who have similar alcohol consumption patterns (Braucht et al., 1973). Interacting with peers who abuse substances is likely to decrease an adolescent's chances of learning appropriate social behavior, moderation strategies, and adaptive coping skills through peer interactions. Ary et al. (1988) examined parent, sibling, and peer influences on the substance use of 173 adolescents (12 to 14 years old), as well as possible mechanisms for the effect of these influences (e.g., behavior modeling, attitudes), over a period of 1 year. Family members provided information regarding their own and other family members' current and past cigarette, alcohol, and marijuana use and their attitudes and behaviors related to use of these substances. In addition, the targeted adolescents were asked to report on their peers' use and endorsement of use of cigarettes, alcohol, and marijuana. Peers were found to be primary influences across both modes of influence and the substances assessed. Siblings influenced the target adolescents' substance use to a significant but more modest extent. Interestingly, while parental attitudes were found to be significant predictors of substance use, behavioral modeling by parents was not.

From a developmental perspective, the appearance of eating disorders among adolescent females appears to be a function of the cultural ideal of thinness, the rapid rate of weight gain and body development experienced during adolescence, and the increasing importance placed on relationships and dating (Streigel-Moore, Silberstein, & Rodin, 1986). Females have been found to rate popularity as a more important goal than other forms of competence, to be more susceptible to evaluations by others, and to vacillate to a greater degree in their self-descriptions than males (Simmons & Rosenberg, 1975). Interestingly, behaviors associated with eating disorders may actually serve to decrease an adolescent's popularity with peers. Eating-disordered adolescents may become secretive in their attempts to hide such socially unacceptable behaviors as vomiting, bingeing, and laxative use. Further, individuals with eating disorders may avoid eating in front of others, steal or hoard food, lie about eating habits, and engage in a high frequency of conflictual interactions with others regarding their weight and eating behaviors (Harris & Phelps, 1985). Peer influences on the development and maintenance of eating disorders are especially strong within boarding schools and colleges (e.g., Hovell, Mewborn, Randle, & Fowler-Johnson, 1985) and activity-oriented groups (e.g., athletes, dancers) that emphasize thinness and stereotypic notions of beauty, or where performance is enhanced by maintaining a low body weight (e.g., Crago, Yates, Beutler, & Arizmendi, 1985; Druss & Silverman, 1979; Yates, Leehey, & Shisslak, 1983).

Family Influences. In addition to the likely genetic and biological influences, socialization processes within the family contribute to the development of a variety of adolescent disorders. For example, aggressive behavior may be modeled and shaped by interactional contingencies provided within the family environment (Patterson, 1982). Adolescents observe aggressive behavior within discordant interactions either between one parent and the other, between parents and siblings, or they may become directly involved in coercive cycles with parents or siblings. In these interactions, each person's aggressive behavior is shaped and maintained through an escalating, reciprocal series of interactions. For example, verbally and physically aggressive behaviors may be positively reinforced by the other person's compliance with demands and negatively reinforced through escape from aversive interpersonal stimuli (Patterson, 1982).

Anxiety disorders also appear to be influenced by familial variables, including heritability. Children of parents with anxiety disorders are significantly more likely to exhibit anxiety disorders themselves than are children of non-anxiety-disordered adults (Crowe, Noyes, Pauls, & Slymen, 1983; Turner, Beidel, & Costello, 1987). This is especially true for female offspring. In one study, 50% of daughters, but only 10% of sons, who had at least one parent with panic disorder were also identified as having a definite or probable diagnosis of panic disorder (Crowe et al., 1983). Although pathology does appear to breed pathology, it is difficult to parcel out the effects of genetics and environment. It is likely that certain individuals may be biologically predisposed to developing anxiety disorders while environmental factors (e.g., modeling of anxious behavior by family members, positive and negative reinforcement of the adolescent's anxious behavior) may be influential in determining whether the disorder is actually manifested.

Substance abuse disorders among adolescents also appear to be highly influenced by the family environment (e.g., Ary et al., 1988; Kandel & Andrews, 1987). O'Leary, O'Leary, and Donovan (1975) present evidence to suggest that parents of individuals who are later identified as problem drinkers typically represent the extremes of alcohol consumptions themselves, thereby failing to provide modeling experiences for moderate drinking. Numerous studies have supported the effects of parental substance use on adolescents' use (e.g., Dishion & Loeber, 1985; Hops et al., 1990; Margulies, Kessler, & Kandel, 1977). Parents with alcohol abuse problems may in fact display approval for their offspring's drinking (Monti, Abrams, Binkoff, & Zwick, 1986). Differences have been found in the problem-solving skills of families with substance-using and non-substance-using adolescents during parent-adolescent interactions (Hops et al., 1990). These differences were found for discussions of both drug-related and non-drug-related conversational topics. In addition, problem-solving strategies of parent-adolescent dyads were found to discriminate between adolescents who engaged in or refrained from substance use 1 year later.

The influence of interactional styles among family members also has been discussed as contributing to the development and maintenance of eating disorders among adolescents. Families of women with anorexia and bulimia tend to evidence higher levels of enmeshment, conflict, and triangulation than those of non-eating-disordered women (see Minuchin, Rosman, & Baker, 1978; Schwartz, Barrett, & Saba, 1985). Parents of adolescents with anorexia nervosa may also be overly concerned with their children, overprotective, highly ambitious, and demanding of obedience, as well as have high standards for performance (Bruch, 1973). The behaviors exhibited by adolescents with eating disorders may be hypothesized to be a means of coping with these dysfunctional family patterns.

Assessment of Social Interaction Problems

Despite the importance and implications of social skills deficits in adolescent psychopathology, little research has been devoted exclusively to the diagnosis and assessment of such deficits in this age group. This section provides a brief review of the extant social skills assessment literature.

Self-Report Inventories

Self-report inventories typically involve asking adolescents to evaluate their own social behavior. The use of self-report inventories with adolescents has been restricted mainly to descriptive research relating general social competence to such factors as divorce, school performance, and depression (e.g., Cauce, 1987; Fauber, Forehand, Long, Burke, & Faust, 1987; Long, Forehand, Fauber, & Brody, 1987). Standardized self-report measures used in such studies include the Matson Evaluation of Social Skills with Youngsters (MESSY; Matson, Rotatori, & Helsel, 1983) and the Perceived Competence Scale for Children (PCSC; Harter, 1982). Self-report measures have also been used to assess social anxiety in children and adolescents (e.g., La Greca, Dandes, Wick, Shaw, & Stone, 1988; Warren, Good, & Velten, 1984). Currently, self-report measures have not been used to identify adolescents or targets for intervention (Foster, Inderbitzen, & Nangle, 1993), and they have been used infrequently as dependent measures for social skills training interventions. A self-report measure with possible applications for social skills training, however, is the Teenage Inventory of Social Skills (TISS; Inderbitzen-Pisaruk & Foster, 1990b). Adolescents are asked to rate how characteristic of their own social behavior each of 40 empirically derived behavioral descriptors are on a 6-point scale. Preliminary investigations suggest that the TISS has adequate psychometric properties (Inderbitzen-Pisaruk, Beyer, Halstenson-Sawyer, & Groene, 1991; Inderbitzen-Pisaruk & Foster, 1990b).

Although self-report inventories are capable of obtaining valuable information about adolescents' perceptions of social competence in a cost- and time-efficient manner, the utility of current measures for social skills assessment is limited (Foster et al., 1993). A key limitation of self-report measures is that they measure perceptions of behavior rather than actual behavior. Children with difficulties in peer relationships might also have deficits in their social perception or self-evaluation skills, or they may wish to present themselves in a more desirable way. Support for this hypothesis has been found in research with younger children (e.g., Boivin & Begin, 1989). An additional limitation of self-report inventories is their global, summative nature which decreases their utility for identifying specific intervention targets.

Peer Ratings and Nominations

Instead of assessing actual social behavior, peer ratings and nominations (i.e., sociometric procedures) assess the adolescent's social standing or acceptance within a peer group or the peers' thoughts or feelings about an adolescent (Foster et al., 1993). Peer nominations typically consist of having adolescents nominate a limited number of peers who fit some prespecified criterion (e.g., like most, like least), while peer ratings typically consist of actually rating peers on some similar criterion (e.g., liking) on a Likert-type rating scale. A less frequently used peer-rating procedure is having adolescents rate peers on specific social behaviors (e.g., fights, sharing).

Though used more commonly with younger children, sociometrics have been used to identify adolescents with social skills deficits, to identify and validate targets for intervention by correlating peer status with specific behaviors, to validate other assessment measures, and as dependent measures for social skills training interventions (e.g., Bierman & Furman, 1984; Coie, Dodge, & Coppotelli, 1982; Inderbitzen-Pisaruk et al., 1991). Sociometrics can also be used as measures of social validity for social skills training interventions, as they allow for the assessment of the impact of behavior change on actual peer acceptance (Foster et al., 1993). In fact, the failure of many interventions to document behavioral change and subsequent improvements on sociometric measures has led to concerns about the social validity of social skills training (Gresham, 1981). It should be noted, though, that there are many possible explanations for the failure of interventions to alter sociometric status, including inadequate curricula, insufficient behavioral change, insufficient contact between peers and the target child to allow peers to experience the change in behavior, reputational biases (Foster et al., 1993), or the sensitivity of the measures themselves (Nangle, Ellis, Christopher, & Hansen, 1993).

The utility of sociometric measures for social skills training with adolescents is not clear. While sociometric measures are often touted for their sound psychometric properties and predictive validity, this type of evaluative research has not been conducted with adolescents, and the generalizability of such findings from younger samples is thus questionable. Sociometrics also suffer from other serious limitations, including their (a) inability to determine or monitor specific behavioral deficits, (b) reactivity if used repeatedly, (c) frequent lack of correspondence with direct observation data, and (d) potential ethical problems and difficulty obtaining consent (Foster et al., 1993; Gresham, 1981). Another potential limitation of sociometrics more specific to adolescents is that adolescents tend to be more mobile than younger children and establish friendships in many settings other than the classroom.

Teacher Ratings

The format for teacher ratings varies considerably; however most involve ratings of how frequently children perform specific social behaviors (e.g., Bierman & Furman, 1984). Although a number of teacher-rating scales are available for use with children, including the Teacher's Rating Scale of Child's Actual Competence (TRS; Harter, 1982), the Matson Evaluation of Social Skills for Youngsters (MESSY; Matson et al., 1983), and the Taxonomy of Problem Situations for Children (TOPS; Dodge, McClaskey, & Feldman, 1985), such measures have been used infrequently with adolescents. A number of studies have used the TRS with adolescents (e.g., Fauber et al., 1987; Long et al., 1987). The TRS is a 28-item scale developed in conjunction with the Perceived Competence Scale for Children (PCSC; Harter, 1982) and assesses the teacher's judgment of the adolescent's social competence.

Teacher ratings can be used to identify adolescents with social skills deficits, as dependent measures for interventions, and for the social validation of measures and intervention targets. Teacher ratings are not only time and cost efficient but provide easily quantifiable data on a wide range of child behaviors. These measures do, however, have a number of important limitations, including the failure to separate evaluations of social behaviors directed toward the teacher from those directed toward peers, the use of global scoring methods incapable of isolating specific behaviors, and rater biases (e.g., based on academic skills; Foster et al., 1993). Limitations of teacher ratings that are more specific to adolescents include the mobility of teens and the fact that many key interactions occur outside of the school environment.

Direct Observation in Analogue Situations

Direct observation in analogue situations (e.g., role play) is a commonly used assessment procedure designed to address many of the potential ethical and methodological limitations associated with directly observing behavior in the natural environment. Analogue situations used with adolescents have ranged from highly structured role plays with scripted prompts (e.g., Kirkland, Thelen, & Miller, 1982; Rhodes, Redd, & Berggren, 1979) to unstructured dyadic interactions (e.g., Bierman & Furman, 1984; Bradlyn et al., 1983; Hansen, St. Lawrence, & Christoff, 1988, 1989). For example, Plienis et al. (1987) presented adolescents with 10 social problem-solving scenarios and rated their verbal responses in terms of prespecified component behaviors, number of solutions generated, and ratings of overall effectiveness.

Direct observation in analogue situations has been used to identify adolescents with social skills deficits and social anxiety, as a dependent measure for interventions, and to validate other measures (e.g., Bierman & Furman, 1984; Hansen, St. Lawrence, & Christoff, 1989; Plienis et al., 1987). The use of analogue situations has a number of advantages. For example, role-play tests have been used to assess the social anxiety and behaviors involved in heterosocial interactions—such as date initiation or sexual assertiveness skills (e.g., Schinke, Blythe, & Gilchrest, 1981)—that for ethical and methodological reasons would not otherwise be accessible. Additional advantages of analogue situations include enabling the experimenter to (a) exercise more control of extraneous variables, (b) simulate specific social situations, (c) use precise recording and measurement (e.g., videotape), and (d) create task analyses of effective performance for each specific situation (Foster et al., 1993).

Of course, the major potential limitation of direct observation in analogue situations is the extent to which performance in the test situations corresponds to performance in the natural environment (i.e., external validity). Research has questioned the external validity of role-play assessments (see Bellack, Hersen, & Lamparski, 1979); however, it is likely that less structured role-play assessments (e.g., unstructured dyadic interactions) would have increased external validity (Hansen, St. Lawrence, & Christoff, 1988, 1989). Another problem with analogue assessments is that the social validity of the selected tasks and target behaviors is often questionable (Foster et al., 1993), and these tasks and behaviors vary quite a bit among studies. Clearly, more research is needed to investigate the validity of analogue assessments.

Direct Observation in the Natural Environment

Direct observation of social interactions in the natural environment is frequently used with children to obtain data on the rate, frequency, or percentage of social interactions or behaviors. Due to ethical and methodological concerns, however, this method is used less frequently with adolescents. Hansen, St. Lawrence, and Christoff (1989) assessed for setting generalization by using in-vivo observations of inpatient adolescents' conversational behavior in a hospital cafeteria. Assessments were conducted prior to, during, and following a group training intervention on conversation skills. The assessment consisted of 15-minute videotaped observations of actual conversations between both subject and nonsubject inpatient youths. Trained raters subsequently rated each videotape for overall conversational effectiveness. In a similar assessment, Hansen, MacMillan, and Shawchuck (1990) conducted unobtrusive observations of a socially withdrawn adolescent in a high school cafeteria. A partial 10-second interval recording system was used to obtain data on positive and negative interactions, as well as social initiations. This assessment was used to evaluate a peer-mediated clinical intervention by observing the social interactions of the target adolescent, peer helpers, and other youths.

Although direct observation in the natural environment is theoretically the most ideal assessment procedure, its utility with adolescents is certainly limited. In addition to the many methodological considerations associated with direct observation, there are additional ethical and practical concerns more specific to clinical work with adolescents. Many of the problems associated with the direct observation of children (e.g., getting close enough to observe specific behaviors without being intrusive) are only exacerbated with adolescents because of their increased mobility and independence. Many key social interactions that affect peer acceptance occur outside of school and away from adult surveillance.

Treatment of Social Interaction Problems

Social skills training has been used in the treatment of a wide range of adolescent populations and behavior problems, including substance abuse (e.g., Gilchrest, Schinke, Trimble, & Cvetkovich, 1987), conduct disorders (e.g., Hansen, St. Lawrence, & Christoff, 1989), developmental disabilities (e.g., Bradlyn et al., 1983), and heterosocial anxiety and dating problems (e.g., Arkowitz et al., 1978; Schinke et al., 1981). This section provides a brief overview of social skills training procedures commonly used with adolescents, including communication, assertion, and problem-solving skills training. In addition, a brief overview of some of the more promising and innovative features of adolescent social skills training is provided. Although the procedures are described separately for ease of discussion, interventions with adolescents typically consist of a combination of several social skills training procedures.

Communication and Assertion Skills Training

Communication skills training has been used extensively with adolescents (e.g., Bradlyn et al., 1983; Hansen, St. Lawrence, & Christoff, 1989; Plienis et al., 1987). Communication skills can be viewed as the social skills required to initiate and maintain conversations with other persons. Obviously such skills are integral for success in a number of social interactions; typical intervention targets include eye contact, affect, speech duration, conversational questions, self-disclosing statements, and reinforcing or complimentary comments (Hansen, Watson-Perczel, & Christopher, 1989). As in most skills training programs, specific skill deficits are identified and then a combination of training procedures—including rationale, instruction, modeling, rehearsal, and feedback components—are employed to remediate the targeted deficits.

Assertion-skills training is another commonly used social-skills training procedure with adolescents (e.g., Kirkland et al., 1982; Lee, Hallberg, & Hassard, 1979; Rotherman & Armstrong, 1980; Stake, DeVille, & Pennell, 1983). In addition, assertion skills training has been used extensively in prevention programs targeting adolescent substance abuse (e.g., Englander-Golden, Elconin, & Miller, 1985; Englander-Golden, Elconin, & Satir, 1986; Gilchrest et al., 1987). Assertion and communication skills training procedures are actually quite similar, as assertion skills are often conceptualized as a subset of communication skills and there is a significant overlap in the behaviors targeted for intervention (Hansen, Watson-Perczel, & Christopher, 1989). Most interventions with adolescents have focused on refusal-assertion skills, which are those behaviors required to refuse the unacceptable actions of another and bring about more acceptable behavior in the future. Specific refusal-assertion skills include eye contact, affect, speech loudness, gestures, statements of understanding and/or problems, verbal noncompliance, requests for behavior change, and speech duration (see Hansen, Watson-Perczel, & Christopher, 1989). More research is certainly needed to examine the importance of, and specific skills required in, positive or "commendatory" assertion among adolescents.

Problem-Solving Skills Training

The use of problem-solving training, either as a component of a broader intervention or the focus of intervention, is a current trend in social skills training with adolescents (e.g., Christoff et al., 1985; Hansen et al., 1990; Kazdin, Esveldt-Dawson, French, & Unis, 1987; Plienis et al., 1987; Tisdelle & St. Lawrence, 1988). Most problem-solving procedures follow the general outline suggested by D'Zurilla and Goldfried (1971), which includes the following components: (a) goal definition; (b) generation of alternatives; (c) evaluation of alternatives; and (d) generation of a plan for implementation. When applied specifically to social problems, the focus of training might be helping an individual to plan practical ways to meet others, discriminate when and with whom to initiate interactions, and generate effective methods for resolving interpersonal conflicts (Christoff et al., 1985).

Problem-solving training teaches skills the adolescent can take into other settings. This is a major advantage in the treatment of antisocial adolescents because other potentially effective interventions (e.g., parent training) are often not practical due to severe family dysfunction and lack of intact families (Kazdin et al., 1987). Since problem-solving training combines skills with cognitively based rules and strategies, there is a potential advantage of increased generalization of treatment effects (Hansen, Watson-Perczel, & Christopher, 1989).

Despite the increasing use of problem-solving training, there is a dearth of sound research supporting its effectiveness. Few studies assess for the acquisition of actual problem-solving skills, and even fewer address the issue of social validity (see Kazdin et al., 1987, and Tisdelle & St. Lawrence, 1988, for exceptions). The failure to assess for the use of problem-solving skills to address real-life problems makes it almost impossible to evaluate the generalization and validity of interventions. In addition, there is a significant need for methods to assess whether problem-solving skills actually mediate behavior.

Social Exposure and Anxiety Reduction Strategies

Systematic desensitization and practice dating are commonly discussed anxiety-reduction techniques for heterosocial anxiety (Hansen et al., 1992). Using systematic desensitization, heterosocial fears are treated like any other phobia; a hierarchy of feared heterosocial situations is constructed and systematically paired with relaxation. Social exposure techniques are the most widely used to reduce date-related anxieties (Hansen et al., 1992; Kelly & Hansen, 1987). In projects conducted by Arkowitz and his colleagues (e.g., Arkowitz et al., 1978), date-anxious individuals were assigned to have repeated practice dates with one another. The practice dates, always with another student who also reported heterosocial anxiety, were structured as low-key and for practice only. This allowed participants to become desensitized to date-related anxieties through nonthreatening, nonevaluative "practice socializing" (Kelly & Hansen, 1987). Many anxiety reduction strategies may also function to improve skill deficits through education, practice, and feedback components. Similarly, the strategies designed to reduce skill deficits may also decrease anxiety through repeated exposure and practice with threatening stimuli.

Additional Techniques

This section provides a brief overview of several promising and innovative trends evident in the adolescent social skills literature (see Christopher, Nangle, & Hansen, 1993, for a more comprehensive review).

Group Training. Group training is frequently used in social skills interventions with adolescents (e.g., Bierman & Furman, 1984; Christoff et al., 1985; Hansen, St. Lawrence, & Christoff, 1989; Kirkland et al., 1982; Plienis et al., 1987). Typically, the procedures used for social skills training with individuals (i.e., rationale, modeling, rehearsal, feedback) are applied to the group. The group training format has many potential advantages, including time and cost efficiency, as well as increased opportunities for the modeling and rehearsal of skills (e.g., Bierman & Furman, 1984; Bradlyn et al., 1983; Hansen, St. Lawrence, & Christoff, 1989). The potential limitations of group training include the difficulty of keeping each adolescent actively involved and interested, tailoring interventions to individuals, and evaluating the individual's responses to treatment (Christopher et al., 1993; Hansen, Watson-Perczel, & Christopher, 1989).

Peer-Mediated Interventions. The utility of peer-mediated interventions has been documented with elementary school-aged children (e.g., Christopher, Hansen, & MacMillan, 1991). Peer-mediated interventions are infrequently used but promising additions to adolescent social skills training (e.g., Bierman & Furman, 1984; Hansen et al., 1990). In peer-mediated interventions, a target child's peers become active treatment agents. The major advantage of peer-mediated interventions is their potential ability to facilitate and maintain the generalization of treatment effects in the child's natural environment (Hansen, Watson-Perczel, & Christopher, 1989). Such interventions also allow for the efficient use of therapist time. The use of peers in the intervention, however, makes maintaining confidentiality more problematic (Hansen et al., 1990). In addition, more research is needed to evaluate the effects of participation on the peer helpers themselves.

Training Individuals in the Natural Environment. Conducting interventions in the natural environment is a welcome trend in the adolescent social skills training literature. Interventions have been conducted in varied settings, including school settings (e.g., Bierman & Furman, 1984; Hansen et al., 1990), a sports program (Anderson, Rush, Ayllon, & Kandel, 1987), and a youth club (Jackson & Marzillier, 1982). Intervening in the natural environment might enhance generalization of treatment effects and allow for the treatment of individuals who are unable to come into the clinic.

Self-Management Training. Teaching adolescents the skills necessary for self-management is another promising social skills training technique. For example, adolescents can be trained to evaluate their own behavior, compare self-ratings to teacher ratings, and select appropriate reinforcement for accurate self-ratings (e.g., Smith, Young, West, Morgan, & Rhode, 1988; Young, Smith, West, & Morgan, 1987). Self-management training might facilitate maintenance and generalization of treatment gains. Implementing such training may prove difficult with adolescents with social skills deficits, however, as it is likely that such adolescents will also have deficits in their abilities to monitor and evaluate their own social behavior.

Use of Videotape. Recent advances in video technology offer many exciting opportunities for social skills training with adolescents (e.g., Elias, 1983). Methodological advantages include the standardization of interventions and variables (enhancing replicability and comparison), improved assessment capabilities (including assessment of nonverbal behaviors), and the ability to investigate post-hoc hypotheses (Harwood & Weissberg, 1987). In addition, the use of video can facilitate discussion of topics that make adolescents feel uncomfortable, minimize potential distractions in live modeling, and improve the ability of the trainer to select appropriate models (Harwood & Weissberg, 1987).

Summary

Adolescence is a transitional period marked by a variety of physical, cognitive, emotional, and behavioral changes that are accompanied by changing social contexts and expectations. As a result, it is not surprising that many youths experience social interaction problems. Although most of the social problems are transitory and minor, more extreme social problems also occur.

Problematic social interactions are believed to be associated with a wide range of psychological disorders and problems. While a great deal of theorizing and empirical study of the relationship between social variables and psychological adjustment has been carried out with children and adults, relatively little research has been conducted specifically with adolescent populations. Given the differing developmental tasks, social situations, and social contingencies operating during adolescence relative to childhood or adulthood, it is important to directly study adolescent populations.

More attention should also be directed to what is "normal" for adolescent social behavior. It is likely, given the rapid changes taking place in physical, cognitive, emotional, and social behavior, that there is a relatively wide range of behavioral differences that can be considered normal. It is unlikely that isolated instances of so-called deviant behavior lead to subsequent psychological maladjustment. A consistent pattern over time of displaying a maladaptive behavior or a cluster of many such behaviors, however, may signal the need for concern.

In addition, greater emphasis should be placed on assessing the adolescent's environment. The majority of research in this area has focused on self-reports of social anxiety and the assessment of social skills. It is important to understand how an adolescent's environment (e.g., family, peers, schools, subcultural groups, and the broader social culture) may contribute to the development and maintenance of social interaction problems. Peer group interactions seem like a particularly important place to start, since adolescents spend so much of their time in the company of peers and are subject to strong social contingencies by peers. Many of the behaviors deemed problematic by professionals are likely to be normal responses to the social contingencies operating in an adolescent's environment. It is also important to examine further how the many physiological changes occurring during adolescence affect social interactions and psychological adjustment.

Research designed to empirically determine and validate targets for intervention has lagged far behind the increasing use of social skills training with adolescents. The failure to demonstrate that behaviors targeted for intervention are actually related to successful interpersonal interactions is a general weakness of the adolescent social skills training literature (Hansen, Watson-Perczel, & Christopher, 1989). For example, while most social skills training studies with adolescents focus on conversation and problem-solving skills, there is little support from prior assessment research that these skills are actually related to peer acceptance (Inderbitzen-Pisaruk & Foster, 1990a).

The treatment literature to date has primarily focused on acquisition of social skills, but a more thorough evaluation of the social validity of the behaviors trained, the generalization of improvements to interactions in the natural environment, and the maintenance of effects over time is required (Hansen, Watson-Perczel, & Christopher, 1989). More research is also needed on the treatment of social anxiety and on interventions that address peer and family influences on social interactions.

Social interactions are an everyday occurrence that can be a source of either pleasure and reinforcement or pain and punishment. Although there is much that has been learned about the complex relationships between adolescent social interactions and adjustment, as well as about procedures to assess and remediate adolescent social interaction problems, many important questions remain unanswered.

References

Allen, J. P., Weissberg, R. P., & Hawkins, J. A. (1989). The relation between values and social competence in early adolescence. *Developmental Psychology, 25*, 458–464.

American Psychiatric Association. (1994). *Diagnostic and statistical manual of mental disorders* (4th ed.). Washington, DC: Author.

Anderson, C., Horowitz, L., & French, R. (1983). Attributional style of lonely and depressed people. *Journal of Personality and Social Psychology, 45*, 127–136.

Anderson, C. G., Rush, D., Ayllon, T., & Kandel, H. (1987). Training and generalization of social skills with problem children. *Journal of Child and Adolescent Psychotherapy, 4*, 294–298.

Arkowitz, H., Hinton, R., Perl, J., & Himadi, W. (1978). Treatment strategies for dating anxiety in college men based on real-life practice. *Counseling Psychologist, 7*, 41–46.

Ary, D. V., Tildesley, E., Hops, H., Lichtenstein, E., & Andrews, J. (1988, November). *Family and peer influence on adolescent substance use.* Paper presented at the meeting of the Association for the Advancement of Behavior Therapy, New York.

Bellack, A. S., Hersen, M., & Lamparski, D. (1979). Role-play tests for assessing social skills: Are they valid? Are they useful? *Journal of Consulting and Clinical Psychology, 47*, 335–342.

Berndt, T. J. (1982). The features and effects of friendship in early adolescence. *Child Development, 53,* 1447–1460.

Bierman, K. L., & Furman, W. (1984). The effects of social skills training and peer involvement on the social adjustment of preadolescents. *Child Development, 55,* 151–162.

Boivin, M., & Begin, G. (1989). Peer status and self-perception among early elementary school children: The case of the rejected children. *Child Development, 60,* 591–596.

Borkovec, T. D., Stone, N. M., O'Brien, G. T., & Kaloupek, D. G. (1974). Evaluation of a clinically relevant target behavior for analogue outcome research. *Behavior Therapy, 5,* 503–511.

Bradlyn, A. S., Himadi, W. G., Crimmins, D. B., Christoff, K. A., Graves, K. G., & Kelly, J. A. (1983). Conversational skills training for retarded adolescents. *Behavior Therapy, 14,* 314–325.

Braucht, G. N., Follingstad, D., Brakarsh, D., & Berry, K. L. (1973). Drug education: A review of goals, approaches, and effectiveness, and a paradigm for evaluation. *Quarterly Journal of Studies on Alcohol, 34,* 1279–1292.

Bruch, H. (1973). *Eating disorders: Obesity, anorexia nervosa and the person within.* New York: Basic Books.

Bruch, M. A., & Hynes, M. J. (1987). Heterosocial anxiety and contraceptive behavior. *Journal of Research in Personality, 21,* 343–360.

Cauce, A. M. (1987). School and peer competence in early adolescence: A test of domain-specific self-perceived competence. *Developmental Psychology, 23,* 287–291.

Center, D. B., & Wascom, A. M. (1986). Teacher perceptions of social behavior in learning disabled and socially normal children and youth. *Journal of Learning Disabilities, 7,* 420–425.

Christoff, K. A., Scott, W. O. N., Kelley, M. L., Schlundt, D., Baer, G., & Kelly, J. A. (1985). Social skills and social problem-solving training for shy young adolescents. *Behavior Therapy, 16,* 468–477.

Christopher, J. S., Hansen, D. J., & MacMillan, V. M. (1991). Effectiveness of a peer-helper intervention to increase children's social interactions: Generalization, maintenance, and social validity. *Behavior Modification, 15,* 22–50.

Christopher, J. S., Nangle, D. W., & Hansen, D. J. (1993). Social-skills interventions with adolescents: Current issues and procedures. *Behavior Modification, 17,* 314–338.

Coie, J. D., Dodge, K. A., & Coppotelli, H. (1982). Dimensions and types of social status: A cross-age perspective. *Developmental Psychology, 18,* 557–570.

Coyne, J. C. (1976). Depression and the response of others. *Journal of Abnormal Psychology, 85,* 186–193.

Crago, M., Yates, A., Beutler, L. E., & Arizmendi, T. G. (1985). Height-weight ratios among female athletes: Are collegiate athletics the precursors to an anorexic syndrome? *International Journal of Eating Disorders, 4,* 79–87.

Crowe, R. R., Noyes, R., Pauls, D. L., & Slymen, D. J. (1983). A family study of panic disorder. *Archives of General Psychiatry, 40,* 1065–1069.

Csikszentmihalyi, M., & Larson, R. (1984). *Being adolescent: Conflict and growth in the teenage years.* New York: Basic Books.

Damon, W. (1983). *Social and personality development: Infancy through adolescence.* New York: Norton.

Dishion, T. J., & Loeber, R. (1985). Adolescent marijuana and alcohol use: The role of parents and peers revisited. *American Journal of Drug and Alcohol Abuse, 11,* 11–25.

Dishion, T. J., Loeber, R., Stouthamer-Loeber, M., & Patterson, G. R. (1984). Skill deficits and male adolescent delinquency. *Journal of Abnormal Child Psychology, 12,* 37–54.

Dodge, C. S., Heimberg, R. G., Nyman, D., & O'Brien, G. T. (1987). Daily heterosocial interactions of high and low socially anxious college students: A diary study. *Behavior Therapy, 18,* 90–96.

Dodge, K. A. (1989). Problems in social relationships. In E. J. Mash & R. A. Barkley (Eds.), *Treatment of childhood disorders* (pp. 222–244). New York: Guilford.

Dodge, K. A., McClaskey, C. L., & Feldman, E. (1985). Situational approach to the assessment of social competence in children. *Journal of Consulting and Clinical Psychology, 53,* 344–353.

Druss, R. G., & Silverman, J. A. (1979). Body image and perfectionism of ballerinas: Comparison and contrast with anorexia nervosa. *General Hospital Psychiatry, 1,* 115–121.

D'Zurilla, T. J., & Goldfried, M. R. (1971). Problem solving and behavior modification. *Journal of Abnormal Psychology, 78,* 107–126.

Elias, M. J. (1983). Improving coping skills of emotionally disturbed boys through television-based social problem-solving. *American Journal of Orthopsychiatry, 53,* 61–72.

Englander-Golden, P., Elconin, J., & Miller, K. J. (1985). Say It Straight: Adolescent substance abuse prevention training. *Academic Psychology Bulletin, 7,* 65–79.

Englander-Golden, P., Elconin, J., & Satir, V. (1986). Assertive/leveling, communication, and empathy in adolescent drug abuse prevention. *Journal of Primary Prevention, 6,* 231–243.

Fauber, R., Forehand, R., Long, N., Burke, M., & Faust, J. (1987). The relationship of young adolescent children's Depression Inventory (CDI) scores to their social and cognitive functioning. *Journal of Psychopathology and Behavioral Assessment, 9,* 161–172.

Ford, M. E. (1982). Social cognition and social competence in adolescence. *Developmental Psychology, 18,* 323–340.

Foster, S. L., Inderbitzen, H. M., & Nangle, D. W. (1993). Assessing acceptance and social skills with peers in childhood: Current issues. *Behavior Modification, 17,* 255–286.

Freedman, B. J., Rosenthal, R., Donahue, C. P., Schlundt, D. G., & McFall, R. M. (1978). A social behavioral analysis of skill deficits in delinquent and nondelinquent adolescent boys. *Journal of Consulting and Clinical Psychology, 46,* 1448–1462.

Garrett, M. K., & Crump, W. D. (1980). Peer acceptance, teacher preference, and self-appraisal of the social status of learning disabled students. *Learning Disabilities Quarterly, 3,* 42–48.

Gilchrest, L. D., Schinke, S. P., Trimble, J. E., & Cvetkovich, G. T. (1987). Skills enhancement to prevent substance abuse among American Indian adolescents. *International Journal of the Addictions, 22,* 869–879.

Gresham, F. M. (1981). Validity of social skills measures for assessing social competence in low-status children: A multivariate investigation. *Developmental Psychology, 17,* 390–398.

Hansen, D. J., Christopher, J. S., & Nangle, D. W. (1992). Adolescent heterosocial interactions and dating. In V. B. Van Hasselt & M. Hersen (Eds.), *Handbook of social development: A lifespan perspective* (pp. 371–394). New York: Plenum.

Hansen, D. J., MacMillan, V. M., & Shawchuck, C. R. (1990). Social isolation. In E. L. Feindler & G. R. Kalfus (Eds.), *Casebook on adolescent behavior therapy* (pp. 165–190). New York: Springer.

Hansen, D. J., St. Lawrence, J. S., & Christoff, K. A. (1988). Conversational skills of inpatient conduct-disordered youths: Social validation of component behaviors and implications for skills training. *Behavior Modification, 12,* 424–444.

Hansen, D. J., St. Lawrence, J. S., & Christoff, K. A. (1989). Group conversation-skills training with inpatient children and adolescents: Social validation, generalization, and maintenance. *Behavior Modification, 13,* 4–31.

Hansen, D. J., Watson-Perczel, M., & Christopher, J. S. (1989). Clinical issues in social-skills training with adolescents. *Clinical Psychology Review, 9,* 365–391.

Harris, F. C., & Phelps, C. F. (1985). Anorexia nervosa. In M. Hersen & A. S. Bellack (Eds.), *Handbook of clinical behavior therapy with adults* (pp. 269–290). New York: Plenum.

Harter, S. (1982). The Perceived Competence Scale for children. *Child Development, 53,* 87–97.

Hartup, W. W., & DeWitt, J. (1974). *Determinants and origins of aggression.* New York: Mouton.

Harwood, R. L., & Weissberg, R. P. (1987). The potential of video in the promotion of social competence in children and adolescents. *Journal of Early Adolescence, 7,* 345–363.

Himadi, W. G., Arkowitz, H., Hinton, R., & Perl, J. (1980). Minimal dating and its relationship to other social problems and general adjustment. *Behavior Therapy, 11,* 345–352.

Hops, H., Tildesley, E., Lichtenstein, E., Ary, D., & Sherman, L. (1990). Parent-adolescent problem-solving interactions and drug use. *American Journal of Drug and Alcohol Abuse, 16,* 239–258.

Hovell, M. F., Mewborn, C. R., Randle, Y., & Fowler-Johnson, S. (1985). Risk of excess weight gain in university women: A three-year community controlled analysis. *Addictive Behaviors, 10,* 15–28.

Howes, M. J., & Hokanson, J. E. (1979). Conversational and social responses to depressive interpersonal behaviour. *Journal of Abnormal Psychology, 88,* 625–634.

Inderbitzen-Pisaruk, H., Beyer, R. L., Halstenson-Sawyer, N., & Groene, J. A. (1991). *Identification of social behaviors important for adolescent peer acceptance: Implications for social skills training.* Paper presented at the annual meeting of the Association for Advancement of Behavior Therapy, New York.

Inderbitzen-Pisaruk, H., & Foster, S. L. (1990a). Adolescent friendships and peer acceptance: Implications for social skills training. *Clinical Psychology Review, 10,* 425–439.

Inderbitzen-Pisaruk, H., & Foster, S. L. (1990b, November). *The Teenage Inventory of Social Skills: An investigation of convergent and discriminant validity.* Paper presented at the annual meeting of the Association for Advancement of Behavior Therapy, San Francisco.

Jackson, M. F., & Marzillier, J. S. (1982). The Youth Club Project: A community-based intervention for shy adolescents. *Behavioural Psychotherapy, 10,* 87–100.

Jessor, R., & Jessor, S. L. (1977). *Problem behavior and psychosocial development: A longitudinal study of youth.* New York: Academic Press.

Jones, W. H., Freeman, J. E., & Goswick, R. A. (1981). The persistence of loneliness: Self and other determinants. *Journal of Personality, 49,* 27–28.

Jones, W. H., Hobbs, S. A., & Hockenbury, D. (1982). Loneliness and social skill deficits. *Journal of Personality and Social Psychology, 42,* 682–689.

Kandel, D. B., & Andrews, K. (1987). Processes of adolescent socialization by parents and peers. *International Journal of Addictions, 22,* 319–342.

Katz, R. C. (1990). Psychosocial adjustment in adolescent child molesters. *Child Abuse and Neglect, 14,* 567–575.

Kazdin, A. E., Esveldt-Dawson, K., French, N. H., & Unis, A. S. (1987). Problem-solving skills training and relationship therapy in the treatment of antisocial child behavior. *Journal of Consulting and Clinical Psychology, 55,* 76–85.

Kelly, J. A. (1982). *Social-skills training: A practical guide for interventions.* New York: Springer.

Kelly, J. A., & Hansen, D. J. (1987). Social interactions and adjustment. In V. B. Van Hasselt & M. Hersen (Eds.), *Handbook of adolescent psychology* (pp. 131–146). New York: Pergamon.

Kelly, J. A., Wildman, B. G., & Berler, E. S. (1980). Small group behavioral training to improve the job interview skills repertoire of mildly retarded adolescents. *Journal of Applied Behavior Analysis, 13,* 461–471.

Kirkland, K. D., Thelen, M. H., & Miller, D. J. (1982). Group assertion training with adolescents. *Child and Family Behavior Therapy, 4,* 1–13.

Koenig, M. A., & Zelnik, M. (1982). The risk of premarital pregnancy among metropolitan-area teenagers: 1976 and 1979. *Family Planning Perspectives, 14,* 239–247.

La Greca, A. M. (1981). Social behavior and social perception in learning-disabled children: A review with implications for social skills training. *Journal of Pediatric Psychology, 6,* 395–416.

La Greca, A. M., Dandes, S. K., Wick, P., Shaw, K., & Stone, W. L. (1988). Development of the Social Anxiety Scale for Children: Reliability and concurrent validity. *Journal of Clinical Child Psychology, 17,* 84–91.

Leary, M. R., & Dobbins, S. E. (1983). Social anxiety, sexual behavior, and contraceptive use. *Journal of Personality and Social Psychology, 45,* 1347–1354.

Lee, D. Y., Hallberg, E. T., & Hassard, H. (1979). Effects of assertion training on aggressive behavior of adolescents. *Journal of Counseling Psychology, 26,* 459–461.

Lindquist, C. U., Lindsay, J. S., & White, G. D. (1979). Assessment of assertiveness in drug abusers. *Journal of Clinical Psychology, 35,* 676–679.

Long, N., Forehand, R., Fauber, R., & Brody, G. H. (1987). Self-perceived and independently observed competence of young adolescents as a function of parental marital conflict and recent divorce. *Journal of Abnormal Child Psychology, 15*, 15–27.

MacDonald, N. E., Wells, G. A., Fisher, W. A., Warren, W. K., King, M. A., Doherty, J. A., & Bowie, W. R. (1990). High-risk STD/HIV behavior among college students. *Journal of the American Medical Association, 263*, 3155–3159.

Margulies, R. Z., Kessler, R. C., & Kandel, D. B. (1977). A longitudinal study of onset of drinking among high-school students. *Journal of Studies on Alcohol, 38*, 897–912.

Marks, I. M. (1985). Behavioural treatment of social phobia. *Psychopharmacology Bulletin, 21*, 615–618.

Matson, J. L., Kazdin, A. E., & Esveldt-Dawson, K. (1980). Training interpersonal skills among mentally retarded and socially dysfunctional children. *Behavior Research and Therapy, 18*, 419–427.

Matson, J. L., Manikam, R., Coe, D., Raymond, K., & Taras, M. (1988). Training social skills to severely mentally retarded multiply handicapped adolescents. *Research in Developmental Disabilities, 9*, 195–208.

Matson, J. L., Rotatori, A., & Helsel, W. J. (1983). Development of a rating scale to measure social skills in children: The Matson Evaluation of Social Skills with Youngsters (MESSY). *Behaviour Research and Therapy, 21*, 335–340.

Miller, W. B. (1975). *Violence by youth gangs and youth groups as a crime problem in major American cities.* Washington, DC: National Institute of Juvenile Justice and Delinquency Prevention.

Minuchin, S., Rosman, B. L., & Baker, L. (1978). *Psychosomatic families: Anorexia nervosa in context.* Cambridge, MA: Harvard University Press.

Monti, P. M., Abrams, D. B., Binkoff, J. A., & Zwick, W. R. (1986). Social skills training and substance abuse. In C. R. Hollin & P. Trower (Eds.), *Handbook of social skills training: Vol. 2. Clinical applications and new directions* (pp. 111–142). Oxford, England: Pergamon.

Meuhlenhard, C. L., & Linton, M. A. (1987). Date rape and sexual aggression in dating situations: Incidence and risk factors. *Journal of Counseling Psychology, 34*, 186–196.

Mueser, K. T., Valenti-Hein, D., & Yarnold, P. R. (1987). Dating-skills groups for the developmentally disabled: Social skills and problem-solving versus relaxation training. *Behavior Modification, 11*, 200–228.

Nangle, D. W., Ellis, J. T., Christopher, J. S., & Hansen, D. J. (1993). Sociometric peer nominations: An idiographic examination of temporal stability. *Education and Treatment of Children, 16*, 175–186.

Nangle, D. W., Giacoletti, A. M., Ellis, J. T., Aljazireh, L., & Hansen, D. J. (1994). *A component analysis of inadequate contraceptive behavior among adolescents: Implications for assessment and intervention.* Manuscript submitted for publication.

Nangle, D. W., & Hansen, D. J. (1993). Relations between social skills and high-risk sexual interactions among adolescents: Current issues and future directions. *Behavior Modification, 17*, 113–135.

O'Leary, D. E., O'Leary, M. R., & Donovan, D. M. (1975). Social skills acquisition and psychosocial development of alcoholics: A review. *Addictive Behaviors, 1*, 111–120.

Overholser, J. C., & Beck, S. (1986). Multimethod assessment of rapists, child molesters, and three control groups on behavioral and psychological measures. *Journal of Consulting and Clinical Psychology, 54,* 682–687.

Parker, J. G., & Asher, S. R. (1987). Peer relations and later personal adjustment: Are low-accepted children at risk? *Psychological Bulletin, 102,* 357–389.

Patterson, G. R. (1982). *Coercive family process.* Eugene, OR: Castalia.

Patterson, G. R., Littman, R. A., & Bricker, W. (1967). Assertive behavior in children: A step toward a theory of aggression. *Monographs of the Society for Research in Child Development, 32,* (5, Serial No. 113).

Petersen, A. C., & Hamburg, B. A. (1986). Adolescence: A developmental approach to problems and psychopathology. *Behavior Therapy, 17,* 480–499.

Platt, J. J., Spivack, G., Altman, W., Altman, D., & Peizer, S. B. (1974). Adolescent problem-solving thinking. *Journal of Consulting and Clinical Psychology, 43,* 787–793.

Plienis, A. J., Hansen, D. J., Ford, F., Smith, S., Stark, L., & Kelly, J. A. (1987). Behavioral small group training to improve the social skills of emotionally-disordered adolescents. *Behavior Therapy, 18,* 17–32.

Rhodes, W. A., Redd, W. H., & Berggren, L. (1979). Social skills training for an unassertive adolescent. *Journal of Clinical Child Psychology, 8,* 18–21.

Rotherman, M. J., & Armstrong, M. (1980). Assertiveness training with high school students. *Adolescence, 15,* 267–276.

Sarason, I. G., & Sarason, B. R. (1984). Teaching cognitive and social skills to high school students. *Journal of Consulting and Clinical Psychology, 49,* 908–918.

Schwartz, R. B., Barrett, M. J., & Saba, G. (1985). Family therapy for bulimia. In D. M. Garner & P. E. Garfinkel (Eds.), *Handbook of psychotherapy for anorexia nervosa and bulimia* (pp. 280–307). New York: Guilford.

Schinke, S. P., Blythe, B. J., & Gilchrest, L. D. (1981). Cognitive-behavioral prevention of adolescent pregnancy. *Journal of Counseling Psychology, 28,* 451–454.

Simmons, R. G., & Rosenberg, F. (1975). Sex, sex roles, and self-image. *Journal of Youth and Adolescence, 4,* 229–258.

Smith, D. J., Young, R., West, R. P., Morgan, D. P., & Rhode, G. (1988). Reducing the disruptive behavior of junior high school students: A classroom self-management procedure. *Behavioral Disorders, 13,* 231–239.

Solano, C., Batten, P., & Parish, E. (1982). Loneliness and patterns of self-disclosure. *Journal of Personality and Social Psychology, 43,* 524–531.

Stake, J. E., DeVille, C. J., & Pennell, C. L. (1983). The effects of assertiveness training on the self-esteem of adolescent girls. *Journal of Youth and Adolescence, 12,* 435–442.

Streigel-Moore, R. H., Silberstein, L. R., & Rodin, J. (1986). Toward an understanding of risk factors for bulimia. *American Psychologist, 41,* 246–263.

Sugarman, D. B., & Hotaling, G. T. (1989). Dating violence: Prevalence, context, and risk markers. In M. A. Pirog-Good & J. E. Stets (Eds.), *Violence in dating relationships: Emerging social issues* (pp. 4–32). New York: Praeger.

Tisdelle, D. A., & St. Lawrence, J. S. (1988). Adolescent interpersonal problem-solving skill training: Social validation and generalization. *Behavior Therapy, 19,* 171–182.

Turner, S. M., Beidel, D. C., & Costello, A. (1987). Psychopathology in the offspring of anxiety disordered patients. *Journal of Consulting and Clinical Psychology, 55*, 229–235.

Van Hasselt, V. B., Hersen, M., & Milliones, J. (1978). Social skills training for alcoholics and drug addicts: A review. *Addictive Behaviors, 3*, 221–233.

Warren, R., Good, G., & Velten, E. (1984). Measurement of social-evaluate anxiety in junior high school students. *Adolescence, 19*, 643–648.

Wills, T. A., Baker, E., & Botvin, G. J. (1989). Dimensions of assertiveness: Differential relationships to substance use in early adolescence. *Journal of Consulting and Clinical Psychology, 57*, 473–478.

Withers, L. E., & Kaplan, D. W. (1987). Adolescents who attempt suicide: A retrospective clinical chart review of hospitalized patients. *Professional Psychology: Research and Practice, 18*, 391–393.

Yates, A., Leehey, K., & Shisslak, C. M. (1983). Running: An analogue of anorexia? *New England Journal of Medicine, 308*, 251–255.

Young, K. R., Smith, D. J., West, R. P., & Morgan, D. P. (1987). A peer-mediated program for teaching self-management strategies to adolescents. *Programming for Adolescents With Behavioral Disorders*, 34–47.

Zimring, F. E. (1981). Kids, groups, and crime: Some implications of a well-known secret. *Journal of Criminal Law and Criminology, 72*, 867–885.

4

Intellectual Development and Retardation

Patti L. Harrison
Tommy E. Turner

An understanding of the intellectual development of adolescents provides an important foundation for understanding adolescent psychopathology and working with adolescents who exhibit the specific disorders described in this textbook. As Keating (1990) points out, "Cognitive changes are intimately linked to other developmental dynamics, and it is perilous to ignore them" (p. 56). The intellectual development of adolescents cannot be separated from the many other aspects of their functioning and behavior. And cognitive characteristics of adolescents both influence and are influenced by the latter's development in other areas and by their perceptions of the many social systems in which they participate.

The purpose of this chapter is to present a number of characteristics of adolescent intelligence. Although the literature on this subject is relatively limited in comparison to the volumes of research studies and articles on younger children's intelligence and the recently increasing study of adult intelligence, there are a number of perspectives of intelligence that have a great deal of applicability to development during the adolescent period. This chapter will present an overview of four prevailing perspectives: psychometric, Piagetian developmental theory, cognitive and information processing, and cognitive socialization. The chapter will also describe specific intellectual characteristics that appear to change during the passage from childhood to adolescence. It will conclude with a discussion of two major issues in the study of intellectual development: characteristics associated with intellectual deficits, and the nature and nurture of intelligence.

What Is Intelligence?

Before discussing the characteristics of adolescent intellectual development and retardation, it would seem appropriate to supply an operational definition of intelligence. Yet, as noted by Weinberg (1989), the *definition* of intelligence is one of the many sources of controversy concerning intellectual development. Although there is general agreement that human intelligence does exist and that intelligence can explain some of the ways in which people behave, there is in fact little agreement regarding the definition itself.

An illustration of the lack of consensus in the definition of intelligence was provided by Sternberg and Detterman (1986). Sternberg and Detterman replicated a classic symposium on the definition of intelligence, published in the *Journal of Educational Psychology* in 1921, by asking 24 of the current experts in the field to prepare essays on their conceptualizations of intelligence. The definitions presented by the experts in 1986 showed considerable variability, as did the definitions in 1921. Sternberg and Berg (1986) summarized the many attributes used by the experts in 1986 to define intelligence and tallied the frequency with which the attributes were noted. Sternberg and Berg found that although some of the same attributes were mentioned by several experts, no attribute was mentioned by more than 50% of them. Attributes mentioned most frequently included higher-level reasoning, problem-solving skills, abilities that are valued by culture, executive control processes, knowledge, effective and successful responses, perception, and attention.

Sternberg and Berg found some overlap between attributes named with relative frequency by experts in 1921 and 1986, including adaptation to the environment, basic mental process, and higher-level reasoning. The experts in 1986, however, emphasized such attributes as metacognition and knowledge more than experts in 1921 did. Detterman (1986) described the 1986 definitions as being more elaborate, intricate, and refined than the 1921 definitions and suggested that those in 1986 reflected progress in conceptualizing intelligence. Detterman also noted that definitions of intelligence in 1986 reflected a stronger social, cultural, and real-world emphasis than did definitions in 1921.

Perspectives of Intelligence

The lack of agreement on a single definition of intelligence is probably based in part on the complex nature of intelligence and the many disparate perspectives from which intelligence is studied. A unanimous conclusion about the definition could greatly oversimplify human ability and behavior (Detterman, 1986). A focus on *different* perspectives of intelligence, rather than on a well-agreed-upon definition, may provide a more comprehensive, flexible foundation for understanding the behavior of adolescents, as well as a more useful and relevant framework for working with them. Although there are a number of different perspectives on intelligence, they tend to be complementary, and each adds information about important characteristics of intellectual functioning. Theory and research in four broad categories of perspectives are described below.

Psychometric Perspectives

Psychometric perspectives of intelligence shaped the earliest attempts to describe intellectual ability and behavior systematically, and many theories of intelligence continue to be based on a psychometric viewpoint (Keating, 1990; Weinberg, 1989). Psychometric perspectives focus on the quantifiable aspects of what and how much people know, the aspects of intelligence that can be measured and ranked, and individual differences in intelligence that exist in a population (Siegler & Richards, 1982; Sternberg, 1985b). These perspectives were originally formed through analysis of performance on intelligence tests, and most modern intelligence tests continue to incorporate them into their models and development. Although a number of psychometric perspectives of intelligence have been formulated, the following four have been widely used in the measurement of intelligence: Spearman's two-factor theory, Thurstone's theory of primary mental abilities, Guilford's structure-of-intellect model, and Cattell and Horn's models of fluid and crystallized abilities.

Spearman (1904, 1927) was the first to provide a theory of intelligence based on statistical analyses of intellectual measures. When Spearman analyzed the intercorrelations among scores from a number of intellectual tasks, he found that all of the tasks measured a common factor to some degree. In addition, he observed that each task also measured a specific factor unique to the task. Spearman therefore proposed that intelligence consists of two types of factors: a general (g) factor that is common to and shared by all intellectual tasks, and specific (s) factors, each of which is limited to a specific task. Applications of Spearman's theory are seen in almost all modern intelligence tests that select tasks according to their loadings on the g factor and provide a global intelligence score obtained from a combination of performance on a number of tasks.

In contrast to Spearman's emphasis on the general factor of intelligence, Thurstone (1931, 1938) maintained that the nature of intelligence is better described in terms of several fundamental abilities. Thurstone identified a dozen or so "primary mental abilities" in intelligence, with the following seven being most frequently corroborated in research by Thurstone and other investigators (Anastasi, 1988): verbal comprehension, word fluency, number, space, associative memory, perceptual speed, and induction/general reasoning. Thurstone's multiple-factor theory of intelligence supplied the foundation for a number of multiple aptitude batteries that are used, for example, in career guidance and employment selection.

In his "structure-of-intellect" model, Guilford (1967, 1985) provided one of the most complex psychometric theories of intelligence. Guilford defined intelligence as the collection of abilities needed for processing different kinds of information in a number of forms, and he described three major facets of each basic intellectual ability: the *operation* or mental process of the ability, the informational *content* to be processed, and the informational *product* that results from the process. In one of his latest descriptions of the structure-of-intellect model, Guilford (1985) identified five operations (cognition, memory, divergent production, convergent production, and evaluation), five types of content (visual, auditory, symbolic, semantic, and behavioral), and six types of products (unit, class, relation, system, transformation, and implication). Thus Guilford's model suggests 150 possible intellectual abilities, with each ability utilizing a unique combination of one operation, one type of content, and one type of product (e.g., cognition of semantic implications). Guilford's model has been useful in understanding intelligence in terms of the different mental operations, as well as different types of content and products, required for intellectual tasks. In particular, his concepts of divergent production (producing a number of alternative correct responses to an intellectual task; e.g., providing a list of objects that are both edible and hard), and convergent production (producing the one specific response that correctly satisfies the requirements of an intellectual task; e.g., determining the murderer in a Sherlock Holmes mystery) have been useful in assessment and training of creativity and problem solving (Meeker, 1985)

Although the theories suggested by Spearman, Thurstone, and Guilford have a number of applications for understanding and measuring intelligence, each has been the subject of debate and criticism. Spearman and Thurstone's differing views on the importance of one general factor versus the importance of multiple factors may have been due to the number and nature of tasks analyzed by each researcher (Anastasi, 1988). In fact, later in their careers, Spearman conceded the existence of group factors and Thurstone conceded the existence of a general factor, although each believed that his original conceptualization was predominantly correct (Sternberg & Powell, 1983). Guilford's model has been criticized on a number of grounds, as described by Carroll (1983) and Lohman (1989), including the statistical methodology used by Guilford and the fractionation of ability produced by the model.

The theory of fluid and crystallized intelligence, originally developed by Cattell (1943) and expanded by Cattell (1987) and Horn (1985), has become one of the most popular and applied psychometric perspectives of intelligence. Cattell and Horn's conceptualization that intellectual performance can be summarized as two broad factors of fluid ability and crystallized ability represents a widely accepted resolution of the debate about the dimensions of intelligence (Lohman, 1989). In Cattell and Horn's model, *fluid ability* is identified as the ability to solve novel problems when the solutions have not already been stored in memory. *Crystallized ability* is described as acquired ability, or the ability to operate in areas that have been experienced before or where one has been taught.

Cattell and Horn's distinction between fluid and crystallized abilities has important implications for understanding intelligence. For example, differences in intellectual performance in a group of people may be attributable to varied backgrounds, prior experiences, and formal education, rather than differences in ability to solve new problems. The distinction between fluid and crystallized abilities also has a number of applications in the development and use of most modern intelligence tests (Kaufman & Harrison, 1991). In the past, intelligence tests have been criticized because of their overemphasis on crystallized abilities (e.g., verbal comprehension and quantitative skills), which may be influenced by past learning, culture, and education. Many of the current intelligence tests—for example, the latest edition of the Stanford-Binet Intelligence Scale (Thorndike, Hagen, & Sattler, 1985) and the Kaufman Assessment Battery for Children (Kaufman & Kaufman, 1983)—were developed to place less emphasis on crystallized abilities and more emphasis on fluid skills, as well as to provide separate scores on measures of fluid and crystallized abilities.

Both Horn and Cattell have extended the initial model of fluid and crystallized ability. Cattell (1987) described three broad factors in addition to fluid ability and crystallized ability: power of visualization, retrieval from memory storage, and cognitive speed. Horn (1985) identified three perceptual organization factors (broad visualization, clerical speed, and broad auditory speed), three association-processing factors (correct decision speed, short-term acquisition, and long-term storage retrieval), and two sensory reception factors (visual sensory detectors and auditory sensory detectors), in addition to the two deep-processing factors of fluid ability and crystallized ability.

Piaget's Developmental Theory

Although psychometric perspectives of intelligence provide a description of generalities among intellectual skills, these perspectives are limited by their focus on the quantifiable, measurable aspects of intelligence and their lack of description about how intelligence develops (Siegler & Richards, 1982; Sternberg & Powell, 1982). Piaget's theory of cognitive development (Inhelder & Piaget, 1958; Piaget, 1950, 1952, 1962, 1972, 1977) focused on qualitative changes and universal patterns and regularities in intelligence as it progresses across age periods. In comparison to the psychometric perspectives, which focus on what and how much individuals know, Piaget's theory emphasized how individuals think (Weinberg, 1989). This section of the chapter describes Piaget's developmental theory of intelligence, including the basic concepts used in his theory and the characteristics of individuals' intelligence during his four stages of cognitive development.

Piaget defined intelligence in terms of biological adaptation. During development, individuals continuously experience disequilibrium, or inconsistencies between their current cognitive structures and environmental experiences. Individuals' successive adaptations and readaptations throughout development allow them to achieve equilibrium between their perceptions of the environment and their cognitive structures. According to Piaget, two complementary processes—assimilation and accommodation—allow individuals to adapt to their environment. Assimilation occurs when new environmental experiences are incorporated into existing cognitive structures, such as when a child sees an elephant for the first time and refers to it as a horse, the cognitive structure she has for large animals. Accommodation occurs when cognitive structures are changed in response to an environmental experience, such as when a child sees an elephant for the first time and develops a new cognitive structure for elephants, which is different from her existing cognitive structure for horses.

Piaget noted several characteristics of intellectual development. First, he indicated that individuals play active roles in their development and are not merely passive recipients of external, environmental experiences; he emphasized that individuals regulate the interaction between their cognitive structures and environment. Second, Piaget incorporated the concept of readiness into his theory of intellectual development. Adaptation and the achievement of equilibrium will not occur through training or teaching, according to Piaget; an individual must be developmentally ready to experience disequilibrium between the perceived environment and cognitive structures, to adapt, and to achieve equilibrium. Finally, Piaget emphasized that equilibrium is dynamic and that adaptation continuously occurs and reoccurs throughout life.

Piaget identified four major mechanisms by which individuals develop: maturation, experience, social transmission, and equilibration. He viewed equilibration as the most important mechanism of intellectual development, hypothesizing it to be the process by which individuals organize the other three mechanisms for broad transitions in intellectual development. Piaget noted that equilibration is the primary process that accounts for individual variations in intellectual development.

Piaget divided the transitions in intellectual development into four general periods or stages. The first, the *sensorimotor period*, extends from infancy to the age of approximately 2 years. During the sensorimotor period, children gradually change from reflexive organisms (who use sensory and motor responses to interact with their environments) to reflective organisms (who are able to form mental, symbolic representations of their environment). Piaget indicated that object permanence, or an understanding that an object exists even when it cannot be seen, is an important accomplishment during the sensorimotor period and accounts for the ability to form mental representations.

Piaget's second developmental stage is the *preoperational period,* which he estimated occurs between the ages of 2 and 7 years. Because children during this period are able to form mental, symbolic representations of their environment, the primary aspect of development is the growth of representational skills, such as language and symbolic play. The preoperational period is also characterized by several limitations in children's thinking, including egocentrism (the inability to take another person's perspective), centration (the focus on one quality or attribute of an object while ignoring others), and irreversibility (the inability to change or reverse the direction of the thought process).

Piaget's third stage of development, the *concrete operational period,* occurs between the ages of about 7 to 11 years. The major limitations of thought during the preoperational period disappear, and children in the concrete operational period are characterized by mobile and flexible thinking. During this period, children are able to perform a number of operations on objects and experiences that are concrete and exist in reality.

The fourth and final period of intellectual development, according to Piaget, is the *formal operational period,* which begins around 12 years of age. During this stage adolescents are able to use hypothetico-deductive reasoning. They develop hypotheses about possible solutions to problems, test the hypotheses against the information they have, and determine if their hypotheses can be accepted or rejected, or if more information is needed. While children in the previous stage are limited to operations on concrete objects and experiences that exist in reality, adolescents in the formal operational period are able to use logical rules that are not necessarily based on reality. Thus the thinking of adolescents during the latter period can be abstract and systematic and take the form of testing mental hypotheses.

Formal operational thinking may be displayed through many overt changes in adolescents' behavior. Adolescents may become engrossed in systematic, theoretical speculation about subjects such as poverty, war, and politics. They may spend a great amount of time pondering the mysteries of life and making inferences, predictions, and idealistic claims.

According to Piaget, the mark of formal thought is the use of a combinatorial system in which all logical combinations of propositions are considered and coordinated. For example, two propositions, p and q, can form four elements: p and q can occur together, neither p or q can occur, p can occur alone without q, and q can occur alone without p. The four elements can result in 16 possible combinations; if the four elements are labeled A, B, C, and D, the 16 possible combinations are ABCD, ABC, ABD, ACD, BCD, AB, AC, AD, BC, BD, CD, A, B, C, D, and 0 or the null set (Keating, 1980). Piaget further identified four operators that are a part of the combinatorial system: identity, negation, reciprocal, and correlative. Thus Piaget indicated that the characteristics of intelligence during the formal operational period are due to a basic reorganization of cognitive structures into a system of propositional logic.

Piaget's theory has been heralded as one of the most comprehensive and systematic explanations of the complex nature of intellectual development (Case, 1981; Gruen, 1985), and his work is recognized as making a number of significant contributions to the study of intelligence (Flavell, 1979; Keating, 1980, 1990). There are numerous criticisms of Piaget's theory, however, and many questions about its validity. For example, Siegler and Richards (1982) claimed research support for the view that tasks typical of the concrete and formal operational periods can be effectively taught to children at a younger age. They also noted that knowledge obtained through the training appears to be generalizable to new tasks and durable over time. Piaget's age norms for the four periods of cognitive development have been questioned, particularly for the formal operational period (Keating, 1980), and a number of investigations have found that many adolescents and adults never attain formal operations (e.g., Capon & Kuhn, 1979; Grinder, 1975; Neimark; 1975). Later in his career, Piaget (1972) himself noted that the formal operational period may not begin until 15 to 20 years of age and that many of the characteristics of formal operational reasoning may only be displayed in areas of interest and expertise.

One of the most serious criticisms of Piaget's views of intellectual development during adolescence concerns his premise that propositional logic accounts for the changes in thought from the concrete to the formal operational period. Keating (1980) conducted a comprehensive and excellent review of research concerning formal operational reasoning. He concluded that although Piaget's theory provided a relatively accurate description of the characteristics of adolescent intelligence, there is little evidence to support Piaget's explanation that propositional logic (a) forms the basis for cognitive structures during the formal operational period and (b) accounts for changes between the thinking of children and adolescents.

Cognitive/Information-Processing Perspectives

Psychometric perspectives and Piaget's developmental theory provide a number of descriptions of intellectual functioning but very little information about specific cognitive processes. Cognitive and information-processing perspectives of intelligence focus on identifying and describing specific ways that symbols are represented and manipulated during mental activities (Siegler & Richards, 1982). Sternberg (1985b) noted several goals of information-processing perspectives of intelligence, including identification of the mental representations and processes used in intellectual tasks, description of the speed and accuracy of the processes, and determination of strategies into which mental processes are combined for task performance.

The study of intelligence from information-processing perspectives has increased substantially over recent years. Although each perspective typically focuses on a single or a few cognitive processes, with few attempts to describe the system as a whole (Keating, 1990), these perspectives have added a great deal to the understanding of intelligence. This section of the chapter focuses on the following four perspectives: Case's neo-piagetian perspective, Brown and Campione's perspective on metacognitive and cognitive processes, Sternberg's componential and triarchic models, and a cognitive and neuropsychological approach advanced by Das and Jarman.

Case (1978, 1981, 1985) explored Piaget's stage theory of development from an information-processing perspective and explained the qualitative changes in intellectual development in terms of utilization of mental processing space. According to Case, intellectual development as described in Piaget's theory is dependent on the use of an increasing number of and more sophisticated mental strategies. The capacity of the system for processing mental strategies remains constant from early childhood on. As children develop, however, their processing of the strategies becomes faster and more efficient and automatic, and less processing space is required. More space is then available for processing additional strategies and refining and expanding old strategies. Case suggested that individuals' increasing capability to process a larger number of strategies and more complex strategies allows them to progress through Piaget's stages. For example, Case's theory implies that the testing of hypotheses by adolescents during Piaget's formal operational period is explained by the ability of adolescents to process several hypotheses at once.

Other cognitive and information-processing researchers have focused on identifying and classifying specific mental processes that develop. Brown, Campione, and colleagues (e.g., Brown, Bransford, Ferrara, & Campione, 1983; Brown & Campione, 1978; 1988; Campione, Brown, & Bryant, 1985; Campione, Brown, & Ferrara, 1982) identified two processes of cognition: cognitive (the skills used to implement strategies) and metacognitive (the knowledge and control of cognitive processes). They further described two distinct types of metacognitive processes: metacognition (individuals' knowledge about their own cognition) and executive control (the processes individuals use to regulate their cognitive activities). Executive control processes, which are considered more important, include planning, monitoring, testing, revising, and evaluating cognitive activities.

Sternberg (1980, 1985a, 1988a, 1991) offered an expanded view of cognitive processes in a componential model of information processing. According to Sternberg, components are elementary processes that operate on mental representations. He identified three types of components: metacomponents, performance components, and knowledge-acquisition components. Metacomponents, which are similar to the executive control processes described by Brown and Campione, are used for the regulation of cognitive performance (e.g., recognition that a problem exists, recognition of the nature of the problem, selection of a strategy for task performance, and monitoring task performance). Performance components are processes used to execute strategies for task performance, including encoding a stimulus, inferring the relations between two or more stimuli, and applying a relation to another situation. Knowledge-acquisition components are processes used to learn and store new information; they include selective encoding of relevant (instead of irrelevant) information, selective combination of relevant information, and selective comparison of new information with information previously stored in memory.

Sternberg (1985a, 1988b, 1991) used his componential theory of information processing to formulate a general triarchic theory of intelligence based on three subtheories: componential, experiential, and contextual. The componential subtheory describes the internal world of the individual, or the mental components of intelligent behavior. The experiential subtheory describes the degree of familiarity individuals have for tasks and their ability to cope with novelty. The contextual subtheory describes the external world of the individual, or the ability to use mental processes in a practical way to adapt or shape environments or to select new environments.

A model described by Das, Jarman, and colleagues (e.g., Das & Jarman, 1991; Das, Kirby, & Jarman, 1979; Naglieri, Das, & Jarman, 1991) attempts to integrate the neuropsychological work of Luria with current conceptualizations of cognitive processes to explain specific cognitive functions. Das and Jarman's model identified four major cognitive functions. The first function, arousal-attention, includes the processes that allow individuals to maintain a state of cortical tone (or arousal) and to focus and direct attention. Insufficient arousal and attention leads to ineffective processing in the other three functions. The second and third cognitive functions—simultaneous and successive processing—are known as coding functions; they are responsible for receiving, processing, and storing of information. Simultaneous processing involves syntheses or integration of stimuli into groups, often by recognizing the common or shared characteristics of different stimuli. (An example of a task that requires simultaneous processing is completing an analogy such as "car is to road as train is to.") Successive processing involves the processing of stimuli into serial order, often by determining the linear relationship between stimuli. (An example of a task that requires successive processing is the arrangement of historical events into chronological order.) The fourth function is planning: using the information from the simultaneous and successive functions to form plans of action, implement them, and evaluate the performance of the action.

Das, Jarman, and colleagues also acknowledged the importance of an individual's knowledge base (the information available at the time of processing, including past experiences and information just received about a particular task) in the execution of the four functions.

Cognitive Socialization Perspectives

The psychometric, Piagetian, and information-processing perspectives each identify a number of general and specific aspects of intelligence. These three perspectives, however, place little emphasis on the role of other people (e.g., parents, teachers, and peers) on intellectual development. Cognitive socialization perspectives emphasize the development of intelligence within the larger social worlds of individuals, and they describe the important influence that other people have on the growth of intelligence (Campione et al., 1985). Two cognitive socialization approaches will be discussed in this section: Vygotsky's model of the zone of proximal development, and Feuerstein's learning potential model.

Vygotsky (1962, 1978) indicated that intellectual development is based initially on social processes and the gradual internalization of the social processes. Vygotsky used the model of the "zone of proximal development" to explain the growth of intelligence. The zone of proximal development is the range between an individual's current developmental level (i.e., the level at which the individual can perform on his or her own) and his or her potential developmental level (i.e., the level at which the individual can perform tasks with assistance and guidance from other people). Skills beyond an individual's current developmental level are acquired only through social interactions at the potential developmental level. According to Vygotsky's model, another person initially guides and controls an individual's activity. Then, the other person and the individual share the activity. Finally, the individual gradually internalizes the skill and is able to perform the activity alone, with the other person only providing support as needed.

Feuerstein's learning potential model (Feuerstein, 1980; Feuerstein, Rand, & Hoffman, 1979) is very similar to Vygotsky's model. Feuerstein indicated that intellectual growth is based on incidental and mediated learning. Incidental learning occurs through simple exposure to the environment. Mediated learning, the more important influence, occurs when another person in an individual's environment frames, selects, focuses, and provides feedback about an environmental experience in order to create relevant learning sets for the individual. Through the training provided by another person, individuals develop the cognitive structures necessary for further independent learning.

Specific Characteristics of Adolescent Intelligence

The four perspectives on intellectual development presented above describe a number of characteristics of intelligence. Keating (1980) noted that regardless of the perspective from which intelligence is studied, there are obvious qualitative differences between the intelligence of children and adolescents. He summarized these differences as follows:

1. Adolescents are able to consider abstract concepts and possibilities not immediately present.
2. Adolescents are able to generate and evaluate hypotheses, including hypotheses that may be impossible in the real world.
3. Adolescents are able to think ahead, plan, and anticipate.
4. Adolescents are able to think about their thoughts, can be aware and knowledgeable about their cognitive activities, and are able to direct and regulate their cognitive activities.
5. Adolescents are able to think beyond old limits.

Keating pointed out that two cautions are necessary when reviewing the characteristics of adolescent intelligence that differentiate adolescents from children. First, the characteristics occur with higher frequency in adolescents than in younger children, but may not be impossible for the latter. Second, the characteristics in the above list represent aspects of intellectual functioning in which many adolescents are *capable*; however, adolescents may not exhibit the characteristics in all circumstances or contexts. It is probably better to consider the characteristics as potential aspects of intellectual functioning for adolescents in some circumstances and contexts.

Keating's summary of characteristics describes the qualitative differences in intelligence found between adolescents and children. Cognitive and information-processing researchers have attempted to identify the specific cognitive processes that actually change or develop from childhood to adolescence. Brown et al. (1983), Campione et al. (1982, 1985), Keating (1990), and Sternberg and Powell (1983) have summarized the specific processes that appear to develop as follows:

1. Broad and spontaneous use of metacognitive and executive control processes
2. Number and complexity of strategies used for problem solving
3. Content and structure of the knowledge base, including new knowledge structures that have the potential to be abstract, multidimensional, relative, and self-reflective

4. Flexibility in transferring information and applying it to new situations

5. Speed, efficiency, and automaticity in processing information

6. Mental representations of information that allow new information to be more easily related to previously learned information

7. Simultaneous representation of different types of knowledge

8. Specialized abilities and skills.

Keating's (1980) description of qualitative differences between children and adolescents, as well as information-processing researchers' description of the development of specific cognitive processes, emphasize the definite and identifiable changes that can occur in intellectual functioning from childhood to adolescence. Thus typical adolescent intellectual functioning can be characterized as quite distinct from that of children. The growth of a number of cognitive processes and increasing flexibility in using them appear to allow adolescents to engage in broader and more abstract and systematic intellectual activities.

Characteristics Associated with Developmental Disorders

Previous sections of this chapter have focused on the development of intelligence and aspects of "normal" intellectual functioning. Individuals with developmental disorders, however, may not exhibit a number of the characteristics of typical intellectual growth. Two developmental disorders commonly associated with intellectual deficits are mental retardation and learning disabilities (also referred to as specific developmental disorders). Mental retardation and specific developmental disorders are described in the *Diagnostic and Statistical Manual of Mental Disorders*, including the revised third edition (American Psychiatric Association, 1987) and the upcoming fourth edition (American Psychiatric Association, 1993). In addition, under the *Individuals with Disabilities Education Act* (1991), adolescents with these conditions are diagnosed and placed in special education programs for children with disabilities.

The development of the first intelligence tests in the early 1900s led to a pervasive practice of defining mental retardation according to a person's IQ (Harrison, 1990). Official definitions of mental retardation by the American Association on Mental Retardation (previously the American Association on Mental Deficiency; e.g., Grossman, 1983; Heber, 1961), however, de-emphasized the use of low IQ as the sole criterion, instead listing three components of mental retardation: low intelligence, deficits in adaptive behavior, and manifestation during the developmental period. The most current definition of mental retardation by the American Association on Mental Retardation (1992) places much less emphasis on measured intelligence and more emphasis on the following characteristics: functional limitations in a person's ability and behavior; adaptive skill deficits in areas such as communication, self-care, community use, social skills, and work; and a person's need for services.

Short and Evans (1991) suggested that according to a Piagetian perspective, individuals with mental retardation may progress through the stages of development at a slower pace than other individuals. Cognitive and information-processing research, though, has found a number of specific cognitive deficits associated with mental retardation. Short and Evans (1991), Campione et al. (1982), and Sternberg and Spear (1985) reviewed a number of studies investigating the differences in cognitive processing between individuals who are and are not mentally retarded. They found that persons with mental retardation are typically deficient in the use of metacognitive and executive control strategies. Campione et al., for example, noted that individuals with mental retardation experience a number of problems when they are required to monitor and evaluate their own intellectual activities. Other processing deficits associated with mental retardation involve efficiency, speed, and accuracy in carrying out mental operations, speed of learning, transfer of learning to new situations, and spontaneous and flexible use of strategies. Campione et al. (1982) found that individuals with mental retardation typically have a less extensive knowledge base than individuals who are not mentally retarded, but the researchers suggested that the limited extent of the knowledge base is a symptom of processing deficits rather than a cause.

Learning disabilities have typically been characterized by underachievement in academic areas and a presumption of some type of central nervous system dysfunction (Hammill, 1990). Operational definitions of learning disabilities, however, have primarily included academic underachievement and discrepancies between ability and achievement. For example, the accompanying regulations (34 CFR 300) for the *Individuals with Disabilities Education Act* (1991) include the following in the criteria for determining the existence of a specific learning disability:

(a)   A team may determine that a child has a specific learning disability if

(1)   The child does not achieve commensurate with his or her age and ability levels in one or more of the areas listed in paragraph (a) (2) of this section, when provided with learning experiences appropriate for the child's age and ability levels; and

(2)   The team finds that a child has a severe discrepancy between achievement and intellectual ability in one or more of the following areas:

(i)   Oral expression;

(ii) Listening comprehension;

(iii) Written expression;

(iv) Basic reading skill;

(v) Mathematics calculation; or

(vii) Mathematics reasoning. (34 CFR 300.541)

Sattler (1988) summarized specific intellectual and processing deficits associated with children with learning disabilities. He indicated that children with learning disabilities may have difficulty in applying efficient task strategies and executive control functions, focusing attention, and encoding and retrieving information. Sattler also suggested that problems in processing verbal language, slower development of strategy use, a teaching-learning environment that does not adequately prepare children, and the negative effects of early school failure on motivation and self-concept may all account for the intellectual deficits of children with learning disabilities.

Nature and Nurture of Intelligence

One of the most controversial aspects of the study of intellectual development and retardation concerns the relative contributions of nature (heredity) and nurture (environment) to intellectual variation in a population. While it is assumed that a genotype (or underlying genetic composition) for intelligence exists, the phenotype (or set of visible or observable characteristics) is assumed to be affected by both genetic and environmental influences (Benson & Weinberg, 1990; Weinberg, 1989). Thus intellectual variation cannot be explained simply by heredity or environment, but by the dynamic interplay between heredity and environment influences.

The heritability index is used to describe the proportion of variation in observed intelligence that can be attributed to genetic differences in a population (Plomin, 1989). It can range from 0 to 1.0; for example, a heritability index of .60 means that 60% of the intellectual variation in intelligence is estimated to be attributable to genetic variation, while 40% is estimated to be the result of nongenetic influences.

Numerous studies have attempted to estimate the heritability index for intelligence using a variety of research strategies for samples of individuals with varying degrees of genetic and environmental similarity. Vandenberg and Vogler (1985) and Benson and Weinberg (1990) summarized the research strategies: correlations between identical and fraternal twins reared together and apart, correlations between parents and children, correlations between adoptive and nonadoptive children, and correlations between various relatives. Plomin (1988, 1989) and Vandenberg and Vogler (1985) reviewed a number of studies and concluded that more recent investigations using sophisticated methodology yield estimates of the heritability indexes that are somewhat lower than older estimates.

More current estimates tend to be from about .30 to .50, compared to older estimates of .70 to .80. Research suggests that genetic variation is the single most important influence on intelligence and is assumed to account for a large proportion of the population variance in intelligence. Even estimated heritability indexes from about .30 to .50, however, indicate that 50% to 70% of intellectual variation may be attributed to environmental influences.

Bouchard and Segal (1985) reviewed a number of studies that examined the relationship between various environmental factors and intelligence. They found that a number of environmental characteristics appear to be related to intelligence, including family background characteristics (e.g., parental education and occupation) and home factors (e.g., press for achievement). Bouchard and Segal concluded, however, that environmental effects on intelligence are multifactorial and that no single environmental factor appears to have a substantial effect on intelligence.

It is emphasized that research concerning the nature and nurture of intelligence, as described above, is directed toward investigating the genetic and environmental contributions to variance in intelligence within a *population*, rather than the intellectual functioning of *individuals* (Anastasi, 1988). A population heritability index will provide no information regarding the causes of a specific person's intellectual functioning. The potential contributions of both genetic and environmental factors, along with descriptions of intelligence provided by psychometric, Piagetian, information-processing, and cognitive socialization perspectives, must all be considered in order to understand the unique aspects of a person's intelligence. Assessment and interpretation of an adolescent's intellectual functioning should take into account the multifaceted nature of intelligence and the many factors that can contribute to intellectual functioning.

Summary

This chapter has attempted to provide a basic foundation for understanding adolescent intelligence. A number of aspects of intelligence were described, and characteristics of intellectual functioning that are applicable to the adolescent period were identified. Key points are summarized below.

1. There is little agreement on a definition of intelligence; however, current experts in the field have identified a number of possible attributes of intelligence and emphasize the social, cultural, and real-world implications of intellectual functioning.

2. Psychometric perspectives of intelligence attempt to identify the quantifiable components of intelligence. Cattell and Horn's two broad fac-

tors of intelligence, fluid ability and crystallized ability, probably represent the best summary of the measurable components of intelligence.

3. Piaget's developmental theory of intelligence focused on equilibration as the primary mechanism for intellectual growth. Piaget identified a number of characteristics of intelligence that develop during four broad periods, with the formal operational period of adolescence being characterized by more abstract, hypothetico-deductive reasoning. Although Piaget's theory has been criticized on many grounds, including his premise that changes in the formal operational period are due to the reorganization of cognitive structures into a system of propositional logic, his description of the many qualitative changes from childhood to adolescence has been supported.

4. Cognitive/information-processing perspectives of intelligence focus on specific mental processes associated with intellectual functioning. Case explained the qualitative changes in intelligence described by Piaget as resulting from more efficient use of mental processing space. Brown and Campione, Sternberg, Das and Jarman, and others have identified a number of specific mental processes, including coding, metacognitive, performance, and knowledge-acquisition processes.

5. Cognitive socialization perspectives of intelligence emphasize the influence of other people on intellectual development. Vygotsky and Feuerstein, among others, explained intellectual development as the gradual internalization of mental activities that are first learned through social processes.

6. A number of specific components of intelligence characterize the adolescent period, regardless of the perspective from which intelligence is studied. These components include the ability to use abstract concepts, to think in terms of possibilities, to generate and evaluate hypotheses, and to plan and regulate cognitive activities. Cognitive and information-processing research has identified several specific processes that develop from childhood to adolescence, including metacognitive processes, problem-solving strategies, knowledge structures, transferring of strategies to new tasks, and efficiency of mental processing.

7. Individuals who are mentally retarded or learning disabled have been found to have a number of deficits in mental processing, including in use of metacognitive processes, transfer of learning to novel tasks, and processing speed.

8. Intellectual development is influenced by both genetic and environmental factors. Genetic factors have been estimated to account from 30% to 50% of intellectual variation in a population and are seen as the single most important influence on intelligence. This means that 50% to 70% of intellectual variation in a population is not accounted for by genetic factors, though, and the interaction of many environmental factors may also influence intelligence.

As noted by Keating (1980, 1990) there is relatively little consensus about either the cognitive changes that occur in adolescence or the reasons for these changes, beyond some obvious descriptive characteristics of intellectual performance. Perhaps we will never learn a great deal about this complex human construct called intelligence. Researchers in a wide variety of fields (including cognitive psychology, developmental psychology, neuropsychology, and educational psychology), however, continue to investigate the puzzle of intelligence and the relationship between it and a host of other aspects of human functioning. The future is likely to see an increase in our understanding of adolescent intelligence and in our ability to use this understanding to affect adolescents' lives.

It must be pointed out that the scope of this chapter is quite limited. In the small space of a single chapter it is impossible to include a discussion of all perspectives of intelligence that could be related to the adolescent period. We have selected the key perspectives that we felt were important for a basic foundation for understanding adolescent intelligence. The chapter does not attempt to resolve a number of controversial issues concerning intelligence (e.g., the definition or heritability of intelligence). These issues simply cannot be resolved at the present time and probably will never be resolved. Finally, because we have focused on the characteristics of intelligence and not on testing, the chapter contains almost no discussion of intelligence tests and the many issues associated with intelligence testing, including bias in test scores and the use and misuse of test scores for selection and placement. Interested readers may refer to sources such as Anastasi (1988), Kaufman (1990), and Sattler (1988) for excellent information pertaining to intelligence testing.

References

American Association on Mental Retardation. (1992). *Mental retardation: Definitions, classifications, and systems of supports* (9th ed.). Washington, DC: Author.

American Psychiatric Association. (1987). *Diagnostic and statistical manual of mental disorders* (3rd ed. rev.). Washington, DC: Author.

American Psychiatric Association. (1993). *DSM-IV draft criteria*. Washington, DC: Author.

Anastasi, A. (1988). *Psychological testing* (6th ed.) New York: Macmillan.

Benson, M. J., & Weinberg, R. A. (1990). Contributions of the psychology of individual differences to school psychology: Different drummers—one beat. In T. B. Gutkin & C. R. Reynolds (Eds.), *The handbook of school psychology* (2nd ed., pp. 218–243). New York: Wiley.

Bouchard, T. J., & Segal, N. L. (1985). Environment and IQ. In B. B. Wolman (Ed.), *Handbook of intelligence: Theories, measurements, and applications* (pp. 391–464). New York: Wiley.

Brown, A. L., Bransford, J. D., Ferrara, R. A., & Campione, J. C. (1983). Learning, remembering, and understanding. In J. H. Flavell & E. M. Markman (Eds.), *Handbook of child psychology* (Vol. 3, pp. 77–166). New York: Wiley.

Brown, A. L., & Campione, J. C. (1978). Permissible inferences from cognitive training studies in developmental research. *Quarterly Newsletter of the Laboratory of Comparative Human Cognition, 2,* 46–53.

Campione, J. C., Brown, A. L., & Bryant, N. R. (1985). Individual differences in learning and memory. In R. J. Sternberg (Ed.), *Human abilities: An information processing approach* (pp. 103–126). New York: Freeman.

Campione, J. C., Brown, A. L., & Ferrara, R. A. (1982). Mental retardation and intelligence. In R. J. Sternberg (Ed.), *Handbook of human intelligence* (pp. 392–490). Cambridge, England: Cambridge University Press.

Capon, N., & Kuhn, D. (1979). Logical reasoning in the supermarket: Adult females' use of a proportional reasoning strategy in everyday context. *Developmental Psychology, 15,* 450–452.

Carroll, J. B. (1983). The measurement of intelligence. In R. J. Sternberg (Ed.), *Handbook of human intelligence* (pp. 29–120). Cambridge, England: Cambridge University Press.

Case, R. (1978). Intellectual development from birth to adulthood: A neo-Piagetian approach. In R. S. Siegler (Ed.), *Children's thinking: What develops?* (pp. 37–71). Hillsdale, NJ: Erlbaum.

Case, R. (1981). Intellectual development: A systematic reinterpretation. In F. F. Farley & N. J. Gordon (Eds.), *Psychology and education: The state of the union* (pp. 142–177). Berkeley, CA: McCutchan.

Case, R. (1985). *Intellectual development: A systematic reinterpretation.* New York: Academic Press.

Cattell, R. B. (1943). The measurement of adult intelligence. *Psychological Bulletin, 40,* 153–193.

Cattell, R. B. (1987). *Intelligence: Its structure, growth, and action.* Amsterdam: North Holland.

Das, J. P., & Jarman, R. F. (1991). Cognitive integration: Alternative model for intelligence. In H. A. H. Rowe (Ed.), *Intelligence: Reconceptualization and measurement* (pp. 163–181). Hillsdale, NJ: Erlbaum.

Das, J. P., Kirby, J. R., & Jarman, R. (1979). *Simultaneous and successive cognitive processes.* New York: Academic Press.

Detterman, D. K. (1986). Qualitative integration: The last word? In R. J. Sternberg & D. K. Detterman (Eds.), *What is intelligence? Contemporary viewpoints on its nature and definition* (pp. 163–166). Norwood, NJ: Ablex.

Feuerstein, R. (1980). *Instrumental enrichment: An intervention program for cognitive modifiability.* Baltimore, MD: University Park Press.

Feuerstein, R., Rand, Y., & Hoffman, M. B. (1979). *The dynamic assessment of retarded learners: The Learning Potential Assessment Device theory, instruments, and techniques.* Baltimore, MD: University Park Press.

Flavell, J. H. (1979). Metacognition and cognitive monitoring: A new area of cognitive developmental inquiry. *American Psychologist, 34,* 906–911.

Grinder, R. E. (Ed.). (1975). *Studies in adolescence* (3rd ed.). New York: Macmillan.

Grossman, H. J. (1983). *Classification in mental retardation*. Washington, DC: American Association on Mental Deficiency.

Gruen, G. E. (1985). Genetic epistemology and the development of intelligence. In B. B. Wolman (Ed.), *Handbook of intelligence: Theories, measurements, and applications* (pp. 159–200). New York: Wiley.

Guilford, J. P. (1967). *The nature of human intelligence*. New York: McGraw-Hill.

Guilford, J. P. (1985). The structure-of-intellect model. In B. B. Wolman (Ed.), *Handbook of intelligence: Theories, measurements, and applications* (pp. 225–266). New York: Wiley.

Hammill, D. D. (1990). On defining learning disabilities: An emerging consensus. *Journal of Learning Disabilities, 23*, 74–84.

Harrison, P. L. (1990). Mental retardation, adaptive behavior assessment, and giftedness. In A. S. Kaufman (Ed.), *Assessing adolescent and adult intelligence* (pp. 533–585). Boston: Allyn and Bacon.

Heber, R. F. (1961). A manual on terminology and classification in mental retardation. *American Journal of Mental Deficiency, 64*, Monograph Supplement. (Rev. ed.).

Horn, J. L. (1985). Remodeling old models of intelligence. In B. B. Wolman (Ed.), *Handbook of intelligence: Theories, measurements, and applications* (pp. 267–300). New York: Wiley.

Individuals with Disabilities Education Act. (1991). 20 U.S.C. Chapter 33.

Inhelder, B., & Piaget, J. (1958). *The growth of logical thinking from childhood to adolescence*. New York: Basic Books.

Kaufman, A. S. (1990). *Assessing adolescent and adult intelligence*. Boston: Allyn and Bacon.

Kaufman, A. S., & Harrison, P. L. (1991). Individual intellectual assessment. In C. E. Walker (Ed.), *Clinical psychology: Historical and research foundations* (pp. 91–119). New York: Plenum.

Kaufman, A. S., & Kaufman, N. L. (1983). *Kaufman assessment battery for children*. Circle Pines, MN: American Guidance Service.

Keating, D. P. (1980). Thinking processes in adolescence. In J. Adelson (Ed.), *Handbook of adolescent psychology* (pp. 211–246). New York: Wiley.

Keating, D. P. (1990). Adolescent thinking. In S. S. Feldman & G. R. Elliott (Eds.), *At the threshold: The developing adolescent* (pp. 54–89). Cambridge, MA: Harvard University Press.

Lohman, D. F. (1989). Human intelligence: An introduction to advances in theory and research. *Review of Educational Research, 59*, 333–373.

Meeker, M. (1985). Toward a psychology of giftedness: A concept in search of measurement. In B. B. Wolman (Ed.), *Handbook of intelligence: Theories, measurements, and applications* (pp. 787–799). New York: John Wiley.

Naglieri, J. A., Das, J. P., & Jarman, R. F. (1991). Planning, attention, simultaneous, and successive cognitive processes as a model for assessment. *School Psychology Review, 19*, 423–442.

Neimark, E. D. (1975). Intellectual development during adolescence. In F. D. Harowitz (Ed.), *Review of child development research* (Vol. 1, pp. 541–594). Chicago: University of Chicago Press.

Piaget, J. (1950). *The psychology of intelligence*. New York: Harcourt Brace.

Piaget, J. (1952). *The origins of intelligence in children.* New York: International Universities Press.

Piaget, J. (1962). *Play, dreams, and imitation in childhood.* New York: Norton.

Piaget, J. (1972). Intellectual evolution from adolescence to adulthood. *Human Developments, 15,* 1–12.

Piaget, J. (1977). *The development of thought: Equilibrium of cognitive structures.* New York: Viking.

Plomin, R. (1988). The nature and nurture of cognitive abilities. In R. J. Sternberg (Ed.), *Advances in the psychology of human intelligence* (Vol. 4, pp. 1–33). Hillsdale, NJ: Erlbaum.

Plomin, R. (1989). Environment and genes: Determinants of behavior. *American Psychologist, 44,* 105–111.

Sattler, J. M. (1988). *Assessment of children* (3rd ed.). San Diego, CA: Sattler.

Short, E. J., & Evans, S. W. (1990). Individual differences in cognitive and social problem-solving skills as a function of intelligence. In N. W. Bray (Ed.), *International review of research in mental retardation* (Vol. 16, pp. 89–123). San Diego, CA: Academic Press.

Siegler, R. S., & Richards, D. D. (1982). The development of intelligence. In R. J. Sternberg (Ed.), *Handbook of human intelligence* (pp. 897–971). Cambridge, England: Cambridge University Press.

Spearman, C. (1904). General intelligence, objectively determined and measured. *American Journal of Psychology, 15,* 201–293.

Spearman, C. (1927). *The abilities of man.* New York: Macmillan.

Sternberg, R. J. (1980). Sketch of a componential subtheory of human intelligence. *Behavioral and Brain Sciences, 3,* 573–614.

Sternberg, R. J. (1985a). *Beyond IQ: A triarchic theory of human intelligence.* Cambridge, England: Cambridge University Press.

Sternberg, R. J. (1985b). Introduction: What is an information processing approach to human abilities? In R. J. Sternberg (Ed.), *Human abilities: An information processing approach* (pp. 1–4). New York: Freeman.

Sternberg, R. J. (1988a). Intelligence. In R. J. Sternberg & E. E. Smith (Eds.), *The psychology of human thought* (pp. 267–308). Cambridge, England: Cambridge University Press.

Sternberg, R. J. (1988b). *The triarchic mind.* New York: Viking.

Sternberg, R. J. (1991). Theory-based testing of intellectual abilities: Rationale for the Triarchic Abilities Test. In H. A. H. Rowe (Ed.), *Intelligence: Reconceptualization and measurement* (pp. 183–202). Hillsdale, NJ: Erlbaum.

Sternberg, R. J., & Berg, C. A. (1986). Quantitative integration: Definitions of intelligence: A comparison of the 1921 and 1986 symposia. In R. J. Sternberg & D. K. Detterman, D. K. (Eds.), *What is intelligence? Contemporary viewpoints on its nature and definition.* Norwood, NJ: Ablex.

Sternberg, R. J., & Powell, J. S. (1983). The development of intelligence. In J. H. Flavell & E. M. Markman (Eds.), *Handbook of child psychology* (Vol. 3, pp. 341–419). New York: Wiley.

Sternberg, R. J., & Spear, L. C. (1985). A triarchic theory of mental retardation. In N. R. Ellis & N. W. Bray (Eds.), *International review of research in mental retardation* (Vol. 13, pp. 301–326). Orlando, FL: Academic Press.

Thorndike, R. L., Hagen, E. P., & Sattler, J. M. (1985). *Stanford-Binet Intelligence Scale* (4th ed.). Chicago: Riverside.

Thurstone, L. L. (1931). Multiple factor analysis. *Psychological Review, 38,* 406–427.

Thurstone, L. L. (1938). *Primary mental abilities.* Chicago: University of Chicago Press.

Vandenberg, S. G., & Vogler, G. P. (1985). Genetic determinants of intelligence. In B. B. Wolman (Ed.), *Handbook of intelligence: Theories, measurements, and applications* (pp. 3–57). New York: Wiley.

Vygotsky, L. S. (1962). *Thought and language.* Cambridge: MIT Press.

Vygotsky, L. S. (1978). *Mind and society: The development of higher psychological processes.* Cambridge, MA: Harvard University Press.

Weinberg, R. A. (1989). Intelligence and IQ: Landmark issues and great debates. *American Psychologist, 44,* 98–104.

Part II
Assessment Issues and Strategies

5
Diagnostic Classification of Adolescents

Richard H. Mesco, Kavitha Rao, Lisa Amaya-Jackson, and Dennis P. Cantwell

T his chapter presents a discussion of the classification of adolescent mental disorders. The reasons for and against specifying a uniform method of diagnostic classification are reviewed, with reference to the particular issues that arise in making and communicating diagnostic judgments about adolescents and the uses to which such judgments may be put. The advantages and disadvantages of various types of classificatory systems are reviewed briefly in an historical context, followed by a detailed look at the categorical, multiaxial system as it exists in DSM-IV. An examination of each axis is undertaken with specific reference to current standards of use, as well as dilemmas and controversies as they apply in the case of adolescence. The review of Axis I outlines the salient changes in DSM-IV for most of the major diagnostic categories as they apply to adolescents. Included in the overview of Axis II is an extensive look at the diagnosis of personality pathology in adolescents. In addition to highlighting the differences between DSM-IV and DSM-III-R, the discussion of each axis contains a comparison to the recently published ICD-10 system, and suggestions for future research.

Purposes of Classification

Any system of diagnostic classification must be clinically useful in order to be used. It must allow for the orderly collection and meaningful organization of clinical data and the communication of this information between health professionals, even those of different medical specialties or theoretical orientations. It must be sufficiently lucid to allow for use by those who deal with commonly encountered disorders, including people from such disparate disciplines as health, education and law. It must facilitate the interdisciplinary communication that occurs routinely in the process of treatment planning, and which is required for the storage and retrieval of information to subserve legal, financial, and other special service needs.

A comprehensive system of diagnostic classification is fundamental to the development of an epidemiological data base. Establishing the prevalence and types of mental disorder in a population of children or adolescents on local, state, national, and international levels is the first step toward convincing funding agencies of the existence, nature, and severity of a problem, and ultimately obtaining financial support for a specific intervention. On an individual level, determining whether an adolescent has a particular diagnosis may make him or her eligible for certain programs (e.g., special educational or language services, physical or occupational therapies, or in-home respite care). It may also allow for the mitigation of charges, or influence disposition, in the adjudication of criminal cases.

Perhaps the most traditional use of any system of diagnostic classification is for prognosis: the prediction of future patterns in an individual, either by comparison with previously observed natural histories in other individuals, or from the development and application of predictive and explanatory scientific theories. In the past, the use of often idiosyncratic terminology and varying criteria for the inclusion of children and adolescents in certain research studies has frequently prevented the direct comparison of related findings between different centers. This is probably most evident in child and adolescent psychiatry in the the fields of childhood psychosis and schizophrenia, autism, and related disorders. This problem has hampered scientific advancement in child and adolescent psychiatry and consequently has impeded both the refinement of methods of treatment and the provision of services to young people in need. The development of an understanding of etiology and treatment response within a consistent framework of diagnostic classification, however imperfect, is an indispensable prerequisite for continued progress in the field of child and adolescent mental health.

One criticism that is levied against the process of diagnostic labeling in general is that it fails to recognize the special characteristics of an individual and the unique aspects of his or her suffering. It is true that treating a patient as an individual requires the clinician to learn about that particular person and develop both a unique diagnostic formulation and a specific treatment plan. Nevertheless, learning about the psychiatric disorders from which a person may suffer requires a useful system of classification. Individual case formulation and systematic diagnostic classification are not mutually exclusive endeavors. Abandoning classification would require each patient to be viewed as an anecdotal research subject, having no shared characteristics with any other patient. There would be no body of knowledge based on the cumulative experience of clinicians who have investigated and treated certain kinds of problems. This would render communication between professionals a process of impressionistic narrative alone, and reduce scientific inquiry to a series of idiosyncratic case reports.

The stigma resulting from diagnostic labels has also been advanced as a reason to avoid the use of any system for classifying psychiatric disorders. The consequences of the stigma thought to result from applying diagnostic terminology includes interpersonal prejudice in the form of rejection and negative expectations and/or interpretations of behavior. To the contrary, several studies suggest that while these assumptions may reflect elements of common belief, neither prejudice nor rejection are automatic consequences of diagnostic classification. Accurate rather than negative expectations can be fostered by careful and detailed diagnosis. One study of young adolescents (Budoff & Siperstein, 1978) found that sixth graders who were labeled as mentally retarded and performed poorly in school were viewed more positively by other sixth graders than were children who performed similarly but who were not labeled as retarded. This finding suggests that the label carried with it an explanation for the relatively poor academic performance and thus resulted in greater tolerance.

Social and political deprivation have also been put forth by Szasz (1961) as the causes for, as well as the inevitable consequences of, psychiatric classification. According to this approach, the act of applying a diagnostic label is itself detrimental, causing psychological maladjustment and economic harm. It is undeniable that economic harm can and does occur to an individual by virtue of having been given a certain psychiatric diagnosis. This may happen, for example, in the context of making an application for insurance or employment. Such an occurrence most often constitutes an abuse of psychiatric classification, rather than its proper use. In the United States, as advancements are made in the understanding of mental disorders, concomitant efforts toward public education and political action are being undertaken by groups like the National Alliance for the Mentally Ill (NAMI) and Children with Attention Deficit Disorders (CHADD). In part through the work of such organizations, there is a trend toward greater legislative protection of the rights of psychiatric patients. Tolerant and informed attitudes are increasingly becoming those of the mainstream.

History of Adolescent Psychiatric Diagnosis

Psychiatric nosology as it exists today in the ICD and DSM systems has its roots in the work of Emil Kraepelin. Born in 1855, Kraepelin followed the best medical model of his time, painstakingly recording and cataloguing extensive clinical histories together with careful and detailed observations of signs and symptoms. By comparing cases, Kraepelin defined symptom complexes, or syndromes. Treating the syndrome as representative of a disease entity, the search could then be undertaken to discover a common etiology presumed to underlie a given syndrome. Kraepelin, who asserted that psychoses were the result of specific brain lesions (Goshen, 1967), was a proponent of the theory of organic causes of psychiatric conditions during a time when psychoanalytic theory was more influential. His widely translated textbook of psychiatry (Kraepelin, 1883, 1893, 1899, 1915) was published in several revised editions over four decades. Although the modern ICD and DSM nomenclatures have been rewritten many times, both take the same basic phenomenological approach to classification and still contain several major categories of disorders that were clinically defined by Kraepelin.

Dementia praecox was a term coined by Morel and redefined by Kraeplin to encompass Clouston's "secondary dementia of adolescence" (Robertson, 1919). This diagnostic cluster which included paranoia, catatonia, and hebephrenia, formed the category of mental disorders known today as the schizophrenias. These disorders were called the "insanity of adolescence" because of the typical age of onset and because masturbation was presumed to be the cause (these disorders were also referred to as the "insanity of onanism"). Kraepelin (1894, 1967) made epidemiologically-based arguments ruling out masturbation as a causal agent in dementia praecox, stating it was nothing but a nonspecific symptom. Kraepelin later distinguished dementia praecox from a similar set of disorders by developing the category of manic-depressive psychoses.

Anorexia nervosa was first named as such by Sir William Gull (1874) in his case reports of two female adolescents. Gull spoke about the psychological and physiological components of anorexia nervosa, as well as its prognosis and treatment; he noted that the typical onset of the condition is in adolescence and that it occurs predominantly among females. His work grew out of that of Lasegue (Hunter & Macalpine, 1982) and was followed 5 years later by a review of the literature dating back to the Middle Ages in William Hammond's monograph "Fasting Girls: Their Physiology and Pathology" (Strober, 1984).

During the first half of the twentieth century, though, little specific attention was paid to the classification of psychiatric disorders in adolescents. The earliest official psychiatric nomenclature in the United States was the first *Diagnostic and Statistical Manual of Mental Disorders*, or DSM-I (American Psychiatric Association [APA], 1952). It was grounded in psychoanalytic theory, listing adjustment reactions and special symptom reactions as the only diagnostic entities distinct to childhood or adolescence, and it did not have a separate section for childhood or adolescent disorders. Since then a number of methods have been proposed for classifying child and adolescent psychopathology. These include the Metapsychological Diagnostic Profile of Anna Freud (1965), the Group for the Advancement of Psychiatry reports (1966, 1974), the dimensional, multivariate factorial approach of the Child Behavior Checklist (Achenbach,

1980), the categorical systems contained in the International Classification of Diseases (World Health Organization, 1978, 1991), and the revised editions of the DSM (APA, 1968, 1980, 1987, 1991, 1993). DSM-II included a small section for "behavior disorders of childhood and adolescence," which specified six childhood disorders and one catchall "other reactions of childhood" category. In DSM-III, DSM-III-R, and DSM-IV the section covering disorders of childhood and adolescence is placed in the front of the manual.

DSM-IV includes approximately 40 childhood-onset disorders, a slight decrease over the number of categories in DSM-III-R. The decrease is primarily due to the removal from this section of the gender identity disorders, all but one of the childhood anxiety disorders, and the eating disorders, all of which were moved to the main body of the manual (with age-specific criteria developed for the first two disorder groups). There has been a concomitant expansion of diagnostic categories for the developmental disorders, though, and the addition of several ADHD subtypes. Despite this extensive coverage, the division of the classification into disorders of childhood and adolescence, as compared to those of adulthood, is not absolute. Individuals with disorders that are typically "first evident in childhood and adolescence" may not present clinically until adulthood. Conversely, many disorders not placed in the DSM-IV child and adolescent section—such as the substance-related disorders, the anxiety disorders (including obsessive-compulsive disorder and posttraumatic stress disorder), the mood disorders, the schizophrenias and other psychotic disorders, the eating disorders and the adjustment Disorders—are all routinely diagnosed during childhood or adolescence.

The International Classification of Diseases (ICD), now in its tenth revision, is a statistical system for classifying diseases that has been accepted by most countries of the world. Created under the auspices of the World Health Organization of the United Nations, the ICD-10 is used to provide statistical data about groups of disorders. The different subsections of the ICD-10 are organized along etiological, situational, or topographic lines. For example, infectious diseases are classified etiologically, by pathogen; complications of pregnancy represent situational organization; and diseases of the nervous, endocrine, or respiratory systems are classified by topography.

The ICD-10 classification of mental, behavioral, and developmental disorders was developed through a series of field trials, conducted at nearly 200 institutions in more than 50 countries. In the early 1980s, the World Health Organization entered an international collaboration with the U.S. Alcohol, Drug, and Mental Health Administration (ADAMHA) to review intensively the existing state of psychiatric diagnosis and classification in the world. This project led to the development of new instruments for epidemiological assessment that were used to conduct multicenter clinical research studies (Loranger, Hirschfeld, Sartorius, & Regier, 1994; Robins et al., 1988; Wing et al., 1990; Wittchen et al., 1991). Clinicians and researchers from several disciplines, representing many schools of psychiatric thought, cooperated to develop a proposal for classification. It was then tested simultaneously in the 10 languages spoken by a combined majority of the world's population: Arabic, Chinese, English, German, French, Italian, Japanese, Portuguese, Russian, and Spanish (Sartorius, 1989). As a result of this process, the number of diagnostic categories was increased from 300 to 1,000, and a multiaxial system for coding diagnoses similar to that in the DSM was introduced and is now being implemented in member nations of the World Health Organization. ICD-10 will ultimately be available in equivalent versions in several different languages and will have additional congruent versions: one designed for use by general practitioners, another for psychiatrists and mental health clinicians, and one for use in research.

As a result of this international collaborative effort, DSM-IV is closely correlated and cross-referenced with ICD-10 as to the arrangement of the major diagnostic category headings. Sponsored by the National Institute of Mental Health, the DSM-IV field trials were undertaken at more than 70 sites in the United States and involved more than 6,000 subjects, comparing DSM-III, DSM-III-R, ICD-10, and the proposed DSM-IV criteria sets. Bound by treaty obligation to adopt the same coding scheme, the DSM-IV nevertheless remains as a separate document and typically employs an alternative sequential structure and different diagnostic criteria. Diagnoses in DSM-IV can generally be correlated with ICD-10 as to the specific subcategories on Axis I, but there are many diagnoses in ICD-10 that have no counterparts in DSM-IV. There is less congruence with regard to the structure and use of Axes II through V, which exist in different forms in the ICD and DSM nomenclature. A multiaxial format was developed as an optional component of ICD-10. In DSM-IV there are now instructions provided for the coding of diagnoses according to an optional *non*axial format (APA, 1993).

Some authors (Katschnig & Simhandl, 1986) suggest that the field of psychiatry today cannot afford two rival systems of classification. The perception of a need for significant changes from ICD-9 to ICD-10 arose in part from the growing use of DSM-III and III-R by clinicians and researchers in many countries. Now DSM-IV makes its debut only 6 years after DSM-III-R, its appearance due in part to pressure felt in the United States as a result of the publication of ICD-10. (DSM-III was published 12 years after DSM-II, and DSM-III-R just 8 years after DSM-III.) Cantwell and Baker (1988) have argued that changes continue to be made that reflect individual opinions and the desire for revision rather than the results of ongoing research—results that may in fact be outpaced and rendered obsolescent by the very rapidity of change in the diagnositic criteria.

Other researchers (e.g., Brockington and Helzer, 1983) have advocated a polydiagnostic approach that would allow comparison of the validity of different systems in order to provide a basis for the establishment of an ultimate classification system. Any future modifications of the current diagnostic criteria should be based on empirical research rather than the advocacy of personal opinions or political or economic pressure. Future diagnostic classification systems successive to DSM-IV should thus represent genuine improvements in the knowledge of child and adolescent psychopathology, and therefore in the classification of these disorders.

The Phenomenological Approach

Currently, although there are two similar "official" systems of classification for mental, behavioral, and developmental disorders, there is no single framework that is recognized as the natural or correct system. There are, however, certain objective criteria by which the effectiveness of classification systems can be judged (Cantwell, 1987, 1988; Rutter, Tuma, & Lann, 1987). Traditionally, these criteria have included reliability, validity, coverage, and feasibility.

Both DSM-III-R and DSM-IV were constructed mainly on a phenomenological basis. As a rule, the disorders listed in DSM-IV are described in terms of clinically observable features. Both essential and associated features are described for each disorder; exclusionary criteria are given for the various categories as well. With few exceptions, references to any theories or notions about causes (whether biological, psychological, social, or environmental) and conditions underlying developmental psychopathological processes are intentionally avoided. This purely descriptive, atheoretical approach was a significant departure from previous classificatory systems, including the first two editions of the DSM and those of both Anna Freud and the Group for the Advancement of Psychiatry. Although for many clinicians this lack of causal criteria constituted perhaps the greatest strength of the DSM system of diagnostic classification (especially given the relative paucity of our present knowledge about the etiological bases of mental disorders), it has been disparaged and even denied. Denial that the existing framework is atheoretical has been argued by Salzinger (1986), who points to the assumptions underlying the medical model. Salzinger's criticism is valid in the case of etiologically organized sections like the one for *substance-related disorders*. It is particularly true on Axis I in DSM-IV in the categories listed under the *dementias* (e.g., *vascular dementia, dementia due to HIV*, and in the cases of *dementia due to Parkinson's, Huntington's, Pick's, or Creutzfeldt-Jakob* diseases), where the etiology is to be specified on Axis III. Further such assumptions have been made more explicit in the main text for the Axis I disorders of DSM-IV. After the sections that clarify the clinical description of each disorder (titled "*Diagnostic Features*") and that describe *associated features and disorders*, DSM-IV includes sections listing "*associated laboratory findings* and *associated physical examination signs, symptoms, and general medical conditions.*" Examples of three subtypes of associated laboratory findings included in DSM-IV are as follows:

1. Those associated laboratory findings that have sufficient sensitivity and specificity to be considered diagnostic of the disorder (e.g., polysomnographic findings in certain sleep disorders)

2. Those associated laboratory findings that are confirmatory of the construct of the disorder but that do not have sufficiently documented sensitivity and specificity to be useful in the diagnosis of a given individual (e.g., ventricle size on a CT scan as a validator of the construct of schizophrenia)

3. Those laboratory findings that are associated with the complications of a disorder (e.g., electrolyte imbalances in individuals with anorexia nervosa)

There were already psychological criteria previously implicit or explicit in DSM-III-R that have been carried over into DSM-IV. This is evident in the category of separation anxiety disorder, the only one of the anxiety disorders remaining in the DSM-IV section on disorders of infancy, childhood, or adolescence: attachment theory is implicit in the name of the disorder itself, as well as in several of the diagnostic criteria. More explicit, though less specific, allusions to inferred psychological etiologies occurred in DSM-III-R. In the case of factitious disorder with psychological symptoms, a major criterion of the diagnosis was a "psychological need to assume the sick role," (DSM III-R, p. 315) which has been changed in DSM-IV to more strictly phenomenological criteria ("the motivation of the behavior is to assume the sick role" and "psychological signs and symptoms predominate in the clinical presentation"). In the case of conversion disorder, a major criterion in DSM-III-R ("psychological factors are judged to be etiologically related to the symptom") has been expanded in DSM-IV to be more explicit ("psychological factors are judged to be associated with the symptom or deficit because the initiation or exacerbation of the symptom or deficit is preceded by conflicts or other stressors"; APA, 1987, 1993) (DSM IV, p. 457). Such changes, along with the inclusion of laboratory results and physical findings (e.g., hepatic cirrhosis as a consequence of alcohol dependence; Frances & First, 1991), will have the effect of making the presence of the medical model more explicit where it is operative. They also move further in the direction toward an at least partially etiological classification system as our knowledge base expands.

Categorical Versus Dimensional Approaches

The specific diagnostic criteria in DSM-III-R and DSM-IV are convention-ally referred to as operational diagnostic criteria. While the criteria are spe-cific in that they specify the essential features of the disorders, they are *not* operational, because they do not specify the operation that must be per-formed in order to make the diagnosis. Proponents of the multivariate dimensional approach to psychiatric classification consider the absence of operational criteria in the DSM system to be among its major failings. Under a dimensional system, the definitions of disorders are linked to sta-tistically determined threshold scores on specified assessment instruments. Although such criteria are absent on Axis I, the DSM framework does not preclude the establishment of operational criteria for specific diagnoses. In fact, it is a requirement that standardized test scores be used in the determi-nation of certain Axis I and II conditions in both DSM-III-R and DSM-IV (e.g., mental retardation, developmental expressive language disorder, developmental reading and arithmetic disorders). Due to a lack of univer-sally accepted standardized tests that span the entire age range from child-hood to adolescence, particular intelligence and educational diagnostic tests are still not specified in DSM-IV for these diagnoses.

As was the case for its Kraepelinian forerunners, the classificatory sys-tem for child and adolescent psychiatric disorders contained in DSM-IV consists of categories that were derived from clinical impressions. This sole reliance on organized observation and the cataloguing of reported symp-toms under clinically meaningful categories significantly enhances aspects of the validity of our diagnoses. Conversely, this approach may have an adverse impact upon diagnostic reliability. This is particularly so in the case of adolescents, where the thresholds separating normal from pathological behavior and functioning are often less clearly defined, where the natural history of many disorders is uncertain, and where the transition from child-hood to adult phenomenology is in most rapid flux.

In contrast to the clinically determined categorical approach, the dimen-sional method employs mathematical and statistical procedures to measure the tendencies of specific items of behavior to occur together. These dimensions of behavior are selected by the mathematical technique of fac-tor analysis and are then associated into mutually exclusive groups using the technique of cluster analysis. Using this method to classify patients the-oretically raises the reliability of two observers making the same diagnosis on a given patient to 100%. Different results can still be obtained in dimensional systems; depending on the various mathematical criteria selected and the methods of mathematical analysis used, the same patients can be classified into different groupings (Pfohl & Andreasen, 1978).

Achenbach, a leading proponent of the dimensional approach, reports that syndromes derived from multivariate statistical studies can be divided into broad-band and narrow-band syndromes (Achenbach, 1980; Achenbach & Edelbrock, 1983). Broad-band syndromes are analogous to general categories in the DSM-IV system (e.g., disruptive behavior and attention-deficit disorders), and the narrow-band syndromes resemble the more specific subcategories (e.g., attention-deficit hyperactivity disorder). Previous detailed comparisons between DSM-III categories and the empirically defined narrow-band syndromes indicated that (a) there were DSM disorders that did not seem to have empirical counterparts; (b) there were empirically derived syndromes that did not have apparent DSM categorical counterparts; and (c) there were a considerable number of corresponding syndromes that occurred in both the multivariate dimensional studies and in the categorical DSM system. Thus dimensional measures lend empirical support for certain DSM categories, but not all of them.

Proponents of the dimensional approach offer as a major argument in favor of their system that all of its syndromes are empirically derived. Due to this method, the dimensional groupings are more homogenous and more reliably arrived at by different clinicians. The fact that the syndromes are closely and inextricably tied to specific assessment instruments may be seen as either an advantage or a disadvantage in varying circumstances. Because the syndromes are defined by numerical scores obtained on the specific assessment tools, a patient's response to treatment can be readily assessed, but only insofar as it is reflected by measurable changes in the same dimensional scores.

Perhaps the most troublesome aspect of the dimensional approach is that the statistically significant groupings of behavior created may not be clinically or theoretically meaningful. For example, it has been demonstrated that cluster analysis can create homogeneous groupings even when applied to random data (Achenbach, 1980). Another problem with the dimensional approach is that its categories require cumbersome mathematical definitions that are difficult to employ in many clinical settings. Not being tied to clinical judgment or intuition, the dimensional categories are also difficult to remember and thus are less likely to facilitate professional communication. Multivariate statistical techniques can be used in combination with more clinically based approaches to enhance diagnostic reliability within a categorical system of classification, but it is likely that clinical judgment will continue to play an indispensable role in the creation and use of diagnostic systems (APA, 1993; Robins, 1976; Pfohl & Andreasen, 1978).

Reliability

The reliability of a classification system refers to the degree to which all clinicians using that system can arrive at the same diagnosis for a given patient. The general procedures for testing diagnostic reliability involve either one clinician diagnosing the same patients more than once or several clinicians diagnosing the same patients at the same time. The latter result is reported as *interrater reliability*, and there are several statistical methods that can be used to compute the degree of agreement between the diagnoses. The reliability of a classificatory system may vary according to the information provided (known as *information variance*), the interpretation of information (called *observation* or *interpretation variance*), and/or the criteria used to summarize the data collected into diagnoses (*criterion variance*; Spitzer & Williams, 1980). The reliability of diagnoses made under a dimensional system is generally higher because the only source for disagreement is in the selection of the various algorithms to be used; once these are selected, the reliability should be 100%.

Validity

Validity refers to the extent to which an instrument or procedure measures what it claims to be measuring. Four types of validity describe the utility of a psychiatric diagnostic classification's categories: *face validity*, the correspondence with clinical judgment and intuition; *descriptive validity*, the uniqueness of each category; *predictive validity*, measured by usefulness at predicting outcome; and *construct validity*, the relationship of the diagnostic categories to psychiatric and psychological theories (Weiner, 1982).

Several models have been described for testing the validity of psychiatric diagnostic systems. Feighner, Robins, and Guze (1972) published the Washington University criteria for the diagnosis of certain adult disorders in the context of psychiatric research. Validation of these criteria was presented according to the following five-stage scheme: (a) clinical description; (b) delimitation from other disorders; (c) laboratory studies; (d) family studies; and (e) follow-up studies. The delineation in the first stage of the Washington University schema of a precise clinical picture (which includes essential as well as associated symptoms, age of onset, demographic factors, etc.) is equivalent to establishing face validity.

This model was subsequently expanded into a six-stage model designed specifically for the validation of childhood and adolescent psychiatric disorders (Cantwell, 1975). The six stages outlined by Cantwell are (a) overall clinical picture, consisting of essential and associated features of the disorder as well as exclusionary criteria; (b) physical and neurological features; (c) laboratory findings; (d) family psychopathology and interaction studies; (e) follow-up studies; and (f) treatment studies. The first step in the six-stage model combines the first two steps of the Washington University scheme: clinical description (or face validity) and clinical delimitation from other disorders (one aspect of descriptive validity).

The six-stage model is based on the premise that child and adolescent psychiatric disorders, with rare exception, are of multifactorial etiology. Thus children or adolescents who meet strict diagnostic criteria for any condition probably form a heterogenous group etiologically. Until recently, family studies have been little used in child and adolescent psychiatric research compared to research with adults. Finding that the same disorders occur in close family relatives of children with a given disorder more often than in unrelated individuals or in families of children with other types of psychiatric disorder can add support to the descriptive validity, and in some cases to the construct validity, of a diagnostic entity. From a clinical point of view, predictive validity is probably the most important type of validity since, as noted earlier, diagnosis is most often used clinically for the purpose of prognosis. A clinician needs to be able to predict untreated natural history, likely responses to different interventions, and family patterns of psychiatric illness.

The fifth stage of the model concerns natural history studies. Prospective and retrospective studies tracing the course of a disorder in an index population of children or adolescents can help determine whether the original group represented a homogenous diagnostic category. In this model, long-term studies of a large number of youngsters who match a precise clinical description (e.g., for a major depressive disorder) are likely to demonstrate subgroups of the initial population over time. It is unreasonable to expect that children who meet criteria at one time for a distinct psychiatric disorder will necessarily exhibit the same untreated natural history. There are too many variables in young people's lives to expect similar outcomes; younger children also have a limited repertoire of behaviors. Those who fit a defined clinical picture early on (e.g., in the preschool years) will more likely represent a heterogenous grouping than will an older group of adolescents or adults who present with similar clinical pictures. Marked differences in outcome may suggest the existence of etiologically distinct subgroups among the initial sample population.

Finally, response to treatment—particularly to psychopharmacological treatment—has been proposed as an additional way of validating psychiatric diagnostic constructs. There are several problems with this approach in children and adolescents at the present time. One is the similar responses to treatment for a given diagnostic entity that may occur with each of a variety of pharmacological agents (e.g., the use of stimulants, heterocyclic antidepressants, or alpha-adrenergic agonists in the treatment of attention-deficit hyperactivity disorder). There is also a lack of diagnostic specificity of many target symptoms that are often the measurable focus of psychopharmacological treatment, and that may frequently cut across diagnostic categories. At the present time, therefore, medication trials are likely to enhance diagnostic validity in the case of children and adolescents only in carefully chosen circumstances.

Feasibility

Feasibility refers to the extent to which a classification system can be successfully used by the professionals for whom it is designed. To be feasible, a classificatory system must use routinely available information; have clear, simple, and unambiguous instructions for use; and be in a form convenient for statistical manipulation (Rutter & Gould, 1985). There is little question that the DSM-IV diagnostic criteria require only routinely available information. This will be increasingly true as more assessment instruments (e.g., interviews, questionnaires, and rating scales) are updated for use with DSM-IV and become widely disseminated. The lists of diagnostic criteria have been revised to decrease ambiguity, and they are organized in DSM-IV Appendix A to correlate with decision trees for differential diagnosis. These devices, which were introduced in DSM-III, aim to aid the clinician in arriving at an Axis I diagnosis; however, their utility is open to question. They have been validly criticized by Millon (1983) as encumbrances imposing unnecessary complexity on an otherwise expedient process. The establishment of diagnostic trees may be premature, as little is known at the present time about how clinicians integrate data to arrive at specific diagnoses.

A classification scheme represents a way of seeing the world; it is the codification of an ideological position with regard to a body of knowledge. Classifying requires the creation and definition of conceptual boundaries and the territory of our discipline (Sartorius, 1989). Thus the widespread (if not uncritical) acceptance and use of the DSM-III and DSM-III-R framework in African, Asian, Australian, European, North and South American countries is probably the best measure of its feasibility (Spitzer, Williams, & Skodol, 1983).

Coverage

Coverage describes the degree to which a system is able to provide diagnoses for all patients. In psychiatric classification, coverage is measured against the proportion of patients with undiagnosed mental disorder. DSM-III-R specified 46 disorders that are "usually first evident in infancy, childhood or adolescence"; although the number of categories in the corresponding section of DSM-IV has shrunk to 41, this is due to the shifting or merging of several categories into corresponding sections in the main body of the manual, coupled with a general increase in the number of subcategories that remain (e.g., the number of specified pervasive developmental disorders has increased from two to five). This relatively large number of categories has resulted from the general splitting, as opposed to lumping, approach taken by the framers of the DSM. In this manner, subdivisions of a disorder are specified whenever face validity can be established. While increasing the number of categories improves coverage, it has the effect of lowering reliability and external validity in many cases.

As has been discussed, coverage of psychiatric disorders occurring during childhood and adolescence is not solely within the section so named. While the DSM-IV system ostensibly follows a phenomenological principle of organization, there are etiologically organized sections that employ various medical or psychological constructs. Furthermore, certain disorders have been placed into groupings defined primarily by age of onset. This continued partition in DSM-IV of a section entitled "Disorders Usually First Diagnosed in Infancy, Childhood, or Adolescence," set off from the ostensibly adult diagnostic section, can be misleading. The age of onset, age at clinical presentation and at the time of initial diagnosis of many disorders not contained within the infancy, childhood, and adolescent section often occurs in those very age ranges. Thus, although a system which groups disorders together based upon age of onset may facilitate its use by clinicians who see only adults—or primarily infants, children, or adolescents—such a separation may mislead users of the system into ignoring appropriate diagnoses listed in other sections. In this way, major depression in a child may be missed due to a failure to include mood disorder in the differential diagnosis. Similarly, an adult presenting with an attention-deficit disorder may go unrecognized as such because of a clinician's lack of familiarity with the criteria or misapprehension about its applicability to adults as a diagnostic entity.

There were some efforts made in DSM-IV to attempt to address these problems. While the age-specific section persists, greater effort has been made in the remainder of the manual to include developmental age or stage-specific criteria sets applicable throughout the life span. In most cases these are presented directly within the criteria sets, and then elaborated upon in the new section following each category entitled "Specific Age-Related or Culturally-Related or Gender-Related Features." Additional such information may also be found in the subsequent new section entitled "Course," which is intended to detail "typical lifetime presentation and evolution of the disorder" (DSM-IV, p. 9), including the typical age of onset and mode of onset, episodic versus continuous nature, duration, and progression of the disorder (APA, 1994).

Multiaxial Approach

Multiaxial diagnostic systems have appeared in at least 20 different forms in nearly a dozen countries in the latter half of the twentieth century (Mezzich, 1988). Most of these systems include one or more axes for phenomenologically based diagnoses, as well as additional axes for the specification of pathogenic or etiological related biological and psychosocial causes and conditions (e.g., personality factors, cognitive development, physical illness, premorbid condition, stressors, or adaptive functioning). Implementing such a multiaxial method of diagnosis was a major change from DSM-II to DSM-III. It has been continued with some significant modifications in DSM-IV, particularly with regard to coding changes on Axis II, and also with the inclusion of instructions for the optional coding of all pertinent diagnoses (psychiatric and nonpsychiatric) using a nonaxial format.

Criticisms of multiaxial systems have been made on both theoretical and practical bases. Axes I and II encompass the entire classification of mental disorders in DSM-III, DSM-III-R, and DSM-IV. Until DSM-IV, the disorders listed on Axis II were supposed to represent those particular mental disorders that generally begin in childhood or adolescence and persist in a stable form without periods of remission or exacerbation into adult life (APA, 1987). Many clinicians and researchers have disagreed with this premise. It has been claimed on theoretical grounds that the distinctions among Axes I, II, and III are arbitrarily made, unclear, or false. There are concerns that listing personality disorders on Axis II incorrectly implies fundamental differences (including relative immutability) compared to Axis I disorders; this distinction has been used by some insurance companies to deny reimbursement for treatment of personality disorders. Additionally, it can be argued that the existence of Axis III creates an unnecessary separation between mental disorders and nonpsychiatric medical disorders, with a number of implications that may include stigma as well as denial of insurance reimbursement. Axes IV and V have been viewed as "nondiagnostic" and therefore inappropriate to be included in a diagnostic manual. Some have argued that multiple axes are too complicated and cumbersome for general clinical use in a variety of settings. ICD-10 does not include a multiaxial system for clinical use, although a separate manual of additional axes is available for research purposes.

Each of the five DSM-IV axes requires the clinician to assess an individual with regard to putatively different domains of information, with the purpose of arriving at a comprehensive evaluation. To be feasible, such a system should be relevant to prognosis and treatment planning, be clear in its organization, be succinctly recordable, and facilitate communication among clinicians and researchers. After more than a dozen years of sporadic use, including two revisions, the DSM multiaxial system has not yet proven to be so feasible in these terms.

A major rationale for retaining the multiaxial system in DSM-IV is that it requires the clinician to consider factors other than diagnosis in formulating a treatment plan and prognosis, despite the complexity of doing so. The descriptions of psychiatric comorbidity, personality and developmental factors, other medical information, stressors, supports, and level of functioning are necessary to evoke and explain the clinical heterogeneity of patients who may have the same primary diagnosis, but who require different interventions and treatment modalities and experience markedly different clinical courses. Following is a detailed discussion of the salient changes in the Axis I diagnostic categories to be found in DSM-IV, as well as a review of the changes made for Axes II through V as they pertain to adolescents.

Axis I Changes in DSM-IV

Disruptive Behavior and Attention-Deficit Disorders

Attention-Deficit Hyperactivity Disorder. In DSM-IV there are a number of changes in the organization of the disruptive behavior disorders. Previously, the three subtypes of attention-deficit disorder (ADD) that existed in DSM-III had been consolidated as attention-deficit hyperactivity disorder (ADHD) and undifferentiated attention-deficit disorder in DSM-III-R. As the nature of the criteria changed from monothetic to polythetic (meaning that no specific symptom or set of symptoms could constitute necessary and sufficient criteria for making the diagnoses), the number of children and adolescents covered by the ADHD diagnosis increased significantly (Lahey, Schaughency, Frame, & Strauss, 1985). This came with a concomitant potential loss in validity, as up to one-quarter of the children diagnosed with ADHD under DSM-III-R might qualify more specifically for ADD without hyperactivity under DSM-III criteria. DSM-IV presents a change in the ADHD construct by collapsing the three conceptual domains of inattention, motoric hyperactivity, and impulsivity (first noted in DSM-III) into two domains of inattention and hyperactivity-impulsivity, now the A(1) and A(2) criterion sets. In this manner, the category of ADD without hyperactivity has been effectively restored as *314.00 Attention Deficit Hyperactivity Disorder, Predominantly Inattentive Type*, where criterion A(1) but not A(2) has been met for the previous 6 months. This new version of 314.00 in DSM-IV, when compared to its predecessors—ADD without hyperactivity in DSM-III and undifferentiated ADD in DSM-III-R—will differ with regard to gender ratios, associated problems and conditions, and possibly medication response and outcome.

The now-familiar *314.00 Attention Deficit Hyperactivity Disorder* has been split in DSM-IV into two subtypes, both with the same numerical code. Predominantly hyperactive-impulsive type is indicated where the A(2) but not the A(1) criterion has been met for the prior 6 months; and Combined type is the diagnosis made when both A(1) and A(2) criterion sets have been satisfied for the preceding 6 months.

Conduct Disorder. The high comorbidity of conduct disorder with ADHD had led to suggestions that the two disorders should be combined into one diagnostic entity. Most DSM studies of transmission and outcome, though, supported maintaining the distinction between conduct and attention-deficit disorders. Etiological factors such as parental antisocial personality disorder and substance abuse, as well as increased risk for later adult criminality, are present in conduct-disordered children with or without concomitant ADHD, but significantly not in children with ADHD alone (Lahey et al., 1988). Nevertheless, the rate of co-occurrence is significant, especially among males, and continues to warrant further research.

ICD-10 has one category termed hyperkinetic conduct disorder, and a related category of depressive conduct disorder, which grew out of the WHO/ADAMHA epidemiological studies and field trials. Several subtypes thus exist for conduct disorder between the ICD and DSM schemata, which generally take into account levels of aggression and the capacity for social relationships. As there is no research that clearly supports one method of organization over another, the issue of subtyping has been simplified for DSM-IV. The various subtypes of conduct disorder in DSM-III-R have been collapsed into the one polythetic category *312.8 Conduct Disorder* with a single exclusionary criterion ("B. If age 18 or older, criteria are not met for Antisocial Personality Disorder"). One may now also specify either childhood onset (prior to age 10) or adolescent onset (not evident prior to age 10), as well as the usual three degrees of severity.

Oppositional Defiant Disorder. The additional DSM diagnosis of *313.81 Oppositional Defiant Disorder*, not found in either ICD-9 or ICD-10, has undergone some changes in DSM-IV aimed at addressing previously recognized problems with the construct validity of this entity, as to whether it is truly representative of pathology, or rather of developmentally normal behaviors. This was especially true in the case of adolescents (APA, 1991). Changes in DSM-IV include dropping the use of obscene language and swearing from the list of behavioral criteria, as well as the addition of a second major criterion requiring evidence of "significant impairment in social, academic, or occupational functioning" to improve the construction of the disorder. A preexisting code has been appended to a new entity, *312.9 Disruptive Behavior Disorder Not Otherwise Specified*, meant to encompass subthreshold presentations of conduct disorder or oppositional defiant disorder, as well as to facilitate congruence with the previously mentioned ICD-10 categories.

Anxiety Disorders of Childhood and Adolescence

The listing of anxiety disorders of childhood and adolescence separately from adult anxiety disorders in DSM-III-R was inconsistent with the DSM approach to childhood and adolescent presentations of mood disorders and schizophrenia. As a result, none of the instruments currently available for assessing children or adolescents measures anxiety symptoms according to the adult model, and so the prevalence of these disorders in younger populations is unknown. Epidemiological studies of even the specific anxiety disorders as defined for adolescents and children are limited, and a strong link between anxiety disorders occurring at younger ages and those in adulthood has not been established. Early data suggested that most emotional disorders do not persist into adult life, and that most specific anxiety disorders in adults cannot be traced to an onset in childhood (Robins, 1966). More recent research indicates the stability of anxiety symptoms generally over time, without yet establishing links between specific childhood, adolescent, and adult disorders (Orvaschel & Weissman, 1986). One notable exception is *300.30 Obsessive Compulsive Disorder*, which demonstrates strong temporal continuity (Zietlin, 1983). Thus, an adolescent with a history of separation anxiety as a child is more likely than other individuals to present again with an anxiety disorder, panic disorder, and agoraphobia as opposed to generalized anxiety disorder.

To facilitate research aimed at greater clinical understanding of the phenomenological continuity and discontinuity of the anxiety disorders over time, DSM-IV promotes the use of a single set of diagnostic criteria across the lifespan by including sections of text that specify age-related features for each anxiety-related diagnosis. Therefore there is no section on anxiety disorders whatsoever among the disorders of infancy, childhood, or adolescence in DSM-IV; *309.21 Separation Anxiety Disorder* has been placed under the section entitled "Other Disorders," and the DSM-III-R categories of overanxious disorder and avoidant disorder of childhood have been eliminated from DSM-IV in favor of modified criteria in the corresponding diagnostic listings of *300.02 Generalized Anxiety Disorder (includes Overanxious Disorder of Childhood)* and *300.23 Social Phobia (Social Anxiety Disorder)*, under which they have been subsumed (APA, 1994).

Mood Disorders

Depressive Disorders. The classification of depression and the identification and meaning of depressive symptoms in adolescence has been controversial. The old concept of "masked depression," which grouped many socially maladaptive behaviors (e.g., impulsivity, sexual promiscuity, risk taking, and substance abuse) together in some cases with eating disorders, sleep disorders, hypochondriasis, poor school performance, and self-destructive behaviors, has been shown to lack constructional validity (Carlson & Cantwell, 1980). Several studies indicate that the general phenomenology of depressed mood, diminished concentration, insomnia, and suicidal ideation occurs with similar frequency across the developmental age span in psychiatrically referred populations. Features such as anhedonia, diurnal variation, hopelessness, psychomotor retardation, and delusions increase in frequency with developmental age, while depressed appearance, low self-esteem, and somatic complaints are seen less frequently with increasing age (Carlson & Cantwell, 1980; Carlson & Kashani, 1988). Among adolescents, the general picture is similar to that for adults, but with a tendency for dysphoric mood to present as irritability more frequently at younger ages and for low self-esteem to give way to guilt with increasing age. In light of these findings, the DSM-IV criteria set for depression for children and adolescents specifies "irritable mood" as an alternative presentation to the major adult criterion of "depressed mood."

DSM-III-R presented a confusing picture by listing different criteria sets for "major depressive episode" and "major depressive syndrome." DSM-IV continues this pattern by subsuming the complete set of criteria for a major depressive episode as the A criterion under the disorder definitions, adding additional exclusionary criteria. One new addition in DSM-IV to the available modifiers for mood disorders that has face validity and probably some predictive validity is the designation "with atypical features," which includes the criteria of significant weight gain or increase in appetite, and hypersomnia. Incorporated in the construct are a tendency toward chronicity and the clinical presumption of preferential treatment response to MAO inhibitors over heterocyclic antidepressants. The DSM-IV section on depressive disorders also presents an extensively revised and expanded construct for *300.40 Dysthymic Disorder*. Two proposed new diagnoses, minor depressive disorder and recurrent brief depressive disorder, were relegated to DSM-IV Appendix B for further study.

Bipolar Disorders. The presentation of mania and bipolar disorders in adolescence is a matter of even greater dispute than is the case with depression. Current data indicate that in one-third of adults diagnosed with bipolar affective disorder, onset occurred prior to age 20 (Werry, McClellen, & Chard, 1991). Although it is believed to have a higher incidence than schizophrenia in adolescents, the diagnosis of bipolar disorder is less commonly made. Studies have shown that the frequency of psychotic symptoms is higher in bipolar adolescents compared to bipolar adults (Carlson & Cantwell, 1980). This has led some authors to suggest that a florid mania (which is the initial presentation of bipolarity in adolescence more frequently than a depressive episode), together with a clinical tendency to minimize or overlook mood symptoms (e.g., euphoria, depression, or irritability) that may accompany a psychosis, accounts for the disproportionate diagnosis of schizophrenia over bipolar disorder in adolescence (Carlson & Strober, 1978; Strober & Carlson, 1982). Further epidemiological research is needed to determine the full extent of any phenomenological differences between adult and adolescent bipolar disorder and to devise developmentally appropriate diagnostic criteria.

Substantial changes in the classification of the bipolar disorders are presented in DSM-IV, with six subtypes (296.0 and 296.4 through 296.7) listed for bipolar I disorder, along with the new category *296.89 Bipolar II*

Disorder (Recurrent Major Depressive Episodes with Hypomanic Episodes). There had been an attempt to specify criteria for treatment-induced manic episodes, believed to be precipitated by the use of antidepressant medication, electroconvulsive therapy, or phototherapy. These do not appear in DSM-IV, but a related new construct which does is *293.83 Mood Disorder Due to a General Medical Condition*, where "there is evidence from the history, physical examination, or laboratory findings that the disturbance is the direct physiological consequence of a general medical condition [and] the disturbance is not better accounted for by another mental disorder (e.g., Adjustment Disorder with Depressed Mood, in response to the stress of having a general medical condition)" (DSM-IV, p. 370). Three new general course specifiers for the mood disorders include rapid cycling, seasonal pattern, and postpartum onset. DSM-IV also features a dozen longitudinal course specifiers, which are accompanied by two-dimensional graphic depictions of the corresponding mood variations as a function of time.

Psychotic Disorders and Schizophrenia

The phenomenology of schizophrenia with an onset in late childhood or during adolescence is generally distinguishable from autism as described by Kanner (Kydd & Werrry, 1982) and shares enough features in common with adult schizophrenia to warrant use of a single set of diagnostic criteria (Beitchman, 1985; Werry et al., 1991). While the distribution of various symptoms with regard to their frequency prepubertally and postpubertally is not fully described, the differences are quantitative in nature. In schizophrenia with onset prior to age 18 there is likely to be a male predominance, more insidious onset, higher rates of neurodevelopmental abnormalities, increased refractoriness to antipsychotic medication, poorer outcome, and less differentiated symptomatology (Werry et al., 1991).

Although the specific categories have remained generally intact, most of the criteria and constructs for schizophrenia and related disorders have undergone significant changes in DSM-IV. A major proposal that was rejected would have divided the criteria into two sets of positive and negative symptoms. It had been suggested that this would improve feasibility by increasing the user-friendliness and educational utility of the criteria. Delusions, hallucinations, and disorganized speech would thus have been listed as positive symptoms, in contrast to the negative symptoms of flat affect, avolition, alogia, and anhedonia. In keeping with this construct, a revised subtyping scheme would have included positive (in lieu of paranoid) and deficit types, in addition to retaining disorganized, catatonic, undifferentiated, and residual types. Rather, all of the DSM-III-R subtypes were left standing in DSM-IV, albeit with substantial revisions in many of the criteria. The positive-versus-negative symptom schema was only partially adopted, as reflected in the addition of criterion *(5) negative symptoms, i.e., affective flattening, alogia, or avolition* (DSM-IV, p. 285) under the general definition of the A criterion set for schizophrenia. Another significant change in DSM-IV is the increase from 1 week to 1 month of the duration required for the active phase of symptoms for schizophrenia but not schizophreniform disorder. This change enhances compatibility with ICD-10 and improves the reliability of the DSM-IV diagnosis of schizophrenia. This is particularly the case with reference to the number of false positives that have arisen from an increase in the frequency of substance-induced psychotic disorders, a significant problem in the adolescent population. Finally, the proposed diagnoses of postpsychotic depressive disorder of schizophrenia and simple schizophrenia were remanded to Appendix B for further study, due to concerns that diagnostic overlap could prove to be a problem for the category and that aspects of reliability, validity, and feasibility would suffer for the sake of improved coverage.

Eating Disorders

Since they were first described clinically by Sir William Gull in the late nineteenth century, the eating disorders, the phenomenology of which comprises one or more syndromes with a high incidence and prevalence during adolescence, have been a subject of sustained study and interest. Nevertheless, in DSM-IV the section titled "Eating Disorders," including both *307.1 Anorexia Nervosa* and *307.51 Bulimia Nervosa*, has been shifted out of the section covering disorders usually first diagnosed in adolescence into the main body of the manual. A reversion to the former DSM-III exclusionary criterion that precludes making the diagnosis of both anorexia and bulimia simultaneously has been added under the definition of the latter disorder. Further DSM-IV refinements of the syndromal descriptions include the division into restricting and binge eating/purging types for anorexia, and purging and nonpurging types for bulimia.

A multisite study was conducted to determine the reliability, face validity, and feasibility of binge eating disorder, a proposed additional category. This construct represents a less severe form of bulimic behavior and is defined by rapid bingeing beyond satiety and resulting in marked distress that occurs at least twice a week for a period of 6 months. Exclusionary criteria are either satisfaction of the diagnostic criteria for bulimia nervosa or regular use of inappropriate compensatory behaviors (e.g., purging, fasting, excessive exercise), or the abuse of medication (e.g., diet pills, thyroid medication) in an attempt to avoid weight gain (DSM IV, p. 731). This diagnosis is dually listed in DSM-IV, appearing in Appendix B for further study, as well as under *307.50 Eating Disorder Not Otherwise Specified*, which also provides several examples of subthreshold presentations of anorexia and bulimia.

Substance-Related Disorders

The distinction which was drawn in DSM-III-R between substance use and substance-induced disorders has been eliminated in DSM-IV. This has occurred along with a marked expansion of the number and types of conditions or disorders judged to be etiologically related to the use of the particular substance under which they are listed. Some representative examples of DSM-IV substance use disorders with the same code (292.89) are alcohol sleep disorder, cannabis anxiety disorder, cocaine sexual dysfunction, hallucinogen persisting perception disorder, and hallucinogen anxiety disorder.

Gender Identity Disorders

In DSM-IV there is one broad category of gender identity disorder with a criteria set that is applicable across the span of age, sex, and developmental levels. Coding is based on current age: 302.6 in childhood, or 302.85 if adolescent or adult. The major criteria for adolescents include a "strong and persistent cross-gender identification . . . manifested by symptoms such as a stated desire to be the other sex, frequent passing as the other sex, desire to live or be treated as the other sex, or the conviction that he or she has the typical feelings and reactions of the other sex." (DSM-IV, p. 537) The second major criterion for adolescents is "persistent discomfort with his or her sex, or sense of inappropriateness in the gender role of that sex . . . manifested by symptoms such as preoccupation with getting rid of primary and secondary sex characteristics" (APA, 1994 pp. 537–8). In the case of children, a boy may assert that his penis or testes are disgusting or will disappear, or that it would be better not to have a penis. A girl may reject urinating in a sitting position or assert that she does not want to grow breasts or menstruate. Subtyping restricted to use for sexually mature individuals allows specification of sexually attracted to males, females, both, or neither.

Under *302.6 Gender Identity Disorder Not Otherwise Specified*, examples given that "are not classifiable as a specific Gender Identity Disorder" include individuals with "intersex conditions (e.g., . . . congenital adrenal hyperplasia) and accompanying gender dysphoria," "transient, stress-related cross-dressing behavior," or "persistent preoccupation with castration or penectomy without a desire to acquire the sex characteristics of the other sex" (APA, 1994, p. 538). As in the case of the eating disorders, the framers of DSM-IV have moved this category outside of the section on disorders of childhood or adolescence into the main body of the manual, in this case under the heading "Sexual and Gender Identity Disorders." Placement alongside other thematically related diagnoses is meant to highlight for clinicians that many individuals who meet criteria for eating or gender disorders are beyond adolescence (APA, 1991).

Specific and Pervasive Developmental Disorders

Although these disorders are most typically diagnosed prior to adolescence, brief mention will be made of the diagnostic changes that have been implemented in DSM-IV. The DSM-III-R specific developmental disorders, which were coded on Axis II, have been reorganized into categories of learning disorders, communication disorders, and motor skills disorder and are to be coded on Axis I in DSM-IV. All of these modifications should result in improved feasibility.

The two pervasive developmental disorders that were listed in DSM-IIIR and coded on Axis II have been moved to Axis I in DSM-IV and expanded in number to five. Two added disorders of somewhat less relevance to a discussion of diagnostic issues in adolescents are *299.80 Rett's Disorder*, which specifies that the onset of all symptoms must occur between the ages of 5 and 48 months, and *299.10 Childhood Disintegrative Disorder*. Along with the familiar *299.00 Autistic Disorder*, of interest in the diagnosis and treatment of adolescents is the addition of two new clinical descriptions, *299.80 Asperger's Disorder* and *299.80 Pervasive Developmental Disorder Not Otherwise Specified (including Atypical Autism)*, which together should help to improve the validity, feasibility, and coverage of the diagnosis of pervasive developmental disorders generally. The repetition of the 299.80 numerical code was required for congruence with ICD-10.

V Codes

Several new V codes for relational problems, in addition to the familiar *V61.20 Parent-Child Problem*, have been made available in DSM-IV. These will improve both feasibility and coverage for the clinician seeking a way to include as part of the diagnostic record the following important issues: *V61.21 Physical Abuse of Child, V61.21 Neglect of Child, V61.22 Sexual Abuse of Child*, and *V61.8 Sibling Relational Problem*. There are also a number of new "additional conditions" codes that will constitute welcome modifications for many clinicians. Some of these with particular relevance to clinical practice with adolescents are *313.82 Identity Problem, V62.61 Religious or Spiritual Problem, V62.4 Acculturation Problem*, and *V62.3 Academic Problem*.

Axis II Changes in DSM-IV

The placement of specific disorders in either Axis I or Axis II continues to be a matter for ongoing research and discussion. In DSM-III-R the personality disorders, the pervasive and specific developmental disorders, and mental retardation were all coded on Axis II. This represented a change from DSM-III, in which the pervasive developmental disorders and mental retardation were coded on Axis I, and only the specific developmental disorders were coded on Axis II. The rationale for moving all three classes of disorders onto Axis II was that they "share all the features of generally having an onset in childhood or adolescence and usually persisting in a stable form without periods of remission or exacerbation into adult life" (APA, 1987). In DSM-IV Axis II has been reconceived yet again, with an entirely new face that now includes only mental retardation and the personality disorders. The pervasive developmental disorders have been returned to Axis I from whence they originated, and the specific developmental disorders have been placed there for the first time since the DSM multiaxial system was developed. To cloud further any sense of the conceptual and practical distinctions to be drawn between Axes I and II, DSM-IV offers the following explanation/disclaimer concerning Axis II:

> The listing of Personality Disorders and Mental Retardation on a separate axis ensures that consideration will be given to the possible presence of Personality Disorders that might otherwise be overlooked when attention is directed to the usually more florid Axis I disorders. The coding of Personality Disorders on Axis II should not be taken to imply that their pathogenesis or range of appropriate treatment is fundamentally different from that for the disorders coded on Axis I. (APA, 1994, p. 26).

Personality Change Disorders in Adolescence

A new class of personality change disorders was proposed for inclusion in DSM-IV to correlate with the category of "enduring personality changes" introduced in ICD-10. The concept had its roots in the DSM-III-R Axis I diagnosis of organic personality disorder, which describes a "persistent personality disturbance, either life-long or representing a change or accentuation of a previously characteristic trait" (APA, 1987, p. 115). Along these lines, the sole example of this class that appears in DSM-IV is *310.1 Personality Change Due to a General Medical Condition*, which provides for specification of the following types: labile, disinhibited, aggressive, apathetic, paranoid, other, combined, and unspecified. Although the other diagnoses in this ICD-10 category of disorders were not included in DSM-IV, clinicians may use and code these diagnoses when ICD-9 is replaced by ICD-10 in the United States.

The availability for use of diagnoses for personality change disorders in the DSM system, particularly in clinical practice with adolescents, would have been a welcome prospect for several reasons. The term *personality change disorder* highlights the fact of ongoing developmental processes and stands in explicit contrast to the relative quality of stasis implicit in the term *personality disorders*. It also presents an opportunity for greater diagnostic specificity than is allowed by the two options still available on Axis

II in DSM-IV: simply listing pathological personality traits (which is only sporadically done by most clinicians and of limited research value), or making the diagnosis of a specific personality disorder on Axis II (not a diagnostic option for persons under 18 years of age prior to DSM-III-R, and a diagnostic judgment that most clinicians are still reluctant to make with regard to adolescents). Thus the various personality change disorders could prove to be particularly useful in clinical case formulation and longitudinal research with adolescents in that they allow for particular reference to putative causes or conditions underlying observed changes in personality, all of which may be tracked independently over time. Clinically, the diagnosis of personality change disorder would allow an explicit and detailed recognition of what is often the major goal in psychotherapy with adolescents, namely, the prevention of a full-blown personality disorder. For the above reasons, we believe that the general failure to include the diagnoses of the personality change disorders in DSM-IV has limited the face, predictive, and construct validities of the available options for the diagnosis of personality pathology in adolescents. We also believe that the addition of these diagnoses to the manual in future years would represent a significant improvement in feasibility and coverage for the DSM classification system in general as it applies to children and adolescents.

In addition to *310.1 Personality Change Due to a General Medical Disorder*, the new DSM-IV category adapted from the ICD-10 *F07.0 Secondary Personality Change*, the etiologically organized section of personality change disorders adapted from ICD-10 and proposed for DSM-IV included the following categories. The first two disorders might find inclusion in a future revision of the DSM-IV.

F62.0 Personality Change Resulting from Catastrophic Experience. This disorder, as it appears in ICD-10, describes individuals who have experienced significant changes in personality functioning (e.g., becoming avoidant, distrustful, hopeless, hostile, or irritable) enduring for at least 3 years following exposure to a severe stressor. As conceptualized for the DSM, it would require that a young person has experienced or witnessed an event that involves actual or threatened death or injury, or a threat to the physical integrity of self or others. This must be followed by a persistent personality disturbance resulting in a disruption in development and impaired social or occupational functioning, or significant distress. Exclusionary criteria include occurrence during posttraumatic stress disorder (PTSD) or accentuation of a premorbidly existing personality disorder. The criteria as proposed would permit personality change resulting from catastrophic experience ultimately to supplant the diagnosis of PTSD, in that the former represents chronic sequelae of the latter (APA, 1991).

F62.9 Personality Change Not Otherwise Specified. An example of this category that would apply to adolescents would be changes due to bereavement.

F62.1 Personality Change Resulting from Another Mental Disorder. This category specifies enduring changes in personality functioning (e.g., dependency, social withdrawal, passivity, demanding attitude, mood lability) following an episode of "another mental disorder from which the individual has recovered without residual symptoms" (WHO, 1991). This criterion would seem to lack both face and construct validity. Due to its somewhat oxymoronic definition, it also appears to lack feasibility.

Personality Disorders in Adolescents

The placement of personality disorders on Axis II is not meant to imply that the pathogenesis or range of appropriate treatments for these disorders is fundamentally different from those coded on Axis I (APA, 1994). Thus there are a number of diagnostic entities, including some of the personality disorders and personality change disorders, that could reasonably be placed on either Axis I or Axis II.

Paranoid, Schizoid and Schizotypal Personality Disorders (Cluster A). With particular reference to the phenomenology of childhood and adolescence, the relevant work groups of the DSM-IV task force considered the placement of schizotypal personality disorder in the schizophrenia section on Axis I. This would have been in keeping with its placement in ICD-10 and with epidemiological data that can be interpreted as suggesting a genetic link between schizotypal personality disorder and schizophrenia. Such a placement would have also improved its face and construct validity, as well as feasibility, given that a diagnosis of schizotypal personality disorder is frequently employed in child and adolescent settings to indicate a less severe and possibly prodromal form of schizophrenia. Recognizing this, in DSM-IV the designation "pre-morbid" may be appended to the diagnosis of either paranoid, schizoid or schizotypal personality disorder "if criteria are met prior to the onset of Schizophrenia" (APA, 1994) (DSM-IV pp. 638, 641, 645).

Borderline Personality Disorder (Cluster B). Changing the age criterion to allow the diagnosis of borderline personality disorder in adolescents improved face validity and feasibility by bringing the DSM-III-R into greater accordance with clinical experience and practice. Adolescents with borderline personality organization typically present with a history of self-mutilation and multiple suicide attempts or gestures, and they usually demonstrate the patterns of splitting, overvaluation, devaluation, and manipulation that characterize borderline adults. In addition to face validity and feasibility, studies have shown that the diagnosis of borderline personality in adolescents exhibits reliability and construct validity (Westen et al., 1990). One study of preadolescent children failed to show predictive validity with regard to the borderline diagnosis specifically but did demonstrate that it was predictive of adult personality disorder in general. This supports the construct of borderline personality as occurring at a primitive level of ego functioning, which in these early cases may have developed over time into more differentiated forms (Lofgren et al., 1991). One of the few major changes proposed in the DSM-IV criteria for borderline personality was the inclusion of a new criterion noting cognitive distortions, which would have taken into account the transient, stress-related, psychotiform episodes experienced by some individuals with borderline personality functioning. The possible decrease in reliability that could have resulted from this increased overlap of the diagnosis with schizotypal personality disorder was one reason for rejecting its inclusion in DSM-IV.

Antisocial Personality Disorder (Cluster B). This diagnosis is applicable only in late adolescence, given the age criterion of 18 years. It is typically seen as the later phase of an often intermittently evidenced pathological developmental process first occurring in the form of childhood or adolescent conduct disorder (Mesco & Cantwell, 1991). Recognition of this developmental pattern underlies the requirement of criterion B ("Evidence of Conduct Disorder with onset before age 15") (DSM-IV, p. 650). As specified in DSM-III-R, antisocial personality disorder had the highest diagnostic reliability of any of the personality disorders (APA, 1991). An effort to improve its construct validity and distinguish it from simple criminality resulted in a proposal to add a list of psychopathy items to the criteria set. These included such traits as glibness or superficiality, arrogance, deceitful or manipulative behavior, a lack of empathy or remorse, and several other items that were subjected to field trials. As a result of these trials, the construct of psychopathy per se does not appear, but the items of deceitfulness and lack of remorse remain in the polythetic list of criteria for this disorder.

Avoidant Personality Disorder (Cluster C). As was the case with avoidant disorder of childhood, avoidant personality disorder is subject to substantial diagnostic overlap with social phobia, generalized type. The proposal to subsume both avoidant categories under social phobia on Axis I was rejected in the case of avoidant personality disorder, which remains on Axis II.

Categorical Versus Dimensional Models of Personality Classification. The relative lack of useful modifiers that may be applied systematically when coding personality functioning was noted in the previous discussion on personality change disorders. In addition to the coding of personality traits, a little-used option in DSM-III-R provided for the clinician to specify severity on Axis II in the same manner as with Axis I disorders, using mild, moderate, or severe ratings for the personality disorders. DSM-IV retains this option, the drafters having rejected the adoption of a proposed dimensional scale with instructions for specifying six levels of personality pathology (absent, trait, subthreshold, threshold, moderate, or prototypical). The validity and feasibility of this particular dimensional scale were not demonstrable, and neither it nor any other alternative Axis II systems were adopted nor included in Appendix B for further study, as had been proposed (APA, 1991, 1993).

Developmental Disorders and Mental Retardation in Adolescents

Two significant changes occurred in DSM-IV with the removal of the specific and pervasive developmental disorders from Axis II and their placement on Axis I. Mental retardation remains on Axis II, where it had been moved in DSM-III-R. While this range of diagnoses is typically determined by late childhood, there are some notable exceptions that often first present clinically during adolescence. Frequently children with mild mental retardation, and more rarely high-functioning children with autisticlike syndromes, may go unreferred and unrecognized until near the end of elementary school or entrance into middle school. It is at this time when a marked deterioration in social and academic functioning often occurs for individuals in this population. Such a deterioration can result in the onset of Axis I problems, which in turn precipitate the concern of parents or teachers, culminating in a referral for diagnostic evaluation.

The comorbid population of psychiatrically disturbed and mentally retarded adolescents has been virtually unstudied from a diagnostic standpoint in the epidemiological literature. Adolescents with mild or even unobservable levels of handicaps may be especially vulnerable to developmental stressors that occur during adolescence, when there is intense self-consciousness and scrutiny by peers. While there is a substantial and well-documented increase in the onset of major mental disorders in adolescence, the onset, nature, and full extent of psychiatric comorbidity in mentally retarded adolescents is not well known. Preliminary diagnostic surveys using the Schedule for Affective Disorder and Schizophrenia in Children, the Depression Self-Report Scale, and the Beck Depression Inventory show that adolescents with IQs as low as 50 are able to give clinically valid responses, and these surveys reveal a diagnostically heterogenous group (Russel, 1987). The increase in the frequency and severity of seizure disorders in adolescence may be of particular relevance in those cases where there is underlying premorbid or ongoing damage to the central nervous system (Myers, 1987).

The specific dimensional criteria for each severity rating of mental retardation have remained unchanged in DSM-IV. The only proposed DSM-IV change in this classification group concerned individuals who develop a late-onset decrement in cognitive functioning prior to age 18. Options considered were whether and when to diagnose dementia, mental retardation, or both. The answer seems to be that when an identifiable dementing etiology can be specified, then that should take diagnostic precedence, as, for example, in the cases of *294.1 Dementia Due to Head Trauma, 294.9 Dementia Due to HIV Disease*, or *292.82 Inhalant-Induced Persisting Dementia.*

AXIS III Changes in DSM-IV

"General medical disorders" is the DSM-IV replacement for the old Axis III designation of "physical disorders or conditions" in DSM-III-R. Many felt this gave the unintended and incorrect impression that there are no physical components to Axis I and Axis II disorders. The intention behind the new terminology is to indicate more clearly that Axis III is for all nonpsychiatric ICD medical disorders—that is, all conditions except those coded in ICD-10 Chapter V (the F codes), which in the United States is supplanted by DSM-IV.

The use in DSM-IV of modifying terms that could be applied to nonpsychiatric medical conditions on Axis III had been proposed as a means to enhance the clinical relevance of the axis and to encourage its use in the development of a comprehensive diagnostic formulation. Modifiers such as *exacerbating, treatment relevant*, or *coexisting* would have been applied to Axis III medical disorders as they pertained to Axis I or Axis II conditions. These changes were rejected, but a related modification on Axis I that reinforces this biopsychosocial model is the use of the terminology "mental disorders due to a general medical condition" in place of the former "organic mental disorders" terminology.

AXIS IV Changes in DSM-IV

Axis IV was one of two dimensional axial components in the DSM-III-R multiaxial system. It was essentially a rating scale for quantifying the severity of psychosocial stressors that were thought to have played a part in the precipitation or exacerbation of the mental disorders coded on Axes I and II. This coding was based on the severity of stress an "average person in similar circumstances and with similar sociocultural values would experience" (APA, 1987) (DSM-III p. 19). The severity rating was therefore based on the stressor itself and not on an individual patient's particular vulnerability to that stressor. Additionally, DSM-III-R required the distinction to be made between acute stressors (those with a duration of less than 6 months) and predominantly enduring stressors (those persisting longer than 6 months). The clinician was then expected to calculate a sum of the severity of all stressors over the previous 12 months, based on the presumed amount of stress an "average person" would experience, and rate them on a scale from 0 to 6.

While there is research literature to support the role of stress in the pathogenesis or exacerbation of various mental disorders, the validity of the DSM-III-R Axis IV rating scale in aiding prognosis had never been demonstrated. One reason for this was that Axis IV was not routinely utilized by either clinicians or researchers (Mezzich, Coffman, & Goodpastor, 1982). While many of its potential users have found it too complex or confusing to be feasible, there are other sets of data that may be more useful to record, such as social supports or personal resources.

Several proposals were made for replacing the Axis IV scale in DSM-IV with ratings to assess the adequacy of a person's social supports, to assist in treatment planning and predicting outcome. Options that were not very user-friendly, and therefore less feasible, included rating personal resources on multiple dimensional scales for social, occupational, and environmental resources. The simplest social support checklist for children and adolescents was scaled from 1 to 5, and the extremes of the descriptive range were as follows:

> Very Deficient: The family unit is habitually hostile and/or neglecting; overt child neglect or abuse are present; and the extrafamilial network either provides little significant compensation or is itself largely detrimental to the child.

> Optimal: The family unit is generally warm, secure, and sensitive. Parental supervision and guidance is consistent and appropriate to the child's age. The family is itself supported by a wider social network and the child enjoys a supportive peer group. Any failures by the family unit to provide support are well compensated for by other elements in the support network. (APA, 1991)

The simplest proposal was to replace the current scale with a psychosocial problem checklist. The final form of Axis IV in DSM-IV is entitled "Psychosocial and Environmental Problems" and allows for the use of any such problem checklist of the individual clinician's choosing. DSM-IV also includes a new list of V codes to be used on Axis IV, specifying such problems as educational (V62.3), housing (V60.9), and economic (V60.9) difficulties, as well as problems with access to health care services (V63.9), those related to interaction with the legal system/crime (V62.5), and problems with primary support group (childhood, V61.9; parent-child, V61.2; etc.). The last of these examples provides evidence of the kind of diagnostic and coding overlap with Axis I that may very well increase the already existing confusion on the part of clinicians as to the proper the uses of Axis I versus Axes IV and V (see below).

Axis V Changes in DSM-IV

The Global Assessment of Functioning (GAF) scale that constitutes Axis V is the other dimensional component to the multiaxial DSM scheme. It was derived from the Global Assessment Scale and its version for children (Shaffer et al., 1983), the reliability and validity of which have been well established. The GAF scale on Axis V in DSM-IV "is to be rated with respect only to psychological, social, and occupational functioning" (APA, 1994, p. 30) and/or educational functioning in adolescents or adults, with school only in lieu of occupational functioning in the case of children. In DSM-III-R two such ratings were to be coded, one current and one to represent the highest level of functioning in the past year. The DSM-IV has simplified this somewhat by suggesting that in "most instances, ratings for the GAF Scale should be for the current period (i.e., the level of functioning at the time of the evaluation) because ratings of current functioning will generally reflect the need for treatment or care." In some settings, the GAF scale may also be rated for other time periods (APA, 1994, p. 30).

Besides the complexity of making two similar dimensional ratings over different time periods—which has been partially resolved by making it optional in DSM-IV—there are conceptual as well as practical problems with the current Axis V scale that adversely affect its construct validity and feasibility. First, the GAF scale combines measures of mental disorder symptom severity with an assessment of social and occupational adaptive functioning. Theoretically, the rating of symptom severity is restricted to Axis I. In the case of Mood Disorders, symptom severity is coded by the fifth digit, which rates the severity of the current state. For example, with *296.3x Major Depression, Recurrent* there are respective scales of symptom severity ranging from 0 (unspecified), to 1 through 4 (mild, moderate, and severe without or with psychotic features), and 5 or 6 (partial or full remission). There is thus redundancy, and a source of potentially discrepant ratings data, between the information required by Axis I and the dimensional scale on Axis V. This, as well as some internal redundancy within the Axis V scale itself, can clearly be seen in examples from DSM-IV that list symptom severity criteria alongside numerical ratings, which on the revised Axis V now range from 1 to 100:

100. . . No symptoms.

90 Absent or minimal symptoms . . .

70 Some mild symptoms . . .

60 Moderate symptoms . . .

50 Serious symptoms . . .

30 Behavior is considerably influenced by delusions or hallucinations (APA, 1994, p. 32)

Secondly, there is a specific instruction to avoid any input to the measure that stems from the consideration of physical impairment or environmental limitations. This constriction can require impossible clinical judgments to be made, especially in primary care or consultation liaison settings. Any future Axis V thus will still require substantial revision in order to achieve descriptive validity with regard to Axes I, II, and III and to attain feasibility across clinical settings. Toward this end, three proposed alternates—the Social and Occupational Functioning Assessment Scale (SOFAS), the Global Assessment of Relational Functioning (GARF), and the Defensive Functioning Scale—are included in Appendix B for further study, or for current use "in some settings" (APA, 1994, p. 704).

Conclusions

This chapter began with a discussion of the purposes of systematic psychiatric diagnostic classification. Arguments for and against specifying a uniform system for the classification of mental disorders were reviewed with reference to some of the issues especially pertinent to adolescents. Among these, the possibility of stigma arising from the process of diagnostic labeling was contrasted with specific benefits that can ensue from appropriate diagnosis, such as increased tolerance due to improved understanding and realistic expectations.

A historical account of the evolution of psychiatric diagnostic thought with reference to adolescents was followed by a discussion of various methods for determining psychiatric classification. The phenomenological approach to syndrome description generally used in DSM-III, DSM-III-R, and DSM-IV was compared to etiological, topographical, and situational organizational schemes. The pros and cons of categorical versus dimensional methods of syndrome or case definition were reviewed, with emphasis on the importance of maintaining clinical relevance. The various types of diagnostic reliability and validity were presented together with a six-stage model for the validation of psychiatric diagnostic categories pertaining to children and adolescents, and practical and theoretical concerns regarding feasibility and coverage were discussed.

A review of multiaxial systems in general was undertaken prefatory to an examination of the major changes that have been instituted on each of the five axes in DSM-IV. Important revisions occurring in several major Axis I diagnostic categories of DSM-IV were detailed as they relate to the diagnosis of adolescents. Of ongoing interest to clinicians working with adolescents is a new category of personality change disorders that has been added to ICD-10 and only partially adopted in DSM-IV. With its proposed developmental perspective, this category offers a potential improvement in face, descriptive, and construct validity for the diagnosis of personality pathology in adolescents. By facilitating the formulation of therapeutic goals regarding personality pathology occurring prior to adulthood, as well as allowing for the monitoring of personality change over time, the category of personality change disorders could enhance both the coverage and feasibility of the current system of diagnostic classification of adolescent psychopathology. Only further empirical research can determine whether these preliminary opinions will be proven correct.

We believe that reliability and face validity together are not sufficient grounds to support the existence of a given diagnostic category. More empirical research is needed to establish the predictive and descriptive validity, as well as the construct validity, for each existing and newly proposed category. This is especially true in the case of disorders of childhood and adolescence, most particularly so where comorbidity exists with such Axis II conditions as mental retardation or personality disorder. The results of research should be used to support any future changes in the diagnostic categories, as well as the nature and structure of the axes themselves, in any systems of diagnostic classification that may succeed DSM-IV.

References

Achenbach, T. (1980). DSM-III in light of empirical research on the classification of child psychopathology. *Journal of the American Academy of Child & Adolescent Psychiatry, 19,* 395–412.

Achenbach, T., & Edelbrock, C. S. (1983). *Manual for Child Behavior Checklist and revised behavior profile.* Burlington: University of Vermont.

American Psychiatric Association. (1952). *Diagnostic and statistical manual of mental disorders* (1st ed.). Washington, DC: Author.

American Psychiatric Association. (1968). *Diagnostic and statistical manual of mental disorders* (2nd ed.). Washington, DC: Author.

American Psychiatric Association. (1980). *Diagnostic and statistical manual of mental disorders* (3rd ed.). Washington, DC: Author.

American Psychiatric Association. (1987). *Diagnostic and statistical manual of mental disorders* (rev. 3rd. ed.). Washington, DC: Author.

American Psychiatric Association. (1991). *DSM-IV options book.* Washington, DC: Author.

American Psychiatric Association. (1993). *DSM-IV draft criteria 3/1/93.* Washington DC: Author.

Beitchman, J. H. (1985). Childhood schizophrenia: A review and comparison with adult-onset schizophrenia. *Psychiatric Clinics of North America, 8,* 793–814.

Brockington, I. F., & Helzer, J. E. (1983). Future directions in research comparing diagnostic systems. In R. L. Spitzer, J. B. W. Williams, & A. E. Skodol (Eds.), *International perspectives on DSM-III* (pp. 327–336). Washington DC: American Psychiatric Press.

Budoff, M., & Siperstein, G. N. (1978). Low-income children's attitudes toward mentally retarded children: Effects of labeling and academic behavior. *American Journal of Mental Deficiency, 82,* 474–479.

Cantwell, D. P. (1975). A model for the investigation of psychiatric disorders of childhood: Its application in genetic studies of the hyperkinetic syndrome. In E. J. Anthony (Ed.), *Explorations in child psychiatry* (pp. 57–79). New York: Plenum.

Cantwell, D. P. (1987). Clinical child psychopathology: Diagnostic assessment, diagnostic process, and diagnostic classification DSM-III studies. In M. Rutter, A. H. Tuma, & I. Lann (Eds.), *Assessment and diagnoses in child psychopathology.* New York: Guilford.

Cantwell, D. P. (1988). Classification of childhood and adolescent disorders. In C. J. Kestenbaum & D. T. Williams (Eds.), *Clinical assessment of children and adolescents* (Vol. 1, pp. 3–18). New York: NYU Press.

Cantwell, D. P., & Baker, L. (1988). Issues in the classification of child and adolescent psychopathology. *Journal of the American Academy of Child and Adolescent Psychiatry, 27, 5,* 521–533.

Carlson, G. A., & Cantwell, D. P. (1980). Unmasking masked depression in children and adolescents. *American Journal of Psychiatry, 137,* 445–449.

Carlson, G. A., & Kashani, J. H. (1988). Phenomenology of major depression from childhood through adulthood: Analysis of three studies. *American Journal of Psychiatry, 145,* 1222–1225.

Carlson, G. A., & Strober, M. (1978). Manic depressive illness in early adolescence: A Study of clinical and diagnostic characteristics in six cases. *Journal of the American Academy of Child and Adolescent Psychiatry, 17,* 138–153.

Feighner, J. P., Robins, E., & Guze, S. B. (1972). Diagnostic criteria for use in psychiatric research. *Archives of General Psychiatry, 26,* 57–63.

Frances, A., & First, M. (1991, April 3). *Memorandum: Issues regarding the DSM-IV text.* Washington DC: American Psychiatric Association.

Freud, A. (1965). *Normality and pathology in childhood: Assessments of development.* New York: International Universities Press.

Goshen, C. E. (1967). *Documentary history of psychiatry.* New York: Philosophical Library.

Group for the Advancement of Psychiatry. (1966). *Psychopathological disorders in childhood: Theoretical considerations and a proposed classification.* New York: Author.

Group for the Advancement of Psychiatry. (1974). *Psychopathological disorders in childhood: Theoretical considerations and a proposed classification.* New York: Aronson.

Gull, W. W. (1874). Anorexia nervosa (apepsia hysterica, anorexia hysteria). *Transactions of the Clinical Society of London, 7,* 22–28.

Hunter, R., & Macalpine, I. (1982). *Three hundred years of psychiatry, 1535–1860.* Hartsdale, NY: Carlisle.

Katschnig, H., & Simhandl, C. (1986). New developments in the classification and diagnosis of functional mental disorders. *Psychopathology, 19,* 219–235.

Kraepelin, E. (1883, 1893, 1899, 1915). *Compendium dar Psychiatrie.* Leipzig: Abel.

Kraepelin, E. (1967). Lectures on clinical psychiatry: Dementia praecox (insanity of adolescence). In C. E. Goshen (Ed.), *Documentary history of psychiatry* (pp. 200–201). New York: Philosophical Library. (Original work published 1894).

Kydd, R. R., & Werry, J. S. (1982). Schizophrenia in children under 16 years. *Journal of Autism and Developmental Disorders, 12*, 343–357.

Lahey, B. B., Piacentini, J. C., McBurnett, K., Stone, P., Hartdagen, S., & Hynd, G. (1988). Psychopathology in the parents of children with conduct disorder and hyperactivity. *Journal of the American Academy of Child & Adolescent Psychiatry, 28*, 163–170.

Lahey, B. B., Schaughency, E. A., Frame, C. L., & Strauss, C. C. (1985). Teacher ratings of attention problems in children experimentally classified as exhibiting attention deficit disorders with and without hyperactivity. *Journal of the American Academy of Child & Adolescent Psychiatry, 24*, 613–616.

Lofgren, D. P., Bemporad, J., King, J., Lindem, K., & O'Driscoll, G. (1991). A prospective follow-up study of so-called borderline children. *American Journal of Psychiatry, 148*, 1541–1547.

Loranger, A., Hirschfeld, R. M. A., Sartorius, N., & Regier, D. A. (1994). *The International Personality Disorder Examination: A semistructured clinical interview for use with DSM-III-R and ICD-10 in different cultures.* Manuscript in preparation.

Mesco, R. H., & Cantwell, D. P. (1991). Risk factors outlined for antisocial behaviors in children with ADHD and conduct disorder. *Psychiatric Times, 8*, 34–35.

Mezzich, J. E. (1988). On developing a psychiatric multiaxial schema for ICD-10. *British Journal of Psychiatry, 152*(5, Suppl. 1), 38–43.

Mezzich, J. E., Coffman, G. A., & Goodpastor, S. M. (1982). A format for DSM-III diagnostic formulation: Experience with 1,111 consecutive patients. *American Journal of Psychiatry, 139*, 591–602.

Millon, T. (1983). The DSM-III: An insider's perspective. *American Psychologist, 38*, 804–814.

Myers, B. A. (1987). Psychiatric problems in adolescents with developmental disabilities. *Journal of the American Academy of Child and Adolescent Psychiatry, 26*, 74–79.

Orvaschel, H., & Weissman, M. (1986). Epidemiology of anxiety disorders in children: A review. In R. Gittelman (Ed.), *Anxiety disorders of childhood* (pp. 58–72). New York: Guilford.

Pfohl, B., & Andreasen, N. C. (1978). Development of classification systems in psychiatry. *Comprehensive Psychiatry, 19*, 197–207.

Robertson, G. M. (1919). Editor's preface. In E. Kraepelin, *Dementia praecox and paraphrenia* (8th ed., pp. i–ii). Edinburgh: E & S Livingstone.

Robins, E. (1976). Categories versus dimensions in psychiatric classification. *Psychiatric Annals, 6*, 39–55.

Robins, L. N. (1966). *Deviant children grown up.* Baltimore, MD: Williams & Wilkins.

Robins, L. N., Wing, J., Wittchen, H. U., Helzer, J. E., Babor, T. F., Burke, J., Farmer, A., Jablenski, A., Pickens, R., Regier, D. A., Sartorius, N., & Towle, L. (1988). The Composite International Diagnostic Interview: An epidemiologic instrument suitable for use in conjunction with different diagnostic systems and in different cultures. *Archives of General Psychiatry, 45*, 1069–1077.

Russel, A. T. (1987, June). *The mentally retarded and psychiatrically disturbed adolescent*. Paper presented to International Research Conference on Mental Health Aspects of Mental Retardation, Evanston, IL.

Rutter, M., & Gould, M. (1985). Classification. In M. Rutter & L. Hersov (Eds.), *Child and adolescent psychiatry: Modern approaches* (2nd ed., pp. 304–321). Boston: Blackwell Scientific.

Rutter, M., Tuma, A. H., & Lann, I. (Eds.). (1987). *Assessment and diagnoses in child psychopathology*. New York: Guilford.

Salzinger, K. (1986). Diagnosis: Distinguishing among behaviors. In T. Millon & G. L. Klerman (Eds.), *Contemporary directions in psychopathology: Toward the DSM-IV* (pp. 115–134). New York: Guilford.

Sartorius, N. (1989). Making of a common language for psychiatry: Development of the classification of mental, behavioural and developmental disorders in the 10th revision of the ICD. *World Psychiatry Association Bulletin, 1*, 3–6.

Sartorius, N., Jablensky, A., Cooper, J. E., Burke, J. D. (Eds.). (1988, May). Psychiatric classification in an international perspective. *British Journal of Psychiatry* (Suppl. 1), 152.

Shaffer, D., Campbell, M., Cantwell, D., Bradley, S., Carlson, G., Cohen, D., Denckla, M., Frances, A., Garfinkel, B., Klein, R., Pincus, H., Spitzer, R. L., Volkmar, F., & Widiger, T. (1989). Child and adolescent psychiatric disorders in DSM-IV: Issues facing the work group. *Journal of the American Academy of Child and Adolescent Psychiatry, 28*, 830–835.

Shaffer, D., Gould, M. S., Brasic, J., et al. (1983). Children's Global Assessment Scale (CGAS). *Archives of General Psychiatry, 40*, 1228–1231.

Spitzer, R. L., Endicott, J., & Robins, E. (1978). Research Diagnostic Criteria: Rationale and reliability. *Archives of General Psychiatry, 35*, 773–782.

Spitzer, R. L., & Williams, J. B. W. (1980). Classification of mental disorders and DSM-III. In H. Kaplan, A. M. Freedman, & B. J. Sadock (Eds.), *Comprehensive textbook of psychiatry* (Vol. 4, pp. 1035–1072). Baltimore, MD: Williams & Wilkins.

Spitzer, R. L., Williams, J. B. W., & Skodol, A. E. (Eds.). (1983). *International perspectives on DSM-III*. Washington DC: American Psychiatric Press.

Strober, M. (1984). Anorexia nervosa: History and psychological concepts. In K. D. Brownell & J. P. Foreyt (Eds.), *Handbook of eating disorders: Physiology, psychology, and treatment of obesity, anorexia, and bulimia* (pp. 231–246). New York: Basic Books.

Strober, M., & Carlson, G. A. (1982). Bipolar illness in adolescents with major depression: Clinical, genetic and psychopharmacological predictors in a three to four year prospective follow-up investigation. *Archives of General Psychiatry, 39*, 549–555.

Szasz, T. S. (1961). *The myth of mental illness*. New York: Harper & Row.

Weiner, I. B. (1982). *Child and adolescent psychopathology*. New York: Wiley.

Werry, J. S., McClellen, J. M., & Chard, L. (1991). Childhood and adolescent schizophrenic, bipolar, and schizoaffective disorders: A clinical and outcome study. *Journal of the American Academy of Child and Adolescent Psychiatry, 30*, 457–465.

Westen, D., Ludolph, P., Lerner, H., Ruffins, S., & Wiss, C. (1990). Object relations in borderline adolescents. *Journal of the American Academy of Child and Adolescent Psychiatry, 29,* 338–348.

Wing, J. K., Babor, T., Brugha, T., Burke, J., Cooper, J. E., Giel, R., Jablensky, A., Regier, D., & Sartorius, N. (1990). SCAN: Schedules for Clinical Assessment in Neuropsychiatry. *Archives of General Psychiatry, 47,* 589–593.

Wittchen, H. U., Robins, L. N., Cottler, L. B., Sartorius, N., Burke, J. D., & Regier, D. (1991). Cross-cultural feasibility, reliability and sources of variance of the Composite International Diagnostic Interview (CIDI). *British Journal of Psychiatry, 159,* 645–653.

World Health Organization. (1978). *The international classification of diseases, 9th revision.* Geneva, Switzerland: Author.

World Health Organization. (1991). *The international classification of diseases, 10th revision.* Geneva, Switzerland: Author.

Zietlin, H. (1983). *The natural history of psychiatric disorder in childhood.* London: University of London.

6
Clinical Interviewing

Eileen P. Ryan

> When students begin, they either suggest to the child all they hope to find, or they suggest nothing at all, because they are not on the lookout for anything, in which case, to be sure, they will never find anything.
>
> —Piaget, 1929

Novice clinicians (and those whose primary interview experience has been with adults or younger children) frequently approach their first adolescent interview with some anticipatory dread. Texts devoted to interviewing in both the child and adult fields may include a chapter on adolescents. However, the implication that a developmental "nip and tuck" is sufficient to skillfully adapt to the challenges of interviewing this group is hardly reassuring to the anxious clinician who may imagine adolescents to be harsher critics than either children or adults—ready to pounce on their fledgling efforts with indifference or surly contempt.

Until recently, the notion of adolescence as a tubulent, tumultuous period of emotional upheaval, in which a lack of regression was considered abnormal (Freud, 1952), was both influential and pervasive. Coleman (1961) described adolescents as "cut off" from the rest of society, "maintaining only a few threads of connection with the outside adult society." Feelings of misery, self depreciation, and ideas of reference or "inner turmoil" (Rutter, Graham, Chadwick, & Yule, 1976) are common during adolescence. Yet, whereas teenagers may have similar conflicts, the level of symptomatology differs greatly. Normal adolescents may experience subclinical or mild, transient symptoms, but do not suffer impaired functioning because of them. They do not begin to fail grades, withdraw from family and friends, or engage in illegal activities. Those adolescents who are symptomatic need to be taken very seriously by the clinical interviewer. Until recently, diagnostic "labeling" was avoided in child and adolescent psychiatry with the result that diagnoses such as "adjustment reaction" became meaningless and encompassed everything from mild, transient situational crises to incipient affective and psychotic disorders. Clearly, the needs of many adolescents were not being served.

The work of Offer and colleagues (Offer & Offer, 1975; Offer, Ostrov, & Howard, 1989) challenged the belief shared by a surprisingly large proportion of mental health professionals that normal adolescence is a necessarily tumultuous period with hostility toward parents and other authority figures. Their findings indicate that most adolescents are neither alienated nor anguished. Most (about 80%) are free of psychopathology and demonstrate good coping skills. For these adolescents, the transition into adulthood is relatively smooth. An inappropriately high threshold for diagnosing psychopathology in adolescents may rob seriously disturbed teens and their families of the opportunity to receive the benefits of early intervention and treatment. The differentiation between mild normative developmental "crises" and psychopathology requires continued study. However, it is apparent that we do not help adolescents and their families when we minimize or dismiss psychiatric symptomatology as part of a phase or something that the adolescent will "grow out of."

From the illness or disorder concept of psychopathology follows the premise that diagnosis is one of the primary goals of clinical assessment. The quality of the psychiatric assessment is a reflection of how skillfully and knowledgeably the clinician conducts the clinical interview. Acquiring and building on these skills is the subject of this chapter. Empathy (and the ability to convey it to the patient), sensitivity, tenacity, skepticism, and flexibility, a solid knowledge base in psychopathology and differential diagnosis, and an understanding of child and adolescent development and phenomenology all combine to distinguish skillful clinical interviewing from comprehensive questioning.

Overview of the Clinical Interview

There are eleven general "goals" to consider when performing a clinical interview:

1. Establish rapport with the adolescent and family.
2. Determine the most crucial question(s) or problem(s) to address during the evaluation (i.e., Is this adolescent psychotic, suicidal, and in need of hospitalization?). Others might include: (a) Can this adolescent return home with his or her parents? (b) Is there an organic component to this presentation? (c) What is the diagnosis (i.e., Bipolar Disorder versus Borderline Personality Disorder)? (d) Is the current school placement appropriate? (e) Should medication be considered (i.e., for an adolescent already in treatment)?

3. Establish an atmosphere in which the adolescent feels safe to discuss sensitive, sometimes painful material. The *experience* of the interview should encourage the liklihood of follow-up with treatment, if indicated.

4. Determine the "crisis" that precipitated evaluation. Often this crisis will differ from the chief complaint or presenting problem.

Consider a 17-year-old girl with a history of mood lability, self-mutilation, recurrent suicidal threats, impulsivity, and unstable and intense relationships, who carries a diagnosis of Borderline Personality Disorder. She presents to the emergency department with the complaint of "depression" and suicidal ideation. Skillful probing by the clinician reveals that several hours ago she called her mother at work. The adolescent wanted to talk about an incident at school that left her feeling somewhat anxious and uncertain. The secretary informed her that her mother was "unavailable" and would be busy for the remainder of the afternoon. If the clinician focuses exclusively on depression as a diagnostic entity, an important opportunity to address this girl's feelings of abandonment and focus her awareness on these feelings as well as her response to them will be missed.

5. Determine whether a psychiatric disorder (or combination of several disorders) exists. Is there sufficient disturbance in emotions, behavior, or cognition to cause dysfunction?

6. Determine whether the psychopathology meets criteria for a disorder (or several) as defined by an accepted classification system. DSM-IV became the official classification system in the United States in 1994. Some adolescents may have a psychiatric disorder which defies precise categorization. Others, although seriously impaired, may have symptoms which fall short of meeting the criteria required for diagnosis of a disorder. Diagnosis (even if only provisional) is a primary goal of clinical assessment. Symptoms overlap among disorders, and the presence or absence of various symptoms can greatly alter the treatments prescribed, and their efficacy, as well as prognosis. However, as Cantwell (1980) noted, DSM-IV is a book of disorders, not a book that describes children.

The ability to quickly tease out the most crucial elements for consideration during an evaluation is acquired through clinical experience. It is an especially essential skill in the emergency setting or in any clinical setting where the initial evaluation or interview may be constrained by limitations of time, privacy, space, lack of cooperative or knowledgable informants, or patient cooperation. It remains crucial to recognize, however, that a truncated evaluation should never be allowed to stand as the comprehensive psychiatric evaluation. At some point, a more thorough evaluation must be completed.

7. Consider the relative contribution of intrapsychic, biologic, familial, societal, and cultural factors in the genesis of the disorder(s). Most child and adolescent psychopathology is multi-determined.

8. Consider the intrapsychic, biologic, familial, societal, and cultural forces maintaining the current problems.

9. Consider the ameliorating forces (strengths) in the adolescent's life which promote healthy development.

10. Evaluate the role of organic factors in the adolescent's presentation. This is related to item number 6 above, but deserves special emphasis especially in new-onset psychiatric symptomatology and unusual exacerbations of more chronic disorders (i.e., visual hallucinations in an adolescent whose previous psychotic psychiatric episodes did not include visual hallucinations).

11. Develop an appropriate treatment plan with consideration given to the intrapsychic, biologic, familial, societal, and cultural aspects of the disorder, as well as the prognosis with and without treatment.

Confidentiality

Clinicians are frequently more preoccupied with confidentiality in the clinical interview than are adolescents. Adolescents (and younger children) present special problems regarding the issue of confidentiality. Unlike adults, they are legally minors. Also, most adolescents do not initiate mental health contact. They are referred by adults with whom they may have good, poor, or indifferent relationships, and sometimes are brought to the evaluation against their wishes.

During the interview, the clinician must be clear about the limits of confidentiality. The adolescent (and his or her parents) must be informed if the results of an evaluation (and/or a report) will be made known to a third party, such as a judge. Parents should be neither ignored nor treated as patients by the clinician. They have a right to be informed about impressions or diagnosis, treatment recommendations, and general prognosis with and without treatment (if such data are available). Keeping suicidal ideation or drug and alcohol abuse from parents for fear of breaching confidentiality is misguided and dangerous. Blanket promises of confidentiality at the initiation of an interview are rarely if ever successful at eliciting crucial information that would not have been revealed otherwise. Once false assurances are given, however, the sense of betrayal experienced by the adolescent when the clinician is forced to reveal suicidal behavior, sexual abuse, etc. may be immense. The clinician's ability to create an atmosphere of respect and trust is much more likely to encourage an ambivalent adolescent to share sensitive material during the clinical interview than any generic promises of secrecy.

Establishing Goals and Priorities

Ideally, the initial diagnostic assessment should be thorough and comprehensive and carried out over several sessions. The interviewer should obtain the adolescent's consent (and parents' consent when appropriate) to garner information from as many significant sources as are available and relevant (teachers, child welfare workers, guidance counselors, etc.). Other diagnostic modalities should be readily available and the results secured in a timely manner. However, failure to recognize and cope adaptively with less than ideal clinical situations may lead to woefully inadequate or even dangerous practices. Many clinicians are faced daily with the demands of the "intake" interview, in which a provisional diagnosis and treatment plan are expected after a 60- to 90- minute evaluation. The shortened time available for assessment makes the clinician's task more difficult; here interviewing skills assume even greater significance.

The clinician must have a very clear sense of what needs to be accomplished during the interview and how much time there is in which to accomplish it. Obviously, an adolescent who makes a suicidal statement and is brought to the emergency department by his anxious parents who found a suicide note is no less complex than the adolescent being evaluated for school refusal in a private practice setting. The initial interview for the first boy, however, will be largely shaped by the urgency of the primary goal, which is to evaluate lethality. Diagnostic assessment also will be an important component of the evaluation, as it frequently relates to suicidal risk and the level of treatment required. The adolescent with a substance abuse, psychotic, mixed state bipolar disorder, or severe depression or conduct disorder is at greater risk for completed suicide (Brent et al., 1989). And the presence diagnosis of any of these disorders in this boy is an indication for psychiatric hospitalization.

The clinician must be flexible and practical, yet capable of resisting inappropriate compromise. Emergency settings frequently strain the boundary between necessary efficiency and dangerous expediency. Clinicians must rapidly determine their role in the evaluation setting, establish a hierarchy with respect to the importance of what needs to be accomplished, and be firm about the limits of what they can and cannot do given the clinical situation. Consider the following example.

> Joe is a 15-year-old male brought to the busy emergency department (ED) of an over-burdened inner city hospital by his swimming coach secondary to the abrupt onset of bizarre behavior two days before. The team has been in town for several days for a championship swim meet which it lost; the team is due to return home in the morning. The boy's parents are 500 miles away. Joe is quite guarded and only barely cooperative and at times appears to be preoccupied. He terminated the interview with the ED physician after about five minutes, but the physician spoke with the coach for about 10 minutes. Vital signs are stable. The ED physician is pushing for involuntarily commitment to the psychiatric unit, having diagnosed a "schizophrenic break;" he wants Joe out of the emergency department as soon as possible; the ED physician's expects the psychiatric consultant to facilitate this admission. The coach wants to take Joe back to the hotel

now; they have been in the ED for over 6 hours. He describes Joe as always having been a "tense, high-strung kid" and believes that Joe is having a hard time dealing with the stress of losing the championship. He promises that Joe will be seen by a physician at home if he continues to have problems.

No clinician looks forward to negotiating the mine fields present in a case like this. The psychiatric consultant's first priority here is the *physical safety* of the adolescent and to determine what immediate action *must* be taken.

1. *Is further medical evaluation or intervention required?* It is absolutely crucial for the psychiatric consultant to be actively involved in the adolescent's overall evaluation. The more integrated the psychiatric consultant is into the evaluation team, the more respect accorded the consultant's recommendations. Flippant directives to complete a more extensive "medical" work-up prior to consultation are frequently perceived as avoidant and obstructionistic, especially if the psychiatric clinician has not yet evaluated the patient. In the case of Joe, however, even the scanty information available (new and abrupt onset of psychosis) raises suspicion of an organic etiology. Here the psychiatric consultant most appropriately considers at the outset conditions which if incorrectly diagnosed as a "schizophrenic break" could be life threatening (i.e., intoxication or withdrawal syndromes, intracerebral or intracranial pathology, metabolic disturbances, and infectious processes) and actively becomes involved with the evaluation team.

2. *Is constant observation required to prevent harm to self or others?* Delirious individuals are at risk for serious self injury. The waxing and waning nature of their confusion, disorientation, and perceptual abnormalities place these adolescents at risk for underestimation of and inattention to their capacity for impulsive suicidal behavior. A psychotic adolescent is incapable of making a valid no-suicide contract.

If immediate hospitalization is not necessary or indicated, are the adolescent's caretakers willing and able to provide constant supervision as well as detect and respond appropriately to changes in clinical status?

3. *Is the adolescent at risk for being prematurely removed from the evaluation setting by caretakers or running away?* A more systematic and thorough psychiatric evaluation should be conducted (or at the very least attempted) only after the adolescent's physical safety is assured.

Let us return to our consultant's dilemma. It is important to be open and forthright with adolescents and families (without causing undue alarm). In this particular case, the clinician's concerns about an organic etiology may dovetail with the adolescent's and coach's resistance to seeing

Joe's problems as "psychological." Deflecting the focus from "bizarre" behavior and shifting it to the more familiar and less stigmatizing arena of physical illness may help decrease this adolescent's anxiety and perhaps elicit his cooperation, however briefly, for additional assessment.

Clinician (after introduction): I understand that you have been here a long time, and have probably had it with people asking you questions. But I hope you'll let me talk with you for a little while. I'd like to explain why people like your coach, are worried about you, and what I'm most concerned about now.

Joe: (no response, but appears to be listening)

Clinician: From what I know, it seems like a couple of days ago you began to seem confused—not at all like yourself. That can be a pretty frightening experience (pause). What has it been like for you, Joe (very gently)?

Joe: (nods, eyes downcast) It's strange, like I'm not really me sometimes. I know something's different, but I'm not sure what.

Clinician: Um Hmm (nodding) What ideas have you had about what's different?

Joe: (says nothing; shakes head and shrugs)

Clinician: Joe, the fact that things seem to have happened so quickly makes it even more important that we make sure we're not overlooking something very basic and easy to treat, like an infection. Sometimes, confusion and feeling strange can have physical causes. So I'd like you to try and help me understand what's been happening over the past few days. Tell me when you first started to notice that things were different.

It is no easy task for the clinician to focus on the most essential areas without disengaging the adolescent. A brief cognitive screening exam, perhaps a Folstein Mini Mental State (Folstein, Folstein, & McHugh, 1975) is crucial to this particular evaluation. However, if approached prematurely, it may make a bad situation worse, especially if part of Joe's guardedness is an attempt to hide his cognitive deficits. The clinician may wish to lead into the cognitive exam more gradually.

Clinician: Tell me what else you remember about the headache, Joe.

Joe: I don't know, just that it was pretty bad.

Clinician: How long did it last?

Joe: I guess almost two days.

Clinician: I bet you felt pretty miserable. Did you notice any problem with your memory?

Joe: (suspiciously) How do you mean?

Clinician: Well, you know how it is when you're in a lot of pain; it can be really hard to concentrate on things—to pay attention and to remember the way you usually do. Was it that kind of a headache?

Joe: Oh, yeah . . . kind of.

Clinician: Tell me what that was like.

Joe: Well, my head just felt kind of messed up like after a hangover only I wasn't drinking or doing any drugs. That's what really makes me mad about the coach and everybody; they . . . (trails off).

Clinician: Go on (nodding).

Joe: Forget it (grins).

At this point the clinician has a choice. The grinning, clearly inappropriate given the situation, should clue the clinician to the possible presence of psychotic symptomatology (hallucinatory phenomena, bizarre thoughts, delusional ideation, etc). The interviewer may choose to pursue this lead and ask "What are you thinking now?" which may be perceived as less judgmental than "Why are you smiling?" "Why" questions frequently convey a more critical attitude, especially to the suspicious or paranoid patient; they imply that the adolescent should know and be able to articulate the "correct" answer. If Joe requires further clarification, the clinician can calmly state, perhaps also smiling gently, that he or she noticed a smile and wondered what he was thinking about. This is a rather innocuous, benign query, and further evasiveness on Joe's part may be an additional indication of aberrant thought process. The clinician may also choose to continue with the cognitive examination, which was the initial reason for bringing up memory problems in the first place. Clinicians sometimes find the cognitive examination awkward and disengaging, but it need not be. The clinician should be matter-of-fact about its inclusion and not at all apologetic (i.e., "Joe I'm going to ask you some attention and memory questions now" or "Earlier you mentioned having trouble concentrating in school. Have you noticed any problems with your memory?"). Some readers may be surprised by the notion of routinely considering a cognitive examination with adolescents. Remember that one of the principal advantages of the clinical interview is that it allows for the flexibility to follow the adolescent's lead, advancing or retreating as clinically appropriate. For example, it is not necessary to check the orientation of an adolescent who after 30 minutes of interviewing is clearly in good contact. However, a check of memory, concentration, and attention, revealing subtle cognitive abnormalities in an uncooperative adolescent, might be one more reason to seriously consider that drug use or some other organic process is involved in the clinical picture. Also, observing the response to the challenge of a cognitive examination may provide a useful look into how problems are solved and challenges met or dealt with in other areas of the adolescent's life.

With an uncooperative, witholding individual, closed-ended questions (questions which lend themselves to a brief one- or two-word answer) usually compound the problem by encouraging or reinforcing minimum spontaneity. Examples of closed ended questions include: "What medications are you taking?" "Are you feeling depressed?" and "Do you think you and your friend will be able to work this out?" The clinician in the above situation, however, must carefully consider the need to obtain specific information (about Joe's headache for example). The adolescent's ability to tolerate the interview must also be weighed. In this interview, closed-ended questions can be carefully juxtaposed with commands ("Tell me about . . .") and open-ended questions ("What ideas have you had?") in order to avoid a rigid question-answer format. Open-ended questions are more difficult to answer with a one- or two-word or "yes" or "no" response. Other examples of open-ended questions include: "How will you cope with this?" "What are some of your thoughts about this situation at school?" and "What are your plans after leaving school?" Empathic statements and maneuvers should be used liberally. Psychosis is an extremely painful state for any individual. Frequently, especially in the early stages of psychotic process, adolescents and adults are exquisitely aware of how different their reality has become from that of others—how alone they really are. Keeping empathic statements brief and avoiding interpretive elements is advised for psychotic patients, especially paranoid individuals. The clinician's ability to covey to the adolescent that others have experienced similar problems and that the clinician is comfortable with the discussion can be a powerful interviewing tool.

Conduct of the Clinical Diagnostic Interview

Introduction

An adolescent psychiatric evaluation should include interviews with the adolescent alone as well as the parents without the child present. It is often invaluable to meet briefly with the family (including the adolescent) at the outset. Rigid "rules" regarding who should be seen first are seldom useful. The clinician must be flexible, but should have a "usual" manner of conducting the evaluation and be ready to deviate from usual procedure as the clinical situation warrants. If the referral source is someone other than a parent, information should be obtained directly from that source also.

A brief initial meeting with the family (including the adolescent) may be useful in a variety of ways:

1. Conflicting agendas and goals among family members may become obvious, and the clinician is quickly alerted to them.

2. Blatant hostility and resistance on the part of either the parents or the adolescent (e.g., in court-ordered evaluations) may dictate a change in the clinician's usual approach.

3. Family interactions can be observed. Alliances and tensions between and among family members may be detected even in brief encounters. The clinician may have the opportunity to observe some of the genuine warmth and concern that binds the family together as well as some of the devisive factors (i.e., minimizing drug or alcohol abuse) perhaps contributing to the adolescent's problem.

4. Erroneous information and fantasies may become apparent and can be corrected immediately. An adolescent threatened with hospitalization may be relieved to hear the clinician directly address this issue in front of his or her parents.

5. The clinician can begin to establish rapport. Warmth, empathy, and genuineness conveyed early to the family as a group can set the tone for the entire assessment. It may also help to allay fears that the clinician will be "taking sides."

It has been generally advised that the adolescent be interviewed individually prior to meeting alone with the parents. The basis for interviewing the adolescent first is to convey that the adolescent's concerns are being taken seriously (Rutter & Cox, 1981). Although no systematic study with adolescents has been undertaken, it has been demonstrated that teachers can be biased by prior information regarding students even when it conflicts with their own experience of the children (Foster, Ysseldyke, & Reese, 1975). Clinicians should be aware of the potential negative effects of bias on the interview, but not allow these concerns to rigidly dictate their clinical practice.

Adolescent Interview

Opening phase. From the moment of introduction, the adolescent begins to evaluate the clinician—Is the clinician "okay" to talk to? Can I trust this person? The first five to 10 minutes of the interview are often crucial to this process, and the adolescent's first impressions can "make or break" the interview. During the first five to 10 minutes, the adolescent is encouraged to describe his or her perception of the reason(s) for evaluation with minimal interruption. Open-ended questions, empathic maneuvers (i.e., "Uh-huh," "Go on," head nodding, facial expressions), and empathic statements (i.e., "It sounds like things have been very difficult for you lately" or "It must be very hard to have so much responsibility when you've been feeling so depressed") are the mainstays of the clinician's participation during this phase. Clinicians should particularly avoid prematurely structuring or focusing of the adolescent during these first five to 10 minutes. There will be opportunities later in the interview for obtaining more specific information; however, premature structuring may compromise the objectives of this early phase of the interview. Those objectives include:

1. Decreasing the adolescent's anxiety.
2. Providing the adolescent the opportunity to describe the reasons for evaluation from his or her own perspective.
3. Gaining valuable mental status information which will assist the clinician to focus more effectively later on in the interview.
4. Developing a sense of the process of the interview itself. Does the adolescent seem guarded, anxious, or bored? Is the adolescent relatively easy or difficult to engage? Is the adolescent loquacious and circumstantial or hostile and/or evasive, providing brief, minimal responses. An early sense of potential problems in the interview enables the clinician to better adapt his or her technique to the needs of the adolescent. For example, if a hostile, uncooperative adolescent is brought involuntarily for an evaluation, the clinician will want to utilize more open-ended questions and commands. The pressured, hypomanic adolescent will probably require a higher ratio of closed-ended questions and more structure after the opening phase.
5. Developing an early awareness of concerns and goals of which the adolescent may be only minimally aware. For example, an adolescent experiencing panic attacks may ostensibly present for treatment, but may also want reassurance that she is not "crazy." This concern may begin to reveal itself in the adolescent's brief, seemingly unrelated reference within the first 10 minutes of the interview to an aunt who has spent the last 30 years in a state hospital.

Presenting problem. After the opening phase, the clinician and adolescent move into the body of the diagnostic interview, where the history of the presenting problem is clarified in detail. Information must be sensitively obtained about the chronology, type, characteristics, and severity of symptoms and their impact on functioning (including relationships, school, employment, and leisure activities). In this phase of the interview, active exporation is necessary, but must be skillfully combined with empathic listening.

The interviewer must accomplish much more than provide the adolescent with a willing "ear" or a "chat." Herein lies the challenge of clinical interviewing—to reconcile an inquiring mind, thoroughness, and tenacity with warmth, empathy, and flexibility. The clinician must thoroughly investigate the presence (and absence) of psychopathology and skillfully elicit detailed information concerning the nature of the psychopathology present, while never losing an appreciation for the adolescent as a person, an individual with hopes, dreams, ambitions, fears, and hurts, not just a "case" or a collection of disorders. One of the major advantages offered by the clinical interview is its flexibility, enabling the skillful interviewer and astute clinician to tailor questions to the specific situation of the individual adolescent. For example, consider the adolescent referred for evaluation of fighting, failing grades, and several school suspensions of recent onset, who mentions during the opening phase that he is frequently in a "bad mood." In the body of the interview, the clinician will want to more actively investigate the presence of depression.

> Clinician: Earlier you mentioned frequently being in a bad mood. Tell me more about that.
>
> Adolescent: I don't know; I guess I've been feeling pretty depressed.
>
> Clinician: Well, depression is different for everyone who experiences it. Tell me how it's affected you.
>
> Adolescent: I feel pretty awful all the time; I don't feel like doing anything except sitting around watching MTV. I can't stand it anymore.

Here the clinician was rewarded with a response which suggests that this adolescent may be experiencing anergia and/or anhedonia, two cardinal symptoms of a major depressive disorder. Also the statement "I can't stand it anymore" should immediately alert the clinician to the possible presence of severe hopelessness and despair. Hopelessness is a crucial area to explore, as completed suicide may be more closely related to the level of hopelessness than to the severity of depressed mood (Pfeffer, 1989). The clinician may wish to immediately follow up on this clue and begin to explore hopelessness, and from there gently move into the region of suicidality. Another clinician may choose to collect information about the presence of additional depressive symptoms (e.g., sleep and appetite disturbances, weight change, decreased concentration) before returning to the areas of hopelessness and lethality.

Sometimes novice clinicians worry that an active interview style is incompatible with empathic listening—that somehow the interview is compromised or distorted when information is actively elicited. Nothing could be further from the truth. Familiarity with psychopathology, diagnostic classification, child and adolescent development, and phenomenology enables the clinician to listen with a discriminating ear and structure the interview sensitively and skillfully. The ultimate interview "skill" is the ability to negotiate the delicate balance between collecting data and engaging the patient in a therapeutic alliance. Shea (1988) defines the engagement process as those "verbal and nonverbal behaviors demonstrated by the interviewer that create an atmosphere of increasing trust, safety, and calmness in the interviewee." A stiff, formal quality, as though the clinician is running down a checklist of "items" is present in the following (about 10 minutes into the interview):

Adolescent: I've been really down lately.

Clinician: How's your appetite?

Adolescent: Okay

Clinician: Sleep?

Adolescent: Alright.

Clinician: Any problems with concentration?

Adolescent: Not really.

Clinician: Have you thought about suicide?

Adolescent: Nope.

The dialogue above conveys little more intimacy or shared purpose than a shopping mall survey. The clinician is clearly *conducting* an interview; the adolescent has little control, and there is no real sense of shared purpose. The validity of sensitive information (i.e., about drug and alcohol use, lethality, psychotic process) obtained in such a manner is of course highly questionable.

Contrast such rigid structuring with the following dialogue in which the clinician manages to elicit information about mood, social withdrawal, anhedonia, suicidal ideation, and possible excessive guilt and feelings of worthlessness without adhering to a rigid question and answer format.

Adolescent: My parents think I'm depressed. Maybe they're right.

Clinician: How do you see it?

Adolescent: I'm bored; I'm sick and tired of everything.

Clinician: Um hmm (nodding) Go on.

Adolescent: That's all there is to it. I'm bored.

Clinician: In what ways has the boredom changed things in your life?

Adolescent: Well, I'm really not into being with people anymore. My friends gave up on me a while ago; I guess I was boring them as much as they were boring me.

Clinician: Uh-huh. Did you notice they were getting on your nerves a lot more than usual?

Adolescent: Oh yeah. Little stuff like my girlfriend wanted to go to some stupid movie I didn't want to see, and I just flipped out on her.

Clinician: Flipped out?

Adolescent: Yelling, screaming; I called her an idiot. That's about it. Worst mistake I ever made; she broke up with me, said she'd had enough.

Clinician: Sounds like that's been hard on you.

Adolescent: Nods.

Clinician: When you were still seeing Julie, did you enjoy being with her as much as you used to.

Adolescent: I guess so.

Clinician: Often when people are feeling as badly as you've been feeling, they notice that they just don't get the same enjoyment out of life that they used to. For example, a guy may notice that he's not as interested in girls as he use to be.

Adolescent: Well, lately I stopped calling Julie anymore; I guess I just didn't care anymore, except I wasn't interested in anyone else either. Everything seems like just too much effort.

Clinician: What else did you lose interest in?

Adolescent: Shrugs.

Clinician: What about school work. You used to make good grades. During the last reporting period you got 2 Ds.

Adolescent: Yeah, well like I said, I've got other things on my mind when I'm in class.

Clinician: What kinds of things do you find yourself thinking about in class?

Adolescent: Mostly about Julie and how I've screwed everything up, how I'm a loser.

Clinician: Do you ever feel so down on yourself that you wish you were dead?

Adolescent: Nods.

Clinician: What thoughts have you had?

Psychiatric symptom inventory. Another very important aspect of the clinical interview is the psychiatric review of symptoms, or symptom inventory. Through the skillful use of probe questions (Roberts, 1984; Shea, 1988), the interviewer explores the presence of current and past symptomatology associated with broad areas of psychopathology (i.e., depression, psychosis, anxiety). Depending on the adolescent's response to the probe questions, the interviewer may explore further or move on. The following dialogue illustrates routine probing for psychotic symptoms in an adolescent girl who thus far in the interview has not aroused any suspicion for the presence of psychotic thinking.

> Clinician: Sometimes when people are feeling as depressed as you've been over the past few months, they begin to notice unusual thoughts or feelings. Has that happened to you?
>
> Jean: No, not really (hesitantly).
>
> Clinician: What thoughts have you had?
>
> Jean: Well, just thinking that I'm no good at anything, that I ruin everything.
>
> Clinician: Have those thoughts ever seemed so intense that they were almost like voices?
>
> Jean: No (shaking her head), never anything like that.
>
> Clinician: You mentioned thinking that you're not good at anything, that you ruin everything. Do you ever think that anyone is purposely trying to trick you up or hurt you?
>
> Jean: No. My friends really try to help; even my brother has been nice to me. It only makes me feel worse—more guilty about ruining everything.

Answers such as "not really," hesitancy, nonverbal behaviors such as nervous mannerisms (biting lips, picking at fingers) or a change in the level or intensity of eye contact, may clue the clinician into the need for further exploration and follow-up probe questions.

The review of symptoms should include queries about affective symptoms (including hypomania which is too frequently not well explored even in adolescents who clearly meet, or have met in the past, criteria for a major depression), suicidal behavior, psychotic symptoms, dissociative symptoms, anxiety disorder (including obsessive-compulsive) symptoms, drug and alcohol use (past and current), eating disorder symptoms, and conduct and attentional problems (including a history of aggression). Pathologic personality traits may be more easily explored when discussing the quality of present and past relationships with individual family members and friends.

The presence of psychopathology must be sought before it can be eliminated. Neglecting to directly question an adolescent about suicidal thoughts, psychotic symptomatology, or obsessive-compulsive thoughts and behaviors is as dangerous and ludicrous as overlooking auscultation of the heart during a physical examination because the patient does not "look sick."

The pertinent details of any previous psychiatric or psychologic evaluations (diagnosis or impressions, recommendations, follow-up) and treatment obtained (type of therapy or medication, duration, success) for the current problem or past difficulties should also be elicited. Clinical sophistication is invaluable in sifting through confusing and complicated information. For example, the more knowledgeable the clinician is regarding behavior therapy, the more capable he or she is of determining whether an appropriate program was designed and whether it was implemented properly. Was a previous trial of antidepressant medication conducted with an adequate dose, monitored with serum levels, and continued for a sufficient period of time?

Social and developmental history. The quantity of social and developmental history obtained must be tailored to the specific adolescent and clinical situation. The quality of information obtained is a function of the skill and knowledge of the interviewer. There is no formula for what to include and what to explore in some detail, any more than there is a set method for predicting what historical incidents will be crucially significant for one adolescent yet much less so for another. Much of the early history will be best provided by the parents. Areas to consider include:

1. Pregnancy and birth (including any prescription medications as well as illicit drugs and alcohol consumed during pregnancy).

2. Infancy, toddler, preschool, school-age, and adolescent development thus far with specific inquiries made about losses, separations (including hospitalizations of caretakers or child) and accidents. The specific ages at which developmental milestones (crawling, walking, talking) were achieved might be useful to obtain if developmental delays or cognitive deficits are present or part of the differential diagnosis. In such cases, however, far more specific information (i.e., additional birth, pregnancy, and medical history for example) will be necessary.

3. Educational history may include information pertaining to the number of schools attended. Have frequent moves affected the adolescent's ability to perform academically and socially? Special classroom placement should specifically receive attention (when it occurred and for what reasons), as well as psychoeducational testing (dates and results); grades (generally), especially in light of any recent changes; and any information available on his or her relationships with teachers and coaches.

4. The interviewer should attempt to get some sense of the quality of the adolescent's relationships with family members and friends. Does the adolescent maintain close, healthy relationships with same age peers or are the relationships with much older or younger children, intense, volatile, and/or short-lived? Are the "friendships" no more than superficial acquain-

tanceships? The quality of the adolescent's relationships with nonfamilial adults should be explored as indicated by the clinical situation (teachers, coaches, friends, parents).

5. The area of sexual history, including the age of onset of sexual activity and current sexual activity, can be disengaging if not approached sensitively. An emergency clinical interview may not be the appropriate forum to explore the sexual history, but there should be a legitimate clinical reason for omitting attention to this area (i.e., a trade-off in order to explore a more urgent region in depth like psychosis, lethality, or drug and alcohol use) rather than the clinician's discomfort with this material. For sexually active adolescents, specific questions sensitively posed about the use of birth control as well as knowledge of AIDS and "safe sex" practices are also important. Sexual abuse should be approached by the interviewer in all but the most emergent clinical evaluations; like most other crucial regions of exploration it can be entered with a sensitive probe question (i.e., "Have you ever been touched in a private way that made you uncomfortable"?). If the clinician suspects familial or extrafamilial sexual abuse, especially currently, more tenacity may be required. The creation of a safe, calm, sensitive interview environment can encourage an ambivalent adolescent to reveal sensitive and painful information. Respect for the adolescent is conveyed throughout the interview by a nonjudgmental approach as well as the expression of genuine interest in what the adolescent is experiencing and has to say. Note taking, a frequent displacement activity of nervous novice clinicians can quickly develop into a bad habit unless actively curbed early on in a clinician's interviewing training. Most of the clinical interview can and should be conducted without any note taking, and most clinicians will find that with discipline they are able to recall almost all the important specifics relayed to them by the patient. Some notes may be necessary in order to recall dates of outpatient treatment or hospitalizations, or for medications and their doses. Addressing the purpose of notes can prevent misunderstanding and disengagement (i.e., "I'm going to jot down a few notes during this part so I'm sure I don't get these dates confused," or with a guarded patient, "Taking a few notes here will help me keep the dosage changes on your medication straight; is that okay with you?"). As a general rule, notes taken during the interview should be kept to a minimum with all patients, and the clinician should *never* take notes while exploring sensitive areas such as lethality.

6. Information concerning plans including higher education, marriage, career, and family and more importantly, how the adolescent is coping with such pressures, choices, and demands provides a window into negotiating one of the major developmental tasks of adolescence—identity formation. Identity formation begins long before puberty, but by the end of adolescence, most young people are faced with choices and decisions

which will affect the rest of their lives (college, political philosophy, religious affiliation, etc.).

Family history. The family psychiatric history goes well beyond asking the standard question about family members with emotional problems. Terms such as "emotional problems," "psychological problems," and "psychiatric disorders" may have different meanings for adolescents and their families. Adolescents and their parents should specifically be asked about a family history of depression, anxiety, "nervous conditions," and unusual behavior or thinking. Vague terms such as "nervous breakdown" and "nerves" should also be clarified with specific inquires as to the affected relative's *behavior* when ill, which can then further direct the interviewer's questioning. "Nervous breakdown" is a euphemism for many disorders including character pathology, anxiety disorders, major affective disorders with and without psychosis, and schizophrenia. A family history of compulsive behavior may be discovered by asking about any relative who never left the house or was frequently washing his or her hands. Such probes may seem rather heavy handed, but touch on several common psychiatric disorders and syndromes and can be useful in jarring the memory of a patient about a family member whose behavior or "moods" were considered different but not perceived as indicative of psychiatric illness.

Specific inquiries as to a family history of learning disabilities, attention deficit disorder, and drug and alcohol abuse are indicated, especially if the adolescent's presentation or history seems related. A family drug and alcohol history is crucial, and the clinician should consider the possibility of a missed psychiatric disorder in those relatives.

Medical history and medical review of symptoms. The medical history and review of symptoms is another crucial aspect of the initial diagnostic interview. Inattention or neglect of psychotic symptoms in a patient with major depression may have grave consequences. Similarly, failure to distinguish depression from the "quiet" delirium of a smoldering encephalitis or metabolic disturbance or from the incipient subtle dementia of an adolescent infected with HIV may have fatal consequences. The ability to obtain a medical history and review of symptoms and, more significantly, integrate that information knowledgeably requires extensive training and experience.

Allergies as well as negative drug reactions (e.g., dystonia, excessive sedation) should be routinely elicited. In addition to providing clinically relevant information, attention to the adolescent's previous experiences with psychotropic medication indicates that his or her preferences and concerns are being taken seriously and increases the adolescent's sense of autonomy and control. The adolescent (and parents if appropriate) should be questioned about the recent use of all prescription medications as well as over-the-counter remedies (including excessive ingestion of vitamins, herbs, and "health foods"). Almost all medications can have side effects affecting mood, cognition, and behavior. Interviewing about contraception and safe sex practices as well as other information about sexuality in general may more naturally flow from other questions asked or information obtained during the medical history portion of the interview.

Mental status examination. Many elements of the mental status examination are evaluated during the exploration of diagnostic regions while inquiring into the present problem and performing a psychiatric symptom inventory. There are few, if any, aspects of the mental status examination which cannot be smoothly blended into the body of the clinical interview.

The mental status examination is analogous to the physical examination in other branches of medicine and is deserving of a much more extensive treatment than it will be given here. The clinician arrives at the diagnostic formulation by considering the signs and symptoms observed and elicited in the mental status examination in combination with the information obtained from the psychiatric history and review of symptoms, medical history and review of symptoms, and pertinent social/developmental and family history.

Precision in the use of clinical terms to describe psychiatric phenomena is as essential in psychiatry as in any other branch of medicine. Even the most skillful interviewer will be hampered by an inability to describe and communicate the findings elicited during the clinical interview. Signs refer to what is *observed* by the clinician during the evaluation. Symptoms are directly elicited by the interviewer and are "subjective," in that they are based on the patients report. For example, psychomotor retardation is a sign and must be *observed* in order to be documented as present; auditory hallucinations is a symptom based on the patient's report. The mental status examination is described briefly below. An excellent detailed description of the mental status examination is provided by Akiskal (1986).

I. Appearance, attitude, and behavior

A. *general physical appearance* (hygiene, dress, grooming, posture, appear stated age?)

B. *appropriateness of behavior* (overly familiar, intrusive, childish)

C. *facial expression* (placid, vacant, bewildered, apprehensive, eager, sad, annoyed, bored, surly, pleasant, smiling)

D. *adolescent's reaction to the interviewer and evaluation* (cooperative, ingratiating, friendly, hostile, evasive, courteous, overeager, sullen, guarded, suspicious)

E. *motor activity* (hyperactivity, agitation, retardation, restlessness, stereotypies)

F. *mannerisms*

G. *tics* (describe as accurately as possible)

II. Speech includes consideration of the following:

A. *spontaneity*

B. *fluency*

C. *prosody* (the natural music of speech). Gross abnormalities may be picked up by asking the patient to repeat the phrase "no ifs, ands, or buts."

D. *articulation*

E. *"rate"* (halting, slow, rapid, pressured, difficult to interrupt or redirect)

F. Also note the presence of telegraphic speech, perserveration, word approximation, mutism, echolalia (repeating of the examiner's words, often the last word or two spoken by the examiner), and neologisms (words invented by the individual, often with idiosyncratic meanings).

III. Affect and mood. Affect refers to the outward manifestation of mood. Mood refers to the pervasive emotion or feeling state which in the extreme markedly affects an individual's perception of the world. An adolescent may describe his or her mood as "okay," "bored," or even "happy" while presenting a depressed affect to the examiner. Such incongruity should be noted. Affect is inferred from what is said as well as from what is observed during the interview. The interviewer's empathic response may also provide valuable clues. While interviewing a profoundly depressed individual, it is not infrequent for the clinician to notice that he or she "feels depressed." The appropriateness of affect, range of emotional expression, and lability of affect should be noted. Do affective changes occur in response to minor or major shifts in content? Do they seem to take place without any stimulus? The clinician should note pervasive elation, undue optimism, euphoria, pessimism or hopelessness, depression, or anxiety. Euthymia refers to the absence of a disturbance in mood or affect.

IV. Thought process. Thought process refers to the *form* of thought, which is *observed* by the examiner as the individual speaks. The following may be included in a description of the adolescent's thought process:

A. productivity and spontaneity

B. coherence and continuity of thought

C. ability to reach goal ideas (Is circumstantiality or tangentiality present?)

D. relevance of productions

E. character of associations (looseness of associations)

F. thought blocking

V. Thought content includes:

A. areas of preoccupation. Open-ended queries such as "What's been on your mind lately" can be helpful.

B. obsessions

C. fears and phobias

D. overvalued ideas (steadfastly maintained notions; for example, the superiority of one race over another)

E. ideas of reference (idea that one is being talked about or laughed at; in the extreme may become delusions of reference)

F. delusional ideation and type (paranoid, somatic, erotic, hypochondrical, persecutory, jealous, worthlessness, guilt)

G. thought insertion, broadcasting, withdrawal (also known as delusions of control or influence)

H. suicidal and homicidal ideation

Probably nowhere else in the clinical interview is the clinician's sensitivity, skill, and knowledge called more into play than in the evaluation of lethality. Suicidality should *always* be explored during the clinical interview. A thorough knowledge of risk factors associated with suicidal behavior and completed suicide is essential for the clinician interviewing adolescents, but is beyond the scope of this chapter. The reader is referred to an excellent review of child and adolescent suicidality by Brent and Kolko (1990) as well as to Shea's (1988) description of the lethality interview.

There is a spectrum of suicidal ideation from nonspecific thoughts ("I wish I was dead") to specific thoughts with a concrete plan to actual suicidal behavior. During questioning about suicidal behavior, the interviewer should move from general to more specific questions, especially if the answers to the general questions are positive.

Clinician: Given how depressed you've been, how worthless everything seems, have you ever had the thought that life isn't worth living?

Adolescent: A couple of times.

Clinician: Tell me about those thoughts.

Adolescent: I've thought that my parents would be better off without me. They'd be sad for a while, but I actually think they'd be a lot better off.

Clinician: If things really get unbearable, what plans do you have to end the pain?

Adolescent: I'd use a gun. I want it to be over quick, and I wouldn't want to make any mistakes.

Clinician: Do you have access to a gun?

Adolescent: My dad has guns, but they're locked in the gun cabinet.

Clinician: (very gently) How close have you actually come to doing something to kill yourself?

In the above dialogue, the clinician smoothly led the adolescent from a discussion of depression into the lethality evaluation, a natural progression, and very deliberately yet sensitively began to clarify the extent of this adolescent's serious suicidal ideation and risk.

VI. Perceptual experiences

A. The presence of *hallucinations* is always examined. *Auditory* hallucinations may command the patient to perform various acts (including self-injurious, suicidal, or homicidal behavior), discuss the individual in the third person, repeat his or her thoughts aloud, and/or comment on the individual's thoughts and behaviors. *Visual* hallucinations should always raise the examiner's suspicion that an organic process is involved especially if the adolescent has never had visual hallucinations before. *Tactile* and *olfactory* hallucinations also deserve additional attention. Olfactory hallucinations may be difficult to distinguish from delusional ideation in severe depression (i.e., the adolescent who is severely depressed with low self-esteem and is convinced she has bad breath and who misinterprets peers neutral facial expressions as indications of disgust). *Hypnagogic and hypnopompic* hallucinations occur in the twilight period just prior to falling asleep and waking up, respectively. They can occur in normal individuals and must be differentiated from true hallucinations.

B. An *illusion* is a misinterpretation of a real stimulus (i.e., curtains misinterpreted as an intruder climbing into the room).

C. *Depersonalization* is a feeling of unreality or strangeness. An "as if" quality is present; the adolescent feels "as if" he or she is changed in some way. *Derealization* usually refers to feelings that the environment has changed.

D. *Passivity experiences* are Schneiderian first rank symptoms and include made feelings, impulses, or acts inflicted on the passive, often unwilling individual by an outside force. The patient experiences a loss of control and is unable to resist these experiences.

VII. Orientation (person, place, situation, time). If the adolescent is oriented to all four, he or she is described as having a clear sensorium.

VIII. Concentration, attention, and memory

A. recalling four digits forward and backward (attention and concentration)

B. serial sevens—counting back from 100 by seven (attention and concentration)

C. recall of three objects immediately and after five minutes (immediate and short term memory)

Although not specifically studied in this population, the Folstein Mini Mental State is an excellent cognitive screening examination. In adolescents, it may alert the clinician to the presence of a subtle or early delirium especially if those questions testing short-term memory, attention, and concentration are asked several times over the course of an evaluation.

IX. Intelligence (abstraction abilities, vocabulary, general knowledge)

X. Judgment and insight. The history will generally provide information as to whether or not the adolescent demonstrates good or poor judgment. How the adolescent behaves in troublesome situations has been traditionally tested by asking what one would do if the first to observe smoke in a crowded theater. More complex problem-solving abilities may be observed by asking what the adolescent would do if a good friend confided that he was planning suicide. *Insight* refers to the adolescent's awareness of his or her emotional state. In the presence of a psychiatric illness or disorder, is the adolescent aware of its severity and impact on significant others and on important areas of functioning?

Parent Interview

The actual content of the parent/caretaker interview is dictated by the needs of the adolescent and the clinical situation at hand. A family assessment can elucidate interactions among individual family members. The parents should be questioned specifically about the presence or absence of psychiatric signs and symptoms, allowing the review to be guided to some extent by what the clinician already knows and suspects to be of importance. There are generally low levels of concordance between parent and adolescent agreement on the presence of affective symptomatology (Moretti, Fine, Haley, & Marriage, 1975). Parents are frequently unaware of the extent of their child's depression and suicidal ideation, but may be better able than the adolescent to describe the outward (behavioral) manifestations and effects of depression. Neither the parents' failure to note indicators of affective illness or suicidality, nor the adolescent's denial of them are grounds for dismissal of their presence.

Strengths and weaknesses of the family as a unit and as individuals are important to consider. For example, parents may be genuinely invested in their adolescent child's welfare but be completely unable to set limits and provide supervision. The clinician's recognition of this will impact significantly on treatment recommendations. Specific information on how the family has coped with stresses in the past as well as their present coping skills should be obtained.

The parents relationship with the child should be explored, particularly for the presence of genuine concern and empathy. The clinician must be aware of countertransference, and how lack of recognition of the strong emotions that disturbed adolescents and their families engender can undermine the clinician's work and ability to be of help. Frequently parents are angry, confused, and frightened by the time psychiatric evaluation is sought. They may present as furious with the adolescent and appear hostile and negative, or seem apathetic and uninvolved. The clinician must probe beneath the surface and consider that such behavior and emotions may well be a coping mechanism which has, however maladaptively, enabled the parents (and adolescent) to survive in a chaotic environment. Empathy with the adolescent's caretakers and the ability to convey it genuinely without risking confidentiality or alienating the adolescent is a necessary skill for every clinician working with this age group.

Summary

This chapter reviews the basic components of the clinical diagnostic interview, with an emphasis on the brief intake assessment—the 60- to 90-minute intake evaluation, after which provisional diagnosis and initial treatment plan are expected. Skillful technique is important, but a sound knowledge of child and adolescent development and psychopathology is equally essential.

Performing clinical interviews with the supervision of an experienced supervisor who has the opportunity to observe the clinician "in action" (directly or by one-way mirror or videotapes) is one of the best ways to develop and build on interviewing skills. Clinicians should attempt to interview as many adolescents as possible (younger, middle, and older adolescents, as well as "normals") in order to gain an appreciation of the variability in the presentations of both healthy and disturbed adolescents. Interview experience with both younger children and adults is also useful, as familiarity with developmental issues and their impact throughout the life cycle can assist in understanding the transitional nature of adolescence with challenges distinct from and shared with both childhood and adulthood.

References

Akiskal, H. S. (1986). Diagnosis in psychiatry and the mental status examination. In G. Winokur & P. Clayton (Eds.), *Medical basis of psychiatry* (pp. 369–383). Philadelphia: W. B. Saunders.

Brent, D. A., & Kolko, D. J. (1990). Suicide and suicidal behavior in children and adolescents. In B. D. Garfinkel, G. A. Carlson, & E. B. Weller (Eds.), *Psychiatric disorders in children and adolescents* (pp. 372–391). Philadelphia: W. B. Saunders.

Brent, D. A., Perper, J. A., Goldstein, C. E., Kolko, D. J., Allan, M. J., Allman, C. J., & Zelenak, J. P. (1988). Risk factors for adolescent suicide. *Archives of General Psychiatry, 45,* 581–588.

Cantwell, D. (1980). The diagnostic process and diagnostic classification in child psychiatry—DSM-III. *Journal of the American Academy of Child and Adolescent Psychiatry, 19,* 345–355.

Coleman, J. S. (1961). *The adolescent society.* London: Collier-Macmillan.

Folstein, M. F., Folstein, S. E., & McHugh, P. R. (1975). "Mini Mental State," a practical method for grading the cognitive state of patients for the clinician. *Journal of Psychiatric Research, 12,* 189–198.

Foster, G. G., Ysseldyke, J. E., & Reese, J. H. (1975). I wouldn't have seen it if I hadn't believed it. *Exceptional Children, 41,* 469–473.

Freud, A. (1952). Adolescence. *Psychoanalytic Study of the Child, 13,* 255–278.

Hill, P. (1985). The diagnostic interview with the individual child. In M. Rutter & L. Hersov (Eds.), *Child and adolescent psychiatry* (pp. 249–263). Oxford: Blackwell Scientific Publications.

Moretti, M. M., Fine, S., Haley, G., & Marriage, M. B. (1985). Childhood and adolescent depression: Child-report versus parent-report information. *Journal of the American Academy of Child Psychiatry, 24,* 298–302.

Pfeffer, P. (1989). Suicide. In L. K. George Hsu & M. Hersen (Eds.), *Recent developments in adolescent psychiatry* (pp. 115–134). New York: Wiley.

Piaget, J. (1929). *The child's conception of the world.* New York: Harcourt, Brace.

Offer, D., & Offer, J. (1975). *From teenage to young manhood: A psychological study.* New York: Basic Books.

Offer, D., Ostrov, E., & Howard, K. K. (1989). Adolescense: What is normal? *American Journal of Diseases of Children, 143,* 731–736.

Roberts, J. K. A. (1984). *Differential diagnosis in neuropsychiatry.* New York: John Wiley and Sons.

Rutter, M., & Cox, A. (1981). Psychiatric interviewing techniques: I Methods and measures. *British Journal of Psychiatry, 138,* 273–282.

Rutter, M., Graham, P., Chadwick, O. F. D., & Yule, W. (1976). Adolescent turmoil: Fact or fiction? *Journal of Child Psychology and Psychiatry, 17,* pp. 35–56.

Shea, S. (1988). *Psychiatric interviewing: The art of understanding.* Philadelphia: W. B. Saunders.

7
Projective Techniques

Billie S. Strauss
Martin Harrow

Psychological tests present all subjects with the same or similar stimuli to which they must respond, so that responses among them can be compared. In the case of projective techniques, patients are asked to respond to relatively ambiguous stimuli (e.g., blank paper, inkblots, pictures, stems of sentences) but are not told what kinds of answers to give; sometimes they may be told that there are no right or wrong answers. In fact, these stimuli may not have one definite meaning and may be interpreted in several ways. Hence the patient "projects" his or her personality—including dynamics, repressed material, and ego structure—onto the stimuli. Among psychological tests, projective techniques are less structured than psychometric, objective tests (Magnussen, 1979).

When tests are interpreted projectively, the evaluation is based at least in some measure on subjective scoring and interpretation, which has been viewed as a weakness (Magnussen, 1979). Attempts have been made to develop norms for the Rorschach test (e.g., Ames, Metraux, & Walker, 1971; Beck, Beck, Levitt, & Molish, 1961; Exner & Weiner, 1982; Krall et al., 1983), where people of different ages are found to respond differentially. Lanyon and Goodstein (1982) discussed the developmental approach to the interpretation of projective tests (i.e., where indices mean different things at different ages).

A focus on adolescents has become popular in recent years. Several books have been published that have an emphasis on adolescent assessment (e.g., Harrington, 1987; Oster, Caro, Eagen, & Lillo, 1988; Reynolds & Kamphaus, 1990) and adolescent issues (e.g., Van Hasselt & Hersen, 1987). Many works combine child and adolescent assessment (e.g., Kestenbaum & Williams, 1988; Krall, 1989; Rabin, 1986), but they do not always sort out issues unique to adolescents. Archer, Maruish, Imhof, and Piotrowski (1991) described the results of a survey of testing practices of psychologists who evaluate adolescents. Of the 600 questionnaires distributed, 165 (36%) provided usable data and evaluated adolescents. The Rorschach test was the most popular projective test and was ranked second overall, after the Wechsler intelligence scales. Other projective tests, in order of ranking of frequency of use in a standard battery, were the Bender-Gestalt, Thematic Apperception Test (TAT), Sentence Completion Test, human figure drawings, House-Tree-Person, Kinetic Family Drawing, and Roberts Apperception Test. Several factors, including short administration time, may account for the popularity of some of these projective techniques.

Rorschach Test

The Rorschach test involves presenting the patient with 10 standard inkblots, having the patient describe associations to what he or she sees, and then inquiring about thought processes that went into those associations. Responses can be interpreted both projectively as well as according to scoring systems that have been normed. Current norms for adolescents are provided by Exner (1990); previous norms were established by Ames et al. (1971), Beck et al. (1961), Exner and Weiner (1982), and Hertz (1970). Ames et al. (1971) provide a brief history of the use of Rorschach with adolescents, citing Hertz (1935) as the forerunner in this area.

Administration of the Rorschach involves a free-association phase (in which the subject gives associations to the inkblots for each of the 10 cards) followed by an inquiry phase (where the examiner inquires about each response; e.g., Exner, 1986). Modifications or variations of this technique include conducting the inquiry at the end of each card (e.g., Ames, Metraux, Rodell, & Walker, 1974; Exner & Weiner, 1982; Rapaport, Gill, & Schafer, 1968), a brief Rorschach (Klopfer, 1984) where the inquiry is done immediately after each response to yield one response per card, and a five-card Rorschach (Beck & Worland, 1983), in which cards I, II, IV, VII, and IX are given. The Rorschach generally is administered last in the test battery (Exner, 1974), although order of administration has little effect on this test (McCraw & Pegg-McNab, 1981). The Rorschach is scored for many variables, including length of record, location of responses on the blot, developmental quality or synthesis, determinants of the response such as use in the response of movement, color, shading, reflections and pair, popular responses, organizational activity, "special scores" (which are manifestation of primary process thinking), and a variety of ratios (Berg, 1986; Exner & Weiner, 1982). Ames et al. (1971) and Exner and Weiner (1982) report on how these variables differ for different age groups.

Archer et al. (1991) noted that the Rorschach test was the most popular personality assessment measure with adolescents. These authors suggest several factors that may have contributed to its popularity: (a) administration of the Rorschach test does not depend on reading level, as does successful administration of many objective personality inventories; (b) the stimuli and task demands of the Rorschach are more likely to hold an adolescent's interest and attention, as compared to objective tests; (c) the Rorschach has a standardized administration and scoring procedure and adolescent norms; and (d) considerable research has been conducted with adolescent populations (e.g., Exner & Weiner, 1982).

Clinical Uses

Clinical interpretation of the Rorschach involves forming hypotheses based on variables in the structural summary as well as on the content and sequence of responses. Rorschach variables refer to intrapsychic functioning rather than to actual behavior; hence normative data provide support for or against hypotheses, rather than certainty about personality characteristics (Exner & Weiner, 1982). Moreover, variables and ratios derived on the Rorschach must be integrated with each other and with other test and interview data. A "cookbook" approach to interpretation may lead to contradictory or erroneous conclusions.

Berg (1986) reviews literature relating the transitional, chaotic turmoil of adolescence to turmoil, regressive and disordered thinking, and shifts in the Rorschach records of adolescents (Ames et al. 1971; Beck & Molish, 1967; Hertz, 1960; Rychlak & O'Leary, 1965; Schimek, 1974; Weiner & Exner, 1978). Other studies, however, suggest that adolescents do not show much turmoil or lability, either clinically or on the Rorschach (Exner, Armbruster & Viglione, 1978; Ostrov, 1975). Rather, psychological health during adolescence has been shown to predict the same during adulthood (Mellsop, 1972). Berg (1986) noted that use of the Rorschach with adolescents is especially difficult because the criteria for health in this age range in our society is unclear; and some degree of turmoil probably will be present.

Exner (1990; Exner & Weiner, 1982) provided normative data as well as qualitative interpretation for evaluating protocols of different age groups. Previously, Ames et al. (1971) examined 700 Rorschach records given by 398 different children, providing normative data for ages 10 through 16 and qualitative descriptions of the nature of responses. These authors also relate developmental characteristics of adolescents at various ages with responses on the Rorschach test. For example, at 13 years, Rorschach mean $H\%$ is low, and developmentally adolescents tend to be unresponsive toward others (p. 188), whereas at 16 years, Rorschach tests show a high point for human responses, and developmentally, adolescents tend to be warmly interested in and responsive to other people (p. 257). Thus clinicians may compare both summary data and qualitative data with a normative sample. Berg (1986) pointed out that normative data of the

Rorschach must be used cautiously in evaluating adolescents. Norms by age groupings are heterogeneous, and assessment of a particular individual is difficult; the use of norms may result in a "sign approach."

Exner and Weiner (1982) discuss how the Rorschach may be used in assessing youngsters for schizophrenia. They include consideration of disordered thinking, such as the "special scorings" in their system; inaccurate perception, measured by poor form quality and few popular responses; interpersonal ineptness, measured by limited *M* (human movement) and *H* (human content); and inadequate controls, measured by disturbed content (e.g., blatant aggressive or sexual material) and by poor integration of color (including pure *C*, or color, unmodulated by form). Exner and Weiner (1982) also discuss assessment of paranoia on the Rorschach using both structural variables—such as unusual location choice (e.g., white space and rare details), introversiveness (experience balance), and constriction (reduced number of responses; high lambda, or ratio of form to nonform responses; and high *A%*, or animal content)—and content variables, such as experience of external threat and need for protection.

Over the years, the Rorschach has provided a valuable technique to help evaluate theoretical formulations about paranoia in schizophrenia (Kwawer, 1977; Lazar & Harrow, 1985). The Rorschach also has been used to evaluate a wide range of formulations about other proposed aspects of schizophrenia, including hypotheses about primitive-drive-dominated thinking, boundary disturbance, object relations, and thought disorder. In relation to diagnostic systems such as DSM-IV (American Psychiatric Association, 1993), the older Rapaport, Gill, and Schafer (1968) framework and the more recent system of assessing thought disorder (Exner, 1974) get accurate estimates that can be used in diagnostic schemes for schizophrenia.

Among the measures that have been linked to schizophrenia are drive-dominated thinking and primitive-drive-dominated thinking. The Rorschach technique has been used to measure these constructs. The construct validity of measures of primitive-drive-dominated thinking has been assessed in research by Harrow, Quinlan, and colleagues (Harrow & Quinlan, 1985; Harrow, Quinlan, Wallington, & Pickett, 1976). Lazar and Harrow (1980) have discussed the broader uses of measures centered around concepts concerning primitive-drive-dominated thinking to assess schizophrenia. These concepts and the development of associated measures are based on earlier formulations by Rapaport et al. (1968) and by Holt (1977).

Similarly, another important measure used to assess schizophrenia with the Rorschach involves disordered boundaries. This concept also is derived from earlier research with the Rorschach technique by Rapaport et al. (1968). A theoretical framework emphasizing the importance of boundary disturbance in schizophrenia has been proposed by Blatt and colleagues (Blatt & Ritzler, 1974; Blatt & Wild, 1976). Some empirical evidence from

Rorschach responses supporting the importance of boundary disturbance in schizophrenia was reported by Blatt's group and by Quinlan and Harrow (Harrow & Quinlan, 1985; Quinlan & Harrow, 1974).

Krall (1989) used the Rorschach test to assess the development of object relations for various disorders. For example, she used the Rorschach with some autistic adolescents who have language and minimal symbiotic features and noted that when there is sufficient language for use of the Rorschach test, the patient probably has moved from an autistic to a symbiotic level of development, or secondary autism with autistic features. Krall (1989) used the Rorschach to evaluate cohesive sense of self, illogical thought processes, and primary process intrusion. She noted that characteristics of patients who function at a preoedipal level include low overall reality testing (accuracy), deviant thought processes (special scorings in the Exner, 1990, system), idiosyncratic or no human responses, or human responses with minus form quality.

Among character-disordered children and adolescents, Krall (1989) noted that Rorschach responses may include omnipotent content, limited number of determinants, or limited empathic ability (e.g., human movement, *M*, such as clowns or fairies). Among hysterical neurotic children and adolescents, she noted that the Rorschach record would be constricted with no obvious failure of repression, phobic objects, somatic preoccupation, or shading determinants that suggest anxiety. Berg (1986) suggested that the Rorschach can contribute to diagnosis of neurotic disorders by ruling out more severe psychopathology.

Exner and Weiner (1982) noted that borderline patients show a need for structure that is often manifested by the discrepancy between performance on the unstructured Rorschach and that on the structured Wechsler tests, as well as by tolerance for their disturbed responses. Rorschach manifestations of borderline personality in adolescents include few responses or content variables, splitting, symbiotic preoccupation, deadness or emptiness, oral or oral-aggressive content, and compliance (Rubenstein, 1980; Sugarman, Bloom-Feshbach, & Bloom-Feshbach, 1980).

Among male outpatients aged 8 to 16, boys who had a positive relationship with their mothers had more human movement (*M*) on the Rorschach than boys who had an ambivalent or negative relationship with their mothers (Bene, 1975). Findings suggest that for boys, ability to give *M* responses (which may reflect acceptance of fantasy and empathy with others) develops at an early age when the relationship with the mother is important.

Viglione (1990) presented the case of an 11-year-old child who was administered the Rorschach test at the time of a trauma (placement in a shelter following his mother's unsuccessful suicide attempt) 7 months later, and 4 years later (at the age of 15, when indices of severe psychopathology found during the first administration did not appear). The author discussed understanding of Rorschach data and suggested that these data serve as a representation of the child's intrapsychic world in the context of the child's environment and behavior. To differentiate severe psychopathology from response to trauma on the Rorschach, Viglione suggests that elevations in *m* and *Y* represent acute stress, and complexity in the record and reference to trauma reflect openness to stressful experience and ability to tolerate some disorganization.

Cates and Lapham (1991) reviewed literature suggesting that the Rorschach may be used with deaf adolescents. Narayan (1983) found that Rorschachs of deaf adolescents suggest that they are conventional, have low self-esteem and high fantasy life, use simple cognitive operations, show emotional distress, and have limited awareness of others. Some difficulties were found in using American Sign Language (ASL) during the inquiry, although scoring systems often can be used, and content analysis usually can be employed.

Research Findings

Exner, Thomas, and Mason (1985) found that among normal children tested every 2 years from ages 8 through 16, except for use of good form (X+%), consistency of Rorschach variables does not begin until age 14. Among children with psychopathology, Rorschach indices reflecting this pathology tend to be stable over time.

Many formulations have evolved concerning the use of Rorschach responses to distinguish between major diagnostic groups (e.g., schizophrenia and depression). Some evidence has been provided to support these formulations (Harrow & Quinlan, 1985), but more mixed evidence has emerged as well. The original formulations concerning use of the Rorschach technique as a sensitive diagnostic instrument are based on earlier works of Rapaport, Gill, and Schafer (1948) and Schafer (1948). With more recent research, however, (a) views about the types of major psychopathology associated with specific diagnostic groups have changed, and (b) views about diagnoses such as schizophrenia and depression have shifted.

At one time, clinicians believed that thought disorder and boundary disturbances were unique to schizophrenia. The Rorschach test, which is one of the better instruments to assess thought disorder, was viewed as a strong diagnostic tool in this area. Recent research (Andreasen, 1979; Harrow & Quinlan, 1977; Johnston & Holzman, 1979), though, has produced evidence indicating that most schizophrenics do have thought disorder during the acute phase, but that other diagnostic groups, and especially manic patients, also are extremely thought disordered (Andreasen & Powers, 1974).

Investigators such as Holzman (Holzman, Shenton, & Solovay, 1986) have attempted to deal with these newer findings (i.e., that severe thought disorder is common in mania as well as in schizophrenia) by developing indices to distinguish between the type of thought disorder found in schizophrenic patients and that found in manic patients. In initial efforts using the Rorschach technique, Holzman et al. (1986) reported successful discrimination between the type of thought disorder found in schizophrenic patients and that found in manic patients. Further investigation is needed in this area.

In addition, as views of clinical psychopathology have become more sophisticated, issues have arisen concerning the phase of the disorder in which one can expect to find a particular type of psychopathology associated with specific types of disordered diagnostic groups or certain types of disordered personalities. In other words, do the psychopathological features found in a diagnostic group persist forever, or are many of them a function of the acute phase of psychopathology? Research over time on thought disorder in both schizophrenia and bipolar affective disorders has provided evidence that the flagrant thought disorder found during the acute phase of schizophrenia or mania diminishes as patients emerge from that phase (Harrow, Grossman, Silverstein, Melzer, & Kettering, 1986; Harrow & Marengo, 1986; Marengo & Harrow, 1987). Investigations of this type point to the importance of such factors as acute-phase psychopathology in shaping our view of a number of major disorders. They also pose a problem for diagnostic assessment, since they point to the importance of recognizing which phase of disorder a patient is experiencing.

The clinical pictures that clinicians should look for when assessing both adolescents and adults have become complicated by other factors as well. Views about the diagnosis of schizophrenia and of depression have shifted with the publication of DSM-III (American Psychiatric Association, 1980) and the emergence of its successors, DSM-III-R and DSM-IV. These more modern outlooks define schizophrenia in terms of narrower criteria, and some psychotic patients who once would have been seen as schizophrenic under older criteria now are viewed as having affective disorders. In general, while schizophrenics no longer are seen as being the only thought-disordered patients, most schizophrenics are thought-disordered during the acute phase, and the Rorschach (along with other assessment methods) is a good, although imperfect instrument for assessment of this diagnosis.

The Rorschach test by itself may not always accurately provide diagnosis of major psychopathology such as schizophrenia and depression, but it is useful as one of a battery of diagnostic instruments. Archer and Gordon (1988) administered Rorschachs and MMPIs to 134 adolescents at hospital admission, and DEPI (Depression Index) and SCZI (Schizophrenia Index; Exner & Weiner, 1982) scores were calculated. The SCZI had an accuracy rate of .69, but it correctly identified only 47% of the schizophrenic adolescents, and was a less accurate predictor of schizophrenic diagnosis than the *Sc* scale of the MMPI. The DEPI had an accuracy rate of .49, but it correctly identified only 10% of the depressed adolescents and is a poor predictor of depressive diagnoses. In a sample of 33 adolescents referred to a community mental health center, a correlation between MMPI scale A and Exner's m (inanimate movement) was found when one outlier was eliminated. The results were not significant, however, when the outlier was not removed (Zgourides, Frey, Camplaire, Tilson, & Ihli, 1989).

Beck and Worland (1983) looked at the developmental level (DL) scores (an index of maturity of visual perception and analysis) of 267 children between the ages of 4 and 20 at two time periods, 3 to 11 years apart. The authors found that DL scores did not differentiate those who later received psychiatric treatment from those who did not receive such treatment. The DL scores in early childhood, however, differentiated children of parents with DSM-III diagnoses of schizophrenia or schizoaffective disorders from children of parents with affective disorders, physical illness, or no diagnosed disorder; this result was not replicated with the adolescents.

In a sample of 46 normal children and adolescents, ranging in age from 6 to 16, the Egocentricity Index (Exner, 1974, 1978) substantiated interpretation of this index as a measure of self-esteem, interpersonal openness, and interest in others (Duricko, Norcross, & Buskirk, 1989). In a sample of 50 adolescent patients with various psychiatric disorders, Caputo-Sacco and Lewis (1991) found that EI was negatively related to Depression scale (2) of the MMPI. EI is based on the number of reflection, pair, and total responses $(3r+2)/R$, and has been related to self-concern (Exner, 1986). These findings were consistent with the conceptual notion that adolescents with lower EI are likely to be withdrawn and depressed. No relationship was found between EI and MMPI scales 4 (Psychopathic Deviance) and 9 (Mania). Exner and Weiner (1982) report on findings from studies of depression. They noted that a low EI and a lower right side of eb (Sum Grey-Black + Shading > Sum FM + m) also are associated with depression for children and adolescents. In addition, use of morbid content (seeing objects as dead or destroyed, injured, broken, or damaged, or attribution of a depressive characteristic) also was related to depression in their study. Exner and Weiner (1982) noted that Rorschach variables do not differentiate distress from depression. Lipovsky, Finch, and Belter (1989) found that self-report measures were more accurate than Rorschach measures in distinguishing depressed from nondepressed hospitalized adolescents. Using the Rorschach test, only shading variables differentiated the two groups.

Arffa (1982) administered Rorschachs to 48 hospitalized adolescents. Using a composite score of signs reflecting suicide potential, she was able to differentiate subjects who had attempted suicide from those who had not; 92% of the suicidal subjects correctly were identified, while 25% of the non-suicidal subjects were incorrectly identified. Individual signs did not significantly differentiate the groups.

Using various scoring systems of the Rorschach test, Leifer, Shapiro, Martone, and Kassem, (1991) found that sexually abused girls, ages 5 to 16, showed more disturbed thinking, had a higher level of stress, described interpersonal relationships more negatively, and showed more preoccupation with sexuality than a control group of girls who had not been sexually abused.

A group of 45 male adolescent sex offenders was compared with a matched group of nonsex offenders on the Rorschach test (McCraw & Pegg-McNab, 1989). Findings suggested that the sex-offender group averaged three more responses per protocol and more anatomy responses than the nonsex offender group. The two groups did not differ on other Rorschach variables, and the authors suggest that adolescent sex offenders are similar to adolescents who commit nonsex crimes.

Using 60 adolescent inpatients and outpatients, Urist and Shill (1982) found that an object relations scale on the Rorschach, called a mutuality of autonomy scale, had a high level of correlation with an independent clinical mutual of autonomy scale.

The Rorschach test has been used with nonclinical samples. Ninety children ages 11 to 16 with IQ greater than 135, and 27 children ages 12 and 13 with average intelligence were administered the Rorschach test (Gallucci, 1989). Children with IQ's greater than 150 did not differ from children with IQ's between 136 and 140, suggesting that gifted children are no less psychologically healthy than very bright children. As compared to the average children, gifted children gave more responses on the Rorschach, more M (human movement), as well as more special scorings which reflect primary process thinking, Dd (rare detail), lower X+% and F+% (indices of reality testing), and higher X-% (index of poor reality testing). Over 70% of the gifted children were inaccurately identified as schizophrenic, although Child Behavior Checklists did not indicate such psychopathology.

A Barrier score (measure of psychological protectiveness) on the Rorschach was found to correlate with values (measured by a semantic differential) of 9th grade students (Stevens, 1981)

Drawing Tests

Drawing tasks (e.g., Cummings, 1986) are useful because they do not involve verbal or reading skills and may be used with adolescents from various cultural groups (Hammer, 1986). Some adolescents, however, are reluctant or embarrassed to draw. Drawing tests used to evaluate adolescents include the Bender-Gestalt, human figure drawings or Draw-A-Person (DAP; Koppitz, 1968; Machover, 1949, 1953), Kinetic Family Drawing (Burns & Kaufman, 1970, 1972), and House-Tree-Person tests (Buck, 1948).

A collaborative drawing technique (Smith, 1985) in which each member of a family sequentially contributes to a drawing has been used to assess the functioning and perception of a child or adolescent within a family. Some research has been conducted using figure drawings to assess European and African adolescents' perception of their body and bodily functions (Amman-Gainotti & Antenore, 1990; Amman-Gainotti, Di Prospero, & Nenci, 1989; Amman-Gainotti & Grazioso, 1991).

Human Figure Drawings

Administration of Human Figure Drawings (Koppitz, 1968; Machover, 1949, 1953) involve having the patient draw a picture of a person, then having him or her draw a picture of a person of the opposite sex. After both drawings have been completed, questions are asked about the drawings (e.g., about the ages of the figures, or what they are thinking or doing).

Clinical Uses. Human figure drawings have been used both as a projective test to assess personality functioning and as a test of cognitive development (Goodenough, 1926; Harris, 1963; Koppitz, 1968; Machover, 1949). Supporting empirical evidence for claims is variable. Projective drawings may reflect self- or ideal representations, representations of meaningful figures in the patient's life, or combinations of these representations.

Among the more central concepts studied with the figure drawing technique is *body image*. The notion that the figure drawing test assesses the concept of body image was formulated in the very early work of Machover (1949). While this construct is extremely important, though, it still is not completely understood. One of the central issues in is that of construct validity, since we have no absolute method of determining what a true measure of body image should be. One way to approximate the construct validity measures is to obtain independent measures of body perception or expression (Maloney & Payne, 1969). Further study of such potentially important constructs as body image, both by use of the figure drawing test and by other means, would advance knowledge and provide valuable information for techniques about projective testings and for our understanding of human personality.

In interpreting drawings to assess body image or other personality constructs, artistic skill and visual-spatial skills must be taken into account (Siegel, 1988). A series of investigations (Carlson, Quinlan, Tucker, & Harrow, 1973) point to the potential confounding influence of artistic skill in assessing psychopathology with the use of the figure drawing test. Carlson et al. used the figure drawing test to evaluate body disturbance and sexual elaboration factors in schizophrenics. Results suggested that artistic skill and sophistication can influence figure drawings and lead to interpretation of greater psychopathology for people with less advanced artistic skills ($r = 0.53$).

Hammer (1986) noted that normal adolescents draw pictures that reflect what they would like to be, so their self-representations often are bigger, stronger, more important, or older than the patient is in reality. Hammer (1986) further observed that adolescent boys often draw aggressive figures (e.g., soldiers), whereas adolescent girls emphasize femininity or attractiveness (e.g., figures in bathing suits).

Krall (1989) noted that the ability to draw a human figure suggests bodily awareness and internal representation of the self. She used human figure drawings to assess development of object relations for a variety of categories of psychopathology. For example, she evaluated autism by looking at the difference between scores on intelligence tests and the Harris-Goodenough score (Harris, 1963) on the figure drawings and suggested that much higher intelligence scores relative to Harris scores imply a deficit in the development of object representation. She noted that autistic children may draw animals, mechanical objects, or parts of human figures. Patients with symbiotic psychosis may draw unusual features.

Among neurotic children and adolescents, human figure drawings show awareness of the human body and show sexual differentiation in drawings of males and females. Omissions of body parts reflect specific anxieties. Among adolescents, figure drawings may be used to assess acting-out potential and impulsivity through consideration of such features as size, nature of pencil strokes, and placement on the page (Hammer, 1986).

Cates and Lapham (1991) summarized literature suggesting that figure drawings are an appropriate instrument for use with deaf subjects.

Research Findings. Machover (1949) hypothesized that size of figure drawings is related to the self-esteem of the subject. Using high school seniors aged 16 to 18, DeLatte and Hendrickson (1982) related self-esteem as measured by Rosenberg (1965) Self-Esteem Scale to size (height, width, and area) of human figure drawings. Among males, they found a positive relationship between both width and area of figure drawings and self-esteem; no relationship was found between any of the size dimensions and self-esteem for females. Sims, Dana, and Bolton (1983) reviewed a variety of scoring systems and literature that provide mixed evidence for DAP as a measure of anxiety (e.g., Handler & Reyher, 1965; Jones & Thomas, 1961; Roback, 1968; Swenson, 1968).

Saarni and Azara (1977) developed a sign-approach measure of two kinds of anxiety: one related to aggression-hostility, and the other related to insecurity-lability. Anxiety related to aggression-hostility was indicated by 10 signs, including transparencies and use of teeth and genitals; anxiety related to insecurity-lability was indicated by 14 signs, including lack of hands and arms at side of body. They found more anxiety related to aggression-hostility among males, but no sex differences in anxiety related to insecurity-lability. Using Saarni and Azara's system with adolescent girls, Rierdan and Koff (1980) suggested that sex of drawing was pertinent in differentiating these two kinds of anxieties. In a study of youngsters aged 9 to 22 years, Rierdan, Koff, and Heller (1982) found that males showed more anxiety about both aggression-hostility and insecurity-lability than did females and that both males and females drew male figures with higher aggression-hostility indices than female figures, which suggests that both sexes have greater anxiety around males. Overall, these results suggest that males have more concern about aggression and dependency issues than do females. No differences were found among students in the fifth, seventh, and ninth grades, in contrast to Schildkrout, Shenker, and Sonnenblick's (1972) suggestion that differences in anxiety might vary during puberty.

Using figure drawings as a measure of anxiety, Doubros and Mascaren-has (1967) had 14-year-old high school students do figure drawings before and after an examination. Stick figures occurred more frequently following the examination, and inclusion of inanimate objects along with the figures was found more frequently before the examination.

Machover (1949) assumed that the human figure drawing is a valid index of body image. Similarly, sex of the first figure drawn has been viewed by some, but not all psychologists, as reflecting sexual identity (Swensen, 1968). Heinrich and Triebe (1972) reviewed 19 studies of figure drawings made by children ages 5 to 18. They found that most of the subjects drew their own sex first, but beginning at age 11, boys drew same-sex figures more frequently than did girls. Rierdan and Koff (1981) permitted children in grades five through nine to indicate if they were uncertain of the sex of the drawing they produced. Of the 461 children, 8% were uncertain of the sex of their drawing; no differences were found for grade or sex of the child. In this study, 94% of the boys and 82% of the girls drew their own sex first.

Rekers and Rosen (1990) administered figure drawings to 66 boys, ages 3 to 18, who were suspected of having gender identity disturbance. They found a significant correlation between drawing of the opposite-sex figure first and severity of diagnosis, in that the most severely disturbed boys tended to draw the female figure first, and the least severely disturbed boys tended to draw the male figure first. The authors noted that only 33% of the sample drew the female figure first, and a nonsignificant relationship was found between older and younger subjects.

In a study of 174 psychiatric inpatients ranging in age from 7 to 16 (Dickson, Saylor, & Finch, 1990), subjects were more likely to draw a figure of the same sex (71.3%) than of the opposite sex (28.7%). No differences were found between children and adolescents or between males and females, although boys drew same-sex figures 80.5% of the time while girls did so 63% of the time. In a study of 30 black and 30 white adolescents, Khulman (1979) found that whites drew more figure drawings of the same race than did blacks, and that whites drew fewer blacks than blacks drew whites. They interpreted these findings to suggest that blacks are less accepting of their racial identity than are whites.

A sign approach has been used to assess psychopathology in adolescents, using such signs as transparencies (Hiler & Nesvig, 1965) and omission of facial features (Haworth, 1962; Koppitz, 1968; Urban, 1963). In a study of 52 children between the ages of 9 and 15, Tharinger and Stark (1990) found that emotional indicators using the Koppitz system did not differentiate children with mood and anxiety disorders from controls. An integrated system that evaluated drawings for inhumaness, lack of agency (inability of the figure to interact effectively with the world), lack of well-being of the figure, and presence of hollow or stilted sense differentiated mood/anxiety disorder subjects from normal controls.

Daum (1983) looked at the relationship features of figure drawings and aggression and withdrawal in adolescent male delinquents. Although 6 of 16 drawing features distinguished among two groups of delinquents and a control group, and use of all of the drawing features increased predictive power, the author suggests caution in use of this technique. Figure drawings also have differentiated adjudicated from nonadjudicated adolescents, in that the first group showed more serious disturbance and conflict, general ineffectiveness and social withdrawal, impaired social acceptability, and greater somatization and depressive tendencies (Marsh, Linberg, & Smeltzer, 1991).

Kinetic Family Drawing

The Kinetic Family Drawing (KFD; Burns & Kaufman, 1970, 1972) is a technique used to assess a patient's perception of interpersonal relationships within his or her family. The subject is instructed to draw a picture of the whole family, with everybody doing something. This test has been evaluated qualitatively in terms of who is included in the drawing, placement on the paper, and activities, as well according to various scoring systems (e.g., Burns & Kaufman, 1970, 1972; McPhee & Wegner, 1976; Meyers, 1978; Nostkoff & Lazarus, 1983; O'Brien & Patton, 1974; Reynolds, 1978).

Sobel and Sobel (1976) found that male adolescent delinquents, as compared with 20 normal male adolescents, more frequently omitted bodies of figures, omitted most family members from their drawings, and lacked "kinesis" (interaction) between family members. Lack of hands, aggressive interaction, encapsulation, and conflict action did not differentiate the two groups as predicted.

Tharinger and Stark (1990) found that emotional indicators on the Reynolds (1978) system did not differentiate subjects with mood and anxiety disorders from normal controls in a group of 9- to 15-year-olds. A qualitative integrative scoring system that evaluated inaccessibility of family members to each other, degree of engagement of family members, inappropriate underlying family structure, and inhumanness of family figures differentiated subjects with mood disorders from controls.

Bender-Gestalt

Archer et al. (1991) report that the Bender-Gestalt was the third most popular instrument in their survey in assessing adolescents. Their survey does not report the extent to which the Bender-Gestalt is used with adolescents either as a screening measure for neurological dysfunction or as a projective technique.

The Bender-Gestalt is administered by asking the subject to copy nine geometric figures, presented one at a time, on a blank sheet of paper. The test may be interpreted projectively by evaluating degree of precision, erasures, speed of execution, and placement of figures (Siegel, 1988). Discrepancies between performance on the Bender-Gestalt and performance on figure drawings may suggest psychopathology, rather than limited intelligence or visual-spatial abilities.

Picture Story Tests

In picture story tests, the patient is presented with a series of pictures and instructed to tell a story. Patients usually are asked to include who is in the picture, what the characters are doing, what happened before, what will happen, and the feelings of the characters. Test results are influenced by instructions, conditions under which the test is conducted, nature of the examiner, and the order of test administration (Lundy, 1988).

The most common of the picture story tests used with adolescents is the Thematic Apperception test (TAT) (Murray, 1938). Archer et al. (1991) noted that the TAT is among the most frequently used instruments in evaluating adolescents. The TAT is employed with a variety of ages, from children through older adults. Murray's (1938) TAT has 31 pictures, some of which originally were designed specifically for use with males, females, older adolescents and adults, or younger adolescents and children. In practice, any of the cards may be used with any type of subject.

Other story-telling tests used for adolescents include the "Tell-Me-A-Story" technique (TEMAS; Costantino, Malgady, & Rogler, 1988a), the Roberts Apperception Test for Children (RATC; McArthur & Roberts, 1982), the Symonds Picture-Story Test (Symonds, 1948), and a TAT technique for adolescent males (Cooper, 1981). The TEMAS test consists of 23 stimulus cards; both a "minority version" (with minority characters) and a nonminority version are available. The RATC is a set of cards of situations involving parents, peers, and schools. The scoring system has both adaptive and clinical scales.

The TAT is evaluated by considering themes and relationships (or lack of them) among characters in the pictures, including the role authority figures and/or members of the opposite sex, themes of intimacy and/or separation, affect, and ability to structure stories. Clinicians typically do not use scoring systems.

Clinical Uses. Dana (1986) provided a framework for evaluating TAT stories of adolescents. He suggests five areas for consideration: ego strength, needs (self-assertion for males; prosocial behavior for females), sex-role development and identity, psychopathology, and controls/defenses. For example, ego strength may be assessed by extent to which the subject complies with the stimulus demand of the picture, uses Aristotelian logic rather than peculiar types of primary process thinking, and exhibits appropriate behavioral and affective controls. Ability to elaborate on TAT stories is unrelated to intelligence and does not increase from the age of 11 to 15 (Slemon, Holzwarth, Lewis, & Sitko, 1976). A study of 686 children, adolescents, and college students suggested that differentiation of sexual identity of males and females on the TAT is found in children from the 3rd through 10 grades, drops out beginning in 11th grade, and then reemerges during the second half of college (Cramer, 1980).

Krall (1989) used the TAT to evaluate cohesive sense of self, thought disorder, and primary process intrusion. She suggested that stories of children and adolescents with symbiotic psychosis do not relate to the stimulus value of the picture, may reflect a confused thought process, and may have themes of loss and abandonment; sudden shifts in stories may occur. Stories of character-disordered patients may be concrete or circumstantial as a way of avoiding affect and anxiety; most show limited empathy with characters, aggressive or antisocial themes, and deprivation and dependency themes. Among neurotic children, stories are well organized. Hysterical types of neurotic children may give stories that suggest repression (where various stimuli are ignored or misperceived) and may show content of castration fears, oedipal themes, or possibly somatic concerns. In the obsessive type of neurosis, stories may have considerable detail or obsessional indecision. Depressive children's TAT stories may be very short, with sad affect and themes of loneliness, deprivation, loss, and passivity.

Cates and Lapham (1991) suggest use of the TAT with deaf children and adolescents with fluent singing skills. The potential difficulty in administration is the tendency of the deaf to perseverate on the first idea. Despite lack of empirical validity, these authors consider the test to be useful with this population.

Research Findings. Matranga (1976) administered TATs that were scored for hostility of content to 76 male adolescent delinquents. Results suggested that hostile content on the TAT correlated negatively with the aggressiveness of the offense committed, and in a nonsignificant but negative direction with aggression as measured by a behavior rating scale and a behavior checklist.

Costantino, Colon-Malgady, Malgady, and Perez (1991) used the TEMAS technique (Costantino, Malgady, & Rogler, 1988b) to measure attention to pictorial stimuli with Hispanic, black, and white school-age children ranging in age for 7 to 15 (152 normal, and 95 with attention-deficit hyperactivity disorder). Results suggested that the clinical group was more likely than the normal group to omit information about characters and settings; in addition, Hispanic and black children in the clinical group were more likely to omit information about events, and white children in the clinical group were more like to omit information about psychological conflicts. Crowley, Worchel, Olson, and Rae Palomares (1991) conducted a principal component factor analysis of the RATC (McArthur & Roberts, 1982) using the standardization sample (200 clinical and 200 normal subjects, ranging in age from 6 to 15) and a sample of 48 children chronically ill due to cancer ($n = 19$) or diabetes ($n = 29$) and ranging in age from 6 to 17. Results suggested three factors. Two profiles of chronically ill children were identified that differed on adaptiveness of coping style.

Sentence Completion Test

Sentence completion tests involve presenting the subject with stems of sentences, which the subject is instructed to complete. Adolescents usually can be given the sentence stems to read and can write the responses, although the examiner may read stems and the subject can respond orally, particularly if the subject has difficulty writing or spelling.

Many sentence completion tests have been developed for use with adolescents; common ones include the Irvin (1972) Sentence Completion Test and the Rotter and Rafferty (1950) Incomplete Sentence Blank. Early evaluation of sentence completion tests used formal analysis of such nonmeaningful variables as length, use of personal pronouns, and reaction time; current evaluation uses content analysis (Zlotogorski & Wiggs, 1986).

Sentence completion tests are used clinically and for research (Goldberg, 1965; Rabin & Zlotogorski, 1985). Zlotogorski and Wiggs (1986) reviewed three areas of research using sentence completion methods: emotional development, stability of feelings, and ego development. Rabin and Zltogorski (1985) review studies related to personality development and adaptive functioning, as well as those related to maladaptive functioning and psychopathology.

Rabin (1977) retested adolescents after 20 years on a sentence completion test to assess the extent to which positive or negative attitudes or "sentiments" endure over time. He found stability of attitude about family, the past, sex, and work, and lack of stability of attitude about parents, self-concept, and the future.

In a study of 1,017 12- to 14-year olds, Lanyon (1972) found a relationship between behavioral ratings of hostility and hostility on a sentence completion test, but no such relationship between anxiety and dependency. Rabinowitz and Shouval (1977) also found that the Rotter incomplete sentences of 203 high school freshmen reflected the behavioral ratings of hostility given by peers and teachers.

Fuller, Parmelee, and Carroll (1982) compared 30 delinquent adolescent boys with 30 normal high school boys on the Rotter Incomplete Sentence Blank (Rotter & Rafferty, 1950). The two groups were significantly different on a maladjustment score on the Rotter, and 73% of the normals and 60% of the delinquents were correctly identified.

Loevinger (Loevinger & Wessler, 1970; Loevinger, Wessler, & Redmore, 1970) developed the Washington University Sentence Completion Test (WU-SCT) to investigate levels of ego development. She postulates seven levels of development; the sentence completion test is used to determine the "core" level. The scoring system is a complicated one and has been used for research rather than for clinical work; it has been applied to TATs and to unstructured interviews of adolescents and adults (Sutton & Swensen, 1983). In one study, a significant relationship was found between grade (6th or 12th) and level of ego development among 32 lower- and lower-middle-class black subjects (Martin & Redmore, 1978). Other studies have shown relationships between ego development and behavior (Hauser, 1976), beliefs (Lorr & Manning, 1978), symptom patterns as measured by the MMPI (Gold, 1980), and success in employment among retarded adolescents (Sheridan, 1978).

Summary

Test batteries and interview, rather than individual projective techniques, should be used in assessment procedures. The results from a single type of psychological test do not reveal ironclad information that applies uniformly to all patients. Rather, the test typically provides useful information that can be used to generate or lend support for or against particular hypotheses. In addition, projective techniques are useful for elaborating individual dynamics, ego structure, internal representations, affects, and coping mechanisms for individual patients.

Projective tests have been interpreted both projectively and with the use of age-based norms. When interpreted projectively, most of these tests are relatively culture free; however, some scoring systems may show differences between various cultural or racial groups (e.g., Krall et al., 1983).

Overall, as can be seen from the current review, while projective testing has led to many rich formulations and to advances in the field, some problems have emerged as well. Some of these difficulties are related to the use of projective testing, and others are related to the larger issues in the field in general. Part of the problem concerns general issues in the field, such as the lack of knowledge and uncertainty concerning key components of psychopathology (which also are poorly understood).

The revisions of diagnostic classification systems such as DSM-IV (American Psychiatric Association, 1993) are a good example of another type of issue that interpretation of projective techniques must face. There are regular changes in the field's views about certain types of psychopathology and personality disorders (e.g., shifts in concepts of "borderline" psychopathology) that have occurred over the years. Thus many of our traditional concepts have been reformulated as thinking about diagnosis and formal diagnostic systems change. In addition, even the boundaries of our diagnostic categories have changed over time as new knowledge has emerged in the field. Many patients viewed as schizophrenic under DSM-II no longer are viewed as schizophrenic under DSM-IV, and a number of patients who once were not considered as having primarily affective or mood disorder diagnoses now are viewed as having such diagnoses.

At the same time, we should not forget that test findings on boundaries and thought disorders in schizophrenia, and on various other types of psychopathology in schizophrenia and in depression, have contributed positively to the field, and some of the changes and improvements in diagnoses are linked to these test findings. Hence some of our ideas about personality, about various types of psychopathology, and about the boundaries of diagnoses have been influenced in a positive way by contributions from psychological testing. Indeed, since the late 1970s, principles of standardized assessment—including standardized structured interviews—have dramatically altered the field and advanced knowledge. These principles have been derived in part from earlier ideas associated with projective testing and other types of psychological testing, as well as from views about the importance of standardized stimuli that have emerged from the projective testing movement.

The use of objective personality tests and structured interviews has not led clinicians to abandon projective tests. Rather, projective tests add another, richer dimension to psychological assessment.

References

American Psychiatric Association. (1980). *Diagnostic and statistical manual of mental disorders* (3rd ed.). Washington, DC: Author.

American Psychiatric Association. (1993). *DSM-IV draft criteria*. Washington, DC: Author.

Ames, L. B., Metraux, R. W., Rodell, J. L., & Walker, R. N. (1974). *Child Rorschach responses* (rev. ed.) New York: Brunner/Mazel.

Ames, L. B., Metraux, R. W., & Walker, R. N. (1971), *Adolescent Rorschach responses: Developmental trends from ten to sixteen years*. New York: Brunner/Mazel.

Amman-Gainotti, M., & Antenore, C. (1990). Development of internal body image from childhood to early adolescence. *Perceptual and Motor Skills, 71*, 387–393.

Amman-Gainotti, M., Di Prospero, B., & Nenci, A. M. (1989). Adolescent girls' representations of their genital inner space. *Adolescence, 94,* 473–481.

Amman-Gainotti, M., & Grazioso, M. (1991). African adolescents' drawings of the interior of the body: Preliminary findings. *Perceptual and Motor Skills, 72,* 1073–1074.

Andreasen, N. (1979). Thought, language and communication disorders: II. Diagnostic significance. *Archives of General Psychiatry, 36,* 1325–1330.

Andreasen, N., & Powers, P. (1974). Overinclusive thinking in mania and schizophrenia. *British Journal of Psychiatry, 125,* 452–456.

Archer, R. P., & Gordon, R. A. (1988). MMPI and Rorschach indices of schizophrenic and depressive diagnoses among adolescent inpatients. *Journal of Personality Assessment, 52,* 276–287.

Archer, R. P., Maruish, M., Imhof, E. A., & Piotrowski, C. (1991). Psychological test usage with adolescent clients: 1990 survey findings. *Professional Psychology: Research and Practice, 22,* 247–252.

Arffa, S. (1982). Predicting adolescent suicidal behavior and the order of Rorschach measurement. *Journal of Personality Assessment, 46,* 563–568.

Beck, J. T., & Worland, J. (1983). Rorschach developmental level and its relationship to subsequent psychiatric treatment. *Journal of Personality Assessment, 47,* 238–242.

Beck, S. J., Beck, A. G., Levitt, E. E., & Molish, H. B. (1961). *Rorschach's test: I. Basic processes* (3rd ed.). New York: Grune & Stratton.

Beck, S. J., & Molish, H. B. (1967). *Rorschach's test: II. A variety of personality pictures* (2nd ed.). New York: Grune & Stratton.

Bene, E. (1975). An effect on Rorschach M responses of a boy's relationship with his mother. *Journal of Personality Assessment, 39,* 114–115.

Berg, M. (1986). Diagnostic use of the Rorschach with adolescents. In A. I. Rabin (Ed.), *Projective techniques for adolescents and children* (pp. 111–141). New York: Springer.

Blatt, S. J., & Ritzler, B. (1974). Thought disorder and boundary disturbance in psychosis. *Journal of Consulting and Clinical Psychology, 42,* 370–381.

Blatt, S. J., & Wild, C. (1976). *Schizophrenia: A developmental analysis.* New York: Academic Press.

Buck, J. N. (1948). The H-T-P technique: A quantitative and qualitative scoring manual. *Clinical Psychology Monographs, 5,* 1–120.

Burns, R. C., & Kaufman, S. H. (1970). *Kinetic family drawings (K-F-D).* New York: Brunner/Mazel.

Burns, R. C., & Kaufman, S. H. (1972). *Actions, styles, and symbols in Kinetic Family Drawings (K-F-D).* New York: Brunner/Mazel.

Caputo-Sacco, L., & Lewis, R. J. (1991). MMPI correlates of Exner's egocentricity index in an adolescent psychiatric population. *Journal of Personality Assessment, 56,* 29–34.

Carlson, K., Quinlan, D., Tucker, G. J., & Harrow, M. (1973). Body disturbance and sexual elaboration factors in figure drawings of schizophrenic patients. *Journal of Personality Assessment, 37,* 56–63.

Cates, J. A., & Lapham, R. F. (1991). *Journal of Personality Assessment, 56,* 118–129.

Cooper, A. (1981). A basic TAT set for adolescent males. *Journal of Clinical Psychology, 37,* 411–414.

Costantino, G., Colon-Malgady, G., Malgady, R. G., & Perez, A. (1991). Assessment of attention deficit disorder using a thematic apperception technique. *Journal of Personality Assessment, 57,* 87–95.

Costantino, G., Malgady, R., & Rogler, L. H. (1988a). *Tell-Me-A-Story (TEMAS) manual.* Los Angeles: Western Psychological Services.

Cramer, P. (1980). The development of sexual identity. *Journal of Personality Assessment, 44,* 604–612.

Cummings, J. A. (1986). Projective drawings. In H. Knoff (Ed.), *The assessment of child and adolescent personality* (pp. 199–244) New York: Guilford.

Dana, R. H. (1986). Thematic apperception test used with adolescents. In A. I. Rabin (Ed.), *Projective techniques for adolescents and children* (pp. 14–36). New York: Springer.

Daum, J. M. (1983). Emotional indicators in drawings of aggressive or withdrawn male delinquents. *Journal of Personality Assessment, 47,* 243–249.

DeLatte, J. G., Jr., & Hendrickson, N. J. (1982). Human figure drawing size as a measure of self-esteem. *Journal of Personality Assessment, 46,* 603–606.

Dickson, J. M., Saylor, C. F., & Finch, Jr., A. J. (1990). Personality factors, family structure, and sex of drawn figure on the Draw-A-Person test. *Journal of Personality Assessment, 55,* 362–366.

Doubros, S. G., & Mascarenhas, J. (1967). Effect of test produced anxiety on human figure drawings. *Perceptual and Motor Skills, 25,* 773–775.

Duricko, A. J., Norcross, J. C., & Buskirk, R. D. (1989). Correlates of the Egocentricity Index in child and adolescent outpatients. *Journal of Personality Assessment, 53,* 184–187.

Exner, J. E. (1974). *The Rorschach: A comprehensive system* (Vol. 1). New York: Wiley.

Exner, J. E. (1978). *The Rorschach: A comprehensive system. Vol. 2. Current research and advanced interpretation.* New York: Wiley.

Exner, J. E. (1986). *The Rorschach: A comprehensive system. Vol. 1. Basic foundations.* (2nd ed.). New York: Wiley.

Exner, J. E. (1990). *A Rorschach workbook for the comprehensive system* (3rd ed.). Asheville, NC: Rorschach Workshops.

Exner, J. E., Armbruster, G. L., & Viglione, D. (1978). The temporal stability of tone Rorschach features. *Journal of Personality Assessment, 42,* 374–382.

Exner, J. E., Thomas, E. A., & Mason, B. (1985). Children's Rorschachs: Description and prediction. *Journal of Personality Assessment, 49,* 13–20.

Exner, J. E., & Weiner, I. B. (1982). *The Rorschach: A comprehensive system. Vol. 3. Assessment of children and adolescents.* New York: Wiley-Interscience.

Fuller, G. B., Parmelee, W. M., & Carroll, J. L. (1982). Performance of delinquent and nondelinquent high schools boys on the Rotter Incomplete Sentence Blank. *Journal of Personality Assessment, 46,* 506–510.

Gallucci, N. T. (1989). Personality assessment with children of superior intelligence: Divergence versus psychopathology. *Journal of Personality Assessment, 53,* 749–760.

Gold, S. N. (1980). Relations between level of ego development and adjustment patterns in adolescents. *Journal of Personality Assessment, 44,* 630–638.

Goldberg, P. A. (1965). A review of sentence completion methods in personality assessment. *Journal of Projective Techniques and Personality Assessment, 29,* 12–45.

Goodenough, F. (1926). *Measurement of intelligence by drawings.* New York: Harcourt Brace & World.

Hammer, E. F. (1986). Graphic techniques with children and adolescents. In A. I. Rabin (Ed.), *Projective techniques for adolescents and children* (pp. 239–263). New York: Springer.

Handler, L., & Reyher, J. (1965). Figure drawing anxiety indices: A review of the literature. *Journal of Projective Techniques and Personality Assessment, 29,* 305–313.

Harrington, R. G. (1987). *Testing adolescents: A reference guide for comprehensive psychological assessments.* Kansas City, MO: Test Corporation of America.

Harris, D. B. (1963). *Children's drawings as measures of intellectual maturity.* New York: Harcourt Brace & World.

Harrow, M., Grossman, L. S., Silverstein, M. L., Melzer, H. Y., & Kettering, R. L. (1986). A longitudinal study of thought disorder in manic patients. *Archives of General Psychiatry, 43,* 781–785.

Harrow, M., & Marengo, J. T. (1986). Schizophrenic thought disorder at followup: Its persistence and prognostic significance. *Schizophrenia Bulletin, 12,* 373–393.

Harrow, M., & Quinlan, D. (1977). Is disordered thinking unique to schizophrenia? *Archives of General Psychiatry, 34,* 15–21.

Harrow, M., & Quinlan, D. (1985). *Disordered thinking and schizophrenic psychopathology.* New York: Gardner.

Harrow, M., Quinlan, D., Wallington, S., & Pickett, L., Jr. (1976). Primitive drive dominated thinking: Relationship to acute schizophrenia and sociopathy. *Journal of Personality Assessment, 40,* 31–41.

Hauser, S. T. (1976). Loevinger's model and measure of ego development: A critical review. *Psychological Bulletin, 83,* 928–955.

Haworth, M. (1962). Responses of children to a group projective film and to the Rorschach, CAT, Despert Fables and DAP. *Journal of Projective Techniques, 26,* 47–60.

Heinrich, P., & Triebe, J. K. (1972). Sex preferences in children's human figure drawings. *Journal of Personality Assessment, 36,* 263–267.

Hertz, M. R. (1935). Rorschach norms for an adolescent age group. *Child Development, 6,* 69–76.

Hertz, M. (1960). The Rorschach in adolescence. In A. Rabin & M. Haworth (Eds.), *Projective techniques with children* (pp. 29–61). New York: Grune & Stratton.

Hertz, M. R. (1970). *Frequency tables for scoring responses to the Rorschach inkblot test* (5th ed.). Cleveland: Western Reserve University Press.

Hiler, E. W., & Nesvig, D. (1965). An evaluation of criteria used by clinicians to infer pathology from human figure drawings. *Journal of Consulting Psychology, 29,* 520–529.

Holzman, P. S., Shenton, M. E., & Solovay, M. R. (1986). Quality of thought disorder in differential diagnosis. *Schizophrenia Bulletin, 12,* 360–371.

Holt, R. R. (1977). A method for assessing primary process manifestations and their control in Rorschach responses. In M. A. Rickers-Ovsiankina (Ed.), *Rorschach psychology.* (rev. ed., pp. 375–420). Huntington, NY: Krieger.

Irvin, F. S. (1972). *Sentence Completion Test manual.* Jacksonville, IL: Psychologists and Educators.

Johnston, M. H., & Holzman, P. S. (1979). *Assessing schizophrenic thinking.* San Francisco: Jossey-Bass.

Jones, L. W., & Thomas, C. B. (1961). Studies on figure drawings: A review of the literature. *Psychiatric Quarterly Supplement, 35,* 212–262.

Kestenbaum, C. J., & Williams, D. T. (Eds.). (1988). *Handbook of clinical assessment of children and adolescents.* New York: New York University Press.

Khulman, T. L. (1979). A validation study of the Draw-A-Person as a measure of racial identity acceptance. *Journal of Personality Assessment, 43,* 457–458.

Klopfer, W. G. (1984). The use of the Rorschach in brief clinical evaluation. *Journal of Personality Assessment, 48,* 654–659.

Koppitz, E. M. (1968). *Psychological evaluation of children's human figure drawings.* New York: Grune & Stratton.

Krall, V. (1989). *Developmental psychodiagnostic assessment of children and adolescents.* New York: Human Sciences Press.

Krall, V., Sachs, H., Lazar, B., Rayson, B., Growe, G., Novar, L., & O'Connell, L. (1983). Rorschach norms for inner city children. *Journal of Personality Assessment, 47,* 155–157.

Kwawer, J. S. (1977). Male homosexual psychodynamics and the Rorschach test. *Journal of Personality Assessment, 41,* 10–18.

Lanyon, B. J. (1972). Empirical construction and validation of a sentence completion test for hostility, anxiety and dependency. *Journal of Consulting and Clinical Psychology, 39,* 420–428.

Lanyon, R. I., & Goodstein, L. D. (1982). *Personality assessment* (2nd ed.). New York: Wiley.

Lazar, B. S., & Harrow, M. (1980). Primitive drive dominated thinking. In R. H. Woody (Ed.), *Encyclopedia of clinical assessment* (Vol. 1, 497–511). San Francisco: Jossey-Bass.

Lazar, B. S., & Harrow, M. (1985). Paranoid and nonparanoid schizophrenia: Drive dominated thinking and thought pathology at two phases of disorder. *Journal of Clinical Psychology, 41,* 145–151.

Leifer, M., Shapiro, J. P., Martone, M. W., & Kassem, L. (1991). Rorschach assessment of psychological functioning in sexually abused girls. *Journal of Personality Assessment, 56,* 14–28.

Lipovsky, J. A., Finch, A. J., & Belter, R. W. (1989). *Journal of Personality Assessment, 53,* 449–458.

Loevinger, J., & Wessler, R. (1970). *Measuring ego development: Vol. 1. Constructing a sentence completion test.* San Francisco: Jossey-Bass.

Loevinger, J., Wessler, R., & Redmore, C. (1970). *Measuring ego development: Vol. 2. Scoring manual for women and girls.* San Francisco: Jossey-Bass.

Lorr, M., & Manning, T. (1978). Measurement of ego development by sentence completion and personality test. *Journal of Clinical Psychology, 34,* 354–360.

Lundy, A. (1988). Instructional set and Thematic Apperception Test validity. *Journal of Personality Assessment, 52,* 309–319.

Machover, K. (1949). *Personality projection in the drawings of the human figure.* Springfield, IL: Thomas.

Machover, K. (1953). Human figure drawings of children. *Journal of Projective Techniques, 17,* 85–91.

Magnussen, M. G. (1979). Psychometric and projective techniques. In J. D. Call, J. D. Noshpitz, R. L. Cohen, & I. N. Berlin (Eds.), *Basic handbook of child psychiatry* (pp. 553–568). New York: Basic Books.

Maloney, M., & Payne, L. (1969). Validity of the Draw-A-Person test as a measure of body image. *Perceptual and Motor Skills, 29,* 119–122.

Marengo, J. T., & Harrow, M. (1987). Schizophrenic thought disorder as followup: A persistent or episodic course. *Archives of General Psychiatry, 44,* 651–659.

Martin, J., & Redmore, C. (1978). A longitudinal study of ego development. *Developmental Psychology, 14,* 189–190.

Marsh, D. T., Linberg, L. M., & Smeltzer, J. K. (1991). Human figure drawings of adjudicated and nonadjudicated adolescents. *Journal of Personality Assessment, 57,* 77–86.

Matranga, J. T. (1976). The relationship between behavioral indices of aggression and hostile content on the TAT. *Journal of Personality Assessment, 40,* 130–134.

McArthur, D. S., & Roberts, G. E. (1982). *Roberts Apperception Test for Children manual.* Los Angeles: Western Psychological Services.

McCraw, R. K., & Pegg-McNab, J. (1981). Effect of test order on Rorschach human and movement responses. *Journal of Personality Assessment, 45,* 575–581.

McCraw, R. K., & Pegg-McNab, J. (1989). Rorschach comparisons of male juvenile sex offenders and nonsex offenders. *Journal of Personality Assessment, 53,* 546–553.

McPhee, J. P., & Wegner, K. W. (1976). Kinetic Family Drawing styles and emotionally disturbed childhood behavior. *Journal of Personality Assessment, 40,* 487–491.

Mellsop, G. (1972). Psychiatric patients seen as children and adults: Childhood predictors of adult illness. *Journal of Child Psychology and Psychiatry, 13,* 91–101.

Meyers, C. V. (1978). Toward an objective procedure evaluation of the Kinetic Family Drawing (KFD). *Journal of Personality Assessment, 42,* 358–365.

Murray, H. A. (1938). *Explorations in personality.* New York: Grune & Stratton.

Narayan, S. (1983). Some perspectives of institutionalized handicapped. *Psychological Research Journal, 7,* 19–23.

Nostkoff, D. L., & Lazarus, P. J. (1983). The Kinetic Family Drawing: The reliability of an objective scoring system. *Psychology in the Schools, 20,* 16–21.

O'Brien, R. P., & Patton, W. F. (1974). Development of an objective scoring method for the Kinetic Family Drawing. *Journal of Personality Assessment, 38,* 156–164.

Oster, G. D., Caro, J. E., Eagen, D. R., & Lillo, M. A. (1988). *Assessing adolescents: A practitioner's guide.* New York: Pergamon.

Ostrov, E. (1975). Patterns of Rorschach test scores among three groups of adolescents. In D. Offer & J. Offer (Eds.), *From teenage to young manhood* (pp. 109–126). New York: Basic Books.

Palomares, R. S., Crowley, S. L., Worchel, F. F., Olson, T. K., & Rae, W. A. (1991). A factor analytic structure of the Roberts Apperception Test for Children: A comparison of the standardization sample with a sample of chronically ill children. *Journal of Personality Assessment, 56,* 414–425.

Quinlan, D. M., & Harrow, M. (1974). Boundary disturbances in schizophrenia. *Journal of Abnormal Psychology, 83,* 533–541.

Rabin, A. I. (1977). Enduring sentiments: The continuity of personality over time. *Journal of Personality Assessment, 41,* 564–572.

Rabin, A. I. (Ed.). (1986). *Projective techniques for adolescents and children.* New York: Springer.

Rabin, A. I., & Zlotogorski, Z. (1985). The sentence completion method: Recent research. *Journal of Personality Assessment, 49,* 641–647.

Rabinowitz, A., & Shouval, R. (1977). Fantasy as a medium for the reduction of trait versus state aggression. *Journal of Research in Personality, 11,* 180–190.

Rapaport, D., Gill, M. M., & Schafer, R. (1948). *Diagnostic psychological testing* (Vol. 2). Chicago: Year Book.

Rapaport, D., Gill, M. M., & Schafer, R. (1968). *Diagnostic psychological testing* (rev. ed.). New York: International Universities Press.

Rekers, G. A., & Rosen, A. C. (1990). Projective test findings for boys with gender disturbance: Draw-A-Person test, IT Scale, and Make-A-Picture story test. *Perceptual and Motor Skills, 71,* 771–779.

Reynolds, C. R. (1978). A quick scoring guide to the interpretation of children's Kinetic Family Drawings (KFD). *Psychology in the School, 15,* 489–492.

Reynolds, C. R., & Kamphaus, R. W. (Eds.). (1990). *Handbook of psychological and educational assessment of children: Personality, behavior and context.* New York: Guilford.

Rierdan, J., & Koff, E. (1980). The psychological impact of menarche: Integrative vs. disruptive changes. *Journal of Youth and Adolescence, 9,* 49–58.

Rierdan, J., & Koff, E. (1981). Sexual ambiguity in children's human figure drawings. *Journal of Personality Assessment, 45,* 256–257.

Rierdan, J., Koff, E., & Heller, H. (1982). Gender, anxiety, and human figure drawings. *Journal of Personality Assessment, 46,* 594–596.

Roback, H. (1968). Human figure drawings: Their utility in the clinical psychologist's armamentarium for personality assessment. *Psychological Bulletin, 70,* 1–19.

Rosenberg, M. (1965). *Society and the adolescent self-image.* Princeton, NJ: Princeton University Press.

Rotter, J. B., & Rafferty, J. E. (1950). *Rotter Incomplete Sentence Blank.* New York: Psychological Corporation.

Rubenstein, A. H. (1980). The adolescent with borderline personality organization: Developmental issues, diagnostic considerations, and treatment. In J. S. Kwawer, H. D. Lerner, P. M. Lerner, & A. Sugarman (Eds.), *Borderline phenomena and the Rorschach test* (pp. 441–467). New York: International Universities Press.

Rychlack, J., & O'Leary, L. (1965). Unhealthy content in the Rorschach responses of children and adolescents. *Journal of Projective Techniques, 29,* 354–368.

Saarni, C., & Azara, V. (1977). Developmental analyses of human figure drawings in adolescence, young adulthood, and middle age. *Journal of Personality Assessment, 41*, 31–38.

Schafer, R. (1948). *The clinical application of psychological tests*. New York: International Universities Press.

Schildkrout, M. S., Shenker, I. R., & Sonnenblick, M. (1972). *Human figure drawings in adolescence*. New York: Brunner/Mazel.

Sheridan, S. J. (1978, June). Level of moral reasoning and ego development as factors in predicted vocational success with the mental retarded. *Resources in Education, 13*, 77.

Schimek, J. (1974). Some developmental aspects of primary process manifestations in the Rorschach. *Journal of Personality Assessment, 33*, 226–229.

Siegel, M. G. (1988). Cognitive and projective test assessment. In C. J. Kestenbaum & D. T. Williams (Eds.), *Handbook of clinical assessment of children and adolescents*. New York: New York University Press. pp. 59–84.

Sims, J., Dana, R. H., & Bolton, B. (1983). The validity of the Draw-A-Person Test as an anxiety measure. *Journal of Personality Assessment, 47*, 250–257.

Slemon, A. G., Holzwarth, E. J., Lewis, J., & Sitko, M. (1976). Associative elaboration and integration scales for evaluating TAT protocols. *Journal of Personality Assessment, 40*, 365–369.

Smith, G. M. (1985). The collaborative drawing technique. *Journal of Personality Assessment, 49*, 582–585.

Sobel, H., & Sobel, W. (1976). Discriminating adolescent male delinquents through the use of Kinetic Family Drawings. *Journal of Personality Assessment, 40*, 91–94.

Stevens, E. D. (1981). Barrier score and the values ascribed to selected individuals by high school students. *Journal of Personality Assessment, 45*, 352–358.

Sugarman, A., Bloom-Feshbach, S., & Bloom-Feshbach, J. (1980). The psychological dimensions of borderline adolescents. In J. S. Kwawer, H. D. Lerner, P. M. Lerner, & A. Sugarman (Eds.), *Borderline phenomena and the Rorschach test* (pp. 469–494). New York: International Universities Press.

Sutton, P. M., & Swensen, C. H. (1983). The reliability and concurrent validity of alternative methods for assessing ego development. *Journal of Personality Assessment, 47*, 468–475.

Swenson, C. H. (1968). Empirical evaluations of human figure drawings: 1957–1966. *Psychological Bulletin, 70*, 20–44.

Symonds, P. M. (1948). *Manual for the Symonds Picture-Story Test*. New York: Bureau of Publications, Teachers College, Columbia University.

Tharinger, D. J., & Stark, K. (1990). A qualitative versus quantitative approach to evaluating the Draw-A-Person and Kinetic Family Drawing: A study of mood- and anxiety-disorder children. *Psychological Assessment: A Journal of Consulting and Clinical Psychology, 2*, 365–375.

Urban, W. (1963). *The Draw-A-Person catalogue for interpretive analysis*. Los Angeles: Western Psychological Services.

Urist, J., & Shill, M. (1982). Validity of the Rorschach mutuality of autonomy scale: A replication using excepted responses. *Journal of Personality Assessment, 46*, 450–454.

Van Hasselt, V. B., & Hersen, M. (Eds.). (1987). *Handbook of adolescent psychology*. New York: Pergamon.

Viglione, D. J. (1990). Severe disturbance or trauma-induced adaptive reaction: A Rorschach child case study. *Journal of Personality Assessment, 55*, 280–295.

Weiner, I. B., & Exner, J. (1978). Rorschach indices of disordered thinking in patient and nonpatient adolescents and adults. *Journal of Personality Assessment, 42*, 339–343.

Zgourides, G., Frey, P., Camplaire, C., Tilson, M., & Ihli, K. (1989). Anxiety and perceived helplessness as measured by MMPI and Exner-scored Rorschach protocols in a sample of adolescent outpatients. *Perceptual and Motor Skills, 69*, 458.

Zlotogorski, Z., & Wiggs, E. (1986). Story-and-sentence-completion techniques. In A. I. Rabin (Ed.), *Projective techniques for adolescents and children* (pp. 195–211). New York: Springer.

8
Behavioral Assessment in Adolescents

Grace R. Kalfus

The evaluation of effective interventions is dependent on the utilization of developmentally appropriate and methodologically sound behavioral assessment procedures. Increased attention has been directed to the development of behavioral assessment methodology since the early 1980s, and child behavioral assessment has recently been cited as one area of expanded focus (Gross & Wixted, 1988). Unfortunately, procedures developed for use with children or adults often have been employed with adolescents (e.g., Teri, 1982). The publication of several texts (Feindler & Kalfus, 1990; Hersen & Van Hasselt, 1987; Van Hasselt & Hersen, 1987) targeting assessment and intervention approaches for adolescents has begun to address the need for separate and concentrated efforts with this population.

Ollendick and Greene (1990) have described child behavioral assessment as "an exploratory, hypothesis-testing process in which a range of specific procedures is used in order to understand a given child, group, or social ecology, and to formulate and evaluate specific intervention strategies" (p. 403). Early behavioral approaches focused on identification and measurement of specific, discrete, and observable target behaviors (e.g., Ullman & Krasner, 1965). Factors beyond overt behavior—such as cognitions and physiological behavior (e.g., Last, Griest, & Kazdin, 1985; Mizes, 1991), as well as social contexts (e.g., Patterson, 1976; Shapiro, 1988)—have been considered more recently. These developments suggest the utilization of multiple methods that provide data from disparate sources relevant to the presenting problem(s).

The effects of developmental ability and developmental change are primary considerations in the selection of behavioral assessment procedures (Ollendick & Hersen, 1984). Developmental aspects of adolescence include (a) biological changes of puberty, as well as accompanying cognitions and overt behaviors (Brooks-Gunn, 1987; Kendall & Williams, 1986); (b) concerns regarding identity development (McKinney & Vogel, 1987); (c) reduced involvement in family relationships, along with intensified peer participation (Kelly & Hansen, 1987); and (d) the right to be involved in decisions pertaining to treatment (Adelman, Kaser-Boyd, &

243

Taylor, 1984). Careful attention to these considerations in the development and implementation of behavioral assessment methodology can result in enhanced validity of and compliance with data collection.

A second critical issue is the use of methods that are psychometrically sound. Examination of the psychometric properties of specific assessment methodology is crucial when selecting procedures. Experimental evaluation of reliability and validity are important in the development of behavioral assessment methods.

Cone (1978) has provided a framework for conceptualizing behavioral assessment by categorizing methods along a continuum of "directness." Directness refers to how the method of data collection relates to the actual occurrence of the behavior. Strategies that would be identified as direct, along the continuum from most to least, include observations in naturalistic settings, analogue observations, and self-observations. Methods considered to be increasingly indirect include ratings by others, self-reports, and interviews. This chapter will review current adolescent behavioral assessment technology as proposed by Cone's conceptual framework.

Behavioral Observation

Direct observation of behavior involves the use of observers recording operationally defined overt behavior exhibited by the target individual. Observations are conducted in the individual's natural environment. In contrast, analogue observations involve assessment of behavior in an environment specifically designed to occasion the occurrence of the behavior (e.g., role playing).

Several methodological concerns must be considered. First, it is crucial that the observers receive training in the operational definitions of the target behaviors and in the observation procedures; in order to prevent observer drift, retraining may be necessary. Second, so that interobserver reliability can be assessed regularly, observations must be conducted by two or more observers. Third, data may be influenced by characteristics of the observation procedure itself (e.g., time of observations, complexity of the coding system). Finally, the process of observing behavior may produce reactive effects on the behavior.

Interval recording is one technique frequently used in behavioral observations for assessing continuous high-frequency responses. This procedure involves the recording of the occurrence of the target behavior during short time intervals (e.g., 15 seconds). Variations include whole interval (recording occurrence throughout the interval), partial interval (recording occurrence during a specific part of the interval), and momentary interval (recording occurrence at a specific point in time during the interval) sampling. Data are summarized as percentage occurrence or total number of intervals recorded for the occurrence of the target behavior. Sequential coding systems preserve the order of occurrence of multiple behaviors and therefore can be used to obtain data on antecedent and consequent events.

Another common method of data collection in behavioral observation involves counting the frequency of occurrence of the target behavior. Frequency counts are appropriate when the behavior is of short duration, with an identifiable beginning and end. Alternatively, duration recording (which involves identifying onset and termination) may be appropriate when target behaviors are longer in duration. When data on antecedents and consequences are also desirable, event recording in which narrative data are recorded can be used.

Recording of frequency, duration, and events can be conducted through continuous monitoring or time sampling. In continuous monitoring, behaviors are observed at all times. In contrast, time sampling involves observation of behaviors at specific predetermined times. The frequency of the target behavior(s) should be considered in the design of a time sampling procedure: short and frequent observational periods should be used with high-frequency behaviors, while less frequent but longer periods are appropriate for low-frequency behaviors.

Different instrumentation is needed to conduct behavioral observation. Paper and pencil methods are inexpensive, mobile, and useful with a variety of procedures. For example, interval recording strategies often utilize data sheets with intervals clearly delineated and a cueing device (e.g., a stopwatch or audiotape with prerecorded tones) to signal intervals. Counters can be used to measure frequency and stopwatches to measure duration; both instruments are relatively inexpensive. Electromechanical devices such as event recorders and computers, though expensive, are convenient and allow recording of several behaviors, assessment of sequential relations, and summarization of data.

Naturalistic Observation

Behavioral observations in the natural environment are frequently employed at baseline and to assess the impact of training. An interval recording system used to measure social initiations and interactions is described by Hansen, MacMillan, and Shawchuck (1990); previous work often focused on such classroom behavior, as being out of one's seat and aggression (e.g., Kaufman & O'Leary, 1972). Recent reports of frequency data are more prevalent, particularly with mentally retarded or behaviorally disordered adolescents. Such data have been used to measure verbal initiations, expansions, and terminations (Park & Gaylord-Ross, 1989); public telephone use (Test, Spooner, Keul, & Grossi, 1990); packaging and filing tasks (Berg & Wacker, 1989; Wacker, Berg, Choisser, & Smith, 1989); verbal and physical aggression (Dangel, Deschner, & Rasp, 1989);

and punctuality and preparedness (Hutchins, Williams, & McLaughlin, 1989). Cumulative duration recording has been utilized to assess reinforcer preference (Wacker, Wiggins, Fowler, & Berg, 1988).

The Family Interaction Coding System (FICS; Maerov, Brummett, Patterson, & Reid, 1978; Patterson, 1982) is another example of a naturalistic observation coding system. It was designed to assess in-home family interactions of aggressive youngsters (Loeber, Weissman, & Reid, 1983). Continuous and sequential recording are used to monitor both positive (e.g., compliant) and aversive (e.g., destructive) behaviors for the targeted family member and the individual with whom the target was interacting. Moderate test-retest reliability (Patterson, 1974) has been shown for the FICS. This system also has been shown to discriminate between dysfunctional and normal families (Patterson, 1976; Snyder, 1977).

Data collected using naturalistic observation procedures have been considered to be the most ecologically valid (Cone, 1978). Several difficulties, however, must be considered. For example, observers must be able to gain entry into the environment in which the target behavior occurs, and/or the target behavior may occur only in highly specific situations. Additionally, naturalistic observation of low frequency behaviors is very lengthy and costly.

Analogue Observation

Analogue observation involves role-play assessment to evaluate a variety of areas, including parent-adolescent conflict, problem-solving abilities, and social skills. Role-play assessment generally utilizes a semistructured script describing the scene, lead-in narration, and a confederate who provides provocation prompts. The adolescent is then expected to respond as he or she would in the natural environment under typical circumstances.

Analogue observation methods offer several advantages. They are: (a) useful for assessing low frequency behaviors, (b) are less expensive than naturalistic observation, and (c) maintain greater control over environmental variables. Unfortunately, observation in analogue settings may be limited in generalizability to the natural environment (Bellack, Hersen, & Lamparski, 1979). The situational descriptions may omit details that influence the responses emitted (Ammerman & Hersen, 1986), the procedure may be anxiety provoking (Kern, 1982), and role-play situations that utilize lengthy interactions are limited in their degree of standardization (Kern, 1991). Further research on the reliability and validity of these methods also is warranted.

Social skills and assertion are frequently evaluated through role-play assessment. Hansen, St. Lawrence, and Christoff (1988, 1989) describe an unstructured assessment format in which participants are instructed to talk and get to know each other so that researchers may evaluate conversational skills (e.g., questions, speech acknowledgers and reinforcers, eye contact, and response timing). Francis and Ollendick (1990) utilized a social role-playing test to assess giving/receiving compliments, initiating social interactions, and emitting negative assertions. The Adolescent Assertion Test (Kirkland, Thelen, & Miller 1982) is a role-play measure that consists of same-sex, peer-related situations; ratings of assertiveness, response duration, and response latency are recorded using a 5-point scale.

A number of intervention programs have utilized role-play techniques to measure problem solving and interpersonal conflict. The component skills of problem solving—problem identification, goal definition, generation and evaluation of alternatives, and selection of the best alternative—have been assessed by Tisdelle and St. Lawrence (1988). In the anger control training manual by Feindler and Ecton (1986), frequency of verbal (e.g., appropriate and inappropriate requests) and nonverbal (e.g., eye contact) behaviors are coded for a variety of problematic situations, such as conflict with authority, teasing from peers, and peer competition.

Two analogue coding systems have been developed to assess parent-adolescent communication; these have been shown to discriminate between distressed and nondistressed families (Prinz, Foster, Kent, & O'Leary, 1979; Robin & Weiss, 1980). In the procedure designed by Prinz and his colleagues (Prinz & Kent, 1978; Prinz, Rosenblum, & O'Leary, 1978), participants spend 10 minutes discussing something that the adolescent wants to change. Raters evaluate this interaction on 31 positive (e.g., compromising) and 31 negative (e.g., yelling) behaviors in addition to global ratings of degree of insult, friendliness, and problem-solving effectiveness. Adequate interrater reliability has been demonstrated.

Self-Monitoring

Self-monitoring involves the systematic observation and recording of one's own behavior. This procedure is frequently employed to assess baseline levels of the target behavior and to perform outcome evaluation. The observation and monitoring of one's own responding may influence the occurrence of that behavior; reactivity therefore is a methodological concern that must be considered when examining baseline data obtained from a self-monitoring procedure (e.g., Nelson, 1977). Additionally, the accuracy of self-monitored data must be viewed with caution.

Much research has examined the specific variables that influence the reactivity and accuracy of self-monitoring procedures (e.g., Bornstein, Hamilton, & Bornstein, 1986). Factors that affect reactivity include motivation of the target individual, treatment goals, valence of the target behavior, and type of instructions provided. Accuracy is influenced by training in the self-monitoring procedure, use of systematic procedures, effort required, and reinforcement for accuracy. The characteristics of the self-monitoring device or procedure, timing of recording relative to observation, schedule of self-monitoring, number of target behaviors, and nature of the behaviors influence both reactivity and accuracy.

The methods of self-monitoring have been discussed previously as behavioral observation procedures. Frequency counts, duration recording, and event recording often are used in self-observation and recording.

Numerous self-monitoring procedures have been incorporated into assessment and treatment with adolescent populations. A library counter was used in a study by Schloss, Schloss, and Smith (1988) to self-monitor positive comments, a skill targeted in interview skills training. Other instrumentation that has been utilized includes bead stringing (Litrownik & Freitas, 1980), battery-operated mechanical devices (Gajar, Schloss, Schloss, & Thompson, 1984), and such paper and pencil forms as a hassle log (Feindler & Ecton, 1986), headache diary (Chin & Russo, 1990), and food diary (Lachenmeyer, 1990).

Ratings by Others

Behavioral rating scales and checklists are frequently employed to identify potential behavior problems, to form a preliminary diagnosis, to assist in decisions regarding intervention, and/or to evaluate treatment outcome. There are several advantages to using ratings provided by others. Behavioral ratings have been considered to be an important source of social (Kazdin, 1977) and face validity (Jensen & Haynes, 1986). They are cost-efficient since they require limited client training and therapist time, and they can be objectively scored.

Several scales have parallel forms to be used by different informants. Additional sources of data can be provided by the use of multiple informants (e.g., parents, teachers, peers). Unfortunately, because these data are based on client report, they may not reflect actual behavior. One must also recognize that since multiple informants often observe behavior in disparate settings, reports may differ. These data must therefore be viewed cautiously and examined with particular attention to settings and situations, informants and individuals present, and time. Finally, characteristics of the informant (e.g., depression) may affect ratings (Brody & Forehand, 1986; Friedlander, Weiss, & Traylor, 1986).

Behavior scales and checklists involve rating of the behavior(s) on a 3- to 7-point Likert-type scale or identifying the behavior(s) as either present or absent. Some devices are more general by design and assess a variety of behavior problems, while others are very specific and examine dimensions of a single behavior.

General Behavioral Checklists

Two of the more common general behavioral checklists that have been employed with the adolescent population will be discussed in this section. The Revised Behavior Problem Checklist (RBPC; Quay & Peterson, 1987) requires raters to identify the severity of items describing a variety of behavior problems on a 3-point scale. Four major subscales (conduct disorder, socialized aggression, attention problems–immaturity, anxiety-withdrawal) and two minor subscales (psychotic behavior, motor excess) were derived by factor analysis. Reports of its psychometric properties are provided in the manual. Discriminant validity (between adolescents from intact and high-conflict divorced families; Long, Slater, Forehand, & Fauber, 1988) has also been demonstrated, as has the utility of a Spanish translation with Hispanic-American children and adolescents (Rio, Quay, Santisteban, & Szapocznik, 1989).

The Child Behavior Checklist (CBCL; Achenbach & Edelbrock, 1979, 1983) is another measure frequently used to obtain parental report of adolescent behavior. It contains 118 items, which are rated on a 3-point scale. A positive feature of this measure is its focus on both problems and competencies. Problems are further identified as internalizing (e.g., social withdrawal) or externalizing (e.g., aggression), and summary scores within problem areas can be calculated. Separate norms for 12- to 16-year-old boys and girls are available. Test-retest reliability, criterion-related validity, and construct validity are acceptable.

The Teacher's Report Form (TRF; Achenbach & Edelbrock, 1986) is a parallel measure. It contains many of the same items as the CBCL and some that are more relevant for teacher report. This measure was shown to have good test-retest reliability, and to differentiate between clinically referred and nonreferred boys.

Specific Behavioral Checklists

Few specific behavioral checklists that target adolescent behavior have been developed for completion by significant others. Subscale scores derived from administration of general behavioral checklists such as the RBPC or CBCL can be used to obtain data on specific behaviors.

The Eyberg Child Behavior Inventory (ECBI; Eyberg & Ross, 1978; Robinson, Eyberg, & Ross, 1980) has been validated with an adolescent sample (Eyberg & Robinson, 1983). It consists of 36 childhood conduct problem behaviors, which are rated along two dimensions: frequency of occurrence (intensity) and identification as a problem (problem). Normative data for 2- through 16-year-olds are reported, and clinical cutoff scores are suggested. Adequate test-retest reliability and internal consistency have been demonstrated. Further, this device has differentiated clinic-referred and control youngsters. Concurrent validity of the ECBI has also been documented (Boggs, Eyberg, & Reynolds, 1990).

Social behavior is the target of the Matson Evaluation of Social Skills with Youngsters (MESSY; Matson, Rotatori, & Helsel, 1983). The MESSY teacher report form is composed of 64 items, while the self-report form contains 62 items; ratings are provided on a 5-point scale. Factor analysis resulted in two factors for the teacher report: inappropriate assertiveness/impulsivity, and appropriate social skills. Five factors emerged for the self-report: appropriate social skills, inappropriate assertiveness, overconfident, impulsive/recalcitrant, and jealousy/withdrawal. Psychometric properties of the MESSY have been demonstrated with visually handicapped (e.g., Matson, Heinze, Helsel, Kapperman, & Rotatori, 1986), hearing impaired (Matson, Macklin, & Helsel, 1985; Raymond & Matson, 1989), and normal (Matson, Esveldt-Dawson, & Kazdin, 1983) children and youths.

Peer Assessment

Children who are rejected by peers are at risk for behavioral problems later in life (Parker & Asher, 1987). Hartup (1989) suggests that "friends are 'developmental advantages' in socioemotional development" (p. 125). Peer sociometric procedures provide a means for assessing social status and social relationships in children and adolescents. Administration can be relatively inexpensive and time efficient; however, several considerations must be addressed. First, in providing a rationale in obtaining permission to participate from both youths and parents, confidentiality of the identity of the target adolescent must be maintained. Second, decisions regarding who will administer the sociometric procedure must consider the possible effects of reactivity as well as interest, motivation, and concern with procedural control. Third, antecedent and consequent data on social behavior are not provided by sociometric assessment procedures.

Two common peer sociometric methods are the nomination and rating scale procedures. Nomination sociometrics involve the selection of a predetermined number of peers (e.g., 3) from a larger sample (e.g., classmates) for a particular referent situation (e.g., choosing who the adolescent would most like to work with on a class project). The situation may be positive and/or negative, and the adolescent either writes the peers' names down or checks their names off a list. Social status scores derived from positive nominations indicate levels of popularity/acceptance, levels of rejection are indicated from negative nominations, and the extent to which an adolescent is ignored by peers is suggested by the absence of both positive and negative nominations. With the rating scale procedure, a list/roster of all possible peers is provided, and the adolescent rates each one on a 3- to 7-

point scale for a specific referent situation. Social status scores are obtained by calculating the mean of ratings received by each child.

Few studies have examined the psychometric properties of sociometric assessment procedures with adolescents. One investigation reported adequate 4-week and 5-month test-retest reliability for both the rating and nomination methods with seventh and ninth grade school children, with the rating scale procedure appearing more stable (Kalfus & Berler, 1985).

The Adjustment Scales for Sociometric Evaluation of Secondary-School Students (ASSESS; Prinz, Swan, Liebert, Weintraub, & Neale, 1978) is a structured peer assessment procedure designed for use with youngsters in grades 9 through 12. ASSESS is composed of 41 items and is designed in a matrix format; items are listed as rows down the left side of the page, and the names of peers are listed across the top. Respondents check the name of each peer who can be described by each item (e.g., "Those who say they can beat everyone else up"). Scales were derived by consensual discussion and cross-validated: aggression-disruptiveness, withdrawal, anxiety, social competence, and academic difficulty. High internal consistency, item-to-scale correlations, and test-retest reliability have been reported.

Self-Report Ratings

Behavioral rating scales and checklists have been developed for completion by the adolescent himself or herself. They can be a useful source of data in assessing baseline functioning and treatment outcome. Very few have been constructed that are general in function; many are available that examine specific target behaviors.

General Behavioral Checklists

The Jesness Behavior Check List (Jesness, 1971) was developed with institutionalized delinquents to assess personal and interpersonal functioning. It is composed of 80 items, each of which is rated on a 5-point scale. Scores on 11 factor-analytically derived and three rationally derived scales are obtained; these include friendliness versus hostility, enthusiasm versus depression, and sociability versus poor peer relations. Parallel forms for self-report and adult/observer report are available. Adequate interrater reliability has been demonstrated.

Additionally, the Youth Self-Report Form (Achenbach & Edelbrock, 1987), the equivalent of the CBCL for use with 11- to 18-year-olds, is composed of 102 items rated on a 3-point scale of severity. It measures multiple areas of dysfunction (e.g., aggression, anxiety). Further examination of its psychometric properties has been suggested, however, before it is used clinically (Witt, Cavell, Heffer, Carey, & Martens, 1988).

Specific Behavioral Checklists

There are numerous behavioral checklists and rating scales that target specific behaviors. This chapter will offer a brief review of the available measures for each of the following target areas: self-esteem, depression, activity/reinforcement schedules, hopelessness, anxiety, fears, problem solving, parent-adolescent communication, and eating disorders.

Self-esteem. The Piers-Harris Children's Self-Concept Scale (Piers, 1984) was designed for use with youngsters ages 8 through 18 years. Using a dichotomous scale, responses to 80 statements (e.g., "I am a good person") are provided. Factor analysis resulted in six scales: behavior, intellectual and school status, physical appearance and attributes, anxiety, popularity, and happiness and satisfaction. Moderate concurrent and convergent validity, test-retest reliability, and good internal consistency have been demonstrated.

Depression. The Beck Depression Inventory (BDI; Beck, 1967, Beck, Ward, Mendelson, Mock, & Erbaugh, 1961) has good reliability, internal consistency, and discriminant validity. Recent examination of the BDI with adolescents has provided normative data for 14- to 17-year-olds across age and sex (Teri, 1982) and has shown it to be a useful assessment instrument (e.g., Barrera & Garrison-Jones, 1988).

A downward extension of the BDI, the Children's Depression Inventory (CDI; Kovacs, 1980/1981, 1985) was designed for use with youngsters ages 8 to 17 years. It consists of 27 items that describe depressive symptomatology. Each item is rated on severity based on the previous 2 weeks. Adequate internal consistency, 1-month test-retest reliability, and concurrent validity have been demonstrated.

Other investigators have examined psychometric properties of the CDI and have found high internal consistency (Ollendick & Yule, 1990; Saylor, Finch, Spirito, & Bennett, 1984), acceptable 6-week (Finch, Saylor, Edwards, & McIntosh, 1987) and 1-year test-retest reliability (Smucker, Craighead, Craighead, & Green, 1986), and good predictive validity (Mattison, Handford, Kales, Goodman, & McLaughlin, 1990). Shain, Naylor, and Alessi (1990) demonstrated good to excellent concurrent validity with two clinician-completed scales and the Reynolds Adolescent Depression Scale (RADS; Reynolds, 1987). A significant decrease in CDI scores between test administrations has been reported (Finch et al., 1987; Nelson & Politano, 1990), leading to suggestions for utilization of more than one baseline assessment prior to treatment implementation. Negative relationships between CDI scores and cognitive and social functioning also have been demonstrated (Fauber, Forehand, Long, Faust, & Burke, 1987; Slotkin, Forehand, Fauber, McCombs, & Long, 1988).

Activity/Reinforcement Schedules. Several behavioral inventories that measure activities and reinforcers may be useful assessment instruments. The Adolescent Activities Checklist (AAC; Carey, Kelley, Buss, & Scott, 1986; Cole, Kelley, & Carey, 1988) describes 100 pleasant and unpleasant activities. While self-reported depression has consistently been positively related to frequency of unpleasant activities, negative relationships with frequency of pleasant activities have been reported less consistently (Carey et al., 1986; Cole et al., 1988; Kauth & Zettle, 1990). Reinforcement surveys for adolescents are also available, such as the Adolescent Reinforcement Survey Schedule (ARSS; Cautela, 1981; Cautela, Cautela, & Esonis, 1983) and the Survey of Rewards for Teens (Houlihan, Jesse, Levine, & Sombke, 1991).

Hopelessness. The Hopelessness Scale for Children (HSC; Kazdin, French, Unis, Esveldt-Dawson, & Sherick, 1983) contains 17 true/false items designed to measure hopelessness in 8- to 13-year-old youngsters. Moderate test-retest reliability, acceptable internal consistency, convergence between measures of hopelessness and depression, and discrimination between normal adolescents and suicide attempters have been demonstrated (Spirito, Williams, Stark, & Hart, 1988).

Anxiety. The Children's Manifest Anxiety Scale (RCMAS; Reynolds & Richmond, 1978, 1985) was developed for use with 6- to 19-year-olds and contains 37 items, 28 assessing anxiety and 9 constituting a lie scale. Three anxiety factors emerged from factor analysis: physiological, worry/oversensitivity, and concentration. Separate norms are available according to grade and sex. The RCMAS has been shown to possess adequate internal consistency (Reynolds & Paget, 1983; Reynolds & Richmond, 1978), concurrent validity (Reynolds, 1980), construct validity (Reynolds & Paget, 1981; Reynolds & Richmond, 1979), predictive validity (Reynolds, 1981), content validity (Reynolds & Richmond, 1978) and 9-month test-retest reliability (Reynolds, 1981).

Alternatively, the State-Trait Anxiety Inventory (STAI; Spielberger, 1983) consists of 40 items that assess state or trait anxiety; each is rated on a 4-point scale. Normative data for a restricted sample of college students studying introductory psychology and 10th-grade high school students are provided. High internal consistency and moderate test-retest reliability have been demonstrated.

Fear. The Fear Survey Schedule for Children-Revised (FSSC-R; Ollendick, 1983) contains 80 items representing specific stimuli, which are rated on a 3-point scale. Factor analysis resulted in five primary factors: fear of failure and criticism, fear of the unknown, fear of injury and small animals, fear of danger and death, and medical fears (Ollendick, King, & Frary, 1989; Ollendick, Matson, & Helsel, 1985a). The FSSC-R has been shown to have internal consistency (Ollendick, 1983; Ollendick & Yule, 1990), high test-retest reliability, and acceptable convergent and discriminant validity (Ollendick, 1983). Normative data on frequency and intensity for 7- to 18-year-old youngsters are available (Ollendick et al., 1985a). The FSSC-R also has been examined with visually impaired adolescents (Ollendick, Matson, & Helsel, 1985b).

Problem Solving. The Adolescent Problems Inventory (API; Freedman, Rosenthal, Donahoe, Schlundt, & McFall, 1978) involves the presentation of problematic situations to which a single verbal response is required. In contrast to typical role-play assessments, continued responding in each situation is not examined; following the single response, the next item is presented. The API is composed of 44 items that deal with problem situations identified as common and difficult to handle by delinquent boys (e.g., aggressive behavior with peers, peer pressure, teachers, and school-related problems). Each item is read to the adolescent, who describes how he or she would respond in that situation. Responses are rated on a 5-point scale of competence.

The API was found to differentiate between delinquents, nondelinquents, and high school "superstars." Also, the Problem Inventory for Girls (PIAG; Gaffney & McFall, 1981), an extension of the API, was found to discriminate between delinquents and nondelinquents, have good inter-rater reliability, and correlate negatively with reported adjudicated delinquency (Ward & McFall, 1986).

Parent-Adolescent Communication. The Conflict Behavior Questionnaire (CBQ; Prinz et al., 1979) was designed to assess an adolescent's evaluation of his or her parent's interaction style and of the interaction within the dyad. A parallel form is available for parent report. Research has demonstrated that the CBQ has good internal consistency, is able to discriminate between distressed and nondistressed adolescent-mother dyads (Prinz et al., 1979; Robin & Weiss, 1980), and is sensitive to treatment effects (Robin, 1981). The Issues Checklist (IC; Robin, Kent, O'Leary, Foster, & Prinz, 1977) is composed of 44 common problems that respondents rate on intensity. Distressed and nondistressed dyads have been discriminable based on adolescent-reported intensity and mother-reported frequency and intensity (Prinz et al., 1979; Robin & Weiss, 1980).

Eating Disorders. The Eating Disorders Inventory (EDI; Garner & Olmstead, 1984, 1986) is composed of 64 items that are rated on a 6-point scale. Eight dimensions are examined: drive for thinness, bulimia, body dissatisfaction, ineffectiveness, perfectionism, interpersonal distrust, interoceptive awareness, and maturity fears. Normative data for eating-disordered populations and a female comparison group have been reported, as well as adequate internal consistency and criterion-related validity. Rosen, Silberg, and Ross (1988) obtained normative data for a sample of 9th- through 12th-grade boys and girls.

A more specific measure designed to identify behaviors reflected in the diagnosis of bulimia is the Bulimia Test (BULIT; Smith & Thelen, 1984; Thelen, McLaughlin-Mann, Pruitt, & Smith, 1987). It consists of 32 multiple-choice items that, when subjected to factor analysis, resulted in seven factors: bingeing/losing control, feelings following bingeing, vomiting, food preferences during a binge, laxative/diuretic abuse, weight fluctuations, and menstrual regularity. Examination of the psychometric properties of the BULIT has revealed good test-retest reliability and concurrent validity; also, the test discriminated between bulimic and nonbulimic individuals. Replication of nearly all factors (bingeing excluded) and similar prevalence rates have been shown with a sample of rural college, high school, and junior high school students (Stein & Brinza, 1989a, b).

Behavioral Interviewing

The behavioral interview involves the collection of data regarding the adolescent's functioning in a number of different areas. These include information about the presenting problem(s) (e.g., history, frequency, duration, intensity, antecedents, consequences); previous treatment attempts; academic and school functioning; relationships with parents, siblings, and peers; developmental history; and potential reinforcers. The adolescent and his or her parents may participate in the interview. Significant others (e.g., teachers, siblings, peers) may also be involved.

The use of structured interview procedures has been advocated in order to improve diagnostic reliability and develop more explicit criteria for diagnosis (Edelstein & Berler, 1987). Structured and systematic procedures also may take less time than unstructured devices, may be easier to conduct for the beginning therapist, and may provide more reliable data. In a highly structured interview, specific content areas are reviewed in a particular order through use of a set of standardized questions and rules for coding of responses. General guidelines are provided in semistructured interview formats; this permits greater flexibility and clinical judgment in conducting the interview and recording responses. By contrast, unstructured interviews are the most flexible: the behavior of the informant guides the interview.

Several structured and semistructured interview protocols are available for use with adolescents and their parents. All provide a method for obtaining data on historical variables as well as presenting behaviors specific to diagnoses and behavioral observations. The Diagnostic Interview for Children and Adolescents (DICA; Herjanic & Reich, 1982; Reich, Herjanic, Welner, & Gandhy, 1982) is highly structured and takes approximately 60 to 90 minutes to complete. Moderate agreement has been demonstrated between child/adolescent and parental reports when the symptoms discussed were concrete, observable, severe, and unambiguous; adolescent reports were more consistent with maternal reports. In addition, high inter-interview reliability, good agreement with clinician-provided discharge diagnoses, and moderate parent-child agreement have been reported (Welner, Reich, Herjanic, Jung, & Amado, 1987).

An example of a semistructured interview is the Schedule for Affective Disorders and Schizophrenia for school-age children (Kiddie-SADS-Present Episode, or K-SADS-P; Puig-Antich & Chambers, 1986). Administration of the K-SADS-P involves interviews with the youngster and parents(s), each taking 45 to 90 minutes. Adequate to good test-retest reliability, interrater reliability, and mother-child agreement have been demonstrated for many diagnoses (Apter, Orvaschel, Laseg, Moses, & Tyano, 1989; Chambers et al., 1985). The K-SADS-P has also been shown to be sensitive to the effects of drug intervention in a small sample of depressed children (Puig-Antich, Blau, Marx, Greenhill, & Chambers, 1978).

Summary

This chapter has provided an overview of the available measures for behavioral assessment of adolescents. Methods were presented from most direct to most indirect, according to Cone's (1978) conceptual schema. Attention to the psychometric properties of measures in the selection of methodology is suggested, as is the use of multiple methods utilizing different sources and informants in order to obtain the most accurate and valid data. Careful consideration must be used in planning the assessment battery to avoid unnecessary and excessive evaluation. Additional instruction and even role-playing exercises may be needed to ensure accurate data collection.

Future research in a number of areas in adolescent behavioral assessment is warranted. First, there is a need for continued development of specific technology for use with adolescents (e.g., in self-reported anger control and sociometric procedures). Second, assessment of reliability and validity of many of these methods is necessary; research employing adolescents of different ages and diagnoses would contribute to the growth in this field. Third, the impact of development on the normative data base is also critical.

References

Achenbach, T. M., & Edelbrock, C. S. (1979). The Child Behavior Profile: II. Boys aged 12–16 and girls aged 6–11 and 12–16. *Journal of Consulting and Clinical Psychology, 47*, 223–233.

Achenbach, T. M., & Edelbrock, C. (1983). *Manual for the Child Behavior Check-list and Revised Child Behavior Profile.* Burlington: University of Vermont, Department of Psychiatry.

Achenbach, T. M., & Edelbrock, C. (1986). *Manual for the Teacher's Report Form and Teacher Version of the Child Behavior Profile.* Burlington: University of Vermont, Department of Psychiatry.

Achenbach, T. M., & Edelbrock, C. (1987). *Manual for the Youth Self-Report and Profile.* Burlington: University of Vermont, Department of Psychiatry.

Adelman, H. S., Kaser-Boyd, N., & Taylor, L. (1984). Children's participation in consent for psychotherapy and their subsequent response to treatment. *Journal of Clinical Child Psychology, 13,* 170–178.

Ammerman, R. T., & Hersen, M. (1986). Effects of scene manipulation on role-play test behavior. *Journal of Psychopathology and Behavioral Assessment, 8,* 55–67.

Apter, A., Orvaschel, H., Laseg, M., Moses, T., & Tyano, S. (1989). Psychometric properties of the K-SADS-P in an Israeli adolescent inpatient population. *Journal of the American Academy of Child and Adolescent Psychiatry, 28,* 61–65.

Barrera, M., Jr., & Garrison-Jones, C. V. (1988). Properties of the Beck Depression Inventory as a screening instrument for adolescent depression. *Journal of Abnormal Child Psychology, 16,* 263–273.

Beck, A. T. (1967). *Depression: Clinical, experimental, and theoretical aspects.* New York: Harper and Row.

Beck, A. T., Ward, C. H., Mendelson, M., Mock, J., & Erbaugh, J. (1961). An inventory for measuring depression. *Archives of General Psychology, 4,* 561–571.

Bellack, A. S., Hersen, M., & Lamparski, D. (1979). Role-play tests for assessing social skills: Are they valid? Are the useful? *Journal of Consulting and Clinical Psychology, 47,* 335–342.

Berg, W. K., & Wacker, D. P. (1989). Evaluation of tactile prompts with a student who is deaf, blind, and mentally retarded. *Journal of Applied Behavior Analysis, 22,* 93–99.

Boggs, S. R., Eyberg, S., & Reynolds, L. A. (1990). Concurrent validity of the Eyberg Child Behavior Inventory. *Journal of Clinical Child Psychology, 19,* 75–78.

Bornstein, P. H., Hamilton, S. B., & Bornstein, M. T. (1986). Self-monitoring procedures. In A. R. Ciminero, K. S. Calhoun, & H. E. Adams (Eds.), *Handbook of behavioral assessment* (2nd ed.). New York: Wiley.

Brody, G., & Forehand, R. (1986). Maternal perceptions of child maladjustment as a function of the combined influence of child behavior and maternal depression. *Journal of Consulting and Clinical Psychology, 54,* 237–240.

Brooks-Gunn, J. (1987). Pubertal processes: Their relevance for developmental research. In V. B. Van Hasselt & M. Hersen (Eds.), *Handbook of adolescent psychology.* New York: Pergamon.

Carey, M. P., Kelley, M. L., Buss, R. R., & Scott, W. O. N. (1986). Relationship of activity to depression in adolescents: Development of the Adolescent Activities Checklist. *Journal of Consulting and Clinical Psychology, 54,* 320–322.

Cautela, J. R. (1981). *Behavior analysis forms for clinical intervention* (Vol. 2). Champaign, IL: Research Press.

Cautela, J. R., Cautela, J., & Esonis, S. (1983). *Forms for behavior analysis with children*. Champaign, IL: Research Press.

Chambers, W. J., Puig-Antich, J., Hirsch, M., Paez, P., Ambrosini, P. J., Tabrizi, M. A., & Davies, M. (1985). The assessment of affective disorder in children and adolescents by semistructured interview: Test-retest reliability of the K-SADS-P. *Archives of General Psychiatry, 42*, 696–702.

Chin, R. J., & Russo, D. C. (1990). Behavioral medicine treatment of an adolescent with cystic fibrosis: A model of coping with chronic illness. In E. L. Feindler & G. R. Kalfus (Eds.), *Adolescent behavior therapy handbook*. New York: Springer.

Cole, T. L., Kelley, M. L., & Carey, M. P. (1988). The Adolescent Activities Checklist: Reliability, standardization data, and factorial validity. *Journal of Abnormal Child Psychology, 16*, 475–484.

Cone, J. D. (1978). The behavioral assessment grid (BAG): A conceptual framework and taxonomy. *Behavior Therapy, 8*, 411–426.

Dangel, R. F., Deschner, J. P., & Rasp, R. R. (1989). Anger control training for adolescents in residential treatment. *Behavior Modification, 13*, 447–458.

Edelstein, B. A., & Berler, E. S. (1987). Interviewing and report writing. In C. L. Frame & J. L. Matson (Eds.), *Handbook of assessment in child psychopathology: Applied issues in differential diagnosis and treatment evaluation*. New York: Plenum.

Eyberg, S. M., & Robinson, E. A. (1983). Conduct problem behavior: Standardization of a behavior rating scale with adolescents. *Journal of Clinical Child Psychology, 12*, 347–354.

Eyberg, S. M., & Ross, A. W. (1978). Assessment of child behavior problems: The validation of a new inventory. *Journal of Clinical Child Psychology, 7*, 113–116.

Fauber, R., Forehand, R., Long, N., Faust, M., & Burke, J. (1987). The relationship of young adolescent CDI scores to their social and cognitive functioning. *Journal of Psychopathology and Behavioral Assessment, 9*, 161–172.

Feindler, E. L., & Ecton, R. B. (1986). *Adolescent anger control*. New York: Pergamon.

Feindler, E. L., & Kalfus, G. R. (Eds.). (1990). *Adolescent behavior therapy handbook*. New York: Springer.

Finch, A. J., Jr., Saylor, C. F., Edwards, G. L., & McIntosh, J. A. (1987). Children's Depression Inventory: Reliability over repeated administrations. *Journal of Clinical Child Psychology, 16*, 339–341.

Francis, G., & Ollendick, T. H. (1990). Behavioral treatment of social anxiety. In E. L. Feindler & G. R. Kalfus (Eds.), *Adolescent behavior therapy handbook*. New York: Springer.

Freedman, B. J., Rosenthal, L., Donahoe, C. P. J., Schlundt, D. G., & McFall, R. M. (1978). A social-behavioral analysis of skill deficits in delinquent and nondelinquent adolescent boys. *Journal of Consulting and Clinical Psychology, 46*, 1448–1462.

Friedlander, S., Weiss, D. S., & Traylor, J. (1986). Assessing the influence of maternal depression on the validity of the Child Behavior Checklist. *Journal of Abnormal Child Psychology, 14*, 123–133.

Gaffney, L. R., & McFall, R. M. (1981). A comparison of social skills in delinquent and nondelinquent adolescent girls using a behavioral role-playing inventory. *Journal of Consulting and Clinical Psychology, 49*, 959–967.

Gajar, A., Schloss, P. J., Schloss, C. N., & Thompson, C. K. (1984). Effects of feedback and self-monitoring on head trauma youths' conversation skills. *Journal of Applied Behavior Analysis, 17*, 353–358.

Garner, D. M., & Olmstead, M. P. (1984). *Manual for Eating Disorder Inventory (EDI)*. Odessa, FL: Psychological Assessment Resources.

Garner, D. M., & Olmstead, M. P. (1986). *Eating Disorder Inventory (EDI): Manual supplement*. Odessa, FL: Psychological Assessment Resources.

Gross, A. M., & Wixted, J. T. (1988). Assessment of child behavior problems. In A. S. Bellack & M. Hersen (Eds.), *Behavioral assessment: A practical handbook* (3rd ed.). New York: Pergamon.

Hansen, D. J., MacMillan, V. M., & Shawchuck, C. R. (1990). Social isolation. In E. L. Feindler & G. R. Kalfus (Eds.), *Adolescent behavior therapy handbook*. New York: Springer.

Hansen, D. J., St. Lawrence, J. S., & Christoff, K. A. (1988). Conversation skills of inpatient conduct-disordered youths: Social validation of component behaviors and implications for skills training. *Behavior Modification, 12*, 424–444.

Hansen, D. J., St. Lawrence, J. S., & Christoff, K. A. (1989). Group conversational-skills training with inpatient children and adolescents: Social validation, generalization, and maintenance. *Behavior Modification, 13*, 4–31.

Hartup, W. W. (1989). Social relationships and their developmental significance. *American Psychologist, 44*, 120–126.

Herjanic, B., & Reich, W. (1982). Development of a structured psychiatric interview for children: Agreement between child and parent on individual symptoms. *Journal of Abnormal Child Psychology, 10*, 307–324.

Hersen, M., & Van Hasselt, V. B. (Eds.). (1987). *Behavior therapy with children and adolescents: A clinical approach*. New York: Wiley.

Houlihan, D., Jesse, V. C., Levine, H. D., & Sombke, C. (1991). A survey of rewards for use with teenage children. *Child and Family Behavior Therapy, 13*, 1–12.

Hutchins, P., Williams, R. L., & McLaughlin, T. F. (1989). Using group contingent free time to increase punctuality and preparedness of high school special education students. *Child and Family Behavior Therapy, 11*, 59–70.

Jensen, B. J., & Haynes, S. N. (1986). Self-report questionnaires and inventories. In A. R. Ciminero, K. S. Calhoun, & H. E. Adams (Eds.), *Handbook of behavioral assessment* (2nd ed.). New York: Wiley.

Jesness, C. F. (1971). *Jesness Behavior Check List Manual*. Palo Alto, CA: Consulting Psychologists Press.

Kalfus, G. R., & Berler, E. S. (1985). Test-retest reliability of sociometric questionnaires across four grade levels. *Journal of Clinical Child Psychology, 14*, 345–347.

Kaufman, K. F., & O'Leary, K. D. (1972). Reward, cost, and self-evaluation procedures for disruptive adolescents in a psychiatric hospital school. *Journal of Applied Behavior Analysis, 5*, 293–309.

Kauth, M. R., & Zettle, R. D. (1990). Validation of depression measures in adolescent populations. *Journal of Clinical Psychology, 46*, 291–295.

Kazdin, A. E. (1977). Assessing the clinical or applied importance of behavior change through social validation. *Behavior Modification, 1*, 427–452.

Kazdin, A. E., French, N. H., Unis, A. S., Esveldt-Dawson, K., & Sherick, R. B. (1983). Hopelessness, depression, and suicidal intent among psychiatrically disturbed inpatient children. *Journal of Consulting and Clinical Psychology, 51,* 504–510.

Kelly, J. A., & Hansen, D. J. (1987). Social interactions and adjustment. In V. B. Hasselt & M. Hersen (Eds.), *Handbook of adolescent psychology.* New York: Pergamon.

Kendall, P. C., & Williams, C. L. (1986). Therapy with adolescents: Treating the "marginal man." *Behavior Therapy, 17,* 522–537.

Kern, J. M. (1982). The comparative external and concurrent validity of three role-plays for assessing heterosocial performance. *Behavior Therapy, 13,* 666–680.

Kern, J. M. (1991). An evaluation of a novel role-play methodology: The standardized idiographic approach. *Behavior Therapy, 22,* 13–29.

Kirkland, K. D., Thelen, M. H., & Miller, D. J. (1982). Group assertion training with adolescents. *Child and Family Behavior Therapy, 4,* 1–12.

Kovacs, M. (1980/1981). Rating scales to assess depression in school-aged children. *Acta Paedopsychiatry 46,* 305–315.

Kovacs, M. (1985). The Children's Depression Inventory (CDI). *Psychopharmacology Bulletin, 21,* 995–998.

Lachenmeyer, J. R. (1990). Bulimia in adolescence. In E. L. Feindler & G. R. Kalfus (Eds.), *Adolescent behavior therapy handbook.* New York: Springer.

Last, C. G., Griest, D., & Kazdin, A. E. (1985). Physiological and cognitive assessment of a fire-setting child. *Behavior Modification, 9,* 94–102.

Litrownik, A. J., & Freitas, J. L. (1980). Self-monitoring in moderately retarded adolescents: Reactivity and accuracy as a function of valence. *Behavior Therapy, 11,* 245–255.

Loeber, R., Weissman, W., & Reid, J. B. (1983). Family interactions of assertive adolescents, stealers, and nondelinquents. *Journal of Abnormal Child Psychology, 11,* 1–14.

Long, N., Slater, E., Forehand, R., & Fauber, R. (1988). Continued high or reduced interparental conflict following divorce: Relation to young adolescent adjustment. *Journal of Consulting and Clinical Psychology, 56,* 467–469.

Maerov, S. L., Brummett, B., Patterson, G. R., & Reid, J. B. (1978). Coding of family interactions. In J. B. Reid (Ed.), *A social learning approach to family intervention: Vol. 3. Observation in home settings.* Eugene, OR: Castalia.

Matson, J. L., Esveldt-Dawson, K., & Kazdin, A. E. (1983). Validation of methods for assessing social skills in children. *Journal of Clinical Child Psychology, 12,* 174–180.

Matson, J. L., Heinze, A., Helsel, W. J., Kapperman, G., & Rotatori, A. F. (1986). Assessing social behaviors in the visually handicapped: The Matson Evaluation of Social Skills with Youngsters (MESSY). *Journal of Clinical Child Psychology, 15,* 78–87.

Matson, J. L., Macklin, G. F., & Helsel, W. J. (1985). Psychometric properties of the Matson Evaluation Scale of Social Skills with Youngsters (MESSY) with emotional problems and self-concept in deaf children. *Journal of Behavior Therapy and Experimental Psychiatry, 16,* 117–123.

Matson, J. L., Rotatori, A. F., & Helsel, W. J. (1983). Development of a rating scale to measure social skills in children: The Matson Evaluation of Social

Skills with Youngsters (MESSY). *Behaviour Research and Therapy, 21* 335–340.

Mattison, R. E., Handford, H. A., Kales, H. C., Goodman, A. L., & McLaughlin, R. E. (1990). Four-year predictive value of the Children's Depression Inventory. *Psychological Assessment, 2,* 169–174.

McKinney, J. P., & Vogel, J. (1987). Developmental theories. In V. B. Van Hasselt & M. Hersen (Eds.), *Handbook of adolescent psychology.* New York: Pergamon.

Mizes, J. S. (1991). Construct validity and factor stability of the Anorectic Cognitions Questionnaire. *Addictive Behaviors, 16,* 89–93.

Nelson, R. O. (1977). Methodological issues in assessment via self-monitoring. In J. D. Cone & R. P. Hawkins (Eds.), *Behavioral assessment: New directions in clinical psychology.* New York: Brunner/Mazel.

Nelson, W. M., III, & Politano, P. M. (1990). Children's Depression Inventory: Stability over repeated administrations in psychiatric inpatient children. *Journal of Clinical Child Psychology, 19,* 254–256.

Ollendick, T. H. (1983). Reliability and validity of the Revised Fear Survey Schedule for Children (FSSC-R). *Behaviour Research and Therapy, 21,* 685–692.

Ollendick, T. H., & Greene, R. (1990). Behavioral assessment of children. In G. Goldstein & M. Hersen (Eds.), *Handbook of psychological assessment* (2nd ed.). New York: Pergamon.

Ollendick, T. H., & Hersen, M. (1984). An overview of child behavioral assessment. In T. H. Ollendick & M. Hersen (Eds.), *Child behavioral assessment: Principles and procedures.* New York: Pergamon.

Ollendick, T. H., King, N. J., & Frary, R. B. (1989). Fears in children and adolescents: Reliability and generalizability across gender, age, and nationality. *Behaviour Research and Therapy, 27,* 19–26.

Ollendick, T. H., Matson, J. L., & Helsel, W. J. (1985a). Fears in children and adolescents: Normative data. *Behaviour Research and Therapy, 23,* 465–467.

Ollendick, T. H., Matson, J. L., & Helsel, W. J., (1985b). Fears in visually-impaired and normally-sighted youths. *Behaviour Research and Therapy, 23,* 375–378.

Ollendick, T. H., & Yule, W. (1990). Depression in British and American children and its relation to anxiety and fear. *Journal of Consulting and Clinical Psychology, 58,* 126–129.

Park, H. S., & Gaylord-Ross, R. (1989). A problem-solving approach to social skills training in employment settings with mentally retarded youth. *Journal of Applied Behavior Analysis, 22,* 373–380.

Parker, J. G., & Asher, S. R. (1987). Peer relations and later adjustment: Are low-accepted children "at risk"? *Psychological Bulletin, 102,* 357–389.

Patterson, G. R. (1974). Interventions for boys with conduct problems: Multiple settings, treatments, and criteria. *Journal of Consulting and Clinical Psychology, 42,* 471–481.

Patterson, G. R. (1976). The aggressive child: Victim and architect of a coercive system. In E. J. Mash, L. A. Hammerlynck, & L. C. Hardy (Eds.), *Behavior modification and families.* New York: Brunner/Mazel.

Patterson, G. R. (1982). *A social learning approach: Vol. 3. Coercive family process.* Eugene, OR: Castalia.

Piers, E. V. (1984). *Piers-Harris Children's Self-Concept Scale: Revised manual*. Los Angeles: Western Psychological Services.

Prinz, R. J., Foster, S., Kent, R. N., & O'Leary, K. D. (1979). Multivariate assessment of conflict in distressed and nondistressed mother-adolescent dyads. *Journal of Applied Behavior Analysis, 12*, 691–700.

Prinz, R. J., & Kent, R. N. (1978). Recording parent-adolescent interactions without the use of frequency or interval-by-interval coding. *Behavior Therapy, 9*, 602–604.

Prinz, R. J., Rosenblum, R. S., & O'Leary, K. D. (1978). Affective communication differences between distressed and nondistressed mother-adolescent dyads. *Journal of Abnormal Child Psychology, 6*, 373–383.

Prinz, R. J., Swan, G., Liebert, D., Weintraub, S., & Neale, J. M. (1978). ASSESS: Adjustment Scales for Sociometric Evaluation of Secondary-School Students. *Journal of Abnormal Child Psychology, 6*, 493–501.

Puig-Antich, J., Blau, S., Marx, N., Greenhill, L. I., & Chambers, W. (1978). Prepubertal major depressive disorders: A pilot study. *Journal of the American Academy of Child Psychiatry, 17*, 695–707.

Puig-Antich, J., & Chambers, W. J. (1986). *Schedule for affective disorders and schizophrenia for school-age children (6–18 years): Kiddie-SADS-Present Episode (K-SADS-P)*. Unpublished manuscript.

Quay, H. C., & Peterson, D. R. (1987). *Manual for the Revised Behavior Problem Checklist*. (Available from H. C. Quay, Department of Psychology, P. O. Box 248185, University of Miami, Coral Gables, FL 33124)

Raymond, K. L., & Matson, J. L. (1989). Social skills in the hearing impaired. *Journal of Clinical Child Psychology, 18*, 247–258.

Reich, W., Herjanic, B., Welner, Z., & Gandhy, P. R. (1982). Development of a structured psychiatric interview for children: Agreement on diagnosis comparing child and parent interviews. *Journal of Abnormal Child Psychology, 10*, 325–336.

Reynolds, C. R. (1980). Concurrent validity of "What I Think and Feel": The Revised Children's Manifest Anxiety Scale. *Journal of Consulting and Clinical Psychology, 48*, 774–775.

Reynolds, C. R. (1981). Long-term stability of scores on the RCMAS. *Perceptual and Motor Skills, 53*, 702.

Reynolds, C. R., & Paget, K. D. (1981). Factor analysis of the Revised Children's Manifest Anxiety Scale for blacks, whites, males, and females with a national normative sample. *Journal of Consulting and Clinical Psychology, 49*, 352–359.

Reynolds, C. R., & Paget, K. D. (1983). National normative and reliability data for the revised Children's Manifest Anxiety Scale. *School Psychology Review, 12*, 324–336.

Reynolds, C. R., & Richmond, B. O. (1978). "What I Think and Feel": A revised measure of children's manifest anxiety. *Journal of Abnormal Child Psychology, 6*, 271–280.

Reynolds, C. R., & Richmond, B. O. (1979). Factor structure and construct validity of "What I Think and Feel": The Revised Children's Manifest Anxiety Scale. *Journal of Personality Assessment, 43*, 281–283.

Reynolds, C. R., & Richmond, B. O. (1985). *Revised Children's Manifest Anxiety Scale (RCMAS) manual.* Los Angeles: Western Psychological Services.

Rio, A. T., Quay, H. C., Santisteban, D. A., & Szapocznik, J. (1989). Factor-analytic study of a Spanish translation of the Revised Behavior Problem Checklist. *Journal of Clinical Child Psychology, 18,* 343–350.

Robin, A. L. (1981). A controlled evaluation of problem-solving communication training with parent-adolescent conflict. *Behavior Therapy, 12,* 593–609.

Robin, A. L., Kent, R., O'Leary, K. D., Foster, S., & Prinz, R. (1977). An approach to teaching parents and adolescents problem-solving communication skills: A preliminary report. *Behavior Therapy, 8,* 639–643.

Robin, A. L., & Weiss, J. G. (1980). Criterion-related validity of behavioral and self-report measures of problem-solving communication skills in distressed and nondistressed parent-adolescent dyads. *Behavioral Assessment, 2,* 339–352.

Robinson, E. A., Eyberg, S., & Ross, A. W. (1980). The standardization of an inventory of child conduct problem behaviors. *Journal of Clinical Child Psychology, 9,* 22–28.

Rosen, J. C., Silberg, N. T., & Ross, G. (1988). Eating Attitudes Test and Eating Disorders Inventory: Norms for adolescent girls and boys. *Journal of Consulting and Clinical Psychology, 56,* 305–308.

Reynolds, W. M. (1987). *Reynolds Adolescent Depression Scale (RADS): Professional manual.* Odessa, FL: Psychological Assessment Resources.

Saylor, C. F., Finch, A. J., Spirito, A., & Bennett, B. (1984). The Children's Depression Inventory: A systematic evaluation of psychometric properties. *Journal of Consulting and Clinical Psychology, 52,* 955–967.

Schloss, C. N., Schloss, P. J., & Smith, M. A. (1988). Enhancement of employment interview skills using self-monitoring with communicatively impaired youths. *Education and Treatment of Children, 11,* 19–28.

Shain, B. N., Naylor, M., & Alessi, N. (1990). Comparison of self-rated and clinician-rated measures of depression in adolescents. *American Journal of Psychiatry, 147,* 793–795.

Shapiro, E. S. (1988). Behavioral assessment. In J. C. Witt, S. N. Elliott, & F. M. Gresham (Eds.), *Handbook of behavior therapy in education.* New York: Plenum.

Slotkin, J., Forehand, R., Fauber, R., McCombs, A., & Long, N. (1988). Parent-completed and adolescent-completed CDIs: Relationship to adolescent social and cognitive functioning. *Journal of Abnormal Child Psychology, 16,* 207–217.

Smith, M. C., & Thelen, M. H. (1984). Development and validation of a test for bulimia. *Journal of Consulting and Clinical Psychology, 52,* 863–872.

Smucker, M. R., Craighead, W. E., Craighead, L. W., & Green, B. J. (1986). Normative and reliability data for the Children's Depression Inventory. *Journal of Abnormal Child Psychology, 14,* 25–39.

Snyder, J. J. (1977). A reinforcement analysis of interaction in problem and nonproblem families. *Journal of Abnormal Psychology, 86,* 528–535.

Spielberger, C. D. (1983). *Manual for the Stait-Trait Anxiety Inventory (Form Y).* Palo Alto, CA: Consulting Psychologists Press.

Spirito, A., Williams, C. A., Stark, L. J., & Hart, K. J. (1988). The Hopelessness

Scale for Children: Psychometric properties with normal and emotionally disturbed adolescents. *Journal of Abnormal Child Psychology, 16,* 445–458.

Stein, D. M., & Brinza, S. R. (1989a). The Bulimia Test: Factor structure in junior high school, high school, and college women. *International Journal of Eating Disorders, 8,* 225–230.

Stein, D. M., & Brinza, S. R. (1989b). Bulimia: Prevalence estimates in female junior high and high school students. *Journal of Clinical Child Psychology, 18,* 206–213.

Teri, L. (1982). The use of the Beck Depression Inventory with adolescents. *Journal of Abnormal Child Psychology, 10,* 277–284.

Test, D. W., Spooner, F., Keul, P. K., & Grossi, T. (1990). Teaching adolescents with severe disabilities to use the public telephone. *Behavior Modification, 14,* 157–171.

Thelen, M. H., McLaughlin-Mann, L., Pruitt, J., & Smith, M. (1987). Bulimia: Prevalence and component factors in college women. *Journal of Psychosomatic Research, 31,* 73–78.

Tisdelle, D. A., & St. Lawrence, J. S. (1988). Adolescent interpersonal problem-solving skills training: Social validation and generalization. *Behavior Therapy, 19,* 171–182.

Ullman, L. P., & Krasner, L. (Eds.), (1965). *Case studies in behavior modification.* New York: Holt Rinehart & Winston.

Van Hasselt, V. B., & Hersen, M. (Eds.), (1987). *Handbook of adolescent psychology.* New York: Pergamon.

Wacker, D. P., Berg, W. K., Choisser, L., & Smith., J. (1989). Evaluation of the generalized effects of a peer-training procedure with moderately retarded adolescents. *Journal of Applied Behavior Analysis, 22,* 261–273.

Wacker, D. P., Wiggins, B., Fowler, M., & Berg, W. K. (1988). Training students with profound or multiple handicaps to make requests via microswitches. *Journal of Applied Behavior Analysis, 21,* 331–343.

Ward, C. I., & McFall, R. M. (1986). Further validation of the Problem Inventory for Adolescent Girls: Comparing Caucasian and black delinquents and non-delinquents. *Journal of Consulting and Clinical Psychology, 54,* 732–733.

Welner, Z., Reich, W., Herjanic, B., Jung, K. G., & Amado, H. (1987). Reliability, validity, and parent-child agreement studies of the Diagnostic Interview for Children and Adolescents (DICA). *Journal of the American Academy of Child Adolescent Psychiatry, 26,* 649–653.

Witt, J. C., Cavell, T. A., Heffer, R. W., Carey, M. P., & Martens, B. K. (1988). Child self-report: Interviewing techniques and rating scales. In E. S. Shapiro & T. R. Kratchowill (Eds.), *Behavioral assessment in schools: Conceptual foundations and practical applications.* New York: Guilford.

9
Epidemiology and Adolescent Diagnosis

Ada C. Mezzich
Oscar G. Bukstein
Michelle R. Grimm

The principal aim of adolescent psychiatric epidemiology is to determine the overall and specific prevalence of psychiatric disorders and their psychosocial and biological correlates in a given population. Health policy planners, public officials, and clinicians can then use these data to plan prevention and mental health strategies and services. This chapter focuses on methodological advances in the field of adolescent psychiatric epidemiology, including the definitions of mental disorder, variability and reliability of diagnostic classification systems, and ways to reduce variability and increase reliability. It also reviews existing studies on the prevalence, comorbidity, and associated factors of general psychiatric disorders and internalizing (depressive and anxiety disorders) and externalizing (disruptive and substance use disorders) disorders in adolescence.

Epidemiological studies were selected on the basis of (a) their use of large community populations of adolescents and/or children recruited either from high schools or households, and (b) their employment of DSM-III/DSM-III-R or ICD (American Psychiatric Association [APA], 1980, 1987) (World Health Organization [WHO], 1987) diagnostic criteria, with or without impaired adaptive functioning, to define a psychiatric case. Daily or regular use of substances, however, was employed as a criterion to define cases in the substance use disorder investigations. This exception was made due to the scarcity of epidemiological studies of substance use disorders utilizing DSM-III-R diagnostic criteria and the assumption that those who drink alcohol or consume drugs daily probably have a substance abuse disorder.

The epidemiological investigations are organized according to their methodology and results. The methodology section includes geographical location, sampling method, sample size, age range of the adolescents, informants, case definition, and diagnostic instruments used. Research results have been structured according to prevalence of psychiatric disorders, comorbidity, treatment utilization, associative factors, and gender and ethnic differences.

Methodological Issues in Psychiatric Epidemiology in Adolescents

Defining Mental Illness

While psychiatry is often defined as the science that deals with the diagnosis and treatment of mental disorders, arriving at a consensual and precise definition of *mental disorder* is difficult. For some researchers, the essence of the mental disorder resides in interpersonal relationships; for others, the focus seems to be on the individual organism (Klein, 1978; Spitzer, Endicott, & Robins, 1978), a concept with a biological connotation. Still others have characterized mental disorder as an adaptation to stress (Meyer, 1987). This concept emphasizes the differential characteristics of the person rather than the similarities between individuals with the same disorders; further, it does not offer a criterion to distinguish illness from health. Mental disorders also have been defined as variations from the statistical norm, either as an excess or as a deficiency (Cohen, 1953). Other concepts involve the characterization of mental disorder as deviation from an ideal normality, which is illustrated by psychoanalytic theory and the World Health Organization's definition of "a state of complete physical, mental and social well-being" and not merely as an absence of illness. Another important criterion of illness deals with the individual's social integration, a concept frequently expressed in terms of suffering and incapacity (Scadding, 1967).

A notion central to the characterization of mental disorder is phenomenology, which expresses mental illness in terms of psychological dysfunction encompassing cognitive, affective, conative, and motivational factors. Yet another identifier of mental disorder has been described by Taylor and Abrams (1975) as the "therapeutic preoccupation," or "what doctors treat." The main difficulty with this definition, as Kendell (1975) pointed out, is that a mentally disordered person could not be identified as ill until the disorder was recognized by a professional, recognition that could be influenced by changing social attitudes.

This multitude of definitions reflects the complexity of the understanding of mental disorder. Nevertheless, a seemingly reasonable and commonly accepted characterization of mental illness is based on the presence of psychopathological symptoms accompanied by the inability to function adaptively.

Classifying Mental Illness

Diagnostic classification systems are used to represent the psychiatric status of the individual in a summarized manner. These systems have to be reasonably specific but they also must be comprehensive—features that are sometimes in conflict. Finally, these systems should be codifiable to facilitate the documentation, processing, and retrieval of information.

In the interest of obtaining reliable or reproducible evaluative judgments, analyses have identified two main sources of undesirable variability in the evaluation process: the process of obtaining clinical information, and the process of diagnostic formulation. Since the mid-1970s, two major methodological developments have occurred to decrease the variability of these processes: the structured clinical interview, and explicit diagnostic criteria.

Structured clinical interviews can diminish variability in the process of obtaining psychiatric information by specifying the items to be investigated, providing definitions or prompts for these items, specifying questions that explore the items of interest, and providing instructions for rating the presence and severity of the items involved. Structured interviewing has certain advantages over other assessment methods. It provides a better foundation to develop rapport with the respondent, maintain his or her interest, clarify misunderstandings, resolve ambiguous responses, and document the context and chronicity of the symptoms. Interviewing is also one way of obtaining self-report data from adolescents, who are viewed as valuable informants regarding their own feelings, behaviors, and social relationships.

Some interview schedules are semistructured and provide general guidelines for conducting the interview and recording information. Others are highly structured and specify the exact order, wording, and coding of each item. The most widely used interview schedules are the Diagnostic Interview Schedule for Children (DISC; Costello, Edelbrock, Kalas, Kessler, & Klaric, 1982), the Schedule for Affective Disorders and Schizophrenia for school-aged children (K-SADS; Puig-Antich & Chambers, 1978), and the Diagnostic Interview for Children and Adolescents (DICA; Herjanic, Herjanic, Brown, & Wheatt, 1975).

The DISC was developed by the National Institute of Mental Health (NIMH) for use in epidemiological studies of psychopathology in children 6 to 18 years of age. It is a highly structured diagnostic interview in which the order, wording, and coding of all items are specified a priori. Parallel versions have been developed for separately interviewing parents (DISC-P) and children (DISC-C). The evaluation of most items is limited to the past year; more specific information about onset and duration is obtained for many symptoms. Administration and scoring of the DISC requires very little training, although interpretation of the computer-generated output may require clinical expertise.

Interrater reliability for the DISC has been examined by comparing symptom scores for videotaped interviews of 10 children, independently coded by three lay interviewers (Costello, Edelbrock, Dulcan, Kalas, & Klaric, 1984). Reliabilities averaged .98 for symptom scores in 23 of 27 symptom areas. Parent-child agreement was examined in 299 dyads (Edelbrock, Costello, Dulcan, Conover, & Kalas, 1986); correlations between symptom scores derived from separate interviews with parents and children were significant ($p < .05$) but modest ($r = .27$). Across all groups, parents reported significantly more conduct problems than their children, while children reported significantly more affective/emotional problems and alcohol and drug abuse than their parents. Also, agreement was significantly higher among children 14 to 18 years of age than among the 10- to 13-year-olds and 6- to 9-year-olds. Validity of the two parallel versions of the DISC was examined by contrasting 40 pediatric referrals and 40 psychiatric referrals 7 to 11 years of age (Costello, Edelbrock, & Costello, 1985). Based on the parent interview, the psychiatric referrals received 51 diagnoses of severe disorders, compared to only 2 diagnoses in the pediatric group. Combining symptom scores derived from both parent and child interviews in one multiple discriminant analysis yielded a sensitivity of 95% and a specificity of 98%.

The K-SADS (Puig-Antich & Chambers, 1978) is a semistructured diagnostic interview for children ages 6 to 17 and is modeled after the Schedule for Affective Disorder and Schizophrenia (SADS) designed for adults (Endicott & Spitzer, 1978). The K-SADS assesses current psychopathology according to Research Diagnostic Criteria (RDC; Spitzer et al., 1978) DSM-III. The procedure is first to interview the parent concerning the psychiatric status of the child and then to interview the child; during the latter interview, the interviewer tries to solve any reporting discrepancies between parent and child. Interviewers are flexible in selecting the wording of the questions and sequence of inquiring about the disorders. Diagnoses are based on a diagnostician's overview of the interview responses, a different method from the computer programs applied to the K-SADS symptom scores. Test-retest reliability was assessed on a sample of 52 psychiatrically disturbed children ages 6 to 17 (Chambers et al., 1985). Individual symptoms were modestly reliable (average intraclass correlation = 55); higher reliabilities were obtained for the 12 summary scales (average intraclass correlation = .68). The reliability of diagnoses ranged from .24 to .70 using the kappa statistic.

The K-SADS has a strong content validity in that it was designed to tap prespecified diagnostic criteria. Its primary use has been in ascertaining children who qualify for major affective disorders (Puig-Antich, Blau, Marx, Greenhill, & Chambers, 1978). An epidemiological version of the K-SADS, the K-SADS-E, was developed to assess lifetime psychopathology in children between the ages of 6 and 17 (Orvaschel, Puig-Antich, Chambers, Tabrizi, & Johnson, 1982). The K-SADS-E is similar to the K-SADS, except for the time frame for gathering information.

The DICA (Herjanic & Reich, 1982) is a highly structured instrument in which the order, working, and coding of all symptoms are specified. It yields information on the presence or absence of 185 symptoms, as well as their onset, duration, and associated impairments. The DICA yields diagnoses according to ICD-9 and DSM-III diagnostic criteria. Interrater reliability was studied through the use of videotaped interviews (Herjanic & Reich, 1982). In the first investigation, 10 interviewers independently coded two taped interviews with children; agreement on symptom items averaged 85%. In the second study, five psychiatrists coded the same child interview twice over a 2- to 3-month period. Within-interview agreement on individual symptoms averaged 89%; parent-child agreement on individual symptoms averaged 80% (Herjanic et al., 1975). The validity of the DICA is supported by its ability to discriminate significantly between matched samples of children referred to either pediatric or psychiatric clinics ($n = 50$ for each group; Herjanic & Campbell, 1977).

These psychiatric interview instruments, designed to obtain a DSM-III diagnosis, have the limitation of assessing diagnostic categories in which the validity is still questionable. They have the advantage of reducing variability in the evaluation process, however, as well as accelerating the process of improvement of diagnostic categories and operationalization of the diagnostic criteria by collecting information on separate symptoms or behaviors.

The development and use of explicit diagnostic criteria represent the second major methodological development aimed at reducing undesirable variability in the diagnostic evaluation process. Generically, this procedure involves setting clear, denotative, and objective rules for assigning diagnostic categories to individuals under examination. The clinical information used to reach a diagnostic formulation can be obtained through a structured or semistructured interview.

The need for specific diagnostic definitions was first proposed by Stengel (1959) in England for a study sponsored by the World Health Organization. This effort was followed some years later by Horowitz and Marconi (1966) in Latin America. Subsequently, criteria for a vast number of diagnostic categories were developed in the United States. Feighner et al. (1972) developed criteria for psychiatric research and pioneered the design of criteria for a significant number of diagnostic categories. Based on the work of Feighner et al., Spitzer et al. (1978) developed the Research Diagnostic Criteria (RDC) within the framework of a collaborative project on psychobiology of depression sponsored by the National Institute of Mental Health.

The third edition of the *Diagnostic and Statistical Manual of Mental Disorders* (DSM-III), its revision (DSM-III-R), and the new fourth edition

(DSM-IV; APA, 1994), represent one more step in the development of explicit diagnostic criteria. The newly developed DSM-IV has included research results obtained on psychiatric diagnoses employing DSM-III and DSM-III-R across the developmental span. As a consequence, the criteria of a significant number of diagnostic categories are supported by results of empirical studies or available data. Where the literature demonstrated lack of agreement, reanalyses of available data and field trials were used to resolve the discrepancies. Investigators collaborating with DSM-IV conducted 40 reanalyses of the available data. Also, 12 field trials were conducted that included more than 70 sites and assessed more than 6,000 individuals. These field trials evaluated the reliability and performance of diagnostic criteria. Although some improvements have been made to refine diagnostic criteria, the DSM diagnostic system still has not been able to solve the issue of heterogeneity of psychiatric disorders. This limitation suggests that it may be more useful to use a dimensional or prototypical model to organize the realm of mental disorders.

Epidemiological Studies in Adolescent Psychiatric Diagnosis

There are few cross-sectional and longitudinal epidemiological studies investigating the prevalence of general and specific psychiatric disorders in a general adolescent population.

General Psychiatric Disorders

Among the cross-sectional epidemiological investigations in children and adolescents reported in the literature, only two have documented the prevalence of psychiatric disorders in an adolescent population per se (Kashani et al., 1987a; Whitaker et al., 1990). Others have investigated children and adolescents conjointly, usually including subjects between the ages of 4 and 16 years with specification of the prevalence of some psychiatric disorders in those adolescents 12 years and older (Offord, Boyle, Fleming, Blum, & Grant, 1989). Longitudinal research designed to determine the course of psychiatric disorders in children has shown the prevalence of psychiatric disorders in adolescents assessed at follow-up (Esser, Schmidt, & Woerner, 1990; Velez, Johnson, & Cohen, 1989). The reader is referred to studies published by Brandenburg, Friedman, and Silver, (1990), Costello (1989), and Garralda (1991), who reviewed epidemiological investigations of children. This review focuses on studies conducted in Canada (Offord et al., 1989), Germany (Esser et al., 1990), and the United States that report the prevalence of psychiatric disorders in adolescent populations.

Table 9–1 describes the methodology used in the reviewed studies. The

Table 9–1
Psychiatric Disorders in General: Methodology

Author	Sampling Location	Sampling Method	Sample Size	Age Range	Informants	Case Definition	Instruments
Offord et al. (1989)	Ontario, Canada	Multistage probability sample of households	2,679 (194)	12–16	Parent/teacher/ adolescent	DSM-III	Survey Diagnostic Instrument (SID) based on CBCL
Kashani et al. (1987a)	Columbia, MO	Single-stage probability sample of secondary school	150	14–16	Parent/ adolescent	DSM-III/need for treatment, impaired functioning	Diagnostic Interview for Children and Adolescents (DICA)
Velez et al. (1989)	New York, NY	Single-stage random selection of households	776	9–18	Parent/ adolescent	DSM-III/ symptom severity	DISC
Whitaker et al. (1990)	New Jersey	Two-stage; entire 9th–12th grades	5,596 (356)	13–18	Parent	DSM-III/impaired functioning	Eating Symptoms Inventory Eating Attitude Test-26 Leyton Obsessional Scale BDI
Esser et al. (1990)	Mannheim, Germany	Two-stage sampling	1,444 (356)	13	Parent/ adolescent	ICD/symptom severity	Modification of Graham/Rutter structured parent interview

U.S.A. research includes studies in Missouri (Kashani 1987a), New York (Velez et al., 1989), and New Jersey (Whitaker et al., 1990). The Canadian, German, and New Jersey surveys used a two-stage probability sampling method of households (Esser et al., 1990; Offord et al., 1989; Whitaker et al., 1990). The Missouri and the New York studies employed a single-stage approach: the former sampled 14- to 16-year-old high school students (Kashani et al., 1987a), and the latter randomly selected households with children 13 to 18 years of age (Velez et al., 1989). The Canadian, German, and New York investigations examined children and adolescents (Esser et al., 1990; Offord et al., 1989; Velez et al., 1989), while the Missouri and New Jersey studies evaluated adolescents only (Kashani et al., 1987a; Whitaker et al., 1990). The adolescents and their parents were the informants in all studies. A psychiatric case was defined by DSM-III diagnostic criteria alone or in combination with either impaired functioning (Offord et al., 1989; Kashani et al., 1987a; Whitaker et al., 1990) or symptom severity (Velez et al., 1989). In the German study, the ICD criteria defined a psychiatric case (Esser et al., 1990). Among the diagnostic interview schedules, the DISC was the most frequently employed diagnostic instrument (Velez et al., 1989), followed by the DICA (Kashani et al., 1987a), the Survey Diagnostic Instrument (based on the CBCL; Offord et al., 1989), and the Behavior Questionnaire (a modification of the "Conner's Scale"). In addition, the Eating Symptom Inventory, Eating Attitudes Test-26, the Leyton Obsessional Scale, and the Beck Depression Inventory were all used in conjunction with case vignettes by Whitaker et al. (1990).

Table 9–2 presents the results pertaining to the definition of a psychiatric case and the prevalence of psychiatric disorder. Judged solely on the basis of DSM-III criteria, the prevalence of any lifetime psychiatric disorder was 41% (Kashani et al., 1987a). When the definition of a psychiatric case encompassed impaired adaptive functioning or symptom severity, however, the prevalence of any psychiatric disorder decreased to a range of 17% to 26.9% (Kashani et al., 1987a; Velez et al., 1989; Whitaker et al., 1990), approximately one-half of the original rate. The epidemiological studies have documented that conduct disorder, emotional disorders, attention-deficit disorder, and substance use disorders are the most frequent psychiatric disorders in adolescence.

Research points to a number of factors that have been proven to have an association with psychiatric disorders: chronic health problems, single parenthood (Offord et al., 1989), male gender, low socioeconomic status, low level of maternal education, poor family relations, experience of one or more stressful events (Velez et al., 1989), physical abuse, sexual relations with at least one partner, cigarette smoking, verbal and physical violence used to resolve conflicts, low self-concept, noncaring parents, male aggressivity, hyperactivity, and hostility or withdrawal (Kashani et al., 1987a).

Table 9–2
Psychiatric Disorders in General: Prevalence, Comorbidity, and Service Utilization

Psychiatric Disorders	Offord et al. (1989) M%	Offord et al. (1989) F%	Kashani et al. (1987a) %	Velez et al. (1989) %	Whitaker et al. (1990) M%	Whitaker et al. (1990) F%	Esser et al. (1990) M%	Esser et al. (1990) F%
Any disorder								
Diagnostic criteria & impaired functioning	18.1		18.7	17.7			16.2	
Diagnostic criteria alone			41.3					
Attention-deficit disorder	7.3	3.4	2.0	9.9			3.0	0.0
Conduct disorder	10.4	4.1	8.7				9.0	7.0
Oppositional defiant disorder			6.0	18.6				
Emotional disorder	4.9	13.6					8.0	3.0
Functional enuresis			0.7					
Separation anxiety								
Overanxious disorder			7.3	6.8				
Simple phobia			0.7	12.7				
Panic disorder								
Generalized anxiety disorder					0.4	0.7		
Obsessive compulsive disorder					1.8	4.6		
Major depression			4.7		0.6	1.8		
Dysthymia			3.3		2.9	4.5		
Mania			0.7		2.3	5.3		
Substance use disorder			6.0					
Alcohol abuse			3.3					
Drug abuse			5.3					
Somatization	4.5	10.7	1.3					
Anorexia nervosa					0.0	0.3		
Bulimia with anorexia					0.0	0.2		
Bulimia with normal weight					0.2	4.0		
Comorbidity	68				35.1			
Service utilization	16.1							

More specifically, a low level of paternal education was related to attention-deficit disorder and separation anxiety. Overanxious disorder was associated with pregnancy. Oppositional defiant and conduct disorders were correlated with the mother not being married to the child's father and parental sociopathy (Velez et al., 1989).

With respect to gender differences, females in contrast to males had more emotional and somatization disorders and greater tobacco and alcohol use, but fewer conduct disorders (Esser et al., 1990; Offord et al., 1989). A strong association was also found between being female and having depressive and anxiety disorders (Esser et al., 1990; Kashani et al., 1987a; Velez et al., 1989; Whitaker et al., 1990). Treatment utilization was reported to be 16.1% in the Canadian study (Offord et al., 1989) and 53.1% in the effort by Whitaker et al. (1990).

With respect to stability of psychiatric disorders, longitudinal studies have reported that attention-deficit disorder and overanxious disorder in males decreased with age, that conduct disorder and oppositional defiant disorder reached a peak in midadolescence and then declined, and that major depression was rare in children and increased with age (Velez et al., 1989). In a longitudinal study, Esser et al. (1990) examined the course and predictors of the emergence and remission of psychiatric disorders. They observed that among the psychiatric cases found at follow-up (age 13), 50% of the children were new cases, and the remainder corresponded to cases with prior psychiatric disturbance. Overall, the neurotic cases had a good prognosis (45% of the cases recovered by age 13), while nearly all individuals diagnosed with a conduct disorder by age 8 were observed to preserve that diagnosis by age 13. Learning disabilities and adverse familial conditions at age 8 predicted the subsequent development of conduct disorder cases; in general, learning disabilities and stressful life events predicted emergence of psychiatric disorders in initially healthy children. The remission of psychiatric disorder was also influenced by an improved psychosocial environment within the family.

Internalizing Psychiatric Disorders

Depressive Disorders. Among the six studies reviewed, five were conducted in the U.S. (Deykin, Levy, & Wells, 1986; Garrison, Schluchter, Schoenbach, & Kaplan, 1989; Kashani et al., 1987b; Lewinsohn, Rohde, Seeley, & Hops, 1991; Rohde, Lewinsohn, & Seeley, 1991) and one in Ontario, Canada (Fleming, Offord, & Boyle, 1989; see Tables 9–3 and 9–4). The majority of the U.S. studies investigated high school populations and used a single-stage method of sampling; the Canadian investigation used a two-stage method and a probability sample of households. The sample sizes varied from 150 to 677 individuals, and the adolescents in four studies ranged from 14 to 19 years of age (Deykin et al., 1986;

Table 9-3

Depressive Disorders: Sampling Location and Method, Sample Size, Age Range, Informants, Case Definition, and Diagnostic Instruments

Author	Sampling Location	Sampling Method	Sample Size	Age Range	Informants	Case Definition	Instruments
Kashani et al. (1987b)	Columbia, MO	Stratified random sampling of students in the 9th, 10th, & 11th grades	150	14–16	Parent/self	DSM-III/need for treatment/dysfunctional	Diagnostic Interview for Children and Adolescents (DICA)
Deykin et al. (1986)	Boston, MA	Single-stage, college students	424	16–19	Self	DSM-III	DISC
Garrison et al. (1989)	Columbia, SC	7th, 8th, and 9th graders of junior high school	677	11–17	Self	DSM-III	CES-D
Fleming et al. (1989)	Ontario, Canada	Multistage probability sample of households	2,679 (194)	4–16	Parent/self teacher	DSM-III/symptom severity	SID
Lewinsohn et al. (1991)	Eugene, OR	Random sampling of high school students	1,710 (347)	14–18	Self	DSM-III-R	K-SADS
Rohde et al. (1991)	Eugene, OR	Same as above					

Table 9–4
Depressive Disorders: Prevalence, Evaluation Time Frame, Comorbidity, and Treatment Utilization

Author	Current Depressive Disorder	%	Current Comorbidity	%	Lifetime Comorbidity	%	Treatment Utilization	%	Suicidal Attempts %
Kashani et al. (1987b)	MDD D MDD/D	4.7 3.3 8.0	Any disorder Anxiety Oppositional Conduct Alcohol abuse Drug abuse	100 75 50 33 25 25					
Deykin et al. (1987)	MDD	6.8			Alcohol abuse Drug abuse	23 23			
Garrison et al. (1989)	MDD	4.4							
Fleming et al. (1989)	MDD	1.8	Any disorder	95.8				21.5	
Lewinsohn et al. (1991)	MDD D MDD/D Any depressive disorder	17 1.8 1.3 20.29						22.6 28.1 30.4	
Rohde et al. (1991)			Bipolar Anxiety Disruptive Substance use Eating Any disorder	0 18 8 14 4 42	Bipolar Anxiety Disruptive Substance use Eating Any disorder	0.9 21 12 20 3 43	Any depressive disorder Comorbidity of depressive disorder and nondepressive disorder	23.7 45	17.7 24.8

Kashani et al., 1987b; Lewinsohn et al., 1991; Rohde et al., 1991). In the report by Garrison et al. (1989), the age range was 11 to 17; in the investigation by Fleming et al. (1989), it was 14 to 16. In four studies, the informant was the adolescent alone (Deykin et al., 1986; Garrison et al., 1989; Lewinsohn et al., 1991; Rohde et al., 1991). In the remaining investigations one parent and the adolescent were the informants (Fleming et al., 1989; Kashani et al., 1987b). (The teacher was also an informant in the study by Fleming et al., 1989.) The psychiatric cases were usually defined only by DSM-III or DSM-III-R diagnostic criteria (Deykin et al., 1986; Garrison et al., 1989; Lewinsohn et al., 1991; Rohde et al., 1991). Kashani et al. (1987b) defined a case by DSM-III diagnostic criteria and the need for treatment, having had treatment, or impaired adaptive functioning; Fleming et al.(1989) used DSM-III criteria and symptom severity. DICA was the most frequently used diagnostic instrument; however, the DISC, K-SADS, SEC-D, and SID were also employed (Table 9–3).

The prevalence of major depression in adolescents was found to be between 1.8% and 17% (Kashani et al., 1987b; Deykin et al., 1986; Garrison et al., 1989; Fleming et al., 1989; Lewinsohn et al., 1991), dysthymia between 1.8% and 3.3% (Kashani et al., 1987b; Lewinsohn et al., 1991), and major depression coexisting with dysthymia between 1.3% and 8% (Kashani et al., 1987b; Lewinsohn et al., 1991; see Table 9–4). The prevalence of current (within the past 6 months) comorbid psychiatric disorders ranged from 42% to 100% (Fleming et al., 1989; Kashani et al., 1987b; Rohde et al., 1991). The rate of lifetime psychiatric comorbidity was similar to that of current psychiatric comorbidity (43% to 76%; Rohde et al., 1991). The most frequent current comorbid disorders were anxiety disorders, estimated to be 75% of depressed cases in the Missouri study (Kashani et al., 1987b) and 18% in Oregon (Rhode et al., 1991); disruptive disorders, measured at 50% by Kashani et al. (1987b); and substance abuse, measured at 25% by Kashani et al., (1987b). The most frequent lifetime comorbid disorders were also anxiety disorders (21%), followed by substance use disorders (20%) and disruptive disorders (12%; Rohde et al., 1991). Deykin et al. (1986) also found a high rate of lifetime comorbidity between major depression and substance use disorders. Major depression and dysthymia were observed to be comorbid in 6.6% of the cases (Lewinsohn et al., 1991; see Table 9–4).

The impact of current and lifetime comorbid psychiatric disorders on the sequence of appearance of disorders, duration, and recovery rate of depressive disorders has been further examined by Lewinsohn et al. (1991) and Rohde et al. (1991). Results showed that dysthymia nearly always preceded major depression (91% to 100% of the cases; Lewinsohn et al., 1991), while a nondepressive disorder preceded a depressive disorder in 79% of the observations (Rohde et al., 1991). The onset of depressive disorder (79%) was usually preceded by anxiety disorder (79%), followed by disruptive disorder (71%), substance use disorder (64%), and eating disorder (50%; Rohde et al., 1991). Rohde et al. (1991) found more recurrence of major depression in adolescents who had comorbid nondepressive disorders but not an increase in the duration of major depression (see Table 9–4).

Treatment utilization for depressed adolescents was estimated to fall between 18% and 45% (Fleming et al., 1989; Lewinsohn et al., 1991; Rohde et al., 1991). Interestingly, the concurrence between depressive disorder and nondepressive disorders augmented the rate of treatment utilization (Rohde et al., 1991). History of suicide attempts was also investigated by Rohde et al. (1991). They found that the rate of suicide attempts was 17.7% in the presence of any depressive disorder, while the coexistence of any depressive disorder and any nondepressive disorder increased the probability of a suicide attempt to 24.8%.

Characteristics associated with depressive disorders include frequent school absenteeism, poor grade-point average (Fleming et al., 1989; Garrison et al., 1989), seventh-grade status, and lower socioeconomic class (Garrison et al., 1989). Additional factors related to depressive disorders included age, being female (Fleming et al., 1989; Lewinsohn et al., 1991), utilization of mental health services, high psychiatric comorbidity (Fleming et al., 1989; Lewinsohn et al., 1991), need for professional help, problems in getting along with others (Fleming et al., 1989), living with a single parent, and living with a nonbiological parent.

Regarding gender differences, more females than males reported depression comorbid with anxiety disorders (Kashani et al., 1987b). When controlled for gender, the prevalence rates of the depressive disorder did not differ for male and female preadolescents; however, females displayed a higher prevalence of mild depression than did males (Fleming et al., 1989). Prevalence of depressive disorders was highest among black females and lowest among black males and white females, black females exhibited the highest total and persistent depressive scores; males, regardless of race, had the lowest scores. Among white males and females, the absence of a parent was associated with an increased probability of having a high symptom score; among black males and females, absence of a parent was associated with a lower probability of having a high symptom score (Garrison et al., 1989).

Anxiety Disorders

Three investigations of anxiety disorder conducted in the U.S. were reviewed. One study carried out in New York, used a two-stage sampling of high school students (Flament et al., 1988); the other two endeavors (both in Missouri) employed a single-stage method to sample students from public high schools (Kashani & Orvaschel, 1988, 1990). The sample sizes ranged from 150 to 356 subjects between the ages of 12 and 18; both parents and adolescents served as informants. A psychiatric case was defined by Kashani and Orvaschel (1988) according to DSM-III criteria and having had or requiring treatment. The other two studies approached the concept of case using DSM-III diagnostic criteria alone (Flament et al., 1988; Kashani & Orvaschel, 1990). The DICA was the most frequently utilized diagnostic instrument (see Table 9–5).

Based on these reports, prevalence of current anxiety-disorder diagnoses was as follows: overanxious disorders, 7.3% to 12.4%; separation anxiety, 0.6% to 12.9%; phobia, 1.0% to 4.6%; and obsessive-compulsive disorder, 0.35% (Flament et al., 1988; Kashani & Orvaschel, 1988; see Table 9–6). Total prevalence of any anxiety-disorder diagnosis, as defined by DSM-III alone, was 17% to 21% of the adolescents (Kashani & Orvaschel, 1988, 1990). The prevalence of psychiatric comorbidity with anxiety disorders fell between 36% and 38% (Kashani & Orvaschel, 1988, 1990). Depression was the psychiatric disorder that coexisted most often with anxiety disorders in general (34.6%; Kashani & Orvaschel, 1988). Among those individuals with obsessive-compulsive disorder (Flament et al., 1988), 75% had one or more other lifetime psychiatric diagnoses, 50% had at least one other current diagnosis, and 25% coexisted with major depression. Obsessive-compulsive disorder also overlapped with overanxious disorder (20%), panic attacks (20%), bulimia (15%), and personality disorder (17%); 20% of the individuals with this diagnosis had at some time sought treatment, although most rated themselves as having poor emotional health. It was also reported that three out of four treated cases sought help for depression or anxiety, although they had not disclosed their specific obsessive-compulsive symptoms to the therapist (Flament et al., 1988). Anxiety disorder was associated with hostility, concern about behavior, use of fantasy, wishful thinking, denial and displacement to deal with stressful events (Kashani & Orvaschel, 1988), physiological symptoms, oversensitivity, concentration problems, and problems with friends (Kashani & Orvaschel, 1990).

Females were more likely to receive treatment, need professional help, or have impaired adaptive functioning (Kashani & Orvaschel, 1988). In addition, females generally exhibited more anxiety and showed more separation anxiety. Ethnic comparisons showed that whites experienced less anxiety than blacks. Adolescents (aged 12 to 17) had fewer psychophysiological symptoms, more social anxiety, and more worriedness than 8-year-olds (Kashani & Orvaschel, 1990).

Eating Disorders

In an epidemiology study of the prevalence and essential symptoms of anorexia nervosa and bulimia, Whitaker et al. (1989) found that the prevalence of anorexia nervosa was 0.2% in female adolescents and 0.0% in male adolescents when weight was used as a criterion along with DSM-III

Table 9–5
Anxiety Disorders: Sampling Location and Method, Sample Size, Age Range, Case Definition, and Diagnostic Instruments

Author	Sampling Location	Sampling Method	Sample Size	Age Range	Informants	Case Definition	Instruments
Kashani & Orvaschel (1990)	Columbia, MO	Stratified random sample from public schools	4,810 (210)	8, 12, 14	Parent/self	DSM-III	Child Assessment Schedule Parent Assessment Schedule
Kashani & Orvaschel (1988)	Columbia, MO	Single-stage, high school children	150	14–16	Parent/self	DSM-III/ treatment, need for treatment, impaired adaptive functioning	DICA
Flament et al. (1988)	New Jersey	Two-stage study of high school students/ randomly stratified	5,596 (356)	14–17 9–12 graders	Adolescents	DSM-III CGAS	DICA

Table 9–6
Anxiety Disorders: Prevalence and Psychiatric Comorbidity

Author	Anxiety Disorder	Prevalence (Current) %	Psychiatric Comorbidity	%
Kashani & Orvaschel (1988)	Overanxiety	7.3		100.0
	Phobia	0.7		
	Obsessive-compulsive	0.0		
	Any anxiety disorder	8.7		
Kashani & Orvaschel (1990)	Overanxiety	12.4	Anxiety/Anxiety	36.4
	Simple phobia	3.3		
	Social phobia	1.0		
	Separation	12.9		
	Any anxiety	21		
	Non Case	36.4		
	Anxiety/Anxiety			
Flament et al. (1988)	Obsessive-compulsive disorder	0.35	Obsessive-compulsive disorder	
			Major depression	25
			Dysthymia	5
			Bulimia	15
			Overanxiety	20
			Phobia	10
			Panic attack	20
			Personality disorder	17

criteria. When the diagnosis was formulated using DSM-III alone, prevalence of anorexia nervosa increased to 7.6% in females and 0.6% in males. The prevalence of bulimia, with or without the additional weight criterion, was 0.4% in male adolescents and 1.2% in female adolescents.

Many adolescents aspired to be thin and experimented with weight control. A small number of males and females, however, engaged in the type of severe weight control reported by patients with eating disorders. Females reported cosmetic reasons as the primary motivation for weight control, while boys attempted weight control for athletic reasons. Older females were more likely than younger females to be worried about weight gain and to have attempted weight control in the past year. All of the essential attitudes and behaviors of the eating disorder, with the exception of recurrent binge eating, were most common in the heaviest adolescents of both sexes; anorectic and bulimic symptoms among nonreferred adolescents were not strongly associated with the upper social classes, as determined by survey. However, the latter were associated with being female, older, and heavier.

Externalizing Disorders

Substance Use Disorders. Six epidemiological studies—conducted in Canada, the United States (Missouri, Massachusetts, and national), Scotland, and Sweden—were reviewed. For a diagnosis of substance use disorder, two of the U.S. investigations used DSM-III diagnostic criteria (Deykin et al., 1986; Kashani & Orvaschel, 1988). The U.S. national study (Johnston, O'Malley, & Bachman, 1987, 1990) employed daily substance use as a criterion to define cases, and the Canadian study measured the occasional and regular use of substances (Boyle & Offord, 1986). Four of the reports utilized a high school population (Holmberg, 1985; Johnston et al., 1987; Kashani & Orvaschel, 1988; Plant, Peck, & Stuart, 1984); one used a college population (Deykin et al., 1986), and one conducted a stratified random sampling of households (Boyle & Offord, 1986; see Table 9–7).

The prevalence rate of substance use disorders that resulted from the studies using DSM-III for case definition showed a range of 1.8% to 9.1% in males, 0.5% to 6.8% in females, and 6.0% to 9.4% in a mixed group (Deykin et al., 1986; Kashani & Orvaschel, 1988). The U.S. "Monitoring the Future" study (Johnston et al., 1990) indicated that daily use of alcohol was present in 4.2% of the high school seniors; marijuana, 2.9%; cigarette smoking, 18.9%; stimulants, cocaine, hallucinogens, and inhalants, 0.3% each; and heroin, sedatives, and tranquilizers, 0.1% each (see Table 9–8). Alcohol use in the prior 30 days ranged from 42.5% in males and 48.8% in females to 60% in both females and males; marijuana use within a similar period ranged from 13.3% in males and 17.6% in females to 16.7% in

Table 9–7
Substance Use Disorders: Sampling Method, Sample Size, Age, Case Definition, and Instrumentation

Author	Sampling Location	Sampling Method	Sample Size	Age Range	Informants	Case Definition	Instruments
Boyle et al. (1986)	Ontario, Canada	Multistage probability sample of households	2,679 (194)	12–16	Parent/teacher/ adolescent	Occasional and regular substance use	Survey Diagnostic Instrument (SID) based on CBCL
Johnston et al. (1987)	USA	Random sample	17,000	high school seniors	self	Occasional substance use daily marijuana, alcohol & tobacco	Monitoring the Future self-report survey questionnaire
Holmberg (1985)	Guthenburg, Sweden	Random stratified sample	1,047	9th graders	self	Treatment received	
Kashani et al. (1987a)	Columbia, MO	Single-stage probability sample of secondary school	150	14–16	Parent/ adolescent	DSM-III	DICA
Plant et al. (1984)	Scotland		1,036	15–16	self	1 or more among 6 serious consequences	
Deykin et al. (1986)	Boston, MA	Single stage	424	16–19	self	DSM-III	DISC

both males and females. Cigarette smoking in the prior 30 days ranged from 28.6% in both males and females to 45.6% in females (see Table 9–8). Age of onset of alcohol and drug use ranged from 15.5 to 15.8 years; for alcohol and drug abuse, it ranged from 16.3 to 16.5 years. A 4-year follow-up of the Canadian adolescents whose first evaluation was in 1983 (Boyle et al., 1992) indicated a dramatic increase of alcohol and drug consumption. Among males, prevalence of regular alcohol use increased from 7% to 39.3%; regular tobacco use, from 8.9% to 23.6%; marijuana use, from 7.3% to 22.8%, and hard drugs use, from 3.5% to 8.9%. The same pattern of increase of substance use was observed in the female adolescents.

Holmberg[*] (1985a) observed substance abuse trends in the Swedish adolescent population and reported that from 1968 to 1973, substance abuse decreased from 4.2% to 3.3% in males and from 2.4 to 1.8% in females. Between 1973 and 1979, substance use also declined from 3.3% to 1.8% for males; for females it declined from 1.8% to 0.5%.

The studies conducted since 1975 by Johnston et al. (1987, 1990) among high school seniors showed that the trend in daily consumption of substances—especially alcohol, marijuana, and cigarette smoking—has decreased since the 1970s. Between 1979 and 1989, daily alcohol consumption declined from 6.9% to 4.25%, daily marijuana use decreased from 10.3% to 2.9%, daily cigarette smoking diminished from 25.4% to 18.9%, and daily stimulant use dropped from 0.7% in 1982 to 0.3% in 1989. Daily cocaine and inhalant use peaked in the 1980s, and "crack" cocaine appeared during the same period. During the same decade, the daily use of hallucinogens, sedatives, heroin, and other opioids remained approximately the same. Although the daily use of substances was not a criterion to define substance abuse, it is probable that individuals who consumed substances daily met psychiatric diagnostic criteria for substance abuse or dependence. The existing trend shows that the adolescent population has decreased the prevalence of daily use of alcohol, marijuana, and cigarette smoking since 1979. Daily use of alcohol has decreased from 6.9% to 4.2%, marijuana use decreased from 10.3% to 2.9%, and cigarette smoking from 25.4% to 18.9%.

The most frequent factors associated with prevalence of substance abuse are as follows: being part of a family that receives welfare, belonging to a single-parent family (Boyle & Offord, 1986), receiving child psychiatric care, contact with social welfare at early age, truancy, placement in special classes, dropping out of high school, high frequency of self-

---

[*]Holmberg (1985a) studied the development of drug abuse over a period of 10 years. The first evaluation was conducted in 1968 when the subjects were approximately 15 years old. Drug abuse was defined by registers of mental health hospitals, other medical facilities, social welfare, and driver licenses.

Table 9-8
Substance Use Disorders: Prevalence

	Johnston et al (1989)	Boyle et al. (1986, 1992)		Holmberg (1968)		(1973)		(1979)		Plant et al (1984)		Kashani et al (1987a)	Deykin et al (1986)
	M/F %	M %	F %	M %	F %	M %	F %	M %	F %	M %	F %	M/F %	M/F %
Any alcohol/drug abuse	60.0			4.2	2.4	3.3	1.8	1.8	0.5	9.1	6.8	6.0	8.2(A) 9.4(D)
Substance use (frequency)													
Alcohol (past 30 days)													
occasional		42.5	48.8										
regular		10.6	15.9										
daily	4.2												
Marijuana (past 30 days)	16.7	13.3	17.6										
daily	2.9												
Cigarette (past 30 days)	28.6												
occasional		31.1	45.6										
regular		15.8	23.4										
daily	18.9												
1/2 pack daily	11.2												
Inhalants (past 30 days)	2.7	3.8	4.5										
Daily	0.3												
Hard drugs		5.3	7.5										
Hallucinogens (past 30 days)	2.9												
Daily	0.3												
Stimulants (past 30 days)	4.2												
Daily	0.3												
Cocaine (past 30 days)	2.8												
Daily	0.3												
Heroin (past 30 days)	0.3												
Daily	0.1												
Other opioids (past 30 days)	1.6												
Daily	0.2												
Other drugs	4.9		4.5										
Sedatives (past 30 days)	1.6												
Daily	0.1												
Tranquilizers (past 30 days)	1.3												
Daily	0.1												

reported substance use, early registration as an abuser (in males), nervous complaints (in women; Holmberg, 1985b), drinking as a regular activity during free time, feeling like fighting after drinking, stating that "people who do not frequent public houses miss a lot a of fun," recreational use of drugs, and viewing alcohol as an important source of pleasure (Plant et al., 1984). The most common substance abuse consequences are psychiatric care, rehabilitation for alcohol and drug problems, hepatitis, development of psychotic symptoms, delirium tremens, and mortality (Holmberg, 1985b).

With regard to gender differences, cigarette smoking was more prevalent in females than in males in urban but not rural areas. Females also tended to use more substances than males (Boyle & Offord, 1986). Males consumed five or more drinks in a row more often than females (Johnston et al., 1987). Further, use of opioids increased slightly more among males than among females between 1976 and 1985; and the use of prescribed minor tranquilizers decreased more among females than among males between 1976 and 1981 (Johnston et al., 1987).

For duration of substance abuse, Holmberg (1985a) classified durations as short (less than 2 years), long (2 to 10 years), or chronic (more than 10 years). Among females and males, 20% to 39% had a short duration of alcohol abuse, 10% to 30% had a long duration, and 20% of males and 10% of females had a chronic duration (see Table 9–9). A large proportion of males had drug careers of long duration, and the climax of intravenous abuse was reached fairly late in their careers. Females had a shorter abuse duration, and the proportion of intravenous abusers reached its maximum earlier (with the exception of females who had attended special education classes and who started their intravenous abuse late). Males who had attended special education classes or dropped out of school tended to have drug careers of longer duration than women from the same groups (Holmberg, 1985a). Males also had more serious alcohol-related problems than females (Plant, Pecks, & Duffy, 1988).

To study the prediction of substance use in late adolescence, Boyle et al. (1992), as part of the Ontario Child Health Study, conducted a longitudinal study of 726 adolescents between the ages of 12 and 16 who had completed an epidemiologic study in 1983 and were followed up in 1987. Results indicated that prior substance use was strongly associated with subsequent use in 1987. Among the psychiatric disorders assessed in 1983, conduct disorder made an independent contribution to predicting use of marijuana (relative odds = 3.46) and other hard drugs (relative odds = 6.82) in 1987, after prior use of these substances and coexisting attention-deficit and emotional disorders were controlled.

Table 9–9
Substance Use Disorder: Duration and Trends

Author	Age of Onset	Duration Short (<2 yrs.)	Long (2–20 yrs.)	Chronic (>10 yrs.)	Trends
Holmberg (1985)		20–30% M&F	10–30% M&F	20% of Ms 10% of Fs	• Between 1968 and 1973, the abuse of substances decreased in males from 4.2% to 3.3% and in females from 2.4% to 1.8%. • Between 1973 and 1979, substance abuse decreased in males from 3.3% to 1.8% and in females from 1.8% to 0.5%.
Johnston et al. (1990)					• Between 1978 and 1985, daily marijuana use fell by more than half. • Between 1981 and 1985 cigarette smoking remained steady (20%), while alcohol use declined from 41 to 37%. • Between 1981 and 1984, there was a decrease in use of any illicit drug (22% to 15%).
Deykin et al. (1986)					
Alcohol use	15.5				
Alcohol abuse	16.3				
Drug use	15.8				
Drug abuse	16.5				

Conduct Disorders

Conduct disorder is one of the most valid (Robins, 1981) and reliably diagnosed (Mezzich, Mezzich, & Coffman, 1985) psychiatric disorders. Epidemiological studies that have included adolescents in their sample composition estimate the prevalence of conduct disorder at approximately 8.7% in the general adolescent population (Kashani & Offord, 1988), 6.7% in males, and 2.7% in females (Szatmari, Boyle, & Offord, 1989). The prevalence of conduct disorder overlapping with attention-deficit disorder with hyperactivity was 2.9% in males and 1.6% in females (Szatmari et al., 1989); the prevalence in females of attention-deficit disorder alone was also 1.6%. Szamari et al. (1989), who found that the prevalence of attention-deficit disorder with hyperactivity (ADDH) is slightly higher (3.9%) in males, also attended to clarify correlates of attention-deficit disorder and conduct disorder as true etiological risk factors. The sample studied consisted of 2,697 subjects, 4 to 16 years old, who participated in the Ontario Child Health Study (Boyle et al., 1992), the only epidemiological investigation that has addressed this issue with a sample that included adolescents. Results showed that pure conduct disorder was approximately twice as common as pure attention-deficit disorder in adolescents 12 to 16 years of age, and that males outnumber females in the conduct disorder group by 2.5 to 1. Males with ADDH were 14 times more likely to have conduct disorders than other males, while ADDH females were 40 times more likely to have conduct disorder than males in general. Conduct disorder was more prevalent in the 12- to 16-year-old group than in younger groups. Further, conduct-disordered children had experienced greater psychosocial disadvantage and had fewer developmental delays than the ADDH group.

Mitchell and Rosa (1979) reported on the precursors of criminality based on a longitudinal study conducted in Buckinghamshire, Scotland, on a randomly selected school population of 3,258 boys and 3,046 girls between 5 and 15 years of age. Their results, based on information from parents, revealed that stealing, lying, wandering, and destructiveness were positively associated with criminality and recidivism 15 years later, while excessive worrying and food fads were negatively associated.

In the Epidemiological Catchment Area (ECA) project, a large study of adults in the general population, antisocial personality and other psychiatric disorders were assessed (Robins, Tipp, & McEvoy, 1991). The total number of conduct disorder symptoms before age 15 was the most important predictor of whether subjects met criteria for antisocial personality as adults. Those with minimal conduct disorder symptoms (three or four criteria) met adult criteria 3.2% of the time if symptoms began prior to age 6, 1.9% if they began between the ages of 6 and 12, and 0.9% if they began after the age of 12. Antisocial personality developed in 24% of those with moderate conduct disorder (five to seven symptoms) if symptoms began before age 6, in 16% if they began between the ages of 6 and 12, and in 10% if they began after age 12. Those with a high level of conduct disorder (eight or more symptoms) met criteria for antisocial personality in 71% of the cases when symptoms began before age 6, in 53% if they began between the ages of 6 and 12, and in 48% if they began after age 12. Further, only one-quarter of those who reported symptoms prior to age 15 developed antisocial personality disorders. Conduct disorder before age 15 also had a strong association with the development of substance abuse and other psychiatric disorders (e.g., mania, schizophrenia, obsessive-compulsive disorder). Even mild conduct disorder before age 15 was associated with an adult disorder rate higher than when there were no early behavior problems (Robins & Price, 1991).

Summary

Although there have been significant advances in diagnosis, assessment, and classification of psychiatric disorders in children and adolescents, the development of a concept of mental disorder is still pending. In this chapter,The review of epidemiological studies of psychiatric disorders in the general population of adolescents has clarified our understanding of the prevalence, gender and ethnic differences, and associative factors of psychiatric disorders.

The prevalence of any psychiatric case, defined by the presence of DSM-III diagnostic criteria and impaired functioning, has been reported to be approximately 18% in the U.S. and German studies. This similarity in results is probably due to the use of comparable methodologies to examine the epidemiology of psychiatric disorders in adolescents. More than one-half of the studies employed multistage probability sampling of households, DSM-III and symptom severity or impaired functioning as criteria to define a psychiatric case, structured or semistructured psychiatric interview schedules, and parents and adolescents as informants. Diagnostic categories most frequently present among adolescents were conduct disorder, emotional disorder (e.g., depression, anxiety disorders), attention-deficit disorder, and substance use disorder. The factors most frequently associated with psychiatric disorders were education and socieconomic status; male gender, aggressivity, hyperactivity, and hostility; chronic health problems; poor family relations; and physical and sexual abuse.

The prevalence of major depression ranges from 1.8% to 18%; for dysthymia, it ranges from 1.8% to 3.3%. Depressive disorders are highly comorbid with anxiety, conduct, and substance use disorders. Usually, the onset of dysthymia and nondepressive psychiatric disorders precede the onset of major depression. The prevalence of depressive disorders increases with age; among depressive individuals with nondepressive comorbid disorders, there is more recurrence of the major depression, treatment utilization, and history of suicide attempts. In contrast to males, females demonstrate more severe major depression and comorbid anxiety disorders. Specifically, black females, in contrast to white females and black and white males, present a higher prevalence of depressive and anxiety disorders.

Among the anxiety disorders, separation anxiety and overanxious disorder are the most prevalent and tend to decrease with age. There is some discrepancy among the prevalence rates of anxiety disorders reported in the literature; these depend on the criteria used for diagnosis, whether DSM-III criteria alone (17% to 21%) or with impaired functioning (8.7%). In adolescence, the anxiety is related to worriedness and social situations more than to physiological symptoms.

The prevalence of anorexia nervosa in female adolescents is 0.2%; in male adolescents it is 0.0% when weight and DSM-III diagnostic criteria are used as parameters to formulate the diagnosis. The prevalence of anorexia nervosa increases substantially when the eating disorder case is defined by DSM-III alone (7.6% in females and 0.6% in males), whereas the prevalence of bulimia with or without the additional weight criterion remains the same (0.4% in males and 1.2% in females). Many male and female adolescents desire to be thin and experiment with weight control. Females attempt to control their weight for cosmetic reasons, however, whereas males control weight for athletic reasons.

The prevalence of substance use disorder as measured by DSM-III (daily use of receiving treatment for alcohol and drug problems) ranges from 1.8% to 9.1% in males and 0.5% to 6.8% in females. The existing trend has been a decreased prevalence of daily use of alcohol, marijuana, and cigarette smoking since 1979. Females smoke more nicotine than males, however, and in general they seem to be progressing toward prevalence rates obtained by males. Among the predictors of substance use, prior substance use and conduct disorder appear to be strongest.

The prevalence rate of conduct disorder is approximately between 2.7% and 8.7%. Conduct disorder before age 15 is highly associated with criminality and substance abuse and other psychiatric disorders (e.g., mania, schizophrenia, obsessive-compulsive disorder) in adulthood, as well as with depression and attention-deficit disorders in adolescence.

To refine the diagnostic formulation in future research, the definition of mental disorder in adolescence should be clarified, and the use of functional impairment scales (in addition to diagnostic criteria) should be encouraged to define a psychiatric case. Moreover, (a) information should be obtained from multiple sources to evaluate parent and child concordance, (b) item content of the interview schedules should match diagnostic criteria, and (c) use of multiple methods to determine the severity of the psychiatric disorder should be underscored. In addition, prospective longitudinal research is needed to obtain age-specific prevalence rates, to study the natural course of the disorder, and to ascertain associative factors that terminate or facilitate continuation of existing disorders and the development of new difficulties.

References

American Psychiatric Association. (1980). *Diagnostic and statistical manual of mental disorders* (3rd ed.). Washington, DC: Author.

American Psychiatric Association. (1987). *Diagnostic and statistical manual of mental disorders* (rev. 3rd ed.). Washington, DC: Author.

American Psychiatric Association. (1994). *Diagnostic and statistical manual of mental disorders* (4th ed.). Washington, DC: Author.

Boyle, M. H., & Offord, D. R. (1986). Smoking, drinking and use of illicit drugs among adolescents in Ontario: Prevalence, patterns of use and sociodemographic correlates. *Canadian Medical Association Journal, 135,* 1113–1121.

Boyle, M. H., Offord, D. R., Racine, Y. A., Szatmari, P., Fleming, J. E., & Links, P. S. (1992). Predicting substance use in late adolescence: Results from the Ontario Child Health Study follow-up. *American Journal of Psychiatry, 149,* 761–767.

Brandenburg, N. A., Friedman, R. M., & Silver, S. E. (1990). The epidemiology of childhood psychiatric disorders: Prevalence findings from recent studies. *Journal of the American Academy of Child and Adolescent Psychiatry, 29,* 76–83.

Chambers, W., Puig-Antich, J., Hirsch, M., Paez, P., Ambrosini, P. J., Tabrizi, M. A., & Davies, M. (1985). The assessment of affective disorders in children and adolescents by semi-structured interview: Test-retest reliability of the K-SADS-P. *Archives of General Psychiatry, 42,* 696–702.

Cohen, H. (1953). The evolution of the concept of disease. *Proceedings of the Royal Society of Medicine, 48,* 155–160.

Costello, A. J., Edelbrock, C., Dulcan, M. K., Kalas, R., & Klaric, S. H. (1984). *Development and testing of the NIMH Diagnostic Interview Schedule for Children in a clinic population* (Final report, Contract No. RFP-DB-81-0027). Rockville, MD: National Institute of Mental Health, Center for Epidemiologic Studies.

Costello, A. J., Edelbrock, C., Kalas, R., Kessler, M. D., & Klaric, S. H. (1982). *The NIMH Diagnostic Interview Schedule for Children (DISC).* Unpublished manuscript, University of Pittsburgh, Department of Psychiatry.

Costello, E. J. (1989). Developments in child psychiatric epidemiology. *Journal of the American Academy of Child and Adolescent Psychiatry, 28,* 836–841.

Costello, E. J., Edelbrock, C., & Costello, A. J. (1985). The validity of the NIMH Diagnostic Interview Schedule for Children: A comparison between pediatric and psychiatric referrals. *Journal of Abnormal Child Psychology, 13,* 579–595.

Deykin, E., Levy, J. C., & Wells, V. (1986). Adolescent depression, alcohol and drug abuse. *American Journal of Public Health, 76,* 178–182.

Edelbrock, C., Costello, A. J., Dulcan, M. K., Conover, N. C., & Kalas, R. (1986). Parent-child agreement on child psychiatric symptoms assessed via structured interview. *Journal of Child Psychology and Psychiatry and Allied Disciplines, 27,* 181–190.

Endicott, J., & Spitzer, R. L. (1978). A diagnostic interview: The Schedule for Affective Disorders and Schizophrenia. *Archives of General Psychiatry, 35*, 837–844.

Esser, G., Schmidt, M. H., & Woerner, W. (1990). Epidemiology and course of psychiatric disorders in school-age children: Results of a longitudinal study. *Journal of Child Psychology and Psychiatry and Allied Disciplines, 31*, 243–263.

Feighner, J. P., Robins, E., Guze, S. B., Woodruff, R. A., Winokur, G., & Munoz, R. (1972). Diagnostic criteria for use in psychiatric research. *Archives of General Psychiatry, 26*, 57–63.

Flament, M. F., Whitaker, A., Rapoport, J. L., Davies, M., Berg, C. Z., Kalikow, K., Sceery, W., & Shaffer, D. (1988). Obsessive compulsive disorder in adolescence: An epidemiological study. *Journal of the American Academy of Child and Adolescent Psychiatry, 27*, 764–771.

Fabrega, H. (1974). *Disease and social behavior.* Cambridge: MIT Press.

Fleming, J. E., Offord, D. R., & Boyle, M. H. (1989). The Ontario Child Health Study: Prevalence of childhood and adolescent depression in the community. *British Journal of Psychiatry, 155*, 647–654.

Garralda, M. E. (1991). Epidemiology and evaluation of child psychiatric disorders. *Current Opinion in Psychiatry, 4*, 524–528.

Garrison, C. Z., Schluchter, M. D., Schoenbach, V. J., & Kaplan, B. K. (1989). Epidemiology of depressive symptoms in young adolescents. *Journal of the American Academy of Child and Adolescent Psychiatry, 28*, 343–351.

Herjanic, B., & Campbell, W. (1977). Differentiating psychiatrically disturbed children on the basis of a structured interview. *Journal of Abnormal Child Psychology, 5*, 127–134.

Herjanic, B., Herjanic, M., Brown, F., & Wheatt, T. (1975). Are children reliable reporters? *Journal of Abnormal Child Psychology, 3*, 41–48.

Herjanic, B., & Reich, W. (1982). Development of a structured psychiatric interview for children: Agreement between child and parent on individual symptoms. *Journal of Abnormal Child Psychology, 10*, 307–324.

Holmberg, M. B. (1985a). Longitudinal studies of drug abuse in a fifteen-year-old population: Drug career. *Acta Psychiatrica Scandinavica, 71*, 67–79.

Holmberg, M. B. (1985b). Longitudinal studies of drug abuse in a fifteen-year-old population: Antecedents and consequences. *Acta Psychiatrica Scandinavica, 71*, 80–91.

Horowitz, J. E., & Marconi, J. (1966). The issue of definitions in the field of mental health: Applicable definitions to epidemiological studies. *Bulletin of the Pananamican Sanitary Office, 60*, 300–309.

Johnston, L. D., O'Malley, P. M., & Bachman, J. G. (1987). Psychotherapeutic, licit, and illicit use of drugs among adolescents: An epidemiological perspective. *Journal of Adolescent Health Care, 8*, 36–51.

Johnston, L. D., O'Malley, P. M., & Bachman, J. G. (1990). *Report on the 15th annual national survey of American high school seniors and the 10th annual national survey of American college students.* Ann Arbor, NI: Institute for Social Research.

Kashani, J. H., Beck, N. C., Hoeper, E. W., Fallahi, C., Corcoran, C. M., McAllister, J. A., Rosenberg, T. K., & Reid, J. C. (1987a). Psychiatric disorders in a community sample of adolescents. *American Journal of Psychiatry, 144,* 584–589.

Kashani, J. H., Carlson, G. A., Beck, N. C., Hoeper, E. W., Corcoran, C. M., McAllister, J. A., Fallahi, C., Rosenberg, T. K., & Reid, J. C. (1987b). Depression, depressive symptoms, and depressed mood among a community sample of adolescents. *American Journal of Psychiatry, 144,* 931–933.

Kashani, J. H., & Orvaschel, H. (1988). Anxiety disorders in mid-adolescence: A community sample. *American Journal of Psychiatry, 145,* 960–964.

Kashani, J. H., & Orvaschel, H. (1990). A community study of anxiety in children and adolescents. *American Journal of Psychiatry, 147,* 313–318.

Kendell, R. E. (1975). *The role of diagnosis in psychiatry.* Oxford, England: Blackwell.

Klein, D. F. (1978). A proposed definition of mental illness. In R. L. Spitzer & D. F. Klein (Eds.), *Critical issues in psychiatric diagnosis.* New York: Raven.

Lewinsohn, P. M., Rohde, P., Seeley, J. R., & Hops, H. (1991). Comorbidity of unipolar depression: I. Major depression with dysthymia. *Journal of Abnormal Psychology, 100,* 205–213.

Meyer, A. (1987). Fundamental conceptions of dementia praecox. *Journal of Nervous and Mental Disease, 34,* 331–336.

Mezzich, A. C., Mezzich, J. E., & Coffman, G. A. (1985). Reliability of DSM-II in child psychopathology. *Journal of the American Academy of Child Psychiatry, 24,* 273–280.

Mitchell, S., & Rosa, P. (1979). Boyhood behavior problems as precursors of criminality: A fifteen-year follow-up study. *Journal of Child Psychology and Psychiatry and Allied Disciplines, 22,* 19–33.

Offord, D. R., Boyle, M. H., Fleming, J. E., Blum, H. M., & Grant, N. I. (1989). Ontario Child Health Study: Summary of selected results. *Canadian Journal of Psychiatry, 34,* 483–491.

Orvaschel, H., Puig-Antich, J., Chambers, W., Tabrizi, M. A., & Johnson, R. (1982). Retrospective assessment of prepubertal major depression with the Kiddie-SADS-E. *Journal of the American Academy of Child Psychiatry, 21,* 392–397.

Plant, M. A., Peck, D. F., & Duffy, J. C. (1988). Trends in the use and misuse of alcohol and other psychoactive drugs in the United Kingdom: Some perplexing connections. *British Journal of Addiction, 83,* 943–947.

Plant, M. A., Peck, D. F., & Stuart, R. (1984). The correlates of serious alcohol-related consequences and illicit drug use amongst a cohort of Scottish teenagers. *British Journal of Addiction, 79,* 197–200.

Puig-Antich, J., Blau, S., Marx, N., Greenhill, L. I., & Chambers, W. (1978). Prepubertal major depressive disorder: A pilot study. *Journal of the American Academy of Child Psychiatry, 17,* 695–707.

Puig-Antich, J., & Chambers, W. (1978). *The Schedule for Affective Disorders and Schizophrenia for school-aged children.* Unpublished interview schedule, New York State Psychiatric Institute.

Robins, L. N. (1981). Epidemiological approach to natural history research: Antisocial disorders in children. *Journal of the American Academy of Child Psychiatry, 20,* 566–580.

Robins, L. N., & Price, R. K. (1991). Adult disorders predicted by childhood conduct problems: Results from the NIMH Eipidemiologic Catchment Area project. *Psychiatry, 54,* 116–132.

Robins, L. N., Tipp, J., & McEvoy, L. (1991). Antisocial personality. In L. N. Robins & D. Reiger (Eds.), *Psychiatric disorders in America.* New York: Free Press.

Rohde, P., Lewinsohn, P. M., & Seeley, J. R. (1991). Comorbidity of unipolar depression: II. Comorbidity with other mental disorders in adolescents and adults. *Journal of Abnormal Psychology, 100,* 214–222.

Scadding, J. G. (1967). Diagnosis: The clinician and the computer. *Lancet, 2,* 877–882.

Spitzer, R. L., Endicott, J., & Robins, E. (1978). Research Diagnostic Criteria. *Archives of General Psychiatry, 35,* 773–782.

Stengel, E. (1959). Classification of mental disorders. *Bulletin of the World Health Organization, 21,* 601–663.

Szatmari, P., Boyle, M., & Offord, D. R. (1989). ADDH and conduct disorder: Degree of diagnostic overlap and differences among correlates. *Journal of the American Academy of Child and Adolescent Psychiatry, 28,* 865–872.

Taylor, M. A., & Abrams, R. A. (1975). A critique of the St. Louis research criteria for schizophrenia. *American Journal of Psychiatry, 132,* 1276–1280.

Velez, C. N., Johnson, J., & Cohen, P. (1989). A longitudinal analysis of selected risk factors for childhood psychopathology. *Journal of the American Academy of Child and Adolescent Psychiatry, 28,* 861–864.

Whitaker, A., Davies, M., Shaffer, D., Johnson, J., Abrams, S., Walsh, B. T., & Kalikow, K. (1989). The struggle to be thin: A survey of anorexic and bulimic symptoms in a non-referred adolescent population. *Psychological Medicine, 19,* 143–163.

Whitaker, A., Johnson, J., Shaffer, D., Rapoport, J. L., Kalikow, K., Walsh, B. T., Davies, M., Braiman, S., & Dolinsky, A. (1990). Uncommon troubles in young people. *Archives of General Psychiatry, 47,* 487–496.

World Health Organization. (1987). *ICD-10 1987 draft of Chapter V: Mental and behavioral disorders.* Geneva: World Health Organization.

Part III
Specific Disorders

10
Depression

William M. Reynolds

Of the many potential mental health problems that may be experienced during adolescence, those related to mood appear to be among the most common. It is well established that in adults, depressive disorders (along with anxiety disorders) are among the most frequently experienced mental health problems in the United States (Regier et al., 1988; Robins et al., 1984). Since 1980 there has been a great amount of research published regarding the nature, prevalence, assessment, diagnosis, correlates, and biological basis of depressive disorders in adolescents. The study of depression in young people encompasses a great many professional domains of inquiry and orientation (Reynolds & Johnston, 1994)—more than can be reviewed in depth within a single chapter.

This literature suggests the general conclusion that depression in adolescents represents a serious mental health problem. Depressive disorders appear to be among the most prevalent emotional problems in adolescents. Estimates of the prevalence of clinical depressive symptomatology range from roughly 4% to 12% of youngsters in the general population (Kashani et al., 1987a; Kashani et. al., 1987b; McGee et al., 1990; Reinherz, Giaconia, Lefkowitz, Pakiz, & Frost, 1993; Whitaker et al., 1990). Although most epidemiological studies of depression in youngsters suffer from methodological limitations (Fleming & Offord, 1990), the above figures suggest at least that a large number of adolescents are in need of psychological services. Silver (1988), citing unpublished survey data from the National Institute of Mental Health (NIMH), reports that approximately one out of six youngsters under the age of 18 years admitted to psychiatric settings and nonfederal hospitals in the United States had an intake diagnosis of an affective disorder. Thus it is realistic to consider depression as one of the most pervasive forms of psychopathology in young people.

In adolescents, depression may be viewed as particularly insidious. As an internalizing problem, this disorder may go undetected and untreated unless formal procedures are instituted for identification and service delivery. Research suggests that depressive disorders in adolescents are underidentified and undertreated (Reynolds, 1994a). Longitudinal research

297

indicates that for some youngsters, particularly those with a dysthymic disorder, their depression may last for many years; in some cases it may be a precursor for other psychiatric disorders (Kovacs, Feinberg, Crouse-Novak, Paulauskas, Pollock, & Finkelstein, 1984). Longitudinal and retrospective research suggests that depression in youngsters may have long-term consequences. In a retrospective study of symptom summaries from youngsters attending the Maudsley Hospital in London, Harrington, Fudge, Rutter, Pickles, and Hill (1990) examined the adult psychiatric status of 52 subjects who initially demonstrated a significant number of depressive symptoms and 52 matched nonpsychiatric controls. They found that 40% of the depressed group met criteria for depression within 5 years of entering adulthood. In this group 58% of the subjects had a history of an affective disorder at the time of follow-up, compared to 25% of the control sample.

The Study of Depression in Adolescents

Much of the research and clinical interest in depression in adolescents has evolved since the early 1980s. Previously held perspectives considered adolescence as a developmentally tumultuous period in which aberrant internalized emotions were normative or at worst indicative of "adolescent turmoil." Such views limited most clinical insight into depression as a real psychopathology experienced by adolescents. Furthermore, when researchers began to focus on depression in young people in the late 1970s, most of the attention was on children, with few published studies specific to adolescents. For example, the first published control-group treatment study of depression in adolescents did not appear until 1986 (Reynolds & Coats, 1986).

Prior notions of depression as masked (i.e., expressed in symptoms different from those of adults; Reynolds, 1985a) limited the comprehensive study of depression in young people. Depression in youngsters was exemplified by the construct of depressive equivalents (Glaser, 1967; Hollon, 1970; Rie, 1966), in which depression was demonstrated by such overt negative behaviors as acting out, aggression, hyperactivity, and delinquency, or in the form of psychosomatic and hypochondriacal disorders (Lesse, 1981). As contemporary systems for the classification and definition of psychopathology were established (e.g., American Psychiatric Association, 1980) there was a recognition that depression and its associated symptoms occurred in adolescents to a large extent as they did in adults. Christ, Adler, Isacoff, and Gershansky (1981) examined the diagnostic utility of masked depression by examining clinical records of more than 10,000 psychiatrically hospitalized children and adolescents. These authors found that youngsters with diagnoses of depressive disorders showed greater numbers of contemporary symptoms of depression (suicidal behavior, sleep and appetite changes, fatigue, etc.), while masked features (aggression and misbehavior) were negatively related to this diagnosis and occurred at a lower frequency in depressed youngsters as compared to youngsters with other psychopathology.

There is now a general consensus that depression in adolescents consists of many of the same symptoms as are found in adults (American Psychiatric Association, 1987; Carlson & Kashani, 1988a, b; Friedman et al., 1982; Friedman, Hurt, Clarkin, Corn, & Aronoff, 1983; Geller, Chestnut, Miller, Price, & Yates, 1985; Mitchell, McCauley, Burke, & Moss, 1988; Strober, 1985; Strober, Green, & Carlson, 1981a). As in adults, depressive disorders in adolescents are not expressed as a single symptom (e.g., dysphoria or sad mood), but as clusters of symptoms that may include anhedonia, lowered self-esteem, social withdrawal, fatigue, impaired school performance, crying spells or tearfulness, sleeping and eating disturbances, and self-destructive impulses (American Psychiatric Association, 1987). Psychotic symptoms (e.g., hallucinations and delusions) have been found in depressed youngsters (Strober et al., 1981a), and particularly in adolescents with an endogenous form of major depression. The constellations and severity of depressive symptoms and their potential impact on the psychosocial and emotional functioning of adolescents suggest that depression should not be viewed as a normal avenue of their development. Furthermore, there is growing evidence to suggest that depression in adolescence may be associated with greater propensity for psychopathology in adulthood (Harrington et al., 1990).

To understand the nature of depression in adolescents one needs to recognize the relatively high degree of comorbidity that is found with other psychiatric diagnoses in this age group. Disorders such as conduct disorders, substance abuse, and anxiety disorders have been found to coexist relatively often with depression in youngsters (e.g., Alessi & Magen, 1988; Alessi, Robbins, & Dilsaver, 1987; Finch, Lipovsky, & Casat, 1989; Kovacs, 1990; Levy & Deykin, 1989; Strauss, Last, Hersen, & Kazdin, 1988). Another problem associated with depression in adolescents is suicidal behavior, including suicidal ideation, intent, and suicide attempts (Reynolds & Mazza, 1992). The relationship between suicidal behavior and depression is not perfect, in that there is a significant proportion of depressed youngsters who do not demonstrate suicidal behaviors. Likewise, it appears that there are many adolescents who show suicidal behaviors but are not depressed (Reynolds, 1989; 1990; Reynolds & Mazza, 1990). These findings point to the need for viewing depression and suicidal behaviors as two related, but distinct forms of psychopathology in young persons.

Models of Depression

Numerous models and theoretical formulations of depression have been developed over the past two decades. In large part, these models have been developed to account for depression in adults. A number of psychological and biological models, however, have either been tested or appear applicable to depression in adolescents.

Biological Models

Several models of depression have been proposed that focus on biological functions. These vary from genetic models (e.g., Faraone, Kremen, & Tsuang, 1990; Reich, Rice, & Mullaney, 1986) to neuroendocrine studies (e.g., Burke & Puig-Antich, 1990; Schlesser, 1986) and attempt to provide an etiological basis for depression. Biochemical models of depression have been studied for several decades, with a primary focus on noradrenergic functioning and the role of various neurotransmitters. The latter include catecholamines (e.g., norepinephrine) and indoleamines (e.g., serotonin) and their mechanism in the neurochemistry of the brain. The original catecholamine hypothesis of depression described by Schildkraut (1965) suggests that the depletion of norepinephrine results in depression. Recent research on the role of catecholamines has lent support for increased noradrenergic function in youngsters with depression (Rogeness, Javors, Maas, & Macedo, 1990). Unfortunately, a comprehensive description of biological models is beyond the scope of this chapter.

Biological research with depressed adolescents has focused on various psychobiological correlates and markers of depression, including growth hormone secretion during sleep or recovery, and as a response to insulin-induced hypoglycemia (Dahl et al., 1992; Puig-Antich, 1986a, b). Likewise, a number of studies have reported on sleep architecture and disturbance in depressed children (e.g., Emslie, Roffwarg, Rush, Weinberg, & Parkin-Feigenbaum, 1987; Lahmeyer, Poznanski, & Bellur, 1983). Neuroendocrine research has also focused on the relationship between hypothalamic-pituitary-adrenal axis function and major depression in adolescents. Puig-Antich (1987a, b) has provided reviews of these psychobiological markers of depression in children and adolescents.

The involvement of adrenocortical hormone metabolism in endogenous depression (considered a more biologically-based subtype) has received attention in the past decade as researchers have focused on the increased levels of cortisol (hydrocortisone) in depressed persons. Increased levels of this hormone, which is produced by the adrenal glands, have been associated with a number of psychopathologies, as well as with a nonspecific stress response; this association is not a recent finding (e.g., Rubin & Mandell, 1966).

In addition, the development of the dexamethasone suppression test (DST), a biological marker for hypothalamic-pituitary-adrenal axis activity, has increased the research in this area.

The DST was introduced in the late 1960s and 1970s as an episode-specific biological marker for endogenous depression in adults. Since the 1980s, the DST has generated a tremendous interest across adult, adolescent, and child psychiatric populations. Research with the DST has focused on a wide range of clinical topics, including the differentiation of subtypes of depression (Miller & Nelson, 1987; Targum, Byrnes, & Sullivan, 1982; Zimmerman, Stangl, & Coryell, 1985), selection of antidepressant medication (Greden et al., 1981), differential diagnosis (Brown, Johnston, & Mayfield, 1979), prediction of course and relapse (Weller, Weller, Fristad, Cantwell, & Preskorn, 1986), and clinical response and investigation in such other psychopathologies as anxiety disorders (Livingston, Reis, & Ringdahl, 1984), panic disorder (Curtis, Cameron, & Nesse, 1982), and schizophrenia and mania (Baumgartner, Graf, & Kurten, 1986). Investigations of the DST in youngsters have followed the general methodology of adult investigations. A number of studies have used the DST with adolescents (e.g., Crumley, Clevenger, Steinfink, & Oldham, 1982; Emslie, Weinberg, Rush, Weissenburger, & Parkin-Feigenbaum, 1987; Extein, Rosenberg, Pottash, & Gold, 1982; Hsu et al., 1983; Klee & Garfinkel, 1984; Robbins, Alessi, & Colfer, 1989; Robbins, Alessi, Yanchyshyn, & Colfer, 1982), and these represent a growing literature base.

Current Psychological Theories

A brief description of several contemporary theories of depression will be presented below. These theories were developed with adults as the target population, although they translate reasonably well to adolescents. At the time of this writing, however, there does not exist a well-formulated contemporary theory of depression specific to adolescents. Most of the theories described are conceptualized as cognitive or behavioral in their orientation, although most also show an overlap between cognitive and behavioral components and their hypothesized mechanism. Because of this blurring of distinctions, it is sometimes difficult to differentiate a theory as solely behavioral or cognitive.

A partial test of a theory is its application to treatment procedures, with clinical efficacy (assuming adequate administration of therapy) providing limited evidence for the theory. An examination of the adult treatment outcome literature, with particular focus on therapies consistent with cognitive and behavioral theories, suggests relatively comparable therapeutic efficacy across treatments (see Beckham, 1990; Dobson, 1989; Reynolds & Stark, 1983; and Williams, 1984, for reviews of representative treatment studies). Lewinsohn, Hoberman, Teri, and Hautzinger (1985) have formulated an "integrative theory" of depression that subsumes cognitive, behavioral, and environmental components and their interaction. As a working model, their conceptualization provides some interesting insights into the psychological mechanisms and etiology of depression. Although not yet applied to interventions for depression in youngsters, future treatment programs may find components of this model useful.

Social Learning Theory. Lewinsohn and colleagues (Lewinsohn, 1974, 1975; Lewinsohn & Arconad, 1981) delineated a behavioral model of depression consistent with social learning theory. The foundation of this theory is that depression results, in part, from decreased levels of response-contingent positive reinforcement. As an outcome of this, the individual engages in fewer activities that provide positive reinforcement, especially those that may be viewed as pleasant. The decrease in response-contingent positive reinforcement may result from an environment low in such reinforcement or in events or situations that produce such an outcome. It may also be the case that the depressed person actively avoids engagement in such reinforcing activities.

Treatments utilizing a social learning approach might have a primary target of increased engagement in pleasant activities, along with a decrease in negative activities. A number of treatment studies with depressed adolescents have included such treatment components (e.g., Lewinsohn, Clarke, Hops, & Andrews, 1990; Reynolds & Coats, 1986). In a related treatment package, Fine, Forth, Gilbert, and Haley (1991) utilized a social skills treatment for depression in adolescents. Within this approach, social skills are taught with the intention of increasing the level of social reinforcement and engagement in pleasant activities with others.

Self-Control Theory. Self-control as a model of depression was delineated by Rehm (1977, 1981; Fuchs & Rehm, 1977) and includes behavioral and cognitive components. Problems in self-control have been applied to a host of problem behaviors (e.g., Kendall & Braswell, 1985; Pressley, Reynolds, Stark, & Gettinger, 1983) and can be related to the model of self-regulation delineated by Kanfer (1970; Kanfer & Karoly, 1972). Rehm's model suggests that depressed individuals show specific deficits or problems in one or more components of self-control (e.g., self-monitoring, self-evaluation, and self-reinforcement). Within this model, a depressed individual may selectively attend to or monitor negative events and outcomes and fail to monitor accurately or attend to positive events or outcomes. Self-monitoring may also focus on the immediate outcomes of behavior rather than potential delayed outcomes. Likewise, a depressed person may show problems in self-evaluation by setting performance expectations at an unobtainable level, so that failure or poor performance is a result. The depressed person may also make more negative self-statements or attributions for their performance or behavior. Problems in self-reinforcement occur when a low level or rate of response-contingent self-reward (or a high or excessive rate of self-punishment) is provided. In addition to the three domains of self-control, Rehm includes faulty attributions for responsibility of behavior.

The self-control model of depression was originally developed as applicable to adults. The problems of self-control in children have been a long-studied domain, however, particularly as they relate to externalizing behaviors. In this context, components of self-control are closely aligned with social learning theory and modeling. For instance, in their classic book on social learning and personality, Bandura and Walters (1963) report that self-reinforcement behavior in children appears to be influenced to a greater extent by the standard setting and self-reinforcement demonstrated by adults (e.g., parents) than those exhibited by peers. This finding has implications for depression in adolescents, particularly if we also incorporate aspects of Lewinsohn's social learning model of depression, the findings of depression in the offspring of depressed adults (Beardslee, 1986; Beardslee, Bemporad, Keller, & Klerman, 1983; Downey & Coyne, 1990), and problems in standard-setting and self-reinforcement suggested by the self-control model of depression.

Learned Helplessness Theory. The learned helplessness theory of depression in adults was developed as a behavioral model by Seligman (1975) and was predicated on earlier studies with animals. From a behavioral and attributional perspective it soon became viewed as a potential model for understanding depression in young children (e.g., Dweck, 1977; Watson, 1977). Over the past decade the learned helplessness theory has been reformulated to include a heavy emphasis on cognitive components (e.g., faulty attributions for success and failure experiences; Abramson, Seligman, & Teasdale, 1978), and has been applied to the study of depression in children (Seligman & Peterson, 1986). The reformulated learned helplessness theory (Abramson et al., 1978) proposes that depression is in part a result of beliefs that negative outcomes will occur, along with the perception or expectation that the event or outcome is beyond the individual's control. An insidious attributional style specific to the uncontrollability of these negative events results in lowered self-esteem and helplessness. Three domains of causal attributions are delineated: internal versus external, stable versus unstable, and global versus specific. The type of attribution made to events may be either functional or dysfunctional. In this manner, individuals who make internal, stable, and global attributions for negative events are seen as predisposed to become depressed; the individual feels a sense of helplessness, given that nothing he or she can do will change the outcome or occurrence of the event. Revisions and extrapolations of this perspective have been provided by Abramson, Alloy, and colleagues (Abramson & Alloy, 1990; Alloy, Abramson, Metalsky, & Hartlage, 1988).

Cognitive Theories. Cognitive theories of depression developed for adults include those by Ellis (1962) and Beck (1967) and are relevant in their application to adolescents. The cognitive theory of depression formulated by Beck (1967; Beck, Rush, Shaw, & Emery, 1979) has had the greatest influence on the development and research of treatments for depression in adults (see Dobson, 1989, for reviews of studies). Treatment components based on this theory have also been incorporated into most experimental treatment studies of adolescent depression. Beck's theory distinguishes three domains related to depressogenic cognitions or thinking patterns. The first domain, the cognitive triad, includes systematic negative cognitions specific to the individual (self), current experiences (the world), and expectations for the future. A second basic element is that of dysfunctional schemas—stable, distorted thought patterns or frames used by the depressed individual to interpret information. Beck et al. (1979) refer to this element as the "structural organization of depressive thinking." The third component of Beck's model consists of six formal types of cognitive errors made in the processing of information: arbitrary inferences, selective abstraction, overgeneralization, magnification or minimization, personalization, and absolutistic or dichotomous thinking. Beck (1967) considers these depressogenic thought patterns to be relatively stable and to predispose an individual to depression.

Diagnosis and Classification of Depression in Adolescents

Advances in the development of research and clinically based systems of classification and diagnosis of mental health problems and disorders has provided greater clarity and criteria for the description of depression. As continued revisions of such systems show, however, classification systems that are used in formulating diagnoses should not be viewed as complete in their description of inclusion and exclusion criteria for specific disorders. As we learn more about specific disorders through research and clinical descriptions, modifications in systems of classification become necessary. This process is exemplified by ongoing revisions in the *Diagnostic and Statistical Manual of Mental Disorders* (DSM) by the American Psychiatric Association and the International Classification of Diseases (ICD) by the World Health Organization Table 10–1.

Diagnostic Systems and Approaches

Several diagnostic systems and approaches have been used by researchers and clinicians for the classification and description of depression in adolescents. Typically these systems (e.g., DSM) utilize a taxonomic approach for the differentiation of type and subtypes of depression. Forms of depressive

Table 10–1
Diagnostic and Statistical Manual (DSM) Depressive Symptomatology in Adolescents

Symptom	DSM-III-R		DSM-IV	
	Major Depression	Dysthymia	Major Depression	Dysthymic Disorder
Dysphoria	•	•	•	•
Insomnia or hypersomnia	•	•	•	
Change in appetite/weight	•	•	•	
Fatigue/low energy	•	•	•	•
Psychomotor retardation/agitation	•		•	
Recurrent morbid or suicidal ideation or attempt	•		•	
Irritability	•	•	•	•
Excessive anger		•		•
Tearfulness or crying	•	•	•	•
Generalized loss of interest or pleasure	•		•	•
Pessimistic attitude toward the future/hopelessness		•		•
Decreased ability to think/poor concentration	•	•	•	•
Indecisiveness	•	•	•	•
Decreased activity				•
Feelings of worthlessness	•		•	
Feelings of inadequacy, low self-esteem, or self-confidence		•		•
Decreased effectiveness or productivity in school or work	•	•	•	•
Social withdrawal	•	•	•	•
Excessive feelings of guilt	•		•	•

Note: Symptoms delineated above may be combined within one symptom criteria grouping in DSM-III-R and DSM-IV and also include symptoms noted as associated features. Above symptoms do not include symptoms specified for bipolar disorder or cross-sectional symptom features (e.g., "with melancholic features") or course specifiers (e.g., "with seasonal pattern").

disorders are based on particular clusters of symptoms and symptom duration; most systems employ both symptom inclusion and exclusion criteria. In the United States and North America, the revised third edition of the DSM (DSM-III-R; American Psychiatric Association, 1987) is the primary system used for the classification of depressive disorders in children, adolescents, and adults. In 1994, the fourth edition of the DSM (DSM-IV; American Psychiatric Association, 1994) was published. In Europe, the

ICD system is often used to classify depressive disorders in young people. Most DSM-III-R/DSM-IV depressive disorders are classified within the category of mood disorders, an exception being adjustment disorder with depressed mood.

The Research Diagnostic Criteria (RDC) predate DSM-III and were developed by Spitzer, Endicott, and Robins (1978). Differences exist between the RDC and DSM-III-R/DSM-IV criteria for depressive disorders; the RDC, which provide greater specificity of subtypes of depression, were primarily designed for research applications. The RDC disorders may be evaluated using a formal diagnostic clinical interview, the Schedule for Affective Disorders and Schizophrenia (SADS; Endicott & Spitzer, 1978) for adults, and the Kiddie-SADS (K-SADS; Puig-Antich & Chambers, 1978) for children. These interview schedules are specific to the RDC in the diagnoses they provide, although research investigators have developed procedures for extracting DSM diagnoses from SADS interviews.

Diagnostic and Statistical Manual of Mental Disorders (DSM)

In North America, the DSM-III/DSM-III-R has since 1980 been the most often used diagnostic system for clinical and research applications with adolescents. In DSM-IV, depressive disorders are for the most part included under the domain of mood disorders. Mood disorders include major depression, bipolar disorders, mania, cyclothymic disorder, and dysthymic disorder. Disorders are differentiated by their clusters of symptoms, age of onset, and the duration of symptoms. Those disorders that are most likely to be found in adolescents are major depression and dysthymic disorder, along with adjustment disorder with depressed mood. Bipolar disorders demonstrate an onset during adolescence in a significant number of individuals who develop this disorder (Loranger & Levine, 1978; McGlashan, 1988). The depressive disorders subsumed under the domain of mood disorders in the DSM-IV are listed in Table 10–1. Some disorders suggested in early drafts, such as minor depression, were not kept in the last draft of the DSM-IV. Because of the recency of DSM-IV, and to illustrate commonalities and differences, both DSM-III-R and DSM-IV mood disorders are presented in the table.

Major Depression. Major depression as a disorder in the DSM-IV refers to a relatively severe, acute form of depression. The diagnostic disorder of major depression is defined in part by the presence of five out of nine potential symptoms, one of which must be either dysphoric mood (can be irritable mood in adolescents) or anhedonia (loss of interest or pleasure in all or almost all activities). Other symptoms include sleep problems, as manifested by insomnia or hypersomnia; complaints or other evidence of diminished ability to think or difficulty concentrating; loss of energy or general fatigue; eating problems, as manifested by decreased or increased appetite or significant weight (in young children failure to make expected weight gains is symptomatic); psychomotor retardation or agitation; suicidal or morbid ideation, death wishes, or suicide attempts; and feelings of self-reproach, worthlessness, or excessive or inappropriate guilt (which may be delusional). For a diagnosis of major depression, symptoms must be present nearly every day for a period of at least 2 weeks. Exclusion criteria preclude a number of other pathologies (e.g., organic mental disorder) and etiologies (e.g., a normal response to bereavement) as concomitant problems. DSM-IV provides information to assist the clinician in a differential diagnosis of major depression, as opposed to conditions that may include significant depressive symptoms.

Major depression may occur as a single episode (without a history of manic or hypomanic episode) or as recurrent depression, the latter delineating a history of two or more major depressive episodes separated by at least 2 months of normal functioning. Major depression may also be chronic if all criteria have been met for a 2 year period. There are also several possible subtypes of major depression, designated by melancholic features, seasonal pattern, atypical features, catatonic features, or postpartum onset (the last three of which are new to DSM-IV). The melancholic subtype describes an endogenous or biological form of major depression with additional symptoms, including diurnal variation (depressive symptoms typically worse in the morning); significant anorexia or weight loss; loss of pleasure in all or almost all activities, or lack of reactivity to pleasurable stimuli; early morning wakening; excessive guilt; significant psychomotor retardation or agitation; and a distinct quality of depressed mood. The seasonal pattern—sometimes referred to as seasonal affective disorder (SAD)—describes a temporal occurrence and onset of either major depression or bipolar disorder, generally during the late fall or early winter months with full remission in the early spring. For a diagnosis of a seasonal pattern, there must be at least two episodes in the last 2 years without a nonseasonal episode, and seasonal episodes must outnumber nonseasonal depressions that have occurred in the person's life.

Dysthymic Disorder. Dysthymic disorder in DSM-IV (dysthymia in DSM-III-R) is a chronic depressive disorder that is usually less severe in symptom distress than major depression but of greater duration. It may be especially relevant to the study of depression in adolescents. Kovacs and colleagues (Kovacs, Feinberg, Crouse-Novak, Paulauskas, & Finkelstein, 1984; Kovacs, Feinberg, Crouse-Novak, Paulauskas, Pollock, & Finkelstein, 1984) found in a longitudinal study that dysthymic disorder was a long-lasting problem (5 years or longer) for some youngsters. Diagnostic criteria for dysthymic disorder in adolescents include a depressed or irritable mood for most of the day, manifested most of the time over a period of at least 1 year, although there may be periods of up to two months during which symptoms are not present. In addition, at least two of the following symptoms must be present when the adolescent is depressed: poor appetite or overeating, insomnia or hypersomnia, fatigue or low energy level, low self-esteem, poor concentration or problems making decisions, and feelings of despair or hopelessness. Exclusion criteria include the adolescent showing no evidence of a major depressive episode during the initial year of the disorder and never having a manic or hypomanic episode, and the disorder being neither superimposed on a chronic psychosis nor due to or maintained by an organic factor.

The symptom criteria for dysthymic disorder feature several changes from those included in the DSM-III-R category of dysthymia, including the removal of appetite and sleep disturbance as symptoms of the disorder. Diagnostic criteria for dysthymia in adolescents differ from those for adults, for whom symptoms of this disorder must be present for 2 years for a diagnosis. Dysthymic disorder may also occur with atypical features similar to the case of major depression. "Depressive disorder not otherwise specified (NOS)" is also included as a diagnostic classification, with examples provided of premenstrual dysphoric disorder, minor depressive disorder, recurrent brief depressive disorder, and postpsychotic depression of schizophrenia, among others.

Bipolar Disorder. Bipolar disorder is a severe psychiatric condition that presents a diagnostic challenge for clinicians. A number of researchers have noted the difficulties in accurately making this diagnosis, as well as the propensity for misdiagnosis in adolescents (Bowden & Sarabia, 1980; Bowring & Kovacs, 1992; Carlson & Strober, 1978a). The essential feature of bipolar disorder is the occurrence of one or more episodes of mania or hypomania, usually accompanied by a history of one or more major depressive episodes. The DSM-IV describes two primary forms of bipolar disorder. Bipolar I disorder may occur as a single manic episode; if there have been multiple episodes, the most recent episode may be hypomanic, manic, mixed, depressed, or unspecified. Bipolar II disorder represents a condition of recurrent major depressive episodes with a history of at least one hypomanic episode. There is also a classification of "bipolar disorder not otherwise specified (NOS)" that includes features such as recurrent hypomania without associated depressive symptoms.

In DSM-IV, a manic episode is defined as a period of pervasive elevated or irritable mood of at least 1 week (or any time period if hospitalization is required). During this period at least three of the following symptoms need to be present: grandiosity or excessive self-esteem; minimal need for sleep; increased talkativeness, flights of ideas or thoughts racing; easy distractibility to irrelevant stimuli; psychomotor agitation or increased task-related activity; and excessive or unrestrained engagement in pleasurable activities. If the primary quality of the mood is irritability, four of the above symptoms must be present. In addition, the mood disturbance needs to cause significant impairment in occupational or social functioning or require hospitalization to avoid self-harm or harm to others. A manic episode may occur with or without psychotic features, with the former either mood congruent (consistent with inflated self-esteem grandiosity, etc.) or incongruent (paranoid delusions, etc.). A hypomanic episode consists of a period of an elevated or irritable mood of at least 4 days' duration, with at least three of the seven symptoms noted above for manic episodes. As with manic episode criteria, four symptoms need to be present when the quality of mood is expressed as irritability. The hypomanic episode features less severe symptoms than the manic episode and lacks the significant impairment in functioning associated with mania.

It has been suggested that bipolar disorder—or manic-depressive illness or manic-depressive psychosis, as it is sometimes referred to—has been underdiagnosed, with many cases diagnosed as schizophrenia (Bowden & Sarabia, 1980; Campbell, 1952; Carlson & Strober, 1978b; Casat, 1982). Other difficulties, including a low base rate and variability of symptoms, have been noted by Bowring and Kovacs (1992) as creating problems in the reliable diagnosis of mania in adolescents.

Cyclothymic Disorder. In DSM-IV, cyclothymic disorder (referred to as cyclothymia in DSM-III-R) is described as a chronic mood disorder that is symptomatically similar to bipolar disorder but of lesser severity. Criteria for cyclothymic disorder include a period of 1 year in which there have been numerous period of hypomanic symptoms, along with many periods of depressed mood or anhedonia that did not meet criteria for major depression. Cyclothymic disorder is similar to dysthymic disorder in that depressive symptoms are not sufficient for a diagnosis of major depression, and the symptoms must be present for 1 year with periods of up to 2 months in which symptoms are not present.

One of the most comprehensive studies of cyclothymia in children and adolescents was conducted by Klein, Depue, and Slater (1985), who studied offspring of parents with bipolar disorder and of parents with other psychopathology. They reported that 38% of adolescents of bipolar parents had an affective disorder, as compared to 5% of children of parents with nonaffective psychiatric disorders. A diagnosis of cyclothymia was found in 24% of youngsters from bipolar parents, and none of the offspring of the control parents. The age of onset for cyclothymia in the 9 youngsters with this diagnosis was 12.4 years of age, with a range from 7 to 15 years. In the Klein et al. sample, hypomanic episodes had an average duration of 1.8 days, whereas depressive episodes lasted 2.3 days, with an approximately equal number of hypomanic and depressive episodes reported. The distribution of episodes was bimodal, with 20% of the sample experiencing fewer than 6 depressive episodes in their lives and 80% reporting 12 or more episodes per year. This study suggests a relatively high rate of affective disorders (and, in particular, cyclothymia) in the off-spring of parents with bipolar disorder. This investigation may be extrapolated to indicate that cyclothymia is a real and, to some degree, prevalent disorder in youngsters.

Cross-Sectional Symptoms, Features, and Course Specifications. There are a number of noteworthy subtype characteristics associated with DSM-IV depressive disorders. Melancholic features may occur with major depressive episodes in major depression or bipolar I or II disorders. The bipolar disorders may also occur with catatonic features in either the current manic or major depressive episode. In addition, major depression, bipolar I, bipolar II, and dysthymic disorder may be evident with atypical features. DSM-IV delineates specific diagnostic symptoms and characteristics of these cross-sectional features.

In addition to cross-sectional features, some mood disorders may also be characterized as to their course. Course specifiers include rapid cycling, seasonal pattern, and postpartum onset, as well as longitudinal course specifiers for major depression and bipolar I disorder. (Some of these course specifiers have been noted earlier in the description of major depression.) It is useful to note that specifications of the longitudinal course include, among other characteristics, the superimposition of major depression on dysthymic disorder, a situation sometimes referred to as double depression. Similarly, bipolar I disorder may be superimposed on cyclothymic disorder.

Other Mood Disorders. In addition to major depression, dysthymic disorder, bipolar disorder, and cyclothymia, a number of other mood disorder classifications are possible in DSM-IV. These include mood disorder not otherwise specified (mood disorder symptoms that do not fit a specific mood disorder and are not clearly depressive disorder NOS or bipolar disorder NOS); mood disorder due to a general medical condition, with the latter etiologically related to the mood disturbance and causing significant functional impairment or distress; and substance-induced mood disorder, in which persistent mood disturbance is associated with substance intoxication or withdrawal.

Comorbidity of Depression and Other Psychopathology

In recent years there has been an increased recognition of the coexistence of other forms of psychopathology with depression in adolescents. The coexistence of two or more disorders is not a new concept. The use of the term *comorbidity* within the diagnostic nomenclature is considered to originate with Feinstein (1970), although one has only to look to the use of two-point high codes on the MMPI as recognition of potential comorbidity in clinical, if not diagnostic, descriptions of psychopathology. The comorbidity of depression and other disorders and/or problems in children and adolescents has been noted for many years (e.g. Agras, 1959).

Since the mid-1980s there has been a very rapid increase in the literature on comorbidity of depression and other psychiatric disorders in adolescents. Of particular note have been studies of comorbidity that have also studied youngsters from a longitudinal perspective (e.g., Anderson & McGee, 1994; Kovacs, Gatsonis, Paulauskas, & Richards, 1989; Kovacs, Paulauskas, Gatsonis, & Richards, 1988). Research has shown comorbidity of depression with a range of disorders, including eating disorders (Rastam, 1992; Smith & Steiner, 1992), substance abuse (Levy & Deykin, 1989), and conduct disorders (Alessi & Magen, 1988). Because of the extensive research on the array of comorbid disorders, space limitations in this chapter, and recent reviews elsewhere (e.g., Anderson & McGee, 1994) this section will only provide a brief description of comorbidity among depression and other psychiatric disorders. It is interesting to note, however, that both internalizing and externalizing disorders have been found to be comorbid with depression in adolescents (Reynolds, 1992a).

A major focus of research on comorbidity of psychiatric diagnoses has been on anxiety and mood disorders (Maser & Cloninger, 1990). Understanding the phenomenon of comorbidity and how it impinges upon the structure and use of current diagnostic systems is important for research and clinical practice. The interested reader is directed to writings by Klerman (1990), Maser and Cloninger (1990), Mezzich, Ahn, Fabrega, and Pilkonis (1990), and Weissman (1990) for a detailed discussion of these issues. Likewise, the work of Blashfield (1986) on approaches to classification provides a useful foundation for the examination of comorbidity in light of current classification schemes.

The recognition of disorders that accompany depression with some regularity in children and adolescents is important for understanding the potential course, complications, problems in identification, and treatment decisions specific to mood disorders in youngsters. For the most part, this discussion will focus on formal disorders, such as anxiety disorders, conduct disorder, and eating disorders.

In a study of psychiatric disorders among adolescents drawn from the general population (i.e., not from clinical settings), Kashani et al. (1987b) reported both major depression and dysthymia to be comorbid with conduct disorder, anxiety disorder, and oppositional disorder. McGee et al. (1990) found significant overlap between depressive disorders and anxiety disorders and the combined category of conduct oppositional disorder. To date, the majority of research on comorbidity of disorders with depression in adolescents has focused on anxiety disorders. The relationship between depression and anxiety in adolescents, both as formal disorders and as symptom clusters, has been described and reviewed by a number of investigators (e.g., Bernstein & Garfinkel, 1986; Brady & Kendall, 1992; Hershberg, Carlson, Cantwell, & Strober, 1982; Kashani & Orvaschel, 1988, 1990; Kolvin, Berney, & Bhate, 1984; Moreau, Weissman, & Warner, 1989).

It is important to note that in some instances the examination of comorbidity between depression and anxiety in youngsters has been confounded by the assessment approach (e.g., severity versus diagnosis), as well as by syndromal symptom overlap between these two disorders. Likewise, research using self-report scales of depression and anxiety with adolescents often finds moderate to high correlations between measures of these two domains, across samples of psychiatrically referred as well as relatively normal children and adolescents (e.g., Bernstein, Garfinkel, & Hoberman, 1989; Eason, Finch, Brasted, & Saylor, 1985; Reynolds, 1987a). To some extent, this relationship is spurious due to the inclusion of depressive item content on a number of anxiety scales used by researchers (e.g., the item "Other children are happier than I" on the Revised Children's Manifest Anxiety Scale; Reynolds & Richmond, 1978). The correlation found between some of the self-report measures has led a number of investigators to suggest that rather than discrete constructs, self-report depression and/or anxiety scales may be evaluating negative affect or, more generally, emotional distress in children and adolescents (Finch et al., 1989; Wolfe et al., 1987).

A number of investigations have focused on comorbidity in youngsters with formal diagnoses of depression and anxiety disorders. In a clinical investigation of 106 children and adolescents with a DSM-III diagnosis of an anxiety disorder (seen in an outpatient anxiety disorder clinic), Strauss, Last, Hersen, and Kazdin (1988) found that 28% had a concomitant diagnosis of major depression. Overanxious disorder and separation anxiety were among the most frequent anxiety-disorder diagnoses in these cases. Approximately two-thirds of the depressed and anxiety-disordered youngsters had two or more anxiety disorders.

In recent years, panic disorder has become recognized as a viable anxiety disorder in adolescents (see Last, 1992). In a school-based investigation, Hayward, Killen, and Taylor (1989) found greater depressive symptoms in adolescents who had experienced panic attacks than in those without a history of such attacks. In a sample of psychiatrically hospitalized adolescents, Alessi et al. (1987) found that of 26 adolescents with a diagnosis of major depression, 13 (50%) received a concurrent definite or probable RDC diagnosis of panic disorder. Of the 10 youngsters in their sample with a definite diagnosis of panic disorder, 9 had a concomitant depressive disorder (major or minor). In 5 of these youngsters, an additional concurrent psychiatric diagnosis of borderline personality disorder was evident. The coexistence of depression with borderline characteristics in adolescents has also been noted by Stone (1981).

Assessment of Depression in Adolescents

For the clinical evaluation of depression in adolescents, reliable and valid measures are essential. Depression is often viewed as prototypic of internalizing disorders, in that many symptoms that define this disorder are internal to the youngster and not readily observable (Reynolds, 1992b). This can be seen in such cognitive symptoms as self-deprecation, suicidal ideation, and feelings of hopelessness or worthlessness. These are some of the symptoms of depression that are difficult for others to observe in a reliable manner unless a formal evaluation is conducted. Similarly, some somatic symptoms (e.g., insomnia, muscle aches) are not easily detected and may go unobserved by parents and others.

A number of measures have been developed for the assessment of depression in adolescents. For the most part this is a recent development, although there are several measures that have a relatively long history of use with adolescents. The latter include the Minnesota Multiphasic Personality Inventory (MMPI; Hathaway & McKinley, 1943), which has been used with adolescents as well as adults. The MMPI is prototypical of multidimensional personality scales and includes a depression scale among its basic clinical scales. In addition, a relatively new form of this measure, the MMPI-A (Butcher et al., 1992), has been developed for use specifically with adolescents. The Rorschach, a projective measure, has also been used with adolescents (e.g., Finch, Imm, & Belter, 1990)—in combination with age-appropriate scoring systems such as that developed by Exner and Weiner (1982)—for the evaluation of depressive themes and percepts. Recent research, however, suggests that the Rorschach may have limited diagnostic utility for the evaluation of depression in adolescents (Archer & Gordon, 1988).

Tests and procedures for the assessment of depression in adolescents developed since 1980 differ on a number of salient characteristics, including their intent (i.e., assessment of severity of symptoms or provision of a diagnosis), source of information (e.g., parent report, self-report, teacher report), time requirements, and psychometric quality. These measures vary from brief, 5- to 10-minute self-report questionnaires to 40- to 90-minute clinical interviews. Brief self-report measures may be administered individually or simultaneously to large groups of youngsters, while clinical interviews typically require significant time and trained interviewers.

Differentiation Between Symptom Severity and Diagnosis

The evaluation and determination of depression as a clinical state in children and adolescents, as well as in adults, is generally accomplished by one of two measurement perspectives: the assessment of the severity of a range or depth of depressive symptoms to evaluate the "clinical level" of depression experienced by the individual, and the formal diagnosis of depression manifested by the person according to a specified set of rules or classification criteria. These two measurement perspectives typically use different assessment measures and provide different information on the nature of depression in persons. Although these approaches are not mutually exclusive, they are dissimilar in focus and outcome. Both of these approaches are valid and, to some extent, complementary. Both have applications dictated by the type and level of information required to make a specific decision about an adolescent.

The assessment of the depth or severity of depressive symptoms, typically using self-report measures or rater checklists, provides useful information as to the level of depressive symptomatology experienced by the youngster. The assessment of clinical severity typically uses paper and pencil measures, but may also be a semistructured clinical interview such as the Hamilton Depression Rating Scale (Hamilton, 1960). In the severity assessment approach, a cutoff score is typically used to delineate a clinically relevant level of depressive symptomatology. A score at or above this level may result in an adolescent being considered depressed. It is important to note, however, that this cutoff score method is not the equivalent of providing a diagnosis of depression according to recognized classification systems. The formal diagnosis of depression can only be competently made when more extensive evaluation procedures, incorporating structured diagnostic interviews or other in-depth methodologies, are employed. For the most part, the use of self-report, clinical interviews, and other measures that focus on assessment of severity are limited to the perspective of depression as a unipolar mood disturbance that represents an internalizing domain of psychological distress.

Measures of Depression in Adolescents

A number of procedures have been developed for the assessment of depression in adolescents. These include paper and pencil self-report questionnaires, projective tests, reports by significant others (e.g., parents), and clinical interviews of varying structure (i.e., from unstructured to highly structured). Some of the measures described below can be used with both children and adolescents, whereas others are specific to adolescents. The evaluation of an adolescent's current level of depression represents an important procedure, since the outcome may determine whether the youngster receives therapy, is hospitalized because symptoms may suggest life-threatening potentiality, or is told that at times people feel somewhat down but such feelings often past quickly. This section presents descriptions of applied procedures and instruments for the assessment of depression in adolescents.

Self-Report Questionnaires

A popular procedure for the evaluation of depressive symptomatology in adolescents is the use of self-report questionnaires. Paper and pencil questionnaires require minimal time for administration and completion and provide a standard presentation of questions. Self-report measures may be individually or group administered, and they can be adapted for use in school or institutional-setting screening activities (Reynolds, 1986a). Paper and pencil self-report measures are not appropriate or valid for purposes of diagnosis or classification. The specificity and complexities of diagnostic classification systems (e.g., use of inclusion and exclusion criteria; disorders based on different symptom clusters, duration, and severity) precludes the use of current self-report measures for diagnostic applications. Furthermore, self-report measures of depression allow for misinterpretation of symptoms, their duration, and severity by the youngster; the potential for less than candid self-evaluation (e.g., presenting an overly positive or negative self-report); and the inability to determine whether symptom severity is due to depression, other psychopathology (e.g., schizoaffective disorder), or normative and nonclinical events (Reynolds, 1994b). However, this does not minimize the clinical and research utility of such measures. Although self-report measures are not of sufficient sensitivity to be viewed as diagnostic, a formal diagnosis of depression is not the sole reason or purpose for the evaluation of depression in youngsters. Given their brevity, ease of administration, and reasonably high reliability and validity demonstrated by some measures, self-report measures provide a useful avenue for the evaluation of depressive symptomatology in adolescents.

Children's Depression Inventory. The Children's Depression Inventory (CDI; Kovacs, 1979, 1980/1981) is one of the most frequently used research measures of depression in children and has also been used with adolescents. The CDI consists of 27 items, each specific to a symptom of depression. Items use a three-alternative, forced-choice response format where the youngster selects the symptom level that best describes how he or she is feeling. The initial development of this measure was described by Kovacs and Beck (1977) with a small sample of youngsters aged 9 through 15 years. Since the early 1980s a significant body of research with the CDI has been generated. Given the focus of this chapter on adolescents, research specific to the CDI will not be presented. Interested readers are directed to reviews by Reynolds (1993a; 1994a) and Curry and Craighead (1993).

Reynolds Adolescent Depression Scale. The Reynolds Adolescent Depression Scale (RADS; Reynolds, 1986b, 1987a) was designed to assess severity of depressive symptoms in youngsters aged 12 through 18 years. A test manual that accompanies the RADS provides documentation of normative information, reliability, validity, and interpretation of test results. Internal consistency reliability estimates have been high (ranging from .91 to .96) with samples of normal and depressed adolescents (Dalley, Bolocofsky, Alcorn, & Baker, 1992; Reynolds, 1987a, 1989, 1990; Reynolds & Miller, 1989; Schonert-Reichl, 1994). Test-retest reliability in a sample of 104 adolescents tested with a 6-week interval between testings was .80. A 12-week test-retest reliability coefficient of .79 was also found with a sample of 415 high school students (Reynolds, 1987a).

The validity of the RADS has been examined in a number of studies. It has demonstrated strong correlations with other self-report measures of depression, including the Beck Depression Inventory (BDI), Center for Epidemiological Studies-Depression Scale (CES-D), and the Zung Self-Rating Depression Scale (Zung, 1965; $rs = .71$ to .89). With a sample of 1,054 younger adolescents aged 12 to 14, a correlation of .70 was found between the RADS and the CDI (Reynolds, 1987a), while Brown, Overholser, Spirito, and Fritz (1991) found a correlation of .64 in a sample of adolescents who had attempted suicide. In a sample of 45 adolescent inpatients with major depression, Shain, Naylor, and Alessi (1990) reported a correlation coefficient of .87 between the RADS and CDI. In a study of 111 school-based adolescents, Reynolds (1987a) reported a correlation of .83 between the RADS and the Hamilton Depression Rating Scale (HRDS; Hamilton, 1960, 1967). Shain et al. (1990) reported a correlation of .73 between the RADS and the HDRS, and .73 between the RADS and Children's Depression Rating Scale-Revised (Poznanski et al., 1984). With a sample of adolescent psychiatric inpatients, Carey, Finch, and Carey (1991) reported a multiple correlation of .72 between the RADS and subscales of the Differential Emotions Scale (Blumberg & Izard, 1986). A cutoff score developed to designate a clinically relevant level of symptom severity has been validated in several studies, using both HDRS scores and formal diagnosis based on the Schedule for Affective Disorders and Schizophrenia (SADS) as criterion measures (Reynolds, 1987a; Reynolds & Evert, 1991). The RADS has also been used in a number of adolescent depression treatment studies as an outcome measure of treatment efficacy (Kahn, Kehle, Jenson, & Clark, 1990; Reynolds & Coats, 1986). The RADS and the Beck Depression Inventory (listed below) have been noted as among the top 20 assessment instruments used in clinical practice with adolescents (Archer, Maruish, Imhof, & Piotrowski, 1991).

Beck Depression Inventory. The Beck Depression Inventory (BDI; Beck, Ward, Mendelson, Mock, & Erbaugh, 1961) is a self-report measures of depression designed for adults. The BDI consists of 21 items, each using a four-alternative, forced-choice response format. The BDI has been used by a number of investigators for the assessment of depression in adolescents (e.g., Baron & Joly, 1988; Beck, Carlson, Russell, & Brownfield, 1987; Kaplan, Hong, & Weinhold, 1984; Reynolds & Coats, 1986), although the reading requirements and format of this measure are problematic for some youngsters. The internal consistency reliability of the BDI has been reported in the .70s to .80s with adolescents (Kashani, Sherman, Parker, & Reid, 1990; Reynolds, 1985b; Reynolds & Coats, 1982; Strober, Green, & Carlson, 1981b). Strober et al. (1981b) reported a 5-day test-retest reliability of .69 in a sample of adolescent psychiatric inpatients. Barrera and Garrison-Jones (1988), in samples of hospitalized psychiatric patients (*n* = 65) and school-based adolescents (*n* = 49), found reasonable sensitivity and specificity for the BDI in the school sample but poor results for the psychiatric sample. Kashani et al. (1990) also reported a low sensitivity rate (48%) using the traditional BDI cutoff score of 16 in a sample of 100 clinic-referred adolescents.

Center for Epidemiological Studies–Depression Scale. The Center for Epidemiological Studies-Depression Scale (CES–D; Radloff, 1977) is a 20-item measure designed for adults that has been used with adolescents (e.g., Doerfler, Felner, Rowlison, Evans, & Raley, 1988; Garrison, Jackson, Marsteller, McKeown, & Addy, 1990; Hops, Lewinsohn, Andrews, & Roberts, 1990). Research with the CES-D has reported limited validity and reliability (Doerfler et al., 1988; Roberts, Lewinsohn, & Seeley, 1991). Use of the CES–D is problematic given the cutoff score, which identifies between 40% and 50% of nonclinical youngsters as depressed (e.g., Doerfler et al., 1988; Faulstich, Carey, Ruggiero, Enyart, & Gresham, 1986; Gjerde, Block, & Block, 1988; Manson, Ackerson, Dick, Baron, & Fleming, 1990; Roberts, Andrews, Lewinsohn, & Hops, 1990; Roberts et al., 1991).

Adolescent Psychopathology Scales: Major Depression and Dysthymia Scales. The Adolescent Psychopathology Scale (Reynolds, in press) is a multidimensional self-report measure of psychopathology designed for use with adolescents aged 13 through 18. Development of the APS was based on clinical samples of approximately 500 adolescents from inpatient and outpatient treatment settings around the United States and a normative sample of more than 2,400 adolescents from public junior and senior high schools in eight states. The Major Depression scale consists of 29 items reflecting DSM-IV symptoms, with items rated on the basis of their occurrence over the past 2 weeks. The Dysthymic Disorder scale consists of 14 items rated on the basis of their occurrence over the past 6 months. In a preliminary report on the psychometric characteristics of the APS, Reynolds (1993b) found an internal consistency reliability of .95 for both the normal and clinical samples for the Major Depression scale and .89 and .88 for the Dysthymic Disorder scale in clinical and school-based samples, respectively. Validity evidence in the form of content validity, contrasted-groups validity (normal adolescents versus those with a diagnosis of major depression), and criterion-related validity as demonstrated by correlations with other self-report (MMPI, RADS) and clinical interview (SADS, HDRS) measures of depression are presented in the APS manual and support the validity of the Major Depression and Dysthymic Disorder scales of the APS with adolescents.

Ratings by Significant Others

The evaluation of psychological problems in adolescents by significant others is not new, and for many disorders of adolescence this assessment procedure is the norm. For instance, the evaluation of externalizing disorders (e.g., conduct disorders, attention-deficit hyperactivity disorder), is usually based in large part on the reports of significant others as well as observation and behavioral assessment. One issue in the assessment of depression in children and adolescents is the general lack of concordance between youngsters' self-reports of depression and reports of their depression obtained from such significant others as parents, teachers, and peers. Although demonstrating little concordance with child self-reports (either by questionnaire or clinical interview), reports by significant others do represent another perspective on a youngster's affective status. A substantial literature base on the concordance of self-reports of depression and reports by significant others has emerged over the past decade, with most of this research specific to children. The issue and nature of differences among sources of assessment information specific to depression in young people has recently been reviewed by Kazdin (in press), who notes the importance of this topic to the study and understanding of depression in children.

It may be argued that when evaluating depression in adolescents, as compared to children, external sources of information (e.g., parents, peers, and teachers) may be less knowledgeable as to the youngster's affective state. Ratings provided by these significant others are, for the most part, based on observation as well as inference. Many parents have limited face-to-face contact with their adolescent, and many adolescents are reticent to fully disclose their feelings to parents, teachers, or peers. Likewise, teachers in high school settings have only brief contact with youngsters, typically 50 minutes a day in groups of 20 to 30 students. There are clear limitations to the viability of significant others when evaluating depression in adolescents, particularly given the internalizing nature of depression. Some symptoms of depression (e.g., weight loss, dysphoric mood, tearfulness or crying) may potentially be seen by others, however, given that the symptom expression occurs in settings where they may be observed. Such symptoms become most evident when there is a significant change from a usually positive or normal level to a pathological or significantly lower level.

A number of broad-band psychopathology measures have been developed for use with children and adolescents that use parents or teachers as respondents and include a depression subscale. The Personality Inventory for Children (PIC; Wirt, Lachar, Klinedinst, & Seat, 1977) is such a multidimensional parent report. Typically completed by the child's mother, the regular form of the PIC consists of 600 true/false items, including 46 items on the depression subscale. Many of these latter items overlap with other scales (e.g., the anxiety subscale). Much of the reliability and validity information on this measure is specific to children rather than adolescents.

The Child Behavior Checklist (CBCL) and Teacher's Report Form (TRF) by Achenbach and colleagues (Achenbach & Edelbrock, 1983, 1986; Achenbach & McConaughy, 1987, 1992) are multidimensional psychopathology scales that include forms for parent and teacher ratings, respectively. These scales in their various forms have made a valuable contribution by distinguishing between internalizing and externalizing forms of child and adolescent psychopathology. Development of the CBCL scales was based on factor-analytic procedures, resulting in different scales for males and females and for various age groups. CBCL parent rating scales designed for use with adolescents aged 12 to 16 years include a depression subscale for girls; a similar subscale is not provided for adolescent boys in this age group.

Clinical Interview Measures of Depression

Clinical interview methodology is considered one of the most sensitive procedures for the evaluation of depression (Hamilton, 1982). Structured and semistructured clinical interview schedules allow for a trained interviewer to evaluate youngsters' reports of depressive symptoms and their severity and frequency. It also provides an opportunity to determine whether symptom endorsement is due to depression or extraneous to the disorder. Adolescents in particular will report a number of symptoms that are present for reasons other than depression; for example, a youngster reporting sleep difficulty or insomnia may be manifesting a symptom of depression or may be kept up at night due to the crying or feeding schedule of a newborn sibling. It is not uncommon to find a youngster who reports some irritability; is experiencing weight loss; complains of body aches, fatigue, and hypersomnia; manifests cognitive symptoms of distractibility and poor concentration in school; and is self-deprecatory. An interviewer asking about potential reasons for these symptoms may find that the youngster is on the wrestling team, has recently lost an important match, and has been told by the coach to drop to a lower weight class.

Although clinical interviews in general represent a more sophisticated procedure than paper and pencil questionnaires for the assessment of depression, they do have a number of limitations. Interviews typically require between 30 and 90 minutes, depending upon the structure of the interview measure and the youngster's severity of depression. Trained interviewers who can obtain reliable and valid clinical information are also required. For further discussion of clinical interviews for the diagnosis of depression and other psychopathology, the reader is directed to reviews by Gutterman, O'Brian, and Young (1987), Hodges (1994), Hodges and Cool (1990), and Orvaschel (1985).

Several semistructured interviews that have as their focus the assessment of the severity of depressive symptoms, as well as cutoff scores for the identification of a clinical level of depression in youngsters, are presented below. Structured diagnostic interviews, given their broad-based focus and coverage, are not presented.

Bellevue Index of Depression. The Bellevue Index of Depression (BDI) was developed by Petti (1978) to assess depressive symptoms in children aged 6 to 12 years. The BID consists of 40 items that evaluate 10 symptom domains (e.g., dysphoric mood, sleep disturbance). The BID takes between 20 to 40 minutes to administer, although in cases of severe depression it may take longer. The BID has been used with adolescents by a number of investigators (Kahn, et al., 1990; Reynolds & Coats, 1986). Reynolds and Coats (1982) reported an internal consistency reliability coefficient of .96 with a sample of 55 depressed adolescents.

Hamilton Depression Rating Scale. The Hamilton Depression Rating Scale (HDRS; Hamilton, 1960, 1967) is one of the most frequently used outcome measures in psychiatric studies of depression in adults (Kobak, Reynolds, Rosenfeld, & Greist, 1990). There are several versions of the HDRS, the most popular being the 17- and 21-item forms. Items are rated on the basis of their severity, with higher scores indicative of greater pathology. Two items (psychomotor retardation and agitation) are observational in nature. Because of the age of this measure, a number of depressive symptoms included in contemporary diagnostic systems are not included on the HDRS (e.g., low self-esteem, self-deprecation). As a severity measure of depression, however, the HDRS, with minor adjustments for age differences, is a useful clinical interview with adolescents.

Research using the HDRS has included both clinical and nonclinical samples of adolescents (Alessi, McManus, Grapentine, & Brickman, 1984; Alessi et al., 1987; Reynolds, 1987a; Robbins, Alessi, Cook, Poznanski, & Yanchyshyn, 1982; Shain et al., 1990; Yanchyshyn & Robbins, 1983).

Reynolds (1987a) reported an internal consistency reliability coefficient of .91 for the 17-item HDRS with a sample of 111 adolescents. Yanchyshyn and Robbins (1983) reported an interrater reliability of .91 for the HDRS with a nonclinic sample of adolescents, and Robbins, Alessi, Colfer, and Yanchyshyn (1985) obtained an interrater reliability of .90 with a sample of 81 adolescent psychiatric inpatients.

Treatment of Depression in Adolescents

The research literature on empirically tested procedures and techniques for the treatment of depression in adolescents is relatively sparse. There are a number of treatment modalities, ranging from invasive (e.g., electroconvulsive therapy) to noninvasive (psychotherapy). Two primary treatment modalities are pharmacotherapy and contemporary psychotherapies. These two treatment approaches have generated a small body of empirical research that allows for the evaluation of their clinical efficacy. Several studies of electroconvulsive therapy (ECT) with depressed youngsters have been reported; Bertagnoli and Borchardt (1990), who review these studies, suggest that although there are but a few published case reports, there are many adolescents who are treated with ECT. They report that of individuals who received ECT in 1980, approximately 500 were between 11 and 20 years of age.

A number of newer therapeutic procedures have been developed for specific subtypes of depression. One such procedure is phototherapy for seasonal affective disorder (seasonal pattern in DSM-III-R/DSM-IV) as well as for other forms of depression, particularly depression associated with certain sleep problems (Lewy & Sack, 1986). To date, there have been few reports of phototherapy with adolescents (e.g., Rosenthal et al., 1986; Sonis, Yellin, Garfinkel, et al., 1987); although these early studies lack adequate controls, there is some indication of efficacy. The utility of phototherapy (as well as other chronobiological procedures, e.g., changes in the sleep-wake cycle) with depressed youngsters may be an area of worthwhile investigation.

Most of the empirical research on the treatment of depression in adolescents has focused on the use of psychopharmacological agents. Pharmacological agents for the treatment of depression in children and adolescents have been described by Johnston and Fruehling (1994), Puig-Antich, Ryan, and Rabinovich (1985), and Weller and Weller (1984, 1986), among others. Results of several studies suggest the clinical efficacy of several tricyclic antidepressants for children, although controlled group studies report mixed results when compared to placebo. There have been four studies examining the efficacy of psychological treatments designed for the amelioration of depression and depressive symptoms in adolescents; this limited

Table 10–2
Summary Table of Results of Two Adolescent Depression
Treatment Studies

| Study | Condition | Mean RADS Score | | |
		Pretest	Posttest[a]	Follow-up
Reynolds & Coats (1986)	Cognitive-behavioral	85.67	66.74	62.60
	Relaxation training	80.09	65.80	54.73
	Wait-list control	80.70	81.12	72.25
Kahn (1988)	Cognitive-behavioral	85.41	53.44	54.18
	Relaxation training	83.82	61.76	61.58
	Self-modeling	84.27	62.12	64.18
	Wait-list control	86.91	80.12	74.70

Note: In both studies reported above, a preassessment was utilized prior to the pretesting.

[a] Posttest and follow-up RADS scores for the Reynolds & Coats (1986) study are adjusted means based on an analysis of covariance with pretest scores as the covariate.

number of studies is unfortunate, given the potentially large number of youngsters who are in need of treatment for depression.

Pharmacotherapy for Depression in Adolescents

This discussion of pharmacological studies with adolescents includes studies of tricyclic antidepressants (TCAs), monoamine oxidase inhibitors (MAOIs), and lithium. A distinction can be made between the treatment of unipolar and bipolar disorders in adolescents, with lithium generally used for the treatment of bipolar disorder. Research also suggests that lithium may be a useful adjunct to the treatment of adolescents with major depression who respond poorly or not at all to tricyclic antidepressants (Ryan, Meyer, Dachille, Mazzie, & Puig-Antich, 1988).

Other drugs have been used with children and adolescents. Dugas, Mouren, Halfon, and Moron (1985) reported an open trial study of mianserin, a tetracyclic antidepressant, with a sample of 80 children and adolescents in France, and Conners (1976) reported on the use of Iudiomil, an antidepressant, to treat depression in children and adolescents in Europe. In North America, a number of newer antidepressants, such as fluoxetine (a phenylpropylamine), have become popular (and controversial; e.g., Teicher, Glod, & Cole, 1990) for use with adults. Reports of fluoxetine use with youngsters (e.g., Dech & Budow, 1991; Naylor & Grossman, 1991; Simeon, Dinicola, Ferguson, & Copping 1990) have begun to appear.

Riddle, Hardin, King, Scahill, and Woolston (1990), studying fluoxetine use in a sample of 10 youngsters with Tourette's syndrome and obsessive-compulsive disorder, found mixed results (using low dosage) specific to treatment of obsessive-compulsive symptoms. Significant behavioral agitation was noted as a response to fluoxetine in 4 of the 10 subjects, but there were minimal adverse biological side effects due to the general lack of anticholinergic and antihistaminic side effects associated with fluoxetine. Riddle et al. (1989) reported a case of fluoxetine overdose in an adolescent. The issue of emerging suicidal preoccupation or ideation in adolescents treated with fluoxetine has yet to be adequately resolved.

Tricyclic Antidepressants. An extensive amount of the psychopharmacological research on the treatment of depression in children and adolescents has focused on such TCAs as imipramine, amitriptyline, nortriptyline, and desipramine (see Johnston & Fruehling, 1994, for an in-depth review). Reports on TCAs for the treatment of depression in children began to appear in the mid 1960s and early 1970s (e.g., Frommer, 1968; Kuhn & Kuhn, 1971; Lucas, Lockett, & Grimm, 1965; Weinberg, Rutman, Sullivan, Penick, & Dietz, 1973).

Much of the research on TCAs has been with children, although some studies have been specific to adolescents or included both children and adolescents. TCAs, and in particular imipramine, have also been used for a host of child and adolescent problems. Wilson and Staton (1984) report improvement in specific neuropsychological test results in imipramine-treated children and adolescents. In a review of the use of imipramine for a range of disorders in children, Gualtieri (1977) had variable success in finding a basis for the action of imipramine in many of its applications. Zametkin and Rapoport (1983) review the use of antidepressants with children and present a description of TCA clinical and side effects. Reports of TCA treatment of depression in adolescents vary with respect to the pharmacological agent used, dosage levels, and accuracy in reporting true drug levels in subjects. More importantly, studies vary in their research design (e.g., blind, double-blind, crossover), control conditions (e.g., placebo versus other antidepressant), and use of reliable treatment outcome measures.

Differences between studies can also be found in the drug administration schedule, although Ryan et al. (1987), in a treatment study of adolescents with major depression, did not find differences between single and divided doses of imipramine initiated after subjects had undergone a 3-week graduated increase (divided dose) to therapeutic levels. Furthermore, a combination of medications may change TCA plasma levels usually associated with single TCA doses. Geller, Cooper, Farooki, and Chestnut (1985), in a sample of delusionally depressed adolescents, found that the addition of chloropromazine with nortriptyline resulted in lower doses of nortriptyline required to achieve a therapeutic steady-state TCA plasma level as compared to a group of nondelusionally depressed adolescents.

There have been a number of case reports and open-trial studies of TCAs for depression in adolescents. Ryan et al. (1986) conducted an open-trial TCA study with a sample of 34 adolescents with major depression. A significant number of these subjects also showed comorbidity with other psychopathology, including separation anxiety, phobias, and obsessions and/or compulsions. Results showed a 44% TCA response rate, with no difference in plasma levels between responders and nonresponders. In subjects with endogenous depression, 67% did not respond to imipramine. Adolescents with nonendogenous depression also did better, and those with comorbidity with separation anxiety tended to show a worse outcome.

A limited number of reasonably well-controlled treatment outcome studies of TCAs for depression in adolescents have been reported, with generally mixed results. Kramer and Feiguine (1981) in a double-blind study of amitriptyline versus placebo with a sample of 20 depressed adolescents, found mixed results, with both groups demonstrating improvement. Robbins et al. (1989) reported on a multimodal treatment study with 38 inpatient adolescents with major depression, half of whom were also melancholic subtype (DSM-III). Initially, all subjects received a psychosocial treatment program that included a combination of psychodynamic interpersonal, family, group and cognitive-behavioral therapy; the authors indicated that the general nature of this therapeutic procedure was consistent with the interpersonal psychotherapy (IPT) of Klerman and Weissman (1982). On the basis of the psychiatrists' observations, Robbins et al. (1989) report that 18 (47%) subjects responded to the psychotherapy alone. Of the 20 subjects who did not respond to psychotherapy, there were 14 ($p < .05$) whose depression was of a melancholic subtype. This indicates that 5 of the melancholic subjects responded to the psychotherapy alone. Fifteen subjects (permission was not provided for 5 subjects) who failed to respond to the psychotherapy were also treated with a variety of TCAs (desipramine, imipramine, nortriptyline, alone or in combination) along with continued psychotherapy. There were 12 subjects who completed an adequate pharmacological trial; 11 responded to the TCAs, and 1 responded to the TCA augmented with lithium.

Unfortunately, the lack of a control group limits the generalizability of this study. A significant number of adolescents with major depression improved with psychotherapy (delivered in a multimodal inpatient therapeutic milieu), however, and this group included a number of adolescents who were diagnosed as melancholic. TCAs along with psychotherapy were generally effective in a majority of youngsters with melancholic subtype major depression. Although the limitations of the basic design and assessment procedures (among other problems) were recognized by the authors, this study provides a basis for controlled experimental investigations of psychotherapy and antidepressants for the treatment of adolescent depression.

Overall, the experimental evidence for the efficacy of TCAs with adolescents is mixed, with minimal superiority of TCAs over placebo noted in a limited number of controlled studies. Ryan (1992) suggests that there are no data to support the specific efficacy of TCAs for depression in adolescents (i.e., beyond nonspecific treatment or self-efficacy effects).

Monoamine Oxidase Inhibitors. MAOIs (e.g., tranylcypromine, phenelzine) that are used with adults tend not to be used with adolescents in large part because of the negative reaction to certain foods that are high in tyramine and are popular with youngsters (including those with aged cheese, e.g., pizza), as well as possible psychological (Mattsson & Seltzer, 1981) and toxic effects (e.g., Pfefferbaum, Pack, & van Eys, 1989). Early studies (Frommer, 1967, 1968; Soblen & Saunders, 1961) reported clinical improvement with MAOIs in early noncontrolled treatment studies with children and adolescents.

MAOIs may be used to treat adolescents with major depression who are unresponsive to TCAs. Studies have also reported a greater treatment response when MAOIs are combined with TCAs. For example, Ryan et al. (1988) reported an open-trial study of 23 adolescents treated with MAOIs after an initial unsuccessful trial of TCA medication. Results indicated that 74% of youngsters had good or fair treatment improvement irrespective of dietary compliance, with a higher proportion of clinical improvement found among subjects who maintained dietary compliance. Ryan et al. suggested the potential for the combination of TCA with MAOI therapy as providing some "protection" for negative side effects associated with the cheese reaction to MAOI treatment.

Lithium. Lithium carbonate is a frequently used treatment for bipolar disorder (manic-depressive illness), and in particular for manic episodes; it has also been found useful in augmenting other antidepressants with cases of treatment-resistant depression (Jefferson, 1989). The degree to which lithium is used for the treatment of bipolar disorder in adolescents is unknown. Most of the research and literature on the use of lithium for the treatment of manic-depressive illness has used single-subject designs, case descriptive methods, or open-trial designs. In a review of case reports of lithium treatment with children and adolescents, Youngerman and Canino (1978) suggest that lithium is effective in the treatment of mania in this age group. Campbell, Perry, and Green (1984) reviewed studies using lithium with children and adolescents with a range of disorders. They indicated that the existence of few methodologically sound treatment outcome studies with lithium limits its formal acceptance with manic-depressive disorder, although there is some evidence to suggest efficacy.

Lithium can have significant side effects in some youngsters. In addition to renal and endocrine effects, there may also be impairment in memory, learning, and concentration (Jefferson, 1982). Jefferson (1982) suggests that potential side effects of lithium in adolescents must be judged in relation to the severe and disruptive nature of manic-depressive disorder. Contemporary perspectives and guidelines for the use of lithium with adolescents are presented in greater detail by Carlson (1994).

Summary of Pharmacological Interventions. The use of pharmacological agents for the treatment of depression in adolescents should be undertaken with caution and be preceded by a complete medical history and examination. As with adults, not all youngsters respond to pharmacological intervention. Puig-Antich et al. (1985) provide guidelines for the treatment of unresponsive youngsters and note that unlike the existing research with adults, many psychopharmacological studies of depressed youngsters have not been subtype specific. There have been few formal comparisons between pharmacotherapy and psychotherapy with adolescents, although this is not surprising given the paucity of empirical research on psychotherapy. There is also a need for more attention to placebo control groups, similar to those used with children, in treatment designs (e.g., Geller et al., 1992).

Psychological Interventions for Depression in Children and Adolescents

Psychological treatment procedures for depression and depressive symptomatology in adolescents have been reported or suggested since the early 1970s (e.g., Anthony, 1970). Since the early 1980s, several reported studies have utilized cognitive and behavioral approaches for the treatment of depression in adolescents. In addition, a number of published suggestions, anecdotal reports, or case descriptions of treatments using psychoanalytic or dynamic procedures for depressed youngsters have been reported (e.g., Toolan, 1978). For example, Bemporad (1988) describes brief case illustrations of psychodynamic therapy to illustrate the psychodynamic nature and characteristics of depression in adolescents. Bemporad (1978) considers the general psychodynamic mechanism of depression in adolescents to be similar to that in adults, with the therapeutic processes modified for the youngster's developmental level.

Cognitive-Behavioral and Behavioral Treatments of Depression in Youngsters. Most of the behavioral and cognitive-behavioral studies reported below may be viewed as contemporary psychotherapies predicated on procedures originally developed for the treatment of depression in adults. These procedures include treatment components based on several theoretical approaches to depression (e.g., cognitive, learned helplessness, social learning). Clarizio (1989) has reviewed and provided a critique of a number of these theoretical approaches to depression treatments for young people.

Since 1980, there have been a few single-case studies reported of behavioral and cognitive therapies for the treatment of depression in adolescents.

An operant study utilizing contingent reinforcement and other behavioral components to treat a depressed 15-year-old girl was reported by Molick and Pinkston (1982). This single-subject study used a reversal design across a number of treatment component and target behaviors (e.g., increased speech, improved self-care, social skills, use of response-contingent reinforces, appropriate initiation with teachers) and resulted in increased positive response in the targeted behaviors.

Trautman and Rotheram-Borus (1988) outlined a 15-session cognitive-behavioral treatment program for depression in adolescents that incorporates the family in many of the sessions. Suggested treatment components incorporate aspects of self-control (e.g., self-monitoring, self-reinforcement), reattribution and self-instructional training, and interpersonal problem solving, with the last component forming the primary basis for the treatment. At present it does not appear that this program has been formally tested.

There have been four control-group experimental treatment studies that provide data on the efficacy of psychological treatments for depression in adolescents. Reynolds and Coats (1986) published the first group-treatment study for depression in adolescents. These authors compared a cognitive-behavioral treatment for depression to a relaxation training group, and a waiting list control group. Subjects were 30 moderately to severely depressed adolescents based on self-report and clinical interview measures. Both active treatment conditions included 10 one-hour sessions administered over a 5-week period. Depression outcome measures included the RADS, BDI, and BID. Both the cognitive-behavioral treatment and the relaxation training were presented in a structured format, with treatment manuals developed for each condition. The cognitive-behavioral therapy was similar to procedures used in the treatment of depression in adults, with modifications made for developmental and situational (e.g., home, school, peer group) differences of adolescents. Cognitive-behavioral therapy components included elements of self-control (i.e., self-monitoring, self-evaluation, self-reinforcement), cognitive restructuring with components of Beck's cognitive therapy, and procedures for increasing involvement in pleasant activities (Lewinsohn, Munoz, Youngren, & Zeiss, 1978). The relaxation condition included training in progressive relaxation procedures based on the work of Jacobsen (1938), along with some guided imagery procedures. Both active treatment conditions were matched for therapist time and amount of homework assignments.

Significant treatment gains on depression outcome measures were found for both active treatment conditions at the posttest and maintained at a 4-week follow-up evaluation. RADS scores for the experimental and control groups at the pretest, posttest, and follow-up assessment points are presented in Table 10–2. As shown, significant decreases in depression were reported by youngsters in the cognitive-behavioral and relaxation groups at post-test, with minimal change in the waiting-list youngsters. In addition, there were therapeutic effects on subjects' self-concept and level of anxiety.

In a similar study to that of Reynolds and Coats (1986), Kahn et al. (1990) reported a treatment outcome study with 68 moderately depressed youngsters in middle school (grades six, seven, and eight). Several active treatments for depression were investigated, including cognitive-behavioral, relaxation training, and a self-modeling procedures, along with a waiting-list control group. The cognitive-behavioral treatment focused on pleasant-activity scheduling and behavioral components consistent with the approach of Lewinsohn et al. (1978), along with components of cognitive, self-control, and social skills training. The relaxation training group was similar to that of Reynolds and Coats (1986). Both the cognitive-behavioral and relaxation training treatments were group administered over twelve 50-minute sessions. The self-modeling condition was administered individually, with each subject developing a 3-minute videotape in which he or she modeled behaviors that were considered inconsistent with depression (e.g., smiling, positive verbalizations, appropriate eye contact). Assessment measures included the RADS, CDI, and BID.

The three active therapy conditions showed significant treatment gains at posttest and at a 4-week follow-up. The greatest therapeutic benefits were found in the cognitive-behavioral and relaxation training conditions. The results of this study specific to treatment outcome on the RADS are also presented in Table 10–2. As shown in the table, the results of this investigation are similar to those reported by Reynolds and Coats (1986) and suggest treatment generalizability.

The Reynolds and Coats (1986) and Kahn et al. (1990) studies are limited by the lack of formal diagnosis of subjects. In both studies, subject selection and description were based on self-report and clinical interview measures. The assessment data reported by these authors, though, do suggest that the majority of subjects demonstrated moderate to severe levels of depressive symptomatology.

Two other treatment studies of adolescent depression, described below, represent interventions with youngsters with formal DSM-III/DSM-III-R diagnoses. Lewinsohn et al. (1990) reported on the downward extension of the Coping With Depression (CWD) course, a multimodal psychoeducational intervention for depression originally developed for adults (Clarke & Lewinsohn, 1989; Lewinsohn, Hoberman, & Clarke, 1989). The Lewinsohn et al. (1990) report describes the outcome of two related forms of this cognitive-behavioral intervention with a sample of 59 adolescents who met DSM-III criteria for major depression or RDC criteria for current minor or intermittent depressive disorder. Treatment conditions consisted of (a) cognitive-behavioral therapy that was group administered to adolescents only (*n* = 21) and consisted of 14 two-hour sessions over a 7-week period; (b) the same treatment administered to another group (*n* = 19) of adolescents along with group training for parents of these adolescents, with the parent training administered over 7 two-hour sessions; and a waiting-list control group of 19 adolescents.

The cognitive-behavioral treatment (the modified CWD course) was based on a social learning approach to the treatment of depression, and included pleasant-activity scheduling; social skills training; cognitive restructuring, with a focus on identification and modification of irrational beliefs; relaxation training; and a unique component dealing with communication, negotiation, and conflict resolution skills. The parent training included discussions of the components and skills taught to the adolescents and training in negotiation, communication and conflict resolution skills similar to those presented to adolescents. Treatment outcome was reported at posttreatment, and 1-month, 6-month, 12-month, and 24-month follow-up assessments. Unfortunately, the waiting-list condition was only available at the immediate posttesting, thus limiting follow-up comparisons. Outcome measures included a number of self-report and parent-report severity measures in addition to K-SADS diagnosis. At the posttest, both active treatments demonstrated significant change as compared to the waiting-list group. The active treatments did not differ from each other in their efficacy, although there was a trend for the combined adolescent-parent group to show greater improvement. Treatment gains were maintained at follow-up assessments with a trend toward further improvement.

Examination of subjects' clinical response indicated successful treatment (lack of depression diagnosis) at posttest in 43% of the subjects in the adolescent-only CWD course and 47% of those in the adolescent-parent CWD course treatments, and positive clinical change in 5% of youngsters in the waiting-list group. A 24-month follow-up presented by Clarke, Lewinsohn, Hops, and Andrews (1989) showed that 25% of the adolescent-only group and 8% of the adolescent-parent group continued to demonstrate a DSM-III affective disorder. Only 23 of the 40 subjects in the active treatment conditions, were available for the 24-month follow-up assessment. This investigation is noteworthy for a number of reasons. It is the first experimental group intervention study with adolescents who had formal DSM-III/RDC diagnoses of depression. The length of treatment was significantly longer and more intense than previously reported studies, consisting of 28 hours of treatment over a 7-week period. Likewise, the long-term follow-up assessments are noteworthy, although the 24-month assessment is somewhat limited by the significant reduction in sample size and the lack of a control comparison group.

A group treatment study of depressed adolescents was reported by Fine et al. (1991) who compared a social skills training group with a therapeutic support group. Both treatments were group administered to adolescents in an outpatient hospital setting. The social skills training condition consisted of self-monitoring of feelings, perspective taking, assertiveness, conversation skills, social problem solving, and conflict resolution. Treatment was delivered via therapist modeling, role play, and videotaped feedback. The therapeutic support group intervention was designed to provide a milieu for discussing problems with goals of enhancing self-concept and self-worth. The original sample consisted of 66 adolescents with a DSM-III-R diagnosis of major depression or dysthymia. Outcome data were reported for 47 of the subjects who completed 8 or more of the 12 treatment sessions; these data included scores on the CDI, and a 12-item depression subscale derived from the K-SADS. At posttest, within-group differences (from pretest) indicated significant improvement for both treatments on the K-SADS scale. Only the therapeutic support group demonstrated significant posttest change on the CDI. Between-group analyses indicated superiority of the therapeutic support condition on the K-SADS, although no difference was found between groups on the CDI. A 9-month follow-up indicated no differences between groups on the outcome measures.

The results of the Fine et al. (1991) study are mixed. Subjects in the social skills group showed little change in scores on the CDI (pretest $M = 20.3$, posttest $M = 18.4$). At posttesting, a change from clinical to nonclinical levels on the K-SADS was found in 50% of subjects in the therapeutic support group and 40% of subjects in the social skills group. Clinical response data were presented for the 9-month follow-up but are difficult to interpret given the lack of control (i.e., wait list, attention placebo) conditions and the potential changes that might have occurred in the natural course of the disorder. The authors do note the limitations due to the lack of a control condition, as well as the general overlap of therapeutic components across treatment conditions. From this study it appears that social skills training may have some therapeutic benefits. The superiority of the therapeutic support group suggests the potential therapeutic efficacy of interpersonal problem-solving therapies with adolescents.

Summary of Psychological Interventions. Research to date suggests that psychological treatments hold promise for the amelioration of depression in adolescents. For the most part, published experimental psychological treatment studies of depression in adolescents have focused on the efficacy of cognitive-behavioral intervention procedures. Basic treatment components used in these studies were predicated on contemporary cognitive and behavioral theories of depression and adapted from treatment packages designed for use with adults. It is useful to note that the treatment of depression in adolescents requires training and knowledge of affective disorders, psychological and biological models of depression, and associated treatment modalities. Treating a youngster experiencing intense subjective misery, with numerous somatic symptoms (e.g., sleep disturbance, appetite loss) as well as possible suicidal thoughts or intent, should be viewed as a serious undertaking. Treatment failure for some youngsters may increase feelings of hopelessness, helplessness, and despondency.

Similar to many investigations with adults, treatment studies for depression in adolescents support the utility of going beyond the application of an intervention predicated solely on a single theoretical model, such as self-control therapy or cognitive therapy. Comparisons of the efficacy of specific components, however, have not been conducted in treatment studies with adolescents. Based on the above studies, as well as the work of Lewinsohn et al. (1985), it is likely that the inclusion of diverse and theory-driven therapeutic components provides a broad-spectrum treatment approach for the amelioration of depressive symptoms and the modification of dysfunctional cognitive and behavioral mechanisms. The incorporation of treatment components that are predicated on theory-based deficits or dysfunctional cognitions and behaviors is similar to the multiple-target approach for clinical change (e.g., Kanfer, 1985; Kazdin, 1985).

Summary

Numerous research, clinical, and epidemiological investigations suggests that depression and depressive disorders are a significant problem in adolescents. Depression as a psychopathology is an internalizing or inner-directed disorder (Reynolds, 1992b) that results in feelings of subjective misery and despondency and that may cause significant impairment in daily functioning. Research findings suggest that depression in adolescents often occurs in combination with other forms of psychopathology, including other internalizing problems (e.g., anxiety disorders) as well as externalizing problems (e.g., conduct disorder, oppositional defiant disorder). The potential deleterious impact of this form of psychopathology on adolescents may also be realized by the significant risk for suicide and suicidal behaviors found in depressed adolescents (Reynolds, 1991; Reynolds & Mazza, 1994; Shaffi & Shaffi, 1992).

The study of depression in adolescents has been a field of active inquiry during the past several years, particularly in relation to the study of stressors and individual-difference variables. Although the research base on the nature of this problem in adolescents has increased significantly, there have been only a few studies of the efficacy of treatments for this disorder. There is a need for well-controlled psychological and pharmacological treatment studies. Such empirical evidence for the efficacy of therapeutic procedures is important for ensuring adequate and appropriate treatment. Given the estimated 5% prevalence of this disorder in the general adolescent population, a focus on the development and delivery of efficacious treatment procedures should be a priority.

References

Abramson, L. Y., & Alloy, L. B. (1990). Search for the "negative cognition" subtype of depression. In C. D. McCann & N. S. Endler (Eds.), *Depression: New directions in theory, research, and practice* (pp. 77–109). Toronto: Wall and Emerson.

Abramson, L. Y., Seligman, M. E. P., & Teasdale, J. D. (1978). Learned helplessness in humans: Critique and reformulation. *Journal of Abnormal Psychology, 87*, 49–74.

Achenbach, T. M., & Edelbrock, C. (1983). *Manual for the Child Behavior Checklist and Revised Child Behavior Profile*. Burlington: Department of Psychiatry, University of Vermont.

Achenbach, T. M., & Edelbrock, C. (1986). *Manual for the Teacher's Report Form and Teacher Version of the Child Behavior Profile*. Burlington, Department of Psychiatry, University of Vermont.

Achenbach, T. M., & McConaughy, S. H. (1987). *Empirically based assessment of child and adolescent psychopathology: Practical applications*. Newbury Park, CA: Sage.

Achenbach, T. M., & McConaughy, S. H. (1992). Taxonomy of internalizing disorders of childhood and adolescence. In W. M. Reynolds (Ed.), *Internalizing disorders in children and adolescents* (pp. 19–60). New York: Wiley.

Agras, S. (1959). The relationship of school phobia to childhood depression. *American Journal of Psychiatry, 116*, 533–536.

Alessi, N. E., & Magen, J. (1988). Comorbidity of other psychiatric disturbances in depressed psychiatrically hospitalized children. *American Journal of Psychiatry, 145*, 1582–1584.

Alessi, N. E., McManus, M., Grapentine, W. L., & Brickman, A. (1984). The characterization of depressive disorders in serious juvenile offenders. *Journal of Affective Disorders, 6*, 9–17.

Alessi, N. E., Robbins, D. R., & Dilsaver, S. C. (1987). Panic and depressive disorders among psychiatrically hospitalized adolescents. *Psychiatry Research, 20*, 275–283.

Alloy, L. B., Abramson, L. Y., Metalsky, G. I., & Hartlage, S. (1988). The hopelessness theory of depression: Attributional aspects. *British Journal of Clinical Psychology, 27*, 5–21.

American Psychiatric Association. (1980). *Diagnostic and statistical manual of mental disorders (3rd. ed.)* Washington, DC: Author.

American Psychiatric Association. (1987). *Diagnostic and statistical manual of mental disorders (rev. 3rd ed.)*. Washington, DC: Author.

American Psychiatric Association. (1994). *Diagnostic and statistical manual of mental disorders* (4th ed.). Washington, DC: Author.

Anderson, J., & McGee, R. (1994). Comorbidity of depression in childhood and adolescence. In W. M. Reynolds & H. F. Johnston (Eds.), *Handbook of depression in children and adolescents* (pp. 581–601). New York: Plenum.

Anthony, J. (1970). Two contrasting types of adolescent depression and their treatment. *Journal of American Psychoanalytic Association, 18*, 841.

Archer, R. P., & Gordon, R. A. (1988). MMPI and Rorschach indices of schizophrenia and depressive diagnoses among adolescent psychiatric inpatients. *Journal of Personality Assessment, 52*, 276–287.

Archer, R. P., Maruish, M., Imhof, E. A., & Piotrowski, C. (1991). Psychological test usage with adolescent clients: 1990 survey findings. *Professional Psychology: Research and Practice, 22*, 247–252.

Bandura, A., & Walters, R. H. (1963). *Social learning and personality development.* New York: Holt, Rinehart & Winston.

Baron, P., & Joly, E. (1988). Sex differences in the expression of depression in adolescents. *Sex Roles, 18*, 1–7.

Barrera, M., & Garrison-Jones, C. V. (1988). Properties of the Beck Depression Inventory as a screening instrument for adolescent depression. *Journal of Abnormal Child Psychology, 16*, 263–273.

Baumgartner, A., Graf, K. J., & Kurten, I. (1986). Serial dexamethasone suppression tests in psychiatric illness: Part I. A study of schizophrenia and mania. *Psychiatry Research, 18*, 9–23.

Beardslee, W. R. (1986). The need for the study of adaptation in the children of parents with affective disorders. In M. Rutter, C. E. Izard, & P. B. Read (Eds.), *Depression in young people: Developmental and clinical perspectives* (pp. 189–204). New York: Guilford.

Beardslee, W. R., Bemporad, J., Keller, M. B., & Klerman, G. L. (1983). Children of parents with major affective disorder: A review. *American Journal of Psychiatry, 140*, 825–832.

Beck, A. T. (1967) *Depression: Causes and treatment.* Philadelphia: University of Pennsylvania Press.

Beck, A. T., Rush, A. J., Shaw, B. F., & Emery, G. (1979). *Cognitive therapy of depression.* New York: Guilford.

Beck, A. T., Ward, C., Mendelson, M., Mock, J., & Erbaugh, J. (1961) An inventory for measuring depression. *Archives of General Psychiatry, 4*, 561–571.

Beck, D. C., Carlson, G. A., Russell, A. T., & Brownfield, F. E. (1987). Use of depression rating instruments in developmentally and educationally delayed adolescents. *Journal of the American Academy of Child and Adolescent Psychiatry, 26*, 97–100.

Beckham, E. E. (1990). Psychotherapy of depression research at a crossroads: Directions for the 1990s. *Clinical Psychology Review, 10*, 207–228.

Bemporad, J. (1978). Psychodynamics of depression and suicide in children and adolescents. In S. Arieti & J. Bemporad (Eds.), *Severe and mild depression: The psychotherapeutic approach* (pp. 185–207). New York: Basic Books.

Bemporad, J. R. (1988). Psychodynamic treatment of depressed adolescents. *Journal of Clinical Psychiatry, 49*(Suppl.), 26–31.

Bernstein, G. A., & Garfinkel, B. D. (1986). School phobia: The overlap of affective and anxiety disorders. *Journal of the American Academy of Child and Adolescent Psychiatry, 25*, 235–241.

Bernstein, G. A., Garfinkel, B. D., & Hoberman, H. M. (1989). Self-reported anxiety in adolescents. *American Journal of Psychiatry, 146*, 384–386.

Bertagnoli, M. W., & Borchardt, C. M. (1990). A review of ECT for children and adolescents. *Journal of the American Academy of Child and Adolescent Psychiatry, 29*, 302–307.

Blumberg, S. H., & Izard, C. E. (1986). Discriminating patterns of emotions in 10- and 11-year-old children's anxiety and depression. *Journal of Personality and Social Psychology, 51*, 852–857.

Bowden, C. L., & Sarabia, F. (1980). Diagnosing manic-depressive illness in adolescents. *Comprehensive Psychiatry, 21*, 263–269.

Bowring, M. A., & Kovacs, M. (1992). Difficulties in diagnosing manic disorders among children and adolescents. *Journal of the American Academy of Child and Adolescent Psychiatry, 31*, 611–614.

Brady, E. U., & Kendall, P. C. (1992). Comorbidity of anxiety and depression in children and adolescents. *Psychological Bulletin, 111*, 244–253.

Brown, L. K., Overholser, J., Spirito, A., & Fritz, G. K. (1991). The correlates of planning in adolescent suicide attempts. *Journal of the American Academy of Child and Adolescent Psychiatry, 30*, 95–99.

Brown, W. A., Johnston, R., & Mayfield, D. (1979). The 24-hour dexamethasone suppression test in a clinical setting: Relationship to diagnosis, symptoms, and response to treatment. *American Journal of Psychiatry, 136*, 543–547.

Burke, P., & Puig-Antich, J. (1990). Psychobiology of childhood depression. In M. Lewis & S. M. Miller (Eds.), *Handbook of developmental psychopathology* (pp. 327–339). New York: Plenum.

Butcher, J. N., Williams, C. L., Graham, J. R., Archer, R. P., Tellegen, A., Ben-Porath, Y. S., & Kaemmer, B. (1992). *MMPI-A (Minnesota Multiphasic Personality Inventory for Adolescents): Manual for administration, scoring, and interpretation.* Minneapolis: University of Minnesota Press.

Campbell, J. D. (1952). Manic depressive psychosis in children: Report of 18 cases. *Journal of Nervous and Mental Disease, 116*, 424–439.

Campbell, M., Perry, R., & Green, W. H. (1984). Use of lithium in children and adolescents. *Psychosomatics, 25*, 95–106.

Carey, T. C., Finch, A. J., & Carey, M. P. (1991). Relation between differential emotions and depression in emotionally disturbed children and adolescents. *Journal of Consulting and Clinical Psychology, 59*, 594–597.

Carlson, G. A. (1994). Adolescent bipolar disorder: Phenomenology and treatment implications. In W. M. Reynolds & H. F. Johnston (Eds.), *Handbook of depression in children and adolescents* (pp. 41–60). New York: Plenum.

Carlson, G. A., & Kashani, J. H. (1988a). Phenomenology of major depression from childhood through adulthood: Analysis of three studies. *American Journal of Psychiatry, 145*, 1222–1225.

Carlson, G. A., & Kashani, J. H. (1988b). Manic symptoms in a non-referred adolescent population. *Journal of Affective Disorders, 15*, 219–226.

Carlson, G. A., & Strober, M. (1978a). Affective disorder in adolescence: Issues in misdiagnosis. *Journal of Clinical Psychiatry, 39, 59*, 63–66.

Carlson, G. A., & Strober, M. (1978b). Manic-depressive illness in early adolescence: A study of clinical and diagnostic characteristics in six cases. *Journal of the American Academy of Child Psychiatry, 17*, 138–153.

Casat, C. D. (1982). The under- and over-diagnosis of mania in children and adolescents. *Comprehensive Psychiatry, 23*, 552–559.

Christ, A. E., Adler, A. G., Isacoff, M., & Gershansky, I. S. (1981) Depression: Symptoms versus diagnosis in 10,412 hospitalized children and adolescents (1957–1977). *American Journal of Psychotherapy, 35*, 400–412.

Clarizio, H. F. (1989). *Assessment and treatment of depression in children and adolescents*. Brandon, VT: Clinical Psychology Publishing.

Clarke, G., & Lewinsohn, P. M. (1989). The coping with depression course: A group psychoeducational intervention for unipolar depression. *Behaviour Change, 6*, 54–69.

Clarke, G. N., Lewinsohn, P. M., Hops, H., & Andrews, J. (1989, August). *Two-year treatment outcome follow-up of depressed adolescents*. Paper presented at the annual meeting, of the American Psychological Association, New Orleans.

Conners, C. K. (1976). Classification and treatment of childhood depression and depressive equivalents. In D. M. Gallant & G. M. Simpson (Eds.), *Depression: Behavioral, biochemical, diagnostic and treatment concepts* (pp. 181–204). New York: Spectrum.

Crumley, F. E., Clevenger, J., Steinfink, D., & Oldham, D. (1982). Preliminary report on the dexamethasone suppression test for psychiatrically disturbed adolescents. *American Journal of Psychiatry, 129*, 1062–1064.

Curry, J. F., & Craighead, W. E. (1993). Depression. In T. H. Ollendick & M. Hersen (Eds.), *Handbook of child and adolescent assessment* (pp. 251–268). Boston: Allyn and Bacon.

Curtis, G. C., Cameron, O. G., & Nesse, R. M. (1982). The dexamethasone suppression test in panic disorder and agoraphobia. *American Journal of Psychiatry, 139*, 1043–1046.

Dahl, R. E., Ryan, N. D., Williamson, D. E., Ambrosini, P. J., Rabinovich, H., Novacenko, H., Nelson, B., & Puig-Antich, J. (1992). Regulation of sleep and growth hormone in adolescent depression. *Journal of the American Academy of Child and Adolescent Psychiatry, 31*, 615–621.

Dalley, M. B., Bolocofsky, D. N., Alcorn, M. B., & Baker, C. (1992). Depressive symptomatology, attributional style, dysfunctional attitude, and social competency in adolescents with and without learning disabilities. *School Psychology Review, 21*, 444–458.

Dech, B., & Budow, L. (1991). The use of fluoxetine in an adolescent with Prader-Willi syndrome. *Journal of the American Academy of Child and Adolescent Psychiatry, 30*, 298–302.

Dobson, K. S. (1989). A meta-analysis of the efficacy of cognitive therapy for depression. *Journal of Consulting and Clinical Psychology, 57*, 414–419.

Doerfler, L. A., Felner, R. D., Rowlison, R. T., Evans, E., & Raley, P. A. (1988). Depression in children and adolescents: A comparative analysis of the utility and construct validity of two assessment measures. *Journal of Consulting and Clinical Psychology, 56*, 769–772.

Downey, G., & Coyne, J. C. (1990). Children of depressed parents: An integrative review. *Psychological Bulletin, 108*, 50–76.

Dugas, M., Mouren, M. C., Halfon, O., & Moron, P. (1985). Treatment of childhood and adolescent depression with mianserin. *Acta Psychiatrica Scandinavia, 72*(suppl.), 48–53.

Dweck, C. S. (1977) Learned helplessness: A developmental approach. In J. G. Schulterbrandt & A. Raskin (Eds.), *Depression in childhood: Diagnosis, treatment and conceptual models* (pp. 135–138). New York: Raven.

Eason, L. J., Finch, A. J., Brasted, W., & Saylor, C. F. (1985). The assessment of depression and anxiety in hospitalized pediatric patients. *Child Psychiatry and Human Development, 16,* 57–64.

Ellis, A. (1980). Rational-emotive therapy and cognitive behavior therapy: Similarities and differences. *Cognitive Therapy and Research, 4,* 325–340.

Emslie, G. J., Roffwarg, H. P., Rush, A. J., Weinberg, W. A., & Parkin-Feigenbaum, L. (1987). Sleep EEG findings in depressed children and adolescents. *American Journal of Psychiatry, 144,* 668–670.

Emslie, G. J., Weinberg, W. A., Rush, A. J., Weissenburger, J., & Parkin-Feigenbaum, L. (1987). Depression and dexamethasone suppression test in children and adolescents. *Journal of Child Neurology, 2,* 31–37.

Endicott, J., & Spitzer, R. L. (1978) A diagnostic interview: The Schedule for Affective Disorders and Schizophrenia. *Archives of General Psychiatry, 35,* 837–844.

Exner, J., & Weiner, I. B. (1982). *The Rorschach: A comprehensive system. Vol. 3. Assessment of children and adolescents.* New York: Wiley.

Extein, I., Rosenberg, G., Pottash, A. L. C., & Gold, M. S. (1982). The dexamethasone suppression test in depressed adolescents. *American Journal of Psychiatry, 139,* 1617–1619.

Faraone, S. V., Kremen, W. S., & Tsuang, M. T. (1990). Genetic transmission of major affective disorders: Quantitative models and linkage analyses. *Psychological Bulletin, 108,* 109–127.

Faulstich, M. E., Carey, M. P., Ruggiero, L., Enyart, P., & Gresham, F. (1986). Assessment of depression in childhood and adolescence: An evaluation of the Center for Epidemiological Studies Depression Scale for Children (CES-DC). *American Journal of Psychiatry, 143,* 1024–1027.

Feinstein, A. R. (1970). The pretherapeutic classification of co-morbidity in chronic disease. *Journal of Chronic Diseases, 23,* 455–468.

Finch, A. J., Imm, P. S., & Belter, R. W. (1990). Brief Rorschach records with children and adolescents. *Journal of Personality Assessment, 55,* 640–646.

Finch, A. J., Lipovsky, J. A., & Casat, C. D. (1989). Anxiety and depression in children and adolescents: Negative affectivity or separate constructs? In P. C. Kendall & D. Watson (Eds.), *Anxiety and depression: Distinctive and overlapping features* (pp. 171–202). San Diego, CA: Academic Press.

Fine, S., Forth, A., Gilbert, M., & Haley, G. (1991). Group therapy for adolescent depressive disorder: A comparison of social skills and therapeutic support. *Journal of the American Academy of Child Psychiatry, 30,* 79–85.

Fleming, J. E., & Offord, D. R. (1990). Epidemiology of childhood depressive disorders: A critical review. *Journal of the American Academy of Child and Adolescent Psychiatry, 29,* 571–580.

Friedman, R. C., Clarkin, J. F., Corn, R., Aronoff, M. S., Hurt, S. W., & Murphy, M. C. (1982) DSM-III and affective pathology in hospitalized adolescents. *Journal of Nervous and Mental Disorders, 170,* 511–521.

Friedman, R. C., Hurt, S. W., Clarkin, J. F., Corn, R., & Aronoff, M. S. (1983) Symptoms of depression among adolescents and young adults. *Journal of Affective Disorders, 5,* 37–43.

Frommer, E. A. (1967). Treatment of childhood depression with antidepressant drugs. *British Medical Journal, 1,* 729–732.

Frommer, E. A. (1968). Depressive illness in childhood. *British Journal of Psychiatry, 117*, 117–136.

Fuchs, C. Z., & Rehm, L. P. (1977). A self-control behavior therapy program for depression. *Journal of Consulting and Clinical Psychology, 45*, 206–215.

Garrison, C. Z., Jackson, K. L., Marsteller, F., McKeown, R., & Addy, C. (1990). A longitudinal study of depressive symptomatology in young adolescents. *Journal of the American Academy of Child and Adolescent Psychiatry, 29*, 581–585.

Geller, B., Chestnut, E. C., Miller, D., Price, D. T., & Yates, E. (1985). Preliminary data on DSM-III associated features of major depressive disorder in children and adolescents. *American Journal of Psychiatry, 142*, 643–644.

Geller, B., Cooper, T. B., Farooki, Z. Q., & Chestnut, E. C. (1985). Dose and plasma levels of nortriptyline and chlorpromazine in delusionally depressed adolescents and of nortriptyline in nondelusionally depressed adolescents. *American Journal of Psychiatry, 142*, 336–338.

Geller, B., Cooper, T. B., Graham, D. L., Fetner, H. H., Marsteller, R. A., & Wells, J. (1992). Pharmacokinetically designed double-blind, placebo-controlled study of nortriptyline in 6- to 12-year-olds with major depressive disorder: Outcome, nortriptyline and hydroxy-nortriptyline plasma levels, EKG, BP and side effects measurements. *Journal of the American Academy of Child and Adolescent Psychiatry, 31*, 34–44.

Gjerde, P. F., Block, J., & Block, J. H. (1988). Depressive symptoms and personality during late adolescence: Gender differences in the externalization-internalization of symptom expression. *Journal of Abnormal Psychology, 97*, 475–486.

Glaser, K. (1967). Masked depression in children and adolescents. *American Journal of Psychotherapy, 21*, 565–574.

Greden, J. F., Kronfol, Z., Gardner, R., Feinberg, M., Mukhopadhyay, S., Albala, A. A., & Carroll, B. J. (1981). Dexamethasone suppression test and selection of antidepressant medications. *Journal of Affective Disorders, 3*, 389–396.

Gualtieri, C. T. (1977). Imipramine and children: A review and some speculations about the mechanism of drug action. *Diseases of the Nervous System, 33*, 368–375.

Gutterman, E. M., O'Brian, J. D., & Young, J. G. (1987). Structured diagnostic interviews for children and adolescents: Current status and future directions. *Journal of the American Academy of Child and Adolescent Psychiatry, 26*, 621–630.

Hamilton, M. (1960). A rating scale for depression. *Journal of Neurology, Neurosurgery, and Psychiatry, 23*, 56–62.

Hamilton, M. (1967). Development of a rating scale for primary depressive illness. *British Journal of Social and Clinical Psychology, 6*, 278–296.

Hamilton, M. (1982). Symptoms and assessment of depression. In E. S. Paykel (Ed.), *Handbook of affective disorders* (pp. 3–11) New York: Guilford.

Harrington, R., Fudge, H., Rutter, M., Pickles, A., & Hill, J. (1990). Adult outcomes of childhood and adolescent depression: I. Psychiatric status. *Archives of General Psychiatry, 47*, 465–473.

Hathaway, S. R., & McKinley, J. C. (1943). *Minnesota Multiphasic Personality Inventory*. Minneapolis: University of Minnesota Press.

Hayward, C., Killen, J. D., & Taylor, C. B. (1989). Panic attacks in young adolescents. *American Journal of Psychiatry, 146*, 1061–1062.

Hershberg, S. G., Carlson, G. A., Cantwell, D. P., & Strober, M. (1982). Anxiety and depressive disorders in psychiatrically disturbed children. *Journal of Clinical Psychiatry, 43*, 358–361.

Hodges, K. (in press). Diagnostic and clinical interviews. In W. M. Reynolds & H. Johnston (Eds.), *Handbook of depression in children and adolescents*. New York: Plenum.

Hodges, K., & Cools, J. N. (1990). Structured diagnostic interviews. In A. M. La Greca (Ed.), *Through the eyes of the child: Obtaining self-reports from children and adolescents* (pp. 109–149). Boston: Allyn and Bacon.

Hollon, T. H. (1970). Poor school performance as a symptom of masked depression in children and adolescents. *American Journal of Psychotherapy, 24*, 258–263.

Hops, H., Lewinsohn, P. M., Andrews, J. A., & Roberts, R. E. (1990). Psychosocial correlates of depressive symptomatology among high school students. *Journal of Clinical Child Psychology, 19*, 211–220.

Hsu, L. K. G., Molcan, K., Cashman, M. H., Lee, S., Lohr, J., & Hindmarsh, D. (1983). The dexamethasone suppression test in adolescent depression. *Journal of the American Academy of Child Psychiatry, 22*, 470–473.

Jacobsen, E. (1938). *Progressive relaxation*. Chicago: University of Chicago Press.

Jefferson, J. W. (1982). The use of lithium in childhood and adolescence: An overview. *Journal of Clinical Psychiatry, 43*, 174–177.

Jefferson, J. W. (1989). Lithium: A therapeutic magic wand. *Journal of Clinical Psychiatry, 50*, 81–86.

Johnston, H. F., & Fruehling, J. J. (1994). Pharmacotherapy for depression in children and adolescents. In W. M. Reynolds & H. F. Johnston (Eds.), *Handbook of depression in children and adolescents*. (pp. 365–397). New York: Plenum.

Kahn, J. S., Kehle, T. J., Jenson, W. R., & Clark, E. (1990). Comparison of cognitive-behavioral, relaxation, and self-modeling interventions for depression among middle-school students. *School Psychology Review, 19*, 196–211.

Kanfer, F. H. (1970). Self-regulation: Research, issues, and speculations. In C. Neuringer & J. L. Michael (Eds.), *Behavioral modification in clinical psychology* (pp. 178–220). New York: Appleton-Century-Crofts.

Kanfer, F. H. (1985). Target selection for clinical change programs. *Behavioral Assessment, 7*, 7–20.

Kanfer, F. H., & Karoly, P. (1972). Self-control: A behavioristic excursion into the lion's den. *Behavior Therapy, 3*, 398–419.

Kaplan, S. L., Hong, G. K., & Weinhold, C. (1984) Epidemiology of depressive symptomatology in adolescents. *Journal of the American Academy of Child Psychiatry, 23*, 91–98.

Kashani, J. H., Beck, N. C., Hoeper, E. W., Fallahi, C., Corcoran, C. M., McAllister, J. A., Rosenberg, T. K., & Reid, J. C. (1987). Psychiatric disorders in a community sample of adolescents. *American Journal of Psychiatry, 144*, 584–589.

Kashani, J. H., Carlson, G. A., Beck, N. C., Hoeper, E. W., Corcoran, C. M., McAllister, J. A., Fallahi, C., Rosenberg, T. K., & Reid, J. C. (1987). Depression, depressive symptoms, and depressed mood among a community sample of adolescents. *American Journal of Psychiatry, 144*, 931–934.

Kashani, J. H., & Orvaschel, H. (1988). Anxiety disorders in mid-adolescence: A community sample. *American Journal of Psychiatry, 145*, 960–964.

Kashani, J. H., & Orvaschel, H. (1990). Community study of anxiety in children and adolescents. *American Journal of Psychiatry, 147*, 313–318.

Kashani, J. H., Sherman, D. D., Parker, D. R., & Reid, J. C. (1990). Utility of the Beck Depression Inventory with clinic-referred adolescents. *Journal of the American Academy of Child and Adolescent Psychiatry, 29*, 278–282.

Kazdin, A. E. (1985). Selection of target behaviors: The relationship of the treatment focus to clinical dysfunction. *Behavioral Assessment, 7*, 33–47.

Kazdin, A. E. (1994) Informant variability in the assessment of childhood depression. In W. M. Reynolds & H. Johnston (Eds.), *Handbook of depression in children and adolescents*. New York: Plenum.

Kendall, P. C., & Braswell, L. (1985). *Cognitive-behavioral therapy for impulsive children*. New York: Guilford.

Klee, S. N., & Garfinkel, B. D. (1984). Identification of depression in children and adolescents: The role of the dexamethasone suppression test. *Journal of the American Academy of Child Psychiatry, 23*, 410–415.

Klein, D. N., Depue, R. A., & Slater, J. F. (1985). Cyclothymia in the adolescent offspring of parents with bipolar disorder. *Journal of Abnormal Psychology, 94*, 115–127.

Klerman, G. L. (1990). Approaches to the phenomena of comorbidity. In J. D. Maser & C. R. Cloninger (Eds.), *Comorbidity of mood and anxiety disorders* (pp. 13–37). Washington, DC: American Psychiatric Press.

Klerman, G. L., & Weissman, M. M. (1982). Interpersonal psychotherapy: Theory and research. In A. J. Rush (Ed.), *Short-term psychotherapies for depression: Behavioral, interpersonal, cognitive, and psychodynamic approaches* (pp. 88–106). New York: Guilford.

Kobak, K., Reynolds, W., Rosenfeld, R., Greist, J. H. (1990). Development and validation of a computer administered version of the Hamilton Depression Rating Scale. *Psychological Assessment: A Journal of Consulting and Clinical Psychology, 2*, 56–63.

Kolvin, I., Berney, T. P., & Bhate, S. R. (1984). Classification and diagnosis of depression in school phobia. *British Journal of Psychiatry, 145*, 347–357.

Kovacs, M. (1979). *Children's Depression Inventory*. Unpublished manuscript, University of Pittsburg School of Medicine.

Kovacs, M. (1980/1981). Rating scales to assess depression in school-aged children. *Acta Paedopsychiatrica, 46*, 305–315.

Kovacs, M. (1990). Comorbid anxiety disorders in childhood-onset depressions. In J. D. Maser & C. R. Cloninger (Eds.), *Comorbidity of mood and anxiety disorders* (pp. 271–281). Washington DC: American Psychiatric Press.

Kovacs, M., & Beck, A. T. (1977). An empirical-clinical approach toward a definition of childhood depression. In J. G. Schulterbrandt & A. Raskin (Eds.), *Depression in childhood: Diagnosis, treatment and conceptual models* (pp. 1–25). New York: Raven.

Kovacs, M., Feinberg, T. L., Crouse-Novak, M., Paulauskas, S. L., Pollock, M., & Finkelstein, R. (1984). Depressive disorders in childhood: II. A longitudinal study of the risk for a subsequent major depression. *Archives of General Psychiatry, 41* 643–649.

Kovacs, M., Feinberg, T. L., Crouse-Novak, M., Paulauskas, S. L., & Finkelstein, R. (1984). Depressive disorders in childhood: I. A longitudinal prospective study of characteristics and recovery. *Archives of General Psychiatry, 41,* 229–237.

Kovacs, M., Gatsonis, C., Paulauskas, S. L., & Richards, C. (1989) Depressive disorders in childhood: IV. A longitudinal study of comorbidity with and risk for anxiety disorders. *Archives of General Psychiatry, 46,* 776–782.

Kovacs, M., Paulauskas, S. L., Gatsonis, C., & Richards, C. (1988) Depressive disorders in childhood: III. A longitudinal study of comorbidity with and risk for conduct disorders. *Journal of Affective Disorders, 15,* 205–217.

Kramer, A. D., & Feiguine, R. J. (1981). Clinical effects of amitriptyline in adolescent depression: A pilot study. *Journal of the American Academy of Child Psychiatry, 20,* 636–644.

Kuhn, V., & Kuhn, R. (1971). Drug therapy for depression in children: Indications and methods. In A. Annell (Eds.), *Depressive states in childhood and adolescence* (pp. 455–459). Stockholm: Almqvist & Wiksell.

Lahmeyer, H. W., Poznanski, E. O., & Bellur, S. N. (1983). EEG sleep in depressed adolescents. *American Journal of Psychiatry, 140,* 1150–1153.

Last, C. G. (1992). Anxiety disorders in childhood and adolescence. In W. M. Reynolds (Ed.), *Internalizing disorders in children and adolescents* (pp. 61–106). New York: Wiley.

Lesse, S. (1981). Hypochondriacal and psychosomatic disorders masking depression in adolescents. *American Journal of Psychiatry, 35,* 356–367.

Levy, J. C., & Deykin, E. Y. (1989). Suicidality, depression, and substance abuse in adolescence. *American Journal of Psychiatry, 146,* 1462–1467.

Lewinsohn, P. M. (1974) A behavioral approach to depression. In R. J. Friedman & M. M. Katz (Eds.), *The psychology of depression: Contemporary theory and research* (pp. 157–184). New York: Wiley.

Lewinsohn, P. M. (1975). The behavioral study and treatment of depression. In M. Hersen, R. M. Eisler, P. M. Miller (Eds.), *Progress in behavior modification* (pp. 19–64). New York: Academic Press.

Lewinsohn, P. M., & Arconad, M. (1981). Behavioral treatment of depression: A social learning approach. In J. F. Clarkin & A. I. Glazer (Eds.), *Depression: Behavioral and directive intervention strategies* (pp. 33–67). New York: Garland.

Lewinsohn, P. M., Clarke, G. N., Hops, H., & Andrews, J. (1990). Cognitive-behavioral treatment for depressed adolescents. *Behavior Therapy, 21,* 385–401.

Lewinsohn, P. M., Hoberman, H. M., & Clarke, G. N. (1989). The coping with depression course: Review and future directions. *Canadian Journal of Behavioral Science, 21,* 470–493.

Lewinsohn, P. M., Hoberman, H., Teri, L., & Hautzinger, M. (1985). An integrative theory of depression. In S. Reiss & R. R. Bootzin (Eds.), *Theoretical issues in behavior therapy* (pp. 331–359). New York: Academic Press.

Lewinsohn, P. M., Munoz, R. F., Youngren, M. A., & Zeiss, A. M. (1978). *Control your depression.* Englewood Cliffs, NJ: Prentice-Hall.

Lewy, A. J., & Sack, R. L. (1986). Light therapy and psychiatry. *Proceedings of the Society for Experimental Biology and Medicine, 183,* 11–18.

Livingston, R., Reis, C. J., & Ringdahl, I. C. (1984). Abnormal dexamethasone suppression test results in depressed and nondepressed children. *American Journal of Psychiatry, 141*, 106–108.

Loranger, A. W., & Levine, P. M. (1978). Age at onset of bipolar affective illness. *Archives of General Psychiatry, 35*, 1345–1348.

Lucas, A. R., Lockett, H. J., & Grimm, F. (1965). Amitriptyline in childhood depressions. *Diseases of the Nervous System, 26*, 105–110.

Manson, S. M., Ackerson, L. M., Dick, R. W., Baron, A. E., & Flemning, C. M. (1990). Depressive symptoms among American Indian adolescents: Psychometric characteristics of the Center for Epidemiologic Studies-Depression Scale (CES-D). *Psychological Assessment: A Journal of Consulting and Clinical Psychology, 2*, 231–237.

Maser, J. D., & Cloninger, C. R. (1990). Comorbidity of anxiety and mood disorders: Introduction and overview. In J. D. Maser & C. R. Cloninger (Eds.), *Comorbidity of mood and anxiety disorders* (pp. 3–12). Washington, DC: American Psychiatric Press.

Mattsson, A., & Seltzer, R. L. (1981). MAOI-induced rapid cycling bipolar affective disorder in an adolescent. *American Journal of Psychiatry, 138*, 677–679.

McGee, R., Feehan, M., Williams, S., Partridge, F., Silva, P. A., & Kelly, J. (1990). DSM-III disorders in a large sample of adolescents. *Journal of the American Academy of Child and Adolescent Psychiatry, 29*, 611–619.

McGlashan, T. H. (1988). Adolescent versus adult onset of mania. *American Journal of Psychiatry, 145*, 221–223.

Mezzich, J. E., Ahn, C. W., Fabrega, H., & Pilkonis, P. A. (1990). Patterns of psychiatric comorbidity in a large population presenting for care. In J. D. Maser & C. R. Cloninger (Eds.), *Comorbidity of mood and anxiety disorders* (pp. 189–204). Washington, DC: American Psychiatric Press.

Miller, K. B., & Nelson, J. C. (1987). Does the dexamethasone suppression test relate to subtypes, factors, symptoms, or severity? *Archives of General Psychiatry, 44*, 769–774.

Mitchell, J., McCauley, E., Burke, P., & Moss, S. J. (1988). Phenomenology of depression in children and adolescents. *Journal of the American of Child and Adolescent Psychiatry, 27*, 12–20.

Molick, R., & Pinkston, E. M. (1982). Using behavioral analysis to develop adaptive social behavior in a depressed adolescent girl. In E. M. Pinkston, J. L. Levitt, G. R. Green, N. L. Linsk, & T. L. Rzepnicki (Eds.), *Effective social work practice* (pp. 364–375). San Francisco: Jossey-Bass.

Moreau, D. L., Weissman, M., & Warner, V. (1989). Panic disorder in children at high risk for depression. *American Journal of Psychiatry, 146*, 1059–1060.

Naylor, M. W., & Grossman, M. (1991). Trichotillomania and depression [Letter to the editor]. *Journal of the American Academy of Child and Adolescent Psychiatry, 30*, 155–156.

Orvaschel, H. (1985). Psychiatric interviews suitable for use in research with children and adolescents. *Psychopharmacology Bulletin, 21*, 737–745.

Petti, T. A. (1978). Depression in hospitalized child psychiatry patients: Approaches to measuring depression. *Journal of the American Academy of Child Psychiatry, 17*, 49–59.

Pfefferbaum, B., Pack, R., & van Eys, J. (1989). Monoamine oxidase inhibitor toxicity. *Journal of the American Academy of Child and Adolescent Psychiatry, 28*, 954–955.

Poznanski, E. O., Grossman, J. A., Buchsbaum, Y., Banegas, M., Freeman, L., & Gibbons, R. (1984). Preliminary studies of the reliability and validity of the Children's Depression Rating Scale. *Journal of the American Academy of Child Psychiatry, 23*, 191–197.

Pressley, M., Reynolds, W. M., Stark, K. D., & Gettinger, M. (1983). Cognitive strategy training and children's self-control. In M. Pressley & J. R. Levin (Eds.), *Cognitive strategy research: Psychological foundations* (pp. 267–300). New York: Springer-Verlag.

Puig-Antich, J. (1986a). Psychobiological markers: Effects of age and puberty. In M. Rutter, C. E. Izard, & P. B. Read (Eds.), *Depression in young people: Developmental and clinical perspectives.* (pp. 341–381). New York: Guilford Press.

Puig-Antich, J. (1986b). Possible prevention strategies for depression in children and adolescents. In J. T. Barter & S. W. Talbott (Eds.), *Primary prevention in psychiatry: State of the art* (pp. 69–84). Washington, DC: American Psychiatric Press.

Puig-Antich, J. (1987a). Affective disorders in children and adolescents: Diagnostic validity and psychobiology. In H. Y. Melzer (Ed.), *Psychopharmacology: The third generation of progress* (pp. 843–859). New York: Raven.

Puig-Antich, J. (1987b). Sleep and neuroendocrine correlates of affective illness in childhood and adolescence. *Journal of Adolescent Health Care, 8*, 505–529.

Puig-Antich, J., & Chambers, W. (1978). *The Schedule for Affective Disorders and Schizophrenia for school-age children (Kiddie-SADS).* New York: New York State Psychiatric Institute.

Puig-Antich, J., Ryan, N. D., & Rabinovich, H. (1985). Affective disorders in childhood and adolescence. In J. M. Wiener (Ed.), *Diagnosis and psychopharmacology of childhood and adolescent disorders* (pp. 151–178). New York: Wiley.

Radloff, L. S. (1977) The CES-D Scale: A self-report scale for research in the general population. *Applied Psychological Measurement, 1*, 385–401.

Rastam, M. (1992). Anorexia nervosa in 51 Swedish adolescents: Premorbid problems and comorbidity. *Journal of the American Academy of Child and Adolescent Psychiatry, 31*, 819–829.

Regier, D. A., Boyd, J. H., Burke, J. D., Rae, D. S. Myers, J. K., Kramer, M., Robins, L. N., George, L. K., Karno, M., & Locke, B. Z. (1988). One-month prevalence of mental disorders in the United States. *Archives of General Psychiatry, 45*, 977–986.

Rehm, L. P. (1977). A self-control model of depression. *Behavior Therapy, 8*, 787–804.

Rehm, L. P. (1981). A self-control therapy program for treatment of depression. In J. F. Clarkin & A. I. Glazer (Eds.), *Depression: Behavioral and directive intervention strategies* (pp. 68–109). New York: Garland.

Reich, T., Rice, J., & Mullaney, J. (1986). Genetic risk factors for the affective disorders. In G. Klerman (Ed.), *Suicide and depression among adolescents and young adults* (pp. 79–103). Washington, DC: American Psychiatric Press.

Reinherz, H. Z. Giaconia, R. M., Lefkowitz, E. S., Pakiz, B., & Frost, A. K. (1993). Prevalence of psychiatric disorders in a community population of older adolescents. *Journal of the American Academy of Child and Adolescent Psychiatry,* *32,* 369–377.

Reynolds, C. R., & Richmond, B. O. (1978). What I Think and Feel: A revised measure of children's manifest anxiety. *Journal of Abnormal Child Psychology,* *6,* 271–280.

Reynolds, W. M. (1985a). Depression in childhood and adolescence: Diagnosis, assessment, intervention strategies and research. In T. R. Kratochwill (Ed.), *Advances in school psychology* (Vol. 4, pp. 133–189). Hillsdale, NJ: Erlbaum.

Reynolds, W. M. (1985b, March). *Depression and validation of a scale to measure depression in adolescents.* Paper presented at the annual meeting of the Society for Personality Assessment, Berkeley, CA.

Reynolds, W. M. (1986a). A model for the screening and identification of depressed children and adolescents in school settings. *Professional School Psychology,* *1,* 117–129.

Reynolds, W. M. (1986b). *Reynolds Adolescent Depression Scale.* Odessa, FL: Psychological Assessment Resources.

Reynolds, W. M. (1987a). *Reynolds Adolescent Depression Scale: Professional manual.* Odessa, FL: Psychological Assessment Resources.

Reynolds, W. M. (1987b). *Suicidal Ideation Questionnaire.* Odessa, FL: Psychological Assessment Resources.

Reynolds, W. M. (1989). Suicidal ideation and depression in adolescents: Assessment and research. In P. F. Lovibond & P. Wilson (Eds.), *Clinical and abnormal psychology* (pp. 125–135). Amsterdam: Elsevier.

Reynolds, W. M. (1990). Development of a semistructured clinical interview for suicidal behaviors in adolescents. *Psychological Assessment: A Journal of Consulting and Clinical Psychology,* *2,* 382–390.

Reynolds, W. M. (1991). A school-based procedure for the identification of adolescents at-risk for suicidal behaviors. *Family and Community Health,* *14,* 64–75.

Reynolds, W. M. (1992a). The study of internalizing disorders in children and adolescents. In W. M. Reynolds (Ed.), *Internalizing disorders in children and adolescents* (pp. 1–18). New York: Wiley.

Reynolds, W. M. (1992b). Depression in children and adolescents. In W. M. Reynolds (Ed.), *Internalizing disorders in children and adolescents* (pp. 149–253). New York: Wiley.

Reynolds, W. M. (1993a). Self-report methods. In T. H. Ollendick & M. Hersen (Eds.), *Handbook of child and adolescent assessment* (pp. 98–123). Boston: Allyn & Bacon.

Reynolds, W. M. (1993b, March). *The Adolescent Psychopathology Scales: Initial reliability of clinical disorder scales.* Paper presented at the annual meeting of the Society for Personality Assessment, San Francisco.

Reynolds, W. M. (1994a). Depression in adolescents: Contemporary issues and perspectives. In T. H. Ollendick & R. J. Prinz (Eds.), *Advances in clinical child psychology* (Vol. 16, pp. 261–316). New York: Plenum.

Reynolds, W. M. (1994a). Assessment of depression in children and adolescents by self-report questionnaires. In W. M. Reynolds & H. F. Johnston (Eds.), *Handbook of depression in children and adolescents* (pp. 209–234). New York: Plenum.

Reynolds, W. M. (in press). *Adolescent Psychopathology Scales*. Odessa, FL: Psychological Assessment Resources.

Reynolds, W. M., & Coats, K. I. (1982, July). *Depression in adolescents: Incidence, depth and correlates*. Paper presented at Meeting of the International Association for Child and Adolescent Psychiatry, Dublin.

Reynolds, W. M., & Coats, K. I. (1986). A comparison of cognitive-behavioral therapy and relaxation training for the treatment of depression in adolescents. *Journal of Consulting and Clinical Psychology, 54,* 653–660.

Reynolds, W. M., & Evert, T. (1991). *Efficacy of a multiple-gate screening strategy for identification of clinical levels of depressive symptomatology in adolescents.* Unpublished manuscript.

Reynolds, W. M., & Johnston, H. F. (1994). The nature and study of depression in children and adolescents. In W. M. Reynolds & H. F. Johnston (Eds.), *Handbook of depression in children and adolescents.* (pp. 3–17). New York: Plenum.

Reynolds, W. M., & Mazza, J. J. (1990, August). *Suicidal behavior and depression in adolescents*. Paper presented at the annual Convention of the American Psychological Association, Boston.

Reynolds, W. M., & Mazza, J. J. (1992, April). *Suicide attempts and psychopathology in youth*. Paper presented at the annual convention of the American Association of Suicidology, Chicago.

Reynolds, W. M., & Mazza, J. J. (1994). Suicide and suicidal behavior in children and adolescents. In W. M. Reynolds & H. F. Johnston (Eds.), *Handbook of depression in children and adolescents.* (pp. 525–580). New York: Plenum.

Reynolds, W. M., & Miller, K. L. (1989). Assessment of adolescents' learned helplessness in achievement situations. *Journal of Personality Assessment, 53,* 211–228.

Reynolds, W. M., & Stark, K. D. (1983). Cognitive behavior modification: The clinical application of cognitive strategies. In M. Pressley & J. R. Levin (Eds.), *Cognitive strategy research: Psychological foundations* (pp. 221–266). New York: Springer-Verlag.

Riddle, M. A., Brown, N., Dzubinski, D., Jetmalani, A. J., Law, Y., & Woolston, J. L. (1989). Fluoxetine overdose in an adolescent. *Journal of the American Academy of Child and Adolescent Psychiatry, 28,* 587–588.

Riddle, M. A., Hardin, M. T., King, R., Scahill, L., & Woolston, J. L. (1990). Fluoxetine treatment of children and adolescents with Tourette's and obsessive compulsive disorders: Preliminary clinical experience. *Journal of the American Academy of Child and Adolescent Psychiatry, 29,* 45–48.

Rie, H. E. (1966). Depression in childhood: A survey of some pertinent contributions. *Journal of the American Academy of Child Psychiatry, 5,* 553–583.

Robbins, D. R., Alessi, N. E., & Colfer, M. V. (1989). Treatment of adolescents with major depression: Implications of the DST and the melancholic clinical subtype. *Journal of Affective Disorders, 17,* 99–104.

Robbins, D. R., Alessi, N. E., Colfer, M. V., & Yanchyshyn, G. W. (1985). Use of the Hamilton Rating Scale for Depression and the Carroll Self-Rating Scale in adolescents. *Psychiatry Research, 14,* 123–129.

Robbins, D. R., Alessi, N. E., Cook, S. C., Poznanski, E. O., & Yanchyshyn, G. W. (1982). The use of the Research Diagnostic Criteria (RDC) for depression in adolescent psychiatric inpatients. *Journal of the American Academy of Child Psychiatry, 21,* 251–255.

Robbins, D. R., Alessi, N. E., Yanchyshyn, G. W., & Colfer, M. V. (1982). Preliminary report on the dexamethasone suppression test in adolescents. *American Journal of Psychiatry, 139,* 942–943.

Robbins, D. R., Alessi, N. E., Yanchyshyn, G. W., & Colfer, M. V. (1983). The dexamethasone suppression test in psychiatrically hospitalized adolescents. *Journal of the American Academy of Child Psychiatry, 22,* 476–469.

Roberts, R. E., Andrews, J. A., Lewinsohn, P. M., & Hops, H. (1990). Assessment of depression in adolescents using the Center for Epidemiologic Studies Depression Scale. *Psychological Assessment: A Journal of Consulting and Clinical Psychology, 2,* 122–128.

Roberts, R. E., Lewinsohn, P. M., & Seeley, J. R. (1991). Screening for adolescents depression: A comparison of depression scales. *Journal of the American Academy of Child and Adolescent Psychiatry, 30,* 58–66.

Robins, L. N., Helzer, J. E., Weissman, M. M., Orvaschel, H., Gruenberg, E., Burke, J. D., & Regier, D. (1984) Lifetime prevalence of specific psychiatric disorders in three sites. *Archives of General Psychiatry, 41,* 949–958.

Rogeness, G. A., Javors, M. A., Maas, J. W., & Macedo, C. A. (1990). Catecholamines and diagnoses in children. *Journal of the American Academy of Child and Adolescent Psychiatry, 29,* 234–241.

Rosenthal, N. E., Carpenter, C. J., James, C. P., Parry, B. L., Rogers, S. L. B., & Wehr, T. A. (1986). Seasonal affective disorder in children and adolescents. *American Journal of Psychiatry, 143,* 356–358.

Rubin, R. T., & Mandell, A. J. (1966). Adrenal cortical activity in pathological emotional states: A review. *American Journal of Psychiatry, 123,* 387–400.

Ryan, N. D. (1992). Pharmacological treatment of major depression. In M. Shafii & S. L. Shafii (Eds..), *Clinical guide to depression in children and adolescents* (pp. 219–232). Washington, DC: American Psychiatric Press.

Ryan, N. D., Meyer, V., Dachille, S., Mazzie, D., & Puig-Antich, J. (1988). Lithium antidepressant augmentation in TCA-refractory depression in adolescents. *Journal of the American Academy of Child and Adolescent Psychiatry, 27,* 371–376.

Ryan, N. D., Puig-Antich, J., Cooper, T. B., Rabinovich, H., Ambrosini, P., Fried, J., Davies, M., Torres, D., & Suckow, R. F. (1987). Relative safety of single versus divided dose imipramine in adolescent major depression. *Journal of the American Academy of Child and Adolescent Psychiatry, 26,* 400–406.

Ryan, N. D., Puig-Antich, J., Cooper, T. B., Rabinovich, H., Ambrosini, P., Davies, M., King, J., Torres, D., & Fried, J. (1986). Imipramine in adolescent major depression: Plasma level and clinical response. *Acta Psychiatrica Scandinavia, 73,* 275–288.

Ryan, N. D., Puig-Antich, J., Rabinovich, H., Fried, J., Ambrosini, P., Meyer, V., Torres, D., Dachille, S., & Mazzie, D. (1988). MAOIs in adolescent major depression unresponsive to tricyclic antidepressants. *Journal of the American Academy of Child and Adolescent Psychiatry, 27,* 755–758.

Schlesser, M. A. (1986). Neuroendocrine abnormalities in affective disorders. In A. J. Rush & K. Z. Altshuler (Eds.), *Depression: Basic mechanisms, diagnosis, and treatment* (pp. 45–71). New York: Guilford.

Schildkraut, J. J. (1965). The catecholamine hypothesis of affective disorders: A review of supporting evidence. *American Journal of Psychiatry, 122,* 509–522.

Schonert-Reichl, K. A. (1994). Gender differences in depressive symptomatology and egocentrism in adolescence. *Journal of Early Adolescence, 14,* 49–64.

Seligman, M. E. P. (1975). *Helplessness: On depression, development, and death.* San Francisco: Freeman.

Seligman, M. E. P., & Peterson, C. (1986). A learned helplessness perspective on childhood depression: Theory and research. In M. Rutter, C. E. Izard, & P. B. Read (Eds.), *Depression in young people: Developmental and clinical perspectives* (pp. 223–249). New York: Guilford.

Shafii, M., & Shafii, S. L. (1992). Dynamic psychotherapy of depression. In M. Shafii & S. L. Shafii (Eds.), *Clinical guide to depression in children and adolescents* (pp. 157–175). Washington, DC: American Psychiatric Press.

Shain, B. N., Naylor, M., & Alessi, N. (1990). Comparison of self-rated and clinician-rated measures of depression in adolescents. *American Journal of Psychiatry, 147,* 793–795.

Silver, L. B. (1988). The scope of the problem in children and adolescents. In J. G. Looney (Ed.), *Chronic mental illness in children and adolescents* (pp. 39–51). Washington, DC: American Psychiatric Press.

Simeon, J., Dinicola, V. F., Ferguson, H. B., & Copping, W. (1990). Adolescent depression: A placebo-controlled fluoxetine treatment study and follow-up. *Progress in Neuropsychopharmacology and Biological Psychiatry, 14,* 791–795.

Smith, C., & Steiner, H. (1992). Psychopathology in anorexia nervosa and depression. *Journal of the American Academy of Child and Adolescent Psychiatry, 31,* 841–843.

Soblen, R. A., & Saunders, J. C. (1961). Monoamine oxidase inhibitor therapy in adolescent psychiatry. *Diseases of the Nervous System, 22,* 96–102.

Sonis, W. A., Yellin, A. M., Garfinkel, B. D., et al. (1987). The antidepressant effect of light in seasonal affective disorder of childhood and adolescence. *Psychopharmacology Bulletin, 23,* 360–363.

Spitzer, R. L., Endicott, J., & Robins, E. (1978) Research Diagnostic Criteria: Rationale and reliability. *Archives of General Psychiatry. 35,* 773–782.

Stone, M. H. (1981). Depression in borderline adolescents. *American Journal of Psychotherapy, 35,* 383–399.

Strauss, C. C., Last, C. G., Hersen, M., & Kazdin, A. E. (1988). Association between anxiety and depression in children and adolescents with anxiety disorders. *Journal of Abnormal Child Psychology, 16,* 57–68.

Strober, M. (1985). Depressive illness in adolescence. *Psychiatric Annals, 15,* 375–378.

Strober, M., Green, J., & Carlson, G. (1981a) Phenomenology and subtypes of major depressive disorders in adolescents. *Journal of Affective Disorders, 3,* 281–290.

Strober, M., Green, J., & Carlson, G. (1981b). Utility of the Beck Depression Inventory with psychiatrically hospitalized adolescents. *Journal of Consulting and Clinical Psychology, 49,* 482–483.

Targum, S. D., Byrnes, S. M., & Sullivan, A. C. (1982). Subtypes of unipolar depression distinguished by the dexamethasone suppression test. *Journal of Affective Disorders, 4,* 21–27.

Teicher, M. H., Glod, C., & Cole, J. O. (1990). Emergence of intense suicidal pre-occupation during fluoxetine treatment. *American Journal of Psychiatry, 147,* 207–210.

Toolan, J. M. (1978). Therapy of depressed and suicidal children. *American Journal of Psychotherapy, 32,* 243–251.

Trautman, P. D., & Rotheram-Borus, M. J. (1988). Cognitive behavior therapy with children and adolescents. In A. J. Frances & R. E. Hales (Eds.), *Review of psychiatry* (Vol. 7, pp. 584–607). Washington, DC: American Psychiatric Press.

Watson, J. S. (1977). Depression and the perception of control in early childhood. In J. G. Schulterbrandt & A. Raskin (Eds.), *Depression in childhood: Diagnosis, treatment and conceptual models* (pp. 123–133). New York: Raven.

Weinberg, W. A., Rutman, J., Sullivan, L., Penick, E. C., & Dietz, S. G. (1973) Depression in children referred to an educational diagnostic center: Diagnosis and treatment. *Journal of Pediatrics, 83,* 1065–1072.

Weissman, M. M. (1990). Evidence for comorbidity of anxiety and depression: Family and genetic studies of children. In J. D. Maser & C. R. Cloninger (Eds.), *Comorbidity of mood and anxiety disorders* (pp. 349–365). Washington, DC: American Psychiatric Press.

Weller, R. A., & Weller, E. B. (1984). Use of tricyclic antidepressants in prepubertal depressed children. In E. B. Weller & R. A. Weller (Eds.), *Current perspectives on major depressive disorders in children* (pp. 50–63). Washington, DC: American Psychiatric Press.

Weller, R. A., & Weller, E. B. (1986). Tricyclic anti-depressants in prepubertal depressed children: Review of the literature. *Hillside Journal of Clinical Psychiatry, 8,* 46–55.

Weller, R. A., Weller, E. B., Fristad, M. A., Cantwell, M. L., Preskorn, S. H. (1986). Dexamethasone suppression test and clinical outcome in prepubertal depressed children. *American Journal of Psychiatry, 143,* 1469–1470.

Whitaker, A., Johnson, J., Shaffer, D., Rapoport, J. L., Kalikow, K., Walsh, B. T., Davies, M., Braiman, S. & Dolinsky, A. (1990). Uncommon troubles in young people: Prevalence estimates of selected psychiatric disorders in a nonreferred adolescent population. *Archives of General Psychiatry, 47,* 487–496.

Williams, J. M. G. (1984). *The psychological treatment of depression.* New York: Free Press.

Wilson, H., & Staton, R. D. (1984). Neuropsychological changes in children associated with tricyclic antidepressant therapy. *International Journal of Neuroscience, 24,* 307–312.

Wirt, R. D., Lachar, D., Klinedinst, J., & Seat, P. D. (1977). *Multidimensional description of child personality: A manual for the Personality Inventory for Children.* Los Angeles: Western Psychological Services.

Wolfe, V. V., Finch, A. J., Saylor, C. F., Blount, R. L., Pallmeyer, T. P., & Carek, D. J. (1987). Negative affectivity in children: A multitrait-multimethod investigation. *Journal of Consulting and Clinical Psychology, 55,* 245–250.

Yanchyshyn, G. W., & Robbins, D. R. (1983) The assessment of depression in normal adolescents: A comparison study. *Canadian Journal of Psychiatry, 28,* 522–526.

Youngerman, J., & Canino, I. A. (1978). Lithium carbonate use in children and adolescents: A survey of the literature. *Archives of General Psychiatry, 35,* 216–224.

Zametkin, A., & Rapoport, J. L. (1983). Tricyclic antidepressants and children. In G. D. Burrows, T. R. Norman, & B. Davies (Eds.). *Drugs in psychiatry: Vol. 1. Antidepressants* (pp. 129–147). New York: Elsevier.

Zimmerman, M., Stangl, D., & Coryell, W. (1985). The Research Diagnostic Criteria for endogenous depression and the dexamethasone suppression test: A discriminant function analysis. *Psychiatry Research, 14,* 197–208.

Zung, W. W. K. (1965) A self-rating depression scale. *Archives of General Psychiatry, 12,* 63–70.

11
Conduct and Oppositional Disorders

Charles M. Borduin
Scott W. Henggeler
Christopher M. Manley

A ntisocial behavior in adolescents represents a significant social and clinical problem. As a social problem, adolescent antisocial behavior has extremely detrimental emotional, physical, and economic effects on victims, their families, and the larger community (Gottfredson, 1989). Antisocial adolescents also consume much of the resources of the child welfare, juvenile justice, and special education systems and are overrepresented in the "deep end" of these systems (Melton & Hargrove, in press; Melton & Spaulding, in press), with considerable cost to the public and intrusion on family integrity and youth autonomy. As a clinical problem, antisocial behavior encompasses from one-third to one-half of all adolescent referrals for mental health services (Gilbert, 1957; Herbert, 1978; Robins, 1981). The immediate costs for these services and for continued contact with the mental health system well into adulthood are difficult to estimate but are undoubtedly exorbitant (Kazdin, 1987b).

The purpose of this chapter is to discuss important conceptual issues and research findings pertaining to the assessment and treatment of antisocial behavior in adolescents. More specifically, we discuss patterns of adolescent antisocial behavior that are referred to as *conduct disorder* and *oppositional defiant disorder* in the fourth edition of the *Diagnostic and Statistical Manual of Mental Disorders (DSM-IV*; American Psychiatric Association, 1993). Also, we examine whether empirical evidence supports a diagnostic distinction between conduct disorder and oppositional defiant disorder in adolescents.

The chapter begins with a description of conduct and oppositional disorders, followed by a discussion of the historical background and epidemiology of these disorders in adolescents. Next we illustrate the type and severity of problems presented by conduct-disordered adolescents and review research findings pertaining to course and prognosis. Recent empirical work on the correlates and causes of conduct disorder in adolescents is then reviewed; this is followed by a discussion of the complications, differential diagnosis, and clinical assessment of this disorder. The final section examines contemporary research on the evaluation of treatment outcomes with conduct-disordered adolescents.

Description of Disorders

Conduct and oppositional disorders are both contained within the sub-classification of disruptive behavior and attention-deficit disorders in the DSM-IV. This subclassification includes syndromes of externalizing behaviors that are more distressful to others than to the person with the disorder.

Conduct Disorder

Many different terms have been used to denote conduct-disordered behaviors in children and adolescents, including *delinquency, antisocial behavior, acting out, externalizing behavior*, and *conduct problems*. In this chapter, the term *conduct disorder* will be used to refer to a persistent pattern of antisocial behavior that significantly impairs the everyday functioning of children or adolescents on several systemic levels (e.g., family, peers, school, community) and is considered uncontrollable by significant others. In DSM-IV, the criteria for diagnosis of conduct disorder are met when at least three of the following antisocial behaviors occur repeatedly over a period of longer than 6 months: stealing (with or without confrontation of the victim); staying out late at night; running away; lying; setting fires; truancy; breaking into houses, buildings, or cars; destroying property; bullying or threatening others; cruelty to people or animals; forcing unwanted sexual activity on others; using weapons; or fighting. In addition, DSM-IV distinguishes between two subtypes of conduct disorder:

1. *Childhood onset type.* The essential feature is the onset of at least one antisocial behavior prior to age 10.
2. *Adolescent onset type.* The main feature is the absence of antisocial behaviors before age 10.

Research is needed to evaluate the reliability of the DSM-IV diagnostic criteria for conduct disorder. Because these criteria are virtually identical to those used in DSM-III-R, however, it seems likely that the reliability of the conduct disorder category in DSM-IV will be similar to that reported for DSM-III-R. Studies evaluating the DSM-III-R diagnostic criteria for conduct disorder have reported interrater reliabilities (expressed as kappa coefficients) ranging from .53 to .75 for the overall category (Strober, Green, & Carlson, 1981; Werry, Methven, Fitzpatrick, & Dixon, 1983).

Although DSM-IV is the predominant classification system in the United States, other clinically derived systems also include a diagnostic category for coding antisocial behavior in children and adolescents. For example, in the ninth revision of the International Classification of Diseases (ICD-9; World Health Organization, 1979), serious antisocial behavior in childhood and adolescence is usually coded within the category "Disturbance of Conduct Not Elsewhere Classified," which includes four subtypes (unsocialized disturbances of conduct, socialized disturbances of conduct, compulsive conduct disorder, and mixed disturbance of conduct and emotions). The interrater reliabilities for these subtypes in the ICD-9 (see Gould, Shaffer, & Rutter, 1984) are generally lower than those reported for the group (i.e., socialized aggressive) and solitary aggressive subtypes of conduct disorder in the DSM-III-R (see Strober et al., 1981; Werry et al., 1983).

Oppositional Defiant Disorder

The essential feature of this disorder, as defined in DSM-IV, is a pattern of "negativistic, hostile, and defiant behavior" (American Psychiatric Association, 1993, p. 11). The pattern of behavior must persist over a period of six months and must include at least four of the following behaviors: temper tantrums, argumentativeness, defying adult requests or rules, blaming others, irritability, anger or resentfulness, or spiteful or vindictive behavior. The diagnosis of oppositional defiant disorder in DSM-IV also requires that the child or adolescent not meet the criteria for conduct disorder. Unlike DSM-IV, ICD-9 does not include a diagnostic category for oppositional defiant disorder; however, a category for this disorder is included in the forthcoming ICD-10.

Considerable debate exists over the utility of distinguishing between conduct disorder and oppositional defiant disorder. Most of the researchers involved in this debate have challenged the reliability of the oppositional disorder category and have argued that the behaviors included in it are likely to be evident in conduct disorder (Achenbach, Conners, Quay, Verhulst, & Howell, 1989; Anderson, Williams, McGee, & Silva, 1987; Costello, Edelbrock, Dulcan, Kalas, & Kloric, 1984; Reeves, Werry, Elkind, & Zametkin, 1987; Rey et al., 1988). In a recent review of factor analytic studies, however, Loeber, Lahey, and Thomas (1991) concluded that although conduct disorder and oppositional defiant disorder are strongly and developmentally related, they are clearly different. Loeber et al. (1991) also concluded that the symptoms of oppositional disorder have an earlier onset than most of the symptoms of conduct disorder, and that almost all youths with the diagnosis of conduct disorder have a history of oppositional defiant disorder (but not the reverse). Nevertheless, the authors reported that lying and mild forms of physical aggression seem to be related to *both* conduct and oppositional disorders. Thus the distinction between oppositional disorder and conduct disorder can only be maintained if the concept of oppositional disorder is expanded to include lying and mild physical aggression.

At present, little evidence supports the reliability or validity of the oppositional disorder category among adolescents. Of course, the issue of whether conduct disorder and oppositional defiant disorder represent distinct disorders or different manifestations of the same disorder in adolescents can only be resolved in future research. Although some factor analytic studies (e.g., Loeber & Schmaling, 1985a; Quay, 1986b) suggest that there are at least two dimensions or groupings of child and adolescent antisocial behavior (i.e., an aggressive dimension composed of oppositional symptoms and "overt" behaviors such as physical fighting and bullying, and a nonaggressive dimension consisting of "covert" delinquent behaviors such as truancy, theft, and association with deviant peers), other factor analytic work has indicated that diverse adolescent problem behaviors (e.g., delinquency, substance use, school problems, early sexual intercourse) reflect a single underlying dimension of behavior (e.g., Donovan & Jessor, 1985; Donovan, Jessor, & Costa, 1988; Jessor & Jessor, 1977; McGee & Newcomb, 1992). Moreover, evidence also suggests that conduct and oppositional disorders in preadolescents are associated with the same family variables (e.g., low maternal monitoring, high family adversity, parental antisocial personality), but to different degrees, suggesting that these disorders may represent more and less severe forms of the same spectrum of behavioral dysfunction (see Frick et al., 1992; Schachar & Wachsmuth, 1990).

Historical Background

Although children and adolescents have evidenced serious conduct problems throughout history, cultures have differed widely in their response to serious forms of youthful misbehavior (see review by Binder, 1987). In the United States, it was only at the beginning of the twentieth century that societal institutions and agencies were established for the specific purpose of remediating conduct problems in youths. One of the earliest mental health facilities designed for the treatment of antisocial behaviors in adolescents was the Juvenile Psychopathic Institution established by William Healy in 1909 (Martin & Hoffman, 1990). Although the federal government's role in developing correctional facilities and programs for juvenile offenders dates back to the creation of the U.S. Children's Bureau in 1912, it was not until 1974, when Congress enacted the Juvenile Justice and Delinquency Prevention Act, that community-based alternatives to the institutionalization of nonviolent and nondangerous delinquent youths (many of whom were housed in facilities with adult criminal offenders) were mandated (Schwartz, 1989).

With regard to the classification of antisocial behavior in youths, Jenkins and Hewitt (1944; Hewitt & Jenkins, 1946) conducted one of the earliest empirical studies. Using 500 case records of delinquent youths referred for treatment, these investigators identified three behavioral syndromes: unsocialized aggressive, socialized delinquent, and overinhibited. These findings and those of later studies by Quay (e.g., 1964; Quay, Peterson, & Consalvi, 1960) were instrumental in the introduction of separate diagnoses of unsocialized aggressive reaction and group delinquent reaction in DSM-II (American Psychiatric Association, 1968). Subsequent efforts (e.g., Quay, 1986b; Robins, 1981) have contributed to the more recent definitions of conduct disorder in DSM-III, DSM-III-R, and DSM-IV (American Psychiatric Association, 1980, 1987, 1993).

Epidemiology

Epidemiological studies have assessed the prevalence of conduct and oppositional disorders in different types of adolescent samples. Prevalence rates often vary according to such factors as geographic location, age, and gender.

Prevalence

The prevalence of conduct and oppositional disorders in adolescents is difficult to estimate, given variations among studies in the criteria that have been used to define these problems. The following prevalence estimates of conduct disorder among preadolescents and adolescents have been reported: 3.4% among 11-year-olds in New Zealand (Anderson et al., 1987); 4% and 10% among 11-year-olds from rural and urban settings, respectively, in England (Graham, 1979; Rutter, Cox, Tupling, Berger, & Yule, 1975; Rutter, Tizard, Yule, Graham, & Whitmore, 1976); 11.6% among 12- to 16-year-old boys in Canada (Offord, Adler, & Boyle, 1986); and 6% among 14- to 16-year-olds in the United States (Kashani et al., 1987).

Only two studies have reported prevalence figures for oppositional defiant disorder in adolescents, with estimates ranging from 5.7% in New Zealand (Anderson et al., 1987) to 8.7% in the United States (Kashani et al., 1987). Since neither of these studies examined rates of co-occurrence of conduct disorder and oppositional disorder, however, substantial overlap between these disorders was most likely.

Gender Differences

Several studies have demonstrated large gender differences in the prevalence of conduct disorder and antisocial behavior in adolescents. Male adolescents evidence considerably higher rates of conduct disorder and serious antisocial behaviors than female adolescents, with male-female prevalence ratios ranging from 3.0 to 12.0 (American Psychiatric Association, 1980, 1987; Graham, 1979; Quay, 1986b). Similarly, prevalence rates of specific types of antisocial behavior are much higher for males than females. For example, based on National Youth Survey data for white adolescents in 1980, Huizinga and Elliott (1987) reported male-female prevalence ratios of 1.2 for status offenses, 2.5 for minor theft, and 4.5 for robbery. Gender differences are also apparent in the age of onset of antisocial behavior; estimates of the median age range from 8 to 10 years of age for boys and 14 to 16 years of age for girls (Robins, 1966).

Clinical Picture

The clinical picture of adolescent conduct disorder can be quite complex. Indeed, many factors pertaining to the individual adolescent, the family system, and extrafamilial systems (e.g., peers, school, neighborhood) can play a role in the development and maintenance of conduct-disordered behavior. A case description of an adolescent with conduct disorder is provided below to illustrate the severity of the possible problems and the contribution of contextual factors to their development and maintenance.

Case Example

Jason is a bright, socially skilled 14-year-old eighth grader who lives at home with his mother and one of his older brothers. Jason was 11 when his mother and father divorced. His natural father was an alcoholic and was physically abusive toward both Jason and his mother. Before the divorce Jason was disruptive at home, refusing to do chores, stealing money from his parents, lying about his whereabouts, and consistently getting into fights with his brother. Following the divorce, Jason's disruptive behavior began to amplify in spite of efforts by Jason's mother to control his problem behaviors. On several occasions he was cruel to animals (e.g., he poisoned a neighbor's cat), and he set several fires in vacant buildings.

Jason's mother worked hard at two different jobs in an effort to meet the family's financial needs. Unfortunately, her work schedule resulted in her being absent from home for long periods of time each day. She developed an intimate relationship with a male coworkers who was an alcoholic; when he subsequently lost his job, he moved into the family's home. The boyfriend spent most of his time drinking beer and watching television, and Jason's mother also began to drink excessively. Further exacerbating the situation, the boyfriend attempted to control Jason's behavior through physical beatings.

By the time Jason entered the seventh grade he was using alcohol and amphetamines on a daily basis, and his grades in school had declined dramatically. He associated almost exclusively with deviant peers who regularly skipped school, shoplifted at the local mall, used drugs, and stayed out all night. He was first referred to juvenile services at the age of 13 after attempting to stab his mother's boyfriend with a butcher knife. Six months later, Jason was expelled from school for brandishing a loaded .22-caliber pistol that he had hidden in his locker. Shortly thereafter he was arrested for using a stolen credit card to obtain $700 from an automatic teller machine at a local bank. Because his behavior was well beyond what his mother could control, Jason was hospitalized at an acute care psychiatric facility for adolescents while he awaited the court date for his criminal offenses. During his stay in the facility, he spent most of his time in a seclusion room due to repeated fistfights with other adolescents and verbal threats toward staff. Jason received suspended sentences from the court and was placed on formal supervision after he and his mother agreed to seek family therapy at a local mental health center.

Comments

This case illustrates the multidimensional nature of conduct disorder in adolescence and the range and severity of the behavior problems that often are involved. The adolescent's problems did not simply represent a defiance of parental authority or a reaction to some stressful life event but involved a broad range of individual (e.g., impulsivity, aggressive behavior, substance abuse) and systemic factors (e.g., family conflict, economic stress on the family, parental substance abuse, association with deviant peers, school difficulties). In addition, there was a progression in the adolescent's behavior problems, beginning with disruptive behaviors in the home and gradually involving more serious conduct problems in extrafamilial systems. Although some cases of adolescent conduct disorder do not progress to life-threatening behaviors, the range and seriousness of deviant behaviors in this case example are by no means atypical. Finally, we wish to emphasize that the factors responsible for the development of the youth's problem behaviors were not identical to the factors that maintained his difficulties over time. For example, association with deviant peers played an important role in maintaining maladaptive behaviors (e.g., substance abuse, poor school performance) by the time the youth had entered the seventh grade; however, such involvement played little if any role in the behavior problems that were evident prior to the parents' divorce.

Course and Prognosis

Antisocial behaviors, especially those involving aggression, tend to be highly stable in individuals (Loeber, 1982) and across generations (Huesmann, Lefkowitz, Eron, & Walder, 1984). In fact, the stability of aggressive behavior in males is only slightly lower than the stability of intelligence (Olweus, 1979). It follows from the stability of such behavior that the prognosis is likely to be poor (Kazdin, 1987b). It is important to recognize, however, that many individuals who show antisocial behaviors during childhood do not display a pattern of serious antisocial behavior upon reaching adolescence. Indeed, antisocial behaviors can be seen in most children over the course of normal development (Kazdin, 1987a), and the proportion of youths who engage in aggressive behaviors gradually decreases from the preschool years to adolescence (Loeber, 1982). Nevertheless, childhood risk factors can be identified that predict serious antisocial behavior in adolescence.

Since the early 1980s a number of longitudinal studies have evaluated the developmental links between adolescent antisocial behavior (or conduct disorder) and its childhood precursors. In addition, several longitudinal studies have examined the course (i.e., stability) of conduct disorder during adolescence and into early adulthood. In the subsections that follow, we summarize the results of some of the recent work in these areas.

Childhood Precursors

Among the strongest predictors of delinquency and antisocial behavior during adolescence are aggression (Huesmann et al., 1984; Magnusson, Stattin, & Duner, 1983) and stealing (Mitchell & Rosa, 1981) during childhood. As noted above, however, the continuity of aggression and other antisocial behaviors is not the same for all individuals. To understand the persistence and progression of deviant behaviors from childhood to adolescence, it is important to appreciate that particular *patterns* of such behaviors during childhood are also relevant. Indeed, researchers (e.g., Loeber, 1982) have concluded that the risk of a later deviant outcome is higher for those children whose problem behavior (a) is more frequent, (b) is more varied, (c) occurs in multiple settings (e.g., both at home and at school), or (d) occurs at an earlier age. Of course, these risk factors can be intercorrelated. For example, a youth who exhibits a variety of problem behaviors at an early age probably also demonstrates them at a relatively high rate and in multiple settings.

Although researchers have devoted greater attention to the prediction of delinquency in adolescents than to the prediction of adolescent conduct disorder per se, there is some evidence that the predictors of delinquency and of conduct disorder are largely the same. For example, Kelso and

Stewart (1986) reported that the strongest predictors of conduct disorder in preadolescent and adolescent boys included the number of conduct problems exhibited in childhood, as well as the early onset of such problems in childhood. Similarly, in one of the few studies to examine prospectively the onset of conduct disorder, Loeber, Green, Lahey, Christ, and Frick (1992) found that a high level of oppositional behavior during childhood predicted the onset of violent acts, theft, and property damage among preadolescent boys.

It should be understood that more than one developmental path leads to clinically severe antisocial behavior (i.e., conduct disorder) during adolescence. In an excellent review of risk factors that influence the course of antisocial and delinquent behavior, Loeber (1990) noted at least three distinct paths leading to antisocial outcomes in adolescents: an "aggressive-versatile path" beginning in the preschool years and involving a great variety of aggressive and nonaggressive conduct problems, as well as hyperactivity; a "nonaggressive path" beginning in late childhood or early adolescence and primarily involving nonaggressive conduct problems (e.g., theft, lying, truancy, substance abuse) that are often committed in the company of deviant peers; and an "exclusive substance abuse path" beginning in early to middle adolescence and involving no appreciable antecedent conduct problems. Although evidence for the existence of these different developmental paths is far from complete, it seems clear that some youths progress more rapidly in the development of antisocial behavior patterns than do others.

Short- and Long-Term Outcomes

A number of prospective studies have shown that aggression and other conduct problems in early adolescence portend criminal behavior in adulthood. For example, in a community sample of 1,027 subjects, Stattin and Magnusson (1989) found a strong association between teacher ratings of boys' and girls' aggressiveness at age 13 and their involvement in criminal activities at age 26. High ratings of aggressiveness were characteristic of both boys and girls who later committed frequent and serious crimes, especially crimes involving violence against persons or property damage. For both sexes, the relation between aggressiveness and crime was largely independent of intelligence and family education. Similarly, in a community sample of 632 subjects who were followed from ages 8 to 30, Huesmann et al. (1984) found that for both boys and girls, the relation between early aggressiveness (as rated by peers) and serious antisocial behavior (including criminal convictions, spouse abuse, and self-reported physical aggression) in adulthood was still significant after partialing out IQ. Finally, in a community sample of 411 boys, Farrington, Loeber, and Van Kammen (1990) found that a composite measure of conduct problems (based on teacher, mother, and peer ratings) at age 10 significantly predicted criminal convictions at age 25.

Prospective and retrospective studies have also shown significant associations between adolescent antisocial behavior and later substance use and abuse, although it appears that these associations are moderated by gender. Using a representative sample of 10th and 11th graders ($N = 1,004$) from public schools in New York State, Kandel, Simcha-Fagan, and Davies (1986) found that self-reported general delinquency at ages 15 and 16 predicted the use of illicit drugs at ages 24 and 25 among men, but not among women. Similarly, in a more recent prospective study using a national probability sample of 2,411 adolescents, Windle (1990) found that various types of self-reported antisocial behaviors (including status, property, and person offenses) at ages 14 and 15 were uniformly related to substance use (including alcohol, cigarettes, marijuana, and other illicit substances) at ages 18 and 19 in men, but not in women; for women, only property offenses (e.g., vandalism) at ages 14 and 15 were linked to substance use at ages 18 and 19. In another recent study using data from the St. Louis sample ($N = 2,572$) of the NIMH Epidemiological Catchment Area project, Lewis and Bucholz (1991) found that serious antisocial behavior before age 15 (as retrospectively reported by subjects) was significantly associated with alcoholism in early adulthood among both men and women. The odds of developing alcoholism following a childhood history of antisocial behavior, however, were more than twice as high for women as for men.

Correlates and Causes

A large number of studies have evaluated correlates of conduct disorder and delinquency in adolescents (for reviews, see Henggeler, 1989; Kazdin, 1987a; Quay, 1987a). In general, these correlates pertain to the individual adolescent and to the key systems (family, peer, school) in which the adolescent is embedded. A number of other studies have evaluated multidimensional causal models of antisocial behavior in adolescents (see review by Henggeler, 1991). This section reviews the major findings that have emerged in these areas of research.

Individual Adolescent Characteristics

There is a substantial body of empirical research showing that conduct disorder and delinquency in adolescents are associated with lower IQ scores, even after controlling for social class and race (Rutter & Giller, 1983). Evidence also suggests that there is a sizable discrepancy between the performance and verbal IQs of conduct-disordered adolescents, and that the association between conduct disorder and IQ is due to the relatively low verbal IQs of these adolescents (Quay, 1987b). Although some researchers have observed an association between the size of the performance–verbal IQ discrepancy and the seriousness of antisocial behavior in adolescents (e.g., Walsh, Petee, & Beyer, 1987), other researchers have not found such a relationship (e.g., Tarter, Hegedus, Alterman, & Katz-Garris, 1983).

The association of low verbal IQ with conduct-disordered behavior might be a result of the linkage between low verbal IQ and the delayed development of higher-order cognitive abilities. For example, researchers (e.g., Arbuthnot, Gordon, & Jurkovic, 1987) have concluded that delinquents in general, and undersocialized aggressive delinquents in particular, have lower moral reasoning maturity than do nondelinquents.

Several researchers have also suggested that social skills deficits are linked with conduct disorder and delinquency in adolescents. In a recent review of this literature, however, Henggeler (1989) concluded that findings have been inconsistent, especially when the influences of mediating factors such as IQ are considered. In contrast, recent studies of sociocognitive deficits in aggressive adolescents have consistently found evidence of hostile attributional biases (for a review, see Akhtar & Bradley, 1991). The association between hostile attributional biases and aggressive behavior seems to be independent of verbal IQ, social class, and race (see Dodge, Price, Bachorowski, & Newman, 1990; Graham, Hudley, & Williams, 1992). Moreover, such attributional biases are linked to forms of aggression that involve interpersonal deficits (undersocialized aggression) but not to deviant behaviors classified as socialized aggression or socialized delinquency (Dodge et al., 1990).

Family Relations

Investigations of the association between family relations and conduct disorder in adolescents have often focused on the area of family affect. A number of studies have demonstrated that undersocialized aggressive conduct disorder in juvenile offenders is associated with low levels of family warmth and supportiveness (e.g., Borduin & Henggeler, 1987; Borduin, Henggeler, Hanson, & Pruitt, 1985) and high rates of marital and family conflict (e.g., Borduin, Pruitt, & Henggeler, 1986; Mann, Borduin, Henggeler, & Blaske, 1990). Likewise, studies using community samples have found that adolescent conduct problems and self-reported delinquent behavior are linked with low parental acceptance and affection (Loeber & Schmaling, 1985b; Patterson & Stouthamer-Loeber, 1984) and high marital and family conflict (Jouriles, Bourg, & Farris, 1991; Tolan & Lorion, 1988). Evidence also suggests that affective relations in families of female delinquents may be even more dysfunctional than those in families of male delinquents (Henggeler, Edwards, & Borduin, 1987; Roff & Wirt, 1984).

Lax and ineffective parental discipline (Henggeler, 1989; Snyder & Patterson, 1987) and parental criminality (Loeber & Dishion, 1983) also have been linked consistently with conduct disorder and delinquency in adolescents. It is interesting that these same family variables (i.e., maternal parenting, paternal antisocial personality disorder) also seem to be associated with oppositional defiant disorder in preadolescent boys, suggesting that conduct disorder and oppositional defiant disorder may share a common etiology, or that they may represent more and less severe forms of the same spectrum of dysfunction (Frick et al., 1992). It is possible, of course, that conduct and oppositional disorders have similar *effects* on parental discipline. Indeed, other recent research (Vuchinich, Bank, & Patterson, 1992) with preadolescent boys and their parents has indicated bidirectional effects between parental discipline practices and child antisocial behavior (see also Lytton, 1990).

Peer Relations

The peer group is important to psychosocial development because it provides adolescents with a sense of belonging, emotional support, and behavioral norms. Within peer groups of many conduct-disordered (i.e., delinquent) adolescents, the sense of belonging and emotional support are evident; however, the group behavioral norms often conflict with societal norms. Moreover, delinquent behavior often serves an adaptive function for these adolescents because it is collaborative and elicits continued peer support and acceptance. In fact, a high percentage of delinquent behavior is carried out with peers (Emler, Reicher, & Ross, 1987), and the youth's involvement with deviant peers is a powerful predictor of both the frequency and the seriousness of his or her antisocial behavior (e.g., Fagan & Wexler, 1987; Hanson, Henggeler, Haefele, & Rodick, 1984; Smith, Visher, & Jarjoura, 1991).

Although association with deviant peers can clearly contribute to delinquent behavior, positive family relations tend to mitigate the effects of such involvement. For example, Poole and Regoli (1979) found that high involvement with delinquent peers was strongly predictive of antisocial behavior under conditions of low family support, but only slightly predictive of antisocial behavior under conditions of high family support; boys who had highly delinquent friends and nonsupportive family relations reported 500% more criminal activity than boys with highly delinquent friends and supportive family relations. Similarly, other researchers (e.g., Dishion, Patterson, Stoolmiller, & Skinner, 1991) have reported that parental discipline and monitoring practices can also buffer the negative effects of involvement with deviant peers.

Several investigators have found that conduct-disordered delinquents are as closely attached to their deviant peers as well-adjusted youths are to their nondeviant peers (e.g., Conger, 1976; Krohn & Massey, 1980). In a review of this literature, Elliott, Huizinga, and Ageton (1985) concluded that the peer relations of conduct-disordered delinquents are qualitatively similar to the peer relations of nondelinquents. However, it seems more likely that these findings hold only among adolescents with problems of socialized (as opposed to undersocialized) aggressive conduct disorder. Indeed, Panella and Henggeler (1986) found that adolescents with under-socialized aggressive conduct disorder, in comparison with well-adjusted adolescents, evidenced less positive affect and less social competence when interacting with both friends and strangers. Blaske, Borduin, Henggeler, and Mann (1989) reported similarly that conduct-disordered adolescents who had committed violent crimes (aggravated assault or assault/battery) were more aggressive toward their peers than were nondelinquent adolescents. Although neither of these studies assessed the sociometric status of these conduct-disordered adolescents, it seems likely that these youths also showed higher rates of rejection by their classmates (see Coie & Dodge, 1983).

School and Academic Performance

Poor school performance (e.g., low grades, special class placement, general reading problems, retention, suspension) and subsequent dropping out of high school have been consistently linked with antisocial behavior and delinquency (see Elliott & Voss, 1974; Hinshaw, 1992). Further, this linkage seems to be independent of such pertinent mediating variables as conduct problems during childhood (Maughan, Gray, & Rutter, 1985) and IQ (Berrueta-Clement, Schweinhart, Barnett, & Weikart, 1987). Academic underachievement and dropping out of school have also been associated with higher rates of criminal activity during early adulthood (e.g., Thornberry, Moore, & Christenson, 1985).

School characteristics also can contribute to antisocial behavior and delinquency. Hellman and Beaton (1986) reported that antisocial behavior in junior high schools was related to low student attendance and to high student-teacher ratios. Delinquent behavior in senior high schools was associated with instability in the student population (i.e., high rates of transfers and new admissions) and with poor academic quality of the school. These relations between school characteristics and in-school delinquent behaviors emerged even after controlling for crime rates in the local communities.

Multidimensional Causal Models

Although the above studies have contributed significantly to our understanding of the different factors associated with conduct disorder and delinquency in adolescents, it should be noted that these investigations generally possess three important methodological limitations. First, in light of the correlational nature of the research, it is impossible to determine whether observed correlates of conduct disorder (or delinquency) led to the conduct-disordered behavior, whether the conduct-disordered behavior led to the correlates, or whether the association is reciprocal. For example, does parental rejection lead to conduct disorder, does conduct disorder lead to parental rejection, or are parental rejection and conduct disorder part of a reciprocal causal structure, mutually influencing one another over time? Second, the association between a particular psychosocial variable and conduct disorder may be spurious (i.e., the result of their joint association with a third variable). For example, low levels of sociomoral reasoning may be linked with conduct disorder because both sociomoral reasoning and conduct disorder are associated with authoritarian discipline strategies. Third, most of the extant studies have tapped only a small subset of the correlates of conduct-disordered behavior. Thus it is not possible to examine the interrelations among the correlates of conduct-disordered behavior to ascertain which variables have direct versus indirect effects on such behavior, or which variables are no longer linked with conduct-disordered behavior when the effects of other correlates are controlled.

To address the inherent limitations of correlational research, several research groups have developed empirically based multidimensional causal models of antisocial behavior in adolescents. For example, Elliott et al. (1985) used a longitudinal design with a representative national sample of adolescents ($N = 1,725$) to assess the psychosocial determinants of delinquent behavior. Across sexes and types of delinquent behavior, path analyses showed that delinquency at time 1 and involvement with delinquent peers at time 2 (1 year later) had direct effects on delinquent behavior at time 2. In addition, delinquent behavior at time 2 was predicted indirectly by family and school difficulties, which predicted involvement with delinquent peers. Similarly, in a cross-sectional study of 7- and 10-grade boys ($N = 136$), Patterson and Dishion (1985) concluded that delinquent behavior was predicted directly by low parental monitoring, low academic skills, and high association with deviant peers. In addition, low social skills and low parental monitoring were indirectly linked with delinquent behavior through their direct linkage with deviant peers. These and other causal modeling studies reviewed by Henggeler (1991) provide consistent support for the view that variance in adolescent antisocial behavior is contributed to directly or indirectly by variables at the individual, family, peer, and school levels.

It is logical to conclude from the results of the causal modeling studies that conduct disorder and delinquency in adolescents are multidetermined. It is important to recognize, however, that the determinants of conduct disorder probably vary according to the developmental stage of the adolescent. Indeed, in a cross-sectional study that included community samples of

12-year-old (*n* = 122), 15-year-old (*n* = 138), and 18-year-old (*n* = 81) boys, LaGrange and White (1985) found considerable differences between age groups in the strengths of the predictors of delinquent behavior. Results showed that association with delinquent peers was a strong predictor for 12-year-olds and 18-year-olds, whereas family relations and school influences were strong predictors for 15-year-olds; social class was also a strong predictor for 18-year-olds, but not for the other age groups. Although this study had some significant methodological limitations (e.g., samples were quite small and included few chronic offenders; measures were based exclusively on adolescent self-reports), the findings suggest that age is an important mediating variable that must be considered in the development of future causal models of adolescent antisocial behavior.

Complications

Conduct disorder in adolescents can be complicated by a number of other specific disorders, including substance use disorders, attention-deficit hyperactivity disorder, anxiety disorders, and depression. Because each of these disorders is comprehensively addressed in other chapters in this book, the reader should rely on the relevant chapters for information pertaining to the assessment and treatment of each problem. A brief review of recent research pertaining to the comorbidity of conduct disorder and each of these other disorders in adolescents is provided below.

Substance Use Disorders

Although it is difficult to pinpoint how many adolescents at a particular age meet the diagnostic criteria for both conduct disorder and substance abuse, numerous studies indicate that substance abuse is often associated with other antisocial behaviors in adolescents (e.g., Donovan et al., 1988) and young adults (e.g., Jessor, Donovan, & Costa, 1991). In addition, findings from recent multivariate research (e.g., Elliott et al., 1985; Rhodes & Jason, 1990) reveal that the causes and correlates of adolescent substance abuse are quite similar to those identified for adolescent antisocial behavior in general (see reviews by Henggeler, 1989, in press; Kazdin, 1987a).

Attention-Deficit Hyperactivity Disorder

Several studies (e.g., Anderson et al., 1987; Prinz, Connor, & Wilson, 1981) have reported considerable overlap between the symptoms of conduct disorder and those of attention-deficit hyperactivity disorder in children and adolescents. In addition, reviewers have suggested that these disorders share similar etiological factors and have similar prognoses (e.g.,

Taylor, 1986). Recent factor analytic studies (Hinshaw, 1987; Quay, 1986a) have yielded distinct factors corresponding to each disorder, however, and other investigations have pointed to disparate family risk patterns, early background factors, and later criminal behaviors for the two disorders (Faraone, Biederman, Keenan, & Tsuang, 1991; Farrington et al., 1990). Nevertheless, it would be premature to conclude that the two disorders, which overlap by as much as 60% in some samples (e.g., Farrington et al., 1990; Walker et al., 1991), are part of different developmental sequences leading to delinquency and crime.

Anxiety Disorders

Few investigations have evaluated the co-occurrence of conduct disorder and anxiety disorder in children or adolescents. In a recent study of 7- to 12-year-old boys ($N = 177$) referred to a university outpatient clinic, however, Walker et al. (1991) reported that 42 (62%) of the 68 boys who met DSM-III-R criteria for conduct disorder also had a coexisting anxiety disorder (i.e., overanxious disorder). In addition, boys with coexisting conduct disorder and anxiety disorder had fewer police contacts for index offenses (0.2 versus 0.6), fewer school suspensions (1.8 versus 4.7), and fewer "fight most" nominations from peers (3.4 versus 10.8) than did boys with conduct disorder without comorbid anxiety disorder. Walker et al. concluded that their findings, together with prior research (Quay & Love, 1977) showing an inverse relation between levels of anxiety and rates of recidivism in delinquents, indicated that high levels of anxiety tend to inhibit serious antisocial behavior in youths with conduct disorder.

Although high levels of anxiety may inhibit some types of antisocial behavior in youths who are not seriously delinquent, it is dangerous to assume that such anxiety promotes inhibition of serious antisocial behavior in adolescents with severe conduct disorders. Indeed, in a recent study evaluating the characteristics of adolescent sex offenders (each of whom averaged more than three arrests), Blaske et al. (1989) found that these offenders reported higher rates of anxiety and more interpersonal isolation than did demographically matched groups of assaultive offenders, nonviolent offenders, or nondelinquent adolescents.

Depression

The number of children who manifest both conduct disorder and depression is greater than would be expected by chance, ranging from 3.5% of children in community samples (Cole & Carpentieri, 1990) to approximately 20% of children in clinical samples (e.g., Geller, Chestnut, Miller, Price, & Yates, 1985; Puig-Antich, 1982). Although less is known about the comorbidity of conduct disorder and depression in samples of adolescents than in samples of younger children, a recent longitudinal study (Capaldi, 1991) evaluated the temporal relation between these disorders in a community sample of adolescent boys ($N = 203$). Using multiple methods (self-report and direct observation) and informants (teacher, parent, and adolescent), Capaldi reported that 13% of the adolescents evidenced both severe conduct problems and severe depressed mood when the boys were 12 years of age. Longitudinal analyses revealed that boys who showed severe conduct problems but not severe depressed mood at age 12 were at high risk to develop severe depressed mood by age 14. Boys who showed only severe depressed mood at age 12, however, were not at increased risk for developing severe conduct problems by age 14.

Differential Diagnosis

As described in the previous section, conduct disorder in adolescents can be complicated by a number of other disorders. Perhaps the most important differential diagnosis pertains to the distinctions between conduct disorder and attention-deficit hyperactivity disorder (ADHD). The central features of ADHD are developmentally inappropriate degrees of inattention (i.e., short attention span), impulsivity, and hyperactivity (American Psychiatric Association, 1987, 1993). In addition, children and adolescents with ADHD often show negativism, aggressive behavior, and other features of conduct or oppositional disorder. Similarly, youths with conduct-disordered behaviors may also show symptoms of ADHD. In DSM-III-R and DSM-IV, children and adolescents who meet criteria can receive both diagnoses. Because the age of onset of ADHD is typically before age 7 (American Psychiatric Association, 1987, 1993), a detailed history of childhood behavior disorders is essential for distinguishing between conduct disorder and ADHD in an adolescent client.

It is also important to distinguish conduct disorder from adjustment disorder with disturbance of conduct, as well as from other isolated antisocial behaviors. For adjustment disorder with disturbance of conduct, the central feature is conduct that involves a violation of societal norms (e.g., truancy, vandalism) or the rights of others (e.g., fighting) and that can be linked to the onset of a particular stressor or change (American Psychiatric Association, 1987, 1993). The behavior problems must have occurred within 3 months of the stressor and must not have persisted for more than 6 months; problems would be expected to diminish over time as the impact of the stressor decreased. If the disturbance of conduct continues, the diagnosis can be changed to conduct disorder.

Finally, some symptoms related to bipolar disorder (e.g., irritability, antisocial behavior) can be mistaken for conduct disorder symptomatology. Again, however, these behaviors are usually transitory and thus can be distinguished from the more persistent pattern of antisocial behavior that is characteristic of conduct disorder.

Assessment

Traditionally, assessment of conduct-disordered adolescents has focused on a relatively narrow range of adolescent behaviors and personality traits (e.g., impulsiveness, aggressiveness, psychopathy, sensation seeking). In light of recent evidence pertaining to the correlates and causes of conduct disorder in adolescents, however, it has become apparent that the scope of assessment needs to be broadened beyond the individual adolescent. In this section we present some general guidelines pertaining to the assessment of conduct-disordered adolescents and the systems in which they are embedded. For a more extensive discussion of these guidelines and of specific assessment procedures, see Henggeler and Borduin (1990).

It is essential to conceptualize adolescent conduct disorder within a framework that considers the youth's broader systemic context. More specifically, the therapist should attempt to determine how the adolescent's problem behaviors "fit" with the individual characteristics of the adolescent (e.g., intellectual functioning, moral reasoning, attributional processes), the nature of family relations (e.g., affective qualities of parent-adolescent and marital relations), and the many extrafamilial variables (e.g., peer relations, school performance) that can be linked with the presenting problems. The delineation of this fit has direct implications for the interventions that will be selected for implementation.

Key systems should be evaluated through multiple methods, and multiple perspectives should also be assessed. For example, family relations can be assessed through interviews with the entire family or discussions with various family subsystems and individual family members. Interviews with the entire family can provide the therapist with an opportunity to observe parent-adolescent interaction patterns and to obtain important information concerning areas of agreement and conflict in the family. Similarly, discussions with the parental dyad can often provide the therapist with an opportunity to assess marital relations and interparental cooperation.

Information about the adolescent's peer group should be obtained from teachers, parents, siblings, and the adolescent. The assessor should ask the teacher about the general reputations of the adolescent's friends; the parents and siblings should also be asked about their impressions of these friends. (It is a negative sign if the adolescent has kept the parents from having much contact with his or her peers.) Often the adolescent will be quite open about his or her friends: he or she will describe the nature of their social activities, how they are performing in school, what their outside interests are, and what their families are like. In addition to obtaining reports from significant others, the therapist may also arrange to meet the youth's peers to obtain firsthand impressions and information. Such assessment strategies rely heavily on the ability of the therapist to synthesize information (which is sometimes conflicting) and to "read" people.

Although parents often emphasize problems that the adolescent presents within the family, we recommend that the therapist always evaluate the adolescent's academic and social functioning in school. Academic and social difficulties frequently reflect the same underlying systemic dysfunctions; an understanding of one area of difficulty thus can facilitate an understanding of the other. In addition, information provided by the teachers can be used by the therapist to confirm or disconfirm impressions of the family and the peer group. The therapist should always ask the teachers whether the adolescent displays behavior problems in school, and these problems present any special difficulties to the teachers. The therapist should also evaluate the adolescent's relationships with teachers; in some cases, the therapist will find that the adolescent's difficulties are associated with a school environment that does not fully promote the adolescent's motivation and efforts to learn. Hence the process and direction of treatment can vary considerably based on information that is provided by teachers.

To our knowledge, no single measure of antisocial behavior has sufficient validity for identifying clinically significant levels of antisocial activity in adolescents. Although a number of diagnostic interviews can be used to identify subtypes of conduct disorder in adolescents, these measures yield categorical information and do not indicate the severity of specific symptoms or of overall dysfunction. Parent and teacher rating scales can be employed to assess severity along various dimensions of problem behavior in adolescents; however, such scales rely on global judgments and show little or no agreement between raters. These ambiguities, coupled with the wide range of other variables that correlate with conduct disorder and that may be as important as the adolescent's antisocial behavior, make it difficult for us to recommend a circumscribed set of measures for assessment purposes. Moreover, in working with conduct-disordered adolescents for 15 years, we have found that the vast majority of assessment instruments rarely provide information that is not already discernable from the multimethod, multiperspective assessment outlined above. An exception pertains to the evaluation of academic difficulties in school, where information is often required about the adolescent's intellectual strengths and weaknesses as well as his or her actual level of achievement. Intellectual tests and achievement tests are useful toward this end.

Clinical Management

The preceding review has several important implications regarding the design of effective treatments of conduct disorder in adolescents. First, in light of the many ways in which conduct disorder can be expressed (Osgood, Johnston, O'Malley, & Bachman, 1988), treatments should possess the flexibility to address a broad range of antisocial behaviors. Second, the multicausal nature of conduct disorder (Henggeler, 1991) suggests that treatments must consider variables that reflect major determinants of antisocial behavior (e.g., adolescent cognitions, family relations, peer relations, and school performance). Third, the intransigence and stability of conduct disorder (Loeber, 1982) suggest that treatments must be intensive.

As described below, few treatments incorporate each of the aforementioned implications. Hence it is not surprising that Kazdin (1987b) concluded that "the significance of conduct disorder is heightened by the absence of clearly effective treatments" (p. 188). Similarly, Henggeler (1989) argued that historically poor outcomes in the treatment of antisocial behavior may have resulted from the prevailing tendency of most treatments to address only a small portion of the factors that might contribute to a particular youth's antisocial behavior. Indeed, recent evidence suggests that serious conduct disorder can be ameliorated when treatment is intense, broad based, and multifaceted. The following review examines the contemporary outcome literature regarding delinquency and substance abuse, the aspects of conduct disorder expressed most frequently in adolescents.

Delinquency

Reviewers of the delinquency treatment outcome literature have drawn discrepant conclusions. On the one hand, several major reviews published in the late 1970s concluded that "nothing works" (Lipton, Martinson, & Wilks, 1975; Romig, 1978; Wright & Dixon, 1977). Similarly, in a more recent meta-analysis, Whitehead and Lab (1989) concluded that delinquency treatments have little positive impact on recidivism, and that many treatments seem to exacerbate the problem. On the other hand, several reviewers have suggested that promising delinquency treatments have emerged (Basta & Davidson, 1988; Greenwood & Zimring, 1985). As emphasized by Andrews et al. (1990), these treatments tend to focus on identified correlates of antisocial behavior in adolescents.

The present review focuses on these "promising" treatments. In general, we conclude that such treatments have beneficial effects on instrumental outcomes (Rosen & Proctor, 1981) that are the focus of the particular treatment (e.g., role-playing to learn social skills). Because of their narrow focus, however, these approaches have had minimal effects on ultimate outcomes such as recidivism and self-reported delinquency. Broad-based, multifaceted treatments, though, have recently demonstrated considerable success regarding both instrumental and ultimate outcomes.

Cognitive and Behavioral Skills Training. Skills training approaches assume that juvenile offenders lack cognitive and interpersonal skills for managing challenges in family, peer, and school situations. Thus, through techniques such as modeling and behavioral rehearsal, offenders are taught strategies for improving problem solving, moral reasoning, anger control, and interpersonal relations.

Guerra and Slaby (1990) conducted what may be the best-designed evaluation of a cognitive and behavioral skills training approach with juvenile offenders. In contrast with most of the research in this area, the focused on a serious clinical sample of incarcerated adolescents, included an attention placebo condition, and examined the generalization of their results. Findings, however, paralleled the vast majority of outcomes in this area (Henggeler, 1989). Relative to youths in the control conditions, those who received cognitive and behavioral skills training showed (a) greater improvements on instrumental outcomes (e.g., social problem-solving measures), (b) modest changes in behavior problems inside the institutional setting, and (c) no differences in antisocial behavior outside the institution at a 24-month follow-up.

Similarly, well-designed studies of social skills training have failed to demonstrate effects on antisocial behavior in the natural environment (e.g., Sarason & Ganzer, 1973; Spence & Marzillier, 1981), leading reviewers to conclude that the durability of social skills acquired during training has not been established (Gresham & Lemanek, 1983; Henderson & Hollin, 1983). Reviewers also have noted that the effectiveness of problem-solving skills training and moral reasoning training have not been demonstrated with clinical samples of antisocial adolescents (Gordon & Arbuthnot, 1987; Kazdin, 1987b). A multifacted and intense cognitive and skills training approach (i.e., Aggression Replacement Training; Goldstein & Glick, 1987), though, has shown some generalization to the natural environment, and the authors recommended that treatment also encompass factors in the offenders' interpersonal systems that contribute to antisocial behavior.

Family Therapy. Family therapy approaches attempt to change aspects of family relations that correlate with delinquency (e.g., lax parental discipline, conflict, low affection). A growing consensus among reviewers is that to be potentially effective, treatments of conduct disorder should be family based (Henggeler, Borduin, & Mann, 1992; Miller & Prinz, 1990; Mulvey, Arthur, & Reppucci, 1990).

Behavioral parent training (Patterson, 1982) is the best researched family-based treatment for conduct disorder, and this approach has shown considerable success with young children (Miller & Prinz, 1990). Behavioral parent training, however, has had limited success when used with antisocial adolescents. For example, Bank, Marlowe, Reid, Patterson, and Weinrott (1991) evaluated the effectiveness of such training with families of chronic juvenile offenders and found that treatment had minimal influence on family functioning and no long-term effect on recidivism.

Functional family therapy (FFT; Alexander & Parsons, 1982) integrates treatment strategies from systems theory and behavior therapy and has been regarded as one of the most promising treatments of antisocial behavior in adolescents (Kazdin, 1988). The initial evaluation of FFT was a well-designed study conducted with adolescent status offenders; FFT was effective at decreasing subsequent status offenses but not criminal offenses (Alexander & Parsons, 1973; Parsons & Alexander, 1973). More recently, quasi-experimental studies with significant methodological shortcomings have supported its effectiveness in ameliorating more serious antisocial behavior (Barton, Alexander, Waldron, Turner, & Warburton, 1985; Gordon, Arbuthnot, Gustafson, & McGreen, 1988).

Multisystemic therapy (MST; Henggeler & Borduin, 1990) has received the most support as an effective treatment of serious antisocial behavior in adolescents. MST is an individualized and highly flexible family- and home-based treatment that devotes considerable attention to problems experienced by family members and the multiple systems (e.g., peer, school, neighborhood) in which the members are embedded. In an initial outcome study conducted with inner-city delinquents (Henggeler et al., 1986), MST had strong effects on numerous measures of instrumental outcome (reduction in reported behavior problems, decreased association with deviant peers, and improved family relations). In a study of adolescent sexual offenders (Borduin, Henggeler, Blaske, & Stein, 1990), MST was relatively effective at reducing subsequent recidivism for both sexual offenses and nonsexual crimes. Henggeler, Melton, and Smith (1992) likewise established the efficacy of MST in the treatment of serious adolescent offenders with regard to key measures of ultimate outcome at a 59-week follow-up (e.g., rearrests, self-reported delinquency, time incarcerated). Moreover, results from a 2-year follow-up (Henggeler, Melton, Smith, Schoenwald, & Hanley, 1993) further support the long-term efficacy of MST. Similarly, Borduin et al. (1994; see also Mann et al., 1990) demonstrated the relative effectiveness of MST regarding numerous instrumental and ultimate outcomes in the treatment of chronic juvenile offenders. Most importantly, substantial between-groups differences in recidivism were demonstrated at a 4-year follow-up. The success of MST, especially in comparison with results from other treatment approaches, has been attributed to the match between MST intervention foci and empirically identified determinants of antisocial behavior, as well as the individualized and flexible use of well-validated interventions in the natural environment (Henggeler, Borduin, & Mann, 1992).

Peer-based interventions. Guided-Group Interaction (GGI) and its derivatives (e.g., Positive Peer Culture) are the most widely used peer-based treatments for delinquency. In general, GGI provides daily group discussions aimed at confronting negative behavior and reinforcing positive behavior. Gottfredson (1987) concluded that GGI-like approaches have proliferated despite little support for their effectiveness. In fact, based on aforementioned findings that association with deviant peers is a powerful predictor of antisocial behavior, treating delinquents in groups may exacerbate their problems. Feldman, Caplinger, and Wodarski (1983) support this contention; in a well-designed study, they found that antisocial adolescents showed the greatest behavioral gains when placed in groups with prosocial peers. In contrast, behavior frequently deteriorated in antisocial adolescents placed in groups with similar youths.

Substance Abuse

Reviewers have concluded that minimal evidence supports the effectiveness of any particular treatment of adolescent substance abuse when compared with no intervention (Beschner & Friedman, 1985; Martin & Wilkinson, 1989; Newcomb & Bentler, 1989; Schinke, Botvin, & Orlandi, 1991). In fact, few controlled evaluations of treatment effectiveness with adolescent substance abusers have been conducted. Several large-scale, uncontrolled descriptive studies, however, document positive pretest–posttest changes on variables such as criminal activity and alcohol use (Friedman, Glickman, & Morrissey, 1986; Hubbard, Rachel, Graddock, & Cavanaugh, 1984; Rush, 1979; Sells & Simpson, 1979). Unfortunately, the conclusion that treatment produced such changes is mitigated by several inherent design factors, including (a) the limitations on causal inferences from one-group pretest–posttest designs (Cook & Campbell, 1979), (b) the impossibility of ruling out self-selection effects when random assignment is not used, and (c) the inability to control for normative decreases in antisocial behavior (Farrington, 1987) and substance abuse (Jessor, 1982) from adolescence to early adulthood.

This review examines those few studies in which random assignment to treatment conditions has been used. Consistent with conclusions in the delinquency literature, reviewers generally concur that potentially effective treatments of substance abuse should address the identified correlates of substance abuse and should recognize the multiple determinants of the problem (e.g., Dishion, Patterson, & Reid, 1988; Morgan, Wallack, & Buchanan, 1989; Rhodes & Jason, 1990; Tolan, 1990). Thus the review focuses on cognitive-behavioral interventions and family therapy approaches.

Cognitive and Behavioral Skills Training. Several investigators have developed multicomponent intervention approaches that combine cognitive and behavioral skills training (sometimes with social network development) into a curriculum administered to groups of adolescents. The curriculum content generally focuses on improving the adolescent's cognitive and interpersonal skills for managing challenges in family and peer situations, and on selecting peers who will support prosocial skills and drug abstinence. Although the efficacy of such approaches has not been evaluated with substance-abusing adolescents, cognitive and behavioral skills training have proven successful at preventing adolescent substance abuse (Botvin, Baker, Dusenbury, Tortu, & Botvin, 1990; Gilchrist, Schinke, Trimble, & Cvetkovich, 1987; Johnson et al., 1990). The approach, however, has had minimal long-term effects on the substance use of adult drug abusers (Hawkins, Catalano, Gillmore, & Wells, 1989). Thus it remains to be determined whether positive effects obtained in nonclinical samples will generalize to clinical samples.

Family-Based Treatments. Several investigators have conducted well-controlled evaluations of the effectiveness of family-based treatments for adolescent substance abuse. Unfortunately, these studies usually contrasted two different types of family-based interventions rather than contrasting family therapy with a distinctly different approach or with a no-treatment control. Thus, when minimal between-groups differences emerged at posttest or follow-up, interpretations of outcome were subject to the same limitations in causal inferences as noted above for one-group, pretest–posttest designs.

Szapocznik, Kurtines, Foote, Perez-Vidal, and Hervis (1983, 1986) evaluated the relative effectiveness of conjoint brief strategic family therapy (BSFT) versus one-person BSFT and found few between-groups differences in outcome at posttest or follow-up. Lewis, Piercy, Sprenkle, and Trepper (1990) contrasted brief family therapy with a didactic, family-oriented educational intervention and found modest and qualified (32% of adolescents increased drug use) support for the effectiveness of brief family therapy. Friedman (1989) compared functional family therapy with parent groups and found few between-groups differences in outcome at follow-up. Finally, Henggeler et al. (1991) analyzed drug-related outcome data from two independent evaluations of MST with serious juvenile offenders and found significant between-groups differences in self-reported drug use and drug-related arrests. Findings were mitigated, however, by the fact that the adolescents were not identified substance abusers. Clearly, the priority of future investigations should be to contrast family therapy with another viable treatment, including a usual-services comparison if at all possible.

Summary

This chapter has highlighted important conceptual issues and research findings in several areas related to antisocial behavior in adolescents. Although there are still gaps in our knowledge concerning the utility and validity of distinguishing between conduct disorder and oppositional-defiant disorder in adolescents, extant research does not provide strong support for making such a distinction. Further, although our understanding of conduct-disordered behavior in adolescents is far from complete, multidimensional causal models of antisocial behavior in adolescents have pointed to the complex and reciprocal interplay between important characteristics of adolescents and the social systems in which they are embedded. Moreover, in contrast to the conclusions of many reviewers, it is proposed that adolescent conduct disorders can be treated efficaciously. To be effective, however, such treatments should be intensive, should possess the flexibility to address a broad range of antisocial behaviors, and should be capable of addressing the multiple factors that can maintain such behaviors.

References

Achenbach, T. M., Conners, C. K., Quay, H. C., Verhulst, F. C., & Howell, C. T. (1989). Replication of empirically derived syndromes as a basis for taxonomy of child/adolescent psychopathology. *Journal of Abnormal Child Psychology, 17*, 299–320.

Akhtar, N., & Bradley, E. J. (1991). Social information processing deficits of aggressive children: Present findings and implications for social skills training. *Clinical Psychology Review, 11*, 621–644.

Alexander, J. F., & Parsons, B. V. (1973). Short-term behavioral intervention with delinquent families: Impact on family process and recidivism. *Journal of Abnormal Psychology, 81*, 219–225.

Alexander, J. F., & Parsons, B. V. (1982). *Functional family therapy.* Monterey, CA: Brooks/Cole.

American Psychiatric Association. (1968). *Diagnostic and statistical manual of mental disorders* (2nd ed.). Washington, DC: Author.

American Psychiatric Association. (1980). *Diagnostic and statistical manual of mental disorders* (3rd ed.). Washington, DC: Author.

American Psychiatric Association. (1987). *Diagnostic and statistical manual of mental disorders* (rev. 3rd ed.). Washington, DC: Author.

American Psychiatric Association. (1993). *DSM-IV draft criteria.* Washington, DC: Author.

Anderson, J. C., Williams, S., McGee, R., & Silva, P. A. (1987). DSM-III disorders in preadolescent children: Prevalence in a large sample from the general population. *Archives of General Psychiatry, 44*, 69–76.

Andrews, D. A., Zinger, I., Hoge, R. D., Bonta, J., Gendreau, P., & Cullen, F. T. (1990). Does correctional treatment work? A clinically relevant and psychologically informed meta-analysis. *Criminology, 28*, 369–404.

Arbuthnot, J., Gordon, D. A., & Jurkovic, G. J. (1987). Personality. In H. C. Quay (Ed.), *Handbook of juvenile delinquency* (pp. 139–183). New York: Wiley.

Bank, L., Marlowe, J. H., Reid, J. B., Patterson, G. R., & Weinrott, M. R. (1991). A comparative evaluation of parent-training interventions for families of chronic delinquents. *Journal of Abnormal Child Psychology, 19*, 15–33.

Barton, C., Alexander, J. F., Waldron, H., Turner, C. W., & Warburton, J. (1985). Generalizing treatment effects of functional family therapy: Three replications. *American Journal of Family Therapy, 13,* 16–26.

Basta, J. M., & Davidson, W. S. (1988). Treatment of juvenile offenders: Study outcomes since 1980. *Behavioral Sciences and the Law, 6,* 355–384.

Berrueta-Clement, J. R., Schweinhart, L. J., Barnett, W. S., & Weikart, D. P. (1987). The effects of early educational intervention on crime and delinquency in adolescence and early adulthood. In J. D. Burchard & S. N. Burchard (Eds.), *Prevention of delinquent behavior* (pp. 220–240). Newbury Park, CA: Sage.

Beschner, G. M., & Friedman, A. S. (1985). Treatment of adolescent drug abusers. *International Journal of the Addictions, 20,* 971–993.

Binder, A. (1987). An historical and theoretical introduction. In H. C. Quay (Ed.), *Handbook of juvenile delinquency* (pp. 1–32). New York: Wiley.

Blaske, D. M., Borduin, C. M., Henggeler, S. W., & Mann, B. J. (1989). Individual, family, and peer characteristics of adolescent sex offenders and assaultive offenders. *Developmental Psychology, 25,* 846–855.

Borduin, C. M., & Henggeler, S. W. (1987). Post-divorce mother-son relations of delinquent and well-adjusted adolescents. *Journal of Applied Developmental Psychology, 8,* 273–288.

Borduin, C. M., Henggeler, S. W., Blaske, D. M. & Stein, R. (1990). Multisystemic treatment of adolescent sexual offenders. *International Journal of Offender Therapy and Comparative Criminology, 34,* 105–113.

Borduin, C. M., Henggeler, S. W., Hanson, C. L., & Pruitt, J. A. (1985). Verbal problem solving in families of father-absent and father-present delinquent boys. *Child and Family Behavior Therapy, 7,* 51–63.

Borduin, C. M., Mann, B. J., Cone, L., Henggeler, S. W., Fucci, B. R., Blaske, D. M., & Williams, R. A. (1994). *Multisystemic treatment of serious juvenile offenders: Long-term prevention of criminality and violence.* Manuscript submitted for publication.

Borduin, C. M., Pruitt, J. A., & Henggeler, S. W. (1986). Family interactions in Black, lower-class families with delinquent and nondelinquent adolescent boys. *Journal of Genetic Psychology, 147,* 333–342.

Botvin, G. J., Baker, E., Dusenbury, L., Tortu, S., & Botvin, E. M. (1990). Preventing adolescent drug abuse through a multimodal cognitive-behavioral approach: Results of a 3-year study. *Journal of Consulting and Clinical Psychology, 58,* 437–446.

Capaldi, D. M. (1991, April). *Antisocial behavior and depression in young adolescent boys: Longitudinal analyses of family and adjustment variables.* Paper presented at the meeting of the Society for Research in Child Development, Seattle.

Coie, J. D., & Dodge, K. A. (1983). Continuities and changes in children's social status: A five-year longitudinal study. *Merrill-Palmer Quarterly, 29,* 261–282.

Cole, D. A., & Carpentieri, S. (1990). Social status and the comorbidity of child depression and conduct disorder. *Journal of Consulting and Clinical Psychology, 58,* 748–757.

Conger, R. (1976). Social control and social learning models of delinquent behavior: A synthesis. *Criminology, 14,* 17–40.

Cook, T., & Campbell, D. (1979). *Quasi-experimentation*. Skokie, IL: Rand McNally.

Costello, A. J., Edelbrook, C., Dulcan, M. K., Kalas, R., & Kloric, S. H. (1984). Report on the Diagnostic Interview Schedule for Children (DISC). Pittsburgh, PA: University of Pittsburgh.

Dishion, T. J., Patterson, G. R., & Reid, J. R. (1988). Parent and peer factors associated with sampling in early adolescence: Implications for treatment. In E. R. Rahdert & J. Grabowski (Eds.), *Adolescent drug abuse: Analyses of treatment research* (NIDA Monograph, DHHS Publication No. ADM 88-1523, pp. 69–93). Washington, DC: U.S. Government Printing Office.

Dishion, T. J., Patterson, G. R., Stoolmiller, M., & Skinner, M. L. (1991). Family, school, and behavioral antecedents to early adolescent involvement with antisocial peers. *Developmental Psychology, 27,* 172–180.

Dodge, K. A., Price, J. M., Bachorowski, J., & Newman, J. M. (1990). Hostile attributional biases in severely aggressive adolescents. *Journal of Abnormal Psychology, 99,* 385–392.

Donovan, J. E., & Jessor, R. (1985). Structure of problem behavior in adolescence and young adulthood. *Journal of Consulting and Clinical Psychology, 53,* 890–904.

Donovan, J. E., Jessor, R., & Costa, F. M. (1988). Syndrome of problem behavior in adolescence: A replication. *Journal of Consulting and Clinical Psychology, 56,* 762–765.

Elliott, D. S., Huizinga, D., & Ageton, S. S. (1985). *Explaining delinquency and drug use*. Beverly Hills, CA: Sage.

Elliott, D. S., & Voss, H. (1974). *Delinquency and dropout*. Lexington, MA: Heath.

Emler, N., Reicher, S., & Ross, A. (1987). The social context of delinquent conduct. *Journal of Child Psychology and Psychiatry, 28,* 99–109.

Fagan, J., & Wexler, S. (1987). Family origins of violent delinquents. *Criminology, 25,* 643–669.

Faraone, S. V., Biederman, J., Keenan, K., & Tsuang, M. T. (1991). Separation of DSM-III attention deficit disorder and conduct disorder: Evidence from a family-genetic study of American child psychiatric patients. *Psychological Medicine, 21,* 109–121.

Farrington, D. P. (1987). Epidemiology. In H. C. Quay (Ed.), *Handbook of juvenile delinquency* (pp. 33–61). New York: Wiley.

Farrington, D. P., Loeber, R., & Van Kammen, W. B. (1990). Long-term criminal outcomes of hyperactivity-impulsivity-attention deficit and conduct problems in childhood. In L. Robins & M. Rutter (Eds.), *Straight and devious pathways from childhood to adulthood* (pp. 62–81). New York: Cambridge.

Feldman, R. A., Caplinger, T. E., & Wodarski, J. S. (1983). *The St. Louis conundrum: The effective treatment of antisocial youths*. Englewood Cliffs, NJ: Prentice-Hall.

Frick, P. J., Lahey, B. B., Loeber, R., Stouthamer-Loeber, M., Christ, M. A. G., & Hanson, K. (1992). Familial risk factors to oppositional defiant disorder and conduct disorder: Parental psychopathology and maternal parenting. *Journal of Consulting and Clinical Psychology, 60,* 49–55.

Friedman, A. S. (1989). Family therapy vs. parent groups: Effects on adolescent drug abusers. *American Journal of Family Therapy, 17,* 335–347.

Friedman, A. S., Glickman, N. W., & Morrissey, M. R. (1986). Prediction to successful treatment outcome by client characteristics and retention in treatment in adolescent drug treatment programs: A large-scale cross validation study. *Journal of Drug Education, 16,* 149–165.

Geller, B., Chestnut, E. C., Miller, M. D., Price, D. T., & Yates, E. (1985). Preliminary data on DSM-III associated features of major depressive disorder in children and adolescents. *American Journal of Psychiatry, 142,* 643–644.

Gilbert, G. M. (1957). A survey of "referral problems" in metropolitan child guidance centers. *Journal of Clinical Psychology, 13,* 37–42.

Gilchrist, L. D., Schinke, S. P., Trimble, J. E., & Cvetkovich, G. T. (1987). Skills enhancement to prevent substance abuse among American Indian adolescents. *International Journal of the Addictions, 22,* 869–879.

Goldstein, A. P., & Glick, B. (1987). *Aggression replacement training: A comprehensive intervention for aggressive youth.* Champaign, IL: Research Press.

Gordon, D. A., & Arbuthnot, J. (1987). Individual, group, and family interventions. In H. C. Quay (Ed.), *Handbook of juvenile delinquency* (pp. 290–324). New York: Wiley.

Gordon, D. A., Arbuthnot, J., Gustafson, K. E., & McGreen, P. (1988). Home-based behavioral-systems family therapy with disadvantaged juvenile delinquents. *American Journal of Family Therapy, 16,* 243–255.

Gottfredson, G. D. (1987). Peer group interventions to reduce the risk of delinquent behavior: A selective review and a new evaluation. *Criminology, 25,* 671–714.

Gottfredson, G. D. (1989). The experiences of violent and serious victimization. In N. A. Weiner & M. E. Wolfgang (Eds.), *Pathways to criminal violence* (pp. 202–234). Newbury Park, CA: Sage.

Gould, M. S., Shaffer, D., & Rutter, M. (1984, September). *UK/WHO study of ICD-9.* Working paper for the NIMH Conference on the Definition and Measurement of Psychopathology in Children and Adolescents, Washington, DC.

Graham, P. (1979). Epidemiological studies. In H. C. Quay & J. S. Werry (Eds.), *Psychopathological disorders of childhood* (2nd ed., pp. 185–209). New York: Wiley.

Graham, S., Hudley, C., & Williams, E. (1992). Attributional and emotional determinants of aggression among African-American and Latino young adolescents. *Developmental Psychology, 28,* 731–740.

Greenwood, P. W., & Zimring, F. E. (1985). *One more chance: The pursuit of promising intervention strategies for chronic juvenile offenders.* Santa Monica, CA: RAND.

Gresham, F. M., & Lemanek, K. L. (1983). Social skills: A review of cognitive-behavioral training procedures with children. *Journal of Applied Developmental Psychology, 4,* 239–261.

Guerra, N. G., & Slaby, R. G. (1990). Cognitive mediators of aggression in adolescent offenders: II. Intervention. *Developmental Psychology, 26,* 269–277.

Hanson, C. L., Henggeler, S. W., Haefele, W. F., & Rodick, J. D. (1984). Demographic, individual, and family relationship correlates of serious and repeated crime among adolescents and their siblings. *Journal of Consulting and Clinical Psychology, 52,* 528–538.

Hawkins, J. D., Catalano, R. F., Gillmore, M. R., & Wells, E. A. (1989). Skills training for drug abusers: Generalization, maintenance, and effects on drug use. *Journal of Consulting and Clinical Psychology, 57,* 559–563.

Hellman, D. A., & Beaton, S. (1986). The pattern of violence in urban public schools: The influence of school and community. *Journal of Research in Crime and Delinquency, 23,* 102–127.

Henderson, M., & Hollin, C. (1983). A critical review of social skills training with young offenders. *Criminal Justice and Behavior, 10,* 316–341.

Henggeler, S. W. (1989). *Delinquency in adolescence.* Newbury Park, CA: Sage.

Henggeler, S. W. (1991). Multidimensional causal models of delinquent behavior and their implications for treatment. In R. Cohen & A. W. Siegel (Eds.), *Context and development* (pp. 211–231). Hillsdale, NJ: Erlbaum.

Henggeler, S. W. (in press). *Multisystemic treatment of serious juvenile offenders: Implications for the treatment of substance abusing adolescents* (NIDA Research Monograph). Rockville, MD: National Institute on Drug Abuse.

Henggeler, S. W., & Borduin, C. M. (1990). *Family therapy and beyond: A multisystemic approach to treating the behavior problems of children and adolescents.* Pacific Grove, CA: Brooks/Cole.

Henggeler, S. W., Borduin, C. M., & Mann, B. J. (1992). Advances in family therapy: Empirical foundations. In T. H. Ollendick & R. J. Prinz (Eds.), *Advances in clinical child psychology* (Vol. 15, pp. 207–241). New York: Plenum.

Henggeler, S. W., Borduin, C. M., Melton, G. B., Mann, B. J., Smith, L. A., Hall, J. A., Cone, L., & Fucci, B. R. (1991). Effects of multisystemic therapy on drug use and abuse in serious juvenile offenders: A progress report from two outcome studies. *Family Dynamics of Addiction Quarterly, 1,* 40–51.

Henggeler, S. W., Edwards, J., & Borduin, C. M. (1987). The family relations of female juvenile delinquents. *Journal of Abnormal Child Psychology, 15,* 199–209.

Henggeler, S. W., Melton, G. B., & Smith, L. A. (1992). Family preservation using multisystemic therapy: An effective alternative to incarcerating serious juvenile offenders. *Journal of Consulting and Clinical Psychology, 60,* 953–961.

Henggeler, S. W., Melton, G. B., Smith, L. A., Schoenwald, S., & Hanley, J. H. (1993). *Family preservation using multisystemic treatment: Long-term follow-up to a clinical trial with serious juvenile offenders. Journal of Child and Family Studies, 2,* 283–293.

Henggeler, S. W., Rodick, J. D., Borduin, C. M., Hanson, C. L., Watson, S. M., & Urey, J. R. (1986). Multisystemic treatment of juvenile offenders: Effects on adolescent behavior and family interaction. *Developmental Psychology, 22,* 132–141.

Herbert, M. (1978). *Conduct disorders of childhood and adolescence: A behavioural approach to assessment and treatment.* Chichester, England: Wiley.

Hewitt, L. E., & Jenkins, R. L. (1946). *Fundamental patterns of maladjustment: The dynamics of their origin.* Springfield: Green.

Hinshaw, S. P. (1987). On the distinction between attentional deficits/hyperactivity and conduct problems/aggression in child psychopathology. *Psychological Bulletin, 101,* 443–463.

Hinshaw, S. P. (1992). Externalizing behavior problems and academic under-achievement in childhood and adolescence: Causal relationships and underlying mechanisms. *Psychological Bulletin, 111*, 127–155.

Hubbard, R. L., Rachel, J. V., Graddock, S. G., & Cavanaugh, E. R. (1984). Treatment outcome prospective study (TOPS): Client characteristics and behaviors before, during, and after treatment. In F. M. Tims & J. P. Ludford (Eds.), *Drug abuse treatment evaluation: Strategies, progress, and prospects* (NIDA Research Monograph No. 51, pp. 42–68). Rockville, MD: National Institute on Drug Abuse.

Huesmann, L. R., Lefkowitz, M. M., Eron, L. D., & Walder, L. O. (1984). Stability of aggression over time and generations. *Developmental Psychology, 20*, 1120–1134.

Huizinga, D., & Elliott, D. S. (1987). Juvenile offenders: Prevalence, offender incidence, and arrest rates by race. *Crime and Delinquency, 33*, 206–223.

Jenkins, R. L., & Hewitt, L. E. (1944). Types of personality structure encountered in child guidance clinics. *American Journal of Orthopsychiatry, 14*, 84–94.

Jessor, R. (1982). Adolescent problem drinking: Psychosocial aspects and developmental outcomes. In L. H. Towle (Ed.), *Proceedings: NIAAA-WHO Collaborating Center designation meeting and alcohol research seminar* (DHHS Publication No. ADM 85-1370, pp. 104–143). Washington, DC: U.S. Government Printing Office.

Jessor, R., Donovan, J. E., & Costa, F. M. (1991). *Beyond adolescence: Problem behavior and young adult development.* New York: Academic Press.

Jessor, R., & Jessor, S. L. (1977). *Problem behavior and psychosocial development: A longitudinal study of youth.* New York: Cambridge.

Johnson, C. A., Pentz, M. A., Weber, M. D., Dwyer, J. H., Baer, N., MacKinnon, D. P., & Hansen, W. B. (1990). Relative effectiveness of comprehensive community programming for drug abuse prevention with high-risk and low-risk adolescents. *Journal of Consulting and Clinical Psychology, 58*, 447–456.

Jouriles, E. N., Bourg, W. J., & Farris, A. M. (1991). Marital adjustment and child conduct problems: A comparison of the correlation across samples. *Journal of Consulting and Clinical Psychology, 59*, 354–357.

Kandel, D., Simcha-Fagan, O., & Davies, M. (1986). Risk factors for delinquency and illicit drug use from adolescence to young adulthood. *Journal of Drug Issues, 16*, 67–90.

Kashani, J., McGee, R., Clarkson, S., Anderson, J., Walton, L., Williams, S., Silva, P., Robins, A., Cytryn, M., & McKnew, D. (1987). Depression in a sample of 9-year-old children: Prevalence and associated characteristics. *Archives of General Psychiatry, 40*, 1217–1223.

Kazdin, A. E. (1987a). *Conduct disorders in childhood and adolescence.* Newbury Park, CA: Sage.

Kazdin, A. E. (1987b). Treatment of antisocial behavior in children: Current status and future directions. *Psychological Bulletin, 102*, 187–203.

Kazdin, A. E. (1988). *Child psychotherapy: Developing and identifying effective treatments.* New York: Pergamon.

Kelso, J., & Stewart, M. A. (1986). Factors which predict the persistence of aggressive conduct disorder. *Journal of Child Psychology and Psychiatry, 27*, 77–86.

Krohn, M. D., & Massey, J. (1980). Social control and delinquent behavior: An examination of the elements of the social bond. *Sociological Quarterly, 21*, 529–543.

LaGrange, R. L., & White, H. R. (1985). Age differences in delinquency: A test of theory. *Criminology, 23*, 19–45.

Lewis, C. E., & Bucholz, K. K. (1991). Alcoholism, antisocial behavior, and family history. *British Journal of Addiction, 86*, 177–194.

Lewis, R. A., Piercy, F., Sprenkle, D., & Trepper, T. (1990). Family-based interventions and community networking for helping drug abusing adolescents: The impact of near and far environments. *Journal of Adolescent Research, 5*, 82–95.

Lipton, D., Martinson, R., & Wilks, J. (1975). *The effectiveness of correctional treatment: A survey of treatment evaluation studies.* New York: Praeger.

Loeber, R. (1982). The stability of antisocial and delinquent child behavior: A review. *Child Development, 53*, 1431–1446.

Loeber, R. (1990). Development and risk factors of juvenile antisocial behavior and delinquency. *Clinical Psychology Review, 10*, 1–41.

Loeber, R., & Dishion, T. J. (1983). Early predictors of male delinquency: A review. *Psychological Bulletin, 94*, 68–99.

Loeber, R., Green, S. M., Lahey, B. B., Christ, M. A. G., & Frick, P. J. (1992). Developmental sequences in the age of onset of disruptive child behaviors. *Journal of Child and Family Studies, 1*, 21–41.

Loeber, R., Lahey, B. B., & Thomas, C. (1991). Diagnostic conundrum of oppositional defiant disorder and conduct disorder. *Journal of Abnormal Psychology, 100*, 379–390.

Loeber, R., & Schmaling, K. B. (1985a). Empirical evidence for overt and covert patterns of antisocial conduct problems: A meta-analysis. *Journal of Abnormal Child Psychology, 13*, 337–352.

Loeber, R., & Schmaling, K. B. (1985b). The utility of differentiating between mixed and pure forms of antisocial child behavior. *Journal of Abnormal Child Psychology, 13*, 315–336.

Lytton, H. (1990). Child and parent effects in boys' conduct disorder: A reinterpretation. *Developmental Psychology, 26*, 683–697.

Magnusson, D., Stattin, H., & Duner, A. (1983). Aggression and criminality in a longitudinal perspective. In K. T. Van Dusen & S. A. Mednick (Eds.), *Antecedents of aggression and antisocial behavior* (pp. 277–302). Boston: Kluwer-Nijhoff.

Mann, B. J., Borduin, C. M., Henggeler, S. W., & Blaske, D. M. (1990). An investigation of systemic conceptualizations of parent-child coalitions and symptom change. *Journal of Consulting and Clinical Psychology, 58*, 336–344.

Martin, B., & Hoffman, J. A. (1990). Conduct disorders. In M. Lewis & S. M. Miller (Eds.), *Handbook of developmental psychopathology* (pp. 109–118). New York: Plenum.

Martin, G. W., & Wilkinson, D. A. (1989). Methodological issues in the evaluation of treatment of drug dependence. *Advances in Behaviour Research and Therapy, 11*, 133–150.

Maughan, B., Gray, G., & Rutter, M. (1985). Reading retardation and antisocial behaviour: A follow-up into employment. *Journal of Child Psychology and Psychiatry, 26*, 741–758.

McGee, L., & Newcomb, M. D. (1992). General deviance syndrome: Evaluations at four ages from early adolescence to adulthood. *Journal of Consulting and Clinical Psychology, 60,* 766–776.

Melton, G. B., & Hargrove, D. S. (in press). *Planning mental health services for children and youth.* New York: Guilford.

Melton, G. B., & Spaulding, W. J. (in press). *No place to go: Civil commitment of minors.* Lincoln: University of Nebraska Press.

Miller, G. E., & Prinz, R. J. (1990). Enhancement of social learning family interventions for childhood conduct disorder. *Psychological Bulletin, 108,* 291–307.

Mitchell, S., & Rosa, P. (1981). Boyhood behavior problems as precursors of criminality: A fifteen-year follow-up study. *Journal of Child Psychology and Psychiatry, 22,* 19–33.

Morgan, P., Wallack, L., & Buchanan, D. (1989). Waging drug wars: Prevention strategy or politics as usual. In B. Segal (Ed.), *Perspectives on adolescent drug use* (pp. 99–124). New York: Haworth.

Mulvey, E. P., Arthur, M. A., & Reppucci, N. D. (1990). *Review of programs for the prevention and treatment of delinquency* (Office of Technology Assessment). Washington, DC: U.S. Government Printing Office.

Newcomb, M. D., & Bentler, P. M. (1989). Substance use and abuse among children and teenagers. *American Psychologist, 44,* 242–248.

Offord, D. R., Adler, R. J., & Boyle, M. H. (1986). Prevalence and sociodemographic correlates of conduct disorder. *American Journal of Social Psychiatry, 4,* 272–278.

Olweus, D. (1979). Stability of aggressive reaction patterns in males: A review. *Psychological Bulletin, 86,* 852–875.

Osgood, D. W., Johnston, L. D., O'Malley, P. M., & Bachman, J. G. (1988). The generality of deviance in late adolescence and early adulthood. *American Sociological Review, 53,* 81–93.

Panella, D., & Henggeler, S. W. (1986). Peer interactions of conduct-disordered, anxious-withdrawn, and well-adjusted Black adolescents. *Journal of Abnormal Child Psychology, 14,* 1–11.

Parsons, B. V., & Alexander, J. F. (1973). Short-term family intervention: A therapy outcome study. *Journal of Consulting and Clinical Psychology, 41,* 195–201.

Patterson, G. R. (1982). *A social learning approach to family intervention: III. Coercive family process.* Eugene, OR: Castalia.

Patterson, G. R., & Dishion, T. J. (1985). Contributions of families and peers to delinquency. *Criminology, 23,* 63–79.

Patterson, G. R., & Stouthamer-Loeber, M. (1984). The correlation of family management practices and delinquency. *Child Development, 55,* 1299–1307.

Poole, E. D., & Regoli, R. M. (1979). Parental support, delinquent friends, and delinquency: A test of interaction effects. *Journal of Criminal Law and Criminology, 70,* 188–193.

Prinz, R. J., Connor, P. A., & Wilson, C. C. (1981). Hyperactive and aggressive behaviors in childhood: Intertwined dimensions. *Journal of Abnormal Child Psychology, 9,* 191–202.

Puig-Antich, J. (1982). Major depression and conduct disorder in prepuberty. *Journal of the American Academy of Child Psychiatry, 21,* 118–128.

Quay, H. C. (1964). Personality dimensions in delinquent males as inferred from the factor analysis of behavior ratings. *Journal of Research in Crime and Delinquency, 1*, 33–37.

Quay, H. C. (1986a). Classification. In H. C. Quay & I. S. Werry (Eds.), *Psychopathological disorders of childhood* (3rd ed., pp. 1–34). New York: Wiley.

Quay, H. C. (1986b). Conduct disorders. In H. C. Quay & J. S. Werry (Eds.), *Psychopathological disorders of childhood* (3rd ed., pp. 35–42). New York: Wiley.

Quay, H. C. (Ed.). (1987a). *Handbook of juvenile delinquency.* New York: Wiley.

Quay, H. C. (1987b). Intelligence. In H. C. Quay (Ed.), *Handbook of juvenile delinquency* (pp. 106–117). New York: Wiley.

Quay, H. C., & Love, C. T. (1977). The effect of a juvenile diversion program on rearrests. *Criminal Justice and Behavior, 4*, 377–396.

Quay, H. C., Peterson, D. R., & Consalvi, C. (1960). The interpretation of three personality factors in juvenile delinquency. *Journal of Consulting Psychology, 24*, 255.

Reeves, J. C., Werry, J. S., Elkind, G. S., & Zametkin, A. (1987). Attentional deficit, conduct, oppositional, and anxiety disorders in children: II. Clinical characteristics. *Journal of the American Academy of Child and Adolescent Psychiatry, 26*, 144–155.

Rey, J. M., Bashir, M. R., Schwarz, M., Richards, I. N., Plapp, J. M., & Stewart, G. W. (1988). Oppositional disorder: Fact or fiction? *Journal of the American Academy of Child and Adolescent Psychiatry, 27*, 157–162.

Rhodes, J. E., & Jason, L. A. (1990). A social stress model of substance abuse. *Journal of Consulting and Clinical Psychology, 58*, 395–401.

Robins, L. N. (1966). *Deviant children grown up.* Baltimore, MD: Williams & Wilkins.

Robins, L. N. (1981). Epidemiological approaches to natural history research: Antisocial disorders in children. *Journal of the American Academy of Child and Adolescent Psychiatry, 20*, 566–580.

Roff, J. D., & Wirt, R. D. (1984). Childhood aggression and social adjustment as antecedents of delinquency. *Journal of Abnormal Child Psychology, 12*, 111–126.

Romig, D. (1978). *Justice for our children.* Lexington, MA: Lexington.

Rosen, A., & Proctor, E. K. (1981). Distinctions between treatment outcomes and their implications for treatment evaluation. *Journal of Consulting and Clinical Psychology, 49*, 418–425.

Rush, T. V. (1979). Predicting treatment outcomes for juvenile and young-adult clients in the Pennsylvania substance-abuse system. In G. M. Beschner & A. A. Friedman (Eds.), *Youth drug abuse: Problems, issues, and treatment* (pp. 629–656). Lexington, MA: Lexington.

Rutter, M., Cox, A., Tupling, C., Berger, M., & Yule, W. (1975). Attainment and adjustment in two geographical areas: I. The prevalence of psychiatric disorder. *British Journal of Psychiatry, 126*, 493–509.

Rutter, M., & Giller, H. (1983). *Juvenile delinquency: Trends and perspectives.* New York: Guilford.

Rutter, M., Tizard, J., Yule, W., Graham, P., & Whitmore, K. (1976). Research report: Isle of Wight studies, 1964–1974. *Psychological Medicine, 6*, 313–332.

Sarason, I. G., & Ganzer, V. J. (1973). Modeling and group discussion in the rehabilitation of juvenile delinquents. *Journal of Counseling Psychology, 20,* 442–449.

Schachar, R., & Wachsmuth, R. (1990). Oppositional disorder in children: A validation study comparing conduct disorder, oppositional disorder, and normal control children. *Journal of Child Psychology and Psychiatry, 31,* 1089–1102.

Schinke, S. P., Botvin, G. J., & Orlandi, M. A. (1991). *Substance abuse in children and adolescents: Evaluation and intervention.* Newbury Park, CA: Sage.

Schwartz, I. M. (1989). *Injustice for juveniles: Rethinking the best interests of the child.* Lexington, MA: Lexington.

Sells, S. B., & Simpson, D. D. (1979). Evaluation of treatment outcome for youths in the Drug Abuse Reporting Program (DARP): A followup study. In G. M. Beschner & A. A. Friedman (Eds.), *Youth drug abuse: Problems, issues, and treatment* (pp. 571–628). Lexington, MA: Lexington.

Smith, D. A., Visher, C. A., & Jarjoura, C. R. (1991). *Journal of Research in Crime and Delinquency, 28,* 6–32.

Snyder, J., & Patterson, G. R. (1987). Family interaction and delinquent behavior. In H. C. Quay (Ed.), *Handbook of juvenile delinquency* (pp. 216–243). New York: Wiley.

Spence, S. H., & Marzillier, J. S. (1981). Social skills training with adolescent male offenders: II. Short-term, long-term and generalized effects. *Behaviour Research and Therapy, 19,* 349–368.

Stattin, H., & Magnusson, D. (1989). The role of early aggressive behavior in the frequency, seriousness, and types of later crime. *Journal of Consulting and Clinical Psychology, 57,* 710–718.

Strober, M., Green, J., & Carlson, G. (1981). The reliability of psychiatric diagnosis in hospitalized adolescents: Interrater agreement using DSM-III. *Archives of General Psychiatry, 38,* 141–145.

Szapocznik, J., Kurtines, W. M., Foote, F. H., Perez-Vidal, A., & Hervis, O. (1983). Conjoint versus one-person family therapy: Some evidence for the effectiveness of conducting family therapy through one person. *Journal of Consulting and Clinical Psychology, 51,* 889–899.

Szapocznik, J., Kurtines, W. M., Foote, F. H., Perez-Vidal, A., & Hervis, O. (1986). Conjoint versus one-person family therapy: Further evidence for the effectiveness of conducting family therapy through one person with drug-abusing adolescents. *Journal of Consulting and Clinical Psychology, 54,* 395–397.

Tarter, R. E., Hegedus, A. M., Alterman, A. I., & Katz-Garris, L. (1983). Cognitive capacities of juvenile violent, nonviolent, and sexual offenders. *Journal of Nervous and Mental Disease, 171,* 564–567.

Taylor, E. A. (1986). Childhood hyperactivity. *British Journal of Psychiatry, 149,* 562–573.

Thornberry, T. P., Moore, M., & Christenson, R. L. (1985). The effect of dropping out of high school on subsequent criminal behavior. *Criminology, 23,* 3–18.

Tolan, P. H. (1990). Family therapy, substance abuse, and adolescents: Moving from isolated cultures to related components. *Journal of Family Psychology, 3,* 454–465.

Tolan, P. H., & Lorion, R. P. (1988). Multivariate approaches to the identification of delinquency-proneness in adolescent males. *American Journal of Community Psychology, 16,* 547–561.

Vuchinich, S., Bank, L., & Patterson, G. R. (1992). Parenting, peers, and the stability of antisocial behavior in preadolescent boys. *Developmental Psychology, 28*, 510–521.

Walker, J. L., Lahey, B. B., Russo, M. F., Frick, P. J., Christ, M. A. G., McBurnett, K., Loeber, R., Stouthamer-Loeber, M., & Green, S. M. (1991). Anxiety, inhibition, and conduct disorder in children: I. Relations to social impairment. *Journal of the American Academy of Child and Adolescent Psychiatry, 30*, 187–191.

Walsh, A., Petee, J. A., & Beyer, T. A. (1987). Intellectual imbalance and delinquency: Comparing high verbal and high performance IQ delinquents. *Criminal Justice and Behavior, 14*, 370–379.

Werry, I. S., Methven, R. I., Fitzpatrick, I., & Dixon, H. (1983). The interrater reliability of DSM-III in children. *Journal of Abnormal Child Psychology, 11*, 341–354.

Whitehead, J. T., & Lab, S. P. (1989). A meta-analysis of juvenile correctional treatment. *Journal of Research in Crime and Delinquency, 26*, 2.

Windle, M. (1990). A longitudinal study of antisocial behaviors in early adolescence as predictors of late adolescent substance use: Gender and ethnic group differences. *Journal of Abnormal Psychology, 99*, 86–91.

World Health Organization. (1979). *International classification of diseases, injuries, and causes of death* (9th ed.). Geneva: Author.

Wright, W. E., & Dixon, M. C. (1977). Community prevention and treatment of juvenile delinquency: A review of evaluation studies. *Journal of Research in Crime and Delinquency, 14*, 35–67.

12
Substance Use Disorders

Oscar G. Bukstein
Vincent B. Van Hasselt

U se and abuse of drugs and alcohol in the United States have produced significant social costs in terms of crime, health hazards, and economic loss. At the end of the 1980s, most Americans were convinced that drugs represented the gravest threat to the nation's well-being (White House, 1989). A problem that has received particular attention from the general public, as well as from mental health professionals, is the use and abuse of substances by youths. Indeed, the 1980s and early 1990s have witnessed a marked increase in both the public's awareness of alcohol and drug problems among adolescents and clinical and investigative activity concerning the assessment, prevention, and treatment of adolescent substance abuse (see Kaminer, 1994; Bukstein & Van Hasselt, 1993). This chapter will review salient aspects of adolescent substance use disorders or the pathological use of substances among youths.

Description of the Disorder

As with adults, alcohol and other drug use among adolescents presents a continuum of substance use behaviors from abstinence to frank physical dependence. At points in between, an adolescent may engage in one or more episodes of experimentation with one or more substances. Or he or she may increase use to a level that triggers a range of negative physical and/or psychosocial consequences. Unfortunately, defining discrete behaviors and symptoms that constitute specific pathological entities of substance abuse or dependence is difficult; past and current definitions of these disor-

Preparation of this chapter was facilitated in part by the Center for Education and Drug Abuse Research (CEDAR), funded by the National Institute on Drug Abuse (No. DA05605). The authors wish to express their appreciation to Tracey Eck and Charlotte Vanook for their technical assistance in preparation of the manuscript.

ders are based primarily on experience and research with adults. Despite almost universal application of adult diagnostic criteria to adolescents, many differences exist between adolescents and adults on a variety of substance use behaviors and characteristics, including use patterns and consequences (Blane, 1979; Weschler, 1979). The tendency to view adult and adolescent substance abuse as fundamentally the same disorder is questionable in light of evidence of discontinuity in problem-drinker status between adolescence and young adulthood (Jessor, 1984). Frequent heavy drinking in adolescents and ensuing problems appear to be self-limited and not highly predictive of alcoholism in adulthood (Blane, 1979). Similarly, patterns of involvement with marijuana and other illicit drugs peak in late adolescence (Kandel & Logan, 1984).

The DSM-III-R psychoactive substance use disorders (American Psychiatric Association, 1987) of abuse and dependence represents a commonly employed dichotomy. The DSM-III-R category of psychoactive substance dependence broadens the concept over prior diagnostic classification schemes to include clinically significant behaviors, cognitions, and symptoms reflecting a critical and substantial degree of involvement with a psychoactive agent (Rounsaville, Spitzer, & Williams, 1986). Many adolescents formerly meeting DSM-III criteria for substance abuse would achieve DSM-III-R criteria for psychoactive substance dependence. Elimination of reliance on physical parameters of tolerance and/or withdrawal as necessary for a diagnosis of dependence (as in DSM-III) allows consideration of excessive alcohol or other drug involvement by adolescents (a) with insufficient opportunity to use to create physical dependence, or (b) using substances that do not have a withdrawal syndrome (e.g., marijuana, solvents).

DSM-III-R criteria for psychoactive substance abuse (and dependence) are consistent across all types of substances. Psychoactive substance abuse consists of a maladaptive pattern of use, indicated by continued use despite recurrent or persistent social, psychological, or physical problems or by recurrent use in physically hazardous situations. Psychoactive substance dependence involves a cluster of cognitive, behavioral, and physiologic symptoms that reflect impaired control over substance use, preoccupation with use, and continued use despite adverse consequences. Since physical symptoms of addiction and/or withdrawal are rare in adolescents (Vingilis & Smart, 1981), the increased emphasis on substance-seeking and -taking behaviors is more relevant to this population. Research in this area has yet to establish the reliability, validity, or clinical utility of DSM-III-R psychoactive substance use disorders in adolescents.

The recent release of the final draft for the DSM-IV substance-related disorders (American Psychiatric Association, 1993) shows a subtle, but important change in the criteria for dependence and more significant changes in the criteria for abuse. The dependence criteria for DSM-IV eliminate the DSM-III-R criteria for frequent intoxication or withdrawal symptoms when expected to fulfill major role obligations, add subtyping according to the presence or absence of physiological signs of dependence (tolerance or withdrawal), and eliminate duration criteria. While the preservation of behavioral and cognitive criteria in a subtype without physiological dependence allows for substantial numbers of youth to meet dependence criteria, the elimination of the criteria for inability to fulfill role obligations due to substance use may reduce the number of adolescents meeting DSM-IV substance dependence criteria.

The DSM-IV criteria for substance abuse represent a more substantial change from DSM-III-R. DSM-IV expands the criteria of maladaptive pattern of substance use to require clinically significant impairment or distress and provides two additional examples of a maladaptive pattern of use: recurrent use resulting in a failure to fulfill major role obligations (omitted from DSM-IV dependence criteria), and recurrent substance-related legal problems. As with the diagnosis of dependence, DSM-IV no longer includes duration criteria for an substance abuse diagnosis.

Perhaps the most significant change in DMS-IV is the addition of a requirement that the maladaptive pattern of substance use lead to clinically significant impairment or distress. In the past the presence of a maladaptive pattern of use, as determined by whatever subjective criteria, was sufficient to meet diagnostic criteria. The requirement of impairment or distress may present a difficult problem of whether to attribute the impairment or distress to substance use rather than to the variety of problem behaviors, psychopathology, or adverse environmental circumstances that are often seen in adolescents who use psychoactive substances. Failure to meet even a minimal level of impairment or distress despite a perceived maladaptive pattern of use may reduce the number of adolescents who meet criteria for a DSM-IV diagnosis of substance abuse. Elimination of the criteria for frequent intoxication or withdrawal symptoms when expected to fulfill major role obligations at work, home, or school may also reduce the number of adolescents receiving a DSM-IV diagnosis of substance dependence. The essential change in DSM-IV is away from the behaviors associated with substance use toward evidence of psychosocial dysfunction. This change may be more significant in the diagnosis of adolescents, as use and related behaviors may be much more prevalent and obvious among them than dysfunction directly attributable to substance use.

Historical Background

The use and abuse of alcohol and other psychoactive substances have been present since antiquity and throughout the history of the United States (see

Lender & Martin, 1987; Musto, 1987). Only since the middle of the twentieth century, however, have clinical and research efforts focused on the phenomenon of adolescent substance abuse. The explanation for this oversight is simple: until the late nineteenth century there were no "adolescents," and prior to the 1960s substance abuse among youths appeared to be uncommon. Specifically, before the last third of the nineteenth century, society made a distinction only between children and adults. Individuals past the physical changes of puberty were considered adults and were accorded the same legal rights and responsibilities as adults (Kett, 1977). In colonial America, a high level of alcohol consumption was a normal part of life; most Americans over 15 years of age drank. There are only a few references to problem drinking in youths, although, drinking, gambling, and fighting appear to have been common problems in colonial and postcolonial American colleges.

After the mid-nineteenth century, changes in social life and expectations, increasing economic pressures, and the industrial revolution created a desire to protect youths and reduce stress so as to allow them to mature into adults through prolonged education and moral development. With these changes emerged the Victorian controls and increasing power of temperance forces in the United States. As a result there were fewer opportunities for alcohol and other substance use among youths, much less problem use.

Apart from the widespread utilization of patent medicines by the general population until the early twentieth century, alcohol, opiate, and cocaine use by adolescents was concentrated in lower socioeconomic groups in the inner cities. Further, when it was present, repeated substance use or abuse was considered part of a syndrome of delinquency or deviant behavior. Prohibition produced a more profound change in youth drinking practices than in adults, since access to alcohol was sharply diminished. Similarly, the rise of narcotic and other drug control laws in the 1930s further limited both access to and social acceptability of opiat, cocaine, and marijuana use by both adolescents and adults. Covert experimentation with alcohol by many adolescents was the rule following Prohibition, with only a very small percentage using alcohol in an abusive pattern or using other illicit drugs at all.

In the 1960s, the civil rights movement, political assassinations, increasing crime rates, and the Vietnam conflict influenced a profound social upheaval in America. Whether as a part of or as a result of this unrest, many American youths earnestly challenged prevailing social norms, attitudes, and values. Part of this challenge was an increasing use of both legal and illicit substances. By the mid-1970s, though, adolescent perceptions and patterns of substance use had changed dramatically (see Epidemiology section below).

Clinical Picture

Two elements define pathology of any kind: subjective distress, and dysfunction in one or more areas. In a manner characteristic of the substantial denial usually present in adult substance abusers, adolescents who abuse alcohol or other drugs usually have poor insight into the effects of their substance use; they may be bothered only by the consequences—direct and indirect—of their use, not by the use itself. Therefore the primary feature identifying substance abuse in adolescents is psychosocial dysfunction in one or more relevant areas. Given the usually covert nature of substance use in adolescents, the deleterious psychosocial effects often are the only apparent problem. Establishing a relationship between dysfunction and substance use or abuse is most often accomplished via comprehensive assessment.

Table 12–1 lists several areas of dysfunction in a "typical" adolescent substance abuser. A basic sign of dysfunction is the inability to meet role expectations. For the adolescent, role expectations are (a) adequate school performance, (b) satisfactory relationships with family and peers, and (c) meeting general societal rules. While deterioration in one or more of these role expectations is often noted in an adolescent substance abuser, problems in these areas often *precede* the onset of substance use or abuse by several years. These difficulties may be the result of social and environmental circumstances or psychopathology highly correlated with, but not necessarily the direct result of, adolescent substance abuse. The work of Donovan and Jessor (1978), for example, points to problem drinking as only part of a larger syndrome of deviant behavior in adolescents. In addition, substance use in adolescence is almost always illicit. Certain negative sequelae follow from this proscription, rather than from the actual properties of the substance being used or substance use behavior itself.

The clinical picture of adolescent substance abuse behavior typically resembles that of conduct disorder or a deviant behavior syndrome. While substance use is not a criterion for a diagnosis of conduct disorder, it is listed as an associated feature (American Psychiatric Association, 1987). Indeed, the adolescent who abuse substances usually has deviant attitudes regarding society, rules, school, and other social institutions. His or her peers are similarly deviant. The appearance of friends whose dress, attitudes, and behaviors are nonnormative is suggestive of the differential association of an adolescent and his or her adoption of a deviant lifestyle that includes substance use. In addition, the adolescent's behavior often violates a variety of societal norms; overt manifestations of an adolescent substance abuser may include lying, stealing, cheating, vandalism, or even selling illicit substances. Substance use or abuse may be masked by an often severe pattern of antisocial behavior, yet the substance use may serve to potentiate such behavior by diminishing social inhibitions further, or by producing a

Table 12–1
Potential Areas of Dysfunction in Adolescent Substance Abusers

I. Environment

    A. Family
        1. Poor communication
        2. Poor supervision/discipline
        3. Overt conflict

    B. School
        1. Poor academic performance
        2. Behavior problems

    C. Peers
        1. Deviant peer group
        2. Peer conflict

    D. Community delinquency/legal problems

II. Individual

    A. Mood problems
    B. Sleep/appetite problems
    C. Conduct/behavior problems
        1. Lying
        2. Stealing
        3. Running away
        4. Property destruction

need for certain antisocial acts (e.g., stealing to support a drug habit). Moreover, comorbid or coexisting psychopathology often is observed in adolescent substance abusers. For example, studies have identified increased rates of mood disorders, anxiety disorders, attention-deficit hyperactivity disorder, and suicidal behavior in adolescent substance abusers (see reviews by Bukstein, Brent, & Kaminer, 1989; Crumley, 1990).

Adolescents use substances ostensibly for their psychoactive effects. These pharmacological effects include (a) central nervous system (CNS) depression in the case of alcohol, sedative/hypnotics, and opiates (e.g., heroin); (b) CNS stimulation with cocaine, amphetamines, and phencyclidine; (c) hallucinations with use of LSD and mescaline. There often are overlapping drug effects; these are frequently more pronounced in inexperienced adolescents. Changes in mood and behavior also appear to be indirect signs of substance use and abuse.

Knowledge of substance use patterns is the extremely useful in determining status. If the adolescent provides a veridical history of substance use, he or she will report progression from initial experimentation (within a social or peer context) to a range of severity of substance use behaviors. These include incidental negative consequences, due to preoccupation with obtaining and using substances, that are indications of dependence. As frequency of use and amounts used progress, certain negative consequences of substance use—accidents, arrests for public intoxication and/or possession of substances, and certain physical stigmata—become more apparent. Although use of substances producing physical addiction (e.g., heroin, sedative/hypnotics) and physical addiction itself are uncommon in adolescents, psychological characteristics of addiction, particularly preoccupation with obtaining and using substances, often are noted in this population.

Course and Prognosis

Despite the fact that the purchase and use of alcohol and other drugs are illegal for all adolescents in this country, large numbers of youths experiment with one or more substances without harmful consequences. In general, use of alcohol and brief experimentation with certain drugs (e.g., marijuana, stimulants, hallucinogens) are normative behavior. Identifying risk or antecedent factors correlated with increased adolescent use and progression assists in the delineation of the course and development of use patterns. Environmental antecedents are among the most robust predictors of adolescent substance use, with parental attitudes and behavior most significant (Kandel, 1982). In addition to parental role modeling, quality and consistency of family communication and parental behavior management and supervision are strong predictors of adolescent use (Donovan & Jessor, 1978; Kandel, Kessler, & Margulies, 1978).

Peer-related factors predicting adolescent use are peer drug activities and attitudes (Kandel et al., 1978) and perceived use of substances by peers (Jessor & Jessor, 1978). Reported peer drinking has the strongest relationship to adolescent drinking; in fact, individual adolescent drinking behavior resembles that of peers. Further, the more that peers use, the greater the likelihood is that an adolescent will initiate use and progress to higher levels of use (Donovan & Jessor, 1978; White, 1987).

Individual factors, including beliefs, attitudes, substance use expectancies, and preexisting psychopathology, also have been implicated as precursors of adolescent substance use and abuse. Prior and current beliefs concerning alcohol are associated with current drinking patterns (Christiansen, Goldman, & Inn, 1982), and favorable attitudes about drug use prior to initiation appear to facilitate onset of drug use (Kandel et al., 1978). Substance use-related expectancies (i.e., effects that the individual anticipates) also have been related to current (Christiansen, Goldman, & Brown, 1985) and future (Brown, 1985) use patterns.

Preexisting or coexisting psychopathology in the adolescent often increases likelihood of use. For example, antisocial behavior frequently predicts adolescent substance use (Johnston, O'Malley, & Bachman, 1987; Kandel et al., 1978), and adolescents with conduct problems are more likely than nondisordered peers to be exposed to illicit substances. Among substance users, the more conduct problems one has, the earlier substance use begins (Robins & McEvoy, 1990). Early substance use itself is a predictor of substance abuse. Delay in onset appears to be critical, as the more conduct problems an adolescent has, the greater the likelihood of substance use is, regardless of age of initiation of use (Robins & McEvoy, 1990). Results of other studies suggest that depression (Christie et al., 1988; Deykin, Levy, & Wells, 1987) and attention-deficit disorder (Gittleman, Mannuzza, Shenker, & Bonagura, 1985) may precede substance use or abuse.

A number of researchers have employed the aforementioned risk factors to construct theories of initiation and progression of adolescent substance use. For example, Kandel (1982) proposed four developmental stages of use: (a) beer and wine, (b) cigarettes and/or hard liquor, (c) marijuana, and (d) other elicit drugs. Participation in each stage is necessary but insufficient for progression to a subsequent stage. Also, there are stage-specific predictors of use of various legal and illegal drugs. For involvement with alcohol, both peer and especially parental influences (e.g., modeling) are critical. Peer influences are more important in predicting marijuana use. Use of illicit drugs other than marijuana is influenced by parental use, poor family relationships, and psychological distress.

Unfortunately, no comprehensive longitudinal investigations of substance abusers have been conducted. Population studies show that most adolescent and young adult problem drinkers "mature out of" and eventually eliminate their problem use (Blane, 1979; Weschler, 1979). However, number of risk factors, severity of use behavior, consequences of use, and family history of adult substance abuse disorders may predict poorer prognosis in both treated and untreated populations. These hypotheses have yet to be confirmed by research with adolescent populations.

Complications

As mentioned earlier, identification of substance abuse in an adolescent requires assessment of the negative psychosocial consequences of use. It is often difficult to ascertain whether substance abuse is the cause or the symptom of psychosocial dysfunction. Whether the pattern is abusive or not, substance use carries the risk of such short-term consequences as car accidents (and resultant fatalities or injuries), school absence, fighting, and overdose. High levels of adolescent drug use have been associated with a tendency toward precocious development; in early adulthood, they predict early involvement in marriage, family, and the work force (Newcomb & Bentler, 1986). Multiple substance use as an adolescent appears to interfere with developmental tasks of adolescence and leads to dropping out of school or poor role performance. In addition, such use has been related to occupational instability and marital dysfunction in adulthood. Longitudinal research by Newcomb and Bentler (1986) has demonstrated that on an individual level, use of hard drugs by adolescents increased loneliness, psychoticism, and suicidal ideation and decreased social supports.

The adverse health and pharmacological effects of alcohol and other substances are well-known for adults (Jaffe, Babor, & Fishbein, 1988; Mendelson & Mello, 1985). While adolescents do not use substances with the quantity and frequency of adult abusers, the effects of substance use on an organism that is still growing and developing may produce physical sequelae in adulthood (Arria, Tarter, & Van Thiel, 1991). For example, Newcomb and Bentler (1986) found a decrease in "physical hardiness" related to general drug use in adolescence.

Epidemiology

The most accurate estimates of current adolescent substance use patterns are derived from two national surveys. Since 1974, the National Senior Survey (NSS) has provided annual data on drug and alcohol use of high school seniors (Johnston et al., 1987). The National Household Survey, funded by the National Institute on Drug Abuse, is administered every 2 to 3 years. Both are self-report surveys with consistent and reliable results (Oetting & Beauvais, 1990). Unfortunately, NSS does not include 15% to 20% of a class cohort that leaves school early; this group of dropouts contains high-risk youths with elevated rates of substance use and abuse.

Lifetime annual and monthly prevalence data from NSS reveal interesting trends over the 1980s (Johnston, 1992). Specifically, although use of most drugs by high school seniors (as defined by lifetime prevalence) increased from the mid-1970s to the early 1980s, there was a subsequent decline in the proportion of high school seniors using marijuana, cocaine, crack, stimulants, and sedatives. In 1991, less than one-third (29%) of all high school seniors claimed they had taken at least one illicit drug during the past year. This represented a substantial decrease from a peak of 54% in 1979. Daily usage rates for cocaine, stimulants, and marijuana were down an estimated 75% from peak levels. Although seniors reported modest declines in the use of alcohol, its use among youths remained widespread. From a peak of 72% of seniors reporting alcohol use in the prior month in 1980, the rate fell to 54% in 1991. Approximately 32% of 1991 seniors reported at least one occasion of drinking in the prior 2 weeks; this was down from a peak of 41% in 1983. Daily use of alcohol declined from a peak of 6.9% in 1979 to 3.6% in 1991.

Results from the National Adolescent Student Health Survey (Windle,

1991) indicate that many 8th-grade adolescents (75.9%) have used alcohol at least once in their lifetime. Fewer African-American students describe themselves as heavy drinkers: among 12th graders, 48.1% of white students were heavy drinkers, as compared to 24% of African-American students and 41% of Hispanic students (Bachman et al., 1991). The number of male and female students who had ever used alcohol were similar in 8th and 10th grade. And although gender differences among drinking adolescents are decreasing, more male adolescents (45%) were frequent drinkers than females (28%). As previously noted, early age of initiation of use appears to predict abuse. Among 10th grade males, heavy drinkers were more likely than non-heavy drinkers to have had their first drink in grades four through eight (Windle, 1991). Polysubstance use (i.e., use of more than one substance) is often considered the rule rather than the exception with adolescents. Among 10th-grade students, 18.5% reported using alcohol in combination with other drugs in the past month (Windle, 1991).

Familial Pattern

A considerable body of evidence documents the tendency for alcoholism to occur in families (Cotton, 1979). Twin studies comparing the incidence of alcohol abuse in monozygotic (identical) twins with dizygotic (fraternal) twins reveal an approximate twofold increase in concordance in rates of abuse (Kaij, 1960) and drinking habits (Partanen, Bruun, & Markkanen, 1966) in the former. Studies of male children placed in nonalcoholic adoptive homes have shown an increased prevalence rate for alcoholism in sons of alcoholic biological fathers compared with sons of nonalcoholic fathers (Bohman, 1978; Cloninger, Bohman, & Sigvardsson, 1981).

Based on adoption data, Cloninger et al. (1981) postulated two forms of alcoholism: milieu- and male-limited. The milieu-limited form occurs in a majority of cases (in both men and women) when sufficient environmental factors interact with genetic predisposition. Milieu-limited individuals are later-onset alcoholics with low rates of antisocial behavior. The male-limited form is strongly influenced by genetic loading and is seen exclusively in male offspring of alcoholic and antisocial fathers. Male-limited alcoholism has an early onset (usually in adolescence) and is associated with rapid deterioration and antisocial behavior.

Again, the association of early onset of use with antisocial behavior is a strong predictor of a familial or genetic form of alcohol abuse or dependence. And several familial factors may increase an adolescent's risk for substance abuse, including degree of family conflict; modeling of use, abuse, or social deviance; social isolation; and parental neglect (Kumpfer & DeMarsh, 1980).

Differential Diagnosis and Assessment

A clinically relevant and valid assessment is the basis for case management and effective treatment interventions. Assessment should initially determine (a) whether the adolescent uses alcohol and/or other drugs, (b) where use of a substance has occurred, and (c) its effects on psychosocial functioning. At a more complex level, assessment can utilize instrumentation to provide qualitative information concerning variables related to antecedents and consequences of substance use in adolescents.

Given the level of use of alcohol and other psychoactive substances by adolescents, screening for actual abuse should be directed to a population at risk. For the clinician, identification of substance abuse occurs through evaluation of an adolescent with psychosocial dysfunction. Because of the covert and often deviant nature of adolescent substance use, these patients rarely self-refer for evaluation and treatment, and they usually fail to acknowledge substance use. Although self-reports of substance use appear to be reliable in some clinical and nonclinical populations (Barnea, Rahav, & Teichman, 1987; Winters, Stinchfield, Henly, & Schwartz, 1991), certain groups, such as extremely antisocial youths, have much higher levels of invalid reporting (Winters et al., 1991).

Despite several research-based measures, there are no standardized devices linking adolescent substance abuse assessment to treatment (Tarter, 1990). Several investigators have developed questionnaires for use in epidemiology (Singh, Kandel, & Johnson, 1975) and for measuring quantity, frequency and context of drug use (Jessor, 1976). For example, the Adolescent Alcohol Involvement Scale (Mayer & Filstead, 1979) represents an attempt to develop an adolescent-specific screening instrument for alcohol.

There is considerable dissatisfaction with one or more elements of currently available screening and interview instruments (see discussions by Tarter, 1990; Winters, 1990). Several structured and semistructured diagnostic interviews—such as the children's version of the Schedule for Affective Disorders and Schizophrenia (Chambers, Puig-Antich, Hirsh, et al., 1985) and the Diagnostic Interview for Children and Adolescents (Herjanic & Reich, 1982)—cover substance abuse, although the involved sections do not have established psychometric properties.

Several more comprehensive instruments with prospective clinical applications have been developed. The Personal Experience Inventory (Henly & Winters, 1988) measures quantity, frequency, and history of use and evaluates environmental circumstances and personality characteristics of the adolescent. The need for an integrated and broad-spectrum assessment device to facilitate measurement of treatment outcome in adolescent substance abusers prompted the National Institute on Drug Abuse to sponsor development of the Adolescent Assessment/Referral System (AARS). The AARS is multidimensional screening procedure designed to direct the adolescent with significant scores to a more extensive battery of standardized instruments. The Drug Use Screening Inventory (Tarter, 1990) and the Problems Oriented Screening Instrument for Teenagers (Rahdert, 1991) are two similar instruments originating in the AARS effort. Each consists of 10 domains in key areas of health, psychiatric, and psychosocial status. They are constructed to systematically screen and identify areas of disturbance that are frequently concomitant to drug use in adolescence. Once areas of possible dysfunction are identified, more detailed evaluation procedures can be employed to achieve a finer-grained analysis.

The domain model is adhered to by a number of other screening or adolescent assessment instruments which are largely modeled after the Addiction Severity Index (McLellan, Luborsky, Woody, & O'Brien, 1980) for adults. These adolescent measures include the Adolescent Drug Abuse Diagnosis Instrument (Friedman & Utada, 1989), the Adolescent Problem Severity Index (Metzger, Kushner, & McLellan, 1991), and the Teen Addiction Severity Index (Kaminer, Bukstein, & Tarter, 1991). The domain model is a useful way to organize the assessment of adolescents with suspected or confirmed substance abuse.

Substance Use

Whether utilizing a unidimensional instrument measuring quantity, frequency, or age of onset data or a more comprehensive interview or device tapping several domains, the prototypical substance use assessment should examine (a) direct consequences of use, (b) withdrawal or physical symptoms of use, and (c) cognitive and behavioral evidence of dependence. The clinician should obtain information concerning types of agents used and age of onset of use for each substance. In addition to age of first exposure and initial use, the clinician should inquire about the progression and age of regular use. While quantity and frequency data are essential to any thorough evaluation, variability in adolescent substance use often is considerable; the adolescent may report periods of abstinence as well as intervals of rapid acceleration of use and heavy use of particular agents. A time-line drug chart is valuable in eliciting information on quantity, frequency, and variability across time, with important dates, holidays, and other time cues as a guide.

Although reports of heavy alcohol or other drug use may be suggestive of a diagnosis of psychoactive substance abuse or dependence, negative consequences of use are the cardinal sign of pathology. The clinician should be careful to inquire about directly related effects or negative consequences of use without assuming that all problems in an adolescent's life are due to substance use.

Questions regarding control of use generally follow DSM-III-R criteria for psychoactive substance dependence. Does the adolescent view his or her use as a problem? Has he or she made efforts to control or stop it? Does he or she spend more time than planned obtaining, using, and recovering from effects of the substance? Are greater amounts of the substance taken than originally planned? Does the adolescent get drunk or high when expected to fulfill role obligations (e.g., at school or work)? Has he or she terminated previously important and favored activities in order to use? Has use continued despite repeated deleterious consequences? Despite the lower prevalence of physical sequelae of substance use, and the rarity of overt physiological withdrawal symptoms, questions pertaining to these features are also essential and, if answered in the affirmative, reflect a severe level of substance dependency. Further, questions should be substance specific. If use of a particular substance is acknowledged, the clinician should proceed with a more detailed inquiry about negative consequences, context, and control of use for each specific substance.

Psychiatric and Behavioral Problems

In view of the significant comorbidity of adolescent substance abuse with other behavioral and emotional problems (Bukstein et al., 1989), screening for and subsequent detailed assessment of psychopathology is essential. Screening should tap depression, suicidal ideation and behavior, anxiety, aggressive acts, and current and past mental health interventions. Determination as to whether symptoms or behaviors are present during both substance use (or intoxication) and abstinence should be made. Do the symptoms or behaviors exist independently of substance use or intoxication, and even well into significant periods of abstinence?

Obtaining a family history of psychiatric disorder is useful for disentangling an often-confusing constellation of symptoms and behaviors. Past treatment history and established psychiatric diagnoses of family members should be ascertained. In addition, the possible existence of similar but undiagnosed comorbid symptom patterns in other family members should be evaluated.

School and/or Vocational Functioning

Most adolescents are enrolled in school, which is the primary "job" of adolescence. Regular attendance and satisfactory academic progress require many of the same functional skills adults must display in obtaining and maintaining employment. Adequate school performance requires certain interpersonal and cognitive skills, behavioral controls, and at least a minimal level of achievement orientation. Not only can school failure promote substance use and abuse, but academic failure and poor school performance often "identify" the adolescent substance abuser.

Social Competency and Peer Relations

Social competency refers to the ability of the adolescent to function adequately with both peers and adults. Included within the larger concept of social competency are social and communication skills, anger control, and problem-solving skills. Our own work (Van Hasselt, Null, Kempton, & Bukstein, 1993) has provided some of the first empirical evidence of deficits in these areas among adolescent substance abusers. The clinician should be careful to evaluate the social competency of the adolescent in both school and family settings. Peer relations are especially critical, however, given the transfer of interest and influence from family and parents to the adolescent's peer group that occurs at this developmental stage.

Leisure and Recreation

The adolescent's availability and utilization of leisure time may play a role in his or her engagement in deviant behavior and substance use. Consequently, the clinician should evaluate the adolescent's current leisure-time attitudes, interests, and activities; past leisure activities (prosocial and deviant) also should be probed. In addition to interest or disinterest in various activities, the adolescent's physical capability to participate should be assessed. Does the adolescent have any special abilities or talents (e.g., music, sports) that have yet to be identified or, if known, cannot be exhibited due to various environmental limitations (e.g., lack of access)?

Health Status

Every adolescent suspected of substance use or abuse should have a complete medical history and physical examination. Preexisting medical conditions may influence the course of substance use and potential consequences of use, and a number of conditions (e.g., hepatitis, AIDS, lung disease, liver disease) may result from substance abuse. Laboratory testing is a useful adjunct to identify relevant medical problems. Recommended tests include complete blood count with differential, liver function tests, urine drug screening, and a pregnancy test; depending on the adolescent's sexual history, tests for human immunodeficiency virus (HIV-1), syphilis, gonorrhea, and chlamydia may be indicated. Drug screening tests (urine and serum) can be very useful or abused. The clinician should be aware of the indications for employment of drug screens (Gold & Dachis, 1986), as well as factors affecting their reliability and validity (e.g., sample collection, handling and protection against contaminants, mislabeling).

Family

Family variables account for many of the most robust psychosocial determinants of risk for substance abuse in adolescents. Prior research points to a genetic contribution in alcoholism and related problems (Goodwin, 1979); children of alcoholic parents show increased rates of psychopathology and alcoholism (Earles, Reich, Jung, & Cloninger, 1988; West & Printz, 1987). In view of the genetic risks and frequent familial nature of alcoholism, drug abuse, and other forms of psychopathology (e.g., depression, schizophrenia), the clinician should obtain a detailed family history of both psychiatric disorder and substance use patterns. Other areas relevant for family assessment include communication style, conflicts, values, norms, and affective expression and involvement.

Clinical Management

Treatment of adolescents with substance use disorders is often determined by the context and severity of substance use within the adolescent's milieu, as well as other environmental and individual problems. Coexisting deviant behavior or other psychopathology may influence referral or treatment decisions. For example, if substance use is a relatively minor component of a more pervasive deviant syndrome that includes aggression or more serious antisocial behaviors, these responses may be the primary targets for intervention; issues pertaining to substance use or abuse may take a more peripheral role. Severe coexisting psychopathology (e.g., severe depression, bipolar disorder, aggression, psychosis, and/or suicidal behavior) will likely necessitate referral to a mental health setting for primary treatment.

With these basic caveats in mind, the first treatment decision involves site of referral. The rise of managed care has limited referral for residential substance abuse intervention to adolescents who present with severe substance use behaviors, such as those requiring detoxification, treatment failures from less restrictive outpatient treatment, and behavior characteristics (e.g., running away) that reduce the potential efficacy of outpatient services. Although most substance abuse treatment programs offer a unitary treatment plan or program (i.e., the same remedial components for each patient), professionals referring adolescents should be familiar with the basic treatment modalities available within both traditional and alternative treatment programs. These are described briefly in the sections below.

Traditional Approaches

Many, if not most, treatment programs for substance-abusing adolescents are based on the Minnesota Model (Wheeler & Malmquist, 1987). This model incorporates group therapy in a residential setting where patients work through the 12 steps of Alcoholics Anonymous (AA; 1976) or similar self-support groups (e.g., Narcotics Anonymous). Other characteristics of this model include the use of recovered addicts as counselors, provision of aftercare, and intensive and ongoing attendance at self-support group meetings. Similar step-work and self-support group focus can be delivered in partial (day hospital) and outpatient treatment settings. Despite the popularity of the Minnesota Model, though, few studies have demonstrated its effectiveness with adolescent substance abusers. Alford, Koehler, and Leonard (1991) compared subjects who did and did not complete treatment in an AA-based adolescent inpatient program. Although completers demonstrated less substance use and greater abstinence 6 months post discharge, no differences were noted between groups at 1- and 2-year followups. Despite a return to substance use at 2-year follow-up, 17% of treatment completers appeared to be successful in social and behavioral functioning.

Alternative Treatments

The growing awareness among mental health professionals that adolescent substance abusers are highly heterogenous and do not respond equally to the same form of treatment has led to implementation of several alternative or adjunct modalities to the traditional Minnesota Model. Many of these strategies have been incorporated into existing traditional programs in recent years. A few of these approaches are presented in the sections below. (See Bukstein & Van Hasselt, 1993, for a more comprehensive review of treatment methods with adolescent substance abusers.)

Cognitive Therapy. Cognitive therapy (CT) refers to individual or group therapeutic techniques designed to modify patients' irrational belief systems, deficient coping skills, and faulty thinking styles. This is accomplished via systematic training in self-observation to enhance the individual's awareness of the association between thoughts and emotions. Attention is directed to negative and irrational self-statements that occur in particular situations and that are related to depressed or anxious mood (Beck, 1976). Then the validity of these maladaptive thoughts and self-statements are challenged, with more functional cognitions gradually substituted.

The potential value of CT with substance-abusing adolescents is suggested by preliminary evidence from our own research indicating that a significant number of these youths report cognitive distortions and negative internalized self-statements (Kempton, Van Hasselt, Bukstein, & Null, in press). Consequently, we have implemented CT with adolescent substance abusers in an inpatient psychiatric setting (Bukstein & Van Hasselt, 1993) with some success. The clinical utility of CT with this population, however, awaits empirical verification.

Behavioral Family Therapy. Clinicians and researchers have directed increased attention to the role of the family in the etiology and maintenance of adolescent substance abuse (Bry, 1988; Hops, Tildesley, Lichtenstein, Ary, & Sherman, 1990). Results of these efforts have documented an association between parental substance abuse, poor supervision and monitoring of children, coercive parental management practices, and high risk of use or abuse in offspring (Dishion, Patterson, & Reid, 1988). Behavioral family interventions that have been conducted to ameliorate these problems include contingency contracting (Frederikson, Jenkins, & Carr, 1976; Rueger & Liberman, 1984) and problem-solving skills training (Bry, Conboy, & Bisgay, 1986).

Contingency contracting typically involves detailing and operationally defining adolescent target behaviors (e.g., completing chores, doing homework, getting home on time) for which parents consistently provide positive consequences. Problem-solving skills training is a multiple component intervention involving identification of desired areas of change, assessment of maintaining variables, generation of solutions, and reinforcement of positive changes (see Robin & Foster, 1988). While controlled outcome studies of the utility of the abovementioned approaches have yet to be conducted, there is a consensus among practitioners that "intervention with substance-abusing adolescents that fails to proactively involve the family in treatment is unlikely to yield significant short- or long-term improvements" (Bukstein & Van Hasselt, 1993, p. 465).

Social Skills Training. Social skills training has been used with substance abusers since the early 1970s (see reviews by Chaney, 1989; Van Hasselt, Hersen, & Milliones, 1978). The impetus for widespread application of skills training procedures is early research demonstrating that at least some substance abusers have high levels of social anxiety, poor assertion skills, and low perceptions of self-efficacy in interpersonal contexts (Van Hasselt et al., 1978). In response to these findings, numerous skills interventions have been developed for substance abusers to enhance coping, social problem-solving, and assertion skills. As mentioned earlier, we have found corroborating evidence of deficient social skills (particularly assertion deficits) in subgroups of adolescent substance abusers (Van Hasselt et al., 1993).

Social skills training programs specifically geared toward adolescent substance abusers have been developed in recent years. In one of the most comprehensive endeavors in this area, Haggerty, Wells, Jenson, Catalano, and Hawkins (1989) implemented Project ADAPT, a treatment and aftercare program for institutionalized delinquents with significant drug or alcohol problems. ADAPT combines behavioral skill training, supportive social network development, and participation in prosocial activities to facilitate community reintegration of adolescents following residential placement. Use of this program across a variety of skill areas (e.g., self-control, social networking, social problem solving, coping with authority) teaches adolescent patients a wide range of behaviors required for subsequent community adjustment.

Van Hasselt and Christ (1992) designed a Social Problem Solving Skills (SPSS) treatment "package" (direct instructions, modeling, performance feedback, behavior rehearsal, and positive reinforcement) to ameliorate social performance and cognition deficits in dually diagnosed adolescents in an inpatient setting. SPSS training focuses on improving verbal and non-verbal skills, social awareness, positive and negative assertion, negotiation skills, ability to resist peer pressure, and conversational, friendship-making, and dating skills. As with most such efforts in the field, this approach appears to have clinical utility but will require further empirical study before its efficacy can be unequivocally determined.

Psychopharmacological Treatments. While still controversial, use of psychopharmacological agents with both adult and adolescent substance abusers has become increasingly widespread (see review by Fialkov, 1993) For example, antidepressants are commonly being used to treat comorbid depression or to decrease craving of use. Several warnings, however, have been issued with regard to pharmacological intervention: (a) prescription of sedative/hypnotics and stimulants should be avoided due to their abuse potential; (b) the clinician is advised to wait until several weeks of abstinence have been achieved prior to a definitive assessment of mood-related symptoms; and (c) factors such as previous episodes of mood disturbance (especially during periods of abstinence), family history of mood disorder, and severity of mood symptoms (including persistent suicidality) may suggest a more aggressive psychopharmacological approach (Bukstein, 1993).

Summary

Despite survey data indicating reduced levels of substance use by adolescents, abuse of alcohol and other drugs by youths continues to be a major mental and public health problem in the United States. The purpose of this chapter was to provide an overview of salient aspects of adolescent substance use disorders. In particular, strategies and issues in adolescent substance abuse research and treatment were examined and evaluated. Alternatives (cognitive therapy, behavioral family therapy, social skills training, and psychopharmacological treatment) to traditional forms of intervention for adolescents who engage in substance use and abuse and related maladaptive behaviors were presented.

Clinicians and researchers in this area have become increasingly aware that many adolescent substance abusers have additional difficulties or disorders (e.g., conduct disorder, depression). Further, there is a heightened realization among care providers that this population is highly resistant to intervention. Consequently, treatment of severely dysfunctional substance-abusing adolescents demands intensive and comprehensive remediation strategies that integrate traditional, behavioral, psychological, and even biological modalities where needed. Unidimensional approaches to change will likely prove inadequate. Existing treatment programs must avoid biases and strive to develop and implement new, empirically tested interventions that are matched to the specific needs and deficits of substance-abusing adolescents across areas of dysfunction.

Research concerning the diagnosis, assessment, prevention, and treatment of adolescent substance abuse is at the nascent stage at this time. Further, it is clear that this is a major national health problem that will require a convergence of investigative efforts from the behavioral and medical sciences. Given the immediate and long-term deleterious consequences of substance use and abuse by our nation's youths, such concerted and labor-intensive endeavors will be required if significant amelioration of this problem is to be eventually achieved.

References

Alcoholics Anonymous (3rd ed.). (1976). New York: Alcoholics Anonymous World Services.

Alford, G. S., Koehler, R. A., & Leonard, J. (1991). Alcoholics Anonymous–Narcotics Anonymous model inpatient treatment of chemically dependent adolescents: A 2-year outcome study. *Journal of Studies on Alcohol, 52*, 118–126.

American Psychiatric Association (1980). *Diagnostic and statistical manual of mental disorders* (rev. 3rd ed.). Washington, DC: Author.

American Psychiatric Association. (1987). *Diagnostic and statistical manual of mental disorders* (rev. 3rd ed.). Washington, DC: Author.

American Psychiatric Association. (1993). *DSM-IV draft criteria*. Washington, DC: Author.

Arria, A. M., Tarter, R. E., & Van Thiel, D. H. (1991). The effects of alcohol abuse on the health of adolescents. *Alcohol Health and Research World, 15*, 52–57.

Bachman, J. G., Wallace, J. M., O'Malley, P. O., Johnston, L. D., Kurth, C. L., & Neighbors, H. W. (1991). Racial/ethnic differences in smoking, drinking and illicit drug use among American high school students. *American Journal of Public Health, 81*, 372–377.

Barnea, Z., Rahav, G., & Teichman, M. (1987). The reliability and consistency of self-reports on substance use in a longitudinal study. *British Journal of Addiction, 82*, 891–898.

Beck, A. T. (1976). *Cognitive therapy and the emotional disorders*. New York: International Universities Press.

Blane, H. (1979). Middle-aged alcoholics and young drinkers. In H. Blane & M. Chafetz (Eds.), *Youth, alcohol and social policy* (pp. 5–38). New York: Plenum.

Bohman, M. (1978). Some genetic aspects of alcoholism and criminality: A population of adoptees. *Archives of General Psychiatry, 35*, 269–276.

Brown, S. A. (1985). Reinforcement expectancies and alcoholism outcome after a 1 year follow-up. *Journal of Studies on Alcohol, 46,* 305–308.

Bry, B. H. (1988). Family-based approaches to reducing adolescent substance use: Theories, techniques, and findings. In E. R. Rahdert & J. Grabowski (Eds.), *Adolescent drug abuse: Analyses of treatment research* (NIDA Research Monograph No. 77). Washington, DC: U.S. Government Printing Office.

Bry, B. H., Conboy, C., & Bisgay, K. (1986). Decreasing adolescent drug use and school failure: Long-term effects of targeted family problem-solving training. *Child and Family Behavior Therapy, 8,* 43–59.

Bukstein, O. G. (1993). Overview of pharmacological treatment. In V. B. Van Hasselt & M. Hersen (Eds.), *Handbook of behavior therapy and pharmacotherapy for children: A comparative analysis* (pp. 13–32). Boston: Allyn and Bacon.

Bukstein, O. G., Brent, D. A., & Kaminer, Y. (1989). Comorbidity of substance abuse and other psychiatric disorders in adolescents. *American Journal of Psychiatry, 146,* 1131–1141.

Bukstein, O. G., & Van Hasselt, V. B. (1993). Alcohol and drug abuse. In A. S. Bellack & M. Hersen (Eds.), *Handbook of behavior therapy in the psychiatric setting* (pp. 453–475). New York: Plenum.

Chambers, W. J., Puig-Antich, J., Hirsh, M., et al. (1985). The assessment of affective disorders in children and adolescents by semi-structured interview. *Archives of General Psychiatry, 42,* 696–702.

Chaney, E. F. (1989). Social skills training. In R. K. Hester & W. R. Miller (Eds.), *Handbook of alcoholism treatment approaches* (pp. 206–221). New York: Pergamon.

Christiansen, B. A., Goldman, M. S., & Inn, A. (1982). Development of alcohol-related expectancies in adolescents: Separating pharmacological from social learning influences. *Journal of Consulting and Clinical Psychology, 50,* 336–344.

Christiansen, B. A., Goldman, M. S., & Brown, S. A. (1985). The differential development of adolescent alcohol expectancies may predict adult alcoholism. *Addictive Behaviors, 10,* 299–306.

Christie, K. A., Burke, J. D., Regier, D. A., Rae, D. S., Boyd, J. H., & Locke, B. Z. (1988). Epidemiologic evidence for early onset of mental disorders and higher risk of drug abuse in young adults. *American Journal of Psychiatry, 145,* 971–975.

Cloninger, C. R., Bohman, M., & Sigvardsson, S. (1981). Inheritance of alcohol abuse. *Archives of General Psychiatry, 38,* 861–868.

Cotton, N. S. (1979). The familial incidence of alcoholism: A review. *Journal of Studies on Alcohol, 40,* 89–116.

Crumley, F. E. (1990). Substance abuse and adolescent suicidal behavior. *Journal of the American Medical Association, 263,* 3051–3056.

Deykin, E. Y., Levy, J. C., & Wells, V. (1987). Adolescent depression, alcohol and drug abuse. *American Journal of Public Health, 77,* 178–182.

Dishion, T. J., Patterson, G. R., & Reid, J. R. (1988). Parent and peer factors associated with drug sampling in early adolescence: Implications for treatment. In E. R. Rahdert & J. Grabowski (Eds.), *Adolescent drug abuse: Analyses of treatment research* (NIDA Research Monograph No. 77). Washington, DC: U.S. Government Printing Office.

Donovan, J. E., & Jessor, R. (1978). Adolescent problem drinking—psychosocial correlates in a national sample study. *Journal of Studies on Alcohol, 39,* 1506–1524.

Earles, F., Reich, W., Jung, K. O., & Cloninger, C. R. (1988). Psychopathology in children of alcoholic and antisocial parents. *Alcoholism: Clinical and Experimental Research, 12,* 481–487.

Fialkov, M. J. (1993). Substance abuse: Pharmacological treatment. In V. B. Van Hasselt & M. Hersen (Eds.), *Handbook of behavior therapy and pharmacotherapy for children: A comparative analysis* (pp. 291–314). Boston: Allyn and Bacon.

Frederikson, L. W., Jenkins, J. O., & Carr, C. R. (1976). Indirect modification of adolescent drug abuse using contingency contracting. *Journal of Behavior Therapy and Experimental Psychiatry, 7,* 377–378.

Friedman, A. S., & Utada, A. (1989). A method for diagnosing and planning the treatment of adolescent drug abusers. *Journal of Drug Education, 19,* 285–312.

Gittleman, R., Mannuzza, S., Shenker, R., & Bonagura, N. (1985). Hyperactive boys almost grown up: I. Psychiatric status. *Archives of General Psychiatry, 42,* 937–947.

Gold, M. S., & Dachis, G. A. (1986). The role of the laboratory in the evaluation of suspected drug abuse. *Journal of Clinical Psychiatry, 47,* 17–23.

Goodwin, D. W. (1979). Alcoholism and heredity. *Archives of General Psychiatry, 36,* 57–61.

Haggerty, K. P., Wells, E. A., Jenson, J. M., Catalano, R. F., & Hawkins, J. D. (1989). Delinquents and drug abuse: A model program for community reintegration. *Adolescence, 24,* 439–456.

Henly, G. A., & Winters, K. C. (1988). Development of problem severity scales for the assessment of adolescent alcohol and drug abuse. *International Journal of the Addictions, 23,* 65–85.

Herjanic, B., & Reich, W. (1982). Development of a structured interview for children: Agreement between child and parent on individual symptoms. *Journal of Abnormal Child Psychology, 10,* 307–324.

Hops, H., Tildesley, E., Lichtenstein, E., Ary, D., & Sherman, L. (1990). Parent-adolescent problem-solving interactions and drug use. *American Journal of Drug and Alcohol Abuse, 16,* 239–258.

Jaffe, J. H., Babor, T. F., & Fishbein, D. H. (1988). Alcoholics, aggression and antisocial personality. *Journal of Studies on Alcohol, 49,* 211–218.

Jessor, R. (1976). Predicting time and onset of marijuana use: A developmental study of high school youth. *Journal of Consulting and Clinical Psychology, 44,* 125–134.

Jessor, R. (1984). Adolescent problem drinking: Psychosocial aspects and developmental outcomes. In L. H. Towle (Ed.), *Proceedings: NIAAA-WHO Collaborating Center designation meeting and alcohol research seminar.* Washington, DC: Public Health Service.

Jessor, R., & Jessor, S. L. (1978). Theory testing on longitudinal research. In D. B. Kandel (Ed.), *Longitudinal research on drug use: Empirical findings and methodological issues* (pp. 41–71). Washington, DC: Hemisphere-Wiley.

Johnston, L. D. (1992). *Monitoring the future: 1991 National Student Survey.* Ann Arbor: University of Michigan.

Johnston, L. D., O'Malley, P. M., & Bachman, J. G. (1987). Psychotherapeutic, licit and illicit use of drugs among adolescents. *Journal of Adolescent Healthcare, 8,* 36–51.

Kaij, L. (1960). *Alcoholism in twins.* Stockholm: Almquist and Wiksell.

Kaminer, Y., Bukstein, O., & Tarter, R. E. (1991) The Teen Addiction Severity Index: Rationale and reliability. *International Journal of the Addictions, 26,* 219–226.

Kaminer, Y. (1994). *Adolescent substance abuse: a comprehensive guide to theory and practice.* New York: Plenum.

Kandel, D. B. (1982). Epidemiological and psychosocial perspectives on adolescent drug use. *Journal of the American Academy of Child Psychiatry, 21,* 328–347.

Kandel, D. B., & Logan, J. A. (1984). Pattern of drug use from adolescence to young adulthood: I. Periods of risk for initiation, continued use and discontinuation. *American Journal of Public Health, 74,* 660–666.

Kandel, D. B., Kessler, R. C., & Margulies, R. Z. (1978). Antecedents of adolescent initiation into stages of drug use: A developmental analysis. In D. B. Kandel (Ed.), *Longitudinal research on drug use: Empirical findings and methodological issues* (pp. 73–99). Washington, DC: Hemisphere-Wiley.

Kempton, T., Van Hasselt, V. B., Bukstein, O. G., & Null, J. A. (in press). Cognitive distortions and psychiatric diagnosis in dually diagnosed adolescents. *Journal of the American Academy of Child and Adolescent Psychiatry.*

Kett, J. K. (1977). *Rites of passage.* New York: Basic Books.

Kumpfer, K. L., & DeMarsh, J. (1980). Family environmental and genetic influences on children future chemical dependency. In S. Griswold-Ezekoge, K. L. Kempfer, & W. J. Bukoski (Eds.). *Childhood and chemical abuse: Prevention and intervention* (pp. 49–91). New York: Haworth.

Lender, M. E., & Martin, J. K. (1987). *Drinking in America.* New York: Free Press.

Mayer, J. E., & Filstead, W. J. (1979). Empirical procedure for defining adolescent alcohol abuse. *Journal of Studies on Alcohol, 40,* 291–300.

McLellan, A., Luborsky, L., Woody, G., & O'Brien, A. (1980). An improved diagnostic evaluation instrument for substance abuse patients: The Addiction Severity Scale Index. *Journal of Nervous and Mental Disease, 168,* 26–33.

Mendelson, J. H., & Mello, N. K. (1985). *The diagnosis and treatment of alcoholism.* New York: McGraw-Hill.

Metzger, D. S., Kushner, H., & McLellan, A. (1991). *Adolescent Problem Severity Index.* Philadelphia: Biomedical Computer Research Institute.

Musto, D. F. (1987). *The American disease: Origins of narcotic control.* New York: Oxford University Press.

Newcomb, M. D., & Bentler, P. M. (1986). Impact of adolescent drug use and social support on problems of young adults: A longitudinal study. *Journal of Abnormal Psychology, 97,* 64–75.

Oetting, E. R., & Beauvais, F. (1990). Adolescent drug use: Findings of national and local surveys. *Journal of Consulting and Clinical Psychology, 58,* 385–394.

Partanen, J., Bruun, M., & Markkanen, T. (1966). *Inheritance of drinking behaviors: A study on intelligence, personality and the use of alcohol of adult twins.* Helsinki: Finnish Foundation for Alcohol Studies.

Rahdert, E. R. (Ed.) (1991). *The Adolescent Assessment/Referral System manual.*

Washington, DC: U.S. Department of Health and Human Services, Alcohol Drug Abuse and Mental Health Administration.

Robin, A. L., & Foster, S. L. (1988). *Negotiating parent adolescent conflict: A behavioral-family systems approach.* New York: Guilford.

Robins, L. N., & McEvoy, L. (1990). Conduct problems as predictors of substance abuse. In L. Robins & M. Rutter (Eds.), *Straight and devious pathways from childhood to adulthood* (pp. 182–204). Cambridge, England: Cambridge University Press.

Rounsaville, B. J., Spitzer, R. L., & Williams, J. B. W. (1986). Proposed changes in DSM-III substance use disorders: Description and rationale. *American Journal of Psychiatry, 143,* 463–468.

Rueger, D. B., & Liberman, R. P. (1984). Behavioral family therapy for delinquent and substance-abusing adolescents. *Journal of Drug Issues, 14,* 403–418.

Singh, E., Kandel, D., & Johnson, B. (1975). The internal validity and reliability of drug use responses in a large scale survey. *Journal of Drug Issues, 5,* 426–443.

Tarter, R. (1990). Evaluation and treatment of adolescent substance abuse: A decision tree method. *American Journal of Drug and Alcohol Abuse, 16,* 1046.

Van Hasselt, V. B., & Christ, M. A. (1992). *Social problem skills training for adolescent substance abusers: A treatment manual.* Unpublished manuscript, Nova University, Fort Lauderdale, FL.

Van Hasselt, V. B., Hersen, M., & Milliones, J. (1978). Social skills training for alcoholics and drug addicts: A review. *Addictive Behaviors, 3,* 221–233.

Van Hasselt, V. B., Null, J. A., Kempton, T, & Bukstein, O. G. (1993). Social skills and depression in adolescent substance abusers. *Addictive Behaviors, 18,* 9–18.

Vingilis, E., & Smart, R. G. (1981). Physical dependence on alcohol in youth. In Y. Israel, F. B. Gleser, & H. Kalant (Eds.), *Research advances in alcohol and drug problems* (Vol. 6, pp. 197–215). New York: Plenum.

Weschler, H. (1979). Patterns of alcohol consumption among the young: High school, college and general population studies. In H. Blane & M. Chafetz (Eds.), *Youth, alcohol, and social policy* (pp. 39–58). New York: Plenum.

West, M. O., & Printz, R. J. (1987). Parental alcoholism and childhood psychopathology. *Psychological Bulletin, 102,* 204–218.

Wheeler, K., & Malmquist, J. (1987). Treatment approaches in adolescent chemical dependency. *Pediatric Clinics of North America, 34,* 437–447.

White, H. R. (1987). Longitudinal stability and dimensional structure of problem drinking in adolescence. *Journal of Studies on Alcohol, 48,* 541–550.

Windle, M. (1991). Alcohol use and abuse. *Alcohol Health and Research World, 15,* 5–10.

Winters, K. C. (1990). The need for improved assessment of adolescent substance involvement. *Journal of Drug Issues, 20,* 487–502.

Winters, K. C., Stinchfield, R. D., Henly, G. A., & Schwartz, R. H. (1991). Validity of adolescent self-report of alcohol and other drug involvement. *International Journal of the Addictions, 25,* 1379–1395.

White House. (1989). *National drug control strategy.* Washington, DC: U.S. Government Printing Office.

13

Anorexia Nervosa and Bulimia Nervosa

D. Blake Woodside

This chapter reviews the eating disorders of anorexia nervosa and bulimia nervosa. While much has been learned about the nature and etiology of these illnesses, and significant progress has been made in terms of formalizing treatment strategies, these illnesses remain a significant burden on those involved in the care of younger age groups.

Table 13–1 presents the draft DSM-IV diagnostic criteria for anorexia nervosa and bulimia nervosa (American Psychiatric Association, 1993). Anorexia nervosa is characterized by a relentless drive for thinness and a body image distortion that leads individuals to reach very low body weights. Patients achieve these low weights by strict dieting and various forms of purging, including excessive exercising, vomiting, or abuse of laxatives or diuretics.

Bulimia nervosa is characterized by bingeing: that is, the consumption of large quantities of food in a short period of time. Clinicians occasionally confuse the presence of vomiting, a common symptom of bulimia, with bulimia itself. Only about 80% of bulimics actually vomit, however, with the remainder purging through other means, such as those described above. Clinicians should recognize that the symptom of binge eating is a fairly common one in the adolescent age group, and that bulimia nervosa should not be diagnosed unless all diagnostic criteria are met. The typical eating pattern of most patients with bulimia nervosa includes strict dieting in between binges; some patients are sufficiently chaotic in their eating patterns that there are no periods of even relatively normal eating, only continuous bingeing interspersed with desperate attempts to avoid eating. In addition to the presence of bingeing, bulimics share with anorexics an intense preoccupation with weight and shape.

Both anorexia nervosa and bulimia nervosa are subtyped. For anorexia nervosa, a distinction is made between the form in which weight is controlled solely through restricted food intake and the situation where the anorexic individual also binges or purges. It is no longer appropriate to make the diagnosis of both anorexia nervosa and bulimia nervosa together,

Table 13–1
Diagnostic Criteria for Anorexia Nervosa and Bulimia Nervosa

1. Anorexia nervosa

    A. Refusal to maintain body weight at or above a minimally normal weight for age and height (e.g., weight loss leading to maintenance of body weight less than 85% of that expected; or failure to make expected weight gain during period of growth leading to body weight less than 85% of that expected).

    B. Intense fear of gaining weight or becoming fat, even though underweight.

    C. Disturbance in the way in which one's body weight or shape is experienced; undue influence of body weight or shape of self-evaluation, or denial of the seriousness of the current body weight.

    D. In postmenarcheal females, amenorrhea (i.e., the absence of at least three consecutive menstrual cycles). A woman is considered to have amenorrhea if her periods occur only following hormone (e.g., estrogen) administration.

    Specify type:

    Restricting type: During the episode of anorexia nervosa the person does not regularly engage in binge eating or purging behavior (i.e., self-induced vomiting or the misuse of laxatives or diuretics).

    Binge eating/purging type: During the episode of anorexia nervosa, the person regularly engages in binge-eating or purging behavior (i.e., self-induced vomiting or the misuse of laxatives or diuretics).

2. Bulimia nervosa

    A. Recurrent episodes of binge eating. An episode of binge eating is characterized by both of the following:

        1. Eating, in a discrete period of time (e.g., within any 2-hour period), an amount of food that is definitely larger than most people would eat during a similar period of time and under similar circumstances.

        2. A sense of lack of control over eating during the episode (e.g., a feeling that one cannot stop eating or control what or how much one is eating).

    B. Recurrent inappropriate compensatory behavior in order to prevent weight gain, such as self-induced vomiting, misuse of laxatives, diuretics or other medications; fasting; or excessive exercise.

    C. The binge eating and inappropriate compensatory behaviors both occur, on average, at least twice a week for 3 months.

    D. Self-evaluation is unduly influenced by body shape and weight.

    E. The disturbance does not occur exclusively during episodes of anorexia nervosa.

    Specify type:

    Purging type: The person regularly engages in self-induced vomiting or the misuse of laxatives or diuretics.

    Non-purging type: The person uses other inappropriate compensatory behaviors, such as fasting or excessive exercise, but does not regularly engage in self-induced vomiting or the misuse of laxatives or diuretics.

as was the case in DSM-III-R. For bulimia nervosa, a differentiation is made between those individuals who purge via laxatives, vomiting, or diuretics (purging type) and those who do not (nonpurging type).

Historical Background

Anorexia nervosa was first reported in the English literature in the late seventeenth century (Morton, 1694). Sporadic reports continued to appear for the next two hundred years (Parry-Jones, 1985), at which point interest in the disorders was rekindled by Lasegue (1873/1964) and Gull (1874). At this time, anorexia nervosa was considered to be primarily a psychological disorder; however, by the early twentieth century attention had shifted towards dysfunction of the body, particularly the hypothalamus (Simmonds, 1914). Interest in the illness then waned until the 1940s, when psychoanalytic theorists began to reinterpret the symptoms in the light of new psychological theories. By the mid-1960's, clinicians working from an object relations viewpoint (Bruch, 1973) began to focus more on the interpersonal experience of the patient, and the 1970s saw the addition of theories related to family functioning (Selvini-Palazolli, 1974; Minuchin, Rosman, & Baker, 1978). In 1982, Garfinkel and Garner suggested a multidetermined approach to this illness, an approach that has continued to be the accepted mode of viewing the illness.

Bulimia nervosa has a shorter history in terms of formal diagnostic assessment; however, some individuals have suggested that it was reported in the Talmud (Kaplan & Garfinkel, 1984), and there are numerous case reports of illnesses reminiscent of bulimia nervosa in the last few centuries (Parry-Jones & Parry-Jones, 1991). Russell (1979) first proposed a diagnosis separate from anorexia nervosa, and this was followed by clear evidence that distinguished the two syndromes on the basis of clinical symptoms and psychopathology (Garfinkel, Moldofsky, & Garner, 1980). In the last decade there has been an explosion both in the number of individuals identified with bulimia nervosa and in the body of knowledge related to it.

Current controversies in the field include the recognition that nutritional status plays a significant role in almost all aspects of human behavior, psychological and physical, and that studies of eating disorders should probably include comparisons between the stage of active symptoms and a stage of fairly normal eating. The natural histories of the two illnesses is still being clarified, and there is no clear consensus about how to view individuals with symptoms of both disorders. Rigorous studies of response to treatment are generally lacking, and it is unknown how patients respond to treatment in the long run. Finally, even though Morton's (1694) initial report included both a male and a female case, there is still interest in how males and females with these disorders might be similar or different.

Clinical Picture

Anorexia nervosa

The most obvious clinical feature of anorexia nervosa—the emaciation demonstrated by most patients—is occasionally focused on to the exclusion of other symptoms of the disorder. Patients achieve their starved state through dietary restraint accompanied by various methods of purging, as described earlier. Many of the typical features of anorexia nervosa are directly related to the starved state, as has been demonstrated by the work of Keys, Brozek, Henschel, Mickelson, and Taylor (1950) and Fichter and Pirke (1984). These include the intense preoccupation with food that most anorexics experience, the physical symptoms (e.g., bloating, early satiety, bradycardia, amenorrhea), and many psychological changes (e.g., irritability, lability of mood, depression, and exacerbations of premorbid personality traits). Many individuals experience extreme social isolation as a consequence of their starved state. The psychological effects of starvation, while often less well appreciated than the more dramatic physical manifestations of the illnesses, are enormously important because they suggest the nature of treatment that is likely to be successful. Table 13–2 lists some common side effects of starvation.

Despite the plethora of symptoms described above, it must be remembered that the two cardinal psychological signs of the condition, the drive for thinness and the body image distortion, antedate any significant amount of weight loss and persist long after a normal weight has been restored. It is possible that the body image distortion that occurs in anorexia nervosa may be related to the heritability of these disorders: according to A. J. Holland (personal communication), identical twins who are discordant for anorexia nervosa both show a body image distortion, with the

Table 13–2
Common Side Effects of Starvation

Dermatological	*Cardiovascular*	*Gastrointestinal*
Dry skin	Bradycardia	Delayed gastric emptying
Thinning hair	Hypotension	Bloating
Lanugo hair	Dependent edema	Early satiety
Cyanosis	Arrhythmias	Constipation or diarrhea
Carotene pigmentation		
Endocrine	*Musculoskeletal*	*Cognitive and Behavioral*
Amenorhea	Weakness	Depression
Hypothemia	Osteoporosis or	Poor concentration
Oligomenorrhea	Osteopenia	Food preoccupation
		Impaired sleep
		Decreased libido

unaffected twin apparently able to resist acting on the misperception about body size.

Bulimia Nervosa

The cardinal symptom of bulimia nervosa is episodes of binge eating; the very term *bulimia* is derived from an ancient Greek word that translates as "ox-like eating." While most bulimics also vomit, presence of vomiting is not required for the diagnosis of bulimia, and vomiting is a frequent symptom of anorexia nervosa as well. It should be noted that individuals suffering from bulimia nervosa share with anorexic patients an extreme concern about weight and shape and are engaging in similarly intense efforts to restrain eating.

The chaotic eating patterns of bulimia nervosa have a variety of psychological effects, as is the case with the starvation of anorexia nervosa. It should be noted that while patients with bulimia nervosa often present at average chart weight, their premorbid weight typically is slightly above average (Garfinkel et al., 1980). Average weight thus often represents a state of relative starvation for these individuals. Complications of this relative starvation include lability of mood, sleep disturbance, decreased concentration, and irritability. These features can occasionally be confused with depressive episodes; the diagnosis of depression must be made with caution in the patient with active bulimia nervosa. Because of the profound effects of chaotic eating and starvation on mood, significant suicidal ideation may occur in some patients.

Despite the above caution regarding depression, there is considerable lifetime psychiatric comorbidity in these individuals. The majority of patients with bulimia nervosa will report a lifetime history of at least one episode of depression, and nearly 50% will have experienced difficulty with a substance, most commonly alcohol. Diagnoses of anxiety disorders or bipolar affective disorder are less frequent. In the experience of the author, the diagnosis of schizophrenia is rare in patients with either anorexia nervosa or bulimia nervosa. When diagnosed, comorbid illnesses should be actively treated, as will be discussed below.

Etiology

No definitive etiology has been demonstrated for either anorexia nervosa or bulimia nervosa. As of this writing, a multidetermined model, such as that advocated by Garfinkel and Garner (1982) seems most appropriate in assisting our understanding of these complex conditions. In this model each individual experiences a range of specific predisposing factors that may be psychological, biological, social, or familial in nature. Some typical issues that are common contributors to the development of an eating disor-

Table 13–3
Common Contributors to the Development of an Eating Disorder

Individual

Autonomy, identity, and separation concerns manifested as:
  Depression
  Behavioral disturbance

Perceptual disturbances (e.g., body image distortion)

Weight preoccupation

Chronic medical illnesses (e.g., diabetes mellitus)

Family

Inherited biological predisposition (e.g., family history of eating disorders, alcoholism, affective illness, obesity)

Magnification of cultural factors

Parent-child interactions leading to problems with autonomy and separation

Cultural

Pressures for thinness

Pressures for performance

---

der are presented in Table 13–3. The common thread to these issues is the development first of a sense of impaired self-worth, followed by a feeling of ineffectiveness or being out of control. In this model, these feelings may lead some individuals to engage in dieting behaviors as a method of regaining a sense of control and temporarily elevating self-esteem.

In the long run, however, dieting and losing weight are unlikely to be an effective response to psychological difficulties. Figure 13–1 demonstrates the ways in which dieting behaviors can intensify problems for patients with eating disorders. First, since the dieting behavior deflects rather than resolves psychological problems, it must then continue if the affected individual is to go on feeling well. This is in itself a vicious cycle, as the effect of long-term dieting is very often weight gain (for a review, see Ciliska, 1991, pp. 3–21). Second, for a small percentage of individuals, weight loss to the point of emaciation occurs, resulting in anorexia nervosa. Many specific effects of starvation, such as bloating, early satiety, or ankle edema, may directly lead the patient to restrain his or her food intake further in a vain effort to reverse the starvation effect. The severe effects of starvation and chaotic eating on the educational and relationship spheres of these patients contribute even more to their sense of ineffectiveness and low self-esteem.

Why certain individuals are able to continue to suppress their weight to this point is unknown, but it is possible that there is some hereditary effect operating. Eventually, due to the profound effects of starvation on physical and psychological functioning, an individual with anorexia nervosa may come to treatment. It is rare, however, for the core symptom of the illness—the drive for thinness—to be ego dystonic at this stage: rather, the patient will often desire to be rid of the complications of his or her starved state while remaining very thin.

More common is the development of bingeing in response to ongoing dieting. The work of Polivy (1976) on the determinants of normal eating strongly suggests a causal relationship between chronically restrained eating and bingeing behaviors. Once established, the cycle of dieting and bingeing will often lead to purging behaviors, or to more strict dieting to "undo" the effect of the binges. Either of these behaviors simply leads in turn to increased starvation and thus increased bingeing, facilitating the continuation of the cycle. Nor does any of this contribute to a resolution of the initial psychological disturbance; once one has invested one's self-esteem into not eating, the development of binge eating is a devastating blow that, simply feeds into the cycle. Viewed in this light, application of models of addiction to the eating disorders becomes possible. Food is not the addictive substance, however, and eating is not the addictive behavior. Rather, these individuals must be viewed as having become addicted to dieting behaviors, and it must be these behaviors that are targeted in treatment efforts.

The development of an appreciation of the connection between dietary restraint and eating disorders is an essential task for any professional working clinically with patients suffering from anorexia nervosa or bulimia nervosa, regardless of the nature of the primary treatment that is being offered. Failure to have a clear understanding of these interactions may significantly impair the ability of a clinician to provide appropriate care for these patients. Any treatment strategy that is focused on food avoidance almost certainly will make both illnesses worse in the vast majority of cases.

Early Warning Signs of Eating Disorders

One common problem faced by those dealing with a younger age group is the scenario of an unwilling, uncooperative patient being (sometimes literally) dragged in by an anxious, usually rather angry parent. It is often difficult or impossible to obtain a complete history from the patient, and one is thus left with trying to make sense of the parents' suspicions. Table 13–4 presents some of the common early warning signs of anorexia nervosa, most of which can be reported by parents.

Changing Weight Goals. Dieting behaviors per se are extremely common in adolescents, especially adolescent girls. The normal dieter will most typically fluctuate around a fairly narrow range, however, and have a fairly stable goal weight. Ongoing decreases in this goal weight should be viewed

Table 13–4
Early Signs of Anorexia Nervosa and Bulimia

1. Ever-decreasing weight goals
2. Dieting that leads to increasing criticism of one's body
3. Dieting that leads to social isolation
4. Dieting that leads to loss of menstrual periods
5. Hiding foods, or any evidence of purging (e.g., vomiting; misuse of laxatives, diuretics, and diet pills)

with considerable suspicion, especially if the patient appears visibly underweight.

Dieting That Leads to Increasing Criticism of One's Body. Again, in the setting of so-called normal dieting, one would expect the successful dieter to be satisfied with achieving his or her goal weight. Dieting that is associated with increased rather than diminished body dissatisfaction may be an early warning sign of an eating disorder. It should be recognized that the reverse is *not* true, especially for eating disorders at an early stage.

Dieting That Leads to Social Isolation. Many teenage (and older) dieters claim that their main reason for dieting is that social and cultural pressure prevents them from engaging in specific activities because they are too heavy. Dieters who become more socially isolated rather than less so are at risk for developing an eating disorder. Such increased social isolation tends to be related to the increased criticism of the body referred to above; a typical teenage girl with anorexia nervosa will be described as "doing nothing but dieting and schoolwork." A young girl with bulimia nervosa will likely be described as moody and unable to concentrate, and her parents may complain that "she never goes out with her friends anymore."

Dieting That Leads to Loss of Menstrual Periods. The amenorrhea of anorexia nervosa is always related to starvation. While it may also have specific psychological significance for an individual patient, it must be viewed as a medical complication of the illness. Dieting that leads to amenorrhea is never normal and should always be investigated by a complete history and physical examination, including a detailed history of weight and dietary intake. It is also risky for physicians to prescribe oral contraceptives for menstrual irregularity in adolescents without having performed such an examination. The picture is slightly complicated when the eating disorder is accompanied by extreme exercise; it is well recognized that some female athletes will develop menstrual irregularities associated with heavy training regimens. Nevertheless, clinicians should be extremely cautious about accepting secondary amenorrhea as normal under any circumstances.

Hiding Food or Any Evidence of Purging. Evidence of any purging behavior (e.g., vomiting; misuse of laxatives, diuretics, or diet pills) should be addressed by performing a complete eating disorder history and by performing a physical examination. Clinicians should *not* regard purging behavior as normal or as a stage an adolescent will grow out of.

Course and Prognosis

Very little is know about the long-term course of these illnesses. One long-term follow-up study of anorexia nervosa (Theander, 1985) suggests that it is chronic unless treated and that long-term morbidity is considerable even with treatment. In this study, nearly 15% of subjects were dead by 30, and an additional 25% remained at least partially ill. An excellent review of follow-up studies of anorexia nervosa is found in Steinhausen, Rauss-Mason, and Seidel (1991). There are no long-term studies of the natural history of bulimia nervosa; however, most authors suggest that bulimia is a chronic illness with a variable course characterized by periods of partial remission and relapse.

While these illnesses are typically thought of as having their onset almost exclusively in the younger age groups, this is probably not the case. Some data (Woodside & Garfinkel, in press) suggest that only about 50% of individuals with either anorexia nervosa or bulimia nervosa will fall ill by age 18. More importantly, the oft-held impression that bulimia nervosa is a late complication of anorexia nervosa is also not likely true, with Woodside, Rockert, and Garkinkel (1991) demonstrating that the development of bulimia nervosa often *precedes* the development of anorexia nervosa. Clinicians working with adolescent populations would be advised to consider a diagnosis of bulimia nervosa in any young female who has a history of wide weight fluctuations or for whom there is any evidence of purging behavior. As well, individuals who carry another primary diagnosis, such as depression, and are not responding to treatment, may also have a covert eating disorder.

Complications

The majority of the physical and psychological complications of anorexia nervosa are related to starvation, as has been described above. (For a review of the medical complications of eating disorders, see Kaplan & Woodside, 1987.) It must be remembered that anorexic individuals who purge are at the same risk for sudden death as bulimic individuals engaging in the same activities. The long-term effect on ultimate growth potential of an episode on anorexia nervosa is unclear; however, it is now widely acknowledged that even relatively young patients suffer from reduced bone density, and that the vigorous exercise characteristic of these individuals does not mitigate this fact.

There are numerous complications of bulimia nervosa that are related to bingeing and purging behaviors; as mentioned above, purging behaviors are common in anorexia nervosa as well. Swollen parotid glands result from local irritation by gastric acids during vomiting. Russell's sign, a callus or sore on the back of the hand, is secondary to abrasion of the back of the knuckles during the manual induction of vomiting (Russell, 1979). Patients who vomit frequently may develop severe dental caries, as tooth enamel can be quite sensitive to the action of gastric acids. In rare instances, lacerations of the esophagus will occur, resulting in blood appearing in vomitus. Bulimic patients experience the same bloating as patients with anorexia nervosa, but may not have early satiety. Patients who abuse laxatives often experience alternating periods of diarrhea and constipation, and they sometimes have bloody stools. In extreme cases, individuals who are using large numbers of laxatives may become laxative dependent (i.e., unable to have normal bowel movements without the aid of purgative laxatives).

Individuals who purge via vomiting, laxative abuse, or the abuse of diuretics may experience hypokalemia (i.e., a low level of the body salt potassium). Because potassium is critical for normal heart function, hypokalemia can lead to death, sometimes with minimal warning, and it is one of the most serious medical complications of anorexia nervosa or bulimia nervosa. It is imperative that potassium levels be monitored regularly in patients who are purging, whether they are suffering from anorexia nervosa or bulimia. Table 13–5 presents a profile of the high-risk patient suffering from anorexia nervosa or bulimia nervosa.

Table 13–5
The High-Risk Patient

This patient has experienced the following:

- Purging, especially by multiple means
- A very low weight (less than 60% of chart average or expected weight)
- A history of self-harm behaviors
- Ipecac usage
- Use of amphetamines as appetite suppressants
- Use of thyroid medication
- Low potassium

Epidemiology

Anorexia nervosa is thought to occur in approximately 0.5% to 1% of women aged 15 to 40 (Crisp, Palmer, & Kalucy, 1976), although no good epidemiological study has been performed. Bulimia nervosa probably occurs in a slightly higher percentage, perhaps as much as 1% to 2% of the same age grouping (Fairburn & Beglin, 1990). The symptom of binge eating is fairly common in both men and women; however, this symptom alone should not be confused with the full syndrome, which requires the excessive preoccupation with weight and shape described above.

Male cases account for about 5% of most samples, with bulimia nervosa being more prevalent than anorexia nervosa. The reason for the predominance of female cases is unknown; it may well relate to the differing extents to which men and women receive the cultural message to achieve a slim shape. It may also be that other, as yet undetermined constitutional factors play some part. In any event, no significant clinical differences have been demonstrated between male and female cases, and the two situations should be treated in the same manner.

The epidemiology of dieting behaviors is a much more grim affair. Recent studies (Eisele, Hartsgaard, & Light, 1986; Storz, 1982) suggest that very large numbers of young girls are dieting or at least body conscious, and that dieting behavior is so common as to be ubiquitous in the teenage group. In the two studies mentioned above, 78% to 83% of 12- to 18-year-old girls felt that they should be thinner. There is increasing evidence that dieting behaviors and body consciousness are on the rise among boys and young men as well.

Dieting behaviors and weight concerns are also becoming common among the very young. Maloney, McGuire, Daniles, and Speckler (1989) surveyed 7- to 12-year-olds and found that 45% (78% of the girls and 40% of the boys) wished to be thinner; 35% had attempted to lose weight. Such studies should give pause to those who consider eating disorders in adolescents to be a passing fad.

Familial Pattern

There is now clear evidence that both anorexia nervosa and bulimia nervosa cluster in families (for a review, see Woodside, in press). It is presently unclear to what extent this familial clustering is hereditary or due to common environmental influences. The heritability of anorexia nervosa has been estimated at 77% (Holland, Sicotte, & Treasure 1988). Bulimia nervosa appears to be slightly less heritable, with the most recent estimate being between 35% and 55% (Kendler, et al., 1992). Rates of familial aggregation run between 4% and 7% for first-degree relatives in most samples with rates for female relatives alone being somewhat higher, around 10% (Strober, Morrell, Burroughs, Salkin, & Jacobs, 1985). No studies have yet attempted to establish a mode of genetic inheritance or to establish linkage to chromosomal markers.

A link between eating disorders and affective disorders has been postulated by many authors (for a review, see Strober & Katz, 1988) on the basis that (a) there is significant comorbidity between affective disorders and eating disorders, and (b) antidepressant medications are useful as antibulimic treatment in a subgroup of patients. The most recent work in this area (Strober, Lampert, Morrell, Burroughs, & Jacobs, 1990) suggests that for anorexia nervosa, high rates of comorbid depression occur mainly among those who have a strong family history of depression; thus it is unlikely that the two illnesses are one and the same. The situation for bulimia nervosa is still very much undecided at present.

Differential Diagnosis and Assessment

Differential Diagnosis

Numerous other conditions can mimic eating disorders. Because of the obvious low weight of most patients, it is not too difficult for clinicians to suspect the nature of their illness. Clinicians should note, however, that current societal expectations about weight and shape will prevent many individuals (including health care workers, who are not immune to such influences) from perceiving patients in the 85% range as being emaciated; such patients are often described as "slender," or "attractively slim." For anorexia nervosa, the primary goal is to establish whether there has been a body image distortion and a drive for thinness: in the absence of these two symptoms, a diagnosis of anorexia nervosa cannot be made. Emaciated adolescents who lack these two cardinal symptoms should receive a very thorough examination for other possible causes of the loss of weight.

Occasionally, patients will lose their drive for thinness at extremely low weights. This criterion, though, can still be considered met if it can be established that the patient did suffer from such a drive at a higher, but still low, weight. Regardless of the results of the psychiatric examination, a thorough physical examination and a series of appropriate investigations should be a mandatory part of the assessment of such a patient.

The diagnostic criteria of amenorrhea is included as a marker for starvation; in the author's treatment setting, young women taking oral contraceptives are excluded from the need to demonstrate this symptom. It is probable that menstrual irregularity is a common way for early or mild anorexia nervosa to present itself. All clinicians who treat young girls presenting with this symptom should obtain a careful history of eating and dieting practices. Establishing that sufficient weight loss or lack of growth has occurred can be difficult in the adolescent age group, as appropriate charts are not always available, and the stage of puberty is often more important than age in calendar years. One approach to deal with this problem is to attempt to chart a growth curve for the patient using available norms, then examine whether the patient has significantly fallen off from his or her growth curve.

Bulimia can present in in a number of ways that are less obvious than anorexia nervosa. Some patients will admit to vomiting—usually because they have been discovered doing so—but will not volunteer information about bingeing behaviours. Patients abusing laxatives may present with symptoms similar to irritable bowel. Because of the effects of starvation on mood, many patients present with symptoms of depression. In older adolescents, differentiating between syndromal depression and mood lability may be possible; this may not be the case for younger adolescents.

Many patients with bulimia nervosa will complain of symptoms of fatigue, or parents will report poor school performance. A thyroid workup is a common investigation in such cases; however, as the semistarvation of bulimia nervosa causes abnormal thyroid function (for a review, see Kaplan & Woodside, in press), clinicians would be well advised to be cautious in this area. As is probably the case with anorexia nervosa, menstrual irregularity is a common presentation for patients with bulimia nervosa. Laboratory investigations of this situation will show the same mild abnormalities as with thyroid indices.

When faced with one of the above dilemmas, clinicians should take a history of eating, weight, and shape concerns, and, most importantly, ask the patient directly whether he or she is bingeing. As information about eating disorders is available freely to adolescents in the popular press, there is little danger of inducing such a symptom by asking about it. The situation is similar for vomiting. Most patients, if asked directly, will provide relatively accurate information about bingeing and vomiting. A history of very wide weight fluctuations is usually indicative of some dieting efforts and warrants a careful history of other eating behaviors.

It is possible to misdiagnose anorexia nervosa when other psychological problems are active. Patients with schizophrenia will occasionally present with low weights, but they usually have bizarre delusions about food (e.g., that it is poisoned) that explain their lack of eating. Individuals suffering from depressive illness will often experience weight loss but usually will describe the loss of weight as ego dystonic or regard it with indifference; they lack a drive for thinness and a body image distortion. Various types of conversion syndromes may be very difficult to distinguish from anorexia nervosa. Choking and swallowing phobias, and obsessional disorders that reduce food intake because of excessive time spent preparing food in unusual ways, provide an initial clinical picture that is very similar to that of anorexia nervosa in that they include low weight and food avoidance as symptoms. The most helpful course in these cases is to take an extremely careful history of the patient's eating behavior, including their rationale for their eating habits, and to search diligently for evidence of a drive for thinness or a body image distortion.

Finally, many adolescents who present with behavioral disturbances will also have eating disturbances. While the eating disturbance may appear trivial in comparison to other problems, the adult literature has clearly demonstrated that there are very profound changes in the level of functioning of patients once eating is normalized.

Eating Disorders in the Very Young. There is now evidence that eating disorders occur in prepubertal children, although this is fairly rare (for a review see Woodside, 1990). Table 13–6 presents suggested diagnostic criteria for very young children. There is no evidence presently available to suggest that either the course or the prognosis of the illnesses are different in prepubertal children compared to older adolescents. Treasure and Thompson (1988) provide a thorough review of this topic.

Eating Disorders in Males. Eating disorders do occur in males as well as females, if only rarely. Available evidence suggests that male cases are indistinguishable from female cases in terms of both clinical features and prognosis. The issue of more frequent homosexuality in male cases is still somewhat controversial; however, clinicians need to be aware that starvation has a profound effect on male sexual drive, and that starvation-related lack of interest in sexuality should not be confused with homosexual orientation. There is no evidence of excessive femininity in males with eating disorders; while such factors may be important in individual cases, therapists should avoid generalizing these cases to all male patients with eating disorders. An excellent review of this topic is found in Anderson (1989).

Assessment

Table 13–7 presents the components of a basic assessment of the patient with an eating disorder. Individuals working in the field of eating disorders who are not physicians may wish to arrange to have portions of the assess-

Table 13–6
Criteria for Anorexia Nervosa in the Young (Russell, 1985)

Criteria	Symptom
Weight loss or a failure to gain weight	Avoidance of "fattening" foods
Specific psychopathology	An overvalued dread of fatness
Delayed puberty	A delay in the sequence of pubertal events (especially menarche)

Table 13–7
Basic Components of the Assessment
of a Patient with an Eating Disorder

Overview and initiating factors
Weight history
Typical day's eating
Bingeing
Purging
Medical/psychological complications
Past psychiatric history
Family history (and family interview)

ment completed by a physician with whom they feel they have a good working relationship. This is important primarily because both anorexia nervosa and bulimia nervosa may result in serious, life-threatening medical complications. Therapists who are not physicians should not put themselves in a position of feeling responsible for monitoring these complications when they neither are trained to do so nor have access to appropriate diagnostic facilities.

The assessment has two basic parts: (a) assessment of eating behaviors and symptoms, and (b) assessment of other relevant information, including a detailed family assessment. Information specific to the assessment of the family will be provided separately below.

Adolescents with eating disorders may at times be reticent about disclosing their symptoms. The author's own practice is to interview the patient alone for about 45 minutes, followed by a family interview of about 30 minutes. Other formats, such as completing the whole assessment with the family present, may be appropriate for certain age groups, particularly for the very young patient. If there is any evidence of marked conflict between the patient and parents, it might be wiser to interview the patient alone, at least briefly, and state at the outset of the interview what information will be shared with the parents and what will be held in confidence. Such disclosure will occasionally be mandated by law, depending on the locale of practice of a given therapist.

Eating Behaviors. Initially obtaining an overview of the history of the eating disorder is useful, as it will assist the interviewer in focusing his or her questions more effectively. Such an overview includes information on the initiation of dieting behaviors and on significant changes in eating patterns (e.g., the onset of bingeing or purging behaviors) that have occurred since. Beginning in this fashion may also shed significant light on the actual predisposing and initiating factors for the individual in question.

Weight History. A weight history is very important. (It should also be noted that a record of height is an important component of such a history.)

Patients with anorexia nervosa will typically have weight fluctuations between average weight and a low weight, and only rarely will they have a history of obesity. Patients with bulimia nervosa often show dramatic fluctuations in weight, both above and below average. It is important to get an idea of premorbid weight, and this may be a convenient opportunity to get some idea of the size of family members. This may also be an appropriate time to take a menstrual history from female patients, including the documentation of oral contraceptive use. Special charts are available to estimate how the patient's weight compares to population norms; clinicians must, however, take racial differences into account. With younger patients, estimates of weight are often referred to in comparison to expected growth.

Typical Daily Intake. Attempt to assess a typical day's food intake for the patient. Some patients will be reluctant to disclose this information; others, especially patients with severe bulimia nervosa, may have such chaotic eating habits that there is no typical pattern. It is important to be very specific. Enquire about portion sizes as well as the type of food eaten; as some patients will eat very small quantities of a wide variety of foods. Information about foods that are typically avoided will be useful when assessing binge eating.

Bingeing. Because many patients who experience binge eating are profoundly ashamed by the activity, they will not always volunteer information about it. A decision not to ask about binges may serve only to heighten the patient's sense of shame and to drive the behavior further underground. A forthright but empathic approach is best, not only to normalize the process of talking about binge eating but also to promote the patient's self-monitoring ability. The clinician should ask directly about onset, frequency, and initiating and alleviating factors of bingeing, including a description of what constitutes a typical binge.

Purging. A detailed inquiry into methods of purging is a mandatory part of an eating disorder history. Asking a patient about a purging method that he or she has not used is not likely to result in the initiation of the behavior; information about such methods is freely available, and, as is the case with bingeing, failing to ask may simply reinforce the patient's sense of shame and inadequacy.

Particularly dangerous purging behaviors include the use of ipecac to induce vomiting (which may lead to cardiac failure); purging by vomiting, laxatives, and diuretics (all of which cause significant potassium depletion); the use of thyroid medication (which may lead to significant cardiac damage); and the use of amphetamines to suppress appetite (as these substances are highly addictive). It is important to ask about exercise, although there is considerable controversy as to what constitutes normal exercise. One useful guideline that the author employs is to consider any exercise that results in amenorrhea to be abnormal. Clinicians assessing sexually active females need to be aware that purging behaviors may negatively affect the efficacy of oral contraceptives.

Other Relevant Information.

Medical and Psychological Complications. Making a detailed inquiry about these complications is helpful in many ways. First, it may alert the clinician to potentially life-threatening situations. Second, it may help the patient to attribute to the abnormal eating behaviors costs that he or she had not previously identified. This is true not only for physical complications of starvation, such as bloating and early satiety, but also for the psychological complications of abnormal eating, of which most patients are much less aware. This is another convenient point at which to assess the female patient's menstrual history.

Past History of Emotional Disturbance. This should include a history of other emotional disturbances from which the patient has suffered, as well as details of past treatments or counseling that the patient has received for any of these conditions. These are important because of the well-recognized comorbidity between eating disorders and other forms of emotional illness, especially affective and substance use disorders. Some patients with eating disorders will have received numerous other treatments for their illness, and it is usually helpful to discuss their expectations in terms of treatment. Many younger patients may be attending a consultation somewhat reluctantly, and this can be a good point to start building a collaborative relationship with the patient.

Past Medical History. This should include information on significant past and current medical problems, including any current medications. This may provide important information about the initiation of the illness, as numerous physical conditions (e.g., diabetes mellitus, cystic fibrosis) have at times been thought to be predisposing factors for the development of an eating disorder (Garfinkel & Garner, 1982, p. 182).

Other Personal History. A assessment of the growth and development of a patient with an eating disorder is an important part of the assessment procedure. It is particularly important to inquire into any history of sexually abusive experiences, given the high rates of these experiences in this clinical population; most studies report rates in excess of 50% (Bulik, Sullivan, & Rorty, 1989; Hall, Tice, Beresford, Wooley, & Hall, 1989; Waller, 1991).

Recommendations for Physician Versus Nonphysician Therapists. While all health care professionals should be able to perform an assessment similar to the one above, the management of severely medically ill patients may be something that nonphysicians may be reluctant to undertake. Nonetheless, even if arrangements have been made for medical attention to be made available, it is important for nonphysicians to have a basic level of familiarity with the portions of the assessment dealing with medical issues.

Assessment of the Family. Family assessments are an important part of the evaluation of adolescents with eating disorders. While the entire literature regarding family influences in the eating disorders will not be reviewed here, many authors have commented on the role that eating symptoms may play in family functioning. This has included work by therapists working from a dynamic perspective (Bruch, 1973), the Philadelphia group (Minuchin et al., 1978) the Milan group (Selvini-Palazolli, 1974), and numerous others. More recent experimental work, reviewed below, strongly supports the role of family intervention for patients with eating disorders. It should, however, be noted that most of the interventions described in the literature occur either during the process of normalizing eating or during the followup phase after eating has been stabilized. Few if any authors suggest that family therapy should be employed as a first-line treatment for eating disorders, especially for underweight patients with anorexia nervosa.

The assessment components described below are derived from the experience of the author and his coworkers at the Toronto Hospital. The program of family therapy in this setting is described extensively elsewhere (Shekter-Wolfson & Woodside, 1991; Woodside & Shekter-Wolfson, 1991). The author's practice is to assess older adolescents separately first, then perform a family assessment; for younger adolescents, the assessment may be done entirely in the context of the family. There are no clear guidelines available for when to proceed with which method.

Family's Understanding of the Eating Disorder. Families come to assessments with a wide diversity of opinions about the nature of their family member's illness. Some families will be extremely preoccupied with physical symptoms, while others will virtually ignore the physical aspects of the disorder and focus exclusively on psychological concerns. An initial overview of each family member's understanding not only allows for an assessment of the family's level of sophistication regarding the eating disorder but also begins the process of normalizing differences of opinion—a process that may be difficult for highly enmeshed families.

In situations where the family meeting precedes any meeting with the patient, the patient should be asked what his or her view of the illness is; if the patient has already been interviewed, it is probably sufficient to simply ask for his or her thoughts about the opinions of others. This sort of approach will often lead to a varied exchange of ideas about the nature and pathogenesis of the illness in the identified patient. *It* is likely that families who are unable to differ openly have difficulty tolerating the children's efforts toward individuation and autonomy.

Discovery of the Eating Disorder. An initial examination of family communication patterns can be obtained by asking how the family became aware of the patient's eating symptoms. In some cases the discovery will have been by accident (e.g., parents discovering evidence of purging behaviors), or the patient may have been able to inform the parents that he or she was having difficulty. It is not uncommon for adolescents to strenuously resist referral, especially those with anorexia nervosa. An examination of this type of process is of obvious value in a family assessment.

Family's Beliefs about the Eating Disorder. It is useful to evaluate the family's beliefs about the etiology and prognosis of the illness. Some family members will have a very sophisticated understanding, while others will be able to vocalize very little. It is not uncommon for parents to have heard of other adolescents with eating problems, and often what they have heard about the course and outcome of these illnesses is not positive. Sometimes families will have idealized the treatment, and this is important to note as well. Finally, any theories that are stated in general terms (e.g., "girls with eating disorders don't feel good about themselves") should be addressed by asking how the family member thinks the general theory applies specifically to the identified patient.

Family's Eating Patterns. A particularly important part of the family assessment of a patient with an eating disorder is the pattern of eating at home. The idea is not to change these patterns, but simply to see what the patient has to deal with. Families who feel as if their own patterns are being challenged or judged are much less likely to be helpful in the treatment process. The author normally inquires about the following:

- The pattern of meals (timing, who is present)
- Who is responsible for cooking and shopping
- What food preferences members of the family have
- Who else, if anyone, is dieting
- Whether alcohol is consumed at meals

While many families will report dieting behavior, therapists must realize that dieting is endemic is North American society. Dieting per se has not been found to be present excessively in family members of patients with eating disorders when this subject has been examined by carefully controlled studies (Garfinkel et al., 1983).

Family's Attitude Toward Weight and Shape. The family's attitude toward weight and shape should be assessed in the same nonjudgmental fashion as described above. Ask each member of the family about the size of each other member of the family, carefully noting discrepant opinions. As most patients who are treated for an eating disorder will gain some weight, it is important to assess the family's beliefs about the patient's ideal weight, and at what weight the family would begin to feel as if the patient were becoming fat.

Family History. A standard family history should be performed at some stage in the family assessment, whenever the family therapist feels most comfortable.

Clinical Management

This section is meant as a general guide for individuals engaged in the treatment of patients with eating disorders; it should not be considered definitive.

Interventions to Normalize Eating

As the above discussion of etiological factors implies, normalization of eating is the essential first step in recovery from anorexia nervosa or bulimia nervosa. Treatments that do not include a major focus on normalizing eating are unlikely to produce lasting change. Although many other important factors predispose one to, initiate, or perpetuate these conditions, abnormal eating itself is such a significant perpetuator of the illness that correcting it must be the first step in recovery. This is particularly important in the adolescent age group, where persistence of starvation may have a significant impact on ultimate potential for physical growth.

Methods by which eating may be normalized are numerous, and no one method will be appropriate for all patients. The Toronto Hospital has adopted a stepped-care approach where patients are brought into our treatment program at the least intrusive level that is believed helpful, then graduated through more intensive treatments if necessary. While individual treatment programs at the hospital differ in structure and intensity, the basic philosophy is similar across all programs. It does not appear to be the case that any one specific treatment is best for all patients with eating disorders.

Focusing on Nondieting Approach to Eating

This is an essential component of the treatment of patients with eating disorders. Providing patients and family with psychoeducational material that outlines the effects of dieting behaviors on physiological and psychological functioning and describes the connections between bingeing and dieting is particularly important. The intent is not to insist on immediate compliance with a nondieting stance; rather, this should be a shared goal toward which the patient, therapist, and perhaps family will work together.

Consultation with a nutritionist who can provide the patient with a plan for normal eating is often helpful early on in the process. It is important for clinicians to develop a liaison with a dietitian or nutritionist who can accept the need for a nondieting stance with such patients, as this meal plan should be very distinct from a "diet." The meal plan should contain foods from all food groups, with a normal number of calories for the patient's age, height, gender, and activity level. It is usually helpful to de-emphasize calories per se and focus instead on food groups and normal serving sizes. Treatment strategies that collude with the patient's desire to restrict his or her eating are likely to lead only to ongoing illness; the same is true for strategies that attempt to trick the patient into eating, or that involve extensive negotiations with the patient about each mouthful he or she consumes. Such treatment approaches will usually simply develop into a power struggle with the patient and, ultimately, the family.

Facilitating Patient Self-Monitoring

The gradual development of an ability to be aware of overeating and restrictive patterns of eating is an important tool for long-term recovery in patients with eating disorders. In this context, self-monitoring does not refer to the rigid and obsessional calorie counting engaged in by some patients with anorexia nervosa, rather, it is an activity that should lead to an increasing sense of mastery over eating behavior. Adopting an approach that emphasizes normal portioning will help avoid inadvertently encouraging an individual's preoccupation with calories.

The more typical situation in bulimia nervosa is for the patient to be relatively unaware of what he or she is eating, often because of either the intense shame associated with bingeing or the extreme degree to which eating has become chaotic. In these cases, self-monitoring with the use of some type of food diary will assist the patient to identify the precipitants of binge eating (often dietary restriction). As time goes on and eating becomes less restricted, ongoing self-monitoring via diaries or journals may allow for the identification of other environmental and psychological variables associated with either binge eating or restriction. Identification of these variables will help the patient to develop strategies to change his or her behavior, thus facilitating the development of an enhanced sense of effectiveness.

Psychoeducation

Because of the widespread social myths about the effects of dieting behaviors, psychoeducational material is a vital aid in the treatment of individuals with eating disorders. Accurate information about eating, body weight and shape, and the nature of the disorders is an essential tool for any therapist treating these patients. Providing this information to patients helps them to become more active players in their own treatment, increasing compliance in the short term and facilitating an enhanced sense of self-worth and effectiveness in the longer term. Psychoeducation is vitally important for parents of younger patients; many centers run psychoeducational or support groups for parents of patients with eating disorders.

Once the process of normalizing eating has begun, many other issues may become active.

Body Image/Weight and Shape

Most patients, even those who normalize their eating rapidly, will remain preoccupied with their weight and shape for months or years. It is important for therapists to recognize that the course of recovery from these concerns is prolonged. For some patients, the experience of being at a normal weight and eating normally will eventually be associated with a diminution of concern; other patients may require specialized treatment focusing on specific body parts. This latter situation may occur more frequently in cases where there has been severe sexual abuse. It is important for therapists to be aware that the resolution of concerns about weight and shape cannot occur at an emaciated body weight, although many patients will request that their body image problems be cleared up before they attempt to eat more normally.

Sexual/Physical Abuse

Research continues to demonstrate very high levels of sexual and physical abuse in patients with either anorexia nervosa or bulimia nervosa. As is the case with body image problems, sexual abuse issues are likely to persist long after eating has been normalized, and they often become very active during the period of normalization. Therapists who are not comfortable working with these issues may consider referring patients to specialized services (e.g., incest survivor groups). In cases where sexual abuse is ongoing, clinicians will have to take whatever action is mandated by local regulations.

Physician Involvement

Many therapists who are not physicians are involved in the care of patients suffering from eating disorders. Physician involvement in the care of such patients is important, however, in a number of cases. First, patients who engage in regular purging behaviors will need to have their body salts and cardiac function monitored on a regular basis. Patients who are emaciated may require hospitalization from time to time, as well as monitoring. In addition, the involvement of outside physicians may facilitate the counseling process if medical issues have become an unhelpful focus in the counseling. Such involvement by physicians should be viewed as collaborative; nonphysician therapists are urged to develop contacts with physicians who are willing to work in such a fashion.

Medication

Medication prescribed for patients with eating disorders may range from potassium supplementation to major tranquilizers (for a review, see Garfinkel & Garner, 1987). As mentioned above, it is important for physician and nonphysician therapists to work collaboratively in order to avoid therapeutic splitting.

Briefly, the following are the most common scenarios in which medication might be prescribed. When potassium is depleted as a result of purging behaviors, potassium supplementation may be required. This supplementation may be oral or, in extreme cases, require hospitalization. Prokinetic agents (i.e., agents that speed gastric emptying) may be helpful in facilitating the process of normalizing eating, as they help improve the feeling of bloating and early satiety that many starved patients experience. In rare cases, various types of tranquilizers may be prescribed for brief durations to reduce anxiety that patients experience during the initial period of refeeding.

Many patients with bulimia nervosa are prescribed antidepressant medication, usually for one of two reasons. First, antidepressants exert an antibingeing effect in about one-third to one-half of patients. This attenuation of urges to binge may help individuals to feel safer while attempting to adhere to a plan of more normal eating. It is, however, important to be aware that this effect is unlikely to persist in the face of ongoing dietary restriction. Medication should be presented to the patient as an adjunct to other efforts at normalizing eating, rather than as the whole answer.

The second major indication for antidepressants is the existence of syndromal major depression. The relationship between depression and eating disorders is complex (for a review, see Strober, 1988). It is possible that many bulimic patients who complain of depression while actively symptomatic may experience considerable improvement in their mood once their eating is more stable.

There is no evidence that treatment with medication assists patients with anorexia nervosa in gaining weight. Appetite stimulants are contraindicated in the treatment of anorexia nervosa, as there is not normally any impairment of appetite in this condition; moreover, patients who discover that they are being prescribed such drugs are unlikely to view it as helpful or empathic. The best medicine for anorexia nervosa is food.

Tube Feeding

Nasogastric tube feeding is occasionally employed in the treatment of severe anorexia nervosa. This technique should be reserved for life-threatening situations and viewed as a desperate measure. Routine use of nasogastric tube feeding as a first-line treatment is unnecessary and inappropriate; the overwhelming majority of reports from intensive treatment programs suggest that almost all patients can be gradually encouraged to eat over the course of a week or two. Although concerns about the ultimate potential for growth in adolescents mandate aggressive treatment of anorexia nervosa, this does not imply a need for tube feeding in most cases. It is debatable as to whether treatment that consists primarily of nasogastric tube feeding is better than no treatment at all.

Family therapy

There is significant evidence to support the role of family therapy as a primary mode of treatment for weight-restored patients with anorexia nervosa. Russell, Szmuckler, and Dare (1987) examined outcomes of 57 patients who had regained weight in an inpatient treatment unit and then were randomly selected for either individual therapy or family therapy as a follow-up treatment. This study demonstrated a clear advantage of family therapy over individual therapy for patients with early-onset, short-duration anorexia nervosa.

Crisp et al. (1991) describe a similar study where anorexic patients were randomly assigned to a variety of treatment conditions, all of which included a significant focus on family issues. All treatments were associated with significant improvement over the course of 1 year.

Assisting the family to help the child maintain her eating as normal and on other issues that may have become relevant for the family as the child has recovered, such as concerns about autonomy.

Treatment-Resistant Patients

All clinicians involved in the treatment of eating disorders will encounter some patients who are treatment resistant. There are two major groups of such patients. The first is typified by the adolescent who arrives unwillingly for the consultation visit, refuses to participate, and is generally unhelpful and unwilling to cooperate. The second group comprises of individuals who demonstrate at least superficial willingness to engage in treatment but either do not respond or relapse very suddenly and completely.

The management of these cases is a challenge, and the suggestions that follow will not help in every instance. Successful treatment for anorexia nervosa cannot be imposed upon a patient; instead, he or she must appreciate how the illness has become a burden in his or her life. In the first type of situation described above, the author normally asks the patient if he or she wishes to be interviewed. If the answer is no, and the patient appears to be in no imminent danger, the parents are invited in (if they are not already present) and the dilemma is presented for the family to solve. If the patient is older and no family is present, the patient is asked whether he or she wishes to proceed with the consultation; if the answer is no, the interview is concluded and the patient is invited to return when treatment is desired. In the author's experience of assessing nearly 1,000 patients, only a handful of patients have actually left the office.

If the patient appears to be in danger (e.g., is very emaciated) an involuntary hospital admission may be necessary. A useful strategy to get the patient to enter the hospital voluntarily is to limit the purpose of the hospitalization to correcting whatever factor is presently putting the patient at risk. An example of this would be to admit a patient with low potassium solely for potassium repletion. Many patients, once in the hospital, will agree to some form of further treatment.

Occasionally, a patient will be so emaciated that tube feeding is required as a lifesaving measure. If this is imposed on an unwilling patient, though it is usually a very long time before the patient allows himself or herself to be put in that situation again. This resistance sometimes has fatal results. The overwhelming majority of patients with anorexia nervosa can be brought to treatment voluntarily within a few weeks or months at worst. The risks of imposing simple refeeding in the guise of definitive treatment are very large in terms of the overall course of the illness.

The second type of treatment resistance often is a result of the first: a patient who is forcibly refed promptly loses weight after discharge, or manages somehow to manipulate his or her treatment while in the hospital to avoid gaining much weight. Most such patients are extremely suspicious and defensive. The therapist should try to contract with the patient around mutually agreeable goals—which, at first, may involve simply keeping the patient alive—and gradually attempt to build up a trusting relationship in which the patient may eventually agree to definitive treatment. This is often a protracted process, requiring years, and the mortality in this group is substantial. A particular dilemma is faced by therapists involved with a younger patient of this nature, for whom considerations of ultimate growth potential are important. The author has no answer to this problem except to reiterate that the cost of imposing refeeding on a patient simply for the purpose of preserving potential growth may exceed the benefit.

References

American Psychiatric Association. (1987). *Diagnostic and statistical manual of mental disorders* (rev. 3rd ed.). Washington, DC: Author.

American Psychiatric Association. (1993). *DSM-IV draft criteria*. Washington, DC: Author.

Anderson, A. (Ed). (1989). *Eating disorders in males*. New York: Brunner/Mazel.

Bruch, H. (1973). *Eating disorders: Anorexia nervosa, obesity, and the person within*. New York: Basic Books.

Bulik, C., Sullivan, P., & Rorty, M. (1989). Childhood sexual abuse in women with bulimia. *Journal of Clinical Psychiatry, 49*, 7–9.

Ciliska, D. (1991). *Beyond dieting*. New York: Brunner/Mazel.

Crisp, A. H., Norton, K., Gowers, S., Halek, C., Bowyer, C., Yeldham, D., Levett, G., & Bhat, A. (1991). A controlled study of the effect of therapies aimed at adolescent and family psychopathology in anorexia nervosa. *British Journal of Psychiatry, 159*, 335–333.

Crisp, A. H., Palmer, R. L., & Kalucy, R. S. (1976). How common is anorexia nervosa? A prevalence study. *British Journal of Psychiatry, 218*, 549–554.

Eisele, J., Hartsgaard, D., & Light, H. K. (1986). Factors related to eating disorders in young adolescent girls. *Adolescence, 21*, 1492–1497.

Fairburn, C. G., & Beglin, S. J. (1990). Studies of the epidemiology of bulimia nervosa. *American Journal of Psychiatry, 147*, 401–408.

Fichter, M. M., & Pirke, K. M. (1984). Hypothalamic-pituitary function in starving healthy subjects. In K. M. Pirke & D. Ploog (Eds), *The psychobiology of anorexia nervosa*. New York: Springer-Verlag.

Garfinkel, P. E., & Garner, D. M. (1982). *Anorexia nervosa: A multidimensional perspective*. New York: Brunner/Mazel.

Garfinkel, P. E., & Garner, D. M. (Eds.). (1987). *The role of drug treatments for eating disorders*. New York: Brunner/Mazel.

Garfinkel, P. E., Moldofsky, H., & Garner, D. M. (1980). The heterogeneity of anorexia nervosa. *Archives of General Psychiatry, 37*, 1036–1040.

Garfinkel, P. E., Garner, D. M., Rose, I., Darby, P. L. Brandes, J. S., O'Hanlon, J., & Walsh, N. (1983). A comparison of characteristics of families of patients with anorexia nervosa and normal controls. *Psychological Medicine, 13*, 821–828.

Gull, W. W. (1874). Anorexia nervosa. *Transactions of the Clinical Society, 7*, 22–28.

Hall, R., Tice, L., Beresford, T., Wooley, B., & Hall, A. K. (1989). Sexual abuse in patients with anorexia nervosa and bulimia. *Psychosomatics, 30*, 73–79.

Holland, A. J. Sicotte, N., & Treasure, J. (1988). Anorexia nervosa: evidence for a genetic basis. *British Journal of Psychiatry, 32*, 561–571.

Kaplan, A. S., & Garfinkel, P. E. (1984). Bulimia in the talmud [Letter]. *American Journal of Psychiatry, 141*, 721.

Kaplan, A. S. & Woodside, D. B. (1987). Biologic aspects of anorexia nervosa and bulimia. *Journal of Clinical and Consulting Psychology, 55*, 645–653.

Kaplan, A. S., & Woodside, D. B. (in press). The thyroid and eating disorders. In R. Joffe & A. Levitt: (Eds.), *Psychiatric aspects of clinical thyroid disorders*. Washington, DC: American Psychiatric Press.

Kendler, K. S., MacLean, C., Neale, M., Kessler, R., Heath, A., & Eaves, L. (1992). The genetic epidemiology of bulimia nervosa. *American Journal of Psychiatry, 148*, 1627–1637.

Keys, A., Brozek, J., Henschel, A., Mickelson, O., & Taylor, H. L. (1950). *The biology of human starvation*. Minneapolis: University of Minnesota Press.

Lasegue, C. (1964). De l'anorexie hysterique. In R. M. Kaufman & M. Heiman (Eds.), *Evolution of psychosomatic concepts: Anorexia nervosa—a paradigm*. New York: International Universities Press. (Original work published 1873)

Maloney, M. J., McGuire, J., Daniles, S. R., & Speckler, B. (1989). Dieting behaviour and eating attitudes in children. *Pediatrics, 84*, 482–489.

Minuchin, S., Rosman, B. L., & Baker, L. (1978). *Psychosomatic families: Anorexia nervosa in context*. Cambridge, MA: Harvard University Press.

Morton, R. (1694). *Phthisologica: Or a treatise of consumption*. London: Smith and Walford.

Parry-Jones, W. L. (1985). Archival exploration of anorexia nervosa. *Journal of Psychiatric Research, 19*, 95–100.

Parry-Jones, B., & Parry-Jones, W. L. (1991). Bulimia: An archival review of its history in psychosomatic medicine. *International Journal of Eating Disorders, 10*, 129–143.

Polivy, J. (1976). Perception of calories and regulation of intake in restrained and unrestrained subjects. *Addictive Behaviours, 1*, 237–243.

Russell, G. F. M. (1979). Bulimia nervosa: An ominous variant of anorexia nervosa. *Psychological Medicine, 9*, 429–448.

Russell, G. F. M. (1985). Anorexia nervosa in the young. *Journal of Psychiatric Research, 19*, 363–369.

Russell, G. F. M., Szmuckler, G. I., & Dare, C. (1987). An evaluation of family therapy in anorexia nervosa and bulimia nervosa. *Archives of General Psychiatry, 44*, 1047–1056.

Selvini-Palazolli, M. (1974). *Self-starvation*. London: Chaucer.

Simmonds, M. (1914). Ueber embolische prozesse in der hypophysis. *Archives of Pathology and Anatomy, 217*, 226–239.

Shekter-Wolfson, L., Woodside, D. B. (1991). A Family relations group. In D. B. Woodside & L. Shekter-Wolfson (Eds.), *Family approaches in treatment of eating disorders* (pp. 107–122). Washington, DC: American Psychiatric Press.

Steinhausen, H., Rauss-Mason, C., & Seidel, R. (1991). Follow-up studies of anorexia nervosa: A review of four decades of outcome research. *Psychological Medicine, 21*, 447–454.

Storz, N. S. (1982). Body image of obese adolescent girls in a high scholl and clinical setting. *Adolescence, 17*, 667–672.

Strober, M., Morrell, W., Burroughs, J., Salkin, B., & Jacobs, C. (1985). A controlled family study of anorexia nervosa. *Journal of Psychiatric Research, 19*, 239–246.

Strober, M., & Katz, J. L. (1988). Depression in the eating disorders: A review and analysis of descriptive, family, and biological findings. In D. M. Garner & P. E. Garfinkel (Eds.), *Diagnostics issues in anorexia nervosa and bulimia nervosa* (p. 80–111). New York: Brunner/Mazel.

Strober, M., Lampert, C., Morrell, W., Burroughs, J., & Jacobs, C. (1990). A controlled family study of anorexia nervosa: Evidence of familial aggregation and lack of shared transmission with affective disorders. *International Journal of Eating Disorders, 9*, 239–253.

Theander, S. (1985). Outcome and prognosis in anorexia nervosa and bulimia. *Journal of Psychiatric Research, 2/3*, 493–508.

Treasure, J., & Thompson, P. (1988). Anorexia nervosa in childhood. *British Journal of Hospital Medicine, 40*, 362–369.

Woodside, D. B. (1990). Anorexia nervosa and bulimia nervosa. *Current Opinion in Psychiatry, 3*, 453–456.

Woodside, D. B. (in press). Genetics of eating disorders. In A. S. Kaplan & P. E. Garfinkel (Eds.), *Medical aspects of eating disorders*. New York: Brunner/Mazel.

Woodside, D. B., & Garfinkel, P. E. (in press). Age of onset of eating disorders. *International Journal of Eating Disorders*.

Woodside, D. B., Rockert, W., & Garfinkel, P. E. (1991). Natural histories of anorexia nervosa and bulimia nervosa [Letter]. *American Journal of Psychiatry, 148*, 950–951.

Woodside, D. B., & Shekter-Wolfson, L. (1991). Family treatment in the day hospital. In D. B. Woodside & L. Shekter-Wolfson (Eds.), *Family approaches in treatment of eating disorders* (pp. 87–105). Washington, DC: American Psychiatric Press.

14
Anxiety Disorders

Christopher A. Kearney
Wendy K. Silverman

T he study of psychopathology in adolescents has often focused on overt, externalizing problems at the expense of more subtle but equally debilitating disorders. An example of the latter is anxiety, which has traditionally received little research attention with respect to classification, assessment, and treatment. Since the early 1980s, though, the study of adolescent anxiety and its disorders has attracted increased interest, resulting in the development of more sophisticated taxonomic strategies, comorbidity information, and assessment techniques. As is discussed below, however, the treatment of clinical anxiety in adolescents remains largely unresearched.

Before proceeding, some points of clarification are needed. First, the term anxiety will generally refer to a collection of responses and not one reaction per se. The conceptualization of anxiety or fear has gravitated toward a model of three different but interrelated components: subjective cognitions (e.g., aversive thoughts such as "I am going to be embarrassed in front of my classmates"), overt behaviors (e.g., avoidance of social situations), and physiological reactivity (e.g., hyperventilation or increased heart rate). These components, however, are not highly intercorrelated (Barlow, Mavissakalian, & Schofield, 1980; Lang, 1968, 1977). Anxiety is thus considered problematic when a person experiences difficulties in at least one response system.

A second point of clarification involves the many terms used by clinicians and researchers to describe anxiety-related problems, which are variably referred to as fears, phobias, or other aversive clinical "reactions" (e.g., Morris, 1980). Because such distinctions have not contributed to treatment knowledge for anxiety-related problems (Barrios & O'Dell, 1989), we subsume them under the umbrella of anxiety disorders and the purview of this chapter. We recognize, however, that distinctions such as "fear" are comprised of the three response systems indicated above.

The study of adolescent anxiety disorders has centered in recent years on categories established in updated editions of the *Diagnostic and Statisti-*

435

cal Manual of Mental Disorders (DSM) of the American Psychiatric Association (APA). In the second edition of the manual (DSM-II; APA, 1968) only one diagnostic category ("overanxious reaction") was available for youngsters with anxiety. With the publication of DSM-III (APA, 1980) and DSM-III-R (APA, 1987), however, an entire "Anxiety Disorders of Childhood and Adolescence" section was available to describe three anxiety disorders specific to youngsters—avoidant, overanxious, and separation anxiety disorder—each of which presented anxiety as the core problem. Avoidant disorder was characterized by excessive and persistent withdrawal from contact with strangers and interference in social relationships. This was also linked to a desire for "affection and acceptance" from family members. Overanxious disorder was characterized by excessive worrying and fearful behavior not focused on a specific situation or object. Symptoms included worrying about one's competence (e.g., socially) and appropriateness of behavior, a need for reassurance, somatic complaints, increased self-consciousness, and difficulty relaxing.

Psychometric and conceptual difficulties with the taxonomic properties of avoidant and overanxious disorder (e.g., American Psychiatric Association, 1994; Werry, 1991), however, resulted in their modification in DSM-IV (APA, 1994). Avoidant disorder per se no longer exists, although youngsters may be diagnosed with "social anxiety disorder" (from the adult anxiety disorder section). Overanxious disorder is now subsumed under "generalized anxiety disorder," and the broad section of "Anxiety Disorders of Childhood and Adolescence" no longer exists. Separation anxiety disorder, however, has been retained in a section of DSM-IV titled "Other Disorders of Infancy, Childhood, or Adolescence." Separation anxiety disorder is characterized by excessive anxiety upon separation or upon threat of separation from major attachment figures or home. Symptoms include internalizing problems (e.g., undue worry about harm toward oneself or those close to oneself, avoidance of situations involving detachment, somatic complaints) as well as externalizing problems (e.g., tantrums, sleep and school refusal behavior) and nightmares.

Like its predecessors, DSM-IV also allows the application of adult anxiety disorder diagnoses to youngsters if appropriate criteria are met. These diagnoses include those for phobic disorders (agoraphobia without history of panic disorder, social phobia/social anxiety disorder, and specific phobia) and anxiety states (panic disorder with or without agoraphobia; obsessive-compulsive, post-traumatic stress, acute stress, generalized anxiety, and substance-induced anxiety disorders; anxiety disorder due to a general medical condition; and anxiety disorders not otherwise specified). Although diagnoses of adult-criteria phobic disorders in adolescents are common (Last, Strauss, & Francis, 1987), diagnoses of obsessive-compulsive disorder are infrequent (Wolff & Rapoport, 1988), and diagnoses of panic disorder are controversial (Kearney & Silverman, 1992).

Other anxiety-related adolescent problems not specifically outlined in the DSM categorical system include school refusal behavior and test anxiety. School refusal behavior, listed in the DSM-IV as a symptom of separation anxiety disorder, has been advocated as a heterogeneous phenomenon (Atkinson, Quarrington, & Cyr, 1985) deserving of separate attention to prescriptive treatment strategies (Burke & Silverman, 1987). The problem is defined as refusal to attend school or difficulties remaining in school for an entire day (Kearney & Silverman, 1990a). Similarly, test anxiety is more complex than originally thought (Beidel & Turner, 1988), comprising severe fearfulness and anxiety, separation difficulties, and general avoidance of evaluative situations.

Historical Background

From a developmental perspective, the period of adolescence has been typically viewed as one of tumult due to rapid advancement in physical, cognitive, and social capacities. This period was succinctly described by Hall (1904) as a time of "storm and stress." With respect to the cognitive domain, adolescence is marked by an increasing ability to understand abstract concepts and a tendency to challenge those concepts already known (e.g., parental values). These phenomena, while not overly stressful to most youngsters, can be somewhat anxiety provoking to many.

One adolescent phenomenon that has received much attention is identity formation. Erikson (1959) delineated eight stages of psychosocial development during the course of the life span. Each stage is marked by a "crisis," the successful or failed resolution of which serves to facilitate or retard future development. For adolescents, the pertinent stage is identity versus identity confusion or diffusion. Although most individuals successfully integrate various descriptions of themselves (e.g., daughter, student, boyfriend, employee) into a consolidated whole, a subset of adolescents experience anxiety over appropriate gender and occupational roles: in essence, the question "Who am I?" remains unresolved.

Other developmental theorists have also proposed certain adolescent processes that have implications for understanding anxiety in this population. Havighurst (1972) and Marcia (1980) extended Erikson's stage of identity versus identity confusion, stating that difficulties (including anxiety) may result from a failure to accomplish such key tasks as the maintenance of heterosexual relationships, acceptance of physical changes, development of self-reliance, formation of ethical and religious conclusions, preparation of career goals, and composition of ideology. In addition, Marcia (1980) delineated four identity statuses directly related to occupational and ideological decisions: identity achievement, foreclosure, identity diffusion, and moratorium. The first two represent adolescents who have chosen occupational and ideological goals, although these are "parentally chosen" in the foreclosure category (versus personally chosen by the adolescent in identity achievement). The identity diffusion and moratorium categories, respectively, represent youngsters without an occupational/ideological direction versus those with ideas but who are indecisive as to which direction to pursue. According to Marcia (1980), adolescents in an identity crisis (and most anxious) are in the moratoriums category. Such adolescents are likely to score higher on an anxiety scale and show longer response latencies in a game situation (e.g., Podd, Marcia, & Rubin, 1970; Stark & Traxler, 1974).

Marcia's (1980) foreclosure category (i.e., those with parentally chosen goals) also represents a distinction that may have implications for anxiety in adolescents. Adolescents often experience parenting strategies that are highly manipulative or authoritarian, and they may develop anxiety-related problems as a result. For example, Johnson, Falstein, Szurek, and Svendsen (1941) discussed an association between separation anxiety and "school phobia" in children and adolescents. Based on psychodynamic theory, the authors proposed that an overdependent or manipulative mother-child relationship resulted in an anxiety response upon separation and, subsequently, refusal to attend school. Although contemporary views of school refusal (e.g., Blagg & Yule, 1984; Kearney & Silverman, 1990a) incorporate greater etiological heterogeneity (i.e., they recognize that not all youngsters refuse school for home-based reinforcement), the presence of restrictive or manipulative parenting patterns remains a dominant explanation for school refusal and related problems. More empirical research is necessary, however, to argue a causal relationship between these developmental phenomena and adolescent anxiety disorders.

Attention from clinical researchers has supplemented hypotheses from developmental theories related to adolescent fear/anxiety. This research, in particular early classic work, generally referred to children and not adolescents. Still, early studies of fearfulness in children have significant implications for current models of adolescent fear/anxiety. For example, Freud (1909/1953) described the case of 5-year-old Hans, who exhibited fear of injury by a horse. The case spawned the development of psychoanalytic therapy in this area, targeting repressed unconscious conflicts and symbolic representations of anxiety.

Watson and Rayner (1920), in their pioneering research on conditioning theory, described the case of 11-month-old Little Albert. The authors associated a loud, frightening noise with a rat to produce subsequent fearfulness in the child; this fear was later shown to generalize to similar stimuli. In addition, Jones (1924) demonstrated that fearfulness could be reduced via classical conditioning: a 2-year-old boy ate several appealing foods in closer approximation to a feared stimulus (e.g., a dog), thereby reducing the latter's aversiveness.

During the 1960s, Bandura and his colleagues (e.g., Bandura, Grusec, & Menlove, 1967) developed a model of fear/anxiety based on observational learning. Specifically, the researchers hypothesized that persons learn to be fearful of a particular object or situation and may become less fearful by observing others engage the same stimulus without fear. Observed models may be live (in person) or symbolic (presented in films or videotape). Treatment techniques based on this approach have successfully alleviated many types of fears, including those of dogs (Bandura, Grusec, & Menlove, 1967) and upcoming medical or dental procedures (e.g., Melamed & Siegel, 1975).

From early articles (e.g., Eisenberg, 1958) and clinical consensus, the diagnosis of "overanxious reaction of childhood" (or adolescence) was included in DSM-II (APA, 1968). Although little additional research was conducted before 1980, subsequent revised editions of DSM were expanded to include the anxiety disorders described earlier. The DSM classification system has been criticized for a variety of reasons, including its controversial reliability and validity, insensitivity to labeling effects, neglect of developmental factors explaining a relationship between child and adult behavior disorders, and inability to prescribe individualized treatment procedures (Achenback, 1980; Burke & Silverman, 1987; Cantwell, 1980; Rey, Plapp, & Stewart, 1989; Rutter & Shaffer, 1980). The system has served as a focal point for expanded research into preadult anxiety disorders, however, catalyzing investigations into this historically neglected area.

Clinical Picture

The clinical picture of adolescent fear/anxiety has been examined in several ways. Preliminary reports of child and adolescent anxiety from DSM diagnostic criteria have only been recently reported, so a description of clinical observations remains important. Much empirical knowledge of anxiety in this population is based on the work of Achenbach and his colleagues using the Child Behavior Checklist. Several studies have also provided a clinical picture of fearfulness by surveying (via inventories) specific types of fears in adolescents. In addition, recent investigations have examined the relationship between fear/anxiety and other disorders (e.g., depression) in this population. This section outlines these areas to present the evolving clinical picture of adolescent anxiety.

Diagnostically, clinical profiles of anxious children and adolescents have not been extensively compared, although preliminary age differences have been reported. Francis, Last, and Strauss (1987) found differences between children (aged 5 to 12 years) and adolescents (aged 13 to 16 years) with separation anxiety disorder: younger children were more concerned with the welfare of primary caregivers, whereas adolescents were more concerned with somatic complaints. Strauss, Lease, Last, and Francis (1988) also found that adolescents (aged 12 to 19 years) with overanxious disorder reported more symptoms (e.g., worrying about previous behavior) than children (aged 5 to 11 years) with the same disorder.

In our experience with anxious youngsters, we have noted several similarities in clinical symptoms from childhood to adolescence. These include subjective cognitions such as being scared or hurt, inadequacy or incompetence, potential retribution (e.g., verbal reprimands) from others, and consequences of catastrophic events (e.g., nuclear war). Concurrent overt behaviors include avoidance, noncompliance, physical proximity (e.g., to caregivers), and verbalizations of nervousness. Concurrent physiological reactions include increased heart rate, perspiration, palpitations, nausea/vomiting, and stomachaches and headaches (particularly for school refusal). Although these symptoms are not necessarily subsumed under DSM-IV criteria for anxiety disorders relevant to adolescents, they are more often than not present in a particular clinical case.

Achenbach and Edelbrock (1983) conducted an empirical factor analysis of parent ratings of child and adolescent behavior problems, organizing several "narrow-band" factors into two "broad-band" factors of internalizing and externalizing symptoms. The resulting scale was the Child Behavior Checklist. With respect to adolescent anxiety, males and females aged 12 to 18 years are currently described via an "anxious/depressed" factor. Specific symptoms within the factor include "cries a lot, fears he/she might think or do something bad, feels he/she has to be perfect, nervous, highstrung, or tense, too fearful or anxious, self-conscious or easily embarrassed, and worries" (Achenbach, 1991a, pp. 11–12). A separate factor also describes "somatic complaints." Factors for anxiety-related and somatic complaints have been replicated for both genders in adolescents (Achenbach, Conners, Quay, Verhulst, & Howell, 1989).

Achenbach and Edelbrock (1986) also conducted a factor analysis of teacher ratings of child and adolescent behavior problems, from which they created the Teacher's Report Form. As in their previous study, several narrow-band factors across internalizing and externalizing behaviors were outlined. For males and females aged 12 to 18 years, specific anxiety symptoms again are currently listed under an "anxious/depressed" factor. These symptoms include some listed in the parent form in addition to also "overconforms to rules, feels hurt when criticized, overly anxious to please, and is afraid of making mistakes" (Achenbach, 1991b, pp. 8–9). An empirical analysis of parent and teacher ratings of adolescent behavior allows a determination of clinical (i.e., above the 98th percentile; Achenbach, 1991a, 1991b; Achenbach & Edelbrock, 1983, 1986) versus normal ranges of behavior. The scales thus permit a formal, empirically based method of assessing the clinical picture of anxiety in adolescents.

What about the clinical picture for adolescent fearfulness? Although many anxiety symptoms proposed from the diagnostic and empirically derived models are also present in a clinical case of fearfulness (e.g., autonomic arousal), symptoms resulting from fearfulness are often more pronounced. These include extended behavioral avoidance and sudden increased physiological reactivity (e.g., Jablensky, 1985). Adolescents report a wide range of fears, the most common of which include being hit by a vehicle, not being able to breathe, getting burned, falling from a high place, a burglar breaking into one's house, death, poor grades, and snakes (Ollendick, King, & Frary, 1989). Ishiyama and Chabassol (1985) found that in 360 young and older adolescents fears of negative social consequences from academic success were greater for persons (particularly females) in grades seven through nine. Payne (1988), evaluating 657 persons aged 12 to 15 years, reported that common fears involved injury/death, sexual situations, and school failure. In a review of adolescent fear/anxiety studies, Barrios and Hartmann (1988) concluded that teenagers also worry about personal competence and economic/political situations. As discussed earlier, the increased cognitive capacity of adolescents allows them to worry about or fear more abstract concepts in addition to concrete ones learned at earlier ages.

Finally, it is important to note that clinical pictures of adolescent (and younger children's) anxiety and fearfulness substantially overlap with other symptomatologies, most notably those traditionally considered depressive. Correlations between measures of anxiety and depression, somatic complaints, fearfulness, and obsessions in children and adolescents, as well as parent reports of child internalizing problems, have been reported in a number of studies (e.g., Hershberg, Carlson, Cantwell, & Strober, 1982; Jacobsen, Lahey, & Strauss, 1983; Jolly, Aruffo, Wherry, & Livingston, 1993; Norvell, Brophy, & Finch, 1985; Strauss, Last, Hersen, & Kazdin, 1988; Wolfe et al., 1987). Kearney, Silverman, and Eisen (1989) found that more than half their sample of children and adolescents with school refusal behavior and severe symptoms of depression DSM-III-R criteria for overanxious disorder.

These results have prompted several investigators to propose a broad-band construct of "negative affectivity" to represent appropriately the clinical picture of children and adolescents with anxiety or depression (Finch, Lipovsky, & Casat, 1989; King, Ollendick, & Gullone, 1991). Negative affectivity, or a mixed clinical profile, must be closely considered in the design and implementation of accurate assessment and individualized treatment strategies for this population. Overall, the clinical picture of adolescent fear/anxiety is complex, warranting further definition. Particular attention should be addressed to specifying highly correlated groups of symptoms, identifying related maintaining variables (e.g., family attention), and designing appropriate assessment techniques.

Course and Prognosis

Some debate exists as to whether fears and anxieties in preadults are transient or stable over time. Earlier work (e.g., Hagman, 1932) suggested that young children's fears dissipate quickly; treatment outcome research on childhood phobias (e.g., Hampe, Noble, Miller, & Barrett, 1973) has supported this view as well. Agras, Chapin, and Oliveau (1972) conducted a 5-year follow-up study of 10 persons under 20 years of age (a distinction between children and adolescents was not reported) untreated for a variety of phobias. None displayed unchanged or worsened phobic symptomatologies, whereas 6 improved and 4 were symptom free. In comparison, 57% of a sample of similar persons over the age of 20 years showed worsened or unchanged phobic symptomatologies. The investigators concluded that "phobia in adults tends to run a prolonged long-term course" (p. 317), particularly in comparison to younger person, whose course is more transient. A reinterpretation of these data, however, (Ollendick, 1979) indicated that only a minority of the preadult sample were symptom free at follow-up. Indeed, more recent studies (e.g., Ollendick et al., 1989) suggest that several fears (e.g., not being able to breathe) remain stable between the ages of 7 and 16 years.

With respect to anxiety disorders, Cantwell and Baker (1989) conducted a follow-up investigation of 151 children and adolescents (ages 5.2 to 20.6 years at follow-up) 4 to 5 years after an initial outpatient evaluation. A differentiation between children and adolescents was not provided for this sample. At the follow-up period, the most stable anxiety diagnosis was avoidant disorder, where 5 (36%) of the original 14 diagnosed individuals were now reportedly "well" (i.e., without any diagnosis) and 4 (29%) still met criteria for the original problem. This contrasts with 4 (44%) of the 9 cases of separation anxiety disorder sample now being found "well," with 1 person meeting criteria for the original problem. For overanxious disorder, 2 of the original 8 persons were considered "well" at follow-up, whereas 2 maintained the diagnosis. Other problems reported for the groups included attention-deficit and oppositional disorders, major depression, and other anxiety disorders. The authors concluded that anxiety disorders "as a group were characterized by higher rates of recovery, and lower rates of stability than the behavioral disorders" (p. 697). Because little stability was found for individual anxiety syndromes, they hypothesized that subtyping anxiety disorders in children and adolescents may be premature.

Velez, Johnson, and Cohen (1989), in a longitudinal analysis of the prevalence and risk factors for adolescent and adult psychopathology, found that low socioeconomic status and low levels of parental (especially paternal) education were related to extended separation anxiety in preadults. McGee et al. (1990) followed up on a sample of 11-year-old children 4 years after an initial diagnosis. For the now 15-year-olds, the prevalence of anxiety disorders was estimated at 12.6%. Specifically, prevalence increased for overanxious disorder (2.9% to 5.9%), decreased for separation anxiety disorder (3.5% to 2.0%), and remained stable for social phobia (0.9% to 1.1%). These figures are somewhat different from those reported in a more recent but similar study (McGee, Feehan, Williams, & Anderson, 1992) that following 750 adolescents (393 boys and 357 girls) without mental disorders from age 11 to age 15. Prevalence increased for overanxious disorder (2.5 to 5.2%), decreased for separation anxiety disorder (1.9 to 1.7%), and increased for social phobia (0.4 to 1.3%). In another study, Feehan, McGee, and Williams (1993) followed 890 adolescents from age 15 to age 18. Of the 44 15-year-olds diagnosed with an anxiety disorder, 29 (65.9%) were diagnosed with some mental disorder 3 years later; 17 (38.6%) were specifically diagnosed with an anxiety disorder.

Berg, Rapoport, Whitaker, Davies, Leonard, Swedo, Braiman, and Lenane (1989) conducted a 2-year follow-up study of 45 adolescents (ages 16 to 21 years at follow-up) with obsessive-compulsive (OC) problems, including obsessive-compulsive disorder (OCD), subclinical OCD, OC personality, and other psychiatric disorders with OC features. This group was compared to 21 adolescents without a diagnosis followed-up over the same period. At follow-up, 6 (13.3%) persons with obsessive-compulsive problems received no diagnosis, compared to 16 (76.0%) persons in the control group. Comorbid diagnoses for the former group included panic, generalized anxiety, eating, and affective disorders. Overall stability for each subclass of obsessive-compulsive problems was high (e.g., only 1 case progressed from subclinical OCD to OCD). Severity of diagnosis was an important factor in this finding.

Researchers have also conducted long-term follow-up or follow-back studies of adolescents with school refusal behavior to determine influential variables on course and prognosis. Timberlake (1984) examined 74 youngsters (mean age 8.3 years) at time of referral, treatment termination, and follow-up 10 to 20 years later. Treatment primarily consisted of a psychodynamic, family-centered approach for at least 6 months, with all subjects eventually returning to school. At follow-up, 36% evidenced mild to severe anxiety symptoms, 91% engaged in some type of employment, and none reported difficulties in the workplace. In addition, positive findings were found for completed education (97%), participation in outside social activities (100%), and presence of same-sex and heterosexual peer relationships (100%). A multiple regression analysis revealed that several variables predicted positive long-term psychosocial functioning, accounting for 79% of the variance. These included timing (premature versus not) of treatment termination, degree of family stress at intake, parent participation in treatment, frequency of contact with grandparents, timing of school return, parental history of fearfulness or phobia, and degree of child anxiety at intake.

Berg and Jackson (1985) evaluated 168 adolescents with school refusal behavior 10 years after hospitalization in an inpatient psychiatric unit. Almost half (44%) had visited a psychiatrist, received treatment for a psychiatric illness, or been admitted to a hospital for psychiatric treatment during the follow-up period. The researchers concluded that "school refusal in early adolescence severe enough to require inpatient treatment leads to an increased risk for psychiatric disturbance for years to come" (p. 369). Flakierska, Lindstrom, and Gillberg (1988) evaluated 35 youngsters (mean age 9.3 years) 15 to 20 years after receiving therapy for school refusal and compared them to 35 age- and sex-matched controls. Subjects in the school refusal group sought more psychiatric assistance and had more children than the control group, but no other differences (e.g., in degree of social adjustment or psychiatric disorders) were found.

The results generated from follow-up investigations do not allow a definitive conclusion as to whether adolescents with fearfulness or anxiety-related disorders present with stable, long-term syndromes (either from childhood to adolescence or from adolescence to adulthood). For example, fear and obsessive-compulsive behavior appear stable, whereas the individual subtypes of adolescent anxiety disorders do not. The predictive validity of current psychiatric nomenclature for adolescent anxiety disorders thus remains suspect. Childhood anxiety disorders are likely related to adult anxiety disorders on a general level, but diagnostic specificity remains poor (Cantwell & Baker, 1989). Researchers may wish to examine adolescent anxiety disorders that are largely self-corrective versus those that more accurately predict adult psychopathology; such a recommendation has been made for panic disorder (Kearney & Silverman, 1992). In addition, the stability of adult anxiety disorder (e.g., social, generalized anxiety disorder) criteria in adolescents should be evaluated further.

Epidemiology

The prevalence of formally diagnosed anxiety disorders in adolescents has only been recently investigated. Kashani and Orvaschel (1988) evaluated 150 adolescents (75 males and 75 females aged 14 to 16 years) on the Diagnostic Interview Schedule for Children and Adolescents; parents were assessed using the adult version of the same schedule (Herjanic & Reich, 1982). Of the 150 youngsters, 26 (17.3%) met DSM criteria for an anxiety disorder, and 13 (8.7%) displayed "clinically significant functional impairment requiring intervention" (p. 962). Most (84.6%) of the latter group met criteria for overanxious disorder. In addition, 9 (6.0%) subjects met criteria for both an anxiety and depressive disorder.

Flament et al. (1988) conducted an epidemiological study of obsessive-compulsive disorder in more than 5,000 high-school students, using the

Leyton Obsessional Inventory-Child Version (C. Z. Berg, Rapoport, & Flament, 1986) as a screening instrument before conducting a structured interview to derive formal diagnoses. Weighted current and lifetime prevalences were estimated to be 1.0% and 1.9%, respectively, with a minimum prevalence rate of 0.3%. The authors concluded that obsessive-compulsive disorder in adolescents is "both underdiagnosed and under-treated" (p. 764).

Bird et al. (1988) examined children and adolescents (aged 4 to 16 years) from Puerto Rico, finding prevalence rates for separation anxiety disorder (4.7%) and simple phobia (2.6%) after adding a "maladjustment" measure to DSM criteria. An epidemiological study of 1,299 persons aged 12 to 16 years in Ontario, Canada (Bowen, Offord, & Boyle, 1990), indicated the prevalence of overanxious and separation anxiety disorder to be 3.6% and 2.4%, respectively. Whitaker et al. (1990) evaluated 5,596 adolescents using screening devices for eating disorders, depression, obsessions, and anxiety prior to semistructured interviews based on DSM criteria. Weighted prevalence rates for panic (0.6%), obsessive-compulsive (1.9%), and generalized anxiety (3.7%) disorders were reported. Fergusson, Horwood, and Lynskey (1993) evaluated nearly 1,000 New Zealand adolescents via self- and maternal reports. Prevalence rates for overanxious (0.6% to 2.1%), generalized anxiety (1.7% to 4.2%), and separation anxiety (0.1% to 0.5%) disorders, as well as social (0.7% to 1.7%) and simple (1.3% to 5.1%) phobias, were reported.

Kashani and Orvaschel (1990) similarly examined 210 youngsters evenly distributed across gender and the ages of 8, 12, and 17 years. The Child Assessment Schedule and Parents' Child Assessment Schedule (Hodges, Cools, & McKnew, 1989) were used as diagnostic instruments. Among 12- and 17-year-olds, 26 (18.6%) met DSM criteria for an anxiety disorder. Specifically, subjects met criteria for overanxious (20, or 14.3%) and separation anxiety disorder (14, or 10.0%), and simple (5, or 3.6%) and social phobia (2, or 1.4%). Kashani and Orvaschel (1990) concluded that the prevalence of separation anxiety disorder tends to decrease with age and that most youngsters diagnosed with one anxiety disorder are diagnosed with another. Clinical prevalence rates of simple phobias in children and adolescents have been also reported as 6.8% to 6.9% (Graziano & De Giovanni, 1979; Silverman & Kearney, 1992).

Finally, prevalence and incidence rates have varied widely within the school refusal literature due to changing problem definitions (Prince, 1968). Prevalence rates in certain populations have been reported as high as 25%, but a more accurate estimate appears to be 3% to 5% (e.g., Granell de Aldaz, Vivas, Gelfand, & Feldman, 1984); incidence rates have also varied but average close to prevalence rates (e.g., Baker & Wills, 1978). These figures, however, do not usually include so-called truant subjects (i.e., those who refuse school with little fearfulness or anxiety). The clinical prevalence of school refusal in children and adolescents has been preliminary reported as 6.08% (Beasley & Kearney, 1991). The prevalence of test anxiety has been reported as high as 10% (Kondas, 1967).

Epidemiological studies indicate that more than one-sixth of adolescents may meet diagnostic criteria for an anxiety disorder. These data indicate a widespread vulnerability to internalizing psychopathology in this population. This information, and the fact that many adult anxiety disorders purportedly begin during adolescence, means that empirical study of adolescents is likely to receive increased attention in the next several years.

Complications

Several complications are associated with anxiety disorders in adolescents, including (a) comorbid diagnostic conditions, and (b) types of symptomatologies. For clarity, these are discussed separately below.

Comorbid Diagnostic Conditions

Last, Strauss, and Francis (1987) examined 73 children and adolescents (aged 5 to 18 years) referred to an outpatient anxiety disorder clinic. The Interview Schedule for Children, a "semistructured symptom-oriented interview schedule based on DSM diagnostic criteria" (p. 726), was employed. Primary diagnoses included separation anxiety (32.9%) and overanxious disorder (15.1%), social phobia of school (15.1%), major depression (15.1%), and simple phobia (5.5%). Youngsters in the first four groups also tended to meet criteria for an additional disorder (separation anxiety disorder, 79%; overanxious disorder, 73%; social phobia of school, 64%; major depression, 100%). Other comorbid conditions included enuresis, stuttering, and dysthymic, attention-deficit, and oppositional disorders.

Last, Francis, Hersen, Kazdin, and Strauss (1987) similarly compared 48 persons with separation anxiety disorder (mean age 9.4 years) with 19 persons with school phobia (mean age 14.3 years). More than one-half of each group met DSM criteria for another anxiety disorder, and one-third (32.8%) of the total sample met criteria for an affective disorder as well. Only 11 subjects (16.4%) presented with no concurrent disorder. The investigators concluded that separation anxiety and school phobia represent clearly distinct diagnostic groupings, although substantial overlap occurs among the child/adolescent anxiety disorders in clinical and non-clinical youngsters. This latter assertion was also supported in a sample of children and adolescents with school refusal (Last & Strauss, 1990). Strauss and Last (1993) found that 66% of youngsters with social phobia (mean age 14.9 years) and 50% of youngsters with simple phobia (mean age 11.1 years) met criteria for another anxiety disorder.

Bernstein and Garfinkel (1986) evaluated the concurrence of affective and anxiety disorders in 26 persons (mean age 13.6 years) with chronic school refusal (at least a 2-year history of poor school attendance). Subjects were partly evaluated using the Diagnostic Interview Schedule for Children. Eighteen (69.2%) met DSM criteria for an affective disorder, 16 (61.5%) for an anxiety disorder, and 6 (23.1%) for conduct disorder. In addition, 13 (50%) met criteria for both an affective and anxiety disorder, and 4 (15.4%) met criteria for an affective, anxiety, and conduct disorder. Only 3 (11.5%) displayed no concurrent diagnosis. The significant overlap led the authors to suggest that "major depression with anxiety disorder may be a subgroup of depression" (p. 240).

Kearney et al. (1989), in an analysis of adolescents (aged 12 to 16) with acute school refusal behavior, similarly found that many subjects met criteria for an additional DSM disorder. Using the Anxiety Disorders Interview Schedule for Children (Silverman & Nelles, 1988), they found that several met criteria for overanxious (44.4%) and avoidant (22.2%) disorders, social phobia (16.7%), major depression (16.7%), simple phobia (11.1%), and oppositional disorder (11.1%). Other concurrent diagnoses included separation anxiety, sleep terror, posttraumatic stress, and attention-deficit disorders. More than one-quarter (27.8%) did not meet criteria for any mental disorder. The last finding indicates that many adolescents refuse school for reasons other than avoidance of fear/anxiety, a point that must be closely considered in classifying this population.

Comorbid Symptomatology

Symptomatic complications of anxiety disorders in adolescents have also been evaluated. Murray and Clifford (1988), for example, examined 238 Northern Ireland 15- and 16-year-olds and found that state and trait anxiety were significantly correlated with headaches, sleeping and breathing difficulties, sweating, doctor visits, and need for medication. No differences in somatic complaints were found between males and females. These findings support those of other investigators (e.g., Kashani & Orvaschel, 1990), although some researchers (e.g., Livingston, Taylor, & Crawford, 1988) report a higher prevalence of somatic complaints in female youngsters with anxiety disorders. Last (1991) compared 158 children and adolescents (defined as those over the age of 13 years) with anxiety disorders on presence of somatic complaints. More than two-thirds (69%) of adolescents reported somatic complaints, compared to 50% of children; no gender differences were evident. In addition, youngsters with an anxiety disorder and somatic complaints were likely to refuse school. Common somatic complaints included headaches and stomachaches, dry mouth, sweaty hands, trouble catching breath, increased heartbeat, jitteriness, cold hands, and fatigue.

As mentioned earlier, other significant complications of anxiety disorders involve symptoms of depression and related problems. Symptoms of depression with anxiety disorders are reported in several studies (e.g., Bernstein & Garfinkel, 1986). In addition, Bernstein, Garfinkel, and Hoberman (1989) evaluated 988 adolescents using the Revised Children's Manifest Anxiety Scale, comparing 60 teenagers with elevated anxiety scores to the remaining sample across several variables. Adolescents with elevated self-reported anxiety showed more minor or chronic physical illness (51.7%), histories of physical and sexual abuse (30.5 and 22.0%), recent suicide attempts (13.8%), illegal drug use (16.9%), and poor school grades (36.7%) than those with low self-reported anxiety. Adolescents with high self-reported anxiety were also likely to be female. These results complement those of Kashani and Orvaschel (1990), who found that anxious 12- and 17-year-old adolescents (assessed via the Child Assessment Schedule and Revised Children's Manifest Anxiety Scale) displayed not only more depressive symptoms than their nonanxious peers but also fears of strangers and social situations, anxiety concerning past imperfections, and "difficulty with school, self-image, oversensitivity, and concentration" (p. 316).

Other comorbid symptoms include externalizing behavior problems, which are common among adolescents with anxiety disorders (Biederman, Newcorn, & Sprich, 1991). Kashani and Orvaschel (1990) found that anxious adolescents displayed more acting-out and conduct disorder symptoms than nonanxious adolescents. Fergusson et al. (1993) reported a significant relationship between anxiety and conduct/oppositional and substance use disorders in youngsters aged 15 years. Sanders and Giolas (1991) examined 47 adolescents hospitalized in a psychiatric unit for periods ranging from 1 to 13 weeks. Measures of childhood trauma and dissociation were moderately correlated (.44), suggesting that life events in childhood typically outside the range of normal human experience may place one at risk for dissociative symptoms and multiple personality disorder.

A final complication of adolescent anxiety and its disorders is a general interference in daily functioning. Kashani and Orvaschel (1990) found that anxious adolescents had significantly more problems with friends and family than nonanxious adolescents. As an example, Kearney and Silverman (1990b) assessed and treated a 14-year-old male with severe obsessive-compulsive disorder. At pretreatment, the youngster reported a significant loss of friends, deteriorating school performance, increased family conflict, restricted travel, and a growing inability to perform athletically over the previous year. Self-report measures, parent and teacher ratings, and clinician severity ratings substantiated these findings. The presence of severe disruptions in daily functioning was determined to be a major contributing factor to extended treatment length. Of course, interference in daily functioning is likely mediated by a wide range of variables, including social support, coping strategies, parental psychopathology, and level of cognitive development. Empirical research examining these mediating variables and improved methods of assessing impairment remain essential.

To summarize, adolescent anxiety is associated with many other behavior problems. These may include somatic complaints, depression, social interaction difficulties, suicide attempts, poor school performance, externalizing behavior problems, and general interference with normal daily functioning. The reports cited above, which provide evidence for highly comorbid symptomatology, underscore the need to identify diagnoses of adolescent anxiety with increased predictive and discriminant validity. Resolving this need would enhance clinical utility and allow researchers to evaluate strategies for effective, individualized treatment.

Familial Pattern

Although research into childhood and adolescent anxiety disorders is fairly new, several investigators have evaluated familial patterns associated with these problems. The most prevalent method of gathering data in this population is the family history approach (i.e., examining the prevalence of related disorders in relatives of an adult or adolescent proband). For example, Sylvester, Hyde, and Reichler (1987) evaluated 125 offspring (aged 7 to 17 years) of parents with either panic disorder (50), depression (27), or no mental disorder (48); children and parents were evaluated through use of the Diagnostic Interview Schedule for Children, among other measures. Children of parents with panic disorder or depression displayed a significantly higher prevalence of anxiety disorders and major depression than children of parents with no mental disorder. These data supplemented those of Sylvester, Reichler, and Hyde (1986), who reported that youngsters whose parents suffered from major depression or panic disorder were likely to view their families as pathological, showing increased conflict and control and less cohesion and independence as measured by the Family Environment Scale (Moos, 1974).

Silverman, Cerny, Nelles, and Burke (1988) examined 20 adolescents (aged 12 to 16 years) whose families included a parent with agoraphobia with panic attacks (55%), panic disorder (25%), generalized anxiety disorder (10%), or mixed phobias (10%). Dependent measures included the Anxiety Disorders Interview Schedule for Children and the Child Behavior Checklist. Although 8 (40%) subjects met criteria for no mental disorder, 8 (40%) did meet criteria for simple phobia. Other diagnoses included overanxious (20%) and avoidant (15%) disorders, social phobia (10%), and separation anxiety disorder (5%). In addition, compared to Achenbach and Edelbrock's (1983) nonclinical sample, adolescents of parents with anxiety disorders in the Silverman et al. (1988) study displayed significantly more behavior problems. Offspring were also likely to receive a clinical diagnosis if parental avoidance was high, leading the authors to conclude that parental avoidance may contribute to the development of anxiety-related psychopathology in adolescents.

Riddle et al. (1990) examined the family history of 6 adolescents (aged 12 to 16) with obsessive-compulsive disorder. Three fathers and one mother displayed obsessive-compulsive symptoms, and one father and one mother met criteria for obsessive-compulsive disorder. Only one parent per adolescent reported difficulties. The authors concluded that a strong familial component to the onset of obsessive-compulsive disorder is evident in preadults.

Fyer et al. (1991) examined a familial link for fearfulness by assessing 15 probands with simple phobia and 49 first-degree relatives. These were compared to 119 first-degree relatives of a normal control proband group ($n = 38$). Relatives were assessed with the Schedule for Affective Disorders and Schizophrenia. Relatives of probands with simple phobia displayed simple phobia themselves (31%) more often than did relatives of control probands (11%). In addition, 15% of children (27% of daughters and 6% of sons, ages unspecified) of simple phobia probands were diagnosed with simple phobia compared to 8% of children of control probands, a statistically significant difference. The investigators concluded that simple phobia has a strong familial component that is possibly explained by genetic transmission.

In a review of investigations of adolescent panic disorder, Kearney and Silverman (1992) stated that reports of panic were common in family members of diagnosed youngsters. For 40 adolescents allegedly diagnosed with panic disorder across six studies, common familial diagnoses included maternal panic disorder or attacks (22.5%), maternal relative panic attacks (10.0%), major depression in a family member (7.5%), phobic disorder in maternal relatives (5.0%), panic attacks in father or paternal relatives (5.0%), and maternal simple phobia (2.5%). Thus adolescent and adult panic may be related. Proposed mechanisms of transfer include parental avoidance, modeling effects, family environment, diagnostic severity, and cultural factors (e.g., Chambless & Mason, 1986).

Finally, examinations of the familial relationship between adolescent school refusal and parental disorders have been conducted. Hypotheses in this area have been discussed for decades (e.g., Johnson et al., 1941), but empirical investigations became prominent with the work of I. Berg and his colleagues in Britain. For example, Berg, Butler, and McGuire (1972) found that adolescents with school phobia tended to be later in the birth order (i.e., had mothers with a higher age) in families with three or more children. More specific to anxiety disorders, Berg (1976) surveyed 299 women with agoraphobia and at least one child aged 7 to 15 years. Overall incidence of school phobia was reported as 7%, although this increased to 14% for persons aged 11 to 15 years. Again, parental avoidance behavior may have been a key transmission factor.

With the advent of DSM-III and its subsequent revisions, more detailed findings have been reported. Last, Francis et al. (1987) indicated that mothers of adolescents with school phobia met criteria for an anxiety disorder in most cases (57.1%) and affective disorder in others (14.3%). Last and Strauss (1990) reported that mothers of children and adolescents with school refusal were likely to have refused school themselves in the past (33%) compared to mothers of children with no problems (10%). These results complement those of Bernstein, Svingen, and Garfinkel (1990), who evaluated 76 youngsters (aged 7 to 17 years) with school refusal and their parents on measures of depression, anxiety, and family functioning. Parents rated the families as clinically dysfunctional with regard to role definition/integration and agreement on family values. Families were rated as most dysfunctional, however, when the child did not meet criteria for an anxiety or depressive disorder. Least family dysfunction was associated with youngsters with an anxiety disorder only (opposed to those with anxiety and depressive disorders).

Despite a lack of breakdown of adolescent and preadolescent samples in many familial studies, interesting hypotheses have been generated. Findings from studies of familial patterns of functioning in adolescents with anxiety-related problems suggest a relationship between adult and preadult psychopathology and symptoms. Potential mechanisms of transmission have been mentioned, with parental avoidance likely a major contributing factor. Additional research in this area, particularly the use of twin studies, is necessary to delineate fully any possible genetic components.

Differential Diagnosis and Assessment

As mentioned earlier, the anxiety/phobia construct is a complex one, consisting of behavioral, cognitive, and physiological components. Fear or anxiety is considered problematic when a person displays difficulties in one or more response systems; the assessment of anxiety and its disorders in adolescents must therefore focus on each system. Few assessment techniques, however, have been specifically designed for preadults, and even fewer exist for adolescents. In fact, many methods used for anxious children are often employed with adolescents without attending to developmental differences between the two. The lack of developmentally sensitive assessment instruments for anxious adolescents is a major problem that requires future research efforts.

With respect to the behavioral component, several observational rating scales have been developed. These include scales for children with dental fears (Melamed, Weinstein, Hawes, & Katin-Borland, 1975), cancer (Katz, Kellerman, & Siegel, 1980), and separation distress (Glennon & Weisz, 1978). A behavioral method popularly used with youngsters with fear/anxiety is the Behavioral Avoidance Test (BAT), an analogue assessment of limited approach to a fear-provoking object (e.g., a snake). Unfortunately, assessment procedures designed to measure this anxiety component suffer from practical and methodological problems, including the amount of work required in a clinical setting (e.g., training observers) and unknown reliability and validity.

With respect to the cognitive component, interviewing strategies, questionnaire measures, and self-monitoring procedures are commonly used. Among these, the clinical interview is most prevalent, and several structured interviews for youngsters with anxiety-related problems have been developed (see Silverman, 1991, for a review). The interview is helpful for soliciting different types of information, including the nature of an anxiety problem, an adolescent's thoughts and feelings, severity of symptoms, and degree of daily life interference. Unfortunately, not enough methodologically sound evidence exists to conclude that any interview provides clinicians with reliable diagnoses (Silverman, 1991); in addition, differences in response across cultures have not been examined.

Recent evidence (Silverman & Eisen, 1992), however, indicates that the Anxiety Disorders Interview Schedule for Children does display adequate overall test-retest reliability for diagnosing anxious symptomatology in children and adolescents across child and parent versions of the measure. Still, parent-child agreement is notoriously poor (Klein, 1991), and only one interview (the Diagnostic Interview Schedule for Children and Adolescents; Welner, Reich, Herjanic, Jung, & Amado, 1987) consists of separate child and adolescent versions. Despite these problems, interviews remain important clinical research tools and are useful for eliciting cognitive/subjective information.

Another popular method of assessing the cognitive domain is self-report. Common measures, several of which were mentioned earlier, include the revised Fear Survey Schedule for Children (Ollendick, 1983), the revised Children's Manifest Anxiety Scale (Reynolds & Paget, 1981), and the State-Trait Anxiety Inventory for Children (Spielberger, 1973). Others include the Beck Anxiety Inventory, a 21-item self-report measure of somatic, affective, and cognitive anxiety symptoms that possesses good psychometric properties when used with adolescents (Jolly et al., 1993); the Children's Coping Questionnaire, in which youngsters are asked to rate how well they can cope with specified situations (Kendall et al., 1992); and the Children's Anxiety Sensitivity Index, an 18-item measure of expectancies that anxiety symptoms will be aversive (Silverman, Fleisig, Rabian, & Peterson, 1991).

Specialized scales have also been developed to measure social (La Greca & Stone, 1993) and test anxiety (Sarason, Davidson, Lighthall, Waite, & Ruebush, 1960). Although these scales demonstrate adequate reliability, their construct validity remains unclear. Also, as mentioned earlier (e.g., King et al., 1991), many anxiety and depression scales are intercorrelated, suggesting the clinical utility of a broader construct of negative affectivity in this population. Self-ratings of fearfulness via a "fear thermometer" (Melamed, Yurcheson, Fleece, Hutcherson, & Hawes, 1978) may assist in measuring this problem for young children, but the additional usefulness of such instruments in obtaining information from adolescents is unknown.

Eliciting cognitive/subjective information from anxious adolescents may also be accomplished via self-monitoring of behavioral and emotional responses such as avoidance or approach with gradations of measured fearfulness or anxiety, as well as related cognitions. Although promising, this technique suffers from reactivity and unknown reliability. Beidel, Neal, and Lederer (1991) designed a self-monitoring procedure for daily anxiety symptoms that is preliminarily reliable and valid for children, although untested on adolescents. Think-aloud procedures (e.g., Kendall, Pellegrini, & Urbain, 1981), in which verbal responses to fear- or anxiety-provoking situations are audiotaped, have also been used, but knowledge of their psychometric properties remains limited.

Finally, with respect to the physiological component of anxiety, psychophysiological recordings of fear/anxiety are common for adults but not children and adolescents. Examples of such recordings include measures of heart rate, respiration, blood pressure, galvanic skin response, sweet gland activity, and somatic complaints (Beidel, 1988). Cost and technological constraints, however, limit the prevalence of these procedures in clinical settings. Silverman and Kearney (1993) recommended that clinicians and researchers focus their measurement on physiological responses such as heart rate and sweat gland activity (e.g., Beidel, 1988; Melamed & Siegel, 1975). Procedural variations and susceptibility to environmental intrusions, though, remain problematic (Morris & Kratochwill, 1983).

Overall, the assessment of anxiety in adolescents has recently received increased clinical and research attention, yet key practical and theoretical problems remain. The convergent and discriminant validity of the above measures must be more vigorously tested, and developmental and cultural factors should be examined. In addition, the usefulness of these procedures with anxious adolescents is almost completely unknown; this lack of knowledge may hamper research efforts to evaluate potentially critical links (e.g., patterns of change in adolescent anxiety) between child and adult fear, anxiety, and related disorders.

Clinical Management

Research on treatment of adolescents with fear/anxiety problems has primarily focused on the elimination of simple phobias. Common strategies for this purpose include systematic desensitization and its variants, contingency management (e.g., positive/negative reinforcement), implosion/flooding, modeling procedures (including live and symbolic), and cognitive or self-control techniques.

Systematic desensitization is often conceptualized as containing three components: teaching an antagonistic response to fear/anxiety (e.g., relaxation); constructing an anxiety hierarchy (i.e., least to most anxiety-provoking items); and pairing the antagonistic response to each item. Systematic desensitization is the behavioral technique most frequently used to alleviate fear in youngsters (Ollendick, 1979), although its effectiveness has yet to be fully evaluated for adolescents. Examples of adolescent fears successfully treated by systematic desensitization include those of school (Croghan, 1981), tests (Laxer, Quarter, Kooman, & Walker, 1969), separation/travel (Bornstein & Knapp, 1981), social settings (Wolpe, 1961), and needles (Rainwater et al., 1988). Implosion or flooding therapies (Marks, 1975) involve exposing individuals to the most fear/anxiety-provoking stimulus first, relying on extinction for therapeutic efficacy. Investigations in adolescents are almost nonexistent, however, being limited primarily to forced school attendance for those who refuse school (e.g., Kennedy, 1965).

The use of modeling procedures, as mentioned earlier, is based on observational learning. Theoretically, one vicariously learns to be anxious or fearful toward a stimulus, and one may become less so by observing others interact less fearfully with the stimulus. For adolescents, modeling procedures are useful for reducing fears of animals (Bandura, Blanchard, & Ritter, 1969), heights (Ritter, 1969), and medical procedures (Faust & Melamed, 1984). Wehr and Kaufman (1987) assigned 96 anxious ninth-grade adolescents to experimental groups of assertiveness training or control groups of counseling in career development. Experimental groups received "lecture(s), discussion groups, modeling, role playing, behavior rehearsal, coaching, and feedback" (p. 199) over four 1-hour training sessions. At posttest, adolescents in experimental groups scored significantly higher on a measure of assertiveness and lower on a measure of state anxiety than control groups. In general, however, most investigations of modeling have been conducted with young children.

Self-control therapies, often based on cognitive restructuring, assist those with fearfulness/anxiety to identify negative self-statements related to deficits in performance. In addition, self-control therapies encourage individuals to produce positive self-statements and apply adaptive self-statements to everyday situations (Morris & Kratochwill, 1983). Although not extensively investigated, self-control strategies may work well with adolescents, who approach the cognitive developmental level of adults. Cognitive-based therapies are useful for adolescents with fears of school and/or public speaking (Craddock, Cotler, & Jason, 1978), public bowel movements (Eisen & Silverman, 1991), and obsessive-compulsive disorder (Kearney & Silverman, 1990b). Future research should also focus on developing coping techniques based on those that adolescents currently use on an everyday basis; these include exercising, improving peer or child-parent relationships, humor, and listening to music among others (Grace, Spirito, Finch, & Ott, 1993; Kurdek, 1987).

Finally, contingency management procedures, based on operant conditioning, stress the causal relationship between stimuli and behavior (Morris & Kratochwill, 1983) and the modification of consequences of behavior. A typical scenario involves a parent or teacher arranging a youngster's environment to ensure that particular consequences to particular behaviors occur. Contingency management procedures include positive and negative reinforcement, shaping, and extinction. Examples with adolescents include reductions of fears of school (Kearney & Silverman, 1990a) and social settings (Jackson & Wallace, 1974).

Although evaluations of adolescent fearfulness have been conducted, almost no work has examined treatment strategies for formally diagnosed overanxious, separation anxiety, and avoidant disorders in this population. Kane and Kendall (1989) reported on a 13-year-old female (and 3 other children) with overanxious disorder. Treatment consisted of a variety of procedures, including cognitive restructuring, self-reinforcement, modeling, exposure, relaxation training, role play, and contingency management. Treatment over a 9-week period produced moderate improvements in self-reported anxiety. For separation (Thyer & Sowers-Hoag, 1988) and social anxiety disorder, however, experimental studies of adolescents are nonexistent with the exception of treating individual symptoms via the fear reduction techniques mentioned above. The treatment of adolescent fear and anxiety disorders must therefore receive a higher priority among researchers. In addition, issues of uncontrolled investigations, combined interventions, inconsistent criteria for positive therapeutic outcome, and lack of identifying maintaining variables of fear/anxiety (for purposes of prescriptive treatment effectiveness) remain (Silverman & Kearney, 1991).

A common theme to many sections in this chapter is the paucity of investigative work regarding adolescents with anxiety disorders. The need for additional research is particularly acute for classification, assessment, and treatment. Although the advent of the DSM-III categorical system stimulated work in this area, many questions remain unresolved. A critical issue is the extensive overlap of symptoms (internalizing and externalizing) in the clinical picture of adolescent anxiety. As a result, a diagnostic system of classifying this area of psychopathology may not be fully adequate and might be supplemented by alternative nosological models such as those based on empirically derived factors or functional analyses.

A related issue involves appropriate assessment and treatment strategies for this population. With respect to assessment, it must be noted that complex clinical issues during the evaluation phase are often ignored in this population. Depending on their level of cognitive and emotional development, teenagers are likely to greet therapists with greater resistance and noncompliance than young children. Researchers developing appropriate therapeutic strategies for this population must consider effective rapport-building methods. In addition, few assessment techniques are specifically designed for adolescents. With respect to treatment, evidence for effective therapeutic strategies is based primarily on adolescent case studies and not extensive examinations of theory-based hypotheses. As such, clinicians are likely to be unsure as to which clinical procedure is best for a particular adolescent with severe anxiety. Given the complicated clinical picture presented earlier, the task of assessing the utility of treatment for this population is imperative. In conjunction with exploring the efficacy of differential typologies and related assessment techniques, researchers should concentrate on examining individualized, prescriptive treatment strategies.

References

Achenbach, T. M. (1980). DSM-III in light of empirical research on the classification of child psychopathology. *Journal of the American Academy of Child Psychiatry, 19*, 395–412.

Achenbach, T. M. (1991a). *Manual for the Child Behavior Checklist/4–18 and 1991 profile*. Burlington: University of Vermont, Department of Psychiatry.

Achenbach, T. M. (1991b). *Manual for the Teacher's Report Form and 1991 profile*. Burlington: University of Vermont, Department of Psychiatry.

Achenbach, T. M., Conners, C. K., Quay, H. C., Verhulst, F. C., & Howell, C. T. (1989). Replication of empirically derived syndromes as a basis for taxonomy of child/adolescent psychopathology. *Journal of Abnormal Child Psychology, 17*, 299–323.

Achenbach, T. M., & Edelbrock, C. (1983). *Manual for the Child Behavior Checklist and revised Child Behavior Profile*. Burlington: University of Vermont, Department of Psychiatry.

Achenbach, T. M., & Edelbrock, C. (1986). *Manual for the Teacher's Report Form and teacher version of the Child Behavior Profile*. Burlington: University of Vermont, Department of Psychiatry.

Agras, W. S., Chapin, H. N., & Oliveau, D. C. (1972). The natural history of phobia. *Archives of General Psychiatry, 26*, 315–317.

American Psychiatric Association. (1968). *Diagnostic and statistical manual of mental disorders* (2nd ed.). Washington, DC: Author.

American Psychiatric Association. (1980). *Diagnostic and statistical manual of mental disorders* (3rd ed.). Washington, DC: Author.

American Psychiatric Association. (1987). *Diagnostic and statistical manual of mental disorders* (rev. 3rd ed.). Washington, DC: Author.

American Psychiatric Association. (1994). *Diagnostic and statistical manual of mental disorders* (4th. ed.). Washington, DC: Author.

Atkinson, L., Quarrington, B., & Cyr, J. J. (1985). School refusal: The heterogeneity of a concept. *American Journal of Orthopsychiatry, 55*, 83–101.

Baker, H., & Wills, U. (1978). School phobia: Classification and treatment. *British Journal of Psychiatry, 132*, 492–499.

Bandura, A., Blanchard, E. B., & Ritter, B. (1969). Relative efficacy of desensitization and modeling approaches for inducing behavioral, affective, and attitudinal changes. *Journal of Personality and Social Psychology, 13*, 173–199.

Bandura, A., Grusec, E., & Menlove, F. L. (1967). Vicarious extinction of avoidance behavior. *Journal of Personality and Social Psychology, 5*, 16–23.

Barlow, D. H., Mavissakalian, M., & Schofield, L. D. (1980). Patterns of desynchrony in agoraphobia: A preliminary report. *Behaviour Research and Therapy, 18*, 441–448.

Barrios, B. A., & Hartmann, D. P. (1988). Fears and anxieties. In E. J. Mash & L. G. Terdal (Eds.), *Behavioral assessment of childhood disorders* (2nd ed.). New York: Guilford.

Barrios, B. A., & O'Dell, S. L. (1989). Fears and anxieties. In E. J. Mash & R. A. Barkley (Eds.), *Treatment of childhood disorders*. New York: Guilford.

Beasley, J. F., & Kearney, C. A. (1991, April). *Getting Johnny back to school: Treatment of school refusal behavior*. Paper presented at the meeting of the Western Psychological Association, San Francisco.

Beidel, D. C. (1988). Psychophysiological assessment of anxious emotional states in children. *Journal of Abnormal Psychology, 97*, 80–82.

Beidel, D. C., Neal, A. M., & Lederer, A. S. (1991). The feasibility and validity of a daily diary for the assessment of anxiety in children. *Behavior Therapy, 22*, 505–517.

Beidel, D. C., & Turner, S. M. (1988). Comorbidity of test anxiety and other anxiety disorders in children. *Journal of Abnormal Child Psychology, 16*, 275–287.

Berg, C. Z., Rapoport, J. L., & Flament, M. (1986). The Leyton Obsessional Inventory-Child Version. *Journal of the American Academy of Child and Adolescent Psychiatry, 25*, 84–91.

Berg, C. Z., Rapoport, J. L., Whitaker, A., Davies, M., Leonard, H., Swedo, S. E., Braiman, S., & Lenane, M. (1989). Childhood obsessive compulsive disorder: A two-year prospective follow-up of a community sample. *Journal of the American Academy of Child and Adolescent Psychiatry, 28*, 528–533.

Berg, I. (1976). School phobia in the children of agoraphobic women. *British Journal of Psychiatry, 128*, 86–89.

Berg, I., Butler, A., & McGuire, R. (1972). Birth order and family size of school-phobic adolescents. *British Journal of Psychiatry, 121*, 509–514.

Berg, I., & Jackson, A. (1985). Teenage school refusers grow up: A follow-up study of 168 subjects, ten years on average after inpatient treatment. *British Journal of Psychiatry, 147*, 366–370.

Bernstein, G. A., & Garfinkel, B. D. (1986). School phobia: The overlap of affective and anxiety disorders. *Journal of the American Academy of Child Psychiatry, 2*, 235–241.

Bernstein, G. A., Garfinkel, B. D., & Hoberman, H. M. (1989). Self-reported anxiety in adolescents. *American Journal of Psychiatry, 146,* 384–386.

Bernstein, G. A., Svingen, P. H., & Garfinkel, B. D. (1990). School phobia: Patterns of family functioning. *Journal of the American Academy of Child and Adolescent Psychiatry, 29,* 24–30.

Biederman, J., Newcorn, J., & Sprich, S. (1991). Comorbidity of attention deficit hyperactivity disorder with conduct, depressive, anxiety, and other disorders. *American Journal of Psychiatry, 148,* 564–577.

Bird, H. R., Canino, G., Rubio-Stipec, M., Gould, M. S., Ribera, J., Sesman, M., Woodbury, M., Huertas-Goldman, S., Pagan, A., Sanchez-Lacay, A., & Moscoso, M. (1988). Estimates of the prevalence of childhood maladjustment in a community survey in Puerto Rico: The use of combined measures. *Archives of General Psychiatry, 45,* 1120–1126.

Blagg, N. R., & Yule, W. (1984). The behavioral treatment of school refusal: A comparative study. *Behaviour Research and Therapy, 22,* 119–127.

Bornstein, P. H., & Knapp, M. (1981). Self-control desensitization with a multiphobic boy: A A multiple baseline design. *Journal of Behavior Therapy and Experimental Psychiatry, 12,* 281–285.

Bowen, R. C., Offord, D. R., & Boyle, M. H. (1990). The prevalence of overanxious disorder and separation anxiety disorder: Results from the Ontario child health study. *Journal of the American Academy of Child and Adolescent Psychiatry, 29,* 753–758.

Burke, A. E., & Silverman, W. K. (1987). The prescriptive treatment of school refusal. *Clinical Psychology Review, 7,* 353–362.

Cantwell, D. P. (1980). The diagnostic process and diagnostic classification in child psychiatry—DSM-III: Introduction. *Journal of the American Academy of Child Psychiatry, 19,* 345–355.

Cantwell, D. P., & Baker, L. (1989). Stability and natural history of DSM-III childhood diagnoses. *Journal of the American Academy of Child and Adolescent Psychiatry, 28,* 691–700.

Chambless, D. L., & Mason, J. (1986). Sex, sex role stereotyping and agoraphobia. *Behaviour Research and Therapy, 24,* 231–235.

Craddock, C., Cotler, S., & Jason, L. A. (1978). Primary prevention: Immunization of children for speech anxiety. *Cognitive Therapy and Research, 2,* 389–396.

Croghan, L. M. (1981). Conceptualizing the critical elements in a rapid desensitization to school anxiety: A case study. *Journal of Pediatric Psychology, 6,* 165–170.

Eisen, A. R., & Silverman, W. K. (1991). Treatment of an adolescent with bowel movement phobia using self-control therapy. *Journal of Behavior Therapy and Experimental Psychiatry, 22,* 45–51.

Eisenberg, L. (1958). School phobia: A study in the communication of anxiety. *American Journal of Psychiatry, 114,* 712–718.

Erikson, E. H. (1959). *Identity and the life cycle.* New York: International Universities Press.

Faust, J., & Melamed, B. G. (1984). Influence of arousal, previous experience, and age on surgery preparation of same day or surgery and in-hospital pediatric patients. *Journal of Consulting and Clinical Psychology, 52,* 359–365.

Feehan, M., McGee, R., & Williams, S. M. (1993). Mental health disorders from age 15 to age 18 years. *Journal of the American Academy of Child and Adolescent Psychiatry, 32,* 1118–1126.

Fergusson, D. M., Horwood, L. J., & Lynskey, M. T. (1993). Prevalence and comorbidity of DSM-III-R diagnoses in a birth cohort of 15 year olds. *Journal of the American Academy of Child and Adolescent Psychiatry, 32,* 1127–1134.

Finch, A. J., Jr., Lipovsky, J. A., & Casat, C. D. (1989). Anxiety and depression in children and adolescents: Negative affectivity or separate constructs? In P. C. Kendall & D. Watson (Eds.), *Anxiety and depression: Distinctive and overlapping features* (pp. 171–202). San Diego, CA: Academic Press.

Flakierska, N., Lindstrom, M., & Gillberg, C. (1988). School refusal: A 15–20-year follow-up study of 35 Swedish urban children. *British Journal of Psychiatry, 152,* 834–837.

Flament, M. F., Whitaker, A., Rapoport, J. L., Davies, M., Berg, C. Z., Kalikow, K., Sceery, W., & Shaffer, D. (1988). Obsessive compulsive disorder in adolescence: An epidemiological study. *Journal of the American Academy of Child and Adolescent Psychiatry, 27,* 764–771.

Francis, G., Last, C. G., & Strauss, C. C. (1987). Expression of separation anxiety disorder: The roles of age and gender. *Child Psychiatry and Human Development, 18,* 82–89.

Freud, S. (1953). Analysis of a phobia in a five-year-old boy. In J. Strachey (Ed. and Trans.), *The standard edition of the complete psychological works of Sigmund Freud* (Vol. 10). London: Hogarth. (Original work published 1909)

Fyer, A. J., Mannuzza, S., Gallops, M. S., Martin, L. Y., Aaronson, C., Gorman, J. M., Liebowitz, M. R., & Klein, D. F. (1991). Familial transmission of simple phobias and fears: A preliminary report. *Archives of General Psychiatry, 47,* 252–256.

Glennon, B., & Weisz, J. R. (1978). An observational approach to the assessment of anxiety in young children. *Journal of Consulting and Clinical Psychology, 46,* 1246–1257.

Grace, N., Spirito, A., Finch, A. J., Jr., & Ott, E. S. (1993). Coping skills for anxiety control in children. In A. J. Finch, Jr., W. M. Nelson III, & E. S. Ott (Eds.), *Cognitive-behavioral procedures with children and adolescents* (pp. 257–288). Boston: Allyn and Bacon.

Granell de Aldaz, E., Vivas, E., Gelfand, D. M., & Feldman, L. (1984). Estimating the prevalence of school refusal and school-related fears: A Venezualan sample. *Journal of Nervous and Mental Disease, 172,* 722–729.

Graziano, A. M., & De Giovanni, I. S. (1979). The clinical significance of childhood phobias: A note on the proportion of child-clinical referrals for the treatment of children's fears. *Behaviour Research and Therapy, 17,* 161–162.

Hagman, E. R. (1932). A study of fears of children of preschool age. *Journal of Experimental Education, 1,* 110–130.

Hall, G. S. (1904). *Adolescence.* Englewood Cliffs, NJ: Prentice-Hall.

Hampe, E., Noble, H., Miller, L. C., & Barrett, C. L. (1973). Phobic children one and two years posttreatment. *Journal of Abnormal Psychology, 82,* 446–453.

Havighurst, R. (1972). *Developmental tasks and education.* New York: McKay.

Herjanic, B., & Reich, W. (1982). Development of a structured psychiatric interview for children: Agreement between child and parent on individual symptoms. *Journal of Abnormal Child Psychology, 10,* 307–324.

Hershberg, S. G., Carlson, G. A., Cantwell, D. P., & Strober, M. (1982). Anxiety and depressive disorders in psychiatrically disturbed children. *Journal of Clinical Psychiatry, 43*, 358–361.

Hodges, K., Cools, J., & McKnew, D. (1989). Test-retest reliability of a clinical research interview for children: The Child Assessment Schedule. *Psychological Assessment: A Journal of Consulting and Clinical Psychology, 1*, 317–322.

Ishiyama, F. I., & Chabassol, D. J. (1985). Adolescents' fear of social consequences of academic success as a function of age and sex. *Journal of Youth and Adolescence, 14*, 37–46.

Jablensky, A. (1985). Approaches to the definition and classification of anxiety and related disorders in European psychiatry. In A. H. Tuma & J. Maser (Eds.), *Anxiety and the anxiety disorders*. Hillsdale, NJ: Erlbaum.

Jackson, D. A., & Wallace, R. F. (1974). The modification and generalization of voice loudness in a fifteen-year-old retarded girl. *Journal of Applied Behavior Analysis, 7*, 461–471.

Jacobsen, R. H., Lahey, B. B., & Strauss, C. C. (1983). Correlates of depressed mood in normal children. *Journal of Abnormal Child Psychology, 11*, 29–40.

Johnson, A. M., Falstein, E. I., Szurek, S. A., & Svendsen, M. (1941). School phobia. *American Journal of Orthopsychiatry, 11*, 702–711.

Jolly, J. B., Aruffo, J. F., Wherry, J. N., & Livingston, R. (1993). The utility of the Beck Anxiety Inventory with inpatient adolescents. *Journal of Anxiety Disorders, 7*, 95–106.

Jones, M. C. (1924). The elimination of children's fears. *Journal of Experimental Psychology, 7*, 382–390.

Kane, M. T., & Kendall, P. C. (1989). Anxiety disorders in children: A multiple-baseline evaluation of a cognitive-behavioral treatment. *Behavior Therapy, 20*, 499–508.

Kashani, J. H., & Orvaschel, H. (1988). Anxiety disorders in mid-adolescence: A community sample. *American Journal of Psychiatry, 145*, 960–964.

Kashani, J. H., & Orvaschel, H. (1990). A community study of anxiety in children and adolescents. *American Journal of Psychiatry, 147*, 313–318.

Katz, E. R., Kellerman, J., & Siegel, S. E. (1980). Behavioral distress in children with cancer undergoing medical procedures: Developmental considerations. *Journal of Consulting and Clinical Psychology, 48*, 356–365.

Kearney, C. A., & Silverman, W. K. (1990a). A preliminary analysis of a functional model of assessment and treatment for school refusal behavior. *Behavior Modification, 14*, 340–366.

Kearney, C. A., & Silverman, W. K. (1990b). Treatment of an adolescent with obsessive-compulsive disorder by alternating response prevention and cognitive therapy: An empirical analysis. *Journal of Behavior Therapy and Experimental Psychiatry, 21*, 39–47.

Kearney, C. A., & Silverman, W. K. (1992). Let's not push the "panic" button: A critical analysis of panic and panic disorder in adolescents. *Clinical Psychology Review, 12*, 293–305.

Kearney, C. A., Silverman, W. K., & Eisen, A. R. (1989, October). *Characteristics of children and adolescents with school refusal behavior*. Paper presented at the meeting of the Berkshire Association for Behavior Analysis and Therapy.

Kendall, P. C., Chansky, T. E., Kane, M. T., Kim, R. S., Kortlander, E., Ronan, K.

R., Sessa, F. M., & Siqueland, L. (1992). *Anxiety disorders in youth: Cognitive-behavioral interventions.* Boston: Allyn and Bacon.

Kendall, P. C., Pellegrini, D. S., & Urbain, E. S. (1981). Approaches to assessment for cognitive-behavioral interventions with children. In P. C. Kendall & S. D. Hollon, (Eds.), *Assessment strategies for cognitive-behavioral interventions.* New York: Academic Press.

Kennedy, W. A. (1965). School phobia: Rapid treatment of 50 cases. *Journal of Abnormal Psychology, 70,* 285–289.

King, N. J., Ollendick, T. H., & Gullone, E. (1991). Negative affectivity in children and adolescents: Relations between anxiety and depression. *Clinical Psychology Review, 11,* 441–459.

Klein, R. (1991). Parent-child agreement in clinical assessment of anxiety and other psychopathology: A review. *Journal of Anxiety Disorders, 5,* 187–198.

Kondas, O. (1967). Reduction of examination anxiety and "stage fright" by group desensitization and relaxation. *Behaviour Research and Therapy, 5,* 275–281.

Kurdek, L. A. (1987). Gender differences in the psychological symptomatology and coping strategies of young adolescents. *Journal of Early Adolescence, 7,* 395–410.

La Greca, A. M., & Stone, W. L. (1993). Social Anxiety Scale for Children-Revised: Factor structure and concurrent validity. *Journal of Clinical Child Psychology, 22,* 17–27.

Lang, P. J. (1968). Fear reduction and fear behavior: Problems in treating a construct. In J. M. Shlien (Ed.), *Research in psychotherapy* (Vol. 13). Washington, DC: American Psychiatric Association.

Lang, P. J. (1977). Fear imagery: An information processing analysis. *Behavior Therapy, 8,* 862–886.

Last, C. G. (1991). Somatic complaints in anxiety disordered children. *Journal of Anxiety Disorders, 5,* 125–138.

Last, C. G., Francis, G., Hersen, M., Kazdin, A. E., & Strauss, C. C. (1987). Separation anxiety and school phobia: A comparison using DSM-III criteria. *American Journal of Psychiatry, 144,* 653–657.

Last, C. G., & Strauss, C. C. (1990). School refusal in anxiety-disordered children and adolescents. *Journal of the American Academy of Child and Adolescent Psychiatry, 29,* 31–35.

Last, C. G., Strauss, C. C., & Francis, G. (1987). Comorbidity among childhood anxiety disorders. *Journal of Nervous and Mental Disease, 175,* 726–730.

Laxer, M., Quarter, J., Kooman, A., & Walker, K. (1969). Systematic desensitization and relaxation of high test-anxious secondary school students. *Journal of Counseling Psychology, 16,* 446–451.

Livingston, R., Taylor, J. L., & Crawford, S. L. (1988). A study of somatic complaints and psychiatric diagnosis in children. *Journal of the American Academy of Child and Adolescent Psychiatry, 27,* 185–187.

Marcia, J. (1980). Identity in adolescence. In J. Adelson (Ed.), *Handbook of adolescent psychology.* New York: Wiley.

Marks, I. M. (1975). Behavioral treatments of phobic and obsessive-compulsive disorders: A critical appraisal. In M. Hersen, R. M. Eisler, & P. M. Miller (Eds.), *Progress in behavior modification* (Vol. 1). New York: Academic Press.

McGee, R., Feehan, M., Williams, S., & Anderson, J. (1992). DSM-III disorders from age 11 to age 15 years. *Journal of the American Academy of Child and Adolescent Psychiatry, 31,* 50–59.

McGee, R., Feehan, M., Williams, S., Partridge, F., Silva, P. A., & Kelly, J. (1990). DSM-III disorders in a large sample of adolescents. *Journal of the American Academy of Child and Adolescent Psychiatry, 29,* 611–619.

Melamed, B. G., & Siegel, L. J. (1975). Reduction of anxiety in children facing hospitalization and surgery by use of filmed modeling. *Journal of Consulting and Clinical Psychology, 43,* 511–521.

Melamed, B. G., Weinstein, D., Hawes, R., & Katin-Borland, M. (1975). Reduction of fear related dental management problems using filmed modeling. *Journal of the American Dental Association, 90,* 822–826.

Melamed, B. G., Yurcheson, R., Fleece, E. L., Hutcherson, S., & Hawes, R. (1978). Effects of film modeling on the reduction of anxiety-related behaviors in individuals varying in level of previous experience in the stress situation. *Journal of Consulting and Clinical Psychology, 46,* 1357–1367.

Moos, R. F. (1974). *Family environment scale.* Palo Alto, CA: Consulting Psychologists Press.

Morris, R. J. (1980). Fear reduction methods. In F. H. Kanfer & A. P. Goldstein (Eds.), *Helping people change* (2nd ed.). New York: Pergamon.

Morris, R. J., & Kratochwill, T. R. (1983). *Treating children's fears and phobias: A behavioral approach.* New York: Pergamon.

Murray, M., & Clifford, S. (1988). Anxiety and aspects of health behavior among adolescents in Northern Ireland. *Adolescence, 23,* 661–666.

Norvell, N., Brophy, C., & Finch, A. J., Jr. (1985). The relationship of anxiety to childhood depression. *Journal of Personality Assessment, 49,* 150–153.

Ollendick, T. H. (1979). Fear reduction techniques with children. In M. Hersen, R. M. Eisler, & P. M. Miller (Eds.), *Progress in behavior modification* (Vol. 1). New York: Academic Press.

Ollendick, T. H. (1983). Reliability and validity of the revised Fear Survey Schedule for Children (FSSC-R). *Behaviour Research and Therapy, 21,* 685–692.

Ollendick, T. H., King, N. J., & Frary, R. B. (1989). Fears in children and adolescents: Reliability and generalizability across gender, age, and nationality. *Behaviour Research and Therapy, 27,* 19–26.

Payne, M. A. (1988). Adolescent fears: Some Carribean findings. *Journal of Youth and Adolescence, 17,* 255–266.

Podd, M. H., Marcia, J. E., & Rubin, B. M. (1970). The effects of ego identity and partner perception on a prisoner's dilemma game. *Journal of Social Psychology, 82,* 117–126.

Prince, G. S. (1968). School phobia. In E. Miller (Ed.), *Foundations of child psychiatry.* London: Pergamon.

Rainwater, N., Sweet, A. A., Elliott, L., Bowers, M., McNeil, J., & Stump, N. (1988). Systematic desensitization in the treatment of needle phobias for children with diabetes. *Child and Family Behavior Therapy, 10,* 19–31.

Rey, J. M., Plapp, J. M., & Stewart, G. W. (1989). Reliability of psychiatric diagnosis in referred adolescents. *Journal of Child Psychology and Psychiatry, 30,* 879–888.

Reynolds, C. R., & Paget, K. D. (1981). Factor analysis of the revised Children's

Manifest Anxiety Scale for blacks, whites, males, and females. *Journal of Consulting and Clinical Psychology, 49*, 352–359.

Riddle, M. A., Scahill, L., King, R., Hardin, M. T., Towbin, K. E., Ort, S. I., Leckman, J. F., & Cohen, D. J. (1990). Obsessive compulsive disorder in children and adolescents: Phenomenology and family history. *Journal of the American Academy of Child and Adolescent Psychiatry, 29*, 766–772.

Ritter, B. (1969). Treatment of acrophobia with contact desensitization. *Behaviour Research and Therapy, 7*, 41–46.

Rutter, M., & Shaffer, D. (1980). DSM-III: A step forward or back in terms of the classification of child psychiatric disorders? *Journal of the American Academy of Child Psychiatry, 19*, 371–394.

Sanders, B., & Giolas, M. H. (1991). Dissociation and childhood trauma in psychologically disturbed adolescents. *American Journal of Psychiatry, 148*, 50–54.

Sarason, S. B., Davidson, K. S., Lighthall, F. F., Waite, R. R., & Ruebush, B. K. (1960). *Anxiety in elementary school children.* New York: Wiley.

Silverman, W. K. (1991). Diagnostic reliability of anxiety disorders in children using structured interviews. *Journal of Anxiety Disorders, 5*, 105–124.

Silverman, W. K., Cerny, J. A., Nelles, W. B., & Burke, A. E. (1988). Behavior problems in children of parents with anxiety disorders. *Journal of the American Academy of Child and Adolescent Psychiatry, 27*, 779–784.

Silverman, W. K., & Eisen, A. R. (1992). Age differences in the reliability of parent and child reports of child anxious symptomatology using a structured interview. *Journal of the American Academy of Child and Adolescent Psychiatry, 31*, 117–124.

Silverman, W. K., Fleisig, W., Rabian, B., & Peterson, R. (1991). The Childhood Anxiety Sensitivity Index. *Journal of Clinical Child Psychology, 20*, 162–168.

Silverman, W. K., & Kearney, C. A. (1991). The nature and treatment of childhood anxiety. *Educational Psychology Review, 3*, 335–361.

Silverman, W. K., & Kearney, C. A. (1992). Listening to our clinical partners: Informing researchers on childhood fears and phobias. *Journal of Behavior Therapy and Experimental Psychiatry, 23*, 71–76.

Silverman, W. K., & Kearney, C. A. (1993). Behavioral treatment of childhood anxiety. In V. B. Van Hasselt & M. Hersen (Eds.), *Handbook of behavior therapy and pharmacotherapy for children: A comparative analysis* (pp. 33–53). Boston: Allyn and Bacon.

Silverman, W. K., & Nelles, W. B. (1988). The Anxiety Disorders Interview Schedule for children. *Journal of the American Academy of Child and Adolescent Psychiatry, 27*, 772–778.

Spielberger, C. D. (1973). *Manual for the State-Trait Anxiety Inventory for Children.* Palo Alto, CA: Consulting Psychologists Press.

Stark, P. A., & Traxler, A. J. (1974). Empirical validation of Erikson's theory of identity crises in late adolescence. *Journal of Psychology, 86*, 25–33.

Strauss, C. C., & Last, C. G. (1993). Social and simple phobias in children. *Journal of Anxiety Disorders, 7*, 141–152.

Strauss, C. C., Last, C. G., Hersen, M., & Kazdin, A. E. (1988). Association between anxiety and depression in children and adolescents with anxiety disorders. *Journal of Abnormal Child Psychology, 15*, 57–68.

Strauss, C. C., Lease, C. A., Last, C. G., & Francis, G. (1988). Overanxious disorder: An examination of developmental differences. *Journal of Abnormal Child Psychology, 16*, 433–443.

Sylvester, C., Hyde, T. S., & Reichler, R. J. (1987). The Diagnostic Interview Schedule for Children and Personality Inventory for Children in studies of children at risk for anxiety disorders or depression. *Journal of the American Academy of Child and Adolescent Psychiatry, 26*, 668–675.

Sylvester, C., Reichler, R. J., & Hyde, T. S. (1986). Children of depressed patients. In *Syllabus for anxiety and mood disorders*. Seattle: University of Washington, School of Medicine.

Thyer, B. A., & Sowers-Hoag, K. M. (1988). Behavior therapy for separation anxiety disorder. *Behavior Modification, 12*, 205–233.

Timberlake, E. M. (1984). Psychosocial functioning of school phobics at follow-up. *Social Work Research and Abstracts, 20*, 13–18.

Velez, C. N., Johnson, J., & Cohen, P. (1989). A longitudinal analysis of selected risk factors for childhood psychopathology. *Journal of the American Academy of Child and Adolescent Psychiatry, 28*, 861–864.

Watson, J. B., & Rayner, R. (1920). Conditioned emotional reactions. *Journal of Experimental Psychology, 3*, 1–14.

Wehr, S. H., & Kaufman, M. E. (1987). The effects of assertive training on performance in highly anxious adolescents. *Adolescence, 22*, 195–205.

Welner, Z., Reich, W., Herjanic, B., Jung, K. G., & Amado, H. (1987). Reliability, validity, and parent-child agreement studies of the Diagnostic Interview for Children and Adolescents (DICA). *Journal of the American Academy of Child and Adolescent Psychiatry, 26*, 649–653.

Werry, J. S. (1991). Overanxious disorder: A review of its taxonomic properties. *Journal of the American Academy of Child and Adolescent Psychiatry, 30*, 533–544.

Whitaker, A., Johnson, J., Shaffer, D., Rapoport, J. L., Kalikow, K., Walsh, B. T., Davies, M., Braiman, S., & Dolinsky, A. (1990). Uncommon troubles in young people: Prevalence estimates of selected psychiatric disorders in a nonreferred adolescent population. *Archives of General Psychiatry, 47*, 487–496.

Wolfe, V. V., Finch, A. J., Jr., Saylor, C. F., Blount, R. L., Pallmeyer, T. P., & Carek, D. J. (1987). Negative affectivity in children: A multitrait-multimethod investigation. *Journal of Consulting and Clinical Psychology, 55*, 245–250.

Wolff, R., & Rapoport, J. (1988). Behavioral treatment of childhood obsessive-compulsive disorder. *Behavior Modification, 12*, 252–266.

Wolpe, J. (1961). The systematic desensitization treatment of neuroses. *Journal of Nervous and Mental Disease, 132*, 189–203.

15
Schizophrenia

Matcheri S. Keshavan
Petronella Vaulx-Smith
Stewart Anderson

Schizophrenia is a major psychiatric disorder with an approximate worldwide prevalence of 1% that begins in early adulthood. It is associated with massive disturbances in a variety of mental functions (including thinking, emotion, perception, and behavior) and leads to considerable deterioration in functioning, with enormous human and economic consequences. About 2% of the U.S. gross national product is spent on schizophrenia annually; the bulk of this is related to the loss of productivity and the expenses of institutionalization. Approximately one-half of all mental hospital beds in the United States are occupied by schizophrenic patients. Schizophrenia is also one of the most difficult psychiatric disorders, to evaluate and treat. It is a syndrome with variable manifestations, course, and outcome, and it is widely believed to be heterogeneous etiologically. In this chapter, we will review the clinical features, course, outcome, and management of schizophrenia, with special reference to adolescence.

Historical Background

The description of schizophrenialike disorders dates back to antiquity. Early writings from Mesopotamia as well as the Atharvaveda, an ancient Indian scripture (ca. 1000 BC), have reference to mental disorders similar to schizophrenia (Jeste, delCarmen, Lohr, & Wyatt, 1985). Modern descriptions of schizophrenia, however, began to appear in the literature only in the late eighteenth and early nineteenth centuries. An early view was that all mental disorders were expressions of a single entity, the unitary psychosis (*Einheit Psychose*) of Greisinger. Another approach, initially championed by Morel, was to classify the psychosis. Morel coined the term *dementia praecoce* for an illness beginning in adolescence and leading to gradual deterioration. Kahlbaum described a condition with abnormal motor activity, which he termed *katatonia*, several other discrete syndromes of insanity were described subsequent to this. It was Kraepelin who (1898/1971) integrated these separate syndromes into an entity—*dementia praecox* characterized by recurrent bouts of illness—that he distinguished from manic-depressive insanity. Bleuler (1908/1952) coined the term *schizophrenia* to describe the "splitting" of mental functions that he thought was the central disturbance in this disorder. He emphasized that certain symptoms (the "four A's—autism, ambivalence, disturbances in association and affectivity) were "fundamental" to the disorder, and that other symptoms (e.g., delusions, hallucinations) were also found in other disorders and were not characteristic. Bleuler's classification of fundamental symptoms began to be widely used in the United States, where a broad concept of schizophrenia led to a possible overdiagnosis of this disorder. Schneider (1959), though, identified certain types of delusions and hallucinations ("first-rank symptoms") as being characteristic of schizophrenia. These criteria represented a narrow concept of schizophrenia that was more popular in European psychiatry.

Since the 1960s it has been increasingly realized that none of the above conceptualizations led to universally recognized diagnostic criteria for schizophrenia. Indeed, because of different conceptualizations of the illness, there were wide variations in the frequency of diagnosis of schizophrenia in different countries. A two-country diagnostic project (Cooper, Kendell, Sharpe, Copeland, & Simon, 1972) demonstrated that the diagnostic concept of schizophrenia was much wider in the United States than in the United Kingdom. The World Health Organization (WHO) took the initiative to establish a set of criteria that gradually evolved toward the ICD-9 criteria. A multinational study conducted by WHO using these standardized criteria revealed a similar worldwide prevalence of schizophrenia (Sartorius, 1985). The American Psychiatric Association (APA) also developed standardized criteria for inclusion in the *Diagnostic and Statistical Manual of Mental Disorders* (DSM; APA, 1987). The latest revision (DSM-IV, released in May 1994), incorporates several significant changes in the diagnostic criteria for schizophrenia; these will be discussed later in the chapter. As of the early 1990s, overall, there are several (at least 15) competing criteria; there is no general agreement as to which is the best.

Clinical Picture

The symptoms of schizophrenia arise from a variety of disorders in thought, perception, emotion, and behavior. No single finding is pathognomonic, as any of these overall symptoms can be observed in patients suffering from disorders of affect or organic brain disease. The symptom complex may vary over the course of the illness; severely impairing auditory hallucinations may give way to occasional mumblings with merely mild social dysfunction. Furthermore, no single individual will present with the multiplicity of symptoms at any given time or during the course of the illness.

Kurt Schneider (1959) emphasized that certain specific symptoms are pathognomonic of schizophrenia in the absence of gross brain disease: *passivity experiences* (e.g., the feeling that one's thoughts, feelings or actions are controlled by other people or outside agencies); *auditory hallucinations* (e.g., voices in the third person anticipating, commenting on, or repeating the individual's thoughts); and *primary delusions* arising from normal perception (internal, bizarre convictions not shared by others from similar cultural and educational backgrounds). Of these symptoms, the most discriminating have been found to be delusions of control; thought insertion, broadcast, or withdrawal; auditory hallucinations in the third person; and auditory hallucinations addressing the individual independent of an affective state (Steinberg, 1985).

More recently, emphasis has been placed on the classification of schizophrenic symptoms into positive and negative symptomatology (Table 15–1). Positive symptoms are considered to result from an excessive activity of brain processes; in contrast, negative symptoms are suggestive of deficient functioning in specific neuronal systems. Positive symptoms include hallucinations, delusions, "positive" formal thought disorder, and disorganized and bizarre behaviors. Negative symptoms are enduring traits of poverty of speech and thought, affective flattening, inability to experience pleasure, diminution of social contact, inattention, anergia, and lack of persistence in work or social functioning. This distinction has significant implications for diagnosis, prognosis, and treatment of schizophrenia (Cannon, 1990; Carpenter, Buchanan, & Kirkpatrick, 1991; Pogue-Geile & Keshavan, 1991).

Disorder of Thought

Disorder of thought is a hallmark of schizophrenia and considered by many to be its most unifying clinical feature. Thought disorder can be arbitrarily

Table 15–1
Positive and Negative Symptoms in Schizophrenia

Negative Symptoms	Positive Symptoms
Affective blunting	Hallucinations
Alogia	Delusions
Avolition/apathy	Bizarre behavior
Anhedonia/asociality	Positive formal thought disorder
Attentional impairment	

classified as disorders of content, control, form, and stream of thought (Fish, 1984).

Thought Content. A *delusion* is a false, fixed belief that is unaltered in face of contrary evidence and not in keeping with the individual's cultural or religious views. Delusional themes common to schizophrenia involve persecution, nihilism, religion, somatization, sexuality, and grandiosity; these can be either well organized and related or nonsystematized and fragmented. In addition, patients may be preoccupied with esoteric and vague ideas of the meaning of life, philosophy, religion, or psychology. Hypochondriacal thinking about unlikely and bizarre medical conditions may develop as well.

Thought Control. Disturbances of thought control likely emanate from a blurring of ego boundaries. The subjective quality of possessing one's thoughts is disrupted, leading to the misperception of being alienated from one's own thinking. Thought alienation refers to a belief or experience that outside forces control or influence one's thoughts through *thought insertion* (placing thoughts into one's mind), *thought withdrawal* (removing thoughts from one's mind), or *thought broadcasting* (broadcasting one's thought to the external world). Similar to this is the idea that one's own impulses, behaviors, and feelings are alien and likewise under the influence of outside forces (i.e., passivity experiences).

Stream of Thought. Thought blocking is a disturbance wherein an individual's train of thought abruptly halts and a new, unrelated thought begins. This disruption in the flow of ideas may be attributable to interference caused by intrusive thoughts or distracting hallucinations.

Thought Form. Formal thought disorder provides an objective, observable clinical finding. It refers to an impairment of conceptual thinking reflective of underlying dysfunctions in language, abstractions, and association of ideas. A useful clinical approach is the distinction between positive and negative formal thought disorder. Positive formal thought disturbance includes *looseness of association* (tangential and obliquely related ideas that in a severe disturbance, lead to incoherence), *overinclusiveness* (excessive inclusion of irrelevant information), *derailment* (digression of the train of thought), *dereism* (idiosyncratic thinking that defies logic and reality), *neologism* (coining of new terms with idiosyncratic meanings), and *perseverations* (persistent repetition of a response to new and unrelated stimuli). A negative thought disorder includes such clinical features as *poverty of speech* (involving a restriction in the amount of speech, which in its severest form presents as mutism) and *poverty of speech content* (wherein the volume of speech is sufficient but lacks substantive content due to vagueness, repetition, or emptiness).

Disorder of Perception

Disturbances in perception primarily involves illusions and hallucinations. *Illusions* are misperceptions of external sensory stimuli; they are commonly associated with paranoid delusions, as increased suspiciousness may lead the patient to misinterpretations of the environment (Fish, 1984). *Hallucinations* are false sensory perceptions in the absence of external stimuli. Auditory hallucinations characteristically take the form of voices that speak in a derogatory, obscene, threatening, or commentary fashion about the patient. Less commonly, the patient may hear command hallucinations; some patients disinclined to respond to such commands, while others are compelled to do so (occasionally leading to suicidal or homicidal behaviors). Nonverbal hallucinations, ranging from single elementary sounds to complex musical experiences, are also often reported (Keshavan, David, Steingard, & Lishman, 1992).

Tactile hallucinations may present as sensations of tingling, crawling, or electrical pulsations. Olfactory and gustatory hallucinations frequently occur in combination with unpleasant odors and tastes, and visual hallucinations may occur as well. Hallucinations from these various modalities are less frequent than auditory hallucinations in schizophrenia and should raise an index of suspicion for the possibility of an organic disease process.

It is not uncommon for schizophrenic patients to complain of somatic hallucinations, as well as bodily perceptual disturbances of bizarre sensations (e.g., animals climbing through the intestines). Schizophrenic patients also experience kinesthetic hallucinations with sensations of altered states of the body (e.g., a burning sensation in the brain). Other perceptual disturbances may include experiences of depersonalization, derealization, and synesthesia.

Disorder of Emotions

Disturbance in emotions is another hallmark of schizophrenia and becomes increasingly evident as the illness progresses. Mood disturbance may present as anxiety, perplexity, elevation, or depression. With a loss of ego boundaries and the onset of referential thinking, young schizophrenics often experience marked anxiety early in the illness. They are perplexed by a chaotic inner world that they struggle to understand and articulate. Depression may occur at any time during the illness, but it frequently appears as adolescents gain insight into their growing functional impairments—an awareness that not uncommonly leads to suicidal tragedies. Depression occurs in as many as 60% of patients (Roy, 1986) in association with acute shifts of intrusive hallucinations and tormenting delusions. Likewise, expansive mood is not uncommon and may present as an ecstacy or exaltation without the infectious quality and relatedness of the manic state (Fish, 1984).

Impairment of affect is characteristic of schizophrenia and presents either as a poverty of emotional expressiveness or excessively active and inappropriate affect. *Flattening* or *blunting of affect* refers to an impairment in the capacity to use facial and bodily gestures to express an underlying emotional tone. The schizophrenic patient, for example, may show a blunted responsiveness to news concerning a family member's death, or while describing graphic details of tortuous body hallucinations. The patient may also manifest emotional responsiveness incongruous with either the content of speech or ideation. Abrupt and unpredictable emotional outbursts are not uncommon.

Disorder of Behaviors

At any time in the course of their illness, schizophrenic patients may manifest abnormalities in psychomotor performance and social capacity. These behavioral abnormalities have been used in characterizing the subtypes of schizophrenia as well as the course of the illness.

Disorders of psychomotor activity can range from simple isolated movements of posturing, mannerisms, and stereotypies to more complex patterns of motion, as observed in various catatonic states. *Mannerisms* are goal-directed behaviors carried out in an odd or stilted fashion; *stereotypies* comprise nonpurposeful and uniformly repetitive motions (e.g., tapping, rocking); and *parakinesias* consist of irregular muscular movements (e.g., grimacing, twitching, jerking). Other psychomotor abnormalities include *echopraxia* (the repetitive imitation of movements performed by others), *automatic obedience* (the automatic compliance with command instructions), and *waxy flexibility* (in which the patient may assume and maintain any variety of postures, even if awkward, when positioned by the examining physician). *Catatonic stupor*, which is associated with immobility and mutism, presents as a marked decline in responsiveness to the surroundings. In *catatonic rigidity*, the patient assumes a fixed posture and resists any efforts to change. *Catatonic excitement* presents as excited and aimless motor activity, uninfluenced by outside stimuli. The patient with *catatonic posturing* will assume and maintain bizarre postures for indefinite periods of time. The patient may also resist any instructions or all efforts to be moved (*catatonic negativism*).

Disorders of Social Capacity

Over the course of the illness, schizophrenic patients may deteriorate in their appearance, habits, interpersonal relations, and role functioning. Marked decline in personal care may manifest in a disheveled, unkempt appearance with eccentric attire and poor hygiene that can extend to episodes of double incontinence. Their personal habits may defy social convention as they rummage through rubbish, hoard bizarre collectibles, or handle their urine in some ritualistic fashion. Interpersonal relations also suffer with progressive social withdrawal and may worsen as others shy away from their odd behaviors, idiosyncratic thinking, and impulsive intrusions. Antisocial behaviors ranging from taunting trickery to violent homicide may also occur (Fish, 1984). The patient may lose initiative and interests (avolition) and be unable to derive pleasure (anhedonia). These psychological disturbances may impede goal-directed activities and lead to impaired work and role performance. Cessation of productivity may further contribute to the patient's progressive social decline.

Somatic Disturbances

The adolescent schizophrenic often presents with nonspecific somatic complaints, such as constipation, bloating, vague muscle aches, back pain, headaches, disturbed sleep, decreased appetite, loss of sexual drive, fatigue, and listlessness. Objective findings may include avoidance of eye contact, absence or rapidity of eye blinks, staring spells, and a disturbance in eye tracking (i.e., saccades; Andreasen & Black, 1991).

Although gross neurological findings are rare, the patient often presents with subtle neurological disturbances on physical examination. Minor neurological findings have been found to correlate with negative symptomatology, earlier onset, chronicity of illness, and poor prognosis. More than 50% of patients manifest such "soft signs," consisting of abnormalities in motor development (gait, balance, coordination, muscle tone, and mirror movements) and sensory integration (graphesthesia, stereognosis, proprioception, and primitive reflexes). Other soft signs associated with particular localized brain syndromes include inability to carry out tasks (reflective of frontal and parietal lobe disturbances, or apraxias), right-left disorientation and indifference about illness (associated with nondominant parietal lobe deficits), and abnormalities in prosody and inflection of speech (suggestive of a deficit in the dominant parietal lobe; Heinrichs & Buchanan, 1988; Kaplan & Sadock, 1988; Keshavan, Vikram, & Channabasavanna, 1979).

Premorbid Abnormalities

Disturbances in neurological maturation, cognition, emotional capacity, and social competency characterize the premorbid condition of schizophrenia (Beitchman, 1985). Adolescents with chronic schizophrenia since childhood or shortly after puberty are likely to have exhibited marked disturbances in neurological growth, with slower motor development, inferior coordination, echolalia, delayed and unclear speech, tactile sensitivity, and nonpurposeful rituals. Such neurodevelopmental findings are nonspecific and do not meet criteria for a pervasive development disorder (Holzman & Grinker, 1974; Kolvin, Ounsted, Humphrey, & McNay, 1971; Russell, Bolt, & Sammons, 1989). Cognitive disturbances in these youths frequently manifest with intellectual impairments, attention deficits, and distractibility (Freeman, 1971; Russell et al., 1989). Cognitive deficits of this sort commonly give rise to impaired school performance characterized by learning problems, failing grades, truancy, hyperactivity, dropping out of school, and dysfunctional teacher-student relations. Other cognitive abnormalities noted include obsessional manifestations, perfectionistic needs, magical thinking, daydreams, and intellectual preoccupations (Beitchman, 1985; Freeman, 1971).

Preschizophrenic individuals have likewise frequently demonstrated emotional deficits, impaired affective control, angry outbursts, detachment, hypersensitivity, and passivity, as well as depressive features and anxious behaviors (Aarkrog & Mortensen, 1985; Holzman & Grinker, 1974; Steinberg, 1985). Other abnormalities observed in the preschizophrenic adolescent include impairment in establishing and maintaining interpersonal relations, poor peer group adjustment, social withdrawal, shyness, introversion, and diffidence. Social isolation and seclusiveness have been found to result more from the individual being regarded by peers as odd and eccentric than from shyness (Steinberg, 1985). Antisocial behaviors are more likely expressed toward family members rather than as a social delinquency (Steinberg, 1985).

Although premorbid behavioral patterns vary greatly among schizophrenics, clinicians more commonly report these features to be consistent with a schizoid personality type. The schizoid personality of the prepsychotic adolescent is similarly described with traits of passivity, introversion, detachment, and autistic thinking. Preschizophrenic youths are more unlikely to have intimate friends and social dates and will choose solitary activities of watching TV, listening to radio, or playing computer games, often to the exclusion of competitive sports and other social activities (Kaplan & Sadock, 1988). Additional personality types described less commonly include avoidant, paranoid, histrionic, and compulsive disorders. Manifestations of a premorbid personality disturbance, which are associated with a poor prognosis, have been observed more often in the earlier-onset chronic schizophrenic syndromes rather than later-onset acute episodes (Andreasen & Black, 1991; Sands, 1956).

Prodromal Manifestations in Adolescence

The clinical presentation of schizophrenia prior to adulthood depends upon the individual's developmental stage and the mode of onset of the illness (Detre & Jarecki, 1971). Common patterns have been observed where an earlier and more insidious onset is less likely to resemble the core features of adult schizophrenia than is a later and more acute appearance of the disease (Kanner, 1955). Symptomatology among both the youngest age groups and developmentally immature adolescents rarely includes well-formulated, systematized psychotic behaviors (Steinberg, 1985; Russell et al., 1989). Delusional thinking and hallucinations tend to be simplistic and less elaborate, with primitive childhood themes, and can be differentiated from the vivid imaginations of nonschizophrenic youths by the ease with which nonpsychotic adolescents relinquish their fantasies when challenged (Kanner, 1955). In comparison, the clinical picture among adolescents who present at a later age may resemble more an adult-onset schizophrenia, with a greater frequency of first-rank symptoms and the presence of more organized delusions and hallucinations.

For the most part, however, the earliest manifestations of schizophrenia in adolescence appear as an incipient psychosis that does not typically consist of the classical core features, making diagnosis a difficult task (Steinberg, 1985; Easson, 1979). Yet a carefully obtained mental status examination and clinical history can reveal pertinent prodromal signs that characterize this thought disorder prior to the onset of florid psychotic behaviors. The adolescent's general attire, for example, sheds insight into an internal disorganization that lacks cohesion and may suggest a dissociation from any particular peer groups (Easson, 1979). The adolescent may present with physical and emotional attributes that appear less mature than the stated age. Bizarre movements of stereotypies, tics, and ritualistic behaviors may be present. Body movements are awkward and clumsy, with a lack of fluidity that may lead to avoidance of school athletics and gym activities. The emotional state is often one of irritability and anxiety as the adolescent struggles to maintain control over a slipping train of thought and muddled ideas. Depressive episodes may ensue, precipitating unrelenting hopelessness and teenage suicide.

The speech of a schizophrenic adolescent may remain grossly coherent but be marred by subtle changes of pitch and inflection, peculiar use of words, monotone monologues, circumstantial rambling, and tangential, irrelevant answers to clear, concrete questions (Easson, 1979). Preoccupation with religious themes, vague philosophies, or inner thought processes replace the usual adolescent concerns of sexuality, independence, and educational goals (Steinberg, 1985). Even when the content is in keeping with usual teenage interests, the schizophrenic adolescent develops obsessional thinking, with forgetfulness for more routine functions. Somatic ruminations likewise evolve as schizophrenic adolescents are fatigued by the excessive effort and stress associated with integrating their deteriorating thinking process. Disturbances in perception initially manifest as a growing inability to screen selectively from various stimuli presented by inner and outer sensory experiences (Detre & Jarecki, 1971). Increased distractibility impairs the adolescent's concentration, requiring additional time and effort to maintain an adequate academic performance.

The clinical history may reveal a marked disturbance in impulse control, with unpredictable rage toward family members and inappropriate sexual intrusiveness toward peers. Growing interpersonal impairment reinforces a preference for seclusiveness and solitary activities. A history of conduct disturbance is not uncommon, including family discord, academic failure, truancy, theft, and inappropriate aggression. Depressive features are equally reported and color the clinical picture with anhedonia, helplessness, poor esteem, social withdrawal, and recurrent suicidal ideation (Weiner, 1987). As the incipient psychosis evolves, the schizophrenic adolescent will exhibit clear personality changes that give way to a marked deterioration in cognitive, social, and educational functions and the inevitable classical presentation of a schizophrenic psychosis.

Subtypes of Schizophrenia

Schizophrenia has been classified into a variety of subtypes throughout the years. The traditional classification of subtypes, outlined below, is continued in DSM-IV (American Psychiatric Association, 1993).

Catatonic type is characterized by marked psychomotor disturbance involving stupor, negativism, rigidity, excitement and posturing. *Disorganized type* is associated with marked loosening of associations, incoherence, grossly disorganized behavior, and flat or grossly inappropriate affect, as well as fragmented delusions and hallucinations lacking a coherent theme. *Paranoid type* is characterized by preoccupation with one or more systemized delusions or presence of frequent hallucinations related to a single theme; symptoms characteristic of disorganized and catatonic types are absent. *Undifferentiated type* is associated with prominent psychotic symptoms that do not meet criteria for other subtypes. *Residual type* is diagnosed by the occurrence of at least one prior episode of schizophrenia with a current clinical picture absent of prominent psychotic symptoms, although signs of the illness persist.

Not included in DSM-IV are two other types: (a) *simple schizophrenia,* diagnosed by gradual onset of amotivation in the absence of prominent delusions and hallucinations; and (b) *latent schizophrenia,* characterized by marked aloofness and occasional odd behaviors (similar to DSM-III-R schizotypal personality disorder). Both these categories are included in the International Classification of Diseases-tenth revision (ICD-10).

The above classification, though widely used, lacks longitudinal stability (i.e., subtypes change over course of time) and has only modest predictive value for treatment. An alternative classification was proposed by Crow (1980), based on the predominance of positive or negative symptoms. In this system, type I schizophrenia is characterized by prominent positive symptoms, absence of gross brain morphological abnormalities, and favorable response to treatment. Type II, in contrast, is characterized by prominent negative symptoms, presence of brain abnormalities and relatively poor response to treatment. While of considerable heuristic value, this classification is yet to be validated; it is unclear whether types I and II are distinct categories or simply two dimensions of the same disorder.

Course and Prognosis

It is generally agreed that the course and outcome in schizophrenia are variable. This variability may stem from (a) the presumed etiological heterogeneity of this disorder, (b) the influence of diverse extraneous factors that could influence outcome, and (c) the unclear boundaries of this disorder.

Onset of schizophrenia is usually in adolescence (very rarely before puberty), but it may occur in middle or late adult life. While the onset is sudden in some patients, in others it is insidious, with the florid psychotic symptoms preceded by prodromal symptoms for varying lengths of time. Males tend to have an earlier onset and a more protracted course. The typical course of schizophrenia is one of remission and exacerbation, with a lack of return to baseline between exacerbations. Some patients, however, have one or more episodes with return to normal or near normal functioning. It has been suggested that the decline in overall functioning continues up to an average of 5 years, after which the level of deterioration of patients may "bottom out" (McGlashan, 1988). Positive symptoms tend to become less severe, but most patients are left with persistent negative symptoms.

Complications

As many as 40% to 70% of schizophrenic patients attempt suicide; the risk of death from completed suicide is between 10% and 15%. Suicides in schizophrenia tend to be associated with coexistent depression, relatively younger age, male sex, single status, multiple hospitalizations, unemployment, and poor treatment response (Roy, 1986). The risk of completed suicide is highest in the immediate postdischarge period. Mortality in schizophrenia is also increased from medical illnesses and accidents.

Depressive symptoms are also common in schizophrenia, both in the acute and chronic phases. They may be a response to the appearance of insight, an integral part of the schizophrenic illness, or reflective of another disorder (e.g., schizoaffective disorder or major depression; Becker, 1988).

Epidemiology

The prevalence of schizophrenia is probably slightly less than 1% worldwide. The estimates of prevalence are variable, at least partly due to the lack of consensus regarding diagnostic criteria. One of the larger epidemiological studies examining lifetime prevalence, the Epidemiological Catchment Area (ECA) program, has indicated a higher lifetime prevalence for schizophrenia than earlier studies (0.6% to 1.9%). The incidence of schizophrenia appears to be 0.3 to 0.6 per 1,000; incidence estimates, usually based on first hospitalizations, tend to underestimate the true incidence. The incidence is highest in young men and in women from 35 to 39 years old.

Several sociodemographic factors appear to influence incidence and prevalence. Schizophrenia occurs more commonly in lower socioeconomic classes of large cities, the likely explanation being the "downward drift" caused by the illness (Dunham, 1965). The alternative hypothesis—that schizophrenia is caused by the stresses of lower socioeconomic status—has little research support. While schizophrenia is seen worldwide, pockets of high prevalence are seen, for example, in northern Sweden, Finland, and western Ireland; prevalence seems to be somewhat lower in Third World countries. There may be a recent decline in the incidence of schizophrenia, though this issue remains controversial (Der, Gupta, & Murray, 1990). There is no difference in prevalence between males and females, although males tend to have an earlier age of onset (18–25 years) than females (26–35 years).

An association between winter births and schizophrenia is described in several studies. In the northern hemisphere, schizophrenic patients tend to be born more frequently between January and April; in the southern hemisphere, the same is true between July and September. Schizophrenia also tends to occur with a higher frequency among recent immigrants than among native populations. Life stressors are associated with an increased risk of relapse, but there are few data suggesting that stress has more than a modest role in the pathogenesis of the disorder. Schizophrenia tends to be most common in the single, never-married population; this may be because the disorder lessens the chances for getting married. Schizophrenic patients, particularly males, have experienced a higher number of birth complications.

Schizophrenia with early onset (i.e., childhood schizophrenia) is currently considered to be on a continuum with adolescent and adult-onset schizophrenia. The diagnostic criteria are identical in DSM IV, except that children and adolescents may show a failure to reach the expected level of social development rather than deterioration from the existing level. The prevalence of schizophrenia with onset before 12 years of age is estimated to be between 1.75 and 4 per 10,000 (Green, 1989).

Familial Pattern

Early investigators such as Bleuler had noted that relatives of patients with schizophrenia were often "tainted by mental disease." However, the role of genetic factors in the etiopathology of schizophrenia has not yet been fully clarified. The available knowledge can be addressed in terms of the questions below.

Is Schizophrenia Genetically Transmitted?

Family, twin, and adoption studies of schizophrenia strongly indicate that schizophrenia aggregates in families and that a substantial proportion of is aggregation results from genetic factors. Few researchers, however, believe that genes are sufficient for the etiology of schizophrenia. The substantial proportion of identical twins showing discordance for schizophrenia strongly suggest that environmental factors may be important in some cases. The heritability of vulnerability to schizophrenia is estimated as between 60% and 70%; in contrast, nongenetic familial factors, if present, could account for only about 30% of the variance in liability (Kendler, 1987).

How Is It Transmitted?

Despite a half century of research, we remain ignorant about the specific mode of transmission of schizophrenia. Evidence is incompatible with either a simple polygenic model or a single major locus (SML) model; a more complex multifactorial/threshold model and the existence of a major gene against a polygenic/multifactorial background remain possibilities. Progress in clarifying this issue has been limited because of (a) genetic heterogeneity; (b) major environmental determinants that could cause a person with a normal genotype to be affected (phenocopy); (c) nongenetic forms of familial transmission, such as "vertical cultural transmission" or viral factors; and (d) unclear clinical boundaries of schizophrenia (Kendler, 1987).

What Is Transmitted?

On a psychopathological level, current evidence indicates that what is transmitted is not a liability specifically for schizophrenia alone, but also for poor psychosocial functioning, oddness, and nonaffective psychoses in general. In adoption studies, biological relatives of schizophrenic probands tend to have a higher prevalence of schizophrenia and schizotypal personality disorder, and these disorders have been considered to represent "schizophrenia spectrum" disorder. On a biological level, several variables have been proposed for the liability to schizophrenia. Current evidence indicates that smooth-pursuit eye movement dysfunction (Holzman et al., 1988) and deficiencies in sustained attention (Erlenmeyer-Kimling & Cornblatt, 1984) may serve as biological vulnerability markers for schizophrenia. Several other candidates, including late evoked-response potential (ERP) components (Erlenmeyer-Kimling & Cornblatt, 1984), lateral ventricular enlargement (DeLisi & Buchsbaum, 1986), and soft neurological signs (Marcus, Hans, Medrick, Schulsinger, & Michelson, 1985), have been proposed, but their heritability and specificity for schizophrenia remain unclear. Despite earlier promise, platelet MAO enzyme activity (Belmaker, 1984) and autonomic dysfunction (Mednick & Schulsinger, 1968) have not been shown to be vulnerability markers for schizophrenia. A recent study has suggested that smooth-pursuit eye movement dysfunctions may represent expressions of a single underlying trait that is transmitted by an autosomal dominant gene (Holzman et al., 1988).

The advent of new techniques of molecular genetics, such as restriction length polymorphism (RFLP), has raised considerable optimism that psychiatric geneticists might detect major gene effects and resolve genetic heterogeneity in schizophrenia. Early claims for detecting specific linkages, however, have not been confirmed. The possible reasons for these disparities may include genetic heterogeneity and incomplete penetrance.

Differential Diagnosis and Assessment

For an adolescent to be diagnosed as suffering from schizophrenia, his or her behaviors must conform to the guidelines outlined by DSM-IV. As per the DSM-IV draft criteria (American Psychiatric Association, 1993), the patient should have at least two of the following symptoms, each present for a significant part of time during a 1-month period: (a) delusions, (b) hallucinations, (c) disorganized speech, (d) disorganized speech or catatonic behavior, and (e) negative symptoms (e.g., flat affect, alogia, or avolition; criterion A). In addition, the patient should manifest social or occupational dysfunction (criterion B), as well as continued signs of disturbance for at least 6 months, including prodromal or residual symptoms (criterion C). Schizoaffective disorder and mood disorder with psychotic features must be ruled out in that either (a) no major depressive or manic episodes should have occurred simultaneously with the active phase, and (b) mood syndromes, if present during the active phase, are brief in duration relative to the active and residual phases of illness (criterion D). Finally, the disorder must unrelated to the direct effects of a general medical condition or substance abuse (criterion E).

The diagnosis of schizophrenia in adolescents is complicated by the heterogeneity of symptoms with which schizophrenia can present, and by the complex nature of psychiatric evaluation in the developing person. One of the most difficult diagnostic situations occurs when the adolescent presents with a mixture of peculiar, withdrawn, or depressed behavior but is not overtly psychotic. Weiner (1987) suggests that attending to the age-appropriate "normative concerns" can help differentiate the depressed or antisocial adolescent from one who is developing schizophrenia:

> Troubled but non-schizophrenic adolescents usually develop symptoms in the context of such developmental tasks as adapting to bodily changes in early adolescence, attaining independence from parents and gaining skill in relationships during middle adolescence, and making commitments to life goals in late adolescence. However, disturbed adolescents who are becoming schizophrenic are much more likely than their peers to manifest an inability or reluctance to grapple with the usual adolescent concerns. (pp. 330–340)

When psychosis is overtly manifested, differentiating schizophrenia from psychotic mania presents another diagnostic challenge. Werry, McClellan, and Chard (1991) found that approximately one-half of their subjects diagnosed with bipolar disorder had previously received the diagnosis of schizophrenia during adolescence. Symptoms suggestive of a persistent diagnosis of schizophrenia included odd personality, poor premorbid adaptive functioning, a history or evidence of major brain dysfunction, a family history of schizophrenia, insidious onset, psychosis lasting more than 3 months, incomplete recovery, and poor outcome. Despite these generalizations, bipolar disorder and schizophrenia may in some cases be indistinguishable on initial presentation (Carlson, 1990).

A complete discussion of "organic" disease states that can present with schizophrenialike symptoms is beyond the scope of this chapter; the topic has been reviewed by Nasrallah (1986). Psychosis persisting more than 2 weeks after the use of illicit drugs (e.g., amphetamines, LSD, phencyclidine) appears to be quite rare and may well represent a "true" case of schizophrenia unmasked by the drug (Kane & Selzer, 1991). Many medications can produce a psychosis similar to schizophrenia. Common offenders include stimulants, medications with prominent anticholinergic side effects (e.g., tricyclic antidepressants), and glucocorticoids (see Keshavan & Keshavan, 1991). Toxic psychosis in adolescents can also follow the chronic ingestion of lead (McCracken, 1987), and the abuse of inhalants. Schizophrenialike states can also be produced by systemic disorders such as endocrinopathies (e.g., hyperthyroidism, hypothyroidism, pheochromocytoma), metabolic disturbances (e.g., hypercalcemia, hyponatremia), neurological disorders (e.g., central nervous system infections, brain tumors, temporal lobe epilepsy, lupus cerebritis, multiple sclerosis) and genetic disorders (e.g., Wilson's disease, acute intermittent porphyria, Huntington's chorea; Nasrallah, 1986).

Although rare, the potential reversibility of many so-called organic causes of schizophrenialike illnesses mandates that patients for whom a new diagnosis of schizophrenia is being considered receive a thorough medical history and examination. Laboratory studies vary depending on illness history and physical findings, but all "first-episode" psychotic patients should probably receive brain imaging (Andreasen & Black, 1991) by CAT scan or MRI (which may indicate space-occupying lesions, as well as cerebritis due to lupus or multiple sclerosis). Other routine laboratory studies include sleep-deprived EEG, complete blood count, electrolyte levels (including calcium), and thyroid function tests.

It is generally believed that 20% to 30% of schizophrenic patients recover sufficiently to lead relatively normal lives; 20% to 30% continue to suffer from moderate symptoms; and 40% to 60% have permanent impairment. Several factors predicting a good prognosis have been identified, including late onset, presence of obvious precipitating factors, acute onset, good premorbid functioning, presence of prominent affective features, married, paranoid or catatonic features, mainly positive symptoms, and family history of affective disorders. Women in general tend to have a better outcome. Illness expressed in developing countries also tend to have a better prognosis.

Schizophrenia beginning in adolescence may manifest either substantial recovery or continuing impairment (Weiner, 1970). While a family history of affective illness may be associated with a good prognosis, long illness duration may augur a relatively poor prognosis (King & Pitman, 1971). Onset before 10 years of age and premorbid personality abnormalities predict poor outcome; high premorbid intelligence and well-preserved personality are associated with a better prognosis (Eggers, 1978).

In the 1950s and 1960s it was recognized that an understimulating hospital environment is associated with a worsening of the negative symptoms (the so-called defect state, or clinical poverty syndrome). An overstimulating environment, however, can trigger relapse. Vaughn and Leff (1976) have reported an association between increased expressed emotion (EE) in relatives and a higher likelihood of relapse; we will discuss this issue further later in the chapter.

Clinical Management

Current treatment of schizophrenia in adults involves the judicious use of antipsychotic medication to reduce acute symptoms, maintenance medication to sustain the period of recovery, and psychoeducation of both patient and family to ameliorate factors related to relapse. Unfortunately, carefully designed placebo-controlled studies of the efficacy of antipsychotics in treating schizophrenia in adolescence are few, and studies of psychoeducational approaches are essentially nonexistent. This section briefly reviews current approaches to the pharmacological and psychoeducational treatment of schizophrenia, with data derived primarily from studies of adult subjects.

Antipsychotic Medication

Evidence has been accumulating since the late 1960s that antipsychotics (also called neuroleptics), due to their ability to produce neurological side effects, are clearly helpful in treating schizophrenia. They have been shown to reduce symptoms of acute exacerbations (Cole, 1964), shorten hospital stay (May, Tuma, Yale, Potepan, & Dixon, 1976), and decrease the rate of relapse (Davis, 1975). More recently it has been suggested that, either by their direct effects or by reducing the duration and severity of psychotic exacerbations, antipsychotics may positively influence the chronic course of schizophrenia (Crow, MacMillan, Johnson, & Johnstone, 1986; Wyatt, 1991).

Table 15–2 shows commonly used antipsychotic medications. Therapeutically equivalent doses are generally estimated from studies comparing two or more antipsychotics in which doses are blindly titrated to clinical efficacy. Potencies are often described relative to chlorpromazine (CPZ). For example, haloperidol and CPZ have relative values of 2 and 100, respectively; 5 mg of haloperidol are therefore estimated to have roughly the same therapeutic efficacy as 250 mg of CPZ (or 250 CPZ "equivalents"). These studies have many methodological difficulties, but the CPZ-equivalent concept remains central to efforts to determine minimum dosage requirements (Kane, 1989).

In addition to clinical impressions that adolescent schizophrenics (unlike children with psychoses) respond to neuroleptics similarly to adults (Campbell, Green, & Deutch, 1985; Green, 1989), a few studies have demonstrated the effectiveness of antipsychotic medication in adolescence. Poole, Bloom, Mielhe, Runiger, and Gallant (1976) studied 75 adolescent schizophrenics (aged 13 to 18) who were in their first episode or in acute exacerbation. Subjects were randomly assigned to a 4-week trial of haloperidol (average dose 9.8 mg), loxapine (87.5 mg), or placebo and evaluated using the Brief Psychiatric Rating Scale (BPRS) in a double-blind design. Seventy percent (70%) of those receiving haloperidol, 87% of those on loxitane, and 36% of the placebo group improved significantly over the treatment period. Major side effects included extrapyramidal symptoms (EPS; 18 on haloperidol, 19 on loxitane) and sedation (21 on loxitane, 13 on haloperidol). In a double-blind, uncontrolled study, Versiani, da-Silva, Frota, and Mundim (1978) also found haloperidol (average dose 7.6 mg) and loxitane (70 mg) to have similar efficacy in reducing symptoms in 50 acutely ill schizophrenics (aged 13 to 18). As often found in adult studies, BPRS items measuring negative symptoms (e.g., blunted affect, emotional withdrawal) did not improve significantly over the 1-month trial period.

Differences between adult and adolescent response to neuroleptics have been suggested by Realmuto, Erickson, Yellin, Hopwood, and Greenberg (1984). In a rater-blind study comparing schizophrenic inpatients receiving

Table 15–2
Selected Antipsychotic Drugs

Drug (Trade Name)	Class	CPZ Equivalent[1] (Oral Dose)	Side Effects			
			EPS	Sedation	Hypotension	Anticholinergic
Clozaril (Clozapine)	Dibenzazapine	160	X	XXX	XXX	XXX
Chlorpromazine (Thorazine)	Phenothiazine (Aliphatic)	100	X	XXX	XXX	XX
Thioridazine (Mellaril)	Phenothiazine (Piperidine)	100	X	XXX	XXX	XXX
Loxapine[2] (Loxitane)	Dibenzazapine	15	XX	XX	XX	XX
Perphenazine (Trilafon)	Phenothiazine (Piperazine)	10	XX	XX	X	X
Trifluoroperazine (Stelazine)	Phenothiazine (Piperazine)	5	XXX	X	X	X
Thiothixene (Navane)	Thioxanthene	5	XXX	X	X	X
Fluphenazene (Prolixin)	Phenothiazine (Piperazine)	2	XXX	X	X	X
Haloperidol (Haldol)	Butyrophenone	2	XXX	X	X	X

Note: For further details, see AMA (1990); Teicher & Glod (1991); Baldessarini (1990).
1   Estimates for therapeutically equivalent doses vary considerably among sources.
2   Not approved for use under age 16.

thioridazine (8 subjects, average age 16.1 years) or thiothixene (13 subjects, average age 15.1 years), both subject groups showed overall improvement on BPRS, but 75% of the thioridazine group and 54% of those treated with thiothixene showed significant sedation. Optimum therapeutic doses (determined retrospectively as doses resulting in adequate response without substantial side effects) were 16 mg for thiothixene and 178 mg for thioridazine. The same authors studied 11 previously unmedicated first-episode adolescents and compared scores on a continuous performance test before and approximately 35 days into treatment with thioridazine or thiothixene (Erickson, Yellin, Hopwood, Realmuto & Greenberg, 1984). The authors report that in contrast to results with similar adults, both reaction time and error rate increased for adolescents on medication. These studies suggest that adolescents may be more sensitive to the sedative effects of neuroleptics than adults, and therefore higher-potency drugs may be preferable in this age group.

Side Effects

Clinical potency differentiates neuroleptics' tendency to cause certain side effects. Low-potency agents generally produce more antiadrenergic (e.g., hypotension), and anticholinergic (e.g., dry mouth, sedation, blurred vision) effects, while high-potency antipsychotics tend more frequently to result in EPS (e.g., acute dystonia, akathisia, and Parkinsonism).

Dystonia. Dystonia refers to sustained muscular spasms; young male adolescents are at a high risk for developing this disturbing side effect. Dystonic reactions are probably the most acutely distressing of all side effects, and they can even be life threatening when pharyngeal musculature is involved. As might be expected, the experience of acute dystonic reactions may negatively affect a patient's later compliance with medication (Van Putten, 1974), and thus some clinicians will temporarily medicate certain patients (e.g., those with past histories of dystonic reactions) prophylactically with anti-Parkinsonian medications. Fortunately, the risk of this side effect decreases with continued treatment (Baldessarini, 1990).

Akathisia. This refers to a syndrome of subjective and objective restlessness frequently occurring during neuroleptic treatment. Akathisia may be the most difficult symptom to diagnose, particularly when it coexists with (and probably exacerbates) agitation and anxiety associated with psychosis. Symptoms vary from a subjective urge to move to pacing, rocking, or other behaviors that reflect an inability to remain motionless. Anti-Parkinsonian medications, benzodiazepines, and beta-adrenergic blockers have all shown some efficacy at treating akathesia. Apart from lowering the neuroleptic dose, propranolol may present the best risk/benefit profile of these options (Adler et al., 1986).

Parkinsonism. The cardinal features of this syndrome include muscular rigidity, masked facies, tremors, and bradykinesia (slowness of movement). It is a common side effect of antipsychotic drugs. Although cogwheel rigidity is easier to diagnose and can even be helpful in establishing an adequate antipsychotic dose (McEvoy, Hogarty, & Steingard, 1991), more subtle Parkinson-like EPS can also be difficult to identify. Akinesia may be mistaken for improvement when it develops several weeks into the treatment, or in the treatment of a previously agitated patient (Van Putten, Marder, & Mintz, 1990). After acute psychotic symptoms have subsided, psychomotor retardation and blunted affect are sometimes misdiagnosed as postpsychotic depression (Becker, 1988). Anti-Parkinsonian medications such as benztropine, biperiden, or amantadine are generally effective at reducing the Parkinson-like side effects of antipsychotics. Since these agents (with the exception of amantadine) can produce disturbing anticholinergic side effects, they are most useful during the acute phase of treatment and should probably be continued for no more than several months. Dosage reduction remains the mainstay of treatment for long-term EPS (Kane & Lieberman, 1987).

Tardive Dyskinesia. Tardive dyskinesia (TD) is a potentially seriously debilitating side effect of the long-term administration of neuroleptics. Age is clearly a risk factor (Baldessarini, 1990), although children and adolescents are also susceptible (Campbell et al., 1985). One study has estimated that over the first 5 years of treatment, about 4% of young adult patients per year will develop the repetitive involuntary lip, jaw, and tongue movements characteristic of this syndrome (Kane et al., 1984). Anti-Parkinsonian medications tend to exacerbate symptoms, while increasing the dose of neuroleptics may paradoxically suppress them. Although lowering the dose of or withdrawing neuroleptics can initially "unmask" TD, it is the only treatment that may eventually ameliorate TD at least in some cases. However, symptoms may improve very slowly or occasionally not at all. As with EPS, occurrence of TD highlights the necessity of employing the minimum effective antipsychotic dose.

Neuroleptic Malignant Syndrome. The neuroleptic malignant syndrome—characterized by severe muscular rigidity, fluctuating autonomic dysfunction, and delirium—usually occurs within 2 weeks of neuroleptic initiation or increase. Several cases of this potentially fatal condition have been reported, but the incidence of clinically recognized cases appears to be quite rare (Teicher & Glod, 1990). Treatment involves termination of antipsychotic medication, in-hospital supportive care, and possibly the administration of dantrolene or bromocriptine (Baldessarini, 1990).

Other Side Effects. Agranulocytosis, drug-induced hepatitis dysfunction, and seizure disorder are other uncommon side effects of neuroleptics that have been reported to occur in adolescents (Rancurello, Vallano & Waterman, 1992). Neuroleptics have also been shown to affect levels of sex hormones in young adolescent males, although the significance of this finding is unclear (Apter et al., 1983).

Guidelines for Acute Management

Apart from the limited data presented above suggesting that higher-potency neuroleptics may be preferable for adolescents, no evidence exists for either adults or adolescents that clearly favors use of one neuroleptic over any other. Data supporting several guiding principles to neuroleptic use, however, have been accumulating in recent years.

There appears to be no advantage to a high-dose "rapid neuroleptization" approach. Rifkin, Seshagiri, Basawaraj, Borenstein and Wachspress (1991) studied 87 newly admitted schizophrenic patients who were randomized to 10, 30, or 80 mg haloperidol orally per day and treated for 6 weeks in a double-blind trial. Substantial improvement was noted in all three groups, but no additional benefit was found for those receiving more than 10 mg per day.

There appears to be a fairly delicate balance between an antipsychotic's therapeutic and untoward effects. Van Putten et al. (1990) compared 80 newly admitted male schizophrenics randomized to a 4-week trial of 5, 10, or 20 mg haloperidol; only those patients (28%) with histories of severe dystonic reactions were treated with benztropine. As a group, the subjects receiving the 20 mg dose improved more quickly, and those who continued to tolerate the higher dose showed greater improvement throughout the trial. These subjects, however, also scored significantly higher on ratings of blunted affect, social withdrawal, akathesia, and akinesia and had a far greater rate of leaving the hospital against medical advice (35% versus 4% of the 5 mg or 10 mg groups). This study highlights the importance of individualized attention to the concurrent development of symptomatic improvement and side effects, and it is especially relevant to the treatment of adolescents, who may be more sensitive to EPS than adults (Teicher & Glod, 1990).

The majority of studies suggest that most acutely ill schizophrenic patients will obtain maximal benefit from 300 to 700 CPZ equivalents per day (Baldessarini, Cohen, & Teicher, 1988). One recent study has suggested that many patients will respond to even lower doses, given adequate trial length. McEvoy et al. (1991) placed 106 acutely ill schizophrenic or schizoaffective patients on the minimum dose of haloperidol, which produced slight stiffness or cogwheel rigidity (the "neuroleptic threshold"). After 2 weeks the 95 patients that remained in the study were randomized either to continuing their present dose (averaging 3.4 mg, or 175 CPZ equivalents) or to a higher dose (averaging 11.6 mg). Double-blind ratings of patient condition after 4 weeks of treatment at the neuroleptic threshold showed that 72% of the subjects responded. By comparison, the higher-dose group showed greater improvement on measures of hostility (but not psychosis) and experienced significantly worse side effects. This study suggests that many patients may obtain appropriate antipsychotic treatment at a substantially reduced dose than that commonly employed, and the authors recommend a systematic approach for establishing this dose.

There is no clear evidence that certain schizophrenic symptoms respond better to any specific medications. This point becomes particularly relevant in cases of highly agitated patients, where there may be a temptation to utilize low-potency neuroleptics for combined sedative and antipsychotic purposes. Benzodiazapines (e.g., lorazepam) have been shown to be useful in treating agitation associated with psychosis while an antipsychotic response at a sub-sedating dosage is awaited (Guz, Morales & Sartoretto, 1972; Salzman, 1989).

Given an adequate dose, at least 4 to 6 weeks is necessary to establish the efficacy of an antipsychotic trial (Rifkin & Siris, 1987). Pressures from patient, family, and hospital administration may often lead the clinician to raise neuroleptic dosage into uncomfortable, sedating, or pseudo-Parkinsonian levels, to change antipsychotics, or to add adjunctive medications prior to at least a 1-month trial. This tendency should be avoided.

Treatment of Neuroleptic Nonresponders

Approximately 70% of adult schizophrenics respond adequately to antipsychotics. The few studies of response to neuroleptics in adolescent schizophrenics also suggest that a substantial nonresponse rate exists in this age group (Poole et al., 1976; Realmuto et al., 1984; Versiani et al., 1978). Prior to considering alternative treatments, though, several points should be considered. First, the agitated or anxious appearing patient may be suffering from akathisia and respond to lowering the neuroleptic dose or adding propranolol. For partially treated or moderately symptomatic patients, the best approach may simply be to continue treatment, as some individuals require 6 weeks or even longer to respond fully (McEvoy et al., 1991). Occasionally, no rigidity or other signs of EPS are present despite routine dosage (up to 700 CPZ equivalents); in such cases, higher drug levels might be useful to identify "rapid metabolizers" who require unusually high antipsychotic doses (Baldessarini et al., 1988; Meyers, Ture, & Coyle, 1980). In the only controlled study of this issue, increasing medication of nonresponders after 3 weeks of treatment at the neuroleptic threshold did not produce additional improvement at 5 weeks relative to those who had remained on the lower dose, and it resulted in significantly increased side effects (McEvoy et al., 1991).

When a given antipsychotic has been proven ineffective, clinicians often switch to another chemical class, although there is little evidence to support this approach. Adjunctive therapy with non-neuroleptic medication is frequently applied next. A recent review found that lithium, carbamazepine, benzodiazapines, reserpine, and propranolol have been shown in double-blind trials to have potential efficacy as adjunctive agents (Christison, Kirch, & Wyatt, 1991). Since lithium has been best studied, and because bipolar disorder can be very difficult to distinguish from schizophrenia in psychotic adolescents (Werry et al., 1991), it should probably be utilized first in this age group. Data supporting the other adjuncts' effectiveness is at this point quite weak, making the use of these agents appropriate only after the more demonstrably effective options have been ruled out.

Clozapine, an antipsychotic considered unconventional due to its atypical neurochemistry and side effects, appears to benefit at least 30% of patients who do not respond to trials of typical antipsychotics (Lieberman, Kane, & Johns, 1989). Clozapine has the additional advantage producing fewer EPS and little or no TD (Kane, 1989). Agranulocytosis, which can be fatal if unrecognized, occurs in about 1.3% of adult patients treated with this compound but is reversible upon discontinuation of the drug. Although it usually develops 6 weeks to 6 months into treatment, agranulocytosis may occur more than 1 year later, necessitating weekly blood counts for the duration of treatment (Lieberman et al., 1989). Sedation and increased salivation are two other unwanted effects of clozapine that may be particularly disturbing to adolescent patients. Despite these problems, clozapine's potential for improving symptoms makes it an important option in the treatment of schizophrenia in adolescence (Birmaher, Baker, Kapur, Quintana, & Ganguli, 1992), particularly when at least two classes of conventional neuroleptics and adjunctive lithium therapy have been ineffective.

Maintenance Treatment

Continuing antipsychotic medication after maximal improvement of acute symptoms has been achieved reduces the likelihood of relapse (Davis, 1975). One review found that from 0% to 40% of subjects medicated with depot injections (to ensure compliance) relapsed within 1 year, compared to 30% to 80% of placebo controls (Kane & Lieberman, 1987). At the same time the possibility of substantial drawbacks to long-term neuroleptic administration (e.g., chronic EPS and TD) are well recognized. Despite the proven efficacy of maintenance medication, it appears that even with antipsychotics most schizophrenics can be expected to relapse within 2 to 3 years (Crow et al., 1986; Hogarty et al., 1988).

Given the substantial risks and the important, but noncurative, benefits of antipsychotic medication, efforts have been made to establish the minimum effective dose for maintenance pharmacotherapy (see Schooler, 1991, for a review). Not surprisingly, studies have demonstrated a risk/benefit trade-off. Low doses of neuroleptics are associated with higher relapse rates than standard doses (e.g., 5 mg versus 20 mg fluphenazine decanoate every 2 weeks) but result in measurably better psychosocial functioning between symptom exacerbations (Hogarty et al., 1988; Kane, Woerner, & Sarantos, 1986). Furthermore, low-dose subjects who begin to show disorganized or psychotic behavior can in many cases be stabilized without hospitalization by temporarily increasing their medication. An alternative strategy to reduce cumulative doses involves withdrawing neuroleptics several months after symptoms have improved, then "targeting" neuroleptic administration to early indicators of relapse (Carpenter et al., 1990). While some patients may benefit from targeted treatment, the increased risk of serious relapse associated with this approach makes it less appropriate for most patients (Schooler, 1991). In summary, maintenance antipsychotic treatment, like that of acute schizophrenic exacerbations, requires flexible, individualized attention to both its benefits and its limitations.

Psychopharmacological Education of Patient and Family

The pharmacological treatment of schizophrenia involves both the appropriate administration of antipsychotics and the development of a working relationship with the patient and family, who need to be trained to recognize symptom and side-effect trends pertinent to the given stage of illness and treatment. Initial discussions of EPS, TD, and other common side effects are necessary for obtaining informed consent, but time lag before response (2 to 4 weeks), risk of nonresponse (roughly 30%, although it may be higher in younger adolescents), and likelihood of eventual relapse should also be discussed. During the relatively symptom-free maintenance phase, the patient and his or her family should understand the difficult trade-off between antipsychotic dose, the potential for symptom recurrence, and the appearance of side effects. In order to minimize a patient's dose, it is particularly important to obtain the patient and family's help in identifying chronic EPS and the earliest signs of relapse. Prior to the reemergence of frank psychosis, many schizophrenics experience mood and behavior changes noticeable to themselves and to their family (Herz & Melville, 1980). By enlisting their help in recognizing prodromal states, the clinician can attempt to intervene with pharmacological and/or psychosocial manipulations before more damaging symptoms have become apparent or inevitable.

Compliance with medication frequently becomes a major issue during maintenance treatment, and it is especially difficult in the adolescent age group (where compliance is traditionally problematic). The clinician must avoid being caught in a power struggle between patient and parents that may result in treatment recommendations being viewed as a threat to the adolescent's autonomy (Ryan & Puig-Antich, 1987). Seeing the patient alone while allowing for frequent contact with concerned others can help in the development of a therapeutic alliance in which the adolescent feels appropriately empowered. When relapse does happen, it is important for both the clinician and the family to avoid blaming the noncompliant patient. Relapse frequently occurs even when compliance is assured with depot administration (Schooler & Hogarty, 1987), and noncompliance itself may be a result rather than a cause of recurring illness (Schooler, 1991). One goal of the therapeutic alliance is for the adolescent who is contemplating noncompliance to trust his or her clinician to the point where an intention to stop medications can be openly explored. The patient then needs to know that although the unmedicated schizophrenic may experience higher baseline symptoms and is more vulnerable to serious relapse, symptoms may not recur for many months after antipsychotics have been discontinued. Allowing the adolescent to participate openly in treatment decisions can also improve the patient's willingness to continue follow-up and psychosocial interventions whether or not neuroleptics are being taken.

Psychosocial Interventions

The awareness that antipsychotic medication usually improves, but does not cure schizophrenia has encouraged continued efforts to develop psychosocial treatment strategies. Testing the efficacy of such strategies has proven methodologically difficult, particularly from the standpoint of controlling for medication compliance and providing an appropriate psychosocial placebo group. Despite these difficulties, data supporting the benefit of several psychosocial treatment approaches have been accumulating (see Schooler & Hogarty, 1987, for a review). Social skills training (SST), in which patients are taught social skills through instructional sessions incorporating such behavioral education aids as videotaping, modeling, role play, and homework, can help some schizophrenics to interact more appropriately with their social environment (Wallace & Liberman, 1985). Group therapy focusing on communication skills may be a useful addition to SST and antipsychotic treatment (Malm, 1982).

Family therapy also plays an important part in the treatment of schizophrenia. Goldstein, Rodrick, Evans, May, and Steinberg (1978) studied the effect of a 6-week therapy designed to help family members understand the illness and develop their ability to identify and cope with potential stressors. Follow-up at the completion of the course and 6 months later showed less social withdrawal and psychotic relapse in the family therapy–treated group, with patients who had also received standard-instead of low-dose depot prolixin (25 mg versus 6.25 mg every 2 weeks) responding best overall. Hogarty, Anderson, Reiss, Kornblith, and Greenwald (1986) found that patients receiving both SST and psychoeducational family therapy on an ongoing basis had a lower tendency to relapse by the end of 1 year than those who received either psychosocial treatment alone. Subjects receiving only maintenance antipsychotic treatment fared worse (40% relapse versus about 20% of the single psychosocial groups and none of the combined psychosocial treatment group). Insight-oriented psychotherapy, though, does not appear to be beneficial in the treatment of schizophrenia (Stanton et al., 1984).

These studies suggest that psychosocial interventions can have an additive effect with antipsychotic medication in improving the quality of life and forestalling relapse in the schizophrenic patient. Given the heterogenous presentation of this illness, it remains to be established which patients will respond best to which treatments. Individual characteristics such as gender, intelligence, and level of social withdrawal play an important but as yet undetermined role (Schooler & Hogarty, 1987). Characteristics of the family also appear to affect illness course and should thus influence the clinician's approach to psychosocial treatment. Households in which the social environment tends to be high in expressed emotion (EE; e.g., households that are argumentative, critical, loud, overinvolved, high in expectations) may dispose the schizophrenic to earlier relapse (Vaughn & Leff, 1976), and poorer social adjustment (Hogarty et al., 1988). Psychoeducational approaches designed to change families from higher to lower levels of EE have been shown to decrease relapse rates (Leff, Kuipers, Berkowitz, & Sturgeon, 1985), particularly for young adult males living with high EE parents (Hogarty et al., 1986; see Anderson, Reiss & Hogarty, 1986, for details of family psychoeducation workshops).

The fact that adolescents as a group are more exposed to—and more dependent upon—their families than are adults leads one to predict that psychoeducational approaches encompassing SST and EE mitigation would have a crucial role to play in the treatment of schizophrenia in this age group. Unfortunately, controlled studies on the impact of psychosocial treatments specifically in the adolescent age group are unavailable. Case reports have suggested that residential treatment programs encompassing some SST-like qualities have been beneficial in the fostering of independence and vocational skills in severely ill schizophrenic adolescents (Nelson & Condrin, 1987).

Summary

Children and adolescents with schizophrenia manifest psychotic symptoms similar to those seen in adults diagnosed with this disorder. While diagnosis in adults with schizophrenia requires decline in functioning, for children one needs the criterion of failure to achieve the expected level of development. In the differential diagnosis of schizophrenia in adolescence, particular attention needs to be given to pervasive developmental disorder, affective disorders, and personality disorders. The onset of schizophrenia is rare before puberty. Familial predisposition is among the best-established etiological factors, but neurodevelopmental deviation is also considered likely. Antipsychotic drugs are the mainstay of treatment and need to be supplemented by individual, family, and group psychotherapy, as well as education about the illness. Course and outcome are variable, but most patients have some persisting symptoms.

References

Aarkrog, T., & Mortensen, K. V. (1985). Schizophrenia in early adolescence. *Acta Psychiatrica Scandinavica, 72*, 422–429.

Adler, L., Angrist, B., Peselow, E., Corwin, J., Maslansky, R., & Rotrosen, J. (1986). A controlled assessment of propranolol in the treatment of neuroleptic-induced akathisia. *British Journal of Psychiatry, 149*, 42–45.

American Medical Association. (1990). *Drug evaluation.* Chicago: American Medical Association.

American Psychiatric Association. (1987). *Diagnostic and statistical manual of mental disorders* (rev. 3rd ed.). Washington, DC: Author.

American Psychiatric Association. (1993). *DSM-IV draft criteria.* Washington, DC: Author.

Anderson, C. M., Reiss, D. J., & Hogarty, G. E. (1986). *Schizophrenia in the family.* New York: Guilford.

Andreasen, N. C. (1987). The diagnosis of schizophrenia. *Schizophrenia Bulletin, 13*, 9–21.

Andreasen, N. C., & Black, D. (1991). *Introductory text of psychiatry.* Washington, DC: American Psychiatric Press.

Apter, A., Dickerman, Z., Gonen, N., Assa, S., Prager-Lewin, R., Kaufman, H., Tyano, S., & Laron, Z. (1983). Effect of chlorpromazine on hypothalamic-pituitary-gonadal function in 10 adolescent schizophrenic boys. *American Journal of Psychiatry, 140*, 1588–1591.

Baldessarini, R. (1990). Drugs and the treatment of psychiatric disorders. In G. A. Gilman, T. W. Roll, A. S. Nies, & T. Palmer (Eds.), *The pharmacological basis of therapeutics* (pp. 383–435). New York: Pergamon.

Baldessarini, R. J., Cohen, B. M., & Teicher, M. H. (1988). Significance of neuroleptic dose and plasma level in the pharmacological treatment of psychosis. *Archives of General Psychiatry, 45*, 79–91.

Becker, R. B. (1988). Depression in schizophrenia. *Hospital and Community Psychiatry, 39*, 1269–1275.

Beitchman, J. H. (1985). Childhood schizophrenia: A review and comparison with adult-onset schizophrenia. *Psychiatric Clinics of North America, 8*, 793–814.

Belmaker, R. H. (1984). The lessons of platelet monoamine oxidase [Editorial]. *Psychological Medicine, 14*, 249–253.

Birmaher, B., Baker, R., Kapur, S., Quintana, H., & Ganguli, R. (1992). Clozapine for the treatment of adolescents with schizophrenia. *Journal of the American Academy of Child and Adolescent Psychiatry, 31,* 160–164.

Bleuler, E. (1952). *Dementia praecox* (J. Zinkin, Trans.). New York: International Press. (Original work published 1908)

Cannon, T. (1990). Antecedents of predominantly negative- and predominantly positive-symptom schizophrenia in a high risk population. *Archives of General Psychiatry, 47,* 622–632.

Campbell, M., Green, W. H., & Deutch, S. I. (1985). *Child and adolescent psychopharmacology.* Beverly Hills, CA: Sage.

Carlson, G. (1990). Annotation, child and adolescent mania: Diagnostic considerations. *Journal of Child Psychology and Psychiatry and Allied Disciplines, 31,* 331–341.

Carpenter, W., Buchanan, R., & Kirkpatrick, B. (1991). The concept of the negative symptoms of schizophrenia. In J. Greden & R. Tandon (Eds.), *Negative schizophrenic symptoms: Pathophysiology and clinical implications* (pp. 3–20). Washington, DC: American Psychiatric Press.

Carpenter, W. T., Hanlon T. E., Heinrichs, D. W., Summerfelt, A. T., Kirkpatrick, B., Levine, J., & Buchanan, R. W. (1990). Continuous vs. targeted medication in schizophrenic outpatients: Outcome results. *American Journal of Psychiatry, 147,* 1138–1148.

Christison, G. W., Kirch, D. G., & Wyatt, R. J. (1991). When symptoms persist: Choosing among alternative treatments for schizophrenia. *Schizophrenia Bulletin, 17,* 217–245.

Cole, J. O. (1964). NIMH-Psychopharmacology Service Center Collaborative Study Group. Phenothiazine treatment in acute schizophrenia: Effectiveness. *Archives of General Psychiatry, 10,* 246–261.

Cooper, J. E., Kendell, R. E., Sharpe, L., Copeland, J. R. M., & Simon, R. (1972). *Psychiatric diagnosis in New York and London* (Maudsley Monograph No. 10). London: Oxford University Press.

Crow, T. J. (1980). Molecular pathology of schizophrenia: More than one disease process? *British Medical Journal, 280,* 66–68.

Crow, T. J., MacMillan, J. F., Johnson, A. L., & Johnstone, E. C. (1986). The Northwick Park study of first episodes of schizophrenia: II. A randomized controlled study of prophylactic neuroleptic treatment. *British Journal of Psychiatry, 148,* 115–120.

Davis, J. M. (1975). Overview: Maintenance therapy in psychiatry. 1. Schizophrenia. *American Journal of Psychiatry, 132,* 1237–1245.

DeLisi, L. E., & Buchsbaum, M. S. (1986). PET of regional cerebral glucose use in psychiatric patients. In M. R. Trimble (Ed.), *New brain imaging techniques in psychopharmacology* (pp. 49–62). Oxford, England: Oxford University Press.

Der, G., Gupta, S., & Murray, R. M. (1990). Is schizophrenia disappearing? *Lancet, 335,* 513–516.

Detre, T., & Jarecki, H. (1971). *Modern Psychiatric Treatment.* Philadelphia: Lippincott.

Dunham, H. W. (1965). *Community and schizophrenia: An epidemiological analysis.* Detroit: Wayne State University Press.

Easson, W. (1979). The early manifestations of adolescent thought disorder. *Journal of Clinical Psychiatry, 40,* 469–475.

Eggers, C. (1978). Course and prognosis of childhood schizophrenia. *Journal of Autism and Childhood Schizophrenia, 8*, 21–36.

Erickson, W. D., Yellin, A. M., Hopwood, J. H., Realmuto, G. M., & Greenberg, L. M. (1984). The effects of neuroleptics on attention in adolescent schizophrenics. *Biological Psychiatry, 19*, 745–753.

Erlenmeyer-Kimling, L., & Cornblatt, B. (1984). Biobehavioral risk factors in children of schizophrenic parents. *Autism and Developmental Disabilities, 14*, 357–374.

Fish, F. (1984). Fish's schizophrenia. In M. Hamilton (Ed.), *Symptomatology* (pp. 38–77). Boston: Wright-PSG.

Freeman, T. (1971). Symptomatology, diagnosis and course. In K. Bellak & L. Lobe (Eds.), *The schizophrenic syndrome* (pp. 311–342). New York: Grune and Stratton.

Goldstein, M. J., Rodrick, E. H., Evans, J. R., May, P. R. A., & Steinberg, M. R. (1978). Drug and family therapy in the aftercare of acute schizophrenics. *Archives of General Psychiatry, 35*, 1169–1177.

Green, W. H. (1989). Schizophrenia with childhood onset. In H. I. Kaplan & B. S. Sadlock (Eds.), *Comprehensive textbook of psychiatry* (5th ed., pp. 1975–1981). Baltimore, MD: Williams and Wilkins.

Guz, I., Morales, R., & Sartoretto, J. N. (1972). The therapeutic effects of lorazepam in psychotic patients treated with haloperidol: A double-blind study. *Current Therapeutic Research, 14*, 767–774.

Heinrichs, D. W., & Buchanan, R. W. (1988). The significance and meaning of neurological signs in schizophrenia. *American Journal of Psychiatry, 145*, 11–18.

Herz, M. I., & Melville, C. (1980). Relapse in schizophrenia. *American Journal of Psychiatry, 137*, 801–805.

Hogarty, G. E., Anderson, C. M., Reiss, D. T., Kornblith, S. T., & Greenwald, D. P. (1986). Family psychoeducation, social skills training, and maintenance chemotherapy in the aftercare of schizophrenia. *Archives of General Psychiatry, 43*, 633–642.

Hogarty, G. E., McEvoy, J. P., Munetz, M., Dibarry, A. L., Bartone, P., & Cather, R. (1988). Environmental/Personal Indicators in the Course of Schizophrenia Research Group: Dose of fluphenazine, familial expressed emotion, and outcome in schizophrenia. *Archives of General Psychiatry, 45*, 797–805.

Holzman, P., & Grinker, R. (1974). Schizophrenia in adolescence. *Journal of Youth and Adolescence, 3*, 267–270.

Holzman, P. S., Kringlen, E., Matthysse, S., Flanagan, S. D., Lipton, R. B., Cramer, G., Levin, S., Lange, K., & Levy, D. L. (1988). A single dominant gene can account for eye tracking dysfunctions and schizophrenia in offspring of discordant twins. *Archives of General Psychiatry, 457*, 641–648.

Jeste, D. V., delCarmen, R., Lohr, J., & Wyatt, R. J. (1985). Did schizophrenia exist before the eighteenth century? *Comprehensive Psychiatry, 26*, 493–503.

Kane, J. M. (1989). The current status of neuroleptic therapy. *Journal of Clinical Psychiatry, 50*, 322–328.

Kane, J. M., & Lieberman, J. A. (1987). Maintenance pharmacotherapy in schizophrenia. In H. Y. Meltzer (Ed.), *Psychopharmacology: The third generation of progress* (pp. 103–111). New York: Raven.

Kane, J. M., & Selzer, J. (1991). Consideration on "organic" exclusion criteria for schizophrenia. *Schizophrenia Bulletin, 17,* 69–73.

Kane, J. M., Woerner, M., & Sarantos, S. (1986). Depot neuroleptics: A comparative review of standard, intermediate, and low dose regimens. *Journal of Clinical Psychiatry, 47,* 330–333.

Kane, J. M., Woerner, M., Weinhold, P., Wegner, J., Kinon, B., & Borenstein, M. (1984). Incidence of tardive dyskinesia: Five-year data from a prospective study. *Psychopharmacology Bulletin, 20,* 387–389.

Kanner, L. (1955). General concept of schizophrenia at various ages. *Research Publications—Association for Research in Nervous and Mental Disease, 34,* 451–453.

Kaplan, H., & Sadock, B. (1988). *Synopsis of psychiatry.* Baltimore, MD: Williams and Wilkins.

Kendler, K. S. (1987). Genetics of schizophrenia, a current prospective. In H. Y. Meltzer (Ed.), *Psychopharmacology: The third generation of progress* (pp. 705–715). New York: Raven.

Keshavan, M. S., David, A. S., Steingard, S., & Lishman, W. A. (1992). Musical hallucinations: A review and synthesis. *Journal of Psychiatry, Psychology and Behavioral Neurology, 5,* 211–223.

Keshavan, M. S., & Keshavan, A. (1992). Drug induced psychotic disorders. In M. S. Keshavan & J. S. Kennedy (Eds.), *Drug-induced dysfunction in psychiatry.* New York: HPC.

Keshavan, M. S., Vikram, K. Y., & Channabasavanna, S. M. (1979). A critical evaluation of primitive reflexes in neuropsychiatric diagnosis. *Indian Journal of Psychiatry, 21,* 267–270.

King, L. J., & Pitman, G. D. (1971). A follow up of 65 adolescent schizophrenic patients. *Diseases of the Nervous Systems, 32,* 328–334.

Kolvin, I., Ounsted, C., Humphrey, M., & McNay, A. (1971). Studies in the childhood psychoses: II. The phenomenology of childhood psychoses. *British Journal of Psychiatry, 118,* 385–395.

Kraepelin, E. (1971). *Dementia praecox and paraphrenia* (R. Barclay, Trans.). Huntington, NY: Krieger. (Original work published in 1898)

Leff, J., Kuipers, L., Berkowitz, R., & Sturgeon, D. (1985). A controlled trial of social intervention in the families of schizophrenic patients: Two year follow up. *British Journal of Psychiatry, 146,* 594–600.

Lieberman, J. A., Kane, J. M., & Johns, C. A. (1989). Clozapine: Guidelines for clinical management. *Journal of Clinical Psychiatry, 50,* 329–338.

MacMillan, J. F., Gold, A., Crow, T. J., Johnson, A. L., & Johnstone, E. C. (1986). The Northwick Park study of first episodes of schizophrenia: IV. Expressed emotion and relapse. *British Journal of Psychiatry, 148,* 133–143.

Malm, U. (1982). The influence of group therapy on schizophrenia. *Acta Psychiatrica Scandinavica, 297*(Suppl.), 1–65.

Marcus, J., Hans, S. L., Mednick, S. A., Schulsinger, F., & Michelson, N. (1985). Neurobiological dysfunction in offspring of schizophrenics in Israel and Denmark: A replication analysis. *Archives of General Psychiatry, 42,* 753–761.

May, P. R., Tuma, A. H., Yale, C., Potepan, P., & Dixon, W. J. (1976). Schizophrenia—a follow-up study of results of treatment: II. Hospital stay over two to five years. *Archives of General Psychiatry, 33,* 481–506.

McCracken, J. T. (1987). Lead intoxication psychosis in an adolescent. *Journal of the American Academy of Child and Adolescent Psychiatry, 26,* 274–276.

McEvoy, J. P., Hogarty, G. E., & Steingard, S. (1991). Optimal dose of neuroleptic in acute schizophrenia. *Archives of General Psychiatry, 48,* 739–745.

McGlashan, T. H. (1988). A selective review of recent North American long term follow up studies of schizophrenia. *Schizophrenia Bulletin, 14,* 515–542.

Mednick, S. A., & Schulsinger, F. (1968). Some premorbid characteristics related to breakdown in children with schizophrenic mothers. In D. Rosenthal and S. S. Kety (Eds.), *The transmission of schizophrenia* (pp. 267–293). Oxford, England: Pergamon.

Meyers, B., Tune, L. E., & Coyle, J. T. (1980). Clinical response and serum neuroleptic levels in childhood schizophrenia. *American Journal of Psychiatry, 137,* 483–484.

Nasrallah, H. A. (1986). The differential diagnosis of schizophrenia: Genetic, perinatal, neurological, pharmacological and psychiatric factors. In H. A. Nasrallah & D. R. Weinberger (Eds.), *Handbook of schizophrenia* (pp. 49–65). New York: Elsevier.

Nelson, R. R., & Condrin, J. L. (1987). A vocational readiness and independent living skills program for psychiatrically impaired adolescents. *Occupational Therapy in Mental Health, 7,* 23–38.

Pogue-Geile, M., & Keshavan, M. (1991). Negative symptomatology in schizophrenia: Syndrome and subtype status. In R. Greden & R. Tandon (Eds.), *Negative schizophrenia symptoms: Pathophysiology and clinical implications* (pp. 41–61). Washington, DC: American Psychiatric Press.

Poole, D., Bloom, W., Mielhe, D. H., Runiger, J. J., & Gallant, D. M. (1976). A controlled evaluation of loxitane in seventy-five adolescent schizophrenic patients. *Current Therapeutic Research, 19,* 99–104.

Rancurello, M. D., Vallano, G., & Waterman, G. S. (1992). Psychotropic drug-induced dysfunction in children. In M. S. Keshavan & J. S. Kennedy (Eds.). *Drug induced dysfunction in psychiatry* (pp. 75–92). New York: Hemisphere Publishing Corporation.

Realmuto, G. M., Erickson, W. D., Yellin, A. M., Hopwood, J. H., & Greenberg, L. M. (1984). Clinical comparison of thiothixene and thioridazine in schizophrenic adolescents. *American Journal of Psychiatry, 141,* 440–442.

Rifkin, A., Seshagiri, D., Basawaraj, K., Borenstein, M., & Wachspress, W. (1991). Dosage of haloperidol for schizophrenia. *Archives of General Psychiatry, 48,* 166–170.

Rifkin, A., & Siris, S. (1987). Drug treatment of acute schizophrenia. In H. Y. Meltzer (Ed.), *Psychopharmacology: The third generation of progress* (pp. 1095–1103). New York: Raven.

Roy, A. (1986). Suicide in schizophrenia. In A. Roy (Ed.), *Suicide* (pp. 95–112). Baltimore, MD: Williams and Wilkin.

Russell, A., Bolt, L., & Sammons, C. (1989). The phenomonology of schizophrenia occurring in childhood. *American Academy of Child and Adolescent Psychiatry, 28,* 399–407.

Ryan, N. D., & Puig-Antich, J. (1987). Pharmacological treatment of adolescent psychiatric disorders. *Journal of Adolescent Health Care, 8*, 137–142.

Salzman, C. (1989). Use of benzodiazapines to control disruptive behavior in inpatients. *Journal of Clinical Psychiatry, 49*(Suppl.), 13–15.

Sands, D. (1956). The psychosis of adolescence. *Journal of Mental Science, 102*, 308–316.

Schneider, K. (1959). *Clinical psychopathology.* New York: Grune and Stratton.

Schooler, N., & Hogarty, G. (1987). Medication and psychosocial strategies in the treatment of schizophrenia. In H. Y. Meltzer (Ed.), *Psychopharmacology: The third generation of progress* (pp. 1111–1121). New York: Raven.

Schooler, N. (1991). Maintenance medication for schizophrenia: Strategies for dose reduction. *Schizophrenia Bulletin, 17*, 311–324.

Stanton, A. H., Gunderson, J. G., Knapp, P. H., Frank, A. F., Vanicelli, M. L., Schnitzer, R., & Rosenthal, R. (1984). Effects of psychotherapy in schizophrenia. *Schizophrenia Bulletin, 10*, 520–563.

Steinberg, D. (1985). Psychotic and other severe disorders in adolescence. In M. Rutter & L. Hersov (Eds.), *Child and adolescent psychiatry: Modern Approaches* (pp. 567–583). Boston: Blackwell Scientific.

Teicher, M. H., & Glod, C. A. (1990). Neuroleptic drugs: Indications and guidelines for their rational use in children and adolescents. *Journal of Child and Adolescent Psychopharmacology, 1*, 33–56.

Van Putten, T. (1974). Why do schizophrenic patients refuse to take their drugs? *Archives of General Psychiatry, 31*, 67–72.

Van Putten, T., Marder, S., & Mintz, J. (1990). A controlled dose comparison of haloperidol in newly admitted schizophrenic patients. *Archives of General Psychiatry, 47*, 754–758.

Vaughn, C. E., & Leff, J. P. (1976). The influence of family and social factors on the course of psychiatric illness. *British Journal of Psychiatry, 129*, 125–137.

Versiani, M., da-Silva, J. A., Frota, C. H., & Mundim, F. D. (1978). Double-blind comparison between haloperidol and loxitane in the treatment of adolescent schizophrenic patients. *Current Therapeutic Research, 24*, 559–566.

Wallace, C. J., & Liberman, R. P. (1985). Social skills training for patient with schizophrenia: A controlled clinical trial. *Psychiatry Research, 15*, 239–247.

Weiner, I. B. (1970). *Psychological disturbance in adolescence.* New York: Wiley.

Weiner, I. B. (1987). Identifying schizophrenia in adolescents. *Journal of Adolescent Health Care, 8*, 336–343.

Werry, J., McClellan, J., & Chard, L. (1991). Childhood and adolescent schizophrenia, bipolar, and schizoaffective disorders: A clinical and outcome study. *Journal of the American Academy of Child and Adolescent Psychiatry, 30*, 457–465.

Wyatt, R. J. (1991). Neuroleptics and the natural course of schizophrenia. *Schizophrenia Bulletin, 17*, 325–351.

16
Mental Retardation and Developmental Disabilities

M. Christopher Borden
Anne S. Walters
Rowland P. Barrett

Developmental disabilities are a heterogeneous group of emotional, physical, and behavioral disturbances generally associated with mental retardation. Until recently, little systematic attention has been directed to the experience and personality development of mentally retarded persons; as a result, our understanding of their vulnerability to psychopathology is limited. In contrast, much debate has been focused on the boundaries of mental retardation and their implications, both fiscal and conceptual, for the development and implementation of management strategies. The term *management* is chosen carefully, as it reflects the belief that many treatment efforts in the past have suffered from the relative absence of a "psychology of mental retardation." This absence reveals itself in the still widely held belief that concomitant intellectual limitations in mentally retarded individuals serve as a buffer against psychological disturbance. This chapter will provide an overview of advances in the assessment and treatment of developmental disabilities, with necessary attention to historical issues and perspectives on mental retardation. In keeping with the focus of the text, an emphasis will be placed on the period of adolescence.

The most widely accepted and applied definition of mental retardation was formulated by the Grossman (1983) committee of the American Association on Mental Deficiency (AAMD):

> Mental retardation refers to significantly subaverage general intellectual functioning resulting in or associated with concurrent impairments in adaptive behavior and manifested during the developmental period. (p. 11)

Subaverage general intellectual functioning is defined by performance of less than 70 (i.e., 2 standard deviations below the mean) on an individually administered test of intelligence. A notable departure from past definitions of mental retardation pertains to the AAMD provision (Grossman, 1983) for the use of "clinical judgment" in cases where IQ is within a few points of the designated cutoff. Accordingly, an individual who appears to be functioning in the mild range of mental retardation may be eligible for services, despite a measured IQ outside of the defined range (i.e., greater than 70).

Impairments in adaptive behavior refers to delays in general maturation or significant limitations in academic learning, personal independence, and social responsibility (Baroff, 1986; Grossman, 1983). As Sattler (1988) asserts,

> Definitions of adaptive behavior tend to be imprecise, because there is no way of knowing the environments in which individuals will be required to function. Furthermore, adaptive behavior must be considered within a developmental context: maturation during the preschool years, academic performance during the school years, and social and economic independence beginning in early adulthood. (p. 376)

Clearly, the relativity of "adaptive behavior" poses difficulties for the design and use of assessment instruments. There remains confusion about what constitutes adaptive behavior (Foster-Gaitskell & Pratt, 1989; Frame & Matson, 1987); consequently, the more popular available tests designed to measure this illusive construct have received criticism since their introduction and despite revision (see Repp & Deitz, 1983). In fact, some (e.g., Zigler, Balla, & Hodapp, 1984) have argued that the criterion of social adaptation should be dropped while continued research efforts are directed toward understanding the relationship between IQ and level of adaptive functioning.

Finally, the *developmental period* refers to the range from conception (to include chromosomal abnormalities such as Trisomy-21; Baroff, 1986) to age 18 years. Thus the Grossman (1983) committee definition emphasizes the pervasive developmental nature of mental retardation in contrast to disturbances of late onset and those involving degenerative processes (Walters, Feinstein, & Barrett, in press).

Consequent to publication of the ninth edition of the American Association on Mental Retardation (AAMR) manual on definition and classification, changes are anticipated in the conceptualization of mental retardation and the diagnostic/assessment practices which must follow. Specifically, AAMR (1992) views mental retardation as the expression of the interaction between a person with limited intellectual functioning and his or her environment, rather than as an absolute trait. Thus increased emphasis is placed on specifying an individual's adaptive skill deficits and the pattern/intensities of support systems that are required to resolve these deficits. The reader is referred to the AAMR manual for detailed information as to the changing understanding of mental retardation.

Historical Background

As suggested above, there has been controversy as to the definition of mental retardation, with a corresponding impact on the assessment procedures utilized under prevailing sets of diagnostic criteria. Repp and Dietz (1983) noted that early historical societies made no distinction between mental retardation and mental illness and, therefore, had no definition for the former. In fact, the conceptual differentiation of mental retardation (as a biologically based intellectual impairment) and mental illness (as a functionally determined emotional disturbance) was not supported by the scientific community until the late eighteenth and early nineteenth centuries (see Ollendick, Oswald, & Ollendick, 1993). Whereas this distinction represented an important advance, Ollendick et al. (1993) observed that is also "led to the common view that mentally retarded persons were in some way 'immune' to emotional problems" (p. 3). Moreover, the absolute division of groups by organic versus environmental etiology is now known to be erroneous (cf. Ollendick et al., 1993).

In the twentieth century, with advances in the testing movement, definitions of mental retardation became more explicit and empirically based. As Sattler (1988) indicated, Goddard's (1908, 1910) introduction of the Binet-Simon (1905) scale saw its nearly exclusive use for evaluation of mentally retarded individuals. Terman's (1916) refinement and standardization of the Binet-Simon scale resulted in publication of the first version of the Stanford-Binet. Individuals scoring below 80 on the scale were classified as mentally retarded, with distinctions between "borderline," "moron," "imbecile," and "idiot" made on the basis of progressively lower scores (Terman, 1916). Definitions of mental retardation continued to rely on IQ as the sole criterion for inclusion until 1959, at which time the AAMD incorporated the concept of "adaptive behavior" (Heber, 1959). Accordingly, classification of an individual as mentally retarded required evidence of difficulties in adjustment to societal demands and expectations (e.g., the ability to function independently) in addition to subaverage performance on a standardized test of intelligence.

Despite this emphasis on standardized assessment, the boundaries of mental retardation have continued to shift repeatedly. As Edgerton (1991) pointed out, "Who is admitted to the [mild mental retardation] category or excluded from it can be arbitrary, depending on an IQ criterion that slides up or down in response to changing social, economic, and political considerations" (p. 327). Specifically, the Heber (1959) committee of AAMD supported a cutoff IQ score of 85 (1 standard deviation below the mean) as a criterion for inclusion, whereas the Grossman (1973) committee set the upper limit at 70 (2 standard deviations below the mean; Edgerton, 1991). As Zigler et al. (1984) indicated, shifts in the IQ criterion of this magnitude (plus or minus 1 standard deviation) altered prevalence estimates in the United States by around 14%.

Contemporary definitions of mental retardation have varied most significantly with regard to the cutoff point at which nonretarded individuals are distinguished from those with a diagnosable condition. The most recent criteria, with their acknowledgement of the importance of adaptive behavior and allowance for the use of clinical judgment, have refined earlier, unidimensional (i.e., IQ alone) conceptions of mental retardation while maintaining the emphasis on assessment that began early in the twentieth century. The present-day assessment of mental retardation is an inferential process through which data obtained from a variety of sources are integrated into a multidimensional view of an individual's behavior (see Morgenstern & Klass, 1991).

Clinical Picture

The AAMD (Grossman, 1983) distinguished four levels or subtypes of mental retardation based, in theory, on a statistical distribution of IQ (Baroff, 1986). These subtypes, based on deviations from a mean IQ of 100, include mild (between 2 and 3 Standard Deviation's below the mean), moderate (between 3 and 4 Standard Deviation's below the mean), severe (between 4 and 5 Standard Deviation's below the mean), and profound mental retardation (greater than 5 Standard Deviation's below the mean). As the standard deviations of individual tests are not necessarily equal, the specific cutoff scores for degree of impairment may vary slightly depending on the instrument used (Sattler, 1988).

Sloan and Birch (1955) provided a rationale for degrees of mental retardation with emphasis on differences in developmental attainment that may be expected for each group. Specifically, individuals with mild mental retardation may be expected during school age (6 to 21 years) to have attained academic skills up to the sixth-grade level (provided that special education education services have been accessed). Persons with moderate levels of impairment were purported to be capable of functional academic skills up to the fourth-grade level by their late teens if given special education (Sloan & Birch, 1955). In contrast, severe and profound levels of mental retardation were associated with the inability to learn functional academic skills and increased need for supportive services. For example, individuals with severe mental retardation were considered able to benefit from systematic health habit training, whereas the profoundly mentally retarded individual required total care (Sloan & Birch, 1955). It is important to note, however, that "mental age is most predictive of cognitive and academic potential and less so of self-help and motor skills" (Baroff, 1986, p. 51). See Baroff (1986) for a detailed description of adaptive potential based on chronological age and degree of mental retardation. In short, the clinical picture of mental retardation is dependent on the individual's age and level of impairment, with the latter variable defining a range of expectations for academic and adaptive skill attainment. As the following sections will illustrate, however, a variety of additional factors influence the clinical course and prognosis for any given individual.

Course and Prognosis

In considering the course and prognosis of mental retardation, the notion of advocacy is central. Though passage of guidelines such as Public Law 94-142 (the Education for All Handicapped Children Act of 1975) have ensured that mentally retarded individuals have access to special education, the degree to which these services meet a student's specific needs (independent of funding issues and/or service availability) varies widely across school districts. In our experience with dually diagnosed adolescents—admittedly a restricted sample—we are frequently in a position of advising parents to advocate specialized services that we know to be nonexistent in an already financially strapped school system. For example, the provision or availability of social skills training, group psychotherapy services by an experienced consultant, speech and language services that are conducted in a naturalistic setting (e.g., classroom or home), occupational therapy services that emphasize adaptive skills in all relevant contexts, and prevocational and vocational services to enhance skills and provide a sense of competence strongly influence the ability of mentally retarded adolescents to adjust satisfactorily to their communities.

There are no easy answers with regard to financial responsibility and identifying personnel who can provide these services. However, we cannot overemphasize the need for professionals to become familiar with the advocacy movement (see Fiedler & Antorak, 1991) and, while remaining cognizant of administrative/funding realities, to educate parents about how to obtain the combination of services that best meet the particular needs of their child (see Fiedler & Antorak, 1991, for a review of the various levels of advocacy available).

At a more personal/ideographic level, the degree to which families and other relevant contexts (school, peers, community) are able to support the mentally retarded adolescent (and one another) in negotiating developmental challenges significantly influences the affected adolescent's course and prognosis. The notion of transactional processes in development (i.e., those processes by which a child's pattern of relative strengths and weakness interact with contextual expectations, in a nonlinear fashion, to determine outcome; Sameroff, 1982) is applicable here. We have discussed the developmental challenges for mentally retarded adolescents elsewhere (see Walters et al., in press); here we note only that this period involves opportunity for increased community and peer participation, increased independence, and increased awareness of differences. Some adolescents may experience sadness about developmental milestones (e.g., obtaining a driver's license, playing a high school sport) that are visible and yet often inaccessible to those in special education. The ability of adults to respond sensitively to these issues and to provide other compensatory opportunities for independence and personal or social competence is essential to continued psychological adjustment.

Complications

As noted in the introduction to this chapter, little research attention has been directed toward understanding the psychological and affective worlds of individuals with mental retardation. Recent years, however, have seen a heightened awareness and sensitivity to the plight of mentally retarded individuals, whose often fragile constitutions may serve to increase susceptibility to psychiatric disturbance. In fact, psychiatric disorders have been estimated as four to six times more prevalent in the mentally retarded population when compared to the general population (see Matson & Barrett, 1982a). These figures are supported by the renowned Isle of Wight studies, which investigated the rates of psychopathology in a well-defined population of children (e.g., Rutter, Tizard, Yule, Graham, & Whitmore, 1976). Matson and Barrett (1982a) compiled one of the earliest and most comprehensive accounts of psychopathology in the mentally retarded, with individual chapters devoted to anxiety (Ollendick & Ollendick, 1982), affective (Matson & Barrett, 1982b), and psychotic (Romanczyk & Kistner, 1982) disorders. A clear determination was that "mentally retarded people are vulnerable to the same range of behavior and emotional problems as the rest of us" (Gualtieri, 1982, p. ix). An updated version of this volume is now available (Matson & Barrett, 1993).

Given the *increased* vulnerability to psychiatric disturbance and the limitations in coping that often ensue with subaverage intellectual and adaptive functioning, it is not surprising that many mentally retarded individuals require specialized psychological services in addition to their mandated special education. As Seltzer and Seltzer (1991) note, the social status and level of residential care for an individual with mental retardation depend not only on classification (subtype) level but also on maladaptive behavior, the ideology of professionals in the field of mental retardation, and broader social trends and circumstances. The impact of maladaptive behavior is particularly relevant here, as the onset of emotional/behavior problems and the frequently concomitant transitions in community/institutional placement represent a most common complication to mental retardation. Seltzer and Seltzer (1991) provide a thorough review and discussion of classification level, social status, and placement alternatives available to mentally retarded individuals.

Until recently there was a prevailing belief that mentally retarded persons lacked the cognitive sophistication to suffer from major mental illnesses (e.g., depression). In fact, this lack of consensus was borne out in controversies regarding treatment of so-called dual-diagnosis patients. Specifically, the provision of services to those perhaps most in need was hampered by debate among respective state-operated mental health and mental retardation departments as to responsibility. Further, the tendency of clinicians to diagnose mental disorders in the mentally retarded was limited by the view of mental retardation and psychiatric illness as necessarily independent problems. For example, Reiss and his colleagues (Reiss, Levitan, & Szysko, 1982; Reiss & Szysko, 1983) demonstrated empirically that a phenomenon called "diagnostic overshadowing" often occurs in which attention to and diagnosis of psychiatric illness were overshadowed by the presence of mental retardation in case histories presented to a group of clinical psychologists.

In short, the frequent coexistence of emotional/behavior problems with mental retardation necessitates a competent response on the part of treatment providers, mental health and mental retardation specialists alike. The future is likely to see an increase in the number of clinicians and researchers trained specifically to address these numerous cases of *complicated* mental retardation; however, the "psychology of mental retardation" remains in the very early stages of its evolution.

Epidemiology

Estimating prevalence of mental retardation is a difficult undertaking because of historical shifts in diagnostic criteria and consideration of influential factors such as age, sex, degree of intellectual impairment, socioeconomic status, and method of measurement (see Kiely, 1987). For example, a normal distribution of IQ would predict that 2% to 3% of the population function in the mentally retarded range (i.e., more than 2 standard deviations below the mean). Inclusion of "concurrent impairments in adaptive behavior" (Grossman, 1983) as a criterion narrows actual prevalence to 1% or even less (Baroff, 1986), however, since intellectual impairment does not always entail significant limitation in adaptive functioning. Recent studies have estimated prevalence of severe (IQ less than 50) and of mild (IQ between 50 and 70) mental retardation at 3 to 4 each per 1,000 (McLaren & Bryson, 1987); taken together, these figures support Baroff's contention (i.e., combined prevalence is 0.6% to 0.8%). Most agencies and professionals concur with an overall prevalence estimate of 1% (e.g., American Psychiatric Association [APA], 1987, 1994).

Implicit in the foregoing is the common practice of dividing the mentally retarded population into "mild" and "severe" (moderate, severe, and profound levels inclusive) groups during the gathering and reporting of epidemiological data. As Kiely (1987) indicates, "Among persons with mental retardation, there is a considerably higher proportion of mild mental retardation relative to severe mental retardation" (pp. 195); this point will be given fuller attention in the section to follow. In fact, some have argued that an increased contribution of social factors in the etiology of mild relative to severe (i.e., organic) forms of retardation explains this skewed distribution (see Kiely, 1987, for a review). Of the 2.5 million mentally retarded individuals—an estimated 1% of the general population—89% function in the mild range of mental retardation (Sattler, 1988).

As indicated above, there are a number of additional factors that affect prevalence estimates reported in any given study; among these, age and gender seem most relevant to this discussion. A steady increase in prevalence from preschool years through late adolescence has been reported across epidemiological studies, followed by a decline during adulthood (Kiely, 1987). This observation appears to be accounted for by the relatively high proportion of cases identified through school systems, where subaverage intellectual and adaptive functioning is most likely to be detected through an individual's poor adjustment to persistent academic and social demands. With regard to gender, there is an increased representation of males in prevalence estimates (1.5 males to 1 female; APA, 1987, 1994). Researchers have variously attributed this finding to identification bias, differing sex-role expectations, and the greater likelihood of X-linked chromosome disorders in males; the reader should consult McLaren and Bryson (1987) for a more thorough discussion and review of these perspectives.

Familial Patterns

As noted previously, the mentally retarded population is commonly divided into "mild" (IQ between 55 and 70) and "severe" (IQ less than 55) groups for actuarial purposes. Although a distribution of IQ in the general population would predict greater numbers of mildly mentally retarded individuals relative to all other levels combined, an additional reason for the mild/severe distinction is based on a conceptual model of etiology. Although a detailed discussion of etiological factors is beyond the scope of this chapter, it should be understood that the more severe of developmental disabilities have an underlying physiological basis, have associated medical conditions and/or sensory impairments, and are generally identified by the preschool years. In contrast, milder and more subtle forms of mental retardation typically have no known organic basis, may be caused and/or exacerbated by such environmental influences as cultural and economic deprivation, and are usually identified at school age (see Matson & Mulick, 1991, for independent reviews of the broad classes of etiology in mental retardation and developmental disabilities).

Historically there has been variable emphasis placed on the role of environmental factors in the etiology of mental retardation, particularly with regard to milder forms of retardation. For example, Sattler (1988) distinguishes between familial and organic forms of mental retardation. The familial group, while associated with the combined effects of subaverage heredity and significantly below-average environment, is proposed to reflect normal intellectual variability and polygenic inheritance. In contrast, Zigler et al. (1984) describe the etiological mechanism as being particularly weighted on contextual suboptimality.

Several genetic and neurophysiological factors have been identified in the etiology of more severe forms of mental retardation and developmental disability. In fact, it has been estimated that genetic disorders are present in approximately one-half of those cases where IQ is below 50 (Abuelo, 1991). Abuelo (1991) should be consulted for a delineation and discussion of the three major classes of genetic disorder (single gene, multifactorial, and chromosomal) underlying particular forms of mental retardation. Pueschel and Thuline (1991) provide detailed information regarding chromosomal anomalies.

Despite compelling evidence for the unique contribution of genetic and environmental factors, the division of mental retardation into familial/psychosocial and organic groups should not be taken literally to reflect a belief in native versus acquired disability. Among the most significant advances in conceptualizations of developmental disabilities is the incorporation of a transactional perspective wherein respective supportive or unsupportive caretaking environments interact dynamically either to ameliorate or to amplify the effects of early (biological) insults (Sameroff, 1982; Sameroff & Chandler, 1975). Accordingly, all developmental disabilities should be viewed within an environmental context when an attempt is made to understand etiology as well as clinical presentation at any given point in time. The interested reader is referred to Zigler et al. (1984) for a discussion of the two-group model of mental retardation. The following discussion will emphasize the process through which individuals in the larger familial/psychosocial group, particularly adolescents, are identified and evaluated with regard to the need for services.

Differential Diagnosis and Assessment

As noted in the taxonomic guidelines of the APA, "the diagnostic criteria for Mental Retardation do not include an exclusion criterion; therefore, the diagnosis should be made whenever the diagnostic criteria are met, regardless of and in addition to the presence of another disorder" (APA, 1994, p. 45). Diagnoses of other developmental disorders commonly associated with mental retardation include pervasive developmental disorders (PDD), learning disorders, and communication disorders (APA, 1994). Although 75%–80% of individuals with pervasive developmental disorders (autistic disorder, Rett's disorder, childhood disintegrative disorder, Asperger's disorder, pervasive developmental disorder not otherwise specified—including atypical autism) also have mental retardation (APA, 1994), most persons who function in the ranges of mental retardation do not meet criteria regarding the essential features of the PDD diagnoses. Specifically, PDD is characterized by qualitative, severe, and pervasive impairment in several areas of development: reciprocal social interaction skills, communication skills, or the presence of stereotyped behavior, interests, and activities (APA, 1994). Many individuals with moderate to profound levels of mental retardation show deficits in social interaction skills as well as limitations in their ability to communicate. There is generally an interest in and pleasure derived from social contact, however, and little evidence of the *specific* communication impairments (e.g., limited use of eye contact, gesture, and facial expression in social interaction) commonly observed in persons with PDD. Moreover, repetitive, seemingly driven and nonfunctional motor movements (e.g., hand shaking or waving, body rocking, mouthing of objects) and self-injurious behavior (e.g., head banging, self-biting, scratching or picking at skin, self-hitting) are often present in both PDD and severe/profound mental retardation. When such movements are not associated with other characteristic features of PDD and are of sufficient severity to become a focus of treatment, a diagnosis of stereotypic movement disorder is made (APA, 1994).

Diagnoses of learning disorders requires assessment of academic achievement in addition to measurement of intellectual functioning. Several instruments, including the Woodcock-Johnson Psycho-Educational Battery (Woodcock, 1977), Kaufman Test of Educational Achievement (K-TEA, Kaufman & Kaufman, 1985), Peabody Individual Achievement Test (PIAT, Dunn & Markwardt, 1970) and Wide Range Achievement Test-Revised (WRAT-R, Jastak & Wilkinson, 1984) have been designed for this purpose (see Sattler, 1988, for reviews of psychometric properties). Each test provides, at a minimum, a gross measure of academic achievement in reading, mathematics, and spelling. A substantial discrepancy between academic performance in one or more areas (as measured by an individually administered achievement test) and general cognitive ability (as indicated by IQ) would support a second diagnosis of reading disorder, mathematics disorder, disorder of written expression, or learning disorder not otherwise specified in addition to mental retardation provided that age-appropriate education has been provided and that the academic limitations are not accounted for adequately by a sensory deficit (e.g., impaired vision or hearing). It should be noted that learning disorders and their underlying deficits are usually not associated with significant impairments in overall adaptive functioning; however, some impact on academic achievement or activities of daily living which require the specific skills is necessary for their diagnosis. For example, impairment in literacy skills will limit an adolescent's or adult's ability to function in community settings.

Finally, communication disorders involving impaired articulation or expressive/receptive deficits also may be associated with mental retardation. In each case, however, the area of impaired functioning is in excess of that which would be usually attributable to mental retardation (APA, 1994). Expressive language disorder, mixed receptive-expressive language disorder, and phonological disorder involve interference with academic or occupational achievement or with social communication. In expressive language disorder there are significant discrepancies between scores obtained on standardized, individually administered measures of expressive language development and those obtained from standardized measures of both nonverbal intellectual capacity and receptive language development (APA, 1994). These limitations may be observed clinically as limited vocabulary, making errors of tense, word-retrieval problems, or by the production of developmentally immature (either in length or complexity) sentences (APA, 1994). Mixed receptive-expressive language disorder is diagnosed when performance on a battery of standardized, individually administered tests of both receptive and expressive language development are below measured nonverbal intellectual ability (APA, 1994). Importantly, neither of these diagnoses is made when criteria are met for autistic disorder or another pervasive developmental disorder. Finally, the diagnosis of phonological disorder is made when there is a failure to use developmentally expected speech sounds appropriate for age and dialect (APA, 1994). This impairment is in excess of that usually associated with mental retardation, a speech-motor or sensory deficit, or environmental deprivation when any of these conditions are also present (APA, 1994).

In short, speech/language evaluation is recommended as a routine practice in the assessment and differential diagnosis of mental retardation and developmental disabilities. This permits the objective distinction of associated communication disorders from mental retardation and provides useful information for the planning of special educational and treatment interventions.

As the foregoing suggests, differential diagnosis of mental retardation and developmental disabilities must begin with assessment of intellectual and adaptive functioning. The point at which an individual is referred for evaluation varies with the likelihood of organic etiology and, consequently, the severity of impairment.

Intellectual Assessment

A wide variety of standardized instruments is available for the assessment of intellectual functioning. Selection of the appropriate test(s) must take into consideration the child's chronological age, estimated verbal abilities, sociocultural background, and the presence of physical handicaps. In addition, information about the child's predominant behavioral style (e.g., history of hyperactivity), significant behavior problems (e.g., history of aggression or self-injury), and any medical conditions (e.g., history of seizure disorder) will be important for planning and taking necessary precautions. Accordingly, a parent and/or teacher interview, in addition to a review of school/medical records and results of previous educational/psychological testing, should be undertaken prior to initial contact with the child.

The most widely used instruments are the Stanford-Binet Intelligence Scale—either Form L-M (Terman & Merrill, 1960) or the fourth edition (Thorndike, Hagen, & Sattler, 1986)—and the Wechsler Intelligence Scale for Children-Revised (WISC-R; Wechsler, 1974) or WISC-III (Wechsler, 1991). The Form L-M version of the Stanford-Binet, like its predecessor (Terman & Merrill, 1937), measures such aspects of cognitive functioning as verbal ability, fund of information, perception, memory, and logical reasoning. In contrast to the Form L-M version, the fourth edition places "less emphasis on verbal tasks, and all items are grouped into point scales that are administered consecutively. In earlier versions there was a mix of items that were verbal, visual-motor, or both, within age ranges" (Wilson, 1992, p. 81). Wilson (1992) has criticized use of the fourth edition of the Stanford-Binet for assessment of young children with mental retardation for this reason; namely, the lack of variety in task presentation may pose difficulties for maintaining the interest and cooperation of younger children and those with limited attention span. Moreover, the "floor" of the fourth edition is relatively high, resulting in inadequate sampling of behavior for those young children in the lower ranges of ability (Wilson, 1992). It should be noted, however, that Wilson's charges apply mainly to the assessment of children below age 5 who are thought to have mild mental retardation, as well as children of all ages who are thought to have severe mental retardation. Taking into consideration the limitations noted and the group of children/adolescents to whom they apply, both forms of the Stanford-Binet are viewed as potentially useful instruments for the assessment of intellectual functioning in individuals with mental retardation.

The WISC-R and the newest revision, the WISC-III, were designed for use with children and adolescents (aged 6 years to 16 years, 11 months) and consist of subtests divided among verbal and nonverbal domains. Unlike the Stanford-Binet scales, the Wechsler scales yield separate verbal and nonverbal IQs in addition to a full-scale IQ. Both the WISC-R and WISC-III have a relatively high floor; the WISC-R measures IQ in the range from 44 to 160, while WISC-III IQs range from 40 to 160. Consequently, neither instrument adequately samples the range of abilities at a severe/profound level of mental retardation (Morgenstern & Klass, 1991).

All four of these instruments—the two editions of the Stanford-Binet and the two Wechsler scales—are based on the concept of a deviation IQ. Whereas earlier measures of intelligence employed a nonstandard ratio score (i.e., IQ = MA/CA x 100), the deviation IQ is a standard score with a mean of 100 and standard deviation of 15 (Wechsler scales) or 16 (Stanford-Binet scales; Sattler, 1988). This standardization yields IQs that are comparable across age levels.

Morgenstern and Klass (1991) have provided a review of alternative measures that are generally employed when severe/profound impairments are hypothesized and when physical or sensory limitations preclude use of the above instruments. As mentioned, perhaps the greatest limitation of the Stanford-Binet and Wechsler scales is their failure to sample the range of abilities that severely/profoundly mentally retarded children may possess; they provide information about what skills are lacking but tend to overlook important competencies. "In these instances, the examiner might use the Cattell (1950), the Bayley (1969), or the Gesell (1949), all of which investigate the chronological course of growth and development in four major areas: social, adaptive, language, and motor" (Morgenstern & Klass, 1991; p. 205). Morgenstern and Klaas (1991) also note that several brief "screening" devices, including the Peabody Picture Vocabulary Test (PPVT; Dunn, 1965), the Slossen Intelligence Test (Slossen, 1963), and the Columbia Mental Maturity Scale (Burgemeister, Blum, & Lorge, 1959), may be used when physical handicaps or severe language problems limit a child's ability to respond to other indices. They caution, however, that these abbreviated tests by design sample only a narrow range of abilities and do not allow for quantitative analysis of responses (Morgenstern & Klass, 1991).

This latter point raises the issue of the purpose for which an assessment is sought. Specifically, the designation of level of mental retardation requires the attainment of an IQ, whereas this need not be the case when assessment is undertaken to plan for educational and treatment programming. Thus one may consider a more qualitative assessment of abilities that in some instances will justify the use of an abbreviated test, portions of one or more conventional instruments (i.e., Wechsler or Stanford-Binet), and/or modified procedures for test administration. The critical point is that the examiner must decide which approach is the more appropriate. Documentation of specific modifications must follow in order to allow for the interpretation of findings and replication of nonstandard procedures should future comparisons (i.e., assessment of reliability or stability) be desirable.

Additional tests that have proven useful with nonverbal children and adolescents, as well as those for whom severe or profound mental retardation is hypothesized, include the Leiter International Performance Scale (Leiter, 1980) and the Merrill-Palmer Scale of Mental Tests (1948). Morgenstern and Klass (1991) also indicate that the Kaufman Assessment Battery for Children (K-ABC; Kaufman & Kaufman, 1983) has been shown to be an acceptable alternative to the WISC-R, as it places less emphasis on academic/verbal concept abilities than the latter instrument. A limitation exists, however, in that the K-ABC is normed for use only with children through the age of 12 years, 6 months.

Adaptive Behavior Assessment

Inclusion of adaptive behavior in definitions of mental retardation reflects necessary attention to the developmental-social consequences of subaverage general intellectual functioning (see Baroff, 1986). The importance of reliable and valid assessment of adaptive behavior is underscored by the extent to which these consequences are malleable; such assessment provides a basis for selecting targets for intervention, as well as a means of determining progress toward treatment goals. The two most frequently employed measures are the Vineland Adaptive Behavior Scale (VABS; Sparrow, Balla, & Cicchetti, 1984) and the AAMD Adaptive Behavior Scale (ABS; Nihira, Foster, Schellhaas, & Leland, 1974). Both use the responses of familiar informants (generally parents, teachers, or treatment workers) through an interview or questionnaire format and provide norms for comparisons within age groups.

The VABS can be used with normally developing as well as with developmentally disabled persons from birth through the age of 19 years; separate norms are included in the VABS for the assessment of mentally retarded adults. Three versions of the scale (the expanded form, classroom edition, and survey form) are available, each of which provides measures of adaptive functioning in communication, daily living skills, and socialization domains. These domains are further divided into subdomains that assess specific skill areas, such as receptive language and interpersonal relationships. In addition, a motor skills domain is included for assessment of the fine and gross motor development of children below the age of 6 years. Although the survey and expanded forms contain a "maladaptive behavior" section, we have found this portion of the scale less suited to its purpose than other traditional inventories; these will be discussed in a subsequent section. Scores obtained for each of the global domains of the VABS are aggregated to yield an adaptive behavior composite. Norms for each respective age group and age equivalents for the composite and domain scores are utilized to determine level of adaptive functioning, as well as areas of relative strength and weakness. Although limitations to the VABS have been noted (see Sattler, 1988, for a review), it remains one of the most useful and widely applied instruments available to date.

The ABS was developed and normed for use with mentally retarded, emotionally disturbed, and developmentally disabled persons (aged 3 to 69 years) who reside in institutional settings. The scale is divided into adaptive and maladaptive behavioral sections, with individual domains constituting each respective part. The first part of the ABS was designed to measure sequential development of skills and habits across 10 specific domains; the second part consists of 14 domains related loosely to disturbances of personality and behavior. Raw scores obtained in each of the adaptive and maladaptive behavior domains are converted to percentile ranks for comparison to norms in 11 age groups. Sattler (1988) notes that the ABS has proven helpful for describing an individual's daily living and social interactive skills, despite major drawbacks in standardization and psychometric properties. Specifically, the scale provides norms for institutionalized persons exclusively and has a relatively low ceiling for some domains, leading to interpretive difficulties. Furthermore, reliability data are limited, and the validity of the scale has yet to adequately established. In fact, we have found information from the maladaptive behavior section of the scale to be misleading in selected cases due to the nature of the standardization group; as noted earlier, we favor the use of other instruments for such assessment.

Rating Scales and Assessment of Psychopathology

A final step in the assessment process involves the evaluation of personality, emotional, and behavioral functioning. Although it is generally accepted that the manifestation of various psychiatric disorders may deviate from the typical symptom picture, identification of psychopathological conditions in the mentally retarded individual has been almost exclusively influenced by trends in the differential diagnosis of psychopathology in persons of normal intelligence (see Matson & Barrett, 1982b). Accordingly, DSM-IV has served as the principal taxonomy, and assessment procedures have been nearly identical to those accepted and commonly employed with individuals who function near, at, or above the normal range of intelligence. Specifically, behavioral interviewing of the prospective patient and available third-party informants (i.e., parents, siblings, relatives, and teachers) serves as an initial basis for conceptualizing presenting complaints. Barrett, Walters, Mercurio, Klitzke, and Feinstein (1992) provide a description of this process as it applies to developmentally disabled children and adolescents. Next, rating scales designed to measure broad features and classes of psychopathology are administered to verify the nature of the disturbance as well as its quantitative aspects. Instruments commonly employed toward this end include the Child Behavior Checklist (CBCL; Achenbach & Edelbrock, 1983), Revised Behavior Problem Checklist (RPBC; Quay & Peterson, 1983), Aberrant Behavior Checklist (ABC; Aman & Singh, 1983), Reiss Screen for Maladaptive Behavior (Reiss, 1988), and the Psychopathology Inventory for Mentally Retarded Adults (PIMRA; Matson, 1988). Each involves the provision of parent or teacher ratings (generally using a 3- or 4-point Likert scale), may be completed in less that 20 minutes, and yields a relatively comprehensive survey of problem behavior.

The chief limitation of these instruments relates to standardized sampling and, consequently, a restricted range of application. The CBCL and RBPC excluded mentally retarded children from their normative samples, and therefore they may be of limited use for the quantitative assessment of psychopathology in this population. Moreover, the ABC was designed for use only with children who function in the moderate to profound ranges of mental retardation, and the Reiss Screen and PIMRA are appropriate only for the assessment of mentally retarded adolescents and adults. Nonetheless, each of these instruments has proven useful either for identifying areas for more focused assessment or for the evaluation of treatment efficacy (e.g., response to pharmacotherapy regimens).

Following the broad-based assessment of psychopathology, the administration of more syndrome-specific measures—such as the Conners parent and teacher rating scales for the assessment of attention-deficit hyperactivity disorder (Goyette, Conners, & Ulrich, 1979)—may be indicated. Again, the majority of available psychiatric rating scales and behavioral checklists were conceived with the assumption of normal intelligence. Some researchers and clinicians, however, have developed instruments exclusively for the assessment of mentally retarded individuals; for example, the Emotional Disorders Rating Scale (EDRS; Feinstein, Kaminer, Barrett, & Tylenda, 1988) and Affective Behavior Checklist (Barrett, Tylenda, Kaminer, & Feinstein, 1986) were devised specifically for use with this population.

Application of self-report indices has yet to be thoroughly investigated, though preliminary reports suggest that mildly or moderately retarded children and adolescents may provide first-person accounts of their symptoms when items are presented orally (e.g., Knapp, Barrett, Groden, & Groden, 1992). Accordingly, some effort has been made to develop inventories specifically for respondents with mental retardation (e.g., Self-Report Depression Questionnaire; Reynolds, 1989).

Finally, direct behavioral observation methods, including event recording and time sampling, play an important role in the assessment of pathological symptoms as well as their response to treatment protocols. Briefly, the behavioral excesses or deficits that led to initial referral are operationally defined in observable and measurable terms. Subsequently, trained observers record occurrence of the behavior with respect to latency, frequency, duration, or intensity as appropriate (see Barrett et al., 1992, for a detailed review).

In sum, the behavioral assessment of developmentally disabled children and adolescents has borrowed liberally from accepted practices with individuals of normal intelligence. Although the adaptation of extant measures represents an important advance, there remains a formidable task for researchers and clinicians to develop new instruments that may be standardized for the assessment of broad-based as well as syndrome-specific psychopathology in mentally retarded children and adolescents. The reader is referred to Aman (1991) for a comprehensive review of instruments currently available for assessing psychopathology and behavior problems in persons with mental retardation.

Personality Assessment

The assessment of personality structure and functioning is only rarely undertaken with mentally retarded individuals. Although some (e.g., Jura & Sigman, 1985) advocate strongly the employment of projective techniques (e.g. Rorschach, Thematic Apperception Test) with persons of subaverage intellectual functioning, these measures are generally restricted to use when there is a question of poor reality testing or thought disorder in a relatively "high-functioning" individual. The assessment of personality in the mentally retarded, however, need not be limited to these instruments and circumstances. Baroff (1986) recommends use of figure drawings and self-concept measures, including the Piers-Harris Self-Concept Scale (Piers & Harris, 1969) and the Self-Concept Scale for Children (Lipsett, 1958; Simpson & Meaney, 1979). In addition, we have found sentence completion techniques (Hart, 1986) and projective drawings (e.g., Cummings, 1986), such as the House-Tree-Person Technique (Buck, 1948), to be useful in the qualitative assessment of developmentally disabled children and adolescents. While these measures provide information about the individual's developmental level, visual-motor integration, and personality organization, they are also helpful in identifying emotional issues for individual psychotherapy that have not been verbalized for a number of possible reasons, including communication disorder.

Clinical Management

Approaches to the treatment of an individual with mental retardation, reflecting the thorough assessment of intellectual, adaptive, and emotional/behavioral functioning, are first set forth in an individualized education plan (IEP). Consequent to the passage of PL 94-142, the Education for All

Handicapped Children Act of 1975, a broad range of services has been made available to those with special needs. Educational and treatment requirements of these numerous individuals, however, far outweigh present and foreseeable service capacities (Jacobson, 1991). Reasons for this disparity relate, first, to the growing numbers of children and adolescents identified with respect to need, and second, to the cost-cutting demands placed upon public human service agencies (see Jacobson, 1991). Whereas fiscal considerations have significantly altered the structure of service delivery systems, approaches to treatment of individual children and adolescents have remained theoretically unchanged. This section will survey treatment modalities that have proven most effective with mentally retarded children and adolescents, with the understanding that the level of care and setting (i.e., residential, inpatient, day treatment, or outpatient) may vary across individuals. The reader is referred to Jacobson (1991) for a review of administrative and policy dimensions of developmental disabilities services.

Behavior Therapy

Behavioral approaches to treatment are based on the hypothesis that maladaptive response patterns are learned, that is, acquired through realization of their function in achieving some (presumably desirable or appetitive) effect on the environment. This realization need not be a conscious one. Within this perspective, an understanding of the functional significance of a behavior is gained through analysis of the conditions antecedent and consequent to its occurrence. The process of delineating the antecedents, behavior, and consequences is referred to as functional analysis (e.g., Iwata, Dorsey, Slifer, Bauman, & Richman, 1982), and it is undertaken both during the initial interview and through subsequent direct observational assessment. Treatment involves removal of the consequence identified as maintaining the undesirable behavior (extinction), as well as provision of a reward contingent upon the performance of desirable, adaptive behaviors (positive reinforcement).

The procedures noted above are based on well-established principles in traditional behavioral psychology: behavior that is rewarded contingent upon its occurrence will increase in frequency and become successively strengthened (principle of reinforcement), and previously rewarded behavior that is contingently ignored (i.e., unrewarded or unreinforced) will occur with decreased frequency and become successively weakened (Skinner, 1938). In fact, the vast majority of behavior therapy and cognitive-behavioral procedures applied with mentally retarded children and adolescents are derived from these basic principles (See Barrett et al., 1992, for a review). It is important to note that the effective management of contingencies and successful modification of behavior are dependent on an interpersonal context (see Russo, 1990). Accordingly, a strong emphasis should be placed on the person managing contingencies (e.g., teacher, parent, treatment worker) and his or her relationship with the patient (Barrett et al., 1992).

Application of behavior therapy and cognitive-behavioral approaches is predicated on the behavior analyst's ability to observe publicly and reliably the behavior(s) targeted for change. Thus behaviors that may be operationalized in observable, quantifiable terms are most suitable for behavioral treatment (e.g., aggression, self-injury, oppositional behavior). In contrast, some internalizing (e.g., depression) and systemic (e.g., family dysfunction) problems may be difficult to observe or measure reliably and may be best approached through an alternative mode of treatment or through combined use of behavioral, cognitive-behavioral, and other approaches (e.g., pharmacotherapy).

Individual Psychotherapy

Use of individual psychotherapy with mentally retarded persons has been restricted and remains controversial among many professionals. One of the primary sources of criticism relates to limitations of the mentally retarded in using verbal mediators and/or symbolic representational systems. As Sigman (1985) asserts, "this line of argument is faulty for two reasons; first because the delineation of psychotherapy is too narrow and, second, because the description of the abilities of mentally retarded individuals is oversimplified" (p. 260).

Individual psychotherapies encompass a broad range of treatment approaches from the more supportive/directive to the insight-oriented/less directive (see Rockland, 1989). Moreover, alternatives to verbal exploration (e.g., play or art therapy) have proven quite useful with younger or developmentally delayed individuals, as well as those with limited verbal abilities (Jakab, 1982).

In light of the difficulties experienced by many developmentally disabled persons in establishing and maintaining relationships and the profound implications of these difficulties for adjustment and adaptation (Barrett et al., 1992), we view individual psychotherapy as an important and useful mode of intervention. Consistent with many definitions, psychotherapy is conceptualized as a treatment *process* undertaken between the identified patient and mental health professional. Barrett et al. (1992) identified two broad goals for the dually diagnosed, developmentally disabled patient and therapist engaged in this process: to explore and ameliorate patterns of dysfunctional relating in the child's life, and to increase the range of the child's coping abilities.

As implied by the breadth of these aims, the therapeutic process itself may take any number of forms and directions. Indeed, the heterogeneity within this population demands that therapists be flexible in their approaches. Important variables to consider include chronological age, level of cognitive functioning, and level of emotional disturbance (Leland, 1983; Sigman, 1985). With regard to developmental factors, Nuffield (1986) suggested that although some older and higher-functioning individuals can make use of purely verbal methods, the majority of children will respond best to a technique that utilizes play materials. Leland (1983) has proposed a fourfold classification of play therapy approaches based on structure, materials, and methods, with selection of the appropriate technique based on evaluation of the patient variables noted above.

Independent of the specific approach to psychotherapy, transactions among patient and therapist provide the basis for modifying the child's pattern of relating to others while also introducing and demonstrating alternative means of coping with emotional problems (see Nuffield, 1986, and Sigman, 1985, for thorough descriptions of the psychotherapy process). The generalization of psychotherapy goals is often supported by concurrent family and group therapies. Goldenberg (1985) is recommended reading for those interested in issues related to family therapy with developmentally disabled individuals.

Group Therapies

Group therapies with mentally retarded children and adolescents share the goals outlined previously for individual psychotherapy, although these goals exist within the context of a peer group rather than a dyadic relationship. Approaches vary from the more structured, which focus on the training of particular skills (e.g., social skills, problem-solving techniques), to the relatively less structured and more process oriented. As Barrett et al. (1992) observed, developmentally disabled children and adolescents may become isolated from their peer group. Reasons for this social isolation range from a lack of social "know-how" to psychiatric difficulties, both of which limit opportunities for positive interpersonal experiences. Moreover, developmentally disabled individuals are accustomed to seeking support from adults rather than from their peers (Zigler & Burack, 1989).

Group therapies allow participants to experience their peers as sources of support while also providing a forum in which to address feelings related to shared issues (e.g., the experience of feeling different, difficulties associated with establishing and maintaining friendships, family problems; Barrett et al., 1992). Whereas diversity in terms of patient composition (e.g., levels of cognitive functioning, types of presenting complaint, physical disabilities) might be viewed as a major drawback to group process, Sigman (1985) reported that "patients appeared to learn from this amalgam that there are numerous ways in which one can be 'handicapped' and, conversely, that each of them had different areas of competence" (p. 271). Nonetheless, it is important to note that the therapist(s), in attending to group conduct and the heterogeneity among participants, must take a very active role (Berkovitz & Sugar, 1975; Sigman, 1985; Sternlicht, 1965). Accordingly, such facilitative activities as generating topics for discussion, prompting members to participate, repeating and/or reframing statements, and relating material to associated issues are often a necessary part of the therapist's administration of a group session (Sigman, 1985).

This strategy applies equally to the more focused approaches to group treatment; the therapist again must be cognizant of the variability among group members and must assume active leadership in conducting individual sessions. Perhaps the most frequently employed groups of the more struc-tured type focus on the acquisition of social skills necessary for developing friendships. The training of specific behavioral sequences (e.g., introducing oneself, maintaining a conversation) generally involves the differentiation of individual steps or requisite behaviors (e.g., gaining the person's atten-tion, using eye contact, knowing what to say), modeling by the therapist, practice using role play, and feedback from peers and therapist regarding performance (see Schloss & Schloss, 1987, for a thorough review of the research on social skills training with mentally retarded persons).

We have found group training of cognitive-behavioral problem-solving techniques to be quite useful in our work with dually diagnosed, develop-mentally disabled children and adolescents. Briefly, group members are introduced to a four-step procedure for addressing difficult emotions and situations: (a) identifying the problem, (b) generating many alternative courses of action, (c) selecting and enacting a potential solution, and (d) evaluating consequences (efficacy) with respect to self and others. The ini-tial phase of the group focuses on rote memory for the problem-solving steps. Subsequently the four-step process is applied in the discussion and role playing of specific hypothetical scenarios and real-life problems intro-duced by individual group members. Finally, training in the use of particu-lar skills (e.g., ignoring, relaxation) is pursued as an adjunct to the problem-solving program. Our experience has been that the children and adolescents who participate in the problem-solving group derive significant esteem from their ability to self-manage and to assume a more independent role in resolving interpersonal difficulties.

Pharmacotherapy

Pharmacotherapy is among the most prevalent forms of treatment used with developmentally disabled individuals (Aman & Singh, 1988). Within residential institutions, between 50% and 67% of mentally retarded patients receive either psychotropic (i.e., behavior-modifying) or anticon-vulsant medications (Aman & Singh, 1988). As one would expect, pharma-cotherapy is less prevalent among mentally retarded individuals living in the community, where combined estimates of psychotropic and antiepileptic drug use range from 36% to 48% (Aman & Singh, 1988). Importantly, the surveys from which these data were compiled generally involved adult patients. Relatively little information is available with regard to prescribed drug use specifically among developmentally disabled children and adolescents.

As Aman and Singh (1991) note, use of pharmacological agents with the mentally retarded has most often been directed toward suppressing nonspecific symptoms and maladaptive behaviors rather than toward treating well-defined syndromes. This circumstance is likely related to the relative difficulty in establishing clear-cut diagnoses in this population (see Szymanski, 1985, for a review of the diagnostic process with mentally retarded persons). It has been reported (Aman & Singh, 1991) that psychoactive medications are most commonly prescribed for the treatment of aggressiveness (29%), hyperactivity (24%), self-injury (19%), excitability (12%), screaming (10%), and anxiety (8%) in mentally retarded individuals.

Of particular concern is the misuse of medications for *managing* the behavior of mentally retarded persons. Bates, Smeltzer, and Arnoczky (1986) estimated that between 39% and 54% of the psychoactive medications administered to mentally retarded individuals were prescribed inappropriately. Indeed, Barrett et al. (1992) noted that many patients admitted to their program for developmentally disabled children and adolescents present with polypharmacy among their chief complaints.

Despite the criticisms that can be leveled over the misuse of medications with mentally retarded patients, pharmacotherapy remains an effective mode of treatment when administered judiciously. Thus Barrett et al. (1992) support pharmacological treatment when it is "subjected to the same stringent analysis as behavior therapy and involves the routine use of double-blind, placebo-controlled methodology and single-subject experimental designs that allow for the partitioning of relative therapeutic effect" (pp. 142–143).

Summary

The history of mental retardation as a field of scientific inquiry has been punctuated by advances in diagnostic, assessment, and treatment practices, with recent leaps toward dispelling long-lived misconceptions. In particular, the frequent coexistence of emotional disturbance with mental retardation has been recognized (e.g., Matson & Barrett, 1982a, 1993; Szymanski & Tanguay, 1980). Moreover, it is increasingly appreciated that the label "mentally retarded" does *not* capture a consistent set of attributes, nor does it describe a homogeneous population. "In fact, there is a much wider gap between a mildly retarded, self-supporting adult and a profoundly retarded one, than between two randomly picked persons of normal intelligence" (Szymanski, 1985, p. 249).

As suggested earlier, one of the most significant advances in the diagnosis and assessment of mental retardation was the shift from unidimensional (i.e., IQ alone) to multidimensional conceptualization. Correspondingly, it is important that clinicians not limit their treatment approaches to a single modality or to a strict focus on the alleviation of disturbing behaviors/symptoms. Integrative approaches to the treatment of people with developmental disabilities should follow the comprehensive assessment of limitations, competencies, and life circumstances.

References

Abuelo, D. N. (1991). Genetic disorders. In J. L. Matson & J. A. Mulick (Eds.), *Handbook of mental retardation* (2nd ed., pp. 97–114). New York: Pergamon.

Achenbach, T. M., & Edelbrock, C. S. (1983). *Manual for the Child Behavior Checklist and Revised Child Behavior Profile.* Burlington: University of Vermont, Department of Psychiatry.

Aman, M. G. (1991). *Assessing psychopathology and behavior problems in persons with mental retardation: A review of available instruments.* Rockville, MD: U.S. Department of Health and Human Services.

Aman, M. G., & Singh, N. N. (1983). *Aberrant Behavior Checklist.* Canterbury, New Zealand: University of Canterbury.

Aman, M. G., & Singh, N. N. (1988). Patterns of drug use, methodological considerations, measurement techniques, and future trends. In M. G. Aman & N. N. Singh (Eds.), *Psychopharmacology of the developmental disabilities* (pp. 1–28). New York: Springer-Verlag.

Aman, M. G., & Singh, N. N. (1991). Pharmacological intervention. In J. L. Matson & J. A. Mulick (Eds.), *Handbook of mental retardation* (2nd ed., pp. 347–372). New York: Pergamon.

American Association on Mental Retardation. (1992). *Mental retardation: Definition, classification, and systems of supports* (9th ed.). Washington, DC: Author.

American Psychiatric Association. (1987). *Diagnostic and statistical manual of mental disorders* (rev. 3rd. ed.). Washington, DC: Author.

American Psychiatric Association. (1994). *Diagnostic and statistical manual of mental disorders* (4th ed.)

Baroff, G. S. (1986). *Mental retardation: Nature, cause, and management* (2nd ed.). Washington, DC: Hemisphere.

Barrett, R. P., Tylenda, B., Kaminer, Y., & Feinstein, C. (1986). *The Affective Behavior Checklist: A behavioral assessment tool for use in mentally retarded children and adolescents with mood disorders.* Unpublished manuscript, Brown University.

Barrett, R. P., Walters, A. S., Mercurio, A. F., Klitzke, M., & Feinstein, C. (1992). Mental retardation and psychiatric disorders. In V. B. Van Hasselt & D. J.

Kolko (Eds.), *Inpatient behavior therapy for children and adolescents* (pp. 113–149). New York: Plenum.

Bates, W. J., Smeltzer, D. J., & Arnoczky, S. M. (1986). Appropriate and inappropriate use of psychotherapeutic medications for institutionalized mentally retarded persons. *American Journal of Mental Deficiency, 90,* 363–370.

Bayley, N. (1969). *Bayley Scales of Infant Development.* New York: Psychological Corporation.

Berkovitz, I. H., & Sugar, M. (1975). Indications and contraindications for young psychotherapy. In M. Sugar (Ed.), *The adolescent in group and family therapy* (pp. 3–26). New York: Brunner/Mazel.

Binet, A., & Simon, T. (1905). Methodes nouvelles pour le diagnostic du niveau intellectuel des anormaux. *L'Annee Psychologigue, 11,* 191–244.

Buck, J. N. (1948). The H-T-P technique, a qualitative and quantitative method. *Journal of Clinical Psychology, 4,* 317–396.

Burgemeister, B., Blum, L. H., & Lorge, I. (1959). *Columbia Mental Maturity Scale.* New York: Harcourt, Brace, and World.

Cattell, P. (1950). *The measurement of intelligence in infants and young children.* New York: Psychological Corporation.

Cummings, J. A. (1986). Projective drawings. In H. M. Knoff (Ed.), *The assessment of child and adolescent personality.* New York: Guilford.

Dunn, L. M. (1965). *Expanded manual for the Peabody Picture Vocabulary Test.* Minneapolis, MN: American Guidance Service.

Dunn, L. M., & Markwardt, F. C., Jr. (1970). *Peabody Individual Achievement Test.* Circle Pines, MN: American Guidance Service.

Edgerton, R. B. (1991). Perspectives on the prevention of mild mental retardation. In F. J. Menolascino & J. A. Stark (Eds.), *Preventive and curative intervention in mental retardation* (pp. 325–342). Baltimore, MD: Brookes.

Feinstein, C., Kaminer, Y., Barrett, R. P., & Tylenda, B. (1988). The assessment of mood and affect in developmentally disabled children and adolescents: The Emotional Disorders Rating Scale. *Research in Developmental Disabilities, 9,* 109–121.

Fiedler, C. R., & Antorak, R. F. (1991). Advocacy. In J. L. Matson & J. A. Mulick (Eds.), *Handbook of mental retardation* (2nd ed., pp. 23–32). New York: Pergamon.

Foster-Gaitskell, D., & Pratt, C. (1989). Comparison of parent and teacher ratings of adaptive behavior of children with mental retardation. *American Journal of Mental Retardation, 94,* 177–181.

Frame, C., & Matson, J. L. (1987). *Handbook of assessment in childhood psychotherapy.* New York: Plenum Press.

Gesell, A. (1949). *Gesell Developmental Schedules.* New York: Psychological Corporation.

Goddard, H. H. (1908). The Binet and Simon tests of intellectual capacity. *Training School, 5,* 3–9.

Goddard, H. H. (1910). A measuring scale of intelligence. *Training School, 6,* 146–155.

Goldenberg, I. (1985). Family therapy with a dual disability client. In M. Sigman (Ed.), *Children with emotional disorders and developmental disabilities: Assessment and treatment* (pp. 315–324). Orlando: Grune & Stratton.

Goyette, C. H., Conners, C. K., & Ulrich, R. F. (1979). Normative data on revised Conners parent and teacher rating scales. *Journal of Abnormal Child Psychology, 6*, 221–236.

Grossman, H. J. (1973). *Manual on terminology and classification in mental retardation*. Washington, DC: American Association on Mental Deficiency.

Grossman, H. J. (Ed.). (1983). *Classification in mental retardation*. Washington, DC: American Association on Mental Deficiency.

Gualtieri, C. T. (1982). Foreword. In J. L. Matson & R. P. Barrett (Eds.), *Psychopathology in the mentally retarded* (pp. ix–xi). New York: Grune and Stratton.

Hart, D. H. (1986). The sentence completion techniques. In H. D. Knoff (Ed.), *The assessment of child and adolescent personality*. New York: Guilford.

Heber, R. F. (1959). A manual on terminology and classification in mental retardation. *American Journal on Mental Deficiency, 64*(Suppl.).

Iwata, B. A., Dorsey, M. F., Slifer, K. J., Bauman, K. E., & Richman, G. S. (1982). Toward a functional analysis of self-injury. *Analysis and Intervention in Developmental Disabilities, 2*, 3–20.

Jacobson, J. W. (1991). Administrative and policy dimensions of developmental disabilities services. In J. L. Matson & J. A. Mulick (Eds.), *Handbook of mental retardation* (2nd ed., pp. 3–22). New York: Pergamon.

Jakab, I. (1982). Psychiatric disorders in mental retardation: Recognition, diagnosis, and treatment. In I. Jakab (Ed.), *Mental retardation* (pp. 270–322). New York: Kargan.

Jastak, S., & Wilkinson, G. S. (1984). *Wide Range Achievement Test-Revised*. Wilmington, DE: Jastak Associates.

Jura, M., & Sigman, M. (1985). Evaluation of emotional disorders using projective techniques with mentally retarded children. In M. Sigman (Ed.), *Children with emotional disorders and developmental disabilities: Assessment and treatment* (pp. 229–248). Orlando, FL: Grune and Stratton.

Kaufman, A. S., & Kaufman, N. L. (1983). *Kaufman Assessment Battery for Children*. Circle Pines, MN: American Guidance Service.

Kaufman, A. S., & Kaufman, N. L. (1985). *Kaufman Test of Educational Achievement*. Circle Pines, MN: American Guidance Service.

Kiely, M. (1987). The prevalence of mental retardation. *Epidemiologic Reviews, 9*, 194–218.

Knapp, L., Barrett, R. P., Groden, G., & Groden, J. (1992). The nature and prevalence of fear in developmentally disabled children and adolescents: A preliminary investigation. *Journal of Physical and Developmental Disabilities, 4*, 195–203.

Leiter, R. G. (1980). *Leiter International Performance Scale instruction manual*. Chicago: Stoelting.

Leland, H. (1983). Play therapy for mentally retarded and developmentally disabled children. In C. E. Schaefer & K. J. O'Connor (Eds.), *Handbook of play therapy* (pp. 436–454). New York: Wiley.

Lipsett, L. P. (1958). A self-concept scale for children and its relation to the children's form of the Manifest Anxiety Scale. *Child Development, 29*, 463–472.

Matson, J. L. (1988). *The PIMRA manual*. Orland Park, IL: International Diagnostic Systems.

Matson, J. L., & Barrett, R. P. (Eds.). (1982a). *Psychopathology in the mentally retarded.* New York: Grune and Stratton.

Matson, J. L., & Barrett, R. P. (1982b). Affective disorders. In J. L. Matson & R. P. Barrett (Eds.). *Psychopathology in the mentally retarded* (pp. 121–146). New York: Grune and Stratton.

Matson, J. L., & Barrett, R. P. (Eds.). (1993). *Psychopathology in the mentally retarded* (2nd ed.). San Antonio, TX: Psychological Corporation.

Matson, J. L., & Mulick, J. A. (Eds.). (1991). *Handbook of mental retardation* (2nd ed.). New York: Pergamon.

McLaren, J., & Bryson, S. E. (1987). Review of recent epidemiological studies of mental retardation: Prevalence, associated disorders, and etiology. *American Journal of Mental Retardation, 92,* 243–254.

Merrill-Palmer Scale of Mental Tests. (1948). New York: Harcourt, Brace, and World.

Morgenstern, M., & Klass, E. (1991). Standard intelligence tests and related assessment techniques. In J. L. Matson & J. A. Mulick (Eds.), *Handbook of mental retardation* (2nd ed., pp. 195–210). New York: Pergamon.

Nihira, K., Foster, R., Schellhaas, N., & Leland, H. (1974). *AAMR Adaptive Behavior Scale manual.* Austin, TX: Pro-Ed.

Nuffield, E. J. (1986). Counseling and psychotherapy. In R. P. Barrett (Ed.), *Severe behavior disorders in the mentally retarded: Nondrug approaches to treatment* (pp. 207–234). New York: Plenum.

Ollendick, T. H., & Ollendick, D. G. (1982). Anxiety disorders. In J. L. Matson & R. P. Barrett (Eds.), *Psychopathology in the mentally retarded* (pp. 77–120). New York: Grune and Stratton.

Ollendick, T. H., Oswald, D. P., & Ollendick, D. G. (1993). Anxiety disorder in mentally retarded persons. In J. L. Matson & R. P. Barrett (Eds.), *Psychopathology in the mentally retarded* (2nd ed., pp. 41–85). San Antonio: Psychological Corporation.

Piers, E. V., & Harris, D. B. (1969). *The Piers-Harris Children's Self-Concept Scale.* Nashville, TN: Counselor Recordings and Tests.

Pueschel, S. M., & Thuline, H. C. (1991). Chromosome disorders. In J. L. Matson & J. A. Mulick (Eds.), *Handbook of mental retardation* (2nd ed., pp. 115–138). New York: Pergamon.

Quay, H. C., & Peterson, D. R. (1983). *Revised Behavior Problem Checklist.* Coral Gables, FL: University of Miami.

Reiss, S. (1988). *Test manual for the Reiss Screen for Maladaptive Behavior.* Orland Park, IL: International Diagnostic Systems.

Reiss, S., Levitan, G. W., & Szysko, J. (1982). Emotional disturbance and mental retardation: Diagnostic overshadowing. *American Journal of Mental Deficiency, 86,* 567–574.

Reiss, S., & Szysko, J. (1983). Diagnostic overshadowing and professional experience with mentally retarded persons. *American Journal of Mental Deficiency, 87,* 396–402.

Repp, A. C., & Deitz, D. E. (1983). Mental retardation. In T. H. Ollendick & M. Hersen (Eds.), *Handbook of child psychopathology* (pp. 97–122). New York: Plenum.

Reynolds, W. M. (1989). *Self-Report Depression Questionnaire (SRDQ) administration booklet*. Odessa, FL: Psychological Assessment Resources.

Rockland, L. H. (1989). *Supportive psychotherapy: A psychodynamic approach*. New York: Basic Books.

Romanczyk, R. G., & Kistner, J. A. (1982). Psychosis and mental retardation: Issues of coexistence. In J. L. Matson & R. P. Barrett (Eds.), *Psychopathology in the mentally retarded* (pp. 147–194). New York: Grune and Stratton.

Russo, D. C. (1990). A requiem for the passing of the three-term contingency. *Behavior Therapy, 21,* 153–165.

Rutter, M. Tizard, J., Yule, W., Graham, P., & Whitmore, K. (1976). Research report: Isle of Wight studies, 1964–74. *Psychological Medicine, 6,* 313–332.

Sameroff, A. J. (1982). The environmental context of developmental disabilities. In D. Bricker (Ed.), *Intervention with at-risk and handicapped infants: From research to application* (pp. 141–152). Baltimore, MD: University Park Press.

Sameroff, A. J., & Chandler, M. J. (1975). Reproductive risk and the continuum of caretaker casualty. In F. D. Horowitz, M. Hetherington, S. Scarr-Salapatek, & G. Siegel (Eds.), *Review of child development research* (Vol. 4, pp. 187–244). Chicago: University of Chicago Press.

Sattler, J. M. (1988). *Assessment of children* (3rd ed.). San Diego, CA: Author.

Schloss, P. J., & Schloss, C. N. (1987). A critical review of social skills research in mental retardation. *Advances in Developmental Disabilities, 1,* 107–151.

Seltzer, M. M., & Seltzer, G. B. (1991). Classification and social status. In J. L. Matson & J. A. Mulick (Eds.), *Handbook of mental retardation* (2nd ed., pp. 166–180). New York: Pergamon.

Sigman, M. (1985). Individual and group psychotherapy with mentally retarded adolescents. In M. Sigman (Ed.), *Children with emotional disorders and developmental disabilities: Assessment and treatment* (pp. 259–176). Orlando, FL: Grune and Stratton.

Simpson, H. M., & Meaney, C. (1979). Effects of learning to ski on the self-concept of mentally retarded children. *American Journal of Mental Deficiency, 84,* 25–29.

Skinner, B. F. (1938). *The behavior of organisms*. New York: Appleton-Century-Crofts.

Sloan, W., & Birch, J. W. (1955). A rationale for degrees of mental retardation. *American Journal of Mental Deficiency, 60,* 258–264.

Slosson, R. L. (1963). *Slosson Intelligence Test*. New York: Slosson Educational Publications.

Sparrow, S. S., Balla, D. A., & Cicchetti, D. V. (1984). *Vineland Adaptive Behavior Scale*. Circle Pines, MN: American Guidance Service.

Sternlicht, M. (1965). Psychotherapeutic techniques with mentally retarded children: A review and critique. *Psychiatric Quarterly, 39,* 84–90.

Szymanski, L. S. (1985). Diagnosis of mental disorders in mentally retarded persons. In M. Sigman (Ed.), *Children with emotional disorders and developmental disabilities: Assessment and treatment* (pp. 249–258). Orlando, FL: Grune and Stratton.

Szymanski, L. S., & Tanguay, P. E. (Eds.). (1980). *Emotional disorders of mentally retarded persons*. Baltimore, MD: University Park Press.

Terman, L. M. (1916). *The measurement of intelligence*. Boston: Houghton Mifflin.

Terman, L. M., & Merrill, M. A. (1937). *Measuring intelligence*. Boston: Houghton Mifflin.

Terman, L. M., & Merrill, M. A. (1960). *Stanford-Binet Intelligence Scale: Manual for the third revision, Form L-M*. Boston: Houghton Mifflin.

Thorndike, R. L., Hagen, E. P., & Sattler, J. M. (1986). *Stanford-Binet Intelligence Scale: Guide for administering and scoring the fourth edition*. Chicago: Riverside.

Walters, A. S., Feinstein, C. B., & Barrett, R. P. (in press). Borderline intellectual functioning and mild mental retardation. In J. Noshpitz & N. E. Alessi (Eds.), *Handbook of adolescent psychiatry*. New York: Basic Books.

Wechsler, D. (1974). *Manual for the Wechsler Intelligence Scale for Children-Revised*. San Antonio, TX: Psychological Corporation.

Wechsler, D. (1991). *Wechsler Intelligence Scale for Children-third edition manual*. San Antonio, TX: Psychological Corporation.

Wilson, W. M. (1992). The Stanford-Binet: Fourth edition and Form L-M in assessment of young children with mental retardation. *Mental Retardation, 30*, 81–84.

Woodcock, R. W. (1977). *Woodcock-Johnson Psycho-Educational Battery: Technical Report*. Allen, TX: DLM Teaching Resources.

Zigler, E., Balla, D., & Hodapp, R. (1984). On the definition and classification of mental retardation. *American Journal of Mental Deficiency, 89*, 215–230.

Zigler, E., & Burack, J. A. (1989). Personality development and the dually diagnosed person. *Research in Developmental Disabilities, 10*, 225–240.

17
Gender Identity Disorder (Transsexualism) and Transvestic Fetishism

Claire B. Lowry Sullivan
Susan J. Bradley
Kenneth J. Zucker

This chapter examines several psychosexual disorders that can be diagnosed in adolescents. In DSM-III-R (American Psychiatric Association [APA], 1987), these disorders included transsexualism; gender identity disorder of adolescence or adulthood, nontranssexual type (GIDAANT); gender identity disorder not otherwise specified (GIDNOS); and transvestic fetishism. In addition, this chapter will also consider some diagnostic issues pertaining to homosexuality during adolescence. As is well known, homosexuality per se was delisted as a psychiatric diagnosis prior to publication of DSM-III (APA, 1980; see, e.g., Bayer, 1981; Bayer & Spitzer, 1982; Spitzer, 1981). Perhaps less well known has been the course of its two successors. In DSM-III, homosexuality per se was replaced by the diagnosis of "ego-dystonic homosexuality." This diagnosis was delisted in DSM-III-R 7 years later, but a person distressed about his or her sexual orientation could now receive a diagnosis of "sexual disorder not otherwise specified."

Several terms are useful in conceptualizing adolescent psychosexual conditions. Many clinicians and researchers who study psychosexual development accept, at minimum, a scheme consisting of three main terms: *gender identity, gender role,* and *sexual orientation* (e.g., Green, 1974; Money, 1973). This scheme evolved in part from the original work of Money (1952; Money, Hampson, & Hampson, 1955) with physically hermaphroditic children (see also Money, 1985, 1991), which demonstrated the importance of conceptualizing gender identity as a distinct psychological variable. A hermaphroditic child born with ambiguous or anomalous genitalia highlighted the salience of gender as a biosocial category—should the "sex of assignment" be announced as male or female? Despite the abnormal sexual biology of hermaphroditic children, it was concluded that these children could in fact develop a normal gender identity if they were assigned to one gender or the other early in life and then reared in an "unambiguous" manner (Hampson, 1955; Money, Hampson, & Hampson, 1956, 1957). Stoller (1964) later reiterated that ongoing uncertainty about a child's gender status on the part of significant others (e.g., parents, professionals) often resulted in the development of a conflicted or "hermaphroditic" gender identity.

Over the years, *gender identity* has been understood to refer to a person's basic sense of self as a male or a female (Stoller, 1965, 1968a). The reference to a *sense* of self connotes an affective or emotional component to gender identity; clinically, this shows itself most acutely in adolescents and adults requesting sex reassignment surgery because of the felt sense of *gender dysphoria*. But whatever affective appraisal an individual has about his or her gender identity (positive, negative, ambivalent, indifferent), there is good empirical evidence that gender identity begins with the cognitive capacity to discriminate males from females and to apply this knowledge to one self. Although the perceptual basis of gender discrimination may be present in infants under 1 year of age (Serbin, 1991), it is unlikely that this ability is accompanied by conscious awareness.

Between the second and third year of life, however, children develop the capacity for a more conscious type of gender discrimination, which seems to serve an organizing function for the expression of at least some sex-typed behaviors. Fagot, Leinbach, and Hagan (1986), for example, tested toddlers between the ages of 21 and 40 months on a gender-labeling task, in which they were required to discriminate between pictures of boys and girls. Over a 4-week period, these toddlers were subsequently observed in a naturalistic play setting in which several sex-typed behaviors were assessed. It was found that the toddlers (mean age 30 months) who "passed" the gender-labeling task spent more time playing with same-sex peers than did the toddlers (mean age 26 months) who "failed" the task; the girls who passed the task were also less aggressive than were the girls who failed it, even with the age difference controlled. These findings point to the important role of cognition as an organizing variable in the display of sex-dimorphic behaviors (see Maccoby, 1988).

Gender role can be defined as those behaviors, attitudes, and personality traits that a society, in a given culture and historical period, defines as masculine or feminine (i.e., as more appropriate for the male or female social role). By definition, this implies that gender roles are completely arbitrary, a view that would not be universally shared by researchers in the field. The terms *sex-preferred* and *sex dimorphic* are descriptively more neutral with regard to origins, but they run the risk of including behaviors that are relatively unrelated to the use of the term *gender role* in psychology, sociology, and anthropology. For example, art activities seem to be sex-preferred by female preschoolers (Fagot, 1977), yet it is not clear if such behavior is considered to be "feminine" by the culture at large (see also Fagot, 1978).

In any case, among children, the measurement of gender role behavior typically includes several easy-to-observe phenomena: affiliative preference for same- versus opposite-sex peers, interest in rough-and-tumble play, fantasy roles, toy choices, and dress-up play. Normative empirical research has established that these behaviors are strongly sex dimorphic (e.g., DiPietro, 1981; Fagot, 1977; Maccoby & Jacklin, 1987; Zucker, Bradley, Corter, Doering, & Finegan, 1980). In late childhood and adolescence, gender role can also be measured in relation to personality attributes that have stereotypical masculine or feminine connotations (see, e.g., Alpert-Gillis & Connell, 1989; Huston, 1985).

Lastly, *sexual orientation* can be defined as a person's preferred mode of responsiveness to sexual stimuli. In contemporary sexology, sexual orientation is most validly assessed by such psychophysiological techniques as penile plethysmography and vaginal photoplethysmography (e.g., Freund, 1963, 1977; Rosen & Beck, 1988). Becker and Kaplan (1988) have recently described the use of psychophysiological techniques with adolescent sex offenders, but this line of research is beyond the scope of the current chapter. The most salient dimension of sexual orientation is probably the sex of one's partner. This stimulus class is obviously how one defines a person's sexual orientation as heterosexual, bisexual, or homosexual.

There are, however, other stimulus classes that elicit sexual arousal and have relevance in the diagnosis of paraphilic disorders. For example, the stimulus class of age is of importance in determining whether a person's sexual orientation is complicated by an age-atypical sexual preference, as in the cases of pedophilia (prepubertal children) and hebephilia (pubescent children, usually around the age of 11 to 14 years), regardless of whether the superordinate sexual orientation is heterosexual or homosexual (e.g., Freund, Watson, & Rienzo, 1989). The use of fetishistic objects (e.g., women's undergarments), as in the case of transvestic fetishism, is another important stimulus class that needs to be considered in assessing sexual orientation.

It is important to uncouple the concept of sexual orientation from another psychosexual term, *sexual identity*. For example, an adolescent or young adult male might report exclusive sexual fantasies of, and interpersonal sexual experiences with, persons of the same sex (a homosexual orientation), yet not label himself to be a homosexual (a sexual identity). In other words, the self-labeling of one's sexual identity may be quite discrepant from a person's predominant mode of sexual fantasy and overt sexual experience (see, e.g., Meyer-Bahlburg et al., 1992). In general, researchers studying identity formation among homosexual adolescents and young adults have attempted to identify stages that occur in the emergence of the sense of oneself as a homosexual (see, e.g., Cass, 1979, 1984, 1990; Herdt, 1989; Martin, 1982; Roesler & Deisher, 1972; Savin-Williams, 1990; Troiden, 1979, 1988). One can apply this perspective to other psychosexual conditions: for example, what is the process by which an adolescent comes to label himself or herself as a transsexual?

Sociologists, particularly those of the social scripting and social constructionist schools, have articulated these issues in a more broad way, arguing that the incorporation of sexual orientation into one's sense of identity is a relatively recent phenomenon, culturally variable, and the result of a complex interplay of sociohistorical events (e.g., D'Emilio, 1983, 1984; Gagnon, 1990; Gagnon & Simon, 1973; Greenberg, 1989; Herdt, 1990; McIntosh, 1968; Nye, 1989; Simon, 1989).

Transsexualism

Description of the Disorder

From a clinical point of view, transsexualism may be considered the most extreme form of cross-gender identification. Adolescents who present with this disorder describe a long-standing feeling of being uncomfortable with their anatomically designated sex. By this, the adolescent is usually indicating a profound discomfort with the basic sense of maleness or femaleness and the gender role expectations associated with being a male or a female. There is usually a request for some form of physical intervention, such as hormonal therapy and surgical sex reassignment.

Historical Background

The idea that children, adolescents, and adults can show a marked anomaly in their gender identity development has been a controversial one. The reasons for this are no doubt multiple and diverse. Historically, the idea that gender identity represents a distinct aspect of the self is relatively recent, at least in scientific circles. For example, Ferenczi (1914/1980), one of Freud's colleagues, seemed to fuse the concepts of gender identity and sexual orientation in his use of the term *subject homoerotics* to describe men who felt and behaved like women. Freud (1925/1961) himself claimed that prior to the oedipal phase (i.e., about the age of 4 to 5), boys and girls were essentially similar in their psychological makeup and made little differentiation among the components of psychosexual development as they are now understood (see above).

As noted earlier, Money's seminal work with physically hermaphroditic children demonstrated the importance of conceptualizing gender identity as a distinct psychological variable. While the psychology of hermaphroditism was being explored and the concept of gender identity articulated, the syndrome of transsexualism began to attract notice. A major scientific watershed was the publication of the Christine Jorgensen case by a Danish endocrinologist (Hamburger, 1953; Hamburger, Sturup, & Dahl-Iverson,

1953). Although other personal and scientific reports along the same lines were available (e.g., Benjamin, 1954; Cauldwell, 1949; Cowell, 1954; Hoyer, 1933; see also Bullough, 1975; Lothstein, 1983), the Jorgensen case helped crystallize the notion that the adults' discontent with their gender identity might impel them to seek radical physical transformations. The relevance of this adult syndrome for the study of children and adolescents was disclosed by life history interviews in which it appeared that the patients' gender dysphoria, or discontent, originated in childhood. Many transsexual adults recalled an extensive childhood history of behaving like, and wishing to be of, the opposite sex. Such recollections served as one rationale for the idea that children and adolescents "at risk" for transsexualism could be identified and studied *in statu nascendi* (Green, 1968; Stoller, 1968b).

Clinical Picture

Although there is a considerable clinical and research literature on gender identity disorders in childhood (e.g., Coates, 1985; Green, 1974, 1987; Zucker, 1985; Zucker & Bradley, in press; Zucker & Green, 1992) and in adulthood (e.g., Benjamin, 1966; Blanchard & Steiner, 1990; Docter, 1988; Lothstein, 1983; Pfäfflin & Junge, 1992; Steiner, 1985; Stoller, 1968b, 1975; Tully, 1992; Walinder, 1967), there is relatively little systematic work on this phenomenon in adolescence, and much of the available literature consists of case reports (e.g., Davenport & Harrison, 1977; Dulcan & Lee, 1984; Kronberg, Tyano, Apter, & Wijsenbeek, 1981; Lothstein, 1980; Newman, 1970; Philippopoulos, 1964; Westhead, Olson, & Meyer, 1990).

The DSM-III-R criteria for transsexualism are shown in Table 17–1. These criteria emphasize the degree to which a cross-gender identity has become fixed and the entrenchment of a belief that sex reassignment offers the best solution to one's gender dysphoria. Table 17–2 shows the DSM-III-R criteria for the diagnosis of GIDAANT. This diagnosis is used for those persons who present with significant gender dysphoria, but for whom surgical sex reassignment has not become a central preoccupation.

Over the several years following DSM-III-R, the subcommittee on gender identity disorders for DSM-IV considered various diagnostic issues, including the clinical utility of the GIDAANT diagnosis (see Bradley et al., 1991). One of the subcommittee's main recommendations was to retain in DSM-IV only one primary diagnosis—termed "gender identity disorder"—with diagnostic criteria that could be applied to patients at different phases of the life cycle (i.e., childhood, adolescence, and adulthood), thus obviating the necessity of arbitrary age-related delineations (e.g., puberty). The DSM-IV (APA, 1994) diagnostic criteria, which are shown in Table 17–3, were separated for children and adolescents/adults and reflect putative developmental differences in clinical presentation.

Table 17–1
DSM-III-R Diagnostic Criteria for Transsexualism

A. Persistent discomfort and sense of inappropriateness about one's assigned sex.

B. Persistent preoccupation for at least 2 years with getting rid of one's primary and secondary sex characteristics and acquiring the sex characteristics of the other sex.

C. The person has reached puberty.

Specify history of sexual orientation: asexual, homosexual, heterosexual, or unspecified.

Table 17–2
DSM-III-R Diagnostic Criteria for Gender Identity Disorder of Adolescence or Adulthood, Nontranssexual Type

A. Persistent or recurrent discomfort and sense of inappropriateness about one's assigned sex.

B. Persistent or recurrent cross-dressing in the role of the other sex, either in fantasy or actuality, but not for the purpose of sexual excitement (as in transvestic fetishism).

C. No persistent preoccupation (for at least 2 years) with getting rid of one's primary and secondary sex characteristics and acquiring the sex characteristics of the other sex (as in transsexualism).

D. The person has reached puberty.

Specify history of sexual orientation: asexual, homosexual, heterosexual, or unspecified.

Table 17–3
DSM-IV Diagnostic Criteria for Gender Identity Disorder (Adolescent and Adult Criteria)

A. A strong and persistent cross-gender identification (not merely a desire for any perceived cultural advantages of being the other sex).
   In adolescents and adults, the disturbance is manifested by symptoms such as a stated desire to be the other sex, frequent passing as the other sex, desire to live or be treated as the other sex, or the conviction that he or she has the typical feelings and reactions of the other sex.

B. Persistent discomfort with his or her sex or sense of inappropriateness in the gender role of that sex.
   In adolescents and adults, the disturbance is manifested by symptoms such as preoccupation with getting rid of primary and secondary sex characteristics (e.g., request for hormones, surgery, or other procedures to physically alter sexual characteristics to simulate the other sex) or belief that he or she was born the wrong sex.

C. The disturbance is not concurrent with a physical intersex condition.

D. The disturbance causes clinically significant distress or impairment in social, occupational, or other important areas of functioning.

The following two vignettes illustrates the clinical picture of severe gender identity disorder manifested in adolescence:

Frieda, age 16 (verbal IQ 78; performance IQ 90), was referred by her
family doctor. She has an older brother (age 18). Her parents separated
when she was 14, following years of marital discord and an open affair on
the part of her mother. The family had emigrated from an eastern European country to Canada when Frieda was 8 years old. Currently she divided her time living with her mother and with her father. Her parents had a
middle-class socioeconomic status in their country of origin but felt that
they were less well off in Canada.

Frieda confided in her family doctor that she felt very uncomfortable
as a female, and she requested a sex change operation. Frieda attended the
assessment with her father, who had an only minimal understanding of
the issues; discomfort in speaking in English made it somewhat difficult to
communicate with him. Frieda refused to involve her mother, not wanting
her to know how she felt. Frieda stated that since around age 11 she had
felt increasingly different from other girls. Over this time period, she also
became aware of sexual attractions toward other girls. She reported no
sexual attraction toward boys, but socially she felt quite at ease in their
company. After a recent argument with her father, she told him that she
was gay. Frieda stated that she was quite ashamed of being homosexual
and was afraid that no one would accept her as a lesbian. She thought that
having a sex change operation would make her sexual attraction to girls
more socially acceptable. Frieda had no overt sexual experience and had
never masturbated.

By self-report and her father's confirmation, Frieda recalled that as a
child she never played with dolls, did not like wearing "nice" girl's dresses, and enjoyed the company of boys and their games. She would wear her
hair short and remembered being teased by her peers for being a "fag."
She stated that as a young girl she had always wanted to be a boy.

At the time of the assessment, Frieda's physical appearance was gender
ambiguous. She wore a large T-shirt in order to conceal her breasts, wore
no makeup, and had her long-blonde hair cut in a masculine fashion. She
indicated that strangers were never quite sure if she was a male or a
female.

Apart from her gender identity conflict, Frieda had some other difficulties. She attended a vocational high school and was doing poorly. She
acknowledged being depressed secondary to both her parent's separation
and her gender conflicts. She recalled taking up boxing at the time her
parents separated. She did not report suicidal ideation. Socially, she felt
isolated and lonely.

Psychological testing indicated that Frieda had significant behavioral
and intrapersonal difficulties. On the Teacher's Report Form of the Child
Behavior Checklist (Achenbach & Edelbrock, 1986), Frieda's total behavior problem score fell well within the clinical range. There were three narrow-band elevations (Immature, Delinquent, and Aggressive). The
Depressed and Unpopular narrow-band scales approached the clinical cut-

off. In contrast to Frieda's subdued demeanor during assessment, her Rorschach protocol was permeated with violent, aggressive, and damaged percepts. There was evidence of an extremely vulnerable body ego and poor regulation of primary process material. Throughout the protocol, there were numerous references to broken body parts (e.g., broken ribs, sides of animals torn off, "open brain surgery," and "a person's insides blowing up").

DSM-III-R diagnoses were gender identity disorder of adolescence or adulthood (nontranssexual type) and dysthymia. Differential diagnoses were transsexualism (homosexual type) and sexual disorder not otherwise specified. The GIDAANT diagnosis was given primarily because of uncertainty regarding the chronicity of Frieda's gender dysphoria.

Benjamin, age 14 (verbal IQ 101; performance IQ 111), was referred by an endocrinologist whom the parents had consulted. He had a younger sister (age 11). The parents were of a middle-class background.

The precipitant for the endocrine consultation (the results of which were normal) was that Benjamin had been using the girl's washroom since beginning high school about 6 months prior to the assessment. The principal at the school tried to discuss the situation with Benjamin in the presence of a couple of female friends, who constantly referred to him as "she." Benjamin acknowledged that he preferred being perceived by his schoolmates as a girl. Reports provided by his teachers indicated that he was usually withdrawn and quiet. Socially he was considered off-limits to the boys, as he was apparently known in the school as "the transvestite." The girls seemed more accepting of him. His teachers noted that he frequently complained of physical ailments and would ask to leave the room. By the time of the referral, one of his teachers noted that Benjamin was now wearing makeup, curled his hair, and displayed more "feminine" mannerisms.

During the assessment, Benjamin indicated that he wanted a sex change operation "so that I can dress and do the things I want to." His mother wanted to know if he was "on the right track"—that is, whether sex change surgery was appropriate for him. She was very supportive of this possibility; later in the interview, the mother commented that "he could wind up as a very well-known hairdresser." In contrast, Benjamin's father was very distressed by the situation, commenting "I'm not going to commit suicide . . . but it makes me feel sick inside." During an individual interview, Benjamin acknowledged some sexual interest in boys, but indicated that he had only masturbated twice and at those times thought about himself as a girl sexually involved with a boy. He had no overt sexual experience.

Benjamin's mother recalled that he engaged in extensive cross-gender behavior as a child. Prior to the age of 2, he would pretend to have long hair by putting a towel around his head; this habit continued for years. He played with stereotypical girl's toys and often role-played as a female. Benjamin avoided boys as playmates and did not participate in sports. He always sat to urinate. By the time he reached adolescence, he refused to participate in a religious ritual that signified his maleness.

On the Child Behavior Checklist, Benjamin's parents had very different perceptions of his general behavioral functioning. His mother's sum behavior problem score was well within the range of the nonreferred youngsters in the standardization sample; there were no narrow-band or broad-band elevations. In contrast, the father's sum behavior problem score was almost five times higher, falling well within the clinical range. All nine narrow-band scales were elevated, as were the Internalizing and Externalizing *T* scores. It was felt that these divergent perceptions of Benjamin's functioning were related to long-standing differences in the nature of his relationships to his mother and father, respectively.

The DSM-III diagnosis was transsexualism. Although Benjamin did not have overt sexual experience, it was felt that his sexual orientation in fantasy was of the homosexual type.

In both cases, it was apparent that a childhood history of gender identity disorder was present. At the time of presentation, there remained a profound cross-gender identification. Superimposed on the cross-gender identity was a nascent recognition of an attraction to persons of the same biological sex as the patient. According to DSM-III-R, the sexual orientation would be homosexual, since the reference point is the patient's biological sex; however, it is important to note that the two youngsters described above wished to experience their attraction as heterosexual, since *their* reference point was their own sense of a cross-sex identity.

The sexual orientation of transsexuals is, in fact, one of the more complicated diagnostic and conceptual issues that has been debated by clinicians and researchers in the field. Biological females with transsexualism are almost always homosexual, i.e., they are attracted to other biological females (Blanchard, 1990a). Although there have been some very recent case reports describing female transsexuals with a kind of "heterosexual" orientation (e.g., Blanchard, 1990a; Coleman, Bockting, & Gooren, 1993), the extant clinical literature suggests that these are very unusual cases. Among biological males with transsexualism, however, the distribution of sexual orientation is very different. Some men show a homosexual orientation, whereas other men show a nonhomosexual orientation, i.e., they are heterosexual, bisexual, or asexual (see, e.g., Blanchard, 1985, 1988, 1989, 1990b, 1991).

Like their female counterparts, transsexual males with a homosexual orientation invariably recall a childhood history suggestive of a gender identity disorder. In contrast, transsexual males with a nonhomosexual orientation typically do not recall a childhood history of gender identity disorder. What also distinguishes the homosexual and nonhomosexual men is a history in the latter of transvestic fetishism and usually some sexual attraction to women, which often eventuates in cohabitation or marriage. (Transvestism is a clinical phenomenon that appears to be virtually nonexistent in biological females.)

The clinical picture is thus potentially more complex among adolescent males presenting with transsexualism, because one might anticipate more variability along the sexual orientation dimension. In our own clinic, however, this has not proven to be the case in the sense that almost all of the biological males requesting sex reassignment have been of the homosexual type. This appears to be so because the "natural history" of transsexualism in the nonhomosexual type is slower, perhaps because it has been delayed by the effects of the transvestism. Indeed, Blanchard (1988) has shown that homosexual transsexual adult men present clinically for sex reassignment at a considerably earlier age than do nonhomosexual transsexual adult men.

Course and Prognosis

As noted above, homosexual transsexualism is often preceded by a childhood history of gender identity disorder. In a sense, then, transsexualism during adolescence can be understood as simply a continuation of a childhood gender disturbance, although the adolescent probably has a more complex view of the disorder (e.g., regarding potential physical interventions, impact on others, and sexual relationships).

There are, however, some intriguing long-term differences between youngsters first assessed in childhood and those first assessed in adolescence. For example, Green (1987) reported that only 1 of 44 markedly feminine boys evaluated initially at a mean age of 7.1 years appeared strongly gender dysphoric to the extent of considering sex reassignment surgery when followed up at a mean age of 18.9 years. The majority of these boys, though were homosexual in their sexual orientation. Zucker (1985, 1990a), who has reviewed more generally the follow-up literature on children with gender identity disorder, also notes the bulk of children followed prospectively do not develop transsexualism.

In contrast, adolescents who present with the request for sex reassignment surgery—even if the procedure is only vaguely understood—seem to show a much poorer prognosis for relinquishing their gender dysphoria (e.g., McCauley & Ehrhardt, 1984; Zucker, Bradley, & Gladding, 1986). In our own clinic, preliminary follow-up data have indicated that about one-third of the adolescents received some type of formal hormonal and/or surgical procedure, whereas another one-third remained severely gender dysphoric but did not receive any physical intervention. The majority of the remaining youngsters appeared to resolve their gender dysphoria and were no longer contemplating sex reassignment; almost all of these youngsters appeared to have a homosexual orientation (Zucker et al., 1986).

Age at presentation (i.e., childhood versus adolescence) therefore appears to be a very good predictor of long-term outcome. How might this be understood? One possibility is that the kinds of cases seen in childhood include less severe forms of gender dysphoria, and thus one would not expect such youngsters to develop transsexualism later in life. As implicated by Green's (1987) prospective study, childhood cross-gender identification is strongly associated with later homosexuality. Retrospective studies of homosexual men and women have also demonstrated an association with childhood cross-gender identification (see Bailey & Zucker, in press), but it is important to note that the majority of homosexual men and women with a childhood cross-gender history probably would not have met formal diagnostic criteria for a gender identity disorder. Thus, samples of cross-gender-identified children may be more heterogeneous with regard to severity than samples of adolescents who present with the request for sex reassignment.

Another possibility is that clinical assessment and treatment during childhood interrupt the "natural history" of transsexualism. One would think that helping a child feel more comfortable about his or her gender identity would, if successful, reduce the likelihood that severe gender dysphoria would persist into adolescence. Working backward from our own clinical experience with adolescent transsexuals, we have been impressed with how little, if any, therapeutic intervention these youngsters received during childhood for their gender identity problems. It has been our clinical opinion that the unresolved childhood gender identity problem has been a strong perpetuating factor in accounting for these adolescents' current gender identity difficulties. Unfortunately, controlled treatment studies to test this hypothesis have not been conducted. We are then left with the puzzle of how to differentiate children with gender identity disorder who will or will not develop transsexualism in later life.

Complications

Studies of children with gender identity disorder, almost exclusively with boys, have examined the occurrence of associated psychopathology (see Zucker & Bradley, in press; Zucker & Green, 1992). For example, Zucker & Bradley (in press) assessed a sample of boys with gender identity problems with the Child Behavior Checklist (CBCL; Achenbach & Edelbrock, 1983), a parent report measure that has been factor analyzed to identify dimensions of behavioral disturbance. These boys had indices of psychopathology at a level similar to that of the clinic-referred group in Achenbach and Edelbrock's (1983) standardization sample. Boys with gender identity disorder had significantly more behavior problems on the CBCL than did their male siblings, but did not differ when compared to concurrently assessed, demographically matched clinical controls. It was also found that boys with gender identity disorder had significantly higher Internalizing than Externalizing *T* scores on the CBCL. The predominance of overcontrolled psychopathology is consistent with findings from other investigators using a different behavior problem questionnaire (Rekers & Morey, 1989; Sreenivasan, 1985), observational ratings of "body constriction" (Bates, Bentler, & Thompson, 1979), and clinical diagnoses of separation anxiety and dysthymia (Coates & Person, 1985).

Research on gender-dysphoric adults has also yielded evidence of comorbidity, especially in the realm of personality disorders and high levels of depression, suicide or suicide attempts, substance abuse, and encounters with the law. Psychopathology associated with gender dysphoria is more likely among males than among females (e.g., Levine & Lothstein, 1981; Lothstein, 1983).

Unfortunately, little systematic research has examined the psychological functioning of adolescents with severe gender dysphoria. Clinical experience suggests that functioning is often compromised, much as has been observed in children and adults with severe gender identity conflicts. Depression and suicide attempts appear to be particularly common (Bradley & Zucker, 1984; Zucker & Bradley, in press).

The central question, which bears on etiological issues, is why there are high rates of associated psychopathology in individuals with gender identity disorder. In particular, there is debate about whether the associated psychopathology is secondary to the stigma associated with the disorder or whether the associated psychopathology in some way predisposes the individual to develop a disturbance in gender identity. For a discussion of these issues, the reader is referred elsewhere (e.g., Coates & Person, 1985; Lothstein, 1983; Meyer, 1982; Person & Ovesey, 1974a, 1974b; Stoller, 1975, Zucker, 1990b; Zucker & Bradley, in press; Zucker & Green, 1992).

Epidemiology

Prevalence and Incidence. There are no formal prevalence studies of children with gender identity disorder or adolescents with transsexualism. There are also no empirical data regarding changes in the incidence of gender identity disorder over the past several decades. Meyer-Bahlburg (1985) has characterized gender identity disorder as a "rare phenomenon," though, and there is little doubt that this disorder in children and adolescents is closer in relative prevalence to conditions such as autism than to conditions such as conduct disorder.

One summary account of transsexualism in adults suggested an occurrence of 1 in 24,000 to 37,000 men and 1 in 103,000 to 150,000 women (Meyer-Bahlburg, 1985). This may be somewhat of an underestimate, however, since it was based on the number of persons attending clinics that serve as gateways for surgical and hormonal sex reassignment, which may not see all gender-dysphoric adults.

Referral Rates. During childhood, it has been consistently observed that boys are referred more often than are girls for concerns regarding gender identity. Since its inception in 1978, our clinic in Toronto, Canada, has had a boy-girl referral ratio of 6.2 to 1 ($N = 218$). Among our adolescent transsexuals, however, the sex difference in referral rates has been considerably smaller (only 1.4 to 1; $N = 44$).

There are two interrelated questions that need to be answered. First, why is there a sex difference in referral rates? Second, why does the sex difference seem to dissipate in the adolescent transsexual group? Regarding the first question, it may be that the true prevalence of gender identity disorder is greater in males, perhaps due to a greater biological vulnerability. For example, it has been noted that among mammals, development along male lines is dependent on the production of androgen during early fetal development. If appropriate androgen secretion does not occur, or if cell receptors do not respond to circulating androgen, then fetal development proceeds along female lines. The androgen-insensitivity (testicular feminization) syndrome (see, e.g., Perez-Palacios, Chavez, Mendez, Imperato-McGinley, & Ulloa-Aguirre, 1987) in genetic males is the most poignant illustration of this postulate. Accordingly, it has been suggested that male fetal development is more complex and thus more susceptible to errors that may affect postnatal psychosexual genesis (e.g., Eme, 1979; Gadpaille, 1972; Money & Ehrhardt, 1972; Stoller, 1972).

Regardless of the contribution of biological events, social factors also appear to play a role in accounting for the disparity in referral rates. For example, there is less tolerance of cross-gender behavior in boys than in girls, among both peers and adults (e.g., Fagot, 1977, 1985; Green, Williams, & Harper, 1980; Zucker, Wilson, & Stern, 1985). Adults are also more likely to predict atypical outcomes, such as homosexuality, in feminine boys than in masculine girls (Antill, 1987; Martin, 1990). Thus, depending on one's point of view, it could be argued that boys are overreferred or that girls are underreferred. Clinically, there is evidence that girls may be required to display more extreme cross-gender behavior before parents seek out a clinical assessment. For example, Zucker and Bradley (in press) reported that mothers of gender-referred girls ($N = 23$) were significantly more likely to score the two CBCL items pertaining to gender identity as a 2 (on a scale from 0 to 2) than were the mothers of gender-referred boys ($N = 155$; 52.5% versus 27.5%, respectively).

With regard to the second question, the severity factor may well account for the reduced sex difference in referral rates among adolescent transsexuals. At this point in the life course, persistent gender dysphoria is very difficult to overlook; for example, one would be hard-pressed to invoke the notion that extensive masculinity in a girl is still "only a phase" that she will "grow out of"—comments that parents of younger children often report hearing from their family doctor, mental health professionals without extensive experience with gender identity disorders, and friends.

Familial Pattern

Clinical data on children from several centers have yielded virtually no concordance for gender identity disorder among nontwin siblings (e.g., Green, 1987). Case reports of both monozygotic (MZ) twins (Chazan, in press; Green & Stoller, 1971) and dizygotic (DZ) twins (Esman, 1970; Zucker, Bradley, & Hughes, 1987) have all been discordant for gender identity disorder. Zuger (1989) reported an unremarkable prevalence of homosexuality in the first- or second-degree male (4%) and female (1%) relatives of 55 child and adolescent males with gender identity disorder.

Familiality for transsexualism in adults has also not been well studied. Case reports have documented the occurrence of concordance among twins and nontwin siblings (reviewed in Hoenig, 1985; see also Joyce & Ding, 1985), but it is unclear if these represent disproportional rates of occurrence. It is likely, however, that the occurrence of this rare disorder in more than one family member is of great importance in understanding its etiology.

Kallmann (1952a, 1952b) reported a 100% concordance rate for homosexuality among MZ twin males, compared to a 15.4% concordance rate for DZ twin males. Since then, there has been a sprinkling of case reports in the English-language literature of MZ twins reared together, some finding concordance for homosexuality and others finding discordance. Among the discordant male pairs, some reports noted that the homosexual twin had shown behavioral signs of femininity during childhood (e.g., Friedman, Wollesen, & Tendler, 1976; McConaghy & Blaszczynski, 1980; Zuger, 1976). The sporadic nature of the case report literature, the existence of discordant cases, methodological criticisms of Kallmann's data (Rosenthal, 1970, pp. 250–255), and an antipathy toward genetic research in the decades after World War II (see Rosenthal, 1970) all seemed to reduce interest in the potential contribution of genetics to sexual orientation development and, indirectly, gender identity.

More recent studies, however, have sparked renewed attention to genetic factors. Eckert, Bouchard, Bohlen, and Heston (1986) described two pairs of MZ twin males reared apart: one pair of male twins was primarily discordant for homosexuality, but the other pair was concordant (and, when the twins were reunited in adulthood, became sexual partners!). Four female MZ twin pairs, also reared apart, were all discordant for homosexuality. Using substantially larger samples of male and female twins reared together, Bailey and Pillard (1991) and Bailey, Pillard, Neale, & Agyeɪ (1993) have shown significantly greater concordance for homosexuality among MZ than DZ twins. Such findings, coupled with recent evidence for an elevated incidence of homosexuality in the brothers of homosexual men and the sisters of homosexual women (e.g., Bailey, Benishay, & Pyron, 1991; Bailey, Willerman, & Parks, 1991; Pillard & Weinrich, 1986), argue for a fresh examination of the role of genetic factors in sexual orientation development. Given the association between gender identity and sexual orientation, the above studies may eventually be helpful in understanding the contribution of genetic and environmental influences on transsexualism, utilizing quantitative genetic modeling techniques employed by behavior geneticists.

Sibling Sex Ratio and Birth Order. Blanchard and Sheridan (1992) recently reviewed the literature and noted that homosexual men have been shown to have more brothers to sisters and to be born later than their siblings. In a fresh sample, the authors then reported that homosexual men with gender dysphoria (in DSM-III-R terminology, transsexualism, homosexual type) also had a sibling sex ratio that favored brothers over sisters (131 to 100) more than that of the general population (106 to 100); in contrast, the sibling sex ratio of nonhomosexual men with gender dysphoria (117 to 100) was not significantly different from the general population. Blanchard and Sheridan also found that homosexual men with gender dysphoria had a later birth order than either nonhomosexual men with gender dysphoria or the theoretical mean.

Blanchard, Zucker, Bradley, and Hume (in press) attempted to extend these findings to a sample of prepubertal feminine boys (many of whom met DSM criteria for gender identity disorder) and male homosexual and/or gender-dysphoric adolescents referred to a child and adolescent gender identity clinic. The sample had a sibling sex ratio that favored brothers over sisters (141 to 100) significantly more than that of either a clinical control group of boys matched for age at assessment, number of full siblings, and approximate year of birth (104 to 100) or the general population. The birth order of the feminine boy/homosexual adolescent group was also significantly later than that of either the clinical control group or the theoretical mean. Thus these two variables appear to be significantly different among homosexual men, homosexual gender-dysphoric men, and feminine boys/homosexual adolescent males as compared to both concurrent controls and general population samples. The reader is referred to Blanchard and Sheridan (1992) and Blanchard et al. (in press) for a review of both biological and psychosocial hypotheses that have been advanced to account for these findings.

Differential Diagnosis and Assessment

Among adolescents presenting with severe gender dysphoria, there are a couple of differential diagnostic issues that require attention. The first issue involves a judgment of the severity and chronicity of the condition, which will have relevance in deciding whether the youngster meets the complete diagnostic criteria for gender identity disorder. If the youngster does not meet the complete criteria, then the GIDNOS diagnosis is available as a residual category. It should be noted, however, that one is probably dealing with variations on a continuum of severity and not qualitatively distinct phenomena.

One of the vexing issues when working with gender-dysphoric adolescents is to what extent the request for sex reassignment is a way of handling internalized homophobia. Consider the following scenario: an adolescent with a childhood history of cross-gender identification reports that at around age 14 he began to think that he should become a woman and have a surgical sex change. He begins to cross-dress privately, but not publicly. The clinical history shows that the patient became aware of sexual fantasies toward other males about 6 months prior to the onset of the wish to become a woman. The thought of being a homosexual was repulsive to the patient, as it was against his moral and religious beliefs. His parents were also extremely repulsed at the thought of their son being a homosexual. The idea that he "really" was a woman appealed to them.

The question, then, is whether the request for sex reassignment is a way of "normalizing" attraction to same-sex persons (see Hellman, Green, Gray, & Williams, 1981; Leitenberg & Slavin, 1983). As was noted earlier, transsexual adolescents who relinquish the wish for surgery typically remain attracted to same-sex persons and develop a homosexual identity (Zucker et al., 1986). This type of issue usually presents itself only among markedly cross-gender-identified adolescents. It is rare, for example, for a homosexual adolescent with only a mild childhood cross-gender history (or no cross-gender history) to develop sustained gender dysphoria during adolescence.

Clinical Management

It goes without saying that the theoretical lens through which one views psychopathology influences how treatment issues will be conceptualized. In the treatment of children with gender identity disorder, for example, proponents of behavior therapy (e.g., Rekers, 1977) have focused largely on the development of techniques to modify specific sex-typed behaviors (e.g., cross-dressing and exclusive play with opposite-sex toys). In contrast, psychodynamically oriented clinicians have a greater preference to treat gender identity disorder in the context of family pathology and associated personality psychopathology in the child (e.g., Coates & Person, 1985; Meyer & Dupkin, 1985) and to place as much emphasis on treating these problems as on the gender identity symptomatology itself. Thus what (or whom) should be treated is embedded in the complexity of the theoretical frame by which the clinician attempts to understand the psychopathology.

It is beyond the scope of this chapter to discuss treatment issues in detail, so we will restrict our consideration of clinical management to some delimited concerns. As a point of departure, it should be recognized that the prognosis for therapeutic change for severely gender-dysphoric adolescents (of the homosexual type) is quite guarded, if by change one means a shift to a "normal" gender identity and a heterosexual sexual orientation. The likelihood of a homosexual adaptation without severe gender dysphoria is a more feasible outcome of therapeutic intervention. In many respects, this therapeutic outlook mirrors what has been generally observed with gender-dysphoric adults.

After conducting an assessment of a gender-dysphoric adolescent, the clinician is faced with two main options. One option is to conclude that the gender dysphoria is intractable and thus support the adolescent in the complex psychological process of beginning to live in society as a member of the opposite sex. Some gender-dysphoric adolescents do this quite well on their own, but others do not. This treatment path, though, is filled with obstacles. One problem is that adult gender identity clinics tend not to accept minors for any form of hormonal or surgical treatment. Adults with gender dysphoria typically have to go through a "real-life test" of living socially as the opposite sex before physical interventions are introduced, so as to be sure that the patient really finds the "transsexual solution" in his or her best interests (Blanchard & Steiner, 1990; Lothstein, 1983; "Standards of Care," 1985). Adolescents may have to go through a longer period of living socially as the opposite sex before hormonal and physical treatments are introduced. Whether this is in the adolescent's best interest is unclear (see, e.g., Dulcan & Lee, 1984; Newman, 1970), but the concern over introducing an irreversible procedure (e.g., penectomy or mastectomy) is an important one to keep in mind. In the Netherlands, there appears to be a more liberal approach to introducing hormonal therapy prior to the age of 18 (Cohen-Kettenis, 1992). Because this is much less common in North America, the clinician may end up doing a lot of supportive work during the transition period from adolescence to young adulthood. Unfortunately, there is no systematic research comparing the long-term effects of varying the age of introduction of physical interventions.

The second option is to encourage the adolescent to delay making a decision about changing his or her sex. This strategy is based on the premise that the disorder may not be fully consolidated and that therapy can help explore alternative adaptations (e.g., homosexuality). This is the usual option that our clinic selects, since we have noted variation in long-term outcome (Zucker et al., 1986). The extent to which gender-dysphoric adolescents can utilize exploratory therapy is, however, quite variable. The focus of therapy can be quite varied, including helping the adolescent better understand his or her motivations for changing sex, exploring attitudes and feelings about nascent sexuality, and working on family issues. In our experience, gender-dysphoric adolescents are quite diverse in their psychological maturity and sophistication regarding sexuality. Some adolescents have only a crude conception of what sex change actually comprises; others are extremely phobic about sexual issues. Thus the clinician should anticipate encountering gender-dysphoric adolescents who are quite variable in their maturity level and capacity for psychological reflection.

Transvestic Fetishism

Description of the Disorder

The literal meaning of the term *transvestism* is to wear clothing of the opposite sex. In the clinical literature prior to 1960 (and perhaps as late as 1970), the term was used in such diverse ways that without studying the material, one could never be certain if the patient was (by "modern" terminology) a transsexual, a transvestite (cross-dressing accompanied by sexual arousal), or a homosexual cross-dresser or "drag queen" (Person & Ovesey, 1984). In contemporary sexology, the accepted clinical use of the term *transvestism* is to describe biological males who cross-dress as a potent source of sexual arousal (e.g., Blanchard, 1991; Ovesey & Person, 1976; Person & Ovesey, 1978; Stoller, 1971).

Historical Background

Unlike gender identity disorders, which appeared for the first time in DSM-III in 1980, fetishistic disorders such as transvestism have long been on the nosological scene and were included in the 1952 and 1968 editions of the DSM. In DSM-IV, transvestic fetishism is included in the section entitled "Sexual and Gender Identity Disorders" as one of the paraphilias. As noted earlier, some individuals with transvestism develop severe gender identity disturbance, so its classification as a paraphilia is probably not entirely accurate (see, e.g., Blanchard & Clemmensen, 1988).

Clinical Picture

Although there is an extensive adult research and clinical literature on transvestism, there has been very little systematic work on transvestism during adolescence (e.g., Adams, Klinge, Vaziri, Maczulski, & Pasternak, 1976; Spensley & Barter, 1971) and only an occasional case report (e.g.,

Table 17–4
DSM-IV Diagnostic Criteria for Transvestic Fetishism

A. Over a period of at least 6 months, in a heterosexual male, recurrent, intense sexually arousing fantasies, sexual urges, or behaviors involving cross-dressing.

B. The fantasies, sexual urges, or behaviors cause clinically significant distress or impairment in social, occupational, or other important areas of functioning.

Specify if

With Gender Dysphoria: if the person has persistent discomfort with gender role or identity.

Scharfman, 1976; Shankel & Carr, 1956). Our clinic has now assessed more than 80 adolescent males with transvestism; to our knowledge, this is the largest clinical sample ever assembled for this developmental period. Much of what we say about transvestism is based on our own extensive clinical and research experience with these youngsters.

%Pager Place table 17–4 here%

The DSM-IV criteria for transvestic fetishism are shown in Table 17–4. The following is a case vignette describing one of our youngsters with this disorder.

> Kyle, age 16 (verbal IQ 103; performance IQ 128), was referred through his school board. He has one younger brother and sister (ages 9 and 6, respectively). Kyle's parents were middle-class in socioeconomic status. His father had a postgraduate degree, and his mother went to commercial school to become a medical secretary.
>
> Kyle was referred after his mother found him lying on his bed wearing black pantyhose. His father then searched Kyle's room and discovered three additional pairs. Both parents stated that they were shocked by the discovery and were unable to talk about it with Kyle. At the time Kyle was discovered, he became tearful and told his mother that he had just wanted to try them on. He denied to her that he had ever done this before. His mother, however, quickly realized that over the past year she had been finding pairs of pantyhose mixed in with his clothes, but had simply assumed that they had gotten there by accident. She also recalled finding pantyhose hidden under a bookcase with many tissues next to them (suggesting that Kyle had been masturbating). Kyle's mother then recalled that when he was 4 or 5 years old he "very frequently" loved to rub pantyhose, either under her own slacks or those being worn by female friends: he would go under the table, rub their legs, and get an erection. When asked how she could discern that Kyle had an erection, his mother commented that he used to wear shorts and that it was possible to see the bulge in his genital area. The parents recalled that they discouraged Kyle from engaging in this behavior and felt that it had stopped by the time he was 5 or 6 years old.

In an individual interview, Kyle was quite anxious and made little eye contact. He answered questions cordially but did not speak spontaneously. Regarding the cross-dressing, Kyle was visibly uneasy and guarded. He minimized the episode, stating that his grandmother had left the pantyhose after staying in his room. He denied engaging in other episodes of cross-dressing. He also denied associated sexual arousal.

Apart from the parents' concern about his cross-dressing, there were numerous other difficulties with Kyle. He had chronic academic problems, being described as a "bright underachiever." His most recent report card was "disastrous," with grades of Cs, Ds, and Fs in the core academic subjects. The parents also felt that Kyle had had long-standing and severe conflicts with his younger siblings. They experienced Kyle as unmotivated academically, demanding, and moody. Throughout the interview, many of their remarks devalued Kyle: "He's a capable enough kid, he's not brilliant. . . . We haven't said that we are ashamed [of him]. . . . [We] used to anticipate naturally Kyle going to university." Several recent arguments with his father had been quite intense, including one that ended up becoming physical. The parents felt that Kyle was quite unhappy and was a loner.

Regarding his development, his mother had found Kyle extremely difficult, coming to the belief that she was not "cut out to be a mother." She had trouble breast-feeding him and changed quickly to a bottle, to which he seemed to adapt well. He was a very poor sleeper, and she recalled being very exhausted as a result. She felt that Kyle cried and whined a lot but was responsive to soothing (e.g., being carried, going for car rides). She recalled going into the spare room with him in the house so her husband would not have to hear the crying. Kyle did not show separation anxiety as an infant, and when he was admitted to hospital at age 1 because of an ear infection "it was as if he had been there all his life." Kyle suffered from numerous ear infections and then developed asthma at age 5. Prior to this, he had to make numerous emergency room visits because of croup. Kyle's mother felt that he never did very well in school. He had always had problematic peer relationships, tending to be somewhat of a bully, and he had never had a best friend.

By age 10, Kyle's mother felt his behavior had become increasingly problematic. He became more oppositional, moody, and his academics continued to decline. She was becoming more concerned about his aggressive behavior toward his siblings. At present, she found Kyle to be very self-centered, lacking in empathy, and prejudicial against minority groups. She reported that once Kyle was looking at a men's magazine and commented that if he was as ugly as one of the pictured men he would kill himself. She described Kyle as obsessed with medicines and noted that he often complained of aches and pains.

On the CBCL, both parents reported a considerable number of behavioral problems in Kyle. On the form completed by his mother, the total behavior problem score was 111, which fell well within the clinical range. Of the nine narrow-band dimensions, eight were clinically elevated; these spanned the Internalizing and Externalizing dimensions. His father also reported a large number of behavioral difficulties, albeit with less extreme scores than those of his mother. This difference seemed to reflect the mother's greater involvement in Kyle's rearing and her own distressed emotional state. Projective testing indicated a youngster who had become quite interpersonally guarded, as judged, for example, by numerous references to "eyes" and people or animals staring at each other. Kyle's sense of masculinity seemed compromised. For example, on the two Rorschach cards that commonly evoke masculine themes (cards IV and VI), Kyle perceived someone "lying down" or sleeping. An insect was perceived as hurt and unable to fly. A pediatric neurological consultation revealed a normal CT scan, including no evidence for temporal lobe pathology. An EEG was also within normal limits. DSM-III-R diagnoses were transvestic fetishism and oppositional defiant disorder.

Adolescents with transvestism are typically referred when they are discovered, usually by a parent or other adult authority figure (e.g., a group home worker), to be cross-dressing. In some instances, a parent might enter the youngster's room at night and inadvertently find him under the covers wearing his mother's underpants. In other instances, the mother becomes aware that items of her clothing disappear and, often wind up intermingled with her son's laundry. At times, the mother or a sister might discover that her underclothing is stained with semen. In extreme cases, the adolescent transvestite engages in the behavior so compulsively that he winds up stealing underclothing from a store or will break into neighbors' homes to obtain the clothing.

Unlike adolescents with transsexualism, who usually self-refer or do so in agreement with an adult authority figure, adolescents with transvestism rarely self-refer. The initiative is invariably on the part of an adult.

Adolescent transvestites vary in the degree to which they cross-dress, as well as in the extent to which they acknowledge associated sexual arousal. Some adolescents will report that they only hold women's underclothing (e.g., underpants, nylons, stockings) because they like its texture; the report of self-soothing with or without associated erotic arousal has long been part of the clinical picture associated with transvestic fetishism. (It should be noted that many adolescents with this disorder are extremely embarrassed and ashamed when they are discovered. The claim that they are not aroused sexually by the cross-dressing may be true, but they may also be lying. The clinician should recognize that talking about one's sexuality is difficult enough, let alone about a behavioral pattern that the adolescent may recognize is a cause of great concern on the part of his parents. It is very important to give the adolescent time to talk about his sexuality with an interviewer who is comfortable discussing this topic.) Other adolescents will report that they wear women's undergarments, are aroused by them, and will subsequently masturbate. Some adolescents will wear the clothing episodically; others will compulsively wear the clothing under their own masculine apparel. In extreme cases, the adolescent will engage in full cross-dressing, attempting to emulate the phenotype of a woman; however, attempting to pass publicly as a woman is very rare during adolescence. In addition to masturbation, some adolescents will mutilate the female apparel (e.g., cutting it to pieces with scissors) or defecate or urinate on it.

Like adults with transvestism, adolescent transvestites appear to be heterosexual in their sexual orientation. They will report sexual fantasies involving females, and some will have engaged in interpersonal heterosexual experiences. They often report being sexually aroused without the use of female clothing, although some adolescents report being more aroused by a female partner's clothing than by the partner herself.

Because some individuals with transvestism can also experience severe gender dysphoria, it is important to assess the youngster's feelings about being a boy. To some extent, the presence of gender dysphoria in transvestic youngsters is disarming because their physical appearance is stereotypically masculine, as are their behavioral interests. This is in marked contrast to transsexual youngsters, who often shape their physical appearance to reflect their cross-gender identification. Blanchard (1991) has identified some of the gender-dysphoric feelings and fantasies common in adult men with transvestism.

The childhood gender development of adolescent transvestites is typically masculine (e.g., in peer preference, toy and activity interests, involvement in sports; Bradley & Zucker, 1984; Zucker & Bradley, in press). The sole exception to this is that in a minority of youngsters there is a prepubertal onset of cross-dressing (e.g., use of mother's underpants, wearing or stroking of nylons); as suggested earlier, however, the purpose of this is not to enhance a sense of feminine identification but rather some type of self-soothing function, which at times has been observed to be accompanied by penile erection. Cross-dressing of boys with gender identity disorder usually involves outerwear (e.g., dresses, jewelry) to fuel the fantasy of being like a girl or a woman. In other words, the nature of cross-dressing in transvestism and gender identity disorder is qualitatively different.

In our own experience, we have been impressed with the regularity of some other characteristics in our sample of adolescent transvestites. We make no claim that these are representative features of transvestites in general, since our sample is a clinic-referred one. For example, the fact that many of our youngsters have been referred from group homes indicates that they were no longer able to live with their families of origin, often due to extreme psychopathology and dysfunction in these families. This is obviously one type of sampling bias.

Comorbidity in psychiatric status has been common. Although some adolescents are overtly anxious, depressed, and withdrawn, the more common clinical presentation has been of a severely undercontrolled youngster with diagnoses such as conduct disorder or attention-deficit hyperactivity disorder. On the CBCL, our transvestitic group, on average, has shown extremely high levels of behavioral disturbance. Verbal IQ has been significantly lower than performance IQ, and language-related learning disabilities have been common, with attendant school failure. Because of their general behavioral difficulties, the social relations of these youngsters have often been poor (e.g., conflicted or nonexistent peer relations). Although paternal absence has been high, so has maternal absence (e.g., by divorce, separation, or placement in group homes). In fact, the rate of maternal absence has been significantly higher among our group of adolescent transvestites than in our other groups of adolescents with psychosexual problems (transsexuals, homosexuals, etc.).

A small minority of these youngsters have documented neurological dysfunction (e.g., epilepsy). We often request a neurological consultation because of the clinical literature, albeit patchy and inconsistent, that has noted a relation between fetishistic behavior and neurological dysfunction (e.g., Epstein, 1973; Kolarsky, Freund, Machek, & Polak, 1967). For example, one 16-year-old youngster seen in our clinic developed epilepsy at age 10; shortly thereafter, his transvestic behavior seemed to appear for the first time. At age 16 he was also found on occasion to wear diapers to school, a type of fetish that has been noted in the clinical literature on adults.

Course and Prognosis

In our own research (Zucker & Bradley, in press), we have noted two distinct ages of onset for transvestic fetishism. A minority of adolescents report engaging in cross-dressing in female underclothing well before puberty. Sometimes this has been accompanied by penile erection, verified by maternal observation. The self-soothing quality of the cross-dressing has been recalled by many of the youngster's parents and is quite reminiscent of the function of a transitional object. In our own clinic we have assessed three prepubertal males (aged 4 to 6 years) with fetishistic cross-dressing, and their developmental history was similar to that recalled by our adolescent transvestites. In the majority of adolescents, however, the age of onset coincides with puberty.

The prognosis for transvestism is poor; it appears to be a chronic condition. Unfortunately, little is known about the long-term outcome of transvestites who are clinically assessed in adolescence (and possibly treated), presumably at an early phase in the disorder's development.

Complications

Blanchard (1991) has made the point that transvestism interferes with "normal" heterosexual activity, commenting that "the individual is aroused by the appearance of an attractively clad woman, but he locates this image on himself rather than another person" (p. 247). One complication of transvestism, therefore, is that it can affect heterosexual relationships. When transvestism becomes extreme, the person usually focuses less and less on his partner for sexual intimacy, except to use her as prop for certain sexual fantasies (e.g., imagining himself as a woman engaged in lesbian relations with his female partner). Thus it is not terribly surprising that there is a high rate of marital or relationship breakdown; among adolescents, however, the main problem seems to be the lack of social skills to develop intimate relationships with other people.

Another complication is the emergence of gender dysphoria. In some cases, the gender dysphoria appears at the same time as the transvestism, but more often than not, it appears to follow it in time. In extreme cases, these feelings will lead toward the pursuit of sex reassignment surgery.

Epidemiology

No formal epidemiological study has ever been conducted to assess the prevalence and incidence of transvestism. Transvestism appears to be a disorder that is almost exclusively the province of biological males, although Stoller (1982) reported several cases of females whom he felt were transvestic.

Familial Patterns

No systematic research has been conducted to assess familial patterns (e.g., concordance among MZ and DZ twins). Blanchard and Sheridan's (1992) study of nonhomosexual men with gender dysphoria indicated sibling sex ratio and birth order patterns that distinguished them from homosexual men with gender dysphoria (see earlier discussion). Unpublished data from our sample of adolescents with transvestic fetishism confirms these findings—both sibling sex ratio and birth order were similar to what would be expected in the general population.

Differential Diagnosis and Assessment

The diagnosis of transvestic fetishism is not particularly difficult when an adolescent is frank about his sexual behavior. The more difficult cases to diagnose involve youngsters who seem to be engaging in fetishistic cross-dressing but deny co-occurring sexual arousal. We have observed this in several prepubertal youngsters (for one case, see Zucker, 1990a, pp. 11–12) and in youngsters who have just entered puberty; typically, they will report holding or stroking the clothing but deny overt sexual arousal. The residual diagnostic category (GIDNOS) can be used for these cases, although it should be recognized that one is probably dealing with a behavioral pattern that is not qualitatively distinct from transvestic fetishism.

Blanchard and Clemmensen (1988) have discussed the problem of severe gender dysphoria co-occurring with transvestic fetishism. As can be seen in Table 17–4, the presence of gender identity disorder is no longer an exclusionary criterion for transvestic fetishism.

Clinical Management

There are virtually no therapeutic guidelines in the literature regarding the treatment of adolescents with transvestism. One can, however, peruse the adult literature that describes the treatment of transvestism with forms of behavior therapy (e.g., Gelder, 1979; Gelder & Marks, 1969; Langevin, 1983, pp. 211–232) and psychotherapy (e.g., Glasser, 1979; Greenacre, 1979). As with transsexualism, the prognosis for therapeutic change should be considered guarded. In our own clinic, it has been our impression so far that not only is the transvestism itself extremely complex to treat, but that the associated psychopathology and family dysfunction are often so great that multiple forms of intervention (targeted to multiple forms of impairment) are required. Unfortunately, there is very little information on the long-term outcome of this disorder when it is diagnosed and treated during adolescence.

In our own clinic, several forms of therapeutic intervention have been considered. From a sheer informational point of view, we have found it useful to explain to parents and the adolescent what transvestism is. Many parents, particularly mothers, believe that the behavior signifies that their son is homosexual or, less commonly, a "pervert" who is prone to sexual aggression. Many parents do not have a label for their child's behavior, so explaining the term *transvestism* can be helpful.

One therapeutic strategy that we recommend is to see whether the adolescent is able to develop alternative strategies of sexual arousal (e.g., masturbating to imagery without the wearing or thought of female clothing). To some extent, this approach is guided by fundamental assumptions about associative conditioning and operant behavior. A second therapeutic strategy is to identify the factors within the adolescent and the family that activate the need to self-soothe. It has often been our impression that the stressor is related to mother-son conflict that has evolved over an extended period of time (Bradley, 1990). This approach is based on the assumption that the cross-dressing serves some representational function pertaining to the adolescent's relationship with his mother in which issues pertaining to closeness, hostility, and the need for comfort are fused (Bradley, 1990).

Lastly, there has been some consideration of psychopharmacological treatment of transvestism. For example, if the patient shows a documented neurological condition (e.g., temporal lobe epilepsy), then medications such as carbamezapine might be tried. The clinical observation of the anxiety-reducing function of cross-dressing has led to some preliminary study of the effects of buspirone (Fedoroff, 1988, 1992). Lastly, conceptualization of transvestism as a compulsive disorder has led to one controlled trial comparing clomipramine with desipramine; this study yielded mixed evidence of the effectiveness of both medications (Kruesi, Fine, Valladares, Phillips, & Rapoport, 1992).

References

Achenbach, T. M., & Edelbrock, C. (1983). *Manual for the Child Behavior Checklist and Revised Child Behavior Profile*. Burlington, VT: University of Vermont, Department of Psychiatry.

Achenbach, T. M., & Edelbrock, C. (1986). *Manual for the Teacher's Report Form and Teacher Version of the Revised Child Behavior Profile*. Burlington, VT: University of Vermont, Department of Psychiatry.

Adams, K. M., Klinge, V., Vaziri, H., Maczulski, B., & Pasternak, A. (1976). Studies in adolescent transvestism: Life history, psychometric and behavioral descriptors. In D. V. Siva Sankar (Ed.), *Mental health in children* (Vol. 2, pp. 89–112). Westbury, NY: PJD.

Alpert-Gillis, L. J., & Connell, J. P. (1989). Gender and sex-role influences on children's self-esteem. *Journal of Personality, 57,* 97–114.

American Psychiatric Association. (1980). *Diagnostic and statistical manual of mental disorders* (3rd ed.). Washington, DC: Author.

American Psychiatric Association. (1987). *Diagnostic and statistical manual of mental disorders* (rev. 3rd ed.). Washington, DC: Author.

American Psychiatric Association (1994). *Diagnostic and statistical manual of mental disorders* (4th ed.). Washington, DC: Author.

Antill, J. K. (1987). Parents' beliefs and values about sex roles, sex differences, and sexuality: Their sources and implications. In P. Shaver & C. Hendrick (Eds.), *Sex and gender* (pp. 294–328). Newbury Park, CA: Sage.

Bailey, J. M., Benishay, D., & Pyron, A. (1991). *A family study of female homosexuality*. Unpublished manuscript, Northwestern University, Evanston, IL.

Bailey, J. M., & Pillard, R. C. (1991). A genetic study of male sexual orientation. *Archives of General Psychiatry, 48,* 1089–1096.

Bailey, J. M., Willerman, L., & Parks, C. (1991). A test of the maternal stress theory of human male homosexuality. *Archives of Sexual Behavior, 20,* 277–293.

Bailey, J. M., & Zucker, K. J. (in press). Childhood sex-typed behavior and sexual orientation: A conceptual analysis and quantitative review. *Developmental Psychology.*

Bailey, J. M., Pillard, R. C., Neale, M. C., & Agyei, Y. (1993). Heritable factors influence sexual orientation in women. *Archives of General Psychiatry, 50,* 217–223.

Bates, J. E., Bentler, P. M., & Thompson, S. K. (1979). Gender-deviant boys compared with normal and clinical control boys. *Journal of Abnormal Child Psychology, 7,* 243–259.

Bayer, R. (1981). *Homosexuality and American psychiatry: The politics of diagnosis.* New York: Basic Books.

Bayer, R., & Spitzer, R. L. (1982). Edited correspondence on the status of homosexuality in DSM-III. *Journal of the History of the Behavioral Sciences, 18,* 32–52.

Becker, J. V., & Kaplan, M. S. (1988). The assessment of adolescent sex offenders. *Advances in Behavioral Assessment of Children and Families, 4,* 97–118.

Benjamin, H. (1954). Transsexualism and transvestism as psychosomatic somatopsychic syndromes. *American Journal of Psychotherapy, 8,* 219–230.

Benjamin, H. (1966). *The transsexual phenomenon.* New York: Julian.

Blanchard, R. (1985). Typology of male-to-female transsexualism. *Archives of Sexual Behavior, 14,* 247–261.

Blanchard, R. (1988). Nonhomosexual gender dysphoria. *Journal of Sex Research, 24,* 188–193.

Blanchard, R. (1989). The classification and labeling of nonhomosexual gender dysphoria. *Archives of Sexual Behavior, 18,* 315–334.

Blanchard, R. (1990a). Gender identity disorders in adult women. In R. Blanchard & B. W. Steiner (Eds.), *Clinical management of gender identity disorders in children and adults* (pp. 77–91). Washington, DC: American Psychiatric Press.

Blanchard, R. (1990b). Gender identity disorders in adult men. In R. Blanchard & B. W. Steiner (Eds.), *Clinical management of gender identity disorders in children and adults* (pp. 47–76). Washington, DC: American Psychiatric Press.

Blanchard, R. (1991). Clinical observations and systematic studies of autogynephilia. *Journal of Sex & Marital Therapy, 17,* 235–251.

Blanchard, R., & Clemmensen, L. H. (1988). A test of the DSM-III-R's implicit assumption that fetishistic arousal and gender dysphoria are mutually exclusive. *Journal of Sex Research, 25,* 426–432.

Blanchard, R., & Sheridan, P. M. (1992). Sibship size, sibling sex ratio, birth order, and parental age in homosexual and nonhomosexual gender dysphorics. *Journal of Nervous and Mental Disease, 180,* 40–47.

Blanchard, R., & Steiner, B. W. (Eds.). (1990). *Clinical management of gender identity disorders in children and adults.* Washington, DC: American Psychiatric Press.

Blanchard, R., Zucker, K. J., Bradley, S. J., & Hume, C. S. (in press). Birth order and sibling sex ratio in homosexual male adolescents and probably prehomosexual feminine boys. *Developmental Psychology.*

Bradley, S. J. (1990). Gender dysphorias of childhood and adolescence. In B. D. Garfinkel, G. A. Carlson, & E. B. Weller (Eds.), *Psychiatric disorders in children and adolescents* (pp. 121–134). Philadelphia: Saunders.

Bradley, S. J., Blanchard, R., Coates, S., Green, R., Levine, S. B., Meyer-Bahlburg, H. F. L., Pauly, I. B., & Zucker, K. J. (1991). Interim report of the DSM-IV subcommittee for gender identity disorders. *Archives of Sexual Behavior, 20,* 333–343.

Bradley, S. J., & Zucker, K. J. (1984, October). *Gender-dysphoric adolescents: Presenting and developmental characteristics.* Paper presented at the joint meeting of the Canadian Academy of Child Psychiatry and the American Academy of Child Psychiatry, Toronto.

Buhrich, N., Bailey, J. M., & Martin, N. G. (1991). Sexual orientation, sexual identity, and sex-dimorphic behaviors in male twins. *Behavior Genetics, 21,* 75–96.

Bullough, V. L. (1975). Transsexualism in history. *Archives of Sexual Behavior, 4,* 561–571.

Cass, V. V. (1979). Homosexual identity formation: A theoretical model. *Journal of Homosexuality, 4,* 219–235.

Cass, V. C. (1984). Homosexual identity formation: Testing a theoretical model. *Journal of Sex Research, 20,* 143–167.

Cass, V. C. (1990). The implications of homosexual identity formation for the Kinsey model and scale of sexual preference. In D. P. McWhirter, S. A. Sanders, & J. M. Reinisch (Eds.)., *Homosexuality/heterosexuality: Concepts of sexual orientation* (pp. 239–266). New York: Oxford University Press.

Cauldwell, D. O. (1949). Psychopathia transsexualis. *Sexology, 16,* 274–280.

Chazan, S. E. (in press). Paired opposites: Mirror gender identity in a case of identical twins. *Current Issues in Psychoanalytic Practice.*

Coates, S. (1985). Extreme boyhood femininity: Overview and new research findings. In Z. DeFries, R. C. Friedman, & R. Corn (Eds.), *Sexuality: New perspectives* (pp. 101–124). Westport, CT: Greenwood.

Coates, S., & Person, E. S. (1985). Extreme boyhood femininity: Isolated behavior or pervasive disorder? *Journal of the American Academy of Child Psychiatry, 24,* 702–709.

Cohen-Kettenis, P. (1992, March). *A gender clinic for children and adolescents: The Dutch model.* Paper presented at the conference on Gender Identity Development in Childhood and Adolescence, St. George's Hospital, London, England.

Coleman, E., Bockting, W. O., & Gooren, L. (1993). Homosexual and bisexual identity in sex-reassigned female-to-male transsexuals. *Archives of Sexual Behavior, 22,* 37–50.

Cowell, R. (1954). *Roberta Cowell's story by herself.* Melbourne: Heinemann.

Davenport, C. W., & Harrison, S. I. (1977). Gender identity change in a female adolescent transsexual. *Archives of Sexual Behavior, 6,* 327–341.

D'Emilio, J. (1983). *Sexual politics, sexual communities: The making of a homosexual minority in the United States, 1940–1970.* Chicago: University of Chicago Press.

D'Emilio, J. (1984). Capitalism and gay identity. In A. Snitow, C. Stansell, & S. Thompson (Eds.), *Desire: The politics of sexuality* (pp. 140–152). London: Virago.

DiPietro, J. A. (1981). Rough and tumble play: A function of gender. *Developmental Psychology, 17,* 50–58.

Docter, R. F. (1988). *Transvestites and transsexuals: Toward a theory of cross-gender behavior.* New York: Plenum.

Dulcan, M. K., & Lee, P. A. (1984). Transsexualism in the adolescent girl. *Journal of the American Academy of Child Psychiatry, 23,* 354–361.

Eckert, E. D., Bouchard, T. J., Bohlen, J., & Heston, L. L. (1986). Homosexuality in monozygotic twins reared apart. *British Journal of Psychiatry, 148,* 421–425.

Eme, R. F. (1979). Sex differences in childhood psychopathology: A review. *Psychological Bulletin, 86,* 574–595.

Epstein, A. W. (1973). The relationship of altered brain states to sexual psychopathology. In J. Zubin & J. Money (Eds.), *Contemporary sexual behavior:*

Critical issues in the 1970s (pp. 297–310). Baltimore, MD: Johns Hopkins University Press.

Esman, A. H. (1970). Transsexual identification in a three-year-old twin: A brief communication. *Psychosocial Process, 1,* 77–79.

Fagot, B. I. (1977). Consequences of moderate cross-gender behavior in preschool children. *Child Development, 48,* 902–907.

Fagot, B. I. (1978). The influence of sex of child on parental reactions to toddler children. *Child Development, 49,* 459–465.

Fagot, B. I. (1985). Beyond the reinforcement principle: Another step toward understanding sex role development. *Developmental Psychology, 21,* 1097–1104.

Fagot, B. I., Leinbach, M. D., & Hagan, R. (1986). Gender labeling and the adoption of sex-typed behaviors. *Developmental Psychology, 22,* 440–443.

Fedoroff, J. P. (1988). Buspirone hydrochloride in the treatment of transvestic fetishism. *Journal of Clinical Psychiatry, 49,* 408–409.

Fedoroff, J. P. (1992). Buspirone hydrochloride in the treatment of an atypical paraphilia. *Archives of Sexual Behavior, 21,* 401–406.

Ferenczi, S. (1980). The noslogy of male homosexuality (homoeroticism). In S. Ferenczi, *First contributions to psychoanalysis.* New York: Brunner/Mazel. (Original work published 1914)

Freud, S. (1961). Some psychological consequences of the anatomic distinction between the sexes. In J. Strachey (Ed. and Trans.), *The standard edition of the complete psychological works of Sigmund Freud* (Vol. 19, pp. 241–260). London: Hogarth. (Original work published 1925)

Freund, K. (1963). A laboratory method for diagnosing predominance of homo- or hetero-erotic interest in the male. *Behavior Research and Therapy, 1,* 85–93.

Freund, K. (1977). Psychophysiological assessment of change in erotic preference. *Behavior Research and Therapy, 15,* 297–301.

Freund, K., Watson, R., & Rienzo, D. (1989). Heterosexuality, homosexuality, and erotic age preference. *Journal of Sex Research, 26,* 107–117.

Friedman, R. C., Wollesen, F., & Tendler, R. (1976). Psychological development and blood levels of sex steroids in male identical twins of divergent sexual orientation. *Journal of Nervous and Mental Disease, 163,* 282–288.

Gadpaille, W. J. (1972). Research into the physiology of maleness and femaleness. *Archives of General Psychiatry, 26,* 193–206.

Gagnon, J. H. (1990). The explicit and implicit use of the scripting perspective in sex research. In J. Bancroft (Ed.), *Annual review of sex research* (Vol. 1, pp. 1–43). Lake Mills, IA: Stoyles Graphic Services.

Gagnon, J. H., & Simon, W. (1973). *Sexual conduct.* Chicago: Aldine.

Gelder, M. (1979). Behaviour therapy for sexual deviations. In I. Rosen (Ed.), *Sexual deviation* (2nd ed., pp. 351–375). New York: Oxford University Press.

Gelder, M. G., & Marks, I. M. (1969). Aversion treatment in transvestism and transsexualism. In R. Green & J. Money (Eds.), *Transsexualism and sex reassignment* (pp. 383–413). Baltimore, MD: Johns Hopkins Press.

Glasser, M. (1979). Some aspects of the role of aggression in the perversions. In I. Rosen (Ed.), *Sexual deviation* (2nd ed., pp. 278–305). New York: Oxford University Press.

Green, R. (1968). Childhood cross-gender identification. *Journal of Nervous and Mental Disease, 147,* 500–509.

Green, R. (1974). *Sexual identity conflict in children and adults.* New York: Basic Books.

Green, R. (1987). *The "sissy boy syndrome" and the development of homosexuality.* New Haven, CT: Yale University Press.

Green, R., & Stoller, R. J. (1971). Two monozygotic (identical) twin pairs discordant for gender identity. *Archives of Sexual Behavior, 1,* 321–327.

Green, R., Williams, K., & Harper, J. (1980). Cross-sex identity: Peer group integration and the double standard of childhood sex-typing. In J. Samson (Ed.), *Childhood and sexuality* (pp. 542–548). Montreal: Editions Etudes Vivantes.

Greenacre, P. (1979). Fetishism. In I. Rosen (Ed.), *Sexual deviation* (2nd ed., pp. 79–108). New York: Oxford University Press.

Greenberg, D. F. (1989). *The construction of homosexuality.* Chicago: University of Chicago Press.

Hamburger, C. (1953). The desire for change of sex as shown by personal letters from 465 men and women. *Acta Endocrinologica, 14,* 361–375.

Hamburger, C., Sturup, G. K., & Dahl-Iverson, E. (1953). Transvestism: Hormonal, psychiatric, and surgical treatment. *Journal of the American Medical Association, 152,* 391–396.

Hampson, J. G. (1955). Hermaphroditic genital appearance, rearing and eroticism in hyperadrenocorticism. *Bulletin of the Johns Hopkins Hospital, 96,* 265–273.

Hellman, R. E., Green, R., Gray, J. L., and Williams, K. (1981). Childhood sexual identity, childhood religiosity, and "homophobia" as influences in the development of transsexualism, homosexuality, and heterosexuality. *Archives of General Psychiatry, 38,* 910–915.

Herdt, G. (Ed.). (1989). *Gay and lesbian youth.* New York: Haworth Press.

Hoenig, J. (1985). Etiology of transsexualism. In B. W. Steiner (Ed.), *Gender dysphoria: Development, research, management* (pp. 33–73). New York: Plenum.

Hoyer, N. (1933). *Man into woman.* New York: Dutton.

Huston, A. C. (1985). The development of sex-typing: Themes from recent research. *Developmental Review, 5,* 1–17.

Joyce, P. R., & Ding, L. (1985). Transsexual sisters. *Australian and New Zealand Journal of Psychiatry, 19,* 188–189.

Kallmann, F. J. (1952a). Comparative twin study on the genetic aspects of male homosexuality. *Journal of Nervous and Mental Disease, 115,* 283–298.

Kallmann, F. J. (1952b). Twin and sibship study of overt male homosexuality. *American Journal of Human Genetics, 4,* 136–146.

Kolarsky, A., Freund, K., Machek, J., & Polak, O. (1967). Male sexual deviation: Association with early temporal lobe damage. *Archives of General Psychiatry, 17,* 735–743.

Kronberg, J., Tyano, S., Apter, A., & Wijsenbeek, H. (1981). Treatment of transsexualism in adolescence. *Journal of Adolescence, 4,* 177–185.

Kruesi, M. J. P., Fine, S., Valladares, L., Phillips, R. A., & Rapoport, J. (1992). Paraphilias: A double blind cross-over comparison of clomiprimine versus desipramine. *Archives of Sexual Behavior, 21,* 587–593.

Langevin, R. (1983). *Sexual strands: Understanding and treating sexual anomalies in men.* Hillsdale, NJ: Erlbaum.

Leitenberg, H., & Slavin, L. (1983). Comparison of attitudes towards transsexuality and homosexuality. *Archives of Sexual Behavior, 12,* 337–346.

Levine, S. B., & Lothstein, L. (1981). Transsexualism or the gender dysphoria syndromes. *Journal of Sex and Marital Therapy, 7,* 85–113.

Lothstein, L. M. (1980). The adolescent gender dysphoric patient: An approach to treatment and management. *Journal of Pediatric Psychology, 5,* 93–109.

Lothstein, L. M. (1983). *Female-to-male transsexualism: Historical, clinical, and theoretical issues.* Boston: Routledge & Kegan Paul.

Maccoby, E. E. (1988). Gender as a social category. *Developmental Psychology, 24,* 755–765.

Maccoby, E. E., & Jacklin, C. N. (1987). Gender segregation in childhood. *Advances in Child Development and Behavior, 20,* 239–287.

Martin, A. D. (1982). Learning to hide: The socialization of the gay adolescent. In S. C. Feinstein, J. G. Looney, A. Z. Schwartzberg, & A. D. Sorosky (Eds.), *Adolescent psychiatry: Developmental and clinical studies* (Vol. X, pp. 52–65). Chicago: University of Chicago Press.

Martin, C. L. (1990). Attitudes and expectations about children with nontraditional and traditional gender roles. *Sex Roles, 22,* 151–165.

McCauley, E., & Ehrhardt, A. A. (1984). Follow-up of females with gender identity disorders. *Journal of Nervous and Mental Disease, 172,* 353–358.

McConaghy, N., & Blaszczynski, A. (1980). A pair of monozygotic twins discordant for homosexuality: Sex-dimorphic behavior and penile volume responses. *Archives of Sexual Behavior, 9,* 123–131.

McIntosh, M. (1968). The homosexual role. *Social Problems, 16,* 182–192.

Meyer, J. K. (1982). The theory of gender identity disorders. *Journal of the American Psychoanalytic Association, 30,* 381–418.

Meyer, J. K., & Dupkin, C. (1985). Gender disturbance in children: An interim clinical report. *Bulletin of the Menninger Clinic, 49,* 236–269.

Meyer-Bahlburg, H. F. L. (1985). Gender identity disorder of childhood: Introduction. *Journal of the American Academy of Child Psychiatry, 24,* 681–683.

Meyer-Bahlburg, H. F. L., Rotheram-Borus, M. J., Dolezal, C., Rosario, M., Exner, T. M., Gruen, R. S., & Ehrhardt, A. A. (1992, July). *Sexual identity vs. sexual orientation vs. gender of partner among New York City adolescent males.* Paper presented at the meeting of the International Academy of Sex Research, Prague.

Money, J. (1952). *Hermaphroditism: An inquiry into the nature of a human paradox.* Unpublished doctoral dissertation, Harvard University.

Money, J. (1973). Gender role, gender identity, core gender identity: Usage and definition of terms. *Journal of the American Academy of Psychoanalysis, 1,* 397–403.

Money, J. (1985). The conceptual neutering of gender and the criminalization of sex. *Archives of Sexual Behavior, 14,* 279–290.

Money, J. (1991). *Biographies of gender and hermaphroditism in paired comparisons.* Amsterdam: Elsevier.

Money, J., & Ehrhardt, A. A. (1972). *Man and woman, boy and girl: The differentiation and dimorphism of gender identity from conception to maturity.* Baltimore, MD: Johns Hopkins Press.

Money, J., Hampson, J. G., & Hampson, J. L. (1955). Hermaphroditism: Recommendations concerning assignment of sex, change of sex, and psychologic management. *Bulletin of the Johns Hopkins Hospital, 97,* 284–300.

Money, J., Hampson, J. G., & Hampson, J. L. (1956). Sexual incongruities and psychopathology: The evidence of human hermaphroditism. *Bulletin of the Johns Hopkins Hospital, 98,* 43–57.

Money, J., Hampson, J. G., & Hampson, J. L. (1957). Imprinting and the establishment of gender role. *Archives of Neurology and Psychiatry, 77,* 333–336.

Newman, L. E. (1970). Transsexualism in adolescence: Problems in evaluation and treatment. *Archives of General Psychiatry, 23,* 112–121.

Nye, R. A. (1989). Sex difference and male homosexuality in French medical discourse, 1830–1930. *Bulletin of the History of Medicine, 63,* 32–51.

Ovesey, L., & Person, E. (1976). Transvestism: A disorder of the sense of self. *International Journal of Psychoanalytic Psychotherapy, 5,* 219–235.

Perez-Palacios, G., Chavez, B., Mendez, J. P., Imperato-McGinley, J., & Ulloa-Aguirre, A. (1987). The syndromes of androgen resistance revisited. *Journal of Steroid Biochemistry, 27,* 1101–1108.

Person, E., & Ovesey, L. (1974a). The transsexual syndrome in males: I. Primary transsexualism. *American Journal of Psychotherapy, 28,* 4–20.

Person, E., & Ovesey, L. (1974b). The transsexual syndrome in males: II. Secondary transsexualism. *American Journal of Psychotherapy, 28,* 174–193.

Person, E., & Ovesey, L. (1978). Transvestism: New perspectives. *Journal of the American Academy of Psychoanalysis, 6,* 301–323.

Person, E. S., & Ovesey, L. (1984). Homosexual cross-dressers. *Journal of the American Academy of Psychoanalysis, 12,* 167–186.

Pfäfflin, F., & Junge, A. (Eds.). (1992). *Geschlechtsumwandlung: Abhandlungen zur transsexualität.* New York: Stuttgart.

Philippopoulos, G. S. (1964). A case of transvestism in a 17-year-old girl: Psychopathology-psychodynamics. *Acta Psychotherapeutica, 12,* 29–37.

Pillard, R. C., & Weinrich, J. D. (1986). Evidence of familial nature of male homosexuality. *Archives of General Psychiatry, 43,* 808–812.

Rekers, G. A. (1977). Assessment and treatment of childhood gender problems. In B. B. Lahey & A. E. Kazdin (Eds.), *Advances in clinical child psychology* (Vol. 1, pp. 267–306). New York: Plenum.

Rekers, G. A., & Morey, S. M. (1989). Personality problems associated with childhood gender disturbance. *Italian Journal of Clinical and Cultural Psychology, 1,* 85–90.

Roesler, T., & Deisher, R. W. (1972). Youthful male homosexuality: Homosexual experiences and the process of developing homosexual identity in males aged 16 to 22 years. *Journal of the American Medical Association, 219,* 1018–1023.

Rosen, R. C., & Beck, J. G. (1988). *Patterns of sexual arousal: Psychophysiological processes and clinical applications.* New York: Guilford.

Rosenthal, D. (1970). *Genetic theory and abnormal behavior.* New York: McGraw-Hill.

Savin-Williams, R. C. (1990). *Gay and lesbian youth: Expressions of identity.* New York: Hemisphere.

Scharfman, M. A. (1976). Perverse development in a young boy. *Journal of the American Psychoanalytic Association, 24,* 499–524.

Serbin, L. A. (1991, August). *Origins of gender concepts and sex-typed behavior in infants and toddlers*. Paper presented at the meeting of the International Academy of Sex Research, Barrie, Ontario.

Shankel, L. W., & Carr, A. C. (1956). Transvestism and hanging episodes in a male adolescent. *Psychiatric Quarterly, 30*, 478–493.

Simon, W. (1989). Commentary on the status of sex research: The postmodernization of sex. *Journal of Psychology and Human Sexuality, 2*, 9–37.

Spensley, J., & Barter, J. T. (1971). The adolescent transvestite on a psychiatric service: Family patterns. *Archives of Sexual Behavior, 1*, 347–356.

Spitzer, R. L. (1981). The diagnostic status of homosexuality in DSM-III: A reformulation of the issues. *American Journal of Psychiatry, 138*, 210–215.

Sreenivasan, U. (1985). Effeminate boys in a child psychiatric clinic: Prevalence and associated factors. *Journal of the American Academy of Child Psychiatry, 24*, 689–694.

Standards of care: The hormonal and surgical sex reassignment of gender dysphoric persons. (1985). *Archives of Sexual Behavior, 14*, 79–90.

Steiner, B. W. (Ed.). (1985). *Gender dysphoria: Development, research, management*. New York: Plenum.

Stoller, R. J. (1964). The hermaphroditic identity of hermaphrodites. *Journal of Nervous and Mental Disease, 139*, 453–457.

Stoller, R. J. (1965). The sense of maleness. *Psychoanalytic Quarterly, 34*, 207–218.

Stoller, R. J. (1968a). The sense of femaleness. *Psychoanalytic Quarterly, 37*, 42–55.

Stoller, R. J. (1968b). *Sex and gender: Vol. 1. The development of masculinity and femininity*. New York: Aronson.

Stoller, R. J. (1971). The term "transvestism." *Archives of General Psychiatry, 24*, 230–237.

Stoller, R. J. (1972). The "bedrock" of masculinity and femininity: Bisexuality. *Archives of General Psychiatry, 26*, 207–212.

Stoller, R. J. (1975). *Sex and gender: Vol. 2. The transsexual experiment*. London: Hogarth.

Stoller, R. J. (1982). Transvestism in women. *Archives of Sexual Behavior, 11*, 99–115.

Troiden, R. R. (1979). Becoming homosexual: A model of gay identity acquisition. *Psychiatry, 42*, 362–373.

Troiden, R. R. (1988). Homosexual identity development. *Journal of Adolescent Health Care, 9*, 105–113.

Tully, B. (1992). *Accounting for transsexualism and transhomosexuality*. London: Whiting & Birch.

Walinder, J. (1967). *Transsexualism: A study of forty-three cases*. Göteborg, Sweden: Scandinavian University Books.

Westhead, V. A., Olson, S. J., & Meyer, J. K. (1990). Gender identity disorders in adolescence. In M. Sugar (Ed.), *Adolescent sexuality* (pp. 87–107). New York: Norton.

Zucker, K. J. (1985). Cross-gender-identified children. In B. W. Steiner (Ed.), *Gender dysphoria: Development, research, management* (pp. 75–174). New York: Plenum.

Zucker, K. J. (1990a). Gender identity disorders in children: Clinical descriptions and natural history. In R. Blanchard & B. W. Steiner (Eds.), *Clinical management of gender identity disorders in children and adults* (pp. 1–23). Washington, DC: American Psychiatric Press.

Zucker, K. J. (1990b). Psychosocial and erotic development in cross-gender identified children. *Canadian Journal of Psychiatry, 35,* 487–495.

Zucker, K. J., Bradley, S. J., Corter, C. M., Doering, R. W., & Finegan, J. K. (1980). Cross-gender behaviour in very young boys: A normative study. In J. Samson (Ed.), *Childhood and sexuality* (pp. 599–622). Montreal: Editions Etudes Vivantes.

Zucker, K. J., Bradley, S. J., & Gladding, J. A. (1986, September). *A follow-up study of transsexual, transvestitic, homosexual, and "undifferentiated" adolescents.* Poster presented at the International Academy of Sex Research, Amsterdam.

Zucker, K. J., Bradley, S. J., & Hughes, H. E. (1987). Gender dysphoria in a child with true hermaphroditism. *Canadian Journal of Psychiatry, 32,* 602–609.

Zucker, K. J., & Green, R. (1992). Psychosexual disorders in children and adolescents. *Journal of Child Psychology and Psychiatry, 33,* 107–151.

Zucker, K. J., Wilson, D. N., & Stern, A. (1985, April). *Children's appraisals of sex-typed behavior in their peers.* Poster presented at the meeting of the Society for Research in Child Development, Toronto.

Zucker, K. J., & Bradley, S. J. (in press). *Gender identity disorder and psychosexual problems in children and adolescents.* New York: Guilford.

Zuger, B. (1976). Monozygotic twins discordant for homosexuality: Report of a pair and significance of the phenomenon. *Comprehensive Psychiatry, 17,* 661–669.

Zuger, B. (1989). Homosexuality in families of boys with early effeminate behavior: An epidemiological study. *Archives of Sexual Behavior, 18,* 155–166.

18

Impulse Control Disorders

Duane G. Ollendick

D SM-III-R (American Psychiatric Association [APA], 1987) begins its discussion of this group of problematic behaviors by stating that they are a "residual diagnostic class of behaviors or disorders" whose central feature is that of impulse control. Use of the term *residual* suggests a leftover or remaining quality, implying that numerous other DSM-III-R diagnostic disorders also involve problems of impulse control. As noted by Woodcock (1986), impulse control is seen both as a principal diagnostic feature of some disorders (e.g., attention-deficit disorder) or as an associated diagnostic feature of others (e.g., eating disorder) that traverses the majority of clinical entities. As will be seen shortly, this lack of homogeneity leads to a debate as to the best fit of these disorders within our diagnostic nomenclature. Nonetheless, DSM-IV (APA, 1994) retains their separate categorization.

The class of impulse control disorders includes the five specific disorders that will be discussed in this chapter: intermittent explosive disorder, kleptomania, pathological gambling, pyromania, and trichotillomania. At least two of these disorders, pyromania and trichotillomania, have been extensively reviewed in the child and adolescent literature; there is a scarcity of information concerning intermittent explosive disorder in childhood or adolescent areas. Another of these disorders, pathological gambling, is witnessing a burgeoning body of work that reflects the relatively new arrival of mass gambling activities in the United States. Research on kleptomania is scarce, as investigators have either rarely utilized this diagnosis or have not reported it as a diagnosis in their research. The sixth disorder in this— impulse control disorder not otherwise specified—will not be discussed in this chapter. Even less is known about this nonspecific disorder than about the disorders mentioned above.

All disorders of impulse control exhibit the following essential features (APA, 1994):

The author thanks Dee Carlson, Annette Krutsch, Thomas Ollendick, and Harlan Wickre for their comments and review of this manuscript.

1. Failure to resist an impulse, drive, or temptation to perform some act that is harmful to the person or others.
2. An increasing sense of tension or arousal before committing the act.
3. An experience of either pleasure, gratification, or release at the time of committing the act. Immediately following the act there may or may not be genuine regret, self-reproach, or guilt.

While the five specific disorders under discussion by definition will evidence these features, significant diversity remains. As will discussed below, heterogeneity, rather than homogeneity, predominates.

Historical Background

Impulse control disorders were essentially introduced to formal diagnostic nomenclature with the publication of DSM-III (APA, 1980). At that time, the category included a sixth specific condition, isolated explosive disorder, which was subsequently dropped in DSM-III-R. DSM-IV retains the five specific diagnoses as seen in DSM-III-R (APA, 1994). This grouping of these otherwise seemingly unrelated behavior problems was new in DSM-III, as there was no similar category in either DSM-I (APA, 1952) or DSM-II (APA, 1968). Indeed, these specific disorders seem to have followed widely differing routes to their current status as "impulse control disorders."

For example, "dishonest gamblers" were seen as an example of sociopathic personality disorder (dyssocial type) in DSM-I; they were then assigned to the ranks of "conditions without manifest psychiatric disorder and nonspecific conditions" in DSM-II. (Since the earlier DSMs were not phenomenologically based, it can only be assumed that subpopulations such as gamblers bore at least some similarity to those defined by current criteria.) Similarly, individuals with intermittent explosive disorder under DSM-III would likely have been diagnosed as having "explosive personality disorder" in DSM-II (Monopolis & Lion, 1983). By contrast, pyromania and kleptomania seemingly hold their diagnostic origins in conduct disturbance (an adjustment reaction of childhood) in DSM-I and unsocialized aggressive reaction (a behavior disorder of childhood and adolescence) in DSM-II. Trichotillomania has been and is seen by many to have its origins within the obsessive-compulsive spectrum of behaviors (e.g., Karno, Golding, Sorenson, & Burnam, 1988). This condition was first described by the French dermatologist Hallopeau in 1889 as a compulsion to pull out one's hair (cited in Atton & Tunnessen, 1990). As is evident, then, the historical evolution of this group of behaviors varies across significantly different clinical problem areas (e.g., from personality disorders to obsessive-compulsive disorders) and across developmental levels (from child and adolescent to adult).

Review of these disorders from a historical perspective highlights other developmental issues, as well as taxonomic ones. For example, it is known that certain problem behaviors are characteristic of a particular developmental age and can be transient in nature (Campbell, 1983). Many of the behaviors evident in the impulse control disorders have been noted in this regard—for example, the "natural curiosity" that young children have with fire (Wooden & Berkey, 1984), isolated hair fidgeting or twirling (Hamdan, 1991), or episodes of theft or stealing (Loeber, 1990). While factors of developmental concern must be accounted for at the clinical level, this does not necessarily diminish the behaviors as a source of concern to parents (Mesibov, Schroeder, & Wesson, 1977).

Another factor affecting the development of these categories is taxonomic in nature. After critically reviewing the diagnoses of childhood and adolescent psychopathology, Achenbach and Edelbrock (1983a) state that "neither the extensions of traditional, adult-oriented taxonomy to child psychopathology, nor more theoretically based taxonomies designed for childhood disorders have demonstrated satisfactory reliability or validity" (p. 90). Other investigators have similarly critiqued the available nomenclatures and found them to be inadequate (Mattison, Cantwell, Russell, & Will, 1979; Wells, 1981).

Taxonomic shortcomings will become evident as issues of comorbidity and differential diagnosis, as well as other complications, are considered. Therefore, while DSM-III-R represented significant improvement over previous historical taxonomic strategies, much room for improvement remained (Tuma & Elbert, 1990). In that DSM-IV introduces few substantive changes to this particular group of diagnoses, indications are that ample challenges remain in addressing these taxonomic issues.

Clinical Picture

Aside from the essential features that define and unify the five specific categories, the behavioral presentation of each is quite distinct. The more specific features of intermittent explosive disorder include the presence of discrete episodes of loss of control of aggressive impulses that result in serious assaultive acts or destruction of property. The degree of aggressiveness expressed during the episodes is grossly out of proportion to the precipitating psychosocial stressors. DSM-III-R diagnostic criteria mandated that there were no signs of generalized impulsivity between the episodes, although DSM-IV dropped this criteria (APA, 1994). As will be seen with all disorders in this category, the presence of other problems or diagnoses is common (Jenkins & Maruta, 1987; Woodcock, 1986). Moreover, some diagnoses (e.g., conduct disorder) need to be ruled out before the diagnosis of intermittent explosive disorder can be made. Monopolis and Lion

(1983) also stressed the need to recognize the "soft signs" of this disorder to aid diagnosis. These include episodes such as spells or attacks, indices of social impairment, partial amnesia of the episodes, and remission of the episodes within minutes or hours.

Kleptomania is characterized by the recurrent failure to resist impulses to steal objects not needed for personal use or for their monetary value; the stealing is not committed to express anger or vengeance and is not committed in response to a delusion or hallucination. Typically stolen objects are either given away, discarded, returned surreptitionsly, or kept and hidden. While the theft does not occur when immediate arrest is likely, neither is the activity preplanned, nor are the legal consequences fully appreciated. The behavior does not occur as a result of a larger antisocial picture or as part of a manic episode. As with all impulse control disorders, an increasing sense of tension is experienced just before the act; this is followed by intense gratification of relief (APA, 1987). Studies of adolescents in which the formal diagnosis of kleptomania is made are lacking; numerous reports exist, though, on adolescent stealing, theft, or shoplifting (Henderson, 1983; Loeber, 1987; Loeber & Stouthamer-Loeber, 1987; Moore, Chamberlain, & Mukai, 1979; J. B. Reid & Patterson, 1976). Investigations with adults frequently reveal adolescent onset in a preponderance of case (see McElroy, Pope, Hudson, Keck, & White, 1991). Other noted clinical features include the presence of significant life stressors as triggering events (Glover, 1985), as well as specific stealing patterns or rituals, prior legal apprehensions for theft, and reported guilt or remorse (McElroy et al., 1991).

While the other disorders in this category frequently reveal a clinical picture where symptoms wax or wane, pathological gambling is seen as being both chronic and progressive in nature. This behavior compromises, disrupts, and damages personal, family, and vocational pursuits; moreover, as problems arise, the gambling behavior intensifies. Resistance to the impulses to gamble are further lowered, and more time, energy, and money are channeled in pursuit of the behavior (APA, 1994). Investigators frequently note onset factors in adolescence, along with predisposing factors that include significant family disruption (e.g., parental separation or divorce), limited parental discipline and supervision, or a major life stressor (e.g., a family death; Bolen & Boyd, 1968; Griffiths, 1989; Wolkowitz, Roy, & Doran, 1985). Finally, Custer and Custer (1981) report on "soft signs" that may also be part of the clinical picture, including a low threshold for boredom, the presence of other risk-taking behaviors, workaholic behaviors, and being higher in both intelligence and general energy level.

The clinical picture of pyromania includes the deliberate and purposeful setting of fires on more than one occasion. This is clearly differentiated from the natural curiosity or accidental fires typically set by very young children (Fineman, 1980; Kafry, 1980; Kolko & Kazdin, 1986; Nurcombe, 1964; Wooden & Berkey, 1984); in addition, fascination with, interest in, curiosity about, or attraction to fire and its situational context is observed. The fire setting is not undertaken for monetary gain, as an expression of sociopolitical ideology, to conceal criminal activity, to express anger or vengeance, to improve one's living circumstances, or in response to a delusion or hallucination (APA, 1994). As seen with klepto-mania, the diagnosis of pyromania is not made if the instances of fire set-ting are evidenced as part of a larger conduct or antisocial problem nor during a manic episode.

As pointed out by Kazdin and Kolko (1986), however, most fire setters also meet diagnostic criteria for conduct disorder. A theoretical controver-sy continues, in fact, as to whether or not Pyromania is a separate entity or whether it exists as one end on an antisocial behavior continuum (Patter-son, 1982). In any case, the clinical picture will nearly always include severe family problems, negative environmental experiences, and at least other isolated conduct behavior problems (Jayaprakash, Jung, & Panitch, 1984; Larsen, 1982; Lowenstein, 1989; Prentky & Carter, 1984; Ritvo, Shanok, & Lewis, 1983)

With the disorder of trichotillomania, there is recurrent failure to resist impulses to pull out one's own hair. Again, an increasing sense of tension is experienced immediately before the act, with pleasure, gratification, or a sense of relief experienced when the act is occurring. The act is not better accounted for by another mental disorder and not due to a general medical condition (e.g., a dermatological disorder; APA, 1994). The most common area affected is the scalp, although eyebrows, eyelashes, mustaches, or beards are also frequently targeted sites; to a lesser extent, armpits and the chest or pubic areas may be involved. As noted by Hamdan (1991), tri-chotillomania may present as an isolated symptom or as part of a complex clinical picture. Rituals such as the mouthing or eating of the hair (tri-chophagy) are commonly observed, and occasionally trichobezoars (hair masses formed intestinally) are found upon medical evaluations (Lamerton, 1984). Finally, alopecia (hair loss) is most frequently the first recognized symptom of this hidden disorder (Adam & Kashani, 1990; Atton & Tun-nessen, 1990; Swedo & Rapoport, 1991).

Course and Prognosis

According to DSM-IV, "limited data" are available as to the course of development of intermittent explosive disorder. Further, while age of onset may be at 'any age,' the disorder is typically seen as occurring from late adolescence to the third decade of life (APA, 1994). One study of 20 patients had an age range of 17 to 41 years (Monopolis & Lion, 1983), however, while 3 of 8 patients in another study (Jenkins & Maruta, 1987) were in their teens. Mattes and Fink (1987, 1990) also examined subject groups that included a large number of adolescents; subjects in these studies, however, did not fully meet DSM-III-R criteria in that generalized aggressiveness was also present. Familial factors, including parenting strategies, marital distress and stability, economic factors, and exposure to aggressiveness (i.e., spousal/child abuse), are well documented as contributing to later adolescent behavior and temper control problems (Bandura & Walters, 1963; Becker, Peterson, Hellmer, Shoemaker, & Quay, 1959; Forehand, Wells, & Sturgis, 1978; Friedrich, 1990; Loeber, 1990; McCord, 1958; Peed, Roberts, & Forehand, 1977).

Regarding medical factors, Schrier (1979) reported the presence of intermittent explosive disorder in the case of a 12-year-old boy who was recovering from viral encephalitis. While not commenting on the potentially different course of development, DeMilio (1989) reported a diagnosis of intermittent explosive disorder in 7% of an adolescent group referred for inpatient substance abuse treatment. Finally, the work of Woodcock (1986) reflects perhaps the most comprehensive review of this and other impulse control disorders. He indicated that a multimodal approach is necessary that targets developmental and neurological problems, emotional difficulties, cognitive limitations, and character or family pathology. Prognosis rests on the ability of treatment efforts to address the associated pathologies as well as the targeted explosive episodes.

As with intermittent explosive disorder, DSM-IV reports minimal information concerning the development and course of kleptomania. Age of onset is reported to be "as early as childhood," and the condition is thought to wax and wane, with tendencies toward chronicity. Rate of remission is unknown (APA, 1994). Whether a relationship exists between the more purposeful, isolated shoplifting incidences of childhood and the development of kleptomania remains to be determined. Similarly, aside from the stealing—which is a common problematic behavior within the context of a conduct disorder—the presence of this disorder in adolescence as a separate entity remains unknown. As will be recalled, kleptomania is not diagnosed if the stealing is part of a larger pattern of problem behavior. McElroy et al. (1991) reported on 20 adults meeting DSM-III-R criteria, 13 of whom reported onset between the ages of 5 and 20. In reviewing the items stolen by these individuals, it is interesting to note a developmental progression; for example, one person's list included "money, candy, food, socks, cosmetics, jewelry, drugs, [and] toiletries" (age onset of 5 years), while a second person's list included "pens, books, pornography, [and] sporting equipment" (age onset of 9 years; p. 653). The investigators noted that *all* of their subjects had other concurrent psychiatric diagnoses (particularly mood, anxiety, and eating disorders), and they questioned whether "pure" kleptomania exists. Moreover, remission of kleptomania appears favorable when treatment efforts have also focused on associated behaviors

(Woodcock, 1986), such as depression (Goldman, 1991; McElroy et al., 1991; Ramelli & Mapelli, 1979) and eating disorders (Crisp, Hsu, & Harding, 1980; Krahn, Flegel, & Canum, 1989). Interventions targeting stealing with adolescents who have had more generalized patterns of conduct disruption have been discouraging (Azrin & Weslowski, 1974; Jeffery, 1967; Moore et al., 1979).

By definition, pathological gambling frequently involves a course which is both chronic and progressive. Onset typically begins in adolescence and is more evident in males than females (APA, 1994; Bolen & Boyd, 1968; Griffiths, 1990a; Trott & Griffiths, 1991; Wolkowitz et al., 1985). Blume (1992) reports that females comprise one-third of all pathological gamblers and develop problem behaviors later than their male counterparts. Custer (1982a) reported that there were "uniform patterns of development and progression and predictable complication" once the pathological gambler begins to gamble. The pattern begins with small successful bets that, with early lucky wins, prompt more skillful gambling with more and larger winnings. The "winning phase," as described by Custer, continues with the gambler wagering amounts equal to or greater than his or her annual salary. The "losing phase," which is characterized by unrealistic optimism, is almost certain to follow. The gambler then begins to "chase" after larger bets to recoup losses (Lesieur, 1977). This "desperation phase" is followed by the "giving up phase," where gamblers continue their activities despite known, insurmountable losses (Lesieur & Rosenthal, 1991).

Given some of the more general limitations of the teenage years (e.g., limited opportunity and income), the progression of this problem has not been thoroughly examined in adolescents. Recent reports, however, have found it to be a "costly activity in terms of both time and money (Trott & Griffiths, 1991)." It has also been noted that unsupervised adolescents play for higher stakes, prompting the suggestion that parents may actually facilitate the progression of gambling by their uninvolvement (Griffiths, 1990a). Arcuri, Lester, and Smith (1985) reported that 79% of parents revealed "little concern" concerning known gambling activities in a study of 717 14- to 19-year-olds. Griffiths (1990c) found that 28% of adolescent gamblers in England began gambling *with* their parents, and Lesieur and Klein (1987) obtained data showing that high school students who reported that their parents had a gambling problem were more likely to have similar difficulties themselves. Studies of intervention and prognosis are lacking, but several investigators have noted how sociological and environmental factors may actually shape adolescent pathological gambling (Arcuri et al., 1985; Griffiths, 1990b, 1990c; Lesieur & Rosenthal, 1991; McGurrin, 1992).

Pyromania has long been recognized as having its onset during childhood or early adolescence (Fineman, 1980; Heath, Gayton, & Hardesty, 1976; Kolko & Kazdin, 1986; Lowenstein, 1989; Steward & Culver,

1982; Wooden & Berkey, 1984). DSM-IV (APA, 1994) reports no information regarding its developmental course but suggests that when onset is later in life, the fire setting is more deliberately destructive. Wooden and Berkey (1984) describe the earliest acts of fire setting as occurring out of "normal curiosity," while Fineman (1980) describes the "normal child who experiments with firesetting behavior." Kolko and Kazdin (1986) further review several studies in which "early fireplay" is reported in the natural course of development.

The causes and course of this behavioral progression are difficult to disentangle. Fineman (1980) describes pathological fire setting as being motivated by factors of anger and frustration resulting from family or parental loss or abuse, or from antagonism for authority. He suggests that the act of firesetting provides a sense of power and control that is otherwise lacking in the fire setter's life. Kolko and Kazdin (1986) offer a conceptual model that includes such factors as early modeling experiences; cognitive, behavioral, and motivational components; and sources of parental and family influences. Researchers continue to concentrate, though, on the abusive and/or abnormal family environments and painful childhood experiences that occur in children who go on to develop pyromania (Lowenstein, 1989; Wooden & Berkey, 1984). With adolescents, the clinician will need to differentiate those who may have pyromania from those whose fire-setting activities fall within a wider array of antisocial behaviors (Forehand, Wierson, Frame, Kempton, & Armistead, 1991; Kolko, Kazdin, & Meyer, 1985; Patterson, 1982). Several studies describe the successful resolution of this disorder, suggesting a favorable prognosis when early and adequate identification is made (Bumpass, Fagelman, & Brix, 1983; McGrath, Marshall, & Prior, 1979).

The last specific impulse control disorder, trichotillomania, also has an extensive research history pointing to its onset early in the developmental process. It has been described (e.g., Friman & Hove, 1987) as a covariant with other childhood behaviors that waxes and wanes and even disappears when treatment efforts target the collateral behaviors (Friman, Finney, & Christophersen, 1984). Illingworth (1984) suggested that the "habit" wanes as children mature; Adam and Kashani (1990) and Swedo and Rapaport (1991) note that adolescents usually deny the self-induced nature of the disorder, as do their parents (Muller, 1987). Frequently the course of this disorder dictates that first diagnosis is made by medical personnel, including dermatologists or family physicians (Atton & Tunnessen, 1990; H. R. Greenberg & Sarner, 1965). For unexplained reasons, earlier onset (between the ages of 2 and 6 years) is much more common in males (Dawber, 1985; Muller, 1987) while preadolescent or adolescent onset is more prevalent in females (H. R. Greenberg & Sarner, 1965; Mannino & Delgado, 1969; Ratner, 1989). Adolescent onset is also associated with a greater level of pathology (Swedo & Rapoport, 1991). Treatment efficacy is well established utilizing different modalities (e.g., see Azrin, Nunn, & Frantz, 1980; Nelson, 1982; Primeau & Fontaine, 1987; Tarnowski, Rosen, McGrath, & Drabman, 1987) although some have reported on treatment difficulties (Toback & Rajkumar, 1979). In general, prognosis appears favorable for successful resolution.

Complications

Due to the nature of the activities involved in four of the five impulse control disorders (intermittent explosive disorder, kleptomania, pathological gambling, and pyromania), legal interventions and possible incarcerations appear to be the major complications (APA, 1987). Incarceration, however, would certainly be less of a consideration with adolescents. Reid (1989) and Woodcock (1986) further discuss the disruptions that occur in the environments of individuals with intermittent impulse control, including family and home life, school, places of employment, and peer groups. In the McElroy et al. (1991) study of 20 kleptomaniacs, 15 had been apprehended at least once, and 3 served jail terms. Legal intervention resulted in complete remission in 5 individuals, minimally influenced the stealing behavior of 8, and had no effect in 2 cases. If law enforcement agencies do not make psychiatric referral at the time of arrest, it remains unlikely that even the added pain and humiliation of arrest helps individuals with kleptomania decide to get assistance (Goldman, 1991), and their problems often intensify.

Numerous investigators have reported on the disruption of personal, legal, and family aspects of adults with pathological gambling (see review by Wolkowitz et al., 1985), and at least two reports exist on the disruption of sexual functioning (Daghestani, 1987; Schwartz & Schwartz, 1971). Much less is known regarding adolescents; Trott and Griffiths (1991) reported on only one individual who stole regularly to support his gambling, although two other adolescents felt they were "addicted." In contrast, Griffiths (1990b, 1990c) reviewed a number of surveys conducted in England where significant numbers of adolescents admitted to stealing (3% to 23%), regular spending of lunch money (17%), and truancy (1% to 6%) related to gambling activities. Griffiths (1990b) reported finding higher prevalences for stealing (12%), use of lunch money (18%), and truancy (32%) in his own work. The relationship between gambling and chemical addictions has been discussed by several researchers (H. R. Greenberg, 1980; Lesieur & Rosenthal, 1991; Wolkowitz et al., 1985).

Pyromania represents the last disorder where legal interventions may represent the major complication. With adolescents, this may mean that extra care is taken to assure follow-up by social service personnel due to the potential danger of fire setting. For example, in their sample of legally incarcerated adolescent males, Ritvo et al. (1983) reported that 69% of the identified fire setters had been in prior residential psychiatric treatment, compared to 37% of the non–fire setters. As will be seen later, however, this behavior can be successfully managed in the majority of cases.

Neither legal complications nor significant family disruptions are apparent with trichotillomania; instead, alopecia is commonly observed (Atton & Tunnessen, 1990). Trichophagy can lead to life-threatening complications (Muller, 1987), and the formation of trichobezoars can lead to gastric or intestinal bleeding, perforation, intestinal obstruction, acute pancreatitis, and obstructive jaundice (Adam & Kashani, 1990; Lamerton, 1984).

Etiology

Theories regarding the causes of impulse control disorders are varied. As will be seen, specific theories range from early psychoanalytic speculations to more recent multifaceted explanations. For some of the disorders, our understanding is mimimal. Further, many theorists continue to question the placement of these specific disorders within this "residual" diagnostic class (see earlier discussion):

> Disorders of impulse control are often thought of as relatively obscure and unusual. It may be assumed that they are either due to esoteric metabolic or physiologic etiologies or to be seen only in association with other developmental pervasive abnormalities. The characteristic features of the underlying illness may be obvious, but they may also be subtle and masked by the dramatic aspects and disruptive effects of the behavioral dyscontrol. (Woodcock, 1986, p. 341)

Woodcock goes on to differentiate impulsive interactive behaviors of intermittent explosive disorder from behaviors that are less spontaneous (e.g., pathological gambling). He views this distinction as an important differentiation from the other four specific disorders. Others have also focused on the neurological or biochemical underpinnings of this disorder (Jenkins & Maruta, 1987; Mattes, 1985; Monopolis & Lion, 1983; Monroe, 1981a, 1981b; Paulsen & Johnson, 1980; Virkkunen, 1984). Conversely, psychodynamic and behavioral understanding of intermittent explosive disorder stems from more psychological theories on aggressive and behavioral dyscontrol (Bornstein, Shuldberg, & Bornstein, 1987; Doke & Flippo, 1983). These theoretical perspectives have highlighted perspectives that view aggression as an instinctive behavior, an elicited drive, or a learned social behavior (see review by Baron, 1977). Finally, Loeber (1990) has discussed the factors that "reflect decreased levels of impulse control," including familial, developmental, social and environmental factors.

In a review, Goldman (1991) stated that the causes of kleptomania are unknown. Further, McElroy et al. (1991) have added that the literature yields "no systematic studies of a series of rigorously diagnosed kleptomanic individuals" (p. 652). Nonetheless, causation is hypothesized to stem from a number of possibilities that have not been extensively formulated or empirically evaluated. These factors include traitlike psychodynamic variables (Goldman, 1991; Reid, 1989; Tolpin, 1983), as well as more situationally based variables that are behavioral in nature (Glover, 1985; McElroy et al., 1991). Etiological studies of adolescents are lacking.

As noted earlier, studies of pathological gambling are increasing, including those targeting adolescents who gamble. Wolkowitz et al. note that the disorder generally begins in adolescence and results from a number of etiologic considerations. Psychodynamic formulations stem from the early work of Freud, who viewed gambling as a masturbatory equivalent (Fenichel, 1945). Later analysts stressed forbidden unconscious drives (Bolen & Boyd, 1968) and masochistic tendencies (Niederland, 1967) of gambling. Greenson (1947) suggested that acts of gambling warded off depression. Skinner (1953) viewed gambling simply as an operant behavior subject to variable reinforcement, noting that proprietors of gambling establishments have long been aware of how to maintain the behavior. Other maintenance behaviors ("nothing else to do," "for a challenge") are reviewed by Griffiths (1990c). DSM-III-R reported that inappropriate parental discipline, early exposure to gambling activities, and a family emphasis on material and financial symbols are also predisposing factors (APA, 1987), while Zuckerman (1979) conceptualized the behavior as being one form of risk taking and sensation seeking. In a small sample of adult pathological gamblers, however, Allcock and Grace (1988) found patients to be no higher in sensation-seeking or impulsivity than controls; these researchers favor the learned maladaptive behavior perspective. More than any of the other impulse control disorders, however, pathological gambling has often been viewed as an addictive behavior (Greenberg, 1980; Leseiur & Rosenthal, 1991; Reid, 1989). Indeed, many authors have reviewed this association to the point of noting parallel withdrawal reactions, even though no known involved chemical exists (Custer, 1982b; Wray & Dickerson, 1981). The success of treatment programs utilizing "Gamblers Anonymous" principles (see later discussion) lends support to this view.

Natural curiosity or early fascination with fire is viewed as integral to the normal developmental sequence. When it persists into adolescence, however, it is viewed as an expression of stress, anxiety, and anger (Wooden & Berkey, 1984). While early psychodynamic formulations of pyromania were again expounded, noting regressive psychosexual developments, poorly developed ego functions, and oral sadistic drives (Fenichel, 1945; Grunstein, 1952; Macht & Mack, 1968), more recent reviews point to family dynamics as causative factors. For example, Fineman (1980) states that "pathological juvenile firesetters generally come from a confused, disturbed, and unstable family background" (p. 485). Ritvo et al. (1983) conclude that the "most consistent finding seems to be an association between firesetting and broken disturbed families" (p. 259). Lowenstein (1989) reported that the etiological factors "can be broadly categorized as [an] abusive and abnormal family environment" (p. 186).

Even though convincing data appear to exist regarding primary etiological factors, Kolko and Kazdin (1986) have forwarded a more extensive conceptual analysis that considers such other factors as stressful external events and cognitive, behavioral, and motivational components. Early learning and modeling experiences, interpersonal skills, peer influences, availability of adult supervision, and parental uninvolvement and pathology are also examined in the Kolko and Kazdin analysis.

Finally, explanatory theories of trichotillomania have also not been absent from professional literature. Representative of the psychodynamic tradition is the work of Buxbaum (1960), who hypothesized that hair pulling was a form of autoeroticism, while Greenberg and Sarner (1965) viewed it as a result of multiple fixation points at all levels of psychosexual development. As noted earlier, several authors have defined it as a less problematic but nonetheless persistent "habit disorder" (Azrin & Nunn, 1973; Illingworth, 1987; Oranje, Peereboom-Wynia, & DeRaeymaecker, 1986); others (Mannino & Delgado, 1969; Toback & Rajkumar, 1979) have viewed it as occurring within the context of more severe psychopathology. The biochemical considerations are underscored by those who classify trichotillomania as a variant of obsessive-compulsive disorder (Atton & Tunnessen, 1990; Jenike, 1990; Rapoport, 1989). More recently, Rapoport and her colleagues (Swedo & Rapoport, 1991; Swedo, Rapoport, Leonard, Lenane, & Cheslo, 1989) have seen trichotillomania as part of a larger spectrum of pathological grooming behaviors and cleaning rituals. As with all the impulse control disorders, etiological views of trichotillomania continue to prosper, many of them without sufficient empirical support.

Familial Pattern

Just as there is a paucity of research regarding the other facets of intermittent explosive disorder with adolescents, there is also little known concerning familial patterns. This is in contrast, of course, to the familial patterns that exist with adolescent aggression or other conduct disorders (Doke & Flippo, 1983; Forehand, 1990; Hetherington & Martin, 1979; Loeber, 1990). Further, there exists evidence to suggest that the tendency to be hot-tempered is familial (Lefkowitz, Eron, & Walder, 1977; Mattes & Fink, 1987; Stewart & deBlois, 1983). DMS-III-R reported this disorder to be "more common" in first-degree relatives (APA, 1987) and Woodcock (1986) also emphasizes the biological contribution to the impulse disorders. In one study of young adults with intermittent explosive disorder, Mattes and Fink (1990) examined first-degree relatives of adopted and nonadopted patients. Results suggested that the transmission of temper problems is due to genetic factors instead of environmental factors, a finding the authors view as being consistent with that of animal studies (e.g., Eleftheriou, Bailey, & Denenberg, 1974) where genetic transmission of aggression has been demonstrated.

Although a strong association between criminal behavior in children and criminal records of their parents has been found to exist (Belson, 1975; Dunford & Elliott, 1984; Klemke, 1982; Patterson, 1982), little is known about the familial patterns per se of kleptomania (APA, 1987). A recent report in this area revealed that 2 of 20 patients with kleptomania had a first-degree relative with the same disorder (McElroy et al., 1991).

With pathological gambling, exposure to the activity and family values and attitudes are seen as significant etiological contributors. Consequently the "more common" occurrence of a familial pattern would be expected (APA, 1987; Wolkowitz et al., 1985). Griffiths (1990a) observed that "many parents actually facilitate their own children's gambling behavior" (p. 1138); in a separate study, Griffiths (1990c) reported that 28% of adolescents who gamble started doing so with their parents. Surprisingly, few other empirical data illustrating this expected relationship are to be found.

As with kleptomania, no information was reported on the familial patterns of pyromania in DSM-III-R (APA, 1987). Just as Lowenstein (1989) observed that diagnosis of fire setting is rarely made because careful assessment is not completed in this area, others examining familial dynamics either have failed to inquire about like parental behavior or have not reported their findings (Showers & Pickrell, 1987). In Fineman's (1980) review of historical family factors related to adolescent fire setting, no mention of parental pyromania is made. Somewhat relatedly, however, Fineman speculates about parents who play a role in teaching their children that fire play is an "acceptable behavior." An earlier study (Macht & Mack, 1968) also found that the fathers of adolescent fire setters were involved in some way with fire in their occupations (e.g., firemen). In spite of the consistent evidence of significant family psychopathology (see earlier review), however, data regarding the relationship between parent and child pyromanic behavior are lacking.

Specific data concerning the familial pattern of trichotillomania were also absent in DSM-III-R (APA, 1987). However, it was reported that one study found 5 of 19 subjects who had a positive family history for some form of alopecia. Delgado and Mannino (1969) also related a history of alopecia in first-degree relatives of 2 subjects with trichotillomania. Swedo, Leonard, et al. (1989) reported similarly on the increased frequency of obsessive-compulsive disorder in first-degree relatives of individuals with trichotillomania. Hamdan (1991) argues that family history studies are "scant". Swedo and Rapoport (1991) conducted the *only* systematic family study to date; in this study, carried out at the National Institutes of Health, 65 first-degree relatives of 16 trichotillomanic probands were interviewed. Although the authors caution about use of the data because no prevalence studies exist for comparison, an incidence of trichotillomania was found in 5% of the relatives. A "higher rate of severe primary obsessive compulsive disorder" was also found in the first-degree relatives. While data may yet remain "scant," an emerging familial pattern is becoming increasingly evident.

Differential Diagnosis and Assessment

Swedo, Leonard, and Rapoport (1990) comment that a continuum of severity exists with virtually all psychiatric disorders. This is particularly true for children, as developmental stages occur and the differentiation between normal versus pathological behaviors evolves. Further according to DSM-III-R (APA, 1987), "There is no assumption that each mental disorder is a discrete entity with sharp boundaries (discontinuity) between it and other mental disorders, or between it and no mental disorder" (p. xxii). To complicate issues even more, adolescence has been characterized by many to be a time of transition and change (e.g., Montemayor, 1983; Petersen, 1987). It is consistently estimated that 20% of adolescents experience psychological problems in general (Forehand, 1990; Graham, 1979; Montemayor, 1983). These issues of differential diagnosis and evolving developmental factors are, as will be seen, noteworthy with regard to the category of impulse control disorders.

Problems of adolescent aggression (e.g., as reflected in antisocial and delinquent behaviors) have increased dramatically over the past decades (Loeber, 1990). Researchers agree that aggressive adolescents suffer from a disturbance in the development of impulse control (Levine & Jordan, 1987; Loeber, 1990). Learning impulse control and control of aggression remains a developmental task which becomes a "common developmental problem" if not accomplished (Campbell, 1983). Differential diagnosis of intermittent explosive disorder in adolescents is made *after* other DSM-IV disorders associated with loss of control of aggressive impulses have been ruled out; these include attention-deficit hyperactivity or conduct disorder and, to a lesser extent, psychotic, organic, personality, or psychoactive substance disorders (APA, 1994). Incidence figures for intermittent explosive disorder in adolescents are lacking. Assessment of this disorder necessitates a broad-based, multimethod approach, as is commonly completed with other childhood or adolescent disorders (see Ollendick & Hersen, 1984).

The use of structured adolescent interviews, as well as behavioral rating scales, has been well delineated (Achenbach & Edelbrock, 1983b; Edelbrock & Costello, 1984).

Because of the relative infrequency of the behaviors constituting intermittent explosive disorder, monitoring is required over a longer time period (Jenkins & Maruta, 1987). In their study of young adults, Mattes and Fink (1990) utilized a modified version of the Family History Research Diagnostic Criteria to conduct interviews, while DeMilio (1989) utilized the Structured Clinical Interview for DSM-III. Yudofsky, Silver, Jackson, Endicott, and Williams (1986) developed the Overt Aggressive Scale for the objective assessment of verbal and physical aggression. Finally, as with all of the impulse control disorders, Woodcock (1986) highlighted the importance of completing a comprehensive neurological evaluation.

Examination of the other disorders in the impulse control category reveals additional problems of assessment and differential diagnosis. Relative to kleptomania, for example, many adolescents self-report engaging in occasional petty theft (Belson, 1975; Gold, 1970), and Miller and Klungness (1989) report that "isolated incidents" of stealing are not necessarily cause for alarm. Loeber and Schmaling (1985) report that there are no developmental norms from which judgments of severity can be made. Further, the relative absence of standardized assessment methods used to diagnose the more "covert" behaviors has been noted (Canter, 1982; Gove & Crutchfield, 1982). After reviewing related studies, Miller and Klungness (1989) report that 40% to 60% of child referrals to clinical settings have stealing identified as the major problem. Information is lacking, however, regarding the incidence of kleptomania in adolescents. DMS-III-R reports that "fewer than 5%" of shoplifters have histories consistent with the disorder, and that kleptomania is likely more common among females, who are more prone to shoplifting (APA, 1987). Clearly the diagnosis from which kleptomania must be differentiated the most would be that of conduct disorder, where stealing is viewed as the most discriminative diagnostic feature (Miller & Klugness, 1989).

Differential diagnosis of pathological gambling in adolescents consists of defining the severity of the behavior and contrasting it with social gambling, where diagnostic criteria are not met (APA, 1994). In addition to the previously mentioned assessment strategies, observational techniques (Griffiths, 1990a) and structured interviews (Trott & Griffiths, 1991) specific to the investigation of adolescent gambling have been proposed. The South Oaks Gambling Screen (Lesieur & Blume, 1987) was developed to aid diagnosis of problem gambling in adults. Additionally, Wolkowitz et al. (1985) discussed the usefulness of information obtained from Zuckerman's (1979) Sensation Seeking Scale for both social and pathological gamblers. DSM-IV reports a prevalence rate of 1% to 3% in the adult population, with the disorder more common among males (APA, 1994). Greenberg

(1980) obtained data revealing pathological gambling to be five times more common in men than women, although Blume (1992) recently noted that women account for one-third of such gamblers. Still others (Sommers, 1988; Volberg & Steadman, 1988) have found pathological gambling to be only twice as common among males as it is among females.

Among adolescents, Trott and Griffiths (1991) report only a "minority" of gamblers are pathological, while Griffiths (1990a) found evidence that two-thirds of gamblers are male. Jacobs (1989) reported that between 4% and 6% of high school students could be diagnosed as pathological gamblers, and a recent Minnesota study (KTCA Reports, 1992) found that 6.3% of 15 to 18-year-olds were "problem" gamblers. Astonishingly, the Minnesota report also identified 19.9% additional adolescents as being at risk of becoming problem gamblers. At least one investigator (Blake, 1984) has reported that the number of women seeking help for pathological gambling had increased tenfold over recent years and noted that women may account for 40% of all pathological gamblers in America. Whether this trend extends to the adolescent population awaits further inquiry, although the rates are not drastically different from those reported by Griffiths (1990a).

Natural curiosity and normal early fascination with fire play have been noted by several researchers (e.g., Fineman, 1980; Kolko & Kazdin, 1986; Wooden & Berkey, 1984). Differential diagnosis between pyromania and young children's experimentation is necessary (APA, 1994), although such experimentation would normally run its course prior to adolescence (Wooden, 1985). More importantly differential diagnosis is necessary to distinguish pyromanic from intentional fire setting in adolescence, which is frequently seen as a form of retaliation or as an act of vandalism in conduct disorders or other antisocial behavioral patterns (Forehand et al., 1991; Patterson, 1982). For example, Loeber (1990) cites data showing that the pattern of school arson increased 859% between 1950 and 1975 while the number of students increased only 86%. More globally, Mieszala (1981) reported that adolescents account for up to 60% of all fire-setting activity.

While etiological theories do not adequately explain gender differences, pyromania is described in DSM-IV as being "much more" common in males than females (APA, 1994). Lowenstein (1989) cites a male-female prevalence ratio of 6 to 1 while Jacobson (1985) found 87 male and 17 female fire setters in a study of 4,242 clinic-referred children. Showers and Pickrell (1987) reviewed several studies and concluded that females generally constitute less than 10% of fire setters. Several researchers (Fineman, 1980; Tennent, McQuaid, Loughnane, & Hands, 1971), though report that female incidence figures may be on the rise.

While assessment difficulties of the more covert behaviors were noted earlier, at least two scales of recent advance have targeted fire-setting behaviors. Lowenstein (1981) developed the Lowenstein Fire Raising Diagnostic

Test and reported limited data regarding its ability to discriminate positively. More recently, Kolko and Kazdin (1989) reported on the Children's Firesetting Interview, with data reported on 6 to 13-year-olds. Specific measures such as these, will aid the assessment process, although much more extensive study and validation is necessary for their use with adolescents.

As with other disorders in this category, trichotillomania needs to be differentiated from less intensive hair-pulling behavior (Azrin & Nunn, 1973; Friman et al., 1984; Friman & Rostain, 1990). Further, diagnosis is not made with the "normal" activities of either periodic stroking or "fiddling with" the hair (APA, 1987). Atton and Tunnessen (1990) review the primary physical causes from which trichotillomania needs to be differentiated; these include tinea capitis (hair loss resulting from a pathogenic fungi), alopecia areata (hair loss associated with autoimmune disease), and telogen effluvium (premature cessation of normal hair growth). Most investigators concur with the need for concomitant medical evaluation (e.g., pediatrics, dermatology; Adam & Kashani, 1990; Muller, 1987; Price, 1978), and occasionally specific microscopic assessment can be completed (see Atton & Tunnessen, 1990; Steck, 1979; Wright, Schaefer, & Solomons, 1979). Assessment difficulties are enhanced by tendencies of both the adolescent and his or her parents to conceal the behavior (H. R. Greenberg & Sarner, 1965; Swedo & Rapoport, 1991).

Prevalence figures are also lacking for trichotillomania (Swedo & Rapoport, 1991), although Azrin and Nunn (1978) estimated that up to 8 million Americans are affected. In spite of this, clinical samples have yielded low incidence figures (Krishnan, Davidson, & Guajardo, 1985; Mannino & Delgado, 1969); Mehregan (1978) reported a ratio of 7 children/adolescents for every 1 adult. Several authors have noted the disorder to be more prevalent among males in early childhood but among females during the adolescent years (Dawber, 1985; Muller, 1987; Ottens, 1981; Swedo & Rapoport, 1991).

Clinical Management

As has been observed, this residual category of diagnoses applies to a diverse set of problem behaviors and a wide variety of individuals. Effective clinical management rests with treatment strategies targeting presenting symptoms, underlying causes, and associated conditions (e.g., see discussions by Borduin & Henggeler, 1990; Weist, Ollendick, & Finney, 1991; Woodcock, 1986). It is because of the behavioral diversity of this group that treatments range from the multifaceted milieu treatment of pathological gambling to the biological treatment of intermittent explosive disorder; this diversity frequently requires professional teamwork and consultation between disciplines, as observed by Reid (1989).

Specific studies of the clinical management of intermittent explosive disorder with adolescents are lacking. Isolated case studies exist, however, such as that of an 18-year-old by Woodcock (1986) and that of a 12-year-old by Schreier (1979). These reflect treatment efforts consistent with the favored biological, neuropsychiatric explanations of the disorder. A sampling of studies utilizing medications with adults include the use of carbamazepine (Stone, McDaniel, Hughes, & Hermann, 1986), phenytoin (Finkel, 1984), beta-blockers (Elliot, 1978; Jenkins & Maruta, 1987; Mattes, 1985) and lithium carbonate (Reid & Gutnik, 1982; Tupin et al., 1972). Reid (1989) observes that finding episodic violence (which may be significantly decreased or eliminated by medication) as "organic" may ironically limit the overall success of treatment. To this end, he notes that accompanying psychotherapy should be provided; goals of such treatment would be to reinforce desired behavioral changes, help develop coping skills, and assist stabilization.

Quite clearly, the majority of interventions for adolescent stealing have relied on behavioral orientations. These include aversive and positive contingency management, parent training, self-control procedures, and environmental (e.g., school, community) strategies (see reviews by Miller & Klungness, 1986, 1989). The use of individualized behavior therapy techniques, especially covert sensitization, has proved particularly effective when individualized treatment is desired in a clinical setting (Cautela, 1967; Gauthier & Pellerin, 1982; Glover, 1985; Guidry, 1975). Tolpin (1983) and Goldman (1991) discuss the usefulness of psychodynamic approaches in eliminating not only stealing behavior but also accompanying mood states. Finally, a recent study of 20 cases (the majority of whom had adolescent onset) found that *all* individuals met criteria for a current or past major mood disorder. When antidepressant medications were utilized with this group, half revealed either partial or complete remission of their kleptomanic (McElroy et al., 1991). Similarly, Robey (cited in Reid, 1989) described the successful use of antidepressant medication with some individuals.

Wolkowitz et al. (1985) observed that until fairly recently, primarily psychodynamic approaches were utilized in the treatment of pathological gambling despite highly variable and discouraging results (Greenberg, 1980). Management approaches now more frequently involve adjunctive group, family, or couple therapy (Bolen & Boyd, 1965). Custer (1982b) considers those approaches that integrate Gamblers Anonymous to be most successful; Several authors have described successful residential or tightly structured programs employing these same principles (Kellner, 1982; Taber, McCormick, & Russo, 1987). Reports of behavioral treatments have been sparse, with Greenberg and Rankin (1982) finding limited success with a variety of behavioral strategies. Other studies (McConaghy, Armstrong, Blaszczynski, & Allcock, 1983; Rankin, 1982) using behavioral techniques like imaginal desensitization have reported some success.

Pathological gambling also has been treated with pharmacological agents that target associated emotional conditions. The presence of mood disorders has been noted historically, and therefore antidepressants have been utilized (Linden, Jonas, & Pope, 1984; McCormick, Russo, Ramirez, & Taber, 1984). Moskowitz (1980) also successfully administered lithium. These treatment approaches have been utilized with adults; clearly their use and heuristic value remain to be determined with adolescents. Treatment outcome investigation's have been reviewed by Lesieur and Rosenthal (1991) and McGurrin (1992).

Behavioral interventions have been used to a much greater extent with pyromania than with any of the other impulse control disorders. Detailed analyses such as the conceptualization offered by Kolko and Kazdin (1986) have provided more specific intervention strategies that focus on specific behaviors. Fineman (1980) and others, however, have stressed that the "most effective intervention" involves premorbid education about fire during the formative years. Kellner (1982) reported that "no controlled studies" on the treatment of pyromania existed before 1981; fortunately, several have appeared since. Behavioral strategies have included the use of satiation principles (Wolff, 1984), negative practice (Kolko, 1983) and methods combining such behavioral components as relaxation and awareness training (Koles & Jensen, 1985). Lande (1980) used covert sensitization successfully to treat fire-setting behavior associated with sexual dysfunction. Other management strategies have emphasized the correlation between fire-setting behaviors and triggering events and feelings (Bumpass, Brix, & Preston, 1985; Bumpass et al., 1983; Dalton, Haslett, & Baul, 1986), and still others have utilized parents in the treatment process (Baizerman & Emshoff, 1984; Kolko, 1983). Kellner (1982) outlined psychodynamic considerations, while Lowenstein (1989) reviewed the use of therapy directed at confrontation. Obviously, when fire-setting is only part of a greater spectrum of behavior problems (as in the case of conduct disorder), these problems must be addressed as well (Forehand et al., 1991; Loeber, 1990; Patterson, 1982).

The choice of clinical management strategies of trichotillomania remains (as with all the behaviors under consideration) dependent on specific assessment findings. Behavioral techniques appear effective in situations where onset is early and the behavior is seemingly more benign (Friman & Rostain, 1990). More severe, unremitting adolescent-onset cases may require additional pharmacological interventions (Swedo et al., 1990). Friman et al. (1984) provide an extensive review of the treatment literature prior to 1984, including studies on self-management, covert desensitization, and habit reversal. Tarnowski et al., (1987) also reported on the use of habit reversal techniques. After surveying the behavioral literature, Swedo and Rapoport (1991) conclude that habit reversal has produced the best results; they add, however, that the behavioral treatments are the only ones to be systematically examined. Hypnotherapy has also been used as a clinical management tool (Barabasz, 1987; Fabbri & Dy, 1974; Friman & O'Connor, 1984; Hall & McGill, 1986). Ottens (1981) utilized cognitive-behavioral psychotherapy, while others (Buxbaum, 1960; Delgado & Mannino, 1969; Greenberg, 1969; Oguchi & Miura, 1977; Sorosky & Sticher, 1980) have focused on psychodynamic techniques.

Pharmacological treatments for trichotillomania include an isolated report on the use of an antipsychotic (chlorpromazine; Childers, 1958), and the use of antidepressants. Antidepressant trials include studies using the MAO inhibitor izocarboxazid (Krishnan, Davidson, & Miller, 1984), imipramine (Sachdeva & Sidhu, 1987; Weller, Weller, & Carr, 1989), amitriptyline (Snyder, 1980), and fluoxetine (Primeau & Fontaine, 1987; Winchel, Stanley, Guido, Posner, & Stanley, 1989), as well as a controlled study of clomipramine and desipramine (Swedo, Leonard et al., 1989). Advances in the systematic investigation of pharmacological agents (e.g., see Swedo, Leonard, et al., 1989) hold particular importance for those cases that have not remitted through other methods. Further empirical study is necessary, however, before conclusions can be drawn regarding the usefulness of the nonbehavioral techniques in the clinical management of trichotillomania with adolescents.

Conclusion

Examination of these five disorders has indeed revealed that significant heterogeneity exists. To some extent this should not be surprising, given that they are defined as a "residual" class of behaviors. Even the identified unifying diagnostic feature of impaired impulse control, however, continues to be questioned by at least some investigators.

As stated earlier, developmental issues and taxonomic dilemmas characterize the study of the impulse control disorders. The words *adolescent* and *kleptomania* are rarely seen in the same sentence, yet "stealing" is extensively reviewed. When does trichotillohabitus—viewed by some as a common childhood habit behavior—become trichotillomania? Comorbidity and complications of differential diagnosis are heightened with this category of disorders. Why do some of these behaviors remit when treatment targets a coexisting condition? Are they distinct disorders, and should they continue to be classified together? Theoreticians view them as fitting better with other diagnostic considerations, including obsessive-compulsive disorders (trichotillomania), organic or neurological conditions (Intermittent Explosive Disorder), and addictions (pathological gambling). To some, pyromania represents an advanced level of antisocial behavior, while kleptomania is rarely identified separate from stealing behaviors seen in the conduct disorders. Finally, with the majority of these behaviors first evident in childhood and adolescence, one wonders why they were not at least identified at this developmental level within the DSM-III-R (and now DSM-IV) nomenclature.

Review of these disorders leads to an understanding of the multiple factors and complexities of each as an independent yet related entity. In all too many instances, the cited references are only representative of a more extensive body of literature; nevertheless the list of references is lengthy. Issues awaiting further study and evaluation abound. At the time of this writing, DSM-IV diagnostic criteria were just published. Other publications of the results, discussions, and recommendations of the DSM-IV study groups may well direct the future explorations and resolutions of these challenging issues.

References

Achenbach, T. M. & Edelbrock, C. S. (1983a) Taxonomic issues in child psychopathology. In T. H. Ollendick & M. Hersen (Eds.), *Handbook of child psychopathology*. New York: Plenum.

Achenbach, T. M., & Edelbrock, C. (1983b). *Manual for the Child Behavior Checklist and Revised Behavior Profile*. Burlington: University of Vermont, Department of Psychiatry.

Adam, B. S., & Kashani, J. H. (1990). Trichotillomania in children and adolescents. *Child Psychiatry and Human Development, 20*, 159–168.

Allcock, C. C., & Grace, D. M. (1988). Pathological gamblers are neither impulsive nor sensation-seekers. *Australian and New Zealand Journal of Psychiatry, 22*, 307–311.

American Psychiatric Association. (1952). *Diagnostic and statistical manual of mental disorders*. Washington, DC: Author.

American Psychiatric Association. (1968). *Diagnostic and statistical manual of mental disorders: DSM-II*. (2nd ed.). Washington, DC: Author.

American Psychiatric Association. (1980). *Diagnostic and statistical manual of mental disorders* (3rd ed.). Washington, DC: Author.

American Psychiatric Association. (1987). *Diagnostic and statistical manual of mental disorders* (rev. 3rd ed.). Washington, DC: Author.

American Psychiatric Association. (1994). *Diagnostic and statistical manual of mental disorders* (4th ed.). Washington, DC: Author.

Arcuri, A. F. Lester, D., & Smith, F. O. (1985). Shaping adolescent gambling behavior. *Adolescence, 20*, 935–938.

Atton, A. V., & Tunnessen, W. W. (1990). Alopecia in children: The most common causes. *Pediatrics in Review, 12*, 25–30.

Azrin, N. H., & Nunn, R. G. (1973). Habit-reversal: A method of eliminating nervous habits and tics. *Behaviour Research and Therapy, 11*, 619–628.

Azrin, N. H., & Nunn, R. G. (1978). *Habit control in a day*. New York: Simon & Schuster.

Azrin, N. H., Nunn, R. G. & Frantz, S. E. (1980). Treatment of hairpulling (trichotillomania): A comparative study of habit reversal and negative practice training. *Journal of Behavior Therapy and Experimental Psychiatry, 11*, 13–20.

Azrin, N. H., & Weslowski, M. D. (1974). Theft reversal: An overcorrection procedure for eliminating stealing by retarded persons, *Journal of Applied Behavior Analysis, 7*, 577–583.

Baizerman, M., & Emshoff, B. (1984). Juvenile firesetting: Building a community-based prevention program. *Children Today, 13*, 7–12.

Bandura, A., & Walters, R. H. (1963). Aggression. In H. W. Stevenson, J. Kagan, & C. Spiker (Eds.), *Child psychology: The sixty-second yearbook of the National Society for the Study of Education*. Chicago: University of Chicago Press.

Barabasz, M. (1987). Trichotillomania: A new treatment. *International Journal of Clinical and Experimental Hypnosis, 35*, 146–154.

Baron, R. A. (1977). *Human aggression*. New York: Plenum.

Becker, W. C., Peterson, D. R., Hellmer, L. A., Shoemaker, D. J., & Quay, H. C. (1959). Factors in parental behavior and personality as related to problem behavior in children. *Journal of Consulting Psychology, 23*, 107–118.

Belson, W. A. (1975). *Juvenile theft: The causal factors*. London: Harper & Row.

Blake, E. (1984). Women: The new compulsive gamblers. *Glamour, 82*, 168.

Blume, S. B. (1992). Compulsive gambling: Addiction without drugs. *Harvard Mental Health Letter, 8*, 4–5.

Bolen, D. W., & Boyd, W. H. (1968). Gambling and the gambler: A review and preliminary findings. *Archives General Psychiatry, 18*, 617–630.

Borduin, C. M., & Henggeler, S. W. (1990). A multisystemic approach to the treatment of serious delinquent behavior. In R. J. McMahon & R. D. Peters (Eds.), *Behavior disorders of adolescence*. New York: Plenum.

Bornstein, P. H., Schuldberg, D., & Bornstein, M. T. (1987). Conduct disorders. In V. B. Van Hasselt & M. Hersen (Eds.), *Handbook of adolescent psychology*. Elmsford, NY.: Pergamon.

Bumpass, E. R., Brix, R. J., & Preston, B. (1985). A community-based program for juvenile firesetters. *Hospital and Community Psychiatry, 36*, 529–533.

Bumpass, E. R., Fagelman, F. D., & Brix, R. J. (1983). Intervention with children who set fires *American Journal of Psychotherapy, 37*, 328–345.

Buxbaum, E. (1960). Hair pulling and fetishism. *Psychoanalytic Study of the Child, 15*, 243–260.

Campbell, S. B. (1983). Developmental perspectives in child psychopathology. In T. H. Ollendick & M. Hersen (Eds.), *Handbook of child psychopathology*. New York: Plenum.

Canter, R. J. (1982). Sex differences in self-report delinquency. *Criminology, 20*, 373–393.

Cautela, J. R. (1967). Covert sensitisation. *Psychological Reports, 20*, 459–468.

Childers, R. T. (1958). Report of two cases of trichotillomania of long-standing duration and their response to chlorpromazine. *Journal of Clinical and Experimental Psychopathology, 19*, 141–144.

Crisp, A. H., Hsu, L. K. G., & Harding, B. (1980). Clinical features of anorexia nervosa. *Journal of Psychosomatic Research, 24*, 179–191.

Custer, R. L. (1982a). An overview of compulsive gambling. In P. A. Carone, S. F.

Yolles, S. N. Kieffer, & L. Krinsky (Eds.), *Addictive disorders update: Alcoholism, drug abuse, gambling.* New York: Human Sciences.

Custer, R. L. (1982b). Gambling and addiction. In R. J. Craig & S. L. Baker (Eds.), *Drug dependent patients: Treatment and research.* Springfield, IL: Thomas.

Custer, R. L., & Custer, L. F. (1981). *Soft signs of pathological gambling.* Paper presented at Fifth National Conference on Gambling, Reno, NV.

Daghestani, A. N. (1987). Impotence associated with compulsive gambling. *Journal of Clinical Psychiatry, 48,* 115–116.

Dalton, R., Haslett, N., & Baul, G. (1986). Alternative therapy with a recalcitrant firesetter. *Journal of the American Academy of Child Psychiatry, 25,* 715–717.

Dawber, R. (1985). Self-induced hair loss. *Seminars in Dermatology, 4,* 53–57.

Delgado, R. A., & Mannino, F. V. (1969). Some observations on trichotillomania in children. *Journal of the American Academy of Child Psychiatry, 8,* 229–246.

DeMilio, L. (1989). Psychiatric syndromes in adolescent substance abusers. *American Journal of Psychiatry, 146,* 1212–1214.

Doke, L. A., & Flippo, J. R. (1983). Aggressive and oppositional behavior. In T. H. Ollendick & M. Hersen (Eds.), *Handbook of child psychopathology.* New York: Plenum.

Dunford, F. W., & Elliott, D. S. (1984). Identifying career offenders using self-reported data. *Journal of Research in Crime and Delinquency, 21,* 57–86.

Edelbrock, C., & Costello, A. (1984). Structured psychiatric interviews for children and adolescents. In G. Goldstein & M. Hersen (Eds.), *Handbook of psychological assessment.* New York: Pergamon.

Eleftheriou, B. E., Bailey, D. W., & Denenberg, V. H. (1974). Genetic analysis of fighting behavior in mice. *Physiology and Behavior, 13,* 773–777.

Elliot, F. A. (1978). Neurological aspects of antisocial behavior. In W. H. Reid (Ed.), *The psychopath: A comprehensive study of antisocial disorders and behaviors.* New York: Brunner/Mazel.

Fabbri, R., & Dy, A. J. (1974). Hypnotic treatment of trichotillomania: Two cases. *International Journal of Clinical and Experimental Hypnosis, 22,* 210–215.

Fenichel, O. (1945). *The psychoanalytic theory of neurosis.* New York: Norton.

Fineman, K. R. (1980). Firesetting in childhood and adolescence. *Psychiatric Clinics of North America, 3,* 483–500.

Finkel, M. J. (1984). Phenytoin revisited. *Clinical Therapeutics, 6,* 577–591.

Forehand, R. (1990). Early adolescence: Behavior problems, stressors, and the role of family factors. In R. J. McMahon & R. D. Peters (Eds.), *Behavior disorders of adolescence.* New York: Plenum.

Forehand, R., Wells, K. C., & Sturgis, E. T. (1978). Predictors of child noncompliance in the home. *Journal of Consulting and Clinical Psychology, 46,* 179.

Forehand, R., Wierson, M., Frame, C. L., Kempton, T., & Armistead, L. (1991). Juvenile firesetting: A unique syndrome or an advanced level of antisocial behavior? *Behavior Research and Clinical Psychology, 46,* 125–128.

Friedrich, W. N. (1990). *Psychotherapy of sexually abused children and their families.* New York: Norton.

Friman, P. C., Finney, J., & Christophersen, E. (1984). Behavioral treatment of trichotillomania: An evaluative review. *Behavior Therapy, 15,* 249–265.

Friman, P. C., & Hove, G. (1987). Apparent covariation between child habit disorders: Effects of successful treatment for thumb sucking on untargeted chronic hair pulling. *Journal of Applied Behavior Analysis, 20,* 421–427.

Friman, P. C., & O'Connor, W. A. (1984). The integration of hypnotic and habit reversal techniques in the treatment of trichotillomania [Letter to the editor]. *Behavior Therapy, 7,* 166–167.

Friman, P. C., & Rostain, A. (1990). Trichotillomania: Hair pulling [Letter to the editor]. *New England Journal of Medicine, 322,* 471.

Gauthier, J., & Pellerin, D. (1982). Management of compulsive shoplifting through covert sensitisation. *Journal of Behavior Therapy and Experimental Psychiatry, 13,* 73–75.

Glover, J. H. (1985). A case of kleptomania treated by covert sensitization. *British Journal of Clinical Psychology, 24,* 213–214.

Gold, J. (1970). *Delinquent behavior in an American city.* Belmont, CA: Brooks/Cole.

Goldman, M. J. (1991). Is there a treatment for kleptomania? *Harvard Mental Health Letter, 8,* 8.

Gove, W. R., & Crutchfield, R. D. (1982). The family and juvenile delinquency. *Sociological Quarterly, 23,* 301–319.

Graham, P. J. (1979). Epidemiological studies. In H. C. Quay & J. S. Werry (Eds.), *Psychopathological disorders of childhood* (2nd ed.). New York: Wiley.

Greenberg, D., & Rankin, H., (1982). Compulsive gamblers in treatment. *British Journal of Psychiatry, 140,* 364–366.

Greenberg, H. R. (1969). Transactions of hair-pulling symbiosis. *Psychiatric Quarterly, 43,* 662–674.

Greenberg, H. R. (1980). Psychology of gambling. In H. I. Kaplan, A. M. Freedman, & B. J. Sadock (Eds.), *Comprehensive textbook of psychiatry* (Vol. 3). Baltimore, MD: Williams and Wilkins.

Greenberg, H. R., & Sarner, C. A. (1965). Trichotillomania, symptom and syndrome. *Archives of General Psychiatry, 12,* 482–489.

Greenson, R. R. (1947). On gambling. *American Imago, 4,* 61–77.

Griffiths, M. D. (1989). Gambling in children and adolescents. *Journal of Gambling Behavior, 5,* 66–83.

Griffiths, M. D. (1990a). Adolescent gambling: An observational pilot study. *Perceptual and Motor Skills, 70,* 1138.

Griffiths, M. D. (1990b). Addiction to fruit machines: A preliminary study among young males. *Journal of Gambling Studies, 6,* 113–126.

Griffiths, M. D. (1990c). The acquisition, development, and maintenance of fruit machine gambling in adolescents. *Journal of Gambling Studies, 6,* 193–204.

Grunstein, A. (1952). Stages in the development of control over fire. *International Journal of Psychoanalysis, 33,* 1–5.

Guidry, L. S. (1975). Use of a cover punishing contingency in compulsive stealing. *Journal of Behavior Therapy and Experimental Psychiatry, 6,* 169.

Hall, J. R. & McGill, J. C. (1986). Hypnobehavioral treatment of self-destructive behavior: Trichotillomania and bulimia in the same patient. *American Journal of Clinical Hypnosis, 29,* 39–46.

Hamdan, A. G. (1991). Trichotillomania in childhood. *Acta Psychiatrica Scandinavica, 83,* 241–243.

Heath, G. A., Gayton, W. F., & Hardesty, V. Z. (1976). Childhood firesetting. *Canadian Psychiatric Association Journal, 21,* 229–237.

Henderson, J. Q. (1983). Follow-ups of stealing behavior in 27 youths. *Journal of Behavior Therapy and Experimental Psychiatry, 14*, 331–337.

Hetherington, E. M., & Martin, B. (1979). Family interaction. In H. C. Quay & J. S. Werry (Eds.), *Psychopathological disorders of childhood*. New York: Wiley.

Illingworth, R. S. (1987). *The normal child*. New York: Churchill Livingstone.

Jacobs, D. F. (1989). Teenage gambling. In H. J. Shaffer, S. A. Stein, B. Gambino, & T. N. Cummings (Eds.), *Compulsive gambling*. Lexington, MA: Heath.

Jacobson R. R. (1985). The subclassification of child firesetters. *Journal of Child Psychology and Psychiatry and Allied Discipline, 26*, 769–775.

Jayaprakash, S., Jung, J., & Panitch, D. (1984). Multifactorial assessment of hospitalized children who set fires. *Child Welfare, 63*, 74–78.

Jeffery, C. R. (1967). Crime prevention and control through environmental engineering. *Journal of Criminology, 7*, 35–58.

Jenike, M. A. (1990). Trichotillomania: Hair pulling [Letter to the editor]. *New England Journal of Medicine, 322*, 472.

Jenkins, S. C., & Maruta, T. (1987). Therapeutic use of propranolol for intermittent explosive disorder. *Mayo Clinic Proceedings, 62*, 204–214.

Kafry, D. (1980). Playing with matches: Children and fire. In D. Canter (Ed.), *Fires and human behavior*. Chichester, England: Wiley.

Karno, M., Golding, J. M., Sorenson, S. B., & Burnam, M. A. (1988). The epidemiology of obsessive-compulsive disorder in five U.S. communities. *Archives of General Psychiatry, 45*, 1094–1099.

Kazdin, A. E., & Kolko, D. J. (1986). Parent psychopathology and family functioning among childhood firesetters. *Journal of Abnormal Child Psychology, 14*, 315–329.

Kellner, R. (1982). Disorders of impulse control. In J. H. Greist, J. W. Jefferson, & R. L. Spitzer (Eds.), *Treatment of mental disorders*. New York: Oxford University Press.

Klemke, L. W. (1982). Exploring juvenile shoplifting. *Sociology and Social Research, 67*, 59–75.

Koles, M. R., & Jensen, W. R. (1985). Comprehensive treatment of chronic firesetting in a severely disordered boy. *Journal of Behavioral Therapy and Experimental Psychiatry, 16*, 81–85.

Kolko, D. J. (1983). Multicomponent parental treatment of firesetting in a six year boy. *Journal of Behavior Therapy and Experimental Psychiatry, 14*, 349–353.

Kolko, D. J. & Kazdin, A. E. (1986). A conceptualization of firesetting in children and adolescents. *Journal of Abnormal Child Psychology, 14*, 49–62.

Kolko, D. J., & Kazdin, A. E. (1989). The Children's Firesetting Interview with psychiatrically referred and nonreferred children. *Journal of Abnormal Child Psychology, 17*, 609–624.

Kolko, D. J., Kazdin, A. E., & Meyer, E. C. (1985). Aggression and psychopathology in childhood firesetters: Parent and child reports. *Journal of Consulting and Clinical Psychology, 53*, 377–385.

Krahn, D. D., Flegel, P., & Canum, K. K. (1989). Stealing in eating disordered patients. In *New research program and abstracts, 142nd annual meeting of the American Psychiatric Association*. Washington, DC: American Psychiatric Association.

Krishnan, K. R. R., Davidson, J., & Miller, R. (1984). MAO inhibitor therapy in trichotillomania associated with depression: Case report. *Journal of Clinical Psychiatry, 45*, 267–268.

Krishnan, K. R. R., Davidson, J., & Guajardo, C. (1985). Trichotillomania: A review. *Comprehensive Psychiatry, 26,* 123–128.

KTCA Reports. (1992, February 25). Betting in Minnesota [Television broadcast]. Minneapolis, MN: KTCA Television.

Lamerton, A. J. (1984). Trichobezoar: Two case reports. *American Journal of Gastroenterology, 79,* 354–356.

Lande, S. D. (1980). A combination of orgasmic reconditioning and covert sensitization in the treatment of a fire fetish. *Journal of Behavior Therapy and Experimental Psychiatry, 11,* 291–296.

Larsen, K. (1982). Firesetting by children and youngsters. *Skolpsykologie, 19,* 36–47.

Lefkowitz, M. M., Eron, L. D., & Walder, L. O. (1977). *Growing up to be violent: A longitudinal study of the development of aggression.* New York: Pergamon.

Lesieur, H. R. (1977). *The chase: Career of the compulsive gambler.* Garden City, NY: Anchor.

Lesieur, H. R., & Blume, S. B. (1987). The South Oak Gambling Screen: A new instrument for the identification of pathological gamblers. *American Journal of Psychiatry, 144,* 1184–1188.

Lesieur, H. R., & Klein, R. (1987). Pathological gambling among high school students. *Addictive Behaviors, 12,* 129–135.

Lesieur, H. R., & Rosenthal, R. J. (1991). Pathological gambling: A review of the literature. *Journal of Gambling Studies, 7,* 5–39.

Levine, M. D., & Jordan, N. C. (1987). Neurodevelopmental dysfunctions. In J. J. Gallagher & C. T. Ramey (Eds.), *The malleability of children.* Baltimore, MD: Brookes.

Linden, R. D., Jonas, J. M., & Pope, H. G. (1984, May). *Pathological gambling and major affective disorder.* Presented at the annual meeting of the American Psychiatric Association, Los Angeles.

Loeber, R. (1987). The prevalence, correlates, and continuity of serious conduct problems in elementary school children. *Criminology, 25,* 615–642.

Loeber, R. (1990). Development and risk factors of juvenile antisocial behavior and delinquency. *Clinical Psychology Review, 10,* 1–41.

Loeber, R., & Schmaling, K. B. (1985). Empirical evidence for overt and covert patterns of antisocial conduct problems: A metaanalysis. *Journal of Abnormal Child Psychology, 13,* 337–352.

Loeber, R., & Stouthamer-Loeber, M. (1987). Prediction. In H. C. Quay (Ed.), *Handbook of juvenile delinquency.* New York: Wiley.

Lowenstein, L. F. (1981). The diagnosis of child arsonists. *Acta Paedopsychiatrica, 47,* 151–154.

Lowenstein, L. F. (1989). The etiology, diagnosis, and treatment of the firesetting behavior of children. *Child Psychiatry and Human Development, 19,* 186–194.

Macht, L. B., & Mack, J. E. (1968). The firesetter syndrome. *Psychiatry, 31,* 277–288.

Mannino, F. V. & Delgado, R. A. (1969). Trichotillomania in children: A review. *American Journal of Psychiatry, 126,* 505–511.

Mattes, J. A. (1985). Metoprolol for intermittent explosive disorder. *American Journal of Psychiatry, 142,* 1108–1109.

Mattes, J. A., & Fink, M. (1987). A family study of patients with temper outbursts. *Journal of Psychiatric Research, 21,* 249–255.

Mattes, J. A., & Fink, M. (1990). A controlled family study of adopted patients with temper outbursts. *Journal of Nervous and Mental Diseases, 178,* 138–139.

Mattison, R., Cantwell, D. P., Russell, A. T., & Will, L. A. (1979). Comparison of DSM-II and DSM-III in the diagnosis of childhood psychiatric disorders. *Archives of General Psychiatry, 36,* 1217–1222.

McConaghy, N., Armstrong, M. S., Blaszczynski, A. & Allcock, C. (1983). Controlled comparison of aversive therapy and imaginal desensitization in compulsive gambling. *British Journal of Psychiatry, 142,* 366–372.

McCord, J., & McCord, W. (1958). The effects of parental role model of criminality. *Journal of Social Issues, 14,* 66–75.

McCormick, R. A., Russo, A. M., Ramirez, L. F., & Taber, J. I. (1984). Affective disorders among pathological gamblers seeking treatment. *American Journal of British Psychiatry, 141,* 215–218.

McElroy, S. L., Pope, H. G., Hudson, J. I., Keck, P. E., & White, K. L. (1991). Kleptomania: A report of 20 cases. *American Journal of Psychiatry, 148,* 652–657.

McGrath, P., Marshall, P. G., & Prior, K. (1979). A comprehensive treatment programme for a fire setting child. *Journal of Behavior Therapy and Experimental Psychiatry, 10,* 69–72.

McGurrin, M. C. (1992). *Pathological gambling: Conceptual, diagnostic, and treatment issues.* Sarasota, FL: Professional Resource Press.

Mehregan, A. H. (1978). Histopathology of alopecias. *Curtis, 21,* 249–253.

Mesibov, G. B., Schroeder, C. S., & Wesson, L. (1977). Parental concerns about their children. *Journal of Pediatric Psychology, 2,* 13–17.

Mieszala, P. (1981, August). Juvenile firesetters. *Rekindle,* 11–13.

Miller, G. E., & Klungness, L. (1986). Treatment of nonconfrontative stealing in school-age children. *School Psychology Review, 15,* 24–35.

Miller, G. E., & Klungness, L. (1989). Childhood theft: A comprehensive review of assessment and treatment. *School Psychology Review, 18,* 82–97.

Monopolis, M. D., & Lion, J. R. (1983). Problems in the diagnosis of intermittent explosive disorder. *American Journal of Psychiatry, 140,* 1209–1202.

Monroe, R. (1981a). Brain dysfunctions in prisoners. In J. Hays, T. Roberts, & K. Solway (Eds.), *Violence and the violent individual.* New York: SP Books.

Monroe, R. R. (1981b). The problem of impulsivity in personality dissturbances. In J. R. Lion (Ed.), *Personality disorders: Diagnosis and management* (2nd ed.). Baltimore, MD: Williams and Wilkins.

Montemayor, R. (1983). Parents and adolescents in conflict: All families some of the time and some families most of the time. *Journal of Early Adolescence, 3,* 83–103.

Moore, D. R., Chamberlain, P., & Mukai, L. H. (1979). Children at risk for delinquency: A follow-up comparison of aggressive children on children who steal. *Journal of Abnormal Psychology, 7,* 345–355.

Moskowitz, J. A. (1980). Lithium and lady luck. *New York State Journal of Medicine, 80,* 785–788.

Muller, S. A. (1987). Trichotillomania. *Dermatologic Clinics, 5,* 595–601.

Nelson, W. M. (1982). Behavioral treatment of childhood trichotillomania: A case study. *Journal of Clinical Child Psychology, 3,* 227–230.

Niederland, W. G. (1967). A contribution to the psychology of gambling. *Psychoanalytic Forum 2,* 175–179.

Nurcombe, B. (1964). Children who set fires. *Medical Journal of Australia, 1*, 579–584.

Oguchi, T., & Miura, S. (1977). Trichotillomania: Its psychopathological aspect. *Comprehensive Psychiatry, 18*, 177–182.

Ollendick, T. H., & Hersen, M. (1984). *Child behavioral assessment.* New York: Pergamon.

Oranje, A. P., Peereboom-Wynia, J. D. R., & DeRaeymaecker, D. M. J. (1986). Trichotillomania in childhood. *Journal of the American Academy of Dermatology, 15*, 614–619.

Ottens, A. J. (1981). Multifaceted treatment of compulsive hair pulling, *Journal Behavior Therapy and Experimental Psychiatry, 12*, 77–80.

Patterson, G. R. (1982). *Coercive family process.* Eugene, OR: Castalia.

Paulsen, K., & Johnson, M. (1980). Impulsivity: A multidimensional concept with developmental aspects. *Journal of Abnormal Child Psychology, 8*, 269–277.

Peed, S., Roberts, M., & Forehand, R. (1977). Evaluation of the effectiveness of a standardized parent training program in altering the interaction of mothers and their noncompliant children. *Behavior Modification, 1*, 323–350.

Petersen, A. C. (1987). Those gangly years. *Psychology Today, 21*, 28–34.

Prentky, R., & Carter, D. (1984). Examined the predictive values of the triad enuresis, firesetting, and cruelty to animals. *Behavioral Sciences and the Law, 2*, 341–354.

Price, V. (1978). Disorders of the hair in children. *Pediatric Clincs of North America, 25*, 305–321.

Primeau, F., & Fontaine, R. (1987). Obsessive disorder with self-mutilation: a subgroup responsive to pharmacotherapy. *Canadian Journal of Psychiatry, 32*, 699–700.

Ramelli, E., & Mapelli, G. (1979). Melancholia and kleptomania. *Acta Psychiatrica Belgia, 79*, 57–74.

Rankin, H. (1982). Control rather than abstinence as a goal in the treatment of excessive gambling. *Behavior Research and Therapy, 20*, 185–187.

Rapoport, J. L. (1989). The biology of obsessions and compulsions. *Scientific American, 260*, 83–89.

Ratner, R. A. (1989). Trichotillomania. *Treatments of psychiatric disorders: A task force report of the American Psychiatric Association.* Washington, DC: American Psychiatric Association.

Reid, J. B., & Patterson, G. R. (1976). The modification of aggression and stealing behavior of boys in the home setting. In E. Ribes-Inesta & A. Bandura (Eds.), *Analysis of delinquency and aggression.* Hillsdale, NJ: Erlbaum.

Reid, W. H. (1989). *The treatment of psychiatric disorders.* New York: Brunner/Mazel.

Reid, W. H., & Gutnik, B. D. (1982). Organic treatment of chronically violent patients. *Psychiatric Annals, 12*, 526–542.

Ritvo, E., Shanok, S. S., & Lewis, D. O. (1983). Firesetting and nonfiresetting delinquents. *Child Psychiatry and Human Development, 13*, 259–267.

Sachdeva, J. S., & Sidhu, B. S. (1987). Trichotillomania associated with depression. *Journal of the Indian Medical Association, 85*, 151–152.

Schreier, H. A. (1979). Use of propranolol in the treatment of postencephalitic psychosis. *American Journal of Psychiatry, 136*, 840–841.

Schwartz, L. J., & Schwartz, R. (1971). Therapeutic acting out. *Psychotherapy, 8,* 205–207.

Showers, J., & Pickrell, E. (1987). Child firesetters: A study of three populations. *Hospital and Community Psychiatry, 38,* 495–501.

Skinner, B. F. (1953). *Science and human behavior.* New York: Macmillan.

Snyder, S. (1980). Trichotillomania treated with amitriptyline. *Journal of Nervous and Mental Disease, 168,* 505–507.

Sommers, I. (1988). Pathological gambling: Estimating prevalence and group characteristics. *International Journal of the Addictions, 23,* 477–490.

Sorosky, A. D., & Sticher, M. B. (1980). Trichotillomania in adolescence. *Adolescent Psychiatry, 8,* 437–454.

Steck, W. D. (1979). The clinical evaluation of pathological hair loss. *Curtis, 24,* 293–301.

Steward, M., & Culver, K. (1982). Children who start fires: The clinical picture and an follow-up. *British Journal of Psychiatry, 14,* 357–363.

Stewart, M. A., & deBlois, C. S. (1983). Father-son resemblances in aggressive and antisocial behavior. *British Journal Psychiatry, 142,* 78–84.

Stone, J. L., McDaniel, K. D., Hughes, J. R., & Hermann, B. P. (1986). Episodic dyscontrol disorder and paroxysmal EEG abnormalities: Successful treatment with carbamazepine. *Biological Psychiatry, 21,* 208–212.

Swedo, S. E., Leonard, H. L., Rapoport, J. L., Lenane, M. C., Goldberger, E. L., & Cheslow, D. L. (1989). A double-blind comparison of clomipramine and desipramine in the treatment of trichotillomania (hair pulling). *New England Journal of Medicine, 321,* 497–501.

Swedo, S. E., Leonard, H. L., & Rapoport, J. L. (1990) Trichotillomania: Hair pulling [Letter to the editor]. *New England Journal of Medicine, 322,* 471–472.

Swedo, S. E., & Rapoport, J. C. (1991). Trichotillomania. *Journal of Child Psychology and Psychiatry and Allied Disciplines, 32,* 401–409.

Swedo, S. E., Rapoport, J. L., Leonard, H. L., Lenane, M. C., & Cheslow, D. L. (1989). Obsessive-compulsive disorder in children and adolescents. *Archives of General Psychiatry, 46,* 335–341.

Taber, J. I., McCormick, R. A., & Russo, A. M. (1987). Follow-up of pathological gamblers after treatment. *American Journal of Psychiatry, 144,* 757–761.

Tarnowski, K. J., Rosen, L. A., McGrath, M. L. & Drabman, R. S. (1987). A modified habit reversal procedure in recalcitrant case of trichotillomania. *Journal of Behavior Therapy and Experimental Psychiatry, 18,* 157–163.

Tennent, T. G., McQuaid, A., Loughnane, T., & Hands, A. J. (1971). Female arsonists. *British Journal of Psychiatry, 119,* 497–502.

Toback, C., & Rajkumar, S. (1979). The emotional disturbance underlying alopecia areata, alopeciatotalis and trichotillomania. *Child Psychiatry and Human Development, 10,* 114–117.

Tolpin, T. H. (1983). A change in the self: The development and transformation of an idealizing transference. *International Journal of Psychoanalysis, 64,* 461–483.

Trott, J. C., & Griffiths, M. D. (1991). Teenage gambling: A pilot study. *Psychological Reports, 68,* 946.

Tuma, J. M., & Elbert, J. C. (1990). Critical issues and current practice in personality assessment of children. In C. R. Reynolds & R. W. Kamphaus (Eds.), *Handbook of psychological and educational assessment of children.* New York: Guilford.

Tupin, J. P., Smith, D. B., Clannon, T. L., Kim, L. I., Nugent, A., & Groupe, A. (1972). The long-term use of lithium in aggressive prisoners. *Comprehensive Psychiatry, 13,* 209–214.

Virkkunen, M. (1984). Reactive hypoglycemic tendency among arsonists. *Acta Psychiatrica Scandinavica, 69,* 445–452.

Volberg, R. A., & Steadman, H. J. (1988). Refining prevalence estimates of pathological gambling. *American Journal of Psychiatry, 145,* 502–505.

Weist, M. D., Ollendick, T. H., & Finney, J. W. (1991). Toward the empirical validation of treatment targets in children. *Clinical Psychology Review, 11,* 515–538.

Weller, E. B., Weller, R. A., & Carr, S. (1989). Imipramine treatment of trichotillomania and coexisting depression in a seven-year-old. *Journal of the American Academy of Child and Adolescent Psychiatry, 28,* 952–953.

Wells, K. C. (1981). Assessment of children in outpatient settings. In M. Hersen & A. S. Bellack (Eds.), *Behavioral assessment: A practical handbook* (2nd ed.). Elmsford, NY: Pergamon.

Winchel, R., Stanley, B., Guido, J., Posner, K., & Stanley, M. (1989, December). *An open trial of fluoxetine for trichotillomania (hairpulling).* Poster presented at the Meeting of the American College of Neuropsychopharmacology, Maui, HI.

Wolff, R. (1984). Satiation in the treatment of inappropriate firesetting. *Journal of Behavior Therapy and Experimental Psychiatry, 15,* 337–340.

Wolkowitz, M. D., Roy, A., & Doran, A. R. (1985). Pathologic gambling and other risk-taking pursuits. *Psychiatric Clinics of North America, 8,* 311–322.

Woodcock, J. H. (1986). A neuropsychiatric approach to impulse disorders. *Psychiatric Clinics of North America, 9,* 341–352.

Wooden, W. S. (1985). Arson is epidemic—and spreading like wildfire. *Psychology Today, 19,* 23–28.

Wooden, W. S., & Berkey, M. L. (1984). *Children and arson: America's middle class nightmare.* New York: Plenum.

Wray, I., & Dickerson, M. G. (1981). Cessation of high frequency gambling and "withdrawal" symptoms. *Behavioral Journal of Addiction, 76,* 401–405.

Wright, L., Schaefer, A. B., & Solomons, G. (1979). *Encyclopedia of pediatric psychology.* Baltimore, MD: University Park Press.

Yudofsky, S. C., Silver, J. N., Jackson, W., Endicott, J., & Williams, D. (1986). The Overt Aggression Scale for the objective rating of verbal and physical aggression. *American Journal of Psychiatry, 143,* 35–39.

Zuckerman, M. (1979). *Sensation seeking: Beyond the optimal level of arousal.* Hillsdale, NJ: Erlbaum.

19
Attention-Deficit Hyperactivity Disorder

Steven W. Evans
Gary Vallano
William Pelham

The diagnosis and treatment of attention-deficit hyperactivity disorder (ADHD) in children have been taking place for many years. The core symptoms of impulsivity, difficulty sustaining attention, and motor overactivity have been well documented in the childhood population (Barkley, 1990). In addition, many children experience such related problems as learning disabilities, poor peer relations, and family problems. Pharmacological and behavioral interventions have been the most successful treatments for the disorder, while cognitive-behavioral techniques have met with mixed results.

Attention to the disorder in adolescents is a fairly recent phenomenon. Clinicians used to tell parents that their ADHD children would "grow out" of the disorder when they reached adolescence. We now know that for most children the symptoms of the disorder persist. While the manifestations of the disorder change as the children mature, there continue to be significant disturbances in daily living well into adulthood for many individuals. Recent research has sought to clarify the clinical picture and diagnosis as well as identify successful treatment strategies for the ADHD adolescent population.

Historical Background

The emergence of a description of behavior problems associated with ADHD can be traced to the beginning of the twentieth century, when George Still described a group of children who may well have met modern criteria for ADHD (Berkley, 1990). He described them as having problems with rule-governed behavior, impulsive, and volatile.

Since that time the study and treatment of the disorder has continued along the same lines as child psychopathology in general. From the 1930s to 1950s there was a great emphasis on the biological basis of psychopathology, and the research with behaviorally disturbed children reflects this emphasis. The terms *minimal brain damage* and *minimal brain dysfunction* have their roots in this period of research. Treatment with medication began in this period, and the efficacy of amphetamines with these children was reported as early as 1937.

During the 1960s the emphasis was on overactivity, and the focus on brain damage slowly decreased. Research into "hyperactivity" increased greatly, and the work of Virginia Douglas and others led to the inclusion of attentional deficits as a primary symptom with these children. During the 1970s the use of stimulant medication grew, and the development of behavioral interventions for this population emerged. In 1975 PL 94-142 (the Education for All Handicapped Children Act) was passed, mandating special education in the schools. This action reflected the growing importance of research into individual differences between children and the school's potential role in treating them.

With the publication of DSM-II and DSM-III in 1968 and 1980, respectively, the importance of reliably identifying a homogeneous group of children grew. These efforts continued throughout the 1980s and into the 1990s and resulted in refined diagnostic criteria in DSM III-R and DSM-IV. The 1980s witnessed a tremendous increase in public awareness of the disorder, a public outcry against stimulant medication, and a tremendous diversification of research regarding ADHD. Most importantly for the purposes of this chapter, it was discovered that ADHD is not just a childhood disorder, but one that continues into adolescence and adulthood. Research into ADHD in adolescent and adult populations is in its early stages, and most of what has been published is descriptive.

Clinical Picture

Although ADHD is usually easy to recognize in childhood, the clinical picture of the disorder in adolescence is not very clear. The core symptoms of overactivity, impulsivity, and difficulty sustaining attention manifest themselves differently in adolescents than in younger children. While manifestations of the disorder are clearly disabling to the affected adolescents, the symptoms are frequently not as observable as they are with younger children. Because of the developmental nature of attention, impulse control, and activity level, these core symptoms improve as ADHD children mature. A variety of studies, however, have documented that these children continue to have significant problems into adolescence and adulthood (Barkley, Anastopoulos, Guevremont, & Fletcher, 1991; Gittelman, Mannuzza, Shenker, & Bonagura, 1985; Hechtman & Weiss, 1983).

The stability of the diagnosis from childhood to adolescence varies depending on the study being referenced. Follow-up studies have reported that as few as 43% of adolescents diagnosed with ADHD in childhood continue to have the disorder in adolescence (Lambert, Hartsough, Sassone, & Sandoval, 1987), but other studies have reported rates between 68% and 83% (Barkley, Fischer, Edelbrock, & Smallish, 1990; Gittelman et al., 1985; Mendelson, Johnson, & Stewart, 1971). Part of the discrepancy can be attributed to the fact that not all studies used the same diagnostic criteria (DSM-III and DSM-III-R) and procedures at baseline and follow-up.

The diagnosis of ADHD with adolescents is complicated, since the DSM-III-R criteria are intended for children. There have been two proposals for modifying the diagnostic criteria for adolescents. Wender, Wood, and Reimherr (1985) proposed diagnostic criteria (the Utah Criteria) to use with adults and have suggested that these criteria also be applied to adolescents. The criteria include manifestations of the three core symptoms plus such common presenting problems as affective lability, overexcitability, and temper outbursts. In addition, Barkley, Fischer, et al. (1990) recommended that a diagnosis of ADHD be given to adolescents if they meet 6 of the 14 DSM-III-R criteria as opposed to 8. They reported that adolescents who met 6 of the criteria based on structured parent interviews were two standard deviations above the mean. These authors suggest that using a norm-based cutoff score would help account for normal child development and developmental changes in the manifestations of the core symptoms of the disorder.

DSM-IV includes language targeting adolescents and adults in the lists of symptoms, but it does not adjust diagnostic criteria according to age or include symptoms related to affect or temper as described above. The core symptoms of overactivity, impulsivity, and difficulty sustaining attention are individually reviewed below as they pertain to adolescents.

Overactivity

The core symptom most frequently reported as improved when children enter adolescence is overactivity. Many reports refer to adolescent overactivity as "restlessness," as opposed to fidgety behavior or overactivity. Wender (1990) defined hyperactivity for adolescents and adults as follows:

> Hyperactivity: persistent excessive motor activity as manifested by restlessness, inability to relax, "nervousness" (meaning inability to settle down—not anticipatory anxiety), inability to persist in sedentary activities (e.g., watching movies, television, reading a newspaper), being always on the go, and dysphoric when inactive.

Empirical studies addressing overactivity in adolescents are rare. A recent study by Fischer, Barkley, Edelbrock, and Smallish (1990) reported some attempts to measure overactivity in a sample of 100 adolescents between the ages of 12 and 20 who had been diagnosed with ADHD between the ages of 4 and 12. The authors compared these adolescents to a group of controls on a variety of measures, including observation of overactivity while completing a 15-minute videotaped academic task. Observational measures of off-task, fidgety, vocalizing, and out-of-seat behavior revealed group main effects, with the ADHD group being more fidgety, more vocal, and more frequently out of their seats than the controls. There was also a main effect for age for the vocalizing and out-of-seat behaviors, although there were no significant interactions. While overactivity may be less extreme in adolescence than in childhood, these findings document the persistence of overactivity as a core symptom for adolescents with ADHD.

A study by Mannuzza et al. (1991) also reported group differences between ADHD adolescents and controls on diagnostic criteria pertaining to overactivity. Through the use of semistructured interviews, the investigators found that adolescents with a history of ADHD were far more likely to report problems with overactivity than a group of adolescents with no history of psychopathology. Our observations of ADHD adolescents are consistent with these findings and indicate that there is considerable variability in their activity levels. We have seen adults and adolescents who fidget in their chairs and never seem to stand still, as well as other adolescents who demonstrate relatively sedate patterns of behavior. Although there appears to be considerable variability in the manifestation of overactivity in ADHD adolescents, almost all of them have histories of moderate to severe overactivity as children. While most children we have seen experience a reduction in the quantity and severity of symptoms as they reach adolescence, a majority of them still exhibit problematic behaviors related to restlessness and overactivity.

Impulsivity

The manifestation of impulsivity also changes as children with ADHD enter adolescence. As with overactivity, the symptoms generally improve. Adolescents with ADHD are less likely than their childhood counterparts to exhibit behaviors frequently associated with impulsivity (e.g., interrupting conversations, climbing on furniture, and difficulty taking turns), although many adolescents with ADHD do still exhibit these behaviors. Normal maturation into adolescence includes an increase in socialization, independence, and an exposure to many influences in society that younger children do not experience. Manifestations of impulsivity for ADHD adolescents reflect this maturation and the changing environments within which they function.

Clinical researchers generally agree that an impulsive cognitive style persists from childhood into adolescence (Barkley, Fischer, et al., 1990;

Brown & Borden, 1986; Weiss, Minde, Werry, Douglas, & Nemeth, 1971). Behaviors considered to be partly a function of impulsivity that are frequently observed with ADHD adolescents include such delinquent behaviors as vandalism, theft, assault, substance abuse, and use of a weapon (Barkley, Fischer, et al., 1990). These behaviors frequently lead to a diagnosis of conduct disorder. Gittelman et al. (1985) reported that children diagnosed with ADHD are four times as likely as their nondiagnosed peers to be diagnosed with conduct disorder as an adolescent.

Mannuzza, Klein, Konig, and Giampino (1989) reported that ADHD children were also at increased risk for diagnosis with an antisocial personality disorder. Rates of adjudicated antisocial behavior are significantly greater for adolescents who were diagnosed with ADHD as a child than for their nondiagnosed peers across all socioeconomic levels (Mannuzza et al. 1989; Satterfield, Hoppe, & Schell, 1982). This finding may reflect both the increased likelihood of delinquent behaviors in this population and the observation by many clinicians who work with this population that a delinquent ADHD adolescent is more likely than an equally delinquent non-ADHD peer to be apprehended due to the former's impulsive style.

Impulsivity is a difficult concept to assess in a laboratory setting, and not surprisingly, few investigators have attempted this with an adolescent ADHD population. A study by Fischer et al. (1990) employed the Kagan Matching Familiar Figures Test-20 (MFFT-20; Cairns & Cammock, 1984) with a group of adolescents diagnosed with ADHD as children and a group of controls. The authors found no effect for group or age (comparing younger and older adolescent samples). Researchers in previous studies have employed the Matching Familiar Figures tests and found that adults and adolescents with a childhood diagnosis of ADHD performed more poorly on the measure than did their nondiagnosed peers (Cohen, Weiss, & Minde, 1972; Hopkins, Perlman, Hechtman, & Weiss, 1979). They also reported other deficiencies in the diagnosed population and concluded that adolescents and adults with a history of ADHD exhibit an inefficient pattern of problem solving. It should be noted that these earlier studies used an older version of the MFFT, and the childhood diagnoses were based on different diagnostic criteria than those employed in the Fischer et al. (1990) study. Overall, these findings neither prove nor contradict the presence of an impulsive style of responding in ADHD adolescents.

Our work with this population suggests that adolescents do continue to have great difficulty with impulse control. Some of the adolescents we have seen exhibit delinquent behaviors that are frequently characterized by a lack of planning. This frequently leads to the adolescents being caught by parents, school authorities, and police for various acting-out behaviors. Other adolescents we have treated continue to display more immature and relatively benign, but nevertheless annoying, impulsive behaviors (e.g., verbal interruptions and physical intrusions). Overall, while the laboratory data are weak, the clinical evidence suggesting continuation of an impulsive cognitive style is convincing.

Inattention

The final core symptom, inattention, also appears to be stable into adolescence. There have been studies addressing different types of attention, but most research has focused on sustained attention (i.e., the ability to attend to a task efficiently for extended periods of time). Problems with sustained attention manifest themselves as difficulty completing tasks, trouble concentrating, and problems following directions. These problems persist into adolescence for most of the children diagnosed with ADHD in childhood (see Brown & Borden, 1986; Hechtman & Weiss, 1983).

The diagnostic procedures proposed by Wender (1990) include two criteria that directly target difficulties in sustaining attention. Behavioral examples of these two criteria include inability to attend to conversations; inability to attend to reading material; forgetfulness; difficulty organizing time, materials, and tasks at home or on the job; and difficulty completing tasks. These are frequently reported manifestations of difficulty sustaining attention in the adolescent and adult population diagnosed with ADHD.

Mannuzza, Klein, Bonagura, Konig, and Shenker (1988) looked at the status of 16- to 23-year-old people who had been diagnosed with ADHD as a child but did not meet diagnostic criteria for any disorder as adults. Even among those currently without a disorder, subjects who had been diagnosed with ADHD as children reported more difficulties with attention than their nondiagnosed peers. Specifically, the previously diagnosed subjects endorsed the following items more frequently than the controls: mind frequently "somewhere else," trouble concentrating or paying attention, and easily distracted at work or school.

One of the complaints most frequently presented by parents of adolescents with ADHD is the latter's failure to complete homework assignments. The parents report that the adolescents are unorganized, do not know what their assignments are, and/or forget to bring materials home; they frequently claim that if they do not stand over their child continuously, he or she will not get things done when studying. A recent investigation by Barkley et al. (1991) provided data to support this observation. Adolescents with a childhood diagnosis of ADHD were compared to a group of adolescents without an ADHD diagnosis on an academic task completion measure. Subjects were given 15 minutes to complete as many math problems as possible. Control subjects completed significantly more problems than the experimental group, and the accuracy rates were similar. Although the group differences may have partly attributable to differences in math ability, the finding is consistent with the frequently described problems completing tasks.

Laboratory tasks designed to measure sustained attention have been extensively used with children, but there are few reports of their use with adolescents and adults. Two studies have documented deficits in attention with adolescent populations. Klorman, Brumaghim, Fitzpatrick, and Borgstedt (1992) reported an interaction on error rates between diagnostic groups (normal versus ADHD) and memory load. Their data suggest a deficit in the stimulus classification processes of these adolescents that is independent of reaction time. Another study (Nuechterlein, 1983) indicated that ADHD adolescents are initially much less cautious when responding to a vigilance computer task than their nondiagnosed peers. This difference is reduced over time as the ADHD adolescents come to employ a conservative style resembling their peer group (i.e., the ADHD adolescents normalize their style of responding).

Neither of these studies reported data supporting a deficit in sustained attention for ADHD adolescents; however, these studies did find the interactions between a dependent variable and a task characteristic necessary to draw conclusions regarding cognitive deficits. Other studies have reported group differences on vigilance tasks (Barkley et al., 1991; Fischer et al., 1990), but their data do not support a cognitive deficit. Deficits in sustained attention require an interaction between time and response time or accuracy; the difference in performance between a control and an experimental group should grow as a function of time if the ability to sustain attention over time is the distinguishing feature. Differences between two groups on a vigilance task that do not measure the effect of time may have nothing to do with differences in attention processes (see van der Meere & Sergeant, 1988).

In spite of minimal laboratory data to support a deficit in sustained attention, our observations of ADHD adolescents support the indications from the descriptive literature that many do exhibit a set of behavior problems related to such a deficit. We have received many reports of failure to complete assignments, problems organizing and taking notes, difficulty comprehending reading material, and problems following conversations. The difficulties following conversations frequently lead to the adolescent either withdrawing from extended conversations or making irrelevant statements. This can contribute to the difficulties frequently exhibited by the adolescents in terms of interacting with peers.

Course and Prognosis

Very little research is available on the adult outcome of ADHD. Wender and his colleagues have studied the diagnosis of and pharmacological treatments for adults with ADHD (Wender, 1990; Wender et al., 1985). Clinical trials of behavioral and psychosocial interventions with the adult population, though, have not been reported.

Adult outcomes have been reported by Klein, Mannuzza, and colleagues (Mannuzza et al., 1988; Mannuzza et al., 1991), Satterfield and colleagues (Satterfield, 1976; Satterfield et al., 1982), and Weiss, Hechtman, and colleagues (Hechtman & Weiss, 1983; Weiss & Hechtman, 1986; Weiss, Hechtman, Milroy, & Perlman, 1985). Results of the Hechtman and Weiss studies indicate that severe problems persist for many children and adolescents in adulthood. Difficulties interacting with peers and supervisors, especially in opposite-sex relationships, were reported. Approximately one-quarter of the adults with childhood histories of hyperactivity met criteria for a diagnosis of antisocial personality disorder. As many as 20% had been physically aggressive during a 3-year period, compared to only 5% of the control group.

Achievement also continues to be a problem, according to the Hechtman and Weiss studies. ADHD children are less likely than their peers to graduate from high school and to attend college. They tend to do poorly at job interviews, and supervisors rate their work as less satisfactory than that of their peers. Consistent with these problems, the socioeconomic status (SES) of the ADHD adults in the Hechtman and Weiss studies was lower compared to both a control group and their own siblings. Adults with a childhood history of ADHD also reported a continuation of the affective disturbances frequently seen in adolescence, including more problems with anxiety and sadness and much higher rates of suicide attempts than were reported by controls.

While these findings are discouraging, it is important to note that most of the adults followed by Weiss, Hechtman, and colleagues were living independently and gainfully employed. Many were likely to have some degree of the difficulties described above, but a majority were in the mainstream of society. As might easily be expected, childhood histories of a nurturing and supportive home, lack of aggression or psychopathology, middle to upper SES, average or greater intelligence, and positive parenting practices predicted good adult outcomes. The role of various forms of treatment in the prediction of adult outcome, though, is still unclear.

Epidemiology

The prevalence of ADHD in children is estimated to fall between 3% and 5% (Barkley, 1990). The exact number of adolescents that continue to meet the diagnostic criteria for ADHD varies from study to study, but in general, it appears that the prevalence in the adolescent population is between one-third and two-thirds of that reported for younger children. Whether this reflects a true decrease in the prevalence of the disorder by the time a child reaches adolescence or the profession's limitations in accurately assessing adolescents with ADHD is unclear.

ADHD is approximately three times more common in boys than girls, and boys are six times more likely than girls to be referred to an outpatient mental health clinic for the disorder. One explanation for this discrepancy is that females are less likely to display the more disruptive aspects of the disorder than their male counterparts, and therefore they are less likely to come to the attention of mental health professionals (Barkley, 1990).

Familial Pattern

There is a growing body of literature suggesting an important role for genetic transmission in ADHD. Studies have demonstrated that children of parents with depression have a greater risk for externalizing disorders than children of parents without depression (Weissman et al., 1984). Additionally, the prevalence of psychopathology is greater among parents who have a child with ADHD (Cantwell, 1972; Morrison & Stewart, 1971) and the history of childhood hyperactivity is greater in the parents of children with ADHD than in normal controls (Schachar & Wachsmuth, 1990). This implicates a genetic component in the etiology of the disorder, but the pattern of inheritance does not appear to follow simple Mendelian genetics (Deutsch, Matthysse, Swanson, & Farkas, 1990). Therefore, while evidence does suggest that genetics is a factor, the precise extent is unclear.

The biological mechanisms that may contribute to the etiology of ADHD have received considerable attention, although little is known about them. Historically the disorder was thought to be the result of some form of brain injury or damage, in part because of the resemblance between symptoms of some identifiable organic disorders and those of ADHD; thus the original classifications of "brain damage," "minimal brain damage," and "minimal brain dysfunction" were proposed and adopted. It was thought that the areas of the brain primarily involved in attention, impulse control, and motor activity were in some way damaged in these children. This belief resulted in research targeting the premotor cortex and the superior prefrontal cortex areas of the brain, which are involved in the control of attention and motor activity (Zametkin et al., 1990). Zametkin et al. (1990) reported that both global and regional glucose metabolism (primarily in the premotor cortex and superior prefrontal cortex) was lower in adults previously diagnosed with ADHD as children than in a group of nondiagnosed adults. While this group difference is intriguing, there is a great deal of research required before reaching conclusions about anatomical differences between the brains of people without ADHD and the brains of those with ADHD.

Additional research has focused on the neurotransmitters to discover clues as to the biological basis of ADHD. The most prominent theories focus on the role of dopamine and norepinephrine. Central nervous system stimulants commonly used in the treatment of ADHD (e.g., Ritalin) promote release of dopamine and norepinephrine from presynaptic storage sites and may be involved in blocking reuptake (Barkley, 1990; Hunt, Mandl, Lau, & Hughes, 1991). This has led to theories of etiology focusing on deficiencies in the functioning of these neurotransmitter systems; however, the current literature cannot explain the exact role they play (Zametkin & Rapoport, 1987; Levy & Hobbes, 1988).

The various etiological factors can be summarized with the following hypothesis: an individual inherits a certain genetic pattern from his or her biological parents that, once transcribed, results in structural and/or chemical discrepancies in the brain. These discrepancies are likely to be in the areas of the premotor cortex and the superior prefrontal cortex. Altered functioning in these areas of the brain may be the result of—or result in—deficiencies in dopamine and/or norepinephrine at the neurotransmitter level that may lead to difficulties with attention, impulse control, and motor activity. These findings remain speculative until further research in these areas is able to provide more information.

Although the etiology of ADHD is unclear, parents can be reassured that parenting behavior does not cause ADHD in children. Previously proposed notions that diet, food additives, or sugar cause ADHD in children also are not supported by the literature (Gross, Tofanelli, Butzirus, & Snodgrass, 1987; Milich & Pelham, 1986; Milich, Wolraich, & Lingren, 1986).

Complications

Besides the core symptoms described above, adolescents with ADHD frequently present with a variety of other related problems. These problems, many of which may be partially attributed to the core symptoms, are in the areas of academics, peer relations, self-esteem, regulation of affect, and family relations. Many normal adolescents experience problems in these areas (Offer, Ostrov, Howard, & Atkinson, 1990; Rutter, Graham, Chadwick, & Yale, 1976; Walker & Greene, 1987), but those growing up with the symptoms of ADHD typically exhibit greater problems in these areas than their nondiagnosed peers.

Problems at school extend beyond disruptive behaviors and homework compliance. In studies that have controlled for intelligence, ADHD adolescents have been reported to lag behind their peers in the areas of spelling, reading, and arithmetic (Barkley, Fischer, et al., 1990; Fischer, et al., 1990; Hoy, Weiss, Minde, & Cohen, 1978). Children with ADHD also are more likely than their nondiagnosed peers to have a learning disability (Barkley, DuPaul, & McMurray, 1990), although little is known about the prevalence of learning disabilities in the adolescent ADHD population. August and Garfinkel (1990) reported that 36% of 58 consecutive ADHD adolescent referrals met diagnostic criteria for a reading disability. It is unclear whether these deficits are attributable to a basic cognitive deficit associated with ADHD, a result of the cumulative effect of difficulties in paying attention to academic tasks, or some combination of the two. Further research is needed to address these issues.

Relationships with peers have been widely reported as a problem for children with ADHD (Cunningham & Siegel, 1987; Landau & Milich, 1988; Whalen, Henker, & Granger, 1990). Follow-up studies have documented that individuals who were diagnosed with ADHD in childhood continue to have problems with peer relations in adolescence (Barkley et al., 1991; Hechtman & Weiss, 1983; Mannuzza et al., 1988). This finding was consistent across measures including interviews, parent and teacher rating scales, social skills tests, and self-report rating scales. The studies reported that adolescents with an ADHD diagnosis participated in few extracurricular activities, performed poorly on social skills measures, tended to withdraw from social situations, were unpopular, and generally were less socially competent when compared to their nondiagnosed peers.

Another related problem for these adolescents is poor self-esteem. Adolescents with ADHD have reported lower levels of self-esteem than their nondiagnosed peers (Hoy et al., 1978; Weiss & Hechtman, 1986). Sometimes this problem may contribute to a diagnosis of dysthymia or depression. Barkley et al. (1991) presented some self-report data indicating that ADHD-diagnosed adolescents do report greater degrees of sadness and higher rates of life stress than their nondiagnosed peers. Weiss and Hechtman (1986) also describe some ADHD adults with diagnoses of major depression and suicide attempts. While many adolescents experience increased levels of sadness or depression when they enter adolescence (Rutter et al., 1976), ADHD adolescents report greater than normal levels.

Another typical adolescent problem that is exacerbated in ADHD is mood lability. This can take many forms, including problems with anger control, anxiety, and temper outbursts. In Wender's (1990) Utah Criteria for diagnosing adolescent and adult ADHD, three items—affective lability, hot temper, and stress intolerance—focus on mood lability. Each of these criteria refer to fluctuations in affect that may cycle across hours or days and can manifest themselves in angry outbursts, anxiety, or depression. These reactions may be unprovoked or out of proportion to the triggering event.

Follow-up studies have also documented these problems. Reports have indicated that adolescents with a childhood diagnosis of ADHD tend to be more depressed, anxious, aggressive, delinquent, and immature than their nondiagnosed peers (Barkley et al., 1991; Hechtman & Weiss, 1983). Parents and adolescents at our clinic frequently report problems with fluctuations in mood, angry outbursts, and immature behavior. These problems with affect are usually described as becoming increasingly more difficult as the child enters adolescence.

Although empirical data are lacking, these problems may be partially the result of years of failing to meet up to others' expectations, repeated failures with peers, loss of a positive illusory cognitive bias, and consistent poor performance in school. Peer rejection and academic failure are common pathways to depressed mood (Patterson & Stoolmiller, 1991). Adolescence is the age where social comparison is a very active and pivotal process in shaping an adolescent's self-concept; this process is usually not very reinforcing for the ADHD-diagnosed child.

Along with problems with mood regulation, relations have also been reported as being distressed in families of ADHD adolescents when compared to families of adolescents without a psychiatric diagnosis. Robin (1990) reported that mothers of ADHD-diagnosed teens report problems with homework and doing chores as the most frequent family disruptions. Barkley, Fischer, et al. (1990) report some home observational data that document family communication problems in this population. These data revealed that during neutral conversations, adolescents with ADHD tended to direct more commands and verbal abuse toward their mother than did nondiagnosed peers. In addition, ADHD adolescents spoke less than normal controls. During conflict discussions, ADHD adolescents and their mothers also differed from normal control subjects. Mothers generated more commands, verbal abuse, defensive statements, and complaints than mothers in the control group; the ADHD adolescents again spoke less than the adolescent controls and generated more statements categorized as defining and evaluative. These findings are consistent with our observation that communication problems and family distress are present in almost all families of ADHD adolescents who present to our clinic. Given the manifestations of the core symptoms and the related problems discussed in this section, there is plenty of evidence to place these families at risk for serious problems.

In summary, the clinical picture of an ADHD adolescent is extremely troublesome. Adolescence is a time when many parent-child relationships are thoroughly tested even with nondisordered children. Adolescents with ADHD frequently require special education services as problems with truancy, poor grades, peer rejection, and lack of discipline in the classroom escalate. Parents often must request police and psychiatric emergency assistance to deal with their ADHD adolescent. Parents who successfully used time-out procedures and mild restraint with their ADHD children must learn different ways to deal with increasingly oppositional and defiant adolescents who may be physically larger than the parents. Adolescence is a period of life that is described as extremely difficult for many people without ADHD (see Rutter et al., 1976); for adolescents with ADHD, it can be traumatic.

Differential Diagnosis and Assessment

The criteria for diagnosing ADHD in DSM-IV require presence of at least six of nine symptoms of inattention and at least four of six symptoms of overactivity and impulsivity. The symptoms must be present for at least 6 months, be evident by the age of 7, be exhibited more frequently than among most people of the same mental age, impair functioning, and be present in two or more settings. In the adolescent population this requires that one establish a childhood history of symptoms and current functioning difficulties in the core areas of inattention, impulsivity, and motor overactivity. In some ways, establishing the childhood history and current difficulties consistent with ADHD represent two separate but overlapping tasks.

To establish presence of symptoms before the age of 7, a thorough interview should be conducted with the adolescent's primary caregivers, and any relevant material (e.g., records of past treatment and early school reports) should be collected and reviewed. Similarly, presence of current symptoms should be established by conducting a complete psychiatric evaluation with both the adolescent and his or her parents. Unlike younger children with ADHD, adolescents may represent a valid source of diagnostic information about their current difficulties (Conners, 1985). Additionally, collecting information from the parents and current teachers in the form of standardized rating scales such as the Child Behavior Checklist (Achenbach & Edelbrock, 1983), IOWA Conners Rating Scale (Loney & Milich, 1982), SNAP (Swanson & Pelham, 1981), and DBD (Pelham, Gnagy, Greenslade, & Milich, 1992) is essential. Unfortunately, many of these standardized rating scales have established norms only for younger children. In addition, computer-based tasks claiming to assess sustained attention and vigilance are sometimes used as diagnostic adjuncts. These tasks, however, tend to lack useful norms, psychometric properties, and theoretical foundations (see earlier discussion of vigilance tasks in the Clinical Picture section).

Another diagnostic issue that needs to be addressed during the assessment of ADHD in adolescents is the presence of concurrent diagnoses or an identifiable organic cause for the presenting problems. The literature on concurrent diagnoses suggests that conduct disorder and oppositional defiant disorder may be present in a significant number of children with ADHD (Barkley, DuPaul, McMurray et al., 1990), and that learning disabilities may be present in a significant percentage of these children as well (Lambert & Sandoval, 1980). As discussed previously, adolescents with ADHD are at particular risk to develop such problems as illicit substance use, legal difficulties, poor self-esteem, and academic failure (Gittelman et al., 1985; Hechtman & Weiss, 1983; Weiss et al., 1985). Therefore careful exploration of these areas is encouraged at the time of the diagnostic assessment, and strong consideration should be given to having a complete psychoeducational assessment conducted as well.

All children and adolescents presenting for an initial diagnostic assessment should be screened for any medical disorder that may mimic or exacerbate the presenting problems. Specific attention should be paid to details in the medical history that may represent a serious head injury or other CNS insult with subsequent behavioral changes. Examples of these and other medical difficulties that should be reviewed include exposure to lead or materials containing lead toxins, presence of spells interrupting routine behavior (which may represent an underlying absence seizure disorder), symptoms consistent with hyperthyroidism, a history of hearing loss or other sensory impairment, sleep deprivation, and side effects of the patient's current medications (especially those known to potentially result in behavioral changes). Any indications of these difficulties should be thoroughly explored, and any diagnostic tests necessary to help establish or rule out their presence should be completed as part of a comprehensive assessment.

After completing an evaluation, the data should be used to determine absence or presence of each of the diagnostic criteria. When making decisions about absence or presence of each symptom, consideration should be given to the wide range of continuous variables that provide the context for the diagnosis (e.g., family factors, developmental level, school environment). This can be especially difficult for adolescents, given the wide normal range for problems during this developmental period.

Clinical Management

Medications

Treatment should target the manifestations of the core symptoms of the disorder in the adolescent's natural environment—in other words, the difficulties the adolescent is experiencing as an individual, with his or her family, at school, and with peers. Therefore, a primary goal of the treating clinician should be to identify clearly the problems the adolescent is having in daily life functioning.

The most frequently used treatment for ADHD has been pharmacotherapy with central nervous system stimulants. In spite of the previously held notion that children no longer respond to stimulants once they reach adolescence, there has been an increasing body of literature suggesting that stimulants are also effective in the adolescent ADHD population (Cantwell, 1985; Evans & Pelham, 1991; Klorman, Coons, & Borgstedt, 1987, Pelham, Vodde-Hamilton, Murphy, Greenstein, & Vallano, 1991).

Methylphenidate (Ritalin and Ritalin SR), dextroamphetamine (Dexedrine and Dexedrine Spansules), and pemoline (Cylert) represent the three most frequently prescribed stimulants for the treatment of ADHD. Ritalin is the most frequently prescribed and thoroughly studied of the stimulants. Ritalin is effective in approximately 70% of children with ADHD (Barkley, 1977), and in a recent study, 96% of ADHD-diagnosed children responded to either Ritalin or Dexedrine (Elia, Borcherding, Rapoport, & Keysor, 1991). Although the literature involving adolescents indicates a less significant response rate than with children (about 50% to 70%; Wender, Wood, & Reimherr, 1991), stimulants should still be considered the drug of choice for this population. Ritalin has been shown to improve scores on self-report measures and parent and teacher rating scales. Improvements have been reported in dysphoric mood, attention to task, vigilance, rule-following behavior, academic functioning, excitability, and negative social behaviors in the adolescent population (Evans & Pelham, 1991; Klorman et al., 1987; Pelham et al., 1991; Varley, 1985)

The clinical assessment of stimulants in the adolescent population should be similar to the well-established double-blind placebo assessments in younger children, with modifications made in determining age-appropriate dependent variables for the adolescent (Evans & Pelham, 1991; Pelham et al., 1991). These variables should represent the primary areas of difficulty for the adolescents being assessed. For example, the dependent variables in the Evans and Pelham (1991) study included scores on assignments, disruptive behaviors in the classroom, on-task behavior, and quiz scores. It is difficult to employ the measures used in this study outside of a laboratory setting; nevertheless, ratings that specifically target these dimensions could be used effectively in a naturalistic environment.

A clinical assessment may include placebo medication and two separate dosage levels of methylphenidate given twice per day (at the beginning and midpoint of the assessment day, approximately 4 hours apart) in random order over approximately 3 weeks. Information should be collected from parents and teachers that targets the adolescent's problematic behavior(s), as described above. Response is assessed by comparing the reports of the adolescent's behavior on the three medication conditions. Side-effect information should also be collected and compared across the medication conditions.

Doses should be determined based on the clinical history, weight, and medical status of the individual patient, the general dose guidelines, and the amount of any single dose in larger children. The effective dose range for methylphenidate with children is 0.3 to 0.7 mg/kg per dose; for dextro amphetamine it is 0.15 to 0.5 mg/kg per dose (each given two to three times per day; Dulcan, 1990). Pemoline is generally given once per day in the morning, with a manufacturer's maximum recommended dose of 112.5 mg. No clear dose range for stimulants, however, has been established for the adolescent population. There is little information about the side-effect profile of stimulants in the adolescent population except for what can be extrapolated from the drug response studies with adolescence and the side-effect studies with younger children (Barkley, McMurray, Edelbrock, & Robbins, 1990; Rancurello, Vallano, & Waterman, in press).

Other medications for ADHD have been studied, although the findings are much less convincing than the literature on stimulants. After the stimulants, tricyclic antidepressants represent the most commonly studied drugs for ADHD, with imipramine and desipramine being the primary agents studied (Biederman, Baldessarini, Wright, Knee, & Harmatz, 1989; Pliszka, 1987; Zametkin & Rapoport, 1983). Newer agents such as bupropion (Simeon, Ferguson, & Van Wyck Fleet, 1986) and fluoxetine (Barrickman, Noyes, Kuperman, Schumacher, & Verda, 1991) have been suggested as alternatives, but the lack of replicated well-controlled studies at this time would indicate that these agents should be used only after trials with stimulants or tricyclic antidepressants have been explored. In children with concurrent Tourette's syndrome (and possibly others), clonidine has been reported to be an effective alternative (Hunt, Capper, & O'Connell, 1990). Although there has been some reported success with the use of monoamine oxidase inhibitors (Zametkin, Rapoport, Murphy, Linnoila, & Ismond, 1985) it is unlikely that this group of agents will be used extensively because of dietary restrictions and other concerns (Rapoport, Zametkin, Donnely, & Ismond, 1985).

Pharmacological treatment of the adolescent with ADHD begins with stimulants unless relevant clinical issues dictate otherwise. While other medications may be useful in individual cases, the literature supports use of stimulants as the drug of choice; unfortunately, it has been a much too common practice to use stimulants as the sole treatment. Stimulant medication is most effective when used in combination with behavioral and other forms of treatment for ADHD (Barkley, 1990; Pelham & Murphy, 1986).

Psychosocial and Behavioral Treatments

There has been very little research done with behavioral or psychosocial treatments for adolescents with ADHD. Following is a review of a variety of treatments that have received some attention in the literature or have been used by clinicians, but there is very little empirical support for any of these methods. The techniques include family-based treatments, school interventions, anger control, group therapy, individual therapy, and partial hospitalization.

Family-Based Interventions. The ADHD adolescent can be an extremely disruptive force in the functioning of the family. As children enter adolescence their power to defy, damage, and aggress becomes increasingly dangerous and difficult for the parents to manage. And because adolescence also serves as a transitional period between childhood and adulthood, the adolescent with ADHD must be educated about the disorder, become a wise consumer of mental health services, and play an active role in his or her own treatment. A recent integration of a variety of family treatment methods by Robin and Foster (1989) appears to meet the needs of some of the problems described above and has been used with the families of ADHD adolescents.

The approach promoted by Robin and Foster is based on a biobehavioral–family systems model of ADHD. Robin (1990) describes this system as a disruption of the family homeostatic pattern by the development of the ADHD child into an ADHD adolescent. Adolescence significantly alters the goals and needs of the child, and this situation results in family conflict. The degree with which the conflict can be resolved is related to the severity of the core ADHD symptoms in the adolescent and the problem-solving skills, communication skills, cognitive distortions, family structure, and psychopathology of all the family members.

The treatment intervention assesses these family system variables and the behavior problems of the adolescent, then attempts to rectify the conflicts within the family. The treatment follows a sequence focusing on assessment and education, medication issues, parental coalition and basic behavioral techniques, study skills, family problem-solving and communication training, cognitive restructuring, and optional supportive or skills-training individual sessions with the adolescent. These components are specifically described by Robin (1990).

While this treatment is theoretically appealing, it has not been thoroughly tested. Barkley, Guevremont, Anastopoulos, and Fletcher (1992) reported modest improvements in a group of families treated with these methods. The treatment produced effects similar to those found with the behavioral parent training and structured family therapy treatment control groups. The behavioral parent training employed in this project was a version of the Defiant Children (Barkley, 1987) program composed of many standard parent training components (praise, time out, etc.). The structured family therapy was a version of a treatment described by Minuchin and Fishman (1981) that focuses on altering maladaptive family systems or interaction processes. Barkley et al. (1992) concluded that while improvements were not as great as had been hoped, changes in the protocol utilizing the same theoretical format might help to maximize the effectiveness of this approach. For example, families were only seen for eight to ten 1-hour sessions; extending the length of treatment was seen as one mechanism likely to benefit the saliency of the technique.

Our experience with these methods has been encouraging. Parents have been very receptive to the format and process, and many adolescents have become active participants in the procedures. The typical duration of treatment for our patients has been 3 to 4 months of weekly sessions, with many cases extending considerably longer than this on a biweekly or monthly basis.

During the course of treatment we have encountered a recurring cognitive distortion among many adolescents and parents. The distortion has to do with the notion of fairness. Adolescents frequently trace their anger and some of their other problematic behaviors to issues of fairness. Parents often encounter difficulty establishing limits or rules that may result in consequences they believe are not exactly fair in certain exceptional situations. This may lead to the creation of so many exceptions to the rules that the rules are meaningless. These problems implicate cognitive distortions related to fairness as appropriate targets for the cognitive component of this treatment.

Another frequent occurrence during this treatment is the disintegration of problem-solving discussions into arguments about past events, with parents and adolescents frequently falling into accusation and defense modes instead of focusing on a solution. Agreement over past events is usually unnecessary and unachievable. Moving the family toward a constructive focus is a common battle in these sessions, but one that is necessary to successful treatment. Therapists need to train families to recognize and modify this destructive cycle of accusation and defense.

Successful communication and problem solving within families can lead to written contracts between the family members. These agreements describe the responsibilities and contingencies for all people involved; family members sign the contract to verify their commitment to the content. The research literature provides only equivocal support for the use of contracts (see Robin & Foster, 1989, pp. 276–280, for a review), but our experience indicates that they sometimes appear to be helpful and are relatively easy to use. The lessons learned from contracts can be twofold. First, the people signing them learn to abide by their commitment. Second, a contract points out to the adolescent(s) and parents the importance of carefully considering what they are agreeing to *before* they sign it. This second lesson is frequently the more important of the two, especially for the ADHD adolescent.

School Interventions. School problems with classwork, behavior, and homework have been documented for adolescents with ADHD and are some of the most frequent complaints from these children's parents (Fischer et al., 1990). A review of a set of home-situation questionnaires by Robin (1990) found that mothers of ADHD teens reported school and homework as the two most problematic areas for their children. Although the difficulties at school are of paramount concern with this population, very little is known about treatment.

Given the success of behavioral interventions in treating school problems with children (see Pelham & Hinshaw, in press), these techniques are the first treatments of choice with the adolescents. Very little clinical research, however, has been done regarding similar interventions with adolescents.

There are a variety of difficulties in implementing behavioral techniques at school with adolescents that are not present when treating younger children. The structure of junior and senior high schools is less conducive than that of elementary schools to these interventions due to the variety of teachers encountered by the students each day, problems with peers becoming aware of individual behavioral interventions, feelings of embarrassment by the adolescent, and the need to coordinate approaches across a wide variety of classroom settings. We have used three approaches to the school problems experienced by ADHD adolescents; these techniques target task completion, off-task behavior, and disruptive behaviors in the classroom.

The first technique targets the quality and quantity of independent work completed by the students, as well as other individual problems the child may be exhibiting. One of the biggest obstacles to encouraging appropriate and productive behavior at school is communication. This intervention enhances communication through use a weekly report by teachers describing the progress and behavior of the student in the classroom. It is a variation of the daily report card used successfully with younger children (Pelham, 1986; Pfiffner & O'Leary, in press). The therapist, student, and parents, with input from the teachers, identify three to four areas of difficulty for the child (e.g., completion of assignments, achievement on tests). A form is developed using these behaviors to label the rows; the columns are labeled with the class names (algebra, biology, etc.). Every Friday the adolescent takes this sheet to each of his or her teachers, who indicate the student's performance in each area using a prearranged scale (see Figure 19–1). The parents then allow the adolescent weekend privileges or allowance contingent on the completeness of the weekly report (i.e., whether every teacher completed the form) and the marks recorded by the teachers. Development of this intervention is negotiated in the family sessions described previously and is written into a contract. Consultation with teachers before the implementation of the program is critical to its success.

This program has been successful with many adolescents in improving their behaviors at school. As with any behavioral program, one of the key ingredients is the parents' willingness to consistently enforce the weekend or allowance contingencies. A second problem with adolescents is their acceptance of the program. Some adolescents will comply until the first time they want to do something important to them but cannot due to a poor weekly report. They may then defy their parents and leave for the weekend to stay with friends. A typical pattern for some adolescents is to return from the weekends, become verbally abusive toward their parents and claim the contract is unfair, then go to school on Monday without any resolution. Parents can justifiably feel quite helpless in these situations. The therapist may need to work with the parents to develop contingencies (e.g., access to the family car, allowance) that are more difficult for the adolescent to undermine.

Date_____

| Criteria: | 1 | 2 | 3 | 4 | 5 |
| | Poor | | Satisfactory | | Excellent |

Behaviors Classes:	Science	Graphics	English	Math	Social Studies
1. Completes classrooms in class					
2. Classroom Behavior					
3. Brings in homework					
4. Approximate grade for work during the past week					
Teacher's Initials					

Figure 19–1 Example of a weekly behavioral report from school.

A second school intervention that has been successful with many families focuses on the completion of homework. Parents frequently complain that they do not know their children's assignments and cannot enforce homework completion. ADHD adolescents frequently fail at keeping assignment notebooks, and junior and senior high school teachers are usually unwilling to give parents homework information on a daily basis. Discussions between the adolescent and the parents about homework are likely to lead to arguments.

Parents cannot enforce what they cannot monitor. Therefore this intervention first helps the adolescents and parents to switch the focus from the completion of homework to the development of good study habits. The adolescent and his or her parents negotiate an amount of time that the student should spend on schoolwork each night (usually about 1 hour); parents can then monitor this work period each evening. If the adolescent claims that there is no homework or that it has been completed, the parents instruct him or her to read a school text, study, or complete academic tasks the parents develop (e.g., read the section on India in the encyclopedia and write a 2-page paper describing why you would or would not want to live there). The family may set a standard time for the adolescent to study or let him or her fulfill the agreement whenever he or she wishes. The important element is that all home privileges (e.g., using the telephone, leaving the house, watching television) are suspended every evening until the study period is completed according to the predetermined criteria. Defining these criteria can take a great deal of work in the family sessions.

The third intervention for school problems involves teaching the adolescents the skill of note taking. Evans, Pelham, and Grudberg (in press) reported that ADHD adolescents demonstrated improvement on measures of comprehension and increased levels of on-task behavior when they took notes on (rather than simply attending) a lecture-format American history class. The authors surveyed a set of junior high school teachers and found that very few actually taught note taking or required their students to take notes. Of those teachers that did encourage note taking, many defined this merely as copying notes from the board to one's notebook.

The notetaking in the Evans et al. study was taught over a 2- to 3-week period. Instruction and practice lasted 1 hour each day. Subjects were taught to identify the main ideas and details in a lecture and record the information in a notebook without prompts from the teacher (see Spires & Stone, 1989); this is a very active process that requires sustained attention and is incompatible with disruptive behaviors. Not all adolescents were able to benefit from this intervention, but the majority of the ADHD adolescents demonstrated improvements in their school behavior and academic performance using this technique.

While these results are preliminary, the findings are encouraging. These interventions, as with most treatments for adolescents, require the cooperation of the adolescent. This may be one of the greatest hurdles to successful intervention.

Anger Control. Physical and verbal aggression are problems that many parents of adolescents with ADHD report. Anger control treatments are one method of helping adolescents manage this problem. Such treatments usually include education, skills acquisition, and application phases; they are modeled after Meichenbaum's (1977) stress inoculation training and Novaco's (1978) anger management treatment. Patients are taught to recognize the precursors of, problems resulting from, and physiological responses to anger. They are then taught skills to address their own patterns of anger (usually cognitive restructuring and relaxation). Finally, they are helped to use these skills in their everyday life to manage anger. Descriptions of anger control programs are Braswell and Bloomquist (1991) and Feindler and Ecton (1986).

While there is growing interest in these techniques, there is little empirical support for their efficacy. Feindler and colleagues have reported that these techniques may be helpful for an aggressive adolescent population (Feindler, Ecton, Kingsley, & Dubey, 1986; Feindler, Marriott, & Iwata, 1984); but their results were tentative. Direct observation measures used in the natural environment yielded no significant treatment effects, although rating scales and observations in structured role-play assessments did produce significant beneficial treatment effects.

There are no reports describing the efficacy of anger control treatment with an ADHD adolescent population. While anger control techniques have shown some success with children (Hinshaw, Henker, & Whalen, 1984), cognitive-behavioral techniques (e.g., problem solving, anger control) have generally been minimally effective (Abikoff, 1987; Bloomquist, August, & Ostrander, 1991). Given the utility of these techniques with aggressive adolescents, as described above, anger control techniques may demonstrate more usefulness with an adolescent ADHD population.

Our own pilot trials using these techniques have indicated that the combination of cognitive interventions and relaxation training using a sequence of education, skills acquisition, and application phases can be effective with some adolescents. ADHD teens with acute episodes of anger as opposed to constant high levels of agitation responded best to the treatment. Some adolescents had difficulty benefiting from the relaxation techniques due to their fidgety behaviors, and we experienced difficulty with many adolescents in group settings. Adolescent concerns about peers seeing them do unusual movements in progressive muscle relaxation and the breathing exercises interfered with group sessions. Compliance with homework was poor without extensive staff follow-up. In addition, consistent with the high rate of oppositional defiant and conduct disorders in an adolescent ADHD population, we were frequently challenged by treatment refusal. These are preliminary findings; a refinement of the techniques for use in clinical research is needed to determine if anger control techniques are going to be beneficial to adolescents with ADHD.

Partial Hospitalization. Partial hospitalization programs are becoming increasingly popular as a method to treat children and adolescents. The Summer Treatment Program and Adolescent Day Treatment Programs at Western Psychiatric Institute and Clinic are examples of a partial hospitalization programs for children and adolescents with ADHD. These programs have attempted to integrate the behavioral and pharmacological treatments described in this chapter into a comprehensive treatment program for adolescents with ADHD.

The programs operate 5 days per week for 8 weeks. During this time adolescents participate in recreational activities, vocational training, group therapy, and educational interventions. A basic behavioral program is in place for all adolescents, although it is less intensive than ones typically employed with younger children. Adolescents meet with primary counselors and supervisors to identify their own manifestations of the core symptoms of ADHD and to assist in the development of their own individual behavioral program. Most of the behavioral and pharmacological treatments described in this chapter are available and used in the context of the various activities.

The environment is designed to challenge the adolescents' problems directly so the behaviors can be observed and treated. In the summer program the adolescents work on several projects that force them to rely on one another, complete tasks responsibly, communicate effectively with adults and peers, and organize activities and information. They organize and develop a variety of projects, including fundraisers, charitable food drives, exercise programs, weekly newsletters, recreational activities, and business meetings. Some adolescents are placed in leadership positions for these projects and receive consultation from the staff.

In this environment there are a variety of natural consequences for failure to complete tasks and numerous opportunities to test new skills. For example, the fundraiser for adolescents in the summer program has been a nightly food sale to parents of the younger children and staff. If one adolescent fails to do product inventory for the fundraiser, the peer responsible for buying the food does not know what to buy, and this affects sales. Reduced sales mean a loss of income, which typically pays for an overnight trip to an out-of-state amusement park. Therefore a natural consequence of failing to complete a task is the extra burden placed on the peers and the peers' response to this imposition. Peer approval is a very potent form of reinforcement and punishment in the adolescent population.

Summary

ADHD is a set of problems that continue well past childhood, compounding the already difficult developmental period of adolescence. The core symptoms of inattention, impulse control, and overactivity present differently in adolescents than in children; this is in part because the teens are maturing, their environment is changing, and their role in the family is drastically altered. Problems at school and home can be quite serious, often requiring the services of inpatient settings, juvenile courts, and psychiatric emergency rooms. The diagnosis and treatment of ADHD adolescents is difficult, since there is no broad empirical foundation of research. Stimulant treatment appears to be one of the treatments of choice for this population, although no behavioral or psychosocial intervention has been thoroughly studied. Nevertheless, a variety of strategies are good candidates for clinical research and provide treatment alternatives for the ADHD adolescent population.

References

Abikoff, H. (1987). An evaluation of cognitive behavior therapy for hyperactive children. In B. Lahey & A. Kazdin (Eds.), *Advances in clinical child psychology* (Vol. 10, pp. 171–216). New York: Plenum.

Achenbach, T. M., & Edelbrock, C. S. (1983). *Manual for the Child Behavior Checklist and Revised Child Behavior Profile*. Burlington: University of Vermont, Department of Psychiatry.

August, G. J., & Garfinkel, B. D. (1990). Comorbidity of ADHD and reading disability among clinic-referred children. *Journal of Abnormal Child Psychology, 18*, 29–46.

Barkley, R. A. (1977). A review of stimulant drug research with hyperactive children. *Journal of Child Psychology and Psychiatry, 18*, 137–165.

Barkley, R. A. (1987). *Defiant Children: A clinician's manual for parent training.* New York: Guilford.

Barkley, R. A. (1990). *Attention deficit hyperactivity disorder: A handbook for diagnosis and treatment.* New York: Guilford.

Barkley, R. A., Anastopoulus, A. D., Guevremont, D. C., & Fletcher, K. E. (1991). Adolescents with ADHD: Patterns of behavioral adjustment, academic functioning, and treatment utilization, *Journal of the American Academy of Child and Adolescent Psychiatry, 30*(5), 752–761.

Barkley, R. A., DuPaul, G., & McMurray, M. B. (1990). A comprehensive evaluation of attention deficit disorder with and without hyperactivity as defined by research criteria. *Journal of Consulting Clinical Psychology, 58*, 775–789.

Barkley, R. A., Fischer, M., Edelbrock, C. S., & Smallish, L. (1990). The adolescent outcome of hyperactive children diagnosed by research criteria: I. An 8 year prospective follow-up study. *Journal of the American Academy of Child and Adolescent Psychiatry, 29*, 546–557.

Barkley, R. A., Guevremont, D. C., Anastopoulos, A. D., & Fletcher, K. E. (1992). A comparison of three family therapy programs for treating family conflicts in adolescents disorder. *Journal of Consulting and Clinical Psychology, 60*, 450–462.

Barkley, R. A., McMurray, M. B., Edelbrock, C. S., & Robbins, K. (1990). Side effects of methylphenidate in children with attention deficit hyperactivity disorder: A systematic, placebo-controlled evaluation. *Pediatrics, 86*, 184–192.

Barrickman, L., Noyes, R., Kuperman, S., Schumacher, E., & Verda, M. (1991). Treatment of ADHD with fluoxetine: A preliminary trial. *Journal of the American Academy of Child and Adolescent Psychiatry, 30*(5), 762–767.

Biederman, J., Baldessarini, R. J., Wright, V., Knee, D., & Harmatz, J. S. (1989). A double-blind placebo controlled study of desipramine in the treatment of ADD: I. Efficacy. *Journal of the American Academy of Child and Adolescent Psychiatry, 28*(25), 777–780.

Bloomquist, M. L., August G. J., & Ostrander, R. (1991). Effects of a school-based cognitive-behavioral intervention for ADHD children. *Journal of Abnormal Child Psychology, 19*, 591–606.

Braswell, L., & Bloomquist, M. L. (1991). *Cognitive behavioral therapy with ADHD children: Child, family and school interventions.* New York: Guilford.

Brown, R. T., & Borden, K. A. (1986). Hyperactivity at adolescence: Some misconceptions and new directions. *Journal Of Clinical Child Psychology, 15*, 194–209.

Cairns, E., & Cammock, T. (1984). The development of reflection-impulsivity: Further data. *Personality and Individual Differences, 5*, 113–115.

Cantwell, D. P. (1972). Psychiatric illness in the families of hyperactive children. *Archives of General Psychiatry, 27*, 414–417.

Cantwell, D. P. (1985). Pharmacotherapy of ADD in adolescents: What do we know, where should we go, how should we do it? *Psychopharmacology Bulletin, 21*(2), 251–257.

Cohen, N. J., Weiss, G., & Minde, K. (1972). Cognitive styles in adolescents previously diagnosed as hyperactive. *Journal of Child Psychology and Psychiatry, 13*, 203–209.

Conners, C. K. (1985). Issues in the study of adolescent ADD-H/hyperactivity. *Psychopharmacology Bulletin, 21*(2), 243–250.

Cunningham, C. E., & Siegel, L. S. (1987). Peer interactions of normal and attention-deficit disordered boys during free-play, cooperative task, and simulated classroom situations. *Journal of Abnormal Child Psychology, 15*, 247–268.

Deutsch, C. K., Matthysse, S., Swanson, J. M., & Farkas, L. G. (1990). Genetic latent structure analysis of dysmorphology in attention deficit disorder. *Journal of the American Academy of Child and Adolescent Psychiatry, 29*(2), 189–194.

Dulcan, M. K. (1990). Using psychostimulants to treat behavioral disorders of children and adolescents. *Journal of Child and Adolescent Psychopharmacology, 1*(1), 7–20.

Elia, J., Borcherding, B. G., Rapoport, J. L., & Keysor, C. S. (1991). Methylphenidate and Dextroamphetamine Treatments of Hyperactivity: Are There True Nonresponders. *Psychiatry Research, 36*, 141–155.

Evans, S. W., & Pelham, W. E. (1991). Psychostimulant effects on academic and behavioral measures for ADHD junior high school students in a lecture format classroom. *Journal of Abnormal Child Psychology, 19*(5), 537–552.

Evans, S. W., Pelham, W. E. K, & Grudberg, M. V. (in press). The effectiveness of notetaking in a lecture format classroom with junior high school aged ADHD children. *Exceptionality*.

Feindler, E. L. & Ecton, R. B. (1986). *Adolescent anger control: Cognitive-behavioral techniques*. New York: Pergamon.

Feindler, E. L., Ecton, R. B., Kingsley, D., & Dubey, D. R. (1986). Group anger-control training for institutionalized psychiatric male adolescents. *Behavior Therapy, 17*, 109–123.

Feindler, E. L., Marriott, S. A., & Iwata, M. (1984). Group anger control training for junior high school delinquents. *Cognitive Therapy And Research, 8*, 299–311.

Fischer, M., Barkley, R. A., Edelbrock, C. S., & Smallish, L. (1990). The adolescent outcome of hyperactive children diagnosed by research criteria: II. Academic, attentional, and neuropsychological status. *Journal of Consulting and Clinical Psychology, 58*, 580–588.

Gittelman, R., Mannuzza, S., Shenker, R., & Bonagura, N. (1985). Hyperactive boys almost grown up. *Archives of General Psychiatry, 42*, 937–947.

Gross, M., Tofanelli, R. A., Butzirus, S. M., & Snodgrass, E. W. (1987). The effects of diets rich in and free from additives on the behavior of children with hyperkinetic and learning disorders. *Journal of the American Academy of Child and Adolescent Psychiatry, 26*(1), 53–55.

Hechtman, L., & Weiss, G. (1983). Long-term outcome of hyperactive children. *American Journal of Orthopsychiatry, 53*(3), 532–541.

Hinshaw, S. P., Henker, B., & Whalen, C. K. (1984). Self-control in hyperactive boys in anger-inducing situations: Effects of cognitive-behavioral training and of methylphenidate. *Journal of Abnormal Child Psychology, 12*, 55–77.

Hopkins, J., Perlman, T., Hechtman, L., & Weiss, G. (1979). Cognitive style in adults originally diagnosed as hyperactives. *Journal of Child Psychology and Psychiatry, 20*, 209–216.

Hoy, E., Weiss, G., Minde, K., & Cohen, H. (1978). The hyperactive child at adolescence: Cognitive, emotional, and social functioning. *Journal of Abnormal Child Psychology, 6,* 311–324.

Hunt, R. D., Capper, L., & O'Connell, P. (1990). Clonidine in child and adolescent psychiatry. *Journal of Child and Adolescent Psychopharmacology, 1,* 87–102.

Hunt, R. D., Mandl, L., Lau, S., & Hughes, M. (1991). Neurobiological theories of ADHD and Ritalin. In L. L. Greenhill & B. Osman (Eds.), *Ritalin: Theory and patient management.* New York: Liebart.

Klorman, R., Brumaghim, J. T., Fitzpatrick, O. A. & Borgstedt, A. D. (1992). Methylphenidate reduces abnormalities of stimulus classification in adolescents with attention deficit disorder. *Journal of Abnormal Psychology, 101,* 130–138.

Klorman, R., Coons, H. W., & Borgstedt, A. D. (1987). Effects of methylphenidate on adolescents with a childhood history of attention deficit disorder: I. Clinical findings. *Journal of the American Academy Of Child And Adolescent Psychiatry, 26*(3), 363–367.

Lambert, N. M., Hartsough, C. S., Sassone, D., & Sandoval, J. (1987). Persistence of hyperactivity symptoms from childhood to adolescence and associated outcomes. *American Journal of Orthopsychiatry, 57,* 22–32.

Lambert, N. M., & Sandoval J. (1980). The prevalence of learning disabilities in a sample of children considered hyperactive. *Journal Of Abnormal Child Psychology, 8,* 33–50.

Landau, S., & Milich, R. (1988). Social communication patterns of attention deficit-disordered boys. *Journal of Abnormal Child Psychology, 16,* 69–81.

Levy, F., & Hobbes, G. (1988). The action of stimulant medication in attention deficit disorder with hyperactivity: Dopaminergic, noradrenergic, or both? *Journal of the American Academy of Child and Adolescent Psychiatry, 27*(6), 802–805.

Loney, J., & Milich, R. (1982). Hyperactivity, inattention, and aggression in clinical practice. In M. Wolraich & D. K. Routh (Eds.), *Advances In behavioral pedriatrics.* Greenwich, CT: JAI.

Mannuzza, S., Klein, R., Konig, P., & Giampino, T. L. (1989). Hyperactive boys almost grown up: IV. Criminality and its relationship to psychiatric status. *Archives of General Psychiatry, 46,* 1073–1079.

Mannuzza, S., Klein, R., Bonagura, N., Konig, P., & Shenker, R. (1988). Hyperactive boys almost grown up: II. Status of subjects without a mental disorder. *Archives Of General Psychiatry, 45,* 13–18.

Mannuzza, S., Klein, R. G., Bonagura, N., Malloy, P., Giampino, T. L., & Addall, K. A. (1991). Hyperactive boys almost grown up: V. Replication of psychiatric status. *Archives of General Psychiatry, 48,* 77–83.

Meichenbaum, D. (1977). *Cognitive behavior modification: An integrative approach.* New York: Plenum.

Mendelson, W., Johnson, N., & Stewart, M. A. (1971). Hyperactive children as teenagers: A follow-up study. *Journal of Nervous and Mental Disease, 153,* 273–279.

Milich, R., & Pelham, W. E. (1986). Effects of sugar ingestion on the classroom and playgroup behavior of attention deficit disordered boys. *Journal of Consulting and Clinical Psychology, 54*(5), 714–718.

Milich, R., Wolraich, M., & Lingren, S. (1986). Sugar and hyperactivity: Critical review of empirical findings. *Clinical Psychology Review, 6,* 473–513.

Minuchin, S., & Fishman, H. C. (1981). *Family therapy techniques.* Cambridge, MA: Harvard University Press.

Morrison, J. R., & Stewart, M. A. (1971). A family study of the hyperactive child syndrome. *Biological Psychiatry, 3,* 189–195.

Novaco, R. (1978). Anger and coping with Stress: Cognitive-behavioral interventions. In J. Foyert & D. Rathjen (Eds.), *Cognitive-behavior therapy: Research and application.* New York: Plenum.

Nuechterlein, K. H. (1983). Signal detection in vigilance tasks and behavioral attributes among offspring of schizophrenic mothers and among hyperactive children. *Journal of Abnormal Psychology, 92,* 4–28.

Offer, D., Ostrov, E., Howard, K. I., & Atkinson, R. (1990). Normality and adolescence. *Psychiatric Clinics of North America, 13,* 377–388.

Patterson, G. R., & Stoolmiller, M. (1991). Replications of a dual failure model for boys' depressed mood. *Journal of Consulting and Clinical Psychology, 59,* 491–498.

Pelham, W. E. (1986). What is attention deficit disorder? In E. Sleator & W. Pelham (Eds.), *Attention deficit disorders: Vol. 1. Dialogues in pediatric management.* East Norwalk, CT: Appleton-Century-Crofts.

Pelham, W. E., Gnagy, E. M., Greenslade, K. E., & Milich, R. (1992). Teacher ratings of DSM-III-R symptoms for the disruptive behavior disorders. *Journal of American Academy of Child and Adolescent Psychiatry, 31,* 210–218.

Pelham, W. E., & Hinshaw, S. (in press). Attention deficit disorder. In S. M. Turner, K. S. Calhoun, & H. E. Adams (Eds.), *Handbook of clinical behavior therapy.* New York: Wiley.

Pelham, W. E., & Murphy, D. A. (1986). Attention deficit and conduct disorders. In M. Hersen (Ed.), *Pharmacological and behavioral treatment: An integrative approach.* New York: Wiley.

Pelham, W. E., Vodde-Hamilton, M., Murphy, D. A., Greenstein, J., & Vallano, G. (1991). The effects of methylphenidate on ADHD adolescents in recreational peer group and classroom settings. *Journal Of Clinical Child Psychology, 20*(3), 293–300.

Pfiffner, L. J., & O'Leary, S. G. (in press). Psychological treatments: School-based. In J. L. Matson (Ed.). *Hyperactivity in children: A handbook.* New York: Pergamon.

Pliszka, S. R. (1987). Tricyclic antidepressants in the treatment of children with attention deficit disorder. *Journal of the American Academy of Child and Adolescent Psychiatry, 26,* 127–132.

Rapoport, J. L., Zametkin, A., Donnely, M., & Ismond, D. (1985). New drug trials in attention deficit disorder. *Psychopharmacology Bulletin, 21,* 232–266.

Rancurello, M. D., Vallano, G., & Waterman, G. S. (in press). Psychotropic drug induced dysfunction in children. In M. S. Keshavan, A. Prasad, & J. Kennedy, (Eds.) *Drug induced dysfunction in psychiatry: Diagnosis and management.* Washington, DC: Hemisphere.

Robin, A. L. (1990). Training families with ADHD adolescents. In R. A. Barkley (Ed.), *Attention deficit hyperactivity disorder: A handbook for diagnosis and treatment*. New York: Guilford.

Robin, A. L., & Foster, S. L. (1989). *Negotiating parent-adolescent conflict: A behavioral family systems approach*. New York: Guilford.

Rutter, M., Graham, P., Chadwick, O. F. D., & Yule, W. (1976). Adolescent turmoil: Fact or fiction? *Journal of Child Psychology and Psychiatry, 17*, 35–56.

Satterfield, J. H. (1976). The hyperactive child syndrome: A precursor of adult psychopathy. In R. Hare & D. Schalling (Eds.), *Psychopathic behavior: Approaches to research*. Chichester, England: Wiley.

Satterfield, J. H., Hoppe, C., & Schell, A. (1982). A prospective study of delinquency in 110 adolescent boys with attention deficit disorder and 88 normal adolescent boys. *American Journal of Psychiatry, 139*, 795–798.

Schachar, R., & Wachsmuth, R. (1990). Hyperactivity and parental psychopathology. *Journal of Child Psychology and Psychiatry, 31*(3), 381–392.

Simeon, J. G., Ferguson, H. B., & Van Wyck Fleet, J. (1986). Bupropion effects in attention deficit and conduct disorders. *Canadian Journal of Psychiatry, 31*, 581–585.

Spires, H. A., & Stone, D. P. (1989). The directed notetaking activity: A self-questioning approach. *Journal of Reading, 33*, 36–39.

Swanson, J., & Pelham, W. (1988). *A rating scale for the diagnosis of attention deficit disorders: Teacher norms and reliability*. Unpublished manuscript, University of Pittsburgh, Western Psychiatric Institute and Clinic, Pittsburgh, PA.

van der Meere, J., & Sergeant, J. (1988). Focused attention in pervasively hyperactive children. *Journal of Abnormal Child Psychology, 16*, 627–640.

Varley, C. K. (1985). A review of drug treatment efficacy for attention deficit disorder with hyperactivity in adolescents. *Psychopharmacology Bulletin, 21*(2), 216–221.

Walker, L. S., & Greene, J. W. (1987). Negative life events, psychosocial resources, and psychophysiological symptoms in adolescents. *Journal of Clinical Child Psychology, 16*, 29–36.

Weiss, G., & Hechtman, L. (1986). *Hyperactive children grown up*. New York: Guilford.

Weiss, G., Hechtman, L., Milroy, T., & Perlman, T. (1985). Psychiatric status of hyperactives as adults: A controlled prospective 15 year follow up of 63 hyperactive children. *Journal of the American Academy of Child Psychiatry, 24*, 211–220.

Weiss, G., Minde, K., Werry, J., Douglas, V., & Nemeth, E. (1971). Studies on the hyperactive child: VIII. Five year follow-up. *Archives Of General Psychiatry, 24*, 409–414.

Weissman, M. M., Prusoff, B. A., Gammon, G. D., Merikangas, K. R., Leckman, J. F., & Kidd, K. K. (1984). Psychopathology in the children (ages 6–18) of depressed and normal parents. *Journal of the American Academy of Child Psychiatry, 23*, 78–84.

Wender, P. H. (1990). Attention deficit hyperactivity disorder in adolescents and adults. In B. D. Garfinkel, G. A. Carlson, & E. B. Weller (Eds.), *Psychiatric disorders in childhood and adolescence*. Philadelphia: Saunders.

Wender, P. H., Wood, D. R., & Reimherr, F. W. (1985). Pharmacological treatment of attention deficit disorder, residual type (ADD-RT), "minimal brain dysfunction," hyperactivity in adults. *Psychopharmacology Bulletin, 21,* 222–231.

Wender, P. H., Wood, D. R., & Reimherr, F. W. (1991). Pharmacological treatment of attention deficit disorder, residual type (ADD-RT) in adults. In L. L. Greenhill & B. H. Osman (Eds.), *Ritalin: Theory and patient management.* New York: Liebert.

Whalen, C. K., Henker, B., & Granger, D. A. (1990). Social judgement processes in hyperactive boys: Effects of methylphenidate and comparisons with normal peers. *Journal of Abnormal Child Psychology, 18,* 297–316.

Zametkin, A. J., Nordahl, T. E., Gross, M., King, A. C., Semple, W. E., Rumsey, J., Hamburger, S., & Cohen, R. M. (1990). Cerebral glucose metabolism in adults with hyperactivity of childhood onset. *New England Journal of Medicine, 323*(20), 1361–1366.

Zametkin, A., & Rapoport, J. L. (1983). Tricyclic antidepressants and children. In G. D. Burrows, T. R. Norman, & B. Davies (Eds.), *Drugs and psychiatry; Vol. 1. Antidepressants.* Amsterdam: Elsevier Biomedical Press.

Zametkin, A. J., & Rapoport, J. L. (1987). Neurobiology of attention deficit disorder with hyperactivity: Where have we come in 50 years? *Journal of the American Academy of Child and Adolescent Psychiatry, 6*(5), 676–686.

Zametkin, A., Rapoport, J. L., Murphy, D. L., Linnoila, M., & Ismond, D. (1985). Treatment of hyperactive children with monoamine oxidase inhibitors. I. Clinical efficacy. *Archives of General Psychiatry, 42,* 962–966.

Part IV
Special Topics

20
Role of Family and Home Environment

David Reitman
Alan M. Gross
Stephen C. Messer

Lay people, philosophers, and natural scientists have long noted the importance of the family in promoting the development of our youth. Traditionally, the family's influence has been discussed in the context of children, and perhaps no individual has influenced our thinking about the family more than Sigmund Freud. Like many others past and present, Freud placed heavy emphasis on the impact of early family experience on development. Adolescence, in contrast, is often described as a period in which peer groups, school achievement, and other factors outside the home become more salient while family influence declines. Consequently, relatively few researchers have recognized the influence of the family and home environment as it extends into adolescence.

In recent years, though, several investigators have given special attention to the adolescent-family relationship and its role in adolescent psychopathology. For example, Hinde (1988) suggests that family or family-like environments remain predominant in our culture and asks how relationships within the family affect children and other persons living in these environments. Further, researchers across the theoretical spectrum view the quality of adolescent-family interaction as an important variable in adolescent development (Cox & Cox, 1979; Parrish, 1987; Patterson & Forgatch, 1990).

While many agree that the family-adolescent relationship deserves further scrutiny, several obstacles remain to understanding it. The most obvious impediment to good basic research here and elsewhere is definition. What constitutes a family? How do we define *adolescent*? A "family or home environment" might consist of any number of alternatives to a nuclear family. Peterson (1991) estimates that nuclear families are now no more common than single-parent homes.

Preparation of this chapter was supported in part by NIH Grant DEO8641 to Alan M. Gross.

621

Recognizing these limitations of a structural definition of *family*, Radke-Yarrow (1990) provides functional criteria with which to evaluate the rearing environment:

> (1) providing care and protection of the child, (2) regulating and controlling the child's behavior in line with the needs and requirements from internal and external sources, (3) providing knowledge and skills and understanding concerning the physical and social world, (4) giving affective meaning to interactions and relationships, and (5) facilitating the child's self-understanding. (p. 175)

Functional definitions such as this may better equip researchers to capture the dynamic and interactive flavor of the family environment. If adopted, her approach may lead to improved research methodologies and better understanding of the family environment. Interested researchers may opt for either a microscopic (dyadic) or a macroscopic (whole family interaction) level of analysis while employing similar definitional criteria. Consequently, the benefits of functional definitions of the rearing (or home) environment might ultimately include a more coherent family literature.

There is little consensus concerning the definition of *adolescence*. The age range is typically considered to span puberty through the late teens, yet adolescence may sometimes be defined in terms of earliest sexual experience and extend until the individual becomes self-supporting and/or sexually mature (Douvan & Gold, 1966; Lambert, Rothschild, Altland, & Green, 1978). In our review of the literature, we found research samples spanning the range from middle childhood (6 to 8 years) to late adolescence (18 years). While many of these studies incorporated considerations of age within their experimental design, several appeared to treat children and adolescents as a homogeneous population. In the latter cases, the plethora of definitions and nebulous inclusion criteria employed weaken our assertions about the dynamics of adolescent-family relations and may obscure unique aspects of those relations related to age or maturational factors. A recent review warns against considering parent-child relationships "a-developmental," pointing out that pubertal maturation may have an important influence on family relations (Collins & Russell, 1991). Variant conceptualizations of *family* and *adolescent* therefore represent an obstacle to researchers and other professionals seeking to aid adolescents and families in distress.

Another barrier to understanding the family-adolescent relationship and its relevance to the development of adolescent psychopathology is the difficulty of separating genetic from family-environmental influences. Several investigators agree on the importance of discriminating between environmental and genetic influences on psychopathology within the family

(Hinde & Stevenson-Hinde, 1988; Pogue-Geile & Rose, 1987; Rutter, 1985). One method used to distinguish the relative contributions of these factors has been to capitalize on special environmental or genetic conditions—such as adoption, divorce, or death of a parent—in which the variable(s) may be isolated (e.g., Plomin, DeFries, & Fulker, 1988; Rutter, 1985; Rutter et al., 1990). Studies reflecting this approach are typically employed by developmental psychologists; more detail about their methods and findings will be presented later in this chapter.

A final difficulty in the examination of family-adolescent relations is the problem of unidirectional causation. Rutter (1985) has suggested a sizable family influence on behavioral development but asserts that this influence is transactional rather than unidirectional in nature. In other words, Rutter argues that in order to progress beyond a purely descriptive analysis of how families and adolescents interact, it may be necessary to broaden our assumptions regarding these relationships to accommodate their transactional nature.

Several studies have demonstrated that alterations in parenting behavior may effect behavior change in preadolescents (see Patterson, 1982, for a review). Further, research by Patterson (1980) suggests that child characteristics may simultaneously influence parenting behavior. Thus it may also prove valuable to attend to the ways in which changes in the adolescent are associated with changes in parenting styles and in the behavior of other members of the home environment. An analogous argument may be made for interactions between families and the environment, as well as between adolescents and the environment. Neither the family nor the adolescent exists in a vacuum. The adolescent and family or home environment interact with each other and with the community. Theories offered by developmental behavioral geneticists suggest that genotype, too, may play an important part in determining how individuals respond (and are responded to) in the rearing environment. Though the complexity of these relationships may be intimidating to the researcher or clinician, promising techniques employed by Patterson (1982), Rutter et al. (1990), and others to study depression, aggression, and other disorders may point the way toward continued progress in understanding the causes and maintenance of adolescent psychopathology.

This chapter will describe two approaches to understanding the adolescent-family relationship and discuss how this relationship may either lead to psychopathology or buffer against it. A discussion of factors relevant to the family or home environment and believed important to understanding adolescent psychopathology also will be presented. The final portion of the chapter will identify what appear to be the most promising avenues for research and briefly discuss the implications of what is known about the adolescent-family relationship.

Theoretical Models

A variety of models have been proposed to conceptualize the role of the family in adolescent development. Some of the most powerful models employed to date have been learning-based theories and their derivatives, as well as the developmental model. There may be much to be gained by including aspects of each approach in the study of adolescent-family relations (Plomin, Nitz, & Rowe, 1990).

Learning-Based Models

The primary characteristic of behavioral theories of human behavior is the emphasis on learned behavior. According to learning theory, most adaptive and maladaptive behaviors are considered learned responses to the environment. A second important feature of behaviorally based theories is the emphasis on observable events. John B. Watson (1913), the founder of behaviorism, insisted that behavior and the environment in which it occurs become the focus of the psychologist's attention, rather than thoughts, emotions, or needs. Though many behaviorally oriented researchers have since become more receptive to cognitive interpretations of behavior, behavioral approaches remain grounded in a predominantly empiricist tradition. The assertions that behavior is learned and that the investigator should focus on observable events suggest two important things with regard to the study of families and their influence on adolescents. First, they imply that a significant portion of behavior may be altered by controlling the environment. Second, they imply that direct observation of the adolescent-family relationship may yield important information pertaining to the development of adolescent psychopathology.

One learning-based model for studying the adolescent (and other family members) has been social learning theory (SLT). SLT is a derivative of earlier learning-based theories with a particular emphasis on the social aspects of learning and the mutually interactive effects of behavior, person, and environment (Jacob, 1987). Two prominent SLT researchers, Albert Bandura and Gerald Patterson, have proposed similar but distinct distillations of this model. Bandura, building on the initial theories of modeling proposed by Dollard and Miller and others, has deemed his version "social cognitive theory." According to Bandura (1986), "People are neither driven by inner forces nor automatically controlled by external stimuli. Rather, human functioning is explained in terms of a model of triadic reciprocality in which behavior, cognitive and personal factors, and environmental events all operate as interacting determinants of one another" (p. 18). Patterson, in contrast subscribes to a "performance model" of social learning that asserts individuals may learn via modeling or vicarious learning processes; however, their behavioral performance is determined by the interaction of behavior and the environment. According to Jacob (1987), all strains of SLT share the following attributes: a focus on behavioral systems with reciprocal interactions among members of that social system; an emphasis on behavior change as a function of environment and/or cognitions; a preference for naturalistic study of families; a commitment to clinical application; and the use of a rigorous, scientific methodology to study social relationships.

Because of Patterson's vast research program involving children and adolescents and issues of particular relevance to the development of psychopathology (e.g., conduct disorder, depression), our presentation will focus on his model of SLT. Patterson's research program, and the investigative efforts of many of his colleagues at the Oregon Social Learning Center, have examined the utility of the "coercive family process" (CFP) construct (Patterson, 1976). CFP distinguishes the quality of social interactions within the family as an important contributor to the development of psychopathology. In the CFP model, family management practices are highlighted. Specifically, persistent disruptions in the interactions of family members and increasingly entrenched behavior patterns among the involved parties are hypothesized to result in psychopathology in affected adolescents and children. It is believed that stressors may disrupt family management practices and lead to increasingly coercive exchanges among family members.

Consequently, adolescents raised in homes pervaded by disrupted family management practices are believed to be at greater risk for psychopathology. For example, a mother who gives in to a tantruming adolescent's request for a favored item or privilege in order to escape embarrassment or threats from the adolescent may inadvertently train the latter in this undesirable behavior (Patterson, 1982). In this case, the tantrum is considered a form of coercion in which the child manipulates the adult to produce a desired outcome. The aversive behaviors (tantrums) are maintained by the adult's negatively reinforced behavior (compliance)—so named because it temporarily removes the aversive event, but increases the frequency of the behavior that removed the aversive action.

The behavior of parent and child therefore interact, establishing a "coercion trap" in which each conflict becomes an occasion for each to engage in a form of emotional-behavioral one-upmanship. Further, the coercive quality of the interactions may escalate: the child may become increasingly disruptive and belligerent, while the parent may respond by resorting to threats, actual violence, or capitulation. It is hypothesized that this form of parent-child interaction will not only result in a continuation of the problem behavior but severely damage the relationship and, via a complex series interactions involving the adolescent and his or her environment, ultimately lead to psychopathology. Thus the coercive process has not only a behavioral component but an important affective dimension as well.

Patterson (1982) has found that through training in family management practices, negative interactions between parent and child may be substantially decreased, and improvements in child behavior have been noted. For example, in one study, parents of a child accused of lying, stealing, and fire setting were trained to monitor the child's behavior (his compliance or whereabouts). After substantial training, the parents were then instructed to provide reinforcers (e.g., talking, attention) to the boy contingent upon his remaining in the home and initiating conversation with his parents and siblings. After several arduous months of intervention, the boy's behavior had markedly improved, and the family environment had significantly been altered in terms of increased positive reinforcement and family interaction (Patterson & Reid, 1970).

The work of Patterson and his colleagues and their rigorous, scientific approach to the study of adolescents and the family environment continue to hold promise empirically and theoretically. Though it is clear no one perspective will provide all the necessary answers, Patterson's social learning approach remains an important contribution to understanding adolescent psychopathology and its development in the context of family environment.

Developmental Models

Other important contributions to the family-adolescent literature stem from developmental psychology. McGraw (1987) has defined developmental psychology as a "scientific discipline concerned with describing age-related changes in the behavior and mental processes of both humans and animals and then explaining how nature and nurture through their interaction produce these changes" (p. 6). The developmental approach brings several potentially valuable assets to the study of family-adolescent relations. This paradigm offers a wider lens in which to view family interaction, and longitudinal studies characteristic of this approach permit more certainty in elucidation of the long-term impact of variables under study. More specifically, longitudinal at-risk studies such as those undertaken by Rutter and colleagues (detailed later in this chapter), provide a tool for focusing on factors relevant to the future development of psychopathology in adolescents. Further, a developmental approach also emphasizes the importance of age-related and interactive factors to the development of psychopathology. Though obviously not limited to the study of adolescence, a developmental perspective illustrates the importance of studying adolescents uniquely—in relation to their current family environment— while permitting consideration of how developmental factors may facilitate or inhibit the development of psychopathology.

Within the domain of developmental psychology, family, twin, and adoption studies undertaken by developmental behavioral geneticists represent potentially valuable aids to the family researcher or clinician interested in adolescent-family relations and psychopathology (Plomin et al., 1990). Family studies determine the extent to which family members resemble one another on a given trait, while twin studies compare monozygotic and dizygotic twins and their families in order to estimate the role of heredity and environment in creating individual differences. Perhaps the behavioral geneticists' most powerful research tool is the adoption study, which compares adopted children to their adoptive and biological families to assess the relationship between genes and environment and the role of each in establishing individual differences. One goal of developmental behavioral geneticists—to address the causes of differences among individuals in a population—may prove particularly relevant to adolescent-family researchers interested in psychopathology.

Significant conceptual and empirical contributions to the study of adolescent psychopathology and family relations have been made by behavioral geneticists via the concepts of shared versus nonshared environments and genotype-environment interaction. Briefly, shared environmental factors are variables that all members of a family experience equally (e.g., socioeconomic status). Nonshared factors are not experienced by all members of the home (e.g., a handicapping condition, or preferential treatment by a parent). Many researchers believe nonshared factors may be so powerful that after controlling for genetic similarity, two children of the same family would be no more alike (in terms of psychopathology) than children selected at random from the population (Plomin & Daniels, 1987; Rowe & Plomin, 1981). It is also possible that shared environment may be more important for some forms of psychopathology than others.

How do genes and environment interact to influence adolescent development? The theory of genotype-environment interaction suggests that genetic propensities toward certain kinds of behavior may interact with the environment to produce different behavioral outcomes (Plomin et al., 1990). According to the theory, for example, two children with dissimilar propensities toward depressive behavior might respond differently to maternal depressive behavior. A child with a genetic propensity (established via physiological, not behavioral, genetic mechanisms) might therefore be more likely exhibit depressive behavior, perhaps via modeling and/or coercive processes operating within the home.

A subtype of this theory, genotype-environment correlation, posits passive, reactive, and active correlations between genes and environments (Plomin, DeFries, & Loehlin, 1977). *Passive correlation* refers to inheritance of both genes and the rearing environment, which is indirectly influenced by the parents' genotype. *Reactive correlation* refers to responses of nonfamily members to genotypical differences among children. *Active correlation* refers to the child's selection of environments, or "niche-building" (Scarr & McCartney, 1983). This form of genotypical expression may be of particular importance to adolescence, as it is believed to be the most powerful and direct expression of genotype and is dependent on the individual having become relatively autonomous for its expression.

Ultimately, one need not assume the learning-based and developmental models to be mutually exclusive. In fact, the developmental model has been referred to as a "macroparadigm" capable of accommodating views from any number of theoretical orientations (e.g., behavioral, biological, family systems) (Achenbach, 1974; Lewis & Miller, 1990). At present, the door seems open to increased communication between learning-based and developmental approaches. On an operational and procedural level, Plomin et al. (1990) recommend "multimethod approaches that consider and compare interviews and questionnaires for self-report, parental ratings, and peer ratings. Additional observational studies are especially needed" (p. 128).

The learning-based and developmental models have been presented as a framework in which one might attempt to integrate the empirical data presented within this chapter. Bear in mind, however, that the data presented herein do not necessarily derive exclusively from the theoretical models presented.

Family Management and the Family and Home Environment

Assessment of the family and home environment may take many different forms. For some, the variables of interest may be broadly defined and structural (e.g., socioeconomic or educational status). For others, a functional approach stressing the relationship between behavior and its consequences might be preferable. In the present analysis a functional approach is taken, and family management practices are the focus of attention.

Inherent in the practice of family management is the notion of control. Patterson (1982), however, has suggested that a parent's affective or emotional disposition (e.g., irritability) may also have an impact on child and adolescent behavior. In a longitudinal study, Greenwald (1990) found that high-risk children (offspring of previously hospitalized adults) raised in families characterized by warmth and healthy communication styles were less likely to evidence emotional-behavioral disturbance at 3-year follow-up than children from families that lacked these qualities. Patterson (1982) has identified warmth and control as two key elements of the family management process, suggesting that parents—and mothers in particular—become less attached to problem children and less likely to follow through on threats of discipline: "It is not lack of warmth, per se, lowering the impact of parental punishment; it is that unskilled and unattached parents do not back up their threats" (p. 123).

Family management practices are frequently described in terms of dyadic exchange, or as a series of dyadic exchanges between members of the family environment. Consequently this analysis, where possible, will frame the data in terms of reciprocal exchanges among family members. Finally, consideration will be given to how the principles of developmental behavioral genetics may inform conclusions drawn from the available research on adolescent-family relations and psychopathology.

Parental Discipline Practices

Initial interest in the role of parental discipline practices in adolescent psychopathology focused on the effect of inconsistent discipline. Glueck and Glueck's (1950) breakthrough work on the effect of inconsistent discipline suggested that severe paternal punishment combined with lax maternal discipline could result in delinquent behavior. Further refinement of this concept revealed that punitive parents who are consistent in their discipline practices are less likely to have antisocial children than inconsistently punitive parents (McCord, McCord, & Zola, 1959). Several investigators have since pointed out that one form of inconsistent discipline—providing positive consequences for problem behavior—has failed to distinguish normal from conduct-disordered children (Gardner, 1989; Johnson, Wahl, Martin, & Johansson, 1973; Patterson, 1982).

In contrast to these failures, Gardner (1989) demonstrated that mothers of conduct-disordered preschoolers *do* respond more inconsistently to their child's behavior than mothers of normal children. In this study, observational data were collected on normal and behavior-problem children. Rather than focus on discrete instances of conflict as in earlier work, however, Gardner considered the entire conflict episode, with particular attention directed to the initiation (e.g., by mother or child) and resolution (parent consistency or acquiescence) of conflict episodes. It was found that mothers of disordered children were more likely than mothers of nondisordered children to demonstrate inconsistency by not following through with commands, unwittingly providing positive consequences (via negative reinforcement) for undesirable child behavior.

For example, a conflict sequence might begin with a mother asking her child to pick up her toys. After a long and emotional argument in which she repeatedly resists the child's efforts to dissuade her (thus inflating traditional measures of consistency), she gives in, and allows the child to go outside and play. Because of its refinement of the "consistency" measure, this study appears to provide solid support for Patterson's negative reinforcement (or coercive family process) construct, at least as it relates to inconsistent mother-child interactions. Still, it is important to note that Gardner's investigation employed preschool subjects, and it is not yet clear that these data generalize to interactions involving adolescents and their mothers. Long-term follow-up of youths from "inconsistent" households may demonstrate the ontogenic value of such findings.

It has also been asserted that punishing appropriate behavior might be a form of inconsistent discipline that results in adolescent and child behavior problems (Dumas & Wahler, 1985; Johnson et al., 1973; Patterson, 1976). In addition, ignoring or failing to reinforce appropriate behavior has been cited as an important factor in child behavior problems (Patterson, 1982). In the latter scenario, the child engages in appropriate behavior but turns to increasingly disruptive behaviors if no reinforcement is provided for appropriateness. Consequently the parent's attention turns increasingly to the child's deviant behavior, further limiting the child's opportunities to learn and perform more appropriate behaviors.

Patterson (1982) has suggested that four important dimensions of family management practices are associated with child and adolescent behavioral disturbances: (a) lack of house rules, (b) lack of parental monitoring, (c) lack of effective contingencies, and (d) lack of techniques for dealing with family crises. In a study that supports and perhaps extends Patterson's model, Olweus (1980) found that mothers' negativity and permissiveness, parent's power-assertive parenting style, and child factors all contributed to the development of a male adolescent's aggressive reaction pattern.

Clearly the role of discipline in adolescent psychopathology is multiply determined and complex. As Rutter (1985) points out, "We need to focus on an awareness of what children are doing, the process of disciplinary management (including problem-solving methods), and the efficiency of the techniques used" (p. 357).

Parental Depression

In a review by Forehand, McCombs, and Brody (1987), it was suggested that "depressive mood states rank foremost among the parental characteristics that have been hypothesized to be associated with children's functioning" (p. 1). Several studies have documented the impact of parental depression on family interaction, and many cite the quality of interaction between parents and children as especially significant (Downey & Coyne, 1990).

There exist a number of studies on the behavior of depressed parents toward their children (Forehand et al., 1987; Gelfand & Teti, 1990; Radke-Yarrow, 1990). In their review, Forehand et al. (1987) found that clinically depressed parents appear to be less involved with and affectionate toward their children, to be more guilty and resentful, and to have more difficulty in managing and communicating with their children than nondepressed parents. Similarly, a more recent review associates maternal depression with unresponsive, inattentive, intrusive, and inept parenting behavior, as well as with negative perceptions of the children (Gelfand & Teti, 1990). In a study conducted with a child sample (3 to 8 years old), depressed mothers were found to be more critical of their children's behavior than nondepressed mothers, though no significant differences were detected in child behavior (Webster-Stratton & Hammond, 1988). Ostensibly, in cases in which parents evidence depressive disorders, their dysfunction may be so pervasive as to lead to substantial impairment in their ability to function as a parent.

Forehand et al. (1987) state that while clinical depression in one or both parents may lead directly to child impairment, a more transactional model—in other words, one that involves other elements of the home environment (e.g., child behavior, job stress, marital relationship)—is needed to account for the relationship of milder forms of parental depression to child or adolescent psychopathology. For example, in studies where externalizing or acting-out behaviors are considered, child behavioral characteristics have been shown to influence parental depression (Patterson, 1980). A developmentally oriented study conducted by Hammen, Burge, and Stansbury (1990) found that maternal functioning and child characteristics interacted (i.e., child characteristics contribute to maternal functioning), thus establishing a cycle of negative mutual influence associated with clinical symptomology and dysfunction in children.

The finding that child factors may contribute significantly to subsequent manifestation of disturbance in adolescence and childhood suggests that more within-family studies are needed to ascertain how differences between siblings may result in psychopathology. Because an adolescent may be more capable than a younger child of accessing and soliciting help from external "buffers" (e.g., friends or adults beyond the family unit), Forehand et al. (1987) suggest that siblings should not be assumed to be equally influenced by parental depressive mood. Inasmuch as parents have been shown to respond differentially to their children on the basis of sex (Block, 1983) and even attractiveness (Elder, Nguyen, & Caspi, 1985), these differences may also be within-family factors worthy of examination.

What are the behavioral correlates of parental depression for children and adolescents? Diagnosis of depression in both parents and current maternal depressive symptomology (as opposed to a history of depression) increase the risk for depression and other behavioral disturbances in children and adolescents (Billings & Moos, 1983; Hammen et al., 1987). In a review and discussion of the rate of psychological disturbance in the children of depressed parents, Miller, Birnbaum, and Durbin (1990) found these children to be at increased risk for psychological symptoms, emotional problems, suicidal behavior, and DSM-III diagnosis. The most common diagnosis made was major depression (13.1%), followed by attention-deficit disorder (10.3%; Weissman et al., 1984). In addition, a comprehensive review by Downey and Coyne (1990) suggests children of depressed parents are at risk for the full range of adjustment problems, particularly clinical depression. Moreover, adolescent girls are more likely than adolescent boys to exhibit depressive mood and receive a diagnosis of major depression (Peterson, Ebata, & Sarigiari, 1987; Weissman et al., 1987).

Despite the volumes dedicated to the description of parenting behavior and the behavioral correlates of parental depression, it is estimated that 60% of the children of depressives seem to function normally (Miller et al., 1990). It is apparent that the factors relevant to outcome for children of depressives are multiply determined and complex. Hops, Sherman, and Biglan (1990) have proposed a model based on the coercive family process (Patterson, 1982) construct to account for why some adolescents and children fail to exhibit dysfunction where others do. According to Hops et al. (1990), depressive mood manifested in one or both parents disrupts normal interactions with their children and leads to affective and/or behavior problems in the latter. The response of the child and other family members to the depressive parent, however, may contribute to the outcome variation that has been observed. Maternal depressive behavior was hypothesized to be aversive to other family members, but functional as well "in that it may (a) reduce the probability of attacks by others, and (b) obtain positive consequences" (p. 187). In addition, the influence is likely to be bidirectional, in that there is evidence to suggest that a family member's aggressive affect would suppress a mother's dysphoric mood (Hops et al., 1990). At the same time, a mother's dysphoric affect (e.g., withdrawal) may be functional in that it shelters her from overt aggressive behavior (Radke-Yarrow, 1990).

Hops et al. (1990) illustrate the process by which these behavior problems may arise, paying special attention to differences across sex and age and interpersonal processes that might explain these differences. In their investigation, 52 families were studied using direct observation and a battery of self-report and interview instruments. Children (aged 3 to 16) were assessed for the degree to which they displayed happy or dysphoric affect. Results indicated that older children, and particularly older girls, may be more greatly influenced (either positively or negatively) by their mother's behavior and level of distress. In particular, older girls in "depressed" families were more likely to display dysphoric and less likely to display happy affect.

Coyne, Kahn, and Gotlieb (1987) suggest that while observation of family interaction involving depressed parents and their offspring has been rare (see Radke-Yarrow, 1990), its inclusion in future research designs should prove theoretically and therapeutically useful. It is hoped that growing appreciation of child characteristics that buffer or exacerbate the effects of parental depression, as well as consideration of both child and parent extrafamilial factors (e.g., school performance, peer relations, job stress), will lead to better understanding of the relationship between parental depression and development of psychopathology in adolescents.

Parent Antisocial Behavior

One of the most puzzling, and perhaps most detrimental, of the problems that can afflict a family environment is the presence of one or more parents who abuse their children or themselves. Parent antisocial behavior includes the spectrum of behavior associated with physical and sexual abuse and neglect of one's children, as well as substance abuse on the part of the parent(s). The term *antisocial behavior*, as used here, should not be interpreted as meeting the criteria for DSM-IV diagnosis unless described as such.

Several studies have documented the deleterious effects of antisocial parental behavior on child and adolescent development. Antisocial youths are more likely than normal youths to have antisocial parents (Archer, Sutker, White, & Orvin, 1978; Rutter, Tizard, & Whitmore, 1970), and they are more likely to have been victims of child abuse (Behar & Stewart, 1982). Given the alarming rates of child abuse estimated to occur in the United States, evidence that it is associated with antisocial behavior in adulthood is disturbing. Though the percentage is likely to be an underestimate (Emery, 1989), a reported 81% of the more than 500,000 cases of adolescent physical abuse, sexual abuse, and neglect in 1986 were perpetrated by parents (American Humane Association, 1988). Moreover, while studies of abuse and neglect have usually involved children, Williamson, Borduin, and Howe (1991) suggest that developing emotional, behavioral, and psychological independence in adolescence might lead one to anticipate different patterns of emotional and interpersonal difficulties than those associated with maltreatment in childhood.

Parental Physical Abuse. Physical abuse is an all too common form of parental antisocial behavior. Physically abused adolescents are more likely to live in homes that employ inflexible and inappropriate discipline measures for the child's transgressions (Tricket & Kuczynski, 1986; Williamson et al., 1991). In addition, mothers of physically abused adolescents are frequently less knowledgeable about adolescent developmental milestones, possibly resulting in the inappropriate discipline measures employed in some of these households (Williamson et al., 1991).

Schellenbach and Guerney (1987) point to five factors that characterize families at high risk for adolescent abuse: (a) excessively authoritarian or permissive communication patterns enforced by abusive punishment; (b) a high level of recent family conflict; (c) adolescents who are behaviorally challenging to their parents; (d) adolescents themselves under stress (e.g., drug or alcohol abusers); (e) a parent responding to the adolescent with more discipline and less support. It is interesting to note that these five factors combine three primary elements suspected to influence adolescent development: unique characteristics of the adolescent, family management practices, and affective quality of the home environment.

As noted above, physical abuse of an adolescent is often influenced by factors other than parental characteristics. Bell (1968) points out that aggressive, defiant children elicit harsher discipline from adults. Garbarino, Sebes, and Schellenbach (1984) indicate that families at risk for destructive parent-child relations are typically more stressed by life changes. These findings suggest we must be conservative when assessing the relative causal contributions of variables associated with child abuse. It appears likely that the presence of child abuse within a family results from a complex inter-play of child factors, external influences on the family, and within-family processes.

The research on differences between adolescent and child maltreatment is equivocal. Adolescents have been shown to be less likely to experience physical abuse than children, more likely to self-report abuse, and more likely to have their claims substantiated (Garbarino & Gilliam, 1980). In contrast, Farber and Joseph (1985) found no differences in either family characteristics or behavioral-emotional disturbance among subjects whose abuse began in adolescence versus childhood. Berdie, Berdie, Wexler, and Fisher (1983) found that "maltreating families" share the same characteristics regardless of age of the abused: multiple problems, financial difficulty, high rates of divorce, separation and marital conflict, and inappropriate expectations of the abused. Reid, Kavanagh, and Baldwin (1987) report that children of abusive parents differed significantly from nonabusives on parent report measures of conduct problems, but these differences were usually not detected via direct observation.

Adolescents' responses to physical abuse are extensive. Farber and Joseph (1985) describe six patterns of behavioral-emotional reactions to such abuse: acting out, depression, generalized anxiety, adjustment difficulties, emotional-thought disturbance, and helplessness-dependency. Wolman (1987) found that family violence is associated with subsequent development of antisocial personality disorder, a diagnostic category requiring history of conduct disorder prior to age 15 (American Psychiatric Association, 1993). Significantly, Bandura (1973) pointed out that parental violence (or even threatened violence) contributes to the formation of anti-social and violent behavior on the part of children. In support of Bandura, a study of adult abusers reported that they were more likely than nonabusers to have witnessed family violence as children (Rosenbaum & O'Leary, 1981). Studies such as these suggest that observational learning (modeling) and family management practices may each play an important part in the development of behavioral disorders in children and adolescents.

Parental Alcohol and Drug Abuse. The presence of alcohol or drug abuse in one or both parents of an adolescent has been identified as a significant factor in adolescent development, particularly with respect to increased risk for substance abuse (Halebsky, 1987). In their review of the literature,

Goodwin and Guze (1989) note several studies finding adolescent sons of alcoholics three to four times as prone to alcoholism as sons of nonalcoholics (Bohman, 1978; Cadoret & Gath, 1978; Goodwin, Schulsinger, Hermansen, Guze, & Winokur, 1975). In an investigation involving female subjects, however, the strong relationship between biological parents and their offspring failed to materialize (Goodwin, Schulsinger, Knop, Mednick, & Guze, 1977).

There appears to be a significant genetic contribution to the development of alcoholism in adolescence, at least for males (Jacob, Krahn, & Leonard, 1991). Niven (1984), though, indicates that in several family studies, as many as one-half of the alcoholic subjects did not have an alcoholic parent or other relative. Further, not all offspring of alcoholics become alcoholics themselves. Again, more appears to be involved in alcoholism than genetic influence alone. In addition to increased risk for alcoholism, adolescent offspring of alcoholics have been shown to experience a higher rate of coping difficulties (Werner, 1986) and conduct disorder in males (Cadoret, Cain, & Grove, 1979; Cadoret & Gath, 1978).

Several investigators have studied the influence of parental alcohol abuse on the family environment (Callan & Jackson, 1986; Moos & Moos, 1984; Werner, 1986). Jacob and his colleagues (Jacob et al., 1991; Jacob, Ritchey, Cvitkovic, & Blane, 1981; Jacob & Seilhamer, 1987) have focused on family interaction and conclude that "the environmental impact of alcoholism is of a current and dynamic nature, rather than reflecting fixed and irreversible effects on the child's level of functioning" (Jacob et al., 1991, p. 176). A study by Jacob et al. (1981) illustrates the importance of assessing context and family interaction. In this investigation, families with alcoholic and nonalcoholic fathers were asked to engage in a series of problem-solving tasks in either a drinking or a no-drinking situation. It was found that an alcoholic father's drinking increased the mother's negativity (e.g., criticism, disagreements) toward her children. In other words, the impact of the fathers' drinking was evidenced not between spouses, but between mothers and their children.

A more recent study by Jacob et al. (1991) did not support the hypothesis that parent alcohol consumption influenced problem-solving behavior. The authors attempted to explain the contrasting results by pointing out differences in the extent to which families in each sample remained intact. According to Jacob et al., if alcoholics are able to maintain a positive affective relationship with their family and utilize effective discipline practices, their children would be expected to function normally. Alcohol thus becomes most salient as a factor when normal parenting functions are disrupted by abuse. Wolin and Bennet (1984) support this view in their work on family rituals, asserting that disruption (e.g., a failure to recognize family events such as birthdays and holidays) is associated with adolescent dysfunction. At least for intact families, a general distress factor seems to account for more differences between alcoholic and normal families than do alcohol-specific effects.

Jacob and Seilhamer (1987) have considered maternal factors which have implications for the transmission and maintenance of alcoholism in their offspring. Citing numerous studies, they suggest that (a) wives of abusers are more likely to become abusers themselves (Shuckit & Morrissey, 1976; Wilsnack, Wilsnack, & Klassen, 1982); (b) alcoholic mothers are more concerned about parenting than male alcoholics (Gomberg, 1981); and (c) alcoholic mothers are more likely to experience guilt and depression when sober (Corrigan, 1980). Recognition of the indirect effects of paternal alcoholism on their spouses and the impact of maternal alcoholism on mothers when sober should alert us to the complexity inherent in studying the transmission of alcoholism to their offspring. It is clear that much remains to be discovered concerning the relationship between parental alcohol abuse and the subsequent development of alcoholism and other dysfunction in adolescents.

Some researchers also have considered parental illicit drug use and its impact on the adolescent. As with alcohol, increased adolescent abuse of marijuana has been associated with parental drug usage (Fawzy, Coombs, & Gerber, 1983; Gorsuch & Butler, 1976; G. M. Johnson, Shontz, & Locke, 1984). In contrast, a study by Klinge and Piggot (1986) found no systematic relationship between parental and adolescent drug use. The latter authors suggest that the aversive features characterizing the family environments in their sample (e.g., family dissolution, paternal absence) "forced" their adolescents into closer identification with their peers and increased the likelihood that peers, rather than parents, would serve as role models in drug use. Certainly further investigation of the relationship between family features and adolescent drug use is warranted, and many questions remain unanswered.

McDermott (1984) suggests that adolescent perception of parental permissiveness may be a more important variable than parental drug use. While his findings indicated that parents who used drugs were more likely than those who did not to have drug-using children, they also indicated that regardless of their parents' drug use, adolescents who perceived their parents as more permissive were more likely to use drugs. These results suggest that rules, along with adequate monitoring and enforcement, may have a significant impact on adolescent drug use and abuse. Of course, the establishment and maintenance of house rules is a key component of family management practices. A recent longitudinal study suggested that parental modeling and permissiveness were important but added that parenting style, as measured by warmth and hostility, proved to be the most salient variable influencing adolescent substance abuse (Johnson & Pandina, 1991). Finally, several investigations suggest that adolescent substance abuse may be prevented though early interventions, such as social skills training and parent training (Botvin & Tortu, 1988; Coombs, Paulson, & Palley, 1988; Dishon, Reid, Patterson, 1988).

As a result of legal and perhaps moral concerns, empirical research has gleaned little regarding illicit drugs and how they might affect family interaction. As with alcohol studies, it will be important to differentiate family factors (e.g., modeling by parents and other family members) from genetic or extrafamilial environmental influences (e.g., peers, social conditions). It is not yet clear that the processes at work in substance abuse are homogeneous. Inasmuch as the drugs commonly used in our society may have vastly different physiological and psychological effects, caution regarding assumptions about their impact on the adolescent-family relationship appears warranted.

Parental Sexual Abuse and Neglect. As the sequelae of child abuse have been more clearly articulated, many refinements have taken place. At this point in its evolution, the study of child abuse consists of three categories of maltreatment—physical abuse, sexual abuse, and neglect—and each is distinguished by unique psychosocial correlates (Williamson et al., 1991).

Neglect may be described as having three components: physical, emotional, and educational (U.S. Department of Health and Human Services, 1988). In this chapter we are most concerned with the former two components, as they relate most closely to the role of family in our society. We regard neglect as inattention to the physical or emotional needs of an adolescent or child resulting in harm. Parental features associated with the occurrence of neglect include maternal report of difficulty with everyday stress and inability to deal effectively with stressors (Williamson et al., 1991). Neglected adolescents are typically associated with less aggressive and more passive behavior than physically abused adolescents (Green, 1978; Hoffman-Plotkin & Twentyman, 1984). Finally, while outcome for neglected adolescents has been associated with extrafamilial problems (e.g., stress, social isolation, and participation in a deviant social group; Williamson et al., 1991), much remains to be discovered concerning the impact of neglect on adolescents and the mechanism by which this neglect translates into psychopathology.

The impact of sexual abuse on a child or adolescent has been conceptualized as a posttraumatic stress disorder by Wolfe, Gentile, and Wolfe (1989). Though their study was conducted with adolescents who reported their abuse (and thus the conclusions may not generalize to children and adolescents who do not report their abuse), Wolfe et al. make two important distinctions:

1. Sex-associated fears and intrusive thoughts are common problems associated with sexual abuse; however, expression of these problems is mediated by the child's age (younger children have more problems), abuse severity, and both global and abuse-specific attributions.

2. Children are not likely to report abuse and must be carefully evaluated by parents, teachers, and other observers. Other problems associated with sexual abuse include learning and behavioral dysfunction, as well as anxiety, fear, somatic complaints, guilt, depression, and suicidal ideation and attempts.

Individuals sexually abused as children or adolescents are more likely to exhibit psychopathology later in life, and it behooves us to identify individuals at risk (Brown & Anderson, 1991). In addition, it is apparent that families in which abuse occurs are frequently disturbed in multiple contexts (e.g., social, emotional; Hoagwood, 1990). Feinauer (1989) indicates that sexual abuse involving a trusted relative or friend may be the most devastating form of sexual abuse. Perhaps because the sexual abuse of an adolescent is unlikely to be reported (Everstine & Everstine, 1989), much remains to be discovered about the etiology and maintenance of sexual abuse within the family (and elsewhere). Future attempts to study these kinds of families may do well to pay close attention to the family dynamics that initiate and maintain abusive parental behavior in sexual abuse, as well as other forms of child and adolescent maltreatment.

Divorce

The impact of divorce on the development of an adolescent is perhaps one of the most heavily researched subjects in the family literature. Empirical studies and review articles have distinguished marital conflict and divorce as key, yet distinct, elements in the development of adolescents (Atkeson, Forehand, & Rickard, 1982), but considerable ambiguity remains (Wallerstein, 1991). Currently, more attention is being directed to factors associated with divorce (e.g., conflict) than divorce itself.

Though marital turmoil has long been suspected to have a causal role in child and adolescent dysfunction (Framo, 1975), early studies were relatively unsophisticated and contributed to a lack of consensus (Emery, 1982). Some investigators have concluded more recently that it may be more advantageous to focus on parental conflict than divorce per se (Long, Forehand, Fauber, & Brody, 1987). After controlling for level of parental conflict, Long et al. (1987) found no differences between adolescents from divorced and nondivorced families on measures of adjustment and independently observed competence. Further, Forehand and McCombs (1989) suggest that the incidence of heated arguments and open conflict within families is actually quite low in absolute terms and that differences in conflict frequency observed between married and divorced couples (divorced couples argued slightly more) were negligible. They hypothesized that parental conflict within divorced families created lasting disruptions in parenting practices that might, in turn, lead to a higher probability of adolescent dysfunction.

Experience of divorce for a child or adolescent has been shown to be associated with a variety of social-emotional difficulties. Kalter (1987) proposes that the failure of a marriage may have important symbolic meaning for the maturing adolescent and that identification with the failed marriage may have a lasting negative impact on an adolescent's future attempts to achieve intimacy. Other researchers agree and have asserted that the impact of divorce on adolescent and child functioning is long-lasting and associated with deficits in forming stable attachments later in life. Wallerstein's (1991) review reinforces the belief that the behavioral and social-emotional outcomes are often multiply determined and may be expressed by adolescent dysfunction both in the short term (behavior problems, depression) and long after the divorce is final (dysfunctional relationships).

Divorce is often associated with substantial changes in the adolescent's environment that may have unspecified consequences. Some changes may have a relatively negative timbre, such as decreases in household income, less parental supervision, and change of school and neighborhood (Hetherington, 1982; Stolberg & Anker, 1983). The particular outcomes of such changes for the adolescent, however, are likely idiosyncratic and relative to the predivorce environment. For example, should the divorce result in a substantial decrease in conflict within the home, the custodial parent may find it easier to monitor and establish house rules than it was during the conflictual marital period; hence the adolescent may evidence improved emotional-behavioral functioning. Conversely, loss of a parent with whom the child shared a close emotional relationship may result in a worsening of behavior and/or emotional dysfunction.

The behavioral correlates of divorce have been found to be different for males and females (Hetherington, Cox, & Cox, 1985). For boys, externalizing behavior (aggression, acting out) has been shown to be more stable, while internalizing behaviors (anxiety, withdrawal) are more common among females. In a study by Johnston, Gonzalez, and Campbell (1987), children of divorce appeared vacant, joyless, and withdrawn 2.5 years after custody disputes. Increased incidences of depression and aggression also were observed; moreover, in keeping with the Hetherington et al. (1985) findings, girls were observed to be more depressed and withdrawn. Finally, a longitudinal study of stepfamilies suggests that girls react more negatively (e.g., with avoidance or withdrawal) than boys to a mother's remarriage (Vuchinich, Hetherington, Vuchinich, & Clingempeel, 1991).

Several factors mediating the outcome of divorce for adolescents have been detailed. Children of divorce appear to display fewer problems if placed in the custody of a same-sex parent (Warshak & Santrock, 1983). In an investigation that questioned the utility of joint custodial arrangements in promoting healthy child and adolescent development, children who had not had paternal contact within the past 5 years appeared to be functioning better academically and behaviorally than children who had seen their fathers more frequently or recently (Furstenberg, Morgan, & Allison, 1987). The authors of this study found that the quality of the child's relationship with the custodial mother was a better predictor of postdivorce functioning than noncustodial parental contact. Nevertheless, noncustodial parent-child relations may still be important; adolescents exposed to interparental conflict and perceiving close relationships with noncustodial fathers evidenced fewer internalizing problems than those with poor relationships (Brody & Forehand, 1990). Moreover, male adolescents having a good relationship with both parents appear to be "buffered" against negative parental divorce effects (Wierson, Forehand, Fauber, & McCombs, 1989). Finally, Rutter (1985) suggests that the deleterious fallout of divorce, parental conflict and other factors of the family environment may possibly be overcome through "compensatory good experiences" occurring outside the family or within the family at a later date. Additional data on the relevance and importance of such mediating factors, however, are necessary to elucidate how such "compensatory experiences" might influence adolescent development.

Institutionalization: An Atypical Family Environment?

Over the years, much attention has been focused on the role of traditional or divorced families. It is clear that for many adolescents, though, institutions and variations on these facilities serve as home. For our purposes, any facility or organization carrying out parenting functions (e.g., providing shelter, warmth, food, clothing) may constitute a form of family or home environment, whatever the quality of that environment. Presently little is known about the functional aspects of these environments and the differences between them and more traditional rearing contexts. For our purposes, the most important issue may be framed as a question: can institutions or nonfamilial home environments be studied in a manner consistent with more traditional family methods? In other words, may findings from one environment be generalized to another? If a functional approach is taken, the answer may be yes.

Landesman (1990) has provided some data to examine the question of similarities and differences between institutions and traditional family environments. She proposes that structural improvements in institutions (e.g., adult-child ratio, size of facility) have not resulted in functional improvements or a higher quality of life. In addition, she suggests that the most salient features of the institutionalized environment are such "functional characteristics" as amount and quality of social interaction, developmentally appropriate activities, and opportunities for choice and variety. Similarly, Rutter (1985) states that differences in outcome for institutionalized youths are most often due to the "qualities of the schools as social organizations" (p. 353). Evidence suggests that it is not the structural quality of an institution per se, but its functional characteristics that are most relevant to the outcome of youths raised in these environments. Moreover, these findings suggest that continued attention to process, rather than topographical features of home environments, will lead to a clearer understanding of the adolescent-family relationship.

Landesman (1988) provides a useful framework for the broader study of institutionalized youth by focusing on (a) the flexibility and responsiveness of the administrating organization, (b) the frequency and sensitivity of social interactions, (c) instability and unpredictability in the presence and behavior of staff, and (d) the effects of isolation on institutionalized youth. It is hoped that by capitalizing on these rather controlled environments, much will be learned regarding the effect of different home environments on the development of psychopathology in adolescents.

Extrafamilial Stressors

Though not considered family factors in and of themselves, extrafamilial stressors may have a substantial impact on relations within families. The purpose of this section is to outline how some of these stressors may exert their influence on seemingly internal familial relations.

The concept of "stressor" has been widely subject to abuse, largely due to a lack of definitional consensus. Still, consideration of extrafamilial stressors does provide us with a wide-angle lens to use for studying the environmental impact of interpersonal phenomena occurring within the family context. Additionally, the concept of stress permits integration of several disparate approaches to studying adolescent-family relations and reflects the understanding that stressors frequently coexist (Webster-Stratton, 1990). In keeping with our emphasis on the study of family interaction and its value as a research tool, these extrafamilial stressors (e.g., unemployment, low socioeconomic status) may be conceptualized as having indirect effects on the adolescent via familial relationships and/or family management practices, as well as direct effects on the youth via economic opportunities, crime rate, and quality of educational support. Our focus will remain on the former effects.

In longitudinal studies by Rutter and his colleagues (Rutter, Cox, Tupling, Berger, & Youle, 1975; Rutter & Quinton, 1977), stress, conceptualized as "family adversity," was found to be the key factor in child psychiatric illness in both urban and rural communities. Bronfenbrenner (1986) explains that:

with the degree of family adversity controlled, the difference between London and Isle of Wight in rates of child psychiatric illness all but disappeared. The authors interpret this result as indicating that the main adverse effects of city life on children are indirect, resulting from the disruption of the families in which they live. (p. 731)

Another investigation implicating stress as an important variable in child and adolescent development reported that the major environmental factor distinguishing "resilient" youths in a high-risk community (e.g., poverty, health hazards, family instability, parental mental health problems, poor parental education) was a low number of chronic, stressful life events and extended familial support (Werner & Smith, 1982).

Poverty, unemployment, and negative life events are some of the most frequently cited extrafamilial stressors. All of these variables may have relevance for adolescent development. Several studies have shown that adolescent-parent conflict frequently centers around spending money and privileges (Evans & Warren-Sohlberg, 1988; Ellis-Schwabe & Thornburg, 1986). Thus it seems likely that the confluence of poverty, unemployment, and the presence of an adolescent in the family system may present substantial challenges to the family environment.

Poverty and unemployment have been shown to have deleterious effects on parenting behavior (Webster-Stratton, 1990). Low socioeconomic status (SES) in families has been associated with a variety of maladaptive parenting behaviors. Typically these families appear to employ more coercion and punishment and are less likely to use reason, show support, and allow independence than middle-class families (Gecas, 1979; Hess, 1970). Rutter and Giller (1983) conclude that SES is a moderating variable capable of producing increased susceptibility to other negative influences. Still, it is not clear that financial hardship has an inherently negative impact. Elder (1974) found that adolescents in both middle-class and, to a lesser extent, lower SES groups displayed greater desire for achievement and greater satisfaction in life than nondeprived adolescents in the years of the Great Depression.

In addition to such extrafamilial stressors as unemployment and poverty, within-family developmental issues may also produce stress. Goodyer (1990) points out that adolescents begin to grapple with important developmental issues (e.g., sexuality, independence) at the same time as their parents confront the issues of mid-life. He concludes that little is known about the interaction of these events. Yet we might reasonably expect that adolescent-parent disputes could be different in important ways from child-parent conflict. For example, these differences might be qualitative, reflecting developmental features of both adolescence and adulthood as mentioned above. Or differences could be quantitative, with adolescents perhaps having fewer opportunities to interact with family members due to increased contact with peers; these fewer opportunities for interaction might result in their increased significance. Still, much remains to be discovered regarding these factors.

A substantial proportion of the family stress literature deals with the impact of negative life stress or major stressful life events. In adolescents, drug use and frequency of self-reported antisocial and delinquent behavior have been associated with stressful life events (Bry, McKeon, & Pandina, 1982; Vaux & Ruggiero, 1983). Additionally, frequency of negative life events experienced by families has been related to attachment problems (Vaughn, Egeland, Sroufe, & Waters, 1979), harsher discipline, and physical abuse (Gaines, Sandgrund, Green, & Power, 1978). Finally, Rutter and colleagues (Rutter, 1979, 1986; Rutter et al., 1970) suggest six significant family stressors associated with conduct disorder, of which three are structural (a father who is an unskilled or semiskilled laborer, large family size, and child in care) and three are functional (maternal psychopathology, paternal criminality, and ongoing marital discord). Though none of these factors alone influences the probability of conduct disorder, the combination of two or more has been shown to increase adolescent risk by two to four times (Goodyer, 1990; Shaw & Emery, 1988).

Though much is known about the impact of extrafamilial stressors, much remains to be discovered. As Webster-Stratton (1990) concludes:

> The task for future research in this area is to continue to conceptualize the complex and dynamic relationships between stressors and the family interaction system, as well as to identify those factors that can serve to increase or decrease a maladaptive outcome for the parents and child. For the ultimate challenge is to recognize those families most at risk, those most vulnerable to disruption by life stressors, and to help them develop resources and coping skills that will minimize the disruption. (p. 310)

Summary

Despite a decline in the number of traditional nuclear families relative to single-parent and other alternative family environments, family environment still appears a useful construct for conceptualizing the psychological development of adolescents. With respect to the family environment, disrupted family management practices (e.g., inept or ineffective discipline, poor or nonexistent monitoring) and negative affective environments appear most reliably associated with adolescent dysfunction. Clearly the roads leading to poor family management are complex and interwoven, and it may never be possible to identify all paths leading to adolescent dysfunction. Still, through the use of correlational research designs, substantial progress has been made in describing molar aspects of the family environment. More longitudinal studies, however, are necessary to validate correlational studies and determine whether impaired family management processes predate adolescent maladjustment or whether some other factors within the home (e.g., adolescent characteristics) are implicated. There exists strong support for a transactional model of family interaction, but the specific circumstances under which this interaction results in an adolescent poorly equipped for life beyond the family system—or buffers the adolescent from serious psychopathology—remain unclear.

As has been shown, a wide variety of factors appear to influence family management either directly or indirectly. These include depression (and other forms of adult psychopathology), alcohol and drug abuse, divorce, and extrafamilial stressors. The vast number of elements that may influence family management practices suggests that our children and adolescents are highly vulnerable to these factors over the course of their development. While correlational studies indicate that a close parent-adolescent relationship is associated with better general adjustment and negatively correlated with adolescent self-reports of depression and anxiety (Sarigiani, 1987), it seems difficult to distinguish between the maintenance of warm intrafamilial relations and the exercise of effective family management practices. Future research might address the relationship of these factors.

Of particular concern for clinicians, researchers, and the public at large is the role of modeling and long-term outcomes for individuals developing within dysfunctional family environments. The lay (and sometimes professional) observation that our own parenting practices reflect those of our parents seems rather daunting in this instance. Indeed, from a learning perspective, adolescents would be likely—via observation and direct experience—to learn a substantial portion of their own parenting behaviors from their parents. Without exposure to positive role models (e.g., through formal education, media, or acquaintances), their parenting behavior and family management practices would be likely to resemble those in which they were raised.

Given the powerful influence families appear capable of exerting even into adolescence, the growing evidence that families may be poorly equipped to institute family management practices that will yield healthy and well-adjusted adolescents is disturbing. Failure to address the factors that affect intrafamilial relations (e.g., family management) and that influence the family peripherally (e.g., poverty, substandard education, crime) may only exacerbate the problem and lead to future generations of adolescents poorly equipped for parenting. If continued research supports the supposition that families and family management practices make significant contributions to adolescent development—and, perhaps, later adult maladjustment—government and social agencies may wish to focus more attention on actively promoting parenting education and other programs designed to facilitate better family management practices.

References

Achenbach, T. M. (1974). *Developmental psychopathology*. New York: Ronald.

American Humane Association. (1988). *Highlights of official child neglect and abuse reporting 1986*. Denver, CO: Author.

American Psychiatric Association. (1993). *DSM-IV draft criteria*. Washington, DC: Author.

Archer, R. P., Sutker, P. B., White, J. L., & Orvin, G. H. (1978). Personality relationships between parents and adolescent offspring in inpatient treatment. *Psychological Reports, 42*, 207–214.

Atkeson, B. M., Forehand, R., & Rickard, K. M. (1982). The effects of divorce on children. In B. B. Lahey & A. E. Kazdin, (Eds.), *Advances in clinical child psychology* (Vol. 5). New York: Plenum.

Bandura, A. (1973). *Aggression: A social learning perspective*. Englewood Cliffs, NJ: Prentice-Hall.

Bandura, A. (1986). *Social foundations of thought and action: A social cognitive theory*. Englewood Cliffs, NJ: Prentice-Hall.

Behar, D., & Stewart, M. A. (1982). Aggressive conduct disorders of children. *Acta Psychiatria Scandnavica, 65*, 210–220.

Bell, R. (1968). A reinterpretation of the direction of effects in studies of socialization. *Psychological Review, 75*, 81–95.

Berdie, J., Berdie, M., Wexler, S., & Fisher, B. (1983). *An empirical study of families involved in adolescent maltreatment: Final report* (Grant No. 90-CA-8371/01). Washington, DC: National Center on Child Abuse and Neglect, Department of Health and Human Services.

Billings, A. G., & Moos, R. H. (1983). Comparisons of children of depressed and nondepressed parents: A controlled 1 year follow-up. *Journal of Abnormal Child Psychology, 14*, 149–166.

Block, J. H. (1983). Differential premises arising from differential socialization of the sexes: Some conjectures. *Child Development, 54*, 1335–1354.

Bohman, M. (1978). Some genetic aspects of alcoholism and criminality: A population of adoptees. *Archives of General Psychiatry, 38*, 965–969.

Botvin, G. L., & Tortu, S. (1988). Peer relationships, social competence, and substance abuse prevention: Implications for the family. *Journal of Chemical Dependency Treatment, 1*, 245–273.

Brody, G., & Forehand, R. (1990). Interparental conflict, relationship with the noncustodial father, and adolescent post-divorce adjustment. *Journal of Applied Developmental Psychology, 11*, 139–147.

Bronfenbrenner, V. (1986). Ecology of the family as a context for human development: Research perspectives. *Developmental Psychology, 22*, 723–742.

Brown, G. R., & Anderson, B. (1991). Psychiatric morbidity in adult inpatients with childhood histories of sexual and physical abuse. *American Journal of Psychiatry, 148*, 55–61.

Bry, B. H., McKeon, P., & Pandina, R. J., (1982). Extent of drug use as a function of number of risk factors. *Journal of Abnormal Psychology, 91*, 273–279.

Cadoret, R. J., Cain, C. A., & Grove, W. M. (1979). Development of alcoholism in adoptees raised apart from alcoholic biologic relatives. *Archives of General Psychiatry, 37*, 561–563.

Cadoret, R. J., & Gath, A. (1978). Inheritance of alcoholism in adoptees. *British Journal of Psychiatry, 132,* 252–258.

Callan, V. J., & Jackson, D. (1986). Children of alcoholic fathers and recovered alcoholic fathers: Personal and family functioning. *Journal of Studies on Alcohol, 47,* 180–182.

Collins, W. A., & Russell, G. (1991). Mother-child and father-child relationships in middle childhood and adolescence: A developmental analysis. *Developmental Review, 11,* 99–136.

Coombs, R. H., Paulson, M. J., & Palley, R. (1988). The institutionalization of drug use in America: Hazardous adolescence, challenging parenthood. *Journal of Chemical Dependency Treatment, 1,* 9–37.

Corrigan, E. M. (1980). *Alcoholic women in treatment.* New York: Oxford University Press.

Cox, M., & Cox, R. (1979). Socialization of young children in the divorced family. *Journal of Research and Development in Education, 13,* 58–67.

Coyne, J. C., Kahn, J., & Gotlieb, I. H. (1987). Depression. In T. Jacob (Ed.), *Family interaction and psychopathology.* New York: Plenum.

Dishon, T. J., Reid, J. B., & Patterson, G. R. (1988). *Early drug use and formal intervention strategies.* Unpublished manuscript.

Douvan, E., & Gold, M. (1966). Model patterns in American adolescence. In L. M. Hoffman (Ed.), *Review of child development research* (Vol. 2), New York: Russell Sage.

Downey, G., & Coyne, J. C. (1990). Children of depressed parents: An integrative review. *Psychological Bulletin, 108,* 50–76.

Dumas, J. E., & Wahler, R. G. (1985). Indiscriminate mothering as a contextual factor in aggressive-oppositional child behavior: "Damned if you do, damned if you don't." *Journal of Abnormal Child Psychology, 13,* 1–17.

Elder, G. H., Jr. (1974). *Children of the great depression.* Chicago: University of Chicago Press.

Elder, G. H., Jr., Nguyen, T. V., & Caspi, A. (1985). Linking family hardship to children's lives. *Child Development, 56,* 361–375.

Ellis-Schwabe, M., & Thornburg, H. D. (1986). Conflict areas between parents and their adolescents. *Journal of Psychology, 120,* 59–68.

Emery, R. E. (1982). Interparental conflict and the children of discord and divorce. *Psychological Bulletin, 92,* 310–330.

Emery, R. E. (1989). Family violence. *American Psychologist, 44,* 321–328.

Evans, E. D., & Warren-Sohlberg, L. (1988). A pattern analysis of adolescent abusive behaviors toward parents. *Journal of Adolescent Research, 3,* 201–216.

Everstine, D. S., & Everstine, L. (1989). *Sexual trauma in children and adolescents: Dynamics and treatment.* New York: Brunner/Mazel.

Farber, E., & Joseph, J. (1985). The maltreated adolescent: Patterns of physical abuse. *Child Abuse and Neglect, 9,* 201–206.

Fawzy, F. I., Coombs, R. H., & Gerber, B. (1983). Generational continuity in the use of substances: The impact of parental substance use on adolescent substance use. *Addictive Behavior, 8,* 109–114.

Feinauer, L. L. (1989). Comparison of long-term effects of child abuse by type of abuse and by relationship to victim. *American Journal of Family Therapy, 17,* 48–56.

Forehand, R., & McCombs, A. (1989). The nature of interparental conflict of married and divorced parents: Implications for young adolescents. *Journal of Abnormal Child Psychology, 17,* 235–249.

Forehand, R., McCombs, A., & Brody, G. H. (1987). The relationship between parental depressive mood states and child functioning. *Advances in Behaviour Research and Therapy, 9,* 1–20.

Framo, J. L. (1975). Personal reflections of a therapist. *Journal of Marriage and Family Counseling, 1,* 15–28.

Furstenberg, F. F., Jr., Morgan, S. P., & Allison, P. D. (1987). Parental participation and children's well-being after marital dissolution. *American Sociological Review, 52,* 695–701.

Gaines, R., Sandgrund, A., Green, A. H., & Power, E. (1978). Etiological factors in child maltreatment: A multivariate study of abusing, neglecting, and normal mothers. *Journal of Abnormal Psychology, 87,* 531–540.

Garbarino, J., & Gilliam, G. (1980). *Understanding abusive families.* Lexington, MA: Lexington.

Garbarino, J., Sebes, J., & Schellenbach, C. (1984). Families at risk for destructive parent-child relations in adolescence. *Child Development, 55,* 174–183.

Gardner, F. E. M. (1989). Inconsistent parenting: Is there evidence for a link with children's conduct problems? *Journal of Abnormal Child Psychology, 17,* 223–233.

Gecas, V. (1979). The influence of social class on socialization. In W. R. Burr, R. Hill, F. I. Nye, & I. L. Russ (Eds.), *Contemporary theories about the family* (Vol. 1). New York: Fiel.

Gelfand, D. M., & Teti, D. M. (1990). The effects of maternal depression on children. *Clinical Psychology Review, 10,* 329–353.

Glueck, S., & Glueck, E. (1950). *Unraveling juvenile delinquency.* Cambridge, MA: Harvard University Press.

Gomberg, E. S. (1981). Women, sex roles, and alcohol problems. *Professional Psychology, 12,* 146–155.

Goodwin, D. W., & Guze, S. B. (1989). *Psychiatric diagnosis* (4th ed.). New York: Oxford University Press.

Goodwin, D. W., Schulsinger, F., Hermansen, L., Guze, S. B., & Winokur, G. (1975). Alcohol problems in adoptees raised apart from alcoholic biological parents. *Archives of General Psychiatry, 28,* 238–242.

Goodwin, D. W., Schulsinger, F., Knop, J., Mednick, S., & Guze, S. B. (1977). Alcoholism and depression in adopted-out daughters of alcoholics. *Archives of General Psychiatry, 34,* 751–755.

Goodyer, I. M. (1990). Family relationships, life events and childhood psychopathology. *Journal of Child Psychology and Psychiatry, 31,* 161–192.

Gorsuch, R. L., & Butler, M. C. (1976). Initial drug abuse: A review of pre-disposing social-psychological factors. *Psychological Bulletin, 83,* 120–137.

Green, A. H. (1978). Dimensions of psychological trauma in abused children. *Journal of the American Academy of Child Psychiatry, 17,* 231–237.

Greenwald, D. F. (1990). Family interaction and child outcome in a high risk sample. *Psychological Reports, 66,* 675–688.

Halebsky, M. A. (1987). Adolescent alcohol and substance abuse: Parent and peer effects. *Adolescence, 22,* 961–967.

Hammen, C., Adrian, C., Gordon, D., Burge, D., Jaenicke, C., & Hiroto, D. (1987). Children of depressed mothers: Maternal strain and symptom predictors of dysfunction. *Journal of Abnormal Psychology, 96,* 190–198.

Hammen, C., Burge, D., & Stansbury, K. (1990). Relationship of mother and child variables to child outcomes in a high-risk sample: A causal modeling analysis. *Developmental Psychology, 26,* 24–30.

Hess, R. D. (1970). Social class and ethnic influences on socialization. In P. H. Musser (Ed.), *Carmichael's manual of child psychology* (Vol. 2). New York: Wiley.

Hetherington, E. M. (1982). Effects of divorce on parents and children. In M. E. Lamb (Ed.), *Nontraditional families: Parenting and child development.* Hillsdale, NJ: Erlbaum.

Hetherington, E. M., Cox, M., & Cox, R. (1985). Long-term effects of divorce and remarriage on the adjustment of children. *Journal of the American Academy of Child Psychiatry, 24,* 518–530.

Hinde, R. A. (1988). Introduction. In R. A. Hinde & J. Stevenson-Hinde (Eds.), *Relationships within families: Mutual influences.* New York: Oxford University Press.

Hinde, R. A., & Stevenson-Hinde, J. (1988). Epilogue In R. A. Hinde & J. Stevenson-Hinde (Eds.), *Relationships within families: Mutual influences.* New York: Oxford University Press.

Hoagwood, K. (1990). Parental functioning and child sexual abuse. *Child and Adolescent Social-Work Journal, 7,* 377–387.

Hoffman-Plotkin, D., & Twentyman, C. T. (1984). A multimodal assessment of behavioral and cognitive deficits in abused and neglected preschoolers. *Child Development, 55,* 794–802.

Hops, H., Sherman, L., & Biglan, A. (1990). Maternal depression, marital discord, and children's behavior: A developmental perspective. In G. R. Patterson (Ed.), *Depression and aggression in family interaction.* Hillsdale, NJ: Erlbaum.

Jacob, T. (1987). Family interaction and psychopathology: Historical overview. In T. Jacob (Ed.), *Family interaction and psychopathology.* New York: Plenum.

Jacob, T., Krahn, F. L., & Leonard, K. (1991). Parent-child interactions in families with alcoholic fathers. *Journal of Consulting and Clinical Psychology, 59,* 176–181.

Jacob, T., Ritchey, D., Cvitkovic, J. F., & Blane, H. T. (1981). Communication styles of alcoholic and nonalcoholic families when drinking and not drinking. *Journal of Studies on Alcohol, 42,* 466–482.

Jacob, T., & Seilhamer, R. A. (1987). Alcoholism and family interaction. In T. Jacob (Ed.), *Family interaction and psychopathology.* New York: Plenum.

Johnson, G. M., Shontz, F. C., & Locke, T. P. (1984). Relationships between adolescent drug abuse and parental drug behavior. *Adolescence, 19,* 295–299.

Johnson, S. M., Wahl, G., Martin, S., & Johansson, S. (1973). How deviant is the normal child: A behavioral analysis of the pre-school child and his family. In R. D. Rubin, J. P. Brady, & J. D. Henderson (Eds.), *Advances in behavior therapy,* (Vol. 4). New York: Academic Press.

Johnson, V., & Pandina, R. J. (1991). Effects of the family on adolescent substance use, delinquency, and coping styles. *American Journal of Drug and Alcohol Abuse, 17,* 71–88.

Johnston, J. R., Gonzalez, R., & Campbell, L. L. (1987). Ongoing post-divorce conflict and child disturbance. *Journal of Abnormal Child Psychology, 15*, 493–509.

Kalter, N. (1987). Long-term effects of divorce on children: A developmental vulnerability model. *American Journal of Orthopsychiatry, 57*, 587–600.

Klinge, V., & Piggot, L. R. (1986). Substance use by adolescent psychiatric inpatients and their parents. *Adolescence, 21*, 323–331.

Lambert, B. G., Rothschild, B. F., Altland, R., & Green, L. B. (1978). *Adolescence: Transition from childhood to maturity.* Monterey, CA: Brooks/Cole.

Landesman, S. (1988). Preventing "institutionalization" in the community. In M. P. Janick, M. W. Krauss, & M. M. Seltzer (Eds.), *Community residences for persons with developmental disabilities: Here to stay.* Baltimore, MD: Brookes.

Landesman, S. (1990). Institutionalization revisited: Expanding views on early and cumulative life experiences. In M. Lewis & S. Miller (Eds.), *Handbook of developmental psychopathology.* New York: Plenum.

Lewis, M., & Miller, S. (1990). Preface. In M. Lewis & S. Miller (Eds.), *Handbook of developmental psychopathology.* New York: Plenum.

Long, N., Forehand, R., Fauber, R., & Brody, G. H. (1987). Self-perceived and independently observed competence of young adolescents as a function of parental marital conflict and recent divorce. *Journal of Abnormal Child Psychology, 15*, 15–27.

McCord, W., McCord, J., & Zola, I. K. (1959). *Origins of crime.* New York: Columbia University Press.

McDermott, D. (1984). The relationship of parental drug use and parent's attitude concerning adolescent drug use. *Adolescence, 19*, 89–97.

McGraw, K. O. (1987). *Developmental psychology.* Orlando, FL: Harcourt Brace Jovanovich.

Miller, S. M., Birnbaum, A., & Durbin, D. (1990). Etiologic perspectives on depression in childhood. In M. Lewis & S. Miller (Eds.), *Handbook of developmental psychopathology.* New York: Plenum.

Moos, R. H., & Moos, B. S. (1984). The process of recovering from alcoholism: Comparing functioning in families of alcoholics and matched control families. *Journal of Studies on Alcohol, 45*, 111–118.

Niven, R. G. (1984). Alcohol in the family. In L. J. West (Ed.), *Alcoholism and related problems.* Englewood Cliffs; NJ: Prentice Hall.

Olweus, D. (1980). Familial and temperamental determinants of aggressive behavior in adolescent boys: A causal analysis. *Developmental Psychology, 16*, 644–660.

Parrish, T. S. (1987). Family and environment. In V. B. Van Hasselt & M. Hersen (Eds.), *Handbook of adolescent psychology.* New York: Pergamon.

Patterson, G. R. (1976). The aggressive child: Victim and architect of a coercive system. In L. A. Hamerlynck, L. C. Handy, & E. J. Mash (Eds.), *Behavior modification and families: Theory and research* (Vol. 1). New York: Brunner/Mazel.

Patterson, G. R. (1980). Mothers: The unacknowledged victims. *Monographs of the Society for Research in Child Development, 45*, 1–64.

Patterson, G. R., (1982). *Coercive family process.* Eugene, OR: Castalia.

Patterson, G. R., & Forgatch, M. S., (1990). Initiation and maintenance of process disrupting single-mother families. In G. R. Patterson (Ed.), *Depression and aggression in family interaction.* Hillsdale, NJ: Erlbaum.

Patterson, G. R., & Reid, J. B. (1970). Reciprocity and coercion: Two facets of social systems. In C. Neuringer & J. L. Michael (Eds.), *Behavior modification in clinical psychology*. New York: Appleton-Century-Crofts.

Peterson, A. C., Ebata, A., & Sarigiani, P. (1987). Who expresses depressive affect in adolescence? In Brooks-Gunn & A. C. Peterson (Co-chairs), *The development of depressive affect in adolescence: Biological, affective, and social factors*. Symposium conducted at the Society for Research in Child Development, Baltimore, MD.

Peterson, C. (1991). *Introduction to psychology*. New York: Harper-Collins.

Plomin, R., & Daniels, D. (1987). Why are children in the same family so different from one another? *Behavioral and Brain Sciences, 10*, 1–16.

Plomin, R., DeFries, J. C., & Fulker, D. W. (1988). *Nature and nurture during infancy and childhood*. New York: Cambridge University Press.

Plomin, R., DeFries, J. C., & Loehlin, J. C. (1977). Genotype-environment interaction and correlation in the analysis of human behavior. *Psychological Bulletin, 84*, 309–322.

Plomin, R., Nitz, K., & Rowe, D. C. (1990). Behavioral genetics and aggressive behavior in childhood. In M. Lewis & S. Miller (Eds.), *Handbook of developmental psychopathology*. New York: Plenum.

Pogue-Geile, M. F., & Rose, R. J. (1987). Psychopathology: A behavior genetic perspective. In T. Jacob (Ed.), *Family interaction and psychopathology*. New York: Plenum.

Radke-Yarrow, M. (1990). Family environments of depressed and well parents and their children: Issues of research methods. In G. R. Patterson (Ed.), *Depression and aggression in family interaction*. Hillsdale, NJ: Erlbaum.

Reid, J. B., Kavanagh, K., & Baldwin, D. V. (1987). Abusive parents' perceptions of child problem behaviors: An example of parental bias. *Journal of Abnormal Child Psychology, 15*, 457–466.

Rosenbaum, A., & O'Leary, K. D. (1981). Marital violence: Characteristics of abusive couples. *Journal of Consulting and Clinical Psychology, 49*, 63–71.

Rowe, D. C., & Plomin, R. (1981). The importance of non-shared environmental influences in behavioral development. *Developmental Psychology, 17*, 517–531.

Rutter, M. (1979). Protective factors in children in response to stress and disadvantage. In M. W. Kent & J. E. Rolfe (Eds.), *Primary prevention of psychopathology: Social competence in children* (Vol. 3). Armidale, AL: Hanover.

Rutter, M. (1985). Family and school influence on behavioral development. *Journal of Child Psychology and Psychiatry, 26*, 349–368.

Rutter, M. (1986). The developmental psychopathology of depression. In M. Rutter, C. Tizard, & P. Read (Eds.), *Depression in young people—developmental and clinical perspectives*. New York: Guilford.

Rutter, M., Cox, A., Tupling, C., Berger, M., & Youle, W. (1975). Attachment and adjustment in two geographical areas: I. The prevalence of psychiatric disorder. *British Journal of Psychiatry, 126*, 493–509.

Rutter, M., & Giller, H. (1983). *Juvenile delinquency: Trends and perspectives*. Harmondsworth Middlesex: Penguin.

Rutter, M., Macdonald, H., Le Couteur, A., Harrington, R., Bolton, P., & Bailey, A., (1990). Genetic factors in child psychiatric disorders: II. Empirical findings. *Journal of Child Psychology and Psychiatry, 31*, 39–83.

Rutter, M., & Quinton, D. (1977). Psychiatric disorder: Ecological factors and concepts of causation. In H. McGurk (Ed.), *Ecological factors in human development*. Amsterdam: North-Holland.

Rutter, M., Tizard, J., & Whitmore, K. (1970). *Health education and behavior*. London: Longmans.

Sarigiani, P. (1987, April). *Perceived closeness in relationship with father: Links to adjustment and body image in girls*. Paper presented at the biennial meeting of the Society for Research in Child Development, Baltimore, MD.

Scarr, S., & McCartney, K. (1983). How people make their own environments: A theory of genotype-environment effects. *Child Development, 54*, 424–435.

Schellenbach, C. J., & Guerney, L. F. (1987). Identification of adolescent abuse and future intervention prospects. *Journal of Adolescence, 10*, 1–12.

Shaw, D., & Emery, R. (1988). Chronic family adversity and school age children's adjustment. *Journal of the American Academy of Child and Adolescent Psychiatry, 2*, 200–206.

Shuckit, M. A., & Morrissey, R. R. (1976). Alcoholism in women: Some clinical and social perspectives with an emphasis on possible subtypes. In M. Greenblatt & M. A. Shuckit (Eds.), *Alcoholism problems in women and children*. New York: Grune and Stratten.

Stolberg, A. L., & Anker, J. M. (1983). Cognitive and behavioral changes in children resulting from parental divorce and consequent environmental changes. *Journal of Divorce, 7*, 23–41.

Tricket, P. K., & Kuczynski, L. (1986). Children's misbehaviors and parental discipline strategies in abusive and nonabusive families. *Developmental Psychology, 22*, 115–123.

U.S. Department of Health and Human Services. (1988). *Study of national incidence and prevalence of child abuse and neglect: 1988* Washington, DC: Author.

Vaughn, B. E., Egeland, B. R., Sroufe, L. A., & Waters, E. (1979). Individual differences in infant-mother attachment at twelve and eighteen months: Stability and change in families under stress. *Child Development, 50*, 971–975.

Vaux, A., & Ruggiero, M. (1983). Stressful life change and delinquent behavior. *American Journal of Community Psychology, 11*, 169–183.

Vuchinich, S., Hetherington, E. M., Vuchinich, R. A., & Clingempeel, W. G. (1991). Parent-child interaction and gender differences in early adolescents' adaptation to stepfamilies. *Developmental Psychology, 27*, 618–626.

Wallerstein, J. S. (1991). The long-term effects of divorce on children: A review. *Journal of the American Academy of Child and Adolescent Psychiatry, 30*, 349–360.

Warshak, R. A., & Santrock, J. W. (1983). The impact of divorce on father-custody and mother-custody homes: The child's perspective. In L. A. Kurdek (Ed.), *Children and divorce*. San Francisco: Jossey-Bass.

Watson, J. B. (1913). Psychology as a behaviorist views it. *Psychological Review, 20*, 158–177.

Webster-Stratton, C. (1990). Stress: A potential disrupter of parent perceptions and family interactions. *Journal of Clinical Child Psychology, 19*, 302–312.

Webster-Stratton, C., & Hammond, M. (1988). Maternal depression and its relationship to life stress, perceptions of child behavior problems, parenting behaviors, and child conduct problems. *Journal of Abnormal Child Psychology, 16,* 299–315.

Weissman, M. M., Gammon, G. D., John, K., Merikangas, K. R., Warner, V., Prusoff, B. A., & Sholomskas, D. (1987). Children of depressed parents. *Archives of General Psychiatry, 44,* 847–853.

Weissman, M. M., Prusoff, B. A., Gammon, G. D., Merikangas, K. R., Leckman, J. F., & Kidd, K. K. (1984). Psychopathology in children (ages 6–18) of depressed and normal parents. *Journal of the American Academy of Child Psychiatry, 23,* 78–84.

Werner, E. E. (1986). Resilient offspring of alcoholics: A longitudinal study from birth to age 18. *Journal of Studies on Alcohol, 47,* 34–40.

Werner, E. E., & Smith, R. S. (1982). *Vulnerable but invincible.* New York: McGraw-Hill.

Wierson, M., Forehand, R., Fauber, R., & McCombs, A. (1989). Buffering young male adolescents against negative divorce influences: The role of good parent-adolescent relations. *Child Study Journal, 19,* 101–115.

Williamson, J. M., Borduin, C. M., & Howe, B. A. (1991). The ecology of adolescent maltreatment: A multilevel examination of adolescent physical abuse, sexual abuse, and neglect. *Journal of Consulting and Clinical Psychology, 54,* 449–457.

Wilsnack, R. W., Wilsnack, S. C., & Klassen, A. D., Jr. (1982, September). *Women's drinking and drinking problems: Patterns for a 1981 survey.* Paper presented at the annual meeting of the Society for the Study of Social Problems, San Francisco.

Wolfe, V. V., Gentile, C., & Wolfe, D. A. (1989). The impact of sexual abuse on children: A PTSD formulation. *Behavior Therapy, 20,* 215–228.

Wolin, S. J., & Bennet, L. A. (1984). Family rituals. *Family Process, 23,* 401–420.

Wolman, B. B. (1987). *The sociopathic personality.* New York: Brunner/Mazel.

21
Suicide and Suicidal Behavior

Mary Margaret Kerr
Jake Milliones

Τhis chapter addresses the alarming topic of youth suicide and suicidal behavior. Suicide is the second-leading cause of death in white American teens and the third leading cause of death among African-American teens (Shaffer, 1993). Of specific concern is the increase in suicide among individuals 15 to 19 years of age. The rate of suicide for males in this group *tripled* from 1965 to 1991 (Shaffer, 1993).

This chapter offers three major sections. In order, they review the epidemiology of youth suicide and suicidal behavior, risk factors contributing to youth suicide and the accompanying identification strategies, and therapeutic management issues. Prior to reading this chapter, the reader should carefully review the previous chapters on assessment (i.e., clinical interviewing and semistructured evaluations) and specific disorders (especially depression, conduct disorders, and substance abuse disorders). Moreover, clinicians should familiarize themselves with the relevant local laws and procedures for emergency evaluation and treatment.

Epidemiology

Prevalence

Death by suicide in any age group is rare. It is the dramatic increase in youth suicide, though, that has brought this problem into intense public and professional scrutiny, as evidenced by both scientific and lay publications. Among Americans between the ages of 15 and 24 years, 12.3 per 100,000 take their own lives each year (Kupfer, 1989). Among 15- to 19-year-olds, however, the prevalence is twice as high.

While completed suicides are rare, suicide attempts appear rather common among adolescents. The ratio of suicide attempts to completed suicides is roughly 10 to 1 (Maris, 1985). Smith and Crawford (1986) found that 63% of teenagers in a midwestern high school had seriously considered, planned, or attempted suicide during one school year. In their survey of college students, Meehan, Lamb, Saltzman, and O'Carroll (1990) found that nearly 2% had made a serious suicide attempt within the past year.

European Americans lead in relative number of suicides over other ethnic and racial groups, although African-American and Hispanic suicide rates have climbed in the recent decade (Hawton & Osborn, 1984). Males are more likely than females to die of their self-inflicted injuries, although more females (especially those who are postpubertal) attempt suicide.

Clinical Picture

Antecedent events. Interpersonal conflict, loss, and unresolved disciplinary situations are the most common precipitant events of adolescent suicide (Hawton & Catalan, 1987; Shaffer, 1988). These events alone do not cause suicidal behavior, but in concert with other risk factors, they may heighten an individual's immediate vulnerability. Clinicians need to be fully aware of these issues in an individual's life history, to make an accurate assessment of risk.

Method. The most common method for suicide in the United States is use of a firearm, followed by hanging, jumping, carbon monoxide, and poisoning (Brent, Perper, Goldstein, et al., 1988). Outside the United States, the most common method used in suicide attempts is self-poisoning. Availability of firearms is contributing to the increase in adolescent suicides in this country (Brent, Perper, & Allman, 1987; Brent, Perper, Goldstein, et al., 1988).

Motivation and Intent. As discussed by Brent, Puig-Antich, and Rabinovitch (1991), high suicidal intent (a fervent will to die) is evidenced by suicide victims who arrange their attempt so that they will not be rescued; for example, a teenager may wait until his or her parents leave the house to take an overdose. The assessment of risk for suicide is predicated on an individual's intent, composite risk factors, and lethality of plans. It is to this assessment of risk that we now turn.

Assessing Suicidal Risk

This review of risk factors offers a framework based on those factors most likely to predict suicidal behavior, as well as those that are related but less predictive. Table 21–1 lists risk factors and some respective indicators.

Psychiatric Disorder in the Adolescent or Family

Suicidal behavior alone does not constitute a psychiatric disorder (American Psychiatric Association, 1993). Yet suicidal behavior may be one symptom of a major depressive disorder; the DSM-IV draft criteria cite

Table 21-1
Risk Factors and Indicators of Risk for Adolescent Suicide

Risk Factor	Indicators of Risk
1. Psychiatric disorder	Prior treatment history (although many adolescent suicide victims have never received psychiatric treatment); diagnostic information, especially that indicating depressive illness, conduct problems, and/or substance abuse; school reports that would suggest depression, substance abuse, and conduct problems; peer reports of changes in behavior that would suggest a psychiatric disorder, especially hopelessness, anhedonia, irritability, substance abuse, and social withdrawal.
2. Personality traits	Evidence of hopelessness, impulsivity, cognitive distortions, poor social skills.
3. Prior suicide attempt	Client-reported prior attempt; physical sign of previous attempt; peer reports; family reports of accidents or ambiguous injuries; prior hospital admissions, especially emergency room admission for substance abuse, "reaction to medication," or unexplained accident; DUI reports.
4. Family factors	Evidence of family psychiatric disorders, especially affective disorder, suicidal behavior, conduct disorder, substance abuse; evidence of sexual or physical abuse.
5. Exposure to suicide	Exposure to suicide of schoolmate, peer, or family member; exposure to portrayals of suicide in print or electronic media.
6. Primary medical concerns	Chronic illness (i.e., epilepsy); concerns about pregnancy, sexually transmitted disease.
7. Specific suicidal plan	Individual has a definite plan for taking his life.

"recurrent thoughts of death (not just fear of dying), recurrent suicidal ideation without a specific plan, or a suicide attempt or a specific plan for committing suicide" (p. J1).

The revised Global Assessment of Functioning (GAF) scale also uses suicidal ideation, plans, and behavior to gauge an individual's general impairment. Here suicidal symptoms are listed in order of severity, including a "serious suicidal act with clear expectation of death," "suicide attempts without clear expectation of death," "suicidal preoccupation," and "suicidal ideation" (American Psychiatric Association, 1993, p. D8)

Underlying psychiatric disorders increase an adolescent's risk for suicidal behavior. Most adolescent suicide victims have had "at least one major, debilitating psychiatric disorder, predominantly affective disorder (particularly bipolar disorder), substance abuse, or conduct disorder" (Brent et al., 1991, p. 15). Many adolescents, however, have never received treatment for their psychiatric problems. Absence of treatment may even be considered a risk factor for youth suicide completion (Brent, Perper, Goldstein, et al., 1988). The clinician thus should not equate absence of prior treatment with absence of a psychiatric disorder.

Relatives of those who have completed and attempted suicide also evidence a high rate of psychiatric disorders, although again these disorders may not have been identified or treated (Brent & Kolko, 1990a). An adolescent can probably describe substance abuse problems, family discord, or other manifestations of underlying psychiatric disorders that warrant further exploration.

Personality Traits

Blumenthal and Kupfer (1988) have delineated traits that may increase the risk of suicidal behavior in children and adolescents. These include "hopelessness, impulsivity, cognitive distortion and external locus of control, and poor social skills" (reported in Brent & Kolko, 1990a, p. 266.)

Hopelessness refers to an individual's inability to view the future in a positive way. Adolescents experiencing hopelessness may have no plans for the immediate future (e.g., the coming weekend, evening, or school break). They may express their despair with such statements as "There's no reason to go on," "Things would be better without me around," or "Life is not worth living anymore."

Impulsivity, as cited by Brent and Kolko (1990a), refers to an underlying problem-solving style. Pfeffer et al. (1988) reported that impulsive youths (those who engaged in explosive, aggressive outbursts) were at greatest risk for repeated suicidal behavior (Brent & Kolko, 1990). Orbach et al. (1983) found that "suicidal children, when compared to chronically ill or normal children, tend to be repulsed by life and attracted to death and also tend to be more rigid in their approach to tasks and to generate fewer alternatives for problem-solving" (reported in Brent & Kolko, 1990a, p. 267).

Many have observed that suicidal youths experience poor social relationships with peers and family members (Brent, Perper, Goldstein, et al., 1988). To an adolescent who has difficulty making and keeping friends, even a temporary loss (typical in the fluctuating relationships of adolescents) may be overwhelmingly painful.

Prior Suicide Attempts

At least one-half of suicide victims have threatened or attempted suicide at least once before. Direct questioning about prior attempts, thoughts, and plans is crucial. It takes considerable practice to be comfortable asking such questions, and those training for clinical work should take every opportunity to develop this skill.

Getting an adolescent to acknowledge suicidal behavior is sometimes difficult. Often the best source of information is peers; in one study, 60% of adolescent suicide victims had told a peer of their intent, but that peer had kept the secret (Brent, 1987).

Follow-up studies of suicide attempters reveal a reattempt rate of 6% to 15% per year (Brent et al., 1991). These attempts may go unnoticed, or parents and friends may fail to recognize the seriousness of the situation.

Family Factors

As Table 21–1 shows, suicidal teenagers often experience family discord, including abuse. It may be difficult to obtain accurate information about the family situation, especially if the adolescent is at odds with family members. Nevertheless, it is crucial to notify parents of their child's status, unless one firmly believes that such notification would further jeopardize the clients' welfare. In situations where parental notification and/or cooperation is impossible, the teenager may be able to admit himself or herself voluntarily for mental health treatment. As mentioned earlier, it is important that clinicians have a good understanding of the mental health laws for their area.

Family psychiatric illness (e.g., affective illness, conduct disorder, substance abuse) can complicate the clinician's task. Parents struggling with their own problems may not acknowledge or take action concerning their child's suicidal behavior. Dismissal of the suicidal behavior as "just a way to get attention" is a common response. The clinician, having offered the family accurate information regarding the young person's status, must then evaluate the ability of the family to protect and support the adolescent.

While some adolescents do experience substantial discord at home, others may grossly exaggerate parent-child conflict. The clinician should not assume that a troubled teenager can accurately portray the level of family cooperation or discord. Direct observations of the parents provide a more reliable assessment of their willingness and capacity to seek help for their child.

Exposure to Suicide

Studies have pointed to a clear "suicide contagion" phenomenon among young people, especially those with underlying vulnerabilities. An astute clinician therefore asks about prior exposure. It is important to keep in mind that the suicide victim need not be a close friend; Brent et al. (1989) showed that exposure to the suicide of a mere acquaintance could have detrimental effects in an otherwise vulnerable youth. Even televised and print depictions of suicide may increase suicidal behavior among those with underlying psychiatric disorders (Gould & Shaffer, 1986).

Primary Medical Concerns

Epileptic individuals exhibit suicidal behavior at a rate higher than that of their nonepileptic peers (Brent, 1987). Other studies have shown a correlation between a recent physical or sexual assault, pregnancy concern, or sexually transmitted disease (Robins, 1989; Brent et al., 1991).

Suicidal Ideation

The presence or absence of a concrete suicide plan is a pivotal indicator. If a teenager has a concrete suicide plan, he or she is to be considered at serious risk. This danger increases with the degree of lethality and intent. Other factors also contribute to increased risk, especially the availability of firearms, a feeling of hopelessness, a history of abuse, and use of alcohol and other drugs.

Unfortunately, many lay persons believe and perpetuate the falsehood that those who talk about suicide do not follow through. This belief can lead someone to downplay a teenager's suicide plan as a "bluff."

A skilled interviewer can find out whether suicide has been a fleeting thought or whether the individual at risk has moved from a general ideation to a more specific plan. For example, the clinican may ask questions such as, "Have you ever thought of hurting yourself?" and "When you were having that thought, did you think about how it would happen?" Individuals who refuse to discuss their thoughts should be considered at high risk.

To supplement the clinical interview there are additional valuable sources for assessing a teenager's suicide risk. The school is a rich environment for referral information. Often a student has come to the counselor's attention through the report of a peer who has witnessed suicidal behavior or overheard suicidal threats. Written assignments and diaries produced for English and social studies courses may reveal a troubled teenager's plans. One repeat attempter reported that she had researched her methods and described them as part of a health class project entitled "Stresses in Teenagers Today." A talented art student designed an elaborate miniature crypt shortly before his death. Hours before killing himself with a hunting rifle, a teenager told the school secretary, "You can take me off the rolls, because I am not coming back to this place." A review of the school library files revealed that the student had been reading about suicide for weeks. These illustrations are included to highlight the phenomenon of "veiled threats" that warrant serious review.

Clinicians may use a "no-suicide contract" as a measure of a client's risk. This contract is a verbal and/or written promise that the client will not injure himself or herself and that he or she will contact the clinician or another responsible adult if the urge to self-injure occurs. *If an ado-*

lescent cannot make a no-suicide contract, consider that individual at serious risk of harm. While the contract is not a guarantee, an individual who can make a no-suicide contract is probably safer than one who cannot.[1] To decide whether the individual is merely trying to please the therapist or is trustworthy, you may ask follow-up questions: "On a scale of one to 10, how safe do you feel?", "How confident are you that you can keep this promise?", "What steps could you take if you felt the urge to hurt yourself? To whom would you talk?", or "Let's say you feel things go badly when you leave school. What can you do to let someone know?" It is important to review with the adolescent exactly what steps to take if a precipitating stressful situation occurs prior to your next meeting.

Pending Disciplinary Action

Unresolved disciplinary actions sometimes precede youth suicides. Shaffer (1974) reported that 31% of adolescent suicide completers in his study had been awaiting the outcome of a disciplinary action, usually at school. One theory is that the unresolved situation increases the anxiety of an otherwise vulnerable young person.

Therapeutic Management

Short-Term Management

Safety must be the primary concern of the clinician confronted with a suicidal youth. There are several safety guidelines that override all other short- and long-term concerns.

First, a suicidal adolescent must never be left alone until a thorough assessment shows that the adolescent is safe without supervision. Parents and friends may help in this supervision, if they are responsible. This need for monitoring does not mandate inpatient status, although hospitalization is suggested for those individuals who cannot make a no-suicide contract, who have made a serious attempt, or who appear generally to be at risk in several areas and have no reliable support system.

Of special concern, secondly, are those youths who have access to a firearm. Recent studies have linked access to guns with elevated suicidal risk (Brent, 1987; Brent, Perper, Goldstein, et al., 1988). It is cru-

---

[1] A colleague once received a no-suicide contract from a student who subsequently went home and placed a loaded shotgun in his mouth. He stopped himself and reported to the school social worker the next morning. When asked what had stopped him, he replied, "I remembered my promise to you. I knew you were counting on me."

cial to question the adolescent and those in his support system about firearms. *All firearms must be removed from the surroundings of a suicidal individual.*[2]

Third, adolescents who use alcohol and other drugs are more likely to try suicide. Teenagers who completed suicide were many times more likely to have been using alcohol or other recreational drugs than those who only attempted suicide.

Fourth, the clinician should continue to monitor suicidality and reassess contingency plans. Brent and Kolko (1990a) recommend that suicidality (lethality and intent) be assessed in every clinical session, and 24-hour emergency phone coverage is essential. We suggest daily telephone contact with the suicidal individual.

Finally, clinicians need their own system for consultation and support on difficult cases. Second opinions are invaluable in the ongoing assessment of a potentially suicidal client.

Long-Term Treatment

Compliance with treatment is of primary concern with this difficult population (Brent & Kolko, 1990b). Recommendations to increase compliance include therapist consistency, reminders for appointments, prompt scheduling of follow-up visits after initial assessment, involvement of the client and family in selection of treatment approach, and involving the teenager's social support network in treatment (Brent & Kolko, 1990a, p. 275).

The underlying causes for the suicidal behavior will determine the course of treatment. A thorough clinical assessment will suggest social skills deficits, cognitive distortions, family discord, or other problems that can be addressed through treatment. An underlying psychiatric disorder or substance abuse disorder will require focused treatment (see earlier chapters). Cognitive-behavioral approaches have proven helpful in improving the individual's outlook and expanding his or her problem-solving skills (Asarnow, Carlson, & Guthrie, 1987). In addition to managing chronic discord in the adolescent's relationships, the clinician should offer special help and vigilance during particularly stressful situations (e.g., the loss of a relationship or individual through death, separation, or suicide). Postvention support in the aftermath of a peer or family member's sudden death or suicide, is essential for an already vulnerable teenager (see below).

---

[2] Locking guns in a cabinet is not sufficient. One adolescent client broke into a locked gun cabinet with a crowbar; minutes later, his parents returned home to find him dead from a self-inflicted wound.

The Clinician's Role in Postvention

Several authors have offered accounts of postvention in the aftermath of a suicide (see Adler & Jelinek, 1990; Brent & Kerr, 1992). This kind of work requires special consultation and clinical skills and the ability to work in a multidisciplinary team with lay and professional members. A thorough understanding of the phenomenon of suicide contagion also is useful (see Brent et al., 1989; Gould & Shaffer, 1986; Phillips & Carstensen, 1986). Community-based postvention seeks to do the following:

- Offer information and support in small groups (as opposed to large assemblies, public announcement systems, media features or public gatherings).
- Reduce any tendency to glamorize or romanticize the suicide victim in memorials, public gestures, discussions, or media coverage.
- Offer straightforward answers as rumors emerge, while avoiding lengthy descriptions of the suicide method.
- Screen for those who may experience an unhealthy reaction to the suicide, especially among those already identified as being at risk.
- Reassure professionals and parents with responsible information regarding warning signs for suicide, substance abuse, and depression.
- Offer specific clinical support for those closest to the victim (especially witnesses), who may exhibit posttraumatic stress symptoms, "survivor guilt," or a tendency to engage in self-destructive behavior.
- Maintain therapeutic links with responsible adults (e.g., clergy, coroner, funeral director, youth organization leaders, school staff) who can monitor and refer youths.
- Analyze the circumstances of the suicide and offer recommendations for future prevention. (See Brent, Perper, Kolko, & Zelenak, 1988, for a review of psychological autopsy methodology.)

Summary

This chapter has offered guidelines for the identification, assessment, management, and treatment of suicidal youths. Adolescents, especially those between 15 and 21, are at elevated risk for suicide. Contributing factors include alcohol and other drug use, underlying psychiatric disorders, availability of firearms, and physical or sexual abuse.

Safety is the first priority in dealing with an adolescent who may be suicidal. To ensure safety, the clinician must conduct a thorough and ongoing assessment of the individual's risk factors, including lethality and intent of any specific suicidal ideation. Helpful information may come from peers and others in the individual's support system.

Long-term therapeutic intervention derives from the underlying causes of the suicidal behavior. Cognitive-behavioral approaches, psychopharmacological intervention, and the development of better coping skills have proven effective in decreasing the underlying risk for future suicidal behavior.

A newly emerging role for clinicians is postvention, or the supportive services offered to a community or group in the aftermath of a completed suicide. Postvention—because of the suicide-contagion phenomenon among youths—has as its primary goal the prevention of further suicidal behavior among the survivors.

References

Adler, R. S., & Jelinek, M. S. (1990). After teen suicide: Issues for pediatricians who are asked to consult to schools. *Pediatrics, 86,* 982–987.

American Psychiatric Association. (1993). *DSM-IV draft criteria.* Washington, DC: Author.

Asarnow, J. R., Carlson, G. A., & Guthrie, D. (1987) Coping strategies, self-perceptions, hopelessness, and perceived family environments in depressed and suicidal children. *Journal of Consulting and Clinical Psychology, 55,* 361–366.

Blumenthal, S. J., & Kupfer, D. J. (1988). Overview of early detection and treatment strategies for suicidal behavior in young people. *Journal of Youth and Adolescence, 17,* 1–23.

Brent, D. A. (1987). Correlates of the medical lethality of suicide attempts in children and adolescents. *Journal of the American Academy of Child and Adolescent Psychiatry, 26,* 86–89.

Brent, D. A., Kerr, M. M., Goldstein, C., Bozigar, J., Wartella, M., & Allan, M. J. (1989). An outbreak of suicide and suicidal behavior in a high school. *Journal of the American Academy of Child and Adolescent Psychiatry, 28,* 918–924.

Brent, D. A., & Kolko, D. J. (1990a). The assessment and treatment of children and adolescents at risk for suicide. In D. Kupfer & S. Blumenthal (Eds.), *Suicide over the life cycle: Risk factors, assessment, and treatment of suicidal patients* (pp. 253–301). Washington, DC: American Psychiatric Press.

Brent, D. A., & Kolko, D. J. (1990b). Suicide and suicidal behavior in children and adolescents. In B. Garfinkel, G. Carlson, & E. Weller (Eds.), *Psychiatric disorders in children and adolescents* (pp. 372–391). Philadelphia: Saunders.

Brent, D. A., Perper, J. A., & Allman, C. J. (1987). Alcohol, firearms, and suicide among youth: Temporal trends in Allegheny County, Pennsylvania, 1960 to 1983. *Journal of the American Medical Association, 257,* 3369–3372.

Brent, D. A., Perper, J. A., Kolko, D. J., & Zelenak, J. P. (1988). The psychological autopsy: Methodological considerations for the study of adolescent suicide. *Journal of the American Academy of Child and Adolescent Psychiatry, 27,* 362–366.

Brent, D. A., Puig-Antich, J., & Rabinovitch, H. (1991). Major psychiatric disorders in childhood and adolescence. Unpublished manuscript.

Brent, D., Perper, J. A., Goldstein, C., Kolko, D., Allan, M., Allman, C. & Zelenak, J. (1988). Risk factors for adolescent suicide: A comparison of adolescent suicide victims and suicide inpatients. *Archives of General Psychiatry, 45*, 581–588.

Brent, D. A., Kerr, M. M., Bozigar, J. A., & McQuiston, L. (1987). A school-based response to traumatic student death. In Nader, P. R. (Ed.); *School health: A guide for health professionals*, (Fourth Edition). American Academy of Pediatrics.

Brent, D. A., Puig-Antich, J., & Rabinovich, H. (1992). Major psychiatric disorders in childhood and adolescence. In: Levine, M. D., Carey, W. B., & Crocker, A. C. (Eds.), *Developmental behavioral pediatrics* (569–588). Philadelphia: Saunders Company.

Gould, M. S., & Shaffer, D. (1986). The impact of suicide in television movies: Evidence of imitation. *New England Journal of Medicine, 315*, 690–694.

Hawton, K., & Catalan, J. (1987). *Attempted suicide: A practical guide to its nature and management* (2nd ed.). New York: Oxford University Press.

Hawton, K., & Osborn, M. (1984). Suicide and attempted suicide in children and adolescents. In B. Lahey & A. Kazdin (Eds.), *Advances in clinical child psychology* (pp. 36–57). New York: Van Nostrand Reinhold.

Kupfer, D. (1989). Summary of the National Conference on Risk Factors for Youth Suicide. In Alcohol, Drug Abuse, and Mental Health Administration, *Report of the secretary's task force on youth suicide: Vol. 2. Risk factors for suicide* (DHHS Publication No. ADM 89-1622). Washington, DC: Government Printing Office.

Maris, R. (1985). The adolescent suicide problem. *Suicide and Life Threatening Behavior, 15*, 91–109.

Meehan, P. J., Lamb, J. A., Saltzman, L. S., & O'Carroll, P. (1990). Attempted suicide among young adults: Progress toward a meaningful estimate of prevalence. *American Journal of Psychiatry, 149*, 1, 41–44.

Orbach, I., Feshbach, S., Carlson, G., et al. (1983). Attraction and repulsion by life and death in suicidal and in normal children. *Journal of Consulting and Clinical Psychology, 51*, 661–670.

Pfeffer, C. R., Newcorn, J., Kaplan, G., Mizruchi, M. S., & Plutchick, R. (1988). Suicidal behavior in adolescent psychiatric patients. *Journal of the American Academy of Child and Adolescent Psychiatry, 27*, 357–361.

Phillips, D. P., & Carstensen, L. L. (1986). Clustering of teenage suicides after television news stories about suicide. *New England Journal of Medicine, 315*, 685–689.

Robins, L. N. (1989). In Alcohol, Drug Abuse and Mental Health Administration, *Report of the secretary's task force on youth suicide: Vol. 4. Strategies for the prevention of youth suicide* (DHHS Publication No. ADM 89-1624, pp. 94–114). Washington, DC: Government Printing Office.

Shaffer, D. (1974). Suicide in childhood and early adolescence. *Journal of Child Psychology and Psychiatry, 15*, 275–291.

Shaffer, D. (1988). The epidemiology of teen suicide: An examination of risk factors. *Journal of Clinical Psychiatry, 49*, 36–41.

Shaffer, D. (1993). Advances in youth suicide: Research update. *Lifesavers (Newsletter of the American Suicide Foundation), 5,* pp. 1, 3.

Shaffer, D., & Fisher, P. (1981). The epidemiology of suicide in children and young adolescents. *Journal of the American Academy of Child and Adolescent Psychiatry, 20,* 545–565.

Smith, K., & Crawford, S. (1986). Suicidal behavior among "normal" high school students. *Suicide and Life Threatening Behavior, 16,* 313–325.

22
Psychiatric Disorders In Medically Ill Children

D. Richard Martini
Patrick Burke

S ubstantial numbers of adolescents have a chronic illness. One recent
survey showed that 31.5% of 27.2 million adolescents had one or
more chronic disorders, 7% had at least two such conditions, and 3%
had three or more (Newachek, McManus, & Harriette, 1991). Adolescents
with chronic illnesses are at increased risk of psychological and behavioral
disorders compared to healthy controls (Pless & Roghmann, 1971). Cadman, Boyle, Szatrari, and Offord (1987) reported that children aged 4 to
16 years with a chronic illness were twice as likely as healthy controls to
have one or more psychiatric disorders. The risk was further increased—
particularly for neurosis, attention deficit hyperactivity disorder, and not
doing well at school—if the chronic illness was associated with disability.

Some risk factors have been identified. Weiland, Pless, and Roghmann
(1992) found an increased risk of behavior or emotional disorder in children with a "serious" chronic illness, especially if the disorder involved the
central nervous system. Earlier reports also implicated central nervous system involvement in increasing the risk of psychological disorder (Breslau,
1985, Pless & Roghmann, 1971). Newachek et al. (1991) observed that
the risk of disorder (e.g., depressed mood, antisocial behavior, hyperactivity, peer conflicts, social withdrawal) increased with the number of chronic
conditions. Gortmaker, Walker, Weitzman, and Sobol (1990) reported that
the increased risk of behavior problems was associated with the absence of
either biological parent, male gender, low income, low level of maternal
education, or young maternal age at childbirth. Among pediatric cancer
patients 15 years of age and younger with long-term survival, Mulhern,
Wasserman, Friedman, and Fairclough (1989) noted a rate of school difficulties and somatic complaints of unknown origin four times that of controls; functional impairments rather than cosmetic difficulties posed the
greater risk for psychiatric disorder.

Severity of illness has been an important element when considering the
development of emotional and behavioral problems; its role, however has

665

not been clearly defined. For example, young patients with severe chronic renal disease have an increased risk for psychiatric disorder when compared to children with moderate illness. Those patients with less physical disability, though, demonstrate higher rates of poor school adjustment (Garralda, Jameson, Reynolds, & Postlethwaite, 1988). The measurement of injury severity relative to psychiatric illness has not been standardized, and such measurements may refer to a single point in time or to a broad classification of lifetime illness.

The adolescent's emotional adjustment to medical illness is influenced by the nature of treatment. Invasive medical procedures, particularly when they occur repeatedly during single or multiple hospitalizations, may be accompanied by changes in behavior. Patients may become more oppositional and disruptive, or develop symptoms of mood and anxiety disorders. Occasionally adolescents are plagued by anticipatory or situational anxiety and suffer from a variety of somatic complaints, including headaches, nausea, vomiting, and recurrent pain. medications such as phenobarbital, steroids, and theophylline also may affect mood or behavior.

The perception of the illness by parents is of particular importance. Perrin, MacLean, and Perrin (1989) noted that when parents rated their child's illness as moderately severe as opposed to mild, patients tended to be less well-adjusted. Multiple factors enter into the parental response. Previous experience with medical illness, either personally or with other family members, can affect how the situation is interpreted. Of particular concern are those parents who have suffered significant losses or who have experienced adjustment disorders with emotional upset; these parents are more likely to experience psychiatric distress. Emotional responses also may be determined by severity of the illness, nature of the disease, extent of the disability, frequency of medical intervention, visibility of the illness, and characteristics of the social environment surrounding the child, including family psychiatric history, socioeconomic status, intelligence of the patient, and availability of social supports (Pless & Pinkerton, 1975).

Anxiety and Medical Illness

The causes of anxiety disorders in children with medical illness include situational, social, and biological factors. The concerns of adolescents focus on areas that parallel appropriate developmental milestones. For example, physical integrity is so important in this population that patients may be more concerned about changes in appearance that may result from treatment (e.g., chemotherapy) than the relative success of the intervention. Chronic illness and the demands of treatment occasionally lead adolescents to become dependent upon their parents, preventing normal emancipation. The resentment that develops may lead to a variety of acting-out behaviors, including noncompliance, sexual promiscuity, substance use, and suicidal behaviors. Loss of control is also a persistent fear among adolescents, and interventions require communication among family members as well as with the medical team. Adolescents do not want to be perceived as different from their peers, particularly as they form friendships and sexual relationships; as a result, medically ill adolescents may avoid peers or become noncompliant with treatment recommendations as a form of denial. The ability of the adolescent to understand the complexities of the diagnosis and the life-threatening nature of particular illnesses may further increase the risk of depression or suicidal behavior.

Noncompliance is perhaps the most troubling sign of psychiatric distress in the medically ill child and adolescent. Among girls, the high level of personal anxiety has been the strongest indicator of noncompliance (Lansky, Smith, Cairns, & Cairns, 1983). Although personal anxiety and anger improve compliance among boys, the obsessive-compulsive tendencies of parents also have led to high levels of compliance. This may reflect a belief that boys require a greater degree of parental supervision in medical settings. Noncompliance with treatment, though, may reflect not only individual psychopathology but family dynamics. Families may not appear regularly for appointments or may choose alternative treatment methods despite recommendations. Occasionally the parent and child may disagree on the most appropriate treatment course. Such disagreement will not only affect treatment decisions but create an atmosphere of escalating anxiety in the home.

Studies have begun to examine the base rate of anxiety disorders in medically ill patients. Garber, Zeman, and Walker (1990) studied the prevalence of emotional problems in a population of children and adolescents (aged 8 to 17) with recurrent abdominal pain. The sample included four patient groups: those with organic pathology, those with functional complaints, a control group of psychiatric patients without medical illness, and a group of healthy controls. The children and adolescents with abdominal pain had a high rate of anxiety disorder regardless of the presence of organic disease. Somatic complaints are included in the diagnostic criteria for overanxious disorder and separation anxiety disorder, and this factor may have increased the rate of diagnosis in the medically ill group. When the investigators excluded inquiries about somatic symptoms from the psychiatric assessment, the rates of disorder remained high. Anxiety disorder could not be used as a means of discriminating children with organic pathology from those with functional symptoms. The incidence as a consequence of, or in addition to, medical illness was comparable to the rate in children with concomitant somatoform disorder. In both situations, the problems may be secondary to the emotional distress that accompanies chronic illness (Vaillant, 1985).

Wasserman, Whitington, and Rivara (1988) studied children between the ages of 6 and 16 with recurrent abdominal pain; children with physical complaints were compared to a matched control group without disorder collected from the subjects' classrooms and pediatricians' offices. Children with abdominal pain had higher scores on the Internalizing scale of the Child Behavior Checklist (CBCL; Achenbach & Edelbrock, 1983) and were generally described as more fearful, inhibited, and overcontrolled. Interviews with recurrent abdominal pain patients revealed high levels of anxiety and depressive disorders, with significant rates of comorbidity. Seventy-one percent (71%) of these children frequently worried about their parents and 48% about themselves, rates twice that of controls. In 50% of these children, the psychiatric disorder developed in conjunction with abdominal complaints, indicating a relationship between disease and psychiatric outcome. The functional impact of abdominal pain was evident in the high school absentee rates in the group with recurrent physical complaints. The presence of an anxiety disorder diagnosis was not related to the age of the subject.

Family dynamics were pivotal factors in the abdominal pain group and in the development of anxiety disorders. In the Wasserman et al. study, 30% of the abdominal pain patients experienced the death or separation from a loved one, psychiatric hospitalization of a family member, or other family turmoil. Garber et al. (1990) examined the parent's assessment of the patient as a measure of family functioning. Mothers of children and adolescents with recurrent abdominal pain and psychiatric disorder reported higher internalizing scores on the Child Behavior Checklist that did mothers of either children with organic illness or normal controls. Mothers of recurrent abdominal patients and of psychiatric controls had higher levels of depression (as reported on the Family History Questionnaire) than mothers of healthy controls; the former also were more likely to describe their children as having been "sickly" most of their lives. Clearly the emotional state of the parent affects the adolescent's approach to the illness and may play a role in the choice of medical professionals and in treatment decisions (i.e., families may "doctor shop" for an opinion that conforms to parental expectations). Parents with a psychiatric disorder may also use the health care system as an emotional support in times of stress, choosing their child's illness as a means of entry. Genetic and environmental factors increase the likelihood that parents with a psychiatric disorder will have offspring with behavioral and emotional problems.

The relationship between anxiety symptoms and medical disorders is not well understood. Wells, Golding, and Burnam (1989) utilized the National Institute of Mental Health (NIMH) Epidemiologic Catchment Area (ECA) program to study the presence of medical and psychiatric disorders in an adult population. They noted that patients with a history of any psychiatric disorder (including affective, anxiety, or substance abuse) were more likely to have experienced a chronic medical condition than a comparison group without a positive psychiatric history. Patients with current medical disorders had more recent episodes of anxiety; however, the anxiety may have reflected the stress of dealing with a chronic medical disorder or may have predisposed the patient to medical illness. Wells et al. (1989) recommended that patients with histories of anxiety disorders be carefully screened for the presence of organic disease.

Panic Disorder and Medical Illness

Patients generally begin to experience symptoms of panic disorder between the ages of 17 and 30, with a mean age of approximately 22.5 years (Sheehan, Sheehan, & Minichiello, 1981). Many patients claim that the onset of the disorder was in their pubescent or prepubescent years. The psychodynamic formulation for panic symptoms focuses on the development of symptoms following separations or unpredictable and stressful life events that are beyond the individual's control and result in the loss of self-esteem (Katon, 1984; Roy-Byrne, Gerace, & Uhde, 1986). The positive family histories of anxiety and nervousness among panic patients (Noyes, Clancy, Crowe, Hoenk, & Slymen, 1978) suggest a genetic etiology for the disorder, a notion further supported by studies that demonstrated higher rates of panic in monozygotic twins than in dizygotic twins (Torgerson, 1983). Environmental factors also play a role in the appearance of panic symptoms. Adults with agoraphobia describe their parents as cold and distant and consider this history to be a significant factor in the development of their symptoms (Arrindel, Emmelkamp, Monsma, & Brilman, 1983; Parker, 1979; Silove, 1986). Patients who suffer from panic without agoraphobia have histories of familial dysfunction characterized by conflict, childhood conduct disorder, and truancy.

Panic may develop in conjunction with somatoform disorder. The symptoms of panic disorder include physiological complaints that frequently present in patients with a medical disorder as an exacerbation of their illness. This is particularly true in adults with asthma, diabetes, and angina (Katon & Roy-Byrne, 1989). In previous research with adults, the most common complaints of patients suffering from panic include cardiac symptoms (e.g., chest pains, tachycardia, and irregular heartbeat), gastrointestinal complaints (e.g., epigastric distress), and neurological problems (e.g., headaches, dizziness, vertigo, syncope, or periostosis; Katon, 1984). The overlap between somatization disorder and panic was clearly demonstrated in the NIMH ECA study (Boyd et al., 1984) which found that patients with somatization disorder were 90 times more likely to experience panic than other patients. In a similar study by Sheehan and Sheehan (1982), 71% of panic patients met criteria for somatization disorder. One explanation is that panic disorder increases the sensitivity of patients to physical complaints; they become more aware of their bodies, and their threshold for symptomatic illnesses is lower (Katon, 1984, 1986).

The combination of somatoform symptoms and other psychiatric disorders led Katon (1991) to categorize adult somatic patients into three groups. The first includes patients who have acute episodes in response to stress and suffer psychophysiological symptoms that include headaches, general intestinal distress, and sleep continuity disorders. The second group experiences somatic complaints in conjunction with preexisting depression and anxiety. In the third category, patients with somatic complaints also suffer from more complex psychiatric disorders, including personality problems, substance abuse, and recurrent mood disorders that are unresponsive to treatment. Panic may be a presentation in each of these categories.

Case reports of panic disorder in children and adolescents have described physiological symptoms similar to those noted in adults, including diaphoresis, dyspnea, tachycardia, chest pains, hot and cold flashes, choking, faintness, nausea, headaches, tremulousness, palpitations, and weakness (Moreau & Weissman, 1992). These symptoms are often accompanied by an intense anxiety and a recurrent fear of dying. The association between mitral valve prolapse and panic disorder noted in adults has not been well documented in the pediatric literature. Arkfen et al. (1990) noted a rate of only 4.2% among 813 children between the ages 9 and 14. No difference was noted in the anxiety scores on standardized instruments between those children with or without mitral valve prolapse.

When patients present with somatic complaints, referrals to mental health professionals usually follow either repeated unsuccessful efforts by the physician to address the physical complaints or the discovery of additional psychiatric disorders (e.g., school refusal, conduct disorder) that require treatment. Decisions on the extant of medical evaluations for young patients suspected of panic are often difficult. The clinician must balance the need to assess the presence of organic pathology with the fear of reinforcing psychiatric symptoms in the patient. Parents may consider the physical complaints to have only an organic basis and believe that psychiatric intervention will somehow invalidate the child's symptoms. A thorough medical evaluation should precede assumptions that somatic complaints are part of a panic disorder; this will allow the patient, family, and physician to address psychological factors in the presentation more comfortably. Assessment of these young patients may be helped or hindered by the fact that a multigenerational family history of panic disorder is common.

Panic disorder is associated with a wide range of medical diagnoses. Higher rates of peptic ulcer disease and hypertension have been documented in adult patients (Katon, 1986), and anxiety symptoms will occasionally develop as a complication of insulin use. The list of medical disorders that mimic panic is extensive and includes the following: cardiac arrhythmia, cardiomyopathy, Cushing's syndrome, hyperparathyroidism, hyperthyroidism, hypoglycemia, hypothyroidism, mitral valve prolapse, pheochromocytoma, temporal lobe epilepsy, and vertigo (Katon, 1991). Pheochromocytoma rarely occurs in children and is usually found in cases with a positive family history and a history of multiple endocrine adenomas. In addition, these patients may suffer from neurofibromatosis, panic attacks with throbbing headaches, hyper- or hypotension, tachycardia, or abdominal mass.

Temporal lobe epilepsy and panic disorder share a number of common features. The events occur intermittently and without warning and are accompanied by a number of physiological symptoms such as diaphoresis, flushing, hyperventilation, and tachycardia. The neurological phenomenon associated with temporal lobe epilepsy (e.g., loss of consciousness, progressive seizures, semipurposeful movements and hallucinations) distinguish these episodes from panic (Raj and Sheehan, 1987). Patients with panic attacks will generally be euthyroid, although occasionally laboratory values will be mildly abnormal due to increased central adrenergic activity in cases of psychiatric illness. When hypoglycemic episodes have been induced in patients who suffer from panic attacks, the subjects describe the symptoms of tachycardia, lightheadedness, sweating, and anxiety (as distinct from panic).

The relationships between medical illness and anxiety disorder has been described in the DSM-IV under the diagnosis "anxiety disorder due to a general medical condition." Patients with this diagnosis may experience generalized anxiety, panic attacks, or symptoms of obsessive-compulsive disorder. The medical condition must be etiologically related to the development of psychiatric symptoms, and the patient should not be suffering from another psychiatric disorder that could account for the anxiety symptoms. As with other psychiatric diagnoses, the presentation should be characterized by deficits in social, occupational, or educational skills (American Psychiatric Association, 1993).

Situational Anxiety and Medical Illness

Adolescents may develop situational anxiety or panic after experiencing painful procedures. This has been noted in studies following bone marrow aspirations and spinal taps;the response of the patient is not only tearfulness and distress, but occasionally physical aggression that may prevent completion of necessary medical procedures. Parents and medical professionals may further complicate the situation by becoming impatient or overly sensitive to the child's agitation. Worschel, Copeland, and Barker (1987) investigated the emotional adjustment of pediatric oncology patients (aged 6 to 17) treated on both inpatient and outpatient units. The authors noted that children and adolescents were not adept at using cognitive skills to protect themselves from emotional upset, in part due to the lack of explanations that appropriately targeted the developmental level of the patients. Worschel et al. emphasizes that the quality of the information provided to the child was more important than its quantity in eventual illness adjustment.

Studies of adult cancer patients have shown that earlier traumatic experiences are important determinants in the development of anxiety disorders with medical procedures (Raskin, Peeke, Dickman, & Pisker, 1982). A history of poor adjustment to earlier medical illness may also predispose an adolescent to psychiatric disorder. Such a presentation suggests a need to work aggressively to comfort the young patient early in the treatment process in order to produce a better outcome.

Family patterns may support and reinforce development of anxiety symptoms in the adolescent. When the families of pediatric cancer patients were studied, those that were enmeshed tended to respond to acute stress by becoming more anxious, irritable, confrontational, or withdrawn (Lansky & Gendel, 1978). The young patient is likely to become even more regressed in these circumstances, leading to more dependence, less compliance, and increased agitation. Such situations should be identified early in the course of treatment, and mental health intervention (including family therapy) should be initiated as soon as possible. Young patients who develop adequate coping strategies throughout life tend to be better adjusted to the stresses of chronic illness (Koocher & O'Malley, 1981). The development of coping strategies, however, depends on the age of the patient; adolescents have more cognitive and communicative skills and tend to respond better than their younger counterparts. Use of constructive cognitive strategies also is an important outcome factor in parental adjustment.

Occasionally, as a sign of poor adaptation to medical illness, the pediatric patient will develop symptoms of school phobia. This disorder, when evident in pediatric cancer patients, has been particularly difficult to treat. A regressive and overdependent relationship may develop between parents and patient, requiring family as well as individual therapy (Lansky, Lowman, Vats, & Gyulay, 1975). The physician and family should encourage a level of activity that is as routine as possible for the child. This includes regular school attendance, age-appropriate activities, and family functions.

Posttraumatic Stress Disorder and Medical Illness

Increasing attention has been directed to the reactions of children to severe physical and emotional stress as a consequence of incest, child abuse, physical injury and violence. One of these reactions is the development of posttraumatic stress disorder (PTSD). Using DSM-III-R (APA, 1987) criteria for

PTSD in adults, one can define a "stressor" as a sudden, unexpected event, unique in the victim's experience, that threatens the physical and psychological integrity of the individual or of a major attachment figure. The stressor may isolate a victim from others, or mislead the person about important life circumstances. The event should be real, not imagined, and can take place when the person is alone or in the company of others (Casey, Ludwig, & McCormick, 1986). Acute medical disorders certainly meet these criteria. Chronic medical illness also may lead to the development of PTSD as a result of recurrent inpatient hospitalization, invasive procedures, treatment side effects, and consequences of the disease itself.

The emotional impact of physical injury may also depend on the subjective impressions of the victim. Feinstein and Dolan (1992) studied patients between the ages of 15 and 60 who required admission to an orthopedic ward for surgical correction of a mild injury. Subjects were initially seen 6 weeks after the trauma and followed for 6 months. At the conclusion of the investigation, 16% of the patients met diagnostic criteria for PTSD, compared to incidences of PTSD of 1% in the general population and 3.5% among subjects exposed to physical attack (Pynoos et al., 1987). Extent of injury did not determine psychological adjustment, nor did the presence of premorbid personality traits or disorders. Among the most important risk factors for the presence of a psychiatric disorder (including PTSD) was the initial perception of the accident as stressful; results suggested that subjective factors should be included in the pathogenesis of PTSD.

Few studies have examined the development of PTSD in pediatric populations. Basson et al. (1991) examined the emotional reactions of children aged 18 and younger who had experienced a physical trauma, with categories divided according to the presence of head injury. The control group consisted of patients who had undergone an emergency appendectomy; there were many more boys in the trauma group than in the control group. The project was based on a review of hospital records and the follow-up of those patients who met the criteria for inclusion 2 to 6 years after injury. The patients showed a high level of psychiatric disorder; moreover, 30% of the traumatized children without head injury and 48% of the head-injured children had behavioral changes, based on parental report. No statistically significant difference between the trauma groups existed, however, indicating that factors other than nature of the trauma were determinants.

A propensity for injury has been noted in children with a variety of environmental and behavioral stressors. Family illness, unemployment, low socioeconomic status, negative parental impressions of medical services, premorbid psychiatric illness, and maternal psychiatric disorder have been described as risk factors for injury in the pediatric population. These factors may also predispose a child to posttraumatic adjustment problems (Dikmen, Temkin, & Armsden, 1989; Horwitz, Morgenstern, DiPietro, & Morrison, 1988).

Burn patients have been studied more frequently than other trauma groups, perhaps because of the dramatic nature of the injury and the demanding treatment programs that follow the trauma. Stoddard, Norman, and Murphy (1989) examined 30 children (aged 7 to 19) who had experienced a severe burn requiring reconstructive surgery. The assessments were completed more than 6 months after the burn; only 65% of all possible subjects participated, and the rejections included 3 children with documented depression. Nearly 27% of the sample had either a full or a partial diagnosis of PTSD. The sample had a particularly high level of anxiety disorders, including phobias and overanxious disorders. Extent of injury was a factor in the development of psychiatric disorder: children with larger burns (in terms of percentage of body area) and/or more severe disfigurement, as well as those of lower socioeconomic class and with histories of family turmoil were more likely to suffer PTSD. The multiple medical procedures involved in treating burn patients may complicate the presentation.

Treatment

Behavioral therapies have been tested in children with fears and phobias related to medical and dental procedures. Among the most successful treatments are the classical conditioning techniques of systematic desensitization, implosion, flooding, and modeling. Positive reinforcement has been effective in encouraging children to comply with required medical and social activities and to develop appropriate behavior. These interventions, though, require the child's participation in order to better identify those reinforcers that will guarantee a response. Use of negative consequences in this context is usually discouraged by behavioral psychologists but may be selectively applied when absolutely necessary; the recommendation is for a loss of privilege or some other mild punishment.

Pain management in the face of medical procedures is occasionally maintained through attentional distraction. No systematic investigation of this method has been attempted; however, it has been effective in the control of nausea and vomiting in cancer patients, as well as in cases of pain control. Use of emotive imagery has relieved anxiety in young patients, most effectively in instances when the fears are irrational and not related to averse circumstances. The patient may become desensitized when the cause of the anxiety recurs, as in the case of medical procedures. Hypnosis also distracts the patient and relieves anxiety in those patients who are responsive.

When symptoms become severe and of panic proportions, medication is recommended. Pharmacological interventions have been limited to the use of tricyclic antidepressants, flouoxetine, alprazolam, lorazepam, and clonazepam. Diphenhydramine has been recommended as a means of sedation, and diazepam and alprazolam (0.02 mg/kg/tid) have been effective in relieving the anticipatory anxiety in children undergoing procedures. When the anxiety becomes chronic, trials of antidepressant medications are indicated; imipramine and amitriptyline have been utilized in cases when persistent anxiety is accompanied by symptoms of depression. Pharmacological interventions for adolescents experiencing panic disorder have not been tested in controlled studies, although tricyclic antidepressants and benzodiazepines have been mentioned in case reports as being effective (Pfefferbaum-Levine, Kumor, Cangir, Choroszy, & Roseberry, 1983).

Family therapy may be an essential component of the treatment plan in chronically ill adolescents. Families can become dysfunctional as patients withdraw and regress; parents may respond by becoming overprotective, intense, and occasionally hostile toward their child. Therapy attempts to decrease the intensity of the relationship between parent and patient while avoiding a defensive reaction among family members that may draw them closer together. Essential in this process is the recommendation that the adolescent maintain as many age-appropriate activities as possible (e.g., school attendance).

Depression and Medical Illness

Symptoms of depression can be associated with a wide variety of medical conditions, including endocrine disorders, electrolyte disturbances, central nervous system (CNS) disorders, and numerous systemic diseases and nutritional deficiencies (Hall, 1980; Whitlock, 1982). Moreover, depression has detrimental effects on the course and outcome of illness (Keitner, Ryan, Miller, Kohn, & Epstein, 1991). Despite the widespread attention given to depression in adults with medical illness (see Rodin & Voshart, 1986), however, few investigations have examined depression in physically ill adolescents. Progress in this area has been limited in part by significant methodological problems. In addition, many of the medical conditions classically associated with depression in adults are less common in adolescents and thus would require multicenter studies.

Diagnosis of Depression

Periods of sadness, irritability, or unhappiness commonly occur in adolescents over the course of an illness, but these are not necessarily synonymous with depression. In DSM-III-R (APA, 1987), the two principal depressive disorders are major depression and dysthymia. To meet criteria for a major depressive episode, the adolescent must experience at least five of nine symptoms during the same 2-week period; at least one of the symptoms must be either anhedonia or depressed or irritable mood. Symptoms must also represent a change from previous functioning. Among the remaining manifestations are a variety of somatic and psychological symptoms: change in weight or appetite, insomnia or hypersomnia, psychomotor agitation or retardation, fatigue or loss of energy, feelings of worthlessness or guilt, impaired ability to think or concentrate, recurrent thoughts of death, and recurrent suicidal ideation or a suicide attempt with or without a specific plan. An important point is that symptoms clearly due to a physical condition are not to be included; however, it is not stated how decisions concerning particular signs or symptoms are to be made.

Dysthymia in adolescents refers to depressed or irritable mood present for at least 1 year in association with some of the symptoms of major depression. Symptoms must be present most of the day, more days than not, and without a symptom-free period lasting longer than two months. Demoralization (i.e., a sense of helplessness or powerlessness in the face of stress, Stoudemire, 1989) may be difficult to distinguish from dysthymia.

When a specific organic factor is associated with prominent and persistent depressed mood, a diagnosis of organic mood syndrome can be made. Associated features can include tearfulness, anxiety, irritability, brooding, excessive somatic concerns, panic attacks, suspiciousness, or an unhappy appearance. The distinction between major depression and organic mood syndrome, however, has been questioned. Fogel (1990) argues that excluding causal organic factors in the diagnosis of major depression may be unreliable and invalid because of (a) a lack of operational specificity, (b) a lack of rules to weight various causal factors, (c) arbitrary distinctions between causal and contributory organic factors, (d) instability of the diagnosis of organic mood syndrome over time, and (e) poor correlation of clinical indices of CNS involvement with neurodiagnostic tests. Other possible diagnoses include depressive disorder not otherwise specified (when insufficient symptoms are present to meet criteria for other diagnoses) and adjustment disorder with depressed mood (when depressed mood is associated with identifiable stresses). The distinction between adjustment disorder with depressed mood and organic mood syndrome may be difficult to make if other stressors (e.g., recent change in school, parental conflict) are present.

The proposed DSM-IV (APA, 1993) includes a new category of "mood disorder due to a general medical condition." This diagnosis is characterized by a persistent or prominent disturbance of mood judged to be etiologically related to a medical condition and associated with impairment of function. Again, guidelines are not offered to indicate how etiologic inferences can be made. The diagnosis of organic mood syndrome in DSM-II-R is reflected in DSM-IV as "substance-induced mood disorder." This diagnosis is to be used when depressed mood can be directly attributed to substance intoxication or withdrawal.

The frequent overlap in symptoms between depression and medical illness (e.g., changes in appetite or weight, fatigue) presents a crucial difficulty. Cohen-Cole and Stoudemire (1987) discuss four approaches to this problem: all pertinent somatic symptoms may be counted toward depression regardless of etiology (inclusive approach); only symptoms that cannot be attributed to the illness are counted (etiological approach), psychological symptoms may be substituted in place of somatic symptoms (substitutive approach); or somatic symptoms are not considered (exclusive approach). Each of these approaches presents some difficulty. If all symptoms are counted regardless of etiology, symptom overlap will result in increased sensitivity, however, specificity will be lowered because of the inclusion of false positives. When etiologic inferences are made, interrater reliability is likely to be low because the criteria for making references are not specified. The exclusive approach will decrease false positives; but some truly depressed individuals may be excluded. Cohen-Cole and Stoudemire (1987) suggest that the exclusive approach be employed for research and that the inclusive approach be used for clinical purposes.

Recent studies, however, suggest that somatic symptoms may not be an important confound and may not radically influence diagnosis. For example, Kathol, Mutgi, Williams, Clamon, and Noyes (1990) reported that somatic symptoms were less successful than psychological symptoms in discriminating depression according to diagnostic criteria in cancer patients. In addition, Frank et al. (1992) were able to identify a core factor consisting of cognitive and affective symptoms across two physically ill groups and two nonpatient groups, suggesting that somatic symptoms may be less important to the diagnosis of depression in medically ill groups. Heiligenstein and Jacobsen (1988) found that eliminating the somatic items from the Children's Depression Rating Scale (CDRS-R; Poznanski, Freeman, & Mokros, 1985) did not significantly change the correlation of the score with clinical judgment of depression in children and adolescents with cancer.

Assessment of Depression

The diagnosis of depression is primarily made on the basis of clinical interviews, although self-support rating scales have been utilized for this purpose. A number of clinical interviews and rating scales have been developed for use with adolescents (see Costello, 1986; Kazdin & Petti, 1987; Strober & Werry, 1986). Semistructured interviews combine flexibility in how signs and symptoms are explored while requiring that a basic schema be followed. In contrast, structured interviews limit flexibility and require the interviewer to ask questions as they are written. The Kiddie Schedule for Affective Disorders and Schizophrenia (K-SADS; Chambers et al., 1985) is the most widely used semistructured interview for depression in children and adolescents; the parent and child are interviewed separately, and a summary judgment is made based on the two interviews. An epidemiological version (K-SADS-E) covering past episodes of depression is also available (Orvaschel, Puig-Antich, Chambers, Tabrizi, & Johnson, 1982). The Interview Schedule for Children (ISC; Kovacs, 1985) is a semi-structured interview covering a broader range of psychopathology. Among the structured interviews are the Diagnostic Interview for Children and Adolescents (DICA; Herjanic & Reich, 1982), and the Diagnostic Interview Schedule for Children (DISC; Costello, Edelbrock, Dulcan, Kalas, & Klaric, 1984).

A number of rating scales are available. Clinician-rated scales include the CDRS (Poznanski et al., 1985), the Bellevue Index of Depression (BID; Petti, 1978), and the Children's Affective Rating Scale (CARS; McKnew, Cytryn, Efron, Gershon, & Bunney, 1979). Relatively little attention, however, has been paid to the psychometric properties of these instruments (Strober & Werry, 1986). Among self-report scales, the Children's Depression Inventory (CDI; Kovacs, 1981) is the most widely used, and reasonable data on psychometric properties are available (Costello, 1986).

Kathol, Mutgi, Williams et al. (1990) found that rating scales did not discriminate adult cancer patients with major depression from patients with depressive symptoms except when patients received high scores. Rating scales thus may be more useful as screening devices and indicators of symptom severity rather than for diagnostic purposes. Kathol, Noyes, Williams et al. (1990) showed that while low scores on a rating scale consistently predict that a patient will not be clinically depressed, substantial proportions of patients scoring above scale cutoffs were not clinically depressed. In addition, the predictive value of the scales were not significantly altered if only psychological items were used.

Prevalence of Depression in Chronically Ill Adolescents

Studies of depression in pediatrically ill groups have typically included wide age ranges, small samples, and inadequate controls. Prevalence levels of depression have ranged from 10% to 30% (Burke et al., 1989; Kashani & Hakami, 1982; Kashani, Lahabidi, & Jones, 1982) and thus are substantially different from adult levels. In a 6-year follow-up of 95 children evaluated at the time of initial diagnosis of diabetes, Marsh, Goldston, and Kovacs (1988) reported that 13% of subjects had developed depression or dysthymia by adolescence.

Determinants of Depression

Some studies suggest that risk for depression increases with age (Kashani & Hakami, 1982; Rait, Jacobsen, Lederberg, & Holland, 1988; Viney & Westbrook, 1985), or develops later in the course of illness (Garralda et al., 1988). Currently available data, though, do not allow confounding of age and duration of illness to be separated. Data on sex differences are limited and inconsistent (Burke et al., 1989; Kashani & Hakami, 1982).

Investigations examining the relationship of depression to clinical aspects of illness also are limited. In a few studies, depression or psychiatric functioning was not significantly correlated with medical variables (Garralda et al., 1988; Kaplan, Busner, Weinhold, & Lenon, 1987; Kashani, Konig, Shepperd, Wifley, & Morris, 1988; Kashani, Venzke, & Millar, 1981; Wood et al., 1987). Methodological problems in defining and measuring severity of illness, as well as a lack of prospective or concurrent measurements of illness and depression, obfuscate interpretation of available data. In a small sample of newly diagnosed patients with inflammatory bowel disease, depression was associated with less severe illness (Burke, Kocoshis, Chandra, Whiteway, & Sauer, 1990).

Symptoms developing early in the course of illness may be important predictors of later problems. Marsh et al. (1988) found that children who were given a psychiatric diagnosis during the first 3 months of diabetes were more likely to become depressed by adolescence.

Not surprisingly, family histories of depression (Burke et al., 1990; Kashani, Barbero, & Bolander, 1981; Kashani, Venzke, & Millar, 1981), and stressful life events (Burke et al., 1990; Kashani, Venzke, & Millar, 1981) are associated with depression. Although Kaplan et al. (1987) found that BDI scores were highly correlated with stressful life events in adolescents with cancer, however, a cross-lag panel analysis indicated the relationship was not causal.

Treatment

Successful management and treatment of the underlying disease will often result in remission of dysphoria and other depressive symptoms. Supportive therapy may be required, though, as depressive symptoms sometimes persist after an organic cause has been alleviated. Use of medications to treat depression in the medically ill presents may difficulties including side effects and drug interactions (see reviews by Stoudemire, Fogel, & Gulley, 1991; Stoudemire, Moran, & Fogel, 1990). Research suggests that antidepressants are not superior to placebo in treating depressed physically healthy adolescents (Ryan, 1990); these investigations include double-blind placebo-controlled studies of amitriptyline (Kramer & Feiguine, 1981) and nortriptyline (Geller et al., 1992) and open-label studies of imipramine (Ryan et al., 1986; Strober, Freeman, & Rigali, 1990). Although Pfefferbaum-Levine et al. (1983) reported clinical improvement in a small series of children and adolescents with cancer given low doses of tricyclic antidepressants, there are no systematic studies of the pharmacological treatment of depression in medically ill adolescents. Pfefferbaum (1991) has suggested that stimulants be used in depressed medically ill children, a strategy that has shown some success in adults. Potential advantages include a rapid onset of action and relative lack of serious side effects.

There is a long history of family-based interventions with medically ill adolescents. Early models stressed pathogenic processes in the family that led to dysfunction or somatic responses in the adolescent. Jacobs (1991) has described more recent models that view the illness as a stressor eliciting responses of varying degrees of competence in family members. This approach has led to structured, psychoeducationally based family interventions that have shown some success in helping adolescents and their families cope with illness (Jacobs, 1991). The potential exists to extend this model to the treatment of depression concurrent with illness.

Two widely used forms of psychotherapy for depression are cognitive therapy (Haaga & Beck, 1992) and interpersonal psychotherapy (Klerman & Weissman, 1992). Interpersonal psychotherapy is a brief, time-limited therapy based on the premise that depression occurs in the context of interpersonal relationships; it has been adapted to address developmental challenges facing adolescents (Moreau et al., 1991). These challenges overlap with issues confronting adolescents who become ill (e.g., separation from parents, relationships with members of the opposite sex, autonomy) and thus this therapy would seem appropriate to be adapted for the treatment of depression in medically ill adolescents. Cognitive therapy focuses on specific cognitive aspects of depression and teaches patients to develop alternative beliefs and assumptions using behavioral and verbal procedures; an adaptation of this therapy for use with adolescents has been described by Wilkes and Rush (1988). Since adolescents use problem-based as well as emotion-based coping strategies (Compas, Malcarne, & Fondacaro, 1988), cognitive therapy also appears suited to the treatment of depression in this population. The effectiveness of these modalities in adolescents, however, has yet to be empirically determined.

Summary

Medical illness increases the risk for psychiatric disorder in both adolescents and adults. Psychiatric symptoms may develop as: (a) a consequence of disease, (b) a by-product of treatment, or (c) an extension of the dependency and emotional distress that often accompanies physical disability. The challenge in assessing and treating these patients is acquiring the ability to distinguish aspects of a case that are related to the disease from those that reflect psychological difficulty. The clinician should build collaborative relationships with medical personnel who are treating the patient, and he or she should encourage a free exchange of information. This aids the mental health professional in gauging the role of the medical illness in the patient's presentation. Cooperation between services will also serve to educate medical and surgical staff as to the role of psychiatric illness in the child's prognosis. Development of affective and anxiety disorders in response to physical disease is not part of expected adjustment. These problems should be aggressively treated in order to avoid increasing problems with compliance, greater risk of medical complications, and increasing disability.

References

Achenbach, T. M., & Edelbrock, C. (1983). *Manual for the Child Behavior Checklist and revised Child Behavior Profile.* Burlington: University of Vermont, Department of Psychiatry.

Arkfen, C. L., Lachman, A. S., McLaren, M. J., Schulman, P., Leach, C. N., & Farmish, G. C. M. (1990). Mitral valve prolapse: Associations with symptoms and anxiety. *Pediatrics, 85,* 311–315.

American Psychiatric Association. (1987). *Diagnostic and statistical manual of mental disorders* (rev. 3rd ed.). Washington, DC: Author.

American Psychiatric Association. (1993). *DSM-IV draft criteria.* Washington, DC: Author.

Arrindel, W. A., Emmelkamp, P. K. G., Monsma, A., & Brilman, E. (1983). The role of perceived parental rearing practices in the etiology of phobic disorders: A controlled study. *British Journal of Psychiatry, 143,* 183–187.

Basson, M. D., Guinn, J. R. E., McElligott, J., Vitale, R., Brown, W., & Fielding, L. P. (1991). Behavioral disturbances in children after trauma. *Journal of Trauma, 31,* 1363–1368.

Boyd, J. H., Burke, J. D., Gruenberg, E., Holzer, C. E., Rae, D. S., George, L. K., Darno, M., Stolzman, R., McEvoy, L., & Nestadt, G. (1984). Exclusion criteria of DSM-III. *Archives of General Psychiatry, 41,* 983–989.

Breslau, N. (1985). Psychiatric disorders in children with physical disabilities. *Journal of the American Academy of Child and Adolescent Psychiatry, 24,* 87–94.

Burke, P. M., Meyer, V., Kocoshis, S. A., Orenstein, D. M., Chandra, R., Nord, D. J., Sauer, J., & Cohen, E. (1989). Depression and anxiety in pediatric inflammatory bowel disease. *Journal of the American Academy of Child and Adolescent Psychiatry, 28,* 948–951.

Burke, P. M., Kocoshis, S. A., Chandra, R., Whiteway, M., & Sauer, J. (1990). Determinants of depression in recent onset pediatric inflammatory bowel disease. *Journal of the American Academy of Child and Adolescent Psychiatry, 29,* 608–610.

Cadman, D., Boyle, M., Szatmari, P., & Offord, D. R. (1987). Chronic illness, disability, and mental and social well-being: Findings of the Ontario Child Health Study. *Pediatrics, 79,* 805–813.

Casey, R., Ludwig, S., & McCormick, M. C. (1986). Morbidity following minor head trauma in children. *Pediatrics, 78,* 497–502.

Chambers, W. J., Puig-Antich, J., Hirsch, M., Paez, P., Ambrosini, P., Tabrizi, M. A., & Davies, M. (1985). The assessment of affective disorders in children and adolescents by semistructured interview. *Archives of General Psychiatry, 42,* 697–702.

Cohen-Cole, S. A., & Stoudemire, A. (1987). Major depression and physical illness. *Psychiatric Clinics of North America, 10,* 1–17.

Compas, B. E., Malcarne, V. L., & Fondacaro, K. M. (1988). Coping with stressful events in older children and young adolescents. *Journal of Consulting and Clinical Psychology, 56,* 405–411.

Costello, A. J. (1986). Assessment and diagnosis of affective disorders in children. *Journal of Child Psychology and Psychiatry, 27,* 563–574.

Costello, A. J., Edelbrock, C., Dulcan, M. K., Kalas, R., & Klaric, S. H. (1984). *Report to the National Institutes of Mental Health on the NIMH Diagnostic Interview Schedule for Children.* Bethesda, MD: National Institutes of Mental Health.

Dikmen, S. S., Temkin, N., & Armsden, G. (1989). Neuropsychological recovery: Relationship to psychosocial functioning and postconcussional complaints. In H. S. Levin, H. M. Eisenberg, & A. L. Benton (Eds.), *Mild head injury.* New York: Oxford University Press.

Feinstein, A., & Dolan, R. (1992). Predictors of post-traumatic stress disorder following physical trauma: An examination of the stressor criterion. *Psychological Medicine, 21,* 85–91.

Fogel, B. S. (1990). Major depression versus organic mood disorder: A questionable distinction. *Journal of Clinical Psychiatry, 51,* 53–56.

Frank, R. G., Chaney, J. M., Clay, D. L., Shutty, M. S., Beck, N. C., Kay, D. R., Elliott, T. R., & Grambling, S. (1992). Dysphoria: A major symptom factor in persons with disability or chronic illness. *Psychiatry Research, 43,* 231–241.

Garber, J., Zeman, J., & Walker, L. S. (1990). Recurrent abdominal pain in children: Psychiatric diagnoses and parental psychopathology. *Journal of the American Academy of Child and Adolescent Psychiatry, 29,* 648–656.

Garralda, M. E., Jameson, R. A., Reynolds, J. M., & Postlethwaite, J. R. (1988). Psychiatric adjustment in children with chronic renal failure. *Journal of Child Psychology and Psychiatry, 29,* 79–90.

Geller, B., Cooper, T. B., Graham, D. L., Fetner, H. H., Marsteller, F. A., & Wells, J. M. (1992). Pharmacokinetically designed double-blind placebo-controlled study of nortriptyline in 6- to 12-year-olds with major depressive disorder. *Journal of the American Academy of Child and Adolescent Psychiatry, 31,* 34–44.

Gortmaker, S. L., Walker, D. K., Weitzman, M., & Sobol, A. M. (1990). Chronic conditions, socioeconomic risks, and behavioral problems, in children and adolescents. *Pediatrics, 85,* 267–276.

Haaga, D. A. F., & Beck, A. T. (1992). Cognitive therapy. In E. S. Paykel (Ed.), *Handbook of affective disorders* (2nd ed., pp. 511–523). London: Churchill Livingstone.

Hall, R. C. W. (Ed.). (1980). *Psychiatric presentations of medical illness: Somatopsychic disorders.* New York: Pergamon.

Heiligenstein, E., & Jacobsen, P. B. (1988). Differentiating depression in medically ill children and adolescents. *Journal of the American Academy of Child and Adolescent Psychiatry, 27,* 716–719.

Herjanic, B., & Reich, W. (1982). Development of a structured interview for children—agreement between child and parent on individual symptoms. *Journal of Abnormal Child Psychology, 5,* 127–134.

Horwitz, S. M., Morgenstern, H., DiPietro, L., & Morrison, C. L. (1988). Determinants of pediatric injuries. *American Journal of Diseases in Children, 142,* 605–611.

Jacobs, J. (1991). Family therapy in the context of childhood medical illness. In A. Stoudemire & B. S. Fogel (Eds.), *Medical psychiatric practice* (Vol. 1, pp. 483–506). Washington, DC: American Psychiatric Press.

Kaplan, S. L., Busner, J., Weinhold, C., & Lenon, P. (1987). Depressive symptoms in children and adolescents with cancer: A longitudinal study. *Journal of the American Academy of Child and Adolescent Psychiatry, 26,* 782–787.

Kashani, J. H., Barbero, G. J., & Bolander, F. (1981). Depression in hospitalized pediatric patients. *Journal of the American Academy of Child Psychiatry, 15,* 123–134.

Kashani, J. H., & Hakami, N. (1982). Depression in children and adolescents with malignancy. *Canadian Journal of Psychiatry, 27,* 474–477.

Kashani, J. H., Konig, P., Shepperd, J. A., Wifley, D., & Morris, D. A. (1988). Psychopathology and self-concept in asthmatic children. *Journal of Pediatric Psychology, 13,* 509–520.

Kashani, J. H., Lahabidi, Z., & Jones, R. (1982). Depression in children and adolescents with cardio-vascular symptomology. *Journal of the American Academy of Child Psychiatry, 21,* 187–189.

Kashani, J. H., Venzke, R., & Millar, E. A. (1981). Depression in children admitted to hospital for orthopedic procedures. *British Journal of Psychiatry, 138,* 21–25.

Kathol, R. G., Mutgi, A., Williams, J., Clamon, G., & Noyes, R., Jr. (1990). Diagnosis of major depression in cancer patients. *American Journal of Psychiatry, 147,* 1021–1024.

Kathol, R. G., Noyes, R., Jr., Williams, J., Mutgi, A., Carrol, B., & Perry, P. (1990). Diagnosing depression inpatients with medical illness. *Psychosomatics, 31,* 434–440.

Katon, W. (1984). Panic disorder and somatization: A review of 55 cases. *American Journal of Medicine, 77,* 101–106.

Katon, W. (1986). Panic disorder: Epidemiology, diagnosis and treatment. *Journal of CLinical Psychiatry, 47,* 21–27.

Katon, W., & Roy-Byrne, P. P. (1989). Panic disorder in the medically ill. *Journal of Clinical Psychiatry, 50,* 299–302.

Katon, W. (1991). *Panic disorder in the medical setting.* Washington, DC: American Psychiatric Press.

Kazdin, A. E., & Petti, T. A. (1987). Self-report and interview measures of childhood and adolescent depression. *Journal of Child Psychology and Psychiatry, 23,* 437–457.

Keitner, G. I., Ryan, C. E., Miller, I. W., Kohn, R., & Epstein, N. B. (1991). Twelve-month outcome of patients with major depression and comorbid psychiatric and medical illness (compound depression). *American Journal of Psychiatry, 148,* 345–350.

Klerman, G. L., & Weissman, M. M. (1992). Interpersonal psychotherapy. In E. S. Paykel (Ed.), Handbook of affective disorders (2nd ed., pp. 501–510). London: Churchill Livingstone.

Koocher, G. P., & O'Malley, J. E. (1981). The Domacles syndrome. New York: McGraw-Hill.

Kovacs, M. (1981). Rating scales to assess depression in school-aged children. Acta Paedopsychiatrica, 46, 305–315.

Kovacs, M. (1985). ISC (The Interview Schedule for Children). Psychopharmacology Bulletin, 21, 991–994.

Kramer, A. D., & Feiguine, R. J. (1981). Clinical effects of amitriptyline in adolescent depression: A pilot study. Journal of the American Academy of Child and Adolescent Psychiatry, 20, 636–644.

Lansky, S. B., & Gendel, M. (1978). Symbiotic regressive behavior patterns in children malignancy. Clinical Pediatrics, 17, 133–138.

Lansky, S. B., Lowman, J. T., Vats, T., & Gyulay, J. (1975). School phobia in children with malignant neoplasms. American Journal of Disorders in Children, 129, 42–46.

Marsh, J., Goldston, D., & Kovacs, M. (1988). Psychiatric morbidity in children with insulin-dependent diabetes mellitus: A follow-up. Paper presented at the annual meeting of the American Academy of Child and Adolescent Psychiatry, Seattle, WA.

McKnew, D. H., Cytryn, L., Efron, A. M., Gershon, E. S., & Bunney, W. E. (1979). Offspring of patients with affective disorders. British Journal of Psychiatry, 134, 148–152.

Moreau, D., & Weissman, M. M. (1992). Panic disorder in children and adolescents: A review. American Journal of Psychiatry, 149, 1306–1314.

Mulhern, R. K., Wasserman, A. L. Friedman, A. G., & Fairclough, D. (1989). Social competence and behavioral adjustment of children who are long-term survivors of cancer. Pediatrics, 83, 18–25.

Newachek, P. W., McManus, M. A. & Harriette, B. F. (1991). Prevalence and impact of chronic illness among adolescents.

Noyes, R., Clancy, J., Crowe, R., Hoenk, P. P., & Slymen, D. J. (1978). The familial prevalence of anxiety neurosis. Archives of General Psychiatry, 35, 1057–1059.

Orvaschel, H., Puig-Antich, J., Chambers, W., Tabrizi, M. A., & Johnson, R. (1982). Retrospective assessment of prepubertal major depression with Kiddie-SADS-E. Journal of the American Academy of Child Psychiatry, 4, 392–397.

Parker, G. (1979). Reported parental characteristics of agoraphobics and social phobics. British Journal of Psychiatry, 135, 555–560.

Perrin, J. M., MacLean, W. E., & Perrin, E. C. (1989). Parental perceptions of health status and psychologic adjustment of children with asthma. Pediatrics, 83, 26–30.

Petti, T. A. (1978). Depression in hospitalized child psychiatry patients: Approaches to measuring depression. Journal of the American Academy of Child Psychiatry, 17, 49–59.

Pfefferbaum, B. (1991). Psychopharmacology in medical ill children and adolescents. In A. Stoudemire & B. S. Fogel (Eds.), Medical psychiatric practice (Vol. 1, pp. 455–482). Washington, DC: American Psychiatric Press.

Pfefferbaum-Levine, B., Kumor, K., Cangir, A., Choroszy, M., & Roseberry, E. A. (1983). Tricyclic antidepressants for children with cancer. *American Journal of Psychiatry, 140,* 1074–1076.

Pless, I. B., & Pinkerton, P. (1975). *Chronic childhood disorder: Promoting patterns of adjustment.* London: Kimpton.

Poznanski, E. O., Freeman, L. N., & Mokros, H. B. (1985). Children's Depression Rating Scale-Revised. *Psychopharmacological Bulletin, 21,* 979–989.

Pynoos, R., Frederick, C., Nader, K., Arroyo, W., et al. (1987). Life threat and post-traumatic stress in school-age children. *Archives of General Psychiatry, 44,* 1057–1063.

Rait, D. S., Jacobsen, P. B., Lederberg, M. S., & Holland, J. C. (1988). Characteristics of psychiatric consultations in a pediatric cancer center. *American Journal of Psychiatry, 145,* 363–364.

Raj, A., & Sheehan, D. V. (1987). Medical evaluation of panic attacks. *Journal of Clinical Psychiatry, 48,* 309–383.

Raskin, M., Peeke, H. V. S., Dickman, W., & Pisker, H. (1982). Panic and generalized anxiety disorder. *Archives of General Psychiatry, 39,* 687–689.

Rodin, G., & Voshart, K. (1986). Depression in the medically ill: An overview. *American Journal of Psychiatry, 143,* 696–705.

Roy-Byrne, P. P., Gerace, M., & Uhde, T. (1986). Life events and the onset of panic disorder. *American Journal of Psychiatry, 143,* 1424–1427.

Ryan, N. D. (1990). Heterocyclic antidepressants in children and adolescents. *Journal of Child and Adolescent Psychopharmacology, 1,* 21–31.

Ryan, N. D., Puig-Antich, J., Cooper, T. B., Rabinovich, H., Ambrosini, P., Fried, J., Davies, M., Torres, D., & Suckow, R. F. (1986). Imipramine in adolescent major depression: Plasma level and clinical response. *Acta Psychiatrica Scandinavica, 73,* 275–288.

Sheehan, D. V., Sheehan, K. H., & Minichiello, W. E. (1981). Age of onset of phobic disorders: A reevaluation. *Comprehensive Psychiatry, 22,* 544–553.

Sheehan, D. V., & Sheehan, K. H. (1982). The classification of anxiety and hysterical states: I. Historical review and empirical delineation. *Journal of Clinical Psychopharmacology, 1,* 235–244.

Silove, D. (1986). Perceived parental characteristics and reports of early parental deprivation in agoraphobic parents. *Australian and New Zealand Journal of Psychiatry, 20,* 365–369.

Stoddard, F. J., Norman, D. K., & Murphy, J. M. (1989). Psychiatric study of severely burned children. *Journal of Trauma, 29,* 471–477.

Stoudemire, A., Fogel, B. S., & Gulley, L. R. (1991). Psychopharmacology in the medically ill: An update. In A. Stoudemire & B. S. Fogel (Eds.), *Medical psychiatric practice* (Vol. 1, pp. 29–97). Washington, DC: American Psychiatric Press.

Stoudemire, A., Moran, M. G., & Fogel, B. S. (1990). Psychotropic drug use in the medically ill: Part 1. *Psychosomatics, 31,* 377–391.

Stoudemire, A. (1989). Depression in the medically ill. In J. Cavenar (Ed.), *Psychiatry* (Vol. 2, pp. 1–12). Philadelphia: Lippincott.

Strober, M., Freeman, R., & Rigali, J. (1990). The pharmacotherapy of depressive illness in adolescence: I. An open label trial of imipramine. *Psychopharmacology Bulletin, 26,* 80–84.

Strober, M., & Werry, J. S. (1986). The assessment of depression in children and adolescents. In N. Sartorius & T. A. Ban (Eds.), *Assessment of depression* (pp. 324–342). New York: Springer-Verlag.

Torgerson, S. (1983). Genetic factors in anxiety disorders. *Archives of General Psychiatry, 40,* 1085–1092.

Vaillant, J. S. (1985). Psychological aspects of peptic ulcer disease in childhood. *Psychotherapy and Psychosomatics, 44,* 40–45.

Viney, L. L., & Westbrook, M. T. (1985). Patterns of psychological reaction to asthma in children. *Journal of Abnormal Child Psychology, 13,* 477–484.

Wasserman, A. L., Whitington, P. F., & Rivara, F. P. (1988). Psychogenic basis for abdominal pain in children and adolescents. *Journal of the American Academy of Child and Adolescent Psychiatry, 27,* 179–184.

Weiland, S. K., Pless, I. B., & Roghmann, K. J. (1992). Chronic illness and mental health problems in pediatric practice: Results from a survey of primary care providers. *Pediatrics, 89,* 445–449.

Wells, K. B., Golding, J. M., & Burnam, M. A. (1989). Chronic medical conditions in a sample of the general population with anxiety, affective, and substance use disorders. *American Journal of Psychiatry, 146,* 1440–1446.

Whitlock, F. A. (Ed.). (1982). *Symptomatic affective disorders.* New York: Academic Press.

Wilkes, T. C. R., & Rush, A. J. (1988). Adaptations of cognitive therapy for depressed adolescents. *Journal of the American Academy of Child and Adolescent Psychiatry, 27,* 381–386.

Wood, B., Watkins, J. B., Boyle, J. T., Nogueira, J., Zimand, E., & Carroll, L. (1987). Psychological functioning in children with Crohn's disease and ulcerative colitis: Implications for models of psychobiological interaction. *Journal of the American Academy of Child and Adolescent Psychiatry, 26,* 774–781.

Worschel, F. F., Copeland, D. R., & Barker, D. G. (1987). Control-related copying strategies in pediatric oncology patients. *Journal of Pediatric Psychology, 12,* 25–38.

23

Adolescent Sexuality

Nathaniel McConaghy

A dolescent sexuality usually receives attention only when it produces problems, so that it tends to be regarded as pathological, or at least to be discouraged. Jones et al. (1985) pointed out that the United States, unlike other countries (e.g., Sweden, where adolescents initiate coitus at slightly younger ages than in the United States), has developed official programs—advocated and subsidized by the government—to discourage teenagers from having sexual relations. Jones et al. also stated that powerful public figures have opposed the provision of contraceptive services in the belief that these act as an incitement to premarital sexual activity.

Emphasis on the prevalence of out-of-wedlock pregnancies and sexually transmitted diseases in adolescents has led to research interest being focused on the age at which boys and girls commence intercourse; as a result, possible positive aspects of their sexual activity have not been investigated, and little attention has been accorded to many of their other sexual problems. This lack of notice may also result in part from the reluctance of adolescents to disclose their sexual activities to others, particularly adults. Striking evidence of the significance of such reluctance was the acceptance by experienced research workers who obtained statements from 110 adolescents that only 1 of the latter had experienced homosexual feelings. These statements, at variance with other reports of young adults indicating that from 20% to 50% had experienced such feelings in adolescence, were used to refute the theory that homosexual feelings resulted from exposure to opposite-sex hormones in utero (McConaghy, 1984). A number of the 110 adolescents, when interviewed subsequently in adulthood, reported a high incidence of homosexual feelings; this was interpreted by the researchers as evidence that with aging, the subjects were more prepared to talk about their sexual feelings and behaviors (Money, Schwartz, & Lewis, 1984).

In view of the reluctance of adolescents to reveal their sexual activities, these are usually detected only when they result in conditions requiring medical attention or in behaviors that come to the attention of concerned relatives or legal authorities. Hence only a limited number of the sexual problems classified in the *Diagnostic and Statistical Manual of Mental Disorders* (American Psychiatric Association, 1994) come to attention among adolescents; most of the problems that do come to attention in this population are not included in the classification. A study of the 65 teenagers who committed suicide from 1979 to 1983 in Metro Dade County, Florida, revealed that of the 80% of cases for which a cause could be found, it was a boyfriend/girlfriend problem in 17%, out-of-wedlock pregnancy in 5%, a lover triangle in 5%, and other sexual problems in a further 10% (Copeland, 1985).

Sexual Problems Identified in DSM-IV

Sexual problems are classified in the DSM-IV draft criteria as sexual and gender identity disorders; the category of sexual disorders includes paraphilias and sexual dysfunctions. Studies of the prevalence of sexual disorders in the population are rarely undertaken. It would appear that it was investigated in only one of the National Institute of Mental Health Epidemiologic Catchment Area studies of the prevalence of psychiatric disorders carried out in St. Louis. The only relevant information provided in this study concerning psychosexual disorders appears to have been the statement that their prevalence was 24%, making them the most common psychiatric disorders after tobacco use disorder (Robins et al., 1984). No information concerning sexual disorders was provided in a recent study of the prevalence of DSM-III disorders in adolescents (McGee et al., 1990).

Sexual Dysfunctions in Adolescence

Though there is little information concerning the prevalence of most of the sexual dysfunctions in adolescents, there is evidence of a high rate of failure in girls to achieve orgasm in sexual relationships. In the most representative survey of the sexual behavior of U.S. adolescents available (Sorensen, 1973), 57% of the nonvirgin teenage girls rarely or never reached orgasm in heterosexual relations, though one-third considered it very important to them that they did. One-half of the anorgasmic girls stated they did not get as much physical satisfaction out of sex as they thought they should, as opposed to 16% of the girls who had orgasms frequently or almost always. As the majority of women do not seek treatment for difficulty to reach orgasm, the finding of Kinsey, Pomeroy, Martin, and Gebhard (1953) that the percentage of women who were anorgasmic with intercourse declined from 25% in the first year of marriage to 11% in the twentieth year, suggests that most anorgasmic adolescent girls eventually become orgasmic without treatment. Such gradual increase in women's ability to reach orgasm over time suggests that learning is involved.

The most likely learned ability that brings about this change is the relinquishing of emotional control, allowing sexual arousal to be experienced

(McConaghy, 1993). As Mead (1950) pointed out, adolescent girls are expected to restrict the limits of sexual relationships, and boys to extend them. Girls therefore must attempt to limit their sexual arousal in physical relationships and are likely to experience anxiety if it increases. When they no longer need to restrain their arousal they have to learn to cease to do so, as well as to lose their anxiety at becoming aroused. It also is likely that biological factors make the achievement of orgasm easier in males than in females (McConaghy, 1991). This would account for the high number of female adolescents who experience difficulty in achieving orgasm with masturbation. Clifford (1978) found that of 100 undergraduate women aged 17 to 25 years who agreed to give information, 25 of the 74 who reported having masturbated did not reach orgasm.

Dyspareunia (painful intercourse) of psychological origin and vaginismus (spasm of the muscles of the outer third of the vagina, often accompanied by spasm of the adductor muscles of the thighs if intercourse is attempted) are usually established in adolescence but rarely lead the sufferer to seek treatment until adulthood. An interesting but unexplored statistic in Sorensen's (1973) study was that 21% of adolescent males with masturbatory experience reported masturbation without orgasm in the previous month, with 12% reporting this as occurring five or more times in the period. The incidence in males of coitus without orgasm and the percentage who had difficulty reaching orgasm were not investigated. Certainly some adolescent males must have this difficulty, as adults seeking treatment for inability to ejaculate and/or experience orgasm (either at all or, more commonly, in the vagina) usually report the condition has persisted since adolescence. In his study of adult sexual behavior, Hunt (1974) found that 15% of men under 25 years of age failed to achieve orgasm on at least 25% of occasions. Adults seeking treatment for impotence in middle-age, in whom an organic factor is commonly found to be contributing to their condition, frequently report difficulties in attaining or maintaining erections as early as their initial experiences in adolescence. These usually were resolved sufficiently with further sexual experience, so that treatment was not sought then. Adults with premature ejaculation also usually date its onset from their earliest sexual relationships.

Sexual dysfunctions in adolescents could be expected to respond to treatments used in adults (McConaghy, 1993) that aim to reduce anxiety associated with sexual activity by graduated exposure to situations of increasing sexual intimacy (either real, if possible, or imagined). As pointed out, however, adolescents rarely seek treatment for these problems.

Paraphilias in Adolescence

The DSM-IV retained the replacement in DSM-III-R (American Psychiatric Association, 1987) of the term *sexual deviations* with *paraphilias*. DSM-III-

R stated that paraphilias were characterized by arousal to sexual objects or situations that are not part of normative arousal-activity patterns. DSM-III-R also pointed out, though, that imagery in paraphilic fantasy is frequently the stimulus for sexual excitement in people without a paraphilia—indicating that arousal to such objects or situations *is* part of normative arousal-activity patterns. The term *sexual deviations* would seem more appropriate as indicating that the activities so labeled deviate from those currently considered socially acceptable: for example, masturbation and homosexuality were in the past considered sexual deviations. The DSM-IV provides diagnostic criteria for exhibitionism, fetishism, frotteurism, pedophilia, sexual masochism, sexual sadism, transvestic fetishism, and voyeurism; detailed accounts of these activities are available (McConaghy, 1991, 1993). Telephone scatologia (obscene phone calls), necrophilia (corpses), partialism (exclusive focus on part of the body), zoophilia (animals), coprophilia (feces), klismaphilia (enemas), and urophilia (urine) were listed as examples of paraphilias not otherwise specified.

Sexual deviations are largely carried out by males, and apart from heterosexual pedophilia, the common sexual deviations of exhibitionism, voyeurism, fetishism, transvestism, sexual assaultive behaviors, sadomasochism, and telephone scatologia are usually established in adolescence. These facts have been demonstrated in clinical studies, evidence from investigations of community samples being limited. Of 45 males who sought treatment for compulsive sexuality other than homosexuality (McConaghy, Armstrong, & Blaszczynski, 1985; McConaghy, Blaszczynski, & Kidson, 1988), 6 were adolescents. A further 21 reported that paraphilic behavior had commenced and was repeated often in adolescence. This trend was particularly marked in the 5 fetishists, 3 of whom showed a strong (though apparently not sexual) interest in the fetishistic object some years prior to puberty; in another, the fetishistic interest commenced at age 13. Deviant behavior reportedly commenced in adolescence for 12 of 19 exhibitionists, 7 of 11 homosexual pedophiles, and 2 of 3 voyeurs. Heterosexual pedophiles did not show this trend, with only 2 of 7 reporting the behavior in adolescence.

As information concerning the prevalence of sexual deviations in the adolescent population is not available, studies of young adults provide the most relevant information. Templeman and Stinnett (1991) obtained sexual histories from 60 undergraduate men whose mean age was 21.5 years using the Clarke Sexual History Questionnaire (SHQ), a self-report instrument developed to identify sexual anomalies in sex offenders. Of the 60 subjects, 3 who reported homosexual contacts were excluded; 65% of the remaining 57 had engaged in some illegal sexual offense. Voyeurism (defined in the SHQ as secretly trying to see a man or women having sexual relations or a women undressing) was the most common offense, reported by 42%. Templeman and Stinnett rejected the possibility that these subjects were reporting only acts of sexual curiosity in early adolescence, as the item was worded to exclude activities occurring before the age of 16. Frottage (the rubbing of one's genitals against a nonconsenting victim, or rubbing the victim's genitals, usually in crowded public transportation) was the next most common offensive behavior, reported by 35% of the undergraduates. Eight percent (8%) had made obscene phone calls; 2 of the 57 subjects reported sexual contact with girls under 12, and 1 reported contact with girls aged 13 to 15.

Only 1 subject reported exhibitionism, an anomalous finding in view of its being the most common deviation among convicted sex offenders. The authors pointed out that because the students investigated were raised and educated in primarily rural environments, the results should not be extrapolated too freely. It may be that exhibitionism is less frequently carried out in rural environments, where the possibility of being recognized would presumably be much higher than in cities. Voyeuristic and 7 exhibitionistic desires were expressed, respectively, by 54% and 7% of the subjects; 5% desired sex with girls under 12. Two subjects reported they had been arrested for sexual offenses, and another had been in trouble with authorities for sexual behaviors.

In another study of the sexual activity of university students, 21% of the men and 8% of the women reported having exhibited their genitals in public, 4% in the previous 3 months (Person, Terestman, Myers, Goldberg, & Salvadori, 1989). Lifetime prevalence of other deviant acts was not investigated, but in the previous 3 months, 4% of men and 5% of women had watched others make love, and in presumably consenting sadomasochistic activities, 6% of women and 1% of men had been forced to submit to sexual acts, 4% of women and 3% of men had been tied or bound, and 4% of women and 1% of men had been sexually degraded. Person et al. did not report the prevalence of sexual activity with prepubertal children but found that 21% of women and 53% of men had fantasized about sexual experiences with a much younger partner. About 15% of male and 2% of female university students surveyed in the United States and Australia reported some likelihood of having sexual activity with a prepubertal child if they could do so without risk (Malamuth, 1989; McConaghy, Zamir, & Manicavasagar, 1993).

In the study of Person et al. (1989), sadomasochistic fantasies were also experienced by a significant percentage, with 20% of women and 15% of men commonly having fantasies of being forced to submit or being tied up during sexual activities; 12% to 20% of men having fantasies of beating, whipping, degrading, or torturing sexual partners; and 8% to 10% of women having fantasies either of being the victim of these activities or of being prostitutes. In Malamuth's (1989) studies of male students, 44% to 50% reported some likelihood they would engage in bondage, and 33% to 35% some likelihood they would engage in whipping and spanking a woman if they could do so without risk. A majority of 54 male undergraduates reported pictures of distressed women in bondage to be more sexually stimulating than those of similar women displaying positive affect (Heilbrun & Leif, 1988). Heilbrun and Leif concluded that there was a sadistic component to normal male sexuality.

Sexually Coercive Behaviors

The DSM-IV retained the exclusion in DSM-III-R of most episodes of sexually coercive behaviors from its classification of sexual disorders. DSM-III-R stated that only rape or other sexual assaults where the suffering inflicted on the victim was far in excess of that necessary for compliance and the visible pain of the victim was sexually arousing were expressions of sexual sadism; fewer than 10% of rapists were considered to carry out such rapes. This conclusion, though, seems at variance with the considerable evidence that a significant percentage of normal men find a sexually coerced woman's suffering arousing. Malamuth and Check (1983) found that 20% of male college students indicated some likelihood of raping a woman if they could do so without risk to themselves; these students reported to male experimenters that they experienced greater arousal to descriptions of sexual interactions in which the woman experienced pain than to those descriptions in which she did not. These students compared to the remainder showed greater aggression against women in a laboratory setting (Malamuth, 1981) and reported greater sexual arousal to stories with a sadomasochistic theme (Malamuth, Haber, & Feshbach, 1980).

Thirty-six male undergraduates who volunteered for a study of responsiveness to sexually explicit videos reported moderate levels of sexual arousal and general enjoyment while watching a depiction of several members of a motorcycle gang chasing, catching, and raping a young woman (Pfaus, Myronuk, & Jacobs. 1986). Nineteen of 50 single undergraduate men reported more than one episode where a dating partner had expressed dissatisfaction because the man had exceeded the sexual limits the partner preferred. Compared to the remaining students, these 19 men found women who displayed fear, anger, disgust, and sadness more sexually attractive than women who displayed happiness (Heilbrun & Loftus, 1986). In view of the significant number of men in these community studies who are aroused by some degree of suffering of women in sexual situations, it would seem unlikely that only 10% of rapists would respond in the same manner. Knight and Prentky (1990), in their study of sex offenders, were unable to substantiate the DSM-III-R distinction between sadistic and nonsadistic rape.

The concept of rape advanced by Koss and Oros (1982), which considers rape as an extreme behavior on a continuum with normal male behavior, appears more consistent with available evidence. The authors administered a a Sexual Experiences Survey (SES) to 1,846 male and 2,016 female students at Kent State University (mean age 21 years). In this survey, men were asked if they had carried out sexually coercive acts and women if they had been the victims of such acts, reflecting the generally accepted view that men are not victims and women not perpetrators of sexually coercive acts. McConaghy et al. (1993) modified the SES questionnaire to investigate the possibility that continua also existed on which women were the aggressors and men the victims. The altered questionnaire was administered to 66 male and 51 female medical students in Sydney, Australia; the mean age of the men was 19.5 years, and that of the women was 19.8 years.

In the Koss and Oros (1982) study, 33% of Kent State University women students reported experiences in which their partner was so aroused he "could not stop," though the woman did not want sexual intercourse. Fourteen percent (14%) of female and 13% of male Sydney medical students reported these experiences (McConaghy et al., 1993). Twenty-three percent of the Kent State men reported experiences of being so aroused they could not stop, though their partner did not want intercourse. Eleven percent (11%) of the Sydney men and 6% of the women reported these experiences. Two percent (2%) of the Sydney men and women and the Kent state men reported they used force to attempt to obtain sexual intercourse. Two percent (2%) of Sydney women, as compared to 6% of Kent State women, reported having been raped. No Sydney men reported having raped or been raped. The Kent State men were not asked this question; 3% reported having sexual intercourse with a woman when she did not want to because they used some degree of physical force.

These data support the dimensional concept of sexual aggression. It could be expected that subjects' level of consciousness concerning rape would determine at what point in the continuum they would label as sexual assault the behavior they had experienced as aggressor or victim. It would appear then that there has been little change in the prevalence of sexual coercive behavior by male students in the past few decades. Replication of an 1957 study found that, as in the earlier study, about one-half of the female students reported having experienced sexual coercion in the previous year, with one-quarter having been forced to have intercourse (Kanin & Parcell, 1977).

Christopher (1988) found that the most common pressure reported by women victims was persistent physical attempts at intercourse, which were not classified as the use of physical force. A question investigating this was added to the modified SES administered to a further group of 101 male medical students (mean age 19.9 years) and 81 female medical students (mean age 19.5 years; McConaghy & Zamir, in press). In this study, 14% of the women and 20% of the men reported that they had made constant physical attempts to have sexual activity with a member of the opposite sex; 1% of the women reported they had made constant physical attempts with a woman. Struckman-Johnson (1988) found that 16% of male and 22% of female university students reported at least one episode in which they were forced to engage in sexual intercourse on a date. Most men were coerced by psychological pressure and most women by force, but 28% of men were coerced by both. In their study of psychology students, Muehlenhard and Cook (1988) found that more men (63%) than women (46%) reported experiencing unwanted sexual intercourse. The men's reasons for engaging in unwanted intercourse commonly related to sex-role expectations (i.e., fearing to appear homosexual, unmasculine, inexperienced, or shy). It would seem that both male and female adolescents and young adults engage in a continuum of sexually exploitive behaviors, ranging from verbal pressure to use of physical force and restraint; few of these are reported to authorities as sexual assaults.

Treatments of Sexual Offenses and Deviations

A number of treatments of sexual deviations are currently employed, based on the disparate models held by therapists concerning the motivation of deviant behaviors. Evidence for the comparative efficacy of the various treatments is minimal.

Therapies Based on Stimulus Control Models

The stimulus control model (i.e., sexual arousal to deviant stimuli motivates deviant behaviors) provided the justification for behavioral therapies introduced in the 1960s for sex offenses and nonoffensive deviations for which treatment was sought. The behavioral therapies utilized conditioning procedures to treat the subjects, almost all of whom were male. Aversive techniques in which deviant stimuli were associated with unpleasant levels of electric shocks to the fingers, or with imagined aversive consequences, were employed with the aim of reducing deviant sexual preferences. Associating pictures of nude females with pictures of nude males was employed to increase homosexual men's ability to be sexually responsive to female partners.

The failure of recent studies of penile circumference response (PCR) assessment either to discriminate sex offenders from nonoffenders or to predict treatment outcome (McConaghy, 1989, 1992) has influenced therapeutic procedures. Quinsey and Laws (1990) considered that offenders who show minimal PCRs to deviant cues were less often targeted for interventions aimed at modifying deviant preferences (e.g., aversive therapies), at least partly because any changes that were produced by the interventions would be difficult to detect. Marshall and Barbaree (1990), however, advised that such interventions originally meant to change deviant arousal patterns should be used with offenders whose patterns of sexual arousal were normal, as their behaviors were nevertheless elicited by features of the environment. At the same time, the latter authors considered that it may not be necessary to direct treatment to sexual preferences even when they appeared to be deviant, as such preferences might be a result rather than a cause of deviant sexual behaviors. Despite these indications of change in therapeutic aims, Quinsey and Laws (1990) concluded that modification of inappropriate sexual preferences remains of central concern in many of the treatment programs in North America, and that some form of aversive therapy is the method most commonly used to reduce inappropriate sexual interest.

Evidence that sexual preference was modified by conditioning procedures was mainly obtained in single-case studies carried out in the 1960s and 1970s. These studies reported that the PCRs of homosexual men to pictures of nude men and women changed following the procedures. A detailed review of these studies (McConaghy, 1977, 1993) concluded that due to the lack of validity of PCR assessment, as well as methodological weaknesses, the data could not be regarded as having demonstrated any reduction in the subjects' homosexual interest or increase in their ability to be sexually aroused by stimuli of adult female nudes.

In a series of studies investigating the responses of homosexual subjects to aversive procedures employing the valid penile volume response (PVR) assessment of homosexual and heterosexual arousal (McConaghy, 1992), it was found that aversive therapies as compared to a placebo procedure did not modify the treated subjects' sexual preferences (McConaghy, 1975). Following treatment, subjects did not experience any aversion to the homosexual stimuli that had been paired with the aversive stimuli, and in their everyday experience they continued to be as aware of the same immediate attraction to males they encountered as they were prior to treatment. Despite the failure of aversive therapy to alter the sexual preferences of the subjects treated, it did increase their ability to control homosexual behaviors that prior to treatment they had experienced as compulsive. For example, some subjects sought treatment because they were spending considerable amounts of time in public lavatories or cruising beats for transient homosexual contacts they often found unsatisfactory, yet they could not discontinue these behaviors. Following treatment they had no difficulty ceasing the unwanted activities. Other treated subjects reported they could continue homosexual activities they found acceptable (e.g., relationships with known partners) while ceasing behaviors they found unacceptable but previously experienced as compulsive (e.g., seeking casual contacts on beats). Those subjects who had experienced homosexual fantasies as preoccupying and guilt-inducing because of their religious beliefs could easily dismiss these fantasies following treatment. Though they were still as aware of being attracted to men they encountered as they were before treatment, once these men passed from their field of vision the subjects did not continue to have uncontrollable fantasies concerning them.

Imaginal Desensitization

To account for the paradoxical finding that aversive therapy did not change homosexual subjects' sexual orientation but did allow them to control homosexual urges, a variant of the stimulus control model—the behavioral completion model (BCM) of compulsive sexuality—was advanced (McConaghy, 1983). This model postulated that when subjects' behaviors became habitual, BCMs for the behaviors were established in the subjects' brains. If subjects were exposed to cues for these established behaviors but tried to avoid acting on them, the BCMs activated their brain arousal system so that they experienced a high level of tension or excitement that drove them to complete the behaviors. To test this model, a form of treatment termed *imaginal desensitization* was evaluated and found to be more effective than aversive therapy in giving subjects control over behaviors they experienced as compulsive (McConaghy, Armstrong, Blaszczynski, & Allcock, 1983; McConaghy et al., 1985). With imaginal desensitization, subjects in a relaxed state repeatedly visualize being in situations where they have carried out the compulsive behavior in the past, but instead remain relaxed and leave the situation without having carried out the behavior. Subsequently using the same model, sexually deviant subjects were given medroxyprogesterone for 6 months in a dose that reduced their testosterone level to about 30% of the pretreatment level. At this level subjects still obtained erections with physical stimuli and could continue their acceptable sexual activity, but their sexual interest was sufficiently reduced that they could control their deviant urges. It was hypothesized that over the 6 months BCMs for the deviant behavior would be inhibited by lack of reinforcement, so that when the medroxyprogesterone was ceased the subjects could control the deviant impulses. More than 80% of deviant subjects responded to the procedure of using either imaginal desensitization or medroxyprogesterone initially and adding the alternative if there was not a response of total control of deviant urges (McConaghy, 1990). Adolescents were more likely than adults to require prolongation of therapy (McConaghy, Blaszczynski, Armstrong, & Kidson, 1989).

Therapies Based on Cognitive Models

In the 1980s, with the acceptance by North American behaviorists that attention needed to be paid to subjects' cognitions as well as their behaviors, most programs developed multimodal approaches by adding cognitive therapy components to their behavioral procedures. The content of the components was determined by the cognitive model of sexually deviant behaviors held by the therapist. The best known of the cognitive models is based on a feminist perspective; discussed in more detail elsewhere (McConaghy, 1993), this model in its radical form considers all men as potential victimizers of women and children, ignoring the sexually coercive behavior of women. It therefore had no need to provide an explanation as to why only some men and women offended. It also proposed that rape and possibly all sexual offenses were motivated not by sexual arousal but by wishes to dominate and express hostility.

The cognitive models of sex offenses adopted by most workers modified the feminist concept by accepting that the offenses were motivated by sexual arousal, and by rejecting the belief that all men held equivalent cognitions supportive of sexual offending. Burt (1980) provided evidence that both men and women varied in the extent to which they held rape-supportive cognitions (or "rape myths"). This extent correlated with their degree of acceptance of interpersonal violence, of sex-role stereotyping, and of the belief that the sexual interactions of men and women were adversarial. The degree to which individual men held these related cognitions was considered to determine the likelihood of their sexually victimizing women and children. Ageton (1983) and Koss, Leonard, Beezley, and Oros (1985), in their studies of sexual assaultive male adolescents and university students, were unable to support this theory. Educating subjects in the role such cognitions play in motivating their sexually deviant behavior remains an important part of many treatment programs, however, along with empathy training concerning the impact of sexually offensive behaviors on the victims (Herman, 1990; Murphy, 1990).

A cognitive treatment approach termed *relapse prevention*, developed to treat addictive disorders (George & Marlatt, 1989), has been extended to treat sex offenders. With this approach the sex offender is considered to control his behavior until he encounters high-risk situations, which are identified as emotional states rather than the situations where he has previously offended (the high-risk situations in stimulus control models). Cognitive training is directed at providing strategies for the offender to identify and not relapse in such situations.

Victims of Reported and Unreported Sexual Assault

The study containing the most representative sample of adolescent female victims of sexual assault was carried out by Ageton (1983). It investigated subjects aged 11 to 20 in a national probability sample, of whom the males self-identified as perpetrators and the females as victims of sexual assault. Sexual assault was defined as all forced behavior involving contact with the sexual parts of the body, the force varying from verbal pressure to physical beatings. Generalizing conservatively from her findings, Ageton concluded that in each year from 1978 to 1980, between 5% and 11% of the adolescent female population in the United States (i.e., from 700,000 to 1 million teenage females) experienced at least one sexual assault. There were no significant race or social class differences between victims and nonvictims, but urban girls were more vulnerable. The offenders were mainly boyfriends or dates in the same age range as the victim; the victim did not know the offender in fewer than 20% of cases. The most common form of coercion reported by victims was verbal, but during the 3 years 27% to 40% experienced some minimal physical force. The majority of all victims were successful in deterring the assault. Victims of violent sexual assaults were typically black, lower class urban adolescents. Up to 15% of all victims, that is about 1% of the total sample of adolescent girls, reported physical beating or the presence of a weapon. Ageton calculated this to be twice the prevalence of all forcible rapes and attempted rapes reported in the National Crime Survey, and 20 times that reported in the Uniform Crimes Report.

Ageton did not report the data on male victims or homosexual assaults in her study, on the grounds that these assaults were not typical and could result in misleading conclusions. Kaufman, Divasto, Jackson, Voorhees, and Christy (1980) found that the percentage of male as compared to female victims of male sexual assault presenting to a treatment team in New Mexico increased from 0% to 10% from 1975 to 1978. Male victims were younger than female victims (5 of the 14 being 13 to 18 years old) and were more likely to have sustained greater physical trauma, more reluctant initially to reveal the genital component of their assault, and more likely to use denial and control of their emotions in relation to the assault. The authors considered that male as compared to female victims were far less likely to report being sexually assaulted but may experience major hidden trauma.

Only 5% of the assaults of women recorded by Ageton (1983) were reported to the police, mainly those involving unknown or multiple assailants and use of threats or of actual violence. More than half of those reported were completed assaults. Ageton suggested that attempted nonviolent assaults by dates or boyfriends may not be defined by the victims as legitimate sexual assaults for purposes of reporting to officials, a belief consistent with the findings of other studies. Holmstrom (1985) found that sexual assaults were more likely to be reported when the assailants broke into the victims' homes, attacked them in their automobiles, or abducted them from public places; the assailants were strangers or acquaintances rather than friends or relatives; and the assailants threatened the victims with weapons or seriously injured them.

Burgess and Holmstrom (1980) differentiated "blitz" and "confidence" rapes. Blitz rapes were sudden surprise attacks by an unknown assailant; confidence rapes involved some nonviolent interaction between the rapist and the victim before the attacker's intention to commit rape emerged. A study of 1,000 consecutive rape victims seen at a Boston rape crisis intervention program over a 10-year period found that the assaults could be classified as blitz rapes in 60% of cases and confidence rapes in 36% (Bowie, Silverman, Kalick, & Edbril, 1990; Silverman, Kalick, Bowie, & Edbril, 1988). Though reported sexual assaults are mainly blitz rapes it is apparent from the data reported by Koss and Oros (1982) and Ageton (1983) that confidence rapes are markedly more frequent. Indeed, Ageton concluded that what she termed date rapes were sufficiently common that they could be regarded as almost a standard feature of dating. In Sorensen's (1973) sample of adolescents aged 13 to 19 years, 26% of boys and 25% of girls agreed with the statement that "if a girl has led a boy on, it's all right for the boy to force her to have sex." A survey of adolescents at the end of the 1970s revealed similar attitudes (Burgess, 1985). Four percent of non-virgin girls aged 13 to 15 years in Sorensen's (1973) study reported that the first boy with whom they had intercourse was someone who raped them.

More than one-third of the girls in Ageton's (1983) study who were assaulted experienced at least one further assault in the same year; compared to all female adolescents, they had three to four times the risk of being assaulted in the next year. Comparisons between victim and control groups suggested that involvement in delinquent behavior and with delinquent peers might account for the victims' initial and continuing vulnerability: 2 years prior to any reported sexual assaults, the victims and controls were substantially different in terms of peer networks.

One-third of the victims assaulted by their romantic partners reported no change in the relationship. Victims' reactions to date rapes may not have not changed significantly from those reported by Kanin (1959); the majority of university freshmen he investigated who reported sexual aggression from a partner did not terminate the relationship. Few of the victims assaulted in Ageton's study informed their parents. Approximately 60% of those whose husband or boyfriend was not the offender informed the partner of the assault, with the majority reporting that their subsequent relationship was closer and more affectionate. More than two-thirds of the victims told their friends, but more than three-quarters did not inform their parents. This may reflect their awareness of the parents' likely negative reactions.

The emotional impact of rape of adolescents who sought treatment has been rated by health professionals as more severe on the parents than the victims: in one study, 71% of parents were assessed as showing a severe response, compared with 37% of victims (Mann, 1981). No parents showed a mild response, as compared to 20% of victims, and 80% of the victims complained about increased communication problems with their parents after the rape. Similar findings were reported in relation to 44 victims of exhibitionists most of whom were adolescents at the time of the offense (Gittleson, Eacott, & Mehta, 1978). In 40 cases victims reported the offense, in 32 cases to their families. In 28 cases those told were upset, compared to 25 cases in which the victims were upset. In 17 cases the degree of upset of those told was greater than that of the victims, and in 14 it was more traumatic to the victim than the offense.

Effects of Sexual Assault

Short-Term Effects

In her study of a representative community sample of adolescents, Ageton (1983) reported that in the week following the assault 50% of the victims experienced anger, depression, embarrassment, and guilt; 20% experienced fear of the offender's return, of other men, and of being alone. During the following 6 months these percentages halved, and Ageton concluded that the typical assault in her study—a date rape—did not generate many negative reactions that persisted for this period of time. Neither race, age, social class, number of offenders, relationship to the offender, nor the amount of force experienced appeared to influence the victims' reactions to the assault, although its resulting in coitus was associated with more negative reactions in the following year.

In contrast to Ageton's findings from her community sample, studies of adolescents seeking treatment and investigated clinically found severe effects following sexual assault. Asher (1988) concluded that depression and suicidal attempts were more common in adolescent than child victims. She pointed out that the adolescent girl was at risk of becoming pregnant, either by an incest perpetrator or another male.

Long-Term Effects

Ageton (1983) assessed the reactions of adolescent girls to sexual assault for up to 3 years in a subsample of victims. After the marked decline noted in the first year, 2 to 3 years later a number of subjects reported depression and fear of men and of being alone. These reactions were not related to features of the assault, and Ageton concluded that factors such as support from significant others, history of traumatic events, and personality traits may be more instrumental in affecting long-term reactions. She also suggested that these late-reported reactions might have been artifacts of the repeated interview situation. Certainly if they were not, and many victims of attempted assault by dates or boyfriends experience fear of men and of being alone two to three years later, these symptoms should be very common in adolescent girls, in view of the prevalence of this type of assault by dates or boyfriends. As stated earlier Ageton considered that such assaults could be regarded as almost a standard feature of dating.

Ageton's suggestion that long-term effects following sexual assault may be associated with personality vulnerability was also put forward by Ellis (1983) to account for the finding of her review that severity of the rape victims' reactions showed no consistent relationships with any features of the rape, including the degree of force and whether a weapon was used. Characteristics of the victim (e.g., prior victimization, economic stress, lack of social support) were associated with slower recovery, however, as was a history of prior psychiatric or physical health problems and suicidal ideation or attempts. Ellis considered these findings to be consistent with a crisis theory model of response to rape. In this model, the outcome of a crisis is not solely determined by the nature of the stress; the victim's previous experience and personality or character structure "load the dice" in favor of a positive or negative outcome. This belief of Ellis could explain the inconsistency between studies, some of which found that the majority of rape victims recovered fairly rapidly and others (particularly clinical studies) that a significant number showed slow and minimal recovery. The latter studies of subjects seeking treatment could have contained more subjects with vulnerable personalities.

In regard to individual symptoms following sexual assault, psychosexual dysfunctions were those most commonly reported in clinical studies. A number of these studies found that the victims' satisfaction with sexual behaviors with their partner was significantly reduced, particularly the behaviors forced on the victim during the assault, though not all studies reported that the frequency of these behaviors was reduced (Foley, 1985). Psychosexual disorders were also reported by adolescent males sexually assaulted by women (Sarrel & Masters, 1982) and by men (Groth & Burgess, 1980).

Incest

No episodes of incestuous abuse were reported in Ageton's (1983) study of sexual assaults of adolescent girls, in which they were asked whether in the last year they had been sexually attacked or raped or whether an attempt had been made to do so. Possibly the subjects did not consider that the incestuous relationships they experienced involved the use of force, including verbal pressure. It would seem that some must have experienced incestuous abuse as 4% of the women studied by Russell (1986) reported experiencing initiation of incestuous abuse between the ages of 14 and 18 years (in addition to the 12% of cases in which it was initiated earlier). Ageton's failure to discuss the issue of incestuous abuse unfortunately suggests that researchers as well as victims may not regard such abuse as sexual assault. Consistent with this view, Johnson and Shrier (1987) noted that of male adolescents attending a medical outpatient service, none under the age of 15 years reported being sexually assaulted prior to puberty. A clinical study of adolescent rape (Mann, 1981) also failed to mention incestuous abuse.

Incestuous and nonincestuous abuse were investigated in a study of 34 female and 6 male adolescents who attended a child sexual abuse clinic in Perth, Australia (Gardner & Cabral, 1990). All 17 whose abuse had continued for longer than a month, but only 4 of 23 whose abuse had been of shorter duration, were incest victims. In Russell's (1986) community study of women, 16% reported being victims of incest before the age of 18. The offending relatives were mainly fathers (4.5%), uncles (4.9%), cousins (almost all male; 3%), and brothers (2.2%). Only 2% of the episodes of incest were reported to the police.

Gomes-Schwartz, Horowitz, and Sauzier (1985) investigated 14- to 18-year-old subjects presenting to a family crisis program for sexually abused children in whom the abuse had occurred or been revealed in the preceding 6 months. The majority of cases were of incestuous abuse. Like Ageton (1983) in relation to sexual assault, Gomes-Schwartz et al. (1985) found absence of marked negative reactions persisting for 6 months following sexual abuse of adolescents. Victimized subjects were compared with adolescents in psychiatric treatment, with the authors using the Louisville Behavior Checklist E-3 as a measure of emotional distress. On 10 of the 13 scales, the sexually abused adolescents showed less pathology than those in treatment. Few exhibited severe pathology on most scales according to the criterion proposed by the author of the checklist. Asher (1988) considered that child victims of sexual abuse approaching adolescence, as compared to younger victims, showed more antisocial behaviors, such as petty crime, drug use, promiscuity, and prostitution (often associated with running away from home). Gomes-Schwartz et al. (1985) pointed out that the adolescents evaluated in their study fell predominantly into the anxious, inhibited category. They suggested that their failure to find significant pathology in their teenage victims of sexual abuse could be due to those who were more severely disturbed, running away, or being placed in welfare institutions. Only the less severely disturbed would turn to a family crisis program for help and hence be included in the study.

Herman (1985) noted that as incestuous abuse continued from childhood into adolescence, the distress of girl victims often increased. The father could initiate attempts at intercourse, with the possible risk of pregnancy; also, he frequently responded to the daughter's increased social involvement—normal at this stage of life—with jealousy verging upon paranoia. Frequent consequences were runaway or suicide attempts, indiscriminate sexual activity, and early pregnancy. As the older daughter became more resistant, the father could turn his attentions sequentially to younger daughters.

In view of the evidence of a virtually universal incest taboo (Lester, 1972), one of the most surprising findings of Sorensen's (1973) investigation of a fairly representative sample of U.S. adolescents was the percentage who did not consider a brother and sister or a parent and child having sex to be abnormal or unnatural (22% and 25% of boys and 14% and 13% of girls, respectively). Unlike this equation by adolescents of the two forms of incest, at least on this dimension, health professionals tend to agree in considering brother-sister incest as relatively innocuous (Steele & Alexander, 1981) but disagree concerning the long-term pathogenic effects of father-daughter incest. Attitudes toward the latter vary from the belief that "normal development can never be expected from a child who is lover to her father, sexual rival of her mother, and mistress to the household" (Cantwell, 1983), through the finding that the majority of victims are unaffected, to the conclusion that in some cases the experience is emotionally beneficial (Kroth, 1979). In fact, as Henderson (1983) concluded from his review (entitled "Is Incest Harmful?"), the quality of the present research does not enable the effect of incest to be known. It would seem likely that as with the long-term consequences of rape, the personality vulnerability of the victim may be the major determining factor.

Treatment of Victims of Sexual Coercion

Hochbaum (1987) pointed out that the immediate care of the victim of recent sexual assault required recognition and management of the emotional trauma, assessment and treatment of physical injuries, prevention of venereal disease and pregnancy, and appropriate collection of evidence. Crisis intervention is generally considered to provide the best model for management of the emotional trauma (Burgess & Holmstrom, 1985). Steketee and Foa (1987) reviewed programs treating sexual assault victims with combined or multimodal cognitive-behavioral approaches; these included the victim being encouraged to recall the rape events in imagery and to experience and express emotional reactions to it. Feelings of guilt and responsibility for the rape were reduced by discussion of societal expectations and rape myths. Coping skills (e.g., self-assertion, relaxation, thought stopping, and methods for resuming normal activities) were then taught.

Mann (1981) found that in treating adolescent rape victims, crisis workers spent more time counseling and calming the parents than the adolescents. The workers relied mostly on the parents' information about the victims' reactions and often did not appreciate the victims' feelings of guilt and self-blame and their worries about bodily, mental, and moral integrity.

Only if parents were overtly hostile were parent-child communication problems perceived. Mann felt that this resulted in teenagers perceiving therapists as nonsupportive and therefore refusing counseling. He recommended that professionals treating adolescent rape victims receive specialized training concerning the differences in the rape stresses experienced by adolescents.

A widely reported program for the treatment of incest victims and their families is the Child Sexual Abuse Treatment Program (CSATP), developed by Giarretto (1978, 1981). The goal of the program is to reconstitute and resocialize the incestuous family whenever possible, returning the perpetrator and/or victim to the home when clinically warranted. Kroth (1979), in an independent evaluation of the program, found that this occurred in about three cases out of four. Kroth found a recidivism rate of 0.6% followed the CSATP, compared with an average of 2% reported by other programs. The significance of the finding was rendered questionable, however, by his further finding that at entry to the CSATP, only 18% of perpetrators and spouses believed that they might conceal future abuse; following the CSATP, 40% did. The mean age of the victims treated was 12 to 13 years, well above the mean age of victims in population samples (Russell, 1983). The incestuous sexual assaults of children revealed in community surveys tended to end as the victims approached 13 years of age (Siegel, Sorenson, Golding, Burnam, & Stein, 1987). This suggests that the abuse of children treated in the CSATP would in many cases have ceased without treatment.

Specific treatment of victims of sexual coercion that occurred some time previously has mainly been directed to incest victims. Courtois and Sprei (1988) commented that retrospective incest therapy draws heavily on the feminist perspective, which stresses belief in and support of the survivor and her experience. They argued that the therapy stance should be nurturing and reality based, and that the therapist must be active in view of the denial, shame, stigma, and repression many survivors experience. Behavioral (Rychtarik, Silverman, Van Landingham, & Prue, 1984) and cognitive-behavioral (McCarthy, 1986) approaches have also been advocated. McCarthy noted that one of the most powerful interventions in the latter approach was confrontation of the perpetrator.

Courtois and Sprei (1988) noted that with survivors who suffered the most serious repercussions, the therapist could assume that the therapy was going to take years and that the patients were likely to be discouraged or enraged by the length of treatment. Therapists treating incest victims need to take into account the possible legal implications of Armsworth's (1989) statements that failure to believe a report of incest is a form of abuse of the patient, and that 46% of incest victims are abused by their therapists in this or other ways. A number of subjects treated as victims of incest suffer from borderline personality disorders, and their report of the incest—often made after they had received considerable encouragement to remember the event—provides the basis for the commonly accepted belief that such abuse is a major etiological factor in borderline personality disorder (Mrazek & Mrazek, 1981). Yet it is accepted that subjects with borderline personality have a poor grasp of reality.

My clinical experience with patients previously treated by some therapists as victims of sexual abuse in childhood suggests that the unquestioning acceptance and inappropriate concern shown by the therapists in regard to the subjects' report of sexual abuse (made voluntarily or with probing) was in itself a form of abuse. I believe that it encouraged the patients to adopt the role of perpetual victim and maintained their inability to work or relate to others effectively, a situation that was extremely difficult if not impossible to reverse. There would seem a marked need to evaluate comparatively the forms of treatment currently employed to deal with victims of sexual coercion.

Masturbation

Though in the past masturbation was accepted to be a cause of major psychopathology, there is little evidence concerning whether vestiges of these beliefs trouble adolescents and, if so, whether they produce negative effects. It is likely that masturbation remains the most frequent sexual outlet of adolescent males and a significant number of females, as was found to be the case in Sorensen's (1973) survey. Sorensen commented that of the sex practices he investigated, there seemed to be none about which the adolescents felt more defensive or private than their masturbation. Only 17% of the boys and 22% of the girls in his sample who had masturbated never experienced guilt, anxiety, or concern about the activity.

Most adolescents would appear to be exposed to ambivalent attitudes to masturbation from their parents. Of the stratified sample interviewed by Gagnon (1985), although more than 80% of both mothers and fathers believed that most preteen children masturbated and about 60% believed that this was acceptable, only about 40% wanted their child to have a positive view of masturbation. Gagnon pointed out that fewer than 20% of parents discussed the topic with their child, so that even when parents did approve, their children were unlikely to know about it. About 80% of Sorensen's (1973) sample of adolescents reported that their parents had never talked to them about masturbation; hence there would appear to have been little change in parental behavior in this respect. Lo Presto, Sherman, and Sherman (1985) argued that statements by many researchers and clinicians that masturbation is beneficial to self-awareness and sexual behavior had not significantly modified the views of many young people who retained societal and religious taboos concerning it.

Adolescent Pregnancy and Parenthood

The marked increase in the 1970s in incidence of both sexually transmitted diseases and pregnancy in unmarried teenagers in the United States demonstrated that a major change in adolescent sexual activity had occurred. Investigation of a fairly representative sample of unmarried metropolitan teenagers found that 20% of girls and 35% of boys aged 15, and 45% of girls and 56% of boys aged 17, had experienced coitus (Zelnik, Kantner, & Ford, 1981). This was a striking increase in incidence over that reported 20 years earlier by Kinsey et al. (1948, 1953). By the 1980s, when the increase leveled off, about one-half of white females and three-fourths of black females had commenced intercourse by age 18 (Furstenberg, Brooks-Gunn, & Chase-Lansdale, 1989), as had 60% of white males by age 18 and 60% of black males by age 16 (Brooks-Gunn & Furstenberg, 1989). The relative increase was much greater among girls than among boys.

By the 1980s the greater incidence of adolescent pregnancies in the United States compared to other nations was considered to have reached epidemic proportions (Beck & Davies, 1987). Premarital pregnancies in women aged 15 to 19 increased from 9% in 1971 to 13% in 1976 and 16% in 1979 (Rodman, Lewis, & Griffith, 1984). This increase could be largely attributed to the increased number of unmarried adolescents who were sexually active, since the increase in pregnancies in those sexually active over the same period showed little increase (from 28% to 30%).

It would appear that use of contraception remained at much the same level of relative inadequacy in the unmarried throughout the 1970s. A mid-1980s National Research Council study (Hacker, 1987) found that 40% of black and 20% of white teenagers became pregnant—approximately half the number who were sexually active, a proportion indicating no improvement in the use of contraception. Differences in the outcome of the pregnancies of the black and white girls were not great: respectively, 35% and 40% arranged abortions, and 51% and 46% delivered the baby (of the latter group, 99% and 92% subsequently reared the child). The annual birth rate per 1,000 unmarried girls aged 15 to 19 was 87 for blacks and 19 for whites, giving the United States the highest rate of developed countries for out-of-wedlock childbirth, even among the white teenagers (Hacker, 1987). It also had one of the highest rates of abortions for adolescents (Furstenberg et al., 1989).

Sugar (1984) reported that nearly one-third of married women giving birth before age 16 lived in poverty, and that the marriages of one-third ended in separation or divorce. Of married women first giving birth after age 22, one-tenth lived in poverty, and one-tenth suffered marital breakup. Deliveries in teenagers were associated with a high risk of obstetric complications (Halperin, 1982), and teenage mothers had a high rate of child abuse and a suicide rate ten times that of the normal population (Byrne,

1983). Their children had lower birth weights and the problems associated with this, which included increased incidence of mental illness and cerebral palsy (Halpern, 1990). Two percent of children born to parents younger than 17 died in the first year of life, twice the rate of children in other families (Robinson & Barrett, 1985).

Furstenberg et al. (1989) cited what they termed a monumental review by the National Research Council documenting a host of negative consequences of early childbearing on the educational, economic, and marital careers of young mothers. They argued that the effect of the many ameliorative programs, other than those providing prenatal care, had been modest. Although a number of hospital- and school-based prenatal programs reached teenagers who otherwise would not have sought this care, and those who obtained such care were more likely to have healthy babies than those who did not, Furstenberg et al. emphasized that a significant number did not. With the exception of alternative schools designed specifically for pregnant teenagers, few programs exclusively promoted educational or occupational advance for adolescent parents.

The somewhat negative attitude toward early intercourse reflected in the studies discussed above expressed the tendency in the United States, noted by Jones et al., (1985), to react to the high levels of extramarital teenage pregnancy by aiming to discourage teenage sexual activity. Jones et al. pointed out that the U.S. government has advocated and subsidized a program intervention for this purpose. Furstenberg et al. (1989) commented that most efforts to influence teens' postponement of sexual activity (e.g., school-based health clinics) are recent and innovative, and their impact has yet to be fully evaluated. The governments of other developed countries Jones et al. investigated—in particular, Canada, England and Wales, France, the Netherlands, and Sweden—directed their policies at reducing pregnancy levels, and not sexual activity, by deliberately encouraging the use of contraception. In these countries, apart from Canada, the percentage of teenage girls having intercourse by age 17 was comparable with that in the United States; the percentage in Sweden was higher at all ages. Their levels of adolescent pregnancies, however, were markedly lower.

Sex Education, Clinics, and Contraception

Brooks-Gunn and Furstenberg (1989) reported that about one-half of all teenagers did not use contraceptives the first time they had sexual relations. Younger as compared to older subjects were much less likely to do so. Failure to use contraceptives was not a one-time event. The percentage of teenagers who continued to have intercourse with no or inconsistent contraception was such that one-half of all first pregnancies occurred in the first 6 months following initiation of intercourse; the only group who commenced contraceptive use within the first or second month in large numbers were white teenagers aged 18 and 19. Zelnik et al. (1981) pointed out that the sexual activity of teenagers is irregular, episodic, and unplanned, and that these qualities are not conducive to efficient contraception. Nevertheless, as Jones et al. (1985) emphasized, the evidence from Sweden demonstrated that teenagers can commence sexual activity at a younger age than their U.S. peers and maintain much more effective use of contraception.

A major factor maintaining the prevalence of adolescent pregnancies in the United States would appear to be the reliance on sex education programs rather than provision of contraceptives. Several studies have found no relation between having received sex education and use of contraception (Cvetkovich & Grote, 1983; Durant, Jay, & Seymore, 1990; Howard, 1985). Brown (1983) believed that the decline in both adolescent pregnancy and abortion rates in Sweden resulted from the establishment in 1975 of clinics for adolescents in which school nurses dispensed nonprescription contraceptives, rather than the introduction of improved sex education in 1977. Introduction of services similar to those of the Swedish youth clinics into U.S. high schools were also followed by falls in pregnancy rates (Edwards, Steinman, Arnold, & Hakanson, 1980; Brooks-Gunn, Boyer, & Heim, 1988); however, few such clinics were available for adolescents.

Sexually Transmitted Diseases

The reduction in age of first intercourse that occurred until the early 1980s in the United States was accompanied by a marked increase in incidence in sexually transmitted diseases (STDs) in adolescents. From 1960 to 1981, the incidence of gonorrhea rose from 15 to 25 per 100,000 for boys and 25 to 75 per 100,000 for girls aged 10 to 14 years, and from 490 to 1,000 per 100,000 for boys and 350 to 1,400 per 100,000 for girls aged 15 to 19 (Howard, 1985). Brooks-Gunn and Furstenberg (1989) cited 1985 reports that apart from homosexual men and prostitutes, female teenagers had the highest rates of gonorrhea, cytomegalovirus, chlamydia cervicitis, and pelvic inflammatory disease of any age group. A similar trend was evident in England, where the incidences of new cases of gonorrhea per 100,000 of the population were 145 and 79, respectively, for men and women of all ages, but 277 and 390 for men and women aged 16 to 19 (Peters, 1989). Mascola, Albritton, Cates, and Reynolds (1983) pointed out that twice as many cases in adolescents remained unreported and noted the significance of such future complications in the infected girls as infertility and ectopic pregnancies. Both Mascola et al. and Brooks-Gunn and Furstenberg (1989) emphasized the contribution of the failure to employ protective contraceptive methods to the increased incidence of STDs.

The appearance of HIV infection, with its associated likelihood of producing the acquired immune deficiency syndrome (AIDS), has added a further health risk to sexual activity. Though few adolescents have been reported to have AIDS, Brooks-Gunn and Furstenberg (1989) found that the number had been doubling in recent years. Further, one-fifth of all cases were among 20- to 29-year-olds, so that in view of the long incubation period of the illness, many of these were likely to have been infected in adolescence. Brooks-Gunn and Furstenberg concluded that if the proportion of cases increases significantly in the heterosexual population, adolescents may be at relatively high risk, given their current rates of other STDs and their poor use of contraception.

As of May 1988, 705 AIDS patients (1% of all cases) were aged 13 to 21 years. Compared to the adult patients, a greater percentage of adolescent patients were female (14% versus 7%), members of minority rather than nonminority groups (53% versus 38%), and infected by heterosexual rather than homosexual transmission (9% versus 4%). Heterosexual contact accounted for 46% of the female adolescent cases. Twenty percent of the adolescent AIDS patients were in New York City, where the sex ratio was 2.9 males to 1 female (in contrast to the 7 to 1 male-female ratio for adults). Heterosexual transmission accounted for 52% of the adolescent female patients (Brooks-Gunn et al., 1988). These authors pointed out that as of 1987, only a small percentage of teenagers had received formal instruction about AIDS in school, though the vast majority desired this. Subsequently more than one-half of the large urban schools initiated AIDS education, although the programs tended to be short and nonspecific. Studies revealed that some teenagers reported changes in casual behavior (e.g., "avoiding gays"), but few reported changes in most sexual behaviors that transmitted the virus. Ten percent (10%) used condoms and 10% abstained from sex.

Adolescent Homosexuality

At least 20% of young men and women answering anonymous questionnaires reported having experienced homosexual feelings in adolescence (McConaghy, 1984, 1987, 1993); the majority of these reported at the same time that their interest was predominantly heterosexual. Homosexual activity in adolescence, particularly among boys, is sufficiently frequent that workers attempting to estimate the prevalence of homosexuality ignore it. Fay, Turner, Klassen, and Gagnon (1989) published an analysis of data from a 1970 study of a U.S. national probability sample, emphasizing that although approximately 20% of the male adults reported that they had experienced sexual contact to orgasm with another man, no more than 6.7% had such contacts after age 19. In their estimate, Van Wyk and Geist

(1984) took into account only homosexual behavior occurring after the age of 18. McConaghy (1977) found that male subjects who reported awareness of homosexual feelings, compared to those who did not, were more likely in childhood and adolescence to have shown behaviors labeled as effeminate (e.g., avoiding contact sports and fighting) and to have been called "sissies." They and girls aware of homosexual feelings were more likely to have had wishes to be of the opposite sex and to feel some degree of opposite-sex identity.

It would seem likely, given negative social attitudes toward homosexuality, that these feelings and experiences caused significant distress to many adolescents. In Sorensen's (1973) study, 80% of teenagers considered two boys having sex together abnormal or unnatural, a marginally higher percentage than thought this of either parent-child incest (78%) or two girls having sex together (76%). Seventy-eight percent (78%) of boys and 72% of girls considered the concept of two men having sex together disgusting, a question not asked concerning incest or female homosexuality. There is no information, however, as to how most of the significant percentage of the adolescent population who have homosexual feelings and experiences deal with these. One reason for the lack of information is the unwillingness of adolescents to reveal such feelings or experiences until they reach adulthood. As pointed out earlier, such reluctance led experienced research workers to accept the statements of 109 out of 110 adolescents that they had not experienced homosexual feelings (McConaghy, 1984).

This reluctance may also have been responsible for Hammersmith's (1988) statement that adolescents confused because they either felt both homosexual and heterosexual attractions, or were capable of both types of sexual experience, would maintain a homosexual orientation in adulthood. In fact, the opposite appears to be the case. The majority of medical students reporting homosexual feelings in adolescence reported concurrent predominant heterosexual feelings and identified as heterosexual in adulthood (McConaghy, 1987). In Saghir and Robins' (1973) study, 82% of self-identified homosexual adult men reported experiencing homosexual activity by age 15, compared with 23% of self-identified heterosexual men. As self-identified homosexual men constitute only about 5% of the population, these figures indicated that five times as many men with homosexual experience in adolescence identify as heterosexual than as homosexual. Only 53% of homosexual women in the same study had experienced homosexual activity by age 19.

In counseling adolescents with concerns about their sexual identity, one should bear in mind Remafedi's (1985) comment that to date, no investigator has identified variables that can accurately predict a young person's ultimate sexual preference. Sophie (1988) recommends that the dichotomous view commonly held of sexual orientation should be rejected, and that the question of identity should be left open initially. It would seem likely that adolescents who postpone their identification (at least to others) as homosexual have less traumatic experiences than adolescents who do not; those who identified as homosexual were more likely to have sought psychiatric help and attempted suicide (Remafedi, 1987a, b; Roesler & Deisher, 1972). In Remafedi's study, half of the identified homosexuals had been arrested or appeared in juvenile courts at least once, mainly for substance abuse, truancy, prostitution, or running away for home. Few of their mothers and fathers responded or were expected to respond supportively to disclosure of their homosexuality. Most reported regular abuse from classmates, and a number had experienced "gay bashings."

However, males who have not identified as homosexual but are aware of some degree of homosexual feelings may be at increased risk of sexual coercion. The current ratio of homosexual as compared to heterosexual feelings reported by male but not female medical students correlated significantly with their having been sexually coerced, both by men ($r = 0.5$) and women ($r = 0.24$; McConaghy & Zamir, in press). With adolescents concerned about their sexual orientation and their parents I have found discussion of the possibility that the adolescent's current homosexual behavior may not indicate his or her lifelong sexual preference was often helpful in aiding resolution of the intense family discord that commonly accompanies revelation of an adolescent's homosexuality (Remafedi, 1985). At times it seemed crucial in keeping adolescents from being forced to leave their homes, an eventuality which would seem to increase the likelihood of the negative experiences reported by Remafedi. At the same time, the therapist's first consideration should be to support the adolescent's decision concerning his or her sexual identity, and it is important to establish that the parents will not harass the adolescent into seeking treatment to modify his or her orientation. There may be a role for behavioral treatment (e.g., imaginal desensitization) to help adolescents control homosexual activities or fantasies when (for religious or other reasons) they cannot come to terms with these behaviors that they experience as compulsive. This can be of particular value for adolescents who have a significant or predominant heterosexual component and whose homosexual component may become minimal or disappear with increasing age (McConaghy, 1987).

Prostitution

Gibson-Ainyette, Templer, Brown, and Veaco (1988) reported that from 1967 to 1976 there was a 240% increase in the number of adolescent female prostitutes in the United States. Of the estimated 2 million prostitutes, 600,000 were under the age of 18 years, and the average age for the beginning prostitute was 14, two years after her initial experience of coitus. Schaffer and DeBlassie (1984) stated that the average age of prostitutes was

20 in Boston and 18 in Miami. The number of male adolescent prostitutes in the United States is also believed to be high; Deisher, Robinson, and Boyer (1982) cited an estimate of 300,000. Strommen (1989) claimed there had been a dramatic rise in teenage male prostitution in the United States, which he attributed in part to the casting out of homosexuals by their parents. These studies did not state how the data concerning the number of adolescent male and female prostitutes were obtained.

Potterat, Woodhouse, Muth, and Muth (1990) attempted to calculate the number of female prostitutes in the United States by extrapolating from the number known to their health department in Colorado Springs, and concluded that through the 1980's there were on average 84,000 women working as prostitutes yearly in the United States. They considered FBI reports that from 33,153 to 83,777 women were arrested annually for violation of prostitution laws between 1970 and 1987 supported their estimate. The median age of the prostitutes they investigated was 22 years, with almost three-quarters under 25 years, and only 2.3% over 34 years at their first visit. If the estimate of Potterat et al. and the claimed marked increase in the number of adolescent prostitutes in the last few decades are both correct, the majority of prostitutes must be involved briefly rather than for some years.

Adolescent prostitution does not appear to be regarded as a form of sexual coercion and has failed to attract the strong legal sanctions against its adult organizers or clients equivalent to those against adults involved in noncommercial heterosexual activities with adolescents. In New York, where both prostitution and patronizing a prostitute are crimes, arrests of prostitutes are 100 times more common than arrests of clients. When clients are arrested, it is a common practice to have them testify against the prostitutes so that charges against the former are dropped (Rio, 1991). To determine the degree to which sex crimes against children and adolescents were investigated, questionnaires were sent to 2,383 law enforcement agencies, of which 832 (35%) responded (D'Agostino et al., 1985). Thirty-two percent (32%) of the responding agencies had investigated child sexual assault cases, and 20% child prostitution cases. The mean ages of the youngest female and male prostitutes per agency were between 13 and 14 years, respectively. More than 50% of the agencies that investigated child or adolescent prostitutes cases had made no adult arrests.

Gibson-Ainyette et al. (1988) reviewed evidence indicating that female adolescent prostitutes tended to be from broken homes where they often experienced emotional and physical abuse and early sexual exploitation, at times including incest; they were often runaways and had a history of school absenteeism and dropping out; and in some instances drug use caused them to begin prostitution. Of 200 women prostitutes in the San Francisco area, 60% were reported to have been sexually abused (by an average of two people) prior to the age of 16 (Silbert, 1981). According to Rio (1991), however, theories that prostitutes entered the profession following childhood abuse, life in broken homes, and early sexual activity including incestuous encounters were based on studies of lower-class streetwalkers who were prone to arrest. These factors were also found in nonprostitute matched controls, but not in call girl and house prostitutes, who advanced more middle-class explanations for their entry (e.g., independence and realistic attitudes about morality). Rio recommended that the study of juvenile prostitution be separated from that of adult prostitution, however, and appeared to suggest that virtually all juvenile prostitutes were in the lower-class streetwalker category.

Schaffer and DeBlassie (1984) pointed out that the greatest difference between male and female prostitutes was that the paid contacts of the males were mainly homosexual, including those of the males who identified themselves as heterosexual. These authors considered that like the females, most male prostitutes had been abused or neglected in childhood, but that there were fewer supports for them, whereas the females on the streets formed an elaborate social network. As Rio concluded of female prostitutes, though, Allen (1980) found in a study of 98 male prostitutes contacted through their personal network that there was no specific type. The mean age of those investigated was 16.6 years, ranging from 14 to 24. There were 23 full-time and 48 part-time prostitutes, who mainly made contacts in street or bars; 13 were involved as part of a peer-delinquent subculture in threatening, assaulting, or blackmailing vulnerable male homosexuals, as well as in other criminal activities; 14 were "call" or "kept" boys. By age 18, 35% of the total group had experienced intercourse with a female. The peer-delinquents were the only group considered predominantly heterosexual, and call and kept boys were the most homosexually oriented. The part-time prostitutes had the highest percentage of intact families, and the full-time prostitutes the lowest. Part-time prostitutes also had the least involvement with heavy use of drugs and alcohol, and at average follow-up of 1 year they continued to have the highest educational and work status. They usually worked as prostitutes only when they needed money for some specific purpose.

In a study of young Manhattan male prostitutes, Pleak and Meyer-Bahlburg (1990) excluded escort-service men, call boys, cross-dressing street prostitutes, and boys under 13 (who they commented were predominantly involved in sex rings under the control of pimps). Of the final sample of 50, 25 were from the street and 25 from bars and theaters. Their mean age was 20.7 years, and they had commenced prostitution at a mean age of 17.6 years. None had been involved in sex rings or had pimps. Their mean number of male clients was 495, and of male partners for pleasure, 109. Most street subjects described themselves as heterosexual, and bar and theater subjects, as homosexual. Sixteen had been involved in heterosexual prostitution, with a mean of 3.4 female clients. All but one had heterosexual intercourse with a woman, with a mean of 42 partners.

HIV Infection and Prostitution

Pleak and Meyer-Bahlburg (1990) cited a number of recent studies investigating the prevalence of HIV infection in male prostitutes. Of 194 male street prostitutes in Atlanta, 25% were HIV positive. Of males attending a New York STD clinic, 17 (53%) of 32 who admitted to prostitution with men were seropositive; none of the 17 admitted to IV drug use. Five (10%) of 52 who admitted to prostitution with women were seropositive; 1 of the 5 was using IV drugs, and 3 had engaged in homosexual activity. Ten percent (10%) of street prostitutes and 23% of call men in San Francisco were seropositive. The Manhattan bar/theater and street prostitutes investigated by Pleak and Meyer-Bahlburg (1990) used condoms, respectively, on 16% and 37% of occasions of heterosexual intercourse, but on 80% and 100% of occasions of receptive anal intercourse (whether for money or pleasure). In active anal intercourse, bar/theater subjects used condoms on 25% of occasions with women partners for pleasure, 82% of occasions with male partners for pleasure, and 90% of occasions with male partners for payment; comparable percentages for street subjects were 6%, 4%, and 89%. In receptive fellatio, bar/theater subjects used condoms on 21% of occasions for pleasure and 64% of occasions for payment; street subjects used them in 66% and 59% of these situations, respectively.

The authors commented that the patterns of higher condom use with clients or casual partners than with lovers, and lower use with female than male partners, have been observed in other studies within and outside the United States. It would appear that the prostitutes investigated took significant precautions to avoid HIV infection, particularly from receptive anal intercourse; however, those who became infected posed a very high risk to their women partners. The authors suggested that the intervention programs most likely to succeed in increasing the safety of male prostitutes' sexual practices were those using selected male prostitutes, or former ones, trained to educate their colleagues.

Adolescent Clients

Regular clients of female prostitutes would appear to include a significant number of adolescent males in some cultures, as Primov and Kieffer (1977) found in Peru. In the United States, they are mainly men aged 30 to 60 years (Rio, 1991). Information is lacking to determine whether a significant percentage of male adolescents in the United States continue to have infrequent contacts. Seven percent (7%) of 15-year-old and 49% of 21-

year-old males in Kinsey, Pomeroy, and Martin's (1948) sample reported one or more experiences with prostitutes.

Gender Identity Disorders, Transvestism, and Transsexualism

The DSM-IV abandoned the terms *transvestism* and *transsexualism*, classifying the latter as a gender identity disorder. Transvestites were included in the paraphilias as "transvestic fetishists." Adolescents with transsexualism feel like members of the opposite sex continuously, whereas those with transvestism feel like (or at least wear clothing of) members of the opposite sex periodically. Both commence cross-dressing in childhood. At puberty transvestites, who are almost invariably male, experience sexual arousal with cross-dressing, and this may become a motive for the activity (justifying of this stage their classification as transvestic fetishists). Transsexuals, roughly a quarter of whom are female, continue to cross-dress in conformity with their feeling of belonging to the opposite sex (Buhrich & McConaghy, 1977).

The prevalence of cross-dressing in adolescents has not been established. Person et al. (1989) found 1% of male university students reported to have carried it out in the previous three months. Male adolescents who cross-dress with sexual arousal come to attention only when their behavior is discovered by relatives, either when they are detected using clothes of family members or stealing them from neighbors. Most of these adolescents reveal on questioning that they feel to some extent like girls during the cross-dressing activity. At this stage their behavior is to some extent compulsive, and so it usually responds to imaginal desensitization, though the addition of medroxyprogesterone therapy may be required. Few of these adolescents have been followed up for more than a few years, so it is not known how many develop in later adolescence or adulthood the form of transvestism that seems to require a classification other than transvestic fetishism. At this stage their periodic cross-dressing is usually associated with much less sexual arousal and more acceptance of their opposite-gender identity, and if they cross-dress in the company of other transvestites they usually adopt a female name while doing so.

Transsexuals usually come to attention by seeking sex-conversion by hormones and/or surgery. Most therapists follow the Standards of Care (1985) recommendations that they should have known the patients in a psychotherapeutic relationship for at least 3 months before recommending hormonal sex reassignment and for at least 6 months before recommending surgery, and that prior to surgery the patient should have lived full-time in the social role of the opposite sex for at least 12 months. In the case of adolescents, most therapists attempt to delay surgery until the subject has lived in this role for at least 2 years.

Summary

Because of the reticence of adolescents concerning their sexual activity, it is usually revealed only when it produces problems; thus it tends to be regarded as pathological when it cannot be ignored. Government-sponsored programs have been developed in the United States aimed at postponing the age at which adolescents commence coitus, and there has been little attempt to identify and treat sexual dysfunctions and paraphilias in adolescents, though the prevalence of failure to reach orgasm both in coitus and masturbation is at its highest in adolescent girls, and of paraphilias, in adolescent boys. There has been little effort equally to determine an appropriate response to the recognized high incidence of sexual coercion of adolescent girls by their dates or boyfriends, and the coercion of boys by girls has remained largely uninvestigated. When reactions to sexual coercion of adolescents are treated, more attention is given to the feelings of the parents than those of the adolescents.

Though adolescents in many other developed countries commence coitus at equivalent ages to those in the United States, the prevalence of premarital pregnancies is much higher in the United States. This has led to concern in view of the negative consequences on the educational, economic, and marital careers of the approximately 50% of pregnant adolescents who decide to rear their children. Nevertheless, little interest has been shown in increasing the availability of contraception to adolescents—the technique that appears to have been effective in maintaining the lower rates of adolescent pregnancies in other countries. Ready availability of condoms should also reduce the high incidence of the established sexually transmitted diseases in adolescents and the likelihood of their being infected with HIV. In determining prevalence of homosexuality, it has been customary to ignore its occurrence in adolescents though it appears to be associated with significant distress at least in those who identify as homosexual.

Prostitution is not regarded as a form of sexual coercion, although it would appear the majority of prostitutes are adolescent, with the number involved claimed to approach or exceed 1 million. It remains disputed whether prostitution is associated with more psychopathology when subjects are matched on socioeconomic variables, and its long-term effects appear not to have been investigated. Male prostitutes could be a significant source of transmission of HIV infection to women, as they do not use condoms on most occasions of heterosexual coitus.

It is not established how many male adolescents who cross-dress with sexual arousal develop the adult form of transvestism. Most therapists tend to delay sex conversion of transsexual adolescents seeking the procedure.

References

Ageton, S. S. (1983). *Sexual assault among adolescents*. Lexington, MA: Lexington.

Allen, D. M. (1980). Young male prostitutes: A psychosocial study. *Archives of Sexual Behavior, 9*, 399–426.

American Psychiatric Association. (1987). *Diagnostic and statistical manual of mental disorders* (rev. 3rd ed.). Washington, DC: Author.

American Psychiatric Association. (1994). *Diagnostic and statistical manual of mental disorders* (4th edition). Washington, D.C.

Armsworth, M. W. (1989). Therapy of incest survivors: Abuse or support? *Child Abuse and Neglect, 13*, 549–562.

Asher, S. J. (1988). The effects of childhood sexual abuse: A review of the issues and evidence. In L. E. A. Walker (Ed.), *Handbook on sexual abuse of children* (pp. 3–18). New York: Springer.

Beck, J. G., & Davies, D. K. (1987). Teen contraception: A review of perspectives on compliance. *Archives of Sexual Behavior, 16*, 337–368.

Bowie, S. I., Silverman, D. C., Kalick, S. M., & Edbril, S. D. (1990). Blitz rape and confidence rape: Implications for clinical intervention. *American Journal of Psychotherapy, 44*, 180–188.

Brooks-Gunn, J., Boyer, C. B., & Heim, K. (1988). Preventing HIV infection and AIDS in children and adolescents. *American Psychologist, 43*, 958–964.

Brooks-Gunn, J., & Furstenberg, F. F. (1989). Adolescent sexual behavior. *American Psychologist, 44*, 249–257.

Brown, P. (1983). The Swedish approach to sex education and adolescent pregnancy: Some impressions. *Family Planning Perspectives, 15*, 90–95.

Buhrich, N., & McConaghy, N. (1977). The discrete syndromes of transvestism and transsexualism. *Archives of Sexual Behavior, 6*, 483–495.

Burgess, A. W. (1985). Sexual victimization of adolescents. In A. W. Burgess (Ed.), *Rape and sexual assault* (pp. 199–208). New York: Garland.

Burgess, A. W., & Holmstrom, L. L. (1980). Rape typology and the coping behavior of rape victims. In S. L. McCombie (Ed.), *Rape crisis intervention handbook* (pp. 27–42). New York: Plenum.

Burgess, A. W., & Holmstrom, L. L. (1985). Rape trauma syndrome and post traumatic stress response. In A. W. Burgess (Ed.), *Rape and sexual assault* (pp. 46–60). New York: Garland.

Burt, M. R. (1980). Cultural myths and support for rape. *Journal of Personality and Social Psychology, 38*, 217–230.

Byrne, D. (1983). Sex without contraception. In D. Byrne & W. A. Fisher (Eds.), *Adolescents and contraception* (pp. 1–31). London: Erlbaum.

Cantwell, H. B. (1983). Vaginal inspection as it relates to child sexual abuse in girls under thirteen. *Child Abuse and Neglect, 7*, 171–176.

Christopher, F. S. (1988). An initial investigation into a continuum of premarital sexual pressure. *Journal of Sex Research, 25*, 255–266.

Clifford, R. (1978). Development of masturbation in college women. *Archives of Sexual Behavior, 7*, 559–573.

Copeland, A. R. (1985). Teenage suicide—the five year Metro Dade County experience from 1979 until 1983. *Forensic Sciences International, 28*, 27–33.

Courtois, C. A., & Sprei, J. E. (1988). Retrospective incest therapy for women. In L. E. A. Walker (Ed.), *Handbook on sexual abuse of children* (pp. 270–308). New York: Springer.

Cvetkovich, G., & Grote, B. (1983). Adolescent development and teenage fertility. In D. Byrne & W. A. Fisher (Eds.), *Adolescents, sex and contraception* (pp. 109–123). London: Erlbaum.

D'Agostino, R. B., Burgess, A. W., Belanger, A. J., Guio, M. V., Guio, J. J., Gould, R., & Montan, C. (1985). Investigation of sex crimes against children. In A. W. Burgess (Ed.), *Rape and sexual assault* (pp. 110–122). New York: Garland.

Deisher, R., Robinson, G., & Boyer, D. (1982). The adolescent female and male prostitute. *Pediatric Annals, 11,* 819–825.

Durant, R. H., Jay, S., & Seymore, C. (1990). Contraceptive and sexual behavior of black female adolescents. *Journal of Adolescent Health Care, 11,* 326–334.

Edwards, L. E., Steinman, M. E., Arnold, K. A., & Hakanson, E. Y. (1980). Adolescent pregnancy prevention services in high school clinics. *Family Planning Perspectives, 12,* 6–14.

Ellis, E. M. (1983). A review of empirical rape research: Victim reactions and response to treatment. *Clinical Psychology Review, 3,* 473–490.

Fay, R. E., Turner, C. F., Klassen, A. D., & Gagnon, J. H. (1989). Prevalence and patterns of same-gender sexual contact among men. *Science, 243,* 338–348.

Foley, T. S. (1985). Family response to rape and sexual assault. In A. W. Burgess (Ed.), *Rape and sexual assault* (pp. 159–188). New York: Garland.

Furstenberg, F. F., Jr., Brooks-Gunn, J., & Chase-Lansdale, L. (1989). Teenaged pregnancy and childbearing. *American Psychologist, 44,* 313–320.

Gagnon, J. (1985). Attitudes and responses of parents to pre-adolescent masturbation. *Archives of Sexual Behavior, 14,* 451–466.

Gardner, J. J., & Cabral, D. A. (1990). *Journal of Pediatrics and Child Health, 26,* 22–24.

George, W. H., & Marlatt, G. A. (1989). Introduction. In D. R. Laws (Ed.), *Relapse prevention with sex offenders* (pp. 1–33). New York: Guilford.

Giarretto, H. (1978). Humanistic treatment of father-daughter incest. *Journal of Humanistic Psychology, 18,* 62–76.

Giarretto, H. (1981). A comprehensive child sexual abuse treatment program. In P. B. Mrazek & C. H. Kempe (Eds.), *Sexually abused children and their families* (pp. 179–197). Oxford: Pergamon.

Gibson-Ainyette, I., Templer, D. I., Brown, R., & Veaco, L. (1988). Adolescent female prostitutes. *Archives of Sexual Behavior, 17,* 431–438.

Gittleson, N. L., Eacott, S. E., & Mehta, B. M. (1978). Victims of indecent exposure. *British Journal of Psychiatry, 132,* 61–66.

Gomes-Schwartz, B., Horowitz, J. M., & Sauzier, M. (1985). Severity of emotional distress among sexually abused preschool, school-age, and adolescent children. *Hospital and Community Psychiatry, 36,* 503–508.

Groth, A. N., & Burgess, A. W. (1980). Male rape: Offenders and victims. *American Journal of Psychiatry, 137,* 806–810.

Hacker, A. (1987). American apartheid. *New York Review of Books, 37,* 26–33.

Halperin, M. E. (1982). Teenage pregnancy—myths and facts. In B. N. Barwin & S. Belisle (Eds.), *Adolescent gynecology and sexuality* (pp. 107–111). New York: Masson.

Halpern, S. (1990). The fight over teen-age abortion. *New York Review of Books,* 37, 30–32.

Hammersmith, S. K. (1988). A sociological approach to counseling homosexual clients and their families. In E. Coleman (Ed.), *Psychotherapy with homosexual men and women* (pp. 173–190). New York: Haworth.

Heilbrun, A. B., & Leif, D. T. (1988). Erotic value of female distress in sexually explicit photographs. *Journal of Sex Research, 24,* 47–57.

Heilbrun, A. B., & Loftus, M. P. (1986). The role of sadism and peer pressure in the sexual aggression of male college students. *Journal of Sex Research, 22,* 320–332.

Henderson, J. (1983). Is incest harmful? *Canadian Journal of Psychiatry, 28,* 34–40.

Herman, J. L. (1985). Father-daughter incest. In A. W. Burgess (Ed.), *Rape and sexual assault* (pp. 83–96). New York: Garland.

Herman, J. L. (1990). Sex offenders: A feminist perspective. In W. L. Marshall, D. R. Laws, & H. E. Barbaree (Eds.), *Handbook of sexual assault* (pp. 177–193). New York: Plenum.

Hochbaum, S. R. (1987). The evaluation and treatment of the sexually assaulted patient. *Emergency Medical Clinics of North America, 5,* 601–622.

Holmstrom, L. L. (1985). The criminal justice system's response to the rape victim. In A. W. Burgess (Ed.), *Rape and sexual assault* (pp. 189–198). New York: Garland.

Howard, M. (1985). Postponing sexual involvement among adolescents. *Journal of Adolescent Health Care, 6,* 271–277.

Hunt, M. (1974). *Sexual behavior in the 1970s.* New York: Dell.

Johnson, R. L., & Shrier, D. (1987). Past sexual victimization by females of male patients in an adolescent medicine clinic population. *American Journal of Psychiatry, 144,* 650–652.

Jones, E. F., Forrest, J. D., Goldman, N., Henshaw, S. K., Lincoln, R., Rosoff, J. I., Westoff, C. F., & Wulf, D. (1985). Teenage pregnancy in developed countries: Determinants and policy implications. *Family Planning Perspectives, 17,* 53–63.

Kanin, E. J. (1959). Male aggression in dating-courtship relations. *American Journal of Sociology, 63,* 197–204.

Kanin, E. J., & Parcell, S. R. (1977). Sexual aggression: A second look at the offended female. *Archives of Sexual Behavior, 6,* 67–76.

Kaufman, A., Divasto, P., Jackson, R., Voorhees, D., & Christy, J. (1980). Male rape victims: Noninstitutionalized assault. *American Journal of Psychiatry, 137,* 221–223.

Kinsey, A. C., Pomeroy, W. B., & Martin, C. E. (1948). *Sexual behavior in the human male.* Philadelphia: Saunders.

Kinsey, A. C., Pomeroy, W. B., Martin, C. E., & Gebhard, P. H. (1953). *Sexual behavior in the human female.* Philadelphia: Saunders.

Knight, R. A., & Prentky, R. A. (1990). Classifying sexual offenders. In W. L. Marshall, D. R. Laws, & H. E. Barbaree (Eds.), *Handbook of sexual assault* (pp. 23–52). New York: Plenum.

Koss, M. P., Leonard, K. F., Beezley, D. A., & Oros, C. J. (1985). Nonstranger sexual aggression: A discriminant analysis of the psychological characteristics of undetected offenders. *Sex Roles, 12,* 981–992.

Koss, M. P., & Oros, C. J. (1982). Sexual experiences survey: A research instrument investigating sexual aggression and victimization. *Journal of Consulting and Clinical Psychology, 50,* 455–457.

Kroth, J. A. (1979). Family therapy impact on intrafamilial child sexual abuse. *Child Abuse and Neglect, 3,* 297–302.

Lester, D. (1972). Incest. *Journal of Sex Research, 8,* 268–285.

Lo Presto, C. T., Sherman, M. G., & Sherman, N. C. (1985). The effects of a masturbation seminar on high school males' attitudes, false beliefs, guilt, and behavior. *Journal of Sex Research, 21,* 142–156.

Malamuth, N. M. (1981). Rape proclivity among males. *Journal of Social Issues, 37,* 138–157.

Malamuth, N. M. (1989). The attraction to sexual aggression scale: Part two. *Journal of Sex Research, 26,* 324–354.

Malamuth, N. M., & Check, J. V. P. (1983). Sexual arousal to rape depictions: Individual differences. *Journal of Abnormal Psychology, 92,* 55–67.

Malamuth, N. M., Haber, S., & Feshbach, S. (1980). Testing hypotheses regarding rape: Exposure to sexual violence, sex differences, and the "normality" of rapists. *Journal of Research in Personality, 14,* 121–137.

Mann, E. M. (1981). Self-reported stresses of adolescent rape victims. *Journal of Adolescent Health Care, 2,* 29–33.

Marshall, W. L., & Barbaree, H. E. (1990). Outcome of comprehensive cognitive-behavioral treatment programs. In W. L. Marshall, D. R. Laws, & H. E. Barbaree (Eds.), *Handbook of sexual assault* (pp. 363–385). New York: Plenum.

Mascola, L., Albritton, W. L., Cates, W., & Reynolds, G. H. (1983). Gonorrhea in American teenagers, 1960–1981. *Pediatric Infectious Disease, 2,* 302–303.

McCarthy, B. W. (1986). A cognitive-behavioral approach to understanding and treating sexual trauma. *Journal of Sex and Marital Therapy, 12,* 322–329.

McConaghy, N. (1975). Aversive and positive conditioning treatments of homosexuality. *Behaviour Research and Therapy, 13,* 309–319.

McConaghy, N. (1977). Behavioral treatment in homosexuality. In M. Hersen, R. M. Eisler, & P. M. Miller (Eds.), *Progress in behavior modification* (Vol. 5, pp. 309–380). New York: Academic Press.

McConaghy, N. (1983). Agoraphobia, compulsive behaviors and behavior completion mechanisms. *Australian and New Zealand Journal of Psychiatry, 17,* 170–179.

McConaghy, N. (1984). Psychosexual disorders. In S. M. Turner & M. Hersen (Eds.), *Adult Psychopathology and diagnosis* (pp. 370–405). New York: John Wiley and Sons.

McConaghy, N. (1987). Heterosexuality/homosexuality: Dichotomy or continuum. *Archives of Sexual Behavior, 16,* 11–424.

McConaghy, N. (1989). Validity and ethics of penile circumference measures of sexual arousal: A critical review. *Archives of Sexual Behavior, 18,* 357–369.

McConaghy, N. (1990). Assessment and management of sex offenders: The Prince of Wales Program. *Australian and New Zealand Journal of Psychiatry, 24,* 175–181.

McConaghy, N. (1991). Psychosexual disorders. In M. Hersen & S. M. Turner (Eds.), *Adult psychopathology and diagnosis* (2nd ed., pp. 323–359). New York: Wiley.

McConaghy, N. (1992). Validity and ethics of penile circumference measures of sexual arousal: A response to McAnulty and Adams. *Archives of Sexual Behavior, 21,* 187–195.

McConaghy, N. (1993). *Sexual behavior: Problems and management.* New York: Plenum.

McConaghy, N., Armstrong, M. S., Blaszczynski, A., & Allcock, C. (1983). Controlled comparison of aversive therapy and imaginal desensitization in compulsive gambling. *British Journal of Psychiatry, 142,* 366–372.

McConaghy, N., Armstrong, M. S., & Blaszczynski, A. (1985). Expectancy, covert sensitization and imaginal desensitization in compulsive sexuality. *Acta Psychiatrica Scandinavica, 72,* 1176–1187.

McConaghy, N., Blaszczynski, A., & Kidson, W. (1988). Treatment of sex offenders with imaginal desensitization and/or medroxyprogesterone. *Acta Psychiatrica Scandanavica, 77,* 199–206.

McConaghy, N., Blaszczynski, A., Armstrong, M. S., & Kidson, W. (1989). Resistance to treatment of adolescent sexual offenders. *Archives of Sexual Behavior, 18,* 97–107.

McConaghy, N., Zamir, R., & Manicavasagar, V. (1993). Non-sexist sexual experiences survey and scale of attraction to sexual aggression. *Australian and New Zealand Journal of Psychiatry, 27,* 686–693.

McConaghy, N., & Zamir, R. (in press). Heterosexual and homosexual coercion, sexual orientation and sexual roles. *Archives of Sexual Behavior.*

McGee, R., Feehan, M., Williams, S., Partridge, F., Silva, P. A., & Kelly, J. (1990). DSM-III disorders in a large sample of adolescents. *Journal of the American Academy of Child and Adolescent Psychiatry, 29,* 611–619.

Mead, M. (1950). *Male and female.* London: Gollancz.

Money, J., Schwartz, M., & Lewis, V. G. (1984). Adult erotosexual status and fetal hormonal masculinization and demasculinization: 46, XX congenital virilizing adrenal hyperplasia and 465, XY androgen-insensitivity syndrome compared. *Psychoneuroendocrinology, 9,* 405–414.

Mrazek, P. B., & Mrazek, D. A. (1981). The effects of child sexual abuse: Methodological considerations. In P. B. Mrazek & C. H. Kempe (Eds.), *Sexually abused children and their families* (pp. 235–245). Oxford, England: Pergamon.

Muehlenhard, C. L., & Cook, S. W. (1988). Men's self-reports of unwanted sexual activity. *Journal of Sex Research, 24,* 58–72.

Murphy, W. D. (1990). Assessment and modification of cognitive distortions in sex offenders. In W. L. Marshall, D. R. Laws, & H. E. Barbaree (Eds.), *Handbook of sexual assault* (pp. 331–342). New York: Plenum.

Person, E. S., Terestman, N., Myers, W. A., Goldberg, E. L., & Salvadori, C. (1989). Gender differences in sexual behaviors and fantasies in a college population. *Journal of Sex and Marital Therapy, 15,* 187–198.

Peters, H. (1989). The epidemiology of sexually transmitted diseases. In R. Richmond & D. Wakefield (Eds.), *AIDS and other sexually transmitted diseases.* Sydney: Harcourt, Brace and Jovanovich.

Pfaus, J. G., Myronuk, L. D. S., & Jacobs, W. J. (1986). Soundtrack contents and depicted sexual violence. *Archives of Sexual Behavior, 15,* 231–237.

Pleak, R. R., & Meyer-Bahlburg, H. F. L. (1990). Sexual behavior and AIDS knowledge of young male prostitutes in Manhattan. *Journal of Sex Research, 27,* 557–587.

Potterat, J. J., Woodhouse, D. E., Muth, J. B., & Muth, S. Q. (1990). Estimating the prevalence and career longevity of prostitute women. *Journal of Sex Research, 27,* 233–245.

Primov, G., & Kieffer, C. (1977). The Peruvian brothel as sexual dispensary and social arena. *Archives of Sexual Behavior, 6,* 245–253.

Quinsey, V. L., & Laws, C. M. (1990). The modification of sexual preference. In W. L. Marshall, D. R. Laws & H. E. Barbaree (Eds.), *Handbook of sexual assault,* (pp. 279–295). New York: Plenum.

Remafedi, G. J. (1985). Adolescent homosexuality. *Pediatrics, 24,* 481–485.

Remafedi, G. (1987a). Homosexual youth: A challenge to contemporary society. *Journal of the American Medical Association, 258,* 222–225.

Remafedi, G. (1987b). Adolescent homosexuality: Psychosocial and medical implications. *Pediatrics, 79,* 331–377.

Rio, L. M. (1991). Psychological and sociological research and the decriminalization or legalization of prostitution. *Archives of Sexual Behavior, 20,* 205–218.

Robins, L. N., Helzer, J. E., Weissman, M. M., Orvaschel, H., Gruenberg, E., Burke, J. D., & Regier, D. A. (1984). Lifetime prevalence of specific psychiatric disorders in three sites. *Archives of General Psychiatry, 41,* 949–958.

Robinson, B. E., & Barrett, R. L. (1985). Teenage fathers. *Psychology Today, 19,* 68–70.

Rodman, H., Lewis, S. H., & Griffith, S. B. (1984). *The sexual rights of adolescents.* New York: Columbia University Press.

Roesler, T., & Deisher, R. W. (1972). Youthful male homosexuality. *Journal of the American Medical Association, 219,* 1018–1023.

Russell, D. E. H. (1983). The incidence and prevalence of intrafamilial and extrafamilial sexual abuse of female children. *Child Abuse and Neglect, 7,* 133–146.

Russell, D. E. H. (1986). *The secret trauma: Incest in the lives of girls and women.* New York: Basic Books.

Rychtarik, R. G., Silverman, W. K., Van Landingham, W. P., & Prue, D. M. (1984). Treatment of an incest victim with implosion therapy: A case study. *Behavior Therapy, 15,* 410–420.

Saghir, M., & Robins, E. (1973). *Male and female homosexuality: A comprehensive investigation.* Baltimore, MD: Williams and Wilkins.

Sarrel, P., & Masters, W. (1982). Sexual molestation of men by women. *Archives of Sexual Behavior, 11,* 117–133.

Schaffer, B., & DeBlassie, R. R. (1984). Adolescent prostitution. *Adolescence, 19,* 689–696.

Siegel, J. M., Sorenson, S. B., Golding, J. M., Burnam, M. A., & Stein, J. A. (1987). The prevalence of childhood sexual assault. *American Journal of Epidemiology, 126,* 1141–1153.

Silbert, M. H. (1981). Sexual child abuse as an antecedent to prostitution. *Child Abuse and Neglect, 5,* 307–411.

Silverman, D. C., Kalick, S. M., Bowie, S. I., & Edbril, S. D. (1988). Blitz rape and confidence rape: A typology applied to 1,000 consecutive cases. *American Journal of Psychiatry, 145,* 1438–1441.

Sophie, J. (1988). Internalizing homophobia and lesbian identity. In E. Coleman (Ed.), *Psychotherapy with homosexual men and women* (pp. 53–65). New York: Haworth.

Sorensen, R. C. (1973). *Adolescent sexuality in contemporary America*. New York: World.

Standards of Care. (1985). The hormonal and surgical sex reassignment of gender dysphoric persons. *Archives of Sexual Behavior, 14,* 79–90.

Steele, B. F., & Alexander, H. (1981). Long term effects of sexual abuse in childhood. In P. B. Mrazek & C. H. Kempe (Eds.), *Sexually abused children and their families* (pp. 223–236). Oxford, England: Pergamon.

Steketee, G., & Foa, E. B. (1987). Rape victims: Post-traumatic stress responses and their treatment. *Journal of Anxiety Disorders, 1,* 69–86.

Strommen, E. F. (1989). "You're a what?" Family member reactions to the disclosure of homosexuality. *Journal of Homosexuality, 18,* 37–58.

Struckman-Johnson, C. (1988). Forced sex on dates: It happens to men, too. *Journal of Sex Research, 24,* 234–241.

Sugar, M. (1984). *Adolescent parenthood*. New York: MTP.

Templeman, T. L., & Stinnett, R. D. (1991). Patterns of sexual arousal and history in a "normal" sample of young men. *Archives of Sexual Behavior, 20,* 137–150.

Van Wyk, P. H., & Geist, C. S. (1984). Psychosexual development of heterosexual, bisexual, and homosexual behavior. *Archives of Sexual Behavior, 13,* 505–544.

Zelnik, M., Kantner, J. F., & Ford, K. (1981). *Sex and pregnancy in adolescence*. Beverly Hills, CA: Sage.

Author Index

Douvan, E., 622, 646
Downey, G., 303, 335, 630, 631, 646
Drabman, R.S., 567, 577, 587
Drigotas, S.M., 88, 95
Druss, R.G., 111, 124
Dubas, J.S., 79, 80, 83, 85, 95, 98
Dubey, D.R., 609, 613
Duffy, J.C., 286, 293
Dugas, M., 322, 335
Duke, P.M., 81, 83, 84, 96
Dulcan, M.K., 268, 291, 351, 375, 529,
    541, 552, 603, 613, 678, 682
Dumas, J.E., 630, 646
Duncan, P.D., 85, 96
Duner, A., 354, 379
Dunford, F.W., 571, 581
Dunham, H.W., 476, 492
Dunn, L.M., 505, 520
Dupaul, G., 598, 601, 612
Dupkin, C., 541, 555
Durant, R.H., 708, 718
Durbin, D., 631, 632, 649
Duricko, A.J., 224, 236
Dusenbury, L., 372, 374
Dweck, C.S., 303, 335
Dwyer, J.H., 372, 378
Dy, A.J. 577, 581
Dzubinski, D., 344

Eacott, S.E., 670, 718
Eagen, D.R., 217, 239
Earles, F., 398, 404
Eason, L.J., 312, 335
Easson, W., 473, 492
Eaves, L., 417, 432
Ebata, A.T., 24, 44, 65, 632, 650
Eckert, E.D., 538, 552
Ecton, R.B., 247, 248, 258, 609, 613
Edbril, S.D., 699, 717
Edelbrock, C.S., 164, 187, 249, 251, 256,
    267, 268, 291, 319, 332, 351, 375,
    440, 450, 456, 512, 519, 531, 535,
    550, 561, 573, 579, 581,591, 592,
    593, 595, 598, 600, 601, 604, 606,
    611, 612, 613, 678, 681, 682
Edelstein, B.A., 255, 258
Edgerton, R.B., 499, 520
Edwards, G.L., 252, 258
Edwards, J., 359, 377
Edwards, L.E., 708, 718
Efron, A.M., 678, 684
Egeland, B.R., 643, 651
Eggers, C., 480, 493

Ehrhardt, A.A., 84, 98, 527, 534, 537,
    555
Eichorn, D.H., 73, 81, 94, 96
Eisele, J., 417, 432
Eisen, A.R., 441, 447, 452, 454, 458, 460,
    463
Eisenberg, L., 439, 458
Eisenhower, J.W., 38, 59
Elbert, J.C., 561, 588
Elconin, J., 118, 124
Elder, G.H., 4, 59, 631, 642, 646
Elefthteriou, B.E., 571, 581
Elia, J., 603, 613
Elias, M.J., 120, 124
Elkind, G.S., 351, 381
Elliot, D.S., 44, 60, 354, 361, 362, 363,
    375, 378, 571, 581
Elliot, F.A., 576, 581
Elliott, L., 454, 462
Elliott, T.R., 677, 682
Ellis, A., 304, 336
Ellis, E.M., 701, 718
Ellis, J.T., 108, 114, 127
Ellis-Schwabe, M., 642, 646
Eme, R.F., 537, 552
Emery, R.E., 633, 638, 643, 646, 651
Emery, G., 304, 333
Emler, N., 360, 375
Emmelkamp, P.K.G., 669, 681
Emshoff, B., 577, 580
Emsley, C., 45, 59
Emslie, G.J., 300, 301, 336
Endicott, J., 266, 268, 269, 292, 294,
    306, 336, 346, 573, 588
Englander-Golden, P., 118, 124
Enyart, P., 371, 336
Epstein, A.W., 547, 552
Epstein, H., 79, 96
Epstein, N.B., 675, 683
Erbaugh, J., 252, 257, 317, 333
Erickson, E.H., 10, 16, 18, 19, 23, 59,
    437, 458
Erickson, W.D., 481, 483, 486, 493, 495
Erlenmeyer-Kimling, L., 477, 478, 493
Eron, L.D., 43, 50, 59, 60, 63, 354, 357,
    378, 570, 584
Esman, A.H., 538, 553
Esonis, S., 253, 258
Esser, G., 270, 272, 274, 292
Esveldt-Dawson, K., 106, 118, 119, 126,
    127, 250, 253, 260
Evans, E.D., 317, 335, 642, 646
Evans, J.R., 489, 493

Subject Index

About the Contributors

Lisa Amaya-Jackson   Department of Psychiatry, Division of Child and Adolescent Psychiatry, Duke University Medical Center, Durham, NC 27710

Stewart Anderson   Resident, Department of Psychiatry, Western Psychiatric Institute & Clinic, University of Pittsburgh Medical Center, Pittsburgh, PA 15213

Rowland P. Barrett   Associate Professor, Department of Psychiatry & Human Behavior, Brown University Program in Medicine, Emma Pendleton Bradley Hospital, East Providence, RI 02915

M. Christopher Borden   Clinical Assistant Professor of Psychiatry, Psychiatric Center, Emma Pendleton Bradley Hospital, A Brown University Affiliated Hospital, East Providence, RI 02915

Charles M. Borduin   Professor of Psychology, Department of Psychology, University of Missouri-Columbia, Columbia, Missouri 65211

Susan J. Bradley   Child and Adolescent Gender Identity Clinic, Clarke Institute of Psychiatry, Toronto, Ontario, CANADA M5T 1R8

Jeanne Brooks-Gunn   The Adolescent Study Program, Department of Developmental and Educational Psychology, Teachers College Columbia University, New York, New York 10027

Oscar G. Bukstein   Director of Child and Parent Behavior, Department of Psychiatry, Western Psychiatric Institute & Clinic, University of Pittsburgh Medical Center, Pittsburgh, PA 15213

Patrick Burke   Associate Professor of Psychiatry and Pediatrics, Western Psychiatric Institute and Clinic, University of Pittsburgh Medical Center, Pittsburgh, PA 15213

Dennis P. Cantwell   Department of Psychiatry, University of California at Los Angeles, Los Angeles, CA 90024

Paul Cinciripini   U.T.M.D. Anderson Cancer Center, Department of Behavioral Sciences, Houston, TX 77030

Steven W. Evans   Department of Psychaitry, Western Psychiatric Institute & Clinic, University of Pittsburgh Medical Center, Pittsburgh, PA 15213

Horacio Fabrega, Jr.   Department of Psychiatry, Western Psychiatric Institute & Clinic, University of Pittsburgh Medical Center, Pittsburgh, PA 15213

Angela M. Giacoletti   Department of Psychology, West Virginia University, Morgantown, West Virginia 26506-6040

Julie A. Graber   Senior Research Scientist, The Adolescent Study Program, Department of Developmental and Educational Psychology, Teachers College Columbia University, New York, New York 10027

Michelle R. Grimm   Department of Psychiatry, Western Psychiatric Institute & Clinic, University of Pittsburgh Medical Center, Pittsburgh, PA 15213

Alan M. Gross   Department of Psychology, The University of Mississippi, University, MS 38677

David J. Hansen   Department of Psychology, University of Nebraska-Lincoln, Lincoln, NE 68588-0308

Patti Harrison   Professor and Chair, Educational and School Psychology, The University of Alabama, Tuscaloosa, AL 35487-0231

Martin Harrow   Director and Professor of Psychology, Humana Hospital Michael Reese, Department of Psychiatry, University of Illinois at Chicago, Chicago, IL 60616-3390

Scott W. Henggeler   Family Services Center, Medical University of South Carolina, Charleston, SC 29425

Grace R. Kalfus   Clinical Associate Professor, Westchester Institute for Human Development, New York Medical College and Westchester County Medical Center, Valhalla, NY 10595

Christopher A. Kearney   Department of Psychology, University of Nevada, Las Vegas, Nevada, 89154

Mary Margaret Kerr   Department of Psychiatry, Western Psychiatric Institute & Clinic, University of Pittsburgh Medical Center, Pittsburgh, PA 15213

Matcheri S. Keshavan   Associate Professor, Department of Psychiatry, Western Psychiatric Institute & Clinic, University of Pittsburgh Medical Center, Pittsburgh, PA 15213

Christopher M. Manley   Department of Psychology, University of Missouri-Columbia, Columbia, Missouri 65211

D. Richard Martini   Assistant Professor of Psychiatry and Pediatrics, Children's Hospital, University of Pittsburgh Medical Center, Pittsburgh, PA 15213-2583

Nathaniel McConaghy   Psychiatric Unit, The Prince of Wales Hospital, Randwick, N.S.W. AUSTRALIA 2031

Richard H. Mesco   Albuquerque Indian Health Services, Albuquerque, New Mexico 87102

Stephen C. Messer   Developmental Epidemiology Program, Duke University Medical Center, Durham, NC 27710

Ada C. Mezzich   Assistant Professor of Psychiatry, Female Adolescent Study, Department of Psychiatry, Western Psychiatric Institute & Clinic, University of Pittsburgh Medical Center, Pittsburgh, PA 15213

Barbara Miller   George Washington University, Department of Anthropology, Washington, D.C. 20016

Douglas W. Nangle   Department of Psychology, West Virginia University, Morgantown, West Virginia 26506-6040

Duane G. Ollendick   Department of Psychiatry and Psychology, Olmsted Medical Group, Rochester, MN 55903-4300

William Pelham   Director, Attention Deficit Disorder Program, Department of Psychiatry, Western Psychiatric Institute & Clinic, University of Pittsburgh Medical Center, Pittsburgh, PA 15213

Kavitha Rao   Child Psychiatry Fellow, Division of Child and Adolescent Psychiatry, UCLA Neuropsychiatric Psychiatry, Los Angeles, CA 90024-6967

David Reitman   Department of Psychology, The University of Mississippi, University, MS 38677

Williams M. Reynolds   Director, and Professor, Department of Educational Psychology, Psychoeducational Research and Training Centre, University of British Columbia, Vancouver, B.C. CANADA V6T 1Z4

Eileen P. Ryan   Clinical Assistant Professor of Psychiatric Medicine, Department of Mental Health, Mental Retardation, and Substance Abuse Services, University of Virginia School of Medicine, Commonwealth of Virginia, Staunton, Virginia 24402-2309

Wendy Silverman   Department of Psychology, Florida International University, Miami, Florida 33199

Billie Strauss   Director of Training in Psychology and Outpatient Psychiatric Services, Michael Reese Hospital and Medical Center, Associate Professor of Psychology, Department of Psychiatry, University of Illinois at Chicago, Chicago, IL 60616-3390

Claire B. Lowry   Sullivan Child and Adolescent Gender Identity Clinic, Clarke Institute of Psychiatry, Toronto, Ontario, CANADA M5T 1R8

Tommy E. Turner   Educational and School Psychology, The University of Alabama, Tuscaloosa, AL 35487-0231

Gary Vallano Department of Psychiatry, Allegheny General Hospital, Pittsburgh, PA 15212

Petronella Vaulx-Smith Assistant Professor, Department of Psychiatry, Western Psychiatric Institute & Clinic, University of Pittsburgh Medical Center, Pittsburgh, PA 15213

Anne S. Walters Department of Psychiatry & Human Behavior, Brown University Program in Medicine, Emma Pendleton Bradley Hospital, East Providence, RI 02915

Cindy L. Wigg Associate Professor, Department of Psychiatry and Behavioral Sciences, Medical Director of Adolescent Inpatient Services, The University of Texas Branch at Galveston, Galveston, TX 77555-0425

D. Blake Woodside Eating Disorder Centre, Toronto Hospital, Ontario, CANADA M5G 2C4

Kenneth J. Zucker Head, Child and Adolescent Gender Identity Clinic, Clarke Institute of Psychiatry, Toronto, Ontario, CANADA M5T 1R8

About the Editors

Vincent B. Van Hasselt, Ph, D., is Professor of Psychology and Director of the Interpersonal Violence Program and Nova Southeastern University in Fort Lauderdale, Florida. Dr. Van Hasselt received his M.S. and Ph.D. from the University of Pittsburgh and completed an internship in clinical psychology and Western Psychiatric Institute and Clinic of the University of Pittsburgh Medical Center. He was formerly Program Director of the Adolescent Drug Abuse and Psychiatric Treatment Program at the University of Pittsburgh. Dr. Van Hasselt is co-editor of the *Journal of Child and Adolescent Substance Abuse, Journal of Family Violence, Handbook of Family Violence, Behavior Therapy for Children and Adolescents: A Clinical Approach, Handbook of Behvior Therapy and Pharmacotherapy for Children: A Comparative Analysis,* and *Inpatient Behavior Therapy for Children and Adolescents.* He has published over 130 journal articles, books, and book chapters including several on the prevention, assessment, and treatment of adolescent substance abusers. His Project for a Safe Family Environment, a multiple-component ecobehavioral treatment program directed towards the problem of child maltreatment in inner-city families, has shown promise in reducing levels of abuse and related problems in this population.

Dr. Van Hasselt is the recipient of grants from the National Institute of Mental Health, the National Institute of Handicapped Research, Handicapped Children's Early Education Program, March of Dimes Birth Defects Foundation, Buhl Foundation, and the Pittsburgh Foundation. He has more than 15 years of experience as a clinical practitioner, administrator, consultant, educator, and researcher.

Michel Hersen, Ph.D., is Professor of Psychology at Nova Southeastern University, Fort Lauderdale, Florida. He is Past President of the Association for Advancement of Behavior Therapy; Diplomate, American Board of Professional Psychology; Diplomate, American Board of Medical Psychotherapists; and Distinguished Practitioner in Psychology, National Academies of Practice. He is the author and co-author of 205 papers, 99 books, and 77 book chapters. His current research involves the behavioral assessment and treatment of older adults. He is co-editor of several journals, inlcuding *Clinical Psychology Review, Journal of Clinical Geropsychology, Behavior Modification, Journal of Family Violence,* and *Journal of Anxiety Disorders.* He has bee the recipient of federal grants from the National Institute of Mental Health, the U.S. Department of Education, and the National Institute on Disabilities and Rehabilitaion Research.